贸易政策专业词汇辞典

Dictionary of Trade Policy Terms

6th Edition

[澳]沃尔特·古德（Walter Goode）·著
《贸易政策专业词汇辞典》翻译组　·译

中国商务出版社
·北京·

图书在版编目（CIP）数据

贸易政策专业词汇辞典 = Dictionary of Trade Policy Terms : 英汉对照 / (澳) 沃尔特 · 古德 (Walter Goode) 著 ;《贸易政策专业词汇辞典》翻译组译 . -- 北京 : 中国商务出版社 , 2024.11
ISBN 978-7-5103-5008-5

Ⅰ . ①贸… Ⅱ . ①沃… ②贸… Ⅲ . ①国际贸易政策—词汇—词典—英、汉 Ⅳ . ① F741-61

中国国家版本馆 CIP 数据核字 (2024) 第 054751 号

版权出让方：Cambridge University Press
著作权合同登记号 图字：01-2024-6060 号

贸易政策专业词汇辞典

MAOYI ZHENGCE ZHUANYE CIHUI CIDIAN

[澳] 沃尔特 · 古德 (Walter Goode) 著
《贸易政策专业词汇辞典》翻译组 译

出版发行：中国商务出版社有限公司
地　　址：北京市东城区安外东后巷 28 号　邮编：100710
网　　址：http://www.cctpress.com
联系电话：010-64515150（发行部）　010-64212247（总编室）
　　　　　010-64269744（商务事业部）　010-64248236（印制部）
特约编审：郝宝生
责任编辑：张高平
责任校对：李　阳　孙柳明
排　　版：廊坊市展博印刷设计有限公司
印　　刷：北京密兴印刷有限公司
开　　本：787 毫米 ×1092 毫米　1/16
印　　张：78.25　字　　数：1788 千字
版　　次：2024 年 11 月第 1 版　印　　次：2024 年 11 月第 1 次印刷
书　　号：ISBN 978-7-5103-5008-5
定　　价：168.00 元

中译文译校人员

主　编

韩　勇　陈雨松　鄂德峰

副主编

田　涯　裴文利　海琳娜

翻　译（以姓氏笔划为序）

王才钰　王安琪　方　博　丛　政
宁　夏　朱学韬　任思雨　刘　怡
刘天洋　刘啸辰　齐心怡　江诗琪
孙恺瑞　杨　天　邹　伟　张思钰
张喜嘉　罗　阳　孟　勰　柳安楠
柳欣玥　钟　珂　姚家威　耿子超
高鹏宇　唐瀚文　韩文逸

校　译（以姓氏笔划为序）

王　师　王　坤　王　怡　邓宇思
苏　骁　李东超　吴文昭　余元堂
易姿含　郑茹娜　赵　晨

审　定

索必成

版权声明

翻译说明

本书收录沃尔特·古德 (Walter Goode) 先生编著的 Dictionary of Trade Policy Terms 一书的英文原文和中译文。

该辞典于 1997 年首次出版，先后于 1998 年、2001 年、2003 年、2007 年更新。本书为 2020 年出版的第 6 版。

本书部分词条中译文参考了上海人民出版社出版的《贸易政策术语词典》(第 5 版)，在此特表示感谢。

本辞典采用中英文对照方式排版，对词条的解释以英文为准，中译文仅供参考。

Dictionary of Trade Policy Terms
Sixth Edition

This is an accessible guide to the vocabulary used in trade negotiations. It explains some 3,000 terms and concepts in simple language. Its main emphasis is on the multilateral trading system represented by the agreements under the World Trade Organization (WTO). In addition it covers many of the traderelated activities, outcomes and terms used in other international organizations, such as the United Nations Conference on Trade and Development (UNCTAD), the World Intellectual Property Organization (WIPO), the Food and Agriculture Organization (FAO), Asia-Pacific Economic Cooperation (APEC) and the OECD. The last decade has seen considerable attention devoted to trade and investment facilitation, sustainability and the formation of free-trade areas in all parts of the world. This dictionary allocates generous space to the vocabulary associated with such developments. It offers clear explanations, for example, of the concepts used in the administration of preferential rules of origin. More recently, trade facilitation has received considerable attention. Additional areas covered include emerging trade issues and issues based particularly on developing-country concerns.

WALTER GOODE was for many years an officer of the Australian Department of Foreign Affairs and Trade. In that capacity he acquired wide experience in the formulation of international trade policy and the conduct of bilateral and multilateral trade negotiations. In particular he participated in negotiations and meetings in APEC, GATT, WTO, UNCTAD and OECD. He has held trade-related postings in Geneva, Beijing, Shanghai and Tokyo. He conducted many trade policy training courses particularly under APEC auspices. He is now retired. His publications include Australian Traded Services, Uruguay Round Outcomes: Services and Negotiating Free-Trade Agreements: A Guide.

出版说明

本辞典是一本关于贸易谈判中所用词汇的实用指南。以简练的文字对 3000 余个术语和概念进行了解释。重点关注以世界贸易组织 (WTO) 项下协定为代表的多边贸易体制。还涵盖联合国贸易与发展会议 (UNCTAD)、世界知识产权组织 (WIPO)、联合国粮农组织 (FAO)、亚太经济合作组织 (APEC) 和经济合作与发展组织 (OECD) 等其他国际组织中许多与贸易有关的活动、成果和所用术语。过去十年，人们非常关注贸易与投资便利化、可持续性和遍布世界的自由贸易区。本辞典大量收录与此类发展情况相关的词汇。例如，本辞典对优惠原产地规则管理中所用概念进行了清晰的解释。贸易便利化最近受到广泛关注。其他涵盖领域包括新出现的贸易问题和发展中国家特别关注的问题。

沃尔特 · 古德先生在澳大利亚外交贸易部任职多年。在这一职位上，他在国际贸易政策制定和开展多双边贸易谈判方面获得了丰富经验。 特别参与了 APEC、GATT、WTO、UNCTAD 和 OECD 的谈判和会议。他曾在日内瓦、北京、上海和东京担任与贸易相关的职位，特别是在 APEC 的主持下，举办了多场贸易政策培训课程。古德先生现已退休。他的出版物包括《澳大利亚贸易服务》、《乌拉圭回合成果 : 服务业》和《自由贸易协定谈判指南》。

DISCLAIMER

Any views given in this dictionary on WTO agreements, provisions, panel and Appellate Body reports, or any other information provided by the WTO, are the sole responsibility of the author. They do not necessarily represent the views of WTO Members, the WTO Secretariat or the Appellate Body. As such, the definitions in this dictionary do not constitute authoritative interpretations of the legal texts of the WTO. They are presented for illustrative purposes only.

免责声明

本辞典中关于 WTO 协定、条款、专家组报告和上诉机构报告的任何观点或 WTO 所提供的任何其他信息均由作者自负全责，并不一定代表 WTO 成员、WTO 秘书处或上诉机构的观点。因此，本辞典中的定义仅用于说明目的，不构成对 WTO 法律文本的权威解释。

PREFACE

This *Dictionary of Trade Policy Terms* is now in its sixth edition. It has again grown larger. It now contains well over 3,000 entries and cross-references. Many of these entries are new. In other cases the changes occurring since the preparation of the last edition have required a complete rewriting of the entry. A great many have needed updating to a greater or lesser extent. I have made an attempt at being reasonably comprehensive, but no doubt there is always more that could be included.

The nature of the book has changed over the years. On many occasions it has gone past simply explaining what this or that term might mean. For example, in recent years several comprehensive free-trade agreements have been concluded, such asthe African Continental Free Trade Area, the Comprehensive and Progressive Agreement for Trans-Pacific Partnership and the United States–Mexico–Canada Agreement. The ambit of these and similar agreements goes well beyond what used to be considered the proper content of trade negotiations. I therefore have included summaries of several of these agreements to give the reader an indication of what is involved.

I should stress that this dictionary concerns itself with words and topics likely to occur in trade negotiations. It is definitely not a dictionary of international economic relations. The areas of the two disciplines overlap in some cases, but the distinction between them is clear. Trade policy consists of a mixture of economics, law and politics, with the latter two often the dominating influence in the conduct of negotiations. The economic aspects of an issue of course shape the expectations of the negotiating partners, and they tend to be analysed, often in great detail, before any negotiations start.

International economic analysis in comparison is much more rigorous. Even a brief look at textbooks of international economics suggests that economists are not always convinced of the validity of concepts used by trade negotiators or, indeed, their achievements.

A large number of entries are based on the work of the World Trade Organization (WTO) and its members. It is the pre-eminent forum for the pursuit of multilateral trade policy. I should emphasize that many words and concepts used within the WTO have a precise meaning to participants in proceedings under its auspices. Rendering these exact meanings would sometimes require rather long explanations. This might not always be helpful. I have therefore attempted to convey a picture of such meanings. Accordingly, all interpretations are my own. They have no legal standing within the organization

前言

《贸易政策专业词汇辞典》已经出版第 6 版，篇幅再一次增加。现收录超过 3000 个词条和交叉引用，许多词条为新增内容。自上一版出版以来，发生了很多变化，需要对其他词条进行重新编写。还有许多词条需要或多或少进行更新。我尽力使这一版相对全面，但显然总是有应收录而未被收录在内的内容。

多年来，辞典的性质已经发生变化。许多情况下，本辞典已经超出简单解释词语含义的范畴。近年来，缔结了多项全面自由贸易协定，例如非洲大陆自由贸易区、《全面与进步跨太平洋伙伴关系协定》和《美国—墨西哥—加拿大协定》。这些协定和类似协定的范畴已经远远超出以往界定的贸易谈判本身的内容。因此，我收录了对其中一些协定的简要介绍，以便读者了解其中所涉内容。

需要强调的是，本辞典专注于贸易谈判中可能出现的词语和议题，而绝不是一本关于国际经济关系的辞典。这两个学科在一些情况下有所重叠，但两者之间的区别是明确的。贸易政策包含经济学、法律和政治的内容，而法律和政治通常在开展谈判过程中产生主要影响。当然，一个议题的经济层面可以影响谈判伙伴的预期，在任何谈判启动前，都要对经济层面进行详细分析。

相比之下，国际经济分析更为严谨。只要简单看一下国际经济学教科书，就能发现经济学家并不一定相信贸易谈判人员所用概念的有效性，或他们的成果。

大量词条基于世界贸易组织 (WTO) 及其成员的工作。WTO 是制定多边贸易政策的最重要场所。需要强调的是，WTO 中使用的许多词语和概念对于 WTO 主持下的相关进程的参与者而言有着确切的含义。要表达这些准确的含义有时需要进行很长的解释，而这一点并不一定有所帮助。我因而尝试对这些含义进行概括。因此，所有的解释均为我本人所作，这些解释在 WTO 中并无法律地位。

I have also drawn on the trade-related work of other international organizations. Chief among these are the United Nations Conference on Trade and Development (UNCTAD), the Organisation for Economic Co-operation and Development (OECD) and Asia-Pacific Economic Cooperation (APEC). The work programmes of these organizations have yielded many items of relevance to a dictionary of this kind, but a comprehensive coverage of their activities would have been beyond the scope of this book.

Some entries are longer than is customary in dictionaries. Some are unquestionably longer than they should be. Still, I think that the reader should be offered, for example, a small historical survey of important concepts like the most-favoured-nation principle, the place of developing countries in the multilateral trading system, attempts to deal satisfactorily with agriculture and agricultural products, or major events like the Kennedy, Tokyo and Uruguay Rounds. The aim of these longer items is to offer a broader perspective of the basic issues and concepts inherent in them as well as their achievements.

Other items might be considered obsolete. At first glance the New International Economic Order might fall into this category. I have included it because some of its elements remain of interest to developing countries, though they might be expressed in different language today.

Some entries are idiosyncratic, or at least the reader may think, with a deal of justification no doubt, that they are. That, I am afraid, is in the nature of books. Some entries are of historical significance only. Among these are the Atlantic Charter, the Havana Charter, the Global Negotiations, the Marshall Plan, the Haberler Report and the United Nations Conference on Trade and Employment. One thing these entries do, however, is to show how persistent some of the problems of international trade policy are, and how hard it can be to find lasting solutions for them.

The main focus of trade policy formulation tends to change over the years. This is of course reflected in this dictionary. For example, a major recent achievement in the multilateral trade negotiations has been the conclusion of the WTO Agreement on Trade Facilitation. It will have a positive impact on the global trading environment. Its negotiation has drawn attention to the efforts of many organizations, many of them non-governmental, that have defined and promoted the issues involved, sometimes for many years. The work of the United Nations Economic Commission for Europe (UN-ECE) should be mentioned in particular. I hope that the new entries on this topic reflect some of the diversity of these organizations. In the meantime, some of the focus has shifted to investment facilitation, but it isfar too early to predict how the international community will approach this topic.

I have retained the few brief descriptions of pre-WTO trade disputes. As I said in the preface to the fifth edition, no dictionary covering trade policy could be complete without a mention of *Hatters' fur or Belgian family allowances*.

我还借鉴了其他国际组织与贸易有关的工作，主要包括联合国贸易与发展会议 (UNCTAD)、经济合作与发展组织 (OECD) 以及亚太经济合作组织 (APEC)。这些组织的工作计划产生了许多与此类辞典相关的词条，但是如全面涵盖这些组织的活动则超出了本辞典的范围。

一些词条要比辞典的惯常解释更长一些。其中一些词条显然超出了应有的长度。然而，我认为应该向读者提供一些重要概念的历史发展情况，例如最惠国原则、发展中国家在多边贸易体制中的地位、妥善处理农业和农产品问题的尝试，或者如“肯尼迪回合”“东京回合”和“乌拉圭回合”等重大事件。编写这些较长词条的目的在于对这些词条所包含的基本问题和概念以及成果提供更广阔的视角。

其他一些词条也许会被认为已经过时。“国际经济新秩序”初看即可能属于此类。我之所以将之收录其中，是因为一些所含要素对发展中国家仍然感兴趣，而如今是以另一种语言方式表述。一些词条是独特的，或者至少读者可能如此认为，毫无疑问是有道理的。我想，这可能就是本辞典的性质所在。

有些词条仅具有历史意义，例如“大西洋宪章”“哈瓦那宪章”“全球谈判”“马歇尔计划”“哈伯勒报告”和“联合国贸易与就业会议”。然而，收录这些词条的目的之一是为表明国际贸易政策中的一些问题如何持续存在及找到持久解决办法有多么困难。

贸易政策制定的主要关注点往往随着时间的推移而发生变化。此点当然也体现在本辞典中。例如，多边贸易谈判最近取得的一项主要成果是 WTO《贸易便利化协定》。该协定将对全球贸易环境产生积极影响。这一谈判使人们注意到很多组织所作出的努力，其中很多是非政府组织，这些组织界定和推动了其中所涉议题，有的已经进行数年。联合国欧洲经济委员会 (UN-ECE) 的工作特别值得一提。我希望关于这一议题的最新词条能够反映这些组织的多样性。与此同时，一些关注点已经转向投资便利化，但预测国际社会将如何处理这一议题为时尚早。

我保留了 WTO 建立前的贸易争端的一些简要介绍。正如我在第 5 版序言中所说的，如不提及“裘皮女帽案”或“比利时家庭津贴案”，

Those interested in the full picture of GATT dispute settlement from its beginning to the establishment of the WTO now have access to *GATT Disputes: 1948–1995*, a two-volume compilation of all cases (316 of them at the time of included a few references to disputes brought before the WTO since 1995. These are included in their entirety in Dispute Settlement Reports, published annually by the WTO and Cambridge University Press.

A word about entries concerning the European Union. It appears in GATT and WTO documents as the European Economic Community, European Community, European Communities and, since 2009, definitively as the European Union. In this edition I use European Union wherever possible, except when this clearly would be an anachronistic usage. The differences between the various names matter to international trade lawyers (who know them anyway), but they might make things needlessly complicated for the purpose of this book.

Entries are in alphabetical order, usually in their most common form. Examples are Kyoto Convention for the International Convention on the Simplification and Harmonization of Customs Procedures, UNCTAD for the United Nations Conference on Trade and Development and CITES for the Convention on International Trade in Endangered Species of Wild Fauna and Flora. In each case I have also included the formal version of the entry, with a referral to the main entry.

Entries are mostly self-contained, but in a few cases I thought it useful to duplicate partly an explanation under a different entry. Many entries contain referrals in italic bold to other entries offering additional or related material. Readers should use these referrals as they like. Occasionally they may find something in this way that they had forgotten or didn't know. References to the WTO are so frequent that there seemed little need to provide a crossreference when they occur.

I would like to thank Finola O'Sullivan of Cambridge University Press who encouraged me to consider preparing a new edition, and to Marianne Nield who helped me along in many ways. At the WTO I would like to thank KeithRockwell and Anthony Martin for their continuing support for this book. My special thanks go to Heather Sapey-Pertin for the many suggestions for improvements. Finally I also offer my gratitude to Professor Kenneth Armstrong of Cambridge University who was kind enough to offer some clarifications concerning European Union law.

It is obvious that I have benefited from the efforts of many, but responsibility for any errors of fact, inadequate interpretation or infelicitous expressions is, as authors usually say, entirely mine.

Walter Goode

任何贸易政策辞典都是不完整的。对自 GATT 临时适用到 WTO 建立的争端解决的总体情况感兴趣的人，现在可以查阅 WTO 出版的包含所有争端案件及其程序的 2 卷本《GATT 争端：1948—1995》一书(书籍编写时共有 316 起案件)。还包括了 1995 年以来提交 WTO 的一些争端。这些争端全部收录在 WTO 与剑桥大学出版社每年出版的《争端解决报告》中。

需要对涉及欧洲联盟的词条作出说明。欧洲联盟在 GATT 和 WTO 文件中先后以欧洲经济共同体、欧洲共同体以及自 2009 年起最终以欧洲联盟等表述出现。在本辞典中，我尽可能使用欧洲联盟的表述，除非在这样使用不合时宜的情况下。各名称之间的差别对国际贸易律师而言是有意义的(他们反正知道这些差别)，但就本辞典而言，这些名称可能使事情变得不必要地复杂化。

词条通常以其最常见的形式按字母顺序排序。例如，以《京都公约》代表《关于简化和协调海关业务制度的国际公约》、以 UNCTAD 代表联合国贸易与发展会议、以 CITES 代表《濒危野生动植物种国际贸易公约》。在每一此类词条下，我列出了词条的正式名称，并提及主词条。

大部分词条是自成一体的，但在少数情况下，我认为重复另一词条下的部分解释会有所帮助。许多词条中以斜体加粗字体提及其他词条，以提供补充或相关信息。读者可按自己意愿使用这些参考词条。有时，读者可能会以此种方式找到他们忘记或不知道的信息。WTO 被多次提及，因此似乎不需要提供交叉引用。

感谢剑桥大学出版社的菲诺拉·奥沙利文，她鼓励我编写本辞典的新版本。还要感谢玛丽安娜·尼尔德，她在许多方面给我提供了帮助。感谢 WTO 的基思·罗克韦尔和安东尼·马丁一直以来对本书的支持。特别感谢希瑟·萨佩－珀丁提出的许多改进建议。最后，感谢剑桥大学的肯尼思·阿姆斯特朗教授，他非常友好，为我澄清了涉及欧盟法律的问题。

很显然，我得益于很多人所作的努力。但是就像作者们通常要讲的那样，对任何事实错误、不充分的解释或不恰当的表述，我负全责。

沃尔特·古德

图例

请按照英文字母顺序查找参考词条

主词条(按英文字母排序)

文中参考词条(***斜体加粗***部分)

WTO: World Trade Organization, established on 1 January 1995 as the successor to the ***GATT*** (*General Agreement on Tariffs and Trade*) and its secretariat. Among the agreements it manages are the ***General Agreement on Trade in Services*** (GATS) and the ***Agreement on Trade-Related Aspects of Intellectual Property Rights***. In August 2019 the WTO had 164 members. The WTO is an organization for the discussion, negotiation and resolution of trade issues covering goods, services and intellectual property. Its essential functions are administering and implementing the multilateral and plurilateral trade agreements that constitute it, acting as a forum for ***multilateral trade negotiations***, seeking to resolve trade disputes, overseeing national trade policies and cooperating with other international institutions involved in global economic policy-making. *See also* **WTO Agreement**.

文末参考词条(***斜体加粗***部分)

文中参考词条(***斜体加粗***部分)

图例

请按照英文字母顺序查找参考词条

主词条(按英文字母排序)

文中参考词条(下划线部分)

WTO
世界贸易组织

1995年1月1日作为GATT及其秘书处的后继组织建立。所管理的协定包括《服务贸易总协定》(GATS)和《与贸易有关的知识产权协定》。截至2019年8月，WTO共有164个成员(截至2024年8月，WTO共有166个成员—译注)。WTO中讨论、谈判和解决涵盖货物、服务和知识产权的贸易问题的组织。基本职能是管理和实施多边和诸边贸易协定，作为多边贸易谈判的场所，寻求解决贸易争端，监督各国贸易政策以及与涉及全球贸易政策制定的其他国际组织开展合作。另见*WTO协定(WTO Agreement)*。

文末参考词条(*斜体*部分)

文中参考词条(下划线部分)

目 录

2030 Agenda for Sustainable Development: *see* ***Sustainable Development Goals***.

Abnormal international market conditions: described formally by the ***Agricultural Market Information System*** as "typically characterized by significant price movements in several commodity markets leading to serious negative impacts". It notes that instances of abnormally low prices could also fall into this category. [www.amis-outlook.org]

Absolute advantage: the ability of an individual firm or country to produce a good or service at a lower unit cost than a similar entity that produces the good or service elsewhere. It originates with Adam Smith who argued that international trade allows a greater specialization than would be possible in an autarkic system, thereby permitting resources to be used more efficiently. *See also* ***autarky***, ***comparative advantage***, ***gains-from-trade theory***, ***Heckscher-Ohlin theorem***, ***self-reliance*** and ***self-sufficiency***. [Smith 1991 (1776)]

Absolute standard: *see* ***minimum standard of treatment***.

Absorption: countering the higher tariffs resulting from ***anti-dumping measures*** through lowering the price of the good. The producer or exporter of the good absorbs the additional cost caused by higher tariffs to preserve his place in the market. *See also* ***anti-absorption*** and ***circumvention***.

Absorption principle: also known as "roll-up" principle, used in the administration of ***preferential rules of origin*** under ***free-trade agreements***. It means that in defined cases, usually after they have undergone specific processing requirements in the territory of a free-trade partner, the ***non-originating materials*** forming part of a good to be imported will not be included in the calculation of the ***regional value content*** of that good. They will be deemed to be ***originating materials***. *See also* ***substantial transformation***.

Abuja Treaty establishing the African Economic Community: *see* ***African Economic Community***. Also ***African Continental Free Trade Area*** and ***African regional economic integration***.

Accelerated tariff liberalization: ATL. The final stage of the ***APEC*** initiative for ***Early Voluntary Sectoral Liberalization***. APEC ministers decided in Kuala Lumpur in November 1998 to transfer the tariff elements of the first nine sectors of this initiative to the WTO. The nine sectors were forest products, fish and fish products, toys, gems and jewellery, chemicals, medical equipment and instruments, environmental goods and services, energy, and a telecommunications mutual recognition agreement. ATL then was deemed

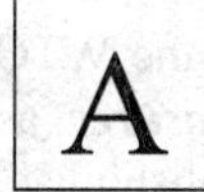

2030 Agenda for Sustainable Development
2030年可持续发展议程
见*可持续发展目标(Sustainable Development Goals)*。

Abnormal international market conditions
国际市场异常情况
农产品市场信息系统将其正式描述为“具有若干商品市场中价格大幅波动导致严重消极影响的典型特征”。同时指出，价格异常低的情况也可属此类情况。

Absolute advantage
绝对优势
指一公司或一国可以低于其他地方生产一货物或服务的类似实体的单位成本生产货物或服务的能力。这一概念源自亚当·斯密，他认为国际贸易与自给自足体制相比可提供的专业化程度更高，因而可使资源得到更有效利用。另见*经济闭关自守(autarky)*、*比较优势(comparative advantage)*、*贸易利得理论(gains-from-trade theory)*、*赫克舍尔-奥林定理(Heckscher-Ohlin theorem)*、*自力更生(self-reliance)*、*自给自足(self-sufficiency)*。

Absolute standard
绝对标准
见*最低待遇标准(minimum standard of treatment)*。

Absorption
吸收
通过降低商品价格以应对反倾销措施所产生的更高关税。货物的生产商或出口商为保住自己在市场中的地位而吸收了高关税所导致的额外成本。另见*反吸收(anti-absorption)*、*规避(circumvention)*。

Absorption principle
吸收原则
又称“总成”原则，在自由贸易协定项下优惠原产地规则的管理中使用。指在明确规定的情况下，部分组成一货物的进口非原产材料在一自由贸易伙伴领土内满足特定加工工序要求后，通常将不再包含在该货物的区域价值成分的计算中。这些材料将被视为原产材料。另见*实质性改变(substantial transformation)*。

Abuja Treaty establishing the African Economic Community
建立非洲经济共同体的阿布贾条约
见*非洲经济共同体(African Economic Community)*。另见*非洲大陆自由贸易区(African Continental Free Trade Area)*、*非洲区域经济一体化(African regional economic integration)*。

Accelerated tariff liberalization
加速关税自由化
ATL。APEC部门自愿提前自由化倡议的最后阶段。APEC各成员部长于1998年11月在吉隆坡决定将该倡议的最初9个部门的关税部分转交WTO。9个部门分别是林产品、水产品、玩具、珠宝、化工、医疗器械、环境、能源和电信

to have been subsumed in the negotiations under the ***Doha Development Agenda***.

Acceptable level of risk: defined in the WTO ***Agreement on the Application of Sanitary and Phytosanitary Measures*** as "the level of protection deemed appropriate by the Member establishing a sanitary or phytosanitary measure to protect human, animal or plant life or health within its territory". The level varies according to country, but it is meant to be based on scientific principles. The ***precautionary principle*** may also apply. This concept is also known as the "appropriate level of sanitary or phytosanitary protection". *See also* ***sanitary and phytosanitary measures***.

Accession: the act of becoming a member of the WTO (World Trade Organization), or another international organization or agreement. Negotiations are usually limited to ensuring that the acceding country or customs territory can meet its membership obligations. Accession to the WTO thus requires negotiations between the applicant and the existing members to ensure that the applicant's trade regime will be in harmony with WTO rules, and that the applicant is able to observe these rules. On accession, the schedules of tariffs and services commitments the new member offers should be broadly comparable to those of existing members which have participated in successive rounds of ***multilateral trade negotiations*** and reduced their trade barriers over the years. In other words, a country or customs territory has to be prepared to offer roughly the same as it will enjoy from membership. Accession to the ***OECD*** requires new members to show that their economic regime is broadly in tune with those of existing members. Membership of ***UNCTAD*** or other United Nations bodies does not entail this sort of obligation. Accession to the ***European Union*** is known as ***enlargement***. *See also* ***Group of Article XII***, ***schedules of specific commitments on services*** and ***schedule of concessions***.

Access to medicines: an aspect of the work on ***intellectual property rights*** in the WTO. It deals with the balance between obligations under the ***Agreement on Trade-Related Aspects of Intellectual Property Rights*** (TRIPS) and the expectations of developing countries for affordable medicines. Developing countries claim that ***compulsory licensing*** and ***parallel imports*** are essential for their governments to carry out effective health policies through affordable medicines. In their view, the TRIPS agreement is biased in favour of pharmaceutical companies residing in developed countries. The differing views on access to medicines show the inherent tension between intellectual property rights (a form of monopoly rights) and public expectations of vigorous competition between companies. The Doha ***Declaration on the TRIPS Agreement and Public Health*** was aimed at reducing this tension. It aimed to make it easier for some developing countries seeking the required authorization to grant a compulsory licence for the purpose of making a pharmaceutical product and exporting it to ***least-developed countries*** and other developing countries which are also members of the WTO. This was subject to the condition that the system would only be used in case of a national emergency or in cases of public

设备相互认可安排。ATL随后被认为已并入多哈发展议程项下的谈判中。

Acceptable level of risk

可接受的风险水平

WTO《实施卫生与植物卫生措施协定》将其定义为“制定卫生与植物卫生措施以保护其领土内的人类、动物或植物的生命或健康的成员所认为适当的保护水平。”该水平因国家不同而不同，但意味着应基于科学原理。预防原则也可适用。该概念又称“适当的卫生或植物卫生保护水平”。另见*卫生与植物卫生措施(sanitary and phytosanitary measures)*。

Accession

加入

成为WTO成员或另一国际组织或协定成员的行为。谈判通常限于保证申请加入国或单独关税区能够遵守其成员义务。因此，加入WTO需要申请方与现有成员进行谈判，以保证申请方的贸易制度将与WTO规则相一致，且申请方能够遵守这些规则。在加入时，新成员提供的关税减让表和服务贸易具体承诺减让表总体上应可与现有成员相比较，这些现有成员已参加多轮多边贸易谈判，并历经多年削减贸易壁垒。换言之，一国或一关税地区需要准备作出大体相同的出价方可享受成员资格。加入经济合作与发展组织(OECD)要求新成员证明其经济制度与现有成员的经济制度大体一致。联合国贸易与发展会议(UNCTAD)或其他联合国机构的成员资格无此类义务。加入欧盟称为扩盟。另见*第12条协调组(Group of Article XII)*、*服务贸易具体承诺减让表(schedules of specific commitments on services)*、*减让表(schedule of concessions)*。

Access to medicines

获得药品

WTO中知识产权工作的一个方面，处理《与贸易有关的知识产权协定》(TRIPS)项下的义务与发展中国家对负担得起药品的期望之间的平衡。发展中国家主张强制许可和平行进口对于政府通过负担得起的药品实施有效健康政策十分必要。在它们看来，《TRIPS协定》偏袒设在发达国家中的制药公司。对获得药品的不同观点表明，知识产权(一种垄断权利)与公司间激烈竞争的公众期望之间存在着内在紧张关系。多哈《关于<与贸易有关的知识产权协定>与公共健康的宣言》旨在缓解这种紧张关系，宣言旨在使一些发展中国家更容易获得它们所寻求的生产药品的强制许可授权，以出口至同属WTO成员的最不发达国家和其他发展中国家。需要满足的条件是，这一制度仅可用于国家紧急

non-commercial use. *See also* ***Paragraph 6 System*** which resolved the matter permanently.

Accordion of likeness: an expression used by the ***Appellate Body*** in *Japan – Taxes on Alcoholic Beverages*. It holds that the meaning of the term ***"like product"*** has to be interpreted more or less generously according to the nature of the product itself. It says that there can be no precise and absolute definition of what is "like". In its words, "[t]he accordion of 'likeness' stretches and squeezes in different places as the provisions of the ***WTO Agreement*** are applied". [WT/DS8/AB/R]

Accounting rate: the charge made by one country's telephone network operator for transporting calls originating in another network to their final destinations within the second network. *See also* ***telecommunications termination services***.

ACP-EC Sugar Protocol: first concluded in 1975 as Protocol 3 to the ***Lomé Convention***, but the concept has a longer history. It later became part of the ACP-EC Partnership Agreement, now the ***ACP-EU Partnership Agreement***. The Protocol gave selected ***ACP states*** guaranteed sugar access quotas to the European Community. It expired in 2009, partly as result of a successful challenge to its legality under the ***WTO*** rules, and also partly in response to changes in the global sugar market. ACP countries as well as the countries benefiting from the European Union's ***Everything But Arms*** initiative now have duty-free and quota-free access to the European Union sugar market.

ACP-EU Partnership Agreement: signed in Cotonou on 23 June 2000 as the successor to the ***Lomé Convention***. The agreement was concluded for twenty years and expired in February 2020. The fundamental principles following its review in 2010 were: (a) equality of the partners and ownership of the development strategies, (b) central governments are the main partners, but the partnership is open also to ACP parliaments, local authorities in ACP states and different kinds of other actors, (c) a pivotal role of dialogue and the fulfilment of mutual obligations and accountability, and (d) differentiation and regionalization so that cooperation arrangements and priorities vary according to the partner's level of development. Negotiations are under way for a new agreement which is expected to build, *inter alia*, on the ***United Nations 2030 Agenda for Sustainable Development***.

ACP states: The African, Caribbean and Pacific states associated with the ***European Community*** through the ***ACP-EU Partnership Agreement***. The group of ACP states was established on 6 June 1975 through the ***Georgetown Agreement***. It now operates under a revised agreement adopted in November 1992. Its General Secretariat is located in Brussels. The main objectives of the group of ACP states are: (a) sustainable development of the member states and their gradual integration into the global economy, (b) activities coordination in the framework of ACP-EU partnership agreements, (c) consolidation of unity and solidarity, and (d) establishment of peace and stability in a free and democratic society. The members of the group are Angola, Antigua and Barbuda, Bahamas, Barbados, Belize, Benin, Botswana, Burkina Faso, Burundi,

状态或公共非商业性使用。另见永久解决这一问题的*第6段制度(Paragraph 6 System)*。

Accordion of likeness

符合同类性

《日本酒类税案上诉机构报告》中使用的表述。上诉机构认为，“同类产品”这一词语的含义需要根据产品本身的性质或多或少加以宽泛解释。上诉机构称，“同类”一词没有准确和绝对的定义。指出，“同类性像手风琴一样随着《WTO协定》条款的适用之处不同而放松或收紧。”

Accounting rate

结算价

一国电话网络运营商将源自另一个网络的通话转接至位于第二网络中的最终目的地的费用。另见*电信终端服务(telecommunications termination services)*。

ACP-EC Sugar Protocol

非加太地区国家与欧共体食糖议定书

最初订于1975年，作为《洛美协定》的《第三个议定书》，而这一概念的历史更为悠久。后成为《非加太地区国家与欧共体伙伴关系协定》的一部分，现称《非加太地区国家与欧盟伙伴关系协定》。议定书保证部分非加太地区国家获得欧洲共同体食糖配额。议定书于2009年失效，部分原因是根据WTO规则对其合法性的挑战获得成功，部分原因是应对全球食糖市场的变化。非加太地区国家及受益于欧盟除武器外的所有产品倡议的国家现在可以免关税和免配额进入欧盟食糖市场。

ACP-EU Partnership Agreement

非加太地区国家与欧盟伙伴关系协定

作为《洛美协定》的后继协定于2000年6月23日在科托努签署。协定在缔结20年后于2020年2月失效。2010年审议后的基本原则为：(a)合作伙伴的平等和发展战略的所有权；(b)中央政府是主要合作伙伴，且该伙伴关系也对非加太地区国家议会、非加太地区国家地方政府和不同类型的其他主体开放；(c)对话具有关键作用，履行相互义务和问责制；以及(d)差异化和区域化，从而使合作安排和优先事项依合作伙伴发展水平而有所不同。目前正在就一项新协定进行谈判，预计该协定将特别以联合国2030年可持续发展议程为基础。

ACP states

非加太地区国家

通过《非加太地区国家与欧盟伙伴关系协定》与欧洲共同体建立联系的非洲、加勒比海和太平洋国家。非加太地区国家集团通过《乔治敦协定》于1975年6月6日建立，目前根据1992年11月通过的修订协定运行。总秘书处设在布鲁塞尔。非加太地区国家集团的主要目标为：(a)成员国的可持续发展及其逐步融入全球经济；(b)在《非加太地区国家与欧盟伙伴关系协定》框架内开展活动协调；(c)巩固团结一致；以及(d)在自由和民主的社会中构建和平与稳定。集团成员包括：安哥拉、安提瓜和巴布达、巴哈马、巴巴多斯、伯利兹、贝宁、博茨瓦纳、布基纳法索、布隆迪、佛得角、喀麦隆、中非共和国、乍得、科摩

Cabo Verde, Cameroon, Central African Republic, Chad, Comoros, Republic of Congo, Democratic Republic of Congo, Cook Islands, Côte d'Ivoire, Cuba, Djibouti, Dominica, Dominican Republic, Eritrea, Eswatini, Ethiopia, Fiji, Gabon, The Gambia, Ghana, Grenada, Equatorial Guinea, Guinea, Guinea-Bissau, Guyana, Haiti, Jamaica, Kenya, Kiribati, Lesotho, Liberia, Madagascar, Malawi, Mali, Marshall Islands, Mauritania, Mauritius, Federated States of Micronesia, Mozambique, Namibia, Nauru, Niger, Nigeria, Niue, Palau, Papua New Guinea, Rwanda, Saint Kitts and Nevis, Saint Lucia, Saint Vincent and the Grenadines, Samoa, Sao Tome and Principe, Senegal, Seychelles, Sierra Leone, Solomon Islands, Somalia, South Africa, Sudan, Suriname, Tanzania, Togo, Tonga, Trinidad and Tobago, Tuvalu, Uganda, Vanuatu, Zambia and Zimbabwe. Cuba is not a party to the ACP-EU Partnership Agreement.

Acquis communautaire*:** all legislation adopted under the treaties establishing the ***European Union, including ***regulations***, ***directives***, ***decisions***, ***recommendations*** and ***opinions***, as well as the judgments handed down by the ***Court of Justice of the European Union*** and international agreements concluded by the European Union from 1959 to the present. Before a country accedes to the European Union, its national legislation needs to be harmonized with the *acquis communautaire*. This can mean revising hundreds of parliamentary acts. European Union law prevails over national law. No member state may derogate permanently from the *acquis*. *See also* ***enlargement***, ***European Union legislation*** and ***European Union treaties***.

Actionable subsidies: a category of subsidies described in the WTO ***Agreement on Subsidies and Countervailing Measures***. Subsidies may be actionable, and therefore illegal, if they cause ***injury*** to the domestic industry of another member, negate other commitments made under the GATT, or cause ***serious prejudice*** to the interests of another member. If such adverse effects exist, the country maintaining the subsidy must withdraw it or remove its adverse effects. *See also* ***non-actionable subsidies***, ***prohibited subsidies*** and ***subsidies***.

Action plan: a list of actions to be carried out individually or collectively. Sometimes it is no more than a device to keep a process going when it has run into difficulties. Too often the plan is far too ambitious to stand any chance of being carried out. At other times it represents a genuine attempt to develop an agenda capable of leading to the solution of a raft of problems.

Action Plan for Boosting Intra-African Trade: issued in 2012 by the ***African Union*** and the United Nations ***Economic Commission for Africa***. One of the stepping stones to the realization of the ***African Continental Free Trade Area***. The Action Plan contains several priority programme clusters: (I) Trade Policy: fast-tracking intra-African trade development, (II) Trade Facilitation: reducing the time it takes to move goods from point A to point B, (III) Productive Capacity: creating regional and continental value chains or complementarity, (IV) Trade-Related Infrastructure: development of innovative legal, financial and other mechanisms for multi-country infrastructural development projects, (V) Trade Finance: develop and strengthen African financial institutions and

罗、刚果(布)、刚果(金)、库克群岛、科特迪瓦、古巴、吉布提、多米尼克、多米尼加、厄立特里亚、斯威士兰、埃塞俄比亚、斐济、加蓬、冈比亚、加纳、格林纳达、赤道几内亚、几内亚、几内亚比绍、圭亚那、海地、牙买加、肯尼亚、基里巴斯、莱索托、利比里亚、马达加斯加、马拉维、马里、马绍尔群岛、毛里塔尼亚、毛里求斯、密克罗尼西亚联邦、莫桑比克、纳米比亚、瑙鲁、尼日尔、尼日利亚、纽埃、帕劳、巴布亚新几内亚、卢旺达、圣基茨和尼维斯、圣文森特和格林纳丁斯、萨摩亚、圣多美和普林西比、塞内加尔、塞舌尔、塞拉利昂、所罗门群岛、索马里、南非、苏丹、苏里南、坦桑尼亚、多哥、汤加、特立尼达和多巴哥、图瓦卢、乌干达、瓦努阿图、赞比亚和津巴布韦，古巴不属《非加太地区国家与欧盟伙伴关系协定》缔约方。

Acquis communautaire
欧盟现行法

根据建立欧盟的条约通过的所有立法，包括条例、指令、决定、建议和意见以及欧洲法院公布的判决和欧盟自1959年至今缔结的国际协定。在一国加入欧盟之前，其国家立法需要与欧盟现行法相协调。这可能意味着需要修改数百项议会法案。欧盟法律优先于国家法律。任何成员国不得永久偏离现行法。另见*扩盟(enlargement)*、*欧洲联盟立法(European Union legislation)*、*欧洲联盟主要条约(European Union treaties)*。

Actionable subsidies
可诉补贴

WTO《补贴与反补贴措施协定》中所描述的一类补贴。如补贴对另一成员的国内产业造成损害，使其在GATT项下所作其他承诺无效，或对另一成员的利益造成严重侵害，则此类补贴可以是可诉的，因而是非法的。如此类不利影响存在，则维持补贴的国家必须撤销补贴或消除其不利影响。另见*不可诉补贴(non-actionable subsidies)*、*禁止性补贴(prohibited subsidies)*、*补贴(subsidies)*。

Action plan
行动计划

一份单独或集体执行的行动清单。有时清单只不过是在遇到困难时保持进程继续的手段。很多时候由于计划过于雄心勃勃而没有任何执行的可能性。其他时候则意味着为制定一项能够解决大量问题的议程而作出的真正尝试。

Action Plan for Boosting Intra-African Trade
促进非洲内部贸易行动计划

非洲联盟和联合国非洲经济委员会于2012年发布，是实现非洲大陆自由贸易区的敲门砖之一。行动计划包含若干优先项目：(1)贸易政策：快速跟踪非洲内部贸易发展情况；(2)贸易便利化：减少将货物从A点运至B点所需时间；(3)生产能力：创建区域和大陆价值链或互补机制；(4)与贸易有关的基础设施：为多国基础设施发展计划设立创新性法律、金融和其他机制；(5)贸易金融：发展和加强非洲金融机构和机制，以促进非洲内部贸易和投资；(6)贸易信息：

mechanisms to promote intra-African trade and investment, (VI) Trade Information: bridging the information gap, and (VII) Factor Market Integration: increase regional mobility of labour. *See also* ***African regional economic integration***.

Act of state doctrine: the principle, as expressed in a United States Supreme Court judgment of 1897, that "every sovereign State is bound to respect the independence of every other sovereign State, and the courts of one country will not sit in judgment on the acts of the government of another, done within its own territory". Other jurisdictions of course also use versions of this doctrine.

Adding-up problem: *see* ***fallacy of composition***.

Additional commitments: the ***General Agreement on Trade in Services*** permits WTO members to make ***commitments*** on trade in services that are additional to those made under ***market access*** and ***national treatment***. Qualifications, standards and licensing matters are mentioned specifically, but additional commitments need not be confined to these areas. *See also* ***schedules of specific commitments on services***.

Additive manufacturing: AM. The technology to build three-dimensional (3D) objects by adding layer upon layer of material in a process analogue to printing, usually called 3D-printing.

Additive regionalism: describes the concurrent membership of several ***free-trade agreements*** by one country. *See also* ***multilateralization of free-trade agreements*** and ***spaghetti-bowl effect***. [Schiff and Winters 2003]

Adjusted value: *see* ***build-down method*** and ***build-up method***.

Adjustment costs: the economic and social costs arising from ***structural adjustment***.

Administered protection: *see* ***contingent protection*** and ***non-tariff measures***.

Administered trade: *see* ***managed trade***.

Administrative guidance: the practice of influencing the activities of an industry by government ministries through formal or informal measures. Guidance may simply consist of advice on how to interpret a government act or decision. It may also be a method of enforcing, for example, voluntary export restraints through the publication of indicative production and export forecasts. Industries are then supposed to work out among themselves how to divide the export cake. Administrative guidance of the second kind probably works best in countries where the enforcement of ***competition policy*** is weak.

Administrative international commodity agreements: these are ***international commodity agreements*** that do not operate a ***buffer stock***, ***export quotas*** or other mechanism designed to influence the price of a commodity through manipulating the amount coming on the market. This type of agreement is concerned with matters such as ***market transparency***, more efficient production, processing and distribution, consumer information, and the collection and dissemination of statistical information. *See also* ***economic international commodity agreements***.

弥合信息差距；以及(7)要素市场一体化：增加劳动力的区域流动性。另见*非洲区域经济一体化(African regional economic integration)*。

Act of state doctrine
国家行为原则

美国最高法院1897年判决中所表述的原则，即“每一主权国家必须尊重其他主权国家的独立性，并且一国的法院无权对另一国政府在其领土内的行为进行裁决”。其他管辖范围也当然适用这一原则的不同版本。

Adding-up problem
总额相符问题

见*合成谬误(fallacy of composition)*。

Additional commitments
附加承诺

《服务贸易总协定》允许WTO成员就服务贸易作出其在市场准入和国民待遇承诺下的附加承诺。具体提及资格、标准和许可事项，但附加承诺不仅限于这些领域。另见*服务贸易具体承诺减让表(schedules of specific commitments on services)*。

Additive manufacturing
增材制造

AM。通过在类似于打印的过程中一层一层添加材料以构建三维(3D)对象的技术，通常称为3D打印。

Additive regionalism
叠加式区域主义

一国同时拥有若干自由贸易协定成员资格的情形。另见*自由贸易协定多边化(multilateralization of free-trade agreements)*、*意大利面碗效应(spaghetti-bowl effect)*。

Adjusted value
调整价格

见*扣减法(build-down method)*、*增值法(build-up method)*。

Adjustment costs
调整成本

因结构性调整产生的经济和社会成本。

Administered protection
行政保护

见*紧急保护(contingent protection)*、*非关税措施(non-tariff measures)*。

Administered trade
管理贸易

见*受管制的贸易(managed trade)*。

Administrative guidance
行政指导

政府部门通过正式或非正式措施影响一产业行为的做法。指导可以仅为关于如何解释一项政府法案或决定的建议，还可以是一种执行的方法，例如通过发布指示性生产和出口预测实施的自愿出口限制。需要各行业自行计算如何切分出口蛋糕。第二种行政指导可能在竞争政策执行薄弱的国家中发挥最佳效果。

Administrative international commodity agreements
国际商品管理协定

不采用旨在通过操纵市场投放数量而影响一商品价格的缓冲储存、出口配额或其他机制的国际商品协定。此类协定关注的事项为市场透明度、更有效生产、加工和分销以及统计信息的收集和传播等。另见*国际商品经济协定(economic international commodity agreements)*。

Administrative protection: *see* ***contingent protection*** and ***non-tariff measures***.

Administrative regulation: *see* ***regulation***.

Administrative ruling of general application: defined in the ***APEC principles on transparency standards*** and some ***free-trade agreements***, such as ***NAFTA***, as "an administrative ruling or interpretation that applies to all persons and fact situations that fall generally within its ambit and that establishes a norm of conduct, but does not include: (a) a determination or ruling made in an administrative or quasi-judicial proceeding that applies to a particular person, good or service of another economy in a specific case, or (b) a ruling that adjudicates with respect to a particular act or practice". In other words, an administrative ruling of general application establishes a norm of conduct applying to all persons, goods, services and practices, as the case may be, in a given economy.

Ad **notes:** the notes and explanatory provisions contained in Annex I to the **GATT**. They amplify and interpret some of the GATT articles proper. They always have to be read together with the relevant article.

Ad referendum **agreement:** provisional acceptance of the outcome of a set of negotiations. Definitive acceptance may depend on the results of related negotiations, approval by the government or the fulfilment of some other condition. *See also* ***bracketed language*** and ***without prejudice***.

Ad valorem**:** a proportion of the value of a good or a transaction. *See* ***ad valorem tariff***.

Ad valorem **equivalent:** a calculation of the level of a ***specific tariff***, which converts a rate expressed as a fixed monetary value per product into a value expressed as a percentage of the value of the product. This gives the ***ad valorem tariff*** rate. For example, a specific tariff of one dollar levied on an item worth ten dollars would give an *ad valorem* equivalent of 10 per cent. On an item worth twenty dollars, a tariff of one dollar would amount to 5 per cent. *See also* ***compound tariff***.

Ad valorem **tariff:** a ***tariff*** rate expressed as a percentage of the value of the goods to be imported or exported. Most tariffs are now expressed in this form. *See also* ***customs valuation*** and ***specific tariff***.

Advance deposit: the requirement to lodge all or part of the cost of the imported good with a government authority, usually at the time it is ordered. *See also* ***non-tariff measures***.

Advance informed consent: an obligation embodied in the ***Cartagena Protocol on Biosafety***. It establishes the need for an exporter to seek consent from an importing country before the first shipment of a ***living modified organism*** intended for intentional release into the environment. *See also* ***prior informed consent***.

Advance rulings: an aspect of customs procedures. Many customs authorities provide advice on request, normally in writing, on how they will treat a good to be imported. Such advice may include the tariff classification, the applicable tariff rate and whether a good qualifies for ***preferential market access***. Such

Administrative protection
行政保护

见*紧急保护(contingent protection)*、*非关税措施(non-tariff measures)*。

Administrative regulation
行政管制

见*管制(regulation)*。

Administrative ruling of general application
普遍适用的行政裁定

APEC透明度标准原则和《北美自由贸易协定》(NAFTA)等部分自由贸易协定中定义为，"适用于通常属于其范围的所有人和事实情况并确立一种行为规范的行政裁定或解释，但不包括：(a)一具体案件中行政或准司法程序作出的适用于另一经济体的特定人、货物或服务的决定或裁定；或(b)对一特定行为或做法作出的裁定"。换言之，普遍适用的行政裁定确立一种适用于一指定经济体中所有人、货物、服务和做法(视情况而定)的行为规范。

***Ad* notes**
补充注释

GATT附录I中所含注释和解释性规定。这些注释和规定对部分GATT条款本身进行了补充和解释，需要与相关条款一起理解。

***Ad referendum* agreement**
待核准协定

对一系列谈判结果的临时性接受。最终接受取决于相关谈判的结果、经政府批准或满足其他一些条件。另见*方括号内文字(bracketed language)*、*不损害(without prejudice)*。

Ad valorem
从价

一商品或一交易的价值比例。另见*从价关税(ad valorem tariff)*。

***Ad valorem* equivalent**
从价税等值

从量关税水平的一种计算方法，将每项产品以固定货币价值表示的税率转换为以产品价值的一定比例表示。由此得出从价关税税率。例如，对价值10美元的物品征收1美元的从量税相当于征收10%的从价关税，对价值20美元的物品，1美元的关税则相当于5%的从价关税。另见*混合关税(compound tariff)*。

***Ad valorem* tariff**
从价关税

以进口或出口货物价值的百分比表示的关税税率。目前大多数关税按此种形式表示。另见*海关估价(customs valuation)*、*从量关税(specific tariff)*。

Advance deposit
保证金

在政府部门寄存进口货物的全部或部分费用的要求，通常是在订货时。另见*非关税措施(non-tariff measures)*。

Advance informed consent
预先知情同意

《卡塔赫纳生物安全议定书》中所含义务。要求出口商首次装运旨在环境中排放的改性活生物体前需要征得进口国同意。另见*事先知情同意(prior informed consent)*。

Advance rulings
预裁定

海关程序的一个方面。许多海关应请求提供关于如何处理拟进口货物的建议，通常以书面形式。这种建议可以包括关税归类、适用关税税率及货物是否有

advice is not always legally binding, but customs authorities usually honour it unless it was based on false information or an error of law. Advance rulings therefore are an important way to bring predictability into the trading system. Importers and exporters alike may apply for them. *See also **trade facilitation***.

Advisory Centre on WTO Law: established on 17 July 2001 in Geneva as an independent ***intergovernmental organization***. The Centre provides legal services and training to developing countries and economies in transition that have contributed to its endowment fund. ***Least-developed countries*** can use the Centre's services without contributing funds.

Advisory opinion: a non-binding opinion by a judicial authority on the interpretation of a law or a constitutional provision. Sometimes these opinions are given upon request, and at other times a court or judicial panel offers its view anyway. Advisory opinions have become an issue in ***WTO*** dispute settlement proceedings because some panels and the ***Appellate Body*** have resorted to them in some cases. Opponents of this practice note that the ***Dispute Settlement Understanding*** makes no mention of this possibility. *See also **judicial activism***.

***A fortiori*:** Lat. with stronger reason; much more so.

African Common Market: *see **African Continental Free Trade Area*** and ***African regional economic integration***.

African Continental Free Trade Area: AfCFTA. A continent-wide ***free-trade area*** for Africa negotiated under the auspices of the ***African Union***. Forty-four of its members signed the Agreement on 21 March 2018. It gives impetus to the aims of the Abuja Treaty establishing the ***African Economic Community***. Consists of a framework agreement and three protocols (trade in goods, services, dispute settlement). It is open to all members of the African Union. The Agreement entered into force on 30 May 2019. Fifty-four of the fifty-five African Union members have signed the Agreement, and twenty-eight members have ratified it. The aims of the Agreement will be realized in stages. Phase I was the negotiation of this Agreement and its three protocols. Negotiations for Phase II (intellectual property rights, investment and competition policy) have been launched. The objectives of the Agreement are (a) to create a single continental market for goods and services facilitated by the movement of persons, (b) create a liberalized market for goods and services through successive rounds of negotiation, (c) contribute to the movement of capital and natural persons and facilitate investments building on the initiatives and developments in the parties and the ***Regional Economic Communities***, lay the foundation for the establishment of a Continental Customs Union, (e) promote and attain sustainable and inclusive socio-economic development, gender equality and structural transformation, (f) enhance the competitiveness of member economies within the continent and the global market, (g) promote industrial development through diversification and regional value chain development and food security, and (h) resolve the challenges of multiple and overlapping memberships and expedite the regional and continental integration processes. The Agreement, when completed, will cover trade in goods, services, investment,

资格获得优惠市场准入。此类建议并不一定具有法律约束力，但海关通常予以尊重，除非建议根据虚假信息或法律错误作出。预裁定因此成为使贸易体制具有可预见性的一个重要途径。进口商和出口商均可申请。另见*贸易便利化(trade facilitation)*。

Advisory Centre on WTO Law
WTO法律咨询中心

作为独立的政府间组织于2001年6月17日在日内瓦成立。中心向捐赠基金捐款的发展中国家和转型经济体提供法律服务和培训。最不发达国家可以使用中心的服务而无需捐款。

Advisory opinion
咨询意见

司法机关对解释一项法律或宪法条款所发表的不具约束力的意见。有时这些意见应请求提供，而其他时候，一法院或司法专家组均会提出意见。咨询意见已成为WTO争端解决程序中的一个问题，因为一些专家组和上诉机构在一些案件中援用这些意见。这种做法的反对者指出，《争端解决谅解》并未提及这种可能性。另见*司法能动主义(judicial activism)*。

A fortiori
更有理由

拉丁语。意为有更强的理由；更是如此。

African Common Market
非洲共同市场

见*非洲大陆自由贸易区(African Continental Free Trade Area)*、*非洲区域经济一体化(African regional economic integration)*。

African Continental Free Trade Area
非洲大陆自由贸易区

AfCFTA。在非洲联盟主持下谈判建立的涵盖非洲大陆的自由贸易区。2018年3月21日，44个成员签署协定。该协定为建立非洲经济共同体的《阿布贾条约》的目标注入动力。由一项框架协定和三项议定书(货物贸易、服务贸易、争端解决)组成。协定对非洲联盟所有成员开放。协定于2019年5月30日生效。非洲联盟55个成员国中已有54个签署协定，28个成员国已批准协定。协定目标将分阶段实现。第一阶段即关于该协定及其三个议定书的谈判。第二阶段的谈判(知识产权、投资和竞争政策)已经启动。协定的目标为：(a)借助人员流动的便利建立一个货物和服务的单一大陆市场；(b)通过连续回合谈判，建立一个货物和服务自由化的市场；(c)在各方和区域经济共同体的倡议和发展的基础上，促进资本和自然人的流动，并便利投资，为大陆关税同盟的建立奠定基础；(e)促进和实现可持续和包容性的社会经济发展、性别平等和结构转型；(f)提高成员经济体在非洲大陆和全球市场内的竞争力；(g)通过多元化、区域价值链发展和粮食安全促进工业发展；以及(h)解决多重成员资格和成员资格重叠问题，并加速区域和大陆一体化进程。协定完成后将涵盖货物、服务、投

intellectual property rights and competition policy. It requires the parties to observe transparency and notify each other of laws, regulations, procedures and administrative rules of general application. It also requires the parties to accord each other, on a reciprocal basis, preferences no less favourable than those given to third parties, and it establishes a dispute settlement mechanism. No reservations may be made on any part of the Agreement. The Agreement will be reviewed every five years to ensure its effectiveness. The *Protocol on Trade in Goods* envisages the progressive elimination of tariffs and non-tariff barriers, enhanced efficiency of customs procedures, trade facilitation and transit, enhanced cooperation in the areas of technical barriers to trade and sanitary and phytosanitary measures, and the development and promotion of regional and continental value chains. It also affords the parties most-favoured nation treatment and national treatment. Quantitative restrictions are only allowed to the extent that that the WTO rules allow them. ***Rules of origin*** are yet to be developed. Anti-dumping and countervailing measures as well as global safeguards may be applied. The *Protocol on Services* (which appears to have taken the ***General Agreement on Trade in Services*** as a broad model) requires the parties to undertake successive rounds of negotiations based on the principle of progressive liberalization. If a party enters into a new preferential agreement with a third party, preferential treatment given to the third country must be extended to all the parties to the Agreement. The parties are to develop schedules of specific commitments. The *Protocol on Rules and Procedures on the Settlement of Disputes* establishes a Dispute Settlement Body, procedures for the work of panels, and it establishes an Appellate Body. Again, the WTO ***Dispute Settlement Understanding*** appears to have informed the provisions of this Protocol. *See also* ***African regional economic integration***.

African Economic Community: AEC. An organization aiming to promote the economic, social and cultural development of Africa. It was established on 12 May 1994 through the Treaty of Abuja. Membership is open to all members of the Organization of African Unity, now the ***African Union***. Its secretariat is located in Addis Ababa. Projected milestones are establishment of a continent-wide ***customs union*** in 2019, a continent-wide ***African Common Market*** in 2023 and establishment of a continent-wide economic and monetary union as well as a parliament in 2028. Current plans call for the completion of these tasks by 2034. *See also* ***African Continental Free Trade Area*** and ***African regional economic integration***.

African Group: a group of forty-three countries active in the WTO. Its members are Angola, Benin, Botswana, Burkina Faso, Burundi, Cabo Verde, Cameroon, Central African Republic, Chad, Congo, Democratic Republic of Congo, Côte d'Ivoire, Djibouti, Egypt, Eswatini, Gabon, The Gambia, Ghana, Guinea, Guinea-Bissau, Kenya, Lesotho, Madagascar, Malawi, Mali, Mauritania, Mauritius, Morocco, Mozambique, Namibia, Niger, Nigeria, Rwanda, Senegal, Seychelles, Sierra Leone, South Africa, Tanzania, Togo, Tunisia, Uganda, Zambia and Zimbabwe.

资、知识产权和竞争政策。协定要求参加方遵守透明度纪律，并相互通报法律、法规、程序和普遍适用的行政规定。还要求参加方在互惠基础上相互给予不低于给予第三方的优惠，并设立争端解决机制。不得对协定的任何部分提出保留。协定将每5年审议一次，以保证其有效性。《货物贸易议定书》设想逐步取消关税和非关税壁垒，提高海关程序、贸易便利化和过境的效率，加强在技术性贸易壁垒和卫生与植物卫生措施领域的合作，并发展和促进区域和大陆价值链。协定还给予参加方最惠国待遇和国民待遇。数量限制仅可在WTO规则允许的限度内实施。原产地规则尚未制定。可以采取反倾销和反补贴措施以及全球保障措施。《服务议定书》(似将《服务贸易总协定》作为模版)要求各参加方在逐步自由化原则基础上进行连续回合谈判。如一参加方与第三方订立新的优惠协定，则给予第三国的优惠待遇必须扩大到协定所有参加方。参加方将制定具体承诺减让表。《关于争端解决规则与程序的议定书》设立争端解决机构、专家组工作程序，并设立上诉机构。同样，WTO《争端解决谅解》似乎对议定书条款产生了影响。另见*非洲区域经济一体化(African regional economic integration)*。

African Economic Community

非洲经济共同体

AEC。以促进非洲经济、社会和文化发展为宗旨的组织。通过《阿布贾协定》于1994年5月12日建立。成员资格对非洲统一组织、现称非洲联盟的所有成员开放。秘书处设在亚的斯亚贝巴。里程碑预期为2019年建立覆盖非洲大陆关税同盟、2023年建立覆盖非洲大陆的非洲共同市场以及2028年建立覆盖非洲大陆的经济和货币同盟和议会。目前的计划为要求在2034年前完成上述任务。另见*非洲大陆自由贸易区(African Continental Free Trade Area)*、*非洲区域经济一体化(African regional economic integration)*。

African Group

非洲集团

活跃在WTO中由43个国家组成的集团。成员包括安哥拉、贝宁、博茨瓦纳、布基纳法索、布隆迪、佛得角、喀麦隆、中非共和国、乍得、刚果(布)、刚果(金)、科特迪瓦、吉布提、埃及、斯威士兰、加蓬、冈比亚、加纳、几内亚、几内亚比绍、肯尼亚、莱索托、马达加斯加、马拉维、马里、毛里塔尼亚、毛里求斯、摩洛哥、莫桑比克、纳米比亚、尼日尔、尼日利亚、卢旺达、塞内加尔、塞舌尔、塞拉利昂、南非、坦桑尼亚、多哥、突尼斯、乌干达、赞比亚和津巴布韦。

African Growth and Opportunity Act: AGOA. A United States Act adopted on 18 May 2000 with an original validity to 30 September 2008. It has since been renewed to 2025. The Act provides significant market access for most products to countries in ***sub-Saharan Africa***, but provision for textiles may be more restrictive in some cases. Only sub-Saharan countries are eligible for benefits under this Act. Countries must meet certain eligibility requirements to benefit from this Act. Among these are that the country (a) has established, or is making progress towards, a market-based economy, (b) enjoys the rule of law and political pluralism, (c) is eliminating barriers to United States trade and investment, (d) has economic policies to reduce poverty, (e) has a system to combat corruption and bribery, and (f) protects internationally recognized ***worker rights***. Activities undermining United States national security or foreign policy interests and engaging in gross human rights violations or international terrorism make a country ineligible for the benefits of this Act. Countries must also have implemented commitments to eliminate the ***worst forms of child labour***.

African regional economic integration: achieving regional economic integration in Africa is a challenge of a high order because of the diversity of the fifty-five countries making up the African continent, as the last fifty years have shown. For example, the Lagos Plan of Action, adopted by the ***Organization of African Unity***, called for the creation of five Regional Economic Communities: North Africa, West Africa, Central Africa, Eastern Africa and Southern Africa. This plan was realized in part. The Treaty of Abuja of 1994 established an ***African Economic Community*** with the goal of free-trade areas, customs unions, a single market, a central bank and a common currency. Some progress towards these aims has been made, but the regional achievements remain uneven. The path forward is now becoming clearer through the efforts of the ***African Union*** (AU) and some of the African regional organizations. The task will require years of patient work. The step-by-step implementation of the AU's ***Agenda 2063***, which has many important aims outside the trade and economic area, should greatly assist the task. The work of the NEPAD Agency in implementing the ***New Partnership for Africa's Development*** should also make a tangible contribution to African regional development. A major step towards continent-wide integration was the signing of an agreement in 2018 establishing the ***African Continental Free Trade Area*** which entered into force on 30 May 2019. A range of regional integration initiatives also exists, most of them with a considerable history behind them. The following is an outline of the principal ones. *A. North Africa.* The ***Arab Maghreb Union*** consisting of Algeria, Libya, Mauritania, Morocco and Tunisia appears to be largely inactive, though member countries are pursuing their own economic initiatives. The ***Community of Sahel-Saharan States***, established in 1998, seeks to establish a comprehensive economic union. *B. East Africa.* The ***East African Community*** established a ***customs union*** in 2004. A ***common market*** followed in 2010, and a monetary union is to be created by 2023. *C. South-East*

African Growth and Opportunity Act
非洲增长与机遇法

AGOA。2000年5月18日通过的一项美国法案，原有效期至2008年9月30日，目前已更新至2025年。该法案为撒哈拉以南非洲国家的大多数产品提供了重要市场准入机会，但在一些情况下对纺织品的规定可能更具限制性。仅撒哈拉以南非洲国家有资格获得该法案项下的利益。有关国家必须满足某些资格要求方可从该法中获益，包括该国(a)已经建立以市场为基础的经济或正在为此取得进展；(b)享有法治和政治多元化；(c)正在消除对美国贸易和投资的壁垒；(d)已经实施减少贫困的经济政策；(e)已经设立反腐败和反贿赂的制度；以及(f)保护国际承认的工人权利。如损害美国国家安全或对外政策利益，以及存在大规模违反人权或国际恐怖主义的行为，一国即无资格从该法案中获益。各国还必须实施消除最恶劣形式的童工劳动的承诺。

African regional economic integration
非洲区域经济一体化

正如过去50年所表明的，由于构成非洲大陆的55个国家的多样性，在非洲实现区域经济一体化是一项艰巨挑战。例如，非洲统一组织通过的《拉各斯行动计划》呼吁建立5个区域经济共同体：北部非洲、西部非洲、中部非洲、东部非洲和南部非洲。这一计划部分实现。1994年的《阿布贾协定》建立了非洲经济共同体，目标为建立自由贸易区、关税同盟、单一市场、中央银行和共同货币。在实现这些目标方面取得了一些进展，但区域进展并不平衡。通过非洲联盟(AU)和一些非洲区域组织的努力，前进的道路现在变得更加清晰。此项任务需要多年的耐心工作。非盟2063年议程的逐步实施将大大有助于这项任务，而议程在贸易和经济领域之外还有许多重要目标。非洲发展新伙伴关系计划(NEPAD)机构在实施NEPAD方面的工作也将为非洲区域发展作出实际贡献。向大陆一体化迈出的重要一步是2018年签署一个建立非洲大陆自由贸易区的协定，协定于2019年5月30日生效。还存在一系列区域一体化倡议，其中大多数都有相当长的历史。以下列出其中的主要倡议：A.北部非洲。由阿尔及利亚、利比亚、毛里塔尼亚、摩洛哥和突尼斯组成的阿拉伯马格里布联盟，很大程度上已经不活跃，尽管成员国正在推行自己的经济倡议。萨赫勒—撒哈拉国家共同体于1998年建立，寻求建立一个全面的经济联盟。B.东部非洲。东非共同体于2004年建立关税同盟，2010年建立共同市场，计划在2023年建立货

Africa. The ***Common Market for Eastern and Southern Africa*** (COMESA) was established in 2000. It is to be transformed into a monetary union by 2025. Its members are Burundi, Comoros, Democratic Republic of Congo, Djibouti, Egypt, Eritrea, Eswatini, Ethiopia, Kenya, Libya, Madagascar, Malawi, Mauritius, Rwanda, Seychelles, Sudan, Uganda, Zambia and Zimbabwe. The proposal for a ***Tripartite Free Trade Area*** to consist of COMESA, SADC and the East African Community is also relevant in this context. The ***Intergovernmental Authority on Development*** (IGAD) is not a trade arrangement, but among its objectives is the promotion of COMESA and the African Economic Community. *D. Southern Africa.* The ***Southern African Development Community*** (SADC) established a free-trade area in 2008. This was to be followed by a customs union by 2013 and a common market by 2015. SADC consists of Angola, Botswana, Democratic Republic of Congo, Eswatini, Lesotho, Madagascar, Malawi, Mauritius, Mozambique, Namibia, Seychelles, South Africa, Tanzania, Zambia and Zimbabwe. The ***Southern African Customs Union*** (Botswana, Eswatini, Lesotho, Namibia and South Africa) was established in 2002 in its current form. *E. West Africa.* The ***Economic Community of West African States*** (ECOWAS) was originally established in 1975 and relaunched in 1993. ECOWAS is establishing a customs union and working towards the implementation of ECOWAS 2020 which envisages, by 2020, a single unified market. Its members are Benin, Burkina Faso, Cape Verde, Côte d'Ivoire, The Gambia, Ghana, Guinea, Guinea-Bissau, Liberia, Mali, Niger, Nigeria, Senegal, Sierra Leone and Togo. The ***West African Economic and Monetary Union*** (WAEMU) or Union Économique et Monétaire Ouest Africaine (UEMOA) was established in 1994. It has a programme of deep integration based on a common market with the free movement of persons, goods, services and capital. Its members are Benin, Burkina Faso, Côte d'Ivoire, Guinea Bissau, Mali, Niger, Senegal and Togo. *F. Central Africa.* The ***Economic Community of Central African States*** was established in 1983, but it remained inactive from 1992 to 1998. Its aim is to promote cooperation and self-supporting development in a wide range of fields. A longer-term aim is to create by 2025 a zone of free movement of people, goods and services. Its members are Angola, Burundi, Cameroon, Central African Republic, Chad, Congo, Democratic Republic of Congo, Equatorial Guinea, Gabon, and Sao Tome and Principe. The United Nations ***Economic Commission for Africa*** has an overall mandate for promoting economic progress in Africa, but it is not party to any regional arrangement.

African Union: established in July 2001 at a meeting in Lusaka of African heads of government as the successor to the ***Organization of African Unity***. It consists of all fifty-five countries making up the African continent. The ***African Continental Free Trade Area*** of 2018 was negotiated under its auspices. The AU's long-term vision is contained in ***Agenda 2063*** adopted in 2013. It is a strategic framework for the socio-economic transformation of Africa over the

币同盟。C.东部和南部非洲。东部和南部非洲共同市场(COMESA)于2000年建立，将于2025年转为货币同盟。成员包括布隆迪、科摩罗、刚果(金)、吉布提、埃及、厄立特里亚、斯威士兰、埃塞俄比亚、肯尼亚、利比亚、马达加斯加、马拉维、毛里求斯、卢旺达、塞舌尔、苏丹、乌干达、赞比亚和津巴布韦。由COMESA、SADC和东非共同体组成的三方自由贸易区提案也与此相关。东非政府间发展机构(IGAD)不是一项贸易安排，但目标之一是促进COMESA和非洲经济共同体。D.南部非洲。南部非洲发展共同体(SADC)于2008年建立了自由贸易区。原定在2013年建立关税同盟，2015年建立共同市场。SADC成员包括安哥拉、博茨瓦纳、刚果(金)、斯威士兰、莱索托、马达加斯加、马拉维、毛里求斯、莫桑比克、纳米比亚、塞舌尔、南非、坦桑尼亚、赞比亚和津巴布韦。南部非洲关税同盟(博茨瓦纳、斯威士兰、莱索托、纳米比亚和南非)于2002年建成现在的形式。E.西部非洲。西非国家经济共同体(ECOWAS)最初于1975年建立，并于1993年重新启动。西共体正在建立关税同盟，并致力于实施西非国家经济共同体2020计划，设想到2020年建立一个单一的统一市场。成员为贝宁、布基纳法索、佛得角、科特迪瓦、冈比亚、加纳、几内亚、几内亚比绍、利比里亚、马里、尼日尔、尼日利亚、塞内加尔、塞拉利昂和多哥。西非经济和货币同盟(WAEMU)于1994年建立。包含一项基于共同市场的深度一体化计划，包括人员、货物、服务和资本的自由流动。成员为贝宁、布基纳法索、科特迪瓦、几内亚比绍、马里、尼日尔、塞内加尔和多哥。F.中部非洲。中部非洲国家经济共同体于1983年建立，但在1992年至1998年期间处于不活跃状态。目的是促进广泛领域的合作和独立发展。更长期目标是到2025年创建一个人员、货物和服务自由流动区域。成员为安哥拉、布隆迪、喀麦隆、中非共和国、乍得、刚果(布)、刚果(金)、赤道几内亚、加蓬和圣多美和普林西比。联合国非洲经济委员会拥有促进非洲经济进步的总体授权，但不是任何区域安排的参加方。

African Union

非洲联盟

2001年7月在卢萨卡召开的非洲政府首脑会议上建立，以取代非洲统一组织。由构成非洲大陆的所有55个国家组成。2018年非洲大陆自由贸易区在其主持下谈判建立。非盟的长期愿景包含在2013年通过的2063年议程中，是未来50年非洲社会经济转型的战略框架。非盟秘书处设在埃塞俄比亚亚的斯亚贝巴。

next fifty years. The secretariat of the AU is in Addis Ababa, Ethiopia. *See also* ***African regional economic integration***.

African Union Convention on Preventing and Combating Corruption: entered into force on 5 August 2006. It requires each party to the Convention to adopt legislative measures to promote and strengthen mechanisms required to prevent, detect, punish and eradicate corruption and related offences in the public and private sectors. As of late 2019 forty-three members of the ***African Union*** had ratified the Convention. *See also* ***corruption***.

AFTA: ASEAN Free Trade Area. Established on 1 January 1993. Intra-ASEAN trade is now largely free of duty, but Cambodia, Laos, Myanmar and Viet Nam, all of whom joined ASEAN later, have further to go. The main mechanism for tariff reductions under AFTA was ***CEPT*** (Common External Preferential Tariff). AFTA was superseded in 2010 by the ***ASEAN Trade in Goods Agreement***.

Agadir Agreement: the ***free-trade agreement*** between Egypt, Jordan, Morocco and Tunisia signed on 11 January 2003 in Amman. It derives its name from the launch of the project in Agadir, Morocco, in 2001. The agreement entered into force in 2007.

Agency for International Trade Information and Cooperation: *see* ***AITIC***.

Agenda 21: The Agenda for the Twenty-First Century. This is a programme of principles and actions relevant to ***trade and environment*** adopted on 14 June 1992 by ***UNCED*** (United Nations Conference on Environment and Development) in Rio de Janeiro. Programme area A seeks to promote ***sustainable development*** through trade. Its objectives are (a) to promote an open, non-discriminatory and equitable trading system that will enable all countries to improve their economic structures and improve the standards of living of their populations through sustained economic development, (b) to improve access to markets for exports of developing countries, (c) to improve the functioning of commodity markets and achieve sound, compatible and consistent commodity policies at national and international levels with a view to optimizing the contribution of the commodity sector to ***sustainable development***, taking into account environmental considerations, and (d) to promote and support domestic and international policies that make economic growth and environmental protection mutually supportive. Programme area B aims (a) at making trade and environment mutually supportive in favour of sustainable development, (b) to clarify the role of ***GATT***, ***UNCTAD*** and other international organizations in dealing with trade and environment-related issues, including, where relevant, conciliation procedure and ***dispute settlement***, and (c) to encourage international productivity and competitiveness and encourage a constructive role on the part of industry in dealing with environment and development issues. *See also* ***commodity policy***, ***Rio Declaration on Environment and Development***, ***trade and environment*** and ***World Summit on Sustainable Development***.

Agenda 2000: the ***European Community*** financial reform plan for 2000–2006 aimed at strengthening the union among European countries to get ready for the new members. The strategy identified three main challenges: (a) how to

另见*非洲区域经济一体化(African regional economic integration)*。

African Union Convention on Preventing and Combating Corruption

非洲联盟预防和惩治腐败公约

2006年8月5日生效。要求公约每一缔约方采取立法措施，以促进和加强预防、侦查、惩罚和根除公共和私营部门中的腐败和相关犯罪所需的机制。截至2019年底，已有43个非洲联盟成员国批准该公约。另见*腐败(corruption)*。

AFTA

东盟自由贸易区

1993年1月1日建立。东盟内部贸易现在大部分免税，但后来加入东盟的柬埔寨、老挝、缅甸和越南还未达到这一水平。AFTA项下关税削减的主要机制为CEPT(共同对外优惠关税)。AFTA于2010年被《东盟货物贸易协定》所取代。

Agadir Agreement

阿加迪尔协定

埃及、约旦、摩洛哥和突尼斯于2003年1月11日在阿曼签署的自由贸易协定。因2001年在摩洛哥阿加迪尔启动谈判而得名。协定于2007年生效。

Agency for International Trade Information and Cooperation

国际贸易信息与合作署

见*国际贸易信息与合作署(AITIC)*。

Agenda 21

21世纪议程

联合国环境与发展会议(UNCED)于1992年6月14日在里约热内卢通过的与贸易与环境相关的原则和行动计划。方案领域A寻求通过贸易促进可持续发展。目标为：(a)促进开放、非歧视和公正的贸易体制，从而使所有国家能够通过持续的经济发展改善经济结构并提高人民生活水平；(b)改善发展中国家出口产品的市场准入；(c)改善商品市场的运作，并在国家和国际层面实现健全、兼容和一致的商品政策，以期优化商品部门对可持续发展的贡献，同时考虑环境因素；(d)促进和支持使经济增长和环境保护相互支持的国内和国际政策。方案领域B旨在(a)使贸易和环境相互支持，以有利于可持续发展；(b)澄清GATT、联合国贸易与发展会议(UNCTAD)和其他国际组织在处理贸易和环境相关问题方面的作用，包括在相关的情况下调解程序和争端解决；以及(c)增强国际生产力和竞争力，并鼓励产业在处理环境和发展问题方面发挥建设性作用。另见*商品政策(commodity policy)*、*里约环境与发展宣言(Rio Declaration on Environment and Development)*、*贸易与环境(trade and environment)*、*可持续发展世界首脑会议(World Summit on Sustainable Development)*。

Agenda 2000

2000年议程

欧洲共同体2000—2006年金融改革计划，旨在强化欧洲国家间的联盟，为吸收新成员作好准备。该战略确定了三项主要挑战：(a)如何增强和改革欧盟政策，使其能够处理扩盟问题，为欧洲公民带来可持续增长、更高的就业率和改善的生活条件；(b)如何在开展扩盟谈判的同时为所有申请加入国的加入时刻作好积极准备；以及(c)如何为扩盟、欧盟内部政策的提前制定和发展提供资金。其结果是对共同农业政策进行了重大调整。另见*欧洲协定(Europe Agree-*

strengthen and reform the ***European Union***'s policies so that they can deal with ***enlargement*** and deliver sustainable growth, higher employment and improved living conditions for Europe's citizens, (b) how to negotiate enlargement while at the same time vigorously preparing all applicant countries for the moment of accession, and (c) how to finance enlargement, the advance preparations and the development of the Union's internal policies. Major changes to the ***common agricultural policy*** have been made as result. *See also* ***Europe Agreements***, ***European Union treaties*** and ***Treaty of Nice***.

Agenda 2030 for Sustainable Development: *see* ***Sustainable Development Goals***.

Agenda 2063: a framework for inclusive growth and sustainable development for Africa to be realized over the next fifty years. It was adopted by the ***African Union*** in 2013. The first ten-year implementation plan is now under way. Agenda 2063 covers many aspects of African development. One of these was the signing of the ***African Continental Free Trade Area*** in March 2018 with the aim of doubling intra-African trade by 2022.

Aggregate measurement of support: a term used in the ***Agreement on Agriculture***. It measures the annual level of support expressed in monetary terms provided in favour of agricultural producers other than support provided under Annex 2 (i.e. ***green box***). It includes product-specific support and support given to agricultural producers in general. *See also* ***Agreement on Agriculture***, ***amber box***, ***blue box***, ***equivalent measure of support***, ***green box***, ***subsidies*** and ***Total Aggregate Measurement of Support***.

Aggressive multilateralism: usually describes the option available to the United States of using the WTO dispute settlement mechanism vigorously, backed up by ***Section 301*** to the extent that that would be legal and desirable.

Aggressive reciprocity: the unilateral action of an economy which seeks to force a trading partner to change its ***trade policy***. Measures used include ***retaliation*** in response to perceived unfair actions, the use of domestic trade legislation, etc. Aggressive reciprocity is capable of solving some trade issues, but often at the expense of considerable political ill-will. It has also been described as the "crow-bar theory of trade policy". *See also* ***bilateralism***, ***passive reciprocity***, ***Section 301***, ***Special 301***, ***unfair trading practices*** and ***unilateralism***.

Aggressive unilateralism: *see* ***unilateralism***.

AGOA: *see* ***African Growth and Opportunity Act***.

Agreement Concerning the International Registration of Marks: *see* ***Madrid Agreement Concerning the International Registration of Marks***.

Agreement for Facilitating the International Circulation of Visual and Auditory Materials of an Educational, Scientific and Cultural Character: *see* ***Beirut Agreement***.

Agreement for the Protection of Appellations of Origin and their International Registration: *see* ***Lisbon Agreement***.

Agreement for the Repression of False or Deceptive Indications of Source on Goods: *see* ***Madrid Agreement for the Repression of False or Deceptive Indications of Source on Goods***.

ments)、*欧洲联盟主要条约(European Union treaties)*、*尼斯条约(Treaty of Nice)*。

Agenda 2030 for Sustainable Development
2030年可持续发展议程

见*可持续发展目标(Sustainable Development Goals)*。

Agenda 2063
2063年议程

将在未来50年实现的非洲包容性增长和可持续发展框架。非洲联盟于2013年通过。第一个10年实施计划正在实施中。2063年议程涵盖非洲发展的许多方面，其中一个方面为2018年3月签署的非洲大陆自由贸易区，目标是到2022年将非洲内部贸易翻一番。

Aggregate measurement of support
综合支持量

《农业协定》中使用的词语。衡量除根据附件2提供的支持(即绿箱)外的、以货币形式表示的有利于农业生产者的年度支持水平。包括特定产品支持和给予一般农业生产者的支持。另见*农业协定(Agreement on Agriculture)*、*黄箱(amber box)*、*蓝箱(blue box)*、*支持等值(equivalent measure of support)*、*绿箱(green box)*、*补贴(subsidies)*、*综合支持总量(Total Aggregate Measurement of Support)*。

Aggressive multilateralism
激进多边主义

通常描述美国可获得的选择办法，即积极使用WTO争端解决机制，同时在合法性和合宜性的限度内得到301条款的支持。

Aggressive reciprocity
主动互惠

一经济体寻求强迫一贸易伙伴改变其贸易政策的单边行动。使用的措施包括对被认为不公平的行为进行报复、使用国内贸易立法等。主动互惠能够解决一些贸易问题，但往往以巨大的政治敌意为代价。也被描述为“贸易政策的撬杆理论”。另见*双边主义(bilateralism)*、*被动互惠(passive reciprocity)*、*301条款(Section 301)*、*特别301条款(Special 301)*、*不公平贸易做法(unfair trading practices)*、*单边主义(unilateralism)*。

Aggressive unilateralism
激进单边主义

见*单边主义(unilateralism)*。

AGOA
非洲增长与机遇法

见*非洲增长与机遇法(African Growth and Opportunity Act)*。

Agreement Concerning the International Registration of Marks
关于国际商标注册的协定

见*商标国际注册马德里协定(Madrid Agreement Concerning the International Registration of Marks)*。

Agreement for Facilitating the International Circulation of Visual and Auditory Materials of an Educational, Scientific and Cultural Character
促进教育、科研和文化性质的视听材料国际流通的协定

见*贝鲁特协定(Beirut Agreement)*。

Agreement for the Protection of Appellations of Origin and their International Registration
保护原产地名称及其国际注册协定

见*里斯本协定(Lisbon Agreement)*。

Agreement for the Repression of False or Deceptive Indications of Source on Goods
制止商品来源虚假或欺骗性标记协定

见*制止商品来源虚假或欺骗性标记马德里协定(Madrid Agreement for the Repression of False or Deceptive Indications of Source on Goods)*。

Agreement on Agriculture: one of the outcomes of the ***Uruguay Round***. It is administered by the WTO. The Agreement provides the first effective multilateral framework specifically aimed at the long-term reform and liberalization of agricultural trade. The Agreement establishes new rules and commitments in ***market access***, ***domestic support*** and ***export competition*** (i.e. the handling of ***subsidies***). It encourages the adoption of domestic support and export-related policies that are less trade-distorting and reduction in protection. It also allows actions aimed at easing domestic adjustment burdens. Some of the measures required by the Agreement were (a) a reduction by developed countries in export subsidy expenditures by 36 per cent over six years in equal instalments, and a 24 per cent reduction over ten years for developing countries; (b) a cut by developed countries in the volume of subsidized exports by 21 per cent over six years, 14 per cent for developing countries over ten years; (c) a cut by 20 per cent over six years in trade distorting domestic support as measured by the aggregate measure of support during the base period 1986–88, and by 13 per cent over ten years by developing country members; and (d) all existing ***non-tariff measures*** have to be converted into tariffs and bound, followed by a reduction by an unweighted average of 36 per cent with a minimal cut of 15 per cent over six years in equal tranches, again with 1986–88 as the base period. For developing countries the cut is 24 per cent with a minimum cut of 10 per cent over ten years. The Agreement entails minimum access commitments where markets were virtually closed before, as well as the commitment to maintain the then existing current access opportunities, and special ***safeguards*** under strictly defined conditions to deal with import surges after ***tariffication***. Negotiations aimed at further liberalization of agricultural trade resumed in 2000. They became part of the negotiations under the ***Doha Development Agenda***. *See also* ***agricultural export subsidies***, ***agriculture and the multilateral trading system***, ***amber box***, ***blue box***, ***continuation clause***, ***green box*** and ***peace clause***.

Agreement on Basic Telecommunications Services: WTO agreement first envisaged in the ***Uruguay Round*** outcome on ***trade in services*** and concluded on 15 February 1997. It contains ***market access*** commitments made by sixty-nine members covering cross-border trade and supply through a ***commercial presence***. The Agreement entered into force on 1 January 1998 through the ***Fourth Protocol to the General Agreement on Trade in Services***. *See also* ***cross-border trade in services***, ***International Telecommunication Union*** and ***reference paper on telecommunications services***.

Agreement on Customs Valuation: formally the WTO ***Agreement on Implementation of Article VII of the General Agreement on Tariffs and Trade 1994***. It sets out a system of non-discriminatory rules to be followed by customs authorities when they assess the value of imports for the levying of ***customs duties***. *See* ***customs valuation*** and ***Customs Valuation Agreement***.

Agreement on Government Procurement: the ***WTO plurilateral trade agreement*** containing rules for the purchase by governments of goods and services

Agreement on Agriculture
农业协定

乌拉圭回合成果，由WTO管理。协定首次为农业贸易的长期改革和自由化规定有效多边框架。协定制定了市场准入、国内支持和出口竞争(即处理补贴)方面的新规则。协定鼓励采取对贸易扭曲作用较小的国内支持和出口相关政策，并减少保护。协定还允许为缓解国内产业调整的负担而采取行动。协定规定的一些措施包括：(a)发达国家在6年内将出口补贴支出削减36%，发展中国家在10年内削减24%；(b)发达国家在6年内将出口补贴量减少21%，发展中国家在10年内削减14%；(c)具有贸易扭曲作用的国内支持在6年内削减20%，以1986—1988年基期综合支持量计算；以及(d)将现有所有非关税措施进行关税化并约束，在6年内均等削减36%，最低削减15%(未加权平均)，基期为1986—1988年，发展中国家在10年内削减24%，最低削减10%。协定对以前实际上封闭的市场规定了最低准入承诺，并规定了维持当时的现行准入机会的承诺，以及在严格规定的条件下使用特殊保障措施处理关税化后的进口激增。旨在推动农业贸易进一步自由化的谈判于2000年恢复，成为多哈发展议程项下谈判的一部分。另见*农产品出口补贴(agricultural export subsidies)*、*农业与多边贸易体制(agriculture and the multilateral trading system)*、*黄箱(amber box)*、*蓝箱(blue box)*、*继续谈判条款(continuation clause)*、*绿箱(green box)*、*和平条款(peace clause)*。

Agreement on Basic Telecommunications Services
基础电信协定

WTO协定，有关设想最初出现在乌拉圭回合服务贸易谈判的结果之中，谈判于1997年2月15日结束。协定包括69个成员作出的市场准入承诺，涵盖跨境贸易和通过商业存在提供服务。协定以《服务贸易总协定第四议定书》的形式于1998年1月1日生效。另见*跨境服务贸易(cross-border trade in services)*、*国际电信联盟(International Telecommunication Union)*、*电信服务参考文件(reference paper on telecommunications services)*。

Agreement on Customs Valuation
海关估价协定

正式名称为WTO《关于实施1994年关税与贸易总协定第7条的协定》。协定规定了海关在为征收关税目的而对进口产品进行估价时需要遵循的一套非歧视规则制度。另见*海关估价(customs valuation)*、*海关估价协定(Customs Valuation Agreement)*。

Agreement on Government Procurement
政府采购协定

WTO诸边贸易协定。1996年1月1日生效，协定包含政府购买自用的货物和服务的规则。后继协定为《政府采购协定修正版》。另见*APEC政府采购非约束*

for their own use which entered into force on 1 January 1996. Its successor is the ***Revised Agreement on Government Procurement***. *See also* ***APEC Non-Binding Principles on Government Procurement***, ***second-level obligations*** and ***Working Group on Transparency in Government Procurement***.

Agreement on Implementation of Article VI of the General Agreement on Tariffs and Trade 1994: the WTO *Anti-Dumping Agreement*. *See also* ***anti-dumping measures*** and ***dumping***.

Agreement on Implementation of Article VII of the General Agreement on Tariffs and Trade 1994: the ***Customs Valuation Agreement***. It sets out the principles and procedures to be followed by WTO members in their assessment of the value of imported goods for the purpose of levying the appropriate amount of ***customs duties***. The primary base for assessing the customs value is the ***transaction value***. Broadly, this is the price actually paid or payable for the goods for export under conditions of competition. *See also* ***customs valuation***, ***identical goods*** and ***similar goods***.

Agreement on Import Licensing Procedures: the agreement setting out the procedures to be followed by WTO members in their administration of ***import licensing*** regimes. It defines import licensing as "administrative procedures used for the operation of import licensing régimes requiring the submission of an application or other documentation (other than that required for customs purposes) to the relevant administrative body as a prior condition for importation into the customs territory of the importing Member". The Agreement has provisions on ***automatic import licensing*** (i.e. approval of the application is always granted) and ***non-automatic import licensing*** (i.e. all cases where licensing is not automatic). The Agreement also establishes a system for notifying import licensing procedures to the WTO.

Agreement on Mutual Acceptance of Oenological Practices: *see* ***World Wine Trade Group***.

Agreement on Preshipment Inspection: a WTO agreement setting out the conditions and procedures under which members may carry out ***preshipment inspections*** to ensure that the cost of goods shipped corresponds to the invoiced cost. Such inspections are used mainly by developing countries to prevent capital flight, commercial fraud, evasion of ***customs duties*** and other similar practices. The Agreement requires user members to apply ***GATT*** principles and obligations to the conduct of inspections. These include ***non-discrimination***, ***transparency***, protection of confidential business information, avoidance of unreasonable delay, the use of specific guidelines for conducting price verification and the avoidance of conflicts of interest by preshipment inspection agencies. Exporting members must apply their laws and regulations concerning preshipment activities in a non-discriminatory way. They must publish promptly all applicable laws and regulations and, if requested, they must afford user members technical assistance. In the case of disputes, the parties have access to independent review procedures mandated by the Agreement. These procedures should be administered by an ***independent entity*** made up of an

性原则(APEC Non-Binding Principles on Government Procurement)、*二级义务(second-level obligations)*、*政府采购透明度工作组(Working Group on Transparency in Government Procurement)*。

Agreement on Implementation of Article VI of the General Agreement on Tariffs and Trade 1994

关于实施1994年关税与贸易总协定第6条的协定

WTO《反倾销协定》。另见*反倾销措施(anti-dumping measures)*、*倾销(dumping)*。

Agreement on Implementation of Article VII of the General Agreement on Tariffs and Trade 1994

关于实施1994年关税与贸易总协定第7条的协定

《海关估价协定》。协定对WTO成员在为征收适当金额的关税为目的而对进口货物进行估价时应遵守的原则和程序。估价的主要根据为成交价格。广义而言，这是供出口货物在竞争条件下实付或应付的价格。另见*海关估价(customs valuation)*、*相同货物(identical goods)*、*类似货物(similar goods)*。

Agreement on Import Licensing Procedures

进口许可程序协定

协定规定了WTO成员在管理进口许可体制方面应遵循的程序。协定将进口许可定义为："用以实施进口许可制度的行政程序，该制度要求向相关行政机关提交申请或其他单证(不同于报关所需单证)，作为货物进入进口成员关税领土的先决条件。"协定包含自动进口许可(即申请在所有情况下均授予)和非自动进口许可(即许可不属自动的所有情况)的条款。协定还规定了进口许可程序通报WTO的制度。

Agreement on Mutual Acceptance of Oenological Practices

关于相互接受酿酒方法的协定

见*世界葡萄酒贸易集团(World Wine Trade Group)*。

Agreement on Preshipment Inspection

装运前检验协定

WTO协定。规定成员据以保证装运货物的价值与发票价值一致而进行装运前检验的条件和程序。此类检验措施主要由发展中国家使用，用以防止资本外流、商业欺诈、偷逃关税和其他类似做法。协定要求用户成员在实施检验时适用GATT原则和义务，包括非歧视、透明度、保护机密商业信息、避免无理迟延、使用明确准则进行价格核实，以及避免装运前检验机构之间的利益冲突。出口成员必须以非歧视的方式适用其关于装运前检验的法律法规，必须迅速公布所有适用的法律法规，应请求还应向用户成员提供技术援助。如发生争端，争端双方可以获得协定规定的独立审查程序。这些程序应由分别代表装

organization representing preshipment inspection agencies and an organization representing exporters. The decision of the three-member review panel is binding on all parties to the dispute.

Agreement on Rules of Origin: an agreement administered by the WTO. It sets out a programme of work by the Committee on Rules of Origin for the long-term harmonization of ***rules of origin***. Rules of origin are defined as laws, regulations and administrative determinations applied by members to determine the country of origin of goods admitted under most-favoured-nation conditions. The country of origin of the goods is either the country where the good has been wholly obtained or, if more than one country is involved, the country where the last ***substantial transformation*** was carried out. The Agreement stipulates that rules of origin should be administered in a consistent, uniform, impartial and reasonable manner. They should not themselves create restrictive, distorting or disruptive effects on international trade. Rules of origin must state what does confer origin rather than what does not. The Agreement contains an annex in the form of a declaration dealing with the administration of rules of origin admitted under preferential conditions. *See also* ***change in tariff classification***, ***preferential rules of origin*** and ***wholly obtained goods***.

Agreement on Safeguards: a WTO agreement setting out and clarifying when and how members may resort to action under ***GATT*** Article XIX, also called ***escape clause***. This Article deals with the possibility of emergency action to protect domestic industry from an unforeseen increase in imports which is causing, or likely to cause, serious ***injury*** to the industry. "Serious injury" is defined as a significant overall impairment in the position of a domestic industry, and "threat of serious injury" means that such injury is clearly imminent. The Agreement notes that a finding of a threat of serious injury must be based on facts, not merely an allegation, conjecture or remote possibility. The Agreement sets out criteria for safeguards investigation which include public notice for hearings and other appropriate means for ***interested parties*** to present evidence. The criteria may include whether a safeguard measure would be in the public interest. If a delay in taking safeguard action would cause damage difficult to repair, ***provisional safeguard measures*** not exceeding 200 days may be taken. Safeguards action must be non-discriminatory. It must be imposed against the product and not against the source of the product. In other words, even though products from country X might be perceived to be the main problem, country X may not be singled out for import reductions. ***Selectivity*** is possible only if (i) it is clear that imports from certain countries have increased disproportionately in the period under consideration, (ii) all the other conditions for taking safeguards action have been satisfied, and (iii) if this would be equitable to other suppliers. Generally, the duration of a safeguards measure should not exceed four years, though this may in some circumstances be extended to a maximum of eight years. Any measure imposed for more than one year must be accompanied by ***structural adjustment*** aimed at liberalizing access. Members taking safeguards action may have to offer ***compensation***.

运前检验机构和出口商的组织组成一个独立实体进行管理。三人审查专家组的决定对争端各方具有约束力。

Agreement on Rules of Origin
原产地规则协定

WTO协定。协定规定了原产地规则委员会长期协调原产地规则的工作计划。原产地规则定义为，成员为确定在最惠国待遇条件下允许进口货物的原产地而适用的法律、法规和行政裁定。货物原产地要么是货物完全获得该货物的国家，要么是进行最后实质性改变的国家，如果涉及一个以上国家的话。协定规定，原产地规则应以一致、统一、公平和合理的方式管理，本身不应对国际贸易产生限制、扭曲或破坏作用。原产地规则必须说明什么授予原产地而非什么不授予。协定包括一个附件，以宣言的形式处理了优惠原产地规则的管理。另见***税则归类改变****(change in tariff classification)*、***优惠原产地规则****(preferential rules of origin)*、***完全获得的货物****(wholly obtained goods)*。

Agreement on Safeguards
保障措施协定

WTO协定。规定和澄清了成员何时以及如何援用GATT第19条采取行动，即所谓的免责条款。这一条款处理采取紧急行动的可能性，以保护国内产业不受不可预见的进口激增的影响，这种激增正在对国内产业造成严重损害或有可能造成此种损害。“严重损害”被定义为对一国内产业状况的重大全面减损，“严重损害威胁”指明显迫近的严重损害。协定指出，严重损害威胁的调查结果应根据事实，而非仅凭指控、推测或极小可能性作出。协定规定的保障措施调查标准包括公开听证和供利害关系方提供证据的其他适当方式。标准可以包括一项保障措施是否符合公共利益。如果采取保障措施的延迟会造成难以弥补的损害，成员可以采取不超过200天的临时保障措施。保障措施必须是非歧视的，必须针对产品而非产品来源实施。换言之，即使来自X国的产品被认定是主要问题，也不能单独针对X国采取进口限制。选择性仅可适用于：(1)明确表明来自特定若干国家的进口在调查期间出现不成比例的增长；(2)采取保障措施的其他所有条件均已满足；以及(3)如果这样做对于其他供应商是公正的。通常，保障措施的期限不应超过4年，但在一些情况下可以最多延长至8年。任何实施超过1年的措施都必须辅以旨在放宽准入的结构性调整。采取保障措施的成员可能需要提供补偿。协定禁止所谓的灰色区域措施，包括自愿限制安

The Agreement prohibits so-called ***grey-area measures***, including ***voluntary restraint arrangements***. All safeguards measures in force on 1 January 1995 had to be phased out within five years. *See also* ***de minimis safeguards rule***, ***Transitional Product-Specific Safeguard Mechanism*** and ***transitional safeguard mechanism***.

Agreement on Subsidies and Countervailing Measures: a WTO agreement which establishes three categories of subsidies and the procedures to be followed in dealing with them. The categories are ***prohibited subsidies*** (subsidies contingent on export performance or the use of domestic rather than imported goods), ***actionable subsidies*** (subsidies which may only be maintained if they do not injure the domestic industry of another member, do not cause ***nullification or impairment*** of benefits, or do not cause ***serious prejudice*** to the interests of another member) and ***non-actionable subsidies*** (subsidies which may be maintained by members). The Agreement details an accelerated timetable for ***dispute settlement*** cases arising from the application of the Agreement. It also sets out the conditions under which countervailing duties may be imposed. It does not apply to ***agricultural subsidies***. *See also* ***Agreement on Agriculture***, ***amber box***, ***blue box***, ***green box***, ***Permanent Group of Experts*** and ***provisional countervailing duties***.

Agreement on Technical Barriers to Trade: the TBT Agreement. A WTO agreement aimed at ensuring that technical regulations and standards, including packaging, marking and labelling requirements, and procedures for assessment of conformity with technical regulations and standards do not create unnecessary obstacles to international trade. It is the successor to the ***Tokyo Round*** Standards Code. The Agreement encourages members to use appropriate international standards, but it does not require them to change levels of protection because of standardization. It covers not only the standards applicable to a product itself, but also related ***processes and production methods***. Prescribed ***notification*** procedures apply. An annex to the Agreement contains a ***Code of Good Practice for the Preparation, Adoption and Application of Standards***. Central government standardizing bodies have to comply with it. Local government and non-government bodies may choose to do so. The administration of this Agreement is assisted by the WTO Technical Barriers to Trade Information Management System. This is a comprehensive database listing all TBT notifications and specific trade concerns raised in the Committee on Technical Barriers to Trade. *See also* ***conformity assessment***, ***ePing SPS and TBT notification alert system***, ***International Electrotechnical Commission*** and ***International Organization for Standardization***.

Agreement on Textiles and Clothing: a WTO agreement succeeding the ***Multi-Fibre Arrangement*** (MFA). It differed from the MFA in that it brought international trade in textiles and clothing again under the normal liberalizing and non-discriminatory WTO trade rules by 1 January 2005. This is also the date when the Agreement itself expired. The Agreement was supervised by the ***Textiles Monitoring Body***.

排。所有在1995年1月1日仍存在的保障措施均应在5年内取消。另见*保障措施微量规则(de minimis safeguards rule)*、*特定产品过渡性保障机制(Transitional Product-Specific Safeguard Mechanism)*、*过渡性保障机制(transitional safeguard mechanism)*。

Agreement on Subsidies and Countervailing Measures
补贴与反补贴措施协定

WTO协定。协定将补贴分为三类，制定了如何处理这些补贴的程序。三类补贴为：禁止性补贴(视出口实绩或使用本国货物替代进口货物而给予的补贴)、可诉补贴(只有在不损害另一成员国内产业、不造成利益的丧失或减损，或不对另一成员的利益造成严重侵害的前提下方可允许保留的补贴)以及不可诉补贴(成员可以保留的补贴)。协定对处理适用协定过程中产生的争端解决案件制定了加快时间表，同时规定了征收反补贴税的条件。协定不适用于农业补贴。另见*农业协定(Agreement on Agriculture)*、*黄箱(amber box)*、*蓝箱(blue box)*、*绿箱(green box)*、*常设专家小组(Permanent Group of Experts)*、*临时反补贴税(provisional countervailing duties)*。

Agreement on Technical Barriers to Trade
技术性贸易壁垒协定

TBT协定，WTO协定，旨在保证包括包装、商标和标识要求在内的技术法规和标准以及技术法规和标准的合格评定程序不对国际贸易造成不必要的障碍。协定是东京回合《标准守则》的后继协定。协定鼓励成员使用适当的国际标准，但不要求各成员因为标准化而改变保护水平。协定不仅涵盖适用于产品本身的标准，还涉及工序和生产方法的标准。需适用所规定的通报程序。协定的附件包含《关于制定、采用和实施标准的良好行为规范》。中央政府的标准机构需要遵守这一规范，地方政府和非政府机构可以选择遵守。协定的管理得到WTO技术性贸易壁垒信息管理系统的支持，这一系统包含所有TBT通报和在技术性贸易壁垒委员会中提出的具体贸易关注。另见*合格评定(conformity assessment)*、*TBT/SPS ePing通报提醒系统(ePing SPS and TBT notification alert system)*、*国际电工委员会(International Electrotechnical Commission)*、*国际标准化组织(International Organization for Standardization)*。

Agreement on Textiles and Clothing
纺织品与服装协定

WTO协定，取代《多种纤维协定》(MFA)。协定与MFA的不同之处在于：到2005年1月1日，将国际纺织品与服装贸易重新纳入正常自由化和非歧视的WTO贸易规则之中。这一日期也是协定终止的日期。协定受纺织品监督机构监督。

Agreement on the Application of Sanitary and Phytosanitary Measures: the SPS Agreement. A WTO agreement aiming to ensure that food safety and animal and plant health regulations are not used as disguised barriers to international trade. The Agreement preserves the right of governments to take ***sanitary and phytosanitary measures***, but they must not be used to discriminate arbitrarily or unjustifiably between WTO members that apply identical or similar measures. It encourages members to base their domestic measures on international standards, guidelines and recommendations where these exist. Members may introduce or maintain higher standards if there is scientific justification, or if a ***risk assessment*** has shown that this is appropriate. An importing country must consider the standards applied by an exporting country as equivalent to its own standards if the exporting country can demonstrate that this is the case. The Agreement sets out detailed procedures governing the ***transparency*** of regulations, ***notifications*** and the establishment of national ***enquiry points***. *See also* ***acceptable level of risk***, ***appropriate level of sanitary or phytosanitary protection***, ***ePing SPS and TBT notification alert system***, ***equivalence***, ***International Plant Protection Convention***, and ***World Organisation for Animal Health***.

Agreement on the Common Effective Preferential Tariff Scheme for the ASEAN Free Trade Area: *see* **AFTA**.

Agreement on the Importation of Educational, Scientific and Cultural Agreements: *see* ***Florence Agreement***.

Agreement on Trade Facilitation: a comprehensive WTO framework for further improvements in the area of ***trade facilitation***. It entered into force on 22 February 2017, but it only applies to members that have accepted it. As of late 2019, 147 WTO members had ratified the Agreement. Section I, i.e. Articles 1 to 12, covers the topics usually understood to make up the trade facilitation agenda. Article 1 requires the prompt publication of all rules, procedures, etc., of interest to traders and governments. Information must be made available, as much as possible, on the Internet. Members must establish ***enquiry points***. Article 2 requires that traders and other interested parties be given an opportunity to comment on the proposed introduction of laws and regulations of general application related to importing and exporting. Article 3 covers ***advance rulings***. Article 4 deals with procedures for appeal or review of administrative decisions. Article 5 specifies the conditions applicable in cases where members maintain a system of controls or inspections at the border in respect of food, beverages or foodstuffs. Notifications for enhanced controls or inspections may be issued based on risk. Importers must be notified promptly of detentions of goods. A second test may be granted where the first test led to an adverse finding. Article 6 covers disciplines on fees and charges imposed in connection with import or export, as well as penalties. Such information must be published. Article 7 deals with the release and clearance of goods. It encourages pre-arrival processing to enable advance lodging of documents in electronic form. It also encourages maintaining a risk management system for customs control.

Agreement on the Application of Sanitary and Phytosanitary Measures
实施卫生与植物卫生措施协定

SPS协定，WTO协定，旨在保证食品安全及动物和植物健康法规不构成对国际贸易的变相壁垒。协定保留政府采取卫生与植物卫生措施的权利，但在使用时不得在WTO成员之间造成任意或不合理的歧视。协定鼓励成员根据现有国际标准、指南和建议制定国内措施。如果有科学依据或风险评估证明适当，成员可以采用或维持更高的标准。进口成员必须将出口成员的标准视为与自身标准等同的标准，如果出口成员能够证明确实如此。协定规定了法规透明度、通报以及国家咨询点建立的具体程序。另见*可接受的风险水平(acceptable level of risk)*、*适当的卫生与植物卫生保护水平(appropriate level of sanitary or phytosanitary protection)*、*TBT/SPS ePing通报提醒系统(ePing SPS and TBT notification alert system)*、*等效(equivalence)*、*国际植物保护公约(International Plant Protection Convention)*、*世界动物卫生组织(World Organisation for Animal Health)*。

Agreement on the Common Effective Preferential Tariff Scheme for the ASEAN Free Trade Area
东盟自由贸易区共同有效特惠关税安排协定

见*东盟自由贸易区(AFTA)*。

Agreement on the Importation of Educational, Scientific and Cultural Agreements
关于教育、科学和文化物品的进口的协定

见*佛罗伦萨协定(Florence Agreement)*。

Agreement on Trade Facilitation
贸易便利化协定

旨在进一步改善贸易便利化领域的全面WTO框架。协定于2017年2月22日生效，但仅适用于已经接受协定的成员。截至2019年底，已有147个WTO成员批准协定(截至本书出版时的数字为160个成员—译注)。协定第一部分，即第1条至第12条，涵盖通常被认为构成贸易便利化议程的主题。第1条要求迅速公布贸易商和政府感兴趣的所有规定和程序等，信息必须尽可能在互联网上提供，成员必须设立咨询点。第2条要求给予贸易商和其他利害关系方对拟议采用的与进口和出口有关的普遍适用的法律法规进行评论的机会。第3条涵盖预裁定。第4条处理对行政决定的上诉或审查程序。第5条规定了适用于成员对食品、饮料或饲料实行边境监管或检查情形的条件。可以根据风险情况作出关于增强监管或检查的通报。必须迅速将扣留货物的情况迅速向进口商进行通报。如果第一次检验产生不利结果，可以进行第二次检验。第6条涵盖对进口和出口征收税费的纪律以及处罚的纪律，此类信息必须公布。第7条处理货物放行和结关。鼓励在抵达前开始处理，从而能够以电子方式提前提交单据，鼓励设立海关

Publication of ***average release times*** is also encouraged. Article 8 requires border control agencies to cooperate with one another and coordinate their activities to facilitate trade. Cooperation may include (a) alignment of working days and hours, (b) alignment of procedures and formalities, (c) development and sharing of common facilities, (d) joint controls, and (e) establishment of ***one-stop border post*** control. Article 9 allows goods imports to be moved from the control of one customs office to another. Article 10 requires members to ensure that, as far as possible, formalities and documentation requirements connected with import, export and transit are aimed at rapid release. A ***Single Window*** is to be established to enable traders to submit documentation through a single entry point. Article 11 deals with ***freedom of transit***. Article 12 promotes customs cooperation. Section II of the Agreement outlines ***special and differential treatment*** provisions for developing country members and ***least-developed country*** members. It establishes three categories of provisions. Category A includes provisions to be implemented on entry into force by developing country members and within a year of entry into force by least-developed country members. Category B includes provisions to be implemented after a transitional period. Category C includes provisions to be implemented after a transitional period and supplemented by the provision of technical assistance. Procedures for the handling of the three categories are outlined in some detail. Section III covers institutional arrangements. Article 24 states that the provisions of the ***Dispute Settlement Understanding*** apply to disputes under this Agreement. It establishes a ***Committee on Trade Facilitation*** to supervise the administration of the Agreement. This part also requires each member to establish a ***National Committee on Trade Facilitation*** to facilitate domestic implementation. The implementation of the Agreement is supported by the WTO ***Trade Facilitation Agreement Database***. The *World Trade Report 2015* provides a detailed analysis of all aspects of the Agreement.

Agreement on Trade in Civil Aircraft: one of the ***WTO plurilateral trade agreements***, originally concluded as part of the ***Tokyo Round***. Members of the Agreement undertake to eliminate all customs duties and other charges on (a) civil aircraft, (b) civil aircraft engines, parts and components, (c) other parts, components and sub-assemblies of civil aircraft, and (d) ground flight simulators. The Agreement requires that purchasers should be free to select suppliers on the basis of commercial and technological factors, and without ***quantitative restrictions***. WTO rules on ***subsidies*** apply. *See also* ***EU–US aircraft agreement*** and ***Large Aircraft Sector Understanding***.

Agreement on Trade in Large Aircraft: *see* ***EU–US aircraft agreement***.

Agreement on Trade-Related Aspects of Intellectual Property Rights: TRIPS. A WTO agreement concluded during the ***Uruguay Round***. It was negotiated to deal with a growing tension in international trade arising from widely varying standards in the protection and enforcement of ***intellectual property rights*** and the lack of multilateral rules on international trade in counterfeit goods. Part I of the Agreement deals with general provisions and basic principles. It states that

监管风险管理制度，鼓励公布平均放行时间。第8条要求边境监管机构相互合作并协调行动以便利贸易。合作可以包括(a)工作日和工作时间的协调；(b)程序和手续的协调；(c)公用设施的建设和共享；(d)联合监管；以及(e)一站式边境口岸的建立。第9条允许将进口货物从入境地海关转移至予以放行或结关的其领土内另一海关。第10条要求成员保证与进出口和过境有关的文件格式和单证要求尽可能以快速放行为目的。设立单一窗口，使交易者能够通过单一接入点提交单证。第11条处理过境自由。第12条旨在促进海关合作。协定第二部分包含发展中国家成员和最不发达国家成员的特殊和差别待遇条款。确立了三类条款。A类条款包括发展中国家成员在协定生效时和最不发达国家成员在协定生效1年内实施的条款。B类条款包括在一定过渡期后实施的条款。C类包括在一定过渡期后实施并辅以技术援助的条款。协定对三类条款的处理程序进行了较为详细的概述。第三部分涵盖机制安排。第24条规定，《争端解决谅解》的规定适用于本协定项下的争端。协定设立贸易便利化委员会以监督协定的管理。此部分还要求每一成员建立国家贸易便利化委员会，以便利国内实施。WTO贸易便利化协定数据库支持协定实施。《世界贸易报告2015》对协定的各个方面进行了详细分析。

Agreement on Trade in Civil Aircraft
民用航空器贸易协定

WTO诸边贸易协定，最初为东京回合成果的一部分。协定参加方承诺取消下列产品的所有关税和其他税费：(a)民用航空器；(b)民用航空器发动机及其零件和部件；(c)民用航空器的所有其他零件、部件及组件；以及(d)所有地面飞行模拟机。协定要求，购买者有权根据商业和技术因素选择供应商，且无数量限制。WTO关于补贴的规则同样适用。另见*欧美航空器协定(EU–US aircraft agreement)*、*民用航空器行业谅解(Large Aircraft Sector Understanding)*。

Agreement on Trade in Large Aircraft
大型航空器贸易协定

见*欧美航空器协定(EU–US aircraft agreement)*。

Agreement on Trade-Related Aspects of Intellectual Property Rights
与贸易有关的知识产权协定

TRIPS。乌拉圭回合达成的一项WTO协定。谈判协定的目的是为了处理知识产权保护和执行标准的巨大差异及缺少国际假冒商标贸易多边规则所导致的国际贸易日益紧张的问题。协定第一部分是总则和基本原则，规定协定适用

the Agreement applies to ***copyright*** and related rights, ***trademarks***, ***geographical indications***, ***industrial designs***, ***patents***, ***layout-design of integrated circuits*** and protection of ***trade secrets***. Standards of protection to be applied are those of the ***Paris Convention*** (1967 revision), the ***Berne Convention*** (1971 revision), the ***Rome Convention*** and the ***Treaty on Intellectual Property in Respect of Integrated Circuits***, but there is no need to accede to these instruments to satisfy the Agreement. Members are free to determine the appropriate method to implement the provisions of the Agreement within their own legal system and practice. Part II covers the standards to be applied to the availability, scope and use of intellectual property rights. Among these are that copyright protection must be for at least fifty years. Initial registration of trademarks must be for at least seven years, followed by an indefinite number of renewals also of at least seven years. Members have to protect geographical indications, and additional protection is available for geographical indications for wines and spirits. Protection must be given for independently created industrial designs that are new and original. Patents must be "available for any inventions, whether products or processes, in all fields of technology, provided that they are new, involve an inventive step, and are capable of industrial application". The term of protection for patents is at least twenty years from the date of filing. The term of protection for lay-out designs (topographies) of integrated circuits is ten years from the date of filing or the date of the first commercial application. Undisclosed information must be protected against unfair competition as provided in the Paris Convention. Special mention is made of undisclosed test or other data submitted as a condition of approving the marketing of pharmaceutical or agricultural chemical products which utilize new chemical entities. The Agreement recognizes that "some licensing practices or conditions pertaining to intellectual property rights which restrain competition may have adverse effects on trade and may impede the transfer and dissemination of technology", and it seeks to minimize such problems through a right to consultations. In January 2017 a new ***Article 31bis*** was added which enables improved access by least-developed countries to generic medicines in circumstances where they do not have suitable production facilities themselves. The means of enforcement of intellectual property rights outlined in Part III of the Agreement include administrative, civil and criminal remedies. Detailed provisions apply to preventing trade in counterfeit or pirated goods. The normal WTO procedures apply to the settlement of disputes. ***Least-developed countries*** had until the end of 2005 to meet the obligations of the Agreement. Finally, the Agreement establishes the ***Council for TRIPS***. *See also* ***access to medicines***, ***industrial property***, ***intellectual property*** and ***Paragraph 6 system***.

Agreement on Trade-Related Investment Measures: TRIMs. A WTO agreement concluded during the ***Uruguay Round***. It aims to eliminate conditions attaching to permission to invest that may distort or restrict trade in goods. The annex to the Agreement contains an illustrative list of TRIMS deemed

于版权和相关权利、商标、地理标志、工业品外观设计、专利、集成电路布图设计和商业秘密的保护。适用的保护标准包括《巴黎公约》(1967)、《伯尔尼公约》(1971)、《罗马公约》和《关于集成电路知识产权的公约》，但无需加入上述法律文件以适用本协定。成员有权决定在其自身法律制度和实践中实施协定条款的适当方法。第二部分涵盖关于知识产权效力、范围和使用的标准。其中规定版权的保护期必须至少为50年。商标首次注册的保护期必须至少为7年，随后的续展不得少于7年。成员必须保护地理标志，对葡萄酒和烈酒的地理标志给予附加保护。必须对独立创造的新的或原创性工业品外观设计给予保护。专利必须授予"所有技术领域的任何发明，无论是产品还是方法，只要它们是新的、包含创造性，且可用于工业应用"。专利的保护期限自提交申请之日起计算至少为20年。集成电路布图设计的保护期限自提交申请之日起或首次进行商业利用之日起为10年。未披露信息必须受到保护以免于《巴黎公约》中所规定的不正当竞争的影响。协定特别提及作为批准销售使用新型化学物质制造的药品或农用化学品的条件而提交的未披露的试验数据或其他数据。协定认识到，"一些限制竞争的有关知识产权的许可行为或条件可对贸易产生不利影响，并会妨碍技术的转让和传播"，并寻求通过磋商权缩小此类问题。2017年1月，新增第31条之二，使最不发达国家在自身没有合适生产设施的情况下能够更好地获得仿制药。协定第三部分列出了知识产权的执行条款，包括行政、民事和刑事救济。对防止假冒商标或盗版货物作出具体规定。WTO正常程序适用于争端解决。最不发达国家可以在2005年底之后履行协定义务。协定最后部分还规定设立与贸易有关的知识产权理事会。另见*获得药品(access to medicines)*、*工业产权(industrial property)*、*知识产权(intellectual property)*、*第6段制度(Paragraph 6 system)*。

Agreement on Trade-Related Investment Measures
与贸易有关的投资措施协定

TRIMs。乌拉圭回合达成的一项WTO协定，旨在取消对投资审批所附加的、可能对货物贸易产生扭曲或限制作用的条件。协定的附件包含被认为不符合GATT第3条(国民待遇)和第11条(普遍取消数量限制)规定的TRIMs例示清单，

inconsistent with Article III (National Treatment) and Article XI (General Elimination of Quantitative Restrictions) of the ***GATT***. These are (a) requirements that an enterprise must use a defined amount of products of domestic origin, (b) permission to import related to export performance, and (c) any requirements related to ***quantitative restrictions*** of imports. The Agreement also raises in Article 9 the possibility that at a later stage it might include provisions on ***investment*** and ***competition policy***. *See also* ***foreign direct investment***, ***investment facilitation***, ***local content requirements***, ***Singapore issues*** and ***trade-balancing requirement***.

Agreement Regarding International Trade in Textiles: *see* ***Multi-Fibre Arrangement***.

Agreement Respecting Normal Competitive Conditions in the Commercial Shipbuilding and Repair Industry: *see* ***OECD shipbuilding agreement***.

Agricultural export subsidies: a subsidy contingent on export performance provided by governments to producers or exporters of agricultural commodities to ensure that their surpluses, usually produced at costs above world market prices, find a market somewhere. At the ***WTO Ministerial Conference*** in Nairobi in 2015 member countries committed to abolish export subsidies for farm exports. Developed countries agreed to do so immediately, developing countries by 2018 with a few exceptions entailing longer phasing out periods. *See also* ***agricultural subsidies***, ***agriculture and the multilateral trading system*** and ***subsidies***.

Agricultural Market Access Database: AMAD. Contains information on tariff and non-tariff measures for more than fifty countries. The database is hosted by the ***OECD***. It uses material supplied by Agriculture and AgriFood Canada, the Directorate-General of Agriculture in the ***European Commission***, the ***Food and Agriculture Organization***, the ***OECD***, the ***World Bank***, ***UNCTAD*** and the Economic Research Service of the United States Department of Agriculture. Updates are done once a year. [www.amad.org]

Agricultural Market Information System: AMIS. Established in 2011 by Ministers of Agriculture of the ***G20*** members. AMIS participants are the G20 members plus Egypt, Kazakhstan, Nigeria, Philippines, Spain, Thailand, Ukraine and Viet Nam. The group concerns itself with wheat, maize, rice and soybeans. Its aims are (a) to improve agricultural market information, analyses and forecasts at national and international levels, (b) to report on abnormal international market conditions and strengthen global early warning capacity, (c) to collect and analyse policy information, promote dialogue and responses, and international policy coordination, and (d) to build data collection capacity in participating countries. The AMIS secretariat is located in the ***Food and Agriculture Organization*** in Rome. *See also* ***Global Food Market Information Group***.

Agricultural products: these are defined in Annex 1 to the WTO ***Agreement on Agriculture*** as mainly the products listed in chapters 1 to 24 of the ***Harmonized Commodity Description and Coding System***. The group includes both raw

包括(a)要求一企业必须使用规定数量的国产品；(b)进口许可与出口实绩相关联；以及(c)与进口数量限制相关联的要求。协定还在第9条中提出了后期纳入投资和竞争政策条款的可能性。另见*外国直接投资(foreign direct investment)*、*投资便利化(investment facilitation)*、*当地含量要求(local content requirements)*、*新加坡议题(Singapore issues)*、*贸易平衡要求(trade-balancing requirement)*。

Agreement Regarding International Trade in Textiles

国际纺织品贸易协定

见*多种纤维协定(Multi-Fibre Arrangement)*（英文误为agreement，应为arrangement—译注）。

Agreement Respecting Normal Competitive Conditions in the Commercial Shipbuilding and Repair Industry

关于商船造修业正常竞争条件的协定

见*OECD造船协定(OECD shipbuilding agreement)*。

Agricultural export subsidies

农产品出口补贴

政府视出口实绩向农产品生产商或出口商提供的补贴，以保证它们的过剩产品在其他地方找到市场，这些产品通常是以高于世界市场成本的价格生产的。在2015年内罗毕举行的WTO部长级会议上，成员承诺取消农产品出口补贴。发达国家同意立即取消，发展中国家在2018年年底前取消，少数成员需要更长的取消时间。另见*农业补贴(agricultural subsidies)*、*农业与多边贸易体制(agriculture and the multilateral trading system)*、*补贴(subsidies)*。

Agricultural Market Access Database

农产品市场准入数据库

AMAD。数据库包含超过50个国家的关税和非关税措施信息，由经济合作与发展组织(OECD)主办。数据库使用加拿大农业及农业食品部、欧盟委员会农业总司长、粮农组织(FAO)、OECD、世界银行、联合国贸易与发展会议(UNCTAD)和美国农业部经济研究服务局提供的材料。每年更新一次。

Agricultural Market Information System

农产品市场信息系统

AMIS。2011年由20国集团成员国农业部长建立。AMIS参加方包括20国集团成员国以及埃及、哈萨克斯坦、尼日利亚、菲律宾、西班牙、泰国、乌克兰和越南。该组织关注小麦、玉米、稻谷和大豆。目标为：(a)在国家和国际层面改善农产品市场信息、分析和预测；(b)报告国际市场异常状况并加强全球预警能力；(c)收集和分析政策信息，促进对话及应对和国际政策协调；以及(d)建设参加国的数据收集能力。AMIS秘书处设在罗马的粮农组织(FAO)中。另见*全球食品市场信息组(Global Food Market Information Group)*。

Agricultural products

农产品

WTO《农业协定》附件1中所定义的产品，主要为商品名称及编码协调制度第1至24章中的产品。包括初级产品和不同程度的加工产品，但不包括林产品和

products and products processed to various degrees, but it excludes forestry and fishery products. *See also* ***common agricultural policy***, ***Food and Agriculture Organization***, ***intermediate agricultural products***, ***International Agreement on Olive Oil and Table Olives***, ***International Cocoa Agreement***, ***International Coffee Agreement***, ***International Cotton Advisory Committee***, ***International Fund for Agricultural Development***, ***International Grains Agreement***, ***International Organisation of Vine and Wine***, ***International Sugar Agreement***, ***International Treaty on Plant Genetic Resources for Food and Agriculture*** and ***market access for agriculture***.

Agricultural subsidies: assistance given to farmers by governments, often through monetary payments, but sometimes in kind. Agricultural subsidies typically include (a) incentives to keep growing a product, grow more of it or switch to producing another, (b) income support to ensure a certain level of standard of living of farmers, and (c) payments to ensure that the farming produce finds a market, either at home or abroad. All of them are funded through national treasuries or directly by the taxpayer. Subsidies related to production are often accompanied by ***import restrictions***, such as high tariffs generally and ***seasonal tariffs***. ***Decoupling*** can be important to reduce trade distortive effects. The farmer still receives a subsidy, but the amount is no longer linked to production quantities, acreages, specific products, or prices. The WTO **Agreement on Agriculture** rules on Domestic Support defined categories of support according to their purpose and impact and constrains the use of trade-distorting support. *See also* ***agricultural export subsidies***, ***box*** and ***domestic support***.

Agriculture and the multilateral trading system: the rules of the GATT do not distinguish between agricultural and other products except in minor ways. Article XI requires the general elimination of all ***quantitative restrictions***, but Article XI:2 permits some import and export restrictions on agricultural products under closely defined conditions. Article XVI (Subsidies) enjoins parties to avoid the use of subsidies on the export of ***primary products***, and Article XX (General Exceptions) allows members to suspend some of their obligations to comply with measures they have accepted as part of their membership of ***international commodity agreements***. Trade under these agreements was effectively not subject to GATT rules. For the first few years of the GATT's existence agricultural production and trade in agricultural products did not cause any real difficulties. Western Europe was still recovering from the effects of the late war, and there were as yet few hints of the persistent surpluses that were to be a feature of world agricultural trade a decade later. In particular, there seemed to be markets for United States domestic surpluses, except for dairy products. By the time of the 1955 ***GATT review session***, there was a feeling among members that the time had come also to bring commodity arrangements under the supervision of the GATT. The United States, however, had run into a problem. Domestic production ran persistently ahead of consumption, and its import market was attractive to foreign suppliers. The 1951

渔业产品。另见*共同农业政策(common agricultural policy)*、*粮食及农业组织(Food and Agriculture Organization)*、*中间农产品(intermediate agricultural products)*、*国际橄榄油和食用橄榄协定(International Agreement on Olive Oil and Table Olives)*、*国际可可协定(International Cocoa Agreement)*、*国际咖啡协定(International Coffee Agreement)*、*国际棉花咨询委员会(International Cotton Advisory Committee)*、*国际农业发展基金(International Fund for Agricultural Development)*、*国际谷物协定(International Grains Agreement)*、*国际葡萄与葡萄酒组织(International Organisation of Vine and Wine)*、*国际糖协定(International Sugar Agreement)*、*粮食与农业植物遗传资源国际条约(International Treaty on Plant Genetic Resources for Food and Agriculture)*、*农产品市场准入(market access for agriculture)*。

Agricultural subsidies

农业补贴

政府给予农民的援助，通常通过货币支付，但有时是实物。农业补贴通常包括(a)继续种植一种产品、增加种植量或转向种植另一种产品的奖励；(b)为保证农民一定生活水平而提供的收入支持；以及(c)保证农产品在国内或国外获得市场的支付。所有这些援助全部由国库或纳税人直接出资。与生产相关的补贴通常伴有进口限制，例如普遍高关税和季节性关税。不挂钩对于减少贸易扭曲作用非常重要。农民仍然获得补贴，但金额不再与产量、种植面积、具体产品或价格挂钩。WTO《农业协定》关于国内支持的规则根据支持的目的和影响定义支持类别，并限制使用具有贸易扭曲作用的支持。另见*农产品出口补贴(agricultural export subsidies)*、*箱(box)*、*国内支持(domestic support)*。

Agriculture and the multilateral trading system

农业与多边贸易体制

GATT规则不区分农产品和其他产品，除了在一些小的方面。第11条要求普遍取消数量限制，但第11条第2款在严格规定的条件下允许对农产品实行一些进口和出口限制。第16条(补贴)要求成员对初级产品的出口避免使用补贴，第20条(一般例外)允许成员暂停履行某些义务，以符合它们作为国际商品协定参加方资格的一部分所接受的措施。这些协定项下的贸易实际上不受GATT规则约束。在GATT存续的最初几年中，农业生产和农产品贸易没有导致任何真正的困难。西欧当时仍在从战争的影响中恢复，当时没有什么迹象表明世界农业贸易在10年后会出现持续过剩。特别是，美国国内生产过剩似乎是有市场的，除奶制品外。到了1955年GATT审议会议时，缔约方感到是时候应该将商品安排纳入GATT管辖之下了。但是，美国遇到了问题。国内生产持续高于消费，而其进口市场对外国供应商具有吸引力。《1951年贸易法》特别规定，新的贸

Trade Act specifically held that new trade agreements could not be made in contravention of existing United States agricultural programmes. The ***import restrictions*** permitted under GATT Article XI:2 appeared insufficient to deal with this problem. In 1951 the United States had been granted a ***waiver*** from the GATT rules to impose import restrictions on dairy products. This was superseded by a request in 1954, and granted in 1955, for a waiver without a time limit until it would be able to bring the provisions of the *Agricultural Adjustment Act* into line with GATT obligations. This was the ***Section 22 waiver***. The United States was now permitted to impose import restrictions on agricultural products as it deemed necessary. This action created a precedent for the treatment of agriculture under GATT rules. For example, when Switzerland acceded provisionally to the GATT in 1958, it obtained a ***carve-out*** for its entire agricultural sector. Nevertheless, the remainder of the GATT membership continued its search for an international regime for trade in commodities. A proposal had emerged in early 1955 for a ***Special Agreement on Commodity Arrangements*** (SACA). It contained a mechanism for dealing with disequilibria between production and consumption of primary commodities, including the possibility of commodity arrangements. Whether this arrangement would have existed side by side with the GATT, or whether it would have been subordinate to it, was never made clear. In any case, whatever the merits of the proposal, this did not matter, since it did not enter into force. There were those who considered that they would fare better under the existing GATT provisions. Others saw no point in proceeding once the United States made it clear that it was not interested in becoming a member of SACA. Attempts over the next three decades to impose GATT disciplines on agricultural trade fell well short of this proposal. An initiative later in 1955 to deal with the problem of surplus disposal, particularly under United States acts such as ***PL 480***, petered out after several years of discussion. The next attempt to deal with the problem of agricultural trade came with the commissioning of the ***Haberler Report*** in 1957. It was aimed particularly at analysing the failure of the trade of developing countries to develop as rapidly as that of industrialized countries, excessive short-term fluctuations in the price of primary products and widespread resort to agricultural protection. The panel report, titled *Trends in International Trade*, was issued in October 1958. It argued, among other things, for a moderation of agricultural protectionism in North America and Western Europe, and its overall tenor was in favour of ***trade liberalization***. Though the Report was universally welcomed, its influence turned out to be quite small. A committee was indeed established to consider the Report's recommendations in detail, and this led some to believe that a solution was nearer. Analysis and discussion there were, but the most that can be said about the longer-term effect of the Haberler Report is that it can be regarded as the first step towards the launch of the ***Dillon Round*** in 1960. In any case, by that time Western Europe's complete recovery from the effects of the war and the establishment of the ***European Economic Community*** (now the ***European Union***) had led to a new

易协定不能与现行美国农业计划相悖。GATT第11条第2款所允许的进口限制似乎不足以处理这一问题。1951年美国被给予对GATT规则的豁免，可以对奶制品实行进口限制。该豁免被在1954年提出并在1955年给予的一项新的豁免请求所取代，新的豁免没有时间限制，直至美国能够使《农业调整法案》条款与GATT义务相一致之时为止，即22条豁免。美国此时被允许可以在其认为必要时对农产品实施进口限制，这一行动创立了根据GATT规则处理农业部门的先例。例如，当瑞士在1958年临时加入GATT时，获得了整个农业部门的例外。尽管如此，其他GATT缔约方继续为商品贸易寻找一种国际体制。1955年初提出了一个商品安排特别协定(SACA)的建议，包含一个处理初级商品的生产与消费不平衡的机制，包括商品安排的可能性。这一安排是否与GATT并行存在，还是纳入GATT之下从未明确。无论如何，该建议无论优点如何也不再重要，因为它没有生效。有些成员认为，它们在现行GATT条款下会过得更好。另外一些则认为，如果美国表明没有兴趣成为SACA成员，就没有必要继续。在随后30年中将GATT规则适用于农业贸易的尝试远不及此建议。1955年稍晚提出的过剩处置问题倡议，特别是根据《480号公法》等美国法律提出的倡议，在经过几年讨论后逐渐淡出。处理农产品贸易问题的下一次尝试源自1957年制定的《哈伯勒报告》。该报告专门分析发展中国家的贸易无法如工业化国家的贸易同样迅速发展、初级产品价格的剧烈短期波动和农业保护的普遍采用等问题。题为《国际贸易趋势》的专家组报告于1958年10月发布。报告中主张改变北美和西欧的农业保护主义，其主旨是倾向于贸易自由化。尽管报告受到了普遍欢迎，但结果是影响非常小。确实设立了一个委员会以详细考虑报告所提建议，这使一些人相信很快要提出解决办法了。虽然进行了分析和讨论，但《哈伯勒报告》最值得一提的长期效果是，报告可以被认为是1960年启动狄龙回合的第一步。无论如何，西欧此时已经完全从战争影响中恢复，欧洲经济

situation in global agricultural trade. The introduction of the ***common agricultural policy*** with its ***variable levies*** and domestic support measures meant that the Community joined the United States in contributing to global trade distortions. Next, the ***Kennedy Round***, launched in 1963, appeared to offer another opportunity to sort out agriculture. One of its objectives was the adoption of measures for access to markets for agricultural and primary products. It began badly with the outbreak of the ***Chicken War***, a dispute between the United States and the European Economic Community over the sudden closure of German and other European markets for poultry through the operation of variable levies. The outcome on agriculture of the Kennedy Round was poor. Its main achievement was creating the impetus for the eventual conclusion of a new *International Grains Arrangement*. The mandate for the ***Tokyo Round*** (1973–79) included negotiations on agriculture, taking into account the special characteristics and problems in this sector. These negotiations again ended in failure. The conclusion of the *Agreement Regarding Bovine Meat* and the *International Dairy Arrangement* introduced a fragile peace into these trades, but they did not deal with the underlying problems of domestic overproduction, ***export subsidies***, import restrictions and other measures characterizing agricultural trade. The Tokyo Round ended with agreement that there should be continuing negotiations on the development of a ***Multilateral Agricultural Framework*** aimed at avoiding endemic political and commercial confrontations in this area. Negotiations were rejoined, but not to any effect. As noted by Hudec, Kennedy and Sgarbossa, there had been 100 disputes in the GATT concerning agriculture between 1947 and the early 1980s, accounting for nearly 43 per cent of all reported disputes. The United States and the European Economic Community had been involved either as a complainant or a respondent in 87 of them. A new start to finding a solution to the problems of agricultural trade was clearly necessary. The 1982 GATT Ministerial Meeting agreed on a work programme for the examination of all matters affecting trade, market access, competition and supply in agriculture. A working party made recommendations in 1984 concerning better market access, greater export competition, clearer rules on quantitative restrictions and subsidies, and more effective special treatment for developing countries. The report containing these recommendations was adopted in the same year. These recommendations then receded into the background as negotiations began for what became the mandate of the ***Uruguay Round***, but they provided in effect a draft set of negotiating objectives for the Round when it was launched in 1986. Ministers agreed at Punta del Este that negotiations should aim to achieve greater liberalization of trade in agriculture and to bring all measures affecting import access and export competition under strengthened and more operationally effective GATT rules and disciplines. Attention would be given to the reduction of import barriers, a better competitive environment and the effects of ***sanitary and phytosanitary measures***. Another new factor now entered into play. In the Kennedy and Tokyo Rounds the negotiations on agriculture were conducted mainly between

共同体(现欧盟) 为全球农业贸易开辟了新局面。共同农业政策及其差价税和国内支持措施的引入，意味着欧共体与美国一起导致了全球贸易扭曲。随后，1963年启动的肯尼迪回合似乎提供了解决农业问题的另一次机会。回合的目的之一是采取进入农业和初级产品市场的措施。鸡肉战的爆发使回合开局不利。这是一起美国与欧共体之间由于德国和其他欧洲禽肉市场因差价税而突然关闭所引发的争端。肯尼迪回合关于农业的成果少得可怜。主要成果是为最终达成一项新的《国际谷物协定》提供了动力。东京回合(1973年至1979年)的授权包括农业谈判，同时考虑该领域的特点和问题。谈判最终还是以失败告终。《国际牛肉协定》和《国际奶制品协定》的达成给这些部门的贸易带来了脆弱的和平，但并不处理国内生产过剩、出口补贴、进口限制和农产品贸易所特有的其他措施的根本问题。东京回合结束时达成协议，即应继续就多边农业框架的制定进行谈判，旨在避免该领域所特有的政治和商业冲突。谈判继续进行，但没有任何成果。正如胡德克、肯尼迪和斯加博萨所指出的，从1947年至20世纪80年代初，在GATT中发生了100起有关农业的争端，占所有有报告争端的43％。美国和欧共体在其中的87个争端中要么是起诉方，要么是被诉方。可以明确的是，有必要重新开始寻找解决农业贸易领域的问题。1982年GATT部长级会议议定了审查所有影响农业贸易、市场准入、竞争和供应问题的工作计划。1984年一工作组就更好的市场准入、更多的出口竞争、更明确的数量限制和补贴规则以及更有效的发展中国家特殊待遇提出了建议。包含这些建议的报告在同年获得通过。这些建议后来随着乌拉圭回合谈判的开始而淡出视线，但是建议实际上为1986年启动的谈判回合提供了一套谈判目标草案。各国部长在埃斯特角城同意，谈判应旨在实现农业领域更大的贸易自由化，并将所有影响进入市场和出口竞争的措施纳入增强的和更有效的GATT规则和纪律之中。特别关注进口壁垒的削减、更好的竞争环境和卫生与植物卫生措施的影响。另一个新的因素出现了。在肯尼迪回合和东京回合中，

the European Economic Community and the United States. Other agricultural traders existed very much at the margin of these negotiations. The formation immediately before the launch of the Uruguay Round of the ***Cairns Group***, a group then consisting of fourteen agricultural producers and exporters, ensured that there would be an influential and moderating third voice. Agriculture was one of the most difficult negotiating subjects during the Uruguay Round. The issues were well understood, but no real progress was made until the European Community had accepted that changes to the ***common agricultural policy*** were necessary for internal budgetary reasons alone, and that reductions in price supports were possible without tearing the Community's social fabric apart. Even then, the ***European Commission*** had great difficulty obtaining a negotiating mandate from the member states. Its difficulties in participating meaningfully in the agricultural negotiations led to the collapse of the Brussels Ministerial Meeting in December 1990. Matters were not helped by adherence by the United States to its objective of zero subsidies, something that observers doubted it would be able to deliver even in respect of its own practices. The Round then effectively marked time until the ***Blair House Accord*** in November 1992. Negotiations remained difficult, and some changes in favour of the European Community were made to this accord in December 1993. This allowed concluding the Round within a few days. Trade in all agricultural products is now covered by GATT rules, but extensive further negotiations will be required to achieve a trade regime resembling that for industrial products. Negotiations on agriculture resumed on 1 January 2000 under ***Article 20*** (the ***continuation clause***) of the WTO ***Agreement on Agriculture.*** These negotiations were then incorporated in the ***Doha Development Agenda***. Achievements in the negotiations so far include decisions at the Bali ***WTO Ministerial Conference*** in 2013 to enlarge the list of ***general services in agriculture*** and an ***Understanding on tariff rate quota administration provisions of agricultural products***. At the 2015 Ministerial Conference in Nairobi WTO members made a commitment to abolish ***agricultural export subsidies*** immediately by developed countries and by 2018 by developing countries. Members also agreed that developing countries will have the right to have recourse to a special safeguard mechanism, to be negotiated in dedicated sessions of the Committee on Agriculture in Special Session. They also agreed to make concerted efforts to agree and adopt a permanent solution on the issue of ***public stockholding for food security***. Separately, the CAP has undergone several revisions by the European Union, *See also* ***Baumgartner proposals***, ***Mansholt proposals*** and ***Ploughshares War***. [Croome 1995, Hudec, Kennedy and Sgarbossa 1993, Ingco, Nash and Cleaver 2004, Josling, Tangermann and Warley 1996, Preeg 1970]

Agriculture Information Management System: Ag-IMS. Provides access to documents and records relevant to the WTO ***Agreement on Agriculture***. It allows users to search and analyse agriculture-related information notified by WTO members as well as questions and responses provided in the ***Committee on Agriculture***. [www.amis-outlook.org]

农业谈判主要在欧共体和美国之间进行。其他农业贸易方在谈判中处于边缘化地位。在乌拉圭回合启动前成立了凯恩斯集团，当时包含14个农业生产国和出口国，保证了将会出现有影响力和协调力的第三个声音。农业是乌拉圭回合中最难谈判的议题之一。问题已经很清楚，但谈判一直没有取得真正进展，直至欧共体接受了仅由于内部预算原因对共同农业政策进行改变是必要的，且削减价格支持而不破坏共同体的社会结构是可能的。即便如此，欧共体委员会自成员国获得谈判授权困难重重。欧共体有效参与农业谈判的困难导致了1990年12月布鲁塞尔部长级会议的失败。美国对零补贴目标的长期坚持并没有起到什么帮助作用，观察者怀疑这一点即使对于美国自身的实践而言能否实现。此后的谈判实际上就是耗时间，直至1992年11月达成《布莱尔宫协议》。谈判仍然困难，1993年12月对该协议作出了有利于欧共体的修改。这样就使这轮回合在几天内结束了。至此所有农产品贸易已为GATT规则所涵盖，但是如果要实现类似工业品的贸易制度仍然需要进行进一步的广泛谈判。农业谈判根据WTO《农业协定》第20条(继续谈判条款)于2000年1月1日恢复。谈判后来纳入多哈发展议程。迄今为止的谈判成果包括2013年巴厘岛WTO部长级会议决定扩大农业一般服务清单以及达成《关于农产品关税配额管理规定的谅解》。在2015年内罗毕部长级会议上，WTO成员承诺发达国家立即取消农产品出口补贴，发展中国家在2018年之前取消。成员们还同意，发展中国家将有权援用特殊保障机制，该机制将在农业委员会特别会议的专门会议上进行谈判。他们还同意共同努力，就粮食安全公共储备问题达成一致并通过永久解决方案。此外，欧盟对共同农业政策(CAP)进行了多次修改。另见*鲍姆加特纳建议(Baumgartner proposals)*、*曼索托建议(Mansholt proposals)*、*犁铧战(Ploughshares War)*。

Agriculture Information Management System
农业信息管理系统

Ag-IMS。提供对与WTO《农业协定》相关的文件和记录的访问。允许用户搜索和分析WTO成员通报的与农业相关的信息以及在农业委员会中提出的问题和答复。

Aid for Trade: assistance to developing countries, and particularly least-developed countries, to enable them to participate more fully in international trade. It gives effect to the ***Aid for Trade Initiative*** led by the WTO. This work is supported by the Aid for Trade Global Review which takes place every two years, prepared jointly by the OECD and the WTO. Assistance in this area is included in ***official development assistance*** programmes. [www.wto.org, www.oecd.org]

Aid for Trade Facilitation Interactive Database: an OECD database created to provide transparency about the support of donors for trade facilitation activities and to enable the matching of supply and demand for support. It is meant to assist developing countries in the implementation of their obligations under the ***Agreement on Trade Facilitation***. [www.oecd.org]

Aid for Trade Initiative: an outcome of the WTO ***Hong Kong Ministerial Conference***. Paragraph 57 of the ministerial declaration states that "Aid for Trade should aim to help developing countries, particularly LDCs, to build the supply-side capacity and trade-related infrastructure that they need to assist them to implement and benefit from WTO Agreements and more broadly to expand their trade". *See also* ***developing countries and the multilateral trading system*** and ***Enhanced Integrated Framework***.

Aid for Trade Monitoring Framework: a framework established jointly by the OECD and the WTO to track progress in the implementation of the ***Aid for Trade Initiative*** and to enhance its credibility. The objective of the monitoring framework is to promote dialogue and encourage all key actors to honour commitments, improve effectiveness and reinforce mutual accountability and to improve the coherence of aid for trade with overall donor strategies.

Aim and effect: a test used in some GATT dispute settlement proceedings to ascertain whether there is possible *de facto national treatment* discrimination. For example, a measure might have the aim of affording protection, but its effect may be to discriminate in favour of the domestic product. [Cossy 2006]

Aircraft: *see* ***Agreement on Trade in Civil Aircraft*** and ***Large Aircraft Sector Understanding***.

AITIC: Agency for International Trade Information and Cooperation. An agency formed in 2002 and funded by Switzerland and others to assist less-developed countries in playing a more active role in the work of the WTO and other trade-related organizations. Dissatisfaction with its operations led to its closure in 2011.

ALADI: Asociación Latinoamericana de Integración. The Latin American Integration Association (LAIA). Formed in 1980 by Argentina, Bolivia, Brazil, Chile, Colombia, Ecuador, Mexico, Paraguay, Peru, Uruguay and Venezuela following the collapse of ***LAFTA*** (Latin American Free Trade Association). The objective of ALADI, as set out in the Treaty of Montevideo, is to pursue the gradual and progressive establishment of a Latin American ***common market***. ***Mercosur*** is seen as a step towards achieving this objective. ALADI's secretariat is located at Montevideo. *See also* ***South American Community of Nations***.

Aid for Trade

促贸援助

给予发展中国家，特别是最不发达国家的援助，使它们能够更充分参与国际贸易。援助使WTO所领导的促贸援助倡议得以生效。这项工作得到了由经济合作与发展组织(OECD)和WTO联合筹备的每2年一次的促贸援助全球审议的支持。这一领域的援助包括在官方发展援助项目中。

Aid for Trade Facilitation Interactive Database

贸易便利化援助互动数据库

经济合作与发展组织(OECD)数据库，设立的目的在于为捐助者对贸易便利化活动的支持措施提供透明度，并实现支持的供需匹配。数据库旨在为发展中国家执行《贸易便利化协定》项下义务提供协助。

Aid for Trade Initiative

促贸援助倡议

WTO香港部长级会议成果。部长宣言第57段指出："促贸援助应旨在帮助发展中国家、特别是最不发达国家，建设它们为实施《WTO协定》并从中获益及更广泛而言扩大其贸易所需的供应能力和与贸易有关的基础设施。"另见*发展中国家与多边贸易体制(developing countries and the multilateral trading system)*、*增强综合框架(Enhanced Integrated Framework)*。

Aid for Trade Monitoring Framework

促贸援助监督框架

经济合作与发展组织(OECD)和WTO联合建立的框架，用于跟踪促贸援助倡议的实施情况并增强其可信度。监督框架的目标是促进对话并鼓励所有关键行为主体履行承诺、提高效率和加强相互问责，并提高促贸援助与总体捐助战略的一致性。

Aim and effect

目标与效果

一些GATT争端解决程序中所使用的测试，用以确定是否存在事实上的国民待遇歧视。例如，一措施可能具有提供保护的目的，但其效果可能因为有利于国产品而具有歧视性。

Aircraft

航空器

见*民用航空器贸易协定(Agreement on Trade in Civil Aircraft)*、*民用航空器行业谅解(Large Aircraft Sector Understanding)*。

AITIC

国际贸易信息与合作署

由瑞士政府等资助于2002年成立的机构，旨在帮助欠发达国家在WTO和其他与贸易相关组织的工作中发挥更加积极的作用。由于运营不佳，该机构于2011年关闭。

ALADI

拉丁美洲一体化协会

在拉丁美洲自由贸易协会(LAFTA)解体后于1980年成立，成员国为阿根廷、玻利维亚、巴西、智利、哥伦比亚、厄瓜多尔、墨西哥、巴拉圭、秘鲁、乌拉圭和委内瑞拉。《蒙得维的亚条约》规定了ALADI的目标，即致力于循序渐进建立拉丁美洲共同市场。南方共同市场(Mercosur)被视为实现这一目标的步骤之一。ALADI秘书处设在蒙得维的亚。另见*南美洲国家共同体(South American Community of Nations)*。

Alliance for Progress: initially a ten-year development plan for Latin America containing economic and social objectives. It was launched by President Kennedy in 1961. Among other aims, it was to find "a rapid and lasting solution to the grave problem created by excessive price fluctuations in the basic exports of Latin American countries" and to accelerate the economic integration of Latin America. Some progress was made over the years, but when the Alliance for Progress was formally ended in 1980, many thought that its achievements fell short of its aims. *See also* ***Andean Trade Preference Act***, ***Andean Trade Promotion and Drug Eradication Act***, ***Caribbean Basin Initiative***, ***Enterprise for the Americas Initiative*** and ***FTAA***.

Alliance for Strategic Products and Special Safeguard Mechanism: a group of developing countries formed at the ***Cancún Ministerial Conference***. It was known as the G-33, but it had more than forty members. The Alliance had three main aims. First, developing countries should be able to nominate a certain number of agricultural ***tariff lines*** as special products. These would not be subject to tariff reductions. Nor would there be any new commitments to liberalize ***tariff rate quotas*** for these products. Second, ***special agricultural safeguards for developing countries*** should be created to protect their markets against cheap and subsidized agricultural imports. Third, products designated as special products should have access to the special safeguard mechanism. *See also* ***Doha Development Agenda***.

Alliance of Small Island States: AOSIS. *See* ***small island developing states***.

Almaty Programme of Action: a list of priority actions to advance the interests of landlocked developing countries adopted in Almaty in 2003. The five priorities are (a) policy improvements – reducing customs bureaucracy and fees and designed to cut costs and travel days for exports of landlocked developing countries, (b) improved rail, road, air and pipeline infrastructure, (c) international trade measures – preferential treatment for goods from landlocked countries, (d) technical and financial international assistance, and (e) monitoring and follow-up on agreements. *See also* ***Vienna Programme of Action for Land-locked Developing Countries for the Decade 2014–2024***. [www.unohrlls.org]

ALOP: *see* ***appropriate level of sanitary and phytosanitary protection***. Also known as ***acceptable level of risk***. *See also* ***precautionary principle*** and ***sanitary and phytosanitary measures***.

Alternative dispute resolution: a method of settling disputes through ***arbitration***, ***consultation***, ***mediation***, etc., outside the formal framework of court proceedings. The parties to the dispute usually appoint a disinterested person who attempts to bring about an outcome based on fairness and equity. Alternative dispute resolution only works if the parties are genuinely committed to finding a solution and to accept a negotiated outcome since such awards are in most cases not enforceable through courts. One such mechanism is ***SOLVIT*** under which natural and legal persons residing in the ***European Union*** can seek redress against the misapplication of internal market rules by another member state. *See also* ***dispute settlement*** and ***International Court of Arbitration***.

Alliance for Progress
进步联盟

最初为拉丁美洲的10年发展计划，其中包含经济和社会目标。由美国总统肯尼迪于1961年发起。除其他目标外，联盟旨在为“拉丁美洲国家基本出口产品价格过度波动所造成的严重问题”寻找快速和持久的解决办法，并加速拉丁美洲的经济一体化。多年来取得了一些进展，但是当进步联盟于1980年正式结束时，许多人认为联盟所取得的成就没有达到目标。另见*安第斯贸易优惠法(Andean Trade Preference Act)*、*安第斯贸易促进与毒品根除法(Andean Trade Promotion and Drug Eradication Act)*、*加勒比盆地倡议(Caribbean Basin Initiative)*、*美洲事业倡议(Enterprise for the Americas Initiative)*、*美洲自由贸易区(FTAA)*。

Alliance for Strategic Products and Special Safeguard Mechanism
战略产品与特殊保障机制联盟

坎昆部长级会议上成立的发展中国家集团，被称为33国协调组(G-33)，但目前成员已经超过40个。联盟有三个主要目标：一是发展中国家应能够提出一定数量的农产品税目作为特殊产品。这些税目免于关税削减。对于这些产品也不作出开放关税配额的任何新承诺。二是应设立发展中国家农产品特殊保障机制，以保护其本国市场免受低价和补贴进口农产品的冲击。三是指定为特殊产品的产品应适用特殊保障机制。另见*多哈发展议程(Doha Development Agenda)*。

Alliance of Small Island States
小岛国联盟

AOSIS。见*小岛屿发展中国家(small island developing states)*。

Almaty Programme of Action
阿拉木图行动纲领

2003年在阿拉木图通过的促进内陆发展中国家利益的优先行动清单。五个优先事项为：(a)政策改进—减少海关官僚和费用，旨在降低内陆发展中国家出口的成本和在途时间；(b)改善铁路、公路、航空和管道基础设施；(c)国际贸易措施—对内陆国家货物的优惠待遇；(d)技术和金融国际援助；以及(e)监测和后继协定。另见*内陆发展中国家2014—2024年十年维也纳行动纲领(Vienna Programme of Action for Land-locked Developing Countries for the Decade 2014–2024)*。

ALOP
适当的卫生与植物卫生保护水平

也称可接受的风险水平。另见*预防原则(precautionary principle)*、*卫生与植物卫生措施(sanitary and phytosanitary measures)*。

Alternative dispute resolution
非诉讼争端解决

在法庭程序的正式框架之外通过仲裁、磋商、调停等解决争端的方法。争端各方通常指定一名无利害关系的人士本着公平和公正的原则尝试达成结果。只有在各方真正致力于找到解决办法且接受谈判结果的情况下，非诉讼争端解决方可奏效，因为此类裁决在大多数情况下是不通过法庭执行的。此种机制之一是欧洲共同体中的非诉讼争端解决机制(SOLVIT)，据此位于欧盟内的自然人和法人可以针对另一成员滥用内部市场规则寻求救济。另见*争端解决(dispute settlement)*、*国际仲裁法院(International Court of Arbitration)*。

Alternative specific tariff: a tariff rate set either at an ***ad valorem*** rate, i.e. expressed as a percentage of the value of the product, or at a specific rate, i.e. set as a fixed monetary rate per article. The customs authorities then usually apply the higher of the two. *See also* ***ad valorem tariff*** and ***specific tariff***.

Amber box: refers to domestic support measures for agriculture that distort production and trade, including price support and subsidies directly related to production quantities. *See also* ***blue box***, ***green box*** and ***Total Aggregate Measurement of Support***.

Amendments to WTO agreements: the following WTO provisions may only be amended by agreement of all members: Article IX (Decision-Making) of the ***WTO Agreement***, Articles I (General Most-Favoured-Nation Treatment) and II (Schedules of Concessions) of the ***GATT 1994***, Article II:1 (Most-Favoured-Nation Treatment) of the ***General Agreement on Trade in Services***, and Article 4 (Most-Favoured-Nation Treatment) of the ***Agreement on Trade-Related Aspects of Intellectual Property Rights*** (TRIPS Agreement). Amendments to other provisions of the WTO multilateral agreements may be made by a two-thirds majority. Each member then has to conclude separate formalities to accept the amendment. The additional Article *31bis* to the TRIPS Agreement was the first change to an agreement administered by the WTO. The Marrakesh Agreement enables the ***WTO Ministerial Conference*** to decide by a three-fourths majority that any member not accepting an amendment within a certain time may be free to withdraw from the WTO or to remain a member anyway. All WTO members have one vote. The ***European Union*** is entitled to a number of votes equalling the number of its member states. Amendments to the ***WTO plurilateral trade agreements*** are made under the provisions contained in these agreements. *See also* ***decision-making in the WTO***.

American Selling Price: ASP. Until 1979 a method under the United States Fordney-McCumber Tariff Act of 1922, and carried over into the Tariff Act of 1930, for valuing some goods at the border for the purpose of levying customs duties. Duty assessments were based on the usual wholesale price, including preparation for shipping, at which an article manufactured in the United States was offered on the domestic market. The effect of this system could be a duty rate two to three times higher than if the method of valuation set out in GATT Article VII (Customs Valuation) had been chosen. The ASP was abolished through the *Trade Agreements Act* of 1979 by which the United States accepted the rules set out in the *Tokyo Round Agreement on Implementation of Article VII [customs valuation]*.

Amicus **brief:** an opinion offered to the court by a disinterested party (called *amicus curiae* or friend of the court) in the hope that this would assist the judges in arriving at the best possible outcomes. Courts do not always welcome being helped in this way.

Amicus curiae**:** *see* ***amicus brief***.

Analogue country: sometimes also called surrogate country. This describes the country selected by anti-dumping authorities for the purpose of price comparison

Alternative specific tariff

选择性从量关税

以从价税率(即以产品价值的百分比表示)或从量税率(即以每件商品的固定货币税率表示)规定的关税税率。海关通常适用两者中较高者。另见*从价关税(ad valorem tariff)*、*从量关税(specific tariff)*。

Amber box

黄箱

指扭曲生产和贸易的农业国内支持措施，包括价格支持和与产量直接挂钩的补贴。另见*蓝箱(blue box)*、*绿箱(green box)*、*综合支持总量(Total Aggregate Measurement of Support)*。

Amendments to WTO agreements

WTO协定的修正

WTO以下条款必须经所有成员同意方可进行修正:《WTO协定》第9条(决策)、GATT 1994第1条(普遍最惠国待遇)和第2条(减让表)、《服务贸易总协定》第2条第1款(最惠国待遇)和《与贸易有关的知识产权协定》第4条(最惠国待遇)。WTO多边协定的其他条款可经成员的三分之二多数通过后进行修正。随后每一成员需完成单独程序以接受修正。新增的《TRIPS协定》第31条之二是对WTO所管理协定的首次修正。《马拉喀什建立世界贸易组织协定》授权WTO部长级会议可以四分之三多数决定，在某一期限内未接受修正的任何成员可以有权退出WTO或仍为成员。每一WTO成员拥有一票。欧盟拥有的票数与其成员国数相等。WTO诸边贸易协定的修正根据这些协定所含条款进行。另见*WTO决策机制(decision-making in the WTO)*。

American Selling Price

美国销售价格

ASP。根据美国《1922年福德尼-麦坎伯关税法》为征税目的在边境对部分货物进行估价的方法，该方法被纳入《1930年关税法》，直至1979年。关税估价根据美国国内制造的物品在国内市场许诺销售的通常的批发价格，包括装运准备的费用。这一制度产生的税率可能比使用GATT第7条(海关估价)估价方法高两至三倍。美国接受了《东京回合关于实施关税与贸易总协定第7条的协定》中的规则，通过《1979年贸易协定法》废止了ASP。

***Amicus* brief**

法庭之友书面陈述

无利害关系的一方(称为法庭之友)为帮助法官达成更好的可能结果而向法庭提供的意见。法院并不总是欢迎得到此种方式的帮助。

Amicus curiae

法庭之友

见*法庭之友书面陈述(amicus brief)*。

Analogue country

类比国

有时也称替代国。指反倾销主管机关在认为可获得的货物原产国的价格信息

when they consider that the price information available from the country of origin of the goods would not yield useful results. *See* ***anti-dumping measures***.

Andean Community: the Cartagena Agreement of 26 May 1969 established the Andean Pact, sometimes known as Andean Group, as a sub-group of ***LAFTA*** (Latin American Free Trade Association). The Agreement aims to coordinate the industry and foreign investment policies of its members. Current members are Bolivia, Columbia, Ecuador, Peru and Venezuela. Chile was a member from 1969 to 1976. An Andean Free Trade Area was established on 1 January 1992, followed by the adoption of a ***common external tariff*** on 1 January 1995. On 1 January 1997 the arrangement evolved into the Andean Community. Its secretariat is located in Lima. *See also* ***Latin American regional integration arrangements***.

Andean Free Trade Area: *see* ***Andean Community***.

Andean Integration System: an umbrella body established by the ***Andean Community*** in 1997 which covers all of the Community's institutions and mechanisms. Its aim is to intensify regional integration.

Andean Pact: *see* ***Andean Community***.

Andean Trade Preference Act: ATPA. A United States act of 1991 which gave trade preferences for ten years to products from Bolivia, Colombia, Ecuador and Peru to encourage the development of licit trade. It was modelled on the ***Caribbean Basin Initiative***. It was renewed and amended in 2002 as the ***Andean Trade Promotion and Drug Eradication Act***. It expired on 31 July 2013.

Andean Trade Promotion and Drug Eradication Act: ATPDEA. Passed by the United States Congress in August 2002 to amend and renew the trade preferences given to Bolivia, Colombia, Ecuador and Peru under the ***Andean Trade Preference Act*** (ATPA) until 31 December 2006. The Act distinguishes between ATPA and ATPDEA status. Separate criteria had to be met to qualify for the latter. It expired on 31 July 2013.

Andriessen Assurance: an arrangement negotiated in 1985 between the ***European Economic Community*** (EEC) and Australia which keeps certain Asian beef markets free of ***subsidies***. Named after Frans Andriessen who was EEC Commissioner for Agriculture at the time.

Animal welfare: a subject proposed at one time by the ***European Union*** and Switzerland with the support of European ***non-governmental organizations*** for inclusion as a ***non-trade concern*** in the WTO negotiations on agriculture. Supporters of this proposal argue that in the absence of a framework in the WTO for discussing farm animal welfare, the domestic animal welfare standards already achieved by them could be undermined by imports from countries where these standards are much lower. One of the solutions offered in response to criticism that such proposals may amount to hidden protectionism is to pay some sort of compensation to producers where these can show additional costs because of the need to maintain higher standards. This could be done through accommodating such payments in the ***green box***.

不会产生有用的结果时为价格比较目的而选定的国家。见*反倾销措施(anti-dumping measures)*。

Andean Community
安第斯共同体

1969年5月26日的《卡塔赫纳协定》确立了安第斯条约组织，有时称为安第斯集团，作为拉丁美洲自由贸易协会(LAFTA)的一个小组。协定旨在协调成员的产业和外国投资政策。目前的成员国为玻利维亚、哥伦比亚、厄瓜多尔、秘鲁和委内瑞拉。智利在1969年至1976年曾为成员国。安第斯自由贸易区于1992年1月1日建立，随后于1995年1月1日采用共同对外关税。1997年1月1日，该安排演变为安第斯共同体。秘书处设在利马。另见*拉丁美洲区域一体化安排(Latin American regional integration arrangements)*。

Andean Free Trade Area
安第斯自由贸易区

见*安第斯共同体(Andean Community)*。

Andean Integration System
安第斯一体化体系

安第斯共同体于1997年建立的一个总括机构，涵盖该共同体的所有机构和机制，目标是增强区域一体化。

Andean Pact
安第斯条约组织

见*安第斯共同体(Andean Community)*。

Andean Trade Preference Act
安第斯贸易优惠法

ATPA。美国1991年的一项法案，给予来自玻利维亚、哥伦比亚、厄瓜多尔和秘鲁的产品10年的贸易优惠，以鼓励发展合法贸易。法案以加勒比盆地倡议为蓝本，2002年更新和修正为《安第斯贸易促进与毒品根除法》。2013年7月31日失效。

Andean Trade Promotion and Drug Eradication Act
安第斯贸易促进与毒品根除法

ATPDEA。美国国会于2002年8月通过修正和更新根据《安第斯贸易优惠法》(ATPA)给予玻利维亚、哥伦比亚、厄瓜多尔和秘鲁的贸易优惠，直至2006年12月31日。该法区分ATPA和ATPDEA的地位。有资格获得后者必须满足单独标准。该法于2013年7月31日失效。

Andriessen Assurance
安德里森保证

1985年欧洲经济共同体(EEC)与澳大利亚谈判的一项安排，保持某些亚洲牛肉市场免于补贴。以当时的欧共体农业委员Frans Andriessen命名。

Animal welfare
动物福利

欧盟和瑞士在欧洲非政府组织支持下，曾经提出的一项议题，建议将动物福利作为一项非贸易关注纳入WTO农业谈判。建议的支持者认为，WTO没有讨论农场动物福利的框架，这些国家已经达到的国内动物福利标准可能受到来自标准低得多的国家进口的损害。对于此类建议可能成为隐性保护主义的批评，提出的解决办法之一是向为维持更高标准而显示额外成本的生产者支付某种形式的补偿。此点可通过将此类支付归入绿箱实现。

Annecy Tariff Conference: the second of the nine rounds of ***multilateral trade negotiations***. It was held at Annecy, France, from April to August 1949. It primarily aimed to facilitate accession to the GATT by ten countries (Denmark, Dominican Republic, Finland, Greece, Haiti, Italy, Liberia, Nicaragua, Sweden and Uruguay) which had not participated in the 1947 Geneva tariff negotiations. In the event, Uruguay did not accede until 1953. *See also* ***Tariff Conference***.

Annex I countries: so named after their inclusion in Annex I of the ***United Nations Framework Convention on Climate Change***. They are Australia, Austria, Belarus, Belgium, Bulgaria, Canada, Croatia, Czech Republic, Denmark, Estonia, European Union, Finland, France, Germany, Greece, Hungary, Iceland, Ireland, Italy, Japan, Latvia, Liechtenstein, Lithuania, Luxembourg, Monaco, Netherlands, New Zealand, Norway, Poland, Portugal, Romania, Russian Federation, Slovakia, Slovenia, Spain, Sweden, Switzerland, Turkey, Ukraine, United Kingdom and the United States.

Annex II countries: in the ***United Nations Framework Convention on Climate Change*** the ***OECD*** member countries.

Annex VII countries: refers to the countries listed in Annex VII to the WTO ***Agreement on Subsidies and Countervailing Measures***. They are (a) the ***least-developed countries*** so designated by the United Nations that are members of the WTO and (b) Bolivia, Cameroon, Congo, Côte d'Ivoire, Dominican Republic, Egypt, Ghana, Guatemala, Guyana, India, Indonesia, Kenya, Morocco, Nicaragua, Nigeria, Pakistan, Philippines, Senegal, Sri Lanka and Zimbabwe. The least-developed countries are exempt from the prohibition on export subsidies. The others are exempt until their GNP per capita reaches $1,000 per year.

Annexes to the General Agreement on Trade in Services: *see* ***General Agreement on Trade in Services***.

Annex on Telecommunications: an annex to the ***General Agreement on Trade in Services*** which requires WTO members (a) to ensure ***transparency*** in their regulation of telecommunications, (b) give access to other members to public telecommunications transport networks and services on reasonable and non-discriminatory terms and conditions, and (c) to encourage and engage in technical cooperation.

Anti-absorption: measures taken by the relevant authority to prevent perceived ***absorption*** of ***anti-dumping measures*** by the producers or exporters of the good in question. In other words, if the producer or exporter is thought to carry the burden of anti-dumping duties, the authorities may in some cases decide to increase these duties. *See also* ***anti-circumvention***.

Anti-circumvention: measures by governments to prevent ***circumvention*** of measures they have imposed, such as definitive ***anti-dumping duties***. Sometimes firms seek to avoid such duties through, for example, assembly of parts and components either in the importing country or a third country, or by shifting the source of manufacture and export to a third country. The term as

Annecy Tariff Conference
安纳西关税会议

9轮多边贸易谈判中的第2轮。1949年4月至8月在法国安纳西举行。主要目的为便利未参加1947年日内瓦关税谈判的10个国家(丹麦、多米尼加、芬兰、希腊、海地、意大利、利比里亚、尼加拉瓜、瑞典和乌拉圭)加入GATT。结果，乌拉圭直至1953年才加入。另见*关税会议(Tariff Conference)*。

Annex I countries
附件1国家

因被列入《联合国气候变化框架公约》附件1而得名。这些国家为澳大利亚、奥地利、白俄罗斯、比利时、保加利亚、加拿大、克罗地亚、捷克、丹麦、爱沙尼亚、欧盟、芬兰、法国、德国、希腊、匈牙利、冰岛、爱尔兰、意大利、日本、拉脱维亚、列支敦士登、立陶宛、卢森堡、摩纳哥、荷兰、新西兰、挪威、波兰、葡萄牙、罗马尼亚、俄罗斯、斯洛伐克、斯洛文尼亚、西班牙、瑞典、瑞士、土耳其、乌克兰、英国和美国。

Annex II countries
附件2国家

《联合国气候变化框架公约》中的经济合作与发展组织(OECD)成员国。

Annex VII countries
附件7国家

指WTO《补贴与反补贴措施协定》附件7中所列国家。这些国家为：(a)联合国指定属最不发达国家的WTO成员；(b)玻利维亚、喀麦隆、刚果(布)、科特迪瓦、多米尼加、埃及、加纳、危地马拉、圭亚那、印度、印度尼西亚、肯尼亚、摩洛哥、尼加拉瓜、尼日利亚、巴基斯坦、菲律宾、塞内加尔、斯里兰卡和津巴布韦。最不发达国家免于禁止使用出口补贴的规定，其他国家在人均国民生产总值达到每年1,000美元之前免于限制。

Annexes to the General Agreement on Trade in Services
服务贸易总协定附件

见*服务贸易总协定(General Agreement on Trade in Services)*。

Annex on Telecommunications
关于电信服务的附件

《服务贸易总协定》附件，要求WTO成员：(a)保证电信法规的透明度；(b)允许其他成员按照合理和非歧视的条款和条件接入公共电信传输网络和服务；以及(c)鼓励和开展技术合作。

Anti-absorption
反吸收

有关主管机关为防止其认为的所涉货物的生产商或出口商对反倾销措施的吸收而采取的措施。换言之，如果生产商或出口商被认为承担了反倾销税的负担，主管机关在某些情况下可以决定增加这些关税。另见*反规避(anti-circumvention)*。

Anti-circumvention
反规避

政府为防止其实施的最终反倾销税等措施受到规避而采取的措施。有时公司寻求避税，例如，在进口国或一第三国组装零部件或将制造和出口来源转移

used in the WTO does not refer to cases of fraud. These would be dealt with under normal legal procedures of the countries concerned. The ***Agreement on Agriculture*** contains an anti-circumvention provision. It stipulates that export subsidies not listed in the Agreement must not be used to circumvent export subsidy commitments. Nor must non-commercial transactions be used in this way. *See also* ***anti-dumping measures***, ***carousel effect***, ***dumping*** and ***screwdriver operations***.

Anti-collusion duties: proposed at one time by some as duties small developing countries could impose on developed-country suppliers found to engage in ***price collusion***. Such duties would apparently be aimed at depriving colluding foreign suppliers of some unearned profits. The idea appears to be flawed. First, the proposed remedy would mainly be at the expense of users in the importing country and quite possibly to the benefit of other suppliers. Second, it is not clear how small developing countries, which often do not have adequate resources to fight collusion among domestic companies, could satisfactorily detect collusion among suppliers abroad. Price collusion is more likely to occur where there are substantial barriers to entry, where industries are protected or where markets are not transparent. Therefore, if collusion is suspected, the first step might usefully be to ascertain how the relevant market might be made more competitive and transparent. *See also* ***antitrust laws*** and ***competition policy***.

Anti-competitive practices: often called ***restrictive business practices*** or unfair business practices. These are used by firms to limit their exposure to price mechanisms. This is possible when firms, or groups of firms, have ***market dominance*** or ***market power***. In some cases, it may involve collusion among firms. *See also* ***antitrust laws***, ***cartel***, ***competition law***, ***conduct*** and ***trade and competition***.

Anti-corruption: the seemingly never-ending fight to stop corruption, though not for want of international efforts. *See*, for example, ***African Union Convention on Preventing and Combating Corruption***, ***Convention on Combating Bribery of Foreign Public Officials in International Business Transactions*** and ***United Nations Convention Against Corruption***.

Anti-Counterfeiting Trade Agreement: ACTA. Concluded in November 2010, but not yet in force. The Agreement aims to provide an international framework for improving the enforcement of ***intellectual property rights*** laws. It does not create new intellectual property rights. Parties must ensure that enforcement procedures are available to permit effective action against any infringement of intellectual property rights covered by the Agreement. Basic means are civil enforcement, border measures and criminal enforcement. Parties also agree to cooperate internationally to bring about the aims of the Agreement. The Agreement ran into a great deal of opposition from non-governmental organizations, based partly on what they knew of the content of the Agreement or what they guessed it might contain, and based partly on the perceived secrecy of the negotiations. Some developing countries also objected to the apparent exclusion of developing countries from the negotiations. The prospects for the entry

至一第三国。WTO中所用词语并不指欺诈案件，这些案件将根据有关国家的正常法律程序加以处理。《农业协定》包含反规避条款，规定未列入协定的出口补贴不得用以规避出口补贴承诺，也不得使用非商业交易加以规避。另见*反倾销措施(anti-dumping measures)*、*旋转木马效应(carousel effect)*、*倾销(dumping)*、*螺丝刀式经营(screwdriver operations)*。

Anti-collusion duties

反串通关税

以往由部分国家提出的一些发展中小国对发现参与价格串通的发达国家供应商征收的关税。此类关税显然是为了剥夺相互串通的外国供应商不劳而获的利润。这一想法存在缺陷。首先，拟议补救将主要以进口国中的用户为代价，而且很可能有利于其他供应商；其次，发展中小国往往缺乏足够资源打击国内公司之间的串通，不清楚它们如何能够明确发现国外供应商之间的串通。在存在实质性准入壁垒、行业受到保护或市场不透明的情况下，价格串通更有可能发生。因此，如果怀疑存在串通，可能有效的第一步是如何使相关市场更具竞争和透明。另见*反垄断法(antitrust laws)*、*竞争政策(competition policy)*。

Anti-competitive practices

反竞争行为

通常被称为限制性商业惯例或不正当商业做法。公司用以限制受到价格机制影响程度的做法。这一点在企业或企业集团拥有市场支配地位或市场支配力时是可以实现的。某些情况下，可能涉及企业之间的串通。另见*反垄断法(antitrust laws)*、*卡特尔(cartel)*、*竞争法(competition law)*、*行为(conduct)*、*贸易与竞争(trade and competition)*。

Anti-corruption

反腐败

似乎永无止境的打击腐败的斗争，尽管国际努力并不缺乏。例如，见*非洲联盟预防和惩治腐败公约(African Union Convention on Preventing and Combating Corruption)*、*关于打击国际商业交易中行贿外国公职人员行为的公约(Convention on Combating Bribery of Foreign Public Officials in International Business Transactions)*、*联合国反腐败公约(United Nations Convention Against Corruption)*。

Anti-Counterfeiting Trade Agreement

反假冒贸易协定

ACTA。2010年11月达成，但尚未生效。协定旨在为改善知识产权法律的执行提供国际框架。不创设新的知识产权。参加方必须保证制定执行程序，允许针对任何侵犯本协定所涵盖的知识产权的行为采取有效行动。基本手段包括民事执法、边境措施和刑事执法。参加方还同意进行国际合作，以实现协定目标。协定遭到非政府组织的很大反对，这些组织部分是由于对协定内容的了解或对协定可能内容的猜测，部分是由于感到谈判包含秘密。一些发展中国家也反对将发展中国家明显排除在谈判之外。本协定的生效前景尚不明确。

into force of this Agreement are not clear. One indicator may be that in 2012 the European Parliament declined to consent, i.e. to support it.

Anti-dilution doctrine: *see* ***dilution doctrine***.

Anti-Dumping Act of 1916: enacted by the United States Congress under the heading of "Unfair Competition" in Title VIII of the Revenue Act of 1916. The Act makes unlawful the import into the United States of any article at a price substantially less than the actual market price, if this is done with the intent of destroying or injuring an industry, preventing the establishment of an industry or restraining or monopolizing any part of trade and commerce in such articles in the United States. The penalty can be a fine, imprisonment or both. Persons injured by such imports may sue for ***treble damages***. The Act is drafted in the form of an ***antitrust law***, but its intent is to permit the imposition of ***anti-dumping measures*** against a practice usually considered ***dumping***. This question was considered by the ***panel*** in a dispute about the conformity of this Act with the WTO anti-dumping provisions. The panel found that the trans-national price discrimination test met the GATT definition of dumping, but that its remedies violated the WTO rules. [WT/DS136/R, WT/DS136/AB/R, WT/DS136/ARB]

Anti-Dumping Agreement: formally the *Agreement on Implementation of Article VI of the General Agreement on Tariffs and Trade 1994*. GATT Article VI and the Anti-Dumping Agreement together form the set of rules governing the imposition of ***anti-dumping measures***. In other words, the two have to be read together. Article VI states that "dumping, by which products of one country are introduced into the commerce of another country at less than the normal value of the products, is to be condemned if it causes or threatens to cause ***material injury*** to an established industry in the territory of a contracting party or retards the establishment of a domestic industry". Although ***dumping*** has been clearly understood as a trade policy issue for a long time, the assessment of whether dumping causing ***injury*** has occurred remains a cause of friction. At issue are the evidence for the occurrence of dumping, whether it has caused or threatened injury and if so, what remedies should be used. The *Anti-Dumping Agreement* is meant to clarify the provisions of GATT Article VI in this regard. Article 2 details the way a determination of dumping must be made. Several methods are available. The first is where prices for the ***like product*** (a crucial concept in anti-dumping procedures) in the exporting and importing country can be compared directly. This is the simplest case. The second is a situation where the product is not sold within the exporting country or only in low volumes and a proper comparison is not possible. The third is where there is no export price or where it may be that the export price is unreliable because of an association between the exporter and the importer or a third party, i.e. there may not be ***arm's-length pricing***. Relevant in this case also is an ***ad note*** to GATT Article VI which states that "in the case of imports from a country which has a complete or substantially complete monopoly of its trade and where all domestic prices are fixed by the State, special difficulties may exist in determining

一个标志是在2012年欧洲议会在2012年拒绝同意支持协定。

Anti-dilution doctrine

反淡化理论

见*淡化理论(dilution doctrine)*。

Anti-Dumping Act of 1916

1916年反倾销法

美国国会在《1916年财政收入法》第8编中的"不正当竞争"标题下制定。对于以大幅低于实际市场价格进口至美国的任何物品，如果目的是摧毁或损害一产业，阻碍一产业的建立或限制或垄断美国国内此类物品的贸易和商业的任何部分，该法将此种进口视为非法。处罚可以是罚款、监禁或两者同时实施。受到此类进口损害的人可以请求三倍赔偿。该法以反垄断法的形式起草，但其目的是允许对通常被视为倾销的做法实施反倾销措施。一争端解决案专家组曾对该法与WTO反倾销条款的一致性进行了审议。专家组认为，跨国价格歧视测试符合GATT倾销定义，但其救济措施违反了WTO规则。

Anti-Dumping Agreement

反倾销协定

正式称为《关于实施1994年关税与贸易总协定第6条的协定》。GATT第6条与《反倾销协定》共同构成管辖实施反倾销措施的一套规则。换言之，两者需要一起理解。第6条规定"通过倾销将一国的产品以低于其正常价值的价格引入另一国的商业，如因此对一缔约方领土内已建立的产业造成或威胁造成实质损害或阻碍一国内产业的建立，则应对倾销予以谴责"。尽管倾销长期以来被认为是贸易政策问题，但是倾销是否造成损害仍存在分歧。争论焦点是发生倾销的证据、倾销是否造成或威胁造成损害，如果造成损害应使用何种救济措施。《反倾销协定》旨在澄清GATT第6条在这方面的规定。协定第2条详细规定了确定倾销的方式。可使用几种方法：第一种是可以与出口国和进口国的同类产品(反倾销程序中的一个关键概念)价格进行直接比较。这是最简单的情况。第二种是产品不在出口国销售或销量很小而无法进行适当的比较的情况。第三种是无出口价格或由于出口商与进口商或与第三方之间的联合，导致出口价格不可靠的情况，即可能没有公平定价。同样与此种情况相关的是GATT第6条的补充注释，规定"在进口产品来自贸易被完全垄断或实质上完全垄断的国家，且所有国内价格均由国家确定的情况下，确定价格可比较性时

price comparability . . . and in such cases importing contracting parties may find it necessary to take into account the possibility that strict comparison with domestic prices in such a country may not always be appropriate". Article 3 deals with the determination of ***injury***. This has to be based on positive evidence and involve an objective examination of both (a) the volume of the dumped imports and the effect of the dumped imports on prices in the domestic market for the products and (b) the consequent impact of these imports on domestic producers of such products. Article 4 defines domestic industry. Broadly, this means the domestic producers as a whole of the like products or those for which the collective output of the product constitutes a major proportion of the total domestic production of those products. Articles 5 and 6, respectively, cover the investigation to determine the existence, degree and effect of the alleged dumping and the evidence for it. An application for an investigation must be supported by more than 50 per cent of the local industry producing the like product and may not proceed if less than 25 per cent support it. If the margin of dumping is *de minimis* (i.e. less than 2 per cent), the investigation must be terminated. Evidence may be collected from a wide variety of sources. Article 7 permits provisional measures where the authorities judge that they may be necessary to prevent injury being caused during the investigation. Article 8 states that proceedings may be suspended or terminated if the exporter provides a voluntary undertaking to revise its prices or to cease exports to the area in question at dumped prices, but only where this is practicable. Article 9 covers the imposition and collection of anti-dumping duties. The anti-dumping duty must not exceed the margin of dumping. Article 10 permits some retroactivity in specified situations. Article 11 states that an "anti-dumping duty shall remain force only as long as and to the extent necessary to counteract dumping which is causing injury". Reviews are to be conducted as required, and an anti-dumping duty terminated no later than five years from its imposition. Article 12 requires public notice of an investigation and an explanation of determinations. WTO members with legislation on anti-dumping must maintain judicial, arbitral or administrative tribunals or procedures for the review of decisions.

Anti-dumping duties: GATT Article VI allows anti-dumping duties to be imposed on goods that are deemed to be dumped and causing ***injury*** to competing products in the importing country. These duties are equal to the difference between the export price of the goods and their ***normal value***, if dumping caused injury. *See also* ***determination of dumping***.

Anti-dumping measures: laws and regulations designed to counter ***dumping***. In the United States anti-dumping laws originated as part of the early ***antitrust laws***. One of these is the ***Anti-Dumping Act of 1916***. These laws were aimed at pulling into line foreign firms perceived to be undercutting United States firms through anti-competitive practices described as ***dumping***. Gradually, however, firms began to understand the value of anti-dumping measures in restricting imports, and the two regimes diverged. In other countries the main reason for

可能存在特殊困难……在此类情况下，进口缔约方可能认为有必要考虑与此类国家中的国内价格进行严格比较不一定总是适当的可能性”。第3条处理损害的确定。必须根据肯定性证据，并包含对以下内容的客观审查：(a)倾销进口产品的数量和倾销进口产品对国内市场同类产品价格的影响和(b)这些进口产品对此类产品国内生产商随之产生的影响。第4条定义了国内产业。总体上，指同类产品的国内生产者全体或指该产品总产量构成同类产品国内总产量主要部分的国内生产者。第5条和第6条分别涵盖确定被指控的倾销的存在、程度和影响的调查及其证据。调查申请必须得到生产同类产品的国内产业50%以上的支持，如果支持率低于25%，则不得发起调查。如倾销幅度为微量(即小于2%)，则必须终止调查。证据可以从广泛的来源收集。第7条允许主管机关在认为防止调查期间造成损害是必要时采取临时措施。第8条规定，如果出口商自愿承诺修改其价格或停止以倾销价格向所涉地区出口，调查程序可以中止或终止，前提是出口商的做法是可行的。第9条涵盖反倾销税的征收。反倾销税不得超过倾销幅度。第10条允许在特定情况下的追溯效力。第11条规定，“反倾销税仅在抵消正在造成损害的倾销所必需的时间和范围内保持有效”。应按要求进行审议，且反倾销税从征收之日起不迟于5年终止。第12条要求对调查发布公告，并对决定作出说明。拥有反倾销立法的WTO成员必须设立审查决定的司法、仲裁或行政庭或程序。

Anti-dumping duties
反倾销税

GATT第6条允许对被认为倾销并对进口国中竞争产品造成损害的货物征收反倾销税。如果倾销造成损害，征收的关税应等于货物出口价格与其正常价值之间的差额。另见*倾销的确定(determination of dumping)*。

Anti-dumping measures
反倾销措施

为应对倾销而制定的法律法规。在美国，反倾销法源自早期的反垄断法。其中之一是《1916年反倾销法》。这些法律旨在限制被认为通过倾销这一反竞争行为削弱美国公司的外国公司。然而，企业逐渐意识到反倾销措施在限制进口方面的价值，而将两种制度分开设立。在其他国家，制定反倾销法的主要原因

enacting anti-dumping laws always was an intent to afford protection to domestic firms. Article VI of the GATT 1994 permits the imposition of anti-dumping duties against dumped goods, if dumping causes ***material injury*** to producers of competing products, described as ***like products***, in the importing country. This is known as ***causality***. The WTO ***Anti-Dumping Agreement*** (formally the *Agreement on Implementation of Article VI of the General Agreement on Tariffs and Trade 1994*) lays down precise and transparent procedures for the adoption of anti-dumping measures. Some sophisticated methods have been developed to measure alleged differences in prices and to determine injury. Anti-dumping measures may be instituted if the price charged to the importing country by a foreign firm is below ***normal value*** in its home country. Normal value is made up of fixed and variable costs of production, plus a range of other costs normally associated with production and trade. If there are too few domestic sales, normal value is to be taken to be the highest comparable charge in third markets or the exporting firm's estimated costs of production plus a reasonable amount to cover other expenses, as well as imputed profits. If there is no export price or if trade is between related parties and therefore considered unreliable as a price indicator, the export price may be constructed on the basis of what would have been charged to an independent buyer, or on some other reasonable basis. The scope for disputes about the right level of normal value is readily apparent. The concept of material injury to industries producing like products is equally fruitful of controversies. Neither the GATT nor the Anti-Dumping Agreement define material injury, but the latter contains an illustrative list of factors to be taken into account in an assessment of whether material injury has occurred. The list, which is not considered exhaustive, includes actual and potential decline in sales, profits, output, market share, productivity, return on investments, or utilization of capacity; factors affecting domestic prices; the magnitude of the ***margin of dumping***; actual and potential negative effects on cash flow, inventories, employment, wages, growth, ability to raise capital or investments. Much has been written about the meaning of "like products", and whether it should be interpreted as the same product, a similar product or a different product put to the same use or achieving the same purpose. The Anti-Dumping Agreement now leaves no doubt on this point. The like product must be identical, i.e. alike in all respects. If there is no such product, another may be chosen for comparison which, even though not alike in all respects, has characteristics closely resembling the product under consideration. Anti-dumping measures may only be taken to the extent that they cover the margin of dumping, i.e. the difference between normal value and the price at the border in the importing country, adjusted for specified normal costs associated with international trade. If the investigating authority finds that there has been dumping, the resulting protection for domestic industries on the basis of anti-dumping measures can be quite limited. Under the WTO rules, a good case for them has to be made, and there is provision for appeals by the affected parties. The Anti-Dumping Agreement

一直是为国内企业提供保护。GATT 1994年第6条允许如倾销对进口国竞争产品(被称为同类产品)的生产者造成实质损害的情况下，对倾销货物征收反倾销税。这被称为因果关系。WTO《反倾销协定》(正式称为《关于实施1994年关税与贸易总协定第6条的协定》)对采取反倾销措施规定了明确和透明的程序。规定了用以衡量价格差异和确定损害的一些复杂的方法。如果一家外国公司向进口国收取的价格低于本国正常价值，可以采取反倾销措施。正常价值由固定和可变生产成本加上一系列通常与生产和贸易相关的其他成本组成。如果国内销售量过少，则正常价值应将采用第三国市场中的最高可比价格或出口公司的估计生产成本加上合理数额的其他费用及估计利润。如果没有出口价格，或者如果贸易是在各相关方之间进行的而被认为是不可靠的价格指标，则可以根据向独立买方收取的价格或其他合理的基础确定出口价格。关于正常价值正确水平的争议范围是显而易见的。对生产同类产品的产业造成的实质损害概念也同样充满争议。GATT和《反倾销协定》均未定义实质损害，但是后者包含一份评估是否发生实质损害时可以考虑因素的例示清单。清单不是穷尽的，包括销售、利润、产量、市场份额、生产力、投资收益或产能利用率的实际和潜在的下降；影响国内价格的因素；倾销幅度的大小；对现金流动、库存、就业、工资、增长、筹措资金或投资能力的实际和潜在的消极影响。关于“同类产品”的含义以及是否应将其解释为相同产品、类似产品或相同用途或达到相同目的的不同产品，已有许多论述。《反倾销协定》对其进行了明确。同类产品必须是相同的产品，即在各方面均相同。如果没有此种产品，可以选择另一种产品进行比较，尽管此种产品并非在各方面均相同，但具有与考虑中的产品极为相似的特点。反倾销措施只有在涵盖倾销幅度的限度内方可采取，即正常价值与进口国边境价格之间的差额，边境价格根据与国际贸易有关的特定正常成本进行调整。如果调查主管机关发现存在倾销，由此产生的根据反倾销措施而对国内产业的保护可能十分有限。根据WTO规则，反倾销措施必须具备充分的理由，并且规定受影响的各方可以提出上诉。《反倾

stresses that an application for the imposition of anti-dumping measures must include evidence of dumping, injury and a causal link between the two. A simple assertion, unsubstantiated by relevant evidence, cannot be considered sufficient to meet the requirements. An application has to be made by domestic industry. No action may be taken if it is supported by firms representing less than 25 per cent of total production of the like product. Under the rule on ***de minimis dumping margins***, no action may be taken if the margin of dumping is less than 2 per cent. Anti-dumping actions remain controversial. Affected firms and their home countries sometimes see them mainly as a means to restrain unwelcome imports. Doubtless, there is some truth in this. Some petitions are frivolous and nothing more than ***trade harassment***. As a form of ***contingent protection***, they enable governments to restrict the flow of imports. This is understood clearly by petitioners. A particularly disliked practice is the ***cumulative assessment of dumping***. This means that the country taking action may under defined conditions investigate alleged dumping by several countries at the same time. Hoekman, commenting on the detailed procedural requirements set out in the Anti-Dumping Agreement, notes that this has become a lucrative area of specialization for the legal profession in territories that actively use anti-dumping measures. Anti-dumping enquiries can serve ***transparency*** by demonstrating to the exporting company suspected of dumping what its real cost structure is. This can lead to alternative approaches to production and trade regimes which might reduce or eliminate the need for anti-dumping measures. Marceau points out that dumping and anti-dumping laws are not just about price discrimination and predation. They are "buffers" between national systems of competition. Other analysts are more severe. J. Michael Finger says that "antidumping is ordinary protection with a grand public relations program", and that "antidumping is a trouble-making diplomacy, stupid economics and unprincipled law". That said, all mechanisms enabling governments to influence the flow of imports create ill-will. In the case of anti-dumping measures, exporters complain of their trade-restrictive impact, but industries in the importing country tend to see them as a cumbersome and onerous means to fix urgent problems. In some cases, a company asking for anti-dumping measures may at the same time be accused of dumping in another market. Consumers seldom call for anti-dumping measures. There will always be some contradictions inherent in the taking of anti-dumping measures. Today, there is a view among some trade policy makers that ***competition policy*** could be a better instrument to deal with dumping issues. This supposes that all WTO members would be willing to pursue effective competition policies, or that they would be willing to enforce each other's competition rulings. Reconciling the different outcomes caused by anti-dumping measures and competition enforcement is an argument for negotiations on ***trade and competition***, but those who are comfortable with their anti-dumping regimes do not find the argument persuasive. In the United States anti-dumping laws and antitrust laws have a common origin. Many argue that until the two are re-united, the anti-dumping

销协定》强调实施反倾销措施的申请必须包括倾销、损害的证据以及两者之间的因果关系。不能为相关证据支持的简单断言不能被视为满足要求。申请必须由本国产业提出。如果支持申请的企业占同类产品总产量不足25%，则不采取任何行动。根据微量倾销幅度规则，如果倾销幅度小于2%，则不采取任何行动。反倾销行动仍存在争议。受影响的公司及其母国有时将其视为限制不受欢迎的进口产品的一种手段。毫无疑问，这种观点有一定道理。有些申请是轻率的，只不过是一种贸易干扰。作为紧急保护的一种形式，反倾销措施使政府能够限制进口流动。申请者对此非常明了。一个特别不受欢迎的做法是倾销累积评估。这意味着采取行动的国家可以在特定条件下同时调查对多个国家的倾销指控。霍克曼在评论《反倾销协定》规定的详细程序要求时指出，此点在积极采用反倾销措施的地区已经成为法律专业人士谋利的专门领域。反倾销调查可以通过向涉嫌倾销的出口公司展示其实际成本结构以提高透明度，对于生产和贸易制度而言可能是替代方式，可能会减少或消除采取反倾销措施的需要。马索指出，倾销和反倾销法律不只关于价格歧视和掠夺，而是国家竞争制度之间的“缓冲器”。其他分析家则更为严厉。迈克尔·芬格表示，“反倾销是具有宏大公共关系计划的普通保护措施”，“反倾销是一种制造麻烦的外交、愚蠢的经济学和无原则的法律”。即便如此，所有使政府能够影响进口流动的机制都会产生敌意。就反倾销措施而言，出口商抱怨这些措施的贸易限制作用，而进口国产业则往往将其视为解决紧迫问题的一种复杂而繁琐的手段。在某些情况下，要求采取反倾销措施的公司可能同时被指控在另一个市场进行倾销。消费者很少要求采取反倾销措施。采取反倾销措施本身总是存在一些固有矛盾。今天，一些贸易政策制定者认为，竞争政策可以成为处理倾销问题的一种更好的工具。这种观点认为，所有WTO成员都愿意推行有效的竞争政策，或愿意执行彼此的竞争裁决。协调反倾销措施和竞争执法所产生的不同结果是贸易与竞争谈判的一个论点，但那些对自己的反倾销制度感到满意的人认为这一论点不具说服力。在美国，反倾销法和反垄断法有相同起源。许多人认为，在两者重新统一之前，反倾销规则如果合法的话，可提

rules offer a somewhat transparent, if legalistic and sometimes flawed, mechanism to deal with some of the concerns raised by producers. The anti-dumping rules are to be clarified as part of the multilateral trade negotiations launched at Doha in November 2001. *See also* ***accordion of likeness***, ***Agreement on Safeguards***, ***analogue country***, ***boomerang clause***, ***competition policy and anti-dumping measures***, ***de minimis dumping margins***, ***lesser-duty principle***, ***negligible imports*** and ***predatory pricing***. [Dam 2001, Finger 1993, Hoekman 1995, Jackson and Vermulst 1990, Marceau 1994, Neufeld 2001, Sykes 1998]

Anti-globalization: a complex, often contradictory, view apparently based on the proposition that it is possible, through a combination of international economic cooperation and the pursuit of ***autarky***, to assist the development of ***developing countries*** and to preserve jobs at home. Views abound on how this should be done, and there is no unanimity among its proponents on the best way to achieve this aim. Some see the matter mainly in terms of a race to the bottom as production of some goods moves to developing countries. In this sense anti-globalization is a type of ***protectionism***. Others complain that not enough is done to help developing countries to promote their economic development. This view would appear to support ***trade liberalization***. Many adherents of anti-globalist views seem to be convinced that, but for the efforts of the WTO, the ***IMF***, the ***World Bank***, the ***G7***, ***G8*** and other economic groupings, their aims, however defined, would be realized speedily. Anti-globalists also tend to overstate, intentionally or otherwise, the ability of ***transnational corporations*** to influence public opinion. Some of these corporations, of course, are quite adept at influencing political power. *See also* ***globalization*** and ***hyperglobalization***. [Deardorff 2003, Stiglitz 2002, Wolf 2004]

Antitrust guidelines for international enforcement and cooperation: last reissued by the United States Department of Justice and the ***Federal Trade Commission*** in January 2017. They provide guidance to businesses engaged in international activities on questions concerning the enforcement policy of the Justice Department and the Federal Trade Commission as well as their investigative tools and cooperation with foreign authorities. The guidelines cover relevant United States antitrust and related statutes, such as the ***Sherman Act***, Federal Trade Commission Act, the Hart-Scott-Rodino Antitrust Improvements Act of 1976, the ***Webb-Pomerene Act***, the ***Wilson Tariff Act***, ***Section 301*** and the Tariff Act of 1930 (the ***Smoot-Hawley Tariff Act***) among others. The remainder of the guidelines covers ***conduct*** involving foreign commerce, ***comity***, foreign government involvement and international cooperation. *See also* ***effects doctrine***, ***extraterritoriality***, ***negative comity*** and ***positive comity***. [justice.gov]

Antitrust laws: often known as ***competition laws***. These laws are a subset of the rules making up ***competition policy***. They aim to promote a competitive environment for firms through ensuring that they do not abuse ***market power*** in domestic markets. In some countries, especially the United States, antitrust laws have an extraterritorial dimension. The term "antitrust" derives its origin from a perception in the United States in the 1880s and 1890s that some industries,

供一个处理生产者所提部分关注的某种程度上透明的机制，同时也存在一定缺陷。作为2001年11月启动的多哈多边贸易谈判的一部分，反倾销规则将得到澄清。另见*符合同类性(accordion of likeness)*、*保障措施协定(Agreement on Safeguards)*、*类比国(analogue country)*、*回旋镖条款(boomerang clause)*、*竞争政策与反倾销措施(competition policy and anti-dumping measures)*、*微量倾销幅度(de minimis dumping margins)*、*低税原则(lesser-duty principle)*、*可忽略不计的进口量(negligible imports)*、*掠夺性定价(predatory pricing)*。

Anti-globalization

反全球化

一种复杂的、经常自相矛盾的观点。该观点的基础是，通过国际经济合作和追求经济闭关自守相结合，有可能有助于发展中国家的发展和保持国内就业。关于应该如何实现这一目标的观点比比皆是，支持者对于实现这一目标的最佳方式并无一致意见。一些人将这一问题理解为低成本竞争，理由是一些货物的生产转移到了发展中国家。从这个意义上讲，反全球化是一种保护主义。另一些人则抱怨在帮助发展中国家促进经济发展方面作得不够。这种观点似乎支持贸易自由化。许多反全球主义观点的支持者似乎相信，如果没有WTO、国际货币基金组织(IMF)、世界银行、7国集团、8国集团和其他经济集团的努力，它们的目标，无论如何确定，都会很快实现。反全球主义者也倾向于有意或无意地夸大跨国公司影响公众舆论的能力。当然，一些公司非常擅长影响政治权力。另见*全球化(globalization)*、*超全球化(hyperglobalization)*。

Antitrust guidelines for international enforcement and cooperation

国际执法与合作反垄断指导原则

最新由美国司法部和联邦贸易委员会于2017年1月重新发布。指导原则对司法部和联邦贸易委员会的执法政策以及它们的调查工具和与外国主管机关的合作等问题向从事国际活动的企业提供指导。指导原则涵盖相关美国反垄断法律和有关法规，例如《谢尔曼法》、《联邦贸易委员会法》、《1976年哈特-斯科特-罗迪尼反垄断改进法》、《韦布-波默林法》、《威尔逊关税法》、301条款和《1930年关税法》(《斯穆特-霍利关税法》)等。指导原则其余部分涵盖包括涉及外国商业、礼让、外国政府参与和国际合作的行为。另见*效果原则(effects doctrine)*、*治外法权(extraterritoriality)*、*消极礼让(negative comity)*、*积极礼让(positive comity)*。

Antitrust laws

反垄断法

通常称为竞争法。这些法律是构成竞争政策的规则的一个子集。旨在通过保证企业不在国内市场滥用市场支配力以促进企业的竞争环境。在一些国家，特别是在美国，反垄断法具有域外效力。“反垄断”一词源于美国在19世纪80年代和90年代的一种观念，当时一些产业组织形成大规模的托拉斯公司，拥有

then organized into large-scale trusts with interlocking directorships, were undermining price mechanisms. The ***Sherman Act***, passed in 1890, remains the cornerstone and symbol of United States antitrust laws. A 1994 House of Representative committee report notes that "first and foremost, antitrust is rooted in the distinctive American preference for pluralism, freedom of trade, access to markets, and – perhaps most important of all – freedom of choice". Penalties in proven cases of antitrust law infringement tend to be severe in many countries. In the United States, for example, the courts can impose ***treble damages*** on the offenders. *See also* ***antitrust guidelines for international enforcement and cooperation***, ***cartel***, ***Clayton Act***, ***essential facilities doctrine***, ***extraterritoriality***, ***Webb-Pomerene Act*** and ***Wilson Tariff Act***. [Dabbah 2003]

ANZCERTA: *Australia New Zealand Closer Economic Relations Trade Agreement*, usually referred to as CER. Entered into force on 1 January 1983. Trade in goods between the partners is free of ***tariffs***, and there are no ***quantitative restrictions***. The partners do not use ***anti-dumping measures*** against each other and rely on ***competition laws*** instead to the extent that dumping may be caused by anti-competitive behaviour. Countervailing duties may still be imposed. The parties accord each other ***national treatment*** in ***government procurement***. Services were brought under the ambit of the free-trade agreement in 1988 through the ***ANZCERTA Protocol on Trade in Services***.

ANZCERTA Protocol on Trade in Services: adopted in 1988 to bring ***trade in services*** within the ***ANZCERTA*** framework. The Protocol covers all services trade between Australia and New Zealand, except for a small number of specified activities listed in the two annexes where restrictions apply. No new activities may be added to the annexes. Periodic bilateral discussions have led to the removal or tightening of the inscriptions. *See also* ***negative listings***.

APEC: Asia Pacific Economic Cooperation [forum]. Established in 1989. Its members are described as "economies". The objectives of APEC include (a) sustaining growth and development in the region, (b) strengthening an open ***multilateral trading system*** rather than the formation of a regional trading bloc, (c) a focus on economic rather than security issues, and (d) to foster constructive interdependence by encouraging the flow of goods, services, capital and technology. APEC objectives are defined further in the ***Seoul Declaration***. Following the terrorist attack on New York in 2001 APEC adopted a small security agenda and established a Counter-Terrorism Task Force. APEC's membership criteria adopted in 1997 are: (a) an applicant economy should be located in the Asia-Pacific region, (b) it should have substantial and broad-based economic linkages with the existing APEC members; in particular, the value of the applicant's trade with APEC members, as a percentage of its international trade, should be relatively high, (c) it should be pursuing externally oriented, market-driven economic policies, and (d) a successful applicant will be required to produce an ***individual action plan*** (IAP) for implementation and to commence participation in the ***Collective Action Plans*** across the APEC work programme from the time of its joining APEC. APEC's main agenda is to dismantle trade and investment barriers among all members by 2020. Developed economy members have undertaken to do so by 2010. Several working groups have also been established to advance cooperation across a range of issues, especially in the areas of business facilitation and information exchange. Members of APEC are Australia, Brunei Darussalam, Canada, Chile, China, Hong Kong (China), Indonesia, Japan, Republic of Korea, Malaysia, Mexico, New Zealand, Papua New Guinea, Peru, Philippines, Russia, Singapore, Chinese Taipei, Thailand, the United States and Viet Nam. APEC is supported by a small secretariat based in Singapore. APEC's main meetings are hosted by one of the member economies for an entire year. This is APEC's main coordination mechanism. *See also* ***Auckland Challenge***, ***Bogor Declaration***, ***Manila Action Plan for APEC***, ***open regionalism***, ***Osaka Action Agenda***, ***Shanghai Accord*** and other entries beginning with ***APEC***.

APEC Action Agenda for the Digital Economy: a plan adopted in 2018 to help the further implementation of the ***APEC Internet and Digital Economy Roadmap*** (the Roadmap). Its work programme is to prepare by the end of 2019 (a) a comprehensive work programme on the future implementation of the Roadmap which will examine the broad potential opportunities and challenges presented by digital technologies, and (b) develop a programme for future data and analytical support for this work, including the preparation of the 2019 APEC Economic Policy Report on the topic of Structural Reform and the Digital Economy. [www.apec.org]

APEC Alliance for Supply Chain Conductivity: adopted in 2014 with the aims of (a) developing a capacity-building plan, (b) identifying readily available tools and methodologies for implementation, (c) contributing to APEC's work on choke points, (d) identifying expertise to deliver technical assistance, and (e) identifying resources for the effective implementation of projects. This initiative will be reviewed in 2020 for its effectiveness.

APEC Blueprint for Action on Electronic Commerce: adopted in 1999. It established a detailed work programme on electronic commerce based on the principle that governments, *inter alia*, would promote the development of electronic commerce by providing a favourable legal and regulatory environment. This environment is assumed to be predictable, transparent and consistent. The blueprint also contains the ***APEC paperless trading initiative***. *See also* ***electronic commerce***.

APEC Business Advisory Council: ABAC. Established at the November 1995 ***APEC*** Ministerial Meeting in Osaka to ensure the continued cooperation and active involvement of the business and private sectors in all APEC activities. Each economy has three ABAC members.

APEC Business Travel Card: ABTC. A scheme enabling *bona fide* business people from participating ***APEC*** economies to travel to other participating economies without the need to obtain visas. Holders of the card are given preferential immigration clearance in the form of a separate gate.

相互联系的董事职位，对价格机制造成破坏。1890年通过的《谢尔曼法》成为美国反垄断法的基石和象征。1994年众议院委员会的一份报告指出，“首先，反垄断植根于美国对多元化、贸易自由、市场准入以及或许是最重要的、对选择自由的独特偏好”。对经证实违反反垄断法的案件在许多国家的处罚是往往是严厉的。例如在美国，法院可以对违法者施加三倍赔偿。另见***国际执法与合作反垄断指导原则**(antitrust guidelines for international enforcement and cooperation)*、***卡特尔**(cartel)*、***克莱顿法**(Clayton Act)*、***必要设施原则**(essential facilities doctrine)*、***治外法权**(extraterritoriality)*、***韦布-波默林法**(Webb-Pomerene Act)*、***威尔逊关税法**(Wilson Tariff Act)*。

ANZCERTA

澳大利亚与新西兰更紧密经济关系贸易协定

通常称CER。1983年1月1日生效。贸易伙伴之间的货物贸易免关税，且无数量限制。贸易伙伴不相互使用反倾销措施，而是在倾销可能因反竞争行为引起时使用竞争法。反补贴税仍可以征收。双方在政府采购中相互给予国民待遇。通过1988年的《ANZCERTA服务贸易议定书》，服务被纳入自由贸易协定的范围。

ANZCERTA Protocol on Trade in Services

ANZCERTA服务贸易议定书

1988年通过，将服务贸易纳入《澳大利亚与新西兰更紧密经济关系贸易协定》(ANZCERTA)框架。议定书涵盖了澳大利亚与新西兰之间的所有服务贸易，除了两个附件中列出的实施限制的少数特定活动。不得在附件中增加新的活动。定期的双边讨论已经使清单内容删除或缩短。另见***负面清单**(negative listings)*。

APEC

亚太经济合作组织[论坛]

1989年成立。成员称为“经济体”。APEC的目标包括：(a)维持区域的增长和发展；(b)增强开放的多边贸易体制而非形成区域贸易集团；(c)注重经济而非安全问题；以及(d)通过鼓励货物、服务、资本和技术的流动促进建设性相互依存关系。APEC目标在《首尔宣言》中得到进一步界定。2001年纽约遭受恐怖袭击后，APEC通过了一项小型安全议程，并成立了反恐特别工作组。1997年通过的APEC成员标准为：(a)申请经济体应位于亚太区域；(b)申请经济体应与现有APEC成员拥有实质和广泛的经济联系，特别是申请经济体与APEC成员的贸易额占其国际贸易的百分比应相对较高；(c)申请经济体应推行以外部为导向的市场驱动经济政策；(d)申请成功的经济体必须提出一项单独行动计划(IAP)以供执行，并自加入时起参与APEC工作计划下的集体行动计划。APEC

的主要议程是在2020年前消除所有成员之间的贸易和投资壁垒。发达经济体已经承诺到2010年实现这一目标。已成立若干工作组以推动在一系列问题上的合作，特别是在商业便利化和信息交流领域。APEC成员包括澳大利亚、文莱、加拿大、智利、中国、中国香港、印度尼西亚、日本、韩国、马来西亚、墨西哥、新西兰、巴布亚新几内亚、秘鲁、菲律宾、俄罗斯、新加坡、中国台北、泰国、美国和越南。APEC秘书处设在新加坡。APEC主要会议由其中一个成员经济体主办一整年。以上为APEC的主要协调机制。另见***奥克兰挑战****(Auckland Challenge)*、***茂物宣言****(Bogor Declaration)*、***APEC马尼拉行动计划****(Manila Action Plan for APEC)*、***开放的区域主义****(open regionalism)*、***大阪行动议程****(Osaka Action Agenda)*、***上海协议****(Shanghai Accord)*及其他以APEC开头的词条。

APEC Action Agenda for the Digital Economy

APEC数字经济行动议程

该计划于2018年通过，旨在协助进一步落实APEC互联网和数字经济路线图(简称路线图)。工作计划是在2019年底前(a)编写一份关于未来实施路线图的全面工作计划，将审查数字技术带来的广泛潜在机遇和挑战；及(b)制定支持此项工作的未来数据和分析计划，包括编写2019年AEPC关于结构改革和数字经济专题的经济政策报告。

APEC Alliance for Supply Chain Conductivity

APEC供应链传导性联盟

2014年通过，目标为：(a)制订能力建设计划；(b)确定便捷可获得的实施工具和方法；(c)促进APEC针对瓶颈问题的工作；(d)确定提供技术援助的专业知识；以及(e)确定用于有效实施项目的资源。将在2020年对该计划有效性进行评估。

APEC Blueprint for Action on Electronic Commerce

APEC电子商务行动蓝图

1999年通过。蓝图制订了详细的电子商务工作计划，所根据的原则是各国政府通过提供有利的法律和监管环境以促进电子商务的发展。这种环境应当是可预测、透明和一致的。该蓝图还包含APEC无纸贸易倡议。另见***电子商务****(electronic commerce)*。

APEC Business Advisory Council

APEC工商咨询理事会

ABAC。1995年11月在大阪举行的APEC部长级会议上成立，旨在保证商业和私营部门在APEC所有活动中的持续合作和积极参与。每一经济体有3名ABAC成员。

APEC Business Travel Card

APEC商务旅行卡

ABTC。使APEC经济体的商务人士无须申请签证即可前往其他经济体的计划。以单独通道形式给予持卡人通关便利。

APEC Comparative Tool Database on RTAs/FTAs: a searchable database listing ***free-trade agreements*** in the APEC region by economy, agreement and chapter. [fta.apec.org]

APEC Cooperation Network on Green Supply Chain: also APEC Green Supply Chain Network. Established in 2011 with the objectives (a) of raising awareness and understanding on trade and investment-related policies that support the development of green supply chains, and (b) to share information, experiences and successful practices as they relate to the cross-border movement of goods and services. [apecgsc.org]

APEC Cross-Cutting Principles on Non-Tariff Measures: adopted in 2018 as a reference guide for ***APEC*** economies. The principles are (a) the processes to develop ***non-tariff measures*** should be transparent, consultative and timely, resulting in predictable, coherent and non-discriminatory application; and the information about non-tariff measures should be publicly available, (b) non-tariff measures should be consistent with member economies' commitments to obligations as members of the WTO, (c) non-tariff measures should be no more trade-restrictive than necessary to meet a legitimate objective, and where appropriate, should focus on outcomes, rather than mandating prescriptive approaches, (d) non-tariff measures should be based on relevant international standards, where appropriate, and should be developed in accordance with the WTO ***Agreement on the Application of Sanitary and Phytosanitary Standards*** and the WTO ***Agreement on Technical Barriers to Trade***, (e) non-tariff measures should not arbitrarily or unjustifiably discriminate against imported products, (f) they should not pose unwarranted barriers to the development of new technologies that drive innovation, and (g) a regulatory impact analysis could be considered as a possible tool to assess consistency with these principles. [www.apec.org]

APEC Economic and Technical Cooperation: ECOTECH. One of the three pillars of the ***APEC*** work agenda. It aims to support the achievement of the APEC goals by developing common policy concepts, implementing joint activities and engaging in policy dialogue. It was established at the November 1995 APEC Ministerial Meeting. Cooperation activities take place in the areas of human resources development, industrial science and technology, small and medium enterprises, economic infrastructure, energy, transportation, tourism, telecommunications and information, trade and investment data, ***trade promotion***, marine resource conservation, fisheries, and agricultural technology. *See also* ***Bogor Declaration*** and ***Osaka Action Agenda***.

APEC Economic Leaders' Meetings: informal meetings of APEC leaders enabling them to share their visions for the Asia-Pacific region and provide directions for APEC's long-term development. Leaders' meetings have been held at Seattle (1993), Bogor (1994), Osaka (1995), Manila (1996), Vancouver (1997), Kuala Lumpur (1998), Auckland (1999), Brunei Darussalam (2000), Shanghai (2001), Mexico (2002), Bangkok (2003), Santiago (2004), Busan (2005), Hanoi (2006), Sydney (2007), Lima (2008), Singapore (2009), Yokohama (2010), Honolulu (2011), Vladivostok (2012), Bali (2013), Beijing (2014),

APEC Comparative Tool Database on RTAs/FTAs
APEC区域贸易协定/自由贸易协定比较工具数据库

按经济体、协定和章节列出APEC区域自由贸易协定的可检索数据库。

APEC Cooperation Network on Green Supply Chain
APEC绿色供应链合作网络

又称APEC绿色供应链网络。成立于2011年，目标为：(a)提高对支持绿色供应链发展的贸易和投资相关政策的认识和理解；及(b)分享与货物和服务跨境流动有关的信息、经验和成功做法。

APEC Cross-Cutting Principles on Non-Tariff Measures
APEC非关税措施交叉原则

2018年通过，作为APEC经济体的参考指南。原则为：(a)制定非关税措施的过程应透明、经过协商和及时，使实施可预测、一致和非歧视；有关非关税措施的信息应可公开获得；(b)非关税措施应符合成员经济体的WTO成员义务；(c)非关税措施对贸易的限制不应超过实现合法目标的必要限度，且如适当，应注重结果，而非授权采取规定性方式；(d)非关税措施在适当时以相关国际标准为基础，并应依照WTO《实施卫生与植物卫生措施协定》和WTO《技术性贸易壁垒协定》制定；(e)非关税措施不应任意或无理歧视进口产品；(f)不应对推动创新的新技术开发设置不合理的壁垒；以及(g)可考虑将对监管影响分析作为评估与这些原则一致性的可能工具。

APEC Economic and Technical Cooperation
APEC经济技术合作

ECOTECH。APEC工作议程三大支柱之一。旨在通过发展共同政策概念、开展联合活动和参与政策对话，支持APEC目标的实现。设立于1995年11月APEC部长级会议。开展合作活动的领域包括人力资源开发、产业科学和技术、中小企业、经济基础设施、能源、运输、旅游、电信和信息、贸易和投资数据、贸易促进、海洋资源保护、渔业和农业技术等。另见*茂物宣言(Bogor Declaration)*、*大阪行动议程(Osaka Action Agenda)*。

APEC Economic Leaders' Meetings
APEC领导人会议

APEC领导人非正式会议使领导人能够分享对亚太地区的愿景，并为APEC的长远发展提供指导。会议曾分别在西雅图(1993年)、茂物(1994年)、大阪(1995年)、马尼拉(1996年)、温哥华(1997年)、吉隆坡(1998年)、奥克兰(1999年)、文莱(2000年)、上海(2001年)、墨西哥(2002年)、曼谷(2003年)、圣地亚哥(2004年)、釜山(2005年)、河内(2006)、悉尼(2007年)、利马(2008年)、新加坡(2009年)、横滨(2010年)、檀香山(2011年)、符拉迪沃斯托克(2012年)、巴厘岛(2013年)、

Manila (2015), Lima (2016), Da Nang (2017) and Port Moresby (2018). Chile was due to host APEC in 2019, but internal developments prevented this. Malaysia will host APEC in 2020, New Zealand in 2021 and Thailand in 2022. *See also* ***Bogor Declaration*** and ***Osaka Action Agenda***.

APEC Environmental Services Action Plan: adopted in 2015. An umbrella framework to coordinate and promote services work in APEC's trade and investment liberalization and facilitation agenda.

APEC framework for liberalization and facilitation: the APEC process of liberalization and facilitation is to achieve the goals set out in the ***Bogor Declaration***, as described in the ***Osaka Action Agenda***. It comprises (a) actions by individual APEC economies, (b) actions by APEC fora and APEC actions related to multilateral fora. *See also* ***Manila Action Plan for APEC***.

APEC individual action plans: IAPs. These describe the voluntary actions by which APEC economies expect to reach the targets of the ***Bogor Declaration***. IAPs contain each economy's proposed action and, where appropriate, proposed collective action on trade and investment liberalization and facilitation. They contain steps to be taken in seventeen areas: tariffs, non-tariff measures, services, investment, standards and conformance, customs procedures, intellectual property rights, competition policy, government procurement, deregulation, rules of origin, dispute mediation, mobility of business people, implementation of the ***Uruguay Round*** outcomes, transparency, free-trade agreements and information-gathering and analysis. IAPs contain more detail on near-term actions. They are less specific on policies or directions for the long term. They are updated regularly. *See also* ***e-IAP*** and ***rolling specificity***.

APEC Information Notes on Good Practice for Technical Regulation: a compendium of resource and reference materials suitable for preparing, adopting or reviewing regimes for the regulation of products according to the ***APEC Principles and Features of Good Practice for Technical Regulation***. It was first issued in September 2000. One of its aims is to help ***APEC*** economies in meeting their obligations under the WTO ***Agreement on Technical Barriers to Trade***. [www.apec.org]

APEC Internet and Digital Economy Roadmap: adopted by ***APEC*** economies in 2017. Its signposts are (1) development of digital infrastructure, (2) promotion of interoperability, (3) achievement of universal broadband success, (4) development of holistic government policy frameworks for the Internet and the Digital Economy, (5) promoting coherence and cooperation of regulatory approaches affecting the Internet and Digital Economy, (6) promoting innovation and adoption of enabling technologies and services, (7) enhancing trust and security in the use of ICTs (information and communication technology), (8) facilitating the free flow of information and data for the development of the Internet and Digital Economy, while respecting applicable domestic laws and regulations, (9) improvement of baseline Internet and Digital Economy measurements, (10) enhancing inclusiveness of Internet and Digital Economy, and (11) facilitation of e-commerce and advancing cooperation on digital trade.

北京(2014年)、马尼拉(2015年)、利马(2016年)、岘港(2017年)和莫尔斯比港(2018年)举行。智利原定于2019年主办会议，但因国内因素而停办。马来西亚将于2020年主办APEC领导人会议，新西兰将于2021年主办，泰国将于2022年主办。另见*茂物宣言(Bogor Declaration)*、*大阪行动议程(Osaka Action Agenda)*。

APEC Environmental Services Action Plan

APEC环境服务行动计划

2015年通过。在APEC贸易和投资自由化便利化议程中协调和促进服务工作的总括框架。

APEC framework for liberalization and facilitation

APEC自由化便利化框架

如《大阪行动议程》所述，APEC自由化便利化进程旨在实现《茂物宣言》中规定的目标。包括(a)APEC各经济体的行动；(b)APEC论坛的行动以及APEC与多边论坛有关的行动。另见*APEC马尼拉行动计划(Manila Action Plan for APEC)*。

APEC individual action plans

APEC单边行动计划

IAPs。指APEC经济体为实现《茂物宣言》的目标而采取的自愿行动。IAPs包含每一经济体提议的行动，以及在适当时提议的关于贸易和投资自由化便利化的集体行动。包括将在17个领域采取的步骤：关税、非关税措施、服务、投资、标准和合规、海关程序、知识产权、竞争政策、政府采购、放松管制、原产地规则、争端调停、商务人员流动、乌拉圭回合成果执行、透明度、自由贸易协定以及信息收集和分析。IAPs包含关于短期行动的更多细节，而对长期政策或方向则不太具体。IAPs定期更新。另见*电子版单边行动计划(e-IAP)*、*滚动式明确性(rolling specificity)*。

APEC Information Notes on Good Practice for Technical Regulation

APEC技术法规良好实践信息摘要

资源和参考资料的汇编，适用于根据《APEC技术法规良好实践的原则和特点》拟定、采用或审议产品监管制度。2000年9月首次发布。目的之一是帮助APEC经济体履行WTO《技术性贸易壁垒协定》项下的义务。

APEC Internet and Digital Economy Roadmap

APEC互联网和数字经济路线图

APEC经济体于2017年通过。主要包括：(1)发展数字基础设施；(2)促进互操作性；(3)实现宽带普及；(4)为互联网和数字经济制定全面政府政策框架；(5)促进影响互联网和数字经济的监管方法的一致性和合作；(6)促进创新以及为技术和服务赋能；(7)加强信息通信技术使用中的信任和安全；(8)促进信息和数据的自由流动，以促进互联网和数字经济的发展，同时尊重适用的国内法律法规；(9)改善基准互联网和数字经济测量；(10)增强互联网和数字经济的包容

The ***APEC Action Agenda for the Digital Economy*** is intended to help implementation of the Roadmap. [www.apec.org]

APEC Investment Facilitation Action Plan: IFAP. Adopted in 2008. Its principles, not exhaustive, are (a) promote accessibility and transparency in the formulation and administration of investment-related policies, (b) enhance stability of investment environments, security of property and protection of investments, (c) improve the efficiency and effectiveness of investment procedures, (d) build constructive stakeholder relationships, (e) use new technology to improve investment environments, (f) establish monitoring and review mechanisms for investment policies, and (g) enhance international cooperation. These principles are supported by an extensive menu of actions, in some cases with timetables. *See also* ***investment facilitation***.

APEC List of Environmental Goods: adopted in 2012. It contains fifty-four environmentally friendly goods on which members undertook to reduce applied tariffs by 5 per cent by 2015. The goods are listed at the six-digit level of the ***Harmonized Commodity Description and Coding System***.

APEC ministerial meetings: the annual meetings of trade and foreign ministers of APEC economies just preceding the ***APEC Economic Leaders' Meeting***. *See also* ***APEC sectoral ministerial meetings*** and ***Meeting of APEC Ministers Related to Trade***.

APEC Model Chapter on Transparency for RTAs/FTAs: adopted in 2012. Seen as an APEC contribution to the promotion of high-quality and comprehensive free-trade agreements (FTAs) and regional trade agreements (RTAs). It is based on existing provisions in free-trade agreements, Article X of the ***GATT*** (Publication and Administration of Trade Regulations) and Article III of the ***General Agreement on Trade in Services*** (Transparency). *See also* ***model measures for RTAs/FTAs***.

APEC model measures for RTAs/FTAs: *see* **model measures for RTAs/FTAs**.

APEC Mutual Recognition Arrangement for Conformity Assessment of Telecommunications Equipment: a non-binding arrangement which entered into force on 1 July 1999. It aims to streamline conformity assessment procedures for telecommunications and telecommunications-related equipment. It provides for the mutual recognition of conformity assessment bodies by the importing countries and mutual acceptance of testing and equipment certification procedures undertaken. APEC members can make the arrangement binding between themselves through an exchange of letters.

APEC New Strategy for Structural Reform: ANSSR. A work programme adopted in 2010 with a target year of 2015 to promote (a) more open, well-functioning, transparent and competitive markets, (b) better functioning and effectively regulated financial markets, (c) labour market opportunities, training and education, (d) sustained SME development and enhanced opportunities for women and for vulnerable populations, and (e) effective and fiscally sustainable social safety net programmes. *See also* ***Leaders' Agenda to Implement Structural Reform*** and ***Renewed APEC Agenda for Structural Reform***. [www.apec.org]

性；以及(11)便利电子商务和推动数字贸易合作。APEC数字经济行动议程旨在协助实施该路线图。

APEC Investment Facilitation Action Plan

APEC投资便利化行动计划

IFAP。2008年通过。原则主要包括：(a)促进与投资有关政策的制定和管理方面的可获性和透明度；(b)加强投资环境的稳定性、财产安全和投资保护；(c)提高投资程序的效率和效力；(d)与利益相关方建立建设性关系；(e)利用新技术改善投资环境；(f)建立投资政策监督审查机制；以及(g)加强国际合作。这些原则得到一份内容广泛的行动清单的支持，其中一些附有时间表。另见*投资便利化(investment facilitation)*。

APEC List of Environmental Goods

APEC环境产品清单

2012年通过，包括54种环境友好产品，成员承诺到2015年将这些产品的实施关税削减5%。这些产品按商品名称及编码协调制度6位编码列出。

APEC ministerial meetings

APEC部长级会议

在APEC经济领导人会议之前举行的APEC经济体贸易和外交部长年度会议。另见*APEC部门部长级会议(APEC sectoral ministerial meetings)*、*APEC贸易部长会议(Meeting of APEC Ministers Related to Trade)*。

APEC Model Chapter on Transparency for RTAs/FTAs

APEC区域贸易协定/自由贸易协定透明度示范章节

2012年通过。被视为APEC对促进高质量全面自由贸易协定和区域贸易协定所作贡献。以自由贸易协定、GATT第10条(贸易法规的公布和实施)以及《服务贸易总协定》第3条(透明度)的现有条款为基础。另见*区域贸易协定/自由贸易协定示范措施(model measures for RTAs/FTAs)*。

APEC model measures for RTAs/FTAs

APEC区域贸易协定/自由贸易协定示范措施

见*区域贸易协定/自由贸易协定示范措施(model measures for RTAs/FTAs)*。

APEC Mutual Recognition Arrangement for Conformity Assessment of Telecommunications Equipment

APEC电信设备合格评定互认安排

1999年7月1日生效的非约束性安排。旨在简化电信和电信相关设备的合格评定程序。规定进口国相互承认合格评定机构，并相互接受所进行的测试和设备认证程序。APEC成员可通过换文使该安排对彼此具有约束力。

APEC New Strategy for Structural Reform

APEC结构性改革新战略

ANSSR。2010年通过的一项工作计划，目标年份为2015年，以促进(a)更开放、运作良好、透明和竞争的市场；(b)更好运转和有效监管的金融市场；(c)劳动力市场机会、培训和教育；(d)中小企业可持续发展和增加妇女和弱势群体的机会；以及(e)有效和财政可持续的社会安全网计划。另见*领导人实施结构性改革议程(Leaders' Agenda to Implement Structural Reform)*、*APEC结构性改革新议程(Renewed APEC Agenda for Structural Reform)*。

APEC Non-Binding Investment Principles: a voluntary code containing principles to be applied to investment flows, adopted in 1994. It aims to promote a policy environment characterized by increased confidence, reduced uncertainty and the liberalization and simplification of investment rules and policies. The principles include transparency, most-favoured-nation (MFN) treatment, establishment, national treatment, transfers, nationalization and compensation, performance requirements, taxation and investment incentives, dispute resolution, etc. *See also* ***investment***, ***investment facilitation*** and ***World Bank Guidelines on the Treatment of Foreign Direct Investment***.

APEC Non-Binding Principles for Domestic Regulation of the Services Sector: adopted in November 2018 from the perspective of the WTO negotiations on ***domestic regulation***. The principles are listed in seven sections. *A*. General Principles. The principles apply to licensing requirements and procedures, qualification requirements and technical standards. Persons granted permission to supply a service must demonstrate compliance with these requirements. Measures must be administered in a reasonable, objective and impartial manner. *B*. Administration of Measures. APEC economies should, to the extent practicable, avoid requiring an applicant to approach more than one competent authority for each application or authorization. Applications should be permitted at any time throughout the year. Applications in electronic form should be accepted where an authorization is required to supply a service. Applications should be processed without undue delay and applicants advised of any reason for rejection. Authorization fees should be reasonable and transparent. *C*. Independence. Competent authorities should reach and administer their decisions in an independent manner. *D*. Transparency. Each APEC economy should ensure that its laws, regulations, procedures and ***administrative rulings of general application*** are promptly published to enable interested persons to have access to them. An enquiry point should be maintained or established. To the extent possible, each economy should give interested persons a reasonable opportunity to comment on proposed measures. *E*. Technical Standards. Economies should adopt technical standards developed through open and transparent processes. *F*. Development of Measures. If an economy adopts or maintains measures relating to the authorization for the supply of a service, they should be based on objective and transparent criteria, consistent with Article VI of the ***General Agreement on Trade in Services***, impartial and without unjustifiable impediments. *G*. Other Areas. Economies should consider supporting dialogues related to the recognition of qualifications. Service providers from other economies should be permitted to use the business names under which they ordinarily trade, and the use of business names should not be arbitrarily restricted.

APEC Non-Binding Principles on Government Procurement: adopted in 1999. The set consists of six main principles. 1. *Elements of transparency:* sufficient and relevant information should be made available to all interested parties consistently and in a timely manner through a readily accessible medium at no more than reasonable cost. 2. *Elements of value for money:* government

APEC Non-Binding Investment Principles

APEC投资非约束性原则

1994年通过，包含适用于投资流动原则的自愿守则。旨在促进一个以增加投资信心、减少不确定性以及投资规则和政策自由化和简化为特征的政策环境。这些原则包括透明度、最惠国待遇、设立、国民待遇、转让、国有化和补偿、绩效要求、税收和投资激励、争端解决等。另见*投资(investment)*、*投资便利化(investment facilitation)*、*世界银行外国直接投资待遇指南(World Bank Guidelines on the Treatment of Foreign Direct Investment)*。

APEC Non-Binding Principles for Domestic Regulation of the Services Sector

APEC服务部门国内规制非约束性原则

从WTO国内规制谈判的角度于2018年11月通过。这些原则分为7部分。A. 总体原则。这些原则适用于许可要求和程序、资质要求和技术标准。获准提供服务者必须证明符合这些要求。国内规制措施必须以合理、客观和公正的方式实施。B. 措施管理。APEC经济体应在切实可行的限度内，避免要求申请人就每项申请或授权向一个以上主管当局提出申请。申请的许可应在全年任何时间审批。如果提供服务需要授权，应接受电子形式的申请。申请的处理不应受到不当延误，如拒绝申请应告知申请人原因。授权费用应合理透明。C. 独立性。主管机关应以独立方式形成和管理其决定。D. 透明度。每一APEC经济体应保证迅速公布其法律、法规、程序和普遍适用的行政裁定，使利害关系人可获得。应设立或建立一咨询点。在可能的情况下，每一经济体应给予利害关系人就拟议措施进行评论的合理机会。E. 技术标准。经济体应采用通过开放和透明的程序制定的技术标准。F. 措施制定。如果一个经济体采用或维持与提供服务的授权有关的措施，这些措施应根据客观和透明的标准，符合《服务贸易总协定》第6条的规定，公正且无不合理的障碍。G. 其他领域。各经济体应考虑支持与资质认证有关的对话。应允许来自其他经济体的服务提供者使用其常用企业名称，且不应任意限制企业名称的使用。

APEC Non-Binding Principles on Government Procurement

APEC政府采购非约束性原则

1999年通过。包括6项主要原则：1. 透明度要素：通过易获取的媒介并以合理价格，使所有利害关系方以一致和及时的方式获得充足和相关的信息。2. 物有所值要素：政府采购做法和采购应实现资金的最佳可获价值。比较报价的

procurement practices and procurement should achieve the best available value for money. The basis for comparison of offers should be benefits and costs on a whole-of-life basis, not simply the lowest price. *3. Elements of open and effective competition:* the government procurement regime should be open, and procurement methods should suit market circumstances and facilitate levels of competition commensurate with the benefits received. *4. Elements of fair dealing:* the design of the procurement system and the conduct of buyers should ensure that procurement is conducted in a fair, reasonable and equitable manner and with integrity. *5. Elements of accountability and due process:* procuring (buying) agencies and individual procuring personnel should be accountable to their governments, the end users, the public and suppliers for the efficient, cost-effective and fair conduct of their procurement. Mechanisms for scrutiny of the procurement process and avenues for review of complaints should be available. *6. Elements of non-discrimination:* procurement laws, rules and regulations should not be applied to favour the suppliers of any particular economy. *See also* ***Revised Agreement on Government Procurement***.

APEC paperless trading initiative: adopted in 1999 as part of the ***APEC Blueprint for Action on Electronic Commerce***. Members agreed to endeavour to reduce or eliminate the requirement for paper documents needed for customs and other cross-border trade administration by 2005 for developed economies and 2010 for developing economies. This initiative applies to sea, air and land transport. *See also* ***electronic commerce***.

APEC Pathfinders: adopted in 2001 as one of the ways in which APEC could move towards achieving the ***Bogor Goals***. The idea is that smaller groups of economies would develop cooperative arrangements with obligations they are ready to take on, and other economies would join the initiative as they felt ready for it. Though eight pathfinder initiatives are now in force, they have not on the whole met expectations of the initiators. Some pathfinders have not been able to add to the original proponents. Current guidelines require first the creation of an interim pathfinder having at least three members, and participation by at least 25 per cent of APEC economies before it can become a full pathfinder. It is possible for pathfinders to be terminated if they prove incapable of attracting new members.

APEC Principles and Features of Good Practice for Technical Regulation: adopted in September 2000. This document contains two principles held to show good regulatory practice. First, economies should consider alternatives to mandatory requirements. Alternative mechanisms could include reliance on systems of legal recourse, liability laws and liability insurance schemes, taxes, fees and other charges, education programmes, co-regulation, voluntary standards, self-regulation and codes of practice. Second, the least interventionist and least trade-restrictive compliance regime necessary should be used to achieve the regulatory objective. Good regulations are described as transparent and non-discriminatory, performance-based, reflecting international standards or internationally aligned standards, reflecting only the standards necessary

基础应为全周期的收益和成本，而不仅是最低价格。3. 公开和有效竞争要素：政府采购制度应公开，采购方法应适合市场状况，促进与所获利益相称的竞争水平。4. 公平交易要素：采购制度的设计和买方行为应保证采购以公平、合理、公正和诚实的方式进行。5. 责任与正当程序要素：采购机构(买方)和采购个人应对其政府、最终用户、公众和供应商负责，进行高效益、低成本和公平的采购。应提供采购过程的监督机制和审查投诉的场所。6. 非歧视要素：采购法律、规定和法规不得优惠任何特定经济体的供应商。另见*政府采购协定修正版(Revised Agreement on Government Procurement)*。

APEC paperless trading initiative

APEC无纸贸易倡议

作为APEC电子商务行动蓝图的一部分于1999年通过。成员们同意努力减少或取消海关和其他跨境贸易管理所需的纸质单证，发达经济体在2005年前实现，发展中经济体在2010年前实现。倡议适用于海运、空运和陆运。另见*电子商务(electronic commerce)*。

APEC Pathfinders

APEC探路者

2001年作为APEC可以实现茂物目标的途径之一获得通过。其构想为，先由较小规模经济体制定合作安排，承担愿意承担的义务，其他经济体在准备好后再加入倡议。虽然目前已有8个探路者倡议生效，但并未完全达到倡议者的期望。一些探路者还未能加入到最初的支持者中。目前的指导方针首先要求建立一个至少有3个成员的临时探路者，并要求至少25%的APEC经济体参与方可成为正式的探路者。如被证明无法吸引新成员，探路者可能被终止。

APEC Principles and Features of Good Practice for Technical Regulation

APEC技术法规良好实践的原则和特点

2000年9月通过。文件包含良好监管实践的两项原则。第一，经济体应考虑强制性要求的替代方案。替代机制可包括依靠追索制度、责任法和责任保险计划、税收、费用和其他收费、教育计划、共同监管、自愿标准、自我监管和业务守则。第二，为实现监管目标，应使用最少干预和具有最少贸易限制作用的合规体制。良好的法规应是透明和非歧视的、基于绩效的、反映国际标准或国

to achieve the legitimate regulatory objective and being subject to review. [www.apec.org]

APEC Principles of Interconnection: adopted on 14 May 1999. This set of eight principles requires major suppliers of ***basic telecommunications services*** (i.e. those able to set prices and control facilities) to establish conditions enabling users of one public telecommunications transport network to communicate effectively with users of another. The first five principles govern the conditions applying to interconnection which is to be provided at any technically feasible point in the network, under non-discriminatory and transparent conditions, to non-affiliated service suppliers at non-discriminatory rates and of a quality no less favourable than that provided to its affiliates, in a timely fashion and negotiations in good faith, and at cost-oriented rates. The remaining principles are that a major supplier may not engage in anti-competitive practices, that all interconnection agreements must be published, and that a service supplier requesting interconnection with a major supplier may resort to applicable dispute settlement mechanisms regarding appropriate terms, conditions and rates for interconnection within a reasonable time. *See also* ***reference paper on telecommunications services***. [www.apec.org]

APEC Principles on Trade Facilitation: a non-binding set of principles adopted in Shanghai in 2001. The principles are: (a) transparency (information on laws, rules, regulations, etc.), (b) communication and consultations, especially with the business and trading community, (c) simplification, practicability and efficiency by ensuring that rules and procedures are no more burdensome or restrictive than necessary to achieve their objectives, (d) non-discrimination, (e) consistency and predictability to minimize uncertainty to the trade and trade-related parties, (f) harmonization, standardization and recognition on the basis of international standards where possible, (g) modernization and the use of new technology, (h) access to due process to enable seeking redress with respect to the administration of rules, and (i) cooperation among government authorities and business and trading communities. *See also* ***trade facilitation***.

APEC principles on transparency standards: formal name *Leaders' Statement to Implement APEC Transparency Standards*, adopted on 27 October 2002. The Statement commits APEC economies to the following principles on transparency in trade and investment liberalization and facilitation: (1) each economy will ensure that its laws, regulations, procedures and ***administrative rulings of general application*** will be published promptly either through official journals or the Internet, (2) each economy will publish relevant information in advance and give interested persons a reasonable opportunity to comment on them, (3) economies will endeavour to provide responses promptly to questions on its laws and regulations, (4) persons of another economy directly affected by administrative proceedings should be notified and given an opportunity to present facts and arguments concerning their positions, (5) each economy to ensure that domestic procedures are in place to enable prompt review and correction of final administrative matters, other than those taken for

际一致标准的、仅反映实现合法监管目标的必要标准，并应接受审查。

APEC Principles of Interconnection

APEC互连原则

1999年5月14日通过，包含八项原则。要求主要基础电信服务提供者(即能够定价和控制设施)创造条件，使一公共电信运输网络的用户与另一公共电信运输网络的用户进行有效通信。前五项原则适用于互连的条件，此种互连应在网络中任何技术可行点，在非歧视和透明的条件下，以非歧视的费率和不低于向其附属服务提供者提供的质量，以及时的方式，通过真诚的谈判，且以成本导向的费率，向无附属关系的服务提供者提供。其他原则为，主要提供者不得从事反竞争做法，必须公布所有互连协议，要求与主要供应商互连的服务提供者可在合理时间内就互连的适当条款、条件和费率诉诸适用的争端解决机制。另见*电信服务参考文件(reference paper on telecommunications services)*。

APEC Principles on Trade Facilitation

APEC贸易便利化原则

2001年在上海通过的一套非约束性原则。这些原则为：(a)透明度(法律、规定、法规的信息)；(b)沟通和协商，特别是与工商界、贸易团体；(c)简化、实用性和效率，以保证规定和程序的负担和限制作用不得超过实现其目标的必要限度；(d)非歧视；(e)一致性和可预测性，将对贸易和与贸易相关方的不确定性减至最小；(f)如可能，根据国际标准进行协调、标准化和认证；(g)现代化和使用新技术；(h)可获得针对管理规定寻找救济的适当程序；以及(i)加强政府主管机关与工商业界和贸易团体之间的合作。另见*贸易便利化(trade facilitation)*。

APEC principles on transparency standards

APEC透明度标准原则

2002年10月27日通过，正式名称为《关于实施APEC透明度标准的领导人声明》。声明中各APEC经济体承诺在贸易和投资自由化便利化方面遵守下列透明度原则：(1)每一经济体将保证其法律、法规、程序和普遍适用的行政裁定通过官方刊物或互联网迅速公布；(2)每一经济体将提前公布相关信息，并给予利害关系人进行评论的合理机会；(3)经济体将致力于迅速回复就其法律法规所提问题；(4)应通知受到行政程序直接影响的另一经济体的人，给予他们提出就其立场的提供事实和论点的机会；(5)每一经济体应保证设有国内程序，能够迅速审查和纠正最终行政事项，由于敏感审慎原因而采取的措施除外；以

sensitive prudential reasons, and (6) "administrative rulings of general application" are defined as administrative rulings or interpretations that apply to all persons and situations that fall generally within their ambit and that establish a norm of conduct. Confidential information is exempt from action under the Statement.

APEC Principles to Enhance Competition and Regulatory Reform: a non-binding set of five principles adopted in Auckland in 1999. The principles are: (1) *non-discrimination* (competition and regulatory principles not to discriminate between economic entities, whether these are foreign or domestic), (2) *comprehensiveness* (broad application of the principles to goods and services, and private and public business activities), (3) *transparency* in policies and rules, (4) *accountability* (clear responsibility within domestic administrations for the implementation of the competition and efficiency dimension in the development and administration of policies and rules), and (5) *implementation* (take, *inter alia*, practical steps to promote consistent application of policies and rules, eliminate unnecessary rules and regulatory procedures, and improve the transparency of policy objectives). *See also* ***competition policy***.

APEC Regulatory Cooperation Advancement Mechanism on Trade-Related Standards and Technical Regulations: ARCAM. A process adopted in 2010 under which trade officials and regulators would conduct work on one emerging regulatory issue per year having relevance to APEC's agenda to strengthen regional economic integration. Criteria to identify an "emerging regulatory issue" would include (a) its relevance to a significant number of APEC economies, (b) strong correlation between the issue and priority trade and investment issues, and (c) relevance of the issue from a trade and investment perspective.

APEC Second Trade Facilitation Action Plan: adopted in 2007. It superseded the ***APEC Trade Facilitation Action Plan*** and called for a further reduction of trade transaction costs by 5 per cent in the period 2007 to 2010. It stressed customs procedures, business mobility, standards and conformance, and electronic commerce. *See also* ***trade facilitation***.

APEC sectoral ministerial meetings: meetings of ministers other than those responsible for foreign affairs or trade at irregular intervals under APEC auspices. Examples are mining or education. *See also* ***APEC ministerial meetings*** and ***Meeting of APEC Ministers Related to Trade***.

APEC Services Competitiveness Roadmap: adopted in November 2016 in Lima. The Roadmap gives effect to the ***APEC Services Cooperation Framework*** adopted in 2015. It consists of a wide-ranging list of actions APEC economies can undertake to improve their competitiveness in the services sector. A mid-term review will be held in 2021, and the objectives of the Roadmap are to be completed by 2025.

APEC Services Cooperation Framework: ASCF. A programme adopted in 2015 to advance work on services among APEC economies. Desired outcomes of the ASCF include an increased services value-adding capacity of APEC

及(6)“普遍适用的行政裁定”定义为适用于属其司法辖区的所有人和情况并确立一种行为规范的行政裁定或解释。机密信息免受该声明行动影响。

APEC Principles to Enhance Competition and Regulatory Reform

APEC增强竞争和监管改革原则

1999年在奥克兰通过的一套5项的非约束性原则。这些原则为：(1)非歧视(不在经济实体之间进行歧视的竞争和监管原则，无论实体来自国内还是国外)；(2)全面性(原则全面适用于货物和服务及私营和公共商业活动)；(3)政策和规定的透明度；(4)问责(国内管理部门在政策和规定制定和管理过程中在竞争和效率实施方面的明确责任)；以及(5)实施(特别采取实际步骤促进政策和规定的一致适用，消除不必要的规定和监管程序，并提高政策目标的透明度)。另见*竞争政策(competition policy)*。

APEC Regulatory Cooperation Advancement Mechanism on Trade-Related Standards and Technical Regulations

APEC贸易相关标准和技术法规监管合作促进机制

ARCAM。2010年通过的进程。根据该进程，贸易官员和监管机构将每年就APEC加强区域经济一体化议程相关的一个新出现的监管问题开展工作。确定“新出现的监管问题”的标准包括：(a)该问题与众多APEC经济体的相关性；(b)该问题与优先贸易和投资问题之间关系密切；以及(c)从贸易和投资角度看这一问题的相关性。

APEC Second Trade Facilitation Action Plan

APEC第二个贸易便利化行动计划

2007年通过。取代APEC贸易便利化行动计划，呼吁在2007年至2010年期间将贸易交易费用进一步降低5%。强调海关程序、商务流动、标准和一致性以及电子商务。另见*贸易便利化(trade facilitation)*。

APEC sectoral ministerial meetings

APEC部门部长级会议

在APEC主持下不定期召开的负责外交或贸易事务以外事务的部长级会议，例如矿产和教育。另见*APEC部长级会议(APEC ministerial meetings)*、*APEC贸易部长会议(Meeting of APEC Ministers Related to Trade)*。

APEC Services Competitiveness Roadmap

APEC服务业竞争力路线图

2016年11月在利马通过。路线图旨在使2015年通过的APEC服务合作框架生效。包括一份APEC经济体为提高服务部门竞争力可采取行动的内容广泛的清单。路线图计划于2021年进行中期审议，路线图的目标定于2025年完成。

APEC Services Cooperation Framework

APEC服务合作框架

ASCF。2015年通过，旨在推动APEC经济体之间关于服务的工作。ASCF的预

economies, expansion of trade and investment in services through improvements in physical, institutional and people-to-people connectivity, and wider access to more efficient and greater variety of services for APEC and its people. *See also* ***APEC Services Competitiveness Roadmap***.

APEC Single Window Strategic Plan: adopted in 2007 to provide the framework for the development of a ***Single Window*** in each APEC economy. Stage 2 envisaged establishment of links between them to allow data sharing.

APEC Statement on Trade and the Digital Economy: adopted by APEC economic leaders on 27 October 2002. Its general objectives are (a) to have the digital economy continue to flourish in a liberal and open trade environment, (b) market access and national treatment commitments across a broad range of relevant goods and services, (c) transparent, non-discriminatory and least restrictive regulations, (d) a long-term ***moratorium on customs duties on electronic transmissions***, and (e) economies to support demand-driven capacity-building projects to ensure that developing economies benefit fully from the ***new economy***. Specific objectives are for APEC economies to encourage others to pursue the same degree of openness as they are aspiring to through (a) liberalization of trade in services, (b) enforcing the WTO ***Agreement on Trade-Related Aspects of Intellectual Property Rights*** and joining the ***WIPO Copyright Treaty*** and the ***WIPO Performances and Phonograms Treaty*** as soon as possible, and (c) to join the WTO ***Information Technology Agreement***. [www.apec.org]

APEC Strategic Blueprint for Promoting Global Value Chains Development and Cooperation: in 2014 APEC economies agreed on the objectives of this blueprint: (1) addressing trade and investment issues that impact on ***global value chains*** (GVCs), (2) cooperate on improving statistics related to GVCs, (3) realize the critical role of services within GVCs, (4) enable developing countries to better participate in GVCs, (5) assist SMEs to benefit from GVCs, (6) improve the investment climate for GVCs development, (7) adopt effective ***trade facilitation*** measures, (8) enhanced resilience of GVCs, (9) enhance public–private partnerships for GVCs, and (10) strengthen collaboration with other stakeholders in GVCs.

APEC Trade Facilitation Action Plan: a framework adopted in 2002 to reduce the cost of ***trade facilitation*** by 5 per cent across the ***APEC*** region by the end of 2007. Actions and measures, which are voluntary, are to be taken under one of the following categories: movement of goods (includes customs, port, health and quarantine and similar procedures), standards, business mobility and e-commerce. The plan was extended for another five years in 2006 with a similar cost-cutting target. *See also* ***APEC Second Trade Facilitation Action Plan***.

APEC Trade Repository: APECTR. An online source of ***APEC*** members' trade and tariff information launched in 2015. It includes the following categories: MFN tariff rates, preferential tariff rates, rules of origin for existing regional trade agreements and free-trade agreements, best practices in trade facilitation, domestic trade and customs laws and regulations, procedures and documentary

期成果包括提高APEC经济体的服务增值能力，通过提高有形、机构和人与人之间的联系扩大服务贸易和投资，以及使APEC及其人民获得更有效和更多样化服务的机会。另见*APEC服务竞争力路线图(APEC Services Competitiveness Roadmap)*。

APEC Single Window Strategic Plan

APEC单一窗口战略计划

2007年通过，为在每一APEC经济体中发展单一窗口提供框架。第二阶段设想在这些单一窗口之间建立联系，以实现数据共享。

APEC Statement on Trade and the Digital Economy

APEC关于贸易和数字经济的声明

APEC经济领导人于2002年10月27日通过。总体目标为：(a)促进数字经济在自由开放的贸易环境中继续蓬勃发展；(b)对范围广泛的货物和服务作出市场准入和国民待遇承诺；(c)透明、非歧视和限制性最小的监管；(d)长期对电子传输暂免关税；以及(e)各经济体支持由需求驱动的能力建设项目，以保证发展中经济体自新经济中充分受益。具体目标为，APEC经济体鼓励其他经济体通过下列途径达到与它们同样程度的开放：(a)服务贸易自由化；(b)执行WTO《与贸易有关的知识产权协定》，并尽快加入《世界知识产权组织版权条约》和《世界知识产权组织表演和录音制品条约》；　以及(c)加入WTO《信息技术协定》。

APEC Strategic Blueprint for Promoting Global Value Chains Development and Cooperation

APEC促进全球价值链发展与合作战略蓝图

APEC经济体于2014年同意这一蓝图的目标为：(1)处理影响全球价值链的贸易和投资问题；(2)合作改进与全球价值链有关的数据统计；(3)认识到服务在全球价值链中的关键作用；(4)促进发展中国家更好地参与全球价值链；(5)帮助中小企业自全球价值链中获益；(6)改善发展全球价值链的投资环境；(7)采取有效贸易便利化措施；(8)加强全球价值链的韧性；(9)加强全球价值链的公私伙伴关系；以及(10)加强与全球价值链其他利益相关方的合作。

APEC Trade Facilitation Action Plan

APEC贸易便利化行动计划

2002年通过的框架，旨在到2007年底将整个APEC区域的贸易便利化成本降低5%。自愿行动和措施将在下列类别中的一个项下采取：货物移动(包括海关、港口、卫生和检疫及类似程序)、标准、商务流动和电子商务。该计划在2006年再次延长5年，具有类似的成本削减目标。另见*APEC第二个贸易便利化行动计划(APEC Second Trade Facilitation Action Plan)*。

APEC Trade Repository

APEC贸易资料库

APECTR。2015年推出的APEC成员贸易和关税信息在线资源。包括以下类别：最惠国关税税率、优惠关税税率、现有区域贸易协定和自由贸易协定的原产地规则、贸易便利化最佳实践、国内贸易和海关法律法规、进出口程序和单证

requirements for imports and exports, a list of authorized economic operators and information on mutual recognition arrangements. *See also* ***ASEAN Trade Repository***. [tr.apec.org]

Appellate Body: an independent standing body of seven persons established under the WTO ***Dispute Settlement Understanding*** (DSU) to hear appeals arising from ***panel*** decisions. The grounds for such appeals are confined to points of WTO law. Appellate Body members are persons of recognized authority with demonstrated expertise in law, international trade and relevant WTO agreements who are not affiliated with any government. At least three persons are needed to hear an appeal. When it was established, many trade law experts thought appeals would be brought only occasionally. But over time it became clear that on many cases, particularly those that were politically sensitive, WTO members seek to pursue all means of legal recourse provided in the system. In fact, most WTO members appealed adverse panel decisions. The workload facing the Appellate Body has been huge, and for various reasons it has taken several years for complex cases to be concluded, even though the DSU sets a deadline of a maximum of 90 days for each appeal. For many years, the United States has raised concerns about the operations of the Appellate Body. The US concerns are broad and centre on several elements of AB work. One pertains to the four-year terms renewable once, that are assigned to AB members. Over time, the Appellate Body adopted a procedural rule enabling its members to continue working on unfinished appeals even if their term had expired. Washington has objected to this practice stating that only WTO members can extend the term of an outgoing AB member. Another, broader, issue may have more substantial ramifications. It is that of perceived ***judicial activism*** and what may lead to the creation of new obligations. WTO members are intensely jealous of the system of rules they have created, and they have established a solid tradition of having the rules interpreted by the membership. How these matters will be resolved is not clear. The impasse points, however, to the difficulty of managing an effective dispute settlement system in a large organization. A lack of consensus among WTO members on the appointment of new Appellate Body members to fill current vacancies brought the work of the Appellate Body to a halt effectively in December 2019. *See also* ***dispute settlement*** and ***Dispute Settlement Body***.

Appellation d'origine contrôlée: AOC. Under the French *Code Rural* and the *Code de la Consommation* an ***appellation of origin*** which has been given legal protection following an examination by the *Institut national des appellations d'origine*. "Appellation of origin" is defined as "denomination of a country, a region or a locality which serves to designate a product originating therein, the quality and characteristics of which are due to the geographical environment, including natural and human factors". An *appellation*, once granted, does not attest to the quality of the wine, but it emphasizes the strong connection between the product and the locality in which it was grown. Once an AOC has been granted, it can never become generic and fall into the public

要求、经认证的经营者名单及互认安排信息。另见*东盟贸易资料库(ASEAN Trade Repository)*。

Appellate Body
上诉机构

根据WTO《争端解决谅解》(DSU)设立的由7人组成的独立常设机构，负责审理对专家组裁决进行的上诉。此类上诉的理由仅限于WTO法律点。上诉机构成员为在法律、国际贸易和WTO相关协定方面具有公认权威的人员，且不附属于任何政府。一上诉案件的审理至少需要3名法官。在上诉机构设立时，许多贸易法专家认为提起上诉的次数会有限。但随着时间的推移，人们清楚地看到，在许多案件中，特别是政治敏感案件，WTO成员寻求该制度中所提供的所有法律追索手段。事实上，大多数WTO成员均对不利的专家组裁决提出上诉。上诉机构面临的工作量巨大，由于各种原因，尽管《争端解决谅解》规定每一上诉的最后期限最多为90天，但复杂案件往往需要几年时间才能结案。多年来，美国一直对上诉机构的运作提出关注。美国的关注广泛，且主要集中在上诉机构工作的几个要素方面。其中一个涉及到上诉机构成员的4年任期可延长一次的问题。随着时间的推移，上诉机构通过了一项规则，使其成员在任期已满后继续处理未完成的上诉案件。华盛顿反对这种做法，称只有WTO成员才能延长即将离任的上诉机构成员的任期。另一个更为广泛的问题可能产生更多实质性影响。即被认为存在的司法能动主义及可能导致新义务的产生。WTO成员非常珍惜它们所创设的规则体系，并且创设了由成员解释规则的牢固传统。将如何解决这些问题尚不清楚。然而，僵局指向了在一个大型组织中管理有效的争端解决体系的困难。由于WTO成员无法就任命新的上诉机构成员以填补现有空缺达成共识，上诉机构的工作在2019年12月实际上陷入停摆状态。另见*争端解决(dispute settlement)*、*争端解决机构(Dispute Settlement Body)*。

Appellation d'origine contrôlée
原产地命名控制

AOC。根据法国《农村法》和《消费法》，一项原产地名称在经国家原产地名称管理局审查后给予法律保护。"原产地名称"的定义为"一个国家、地区或地方的名称，用于指示一项产品来源于该地，其质量和特征取决于地理环境，包括自然和人为因素"。名称一旦授予，虽不能证明葡萄酒的质量，但表明产品与产地之间的紧密联系。一旦授予一项AOC，这一命名永远不能成为通用名

domain. The labels of products granted this status must conform to prescribed legal requirements. *See also* ***generic geographical indications*** and ***geographical indications***.

Appellations of origin: a category of ***indications of source*** which enjoys domestic protection under ***intellectual property*** laws. International protection can be achieved through multilateral treaties, such as the ***Paris Convention*** and the ***Lisbon Agreement***, or bilateral agreements. Protection in other countries is only available if the name is protected at home. Article 1 of the Paris Convention protects, among other types of industrial property, appellations of origin. It does not define the term, but it says that "industrial property shall be understood in the broadest sense . . . and shall apply to agricultural and extraction industries, and to all manufactured or natural products, for example, wines, grain, tobacco leaf, fruit cattle minerals, mineral waters, beer, flowers and flour". Article 2(1) of the Lisbon Agreement defines an appellation of origin as "the geographical name of a country, region, or locality, which serves to designate a product originating therein, the quality and characteristics of which are due exclusively or essentially to the geographical environment, including natural and human factors". Article 2(2) defines the country of origin as "the country whose name, or the country in which is situated the region or locality whose name constitutes the appellation of origin which has given the product its reputation". In other words, protection for an appellation of origin is available under the Lisbon Agreement if the product bearing it has characteristics which can be ascribed exclusively or essentially to the place where it comes from. These characteristics may be due to natural and human factors. Article 3 of the Lisbon Agreement requires protection "against any usurpation or imitation, even if the true origin of the product is indicated or if the appellation is used in translated form or accompanied by terms such as 'kind', 'type', 'imitation' or the like". Expressions such as "konjak" or "Bordeaux-type wine" would therefore not be acceptable under this Agreement. The 2015 ***Geneva Act of the Lisbon Agreement on Appellations of Origin and Geographical Indications*** now allows the registration of geographical indications under the Lisbon Agreement also. Under United States law the appellations of origin available for wine are (a) the United States, (b) a state, (c) two or no more than three adjoining states, (d) a county, (e) two or no more than two or three adjoining counties in the same state, and (f) a wine-growing area which can be distinguished by geographical features and which has recognized and defined boundaries. Ownership of appellations of origin is collective, either through a private or a public body. All farmers belonging to the specified geographical area and respecting the applicable specifications have the right to use the geographical name recognized by the appellation of origin. *See also* ***protected geographical indications*** and ***designation of origin***.

Applied MFN tariff rate: the tariff rate actually used for imports from countries enjoying ***most-favoured-nation treatment***, often the same as the ***applied tariff rate***. Sometimes it is much lower than the ***bound tariff rate***.

称并进入公有领域。被授予AOC地位产品的标签必须符合规定的法律要求。*另见通用地理标志(generic geographical indications)*、*地理标志(geographical indications)*。

Appellations of origin

原产地名称

根据知识产权法受到保护的一类产地标志。国际保护可以通过《巴黎公约》和《里斯本协定》等多边协定或双边协定实现。只有名称在本国受到保护，在其他国家方可得到保护。《巴黎公约》第1条保护原产地名称，还保护其他类型的工业产权。公约未对这一词语进行定义，但规定"对工业产权应作最广义的理解……也应同样适用于农业和采掘业，适用于一切制成品或天然产品，例如酒类、谷物、烟叶、水果、牧畜、矿产品、矿泉水、啤酒、花卉和谷类的粉"。《里斯本协定》第2条第1款将原产地名称定义为"指一个国家、地区或地方的地理名称，用于指示一项产品来源于该地，其质量或特征完全或主要取决于地理环境，包括自然和人为因素"。第2条第(2)款将原产地定义为"原属国系指其名称构成原产地名称而赋予产品以声誉的国家或者地区或地方所在的国家"。换言之，如果含有原产地名称的产品具有可以完全或主要归因于其产地的特征，则可根据《里斯本协定》对原产地名称提供保护。这些特征可以取决于自然和人为因素。《里斯本协定》第3条要求保护"旨在防止任何假冒和仿冒，即使标明了产品的真实来源或者使用名称的翻译形式或附加'类'、'式'、'样'、'仿'字样或类似字样"。因此，诸如"konjak"(即Cognac，干邑的同音词)或"波尔多类型葡萄酒"等表达方式在该协定项下是不被接受的。2015年《原产地名称和地理标志里斯本协定日内瓦文本》现在也允许根据《里斯本协定》注册地理标志。根据美国法律，可用的葡萄酒的原产地名称包括：(a)美国；(b)一个州；(c)两个或不超过三个毗连州；(d)一个县；(e)同一个州的两个或不超过三个毗连县；以及(f)可通过地理特征进行区分且边界认定和确定的葡萄酒产区。原产地名称所有权为集体所有，或是通过私营机构或是通过公共机构。属于特定地理区域且遵守适用规定的所有农民有权使用经原产地名称所认定的地理名称。*另见地理标志保护(protected geographical indications)*、*原产地命名(designation of origin)*。

Applied MFN tariff rate

最惠国实施税率

对源自享受最惠国待遇的国家的进口产品实际使用的税率，通常与实施税率相同。有时大大低于约束税率。

Applied tariff rates: the tariff rates imposed by a customs administration when a good crosses the border. These rates are often considerably lower than the bound rates arrived at as a result of trade negotiations or the rates listed in national ***tariff schedules***. *See also* ***binding*** and ***nominal tariff***.

Appropriate level of sanitary or phytosanitary protection: ALOP. Defined in the WTO ***Agreement on the Application of Sanitary and Phytosanitary Measures*** as the "level of protection deemed appropriate by the Member establishing a sanitary or phytosanitary measure to protect human, animal or plant life or health within its territory". Views on what constitutes an appropriate level of protection vary greatly. This concept is also known as the "acceptable level of risk".

A priori **limitation:** a quantitative ceiling on imports enjoying preferential treatment under a ***GSP*** scheme.

Arab Common Market: A project launched in 2015 for completion by 2020. Negotiations for its establishment are under way. An earlier Arab Common Market, established in 1964, is no longer operational. *See also* ***Greater Arab Free Trade Area***.

Arab Customs Union: announced in 2009 for realization by 2015. Work on full implementation is under way. *See also* ***Arab Common Market***.

Arab League: *see* ***League of Arab States***.

Arab Maghreb Union: consists of Algeria, Libya, Mauritania, Morocco and Tunisia. It was formed in 1989 with political, economic and social objectives, including the aim of achieving a Common Market. Its secretariat is located at Rabat. *See also* ***Maghreb region***.

Arbitrary or unjustifiable discrimination: a term used in several of the agreements administered by the WTO where it is, however, not further defined. A hypothetical example of such discrimination would be where a country discriminates perfectly legally between trading partners that meet its ***sanitary and phytosanitary measures*** and those that cannot satisfy them. If it then discriminates further for whatever reason between those that meet the requirements, this could well be a case of arbitrary or unjustifiable discrimination.

Arbitration: a way of settling disputes. It is more formal than ***mediation*** which is aimed at bringing the parties together, and less legalistic than formal court proceedings which are adversarial. The parties agreeing to arbitration often bind themselves to well-defined rules of procedure. They also usually agree in advance that the award handed down by the arbitrator is binding on them. Arbitration proceedings are especially helpful when the parties to a dispute seek an equitable and definitive solution to a problem. They may also be cheaper to conduct because appeals to a higher authority are usually not possible. Article 25 of the WTO ***Dispute Settlement Understanding*** enables members to solve disputes by arbitration if that is their preference. They have to notify all other members before the start of the arbitration and also of the outcome. Other members may participate in the arbitration proceedings only with the agreement of the parties seeking arbitration. Many ***free-trade***

Applied tariff rates
实施税率

货物过境时海关征收的税率，这些税率通常大大低于作为贸易谈判结果达成的约束税率或国别关税减让表中所列税率。另见*约束(binding)*、*名义关税(nominal tariff)*。

Appropriate level of sanitary or phytosanitary protection
适当的卫生与植物卫生保护水平

ALOP。WTO《实施卫生与植物卫生措施协定》将其定义为"制定卫生与植物卫生措施以保护其领土内的人类、动物或植物的生命或健康的成员所认为适当的保护水平"。对于适当的保护水平的构成意见分歧很大。这一概念也被称为"可接受的风险水平"。

***A priori* limitation**
预定限额

在普惠制(GSP)方案下享受优惠待遇的进口产品的数量上限。

Arab Common Market
阿拉伯共同市场

2015年启动的计划，2020年前完成。建立共同市场的谈判正在进行中。先前在1964年建立的阿拉伯共同市场已停止运作。另见*大阿拉伯自由贸易区(Greater Arab Free Trade Area)*。

Arab Customs Union
阿拉伯关税同盟

2009年宣布于2015年实现。全面实施工作正在进行中。另见*阿拉伯共同市场(Arab Common Market)*。

Arab League
阿拉伯联盟

见*阿拉伯国家联盟(League of Arab States)*。

Arab Maghreb Union
阿拉伯马格里布联盟

由阿尔及利亚、利比亚、毛里塔尼亚、摩洛哥和突尼斯组成。该联盟成立于1989年，包含政治、经济和社会目标，包括实现共同市场的目标。秘书处设在拉巴特。另见*马格里布地区(Maghreb region)*。

Arbitrary or unjustifiable discrimination
任意或不合理的歧视

WTO管理的若干协定中使用的词语，但没有进一步定义。一个假设的例子为，一国在能够满足其卫生与植物卫生措施要求的贸易伙伴与不能满足要求的贸易伙伴之间以完全合法的方式进行歧视。如果该国进一步以任何原因在那些能够满足措施要求的贸易伙伴之间进行歧视，则是一种任意或不合理的歧视的情况。

Arbitration
仲裁

解决争端的一种方式。相对于撮合各当事方的调停，仲裁更正式，而对于具有对抗性的正式法庭程序，仲裁又不那么死扣法律条文。同意仲裁的当事方往往遵守明确规定的议事规则。当事方也通常事先同意仲裁人下达的裁决对他们具有约束力。如果争端各方寻求对一问题的公正的和最终的解决方案，仲裁程序则会特别有帮助。仲裁成本可能更低，原因是不能向上一级机关提出上诉。WTO《争端解决谅解》第25条使成员在愿意的情况下能够通过仲裁解决争端。在仲裁开始前成员必须通报其他所有成员并通报仲裁结果。其他成

agreements contain arbitration rules. ***NAFTA***, for example, contains two arbitration provisions. Article 20 establishes the procedures to be followed in the arbitration of disputes between the parties generally. Article 11 permits investors of a NAFTA party to seek arbitration in disputes with the NAFTA parties, but only concerning alleged breaches of some of the obligations set out in Chapters 11 and 15. *See also* ***Article 22.6 arbitration***, ***dispute settlement***, ***Inter-American Convention on International Commercial Arbitration***, ***International Court of Arbitration***, ***Model Arbitration Clause***, ***NAFTA Chapter 11***, ***New York Convention*** and ***UNCITRAL Arbitration Rules***.

Area freedom: the concept of pest- or disease-free areas and areas of low pest or disease prevalence outlined in Article 6 of the WTO ***Agreement on the Application of Sanitary and Phytosanitary Measures***. A determination of such areas has to take into account factors such as geography, ecosystems, epidemiological surveillance and the effectiveness of sanitary or phytosanitary controls. Exporting countries claiming that some areas within their territories fall into this category have to be able to provide the necessary evidence to the importing country. A demonstration of area freedom means that a country can export products from the area concerned even though the same product may be subject to disease in another area of the country. *See also* ***regionalization***.

Areeda-Turner test: a method proposed by Phillip Areeda and Donald Turner in 1975 "to examine the relationship between a firm's prices and its costs in order to define a rational dividing line between legitimately competitive prices and prices that are properly regarded as predatory". Areeda and Turner concluded that unless at or above average cost, a price below reasonably anticipated (1) short-run marginal costs or (2) average variable costs should be deemed predatory, and the monopolist may not defend it on the grounds that his price was "promotional" or merely met an equally low price of a competitor. They say that although marginal cost data are nearly always unavailable, a price below reasonably anticipated average variable cost should conclusively be presumed unlawful. This proposition by Areeda and Turner has spawned a considerable literature questioning and refining its assumptions, but the basic approach is considered to remain valid. *See also* ***antitrust laws*** and ***predatory pricing***. [Areeda and Turner 1975]

Arguendo**:** Latin meaning "for the sake of argument", as in "assuming *arguendo* that the drafters of Article 12 intended it to mean . . .".

Arm's-length pricing: a principle designed to assess whether the market price charged for goods and services traded internationally has been manipulated. The arm's-length price is usually defined as the price that would have been charged between independent firms dealing at arm's length in comparable circumstances. The methods to assess whether this criterion has been satisfied can be complex. *See also* ***customs valuation*** and ***transfer pricing***.

Arrangement on Officially Supported Export Credits: *see* ***OECD Arrangement on Officially Supported Export Credits***.

员只有在寻求仲裁的当事方同意的情况下方可参与仲裁程序。许多自由贸易协定包含仲裁规则。例如，《北美自由贸易协定》(NAFTA)包含两个仲裁条款。第20条总体上规定了当事方争端仲裁应遵循的程序。第11条允许一NAFTA参加方的投资者在与其他参加方的争端中寻求仲裁，但仅涉及涉嫌违反第11章和第15章规定的部分义务。另见*第22.6条仲裁(Article 22.6 arbitration)*、*争端解决(dispute settlement)*、*美洲国家国际商事仲裁公约(Inter-American Convention on International Commercial Arbitration)*、*国际仲裁法院(International Court of Arbitration)*、*示范仲裁条款(Model Arbitration Clause)*、*北美自由贸易协定第11章(NAFTA Chapter 11)*、*纽约公约(New York Convention)*、*联合国国际贸易法委员会仲裁规则(UNCITRAL Arbitration Rules)*。

Area freedom

无疫区

WTO《实施卫生与植物卫生措施协定》第6条规定的病虫害非疫区和低度流行区。这类地区的确定应考虑地理、生态系统、流行病监测以及卫生或植物卫生控制的有效性等因素。声明其领土内的地区属此类地区的出口国应能够向进口国提供必要证据。证明存在无疫区意味着一国可以从有关地区出口产品，即使相同产品在该国另一地区可能遭受病害。另见*区域化(regionalization)*。

Areeda-Turner test

阿瑞达-特纳检验

菲利普·阿瑞达和唐纳德·特纳在1975年提出的一种方法，“用以审查一公司的价格与其成本之间的关系，从而在合法的竞争价格与被适当地视为掠夺性价格之间确定一条合理界线”。阿瑞达和特纳的结论是，除非达到或超过平均成本，否则如一价格低于合理预期的(1)短期边际成本或(2)平均可变成本，则应被视为掠夺性价格，垄断者不得以价格属“促销性质”或仅为达到与竞争对手相同的低价格为由进行辩护。他们表示，尽管边际成本数据常常难以获得，但是低于合理预期的平均可变成本的价格应最终被认定属非法。阿瑞达和特纳主张引发了大量的文献对这一假设提出质疑和改进，但其基本方法被认为仍然有效。另见*反垄断法(antitrust laws)*、*掠夺性定价(predatory pricing)*。

Arguendo

在论证中

拉丁语。意为“为了辩论起见”。例如，“为了辩论起见，假设第12条的起草者意在……”。

Arm's-length pricing

公平定价

一项旨在评估国际贸易中对货物和服务收取的市场价格是否受到操纵的原则。公平定价通常被定义为在可比情况下独立公司之间进行公平交易所收取的价格。评估这一标准是否得到满足的方法可能很复杂。另见*海关估价(customs valuation)*、*转让定价(transfer pricing)*。

Arrangement on Officially Supported Export Credits

官方支持出口信贷的安排

见*OECD 官方支持出口信贷的安排(OECD Arrangement on Officially Supported Export Credits)*。

Arrangement Regarding Bovine Meat: *see* ***International Bovine Meat Agreement***.

Arrangements for Consultations on Restrictive Business Practices: a GATT mechanism adopted on 18 November 1960 aimed at ensuring that ***restrictive business practices*** do not frustrate the benefits of tariff reductions and the removal of ***quantitative restrictions***. This mechanism lay dormant until 1996 when the United States invoked it in a dispute with Japan concerning photographic materials, the so-called ***Kodak–Fuji case***.

Article V: the provision in the ***General Agreement on Trade in Services*** which establishes the conditions for ***free-trade agreements*** covering services.

Article XII members: countries and customs territories that have joined the WTO since its establishment in 1995. *See also see* ***Group of Article XII***.

Article XIX: the GATT article permitting the use of ***safeguards*** against import surges, but only if certain conditions have been met. It is better known as the ***escape clause***. *See also* ***Agreement on Safeguards***.

Article XX: the GATT article listing allowed ***general exceptions*** to the trade rules under defined conditions.

Article XXIV: the GATT article describing the basic multilateral requirements for ***customs unions***, ***free-trade areas***, ***free-trade agreements*** and ***regional trade agreements***.

Article 20 of the WTO Agreement on Agriculture: the clause authorizing the resumption of agricultural negotiations by 1 January 2000. *See* ***continuation clause***.

Article 21.5 panel: a ***panel*** established under this article of the ***Dispute Settlement Understanding*** to rule on disagreements over the implementation of recommendations or rulings of a dispute settlement panel. Where possible, the panel hearing the original complaint will examine the disagreement over its ruling. It normally has ninety days to produce its report. Also known as ***compliance panel***.

Article 22.6 arbitration: a procedure available under this article of the ***Dispute Settlement Understanding***. When a WTO member refuses to comply with a ***panel*** ruling, the aggrieved party can ask for a new ***panel*** to rule on whether the original panel ruling has been implemented to satisfy the WTO rules. This is the ***Article 21.5 panel***. If there is a new adverse ruling, the parties are then supposed to enter into discussion concerning mutually acceptable ***compensation***. If this does not lead to any agreement, the complaining party may ask for authorization from the ***Dispute Settlement Body*** to suspend ***concessions*** or other obligations no later than the expiry of the ***reasonable period of time*** (usually a maximum of fifteen months from the adoption of the panel or ***Appellate Body*** report). If the member which is the target of these actions complains about their level, the matter may be referred to ***arbitration***. Generally, the original panel will act as arbitrator, but the WTO Director-General may decide to appoint a different arbitrator. Concessions or obligations may not be suspended during the course of the arbitration. The arbitrator's decision is final. *See also* ***suspension of concessions or other obligations***.

Arrangement Regarding Bovine Meat
牛肉安排

见*国际牛肉协定(International Bovine Meat Agreement)*。

Arrangements for Consultations on Restrictive Business Practices
关于限制性商业惯例磋商的安排

1960年11月18日通过的GATT机制，旨在保证限制性商业惯例不使关税削减和数量限制取消的利益无效。该机制处于休眠状态，直至1996年在美国与日本的"柯达-富士案"中援引。

Article V
第5条

《服务贸易总协定》第5条，规定涵盖服务的自由贸易协定的条件。

Article XII members
第12条成员

自1995年WTO成立以来加入WTO的国家和单独关税区。另见*第12条协调组(Group of Article XII)*。

Article XIX
第19条

GATT条款，允许针对进口激增使用保障措施，但仅在满足某些条件的情况下。这一条款更为人所知的名称为免责条款。另见*保障措施协定(Agreement on Safeguards)*。

Article XX
第20条

GATT条款，列出在规定条件下对贸易规则的一般例外。

Article XXIV
第24条

GATT条款，描述了关税同盟、自由贸易区、自由贸易协定和区域贸易协定的基本多边要求。

Article 20 of the WTO Agreement on Agriculture
WTO农业协定第20条

授权在2000年1月1日前恢复农业谈判的条款。另见*继续谈判条款(continuation clause)*。

Article 21.5 panel
第21.5条专家组

根据《争端解决谅解》第21.5条设立的专家组，对执行争端解决专家组的建议或裁决产生的异议作出裁决。在可能的情况下，听取最初起诉方意见的专家组将审查对其裁决的异议。专家通常应在90天内提交报告。也被称为执行之诉专家组。

Article 22.6 arbitration
第22.6条仲裁

根据《争端解决谅解》第22.6条可获得的程序。如一WTO成员拒绝遵守专家组裁决，受损害方可以要求设立一个新的专家组裁决原专家组裁决是否得到执行以符合WTO规则，即第21.5条专家组。如产生新的不利裁决，各方随即应就双方均可接受的补偿进行讨论。如果不能达成任何协议，起诉方可要求争端解决机构授权在合理期限失效前(通常最长为自专家组或上诉机构报告通过后的15个月)中止减让或其他义务。如果这些行动所针对的成员对措施的水平提出质疑，可以将此事项提交仲裁。通常，原专家组将担任仲裁人，但WTO总干事可以决定指定另一仲裁人。在仲裁过程中，减让或其他义务不得中止。仲裁人的决定将是最终决定。另见*中止减让或其他义务(suspension of concessions or other obligations)*。

Article 25 arbitration: *see* ***arbitration***.

Article 31*bis*: see ***Declaration on the TRIPS Agreement on Public Health*** and ***Paragraph 6 system***.

Article 50 procedure: the article of the ***Treaty on European Union*** setting out the procedure to be followed by countries wishing to leave the ***European Union***. Introduced as an amendment by the ***Treaty of Lisbon***. It says that any member state may withdraw by notifying its intention to the ***European Council***. This then leads to negotiations of the arrangements for withdrawal. Membership ceases from the date of entry into force of the withdrawal agreement. If agreement cannot be reached, membership will cease two years after notification, unless the Council and the member state wishing to leave unanimously decide to extend the period. *See also* ***Brexit***.

Article 113 Committee: the predecessor of the ***Article 133 Committee***. It took its name from Article 113 of the ***Treaty of Rome***. Its modern form is the ***Trade Policy Committee***.

Article 133 Committee: often referred to as the 133 Committee. It takes its name from Article 133 of the ***Treaty of Amsterdam***, one of the treaties amending the ***Treaty of Rome***, now Article 207 of the consolidated version of the Treaty of Rome, the ***Treaty on the Functioning of the European Union***. This article is the legal basis for the ***European Union***'s ***common commercial policy***. Its modern form is the ***Trade Policy Committee***. *See also* ***competence***, ***shared competence*** and ***subsidiarity***.

Arusha Declaration: originally adopted in July 1993 by the Customs Co-operation Council, now the ***World Customs Organization***, to promote an effective customs service free of corruption. The revised declaration of July 2003 lists the following as key factors in the fight against corruption: (a) prime responsibility for corruption prevention must rest with the head of customs and the executive management team, (b) customs laws, regulations, etc., should be harmonized and simplified to the greatest possible extent, (c) a high degree of certainty and predictability is needed, (d) automation of customs functions will remove many opportunities for corruption, (e) systems should be reformed and modernized, (f) appropriate monitoring and control mechanisms should be in place, (g) customs services should adopt a code of conduct, (h) need for sound human resource management practices, (i) high morale among officers should be promoted, and (j) foster an open, transparent and productive relationship with the private sector. *See also* ***bribery*** and ***corruption***.

ASEAN: Association of South-East Asian Nations. Established on 8 August 1967 with Indonesia, Malaysia, Philippines, Singapore and Thailand as its members. Brunei Darussalam joined in 1984, Viet Nam in 1995, Laos and Myanmar in 1997 and Cambodia in 1999. The last four are known collectively as the CLMV countries. On 20 November 2007 ASEAN Leaders adopted the ASEAN Charter, and they launched it on 15 December 2008. Article 1 of the Charter lists the purposes of ASEAN. They are: to (1) maintain and enhance peace, security and stability and further strengthen peace-oriented values in the

Article 25 arbitration

第25条仲裁

见*仲裁(arbitration)*。

Article 31 bis

第31条之二

见*关于与贸易有关的知识产权协定与公共健康的宣言(Declaration on the TRIPS Agreement on Public Health)*、*第6段制度(Paragraph 6 system)*。

Article 50 procedure

第50条程序

《欧洲联盟条约》条款，规定了希望脱离欧盟的国家应遵循的程序。作为《里斯本条约》的修正案引入。该条规定，任何成员国可以通过向欧洲理事会通报其意见而退出欧盟。此后将进行关于退出安排的谈判。成员资格自退出协定生效之日起终止。如果不能达成协议，成员资格将在通报2年后终止，除非理事会和希望退出的成员国一致决定延长该期限。另见*英国脱欧(Brexit)*。

Article 113 Committee

第113条委员会

第133条委员会的前身。名称源自《罗马条约》第113条。其现代形式为贸易政策委员会。

Article 133 Committee

第133条委员会

通常称为133委员会。名称源自《阿姆斯特丹条约》第133条，该条约是修正《罗马条约》的条约之一，现在是《罗马条约》合并本《欧洲联盟运行条约》第207条。该条是欧盟共同商业政策的法律基础。其现代形式是贸易政策委员会。另见*权限(competence)*、*共享权限(shared competence)*、*辅助原则(subsidiarity)*。

Arusha Declaration

阿鲁沙宣言

最初于1993年7月由海关合作理事会(现为世界海关组织)通过，旨在促进高效海关服务，杜绝腐败。2003年7月的修订宣言将下列因素列为反腐败斗争的关键：(a)预防腐败的主要责任由海关负责人和行政管理团队承担；(b)海关法律法规等应在最大可能限度内协调和简化；(c)需要高程度的确定性和可预测性；(d)海关职能的自动化将消除许多腐败机会；(e)系统应改革和实行现代化；(f)应建立适当的监测和管控机制；(g)海关服务应采用行为守则；(h)需要健全的人力资源管理做法；(i)应提高官员士气；以及(j)与私营部门建立公开、透明和富有成效的关系。另见*贿赂(bribery)*、*腐败(corruption)*。

ASEAN

东南亚国家联盟

1967年8月8日成立，成员国包括印度尼西亚、马来西亚、菲律宾、新加坡和泰国。文莱于1984年加入，越南于1995年加入，老挝和缅甸于1997年加入，柬埔寨于1999年加入。后加入的4国统称CLMV(柬老缅越)国家。2007年11月20日，东盟领导人通过了《东南亚国家联盟宪章》，并于2008年12月15日发布。宪章第1条列出了东盟的宗旨即：(1)维护和加强本地区的和平、安全和稳定，进一

region, (2) enhance regional resilience by promoting greater political, security, economic and socio-cultural cooperation, (3) preserve South-East Asia as a Nuclear Weapon-Free Zone and free of all other weapons of mass destruction, (4) ensure that the peoples and Member states of ASEAN live in peace with the world at large in just, democratic and harmonious environment, (5) create a single market and production base which is stable, prosperous, highly competitive and economically integrated with effective facilitation for trade and investment in which there is a free flow of goods, services and investment, facilitated movement of business persons, professionals, talents and labour, and free flow of capital, (6) alleviate poverty and narrow the development gap within ASEAN through mutual assistance and cooperation, (7) strengthen democracy, enhance good governance and the rule of law, and promote and protect human rights and fundamental freedoms, with due regard to the rights and responsibilities of the Member States of ASEAN, (8) respond effectively, in accordance with the principle of comprehensive security, to all forms of threats, international crimes and transboundary challenges, (9) promote sustainable development so as to ensure the protection of the region's environment, (10) develop human resources, (11) enhance the well-being and livelihood of the peoples of ASEAN, (12) strengthen cooperation in building a safe, secure and drug-free environment, (13) promote a people-oriented ASEAN, (14) promote an ASEAN identity, and (15) maintain the centrality and proactive role of ASEAN. Article 7 establishes the ***ASEAN Summit*** as the supreme policymaking body of ASEAN. *See also* ***ASEAN Economic Community***, ***ASEAN Comprehensive Investment Agreement***, ***ASEAN Trade in Goods Agreement*** and ***ASEAN Trade in Services Agreement***.

ASEAN-5: Indonesia, Malaysia, Philippines, Singapore and Thailand. Used mainly for statistical purposes.

ASEAN-6: Brunei Darussalam, Indonesia, Malaysia, Philippines, Singapore and Thailand. Used mainly for statistical purposes.

ASEAN+3: the ***ASEAN*** countries plus China, Japan and the Republic of Korea. Its first summit meeting was held in Kuala Lumpur in December 1997. *See also* ***East Asia Vision Group***.

ASEAN+6: roughly equivalent to the participants in the ***East Asia Summit***, i.e. the ***ASEAN*** members plus Australia, China, India, Japan, Republic of Korea and New Zealand. An informal study for a possible ASEAN+6 ***free-trade agreement*** was launched in 2006.

ASEAN–x: a method used within ***ASEAN*** to indicate that not all of its members are participating in a programme or activity. The magnitude of *x* varies.

ASEAN Charter: the fundamental document for the aims and work of ***ASEAN***.

ASEAN-China Free Trade Area: ACFTA. Came into force on 1 January 2010. It covers goods, trade in services and investment.

ASEAN Community: launched in 2015. It consists of three community pillars: Political-Security Community, Economic Community and Socio-Cultural Community. *See also* ***ASEAN Economic Community***.

步加强以和平为导向的价值观；(2)通过加强政治、安全、经济和社会文化合作，加强地区韧性；(3)维护东南亚无核武器区地位，无任何其他大规模杀伤性武器；(4)保证东盟各国人民和成员国在公正、民主、和谐的环境中与世界和平共处；(5)建立稳定、繁荣、高度竞争和经济一体化的单一市场和生产基地，有效促进贸易和投资，商品、服务和投资自由流动，便利商务人员、专业人员、人才和劳动力的流动，以及资本自由流动；(6)通过相互援助与合作减轻贫困，缩小东盟内部的发展差距；(7)加强民主，促进良政和法治，促进和保护人权和基本自由，并适当考虑东盟成员国的权利和责任；(8)依照全面安全原则，有效应对各种形式的威胁、国际犯罪和跨境挑战；(9)促进可持续发展，以保证地区环境得到保护；(10)开发人力资源；(11)增进东盟各国人民福祉和生活；(12)加强合作，以建立安全、有保障和无毒品的环境；(13)促进以人为本的东盟；(14)促进东盟身份认同；以及(15)保持东盟的中心地位和积极作用。第7条规定东盟领导人会议为东盟最高决策机构。另见*东盟经济共同体(ASEAN Economic Community)*、*东盟全面投资协定(ASEAN Comprehensive Investment Agreement)*、*东盟货物贸易协定(ASEAN Trade in Goods Agreement)*、*东盟服务贸易协定(ASEAN Trade in Services Agreement)*。

ASEAN-5
东盟5国
印度尼西亚、马来西亚、菲律宾、新加坡和泰国。主要用于统计目的。

ASEAN-6
东盟6国
文莱、印度尼西亚、马来西亚、菲律宾、新加坡和泰国。主要用于统计目的。

ASEAN+3
东盟+3
东盟国家加中国、日本和韩国。首次峰会于1997年12月在吉隆坡举行。另见*东亚展望小组(East Asia Vision Group)*。

ASEAN+6
东盟+6
大致等同于东亚峰会的参加国，即东盟成员国加澳大利亚、中国、印度、日本、韩国和新西兰。2006年启动一项关于东盟+6自由贸易协定的非正式研究。

ASEAN-x
东盟-x
在东盟内使用的用以表明并非所有成员国均参与一项计划或活动的方法。x的范围并不确定。

ASEAN Charter
东盟宪章
关于东盟目标和工作的基本文件。

ASEAN-China Free Trade Area
东盟—中国自由贸易区
ACFTA。2010年1月1日生效，涵盖货物贸易、服务贸易和投资。

ASEAN Community
东盟共同体
2015年启动。由三个共同体支柱组成：政治安全共同体、经济共同体和社会文化共同体。另见*东盟经济共同体(ASEAN Economic Community)*。

ASEAN Comprehensive Investment Agreement: ACIA. Entered into force 29 March 2012. Superseded the ASEAN Investment Area. Its objectives are: (a) progressive liberalization of the investment regimes of member states, (b) provision of enhanced protection to investors of member states and their investments, (c) improvement of transparency and predictability of investment rules, (d) joint promotion of the region as an integrated investment area, and (e) cooperation to create favourable conditions for investors of a member state in the territory of another. ACIA permits reservations where a measure does not conform to the obligations on (a) national treatment or (b) senior management and board of directors. ACIA has been amended three times, the last time in 2017. *See also **ASEAN*** and ***investment***.

ASEAN Economic Community: AEC. After several years of preparatory work the AEC was formally established on 31 December 2015 with a blueprint for actions up to 2025. AEC seeks to make the ASEAN area into a globally competitive single market and production base through a free flow of goods, services and investment between ASEAN members. The AEC Blueprint 2025 envisages that by 2025 the AEC is (a) a highly integrated and cohesive economy, (b) a competitive, innovative and dynamic ASEAN, (c) has enhanced connectivity and sectoral cooperation, (d) a resilient, inclusive and people-oriented and people-centred ASEAN, and (e) a global ASEAN. The ***ASEAN Trade in Goods Agreement*** and the ***ASEAN Comprehensive Investment Agreement*** will be major parts of the AEC, as will be the yet-to-be completed ***ASEAN Trade in Services Agreement***. A raft of other activities will promote the growth of the AEC.

ASEAN Economic Community Blueprint 2025: *see **ASEAN Economic Community.***

ASEAN Framework Agreement on Intellectual Property Cooperation: concluded on 15 December 1995 in Bangkok. It aims to strengthen cooperation among ***ASEAN*** countries in ***intellectual property*** to promote regional and global trade liberalization. It envisages the possibility of an ASEAN patent system and an ASEAN Patent Office, an ASEAN trademark system and an ASEAN Trademark Office as well as an ASEAN Intellectual Property Association (formed in 1996). The Agreement also establishes an extensive programme of cooperative activities in all main areas of intellectual property. It is not yet in force.

ASEAN Framework Agreement on Services: adopted by ***ASEAN*** governments on 15 December 1995. The Agreement seeks (a) to enhance cooperation in services among member states to improve the efficiency and competitiveness of ASEAN services providers and to diversify production capacity and supply and distribution of services within and outside ASEAN, and (b) to eliminate substantially restrictions on trade in services among member states and to liberalize trade in services by expanding the depth and scope of liberalization beyond the commitments made under the ***General Agreement on Trade in Services*** (GATS) with the aim of realizing a ***free-trade area*** in services. Article II seeks

ASEAN Comprehensive Investment Agreement
东盟全面投资协定

ACIA。2012年3月29日生效。替代原东盟投资区。目标为：(a)逐步放宽成员国的投资体制；(b)对成员国投资者及其投资提供增强保护；(c)改善投资规则的透明度和可预测性；(d)共同促进本地区形成一体化投资区域；以及(e)合作为成员国的投资者在另一成员国领土内创造有利条件。如果一项措施不符合(1)国民待遇义务或(2)高级管理人员和董事会义务，则ACIA允许保留该措施。ACIA已进行三次修正，最近一次是在2017年。另见*东盟(ASEAN)*、*投资(investment)*。

ASEAN Economic Community
东盟经济共同体

AEC。经过数年筹备工作，AEC于2015年12月31日正式建立，制定了到2025年的行动蓝图。AEC旨在通过东盟成员国之间货物、服务和投资的自由流动，使东盟地区成为一个具有全球竞争力的单一市场和生产基地。《2025年东盟经济共同体蓝图》设想到2025年AEC将成为：(a)一个高度一体化和融合的经济体；(b)一个竞争、创新和充满活力的东盟；(c)增强的互联互通和部门合作；(d)一个具有韧性、包容、以人为本和以人为中心的东盟；以及(e)全世界的东盟。《东盟货物贸易协定》和《东盟全面投资协定》将是AEC的主要组成部分，尚未完成的《东盟服务贸易协定》同样如此。一系列其他活动将促进AEC的形成。

ASEAN Economic Community Blueprint 2025
2025年东盟经济共同体蓝图

见*东盟经济共同体(ASEAN Economic Community)*。

ASEAN Framework Agreement on Intellectual Property Cooperation
东盟知识产权合作框架协定

1995年12月15日在曼谷缔结。旨在加强东盟国家在知识产权领域的合作，以促进区域和全球贸易自由化。协定设想建立东盟专利系统和东盟专利局、东盟商标系统和东盟商标局以及东盟知识产权协会(成立于1996年)的可能性。协定还在知识产权的所有主要领域建立了一项广泛合作计划。协定尚未生效。

ASEAN Framework Agreement on Services
东盟服务框架协定

东盟各国政府于1995年12月15日通过。协定寻求(a)加强成员国之间服务领域合作，以提高东盟服务提供者的效率和竞争力，使东盟内外服务业的生产能力、供应和分销多样化；及(b)消除对成员国之间服务贸易的实质性限制，并通过在WTO《服务贸易总协定》(GATS)项下所作承诺基础上扩大自由化的深度和范围以进一步开放服务贸易，从而实现服务自由贸易区。第2条要求通过

cooperation through establishing or improving infrastructural facilities, joint production, marketing and purchasing arrangements, research and development, and exchange of information. Article III requires member states to liberalize trade in services in a substantial number of sectors within a reasonable timeframe through the removal of discriminatory measures and market access limitations and a prohibition of new restrictive measures. Under Article IV, member states are to enter into negotiations on measures affecting specific services sectors. Article V permits the mutual recognition of qualifications, education, experience and licences, but it does not require any member state to do so. The Agreement stipulates that the provisions of the GATS will apply on matters where it is silent. Several rounds of negotiations under this Agreement have been completed. The target is a for a free flow of services by 2020. The next step is to negotiate the ***ASEAN Trade in Services Agreement***. *See also* ***ASEAN Economic Community*** and ***ASEAN Investment Area***.

ASEAN Framework for Regional Comprehensive Economic Partnership: a declaration adopted by ASEAN Heads of Government in 2012 which sets out general principles for a regional comprehensive economic partnership. These principles are (a) a comprehensive mutually beneficial economic partnership agreement, (b) to be achieved either sequentially, a single undertaking or an agreed other method, (c) open accession mechanism to permit later accession by ASEAN or external partners, (d) transparency, (e) economic and technical cooperation among the parties, (f) economic integration and equitable economic development, (g) special and differential treatment for Cambodia, Laos, Myanmar and Viet Nam, (h) consistency with the WTO rules and (i) periodic reviews to ensure effective and beneficial implementation. *See also* ***Regional Comprehensive Economic Partnership***.

ASEAN Free Trade Area: *see* ***AFTA***. Now superseded by the ***ASEAN Trade in Goods Agreement***.

ASEAN Industrial Cooperation Scheme: AICO. An industrial development programme adopted in 1996 by the ***ASEAN*** countries to promote investment in technology-based industries and to enhance value-adding activities in goods and services production. It replaced the ASEAN Industrial Joint Venture Scheme. To be eligible for the benefits under AICO, a cooperative venture must consist of at least two companies located in different ASEAN countries, and the companies must have at least 30 per cent of equity owned by ASEAN nationals.

ASEAN Industrial Joint Venture Scheme: *see* ***ASEAN Industrial Cooperation Scheme***.

ASEAN Integration System of Preferences: entered into force on 1 January 2002. This scheme enables the six original members of ***AFTA*** (Brunei Darussalam, Indonesia, Malaysia, Philippines, Singapore and Thailand) to extend voluntary tariff preferences to the four newer members (Burma, Cambodia, Laos and Viet Nam).

ASEAN Investment Area: AIA. Superseded by the ***ASEAN Comprehensive Investment Agreement*** which entered into force on 24 February 2012.

建立或改善基础设施、联合生产、销售和采购安排、研究和开发以及信息交流开展合作。第3条要求成员国通过取消歧视性措施和市场准入限制，并禁止采取新限制措施，在合理时限内在相当数量的部门实现服务贸易自由化。根据第4条，成员国将就影响特定服务部门的措施进行谈判。第5条允许相互承认资格、教育、经历和执照，但并不要求任何成员国这样作。协定规定，GATS条款将适于本协定未涉及的内容。在协定项下已经完成数轮谈判。目标为到2020年实现服务自由流动。下一步是谈判《东盟服务贸易协定》。另见*东盟经济共同体(ASEAN Economic Community)*、*东盟投资区(ASEAN Investment Area)*。

ASEAN Framework for Regional Comprehensive Economic Partnership
东盟区域全面经济伙伴关系框架

东盟政府首脑于2012年通过的一份宣言，列出了区域全面经济伙伴关系的总体原则。这些原则为：(a)一项全面互利经济伙伴关系协定；(b)逐步实现或以议定的其他方式实现一揽子协议；(c)开放型加入机制，以允许东盟或外部伙伴稍后加入；(d)透明度；(e)参加方之间的经济和技术合作；(f)经济一体化和公正经济发展；(g)给予柬埔寨、老挝、缅甸和越南特殊和差别待遇；(h)与WTO规则的一致性；以及(i)定期审查以保证有效和有益实施。另见*区域全面经济伙伴关系协定(Regional Comprehensive Economic Partnership)*。

ASEAN Free Trade Area
东盟自由贸易区

见*东盟自由贸易区(AFTA)*。现已被《东盟货物贸易协定》所取代。

ASEAN Industrial Cooperation Scheme
东盟产业合作计划

AICO。东盟国家于1996年通过的一项产业发展计划，目的在于促进对技术型产业的投资，并加强货物和服务生产方面的增值活动。替代东盟产业合资计划。为有资格获得AICO项下的优惠，一合作企业必须由至少两家设在不同东盟国家的公司组成，且这些公司必须至少有30%的股权为东盟国家国民拥有。

ASEAN Industrial Joint Venture Scheme
东盟产业合资计划

见*东盟产业合作计划(ASEAN Industrial Cooperation Scheme)*。

ASEAN Integration System of Preferences
东盟一体化优惠体系

2002年1月1日生效。该计划使东盟自由贸易区(AFTA)6个创始成员国(文莱、印度尼西亚、马来西亚、菲律宾、新加坡和泰国)能够向4个新成员国(柬埔寨、老挝、缅甸和越南)提供自愿关税优惠。

ASEAN Investment Area
东盟投资区

AIA。已被2012年2月24日生效的《东盟全面投资协定》所取代。

ASEAN–Japan Comprehensive Economic Partnership: an agreement signed on 8 October 2003 to strengthen economic integration between the ***ASEAN*** countries and Japan. Entered into force on 1 December 2008. It established the framework for the creation of a Comprehensive Economic Partnership (CEP), i.e. a ***free-trade agreement*** covering trade in goods, trade in services and investment

ASEAN Priority Integration Sectors: refers to eleven sectors identified by the ***ASEAN*** countries for early liberalization among themselves. They are (i) agro-based products, (ii) air travel, (iii) automotives, (iv) e-ASEAN, (v) electronics, (vi) fisheries, (vii) healthcare, (viii) rubber-based products, (ix) textiles and apparel, (x) tourism, and (xi) wood-based products.

ASEAN Summit: the highest policy organ of ***ASEAN***.

ASEAN Trade in Goods Agreement: ATIGA. A comprehensive ***free-trade agreement*** which entered into force on 17 May 2010. It supersedes ***AFTA*** and provides for further liberalization of trade in goods among the ASEAN members. All duties on intra-ASEAN trade had to be eliminated by 2010 for the ***ASEAN-6*** and 2015 for Cambodia, Laos, Myanmar and Viet Nam. All ***tariff rate quotas*** have been abolished. The Agreement establishes a work programme for ***trade facilitation***. ATIGA is one of the building blocks for the ***ASEAN Economic Community***.

ASEAN Trade in Services Agreement: ATISA. An agreement intended to supersede the ***ASEAN Framework Agreement on Services*** and serve as a building block for ***ASEAN Economic Community***. Negotiations have not yet begun.

ASEAN Trade Repository: ATR. A database listing the trade and customs laws and procedures of ***ASEAN*** members. It provides information on tariff nomenclatures, MFN tariffs and preferential tariffs, rules of origin, non-tariff measures, national trade and customs laws and procedures and documentary requirements, administrative rulings, best practices in trade facilitation and a list of ***authorized economic operators***.

ASEAN Vision 2020: adopted on 28 June 2012. It envisages ASEAN as zone of peace, freedom and neutrality, a partnership in dynamic development, a community of caring societies and an outward-looking ASEAN. *See also* ***ASEAN Economic Community***.

ASEM: Asia-Europe Meeting. Inaugurated in 1996. An informal process of dialogue and cooperation. It consists of the twenty-seven members of the ***European Union*** plus Norway and Switzerland on the European side and the ten ***ASEAN*** countries plus Australia, Bangladesh, China, India, Japan, Kazakhstan, Republic of Korea, Mongolia, New Zealand, Pakistan and Russia on the Asian side, fifty countries in total. ASEM has no secretariat. It is coordinated through the foreign ministries and senior officials. ASEM has a wide-ranging agenda. Issues discussed have included connectivity, trade and investment, climate change and broader security issues such as counter-terrorism, migration and maritime security. Summit meetings are held every two years, but the

ASEAN–Japan Comprehensive Economic Partnership

东盟—日本全面经济伙伴关系协定

2003年10月8日签署的协定，旨在加强东盟国家与日本之间的经济一体化。2008年12月1日生效。协定建立了产生《全面经济伙伴关系》的框架，即一项涵盖货物贸易、服务贸易和投资的自由贸易协定。

ASEAN Priority Integration Sectors

东盟优先一体化部门

指东盟国家确定的相互间实现提前自由化的11个部门。这些部门包括：(1)农产品；(2)航空旅行；(3)汽车；(4)电子东盟；(5)电子产品；(6)渔业、(7)医疗保健；(8)橡胶制品；(9)纺织品和服装；(10)旅游业；以及(11)木制品。

ASEAN Summit

东盟领导人会议

东盟最高政策机关。

ASEAN Trade in Goods Agreement

东盟货物贸易协定

ATIGA。2010年5月17日生效的全面自由贸易协定。取代东盟自由贸易区(AFTA)，并规定东盟成员国之间的货物贸易进一步自由化。东盟6国到2010年取消所有东盟内部关税，柬埔寨、老挝、缅甸和越南到2015年取消。所有关税配额已经取消。协定确定了贸易便利化工作计划。ATIGA是东盟经济共同体的组成部分。

ASEAN Trade in Services Agreement

东盟服务贸易协定

ATISA。该协定旨在取代《东盟服务框架协定》，成为东盟经济共同体的组成部分。谈判尚未开始。

ASEAN Trade Repository

东盟贸易资料库

ATR。列出东盟成员国贸易和海关法律和程序的数据库。提供关税税则、最惠国关税和优惠关税、原产地规则、非关税措施、国别贸易及海关法律和程序、单证要求、行政裁定、贸易便利化最佳实践以及经认证的经营者名单。

ASEAN Vision 2020

东盟2020愿景

2012年6月28日通过。设想东盟成为一个和平、自由和中立的地区，一个蓬勃发展中的伙伴，一个关爱社会的共同体和一个外向型的东盟。另见***东盟经济共同体****(ASEAN Economic Community)*。

ASEM

亚欧会议

创立于1996年。非正式的对话与合作进程。欧洲方面包括欧盟27个成员国及挪威和瑞士，亚洲方面包括10个东盟国家及澳大利亚、孟加拉国、中国、印度、日本、哈萨克斯坦、韩国、蒙古、新西兰、巴基斯坦和俄罗斯，共计50个国家。亚欧会议没有秘书处，通过外交部和高级官员进行协调。亚欧会议议程广泛。讨论的议题包括互联互通、贸易和投资、气候变化和更广泛的安全问题，如反恐、移民和海上安全。峰会每2年举行一次，但亚欧会议进程得到多层级的专

ASEM process is supported by more specialized meetings at many levels. Summit meetings held so far are ASEM-1 in Bangkok in 1996, ASEM-2 London 1998, ASEM-3 Seoul 2000, ASEM-4 Copenhagen 2002, ASEM-5 Hanoi 2005, ASEM-6 Helsinki 2006, ASEM-7 Beijing 2008, ASEM-8 Brussels 2010, ASEM-9 Vientiane 2012, ASEM-10 Milan 2014, ASEM-11 Ulaanbaatar 2016 and ASEM-12 Brussels 2018. ASEM-13 will be held in Phnom Pen in 2020.

ASEM Investment Promotion Action Plan: IPAP. *See* ***Investment Promotion Action Plan***.

Asia-Europe Meeting: *see* ***ASEM***.

Asian developing members: a group of thirty-one WTO members established in 2012. Members are Bahrain, Bangladesh, Brunei Darussalam, Cambodia, China, Hong Kong (China), India, Indonesia, Jordan, Republic of Korea, Kuwait, Kyrgyz Republic, Laos, Macao (China), Malaysia, Maldives, Mongolia, Myanmar, Nepal, Oman, Pakistan, Philippines, Qatar, Saudi Arabia, Singapore, Sri Lanka, Chinese Taipei, Thailand, Turkey, United Arab Emirates and Viet Nam.

Asian Development Bank: ADB. An international development finance institution dedicated to reducing poverty in Asia and the Pacific through loans, technical assistance, grants and equity investments. It has sixty-seven members, forty-eight of which are from the Asia-Pacific region. *See also* ***Asian Infrastructure Investment Bank***. [www.adb.org]

Asian Infrastructure Investment Bank: AIIB. A multilateral development bank launched in January 2016 with the aims of (a) fostering sustainable economic development, creating wealth and improving infrastructure connectivity in Asia by investing in infrastructure and other productive sectors, and (b) promoting regional cooperation and partnership in addressing regional development challenges by working in close collaboration with other multilateral and bilateral development institutions. It has sixty-eight members and is located in Beijing. *See also* ***Asian Development Bank*** and ***New Development Bank***. [www.aiib.org]

Asia-Pacific Trade Agreement: the name since December 2005 for the Bangkok Agreement (formally *First Agreement on Trade Negotiation Among Developing Countries of ESCAP*). It aims at trade expansion among developing country members of the Economic and Social Commission for the Asia-Pacific (***ESCAP***) through mutually beneficial trade measures. It was signed on 31 July 1975. Members are Bangladesh, China, India, Laos, Republic of Korea and Sri Lanka. Mongolia is expected to become the seventh member.

Asia-Pacific Trade Facilitation Forum: APTFF. An annual event organized by ***ESCAP*** and the ***Asian Development Bank*** which provides a platform for the exchange of information on ***trade facilitation***.

Asset-based definition of investment: *see* ***investment***.

Assistance: a more genteel term than ***protection*** or ***subsidies***, but it means the same and has the same effect.

门会议支持。迄今举行的首脑会议有：1996年第1届曼谷会议、1998年第2届伦敦会议、2000年第3届首尔会议、2002年第4届哥本哈根会议、2005年第5届河内会议、2006年第6届赫尔辛基会议、2008年第7届北京会议、2010年第8届布鲁塞尔会议、2012年第9届万象会议、2014年第10届米兰会议、2016年第11届乌兰巴托会议、2018年第12届布鲁塞尔会议，第13届亚欧会议定于2020年在金边举行。

ASEM Investment Promotion Action Plan
亚欧会议投资促进行动计划

IPAP。见*投资促进行动计划(Investment Promotion Action Plan)*。

Asia-Europe Meeting
亚欧会议

见*亚欧会议(ASEM)*。

Asian developing members
亚洲发展中成员

2012年成立的由31个WTO成员组成的集团。成员为巴林、孟加拉国、文莱、柬埔寨、中国、中国香港、印度、印度尼西亚、约旦、韩国、科威特、吉尔吉斯斯坦、老挝、中国澳门、马来西亚、马尔代夫、蒙古、缅甸、尼泊尔、阿曼、巴基斯坦、菲律宾、卡塔尔、沙特阿拉伯、新加坡、斯里兰卡、中国台北、泰国、土耳其、阿拉伯联合酋长国和越南。

Asian Development Bank
亚洲开发银行

ADB。国际发展融资机构，致力于通过贷款、技术援助、赠款和股权投资减少亚太地区的贫困。有67个成员，其中48个来自亚太地区。另见*亚洲基础设施投资银行(Asian Infrastructure Investment Bank)*。

Asian Infrastructure Investment Bank
亚洲基础设施投资银行

AIIB。2016年1月创设的多边开发银行，目的为：(a)通过基础设施和其他生产部门投资，促进亚洲可持续经济发展、创造财富和改善基础设施连通性；及(b)通过与其他多边和双边发展机构密切合作，促进区域合作和伙伴关系，以应对区域发展挑战。共有68个成员，设在北京。另见*亚洲开发银行(Asian Development Bank)*、*新开发银行(New Development Bank)*。

Asia-Pacific Trade Agreement
亚太贸易协定

2005年12月起，《曼谷协定》改用此名，正式名称为《亚太经社会发展中成员国之间贸易谈判第一协定》。协定旨在通过互利贸易措施，扩大亚太经社会(ESCAP)发展中成员国之间的贸易。协定于1975年7月31日签署。成员包括孟加拉国、中国、印度、老挝、韩国和斯里兰卡。蒙古有望成为第7个成员国。

Asia-Pacific Trade Facilitation Forum
亚太贸易便利化论坛

APTFF。亚太经社会(ESCAP)和亚洲开发银行举办的年度活动，为贸易便利化信息交流提供平台。

Asset-based definition of investment
基于资产的投资定义

见*投资(investment)*。

Assistance
援助

一个比保护或补贴更文雅的词语，但含义相同且效果相同。

Associated foreign direct investment: defined by ***UNCTAD*** as ***foreign direct investment*** triggered either by the establishment of an affiliate or the expansion of existing affiliates. *See also* ***sequential foreign direct investment***.

Association Agreement: a bilateral agreement between the ***European Union*** and a third country. This type of agreement is aimed at fostering a close relationship between the European Union and the country concerned, but economic cooperation is its dominant aspect. Association Agreements usually contain a free-trade agreement. Three categories of countries are addressed through such an agreement: (a) countries that have a special historical bond with European Union member states, including former colonies, but also some developing countries, (b) members of ***EFTA*** (European Free Trade Area), and (c) prospective members of the European Union.

Association of Caribbean States: entered into force in August 1995. It consists of thirty-two Latin American and Caribbean countries. They are Antigua and Barbuda, Bahamas, Barbados, Belize, Colombia, Costa Rica, Cuba, Dominica, Dominican Republic, El Salvador, Grenada, Guatemala, Guyana, Haiti, Honduras, Jamaica, Mexico, Nicaragua, Panama, Saint Kitts and Nevis, Saint Vincent and the Grenadines, Suriname, Trinidad and Tobago, and Venezuela. Its five main areas of concern are (a) preservation and conservation of the Caribbean Sea, (b) sustainable tourism, (c) trade and external relations, (d) natural disasters, and (e) transport. *See also* ***CARICOM Single Market and Economy***.

Association of Tin Producing Countries: ATPC. Established in 1983 with the objective of obtaining remunerative and equitable returns to tin producers and adequate to consumers at fair and stable prices. Disbanded in 2001. Members in the final years included Brazil, Bolivia, China, Democratic Republic of Congo, Indonesia, Malaysia, Nigeria and Thailand. Its secretariat was in Kuala Lumpur until 1997, when it moved to Rio de Janeiro.

ASYCUDA: UNCTAD Automated System for Customs Data. An integrated customs management system for international trade and transport operations in an automated environment. The aims of the system are: (a) modernizing customs operations and helping to improve revenue collections, (b) facilitating trade efficiency and competitiveness by substantially reducing transaction time and costs, (c) improving security by streamlining procedures of cargo control, transit of goods and clearance of goods, (d) helping fight corruption by enhancing the transparency of transactions, and (e) promoting sustainable development by cutting down on the use of paper through electronic transactions and documents. *See also* ***paperless trading*** and ***trade facilitation***. [www.unctad.org, www.asycuda.org]

Asymmetrical preferences: an arrangement whereby a country gives trade preferences to another country without expecting reciprocity. *See also* ***asymmetrical trade agreements***.

Asymmetrical price comparison: occurs, for example, when the investigators in an anti-dumping case use different methods to calculate the ***normal value*** and the ***export price***. *See also* ***dumping*** and ***anti-dumping measures***.

Associated foreign direct investment
关联外国直接投资

联合国贸易与发展会议(UNCTAD)将其定义为通过建立附属公司或通过扩大现有附属公司而产生的外国直接投资。另见*连续外国直接投资(sequential foreign direct investment)*。

Association Agreement
联系协定

欧盟与一第三国签署的双边协定。此类协定旨在促进欧盟与有关国家之间的紧密关系，但经济合作是其主要方面。联系协定通常包含一项自由贸易协定。此种协定处理三类国家的情况：(a)与欧盟成员国有特殊历史关联的国家，包括前殖民地，也包括一些发展中国家；(b)欧洲自由贸易联盟(EFTA)成员国；以及(c)潜在欧盟成员国。

Association of Caribbean States
加勒比国家联盟

1995年8月生效。由32个拉丁美洲和加勒比国家组成，即安提瓜和巴布达、巴哈马、巴巴多斯、伯利兹、哥伦比亚、哥斯达黎加、古巴、多米尼克、多米尼加、萨尔瓦多、格林纳达、危地马拉、圭亚那、海地、洪都拉斯、牙买加、墨西哥、尼加拉瓜、巴拿马、圣基茨和尼维斯、圣文森特和格林纳丁斯、苏里南、特立尼达和多巴哥以及委内瑞拉。五个主要关注领域为：(a)加勒比海的保护和养护；(b)可持续旅游业；(c)贸易和对外关系；(d)自然灾害；以及(e)运输。另见*加勒比共同体单一市场和经济(CARICOM Single Market and Economy)*。

Association of Tin Producing Countries
锡生产国协会

ATPC。成立于1983年，目的是使锡生产者获得有报酬且公正的回报并以公平和稳定的价格向消费者充足供应。2001年解散。最后几年的成员包括巴西、玻利维亚、中国、刚果(金)、印度尼西亚、马来西亚、尼日利亚和泰国。秘书处直至1997年设在吉隆坡，此后迁往里约热内卢。

ASYCUDA
海关数据自动化系统

联合国贸易与发展会议(UNCTAD)海关数据自动化系统。自动化环境下国际贸易和运输业务的综合海关管理系统。该系统的目标为：(a)使海关业务实现现代化，帮助改善税收征收；(b)通过大幅减少交易时间和成本，提高贸易效率和竞争力；(c)通过简化货物管控、货物过境和货物清关程序改善安全；(d)通过提高交易透明度打击腐败；以及(e)通过使用电子交易和单证减少纸质单证，促进可持续发展。另见*无纸贸易(paperless trading)*、*贸易便利化(trade facilitation)*。

Asymmetrical preferences
非对称优惠

一国给予另一国贸易优惠而不要求互惠的安排。另见*非对称贸易协定(asymmetrical trade agreements)*。

Asymmetrical price comparison
非对称价格比较

出现在反倾销案件的调查人员使用不同方法计算正常价值和出口价格时。另见*倾销(dumping)*、*反倾销措施(anti-dumping measures)*。

Asymmetrical trade agreements: these are in the main bilateral trade agreements with unequal sets of obligations for the partners. This might mean different timetables for tariff reductions or the phasing out of ***non-tariff measures***. In other cases, one party might give free entry to the products of the other party without expecting similar treatment in return.

Asymmetrical trade openness: describes a situation in which an exporting country with relatively closed markets can take advantage of relatively open markets elsewhere.

ATA Carnet: *see* ***Customs Convention on the ATA Carnet for the Temporary Admission of Goods***.

ATC: the WTO ***Agreement on Textiles and Clothing*** which integrated trade in this sector back to GATT rules within a ten-year period. It expired on 1 January 2005.

Atlantic Charter: agreed at the August 1941 Atlantic Conference between President Roosevelt and Prime Minister Churchill. The Charter set out in paragraphs four and five an early definition of the ***multilateralism*** that was to guide post-war reconstruction. It expressed the wish of the United States and the United Kingdom "with due respect for their existing obligations, to further the enjoyment by all States, great or small, victor or vanquished, of access, on equal terms, to the trade and the raw materials of the world which are needed for their prosperity". The words "existing obligations" were meant to give comfort to the United Kingdom regarding the ***imperial preferences arrangement***. Paragraph five read ". . . they desire to bring about the fullest collaboration between all nations in the economic field with the objective of ensuring, for all, improved labour standards, economic development and social security". In time, these sentiments led to the ***Bretton Woods agreements*** and, ultimately, the ***GATT***.

At-the-border barriers: these consist in the main of ***tariffs*** and ***non-tariff measures***, including ***import quotas***. Some add exchange rates to this category, but these are not usually the responsibility of trade ministries. *See also* ***behind-the-border issues***.

Attraction-aversion dilemma: defined by William A. Stoever as "the dilemma of desiring the benefits that foreign investors could bring while wanting to limit the intrusion of foreign entities". *See also* ***anti-globalization***, ***foreign direct investment*** and ***globalization***. [Stoever 2002]

Auckland Challenge: the long declaration issued at the ***APEC Economic Leaders' Meeting*** at Auckland in September 1999. The ***APEC Principles to Enhance Competition and Regulatory Reform*** seem to be its only noteworthy part.

Audiovisual Media Services Directive: AVMSD. A ***directive*** adopted by the ***European Union*** in 2013 and revised in 2018. It governs the coordination of national legislation across the European Union on all audiovisual media, both traditional TV broadcasts and on-demand services. Among other changes, the 2018 revision also includes video-sharing platforms. It also has a strengthened ***country of origin principle*** which states that providers only need to abide by

Asymmetrical trade agreements
非对称贸易协定

在主要双边贸易协定中，双方承担不平等的义务。这可能意味着关税削减或非关税措施取消的时间表不同。在其他情况下，一方可能给予另一方的产品自由进入，而不期望作为交换得到类似待遇。

Asymmetrical trade openness
非对称贸易开放

指市场相对封闭的出口国可以利用其他相对开放市场的情况。

ATA Carnet
ATA单证册

见*关于货物暂准进口的ATA报关单证册海关公约(Customs Convention on the ATA Carnet for the Temporary Admission of Goods)*。

ATC
纺织品与服装协定

WTO《纺织品与服装协定》在10年期限内使该部门贸易回归GATT规则。协定于2005年1月1日终止。

Atlantic Charter
大西洋宪章

罗斯福总统和丘吉尔首相在1941年8月的大西洋会议上达成。宪章第4条和第5条提出了多边主义的早期定义，用于指导战后重建。宪章表达了美国和英国希望“他们要在尊重他们现有的义务下，努力促使所有国家，不分大小，战胜者或战败者，都有机会在同等条件下，为了实现它们经济的繁荣，参加世界贸易和获得世界的原料”。“现有的义务”一词意在就帝国特惠安排宽慰英国。第5条指出“他们希望促成所有国家在经济领域内最充分的合作，以促进所有国家的劳动水平、经济进步和社会保障”。最后，这些观点促成了布雷顿森林协定，并最终促成了GATT。

At-the-border barriers
边境壁垒

主要由关税和非关税措施组成，包括进口配额。一些国家将汇率归入这一类别，但这些通常不是贸易部门的职责。另见*边境后问题(behind-the-border issues)*。

Attraction-aversion dilemma
吸引与厌恶困境

威廉·A. 斯托弗将其定义为“渴望外国投资者所带来的利益而同时又希望限制外国实体侵入的困境”。另见*反全球化(anti-globalization)*、*外国直接投资(foreign direct investment)*、*全球化(globalization)*。

Auckland Challenge
奥克兰挑战

APEC经济领导人会议1999年9月在奥克兰发表的长篇宣言。APEC增强竞争和监管改革原则似乎是其中惟一值得注意的部分。

Audiovisual Media Services Directive
视听媒体服务指令

AVMSD。欧盟于2013年通过并于2018年修订的一项指令。管辖整个欧盟关于所有视听媒体的国家立法协调，包括传统电视广播和点播服务。在其他修改中，2018年修订版还包括视频共享平台。还包括加强版的原属国原则，规定提

the rules of a member where the action is performed (rather than in multiple countries), and which gives clarity on which member state's rules apply in each case. [ec.europa.eu]

Audiovisual services: the production, distribution and exhibition of films and video tapes. Some sensitive policy areas converge on this sector. They include claims of ***cultural identity***, the protection of ***intellectual property rights*** and the aim to liberalize trade. These competing claims play themselves out against the broader canvas of rapid technological change and the new possibilities for distribution of audiovisual services it offers. Governments sometimes apply screening quotas and cross-ownership limitations on newspapers, radio and television stations in an attempt to preserve the local cultural characteristics. *See also* ***Beijing Treaty on Audiovisual Performances***, ***local content rules in broadcasting*** and ***trade and culture***.

Australian argument for protection: the conclusion drawn in the ***Brigden Report*** that the "evidence available does not support the contention that Australia could have maintained its present population at a higher standard of living under free trade". It continued that "the same average income for the same population could not have been obtained without protection". The Brigden Report did not claim that protection would increase aggregate national income, and therefore it did not undermine the argument for free trade.

Australian subsidy on ammonium sulphate: a ***non-violation*** case brought by Chile against Australia under the GATT in 1950. It resulted from the discontinuation by Australia of its war-time subsidy for the sale of imported nitrate of soda of which Chile was a major supplier. A similar subsidy for ammonium sulphate was continued. The subsidy in both cases had been intended to balance war-time shortages of nitrogenous fertilizers, but it was continued for several years after the war because of a continuing shortage. The working party established to look at this case found that the value of a ***concession*** granted to Chile at the time of the 1947 tariff negotiations had been impaired as the result of a measure which did not otherwise conflict with the provisions of the GATT. This happened because ammonium sulphate and nitrate of soda had for a long time been treated in the same way. Chile therefore had reasonable expectations that the war-time subsidy would be applied to both fertilizers as long as there was a local shortage of nitrogenous fertilizer.

Australia New Zealand Closer Economic Relations Trade Agreement: *see* ***ANZCERTA***.

Autarky: national self-sufficiency in production. Pure autarky is a theoretical construct. It is not attainable in the modern world. Where it has been tried, it has led to misery. The pretended policy of autarky in some countries has only been possible through substantial assistance from friendly countries and humanitarian help from others. The term is now also used loosely for economies that seek to produce the bulk of their requirements at home regardless of the cost through policies aimed at ***self-reliance***, ***self-sufficiency*** and

供商只需遵守采取行动的成员国(而不是多个国家)的规定，并明确了每种情况所适用的成员国的规定。

Audiovisual services

视听服务

电影和录像带的制作、发行和放映。一些敏感的政策领域集中在这一领域。包括文化特性、知识产权保护的主张和贸易自由化的目标。这些相互竞争的主张在快速技术变革和音像服务传播的新可能性这一更广泛的背景下发挥了作用。政府有时会对报纸、广播和电视台实施放映配额和交叉所有权限制，以保护当地文化特色。另见*视听表演北京条约(Beijing Treaty on Audiovisual Performances)*、*广播中的本地内容规则(local content rules in broadcasting)*、*贸易与文化(trade and culture)*。

Australian argument for protection

澳大利亚保护论

《布里格登报告》得出的结论是“现有证据不支持澳大利亚本可以在自由贸易条件下使其现有人口保持更高生活水平的观点”。报告还指出，“没有保护，相同人口不可能获得相同平均收入”。《布里格登报告》没有声称保护会增加国民总收入，因此没有削弱自由贸易的论据。

Australian subsidy on ammonium sulphate

澳大利亚对硫酸铵补贴案

智利于1950年在GATT下对澳大利亚提起的非违反之诉案件。原因是澳大利亚中止了对进口硝酸钠的战时补贴，而智利是主要供应商。对硫酸铵的类似补贴仍继续。这两种情况下的补贴都是为了平衡战时氮肥的短缺，但由于持续短缺，此种补贴在战后持续了若干年。审理该案的工作组认为，1947年关税谈判时给予智利的减让价值因一项在其他方面与GATT条款并无冲突的措施而受到减损。之所以会发生此种情况，是因为长期以来，硫酸铵和硝酸钠一直受到同样的待遇。智利因此有合理预期，只要当地氮肥短缺，战时补贴即适用于这两种肥料。

Australia New Zealand Closer Economic Relations Trade Agreement

澳大利亚与新西兰更紧密经济关系贸易协定

见*澳大利亚与新西兰更紧密经济关系贸易协定(ANZCERTA)*。

Autarky

经济闭关自守

国家生产的自给自足。纯粹的经济闭关自守是一种理论构想。这在现代世界中是不可能实现的。凡尝试过的都带来了痛苦。只有通过友好国家的大量援助和其他国家的人道主义援助，一些国家才有可能实行所谓的经济闭关自守政策。这一词语现在也被不精确地用于指那些通过旨在实现自力更生、自给自足和技术民族主义的政策，不计成本地在国内生产大部分所需产品的经济

techno-nationalism. Some texts use *autarchy* when they mean *autarky*. That is wrong. *Autarchy*, according to the *Shorter Oxford English Dictionary*, means absolute sovereignty.

Authorized economic operator: described by the World Customs Organization (WCO) in its ***SAFE Framework of Standards*** as "a party involved in the international movement of goods, in whatever function, that has been approved by, or on behalf of, a national Customs administration as complying with WCO or equivalent supply chain security standards". This includes, among others, manufacturers, importers, exporters, brokers, carriers, consolidators, ports, airports, terminal operators, warehouses, distributors, etc. *See also* ***Container Security Initiative*** and ***economic operator***. [www.wcoomd.org]

Authorized operators: in the WTO ***Agreement on Trade Facilitation*** persons or enterprises that perform functions similar to ***authorized economic operators*** or ***economic operators***. They have to meet criteria such as (i) appropriate record of compliance with customs and other related laws and regulations, (ii) a system of managing records to allow for necessary internal controls, (iii) financial solvency, and (iv) supply chain security. Authorized operators should have access to at least three of the following trade facilitation measures: (a) low documentary and data requirements, (b) low grade of physical inspections and examinations, (c) rapid release time, (d) deferred payment of duties, taxes, fees and charges, (e) use of comprehensive guarantees or reduced guarantees, (f) a single customs declaration on all imports or exports in a given period, and (g) clearance of goods at the premises of the authorized operator or another place authorized by Customs. *See also* ***trade facilitation***.

Authorized persons: *see* ***authorized operators***.

Automatic import licensing: an ***import licensing*** system where applications are always approved. *See* ***Agreement on Import Licensing Procedures***.

Automaticity: the "automatic" chronological progression in the WTO for settling trade disputes in regard to panel establishment, terms of reference, composition and adoption procedures. *See also* ***dispute settlement*** and ***Dispute Settlement Understanding***.

Automatic termination: *see* ***sunset clause***.

Autonomous liberalization: countries often lower their ***tariffs*** or remove other market access restrictions without being asked by others. They do so because they envisage a flow of benefits for their economies. The extent to which they should be able to claim payment for their autonomous liberalization in ***multilateral trade negotiations*** then becomes an issue for negotiators. A notional credit is created to exact payment from others, sometimes with the use of complicated formulas. The logic of using negotiating credit in this way is not always clear since the country benefiting most from autonomous trade liberalization is the country doing it in the first place.

Autonomous preferential rules of origin: refers to ***rules of origin*** applied, for example, under ***GSP*** schemes to enable the ***donor country*** to determine whether goods imported from a ***beneficiary country*** qualify for preferential

体。一些文本在表示“经济闭关自守”时使用了“专制”一词，这是错误的。根据《精缩牛津英语词典》，“专制”意味着绝对主权。

Authorized economic operator

经认证的经营者

世界海关组织(WCO)在其SAFE标准框架中将其描述为“以任何一种方式参与货物国际流通，并被海关当局认定符合世界海关组织或相应供应链安全标准的一方”。其中包括包括生产商、进口商、出口商、报关行、承运商、理货人、中间商、口岸和机场、货站经营者、综合经营者、仓储业经营者和分销商。另见*集装箱安全倡议(Container Security Initiative)*、*经济运营者(economic operator)*。

Authorized operators

经认证经营者

在WTO《贸易便利化协定》中，履行类似经认证的经营者或经营者职能的个人或企业。必须符合以下标准：(1)遵守海关和其他相关法律和法规的适当记录；(2)允许进行必要内部控制的记录管理系统；(3)财务偿付能力；以及(4)供应链安全。经认证经营者应至少可获得以下贸易便利化措施中的3条措施：(a)降低单证和数据要求；(b)降低实地检查和审查比例；(c)快速放行时间；(d)延迟支付关税、国内税、规费及费用；(e)使用总担保或减少担保；(f)在指定期限内对所有进口或出口进行一次性海关申报；以及(g)在经认证经营者的场所或海关批准的另一地点办理货物结关。另见*贸易便利化(trade facilitation)*。

Authorized persons

经认证人员

见*经认证经营者(authorized operators)*。

Automatic import licensing

自动进口许可

一种申请总是获得批准的进口许可制度。另见*进口许可程序协定(Agreement on Import Licensing Procedures)*。

Automaticity

自动性

WTO贸易争端解决中，对于专家组的设立、职权范围、组成和通过程序的“自动”序时进度。另见*争端解决(dispute settlement)*、*争端解决谅解(Dispute Settlement Understanding)*。

Automatic termination

自动终止

见*日落条款(sunset clause)*。

Autonomous liberalization

自主自由化

各国往往在没有其他国家要求的情况下降低关税或取消其他市场准入限制。它们之所以这样作，是因为它们设想了对本国经济的利益流动。在多边贸易谈判中，它们应该在多大程度上对其自主自由化求得回报就成了谈判者的一个问题。创造出来名义奖励一词，用于从其他国家处索取回报，有时会使用复杂的公式。以这种方式使用谈判奖励的逻辑并不总是那么清晰，因为从自主贸易自由化中获益最多的国家是最先进行贸易自由化的国家。

Autonomous preferential rules of origin

自主优惠原产地规则

指适用的原产地规则，例如，根据普惠制(GSP)方案，使捐助国能够确定从受

tariff treatment. The donor country has no contractual obligation to consult beneficiary countries when it establishes or amends these rules.

Autonomous tariff quota: when a component or a finished good is not produced within the ***European Union***, manufacturers or importers may apply for duty-free entry of that good. If the application is granted in the form of an autonomous quota, the good may be imported duty-free within the quota limit. Other importers may then also make use of the quota. Other customs authorities have similar mechanisms. *See also* ***tariff quota*** and ***temporary tariff suspension***.

Auto pact: *see* ***Canada–United States Automotive Products Agreement.***

Average release time: the average time between the arrival of goods at the border and the time that permission is given for the goods to enter the home market. *See also* ***trade facilitation***.

Average tariff: a device used to give an informative picture at a glance of a complete tariff schedule, which will usually have troughs and peaks, in a single average rate. It is the unweighted mean of either all applied or all bound rates. Such rates are also used for comparing the treatment of product sectors in different countries. *See also* ***applied tariff rates***, ***bindings***, ***peak tariffs*** and ***trade-weighted average tariffs***.

Averaging: a method of inventory management which uses the average cost of goods bought over a given period as the valuation basis. Its main relevance to trade policy stems from the need to calculate a ***regional value content*** under the ***rules of origin*** adopted in some ***free-trade agreements***. *See also* ***first-in, first-out*** and ***last-in, first-out***.

Aviation: *see* ***Agreement on Trade in Civil Aircraft***, ***bilateral air services agreements***, ***bilateral aviation rights***, ***cabotage***, ***Chicago Convention***, ***freedoms of the air***, ***Large Aircraft Sector Understanding***, ***Multilateral Agreement on the Liberalization of International Air Transportation***, ***open-skies arrangements*** and ***seventh-freedom cargo services***.

益国进口的货物是否符合优惠关税待遇。捐助国在制定或修订这些规则时，没有与受益国进行协商的契约义务。

Autonomous tariff quota

自主关税配额

如果某一部件或制成品不是在欧盟内部生产的，制造商或进口商可以申请该产品免税进入。如果申请以自主配额的形式获得批准，该商品可以在配额限额内免税进口。其他进口商因而也可以使用这一配额。其他海关有类似机制。另见*关税配额(tariff quota)*、*暂免关税(temporary tariff suspension)*。

Auto pact

汽车协议

见*加拿大—美国汽车产品协定(Canada–United States Automotive Products Agreement)*。

Average release time

平均放行时间

货物到达边境与允许货物进入国内市场之间的平均时间。另见*贸易便利化(trade facilitation)*。

Average tariff

平均关税

以一简单平均税率直观了解完整关税税则的方法，而完整关税税则中的税率通常有高有低。所有实施税率或所有约束税率的未加权平均值。此类税率也被用于比较产品部门在不同国家中的待遇。另见*实施税率(applied tariff rates)*、*约束(bindings)*、*关税高峰(peak tariffs)*、*贸易加权平均关税(trade-weighted average tariffs)*。

Averaging

平均法

库存管理的一种方法，使用在给定时期内购买商品的平均成本作为估价基础。与贸易政策的主要相关性源于在一些自由贸易协定中采用的原产地规则下计算区域价值成分的需要。另见*先进先出法(first-in, first-out)*、*后进先出法(last-in, first-out)*。

Aviation

航空

见*民用航空器贸易协定(Agreement on Trade in Civil Aircraft)*、*双边航空服务协定(bilateral air services agreements)*、*双边航空权(bilateral aviation rights)*、*国内交通运输权(cabotage)*、*芝加哥公约(Chicago Convention)*、*航空自由(freedoms of the air)*、*民用航空器行业谅解(Large Aircraft Sector Understanding)*、*国际航空运输自由化多边协定(Multilateral Agreement on the Liberalization of International Air Transportation)*、*开放天空安排(open-skies arrangements)*、*货运第七航权(seventh-freedom cargo services)*。

B

B20: also Business 20. The official dialogue of the ***G20*** with the business community. It consists, among other activities, of an annual summit coinciding with the G20 meeting.

Backdoor protectionism: the use of measures such as unreasonable product standards or excessively stringent quarantine rules to reduce the flow of imports. Ostensibly, such requirements are imposed to protect the public interest and, sometimes to their surprise, the consumers. *See also* ***protectionism***, ***sanitary and phytosanitary measures*** and ***technical barriers to trade.***

Backloading: the practice of ensuring that liberalizing commitments do not fall due until late in whatever phase-in period has been agreed in trade negotiations. It may also refer to deferring mandatory trade liberalization under an agreement or arrangement until the last possible legally acceptable moment. *See also* ***frontloading***.

Back-to-back investigation: sometimes used to describe the initiation of an anti-dumping or countervailing investigation immediately after another investigation involving the same product has been terminated. *See also* ***anti-dumping measures***.

Balance of advantages: a principle sometimes used in ***multilateral trade negotiations*** which holds that advantages derived from the ***exchange of concessions*** in trade negotiations should be broadly balanced among participants. The balance is usually achieved through the ***requests-and-offers*** technique. This principle is not based on economic theory. Its ultimate basis is the fallacious assumption that ***trade liberalization*** entails a cost to the liberalizing country. *See also* ***mercantilism***.

Balance of concessions: a judgement WTO members make in the course of negotiations and on their conclusion about the relative value of what they sought and were given. They usually try to ensure that the two are about equal. *See also* ***balance of advantages***.

Balance of payments: BOP. A statistical summary of a country's total trade, other economic transactions and financial inflows and outflows at a given time. The BOP is made up of current account (current transactions), capital account (capital transactions) and a balancing item to even out difficulties in recording international transactions. The current and capital account components of the BOP may each either be in surplus or deficit, but the BOP itself must always show a balance. The current account is the component of the BOP showing trade in goods and services, income and unrequited transfers (e.g. foreign aid

B

B20

20 国集团工商峰会

20 国集团与工商界的官方对话渠道。活动包括在 20 国集团会议期间召开年度峰会。

Backdoor protectionism

后门保护主义

使用不合理的产品标准或过于严格的检疫规定等措施以减少进口流量。从表面上看，此类要求是为保护公众利益，有时甚至还出乎意料地称是为保护消费者。另见*保护主义(protectionism)*、*卫生与植物卫生措施(sanitary and phytosanitary measures)*、*技术性贸易壁垒(technical barriers to trade)*。

Backloading

后期实施

保证自由化承诺在贸易谈判中议定的任何过渡期的后期再予以实施的做法。也可指将一项协定或安排项下的贸易自由化义务推迟至法律上可接受的最后时刻。另见*前期实施(frontloading)*。

Back-to-back investigation

背靠背调查

有时用于描述在涉及同一产品的另一项调查已被终止后，立即启动反倾销或反补贴调查的情况。另见*反倾销措施(anti-dumping measures)*。

Balance of advantages

利益平衡

多边贸易谈判中有时使用的一项原则，认为贸易谈判中交换减让所产生的利益应在参与者之间达到总体平衡。此种平衡通常通过要价和出价技巧实现。这一原则并非基于经济学理论。最终依据是一个错误的假设，即贸易自由化会使自由化国家付出代价。另见*重商主义(mercantilism)*。

Balance of concessions

减让平衡

WTO 成员在谈判过程中对其所求和所得的相对价值的结果作出的一种判断。它们通常会努力保证两者大致相等。另见*利益平衡(balance of advantages)*。

Balance of payments

国际收支

BOP。一国在一定时间内的总贸易、其他经济往来以及资金流入和流出的统计摘要。BOP 由经常账户(经常交易)、资本账户(资本交易)及用以均衡记录国际交易中的困难的平衡项目组成。BOP 的经常账户和资本账户组成部分可处于盈余或赤字状态，但 BOP 本身必须始终保持平衡。经常账户是 BOP 组成部分，显示一定时间内的货物贸易和服务贸易、收入和无偿转移(例如外国援助

payments, workers' remittances, etc.) over a specified period. The capital account records currency inflows and outflows due to international dealings in financial assets, such as investments and loans.

Balance-of-payments basis: trade data conforming with national accounting methods (the value of trade in goods and services changing hands between residents and non-residents sometimes without crossing borders). The figures for trade in goods are derived and adjusted from customs data (the value of goods crossing borders). [www.wto.org]

Balance-of-payments consultations: WTO members may use GATT Article XII (Restrictions to Safeguard the Balance of Payments) in the case of developed countries, Article XVIII:B (Governmental Assistance to Economic Development) in the case of developing countries in some circumstances and Article XII of the ***General Agreement on Trade in Services*** to impose import restrictions to shore up deteriorating foreign exchange reserves. The basic conditions under which restrictions may be taken are almost the same under these articles: the measures taken must be no more than is necessary (i) to forestall the imminent threat of, or to stop, a serious decline in monetary reserves, or (ii) in the case of very low monetary reserves, to achieve a reasonable rate of increase in these reserves. Any WTO member taking this step has to consult the WTO membership, either before or immediately after doing so, on the nature of its balance of payments difficulties, alternative corrective measures that may be available to it and the possible effect of restrictions on other members. Once restrictions have been imposed, they are subject to reviews. Reviews normally use the "full consultation procedures", but the "simplified consultation procedures" apply in the case of ***least-developed countries*** or when developing countries have adopted liberalization programmes in response to earlier consultations and when, in the case of developing countries, the consultations would occur in the same year as a ***trade policy review***.

Balance of trade: in standard usage, this is the balance between exports and imports in an economy. In some countries it refers to the ***balance on merchandise trade*** only. In others it is the ***balance on goods and services trade***. The concept conveys few analytical insights. The term also refers to attempts, rooted deeply in ***mercantilism***, to ensure that the value of imports does not exceed that of exports. Bhagwati has described this attitude as "trade is good, but imports are bad". Adam Smith wrote that "[n]othing, however, can be more absurd than this doctrine of the balance of trade, upon which not only these restraints, but almost all the other regulations of commerce are founded. When two places trade with one another, this doctrine supposes that, if the balance be even, neither of them either loses or gains; but if it leans in any degree to one side, that one of them loses and the other gains in proportion to its declension from the exact equilibrium." Where countries have applied ***import restrictions*** to balance their trade, they have usually only succeeded in reducing the overall amount of trade and thus in reducing welfare. Whether a country imports more goods than it exports depends on many factors, including its stage of economic

支付、工人汇款等)。资本账户记录因国际金融资产交易(例如投资和贷款)而产生的货币流入和流出。

Balance-of-payments basis

国际收支基础

符合国民核算方法的贸易数据(居民与非居民之间货物贸易和服务贸易的易手价值，有时无需跨境)。货物贸易的数据来源于海关数据并经调整(跨境货物的价值)。

Balance-of-payments consultations

国际收支磋商

WTO 发达国家成员可以使用 GATT 第 12 条(为保障国际收支而实施的限制)；发展中国家成员在某些情况下可以使用第 18 条 B 节(政府对经济发展的援助)和《服务贸易总协定》第 12 条实施进口限制，以支撑不断恶化的外汇储备。根据这些条款，据以采取限制的基本条件大致相同：采取的措施不得超过下列必要限度：(1)为防止其货币储备严重下降的迫近威胁或制止其货币储备的严重下降；或(2)对于货币储备很低的情况，为使这些储备达到合理增长率。采取这一步骤的任何 WTO 成员必须在采取这一步骤之前或之后立即就其国际收支困难的性质、可获得的替代纠正措施以及有关限制对其他成员可能产生的影响与 WTO 成员进行磋商。一旦实施限制措施，这些措施就要接受审查。审查通常使用“全面磋商程序”，而“简化磋商程序”适用于最不发达国家，或已根据较早的磋商情况采取自由化计划且磋商与贸易政策审议在同一年进行的情况的发展中国家。

Balance of trade

贸易平衡

在标准用法中，指一经济体的进口和出口之间的平衡。在一些国家，仅指商品贸易平衡。也有一些国家指货物贸易和服务贸易平衡。这一概念所表达的分析性见解很少。这一词语也指深深植根于重商主义的、保证进口价值不超过出口价值的努力。巴格瓦蒂将这种态度描述为“贸易是好的，但进口是坏的”。亚当 · 斯密写道：“然而，这种限制以及许多其他商业条例所根据的整个贸易差额学说，是再荒谬不过的了。这种学说认为，当两地通商时，如果贸易额平衡，则两地各无得失；如果贸易额略有偏倚，就必一方损失另一方得利，得失程度和偏倚程度相当。”如国家已经实施进口限制平衡贸易，它们通常只能减少贸易总量，因而减少福利。一国进口的货物是否多于出口的货物取决于很多因素，包括其经济发展阶段和经济结构。平衡的商品贸易本身并不是成功

development and the structure of its economy. Balanced merchandise trade is not in itself an indicator of successful economic policies. As Schumpeter noted in his *History of Economic Analysis*, "an 'unfavorable' balance may be the symptom of increasing wealth, but also of a process of impoverishment; a 'favorable' one may mean prosperity and employment, but just as well the reverse". *See also* ***beggar-thy-neighbour policies***, ***mercantilism***, ***trade deficit*** and ***trade surplus***. Bhagwati 2002a, Schumpeter 1982 [1954], Smith 1991 [1776]]

Balance on goods and services trade: the difference between exports and imports of goods and services, measured over a given period.

Balance on merchandise trade: the difference between exports and imports of goods, measured over a given period.

Bali Concord: a 1976 ***ASEAN*** declaration setting out objectives and principles in the pursuit of political stability. It also contained a programme of political, economic and other actions.

Bali Concord II: the declaration issued by a meeting of ***ASEAN*** members in Bali on 7 October 2003. It envisages the establishment of an ***ASEAN Community*** consisting of an ASEAN Security Community, an ***ASEAN Economic Community*** and an ASEAN Socio-cultural Community. The Economic Community is to result in the free flow of goods, services and investment and a freer flow of capital by 2020.

Bali Concord III: the declaration issued by ***ASEAN*** Leaders in Bali on 17 November 2011 which adopts an ASEAN common platform based on (a) a more coordinated, cohesive and coherent ASEAN position on global issues of common interest and concern, (b) an enhanced ASEAN capacity to respond to global issues, (c) a strengthened ***ASEAN Community*** centred on ASEAN as a rules-based organization, and (d) a strengthened capacity of the ASEAN Secretariat.

Bali WTO Ministerial Conference: held in 2013. Ministers were able to adopt the ***Agreement on Trade Facilitation***, subject to a legal review for rectifications of a purely formal character. They agreed to put in place an interim mechanism governing ***public stockholding for food security*** and to negotiate a permanent agreement. They also adopted an ***Understanding on tariff rate quota administration provisions of agricultural products*** which deems scheduled tariff quotas as falling within the meaning of "import licensing" under the ***Agreement on Import Licensing Procedures***. The negotiating aims for dealing with agricultural ***export competition*** were strengthened. Ministers also adopted the basic approach for ***preferential rules of origin for least-developed countries***, to initiate the operationalization of the ***LDC services waiver*** and to encourage WTO members to widen as far as possible duty-free and quota-free ***market access*** for ***least-developed countries***. Several other measures relating to existing work programmes were also adopted.

Baltic states: Estonia, Latvia and Lithuania.

Banana cases: this refers to two trade disputes brought for adjudication in the GATT and the WTO. The first was a case launched in 1993 in the GATT by

经济政策的指标。正如熊彼特在《经济分析史》中所指出的，"'不利的'平衡可能是财富增加的征兆，也可能是贫穷的过程；'有利的'平衡可能意味着繁荣和就业，但也可能正好相反"。另见*以邻为壑政策(beggar-thy-neighbour policies)*、*重商主义(mercantilism)*、*贸易逆差(trade deficit)*、*贸易顺差(trade surplus)*。

Balance on goods and services trade

货物贸易和服务贸易平衡

在一定时期内计算的货物和服务的进口与出口之间的差额。

Balance on merchandise trade

商品贸易平衡

在一定时期内计算的货物的进口与出口之间的差额。

Bali Concord

巴厘协约宣言

1976 年东盟的一份宣言，列出实现政治稳定的目标和原则，还包含一份政治、经济和其他行动的计划。

Bali Concord II

巴厘第二协约宣言

2003 年 10 月 7 日东盟成员国在巴厘岛举行的会议发表的宣言。设想建立一个由东盟安全共同体、东盟经济共同体和东盟社会文化共同体组成的东盟共同体。经济共同体的目标是到 2020 年实现货物、服务和投资的自由流动及资本的更自由流动。

Bali Concord III

巴厘第三协约宣言

2011 年 11 月 17 日东盟领导人在巴厘岛发表的宣言，宣言通过了一个基于以下内容的东盟公共平台：(a)东盟在共同关心和关切的全球问题上采取的更加协调、团结和一致的立场；(b)东盟增强的应对全球问题的能力；(c)增强的以东盟为核心的和以规则为基础的东盟共同体；以及(d)职能得到加强的东盟秘书处。

Bali WTO Ministerial Conference

WTO 巴厘岛部长级会议

2013 年举行。部长们得以通过《贸易便利化协定》，需经法律审查以供正式批准。部长们同意设立粮食安全公共储备临时机制，并就此谈判永久协议。还通过了一项《关于农产品关税配额管理规定的谅解》，认为减让表中的关税配额属《进口许可程序协定》范围内的"进口许可"。处理农业出口竞争的谈判目标得以加强。部长们还通过了对于最不发达国家优惠原产地规则的基本方式，启动了最不发达国家服务豁免的实施，并鼓励 WTO 成员尽可能扩大最不发达国家免关税和免配额市场准入。还通过了与现有工作计划相关的其他措施。

Baltic states

波罗的海国家

爱沙尼亚、拉脱维亚和立陶宛。

Banana cases

香蕉案

指先后提交 GATT 和 WTO 裁决的两起贸易争端。第一案于 1993 年在 GATT 下发起，由哥伦比亚、哥斯达黎加、危地马拉、尼加拉瓜和委内瑞拉诉欧洲经

Colombia, Costa Rica, Guatemala, Nicaragua and Venezuela against the European Economic Community (EEC) and decided in early 1994. It arose from a change in the EEC import regime for bananas which resulted in differing ***market access*** depending on whether they originated within the EEC, traditional ***ACP states***, non-traditional ACP states or third countries. The complainants charged that this violated the non-discrimination provisions of the GATT, and that the EEC also had broken its ***tariff bindings***. Altogether, the ***panel*** was asked to find on the consistency of the import regime with about ten GATT articles. On many of them it found that the EEC had no case to answer. Importantly, however, it decided that the manner of the EEC's preferential tariff treatment of banana imports was contrary to the ***most-favoured-nation treatment*** required by GATT Article I. The second case had a wider ambit. It was initiated in early 1996 in the WTO by Ecuador, Guatemala, Honduras, Mexico and the United States concerning the European Community (EC) regime for the import, sale and distribution of bananas. The complainants alleged that the EC was in contravention of its obligations under the ***GATT***, the ***General Agreement on Trade in Services*** (GATS), the ***Agreement on Trade-Related Investment Measures***, the ***Agreement on Agriculture*** and the ***Agreement on Import Licensing Procedures***. The panel found that the EC had breached its commitments under the GATT, GATS and the import licensing provisions. One point of particular interest arising from this panel finding is that it applies aspects of the provisions relating to ***trade in services*** to trade in goods. The European Community lodged an appeal against the decision, but the ***Appellate Body*** upheld most of the contested findings. In 1994 it introduced a new banana regime, but this also was found to be incompatible with WTO obligations. Then followed ten years of negotiations, arbitration, panel proceedings and resort to the ***good offices*** of the WTO Director-General, during which the parties slowly moved towards a resolution of the case. In December 2009 they were successful with the conclusion of the *Geneva Agreement on Trade in Bananas* between the European Union, Brazil, Colombia, Costa Rica, Ecuador, Guatemala, Honduras, Mexico, Nicaragua, Panama, Peru and Venezuela (collectively known as the Latin American MFN banana suppliers). It entailed, *inter alia*, agreement by the European Union to institute phased tariff reductions on bananas, to maintain an MFN tariff regime only for the import of bananas and to bind the tariff cuts. The Latin American MFN banana suppliers agreed that the settlement would constitute the European Union's final market access commitments for bananas in the next multilateral market access negotiations for agriculture products successfully concluded in the WTO, including the ***Doha Development Agenda***.

Banded formula: a method for reducing tariffs proposed during the ***Doha Development Agenda*** negotiations. It divides tariff levels into three bands which could be described roughly as high, medium and low, and it suggests tariff reductions for each band. The biggest reductions would occur at the high level. *See also* ***blended formula*** and ***tiered formula***.

济共同体(EEC)，于 1994 年初作出裁决。案件原因是欧共体改变香蕉进口体制，根据是否原产于欧共体、传统非加太地区国家、非传统非加太地区国家或第三国而适用不同的市场准入。起诉方指控此点违反了 GATT 非歧视条款，且欧共体也突破了关税约束。总之，要求专家组就进口体制与 10 个 GATT 条款的一致性进行审查。对于其中的多个条款，专家组认为欧共体没有理由回答。但是，重要的是，专家组裁决欧共体的香蕉进口优惠关税待遇违反了 GATT 第 1 条所要求的最惠国待遇。第二案涉及的范围更广。1996 年初，厄瓜多尔、危地马拉、洪都拉斯、墨西哥和美国在 WTO 中就欧共体的香蕉进口、销售和分销体制提起诉讼。起诉方指称，欧共体违反了其在 GATT、《服务贸易总协定》(GATS)、《与贸易有关的投资措施协定》、《农业协定》和《进口许可程序协定》项下的义务。专家组裁决，欧共体违反其在 GATT、GATS 及进口许可条款项下的承诺。专家组调查结果中引起特别关注的一点是，将与服务贸易相关条款的某些方面适用于货物贸易。欧共体对这一裁决提起上诉，但上诉机构维持了大部分有争议的裁决。1994 年，欧共体引入了一个新的香蕉体制，但这也被认为与 WTO 义务不符。随后经历了 10 年的谈判、仲裁、专家组审理和 WTO 总干事斡旋，其间各方缓慢地朝着解决该案的方向迈进。2009 年 12 月欧盟、巴西、哥伦比亚、哥斯达黎加、厄瓜多尔、危地马拉、洪都拉斯、墨西哥、尼加拉瓜、巴拿马、秘鲁和委内瑞拉(统称拉丁美洲最惠国香蕉供应商)成功达成《日内瓦香蕉贸易协定》。协定中特别要求，欧盟同意对香蕉实行分阶段关税削减，对进口香蕉维持单一最惠国关税体制，并约束关税削减。拉丁美洲最惠国香蕉供应商同意，这一解决方案在下一轮成功结束的 WTO 农产品多边市场准入谈判中将构成欧盟最终市场准入承诺，包括多哈发展议程。

Banded formula

分层公式

多哈发展议程谈判中提出的关税削减方法。将关税水平大致分为高、中、低三层，并对每层关税削减提出建议。对高层关税进行最大幅度削减。另见*混合公式(blended formula)*、*分层公式(tiered formula)*。

Bangkok Agreement: *see* ***Asia-Pacific Trade Agreement***.

Bangkok Declaration: part of the final report adopted at UNCTAD X in Bangkok on 19 February 2000. Its focus is on ***globalization*** and ***UNCTAD***'s contribution to the international debate on development-related global issues. The declaration is supplemented by a plan of action.

Bangkok Declaration on Partnership for the Future: the declaration adopted on 21 October 2003 at the ***APEC Economic Leaders' Meeting***. It consists of three parts. The first part is a list of actions in support of trade and investment liberalization. The second part is concerned with fighting terrorism and resisting the proliferation of weapons of mass destruction. The third part deals with using ***APEC*** to help people and societies benefit from globalization.

Bank for International Settlements: BIS. Supports central banks in attaining monetary and financial stability, promotes international cooperation in these areas and acts as a bank for central banks. It is located in Basel, Switzerland. [www.bis.org]

BAPA+40: the ***Buenos Aires Plan of Action for Promoting and Implementing Technical Co-operation among Developing Countries*** (1978), forty years later. *See* ***Second High-Level United Nations Conference on South–South Cooperation***.

Barbie doll case: refers to a newspaper report in 1996 which claimed that the economic benefit to China of a Barbie doll made there, bearing its ***mark of origin*** and selling in the United States for $9.99, was only 35 cents. Most of the remainder could be allocated to shipping, ground transport, wholesaling costs, retailing costs and profit. Whatever else the example may demonstrate, it shows clearly the degree to which even the production of relatively simple articles has now been internationalized. *See also* ***globalization***. [UNCTAD/ITCD/TSB/2]

Barcelona Declaration: issued on 28 November 1995 by the ***European Union*** and Mediterranean states. It seeks to establish a common area of peace and stability; create an area of shared prosperity, including a free-trade area; and develop human resources, promote understanding between cultures and exchanges between civil societies. It also set up a work programme, the ***Barcelona process***, to achieve these aims. *See also* ***Euro-Mediterranean Free Trade Area*** and ***pan-Euro-Mediterranean cumulation***.

Barcelona process: a programme of trade and development cooperation between the ***European Union*** and Mediterranean countries which was initiated in 1995 in Barcelona. Its members, in addition to the European Union, are Albania, Algeria, Bosnia and Herzegovina, Egypt, Israel, Jordan, Lebanon, Mauritania, Morocco, Montenegro, State of Palestine, Syria (suspended 2011), Tunisia and Turkey. Libya is an observer. *See also* ***Euro-Mediterranean Association Agreements***.

Bargaining tariff: the name accorded in popular parlance to the United States tariff once it could be used to bargain down the tariffs of others following the adoption of the ***United States Reciprocal Trade Agreements Program*** in 1934. The tariff then in force was the Smoot-Hawley tariff which was unalterable

Bangkok Agreement
曼谷协定
见*亚太贸易协定(Asia-Pacific Trade Agreement)*。
Bangkok Declaration
曼谷宣言
联合国贸易与发展会议(UNCTAD)第 10 届大会于 2000 年 2 月 19 日在曼谷通过的最后报告的一部分。报告聚焦全球化及 UNCTAD 对与发展有关的全球问题国际辩论的贡献。宣言还附有一个行动计划作为补充。
Bangkok Declaration on Partnership for the Future
关于未来伙伴关系的曼谷宣言
APEC 经济领导人会议 2003 年 10 月 21 日通过的宣言。由三部分组成：第一部分是一份支持贸易和投资自由化的行动清单。第二部分关于打击恐怖主义和抵制大规模杀伤性武器的扩散。第三部分涉及利用 APEC 帮助人民和社会从全球化中获益。
Bank for International Settlements
国际清算银行
BIS。支持中央银行实现货币和金融稳定，促进这些领域的国际合作，并充当中央银行的银行。设在瑞士巴塞尔。
BAPA+40
布宜诺斯艾利斯行动计划 40 周年
《促进和实施发展中国家间技术合作的布宜诺斯艾利斯行动计划》(1978) 制定 40 周年。另见*第二届联合国南南合作高级别会议(Second High-Level United Nations Conference on South–South Cooperation)*。
Barbie doll case
芭比娃娃案例
指 1996 年一份新闻报道，称在中国制造的带有原产地标记的芭比娃娃，在美国以 9.99 美元的价格出售，对中国的经济利益仅为 35 美分。价格的其余部分分布在海运、陆运、批发成本、零售成本和利润中。不管这个案例可以证明其他什么内容，它清楚地表明，即使是相对简单物品的生产现在也已经国际化。另见*全球化(globalization)*。
Barcelona Declaration
巴塞罗那宣言
欧盟与地中海国家于 1995 年 11 月 28 日发布。宣言寻求建立一个和平与稳定的共同地区；创建一个包括自由贸易区在内的共同繁荣的地区；以及开发人力资源，促进不同文化之间的理解和公民社会之间的交流。宣言还建立了一个工作计划，即巴塞罗那进程，以实现这些目标。另见*欧洲—地中海自由贸易区(Euro-Mediterranean Free Trade Area)*、*泛欧—地中海累积(pan-Euro-Mediterranean cumulation)*。
Barcelona process
巴塞罗那进程
1995 年在巴塞罗那发起的欧盟与地中海国家之间的贸易和发展合作计划。成员除欧盟外，还包括阿尔巴尼亚、阿尔及利亚、波斯尼亚和黑塞哥维那、埃及、以色列、约旦、黎巴嫩、毛里塔尼亚、摩洛哥、黑山、巴勒斯坦国、叙利亚(2011 年中止)、突尼斯和土耳其。利比亚是观察员。另见*欧洲与地中海联系协定(Euro-Mediterranean Association Agreements)*。
Bargaining tariff
互惠协定关税
曾经对美国关税的一种流行称谓，在 1934 年美国互惠贸易协定计划通过后，美国关税曾用来谈判降低其他国家的关税。当时生效的关税是斯穆特-霍利关

except through congressional amendment. The term is now used more commonly to refer to the practice of keeping an obsolete tariff in the hope that it may be used to exact a tariff reduction from others. Sometimes it works, but it is a poor negotiating tool. *See also* ***autonomous tariff quota***, ***conventional tariff***, ***multi-column tariff*** and ***single-column tariff***.

Barriers to trade: any measures that in some way influence, limit or deny ***market access*** for goods or services. Such measures come in several categories, and many are in place for good reasons. Thus the word "barrier" is not always appropriate, and it might be better to talk of impediments to trade because trade under them is possible, though possibly at less than optimal flows. The main categories of barriers can be listed as (a) governmental measures, (b) ***restrictive business practices***, and (c) barriers facing goods and services because they do not meet the needs of the market for reasons of price, quality, shipping costs, delivery times, etc. The remainder of this entry is not concerned with the third category. The main trade barriers imposed by governments are obviously ***tariffs*** and ***non-tariff measures***. Tariffs are transparent, well understood, and their level clearly determines the extent to which they act as a barrier. ***Tariff quotas*** are intended to be barriers even if imports outside the quota are in theory possible. Other measures usually based on tariff increases are ***trade remedies***, i.e. ***safeguards***, ***anti-dumping measures*** and ***countervailing measures***. Then there is the category of non-tariff measures that can act as trade barriers or impediments. Examples of them are ***import quotas*** and ***export quotas***, foreign exchange restrictions, ***import licensing*** and onerous customs procedures, but this list is by no means complete. Other important measures are ***technical barriers to trade*** (standards) and ***sanitary and phytosanitary measures***. Obviously, the justification for the use of such measures varies greatly, but few would argue that measures to protect health and safety are not needed. A test in these cases is whether a measure is a ***disguised restriction on international trade***. Finally, governments can use the ***general exceptions*** and the ***security exceptions*** as trade barriers under certain conditions. Actions by business can also result in barriers to trade through, for example, import ***cartels*** and other ***anti-competitive practices***. The ***UNCTAD Coding System of Trade Control Measures*** offers a comprehensive overview of measures that might be called barriers to trade.

Barter trade: an exchange of goods or services estimated to have the same value. Each party's contribution may be valued for accounting purposes in terms of a third-country currency, but the principal trait of barter trade is that no money changes hand between the parties to the transaction. *See also* ***compensation trade*** and ***countertrade***.

Basel I: the Basel Capital Accord. A framework adopted in 1988 within the Bank for International Settlements in Basel which called for a minimum ratio of capital to risk-weighted assets of 8 per cent, to be implemented by the end of 1992. [bis.org]

Basel II: the revised capital adequacy framework which replaced ***Basel I***. Released in June 2004. Its three pillars were (a) minimum capital requirements,

税，该关税不可调整，除非通过国会进行修正。这一词语现在更普遍用于指保留过时的关税以期迫使其他国家降低关税的做法。这样作有时候可以奏效，但却是一个糟糕的谈判工具。另见*自主关税配额(autonomous tariff quota)*、*协定关税(conventional tariff)*、*多栏关税(multi-column tariff)*、*单栏关税(single-column tariff)*。

Barriers to trade

贸易壁垒

以某种方式影响、限制或拒绝货物或服务市场准入的任何措施。此类措施可以分为几类，且许多措施的实施都有充分理由。因此“壁垒”一词并不一定恰当，称为贸易障碍可能更好，因为在这些障碍下进行贸易是可能的，尽管可能没有最佳贸易流动那么好。壁垒主要的类别可以分为：(a)政府措施；(b)限制性商业惯例；以及(c)货物和服务面临的壁垒，因价格、质量、运输成本、交货时间等不能满足市场需求所导致。本词条下面部分不涉及第三类。政府设置的主要贸易壁垒显然是关税和非关税措施。关税是透明的、易于理解，关税水平明确确定了它们作为壁垒的限度。关税配额意在成为一种壁垒，尽管配额外进口理论上是可行的。其他通常基于关税提高的措施是贸易救济，即保障措施、反倾销措施和反补贴措施。接下来一类是非关税措施，可以作为贸易壁垒或障碍。例如进口配额和出口配额、外汇限制、进口许可和繁琐的海关手续，这一清单不一而足。其他重要措施包括技术性贸易壁垒(标准)和卫生与植物卫生措施。显然，使用这些措施的理由千差万别，但很少有人会说保护健康和安全的措施是不必要的。测试这些情况的根据是一项措施是否构成对国际贸易的变相限制。最后一点，政府可以将一般例外和安全例外用作某些条件下的贸易壁垒。企业的行动也可能产生贸易壁垒，例如通过进口卡特尔和其他反竞争行为。联合国贸易与发展会议(UNCTAD)贸易管制措施编码系统对可能被称为贸易壁垒的措施提供了全面概述。

Barter trade

易货贸易

交换估价为等值的货物或服务。每一方的供货可为会计记账目的而使用第三国货币计价，但易货贸易的特征是交易双方之间不易手货币。另见*补偿贸易(compensation trade)*、*对销贸易(countertrade)*。

Basel I

第一版巴塞尔协议

巴塞尔资本协议。1988 年在巴塞尔国际清算银行内通过的一个框架，要求资本与风险加权资产的最低比率为 8%，并于 1992 年底之前实施。

Basel II

第二版巴塞尔协议

经修订的资本充足率框架，取代第一版巴塞尔协议。协议的三大支柱为：(a)

(b) supervisory review of institutions' capital adequacy and internal assessment process, and (c) effective use of disclosure. [www.bis.org]

Basel III: an international regulatory framework for banks developed in 2017 under the auspices of the Bank for International Settlements in response to the ***global financial crisis***. Its provisions will be implemented in phases by 2027. [www.bis.org]

Basel Convention: *Basel Convention on the Control of Transboundary Movements of Hazardous Wastes and Their Disposal.* Adopted on 22 March 1989 under the auspices of ***UN Environment Programme*** (UNEP). It entered into force on 5 May 1992. The Convention aims to reduce and control the international movement of hazardous waste and to ensure that these wastes are disposed of in an environmentally sound manner. Its two trade-related provisions state that (a) the parties have the right to ban the import of hazardous wastes, and (b) they may not export to or import hazardous wastes from non-members of the Convention. In September 1995 the parties decided to amend the Convention to include a ban on the movement of hazardous waste for recycling from developed to developing countries starting on 1 January 1998. *See also* ***multilateral environment agreements*** and ***trade and environment***. [www.basel.int]

Basel Convention on the Control of Transboundary Movements of Hazardous Wastes and Their Disposal: *see* ***Basel Convention***.

Base period: the time period, rather like a snapshot, agreed during the ***Uruguay Round*** agricultural negotiations as the basis on which all reductions and commitments were to be made. For market access and domestic support commitments, the base period was 1986–88. For export subsidy commitments, it was 1986–90. *See also* ***Agreement on Agriculture***.

Base rate: a term often used to describe the tariff levels that form the starting point for reductions to be made through tariff negotiations. The levels concerned are those in force on a certain date. A decision whether to use ***bound tariff rates*** or ***applied tariff rates*** is necessary. In ***free-trade agreement*** negotiations it is usually the latter.

Basic agricultural products: defined in the WTO ***Agreement on Agriculture*** as "the product as close as practicable to the first sale". Products are in their original form, or they may have undergone primary processing. Examples include eggs, fruit, vegetables and beef. *See also* ***agricultural products***.

Basic Instruments and Selected Documents: *see* ***GATT Basic Instruments and Selected Documents*** and ***WTO Basic Instruments and Selected Documents***.

Basic Payment Scheme: the system of basic income support for farmers since 2015 under the ***common agricultural policy***. The support is independent of agricultural production and income. Also known as ***decoupled income support***.

Basic telecommunications services: includes voice telephony, telex, facsimile and data transmission. *See also* ***Agreement on Basic Telecommunications Services***, ***International Telecommunication Union***, ***Negotiating Group on Basic Telecommunications***, ***reference paper on telecommunications services*** and ***value-added telecommunications***.

最低资本要求；(b)对机构的资本充足率及内部评估程序进行监管审查；以及(c)有效运用披露的资料。

Basel III

第三版巴塞尔协议

2017 年在国际清算银行主持下制定的国际银行监管框架，以应对全球金融危机。这些条款将在 2027 年前分阶段实施。

Basel Convention

巴塞尔公约

全称为《控制危险废物越境转移及其处置的巴塞尔公约》。在联合国环境规划署(UNEP)的主持下于 1989 年 3 月 22 日通过，1992 年 5 月 5 日生效。公约旨在减少和控制危险废物的国际流动，并保证这些废物以环境友好的方式加以处置。其中有两项条款与贸易有关：(a)缔约国有权禁止危险废物进口；及(b)缔约国不得向非公约缔约国出口或自非成员国进口危险废物。1995 年 9 月，缔约国决定修正公约，自 1998 年 1 月 1 日起禁止发达国家将危险废物转移到发展中国家进行再循环。另见*多边环境协定(multilateral environment agreements)*、*贸易与环境(trade and environment)*。

Basel Convention on the Control of Transboundary Movements of Hazardous Wastes and Their Disposal

控制危险废物越境转移及其处置的巴塞尔公约

见*巴塞尔公约(Basel Convention)*。

Base period

基期

在乌拉圭回合农业谈判中议定的作为所有削减和承诺基础的时期，这更像一张快照。对于市场准入和国内支持承诺，基期为 1986—1988 年。对于出口补贴承诺，基期为 1986—1990 年。另见*农业协定(Agreement on Agriculture)*。

Base rate

基础税率

该词通常用于描述构成关税谈判削减起点的关税水平。有关水平是在某一日期实施的水平。需要就使用约束税率还是实施税率作出决定。在自由贸易协定谈判中，通常为后者。

Basic agricultural products

基本农产品

在 WTO《农业协定》中定义为“尽可能接近第一销售点的产品”。产品为原始形态，或可能经过初级加工。例如，鸡蛋、水果、蔬菜和牛肉。另见*农产品(agricultural products)*。

Basic Instruments and Selected Documents

基本文件资料选编

见 *GATT 基本文件资料选编(GATT Basic Instruments and Selected Documents)*、*WTO 基本文件资料选编(WTO Basic Instruments and Selected Documents)*。

Basic Payment Scheme

基本支付方案

根据欧盟共同农业政策自 2015 年以来实行的农民基本收入支持制度。此种支持与农业生产和收入无关。也称不挂钩的收入支持。

Basic telecommunications services

基础电信服务

包括语音电话、电传、传真和数据传输。另见*基础电信协定(Agreement on Basic Telecommunications Services)*、*国际电信联盟(International Telecommunication Union)*、*基础电信谈判组(Negotiating Group on Basic Telecommunications)*、*电信服务参考文件(reference paper on telecommunications services)*、*增值电信(value-added telecommunications)*。

Basket tariff quota: a ***tariff quota*** covering a range of closely related internationally traded products. If a tariff quota is applied at the four-digit level under the ***Harmonized Commodity Description and Coding System*** (HS), it would still be possible to give additional protection to sensitive products by splitting the four-digit level into six digits or more. ***Quota rights*** could then be allocated selectively within the entire four-digit range. In this way, a tariff quota can be used as a protectionist measure even when it is allocated fully to importers.

Baumgartner proposals: a set of ideas suggested for action in the GATT in 1961 by the then French Minister for Finance and Economic Affairs, M. Baumgartner, for the management of world trade in agricultural products. The essence of the proposals was an extension of the ***common agricultural policy*** model to global markets, supplemented by the United States ***Food for Peace Program***, to dispose of surplus production. The cost of this plan would have been met by the importing countries. The key component of the pricing mechanism was the "normal price" which would have been set at a level well above what then was the price on the open market. *See also* ***agriculture and the multilateral trading system*** and ***PL 480***.

Bay of Bengal Initiative for Multi-Sectoral Technical and Economic Cooperation: BIMSTEC. Attained its current form in 2004. It consists of Bangladesh, Bhutan, India, Myanmar, Nepal, Sri Lanka and Thailand. Its fourteen priority sectors for cooperation are: trade and investment, transport and communications, energy, tourism, technology, fisheries agriculture, public health, poverty alleviation, counter-terrorism and transnational crime, environment and disaster management, people-to-people contact, cultural cooperation and climate change. A Framework Agreement on the BIMSTEC Free Trade Area came into force on 30 June 2004. Negotiations are continuing. Its secretariat is in Dhaka.

Beggar-thy-neighbour policies: also beggar-my-neighbour policies. Trade or economic measures, such as export subsidies, import quotas and tariffs, taken with the aim of improving domestic economic conditions, e.g. raising employment, and the intention of making them a cost to other countries. Such policies may lead to similar measures by others in response. Beggar-thy-neighbour policies are considered to have been a major factor in deepening and prolonging the Great Depression of the 1930s. *See also* ***balance of trade***, ***mercantilism*** and ***Smoot-Hawley Tariff Act***. [Robinson 1947]

Behaviour: a term used in the administration of ***antitrust laws*** or ***competition laws***. It is virtually the same as ***conduct***, and it describes the actions of firms that may fall within the ambit of the applicable laws.

Behind-the-border issues: policies and measures adopted by governments which are aimed primarily at the domestic economy, but which may have an impact on imports and exports. These include domestic ***subsidies***, ***competition policy***, ***standards***, labour conditions, and many others. *See also* ***at-the-border barriers***.

Beijing Agenda for an Integrated, Innovative and Interconnected Asia-Pacific: the 2014 statement issued by the ***APEC Economic Leaders' Meeting***.

Basket tariff quota

一揽子关税配额

涵盖一系列紧密关联的国际贸易产品的关税配额。如果关税配额在商品名称及编码协调制度(HS)4 位编码基础上适用，仍有可能通过将 4 位编码拆分为 6 位或更细编码而给予敏感产品额外保护。配额权因而可以在整个 4 位编码范围内有选择地分配。这样，即使关税配额全部分配给进口商，也可以用作一种保护主义措施。

Baumgartner proposals

鲍姆加特纳建议

时任法国财政和经济事务部长 M. 鲍姆加特纳于 1961 年在 GATT 中提出的管理世界农产品贸易的一系列行动设想。建议的实质是将共同农业政策模式扩展到全球市场，辅之以美国粮食换和平计划，以处置过剩产量。这一计划的成本将由进口国承担。定价机制的关键部分是“正常价格”，定在大大高于当时公开市场价格的水平。另见*农业与多边贸易体制(agriculture and the multilateral trading system)*、*480 号公法(PL 480)*。

Bay of Bengal Initiative for Multi-Sectoral Technical and Economic Cooperation

环孟加拉湾多领域经济技术合作倡议

BIMSTEC。2004 年达成目前的形式。由孟加拉国、不丹、印度、缅甸、尼泊尔、斯里兰卡和泰国组成。14 个优先合作部门为：贸易与投资、运输与通信、能源、旅游、技术、渔业农业、公共卫生、消除贫困、反恐与跨国犯罪、环境和灾害管理、人民之间的联系、文化合作和气候变化。BIMSTEC 自由贸易区框架协定于 2004 年 6 月 30 日生效。谈判仍在继续进行。秘书处设在达卡。

Beggar-thy-neighbour policies

以邻为壑政策

为改善国内经济条件(例如提高就业)而采取的贸易或经济措施，且有意使其他国家为这些措施付出代价，例如出口补贴、进口配额和关税。此类政策可能会导致其他国家采取类似措施作为应对措施。以邻为壑政策被认为是加深和拖延 20 世纪 30 年代大萧条的主要因素之一。另见*贸易平衡(balance of trade)*、*重商主义(mercantilism)*、*斯穆特-霍利关税法(Smoot-Hawley Tariff Act)*。

Behaviour

行为

管理反垄断法或竞争法时使用的词语。实际上与“行为”相同，描述了可能属于适用法律范围的公司的行动。

Behind-the-border issues

边境后问题

政府采取的主要针对国内经济但可能对进口或出口产生影响的政策和措施。包括国内补贴、竞争政策、标准、劳工条件等等。另见*边境壁垒(at-the-border barriers)*。

Beijing Agenda for an Integrated, Innovative and Interconnected Asia-Pacific

构建一体化、创新、联动的亚太北京议程

APEC 经济领导人会议 2014 年发表的声明。包括《APEC 推动实现亚太自由

It includes the ***Beijing Roadmap for APEC's Contribution to the Realization of the FTAAP*** and the ***APEC Strategic Blueprint for Promoting Global Value Chain Development and Cooperation***.

Beijing Roadmap for APEC's Contribution to the Realization of the FTAAP: at the Beijing ***APEC Economic Leaders' Meeting*** in 2014 Leaders agreed that the time had come to take concrete steps towards a ***Free Trade Area of the Asia-Pacific*** based on a common view that (a) the ***multilateral trading system*** would remain a key tenet of APEC, and that an FTAAP should support it, (b) the FTAAP should be comprehensive and of high quality and address ***"next-generation" trade issues***, (c) the FTAAP would contribute to achieving the ***Bogor Goals*** by 2020, (d) the FTAAP would be realized outside of APEC, but parallel with the APEC process, (e) it should aim to minimize any negative effects from the proliferation of regional and bilateral RTAs/FTAs, and (f) APEC should continue to provide economic and technical cooperation activities in support of the FTAAP. The main action to give effect to these views was the launch of a comprehensive study identifying the various issues by the end of 2016. Its results were outlined in the ***Lima Declaration on FTAAP***.

Beijing Treaty on Audiovisual Performances: adopted in 2012. It gives performers four kinds of economic rights for their performances fixed in audiovisual recordings: (a) right of reproduction, (b) right of distribution, (c) right of rental, and (d) right of making recordings available. [www.wipo.int]

Beirut Agreement: *Agreement for Facilitating the International Circulation of Visual and Auditory Materials of an Educational, Scientific and Cultural Character*. Adopted under the auspices of the ***United Nations Educational, Scientific and Cultural Organization*** (UNESCO) in 1948. The agreement provides that the parties do not levy import duties or impose ***quantitative restrictions*** on the import of defined materials.

Belgian family allowances*:** a case brought against Belgium by Norway and Denmark in 1952 under the GATT. It concerned the imposition of a levy on foreign goods purchased by Belgian public bodies when these goods came from a country whose system of family allowances did not meet specific Belgian requirements. The ***panel concluded that, as the levy was charged at the time the purchase was paid by the public body rather than when it was imported, the point at issue was ***national treatment***. It considered, however, that arriving at a very definite ruling would be difficult, partly because it found the concept of a levy to offset the absence of family allowance payments in other countries difficult to reconcile with the spirit of the GATT. It noted with evident relief that in the meantime the Belgian Government had decided to make its measures consistent with the GATT. ***Japanese measures on leather*** deals with another attempt in the GATT to defend a restrictive trade measure through reference to a social policy. *See also* ***social clause*** and ***trade and labour standards***.

Belt and Road Initiative: an initiative launched by China in 2013 under the original name of One Belt and One Road Initiative. It seeks to improve regional

贸易区北京路线图》和《APEC 促进全球价值链发展与合作战略蓝图》。

Beijing Roadmap for APEC's Contribution to the Realization of the FTAAP

APEC 推动实现亚太自由贸易区北京路线图

在 2014 年北京 APEC 经济领导人会议上，领导人同意基于以下共识而认为现在采取具体步骤建立一个亚太自由贸易区的时机成熟：(a)多边贸易体制仍是 APEC 的关键原则，FTAAP 应对此提供支持；(b)FTAAP 应是全面高质量的，并处理下一代贸易议题；(c) FTAAP 将有助于到 2020 年实现茂物目标；(d) FTAAP 将在 APEC 之外实现，但与 APEC 进程并行；(e)APEC 应力求尽量减少区域和双边区域贸易协定/自由贸易协定激增的任何消极影响；以及(f)APEC 应继续提供经济和技术合作活动以支持 FTAAP。落实这些观点的主要行动为启动一项全面研究以在 2016 年底前确定各项问题，《亚太自由贸易区利马宣言》概述了有关结果。

Beijing Treaty on Audiovisual Performances

视听表演北京条约

2012 年通过。条约赋予表演者对其固定在音像制品中的表演 4 种经济权利：(a)复制权；(b)发行权；(c)出租权；以及(d)提供已录制表演的权利。

Beirut Agreement

贝鲁特协定

《促进教育、科学和文化性质的视听材料国际流通的协定》。1948 年在联合国教科文组织(UNESCO)的赞助下通过。该协定规定缔约方不征收进口关税，也不对规定材料进口施加数量限制。

Belgian family allowances

比利时家庭补助案

1952 年挪威和丹麦根据 GATT 规则对比利时提起的争端案件。涉及比利时公共机构购买外国货物征税问题，原因是这些货物所来自国家的家庭补助制度不符合比利时具体要求。专家组的结论是，由于征税是在公共机构支付购买费用时收取，而不是在进口时收取的，因此争议点在于国民待遇。然而，专家组认为很难作出非常明确的裁决，部分原因是，它认为用征税来抵消其他国家没有支付家庭补助的概念难以符合 GATT 精神。专家组欣慰地注意到，与此同时比利时政府已经决定使其措施符合 GATT。"日本皮革措施案"涉及在 GATT 中引用社会政策捍卫一项限制性贸易措施的又一次尝试。另见*社会条款(social clause)*、*贸易与劳工标准(trade and labour standards)*。

Belt and Road Initiative

"一带一路"倡议

中国在 2013 年以"一带一路"倡议的名义发起的一项倡议。共建"一带一路"

connectivity through a land-based Silk Road Economic Belt consisting of several corridors and an ocean-based Maritime Silk Road making use of the South China Sea, the South Pacific Ocean and the Indian Ocean. The investment required for this initiative is huge. *See also* ***Blue Dot Network***.

Beneficiary countries: a term often used to describe the countries receiving preferential treatment under ***GSP*** schemes. It serves to emphasize the unilateral nature of GSP schemes. *See also* ***donor countries***.

Benefit: under the WTO ***Agreement on Subsidies and Countervailing Measures*** this is a criterion necessary to establish whether a ***subsidy*** exists. The Agreement describes six categories of governmental measures that may satisfy the criterion if they confer a benefit. These are (a) a financial contribution by a government or public body, (b) a government practice involving a direct transfer of funds, (c) government revenue forgone or not collected, (d) provision by a government of goods and services other than infrastructure, (e) payments made by a government through a funding mechanism, (f) payments made through a private body on behalf of a government, and (g) any form of income or price support in the sense of GATT Article XVI (subsidies) which confers a benefit.

Benefits of trade: refers to benefits different to the ones postulated in the ***gains-from-trade theory*** which states that two countries with different price structures will get better economic returns if they trade with each other than if they adhere to ***autarky***. The theory of ***comparative advantage*** also points to the benefits of international specialization. There are some other benefits. Trade gives access to capital goods, machinery and raw materials. It leads to the ***transfer of technology*** through the commercial and cooperative spread of new techniques, ideas and skills. Trade promotes the transfer of capital as firms seek to produce in the country best suited to their needs. Trade also brings about an additional benefit not always seen as that: anti-monopolist policies and an environment of competition.

Benelux: a ***customs union*** formed in 1948 between Belgium, the Netherlands and Luxembourg. Plans for the three to enter into an economic union were superseded by their founding membership of the ***European Economic Community*** on 1 January 1958.

Benign mercantilism: *see* ***mercantilism***.

Berne Convention: the *Berne Convention for the Protection of Literary and Artistic Works* protects the rights of authors of literary and artistic works. It was concluded in 1886 and revised several times since, the last time in 1971. The main aim of the latest revisions was to move the convention towards according substantially uniform protection in all member countries. It is administered by ***WIPO***. The 1971 revision of the Berne Convention is one of the standards to be observed under the WTO ***Agreement on Trade-Related Aspects of Intellectual Property Rights***. *See also* **intellectual property**.

Best-endeavour undertakings: conditional promises to take certain actions, or to consider the possibility of taking certain action. If they are part of a trade agreement, they are an aspect of ***soft law***. In trade negotiations best-endeavour

旨在通过多条走廊组成的陆上丝绸之路经济带和依托南中国海、南太平洋和印度洋的海上丝绸之路，促进区域互联互通。这项倡议所需投资巨大。另见*蓝点网络(Blue Dot Network)*。

Beneficiary countries

受益国

经常用于描述在普惠制(GSP)方案中获得优惠待遇的国家。用于强调普惠制方案的单边性质。另见*捐助国(donor countries)*。

Benefit

利益

根据 WTO《补贴与反补贴措施协定》，利益是确定是否存在补贴的必要标准。协定描述了 6 类政府措施，如果这些措施授予了一项利益，即可满足标准。这些包括：(a)政府或公共机构的财政资助；(b)涉及资金直接转移的政府做法；(c)放弃或未予征收的政府税收；(d)政府提供的除基础设施以外的货物和服务；(e)政府通过筹资机构支付的款项；(f)通过代表政府的私营机构支付的款项；以及(g)GATT 第 16 条(补贴)意义上的任何形式的收入或价格支持。

Benefits of trade

贸易收益

指与贸易利得理论所假定的收益不同的收益，该理论认为，比起坚持经济闭关自守，两个价格结构不同的国家如果相互进行贸易，将获得更好的经济效益。比较优势理论也指出了国际专业化的收益。还有一些其他的收益。贸易使人们能够获得资本货物、机器和原材料。它通过新技术、新想法和新技能的商业与合作传播，实现技术转让。贸易促进资本的转移，因为企业寻求在最适合其需要的国家进行生产。贸易还带来了额外的利益：反垄断政策和竞争环境。

Benelux

比荷卢关税同盟

比利时、荷兰和卢森堡之间于 1948 年建立的关税同盟。三国组建经济联盟的计划被 1958 年 1 月 1 日三国成为欧洲经济共同体的创始成员国所取代。

Benign mercantilism

良性重商主义

见*重商主义(mercantilism)*。

Berne Convention

伯尔尼公约

《保护文学艺术作品伯尔尼公约》，保护文学艺术作品作者的权利。公约于 1886 年缔结，此后经多次修订，最后一次修订是在 1971 年。最新修订的主要目的是推动该公约在所有成员国实现实质上的统一保护。公约由世界知识产权组织(WIPO)管理。1971 年修订的《伯尔尼公约》是 WTO《与贸易有关的知识产权协定》项下需要遵守的标准之一。另见*知识产权(intellectual property)*。

Best-endeavour undertakings

最佳努力承诺

有条件承诺采取某些行动或考虑采取某些行动的可能性。如果承诺是贸易协定的一部分，即成为软法的一个方面。在贸易谈判中，最佳努力承诺往往是

undertakings are often the first step towards more binding obligations. *See also* ***nagging rights***.

Best information available: a concept used in the administration of ***anti-dumping measures***. The WTO ***Anti-Dumping Agreement*** states that even though the information provided by a party to a dumping investigation may not be ideal in all respects, this is not a reason for disregarding it, as long as the other party has acted to the best of its ability. If the evidence or information is not accepted, the supplying party should be given the reasons for it. It should also be given an opportunity to supply further explanations, taking account of the time limits for the investigation.

Best practice for RTAs/FTAs in APEC: a set of twelve non-binding principles adopted in November 2004 to assist ***APEC*** economies negotiating ***preferential trade arrangements***. The principles are (1) *consistency with APEC principles and goals*, (2) *consistency with the WTO*, (3) *go beyond WTO commitments*, both in terms of existing obligations and areas covered by the WTO, (4) *comprehensiveness* to deliver maximum economic benefits to all sectors of the economy, (5) *transparency* by ensuring that texts are readily available, in English where possible, on official websites, (6) practical measures in *trade facilitation* to reduce transaction costs, (7) *mechanisms for consultation and dispute settlement* to reduce uncertainty and prevent and resolve disagreements quickly, (8) *simple rules of origin that facilitate trade* by recognizing the increasingly globalized nature of production, (9) commitments on economic and technical *cooperation*, (10) *sustainable development* by recognizing that economic development, social development and environmental protection are mutually supportive, (11) openness to *accession by third parties*, and (12) *provision for periodic review* to ensure full implementation of the terms of the agreement. [www.apec.org]

Bicycle theory: the proposition that the ***multilateral trading system*** must keep moving forward through successive liberalizing rounds and agreements if it is to remain liberal. On this analogy, the system would fall over like a bicycle if long gaps between liberalizing moves were to permit protectionist sentiments and actions to become dominant. *See also* ***protectionism***.

Bid challenge: in ***government procurement*** a complaint by one party that the other party has not followed the agreed rules in awarding a contract. A challenge usually has to be made within a specified period. The parties normally also agree that challenges should be heard by an impartial and independent tribunal, and that the challenger can attend all hearings.

Bilateral air services agreements: air traffic agreements concluded between governments in accordance with Article 6 of the ***Chicago Convention***. They specify, sometimes in great detail, matters such as names of the carriers, the number of scheduled flights and the maximum number of passengers the other country may direct to one's own country. They also list the airports that may be used. *See also* ***freedoms of the air*** and ***open-skies arrangements***.

形成更具约束力义务的第一步。另见*游说权(nagging rights)*。

Best information available

可获得的最佳信息

反倾销措施管理中使用的概念。WTO《反倾销协定》规定，即使倾销调查一方提供的信息并非在各方面均理想，但只要另一方已经尽力而为，主管机关就不能忽略该信息。如果证据或信息未被接受，即应立刻将有关理由告知提供方。考虑到调查的时限，也应该给予其提供进一步说明的机会。

Best practice for RTAs/FTAs in APEC

APEC 区域贸易协定/自由贸易协定最佳实践

2004 年 11 月通过的一系列 12 项非约束性原则，用于协助 APEC 经济体谈判优惠贸易安排。这些原则包括：(1)与 APEC 的原则和目标的一致性；(2)与 WTO 的一致性；(3)在现有义务和 WTO 所涵盖领域方面超越 WTO；(4)全面为各经济部门带来最大经济利益；(5)通过保证在官方网站上可随时获得英文文本而提高透明度；(6)在贸易便利化方面采取实际措施降低交易成本；(7)磋商和争端解决机制，以减少不确定性和迅速防止和解决分歧；(8)认识到生产日益全球化的特点，实施促进贸易的简单原产地规则；(9)关于经济和技术合作的承诺；(10)通过认识到经济发展、社会发展和环境保护相互支持，实现可持续发展；(11)对第三方加入持开放态度；以及(12)规定定期审议以保证协定条款得到充分实施。

Bicycle theory

自行车理论

认为如果多边贸易体制要保持自由，就必须通过连续的自由化回合和协定不断前行。根据这一比喻，如果自由化举措间隔过长就会让保护主义情绪和行动占据上风，这一体制就会像自行车一样翻倒。另见*保护主义(protectionism)*。

Bid challenge

投标质疑

在政府采购中，一方抱怨另一方在授予合同时未遵守议定规则。质疑通常必须在规定时间内提出。当事方通常也同意应由一个公正和独立的法庭来审理质疑，且质疑者可以出席所有听证。

Bilateral air services agreements

双边航空服务协定

政府间依照《芝加哥公约》第 6 条缔结的航空交通协定。协定有时非常详细地规定一些事项，例如航空公司的名称、定期航班的数量以及对方国家可能直接飞往本国的最大乘客人数。协定还列出可以使用的机场。另见*航空自由(freedoms of the air)*、*开放天空安排(open-skies arrangements)*。

Bilateral aviation rights: the rights specified in ***bilateral air services agreements*** for airlines to carry passengers and freight between two countries. *See also* ***open-skies arrangements***.

Bilateral cumulation: used in the administration of ***preferential rules of origin***. For example, the rules may permit country A to use materials imported from country B and, after they have been processed, to re-export them to country B. Such goods are then admitted in country B under its ***preferential tariff***, assuming that any other applicable conditions have been met. *See also* ***diagonal cumulation***.

Bilateral investment treaties: BITs. A name given by many countries to their ***investment promotion and protection agreements***. The model United States agreement contains rights and obligations concerning the application of ***most-favoured-nation treatment*** and ***national treatment***, whichever is the better; fair and equitable treatment more generally; permission for aliens to enter the other party's territory to establish, develop, administer and advise on an investment and to engage top managerial personnel regardless of nationality; an undertaking not to impose performance requirements; the provision of effective means for asserting claims and enforcing rights; transparency of regulation; procedures to be followed in case of expropriation; and freedom to transfer funds. *See also* ***international investment agreement***.

Bilateralism: the conduct of international trade policy mainly through bilateral negotiations, sometimes through ***free-trade agreements***. Bilateralism assumes that results are more easily obtained if only two parties are involved, partly because available economic or political pressure would be less diluted. In principle, fewer diverting factors are involved. This is true in cases where it is possible to isolate the purely bilateral dimension. Often this cannot be done since at least one of the parties may have obligations in the same matter towards third parties. Some advocates of bilateral negotiations see them as the only valid way for achieving results. The history of bilateral negotiations since the mid-1980s casts doubt on the general validity of this proposition, but bilateralism has been used with success for the resolution of some selected issues. The effectiveness of bilateral approaches depends on the amount of ***negotiating coin*** a country has to influence the behaviour of the other. It is largely an approach which works more in favour of the strong and against the interests of small and medium-sized countries. Bilateralism can also introduce additional tensions into the multilateral system. One form of bilateralism is used in the ***multilateral trade negotiations***. WTO members often negotiate tariff ***concessions*** bilaterally, but they apply the results multilaterally in accordance with the ***most-favoured-nation treatment*** obligation.

Bilateral restraint agreement: *see* ***voluntary restraint arrangement***.

Bilateral safeguards: *see* ***bilateral transitional safeguards***.

Bilateral trade agreement: an agreement between two countries setting out the conditions under which trade between them will be conducted. If both parties are already WTO members enjoying the attendant ***non-discrimination***, ***market***

Bilateral aviation rights

双边航空权

双边航空服务协定中规定的航空公司在两国之间运送乘客和货物的权利。另见*开放天空安排(open-skies arrangements)*。

Bilateral cumulation

双边累积

用于优惠原产地规则的管理。例如，原产地规则可能准许 A 国使用自 B 国进口的材料，并在这些材料加工后复出口至 B 国。此类货物随后在假设已经满足其他任何适用条件的情况下准许按优惠关税进入 B 国。另见*对角累积(diagonal cumulation)*。

Bilateral investment treaties

双边投资条约

BITs。许多国家对其投资促进与保护协定的称呼。美国协定范本包含的权利和义务涉及：适用的最惠国待遇和国民待遇，两者取优；更普遍的公平和公正的待遇；允许外国人进入另一方领土建立、发展、管理和咨询投资，并聘用高级管理人员而不区分国籍；承诺不施加业绩要求；提供有效手段主张权利和执行权利；监管透明度；在征收时应遵循的程序；以及转移资金自由。另见*国际投资协定(international investment agreement)*。

Bilateralism

双边主义

主要通过双边谈判实施国际贸易政策的行为，有时通过自由贸易协定。双边主义认为，如果只有两方参与，会更容易取得成果，部分原因是存在的经济或政治压力会减少。原则上，涉及的偏离因素更少。如果有可能将纯粹双边层面分离则是对的。而通常这是作不到的，因为至少其中一方可能在同一事务中对第三方负有义务。一些双边谈判的支持者认为这是取得成果的惟一有效途径。自 20 世纪 80 年代中期以来的双边谈判历史使人对这一主张的普遍有效性产生怀疑，但双边主义已经成功用于解决一些选定的问题。双边方式的有效性取决于一国影响另一国家行为的谈判筹码的多少。在很大程度上，这是一种有利于强国利益而不利于中小国家利益的方式。双边主义也会给多边体制带来额外的矛盾。双边主义的一种形式也用于多边贸易谈判中。WTO 成员经常通过双边形式谈判关税减让，但是它们依照最惠国待遇义务在多边适用这些成果。

Bilateral restraint agreement

双边限制协定

见*自愿限制安排(voluntary restraint arrangement)*。

Bilateral safeguards

双边保障措施

见*双边过渡性保障措施(bilateral transitional safeguards)*。

Bilateral trade agreement

双边贸易协定

两国之间规定双方开展贸易的条件的协定。如果双方已经是 WTO 成员，即可

access and other benefits, the main additional reason for a bilateral agreement may be a programme of bilateral ***trade facilitation*** and ***trade promotion*** activities. Sometimes it may be a ***free-trade agreement*** which offers the prospect of tariff-free trade between the parties. If one party is not a member of the WTO, the agreement will normally provide for ***most-favoured-nation treatment*** and ***national treatment***, protection of ***intellectual property rights***, ***consultation*** and ***dispute settlement***, and other principles and mechanisms necessary for ensuring smooth trade flows and the speedy resolution of problems. Bilateral trade agreements usually contain a provision for periodic reviews of trade developments at ministerial or officials level, such as a ***joint trade committee*** or a ***mixed commission***. *see also* ***trade and investment facilitation agreement*** and ***trade and investment framework agreement***.

Bilateral transitional safeguards: a means available under many ***free-trade agreements*** measures to restrain surges in imports of ***originating goods***, i.e. goods eligible for preferential tariff treatment. These safeguards mechanisms, sometimes simply called bilateral safeguards, are usually modelled on the ***global safeguards*** (safeguards imposed under Article XIX of the GATT), but they can only be used for goods still subject to tariffs. In time the need for the mechanism should disappear. They usually require that a safeguard can only be imposed if (a) the import surge causes, or threatens to cause, ***serious injury*** to domestic industry and (b) the surge in imports has been caused by a tariff reduction under the terms of the agreement. An investigation also has to be conducted to ensure that the safeguard is warranted. Agreements usually set a ceiling for any safeguard tariff. The measure also is time-bound. Compensation in the form of lower tariffs for other goods may be payable. *See also* ***safeguards***.

BIMP-EAGA: Brunei–Indonesia–Malaysia–Philippines East ASEAN Growth Area, proposed at a meeting of ***ASEAN*** economic ministers in October 1993. It covers Labuan, Sabah, Sarawak (Malaysia), North, Central, South and South-East Sulawesi, Maluku, Irian Jaya and East, West and Central Kalimantan (Indonesia), Mindanao and Palawan (Philippines) and all of Brunei. BIMP-EAGA is aimed at developing trade and investment between contiguous under-developed areas of separate countries.

BIMST-EC: *see* ***Bay of Bengal Initiative for Multi-Sectoral Technical and Economic Cooperation.***

Binding: also called ***concession***. A legal obligation not to raise tariffs on particular products above the specified rate agreed in ***WTO*** negotiations and incorporated in a country's ***schedule of concessions***. Bindings are enforceable through the WTO. Their purpose is to provide greater commercial certainty through a ceiling on tariffs which cannot be breached without an offer of ***compensation*** to affected trading partners. These ceilings are often higher than the ***applied tariff rates***.

Binding commitments: binding or bound commitments are a legal obligation not to make ***market access*** conditions for services more restrictive than described

享受由此产生的非歧视、市场准入和其他利益，达成双边协定的一个主要额外原因可能是包含一项双边贸易便利化和贸易促进活动的计划。有时可能是一项自由贸易协定，提出了双方之间免关税贸易的前景。如果一方不是 WTO 成员，协定通常规定最惠国待遇和国民待遇、保护知识产权、磋商和争端解决，以及为保证顺畅贸易流动和迅速解决问题所需的其他原则和机制。双边贸易协定通常包含对贸易发展情况进行部长级或官员级别定期审查的条款，如联合贸易委员会或混合委员会。另见*贸易投资便利化协定(trade and investment facilitation agreement)*、*贸易投资框架协定(trade and investment framework agreement)*。

Bilateral transitional safeguards

双边过渡性保障措施

在许多自由贸易协定项下用以抑制原产货物进口激增的措施，这些货物有资格享受优惠关税待遇。这些保障措施机制，有时简单称为双边保障措施，通常仿照全球保障措施(根据 GATT 第 19 条实施的保障措施)，但这些措施只能用于仍然征收关税的货物。随着时间的推移，使用此种机制的需求将会消失。措施通常要求只有在下列情况下方可实施：(a)进口激增对国内产业造成或威胁造成严重损害；及(b)进口激增是因根据协定条款实施的关税削减造成的。同样需要进行调查，以保证保障措施是合理的。协定通常对任何保障措施关税设定上限。措施也有时间限制。可以使用更低关税的形式对其他货物作出补偿。另见*保障措施(safeguards)*。

BIMP-EAGA

东盟东部增长区

文莱—印度尼西亚—马来西亚—菲律宾东盟东部增长区，东盟经济部长在 1993 年 10 月召开的会议上提出。涵盖马来西亚的纳闽岛、沙巴州、沙捞越州，印度尼西亚的苏拉威西北部、中部、南部和东南部、马鲁古群岛、伊里安加亚岛和加里曼丹的东部、西部和中部，菲律宾的棉兰老岛和巴拉望岛，以及文莱的全部地区。BIMP-EAGA 旨在发展不同国家毗邻的欠发达地区之间的贸易和投资。

BIMST-EC

孟加拉国—印度—缅甸—斯里兰卡—泰国经济合作

见*环孟加拉湾多领域经济技术合作倡议(Bay of Bengal Initiative for Multi-Sectoral Technical and Economic Cooperation)*。

Binding

约束

也称减让。一项法律义务，要求不得将特定产品的关税提高至 WTO 谈判中议定且已并入一国减让表的税率水平以上。约束可以通过 WTO 强制执行。目的是通过设定关税上限提供更大的商业确定性，关税上限如不向受影响的贸易伙伴提供补偿即不得违反。这些上限通常高于实施税率。

Binding commitments

约束承诺

约束承诺是一项法律义务，要求不得使服务市场准入条件比提交 WTO 的一

in a country's schedule of commitments on services submitted to the WTO. Bindings are enforceable under WTO rules and may only be breached through negotiation with affected trading partners. A country breaching a binding may have to offer ***compensation*** to other trading partners in the form of ***commitments*** in other services.

Binding overhang: situations where bound tariffs in a country's tariff system as a whole are significantly higher than applied tariffs. [Francois and Martin 2003]

Binding ratio: the proportion of bound tariffs to unbound ones in a given customs territory.

Biochemical prospecting: *see* ***UNCTAD BioTrade Initiative***.

Biodiversity: short for biological diversity. Defined in Article 2 of the ***Convention on Biological Diversity*** as "the variability among living organisms from all sources, including, *inter alia*, terrestrial, marine and other aquatic ecosystems and the ecological complexes of which they are part; this includes diversity within species, between species and ecosystems".

Biopiracy: the unauthorized search in the wild by biotechnology companies for plants or genes that may be useful for the development of, for example, new pharmaceuticals or improved strains of commercial crops. Some developing countries in particular consider that they are disadvantaged by this practice because they may not receive proper compensation for the use of plants that occur naturally in their territories. The biotechnology companies, on the other hand, are seen by them as benefiting commercially through their application for ***patents*** for discoveries made in this way. This is the basis for the argument that there should be a new class of ***intellectual property rights*** to curb biopiracy. The entire concept remains contentious.

Bioprospecting: the search for plants or genes that may be useful for the development of, for example, new pharmaceuticals or improved strains of commercial crops. Bioprospecting differs from other branches of biotechnology in that it is looking for as yet undiscovered applications. *See also* ***biopiracy***. [Ministry of Economic Development 2002]

BioTrade: defined by ***UNCTAD*** as those activities of collection, production, transformation and commercialization of goods and services derived from native ***biodiversity*** under the criteria of environmental, social and economic sustainability. *See also* ***UNCTAD BioTrade Initiative***. [www.unctad.org]

BioTrade Facilitation Programme: *see* ***UNCTAD BioTrade Initiative***.

Black letter law: laws so well established in the legal system that they are no longer open to argument or interpretation.

Black Sea Economic Cooperation Organization: BSEC. Established on 1 May 1999 as the successor to the Economic Cooperation Area of Black Sea Countries. Its members are Albania, Armenia, Azerbaijan, Bulgaria, Georgia, Greece, Moldova, Romania, Russia, Serbia, Turkey and Ukraine. BSEC runs an extensive intergovernmental work programme on trade cooperation. Its secretariat is located in Istanbul.

国服务承诺减让表中所规定的内容更具限制性。约束可以在 WTO 中强制执行，只有通过与受影响的贸易伙伴谈判方可被违反。违反一项约束的国家可能必须以对其他服务作出承诺的形式向其他贸易伙伴提供补偿。

Binding overhang

约束税率超出

一国关税制度中的全部约束关税大大高于实施税率的情况。

Binding ratio

约束比率

在给定关税地区约束关税与非约束关税的比例。

Biochemical prospecting

生化勘探

见 *UNCTAD 生物贸易倡议(UNCTAD BioTrade Initiative)*。

Biodiversity

生物多样性

生物多样性的简称。《生物多样性公约》第 2 条将其定义为“所有来源的形形色色生物体，这些来源除其他外特别包括陆地、海洋和其他水生生态系统及其所构成的生态综合体；这包括物种内部、物种之间和生态系统的多样性”。

Biopiracy

生物剽窃

生物技术公司未经授权，在野外搜寻可能有助于开发新药物或经济作物改良品种的植物或基因的行为。一些发展中国家特别认为，这种做法使它们处于不利地位，因为它们可能不能获得使用其领土内自然生长植物的适当补偿。另一方面，它们认为，生物技术公司通过为按此种方式取得的发现申请专利可以获得商业利益。这就是应该有一类新的知识产权来遏制生物剽窃的论点的基础。整个概念存在争议。

Bioprospecting

生物勘探

寻找可能有助于开发新药物或经济作物改良品种的植物或基因。生物勘探不同于生物技术的其他分支，是寻找尚未被发现的应用。另见*生物剽窃(biopiracy)*。

BioTrade

生物贸易

联合国贸易与发展会议(UNCTAD)定义为根据环境、社会和经济可持续性标准，收集、生产、转化和商业化源于当地生物多样性的货物和服务的活动。另见 *UNCTAD 生物贸易倡议(UNCTAD BioTrade Initiative)*。

BioTrade Facilitation Programme

生物贸易便利化计划

见 *UNCTAD 生物贸易倡议(UNCTAD BioTrade Initiative)*。

Black letter law

公认的基本法律原则

在法律体系中公认的不再争论或解释的法律。

Black Sea Economic Cooperation Organization

黑海经济合作组织

BSEC。成立于 1999 年 5 月 1 日，是黑海国家经济合作区的后继组织。成员包括阿尔巴尼亚、亚美尼亚、阿塞拜疆、保加利亚、格鲁吉亚、希腊、摩尔多瓦、罗马尼亚、俄罗斯、塞尔维亚、土耳其和乌克兰。BSEC 在贸易合作方面有一个内容广泛的政府间工作计划。秘书处设在伊斯坦布尔。

Blair House Accord: an agreement reached on 20 November 1992 between the United States and the ***European Community*** on three changes to the draft ***Uruguay Round*** outcome on agriculture. First, there would be a reduction in the cutback of the volume of subsidized exports from 24 per cent to 21 per cent. Second, some domestic subsidies paid directly by governments to producers would be exempt from the reduction commitment (*see also* ***blue box***). Third, the ***peace clause*** giving immunity against complaints on subsidies being reduced was extended. These changes left intact the principles to govern trade in agriculture following the conclusion of the Round, but they gave participants greater flexibility in implementing them. The Blair House Accord enabled a restart of the multilateral negotiations, but its initial favourable reception faded away once it became clear that it had not resolved the fundamental differences on ***market access*** between the two parties. The Accord was revised in December 1993, and this removed the final difficulty standing in the way of the Uruguay Round outcome on agriculture. *See also* ***Agreement on Agriculture***, ***agriculture and the multilateral trading system*** and ***market access for agriculture***.

Blended formula: a method for reducing tariffs proposed during the ***Doha Development Agenda*** negotiations. It entails the use of the ***Uruguay Round*** tariff reduction formula for some tariffs, the ***Swiss formula*** for others, and eliminating tariffs altogether on some ***tariff lines***. The formula used during the Uruguay Round combined an average reduction with a minimum reduction per tariff line, and it permitted some measures to protect ***sensitive products*** from increasing competition. *See also* ***banded formula*** and ***tiered formula***.

Blockchain: an electronic decentralized public ledger of financial transactions associated particularly with ***cryptocurrencies***. It allows participants to keep track of transactions without central record-keeping. Records cannot be deleted, revised or tampered with. Many banks, for example, are now assessing how blockchain technology can be used in their work.

Block exemptions: used in the administration of ***competition policy*** to exempt certain sectors or practices from the applicable laws.

Blocking regulation: a ***regulation*** first adopted by the ***European Union*** in 1996 to counteract the effects of extraterritorial application of legislation adopted by third countries. It only applies to persons legally established in the European Union and only when they engage in international trade and/or movement of capital and related commercial activities between the European and third countries. The only "third country" so far has been the United States.

Blocking statutes: national legislation aimed at countering the attempted extraterritorial use of ***antitrust laws*** by others. Such legislation typically forbids nationals of the country concerned to cooperate in antitrust investigations launched by a foreign country. *See also* ***extraterritoriality***.

Blood diamonds: also known as conflict diamonds. *See* ***Kimberley Process Certification Scheme***.

Blue BioTrade: an initiative launched in 2017 under the ***UNCTAD BioTrade Initiative***. Work areas include specialized fisheries and aquaculture and sea

Blair House Accord
布莱尔宫协议

1992 年 11 月 20 日美国与欧共体达成的一项协议，对乌拉圭回合农业成果草案作出三项修改。一是，补贴出口的数量从 24%减至 21%。二是，一些政府直接支付生产商的国内补贴免于削减承诺(另见*蓝箱(blue box)*)。三是，延长免于对正在削减过程中的补贴提起诉讼的和平条款。这些修改没有改动管辖回合结束后农业贸易的原则，但给予参加方在实施方面更大的灵活性。《布莱尔宫协议》使得多边谈判得以重启，但一旦意识到协议并未解决双方在市场准入问题上的根本分歧，最初的良好反响即烟消云散。该协议在 1993 年 12 月进行了修订，消除了阻碍乌拉圭回合农业谈判结果的最后难题。另见*农业协定(Agreement on Agriculture)*、*农业与多边贸易体制(agriculture and the multilateral trading system)*、*农产品市场准入(market access for agriculture)*。

Blended formula
混合公式

在多哈发展议程谈判中提出的一种关税削减方法。需要对部分关税使用乌拉圭回合关税削减公式，对其他关税使用瑞士公式，并完全取消部分税目的关税。乌拉圭回合期间使用的公式将平均削减与每一税目最低削减相结合，并允许采取一些措施保护敏感产品免受日益激烈的竞争。另见*分层公式(banded formula)*、*分层公式(tiered formula)*。

Blockchain
区块链

特别与加密数字货币相关的金融交易的去中心化电子公共分类账。允许参与者在没有中央记录保存的情况下跟踪交易。记录不能被删除、修改或篡改。例如，许多银行目前正在评估如何在其工作中使用区块链技术。

Block exemptions
集体豁免

用于竞争政策的管理中，将某些部门或做法例外于适用法律。

Blocking regulation
阻断条例

欧盟于 1996 年首次通过的一项条例，目的是抵消在域外适用第三国通过的法律的影响。仅适用于在欧盟设立的法人，且仅在其从事欧洲与第三国之间的国际贸易和/或资本流动及相关商业活动时适用。到目前为止，惟一的“第三国”是美国。

Blocking statutes
阻断法

旨在打击其他国家试图在域外使用反垄断法的国家立法。此类立法通常禁止有关国家的国民在一外国发起的反垄断调查中进行合作。另见*治外法权(extraterritoriality)*。

Blood diamonds
血钻

又称冲突钻石。另见*金伯利进程证书制度(Kimberley Process Certification Scheme)*。

Blue BioTrade
蓝色生物贸易

2017 年在联合国贸易与发展会议(UNCTAD)生物贸易倡议下发起的一项倡议。

products, sea-based cosmetics, marine pharmaceuticals, and coastal and marine eco-tourism. Participants in this initiative are ***UNCTAD***, Development Bank of Latin America (CAF), ***CITES*** Secretariat and the International Oceans Institute (IOI).

Blue box: agricultural supports linked to production, but provided under production-limiting programmes and therefore less trade-distorting than ***amber box*** support. The specific rules are: (a) payments are based on fixed area and yields, or (b) payments are made on 85 per cent or less of the base level of production, or (c) livestock payments are made on a fixed number of head. These supports are exempt from the reduction commitments under the WTO ***Agreement on Agriculture***. *See also* ***amber box*** and ***green box***.

Blue Dot Network: an initiative launched by the United States, Japan and Australia in November 2019. It seeks to bring together governments, the private sector and civil society "to promote high-quality trusted standards for global infrastructure development in an open and inclusive framework". The Blue Dot Initiative aims to evaluate and certify nominated infrastructure projects to promote market-driven, transparent and financially sustainable infrastructure development in the Indo-Pacific region and elsewhere. *See also* ***Belt and Road Initiative***.

Bogor Declaration: adopted by the ***APEC Economic Leaders' Meeting*** on 15 November 1994 at Bogor (Indonesia) to achieve free trade in goods and services as well as free investment among APEC members. Developed economy members were expected to achieve the target by 2010, developing economies by 2020. Leaders emphasized their strong opposition to the creation of an inward-looking bloc that would impair the pursuit of global free trade. Leaders also said that they would give particular attention to their trade with non-APEC developing countries to ensure that they would also benefit from APEC's trade and investment liberalization, in conformity with GATT/WTO provisions. *See also* ***APEC*** and ***open regionalism***.

Bogor Goals: the aim of ***APEC*** members to achieve free trade and investment by 2010 for developed economies and by 2020 for developing economies. *See also* ***Bogor Declaration***.

Bolar exception: named after a case in 1983 in the United States District Court launched by Roche Products Inc., a research-oriented pharmaceuticals company, against Bolar Pharmaceutical Co., a manufacturer of generic products. The gist of the case was that Bolar had begun an effort to obtain federal approval for the marketing of a generic drug based on a patent held by Roche before that patent expired. Roche alleged that this violated United States patent law. The court held that Bolar's use of the patented compound federally mandated testing was not an infringement of the law because it was ***de minimis*** and experimental. An appeal by Roche, heard in 1984 by the Court of Appeals, was successful. Later that year the United States Congress passed the *Drug Price Competition and Patent Term Restoration Act* which gave backing to the practice at issue in the Bolar case. It stated that it was not an infringement to

工作领域包括专业渔业、水产养殖和海洋产品、海洋化妆品、海洋药物以及沿海和海洋生态旅游。倡议参加方包括 UNCTAD、拉丁美洲开发银行(CAF)、《濒危野生动植物种国际贸易公约》(CITES)秘书处和国际海洋研究所(IOI)。

Blue box

蓝箱

与生产挂钩的农业支持，但是根据限产计划提供，因此贸易扭曲作用小于黄箱。具体规则为：(a)支付按固定面积和产量给予；或(b)支付按基期生产水平的 85%或以下给予；或(c)牲畜支付按固定头数给予。这些支持免于 WTO《农业协定》项下的削减承诺。另见*黄箱(amber box)*、*绿箱(green box)*。

Blue Dot Network

蓝点网络

美国、日本和澳大利亚于 2019 年 11 月发起的倡议。寻求政府、私营部门和公民社会一起“在一个开放和包容的框架内为全球基础设施发展而促进高质量可信标准的达成”。《蓝点倡议》旨在评价和核证提名的基础设施项目，以促进印太区域及其他地区市场驱动、透明和财政可持续的基础设施发展。另见*“一带一路”倡议(Belt and Road Initiative)*。

Bogor Declaration

茂物宣言

APEC 经济领导人会议于 1994 年 11 月 15 日在茂物(印度尼西亚)通过，旨在 APEC 成员之间实现货物贸易和服务贸易自由化以及投资自由化。发达经济体应到 2010 年实现这一目标，发展中经济体应到 2020 年实现。领导人强调，强烈反对建立一个封闭集团，这将损害全球自由贸易事业。领导人还表示，将特别关注与非 APEC 发展中国家的贸易，以保证这些国家也能以符合 GATT/WTO 条款的方式，自 APEC 贸易和投资自由化中获益。另见*亚太经济合作组织(APEC)*、*开放的区域主义(open regionalism)*。

Bogor Goals

茂物目标

APEC 成员的目标是到 2010 年发达经济体实现贸易和投资自由化，发展中经济体到 2020 年实现。另见*茂物宣言(Bogor Declaration)*。

Bolar exception

博拉例外

因美国地区法院 1983 年的一起案件而得名，研究型制药公司——罗氏制药公司对非专利产品制造商——博拉制药公司提起诉讼。该案的要旨是，博拉公司的一项仿制药是基于罗氏公司的专利生产的，在专利到期前，博拉公司已经开始争取获得联邦政府销售许可。罗氏公司指控此点违反了美国专利法。法院认为，博拉公司使用联邦政府授权进行专利化合物测试并不违法，因其属微量和实验性质。罗氏提起上诉，上诉法院于 1984 年进行审理，罗氏胜诉。1984 年稍晚，美国国会通过了《药品价格竞争与专利期补偿法》，该法支持了

make, use or sell a patented drug if that was done solely for uses reasonably related to the development and submission of information under a federal law regulating the manufacture, use or sale of drugs. The thinking underlying this provision was that if a manufacturer of generic drugs had to wait until the expiry of a patent for a drug before being allowed to start developmental work, the patent term of the drug would be extended *de facto*, probably by several years, until approval could be obtained. *See also* ***generic springboarding*** and ***intellectual property rights***.

Bona fides*:** *Lat. good faith*, often met as *bona fide* (in good faith). *See also* ***mala fides.

Bonus: *see* ***Dairy Export Incentive Program*** and ***Export Enhancement Program***.

Boomerang clause: Article 91.2 of the ***Treaty of Rome*** deals with ***dumping*** practices by member states of the ***European Economic Community*** towards other member states during the twelve-year transition period (1958–70) leading to full implementation of the Treaty. Protective measures against dumping were possible during the transition period, but the ***European Commission*** decided what action to take. One of the possibilities open to companies found to have dumped products was to take them back. Article 91.2 made this possible with minimum friction. It states that products originating or having been entered for consumption in one member state that are exported to another member state had to be admitted free of all charges or ***quantitative restrictions*** when they were reimported into the territory of the first member state. The Article did not prohibit dumping, but it reduced the incentive for doing so. In 1970 the members of the European Community stopped using anti-dumping action against each other. *See also* ***competition policy and anti-dumping measures***.

Boomerang effect: the possibility that policies executed by a government may rebound on it. ***Trade policy*** generally seeks to avoid the boomerang effect by treating exporters from other jurisdictions and their products in a manner equivalent to that given to domestic producers and their products. The boomerang effect is more likely to occur under laws and regulations not subject to the ***national treatment*** provision. *See also* ***beggar-thy-neighbour policies*** and ***retaliation***.

Bootlegging: the unauthorized recording of artistic performances for later broadcasting or other commercial gain. Such recordings are often cheap, and their quality inferior, but this is not necessarily a deterrent for the buyer. *See also* ***copyright***, ***intellectual property*** and ***piracy***.

Borderless world: originally the title of a book written in 1990 by Kenichi Ohmae which is more concerned with ways in which a firm can make the best of competing in an interlinked global economy. It represents an aspect of the literature on ***globalization*** and ***internationalization***. In the meantime, the idea of a world without national borders to trade has taken hold in some quarters. However, like the paperless office, this will take some time to achieve.

Border measures: *see* ***tariff*** and ***non-tariff measures***.

博拉案中存在争议的做法。该法指出，如果制造、使用或销售一项专利药品仅用于根据规范药品制造、使用或销售的联邦法律而与开发和提交信息合理相关的用途，并不违法。此项规定所依据的思路为，如果仿制药制造商必须等到一种药品的专利到期后才能获准启动开发工作，那么该药品的专利期事实上就被延长到获得批准为止。另见*仿制药跳板(generic springboarding)*、*知识产权(intellectual property rights)*。

Bona fides

善意

拉丁语中“善意”之意，经常写作 *bona fide*。另见*恶意(mala fides)*。

Bonus

红利

见*奶制品出口激励计划(Dairy Export Incentive Program)*、*出口增强计划(Export Enhancement Program)*。

Boomerang clause

回旋镖条款

《罗马条约》第 91.2 条处理欧洲经济共同体成员国在全面实施该条约之前的 12 年过渡期内(1958—1970 年)对其他成员国的倾销行为。在过渡期内，针对倾销的保护措施是可能的，但由欧盟委员会决定采取什么行动。一种可能性是被认定倾销产品的公司回收产品。第 91.2 条允许此点而使摩擦最小化。该条指出，原产于一成员国或已经进入一成员国供消费的产品再出口到另一个成员国后，在复进口至第一个成员国领土时，必须免征任何费用或免于数量限制。该条并未禁止倾销，但却减少了这样作的动机。1970 年，欧共体成员国停止相互采取反倾销行动。另见*竞争政策(competition policy)*、*反倾销措施(anti-dumping measures)*。

Boomerang effect

回旋镖效应

政府执行的政策会反作用于政府的可能性。贸易政策通常通过以对待本国生产者及其产品的方式对待其他管辖范围的出口商及其产品，以寻求避免回旋镖效应。回旋镖效应在不受国民待遇条款管辖的法律法规中更有可能出现。另见*以邻为壑政策(beggar-thy-neighbour policies)*、*报复(retaliation)*。

Bootlegging

非法制造

以日后进行广播或其他商业盈利为目的对艺术表演进行未经授权的录音。此类录音通常廉价、质次，但并不一定会使买家止步。另见*版权(copyright)*、*知识产权(intellectual property)*、*盗版(piracy)*。

Borderless world

无国界世界

最初为大前研一写于 1990 年的一本书的书名，该书更关注一家公司如何在一个相互关联的全球经济中进行最佳竞争。代表了关于全球化和国际化的文学侧面。与此同时，关于开展贸易的无国界世界的想法已经在一些地方扎根。然而，就如无纸化办公一样，这需要花一些时间才能实现。

Border measures

边境措施

见*关税(tariff)*、*非关税措施(non-tariff measures)*。

Border prices: the price of goods when they arrive at the border and before they have gone through an assessment of any duty that may be payable. The border price is therefore the equivalent of the ***CIF*** price.

Border protection: any measure which acts to restrain imports at the point of entry.

Border tax adjustments: refunds of, or additions to, indirect taxes (e.g. excise tax) or non-collection of dues borne by an article destined for domestic consumption if that article is exported. Such adjustments are sometimes also called ***drawbacks*** or remissions. Adjustment can also be a charge levied on an imported article that equals indirect taxes (e.g. sales tax) imposed on similar domestic products. Such adjustments are not illegal under the GATT. *See also* ***export incentives***.

Border trade: *see* ***frontier traffic***.

Borocay Action Agenda to globalize MSMEs: an agenda adopted by the 2015 ***Meeting of APEC Ministers Related to Trade***. It consists of a detailed five-year programme to foster the participation of micro, small and medium enterprises in regional and global markets.

Bottleneck facilities: *see* ***essential facilities doctrine***.

Bottom-up approach: preparing an agenda for trade negotiations by agreeing on negotiating subjects item by item. As agreement is reached on each item, the shape of the final agenda gradually becomes apparent. The term is also used to describe the use of positive lists for schedules of commitments in ***free-trade agreements***. *See also* ***top-down approach***.

Bottom-up multilateralism: a negotiating process resulting in bilateral and minilateral outcomes which are extended multilaterally from the bottom up. Cowhey and Aronson, proponents of this process, stress that such deals must encompass the basic principles of the multilateral trade regime, and they must be open to the scrutiny of third parties. They say that multilateral negotiations will only yield slow incremental progress towards liberalization, and that ***regionalism***, and in some cases the sectoral approach, can provide a superior solution to many issues if appropriate consultative mechanisms between regions exist. *See also* ***bilateralism***, ***hub and spokes***, ***minilateralism***, ***multilateralism*** and ***sectoral trade negotiations***. [Cowhey and Aronson 1993]

Bound: *see* ***concession***.

Bound tariff rate: sometimes bound rate or simply ***binding***. The tariff a WTO member undertakes not to exceed. *See also* ***applied tariff rates***.

Bounty: a subsidy available to domestic producers, usually to help an ailing industry. It can be aimed at bridging the gap between domestic and imported prices of a manufacture (e.g. shipbuilding), or the use of a specified input in a production process (i.e. superphosphate for agriculture). Many prefer bounties to tariffs as a method for supporting or protecting industries because the amount paid, and therefore the cost to other industries and consumers, is clearly evident. Budgetary pressures are likely to keep bounties in check. Another argument is that bounties can be targeted more accurately, and they do not become a charge

Border prices
边境价格
货物抵达边境后、在对应缴税费进行估价前的价格。因此边境价格等于到岸价格。
Border protection
边境保护
在入境点采取的限制进口产品的任何措施。
Border tax adjustments
边境税调节
如出口一供国内消费的物品时，退还或加征间接税(如消费税)或免征应缴款。此类调节有时也被称为退税或免税。调节也可以是对进口物品征收相当于对类似国产品所征收的间接税的费用(如销售税)。此类调节根据GATT并不违法。另见*出口鼓励措施(export incentives)*。
Border trade
边境贸易
见*边境贸易(frontier traffic)*。
Borocay Action Agenda to globalize MSMEs
中小微企业全球化长滩岛行动纲领
2015 年 APEC 贸易部长会议通过的一项议程。由一项促进中小微企业参与区域和全球市场的 5 年详细计划组成。
Bottleneck facilities
瓶颈设施
见*必要设施原则(essential facilities doctrine)*。
Bottom-up approach
自下而上方式
通过对谈判议题逐项达成一致的方式制定贸易谈判议程。随着就每项议题达成一致，最终议程的结构逐渐明朗。该词也用来描述自由贸易协定中承诺减让表的正面清单。另见*自上而下方式(top-down approach)*。
Bottom-up multilateralism
自下而上的多边主义
指双边或诸边谈判结果自下而上向多边扩展的谈判过程。该进程的倡导者科威和阿隆森强调，此类交易必须体现多边贸易体制的基本原则，必须接受第三方的审查。他们称多边谈判只能在实现自由化方面取得渐进性进展，而如果区域之间存在适当协商机制，区域主义及在一些情况下的部门方式，可以为许多问题提供更好的解决方案。另见*双边主义(bilateralism)*、*轮轴-辐条(hub and spokes)*、*小多边主义(minilateralism)*、*多边主义(multilateralism)*、*部门贸易谈判(sectoral trade negotiations)*。
Bound
约束
见*减让(concession)*。
Bound tariff rate
约束税率
有时称作约束税率或简称为约束，即 WTO 成员承诺不超过的关税。另见*实施税率(applied tariff rates)*。
Bounty
津贴
国内生产者可获得的补贴，通常用于帮助处境困难的行业。目的可以是弥补制造业(例如造船业)的国内价格与进口价格的差距，或是在生产过程中使用特定投入物(例如农用过磷酸盐)。许多人喜欢津贴多于关税，作为支持或保护产

on inputs to other industries except through the general taxation system. *See also* ***protection*** and ***subsidies***.

Box: under ***WTO*** rules for agriculture, a category of domestic support. ***Green box***: support is considered not to distort trade or only minimally, and therefore permitted without limits. ***Blue box***: permitted supports linked to production, but provided under production-limiting programmes. ***Amber box***: supports considered to distort trade and therefore subject to reduction commitments.

Boycott: the refusal to supply a country or a firm, to import or buy from it, or to deal with it in other ways. This may in certain cases constitute an ***anti-competitive practice*** or a ***restrictive business practice***.

Bracketed language: a section of a negotiating text put in square brackets either because the language is disputed or because its adoption will depend on agreement being achieved elsewhere in the text. *See also* ***ad referendum agreement*** and ***without prejudice***.

Brain drain: *see* ***reverse transfer of technology***.

Branch office economy: the proposition that modern communications technologies enable economic decision-making to be concentrated in a few financial centres, and that smaller economies are no longer their own masters. Holders of this view often expect their governments to take steps to prevent this. They fall into two main groups. The first advocates making the economy more competitive and therefore more attractive to foreign investors through trade and investment liberalization. The second calls for ***protectionism***, though this is usually couched in words like positive intervention, the need for a more modern ***industry policy*** and other devices with this intent. *See also* ***globalization*** and ***internationalization***.

Brandt Report: published in 1980 as *North–South: A Programme for Survival* by the Independent Commission on International Development Issues. This commission was convened in 1977 under the chairmanship of Mr Willy Brandt, a former chancellor of the Federal Republic of Germany. The report covered, among other topics, commodity trade and development, energy, industrialization and world trade, transnational corporations, investment and the sharing of technology, the world monetary order and development finance. It sought greater participation by developing countries in the processing, marketing and distribution of commodities, ***compensatory financing arrangements*** and the conclusion of ***international commodity agreements***. It also advocated a ***rollback*** of ***protectionism*** by the industrialized countries, positive adjustment programmes (***structural adjustment***), an easing of the rules of the ***GSP***, and fair labour standards to prevent unfair competition and to facilitate ***trade liberalization***. The quality of the report, its timeliness and the composition of the commission ensured wide coverage and public discussion of its proposals. Its proposals found their way into the agenda of all important conferences at the time, but the problems giving rise to them evaded a successful resolution. In 1983, the Brandt Commission published *Common Crisis North–South: Cooperation for World Recovery* in response to what members of the commission saw

业的一种方法，因为支付的金额及因此给其他产业和消费者带来的成本是显而易见的。预算压力有可能使津贴受到限制。另一种观点认为，津贴的目标可以更精准，除了通过一般税收制度外，不会构成其他产业投入物的费用。另见*保护(protection)*、*补贴(subsidies)*。

Box
箱

WTO农业规则下，国内支持的类别。绿箱：被认为不会扭曲贸易或扭曲作用很小的支持，因而允许绿箱而无限制。蓝箱：被允许提供的与生产相关的支持，但是要在限产计划下提供。黄箱：被认为扭曲贸易因而受到削减承诺限制的支持。

Boycott
抵制

拒绝向一国或一公司供应，拒绝自一国或一公司进口或购买，或以其他方式处理一国或一公司。这在一些情况下可能构成反竞争行为或限制性商业惯例。

Bracketed language
方括号内文字

放入方括号内的一段谈判案文，要么由于文字存在争议，要么由于这段案文是否采纳取决于案文其他处达成一致的情况。另见*待核准协定(ad referendum agreement)*、*不损害(without prejudice)*。

Brain drain
人才外流

见*反向技术转让(reverse transfer of technology)*。

Branch office economy
分公司经济

关于现代通信技术使得经济决策集中在少数几个金融中心，而较小的经济体不再能自己主宰的一种观点。持这种观点的人通常希望他们的政府采取措施来阻止此种情况的发生。他们又分为两派：第一种主张通过贸易和投资自由化使经济更具竞争力，因而对外国投资者更具吸引力。第二种呼吁保护主义，尽管这通常是以积极干预、需要更现代的产业政策和其他具有类似意图的手段等措辞加以表达的。另见*全球化(globalization)*、*国际化(internationalization)*。

Brandt Report
勃兰特报告

该报告于1980年由国际发展问题独立委员会以《北方和南方：争取生存的纲领》为题发表。委员会于1977年成立，主席为联邦德国前总理维利·勃兰特。该报告涵盖的议题包括商品贸易和发展、能源、工业化和世界贸易、跨国公司、投资和技术共享、世界货币秩序和发展金融等。报告旨在寻求发展中国家更多参与商品加工、市场营销和分销、补偿性融资安排并达成国际商品协定。还主张工业化国家贸易保护主义回退、积极的调整计划(结构性调整)、放宽普惠制(GSP)规定、实行公平的劳工标准以防止不正当竞争以及促进贸易自由化。报告的质量、及时性和委员会的组成保证了其建议引起广泛关注和公众讨论。建议被列入当时所有重要会议的议程，但产生这些建议的问题阻碍了解决办法的达成。1983年，勃兰特委员会出版了名为《南北共同的危机：合作推动世界复苏》的报告，报告是对委员会成员认为未作充分回应的第一份报告中

as an inadequate response to the issues raised in its first report. The commission was formally disbanded in February 1983. *See also* ***Cancún Summit*** and ***North–South dialogue***. [Brandt Commission 1980]

Brazilian unroasted coffee*:** a case brought before the GATT in 1980 which centred on the meaning of ***like product. Brazil complained that changes in the Spanish ***tariff schedule*** meant that Brazilian unroasted non-decaffeinated coffee was now treated less favourably than "mild coffee". The distinction between these coffee types was based on a statistical method used by the International Coffee Organization which broadly graded coffee into mild Arabicas, unwashed Arabicas and Robustas. Brazil claimed that Spain was contravening GATT Article I:1 (General Most-Favoured-Nation Treatment) in that it treated like products from different countries in a discriminatory way. Spain argued that "unwashed Arabica" and "mild coffee" were different products in terms of quality, taste and cultivation methods. The ***panel*** agreed with Brazil. It accepted the existence of different types of coffee, but it held that these differences were not enough to allow for a different tariff treatment. It also found that unroasted coffee was mostly sold in blends, and that "coffee, in its end-use, was universally regarded as a well-defined and single product for drinking". Accordingly, the panel suggested that Spain remove its discriminatory treatment of Brazilian coffee. [GATT BISD 28S]

Bretton Woods agreements: the United Nations Monetary and Financial Conference held at Bretton Woods, New Hampshire, in 1944 produced charters for the ***World Bank*** (International Bank for Reconstruction and Development or IBRD) and the International Monetary Fund (***IMF***). It also proposed the establishment of the International Trade Organization (***ITO***) for which negotiations were held separately, but which ultimately resulted in a less ambitious outcome in the form of the ***GATT***. The three are sometimes called the Bretton Woods institutions. *See also* ***Havana Charter***.

Brexit: short for exit of Britain (formally the United Kingdom of Great Britain and Northern Ireland) or UK from the ***European Union***. The UK joined the European Union (then the ***European Economic Community***) on 1 January 1973. It did not become part of the ***Eurozone***. On 23 June 2016 the UK Government conducted a referendum on whether the country should remain in the European Union. The result was a clear, but not overwhelming, vote in favour of leaving. On 29 March 2017 the UK Government invoked Article 50 of the ***Treaty on European Union***. This article enables member states of the European Union to leave the Union by notifying its intention to the ***European Council***. It also states that membership will cease once a withdrawal agreement between the departing member state and the European Union enters into force or, if agreement cannot be reached, membership will cease anyway two years after notification. The article foresees the possibility of an extension of the negotiating period. Once the notification had been lodged by the UK Government and negotiations set in train, it became obvious that two years were a very short time for getting the negotiations under way for completing

所提问题的一种回应。1983 年 2 月，委员会正式解散。另见*坎昆峰会(Cancún Summit)*、*南北对话(North-South dialogue)*。

Brazilian unroasted coffee

巴西未焙炒咖啡案

1980年提交GATT的案件，争议点是同类产品的定义。巴西抱怨称，西班牙关税税则的变更意味着巴西未烘焙、未浸除咖啡碱咖啡的待遇低于"淡味咖啡"的待遇。这些咖啡类别根据国际咖啡组织使用的一种统计方法进行区分，将咖啡大致分为淡味阿拉比卡咖啡、未洗阿拉比卡咖啡和罗伯斯塔咖啡。巴西指称，西班牙违反了GATT第1条第1款(普遍最惠国待遇)，因其以歧视方式对待来自不同国家的同类产品。西班牙辩称，"未洗阿拉比卡咖啡"与"淡味咖啡"在质量、口味和栽培方法上都是不同的产品。专家组同意巴西的观点，接受不同种类咖啡的存在，但认为这些差异不足以允许不同的关税待遇。专家组还认为，未烘焙咖啡大多以混合形式销售，且"咖啡的最终用途被普遍认为是一种明确界定的单一饮品"。因此，专家组建议西班牙取消对巴西咖啡的歧视性待遇。

Bretton Woods agreements

布雷顿森林协定

联合国货币与金融会议于1944年在新罕布什尔州布雷顿森林举行，制定了世界银行(国际复兴开发银行)、国际货币基金组织(IMF)的章程。会议还提议设立国际贸易组织(ITO)，有关谈判单独举行，但最终以GATT的形式取得了雄心水平较低的成果。三个机构有时被称为布雷顿森林机构。另见*哈瓦那宪章(Havana Charter)*。

Brexit

英国脱欧

英国(全称为大不列颠及北爱尔兰联合王国)退出欧盟的简称。英国于1973年1月1日加入欧盟(当时的欧洲经济共同体)，未成为欧元区一部分。2016年6月23日，英国政府就该国是否应该留在欧盟进行了全民公决。投票结果是明确地、但并非压倒性地赞成脱欧。2017年3月29日，英国政府援引《欧洲联盟条约》第50条，该条允许欧盟成员国通过向欧洲理事会通报其意图而脱离欧盟。该条还规定，一旦拟脱离的成员国与欧盟之间的退出协定生效，成员资格即告终止，或者如未能达成协定，成员资格无论如何将在作出通报2年后终止。该条预见了延长谈判期限的可能性。一旦英国政府作出通报并启动谈判，很明显一点是2年时间不足够以令人满意的方式完成谈判。此外，2018年《退出欧盟法案》要求英国政府获得议会对谈判结果的批准，这是无法实现的。因此，

them satisfactorily. In addition, the *European Union (Withdrawal) Act 2018* required the UK Government to obtain parliamentary approval for the outcome. This it was unable to achieve. The negotiations were accordingly first extended to 31 October 2019 and again to 31 January 2020. In the face of continuing deadlock in parliament, the UK Government decided to call a general election on 12 December 2019. The election outcome removed any doubt over the way forward when a majority of candidates in favour of a speedy Brexit was returned. The United Kingdom accordingly left the European Union on 31 January 2020. A transition period applies between 1 February and 31 December 2020 during which existing trade rules are applied for trade between the two. A new agreement governing trade relations between the United Kingdom and the European Union is to be concluded by 31 December 2020.

Bribery: a form of ***corruption***, usually entailing some payment either in money or kind or a favour. It is defined, for example, in the OECD ***Convention on Combating Bribery of Foreign Public Officials in International Business Transactions*** as "the promise or giving of any undue payment or other advantages, whether directly or through intermediaries to a public official, for himself or for a third party, to influence the official to act or refrain from acting in the performance of his or her official duties in order to obtain or retain business". The practice of paying or receiving bribes is not, of course, confined to international business transactions.

Bribery in international transactions: *see* ***African Union Convention on Preventing and Combating Corruption***, ***Arusha Declaration***, ***Convention on Combating Bribery of Foreign Public Officials in International Business Transactions***, ***Draft International Agreement on Illicit Payments***, ***Recommendation for Further Combating Bribery of Foreign Public Officials in International Business Transactions***, ***trade and illicit payments***, and ***United Nations Convention Against Corruption***.

BRICS: Brazil, Russia, India, China and South Africa when they coordinate their activities in international fora and organizations, originally in the ***G20***. The ***New Development Bank***, operated by the BRICS members, became operational in 2016. *See also* ***Asian Infrastructure Investment Bank***.

Brigden Report: commissioned in 1927 by the Australian Government to report on the effects of the tariff on the economy. It was named after Professor J. B. Brigden of the University of Tasmania who headed the enquiry. The report, published in 1929, recommended moderate levels of protection and warned that protection levels at the time had probably reached their economic limit. In the long run, the influence of the report was much greater on approaches to the assessment of protection levels than the making of tariff policy. *See also* ***Australian argument for protection***.

Broadband services: communications services using still images, video, sound, text and data either separately or in combination. Broadband generally denotes the ability to communicate information at a high transmission rate. *See also* ***audiovisual services***.

谈判首次延长至2019年10月31日，后又延长至2020年1月31日。面对议会的持续僵局，英国政府决定于2019年12月12日举行大选。选举结果消除了对未来道路的任何怀疑，因为大多数候选人赞成迅速脱欧。因此，英国于2020年1月31日脱离欧盟。过渡期为2020年2月1日至12月31日，在此期间，现行贸易规则适用于双方之间的贸易。2020年12月31日之前需缔结一项管辖英国与欧盟贸易关系的新协定。

Bribery

贿赂

腐败的一种形式，通常包含付款，或货币或实物或好处。例如，经济合作与发展组织(OECD)《关于打击国际商业交易中行贿外国公职人员行为的公约》将其定义为："任何人，无论直接还是通过中间方，故意向一外国公职人员，为该官员或为一第三方提供、承诺或给予金钱或其他利益，以使该官员在履行公务方面作为或不作为，从而在从事国际商业过程中获得或保留商业或不当利益。"当然，行贿或受贿的做法并不限于国际商业交易。

Bribery in international transactions

国际交易中的行贿行为

见*非洲联盟预防和惩治腐败公约(African Union Convention on Preventing and Combating Corruption)*、*阿鲁沙宣言(Arusha Declaration)*、*关于打击国际商业交易中行贿外国公职人员行为的公约(Convention on Combating Bribery of Foreign Public Officials in International Business Transactions)*、*关于违法付款的国际协定草案(Draft International Agreement on Illicit Payments)*、*关于进一步打击国际商业交易中行贿外国公职人员行为的建议(Recommendation for Further Combating Bribery of Foreign Public Officials in International Business Transactions)*、*贸易与违法付款(trade and illicit payments)*、*联合国反腐败公约(United Nations Convention Against Corruption)*。

BRICS

金砖国家

巴西、俄罗斯、印度、中国和南非在国际论坛和组织中协调其活动时的名称，最初起源于20国集团。由金砖国家成员经营的新开发银行于2016年投入运行。另见*亚洲基础设施投资银行(Asian Infrastructure Investment Bank)*。

Brigden Report

布里格登报告

1927年受澳大利亚政府委托起草的关于关税对经济影响的报告。报告以此项调查牵头人、塔斯马尼亚大学J. B. 布里格登教授的名字命名。报告于1929年发表，建议保持适度保护水平，并警告当时的保护水平可能已经达到经济极限。从长远看，该报告对评估保护水平方式的影响远大于制定关税政策。另见*澳大利亚保护论(Australian argument for protection)*。

Broadband services

宽带服务

使用静态图像、视频、声音、文本和数据的通信服务，可以单独使用，也可以结合使用。宽带通常指高速传输信息的能力。另见*视听服务(audiovisual services)*。

Broader competition policy: *see* ***competition policy*** and ***wider competition policy***.

Brundtland Commission: *see* ***World Commission on Environment and Development***.

Brussels Convention: *see* ***Convention Relating to the Distribution of Programme-Carrying Signals Transmitted by Satellite***.

Brussels Definition of Value: BDV. A standard for valuing goods at the border to fix the ***customs duties*** to be paid. It was developed under the auspices of the Customs Cooperation Council, now the ***World Customs Organization***, located in Brussels. The BDV is the price goods would fetch on sale in the open market in the importing country at the time and in the place the import occurs. It sets out a number of considerations aimed at arriving at a decision on whether the actual sales price of the product corresponds with the notional standard of value. The BDV has now been superseded by the methods set out in the WTO *Agreement on Implementation of Article VII [customs valuation] of the General Agreement on Tariffs and Trade 1994*, the ***Customs Valuation Agreement***. *See also* **customs valuation**.

Brussels Ministerial Meeting: *see* ***Uruguay Round***.

Brussels Tariff Nomenclature: BTN. A product classification for use in a national tariff. Developed by the Customs Cooperation Council, now the ***World Customs Organization***, based in Brussels. This nomenclature was superseded on 1 January 1988 by the ***Harmonized Commodity Description and Coding System***.

BSE: bovine spongiform encephalopathy, or "mad cow disease".

BTA: *see* ***border tax adjustments***.

Budapest Treaty on the International Recognition of the Deposit of Micro-organisms for the Purposes of Patent Procedure: concluded on 28 April 1977. It aims to simplify patenting procedures for applicants whose invention involves a microorganism or the use of a microorganism not available to the public. In a growing number of countries, ***patent*** procedure not only requires the filing of a written description of the invention, but also a deposit, with a specialized institution, of a sample of the microorganism. This is complex and costly when it has to be repeated in several countries. Parties to this treaty agree that one deposit with any international depository authority is sufficient, regardless of the location of the authority. The Treaty is administered by ***WIPO***. *See also* **intellectual property**.

Buenos Aires Plan of Action for Promoting and Implementing Technical Co-operation among Developing Countries: BAPA. Adopted at the United Nations Conference on Technical Cooperation among Developing Countries in 1978. Its objectives are to (a) foster the self-reliance of developing countries, (b) promote and strengthen collective self-reliance among developing countries, (c) strengthen their capacity to identify and analyse the main issues of their development, (d) increase the quantum and enhance the quality of international cooperation, (e) strengthen existing technological capacities in developing countries, (f) increase and improve communications between them, (g) improve their capacity for the absorption and adaptation of technology and

Broader competition policy
广义竞争政策
见*竞争政策(competition policy)*、*广义竞争政策(wider competition policy)*。

Brundtland Commission
布伦特兰委员会
见*世界环境与发展委员会(World Commission on Environment and Development)*。

Brussels Convention
布鲁塞尔公约
见*关于播送人造卫星传输节目信号公约(Convention Relating to the Distribution of Programme-Carrying Signals Transmitted by Satellite)*。

Brussels Definition of Value
布鲁塞尔估价定义
BDV。在边境对货物进行估价以确定应缴关税的标准。在设在布鲁塞尔的海关合作理事会(现为世界海关组织)主持下制定。BDV 是在进口发生的时间和地点在进口国的公开市场上购买货物的价格。列出了多个考虑因素，旨在就产品的实际销售价格是否与名义价值标准相一致作出决定。现 BDV 已被《关于实施 1994 年关税与贸易总协定第 7 条的协定》(《海关估价协定》)中所列方法取代。另见*海关估价(customs valuation)*。

Brussels Ministerial Meeting
布鲁塞尔部长级会议
见*乌拉圭回合(Uruguay Round)*。

Brussels Tariff Nomenclature
布鲁塞尔税则
BTN。用于国别关税的产品分类方法。由设在布鲁塞尔的海关合作理事会制定，即现在的世界海关组织。税则于 1988 年 1 月 1 日被商品名称及编码协调制度所取代。

BSE
牛海绵状脑病
或称"疯牛病"。

BTA
边境税调节
见*边境税调节(border tax adjustments)*。

Budapest Treaty on the International Recognition of the Deposit of Microorganisms for the Purposes of Patent Procedure
国际承认用于专利程序的微生物保存布达佩斯条约
1977 年 4 月 28 日缔结。旨在简化申请人的专利申请程序，其发明涉及一种微生物或一种不为公众所知的微生物的使用。在越来越多的国家中，专利程序不仅要求提交关于发明的书面说明，而且还要求向专门机构交存微生物样本。如果必须在几个国家重复这种做法就会很复杂且费用高。条约缔约方同意，在任何国际保存单位交存一次即可满足要求，无论该保存单位位于何处。该条约由世界知识产权组织(WIPO)负责管理。另见*知识产权(intellectual property)*。

Buenos Aires Plan of Action for Promoting and Implementing Technical Co-operation among Developing Countries
促进和实施发展中国家间技术合作布宜诺斯艾利斯行动计划
BAPA。联合国发展中国家间技术合作会议于 1978 年通过。目标为：(a)促进发展中国家自力更生；(b)促进和加强发展中国家之间的集体自力更生；(c)加强它们确定和分析其发展主要问题的能力；(d)增加国际合作的数量并提高质

skill, (h) recognize and respond to the problems of the least developed, land-locked, island developing and most seriously affected countries, and (i) enable developing countries to attain a greater degree of participation in international economic activities. *See also* ***Second High-Level United Nations Conference on South–South Cooperation***.

Buenos Aires WTO Ministerial Conference: held in December 2017. Main outcomes at this Conference were a ministerial decision on ***fisheries subsidies***, a work programme on ***electronic commerce***, including an extension of the ***moratorium on customs duties on electronic transmissions*** until the 2020 Ministerial Conference, an extension of the ***moratorium on non-violation cases in intellectual property rights*** until the same Conference and a decision on a continuing ***Work Programme on Small Economies***. The Conference also resulted in declarations by groups of WTO members on ***joint initiatives*** related to trade-related aspects of electronic commerce, development of a multilateral framework on ***investment facilitation*** and the creation of an Informal Working Group on MSMEs (micro, small and medium-sized enterprises. *See also* ***WTO Ministerial Conference***.

Buffer stocks: holdings usually established under some ***international commodity agreements*** to influence and stabilize the price of ***commodities***. Buffer stocks are sold when the price moves above a defined price band. They are accumulated when the price moves below a band reflecting current market prices. Buffer stocks can work when price fluctuations are short-term, and when high prices more or less cancel out low prices within a reasonable period. The price range covered by the agreement normally is structured so that the buffer stock manager must buy when the price is in the lowest band, assuming funds are left to do so. Then follows a band in which the manager may buy. That decision is based on the commercial outlook, available funds, the size of the existing buffer stock, etc. At yet a higher price level, the manager may sell. Once the commodity price enters the highest price band set out in the agreement, the manager must sell, assuming that there are stocks. Buffer stocks are intended to be self-financing. The maximum size of the stock and the method of financing it are usually contentious. Proponents of such mechanisms hold that a large buffer stock operation compared to the size of the market and endowed with strong financial resources can much more easily deal with market fluctuations than a smaller one. A larger stock also would be much more expensive to run. In the case of secular changes to demand and supply, large buffer stocks may hinder production adjustments. Sometimes producers seek to cope with long-term low prices through increasing their production. If the buffer stock continues to buy, it gives producers the wrong signal since at this time producers should be encouraged to limit production. Continued buying could send the operation out of business. If the price band for triggering buffer stock purchases or sales is too wide, the effectiveness of international commodity agreement as a tool for market intervention is greatly diminished. On the whole the record of buffer stocks has been disappointing. Their successes have tended to be temporary. No international

量；(e)加强发展中国家中的现有技术能力；(f)增加和改善发展中国家之间的交流；(g)提高其吸收和适应技术和技能的能力；(h)认识并应对最不发达国家、发展中内陆国、小岛屿发展中国家和受影响最严重国家的问题；(i)促进发展中国家在更大程度上参与国际经济活动。另见*第二届联合国南南合作高级别会议(Second High-Level United Nations Conference on South–South Cooperation)*。

Buenos Aires WTO Ministerial Conference

WTO 布宜诺斯艾利斯部长级会议

2017 年 12 月举行。会议主要成果包括：关于渔业补贴的部长决定；关于电子商务的工作计划，包括将电子传输暂免关税延长至 2020 年部长决定；将知识产权非违反案件暂停起诉的期限延长至 2020 年的部长决定；关于继续实施小经济体工作计划的决定。会议还产生了部分 WTO 成员关于联合倡议的声明，内容涉及与贸易有关的电子商务、制定投资便利化的多边框架以及设立中小微企业非正式工作组。另见 *WTO 部长级会议(WTO Ministerial Conference)*。

Buffer stocks

缓冲储存

通常根据一些国际商品协定设定的持有数量，以影响和稳定商品的价格。当价格高于规定的价格区间时抛售缓冲储存。当价格低于反映当前市场价格区间时，累积缓冲储存。当价格波动是短期的，且高价或多或少在一合理期限内抵消低价时，缓冲储存可以发挥作用。协定所涵盖的价格区间通常是这样构成的，即缓冲储存经理在价格处于最低区间时必须收购，假设所留资金就是用于此目的。接下来是经理可以收购的区间。所作决定取决于商业前景、可用资金、现有缓冲储存规模等。在更高的价格水平上，经理可以抛售。一旦商品价格进入协定规定的最高价格区间，经理必须抛售，假设持有库存的话。缓冲储存设计为资金自筹。库存的最大规模和融资方法通常存在争议。支持此类机制的人认为，相对于市场规模，大型缓冲储存的运行和强大的财政资源要比小型缓冲储存更容易应对市场波动。较大库存的运行成本会更高。在需求和供应发生长期变化的情况下，大量的缓冲储存可能阻碍生产调整。有时生产者寻求通过提高其产量以应对长期的低价格。如果缓冲储存继续收购，就会给生产者一个错误的信号，因为此时是应该鼓励生产者限产。继续收购可能会导致运行停止。如果触发缓冲储存收购或抛售的价格区间过宽，国际商品协定作为市场干预工具的有效性就会大大降低。总体而言，缓冲储存的记录令人失望，奏效往往是暂时的。目前已经没有包含缓冲储存条款的任何国

commodity agreement with provisions for a buffer stock now exists. The ***IMF*** maintained until 2000 a Buffer Stock Financing Facility to assist the financing of member contributions to approved international buffer stocks. It had not been used since 1984. *See also* ***commodity policy***, ***Common Fund for Commodities*** and ***Integrated Programme for Commodities***.

Build-down method: one of the methods used in the administration of ***rules of origin*** to establish whether a good imported from another party to a ***free-trade agreement*** qualifies for the ***preferential tariff***. In the free-trade agreement between Singapore and the United States, and other free-trade agreements to which the United States is a party, the formula is:

$$RVC = \frac{AV - VNM}{AV} \times 100$$

where RVC is the ***regional value content***, expressed as a percentage, AV is the adjusted value, and VNM is the value of ***non-originating materials*** that are acquired and used by the producer in the production of the good. The term "adjusted value" is defined in some detail in the agreement. In essence it means that the following have to be excluded from the customs value of the goods under consideration: any costs, charges or expenses incurred for transport, insurance and related services as part of the international shipment of the good from the country of export to the country of import. This method is a variation of the ***FOB value method***.

Building-block approach: first, building blocks may be the elements ultimately making up a ***free-trade agreement***. Some easy elements, such as ***trade facilitation*** activities, might be tackled first as confidence-building measures. The more difficult trade-liberalizing provisions would come later. Second, ***free-trade areas*** are seen by some as the building blocks for a tariff-free ***multilateral trading system***. Individual areas could ultimately be combined to bring down trade barriers between ever larger areas. *See also* ***multilateralization of free-trade agreements*** and ***stumbling blocks***. [Bhagwati 1991]

Build-up method: one of the methods used in the administration of ***rules of origin*** to establish whether a good imported from another party to a ***free-trade agreement*** qualifies for the ***preferential tariff***. In the free-trade agreement between Singapore and the United States, and other free-trade agreements to which the United States is a party, the formula is:

$$RVC = \frac{VOM}{AV} \times 100$$

where RVC is the ***regional value content***, expressed as a percentage, AV is the adjusted value, and VOM is the value of ***originating materials*** that are acquired or self-produced, and used by the producer in the production of the good. The term "adjusted value" is defined in some detail in the agreement. In essence it means that the following have to be excluded from the customs value of

际商品协定存续。国际货币基金组织(IMF)在2000年之前曾一直保留着缓冲储存融资机制，以帮助成员为经批准的国际缓冲储存供资。该机制自1984年以来一直未使用。另见*商品政策(commodity policy)*、*商品共同基金(Common Fund for Commodities)*、*商品综合方案(Integrated Programme for Commodities)*。

Build-down method

扣减法

用于管理原产地规则的一种方法，以确定从自由贸易协定的另一方进口的货物是否有资格享受优惠关税。在新加坡与美国的自由贸易协定以及美国为参加方的其他自由贸易协定中，公式为：

$$RVC = \frac{AV - VNM}{AV} \times 100$$

其中 RVC 为区域价值成分，以百分比表示，AV 为调整价格，VNM 为生产者在货物生产时获得和使用的非原产材料价格。“调整价格”一词在协定中有详细定义。实质上意味着以下内容需要从考虑中的货物完税价格中排除：运输、保险以及作为货物自出口国至进口国国际航运一部分的相关服务所产生的任何成本、费用或支出。此种方法是离岸价格法的变种。

Building-block approach

积木法

首先，“积木”可能会成为最终形成自由贸易协定的要素。一些容易的要素，如贸易便利化活动，会首先加以解决以作为建立信任的措施。较为困难的贸易自由化条款会稍后处理。其次，自由贸易区被视为构建零关税多边贸易体制的“积木”。单个地区可以最终合在一起以消除与更大地区之间的贸易壁垒。另见*自由贸易协定多边化(multilateralization of free-trade agreements)*、*绊脚石(stumbling blocks)*。

Build-up method

增值法

用于管理原产地规则的一种方法，以确定从自由贸易协定的另一方进口的货物是否有资格享受优惠关税。在新加坡与美国的自由贸易协定以及美国为参加方的其他自由贸易协定中，公式为：

$$RVC = \frac{VOM}{AV} \times 100$$

其中 RVC 是区域价值成分，以百分比表示，AV 为调整价格，VOM 为生产者在货物生产时所使用的获得或自产的原产材料价格。“调整价格”一词在协定中有详细定义。实质上意味着以下内容需要从所考虑的货物完税价格中排除：

the goods under consideration: any costs, charges or expenses incurred for transport, insurance and related services as part of the international shipment of the good from the country of export to the country of import.

Built-in agenda: BIA. The extensive WTO work programme resulting from the provisions contained in the instruments negotiated during the ***Uruguay Round***. The BIA authorized or mandated new negotiations. These later became part of the ***Doha Development Agenda***.

Bunching of tariffs: the practice of carrying out tariff reduction or elimination commitments in batches, often as close as possible to a deadline.

Burden of proof: the obligation of a plaintiff or a defendant to show that an alleged action has or has not occurred, as the case may be. The established procedure in the WTO for approaching burden of proof is described in *EC – Hormones (US) (Article 22.6 – EC)*. It states that "WTO members, as sovereign entities, can be *presumed* to act in conformity with their WTO obligations. A party claiming that a Member has acted *inconsistently* with WTO rules bears the burden of proving that inconsistency" [italics in the original]. The situation changes once the complainant has made a ***prima facie case*** or shown that an inconsistency has occurred. It is then up to the defendant to show that this is not the case. If the evidence were to show that claim and counterclaim are evenly balanced, the plaintiff would lose the case. [WT/DS26/ARB]

Burden-sharing: the idea that the cost of new trade measures should be borne by the widest possible group of affected countries. Some also use the term when they erroneously *see* ***trade liberalization*** as a cost to economies doing so. Burden-sharing is not the same as ***reciprocity***, which demands roughly equivalent action from others. *See also* ***balance of advantages***.

Busan Roadmap to the Bogor Goals: a component of the statement issued by the 2005 ***APEC Economic Leaders' Meeting***. The roadmap among other things stresses APEC support for the multilateral trading system, the promotion of high-quality ***free-trade agreements*** and the key role of business in the trading environment.

Business mobility: the ability of people to travel across borders to promote and undertake business activities. In the ***GATS*** this is known as the ***movement of natural persons***. In a wider sense it also refers to the ability of natural and ***juridical persons*** to establish businesses in other countries and to manage them. This is covered by the GATS under ***commercial presence***. Many ***free-trade agreements*** have chapters covering business mobility to support the cross-border supply of services and investment chapters.

Business process outsourcing: BPO. *See* ***outsourcing***.

But for test: a method adopted, for example, by the WTO ***panel*** in *Canada – measures affecting the export of civil aircraft* to establish whether a link existed between a governmental grant "to the Canadian regional aircraft industry and anticipated exportation or export earnings". The test in this case asks whether assistance would not have been given *but for* anticipated exportation or earnings. The panel found that assistance to the Canadian regional aircraft industry

即运输、保险以及作为货物自出口国至进口国国际航运一部分的相关服务所产生的任何成本、费用或支出。

Built-in agenda

既定议程

BIA。乌拉圭回合中谈判达成的法律文件中所含条款产生的内容广泛的 WTO 工作计划。BIA 批准或授权开展新的谈判。后来成为多哈发展议程的一部分。

Bunching of tariffs

批量调整关税

分批履行削减或取消关税承诺的做法，通常在尽可能接近最后期限时进行。

Burden of proof

举证责任

原告或被告证明所指控的行为发生或未发生(视情况而定)的义务。WTO中关于处理举证责任的既定程序在“美国诉欧共体荷尔蒙案”中有所描述。指出，“WTO成员作为主权实体，可以被推定为以符合其WTO义务的方法行事。声称一成员未以符合WTO规则的方式行事的一方承担证明此种不符性的责任。”一旦原告提出初步证据或证明发生了不符行为，情况即产生变化，因此则需要被告证明情况并非如此。如果证据表明诉求和反诉势均力敌，原告即败诉。

Burden-sharing

责任分担

认为新贸易措施的代价应由尽可能多的受影响国承担的观点。一些人在错误地将贸易自由化视为对经济的代价时也使用该词。责任分担与互惠不同，后者要求其他国家采取大致相同的行动。另见*利益平衡(balance of advantages)*。

Busan Roadmap to the Bogor Goals

茂物目标釜山路线图

2005 年 APEC 经济领导人会议发表声明的组成部分。该路线图中强调 APEC 对多边贸易体制的支持，促进高质量自由贸易协定，以及企业在贸易环境中的关键作用。

Business mobility

商业流动性

人们跨越边境流动促进和开展商业活动的能力。在《服务贸易总协定》(GATS)中，被称为自然人流动。在更广泛的意义上，也指自然人和企业法人在其他国家设立和管理企业的能力。此点为《服务贸易总协定》中的商业存在所涵盖。许多自由贸易协定设有涵盖商业流动性的章节，以支持跨境提供服务和投资章节。

Business process outsourcing

业务流程外包

BPO。见*外包(outsourcing)*。

But for test

若非测试

WTO“加拿大影响民用航空器出口措施案”专家组中采用的一种方法，以确定“对加拿大支线航空器产业的政府赠款与预期出口或出口收入”之间是否存在关联。本案的检验标准为，如果不是为了预期出口或收入，是否不会给予援

constituted ***export subsidies*** inconsistent with the ***Agreement on Subsidies and Countervailing Measures***.

Butter mountain: the name given in common parlance to the dairy product surpluses caused by the ***common agricultural policy*** of the ***European Community***. *See also* ***wine lake***.

Buy American Act: a United States act passed in 1933 and amended significantly in 1979 by the Trade Agreements Act to ensure (a) that only unmanufactured and manufactured articles, materials and supplies produced in the United States would be bought for public use and (b) that in the case of construction of public buildings and public works only articles, materials and supplies produced in the United States would be used at all construction stages. The Act does not apply to goods used outside the United States or not produced domestically. There are some other exceptions, including one where the public interest would demand otherwise or where the cost would be unreasonable if American materials were used. Members of the WTO ***Agreement on Government Procurement*** are exempt from significant aspects this Act. Many of the American states have their own Buy American law. *See also* ***buy-local policies***.

Buy-local policies: a way of giving advantages to domestic producers of goods and services under the ***government procurement*** rules of some countries. Such policies are often expressed in terms of a preference margin favouring the homegrown product, but sometimes they may be limited to a decision to purchase locally if all other things are equal. Buy-local policies at times are used to promote the development of domestic industries.

Buy-Ship-Pay Model: developed by ***UN/CEFACT*** to explain the steps involved in ***trade facilitation***. The model identifies the key commercial, logistical, regulatory and payment procedures involved in the international supply chain. It also provides an overview of the information exchanged between the parties. [tfig.unece.org]

Byrd Amendment: the *Continued Dumping and Subsidy Offset Act* passed by the United States Congress in October 2000 and repealed effective 1 October 2007. Named after Senator Robert Byrd who proposed it as an amendment to an appropriation bill for agriculture. The Act sought to ensure that proceeds from anti-dumping and countervailing duty cases were paid to the United States companies that initiated the cases. Companies receiving such payments could use them for items such as plant modernization and pension expenditures.

助。专家组认为，对加拿大支线航空器产业的援助构成了与《补贴与反补贴措施协定》不符的出口补贴。

Butter mountain

黄油山

对欧洲共同体共同农业政策所导致的奶制品过剩的俗称。另见*葡萄酒湖(wine lake)*。

Buy American Act

购买美国货法

1933年通过的一项美国法，后经《1979年贸易协定法》进行重大修订，以保证(a)仅购买在美国生产的未制成品和制成品、材料和物品用于公共用途；及(b)在建造公共建筑和公共工程时，在所有施工阶段仅使用在美国生产的物品、材料和供应品。该法不适用于在美国境外使用的或不在国内生产的货物。还有一些其他的例外情况，包括公共利益的要求，或如果使用美国材料则成本不合理等。WTO《政府采购协定》参加方在很多方面例外于该法。美国许多州有自己的购买美国货法。另见*购买当地产品政策(buy-local policies)*。

Buy-local policies

购买当地产品政策

根据一些国家的政府采购规定，给予本国货物和服务生产商利益的一种方式。此类政策往往表现为有利于本土产品的优惠幅度，但有时可能仅限于在所有其他条件均相同的情况下作出在当地购买的决定。购买当地产品政策有时被用来促进本国产业发展。

Buy-Ship-Pay Model

购买-运输-支付模型

由联合国贸易便利化与电子商务中心(UN/CEFACT)开发，用于解释贸易便利化所涉及的步骤。该模型确定了国际供应链中涉及的关键商业、物流、监管和支付程序。还概述了各方之间的信息交流。

Byrd Amendment

伯德修正案

美国国会2000年10月通过的《持续倾销与补贴抵消法》，2007年10月1日废除。该法以提议将其作为农业拨款法案修正案的参议员罗伯特·伯德的名字命名。该法旨在保证反倾销税和反补贴税案的收益应支付给发起案件的美国公司。收到此类款项的公司可以将其用于厂房现代化和养老金支出等。

C

Cabotage: reserving the provision of shipping or air services between domestic ports and airports, respectively, in most countries, to ships or aircraft owned and registered locally. Their crews must be hired under local employment conditions. In the United States ships providing cabotage services must also be built in domestic shipyards. *See also* ***freedoms of the air*** and ***Jones Act***.

Cadmium regulation: a ***regulation*** of the ***European Union*** which entered into force on 1 January 2019. It sets maximum levels of cadmium that may be present in vegetables, grains, cocoa and chocolate products, various types of meat, crustaceans, infant formulae, food supplements, etc., placed on European Union markets. [Regulation (EU) No 488/2014]

CAFTA: *see* ***United States–Central American Free Trade Agreement***.

Cairns Group: a group of agricultural exporting nations lobbying for agricultural trade liberalization. It was formed in 1986 at a Ministerial Meeting in Cairns, Australia, just before the start of the ***Uruguay Round***. Current members are Argentina, Australia, Brazil, Canada, Chile, Colombia, Costa Rica, Guatemala, Indonesia, Malaysia, New Zealand, Pakistan, Paraguay, Peru, Philippines, South Africa, Thailand, Uruguay and Viet Nam. *See also* ***Agreement on Agriculture*** and ***agriculture and the multilateral trading system***.

Calvo doctrine: a doctrine at one time prevalent in Latin American legal systems. It holds that foreign nationals, and particularly foreign investors, are not entitled to seek protection from their governments in excess of that available to nationals of host countries. In other words, it rejects any suggestion of privileged treatment for foreign investors. The doctrine in effect prevented countries adhering to it from concluding treaties for the protection of investment, and it therefore was seen as having a direct influence on investment flows. It is named after Dr Carlos Calvo, an Argentinian lawyer and diplomat, who enunciated it in 1885.

Canada – Measures affecting exports of unprocessed herring and salmon: *see* ***Herring and salmon***.

Canada–United States Automotive Products Agreement: entered into force in 1966. It permitted some motor vehicle manufacturers to bring vehicles, parts and accessories into Canada from the United States free of import duties. Some ***performance requirements*** had to be met by companies participating in the scheme. The last time new applicants were given permission to participate in the scheme was on 31 July 1989. The Agreement became an irritant especially for Japanese car manufacturers who had begun operations in the United States

C

Cabotage

国内交通运输权

大多数国家中将在国内港口和机场之间提供航运服务和空运服务仅限于本地拥有或注册的船只或航空器。船员必须按照当地雇佣条件雇佣。在美国，提供国内交通运输服务的船只必须在国内船厂制造。另见*航空自由(freedom of the air)*、*琼斯法案(Jones Act)*。

Cadmium regulation

镉条例

2019 年 1 月 1 日生效的欧盟条例。规定了欧盟市场上蔬菜、谷物、可可和巧克力制品、各种肉类、甲壳类动物、婴儿配方奶粉以及食品添加剂中镉的最高含量。

CAFTA

中美洲自由贸易区

见*美国—中美洲自由贸易协定(United States–Central American Free Trade Agreement)*。

Cairns Group

凯恩斯集团

指游说农产品贸易自由化的农产品出口国集团。在乌拉圭回合开始前，1986 年在澳大利亚凯恩斯举行的一次部长级会议上成立该集团。现任成员为阿根廷、澳大利亚、巴西、加拿大、智利、哥伦比亚、哥斯达黎加、危地马拉、印度尼西亚、马来西亚、新西兰、巴基斯坦、巴拉圭、秘鲁、菲律宾、南非、泰国、乌拉圭和越南。另见*农业协定(Agreement on Agriculture)*、*农业与多边贸易体制(agriculture and the multilateral trading system)*。

Calvo doctrine

卡尔沃主义

曾在拉丁美洲法律体系中盛行一时的理论。认为，外国国民，特别是外国投资者，无权寻求其政府提供超过东道国国民可获得的保护水平。换言之，拒绝任何给予外国投资者特权待遇的建议。这一理论实际上阻止了遵守该理论的国家缔结投资保护条约，因此被视为对投资流动有直接影响。以阿根廷律师和外交官卡洛斯·卡尔沃博士的名字命名，卡于 1885 年阐述了该理论。

Canada – Measures affecting exports of unprocessed herring and salmon

加拿大-影响未加工鲱鱼和鲑鱼出口措施案

见*鲱鱼和鲑鱼案(Herring and salmon)*。

Canada–United States Automotive Products Agreement

加拿大—美国汽车产品协定

协定于1966年生效，允许一些汽车制造商自美国向加拿大输入车辆、零件和配件时免征进口关税。参与该方案的公司必须符合一定的实绩要求。最近一

in the 1980s. In 2000 a WTO ***panel*** ruled that certain elements of the agreement violated Canada's WTO obligations. It was abolished in 2001. *See also* ***United States–Mexico–Canada Agreement*** and ***USMCA rules of origin for automotive products***.

Canada–United States Free Trade Agreement: CUSFTA or CUSTA. Concluded on 2 January 1988. This Agreement was superseded by ***NAFTA***.

Canadian periodicals: a WTO case brought by the United States against Canada in 1996. Canada had maintained measures designed to prohibit the import of certain editions of foreign periodicals or to favour domestic periodicals through lower ***excise duties*** and postal rates. An important element of these measures was the aim of protecting Canadian ***cultural identity***. In June 1997 the ***panel*** found against Canada on most counts, especially in relation to its obligations under GATT Article III (National Treatment) and Article XI (General Elimination of Quantitative Restrictions). This case is relevant to any work on ***trade and culture***.

Cancún Ministerial Conference: the fifth ***WTO Ministerial Conference*** held at Cancún, Mexico, from 10 to 14 September 2003.

Cancún Summit: a meeting of 22 heads of state and heads of government held at Cancún, Mexico, in 1981. It aimed to find a way to restart the stalled ***North–South dialogue***. It was organized in the favourable climate created by the first ***Brandt Report***, issued in 1980. Although the meeting ended in an apparent consensus, it turned out to be a failure in bringing about its stated objective. Like all other North–South initiatives, it was not able to overcome the competing views of the main participants concerning the best way to implement any proposed measures.

Candidate countries: a name for countries that have applied to join the ***European Union***. *See also* ***Copenhagen criteria*** and ***enlargement***.

CAP: the ***common agricultural policy*** of the ***European Union***.

Capacity-building: support mainly for developing countries to improve their ability to implement and observe their international treaty obligations. The ***WTO***, ***UNCTAD***, the ***World Bank***, ***OECD***, ***APEC*** and other multilateral organizations have a range of programmes aimed at ensuring that developing countries can participate as fully as possible in international trade. Many countries and non-governmental organizations offer similar programmes. They range from short workshops to explain, for example, a new policy to long-term programmes aimed at changing an entire system. Providing good technical assistance is not an easy task. Various methods and principles have been devised to make capacity-building more effective. The OECD ***Development Assistance Committee***, for example, has adopted the following principles: (a) coordinate trade capacity-building efforts among donors, both bilateral and multilateral, (b) ensure that trade capacity-building activities are comprehensive in scope and integrated in execution by going, for example, beyond trade ministries, (c) foster local ownership and participation in trade-related development cooperation activities, (d) devise and embrace approaches that will

次加入该方案的申请获得批准是在1989年7月31日。协定特别对日本汽车制造商产生了刺激，他们19世纪80年代开始在美国经营。2000年，WTO专家组裁定，协定某些内容违反了加拿大的WTO义务。协定于2001年废止。另见*美国—墨西哥—加拿大协定(United–States–Mexico–Canada Agreement)*、*USMCA汽车产品原产地规则(USMCA rules of origin for automotive products)*。

Canada–United States Free Trade Agreement
加拿大—美国自由贸易协定

CUSFTA或CUSTA。1988年1月2日签署，被《北美自由贸易协定》(NAFTA)所取代。

Canadian periodicals
加拿大期刊案

美国于1996年对加拿大提起的WTO案件。加拿大维持旨在禁止进口某些版次的外国期刊或通过较低消费税和邮费以支持国内期刊的措施。这些措施的一个重要要素是为了保护加拿大的文化特性。1997年6月，专家组认为加拿大在大多数方面站不住脚，特别是在GATT第3条(国民待遇)和第11条(普遍取消数量限制)的义务方面。该案与关于贸易与文化的工作相关。

Cancún Ministerial Conference
坎昆部长级会议

2003年9月10日至14日在墨西哥坎昆举行的第5届WTO部长级会议。

Cancún Summit
坎昆峰会

1981年在墨西哥坎昆举行的22位国家元首和政府首脑会议。会议旨在为停滞的南北对话寻找重启途径。会议是在1980年发表的第一份《勃兰特报告》所营造的有利氛围中召开的。尽管会议最后达成了明确的共识，但是在实现其所声明的目标方面却失败了。与所有其他南北倡议一样，会议未能克服主要参与方对实施任何拟议措施最佳方式的相互对立观点。

Candidate countries
候选国

对已经申请加入欧盟的国家的称谓。另见*哥本哈根标准(Copenhagen criteria)*、*扩盟(enlargement)*。

CAP
共同农业政策

欧盟共同农业政策。

Capacity-building
能力建设

主要给予发展中国家的支持，以提高它们实施和遵守国际公约义务的能力。WTO、联合国贸易与发展会议(UNCTAD)、世界银行、经济合作与发展组织(OECD)、APEC及其他多边组织有一系列的计划，旨在保证发展中国家能够尽可能充分参与国际贸易。许多国家和非政府组织提供类似计划。范围从解释一项新政策的短期讲习班到旨在改变整个系统的长期计划。提供良好的技术援助并非易事。为使能力建设更加有效，开发了多种方法和原则。例如，OECD发展援助委员会采取了以下原则：(a)协调双边和多边捐助者之间的贸易能力建设努力；(b)保证贸易能力建设活动范围全面，执行统一，例如将范围超越贸易部门；(c)在与贸易有关的发展合作活动中形成当地所有权和参与；(d)设计和接受能够加强可持续性的方式；(e)通过计划和经验信息的系统交流，增强捐助方自身与贸易有关的能力；以及(f)对发展中国家中的贸易政策框架建设努力投入更多财力和人力资源，并有望获得实质回报。另见*WTO法律*

strengthen sustainability, (e) strengthen donors' own trade-related capacities through a systematic exchange of information on programmes and experiences, and (f) commit greater financial and personnel resources to efforts to build trade policy frameworks in developing countries – with the prospect of substantial returns. *See also* ***Advisory Centre on WTO Law***, ***Aid for Trade Facilitation Interactive Database***, ***Aid for Trade Initiative***, ***Aid for Trade Monitoring Framework***, ***APEC Economic and Technical Cooperation***, ***Doha Development Agenda Global Trust Fund***, ***Enhanced Integrated Framework***, ***Hub and Spokes Programme***, ***implementation***, ***International Trade Centre***, ***New Partnership for Africa's Development***, ***Programme of Action for the Least-Developed Countries for the Decade 2011–2020***, ***Standards and Trade Development Facility***, ***Trade Policy Framework Review*** and ***UNCTAD Virtual Institute on Trade and Development***.

Carbon tariff: a tax in the form of a ***tariff*** on goods that produce a high level of carbon-dioxide in their manufacture. Sometimes also called green tariff.

CAREC 2030 Strategic Framework: *see* ***Central Asia Regional Economic Cooperation***.

Caribbean Basin Initiative: CBI. A United States initiative to facilitate the development of a stable Caribbean Basin economy by providing beneficiary countries with duty-free access for goods to the United States. It began on 1 January 1984 with the Caribbean Basin Recovery Act (CBERA). This has no expiration date. CBI was expanded in 2000 by the Caribbean Basin Trade Partnership Act (CBTPA) which is scheduled to expire on 30 September 2025. Coverage under the two acts is not the same. CBERA beneficiaries are Antigua and Barbuda, Aruba, Bahamas, Barbados, Belize, British Virgin Islands, Curaçao, Dominica, Grenada, Guyana, Haiti, Jamaica, Montserrat, Saint Kitts and Nevis, Saint Lucia, Saint Vincent and the Grenadines, and Trinidad and Tobago. CBTPA beneficiaries are Barbados, Belize, Curaçao, Guyana, Haiti, Jamaica, Saint Lucia, and Trinidad and Tobago.

Caribbean Common Market: Consists of all the members of ***Caribbean Community and Common Market*** except The Bahamas.

Caribbean Community and Common Market: CARICOM. Established on 1 August 1973 through the Treaty of Chaguaramas as the successor to the Caribbean Free Trade Association (CARIFTA). The Caribbean Common Market has now been superseded by the ***CARICOM Single Market and Economy***. Its secretariat is located at Georgetown, Guyana.

Caribbean Free Trade Association: *see* ***Caribbean Common Market***.

CARICOM: *see* ***Caribbean Community and Common Market***.

CARICOM Single Market and Economy: CSME. Formed through the *Revised Treaty of Chaguaramas Establishing the Caribbean Community Including the CARICOM Single Market and Economy*, signed at Nassau, Bahamas, on 5 July 2001 by Antigua and Barbuda, The Bahamas, Barbados, Belize, Dominica, Grenada, Guyana, Haiti, Jamaica, Montserrat, Saint Kitts and Nevis, Saint Lucia, Saint Vincent and the Grenadines, Suriname, and Trinidad and Tobago.

咨询中心(Advisory Centre on WTO Law)、*贸易便利化援助互动数据库(Aid for Trade Facilitation Interactive Database)*、*促贸援助倡议(Aid for Trade Initiative)*、*促贸援助监督框架(Aid for Trade Monitoring Framework)*、*APEC 经济技术合作(APEC Economic and Technical Cooperation)*、*多哈发展议程全球信托基金(Doha Development Agenda Global Trust Fund)*、*增强综合框架(Enhanced Integrated Framework)*、*轮轴-辐条计划(Hub and Spokes Programme)*、*实施(implementation)*、*国际贸易中心(International Trade Centre)*、*非洲发展新伙伴关系计划(New Partnership for Africa's Development)*、*2011—2020 年十年期支援最不发达国家行动纲领(Programme of Action for the Least-Developed Countries for the Decade 2011–2020)*、*标准和贸易发展基金(Standards and Trade Development Facility)*、*贸易政策框架审议(Trade Policy Framework Review)*、*UNCTAD 贸易与发展虚拟学院(UNCTAD Virtual Institute on Trade and Development)*。

Carbon tariff
碳关税

对制造过程中产生高水平二氧化碳的货物以关税形式征收的一种税。有时也称为绿色关税。

CAREC 2030 Strategic Framework
CAREC 2030 战略框架

见*中亚区域经济合作组织(Central Asia Regional Economic Cooperation)*。

Caribbean Basin Initiative
加勒比盆地倡议

CBI。美国一项倡议，旨在通过向受益国提供货物进入美国的免关税待遇，促进加勒比盆地经济的稳定发展。始于 1984 年 1 月 1 日的《加勒比盆地经济复苏法》(CBERA)，无失效日期。2000 年，《加勒比盆地贸易伙伴关系法》(CBTPA)扩大了 CBI 的范围，该法定于 2025 年 9 月 30 日失效。两法涵盖范围不同。CBERA 的受益国为安提瓜和巴布达、阿鲁巴、巴哈马、巴巴多斯、伯利兹、英属维尔京群岛、库拉索岛、多米尼加、格林纳达、圭亚那、海地、牙买加、蒙特塞拉特、圣基茨和尼维斯、圣卢西亚、圣文森特和格林纳丁斯以及特立尼达和多巴哥。CBTPA 的受益国为巴巴多斯、伯利兹、库拉索岛、圭亚那、海地、牙买加、圣卢西亚以及特立尼达和多巴哥。

Caribbean Common Market
加勒比共同市场

由除巴哈马外的所有加勒比共同体和共同市场成员组成。

Caribbean Community and Common Market
加勒比共同体和共同市场

CARICOM。1973 年 8 月 1 日通过签署《查瓜拉马斯条约》建立，是加勒比自由贸易协会(CARIFTA)的后继组织。加勒比共同市场现已被加勒比共同体单一市场和经济所取代。秘书处设在圭亚那乔治敦。

Caribbean Free Trade Association
加勒比自由贸易协会

见*加勒比共同市场(Caribbean Common Market)*。

CARICOM
加勒比共同体

见*加勒比共同体和共同市场(Caribbean Community and Common Market)*。

CARICOM Single Market and Economy
加勒比共同体单一市场和经济

CSME。通过 2001 年 7 月 5 日在巴哈马拿骚签署经修订的《关于建立包括加勒比共同体单一市场和经济在内加勒比共同体的查瓜拉马斯条约》建立，成

Associate members are Anguilla, Bermuda, British Virgin Islands, Cayman Islands, and Turks and Caicos Islands. The CSME succeeded the Caribbean Community and CARICOM. The CSME permits the free movement of goods, services, capital and people among its members. The Single Market became effective on 1 January 2006, and it is expected to lead to a common economic space. Its headquarters are in Georgetown, Guyana.

Carousel effect: used to describe some attempts to escape the effects of anti-dumping or ***safeguards***. Some say that manufacturers or exporters will change periodically the make-up of a product subject to these measures to evade ***retaliation***.

Carousel legislation: refers to Section 407 of the United States *Trade and Development Act* adopted on 18 May 2000 to encourage implementation by trading partners of the United States of WTO ***dispute settlement*** decisions that have gone against them. In such cases, the WTO rules permit the ***suspension of concessions or other obligations***, though the procedures for doing so are carefully defined. A list of products is usually prepared and maintained for this purpose. The United States has a different approach. The carousel legislation requires a mandatory and unilateral revision of this list of products 120 days after the application of the first suspension and then every 180 days after that. Many trading partners consider that doing so would go beyond the intentions of the ***Dispute Settlement Understanding***. This provision was suspended in 2009 without having been used.

Carry forward: under the ***Agreement on Textiles and Clothing***, now expired, the use in the current year of part of next year's textiles and clothing export quota. *See also* ***flexibility provisions***.

Carry over: under the ***Agreement on Textiles and Clothing***, now expired, the use in the current year of unused textiles and clothing export quota from the previous year. *See also* ***flexibility provisions***.

Cartagena Agreement: Agreement on Andean Subregional Integration. *See* ***Andean Community***.

Cartagena Protocol on Biosafety: a protocol to the ***Convention on Biological Diversity***, adopted 29 January 2000. The protocol seeks to protect biological diversity from the potential risks posed by living modified organisms resulting from modern biotechnology. It establishes a procedure for ***advance informed consent*** and it refers to the ***precautionary principle*** (principle 15 of the ***Rio Declaration on Environment and Development***). *See also* ***multilateral environment agreements***.

Cartel: a formal or informal agreement between firms to manage domestic or international markets by lessening competition between the firms. Methods include agreement not to compete on price, limitations on the total output by the members to the agreement, market-sharing arrangements, etc. To what extent such activities are legal depends on a country's ***competition policy***. Cartel arrangements work best when few firms dominate an activity. Agreements are divided into public and private cartels. A public cartel is one where

员包括安提瓜和巴布达、巴哈马、巴巴多斯、伯利兹、多米尼克、格林纳达、圭亚那、海地、牙买加、蒙特塞拉特、圣基茨和尼维斯、圣卢西亚、圣文森特和格林纳丁斯、苏里南以及特立尼达和多巴哥。联系成员有安圭拉、百慕大、英属维尔京群岛、开曼群岛、特克斯和凯科斯群岛。CSME 继承了加勒比共同体和 CARICOM。CSME 允许货物、服务、资本和人员在其成员之间自由流动。单一市场于 2006 年 1 月 1 日生效，预计将形成一个共同的经济空间。总部设在圭亚那乔治敦。

Carousel effect
旋转木马效应

用于描述逃避反倾销或保障措施影响的企图。有些人认为，制造商或出口商会定期改变受这些措施影响的产品的加价以逃避报复。

Carousel legislation
旋转木马立法

指 2000 年 5 月 18 日通过的《美国贸易与发展法》第 407 节，鼓励美国的贸易伙伴执行对它们不利的 WTO 争端解决裁决。在此种情况下，WTO 规则允许中止减让或其他义务，尽管这样作的程序是仔细界定的。通常为此目的制定和保留一份产品清单。美国的方式则不同。旋转木马立法要求在实施第 1 次中止后的 120 天内对该清单产品进行强制性单边修改，此后每 180 天修改一次。许多贸易伙伴认为，这样作会超出《争端解决谅解》的意图。这一规定在 2009 年中止未再使用。

Carry forward
借用

根据《纺织品与服装协定》(现已终止)，当年使用下一年度纺织品和服装出口配额。另见*灵活性条款(flexibility provisions)*。

Carry over
留用

根据《纺织品与服装协定》(现已终止)，当年使用上一年度未使用的纺织品和服装出口配额。另见*灵活性条款(flexibility provisions)*。

Cartagena Agreement
卡塔赫纳协定

《安第斯次区域一体化协定》。另见*安第斯共同体(Andean Community)*。

Cartagena Protocol on Biosafety
卡塔赫纳生物安全议定书

《生物多样性公约》的议定书之一，2000 年 1 月 29 日通过。议定书寻求保护生物多样性免受现代生物技术产生的改性活生物体所带来的潜在风险。针对预先知情同意制定了程序，并提及了预防原则(《环境与发展里约宣言》第 15 条原则)。另见*多边环境协定(multilateral environment agreements)*。

Cartel
卡特尔

企业之间达成的正式或非正式协议，以缓和企业之间的竞争，管理国内或国际市场。方法包括同意不进行价格竞争、限制协议参加方的总产量、市场分配安排等。此类活动在多大程度属合法性质取决于一国的竞争政策。卡特尔安排在少数企业控制一项活动时效果最好。协议分为公共卡特尔和私人卡特尔。

the government forms and administers the rules for its own reasons. This may include acceptance of export cartels aimed at strengthening the competitiveness of domestic firms. An example of such rules is the United States ***Webb-Pomerene Act***. *Pure export cartels*, directed exclusively at foreign markets, enjoy considerable freedom from the application of ***competition laws***. *Mixed export cartels* affect domestic and export markets. Import cartels are much rarer. In many cases competition authorities do not approve their formation or operation. Public cartels might also be permitted to promote ***structural adjustment***. Private cartels, or arrangements between firms, are usually kept secret, particularly if they are against the law or if they would lead to higher prices for consumers. *See also* ***antitrust laws***, ***rule of reason*** and ***trade and competition***.

Carve-out: an agreement among participants in negotiations to exempt for the time being a set of measures or a defined economic activity from the application of new or proposed trade rules. An example of a carve-out is the exemption from the ***General Agreement on Trade in Services*** rules of ***bilateral aviation rights***.

Cascading tariffs: sometimes used instead of ***tariff escalation***. It describes the practice of setting low tariffs on relatively simple components of a final product and to increase tariffs as the degree of processing increases. The aim is to add as much value as possible domestically.

Cassis de Dijon* case:** *see* ***mutual recognition arrangements.

Causality: the existence of a causal link between increased imports and serious ***injury*** or the ***threat of serious injury*** to domestic industry producing like or directly competitive products which can be used to impose ***safeguards***. Likewise, members imposing ***anti-dumping measures*** must show that the harm to industry has been caused by ***dumping*** and not some other reason. *See also* ***like product***.

Causal linkage: *see* ***causality***.

CBD: *see* ***Convention on Biological Diversity***.

CEFTA 2006: the free-trade agreement replacing the ***South-East Europe Free Trade Area*** (SEEFTA) from 1 January 2007. Its members are Albania, Bosnia-Herzegovina, Kosovo, Moldova, Montenegro, North Macedonia and Serbia. *See also* ***Stabilization and Association Agreements***.

Ceiling bindings: the practice in the WTO of binding all, or large sections, of a tariff at a specified level, often with a comfortable cushion above the ***applied tariff rates***. Bindings are normally the result of negotiations. Countries that undertake to bind their tariffs are under a legal obligation not to increase these bound levels, but ceiling bindings allow them to make many desired increases up to the level of the ceiling. *See also* ***binding*** and ***peak tariffs***.

Ceiling duties: refers in most cases to the highest possible tariff rate in a national ***tariff schedule***. Often these are the same as ***ceiling bindings***.

Central African Customs and Economic Union: often referred to as UDEAC (Union douanière et économique de l'Afrique centrale). Established in 1964 with the ultimate aim of turning into a ***common market***. Its members were Cameroon, Central African Republic, Chad, Congo, Equatorial Guinea

公共卡特尔由政府形成并根据政府自身原因管理有关规定。可以包括旨在加强国内企业竞争力的出口卡特尔。此类规定的一个例子是美国的《韦伯-波默斯法》。纯出口卡特尔全部针对国外市场，享受免于适用竞争法的相当大的自由。混合式出口卡特尔影响国内和出口市场。进口卡特尔则非常少见，在多数情况下竞争主管机关不批准其形成或运行。公共卡特尔也可能会被允许用于促进结构性调整。私人卡特尔或企业之间的安排，通常是保密的，特别是在违法或会给消费者造成更高价格的情况下。另见*反垄断法(antitrust laws)*、*合理原则(rule of reason)*、*贸易与竞争(trade and competition)*。

Carve-out
例外

谈判参加方关于暂时将一系列措施或一项确定的经济活动例外于新的或拟议贸易规则适用范围的协议。例外的例子是双边航空权例外于《服务贸易总协定》的规则。

Cascading tariffs
阶梯关税

有时用以替代关税升级一词。指对一制成品相对简单的组件设置低关税，而随着加工程度的提升而提高关税。目的是为尽可能在国内增值。

***Cassis de Dijon* case**
第戎黑醋栗酒案

见*相互承认安排(mutual recognition arrangements)*。

Causality
因果关系

指在增加的进口与对生产同类或直接竞争产品的国内产业的严重损害或严重损害威胁之间存在因果关系，可用来采取保障措施。同样，实施反倾销措施的成员必须证明对产业的损害是由倾销而非其他一些原因造成的。另见*同类产品(like product)*。

Casual linkage
因果关系

见*因果关系(causality)*。

CBD
生物多样性公约

见*生物多样性公约(Convention on Biological Diversity)*。

CEFTA 2006
2006 年中欧自由贸易协定

2007 年 1 月 1 日起取代东南欧自由贸易区(SEEFTA)的自由贸易协定。成员国为阿尔巴尼亚、波斯尼亚和黑塞哥维那、克罗地亚、科索沃、摩尔多瓦、黑山、塞尔维亚和北马其顿。另见*稳定与联系协定(Stabilization and Association Agreement)*。

Ceiling bindings
上限约束

指 WTO 中将全部关税或大部分关税约束在规定水平的做法，通常在实施税率之上有足够的缓冲。约束通常是谈判的结果。承诺约束其关税的国家承担不提高这些约束水平的法律义务，但上限约束可以使它们按自己意愿在上限水平之内多次提高关税。另见*约束(binding)*、*关税高峰(peak tariffs)*。

Ceiling duties
上限税率

大多指一国关税税则中可以实施的最高关税税率。通常与上限约束相同。

Central African Customs and Economic Union
中部非洲关税与经济同盟

UDEAC。1964 年建立，最终目标为成为共同市场。成员包括喀麦隆、中非共

and Gabon. UDEAC's secretariat was located at Bangui, Central African Republic. UDEAC was succeeded in June 1999 by the ***Communauté Économique et Monétaire de l'Afrique Centrale***.

Central African Economic and Monetary Union: *see* ***Communauté Économique et Monétaire de l'Afrique Centrale***.

Central American Common Market: CACM. One of the ***preferential trade arrangements*** of the ***first regionalism***. The *General Treaty on Economic Integration* establishing it entered into force on 4 June 1961. Its members are Costa Rica, El Salvador, Guatemala, Honduras and Nicaragua. The secretariat is located in Guatemala City. The task of promoting CACM has now been revitalized through the formation of the ***Secretariat of Central American Economic Integration*** (SIECA).

Central American Free Trade Agreement: *see* ***United States–Central American Free Trade Agreement***.

Central American Integration System: Sistema de la Integracíon Centroamericana (SICA). Established in 1991 as the successor to the Organization of Central American States and the Central American Common Market. Its objectives include (a) consolidate democracy and strengthen its institutions, (b) set up a new model of regional security, (c) achieve a regional system of welfare and economic and social justice, (d) attain economic union and strengthen the Central American financial system, and (e) strengthen the region as a bloc to insert it successfully into the international economy. Its members are Belize, Costa Rica, Dominican Republic, El Salvador, Guatemala, Honduras, Nicaragua and Panama. Its secretariat is in El Salvador. *See also* ***Secretariat of Central American Economic Integration***.

Central American Uniform Customs Code: CAUCA (Código Aduanero Uniforme Centroamericano). First established in 1984 and updated several times since. It establishes harmonized customs procedures for El Salvador, Guatemala, Honduras and Nicaragua. *See also* ***Central American Integration System***. [www.sieca.int]

Central Asian Cooperation Organization: CACO. Established on 28 February 2002 as the successor to the Central Asian Economic Community. It consists of Kazakhstan, Kyrgyz Republic, Tajikistan and Uzbekistan. At the same time it widened its sphere of activity to include security and strategic issues in addition to economic matters. On 7 October 2005 it merged with the ***Eurasian Economic Community*** (EAEC) which in turn joined the ***Eurasian Economic Union***. Tajikistan has not acceded to it.

Central Asian Economic Community: *see* ***Central Asian Cooperation Organization***.

Central Asia Regional Economic Cooperation: CAREC. A partnership of eleven countries (Afghanistan, Azerbaijan, China, Georgia, Kazakhstan, Kyrgyz Republic, Mongolia, Pakistan, Tajikistan, Turkmenistan and Uzbekistan), supported by the ***Asian Development Bank***, European Bank for Reconstruction and Development, ***IMF***, Islamic Development Bank, ***United Nations***

和国、乍得、刚果(布)、赤道几内亚和加蓬。UDEAC 秘书处设在中非共和国班吉。UDEAC 在 1999 年 6 月被中部非洲经济与货币共同体所取代。

Central African Economic and Monetary Union
中部非洲经济与货币同盟

见*中部非洲经济与货币共同体*(Communauté Économique et Monétaire de l'Afrique Centrale)。

Central American Common Market
中美洲共同市场

CACM。第一次区域主义浪潮中的优惠贸易安排之一。建立共同市场的《经济一体化总协定》于 1961 年 6 月 4 日生效。成员国为哥斯达黎加、萨尔瓦多、危地马拉、洪都拉斯和尼加拉瓜。秘书处设在危地马拉城。推进 CACM 的任务目前已经通过成立中美洲经济一体化秘书处(SIECA)而重获动力。

Central American Free Trade Agreement
中美洲自由贸易协定

见*美国—中美洲自由贸易协定(United States-Central American Free Trade Agreement)*。

Central American Integration System
中美洲一体化体系

SICA。成立于 1991 年，是中美洲国家组织和中美洲共同市场的后继组织。目标包括：(a)巩固民主和增强机构；(b)建立新区域安全模式；(c)实现区域福利和经济社会正义体系；(d)实现经济联盟并加强中美洲金融体系；以及(e)加强本地区以集团身份成功融入国际经济。成员包括伯利兹、哥斯达黎加、多米尼加、萨尔瓦多、危地马拉、洪都拉斯、尼加拉瓜和巴拿马。秘书处设在萨尔瓦多。另见*中美洲经济一体化秘书处(Secretariat of Central American Economic Integration)*。

Central American Uniform Customs Code
中美洲统一海关代码

CAUCA。最早于 1984 年创建，此后多次更新。为萨尔瓦多、危地马拉、洪都拉斯和尼加拉瓜建立协调的海关程序。另见*中美洲一体化体系(Central American Integration System)*。

Central Asian Cooperation Organization
中亚合作组织

CACO。2002 年 2 月 28 日建立，是中亚经济共同体的后继组织。由哈萨克斯坦、吉尔吉斯斯坦、塔吉克斯坦和乌兹别克斯坦组成。同时，扩大了活动范围，除经济事务外，还包括安全和战略问题。2005 年 10 月 7 日，与欧亚经济共同体(EAEC)合并，后者又加入欧亚经济联盟。塔吉克斯坦还未加入该组织。

Central Asian Economic Community
中亚经济共同体

见*中亚合作组织(Central Asian Cooperation Organization)*。

Central Asia Regional Economic Cooperation
中亚区域经济合作组织

CAREC。阿富汗、阿塞拜疆、中国、格鲁吉亚、哈萨克斯坦、吉尔吉斯斯坦、蒙古、巴基斯坦、塔吉克斯坦、土库曼斯坦和乌兹别克斯坦等 11 国组成的伙伴关系，由亚洲开发银行、欧洲复兴开发银行、国际货币基金组织(IMF)、伊

Development Programme and the ***World Bank***. Its aim is to facilitate practical results-based regional projects and policy initiatives leading to sustainable economic growth and poverty reduction in the region. Its guiding plan is the CAREC 2030 Strategic Framework.

Central European Free Trade Agreement: CEFTA. An omnibus term for a complex structure of plurilateral and bilateral agreements which linked the Czech Republic, Hungary, Poland, Romania, Slovakia and Slovenia. CEFTA in its original form was made largely redundant by the accession to the ***European Union*** of most of its participants. Its successor is ***CEFTA 2006***.

Centrally-planned economies: CPE. A name until the late 1980s or early 1990s for the countries of Central and Eastern Europe, the USSR, China, Viet Nam and some others in which economic activity was based on yearly plans usually elaborated by a body like the State Planning Commission. These countries were also known as non-market economies. Most CPEs have now turned into ***market economies*** or are on the way towards that goal. *See also* ***economies in transition*** and ***non-market economies***.

CEPAL: Comisión Económica de las Naciones Unidas para América Latina y el Caribe. *See* ***Economic Commission for Latin America and the Caribbean***.

CEPT: Common Effective Preferential Tariff. The mechanism in ***AFTA*** to reduce tariffs. AFTA has now been superseded by the ***ASEAN Trade in Goods Agreement***.

CER: closer economic relations. Originally this referred to the Australia New Zealand Closer Economic Relations Trade Agreement, or ***ANZCERTA***, but it now has become one of the names used for trade and economic agreements.

CER Protocol on Trade in Services: *see* ***ANZCERTA Protocol on Trade in Services***.

Certificate of non-manipulation: a certificate issued by a country through which a good has been transshipped to the effect that the good has not undergone any manipulation in that country. Issuance of the certificate may be accompanied by a requirement that the good was stored in a bonded warehouse before being sent on. One benefit of this certificate is that it provides an assurance that the good has remained unchanged since leaving the original country, and that it has been stored under suitable conditions during its journey. Of course, the procedure adds another documentary requirement. *See also* ***trade facilitation***.

Certificate of origin: a document in paper or electronic form which states that the goods about to be imported are the product of a particular country. Such certificates are often used for goods imported under preferential conditions, such as the ***GSP*** or a ***free-trade agreement***. The ***GATT*** membership agreed as early as 1953 that certificates of origin should only be used where they are strictly indispensable. *See also* ***certificate of non-manipulation*** and ***self-certification***.

Certificate of specific character: now superseded by ***traditional speciality guaranteed***.

Certification mark: sometimes called a guarantee mark. A mark owned or administered by a public or private certifying body. It indicates that the product

斯兰开发银行、联合国开发计划署和世界银行提供支持。旨在促进基于结果的实用区域项目和政策倡议，以实现该地区的可持续经济增长和减少贫困。指导计划是 CAREC 2030 战略框架。

Central European Free Trade Agreement
中欧自由贸易协定

CEFTA。对将捷克、匈牙利、波兰、罗马尼亚、斯洛伐克和斯洛文尼亚联系在一起的复杂诸边和双边协定的总称。最初形式的 CEFTA 因大多数参加方加入欧盟而在很大程度上显得多余。后继协定为《2006 年中欧自由贸易协定》。

Centrally-planned economies
中央计划经济体

CPE。20 世纪 80 年代末或 90 年代初以前对中东欧国家、苏联、中国、越南及其他国家的称谓，这些国家的经济活动根据像计划委员会这样的机构详细制定的年度计划开展。这些国家也称非市场经济体。大多数 CPE 国家目前已经转型为市场经济体或正在向此目标迈进。另见*转型经济体(economies in transition)*、*非市场经济体(non-market economies)*。

CEPAL
拉丁美洲和加勒比联合国经济委员会

见*拉丁美洲和加勒比经济委员会(Economic Commission for Latin America and the Caribbean)*。

CEPT
共同有效特惠关税安排

东盟自由贸易区(AFTA)中的关税削减机制。AFTA 现已被《东盟货物贸易协定》所取代。

CER
更紧密经济关系

最初指《澳大利亚与新西兰更紧密经济关系贸易协定》(ANZCERTA)，现已成为贸易经济协定的名称之一。

CER Protocol on Trade in Services
CER 服务贸易议定书

见 *ANZCERTA 服务贸易议定书(ANZCERTA Protocol on Trade in Services)*。

Certificate of non-manipulation
未再加工证明

由货物过境国签发的证明，证明该货物在该国未经任何加工。签发证书的同时可要求货物在转运前存放在保税仓库。该证明的好处之一是，可以保证货物在离开原产国后未发生任何改变，且在途中一直在适宜条件下存放。当然，该程序又增加了一项单证要求。另见*贸易便利化(trade facilitation)*。

Certificate of origin
原产地证书

纸质或电子形式的单证，表明即将进口的货物是一特定国家的产品。此类证书通常用于在优惠条件下进口的货物，例如普惠制(GSP)或自由贸易协定。早在 1953 年，GATT 缔约方即同意原产地证书只能在绝对不可或缺的情况下使用。另见*未再加工证明(certificate of non-manipulation)*、*自我认证(self-certification)*。

Certificate of specific character
特定品质证书

现在被注册传统特色产品所取代。

Certification mark
认证标志

有时称保证标志。公共或私营认证机构拥有或管理的一种标志。表明带该标

which bears it complies with certain standards, has specific qualities or originates in a certain geographical location. Prospective users of a certification mark have to apply for permission to do so. They usually have to demonstrate that they are able to meet the standards administered by the certifying body. *See also* ***collective mark***, ***geographical indications*** and ***trademarks***. [WIPO SCT/8/4; SCT/9/4]

CGIAR: *see* ***Consultative Group on International Agricultural Research***.

Chaebol **enterprises:** large Korean conglomerate firms of post-war origin. They are characterized by single-family ownership, and control remains concentrated even into the second or third generation of owners. They are prevalent particularly in manufacturing and construction. The share of total Korean economic output of *chaebol* firms appears to have been falling since the 1970s, but they remain significant economic actors. [Chang 2003]

Change in chapter heading: sometimes used interchangeably with ***change in tariff classification*** or change in tariff heading. A method used in the application of ***rules of origin*** to ascertain whether ***substantial transformation*** has occurred. It is based on the ***Harmonized Commodity Description and Coding System*** which divides traded goods into ninety-seven ***chapters***. A chapter has two digits. According to this method an article produced in country A from materials originating in country B is considered a product of country A if it was made into a substantially different product there, i.e. it is now considered to fall under a different chapter of the Harmonized System. Such a system, if applied literally, would be highly restrictive. In practice, all such systems use changes in chapter headings (a change from one two-digit group to another), ***headings*** (four digits) and ***sub-headings*** (six digits), as the case may require.

Change in tariff classification: CTC. Used in the administration of ***rules of origin*** to ascertain whether a good qualifies for entry under a ***preferential tariff*** through having undergone ***substantial transformation***. The classification used is normally the ***Harmonized Commodity Description and Coding System***. Some ***free-trade agreements*** specify that a change in tariff classification means that a product has undergone sufficient transformation in the exporting country to be moved from one four-digit classification to another, but this is not a firm rule. *See also* ***change in chapter heading***.

Change in tariff heading: *see* ***change in chapter heading*** and ***change in tariff classification***.

Change in tariff lines: a concept used in the administration of ***rules of origin*** to determine where a good comes from. A change in tariff lines occurs when a material or good carrying a six-digit classification in the ***Harmonized Commodity Description and Coding System*** is transformed in a production process to a good carrying a different six-digit number. The two numbers may be consecutive, unless the particular regime precludes this, or they may be at some remove. *See also* ***change in tariff classification***.

Chapter: one of the ninety-seven two-digit entries in the ***Harmonized Commodity Description and Coding System***. Examples are: 01 (live animals), 52 (cotton)

志的产品符合某种标准，具有特定质量或源自某一地理位置。认证商标的潜在用户必须申请方可获得许可。他们通常需要证明能够达到认证机构所管理的标准。另见*集体商标(collective mark)*、*地理标志(geographical indications)*、*商标(trademarks)*。

CGIAR

国际农业研究磋商组织

见*国际农业研究磋商组织(Consultative Group on International Agricultural Research)*。

***Chaebol* enterprises**

韩国财阀企业

起源于战后的韩国企业公司。特点是单一家族所有，控制权集中，甚至延续至第二代或第三代所有者。在制造业和建筑业特别常见。财阀在韩国经济总产出中的份额自 20 世纪 70 年代以来一直在下降，但是它们仍然是重要的经济行为者。

Change in chapter heading

章改变

有时可与税则归类改变或税目改变互换使用。实施原产地规则的一种方法，以确定是否发生实质性改变。主要基于商品名称及编码协调制度，该制度将进行交易的货物分为 97 章，各章包含 2 位编码。按照这一方法，使用原产于 B 国的材料在 A 国生产的一物品，如果在 A 国制造形成实质不同的产品，即被认为归入协调制度另一章，则被视为 A 国产品。这种制度如果真正实施则会具有很强的限制性。实践中，所有此类制度视情使用章改变(从一个 2 位编码变为另一 2 位编码)、税目改变(4 位编码)和子目改变(6 位编码)。

Change in tariff classification

税则归类改变

CTC。用于管理原产地规则，以确定一货物是否经过实质性改变而有资格按照优惠关税进口。使用的分类方法通常为商品名称及编码协调制度。一些自由贸易协定规定，税则归类改变意味着一产品在出口国已经发生充分改变，而从一个 4 位编码转为另一个 4 位编码，但这不是固定规则。另见*章改变(change in chapter heading)*。

Change in tariff heading

税目改变

见*章改变(change in chapter heading)*、*税则归类改变(change in tariff classification)*。

Change in tariff lines

税目改变

用于管理原产地规则的一个概念，以确定商品来源地。如归入商品名称及编码协调制度一个 6 位编码的一材料或产品在生产过程中转变为另一个 6 位编码产品时，即发生税目改变。两个编码可以是连续的，除非特定制度排除此种情况，或两个编码有所间隔。另见*税则归类改变(change in tariff classification)*。

Chapter

章

商品名称及编码协调制度 97 个 2 位编码条目之一。例如：01(活动物)、52(羊

and 72 (iron and steel). Many trade agreements are also divided into chapters. The parties to them name and number them as they deem best. *See also* ***heading*** and ***sub-heading***.

Charter for an International Trade Organization: *see* ***Havana Charter***.

Charter of Economic Rights and Duties of States: CERDS. An initiative launched at ***UNCTAD*** III (1972) ostensibly aimed at protecting the economic rights of all countries, but really promoting a change in what was seen as the entrenched lower status of ***developing countries*** in the international economic system. The draft Charter, originally intended to be binding on signatories and to become part of international law, was adopted by the United Nations General Assembly as Resolution 3281 (XXIX) on 12 December 1974. The Charter has thirty-four articles grouped in four chapters. Chapter I sets out fifteen principles that should govern the fundamentals of international economic relations among states. These are: (a) sovereignty, territorial integrity and political independence of states, (b) sovereign equality of all states, (c) non-aggression, (d) non-intervention, (e) mutual and equitable benefit, (f) peaceful coexistence, (g) equal rights and self-determination of peoples, (h) peaceful settlement of disputes, (i) remedying of injustices which have been brought about by force and which deprive a nation of the natural means necessary for its normal development, (j) fulfilment in good faith of international obligations, (k) respect for human rights and fundamental freedoms, (l) no attempt to seek hegemony and spheres of influence, (m) promotion of international social justice, (n) international cooperation for development, and (o) free access to and from the sea by land-locked countries within the framework of these principles. Chapter II contains twenty-eight articles describing the economic rights and duties of states. In abbreviated form they are: (1) the right to choose economic, political, social and cultural systems in accordance with the will of the people, (2) full permanent sovereignty over all wealth, natural resources and economic activities, (3) if two or more countries share natural resources, they must cooperate in their exploitation, (4) the right to engage in international trade and other economic cooperation irrespective of political, economic or social systems, (5) the right to associate in organizations of primary commodity producers, (6) the duty to contribute to the development of international trade of goods, particularly through the conclusion of long-term multilateral commodity agreements, (7) responsibility of the state to promote the economic, social and cultural development of its people, (8) cooperation in achieving a more rational and equitable system of international economic relations, (9) responsibility to cooperate in the economic, social, cultural, scientific and technological fields, (10) the right to participate fully as equals in the international decision-making process to solve world economic, financial and monetary problems, (11) cooperation to improve the efficiency of international organizations, (12) the right to participate in subregional, regional and interregional cooperation in the pursuit of development, (13) the right to benefit from the advances in science and technology, (14) the duty to cooperate in

毛)和 72(钢铁)。许多贸易协定也分成多个章。协定参加方按他们认为最佳的方式对各章命名和编号。另见*税目(heading)*、*子目(sub-heading)*。

Charter for an International Trade Organization

国际贸易组织宪章

见*哈瓦那宪章(Havana Charter)*。

Charter of Economic Rights and Duties of States

各国经济权利与义务宪章

CERDS。联合国贸易与发展会议(UNCTAD)1972 年第 3 届大会上提出的一项倡议，表面上旨在保护所有国家的经济权利，而实际上促成了当时被认为发展中国家在国际经济体系中长期所处较低地位的改变。宪章草案最初意在约束所有签署方而成为国际法的一部分，而最终由联合国大会于 1974 年 12 月 12 日以第 3281(XXIX)号决议通过。宪章共 34 条，分为 4 章。第一章规定了管辖各国国际经济关系基本准则的 15 条原则，即(a)各国的主权、领土完整和政治独立；(b)所有国家主权平等；(c)互不侵犯；(d)互不干涉；(e)公平互利；(f)和平共处；(g)各民族平等权利和自决；(h)和平解决争端；(i)对于以武力造成的、使得一个国家失去其正常发展所必需的自然手段的不正义情况，应予补救；(j)真诚地履行国际义务；(k)尊重人权和基本自由；(l)不谋求霸权和势力范围；(m)促进国际社会正义；(n)国际合作以谋发展；以及(o)内陆国家在上述原则范围内进出海洋的自由。第二章共 28 条，描述了各国的经济权利和经济义务。简述为：(1)依照人民意志选择经济、政治、社会和文化制度的权利；(2)对全部财富、自然资源和经济活动享有充分的永久主权；(3)对于两国或两国以上所共有的自然资源时的开发应合作；(4)每个国家不论政治、经济和社会制度如何，有权进行国际贸易和其他方式的经济合作；(5)有权参加初级商品生产者的组织；(6)有义务对国际货物贸易的发展作出贡献，特别通过在适当情况下缔结长期多边商品协定；(7)各国有促进其人民的经济、社会和文化发展的责任；(8)合作促进较为公平合理的国际经济关系；(9)有责任在经济、社会、文化、科学和技术领域进行合作；(10)有权充分平等参与为解决世界经济、金融和货币问题作出国际决定的过程；(11)合作改进国际组织效能；(12)有权参加分区域、区域和区域间的合作以谋求发展；(13)有权分享科学技术进步和发展的利益；(14)有义务进行合作，促进世界贸易稳定、日益增加的发展

promoting steady and increasing expansion and liberalization of world trade, (15) the duty to promote achievement of general and complete disarmament, (16) the right and duty to eliminate colonialism, racial discrimination, neo-colonialism and all forms of foreign aggression, (17) the duty to cooperate internationally for development, (18) developed countries to improve and enlarge the system of generalized non-reciprocal and non-discriminatory tariff preferences, (19) developed countries to grant generalized, preferential, non-reciprocal and non-discriminatory treatment in fields of international and economic cooperation where it may be feasible, (20) developing countries to increase their trade with socialist countries, (21) developing countries to promote the expansion of their mutual trade, (22) promotion of increased net flows of real resources to the developing countries, (23) developing countries to strengthen their economic cooperation and expand their mutual trade to accelerate their economic and social development, (24) the duty to conduct mutual economic relations through taking into account the interests of other countries, (25) special attention to be paid to the least-developed countries, (26) the duty to coexist in tolerance and live together in peace, (27) the right to enjoy fully the benefits of world invisible trade and to engage in its expansion, and (28) the duty to cooperate in achieving adjustments in the prices of exports of developing countries compared to import prices. Chapter III details in two chapters the common responsibilities of states towards the international community, i.e. towards each other. Article 29 states that the seabed and ocean floor beyond the limits of national jurisdiction, as well as the resources of the area, are the common heritage of mankind. Article 30 makes the protection, preservation and enhancement of the environment for the present and future generations the responsibility of all states. Chapter IV observes, *inter alia*, that the prosperity of the international community as a whole depends upon the prosperity of its constituent parts. The majority of developed countries either abstained or voted against the Charter. The countries refusing to support the Charter were concerned that it did not contain a commitment to international law or a reference to the relevance of international law. Considerable debate developed over the legal standing of the Charter, but it slowly faded away as an international issue in any case. Some are of the view that although the Charter failed to bring about the intended changes in international economic relations, the controversy over it ensured that the concerns of developing countries would be given more attention in future. *See also* ***Global Negotiations***, ***New International Economic Order*** and ***North–South dialogue***.

Charter of the South Asian Association for Regional Cooperation: *see* ***South Asian Association for Regional Cooperation***.

Chemicals: *see* ***advance informed consent***, ***Convention on Persistent Organic Pollutants***, ***Convention on the Prior Informed Consent Procedure for Certain Hazardous Chemicals and Pesticides in International Trade***, ***Globally Harmonized System of Classification and Labelling of Chemicals***, ***London***

和自由化；(15)有义务促进实现在有效国际管制下的全面彻底裁军；(16)有权利和义务消除殖民主义、种族隔离、种族歧视、新殖民主义和各种形式的外国侵略；(17)有义务进行国际合作以谋求发展；(18)发达国家应改进和扩大普遍的、非互惠和非歧视的关税优惠制度；(19)发达国家应在国际经济合作可行领域内给予发展中国家以普遍优惠的、非互惠和非歧视的待遇；(20)发展中国家应扩大它们同社会主义国家的贸易；(21)发展中国家应努力促进它们之间相互贸易的扩展；(22)促进真实资源净额流入发展中国家；(23)发展中国家应加强它们之间的经济合作并扩大相互贸易以加速它们的经济和社会发展；(24)有义务在其相互间的经济关系中考虑到其他国家的利益；(25)应特别注意最不发达国家；(26)有义务宽容相待，和平相处；(27)有权充分享受世界无形贸易的利益，并有权参与这种贸易的扩展；以及(28)有义务为在发展中国家的出口商品价格和它们的进口商品价格之间达成调整而开展合作。第三章细化了前两章中各国对国际社会的共同责任，即相互间的共同责任。第29条规定，国家管辖范围外的海床和洋底以及该海域的资源是人类共同继承的财产。第30条规定，所有国家有责任为了今代和后世而保护、维护和改善环境。第四章特别关注整个国际社会的繁荣取决于其组成部分的繁荣。大多数发达国家对这一宪章投了弃权票或否决票。拒绝支持宪章的国家担心宪章未包含国际法的承诺，或未提及与国际法的关联。宪章的法律地位引发了较大争论，但最终就像任何一个国际问题一样逐渐消失。有人认为，尽管宪章未能给国际经济关系带来预想的变化，但其存在的争议保证了发展中国家的关注会在未来获得更多重视。另见*全球谈判(Global Negotiations)*、*国际经济新秩序(New International Economic Order)*、*南北对话(North-South dialogue)*。

Charter for the South Asian Association for Regional Cooperation
南亚区域合作联盟宪章

见*南亚区域合作联盟(South Asian Association for Regional Cooperation)*。

Chemicals
化学品

见*预先知情同意(advance informed consent)*、*关于持久性有机污染物的公约(Convention on Persistent Organic Pollutants)*、*关于在国际贸易中对某些危险化学品和农药采用事先知情同意程序的公约(Convention on the Prior Informed Consent Procedure for Certain Hazardous Chemicals and Pesticides in International Trade)*、*全球化学品统一分类和标签制度(Globally Harmonized System of Classification and Labelling of Chemicals)*、*关于化学品国际贸易资料交换的伦敦准则(London Guidelines for the Exchange of Information on Chemi-*

Guidelines for the Exchange of Information on Chemicals in International Trade, ***prior informed consent*** and ***REACH***.

Cherry-picking: the attempt to choose from a menu of obligations or negotiating options only those likely to cause one the fewest difficulties. The vigilance of others often prevents this. *See also* ***forum-shopping***.

Chiang Mai Initiative: adopted at a meeting of ***ASEAN+3*** finance ministers in Chiang Mai, Thailand, in May 2000. It created a network out of the currency swap arrangements then in existence among the ASEAN+3 members, with Japan at the centre. *See also* ***New Miyazawa Initiative***.

Chicago Convention: the *Convention on International Civil Aviation*, concluded in 1944 with the aim of promoting a regime for safe and orderly international air services. Its provisions govern the methods of allocating bilateral air traffic rights, a basic feature of the global aviation system. The Convention is administered by the International Civil Aviation Organization (ICAO), located in Montreal. *See also* ***bilateral air services agreements***, ***freedoms of the air*** and ***open-skies arrangements***.

Chicken War: a period of trade tension between the United States and the ***European Economic Community*** lasting from July 1962 to January 1964. It overshadowed the start of the ***Kennedy Round***. It was triggered by the extension of ***variable levies*** under the ***common agricultural policy*** to poultry which trebled German import charges. This led to an immediate and drastic decline in the export of United States poultry to Germany where up to that time United States exporters had been spectacularly successful. Claim and counterclaim for ***compensation*** followed. The establishment of a panel of experts by the GATT in November 1963 provided the basis of a solution. Both parties accepted that poultry trade worth $26 million was affected. To settle the score, the United States then imposed additional import duties affecting mainly French cognac, German trucks and Dutch dextrine and starch, thus ensuring that the United States retaliatory action would be noticed among members of the European Economic Community more broadly. The influence of the Chicken War on the remainder of the Kennedy Round is hard to judge, especially since it was followed by several other difficult periods. It provided a pointer, however, to the increasingly vexing problem of international agricultural trade facing exporters as the common agricultural policy first led to European ***self-sufficiency*** and then to subsidized exports of many products. *See also* ***agriculture and the multilateral trading system*** and ***Ploughshares War***.

Chief supplier provision: one of the main features of the ***United States Reciprocal Trade Agreements Program***. It stipulated that no tariff concession would be made to any country unless it was the chief supplier of the product. The provision was intended to preserve United States bargaining power with countries yet to conclude a reciprocal trade agreement after earlier reductions had been applied to other trade agreement partners under the ***most-favoured-nation treatment*** rule. The chief supplier provision was carried forward into the GATT in the form of the ***principal supplier right***.

cals in International Trade)、***事先知情同意****(prior informed consent)*、***化学品的注册、评估、授权和限制****(REACH)*。

Cherry-picking

精挑细选

试图从义务清单或谈判选项中挑选那些对自己困难最少的项目的做法。其他人的警觉时常阻止这一情况发生。另见***挑选法院****(forum-shopping)*。

Chiang Mai Initiative

清迈倡议

在 2000 年 5 月泰国清迈召开的东盟+3 财政部长会议上通过。以东盟+ 3 成员国之间当时存在的货币互换安排为基础创建一个网络，以日本为中心。另见***新宫泽喜一倡议****(New Miyazawa Initiative)*。

Chicago Convention

芝加哥公约

1944 年达成的《国际民用航空公约》，旨在促进安全有序的国际航空服务体制。公约条款管辖双边航权的分配方法，这是全球航空体系的一个基本特征。公约由设在蒙特利尔的国际民用航空组织管理。另见***双边航空服务协定****(bilateral air services agreements)*、***航空自由****(freedoms of the air)*、***开放天空安排****(open-skies arrangements)*。

Chicken War

鸡肉战

美国与欧洲经济共同体之间自 1962 年 7 月至 1964 年 1 月的一段贸易紧张时期。给肯尼迪回合启动蒙上阴影。贸易战源起于根据共同农业政策征收的差价税扩展到家禽，使德国的进口费用增加两倍。导致美国对德国的家禽出口立即大幅下降，就在此前，美国出口商的业绩十分出色。随后是补偿诉求和反诉求。GATT 于 1963 年 11 月成立专家组，为解决争端提供了基础。双方均承认受影响的家禽贸易额达 2,600 万美元。为解决问题，美国随后加征附加进口税，主要影响法国干邑、德产卡车及荷兰的糊精和淀粉，从而保证美国的报复行动能够在欧共体成员国中引起更广泛关注。鸡肉战对肯尼迪回合剩余阶段的影响难以判断，特别是因为随后又出现了其他若干困难时期。然而，鸡肉战指出了出口商所面临的国际农产品贸易中日益恼人的问题，原因是共同农业政策先是使欧洲自给自足，随后导致许多产品获得出口补贴。另见***农业与多边贸易体制****(agricultural and multilateral system)*、***犁铧战****(Ploughshares War)*。

Chief supplier provision

主要供应方条款

美国互惠贸易协定计划的主要特点之一。规定对任何国家不作出关税减让，除非该国是该产品主要供应方。该条款意在使美国根据最惠国待遇规定已对其他贸易协定伙伴实施削减之后，保留与尚未缔结互惠贸易协定的国家进行讨价还价的能力。主要供应方条款以主要供应方权利的形式借用到 GATT 中。

Child labour: Convention No. 138 (Minimum Age Convention) of the ***International Labour Organization*** states that the minimum age of employment in acceding countries must not be less than fifteen years. This may be lowered to thirteen years for some forms of light work and twelve years for developing countries, provided that employment does not interfere with the child's education. Convention No. 138 aims to raise the minimum age progressively, and ILO Recommendation No. 146 suggests that the minimum age of employment should be sixteen years. *See also* ***Convention Concerning the Prohibition and Immediate Action for the Elimination of the Worst Forms of Child Labour*** and ***core labour standards***.

CHOGM: the ***Commonwealth*** Heads of Government Meeting, usually held every two years. ***Trade policy*** issues are usually on its agenda, but it does not make rules.

CIF: cost, insurance and freight. Denotes that the price of a good as quoted or invoiced consists of the cost of the good itself, plus the cost of insurance and freight by sea or inland waterway to the port of destination. *See also* ***FOB.***

Circumvention: getting around commitments made in the WTO and elsewhere, such as commitments to limit agricultural export subsidies. Other examples are avoiding quotas and other restrictions by altering the country of origin of a product, or measures taken to evade anti-dumping or countervailing duties. *See also* ***anti-circumvention***.

CITES: Convention on International Trade in Endangered Species of Wild Fauna and Flora. Drafted following a resolution adopted in 1963 at a meeting of the International Union for the Conservation of Nature and Natural Resources (IUCN). The text was adopted in 1973, and the Convention entered into force on 1 July 1975. It now has 183 parties. CITES regulates international trade of certain species and places them into three categories. Appendix I to the Convention includes species threatened with extinction. Trade in these species is permitted in exceptional circumstances only. Appendix II includes species not necessarily threatened with extinction, but trade in them must be controlled to avoid utilization incompatible with their survival. Appendix III includes species protected in at least one country and for which the cooperation of others is sought. Where trade is allowed under the Convention, it takes place through a permit system. CITES is administered by ***UN Environment Programme***. Its secretariat is in Geneva. *See also* ***multilateral environment agreements*** and ***trade and environment***.

Civil aircraft code: *see* ***Agreement on Trade in Civil Aircraft***.

Civil society: in the context of trade policy, those who are not directly involved in the discussions and negotiations in ***intergovernmental organizations***, but who may be affected by their decisions or who may have points of view to put across. Most often *civil society* appears to refer to ***non-governmental organizations*** (NGOs), but it is also taken to mean, by ***UNCTAD***, for example, parliamentarians, trade unions and academics. Most intergovernmental organizations now have a website aimed to meet the needs of civil society.

Child labour

童工

国际劳工组织(ILO)《第 138 号公约》(准允就业最低年龄公约)规定，公约加入国中最低就业年龄不得低于 15 岁。对于一些形式的轻工作，最低就业年龄可降至 13 岁，对于发展中国家可降至 12 岁，只要此种雇佣不妨碍儿童的教育。《第 138 号公约》旨在逐步提高最低就业年龄，国际劳工组织《第 146 号建议书》建议最低就业年龄应为 16 岁。另见*禁止和立即行动消除最恶劣形式的童工劳动公约(Convention Concerning the Prohibition and Immediate Action for the Elimination of the Worst Forms of Child Labour)*、*核心劳工标准(core labour standards)*。

CHOGM

英联邦政府首脑会议

会议通常每 2 年举行一次。贸易政策问题经常列入议程，但会议不制定规则。

CIF

到岸价格

成本、保险费和运费。指货物报价或发票价格，由货物本身成本，加上保险和通过海运或内河航道运至目的港的成本组成。另见*离岸价格(FOB)*。

Circumvention

规避

规避在 WTO 中和其他处所作承诺，例如限制农产品出口补贴的承诺。其他例子包括通过改变产品原产国而避开配额和其他限制，或采取措施逃避反倾销或反补贴税。另见*反规避(anti-circumvention)*。

CITES

濒危野生动植物种国际贸易公约

在国际自然及自然资源保护联盟(IUCN)1963 年会议通过决议后起草有关文本。公约于 1973 年获得通过，1975 年 7 月 1 日生效，现有 183 个缔约方。CITES 对某些物种的国际贸易进行管理，并将它们分为三类。公约附录 I 包括濒临灭绝的物种。这些物种的贸易仅在特殊情况下允许进行。附录 II 包括虽未濒临灭绝但必须对其贸易加以管理以防止不利其生存的利用。附录 III 包括至少在一个国家受到保护的物种，并为此寻求其他国家的合作。如公约项下允许进行贸易，贸易需要通过许可证制度进行。CITES 由联合国环境规划署管理。秘书处设在日内瓦。另见*多边环境协定(multilateral environment agreements)*、*贸易与环境(trade and environment)*。

Civil aircraft code

民用航空器守则

见*民用航空器贸易协定(Agreement on Trade in Civil Aircraft)*。

Civil society

公民社会

在贸易政策范围内，指那些未直接参与政府间组织的讨论和谈判，但可能受到这些组织的决定影响或可能有要表达的观点的人。通常公民社会似乎指非政府组织(NGOs)，但联合国贸易与发展会议(UNCTAD)认为指议员、工会和学术界。大多数政府间组织现在设有网站以满足公民社会的需要。

Classifications of goods, services and activities: *see* ***Harmonized Commodity Description and Coding System***, ***International Standard Classification of Occupations***, ***International Standard Industrial Classification of All Economic Activities***, ***SITC*** (Standard International Trade Classification) and ***United Nations Central Product Classification***.

Clawback provisions: the ability of a foreign party ordered to pay ***treble damages*** in extraterritorial proceedings conducted under United States ***antitrust laws*** to recover through the national court system the amount in excess of actual damages. If the party ordered to pay treble damages is successful in its counterclaim, the party receiving the treble damages will be ordered to repay the amount deemed to be excessive. Recovery of damages really is only possible if the company receiving them in the first place has assets in the country conducting clawback proceedings. *See also* ***extraterritoriality***.

Clayton Act: a United States ***antitrust law*** first passed in 1914. It seeks to prohibit a range of restrictive business practices and to "arrest the creation of trusts, conspiracies, and monopolies in their incipiency and before consummation". It also permits the imposition of ***treble damages***. The Act in general applies to foreign trade, but some provisions are limited to interstate commerce. *See also* ***competition policy***, ***Robinson-Patman Act***, ***Sherman Act***, ***Webb-Pomerene Act*** and ***Wilson Tariff Act***.

Clean Development Mechanism: *see* ***Kyoto Protocol***.

Climate change: a term summarizing the concern that increased concentrations of ***greenhouse gases*** in the atmosphere because of human interference will lead to accelerated changes in climate patterns. *See also* ***Global Green New Deal***, ***Kyoto Protocol***, ***Paris Agreement***, ***trade and environment*** and ***United Nations Framework Convention on Climate Change***.

CLMV: Cambodia, Laos, Myanmar (Burma) and Viet Nam. The newer members of ***ASEAN***.

CNUCED: Conférence des Nations Unies sur le Commerce et le Développement. *See* ***UNCTAD***.

CoA*:** *see* ***Committee on Agriculture.

CoASS: ***Committee on Agriculture*** in special sessions, i.e. negotiating meetings.

Cobden-Chevalier Treaty: a commercial treaty concluded in 1860 between England and France. It brought ***most-favoured-nation treatment*** into general use within Europe for a few decades.

Cocktail approach: a term describing the concurrent use of several methods to achieve ***tariff*** reductions. A cocktail could include, for example, ***item-by-item tariff negotiations***, ***linear tariff cuts*** and ***zero-for-zero tariff reductions***. *See also* ***blended formula***.

COCOM: Co-ordinating Committee for Multilateral Export Controls. It was formed in response to a 1951 ***United Nations General Assembly*** recommendation for an embargo on the shipment of "arms, ammunition and implements of war, atomic energy materials, petroleum and items useful in the production of implements of war" to communist countries. In 1958, the list of prohibited

Classifications of goods, services and activities
货物、服务及活动分类

见*商品名称及编码协调制度(Harmonized Commodity Description and Coding System)*、*国际标准职业分类(International Standard Classification of Occupations)*、*全部经济活动国际标准行业分类(International Standard Industrial Classification of All Economic Activities)*、*国际贸易标准分类(Standard International Trade Classification-SITC)*、*联合国中央产品分类(United Nations Central Product Classification)*。

Clawback provisions
回拨条款

在根据美国反垄断法进行的域外诉讼中，被责令支付三倍赔偿的外国当事人通过国家法院系统收回超过实际损失的金额的能力。如果被责令支付三倍赔偿的当事方在其反诉中获胜，收到三倍赔偿的一方将被责令归还被认为超出的金额。只有收到赔偿金的公司首先在进行回拨程序的国家拥有资产的情况下，方有可能真正收回赔偿金。另见*治外法权(extraterritoriality)*。

Clayton Act
克莱顿法

美国的反垄断法，于 1914 年首次获得通过。该法旨在禁止一系列限制性商业惯例，并"在其萌芽阶段和形成之前阻止托拉斯、阴谋和垄断的产生"。还允许施加三倍赔偿。该法一般适用于对外贸易，但一些条款仅限于州际贸易。另见*竞争政策(competition policy)*、*罗宾逊帕特曼法(Robinson-Patman Act)*、*谢尔曼法(Sherman Act)*、*韦布-波默林法(Webb-Pomerene Act)*、*威尔逊关税法(Wilson Tariff Act)*。

Clean Development Mechanism
清洁发展机制

见*京都议定书(Kyoto Protocol)*。

Climate change
气候变化

这一词语概括了对因人类干扰造成的大气温室气体浓度增加将导致气候模式加速变化的担忧。另见*全球绿色新政(Global Green New Deal)*、*京都议定书(Kyoto Protocol)*、*巴黎协定(Paris Agreement)*、*贸易与环境(trade and environment)*、*联合国气候变化框架公约(United Nations Framework Convention on Climate Change)*。

CLMV
柬埔寨、老挝、缅甸和越南

东盟新成员。

CNUCED
联合国贸易与发展会议

见*联合国贸易与发展会议(UNCTAD)*。

CoA
农业委员会

见*农业委员会(Committee on Agriculture)*。

CoASS
农业委员会特别会议

以特别会议形式召开的农业委员会，即谈判会议。

Cobden-Chevalier Treaty
科布登-舍瓦利埃条约

1860 年英国与法国之间缔结的商业条约。使最惠国待遇在欧洲得到普遍使用长达几十年。

Cocktail approach
鸡尾酒方式

描述同时使用几种方法实现关税削减的词语。例如，鸡尾酒可以包括逐税目关税谈判、线性关税削减和零对零关税削减。另见*混合公式(blended formula)*。

COCOM
多边出口管制协调委员会

根据 1951 年联合国大会关于禁止向共产主义国家运送"武器、弹药和兵器、原子能材料、石油和用于生产武器的物品"的建议而成立。1958 年，被禁物品

articles was reduced to strictly strategic goods, and there were several changes afterwards in the list of prohibited articles. COCOM's membership consisted of NATO (North Atlantic Treaty Organization) countries, except Iceland, plus Japan. The ***Wassenaar Arrangement on Export Controls for Conventional Arms and Dual-Use Goods and Technologies***, effective from 1 November 1996, has superseded the COCOM arrangement.

Code-conditioned most-favoured-nation treatment: describes situations where ***most-favoured-nation treatment*** only has to be extended to members of the same GATT code or WTO agreement. An example of this is the WTO ***Agreement on Government Procurement***. *See also* ***conditional most-favoured-nation treatment***.

Code of conduct: usually a non-binding intergovernmental instrument that seeks to regulate certain types of behaviour of governments or private corporations. Codes of conduct are as difficult to negotiate as binding agreements since signatories normally expect to observe them in ***good faith***. Sometimes, codes of conduct are in fact the first step towards a binding agreement. *See also* ***memorandum of understanding***.

Code of Good Practice for the Preparation, Adoption and Application of Standards: this is contained in Annex 3 to the WTO ***Agreement on Technical Barriers to Trade***. Central government standardizing bodies must comply with its provisions, but it is open also to local government and non-government bodies. The Code contains fourteen substantive provisions aimed at the non-discriminatory and transparent preparation and administration of standards. *See also* ***conformity assessment***, ***International Electrotechnical Commission*** and ***International Organization for Standardization***.

Codex Alimentarius*:** a programme managed jointly by the ***Food and Agriculture Organization (FAO) and the World Health Organization for initiating, preparing, publishing and revising international food standards. These standards cover matters such as food labelling, food additives, contaminants, methods of analysis and sampling, food hygiene, nutrition and foods for special dietary uses, food import and export inspection and certification systems, residues of veterinary drugs in foods and pesticide residues in foods. In addition, there are standards applicable to particular commodities. The programme is administered by the ***Codex Alimentarius Commission***. [www.fao.org]

Codex Alimentarius* Commission:** established in 1963. This is the body charged with developing food standards, guidelines, recommendations, etc., under the ***Codex Alimentarius programme. The Commission's work on the harmonization of food standards supports aspects of the WTO work on ***sanitary and phytosanitary measures*** and ***technical barriers to trade***. [www.fao.org]

Código Aduanero Uniforme Centroamericano: CAUCA. *See* ***Central American Uniform Customs Code***.

Collected tariff rate: the tariff rate actually levied and collected by customs authorities when a good is imported. *See also* ***bound tariff rate***.

清单缩减为严格意义上的战略物资，此后被禁物品清单又有几次变化。COCOM的成员包括北大西洋公约组织(NATO)国家，冰岛除外，另包括日本。1996年11月1日生效的《关于常规武器和两用物品及技术出口管制的瓦森纳安排》取代了COCOM的安排。

Code-conditioned most-favoured-nation treatment

以守则为条件的最惠国待遇

描述最惠国待遇只需扩大至同一GATT守则或WTO协定的成员的情况。例如WTO《政府采购协定》。另见*有条件最惠国待遇(conditional most-favoured-nation treatment)*。

Code of conduct

行为守则

通常为一种非约束力的政府间文书，寻求规范政府或私营公司的某些类型的行为。行为守则的谈判难度与具有约束力的协议相同，因为签署方通常期望善意遵守守则。有时，行为守则实际上是达成具有约束力的协议的第一步。另见*谅解备忘录(memorandum of understanding)*。

Code of Good Practice for the Preparation, Adoption and Application of Standards

关于制定、采用和实施标准的良好行为规范

载于WTO《技术性贸易壁垒协定》附件3。中央政府的标准化机构必须遵守其规定，但它也对地方政府和非政府机构开放。该规范包含14项实质性规定，旨在以非歧视和透明的方式制定和管理标准。另见*合格评定(conformity assessment)*、*国际电工委员会(International Electrotechnical Commission)*、*国际标准化组织(International Organization for Standardization)*。

Codex Alimentarius

食品法典

由粮农组织(FAO)和世界卫生组织共同管理的一项计划，用于发起、制定、公布和修订国际食品标准。这些标准涵盖诸如食品标签、食品添加剂、污染物、分析和采样方法、食品卫生、营养和特殊膳食用食品、食品进出口检验和认证系统、食品兽药残留和食品农药残留等事项。此外，还有适用于特定商品的标准。该计划由国际食品法典委员会负责管理。

***Codex Alimentarius* Commission**

食品法典委员会

成立于1963年，负责根据食品法典计划制定食品标准、准则、建议等的机构。委员会在协调食品标准方面的工作支持WTO在卫生与植物卫生措施以及技术性贸易壁垒方面的工作。

Código Aduanero Uniforme Centroamericano

中美洲统一关税税则

CAUCA。见*中美洲统一海关代码(Central American Uniform Customs Code)*。

Collected tariff rate

实征税率

货物进口时海关实际征收的税率。另见*约束税率(bound tariff rate)*。

Collective action: a term used in ***APEC*** to describe activities aimed at liberalizing or expanding trade that can, by definition, only be carried out jointly. This is done through the ***Collective Action Plans***. These include mutual recognition of qualifications and standards, customs cooperation, etc. *See also* ***concerted liberalization action***.

Collective Action Plans: used by the members of APEC to detail actions they have taken jointly under the ***Osaka Action Agenda***. Their purpose is to make progress towards the ***Bogor Goals***.

Collective mark: a mark owned by a cooperative, a trade association, an association of producers or manufacturers, etc. which indicates that the user of the mark is a member of that body. The mark is meant to assure clients of member firms or purchasers of the products made by them that they are dealing with a reputable firm or product. Permission to use a collective mark is usually dependent on compliance with rules concerning production standards or geographical location of the user of the mark. Article 7bis of the ***Paris Convention*** requires member countries to protect collective marks belonging to associations lawfully established in the country of origin. *See also* ***certification mark***, ***geographical indications*** and ***trademarks***. [Paris Convention for the Protection of Industrial Property; WIPO SCT/8/4]

Collective preferences: a concept proposed by M. Pascal Lamy, the then Commissioner for Trade in the ***European Commission***, in 2004 to the effect that collective preferences "synthesize the preferences of individuals through political debate and institutions", and that they are "the end result of choices made by human communities that apply to the community (i.e. any group of persons that have set up institutions capable of forging preferences) as a whole".

Collective rights: *see* ***community rights***.

Colorado Group: a group active in the WTO which sought to develop multilateral principles for ***trade facilitation***. It had Australia, Canada, Chile, Colombia, Costa Rica, European Community, Hong Kong (China), Hungary, Japan, Korea, Morocco, New Zealand, Norway, Paraguay, Singapore, Switzerland and the United States as core members. *See also* ***Agreement on Trade Facilitation*** and ***Global Alliance for Trade Facilitation***.

Columbus Declaration: the ministerial declaration of 21 October 1994 launching the ***Trade Efficiency Programme*** administered by ***UNCTAD***. Its appendix contains recommendations to governments for trade efficiency in banking and insurance, customs, business information for trade, transport, telecommunications and business practices.

Comecon: *see* ***Council for Mutual Economic Assistance***.

COMESA: *see* ***Common Market for Eastern and Southern Africa***.

Comité des Représentants Permanents: a ***European Union*** coordination mechanism. *See* ***Coreper***.

Comity: a term used in international law to signify the reciprocal courtesy or mutual respect which one member of the family of nations owes to the others

Collective action
集体行动

APEC 中用于描述旨在开放贸易或扩大贸易的一系列活动的词语，根据定义，这些活动必须联合实施。这些活动通过集体行动计划实施，包括资格和标准的相互认证、海关合作等。另见*协调的自由化行动(concerted liberalization action)*。

Collective Action Plans
集体行动计划

APEC 成员用于细化已经根据《大阪行动议程》共同采取的行动。行动目标是朝着茂物目标取得进展。

Collective mark
集体商标

由一社团、一贸易协会、一生产商或制造商协会等所拥有的标志，表明标志的用户是该机构成员。该标志意味着使成员企业的客户或成员企业所制造产品的购买者相信，是在与一家有信誉的企业进行交易或购买信誉良好的产品。使用集体商标的许可通常取决于对有关产品标准规定的遵守程度或标志使用者的地理位置。《巴黎公约》第 7 条之二要求成员国保护原属国中依法设立的协会所拥有的集体标志。另见*认证标志(certification mark)*、*地理标志(geographical indications)*、*商标(trademarks)*。

Collective preferences
集体优惠

时任欧盟委员会贸易委员帕斯卡尔·拉米于2004年提出的一个概念，大意是，集体优惠是“通过政治辩论和机构将个人优惠进行综合”，且它们是“人类社会所作选择的最终结果，适用于整个社会(即能够给予优惠的已经建立机构的任何一组人)”。

Collective rights
集体权利

见*社区权利(community rights)*。

Colorado Group
科罗拉多集团

活跃于 WTO 中致力于制定贸易便利化多边规则的集团。核心成员为澳大利亚、加拿大、智利、哥伦比亚、哥斯达黎加、欧共体、中国香港、以色列、日本、韩国、摩洛哥、新西兰、挪威、巴拉圭、新加坡、瑞士和美国。另见*贸易便利化协定(Agreement on Trade Facilitation)*、*全球贸易便利化联盟(Global Alliance for Trade Facilitation)*。

Columbus Declaration
哥伦布宣言

1994 年 10 月 21 日发表的宣言，启动由联合国贸易与发展会议(UNCTAD)管理的贸易效率计划。宣言附录包含在银行和保险、海关、贸易商业信息、交通、电信和商业惯例方面对政府的建议。

Comecon
经互会

见*经济互助委员会(Council for Mutual Economic Assistance)*。

COMESA
东部和南部非洲共同市场

见*东部和南部非洲共同市场(Common Market for Eastern and Southern Africa)*。

Comité des Représentants Permanents
常驻代表委员会

欧盟的一种协调机制。另见*常驻代表委员会(Coreper)*。

Comity
礼让

国际法用语，代表国际大家庭的成员在考虑其官方行为的影响时，对其他成

in considering the effects of its official acts. *See also* ***negative comity*** and ***positive comity***.

Commerce: usually, but by no means exclusively, refers to activities related to the production, sale and distribution of goods and services within the ***internal market***. *See also* ***trade***.

Commercial defence mechanisms: *see* ***contingent protection***.

Commercial displacement: the replacement of sales on commercial terms by gifts or subsidized sales. This occurs, for example, when the granting of food aid takes away opportunities for sales at market prices.

Commercial import: the ***import*** of a product into a ***customs territory*** for the purpose of sale, incorporation in a good for sale or for the production of goods for sale.

Commercial policy: a term now slowly disappearing and in general use being replaced by ***trade policy*** with which it has coexisted for decades. It covers governmental acts, policies and practices which influence trade in goods and services. The drafters of the ***GATT*** thought of commercial policy as the subjects covered in Part II of the GATT which includes, among others, ***national treatment***, anti-dumping and countervailing duties, ***customs valuation***, import and export fees and formalities, ***marks of origin***, ***quantitative restrictions***, ***subsidies***, ***state-trading enterprises***, ***safeguards***, and consultation and ***dispute settlement***. *See also* ***common commercial policy***.

Commercial policy measurement: *see* ***measurement of commercial policy*** and ***non-tariff measures***.

Commercial presence: any type of business or professional establishment within the territory of a member of the ***General Agreement on Trade in Services*** (GATS) for the purpose of supplying a service. This includes subsidiaries, branches and representative offices. *See also* ***modes of services delivery***, ***right of establishment*** and ***right of non-establishment***.

Commercial services trade: *see* ***trade in services***.

Commercial treaty: any agreement between two or more countries which is concerned mainly with the conduct of trade relations between them. For examples of commercial treaties *see* ***bilateral trade agreement***, ***economic framework agreement***, ***free-trade agreement***, ***trade and economic agreement*** and ***trade and investment facilitation agreement***.

Commission of the European Union: *see* ***European Commission***.

Commission on Phytosanitary Measures: established under the auspices of the ***Food and Agriculture Organization*** through the 1997 revision of the ***International Plant Protection Convention*** (IPPC). Its main functions are to (a) review the state of plant protection in the world and the need for action to control the international spread of pests and their introduction into endangered areas, (b) develop and adopt international standards, and (c) establish rules for the resolution of disputes concerning obligations under the IPPC. Until the entry into force of the revised IPPC, the Commission is known as the Interim Commission on Phytosanitary Measures.

员应给予的对等礼遇或相互尊重。另见*消极礼让(negative comity)*、*积极礼让(positive comity)*。

Commerce
商业

通常但并非仅指内部市场中与生产、销售和分销货物和服务有关的活动。另见*贸易(trade)*。

Commercial defence mechanism
商业保护机制

见*紧急保护(contingent protection)*。

Commercial displacement
商业替代

将以商业条件进行的销售以礼物或补贴销售形式加以替代。例如，此种情况发生在给予食品援助即剥夺了以市场价格销售的机会之时。

Commercial import
商业进口

以销售、并入一供销售的货物或生产供销售的货物为目的将一产品进口至一关税领土。

Commercial policy
商业政策

这一词语正在逐渐消失，且在通常使用中已被与其共存几十年的贸易政策一词所取代。涵盖影响货物贸易的政府行为、政策和做法。GATT 的起草者想到的 GATT 第二部分所涵盖的商业政策包括国民待遇、反倾销税和反补贴税、海关估价、进出口规费和手续、原产地标记、数量限制、补贴、国营贸易企业、保障措施以及磋商和争端解决。另见*共同商业政策(common commercial policy)*。

Commercial policy measurement
商业政策测算

见*商业政策测算(measurement of commercial policy)*、*非关税措施(non-tariff measures)*。

Commercial presence
商业存在

《服务贸易总协定》(GATS)一成员领土内为提供服务目的而设立的任何类型的商业或专业机构。包括子公司、分支机构和代表机构。另见*服务提供模式(modes of services delivery)*、*设立权(right of establishment)*、*无需设立商业实体(non-establishment)*。

Commercial services trade
商业服务贸易

见*服务贸易(trade in services)*。

Commercial treaty
商业条约

两个或多个国家之间的任何协定，主要涉及它们之间的贸易关系的处理。商业条约的例子见双边贸易协定、经济框架协定、自由贸易协定、贸易经济协定以及贸易投资便利化协定。

Commission of the European Union
欧盟委员会

见*欧盟委员会(European Commission)*。

Commission on Phytosanitary Measures
植物卫生措施委员会

通过 1997 年修订的《国际植物保护公约》(IPPC)，在粮农组织(FAO)主持下成立。主要职能为：(a)审议世界植物保护状况以及对控制有害生物在国际上扩散及其传入受威胁地区而采取行动的必要性；(b)制定和采用国际标准；以及(c)制定解决涉及 IPPC 义务争端的规则。在修订的 IPPC 生效之前，委员会称为植物卫生措施临时委员会。

Commission on Science and Technology for Development: a subsidiary body of ***ECOSOC***, but serviced by ***UNCTAD***. It has a work programme with a strong development perspective covering technology for small-scale economic activities, gender implications of science and technology, science and technology and the environment, the contribution of technologies to industrialization in developing countries, and information technologies and their role in science and technology. The Commission meets every two years.

Commitment: a legally binding undertaking specific to a country under one of the agreements administered by the WTO. Examples of commitments are tariff ***bindings*** and inscriptions in the schedules of commitments on services. Such commitments usually stem from negotiations between two or more parties and are then made available in a non-discriminatory way to all parties of the agreement concerned. *See also* ***additional commitments***.

Commitment mechanisms: as argued in the *Asian Development Outlook 2002* and elsewhere, preferential trade agreements can hasten or lock in economic policy reforms. Whether an agreement does this depends greatly on the robustness of its provisions, including the credibility of the applicable dispute settlement system. [Asian Development Bank 2002]

Committee of Permanent Representatives: a ***European Union*** coordination mechanism. *See* ***Coreper***.

Committee on Agriculture: CoA. The committee established under Article 17 of the WTO ***Agreement on Agriculture***. Through it its members agree to review progress made in the implementation of commitments negotiated under the ***Uruguay Round*** reform programme, to give due consideration to the influence of excessive rates of inflation and to consult annually on their participation in world trade in agricultural products within the framework of commitments on export subsidies. The negotiations on agriculture under the ***Doha Development Agenda*** take place in special sessions of the Committee on Agriculture (CoASS).

Committee on Regional Trade Agreements: the WTO body charged with examining ***regional trade agreements***, sometimes called preferential trade agreements, concluded by WTO members, as well as developing policy towards such agreements. *See also* ***regional trade agreement*** and ***transparency mechanism for RTAs***.

Committee on Rules of Origin: *see* ***Agreement on Rules of Origin***.

Committee on Specific Commitments: the WTO committee responsible for overseeing the implementation of ***specific commitments*** made by WTO members under the ***General Agreement on Trade in Services***.

Committee on Trade and Development: a WTO committee established on 26 November 1964. It is concerned with developing-country issues. One of its main tasks has long been the administration of ***Part IV of the GATT*** and the ***Enabling Clause***. *See also* ***developing countries and the multilateral trading system***.

Committee on Trade and Environment: a WTO committee established in response to the ***Rio Declaration on Environment and Development*** and

Commission on Science and Technology for Development
科学技术促进发展委员会

联合国经社理事会(ECOSOC)附属机构，但由联合国贸易与发展会议(UNCTAD)提供服务。该委员会的工作计划具有鲜明的发展立场，涵盖小型经济活动所使用的技术、科学技术的性别影响、科技与环境、技术对发展中国家工业化的贡献以及信息技术及其在科学和技术中的作用。委员会每 2 年召开一次会议。

Commitment
承诺

在 WTO 所管理的一项协定项下专门针对一国的具有法律约束力的保证。承诺的例子包括关税约束和服务贸易承诺减让表中的内容。此类承诺通常源自双方或多方之间的谈判，随后以非歧视的方式适用于有关协定的所有参加方。另见*附加承诺(additional commitments)*。

Commitment mechanisms
承诺机制

正如《2002 年亚洲发展展望》等所指出的，优惠贸易协定可加速或锁定经济政策改革。一协定能否实现这一点在很大程度上取决于其条款的力度，包括所适用的争端解决机制的可信度。

Committee of Permanent Representatives
常驻代表委员会

欧盟的协调机制。另见*常驻代表委员会(Coreper)*。

Committee on Agriculture
农业委员会

CoA。根据 WTO《农业协定》第 17 条设立的委员会。通过委员会，成员同意审议在乌拉圭回合改革计划项下谈判承诺的实施进展情况，适当考虑过高通货膨胀率的影响，并在关于出口补贴的承诺框架内，每年就它们参与世界农产品贸易的情况进行磋商。多哈发展议程下的农业谈判在农业委员会特别会议中进行。

Committee on Regional Trade Agreements
区域贸易协定委员会

WTO 负责审议 WTO 成员所缔结的区域贸易协定(有时也称优惠贸易协定)的机构，并针对此类协定制定政策。另见*区域贸易协定(regional trade agreement)*、*区域贸易协定透明度机制(transparency mechanism for RTAs)*。

Committee on Rules of Origin
原产地规则委员会

见*原产地规则协定(Agreement on Rules of Origin)*。

Committee on Specific Commitments
具体承诺委员会

WTO 负责监督 WTO 成员实施在《服务贸易总协定》项下所作具体承诺的委员会。

Committee on Trade and Development
贸易与发展委员会

WTO 中的委员会，最早于 1964 年 11 月 26 日设立。关注发展中国家的问题。长期以来的主要任务之一是管理 GATT 第四部分和授权条款。另见*发展中国家与多边贸易体制(developing countries and the multilateral trading system)*。

Committee on Trade and Environment
贸易与环境委员会

WTO 为回应《里约环境与发展宣言》和《21 世纪议程》而设立的委员会。

Agenda 21. Its task is to identify the relationship between trade measures and environmental measures to promote ***sustainable development*** and to make recommendations on possible changes to the rules of the multilateral trading system concerning goods, services and ***intellectual property rights***. According to the Committee's terms of reference, any suggested changes ought to be compatible with the open, equitable and non-discriminatory nature of the multilateral trading system. *See also* ***multilateral environment agreements*** and ***trade and environment***.

Committee on Trade Facilitation: established under the WTO ***Agreement on Trade Facilitation*** to enable members to consult on any aspect of the operation of the Agreement. It meets at least once a year. *See also* ***National Committee on Trade Facilitation***.

Commodities and Development Report: a report prepared about every two years in the ***UNCTAD*** Secretariat which analyses global commodities trade from the perspective of developing countries. *See also* ***Trade and Development Report***. [www.unctad.org]

Commodity: any article exchanged in trade, but commonly used to refer to raw materials. Examples are wheat, tin, copper, manganese, iron ore, coffee, tea and rubber. *See also* ***buffer stocks***, ***commodity-dependent developing countries***, ***commodity policy***, ***commodity terms of trade*** and ***international commodity agreements***.

Commodity arrangements: a general term for schemes to manage the production and trade of commodities. *See* ***administrative international commodity agreements***, ***buffer stocks***, ***commodity policy***, ***economic international commodity agreements*** and ***Integrated Programme for Commodities***.

Commodity cartels: public or private ***cartels*** formed to maintain the price of a commodity above what it would fetch on open markets. The usual mechanisms are the imposition of ***export quotas*** and collusion to maintain prices above real market levels. Such cartels can only be successful if they include all of the important producers and if no commodity can be readily substituted. ***OPEC*** was a successful cartel for some time, but its ability to keep prices up led to the entry of higher-cost producers into the market. The international diamond cartel based in South Africa also operated profitably for many years. *See also* ***commodity policy***, ***international commodity agreements***, ***international steel cartel*** and ***resources diplomacy***.

Commodity Credit Corporation: CCC. A government corporation within the United States Department of Agriculture charged with stabilizing, supporting and protecting farm incomes. The main functions of the CCC are (a) to assist producers through loans, purchases and payments and through providing materials and facilities needed in the production and marketing of agricultural commodities, and (b) to permit the sale of agricultural commodities to other government agencies and foreign governments as well as to donate food to domestic and international relief agencies. The CCC also has a role in developing new domestic and international markets. Main commodities receiving CCC

任务是确定贸易措施与促进可持续发展的环境措施之间的关系，并就多边贸易体制中有关货物、服务和知识产权的规则可能的变更提出建议。根据委员会的职权范围，任何改革建议都应符合多边贸易体制的开放、公正和非歧视性质。另见*多边环境协定(multilateral environment agreements)*、*贸易与环境(trade and environment)*。

Committee on Trade Facilitation
贸易便利化委员会

根据 WTO《贸易便利化协定》设立，使成员能够就协定运用的任何方面进行磋商。委员会每年至少召开一次会议。另见*国家贸易便利化委员会(National Committee and Trade Facilitation)*。

Commodities and Development Report
初级商品与发展报告

联合国贸易与发展会议(UNCTAD)秘书处大约每 2 年编写一份的报告，从发展中国家的角度分析全球初级商品贸易。另见*贸易与发展报告(Trade and Development Report)*。

Commodity
商品

在贸易中交换的任何物品，但通常指原材料。例如小麦、锡、铜、锰、铁矿石、咖啡、茶叶和橡胶。另见*缓冲储存(buffer stocks)*、*依赖初级商品的发展中国家(commodity-dependent developing countries)*、*商品政策(commodity policy)*、*商品贸易条件(commodity terms of trade)*、*国际商品协定(international commodity agreements)*。

Commodity arrangements
商品安排

管理商品生产和贸易的机制的总称。另见*国际商品管理协定(administrative international commodity agreements)*、*缓冲储存(buffer stocks)*、*商品政策(commodity policy)*、*国际商品经济协定(economic international commodity agreements)*、*商品综合方案(Integrated Programme for Commodities)*。

Commodity cartels
商品卡特尔

公共或私营卡特尔，目的是使一商品的价格维持在公开市场所能买到的价格之上。通常的机制为实施出口配额和串通以保持价格高于实际市场水平。此类卡特尔只有在包括了所有重要生产者且无任何商品可以轻易替代的情况下方能取得成功。石油输出国组织(OPEC)曾一度是成功的卡特尔，但其保持价格上涨能力使成本更高的生产商进入了市场。设在南非的国际钻石卡特尔也多年经营获利。另见*商品政策(commodity policy)*、*国际商品协定(international commodity agreements)*、*国际钢铁卡特尔(international steel cartel)*、*资源外交(resources diplomacy)*。

Commodity Credit Corporation
商品信贷公司

CCC。美国农业部的一家政府企业，负责稳定、支持和保护农业收入。CCC 的主要职能为：(a)通过贷款、收购和支付以及通过提供生产和销售农产品所需的材料和设施帮助生产者；及(b)批准向其他政府机构和外国政府出售农产品，

support are wheat, corn, oilseeds, cotton, rice, tobacco, milk and milk products, barley, oats, grain sorghum, mohair, honey, peanuts and sugar. Farmers can receive commodity loans in return for pledging and storing part of the commodity as a security. This mechanism is called the ***loan rate***. Farmers may also be eligible for ***deficiency payments***. CCC finances sales made under the ***Export Enhancement Program*** (EEP) and the ***Dairy Export Incentive Program*** (DEIP). *See also* ***Food for Progress Program*** and ***PL 480***.

Commodity-dependent developing countries: CDDC. A term used, for example, in the UNCTAD ***Commodities and Development Report*** to refer to developing countries dependent on the production and export of basic commodities for the bulk of their export earnings. The report on *State of Commodity Dependence*, also published by UNCTAD, contains a great deal of relevant information.

Commodity policy: the part of ***trade policy*** dealing with governmental actions affecting international trade in commodities. Its principal objectives are to secure fair and remunerative returns to producers and reliable and competitive supplies to consumers. Neither of these aims can be defined objectively. Commodities have always been classified by some as needing special measures because of unpredictable supply and demand fluctuations and the attendant price changes and export income fluctuations. One reason for this is that in some commodities relatively small changes in supply and demand can lead to considerable price fluctuations. In other cases, particularly agricultural products, the livelihood of large population segments is to a greater or lesser extent influenced by developments in the market. Governments tend to be alert to such concerns and to seek ways and means to alleviate them. Modern international commodity policy began with the drafting of the ***Havana Charter*** which essentially favoured free-market principles. The draft Charter allowed the creation of ***international commodity agreements*** (ICAs) with price and trade controls, called intergovernmental control agreements, only if normal market forces were unable to deal rapidly with adjustments between production and consumption, and widespread unemployment in connection with a primary commodity was either happening or expected to happen. The free-market principle was, however, compromised in many ways as drafting proceeded to permit, for example, government planning by those who saw a need for it. Developing countries were allowed to maintain import restrictions to protect domestic industries. In the end, the Havana Charter did not enter into force. In 1947, ***ECOSOC*** established an Interim Co-ordinating Committee for International Commodity Arrangements (ICCICA) with a mandate to convene commodity study groups and to recommend calling conferences to negotiate commodity arrangements. Several ICAs with stabilization mechanisms were negotiated under its auspices. The ***Haberler Report***, prepared under GATT auspices in 1958, cautiously supported the conclusion of international commodity agreements and limited compensatory financing schemes. When ***UNCTAD*** was established in 1964, ICCICA's functions were transferred to it. In the early 1970s proposals for a ***New International Economic Order*** were

以及向国内和国际救济机构捐赠粮食。CCC 还负责开拓新的国内和国际市场。获得 CCC 支持的主要商品为小麦、玉米、油籽、棉花、大米、烟草、牛奶和奶制品、大麦、燕麦、粒用高粱、马海毛、蜂蜜、花生和食糖。农民可以接受商品贷款，以抵押和储存部分商品作为担保。这一机制称为基准贷款价格。农民也有资格获得差价补贴。CCC 资助在出口促进计划(EEP)和奶制品出口激励计划(DEIP)项下的销售。另见*粮食促进步计划(Food for Progress Program)*、*480 号公法(PL 480)*。

Commodity-dependent developing countries
依赖初级商品的发展中国家

CDDC。指大部分出口收入依赖基本初级商品的生产和出口的发展中国家，联合国贸易与发展会议(UNCTAD)《初级商品与发展报告》中使用该词。UNCTAD 还发布《商品依赖状况报告》，其中包含大量相关信息。

Commodity policy
商品政策

贸易政策中处理影响国际商品贸易的政府行为的部分。主要目标是保证生产者获得公平和丰厚回报及消费者获得可靠和有竞争的供应。这两个目标都难以进行客观定义。商品总是被一些人归入需要特殊措施的类别，理由是无法预测的供求波动及由此导致的价格变化和出口收入波动。其中一条理由是，一些商品相对较小的供求变化即会导致巨大的价格波动。另一个理由是，特别对于农产品，大量人口群体的生计或多或少受到市场中发展情况的影响。政府往往对此类关注保持警惕，并寻求减轻这些关注的途径和手段。现代国际商品政策肇始于《哈瓦那宪章》草案，宪章从根本上支持自由市场原则。宪章草案允许制定实施价格和贸易管制的国际商品协定(ICA)，称为政府间控制协定，条件是在正常市场力量无法快速处理生产与消费之间的调整且与初级商品有关的普遍失业正在发生或预计发生的情况下。然而自由市场原则在起草过程中在许多方面作出妥协，例如允许在认为有必要时实行政府计划。发展中国家被允许维持进口限制以保护国内产业。最终，《哈瓦那宪章》没有生效。1947 年，联合国经社理事会(ECOSOC)设立了国际商品安排临时协调委员会(ICCICA)，授权其召集商品研究小组，并就召开会议谈判商品安排提出建议。在其主持下，对若干设有稳定机制的 ICA 开展了谈判。1958 年在 GATT 主持下编写的《哈伯勒报告》谨慎地支持缔结国际商品协定和有限的补偿性融资方案。1964 年联合国贸易与发展会议(UNCTAD)成立时，ICCICA 的职能转至该组织。在 20 世纪 70 年代早期，讨论了建立国际经济新秩序的提议但

discussed without result. They envisaged a massive transfer of resources to developing countries, partly through commodity arrangements and schemes to deal with export earnings shortfalls. UNCTAD was from the beginning much more interventionist in its views of commodity policy, and at UNCTAD IV (1976) it developed the ***Integrated Programme for Commodities*** and the ***Common Fund for Commodities***. These are mechanisms to regulate and stabilize international commodity trade through ***buffer stocks*** and compensatory financing. Sober assessments of the issues attaching to international commodities trade from the mid-1980s onwards, prompted to some extent by the collapse of the ***International Tin Agreement***, cast increasing doubt on the merits of large-scale market intervention, both from the producer and consumer perspective. The consensus view appears to have returned to basically free-market principles which limit international cooperation to the promotion of ***transparency*** mechanisms and the financing of research and development to make commodities more attractive to manufacturers and users. *See also* ***compensatory financing arrangements*** and ***single commodity producers***.

Commodity terms of trade: an index showing the ratio of commodity prices to prices for manufactured goods. Commodity terms of trade have improved if fewer commodities have to be sold to pay for a given amount of manufactures. They have deteriorated when more commodities have to be sold. *See also* ***Singer-Prebisch thesis*** and ***terms of trade***.

Common agricultural policy: CAP. The basic agricultural policy of the ***European Union***. Originally established in 1962 and redefined several times since. Article 39 of the ***Treaty on the Functioning of the European Union*** gives the objectives of the CAP as (a) to increase agricultural productivity by promoting technical progress and by ensuring the rational development of agricultural production and the optimum utilization of the factors of production, in particular labour, (b) to ensure a fair standard of living for the agricultural community, in particular by increasing the individual earnings of persons engaged in agriculture, (c) to stabilize markets, (d) to assure the availability of supplies, and (e) to ensure that supplies reach consumers at reasonable prices. The operational aims of the CAP have been revised periodically, and they currently are: (a) to support farmers and improve agricultural productivity so that consumers have a stable supply of affordable food, (b) to ensure that European Union farmers can make a reasonable living, (c) to help tackle climate change and ensure the sustainable management of natural resources, (d) to maintain rural areas and landscapes across the European Union, and (e) to keep the rural economy alive by promoting jobs in farming, agri-foods industries and associated sectors. The CAP works in three main ways: (a) income support through direct payments to farmers to ensure income stability, (b) market measures aimed at dealing with difficult market conditions, such as a sudden change in demand through a health scare or temporary oversupply of an agricultural commodity, and (c) rural development measures. Over the years the CAP has been much criticized for distorting world agricultural markets through its use of

无结果，其设想向发展中国家大规模转移资源，部分是通过商品安排和方案处理出口收入缺口。UNCTAD 从一开始即持对商品政策进行更多干预的立场，在 1976 年 UNCTAD 第 4 届大会上，制定了商品综合方案和商品共同基金。这些机制通过缓冲储存和补偿性融资来调节和稳定国际商品贸易。从 1980 年代中期开始对国际商品贸易有关问题进行了清醒的评估，某种程度上是由于《国际锡协定》的失败引发的，对大型市场干预的优点的怀疑态度日渐增加。共识似乎回到了基本上的自由市场原则，这些原则将国际合作限定在促进透明度机制和资助研究与开发，而使商品对制造商和用户更具吸引力。另见*补偿性融资安排(compensatory financing arrangements)*、*单一商品生产国(single commodity producers)*。

Commodity terms of trade
商品贸易条件

显示商品价格与制成品价格比率的指数。如果为支付一给定数量制成品所需出售的商品更少，表明商品贸易条件得到改善。如果需要出售更多商品，表明商品贸易条件恶化。另见*辛格-普雷维什命题(Singer-Prebisch thesis)*、*贸易条件(terms of trade)*。

Common agricultural policy
共同农业政策

CAP。欧盟基本农业政策。最初于 1962 年制定，此后多次修改。《欧洲联盟运行条约》第 39 条规定，CAP 的目标为：(a)通过促进技术进步和保证农业生产的合理发展及生产要素(特别是劳动力)最佳利用，以提高农业生产率；(b)保证农业社区的公平生活水平，特别是通过增加从事农业人员的个人收入的方式；(c)稳定市场；(d)保障供应；以及(e)保证消费者以合理价格获得供应品。CAP 的运行目标几经修改，现行目标为：(a)支持农民，并提高农业生产力，使消费者能够获得负担得起的粮食的稳定供应；(b)保证欧盟农民能够过上合理的生活；(c)帮助应对气候变化和保证自然资源的可持续管理；(d)维护整个欧盟的农村地区和景观；以及(e)通过促进农业、农产品工业和相关部门的就业，保持农村经济活力。CAP 主要通过三种方式发挥作用：(a)通过对农民直接支付的收入支持保证收入稳定；(b)旨在应对困难市场条件的市场措施，例如由于健康恐慌或农产品暂时供给过剩而导致需求突然变化；以及(c)乡村发展措施。多年来，CAP 一直因使用出口补贴扭曲世界农产品市场而受到批评。在

export subsidies. Within the European Union it has attracted criticism for favouring large farms and for its effect on European Union budgets. The ***European Commission*** published proposals in 2018 for the working of the CAP after 2020. These would, *inter alia*, give a higher level of support per hectare to small and medium-sized farms, reward environmental and climate action, and help new generations to become farmers. These new proposals in the administration of the CAP, if adopted, would shift the emphasis from compliance and rules towards results and performance. The CAP is financed by the ***European Agricultural Guarantee Fund*** (EAGF) which finances direct payments to farmers as well as measures regulating or supporting agricultural markets and the ***European Agricultural Fund for Rural Development*** which finances the European Union's contribution to rural development programmes. Together they account for about 40 per cent of the European Union's budget. *See also* ***Basic Payment Scheme***.

Common Arab Market: *see* ***Greater Arab Free Trade Area***.

Common commercial policy: originally introduced through Article 113 of the ***Treaty of Rome*** (amended to Article 133 of the ***Treaty of Amsterdam***), and now Article 207 of the ***Treaty on the Functioning of the European Union***, the member states of the ***European Union*** conduct a common commercial policy based on uniform principles, particularly in regard to changes in tariff rates, the conclusion of tariff and trade agreements, the achievement of uniformity in measures of liberalization, export policy and measures to protect trade, such as those to be taken in the event of dumping or subsidies. Agreements on trade in services and the commercial aspects of intellectual property are subject to the common commercial policy, but only to the extent that they do not go beyond the Community's internal powers. This leaves a degree of uncertainty about the limits of the common commercial policy, but which in practice always gets sorted out. The policy is administered by the ***European Commission***. Member states do not have the authority to change unilaterally the ***common external tariff*** or to enter into trade agreements with other countries. There are highly developed internal consultative mechanisms under which member states may bring forward proposals for changes to the common commercial policy. *See also* ***common agricultural policy*** and ***Trade Policy Committee***.

Common Crisis North–South: Cooperation for World Recovery*:** *see* ***Brandt Report.

Common customs tariff: *see* ***common external tariff***.

Common economic space: an imprecise term indicating that two or more countries have agreed to pursue some common economic policies and possibly form a ***free-trade area***. In its most developed form it probably would be a ***common market***. *See also* ***single economic space***.

Common External Preferential Tariff: CEPT. The mechanism for reducing tariffs that operated under ***AFTA***. Now superseded by the ***ASEAN Trade in Goods Agreement***.

欧盟内部，这一政策因有利于大型农场及其对欧盟预算的影响而招致批评。欧盟委员会于 2018 年公布了关于 2020 年后 CAP 工作的提议。这些措施中包含给予中小型农场每公顷更高支持水平，奖励环境和气候行动，并帮助新一代成为农民。如果这些管理 CAP 的新提议得以采纳，将把重点从合规和规则转移到结果和实绩上。欧洲农业担保基金(EAGF)和欧洲农业发展基金为 CAP 提供资金，EAGF 提供资金的范围包括给予农民的直接支付和监管或支持农产品市场的措施，发展基金为欧盟农村发展方案的拨款提供资金，加在一起占欧盟预算的 40%。*另见基本支付方案(Basic Payment Scheme)*。

Common Arab Market

阿拉伯共同市场

见大阿拉伯自由贸易区(Greater Arab Free Trade Area)。

Common commercial policy

共同商业政策

最初通过经《阿姆斯特丹条约》第 133 条修订的《罗马条约》第 113 条采用，现在为《欧洲联盟运行条约》第 207 条。欧盟成员国在统一原则的基础上实行共同商业政策，特别是在关税税率变更、缔结关税和贸易协定、自由化措施的统一实现、出口政策和贸易保护措施(例如在发生倾销或补贴时采取的措施)等方面。服务贸易和与贸易有关的知识产权的协定受共同商业政策管辖，但仅限于这些协定不超出共同体的内部权力。这就给共同商业政策的界限留下一定程度的不确定性，但在实践中总会得到解决。政策由欧盟委员会进行管理。欧盟成员国无权单方面改变共同对外关税或与其他国家签订贸易协定。在高度发达的内部协商机制下，成员国可以提出修改共同商业政策的提案。*另见共同农业政策(common agricultural policy)、贸易政策委员会(Trade Policy Committee)*。

Common Crisis North–South: Cooperation for World Recovery

南北共同的危机：合作推动世界复苏

见勃兰特报告(Brandt Report)。

Common customs tariff

共同关税

见共同对外关税(common external tariff)。

Common economic space

共同经济空间

一个不确切的词语，表示两个或两个以上国家已同意采取一些共同经济政策，并可能形成自由贸易区。在更深入发展的阶段，可能是共同市场。*另见单一经济空间(single economic space)*。

Common External Preferential Tariff

共同对外优惠关税

CEPT。东盟自由贸易区(AFTA)项下运行的关税削减机制。现被《东盟货物贸易协定》所取代。

Common external tariff: the uniform tariff rates applied by the members of a ***customs union*** against non-members. Members of a customs union agree to eliminate or phase out all tariffs among themselves. At the same time, they replace their individual tariffs with a single tariff applied to third countries. Membership of a customs union may therefore entail an unchanged, higher or lower tariff by individual members on a given product. Under WTO rules, the resulting changes may not be used to increase the level of protection overall. ***Free-trade areas*** do not have a common external tariff. *See also* ***common commercial policy***.

Common fisheries policy: CFP. A ***European Union*** policy that aims to ensure that fishing and aquaculture are environmentally, economically and socially sustainable, and that they provide a source of healthy food for European Union citizens. The update taking effect in 2014 has four main policy areas: fisheries management, international policy, market and trade policy and funding of the CFP. *See also* ***common agricultural policy***. [ec.europa.eu]

Common Fund for Commodities: CFC. Usually known as the Common Fund. An intergovernmental financial institution originally proposed at UNCTAD IV (1976) as the financing mechanism for the ***Integrated Programme for Commodities***. Negotiations on its structure were completed in 1980, and it entered into force in 1989. Its main functions are (a) to contribute through its First Account to the financing of international ***buffer stocks*** and internationally coordinated national stocks, all within the framework of ***international commodity agreements*** (this account does not seem to be operational) and (b) to finance, through its Second Account, measures in the field of commodities other than stocking. The Fund has 101 members. The ***African Union***, ***Andean Community***, ***Caribbean Community and Common Market***, ***Common Market for Eastern and Southern Africa***, ***East African Community***, ***Economic Community of West African States***, ***European Union***, ***Southern African Development Community*** and the ***West African Economic and Monetary Union*** are institutional members. Its secretariat is located in Amsterdam. *See also* ***commodity policy***, ***international commodity bodies*** and ***UNCTAD***.

Common market: a more developed type of ***customs union*** in which, in addition to the free movement of goods between member states, labour, capital and services can also move without restriction. Common markets lead to highly integrated economies. *See also* ***four freedoms***.

Common Market: *see* ***European Economic Community***.

Common Market for Eastern and Southern Africa: COMESA. The treaty establishing COMESA was signed at Kampala on 5 November 1993. It is the successor to the Preferential Trade Area for Eastern and Southern African States (PTA). Its members are Burundi, Comoros, Democratic Republic of Congo, Djibouti, Egypt, Eritrea, Eswatini, Ethiopia, Kenya, Libya, Madagascar, Malawi, Mauritius, Rwanda, Seychelles, Sudan, Uganda, Zambia and Zimbabwe. The aims of COMESA are (a) to attain sustainable growth and development of member states by promoting a more balanced and harmonious

Common external tariff

共同对外关税

关税同盟成员对非成员实施的统一关税税率。关税同盟成员同意取消或逐步取消相互之间的所有关税。同时，成员以单一实施关税替代各自对第三国实施的关税。因此关税同盟成员资格可能意味着各成员对一给定产品的关税保持不变、需要提高或需要降低。根据 WTO 规则，由此产生的变化不得用以提高总体保护水平。自由贸易区没有共同对外关税。另见*共同商业政策(common commercial policy)*。

Common fisheries policy

共同渔业政策

CFP。欧盟的一项政策，旨在保证捕捞和水产养殖环境、经济和社会可持续，且为欧盟公民提供健康食品来源。2014 年生效的更新政策有四个主要政策领域：渔业管理、国际政策、市场和贸易政策以及共同渔业政策的筹资。另见*共同农业政策(common agricultural policy)*。

Common Fund for Commodities

商品共同基金

CFC。通常称为共同基金。最初是在 1976 年联合国贸易与发展会议(UNCTAD)第 4 届大会上提议的政府间金融机构，作为商品综合方案的融资机制。关于共同基金结构的谈判于 1980 年完成，并于 1989 年生效。主要职能为：(a)通过“第一账户”为国际缓冲储存和国际协调的国家储存提供融资，这些均在国际商品协定的框架内进行(该账户似乎未运行)；(b)通过“第二账户”为商品领域储存以外的措施提供融资。基金有 101 个成员。非洲联盟、安第斯共同体、加勒比共同体和共同市场、东部和南部非洲共同市场、东非共同体、西非国家经济共同体、欧盟、南部非洲发展共同体以及西非经济货币联盟为机构成员。秘书处设在阿姆斯特丹。另见*商品政策(commodity policy)*、*国际商品机构(international commodity bodies)*、*联合国贸易与发展会议(UNCTAD)*。

Common market

共同市场

一种更为成熟的关税同盟，内部成员国之间不仅实现货物自由流动，劳工、资本和服务也可以无限制流动。共同市场会形成高度一体化的经济体。另见*四大自由(four freedoms)*。

Common Market

共同市场

见*欧洲经济共同体(European Economic Community)*。

Common Market for Eastern and Southern Africa

东部和南部非洲共同市场

COMESA。建立 COMESA 的条约于 1993 年 11 月 5 日在坎帕拉签署。是东部和南部非洲国家优惠贸易区(PTA)的后继安排。成员包括布隆迪、科摩洛、刚果(金)、吉布提、埃及、厄立特里亚、斯威士兰、埃塞俄比亚、肯尼亚、利比亚、马达加斯加、马拉维、毛里求斯、卢旺达、塞舌尔、苏丹、乌干达、赞比亚和津巴布韦。COMESA 的目标为：(a)通过促进更加平衡和和谐的生产和

development of its production and marketing structures, (b) to promote joint development in all fields of economic activity and the joint adoption of macroeconomic policies and programmes to raise the standard of its peoples and to foster closer relations among members states, (c) to cooperate in the creation of an enabling environment for foreign, cross-border and domestic investment, including the joint promotion of research and adaptation of science and technology for development, (d) to cooperate in the promotion of peace, security and stability among the member states in order to enhance economic development in the region, (e) to cooperate in strengthening the relations between the Common Market and the rest of the world and the adoption of common positions in international fora, and (f) to contribute towards the establishment, progress and the realization of the objectives of the ***African Economic Community***. A COMESA Free Trade Area was established in 2000. It is to be transformed into a monetary union by 2025. COMESA's secretariat is located at Lusaka. *See also* ***African regional economic integration***.

Commonwealth: an association of fifty-three independent states established in its present form in 1949 through the London Declaration. Its members were at one time or another part of the British Empire. It is administered by the Commonwealth Secretariat located in London. Among its many functions, the Secretariat runs programmes aimed at the economic and trade development particularly of developing members. The Commonwealth's current membership consists of Antigua and Barbuda, Australia, The Bahamas, Bangladesh, Barbados, Belize, Botswana, Britain, Brunei, Cameroon, Canada, Cyprus, Dominica, Eswatini, Fiji, The Gambia, Ghana, Grenada, Guyana, India, Jamaica, Kenya, Kiribati, Lesotho, Malawi, Malaysia, Maldives, Malta, Mauritius, Mozambique, Namibia, Nauru, New Zealand, Nigeria, Pakistan, Papua New Guinea, Saint Christopher and Nevis, Saint Lucia, Saint Vincent and the Grenadines, Samoa, Seychelles, Sierra Leone, Singapore, Solomon Islands, South Africa, Sri Lanka, Tanzania, Tonga, Trinidad and Tobago, Tuvalu, Uganda, Vanuatu and Zambia. *See also* ***CHOGM*** (Commonwealth Heads of Government Meeting).

Commonwealth of Independent States: CIS. Formed in December 1991 with many of the republics that had made up the Soviet Union. Its members are Armenia, Belarus, Kazakhstan, Kyrgyz Republic, Moldova, Russia, Tajikistan, Turkmenistan (associate member since 2005), Ukraine (in the process of withdrawing) and Uzbekistan. Azerbaijan and Georgia joined in 1993. In September 1993 its members agreed on the creation of an economic union allowing the free movement of goods, services, labour and capital. This turned out to be more difficult than expected. CIS members then agreed in 1999 that the first stage towards an economic union should be a series of bilateral ***free-trade agreements***. In 2009 the CIS free-trade agreement was established. The CIS's secretariat is located in Minsk, Belarus. *See also* ***Newly Independent States***.

Commonwealth preferences: the name for empire preferences (also known as imperial preferences) used especially in the post-war years, but it was already in

销售结构的发展，实现成员国的可持续增长和发展；(b)促进所有领域经济活动的共同发展及在共同采取宏观经济政策和计划，以提高人民生活水平和促进成员国之间更紧密的关系；(c)合作创造有利于外国、跨境和国内投资的环境，包括共同促进有利于发展的科学技术的研究和适应；(d)合作促进成员国之间的和平、安全和稳定，以增强该区域的经济发展；(e)合作强化共同市场与世界其他地区之间的关系，并在国际场合采取共同立场；以及(f)促进非洲经济共同体的建立、推进和目标的实现。COMESA 自由贸易区建立于 2000 年。到 2025 年，将转为货币联盟。COMESA 秘书处设在卢萨卡。另见*非洲区域经济一体化(African regional economic integration)*。

Commonwealth

英联邦

1949 年通过《伦敦宣言》以现在的形式成立的由 53 个独立国家组成的联盟，成员曾经是大英帝国一部分，由设在伦敦的英联邦秘书处管理。秘书处众多职能中的一项是促进经济和贸易发展，特别是其中的发展中成员。英联邦目前的成员国包括安提瓜和巴布达、澳大利亚、巴哈马、孟加拉国、巴巴多斯、伯利兹、博茨瓦纳、英国、文莱、喀麦隆、加拿大、塞浦路斯、多米尼加、斯威士兰、斐济、冈比亚、加纳、格林纳达、圭亚那、印度、牙买加、肯尼亚、基里巴斯、莱索托、马拉维、马来西亚、马尔代夫、马耳他、毛里求斯、莫桑比克、纳米比亚、瑙鲁、新西兰、尼日利亚、巴基斯坦、巴布亚新几内亚、圣基茨和尼维斯、圣卢西亚、圣文森特和格林纳丁斯、萨摩亚、塞舌尔、塞拉利昂、新加坡、所罗门群岛、南非、斯里兰卡、坦桑尼亚、汤加、特立尼达和多巴哥、图瓦卢、乌干达、瓦努阿图以及赞比亚。另见*英联邦政府首脑会议(CHOGM)*。

Commonwealth of Independent States

独立国家联合体

CIS。1991 年 12 月成立，由曾经组成苏联的众多共和国组成。成员包括亚美尼亚、白俄罗斯、哈萨克斯坦、吉尔吉斯斯坦、摩尔多瓦、俄罗斯、塔吉克斯坦、土库曼斯坦(2005 年起成为联系成员)、乌克兰(正在退出)和乌兹别克斯坦。阿塞拜疆和格鲁吉亚于 1993 年加入。1993 年 9 月，成员国同意建立一个允许货物、服务、劳动力和资本自由流动的经济联盟。事实证明这比预期的要困难得多。CIS 成员国随后于 1999 年同意建立经济联盟的第一阶段应该是形成一系列双边自由贸易协定。2009 年，CIS 自由贸易协定形成。CIS 秘书处设在白俄罗斯明斯克。另见*新独立国家(Newly Independent States)*。

Commonwealth preferences

英联邦特惠制

帝国优惠制(也称为帝国特惠制)这一名称特别用于战后年代，但是在两次世界

use between the wars. *See also* ***historical preferences*** and ***imperial preferences arrangement***.

Communauté Économique de l'Afrique de l'Ouest: *see* ***West African Economic Community***.

Communauté Économique des États de l'Afrique de l'Ouest: *see* ***Economic Community of West African States***.

Communauté Économique des Pays des Grands Lacs: CEPGL. Established in 1976 to promote regional economic cooperation and integration. Its members are Burundi, Democratic Republic of Congo and Rwanda. Its secretariat is located in Gisenyi, Rwanda. *See also* ***African regional economic integration***.

Communauté Économique et Monétaire de l'Afrique Centrale: CEMAC. Entered into force in June 1999 as the successor to the ***Central African Customs and Economic Union*** (UDEAC). Its members are Cameroon, Central African Republic, Chad, Congo, Equatorial Guinea and Gabon. Among its main objectives are (a) promotion of national markets through the abolition of intra-community obstacles to trade, (b) coordinated development programmes, (c) harmonized industrial development and (d) creation of a true African common market. It is located in Bangui. *See also* ***African Economic Community*** and ***African regional economic integration***.

Community: often refers to the ***European Community***, now the ***European Union***, but it can mean any group of countries sharing common characteristics or working towards greater integration, usually under a framework agreement setting out its aims and likely shape.

Community Charter of Fundamental Social Rights for Workers: *see* ***European Social Charter***.

Community exhaustion: the doctrine that once a product embodying ***intellectual property rights*** (IPRs) has been lawfully placed on the market within the ***European Community*** (EC), now the ***European Union***, it can be resold or transferred to any part of the EC without the further consent of the owner of these IPRs. *See also* ***exhaustion doctrine*** and ***parallel imports***.

Community interest clause: this clause is part of a ***regulation*** issued in 1979 by the ***European Community***, now the ***European Union***, which makes the imposition of anti-dumping or countervailing duties dependent on the existence of a Community interest in the matter. Importantly, "Community interest" includes the interests of consumers and processors of the imported product as well as the need for an internal competitive market. *See also* ***anti-dumping measures***.

Community of Andean Nations: *see* ***Andean Community***.

Community of Latin American and Caribbean States: Comunidad de Estados Latinoamericanos y Caribeños (CELAC). The successor since 2010 of the Rio Group. It consists of thirty-three countries in the Latin American and Caribbean region and works as an intergovernmental mechanism for political dialogue. Its work programme encompasses social development, education, nuclear

大战之间即已经使用。另见*历史性优惠(historical preferences)*、*帝国特惠安排(imperial preferences arrangement)*。

Communauté Économique de l'Afrique de l'Ouest
西非经济共同体

见*西非经济共同体(West African Economic Community)*。

Communauté Économique des États de l'Afrique de l'Ouest
西非国家经济共同体

见*西非国家经济共同体(Economic Community of West African States)*。

Communauté Économique des Pays des Grands Lacs
大湖国家经济共同体

CEPGL。1976 年成立，旨在促进区域经济合作和一体化。成员国为布隆迪、刚果(金)和卢旺达。秘书处设在卢旺达吉塞尼。另见*非洲区域经济一体化(African regional economic integration)*。

Communauté Économique et Monétaire de l'Afrique Centrale
中部非州经济与货币共同体

CEMAC。1999 年 6 月生效，作为中部非洲关税与经济同盟(UDEAC)的后继安排。成员包括喀麦隆、中非共和国、乍得、刚果(布)、赤道几内亚和加蓬。主要目标包括为：(a)通过消除共同体内部贸易障碍促进国内市场；(b)协调发展计划；(c)协调产业发展；以及(d)建立一个真正的非洲共同市场。设在班吉。另见*非洲经济共同体(African Economic Community)*、*非洲区域经济一体化(African regional economic integration)*。

Community
共同体

通常指欧洲共同体，即现欧盟，但也可指具有共同特征或致力于更大一体化的任何国家集团，通常根据一个规定目标和可能形式的框架协定建立。

Community Charter of Fundamental Social Rights for Workers
工人基本社会权利共同体宪章

见*欧洲社会宪章(European Social Charter)*。

Community exhaustion
共同体内权利用尽

一项法律原则，即在含有知识产权的产品在欧洲共同体(EC)(现欧盟)内合法投放市场后，即可转售或转让到欧共体任何地方而无需经知识产权所有人进一步同意。另见*权利用尽原则(exhaustion doctrine)*、*平行进口(parallel imports)*。

Community interest clause
共同体利益条款

该条款是欧洲共同体(现欧盟)1979 年颁布的条例的一部分，规定是否征收反倾销税或反补贴税取决于共同体在该问题上的利益。重要的是，“共同体利益”包括消费者和进口产品加工者的利益以及内部竞争性市场的需要。另见*反倾销措施(anti-dumping measures)*。

Community of Andean Nations
安第斯国家共同体

见*安第斯共同体(Andean Community)*。

Community of Latin American and Caribbean States
拉丁美洲和加勒比国家共同体

CELAC。自 2010 年起作为里约集团的后继组织。由拉丁美洲和加勒比地区的 33 个国家组成，作为一个开展政治对话的政府间机制运行。工作计划包括社

disarmament, family farming, culture, finance, energy and the environment. *See also* ***Latin American regional integration arrangements***.

Community of Sahel-Saharan States: established on 4 February 1998. The treaty establishing it seeks the creation of a comprehensive economic union. Member states are Benin, Burkina Faso, Central African Republic, Chad, Comoros, Côte d'Ivoire, Djibouti, Egypt, Eritrea, The Gambia, Ghana, Guinea-Bissau, Libya, Mali, Mauritania, Morocco, Niger, Nigeria, Senegal, Sierra Leone, Somalia, Sudan, Togo and Tunisia. Its headquarters are in Tripoli, Libya. *See also* ***African regional economic integration***.

Community rights: also known as collective rights. The terms describe the fact that communities may develop and/or own aspects of ***traditional knowledge***. There is a view that these rights need new forms of ***intellectual property protection***.

Comparability: a term used in the ***APEC*** discussions denoting arrangements which ensure a broad and perceived equivalence between individual APEC contributions towards the implementation of the ***Bogor Declaration***. *See also* ***comprehensiveness*** and ***Osaka Action Agenda***.

Comparative advantage: the theory first proposed by David Ricardo in 1817 that a country is more likely to export goods that it can produce relatively efficiently. The relative efficiency measure compares production costs of different goods in each country concerned, not the production cost of the same good in different countries. A country's comparative advantage is reflected in its unsubsidized exports to world markets which is then said to be a country's revealed comparative advantage. Comparative advantage is seldom static. Countries can acquire a comparative advantage through, for example, investing in the acquisition of skills by their workforces. Hence the concept of dynamic comparative advantage. *See also* ***absolute advantage***, ***competitive advantage***, ***gains-from-trade theory***, ***Heckscher-Ohlin theorem***, ***kaleidoscopic comparative advantage*** and ***Stolper-Samuelson theorem***. [Brenton, Scott and Sinclair 1997, Krugman 1998, Maneschi 1998]

Compendium of Trade Facilitation Recommendations: a reference guide for those engaged in simplifying, harmonizing and rationalizing trade procedures and practice. Compiled jointly by the United Nations Centre for Trade Facilitation and Electronic Business **(UN/CEFACT)** and ***UNCTAD*** in 1994 and updated 2001.

Compensation: a remedy available to members of the WTO in cases where another member breaks a bound commitment on services or imposes a tariff on a good above its bound rate. Such an action may be possible under the terms of the agreement, but the member taking it must then compensate others in some fashion, usually through making a tariff concession in another product or a commitment on another services activity. *See also* ***binding***, ***binding commitments*** and ***safeguards***.

Compensation trade: a trading arrangement whereby the supplier of raw materials, manufactures or services to a foreign enterprise agrees to be paid in the

会发展、教育、核裁军、家庭农业、文化、财政、能源和环境。另见*拉丁美洲区域一体化安排(Latin American regional integration arrangements)*。

Community of Sahel-Saharan States
萨赫勒—撒哈拉国家共同体

1998 年 2 月 4 日建立。建立共同体的条约寻求建立一个全面的经济联盟。成员国包括贝宁、布基纳法索、中非共和国、乍得、科摩罗、科特迪瓦、吉布提、埃及、厄立特里亚、冈比亚、加纳、几内亚比绍、利比亚、马里、毛里塔尼亚、摩洛哥、尼日尔、尼日利亚、塞内加尔、塞拉利昂、索马里、苏丹、多哥和突尼斯。总部设在利比亚的黎波里。另见*非洲区域经济一体化(African regional economic integration)*。

Community rights
社区权利

也称团体权。该词描述了这样一个事实：社区可以形成和/或拥有传统知识的各个方面。有一种观点认为，这些权利需要新形式的知识产权保护。

Comparability
可比性

APEC 讨论中使用的词语，表示为保证实施《茂物宣言》的 APEC 各项努力之间具有广泛和可感知的等同性安排。另见*全面性(comprehensiveness)*、*大阪行动议程(Osaka Action Agenda)*。

Comparative advantage
比较优势

大卫·李嘉图在 1817 年首次提出的理论，即一国更有可能出口其生产效率相对较高的货物。相对效率指标比较每一相关国家中不同货物的生产成本，而不是相同货物在不同国家的生产成本。一国的比较优势反映在其对世界市场的无补贴出口产品上，这因而被称为一国的显性比较优势。比较优势很少是静止不变的。国家可以通过例如投资使其劳动力获得技能而获得比较优势。因此有了动态比较优势的概念。另见*绝对优势(absolute advantage)*、*竞争优势(competitive advantage)*、*贸易利得理论(gains-from trade theory)*、*赫克舍尔-奥林定理(Heckscher-Ohlin theorem)*、*万花筒式比较优势(kaleidoscopic comparative advantage)*、*斯托尔珀-萨缪尔森定理(Stolpher-Samuelson theorem)*。

Compendium of Trade Facilitation Recommendations
贸易便利化建议汇编

一份供参与简化、协调和合理化贸易程序和实践的人士使用的参考指南。由联合国贸易便利化与电子商务中心(UN/CEFACT)与联合国贸易与发展会议(UNCTAD)于 1994 年编制，并于 2001 年更新。

Compensation
补偿

在一成员违反约束服务承诺或对一货物征收的关税高于约束税率的情况下，WTO 成员可以使用的一种救济。此种行动根据协定条款是可以采取的，但采取行动的成员必须以某种方式补偿其他成员，通常是对另一种产品作出关税减让或对另一种服务活动作出承诺。另见*约束(binding)*、*约束承诺(binding commitment)*、*保障措施(safeguards)*。

Compensation trade
补偿贸易

一种贸易安排，即向外国企业提供原材料、制成品或服务的供应商同意以该

form of part of the output of that enterprise. For the buyer enterprise, the advantages are that it does not need foreign exchange to import production components, that repayments are not due until the operation is up and running, and that it has a ready market for some of its products. A disadvantage may be that it will almost certainly have to sell its output at a discount. *See also* ***barter trade*** and ***countertrade***.

Compensatory financing arrangements: intergovernmental schemes designed to minimize the effects of shortfalls in commodity export earnings and export earning fluctuations, particularly those of developing countries heavily dependent on commodity exports. *See also* ***Common Fund for Commodities***.

Competence: the constitutional empowerment given to governments to enact laws and enter into binding international commitments. In federated states, there is usually a division of power between the central government and the states or provinces, but in all cases the central government has control over foreign affairs and defence matters, including ***international economic relations***. The ***European Union*** is a particularly interesting example of a division of power. It has explicit powers where these are specified in its treaties. Article 3 of the ***Treaty on the Functioning of the European Union*** gives the Union exclusive power in the following areas: (a) customs union, (b) the establishing of competition rules necessary for the functioning of the internal market, (c) monetary policy for the member states whose currency is the ***euro***, (d) conservation of marine biological resources under the ***common fisheries policy***, and (e) ***common commercial policy***. The Union also has exclusive competence for the conclusion of an international agreement when it is based on a legislative act of the Union, is necessary to enable the Union to exercise its internal competence or if its conclusion may affect common rules. The Union has competence to carry out actions to support, coordinate or supplement activities in (a) protection and improvement of human health, (b) industry, (c) culture, (d) tourism, (e) education, youth and sport, (f) civil protection, and (g) administrative cooperation. Competence in other areas is shared. *See also* ***shared competence*** and ***subsidiarity***.

Competition: the way firms behave in the marketplace and how they respond to the actions of other suppliers and consumers. Underlying the idea of competition is the assumption that supply and demand are limited, at least in the short term, and that firms must strive obtain their share of the available resources. In ideal conditions, competition between firms would be based on price and the ability to innovate and respond to changes in the market. There would be no impediments to the operation of the price or market systems. In a real situation, human ingenuity, high entry barriers to some industries, efficiencies of scale obtainable from large-scale operations and other factors combine to impair competition in various ways. This may lead to economic rents being accorded to some firms, but without any obligation on their part to let the consumer benefit from this situation. Governments recognize this, and in many countries they seek to protect, where necessary, competition through ***antitrust laws*** and

外国企业的部分产出作为支付形式。对于买方企业，补偿贸易的优点是进口生产组件无需外汇，直到正式投入运营之时才需还款，且其部分产品已有现成的市场。缺点之一可能是，几乎肯定会以折扣价出售产品。另见*易货贸易(barter trade)*、*对销贸易(countertrade)*。

Compensatory financing arrangements
补偿性融资安排

旨在减少商品出口收入缺口和出口收入波动影响的政府间方案，特别是对严重依赖商品出口的发展中国家。另见*商品共同基金(Common Fund for Commodities)*。

Competence
权限

给予政府颁布法律和订立具有约束力的国际承诺的宪法授权。在联邦制国家，中央政府与各州或各省之间通常有权力划分，但在任何情况下中央政府对外交事务和国防事务拥有控制权，包括国际经济关系。欧盟是权力划分的一个特别有趣的例子。如果其条约中有明确规定，欧盟即有明确的权力。《欧洲联盟运行条约》第3条赋予欧盟在下列领域的专属权力：(a)关税同盟；(b)制定内部市场运作所必需的竞争规则；(c)对货币使用欧元的成员国实行的货币政策；(d)根据共同渔业政策保护海洋生物资源；以及(e)共同商业政策。欧盟还拥有缔结一项协定的专属权限，如果该国际协定是根据欧盟的一项立法行动缔结的，或者是欧盟行使其内部权限所必需的，或者缔结协定可能影响共同规则。欧盟有权采取行动加以支持、协调或补充以下活动：(a)保护和改善人类健康；(b)产业；(c)文化；(d)旅游；(e)教育、青年和体育；(f)民事保护；以及(g)行政合作。其他领域的权限是共享的。另见*共享权限(shared competence)*、*辅助原则(subsidiarity)*。

Competition
竞争

企业在市场中的行为方式及企业如何对其他供应商和消费者的行动作出反应。竞争概念所基于的假设是，供应和需求是有限的，至少在短期内，且企业必须努力获得可用资源的份额。在理想情况下，企业之间的竞争将基于价格、创新能力以及对市场变化的反应。价格或市场体系的运行不会受到任何阻碍。但在实际情况中，人类的创造性、某些行业的高准入壁垒、大规模经营可获得的规模效益以及其他因素结合起来，以各种方式损害竞争。这可能导致一些企业获得了经济租金，但自身却没有任何义务让消费者从中获益。政府认识到这一点，且在许多国家中，政府寻求在必要时通过反垄断法和竞争政策保护

competition policy. Most economies are becoming internationalized, and government approaches to ***trade policy***, i.e. their assessment of the extent to which foreign firms and their products should be allowed to compete in the market, therefore can be of critical importance to the level of competition prevailing in the market.

Competition law: rules and regulations, also known as ***antitrust laws***, to foster the competitive environment in an economy, partly through the more efficient allocation of resources. The competition laws of most countries deal with four main groups of behaviour by firms: (a) horizontal arrangements (mainly arrangements between firms to maintain and control prices), (b) vertical arrangements (can include exclusive dealing, resale price maintenance, geographical limitations on activities and tied dealing), (c) misuse of market power by monopolies and large firms, and (d) control of mergers and acquisitions to ensure that they do not impair competitive overall conditions in the market. Measures dealing with horizontal and vertical restraints as well as the enforcement of laws concerning them are sometimes called ***conduct*** policies. Those dealing with mergers may be known as structural policies. Rules covering these matters are sometimes described as ***narrow competition policy***. Many say that four variables affect the relative strength or weakness of competition laws: (a) scope of application to governmental entities and to government-encouraged or sanctioned conduct of state enterprises and private firms, (b) substantive rules governing specific business practices and arrangements, (c) scope of sectoral coverage, and (d) enforcement. *See also* ***wider competition policy***.

Competition policy: approaches of governments to the promotion and protection of competition. It consists of ***competition laws*** and policies achieving similar aims. Since the 1980s the term "competition policy" has broadened in scope in many industrial economies. It now may be concerned also with the welfare-enhancing effects of opening non-tradable sectors to competition, the so-called ***wider competition policy***. This includes gas, water and electricity utilities which once were considered natural monopolies. Competition policy is often seen as promoting especially the interests of the consumer, and comparisons are made with ***trade policy*** which, especially in the case of ***trade remedies***, tends to favour the producer. *See also* ***antitrust laws*** and ***trade and competition***.

Competition policy and anti-dumping measures: an issue relevant to a study of the feasibility of multilateral rules on ***trade and competition***. Some say that there is a fundamental conflict between the concurrent administration by a government of anti-dumping laws and competition or ***antitrust laws***. This view is based partly on the assumption that trade policy may confer benefits to domestic producers through ***anti-dumping measures*** that allow them to secure additional returns by enabling them to raise prices. Exporters who make price undertakings to evade the imposition of anti-dumping duties may in this way also be able to obtain economic rents. The contention is that such actions are legal under trade policy, but illegal under ***competition policy***. Another conflict is seen as resulting from an underlying principle that anti-dumping laws are

竞争。大多数经济体正在越来越国际化，因而政府处理贸易政策的方式，即评估应在多大程度上允许外国公司及其产品在本国市场中竞争，对于市场上普遍存在的竞争水平至关重要。

Competition law
竞争法

旨在培育经济中的竞争环境的规则和规定，也称反垄断法，有时通过更有效的资源分配。大多数国家的竞争法主要处理公司的四类行为：(a)横向安排(主要是公司之间维持和控制价格的安排)；(b)纵向安排(可包括独家交易、维持转售价格、对活动的地域限制以及捆绑交易)；(c)垄断公司和大公司滥用市场支配力；以及(d)控制兼并和收购，以保证它们不损害市场的整体竞争条件。处理横向和纵向限制的措施以及相关法律的执行有时被称为行为政策。处理兼并的政策可称为结构性政策。涉及这些问题的规定有时被称为狭义竞争政策。许多人说，有四个变量影响竞争法的相对强度：(a)对政府实体及对政府鼓励或批准的国有企业和私营公司的行为的适用范围；(b)管辖具体商业惯例和安排的实质性规定；(c)部门覆盖范围；以及(d)执法。另见*广义竞争政策(wider competition policy)*。

Competition policy
竞争政策

政府促进和保护竞争的方式，包括竞争法和实现类似目标的政策。自 20 世纪 80 年代以来，“竞争政策”一词的范围在许多工业化经济体中已经扩大。现在可能还涉及开放非贸易部门竞争所带来的福利增强效应，即所谓广义竞争政策。包括曾被认为属自然垄断的天然气、水、电等公用事业。与贸易政策相比，特别是对于贸易救济，竞争政策通常被视为特别有利于消费者利益，而贸易政策往往有利于生产者。另见*反垄断法(antitrust laws)*、*贸易与竞争(trade and competition)*。

Competition policy and anti-dumping measures
竞争政策与反倾销措施

与贸易与竞争多边规则可行性研究相关的问题。一些人认为，一政府同时管理反倾销法和竞争或反垄断法之间存在根本冲突。此观点部分基于这样一种假设，即贸易政策可以通过反倾销措施给国内生产者带来好处，这样可使国内生产者能够通过提高价格获得额外回报。作出价格承诺以逃避征收反倾销税的出口商也可以通过这种方式获得经济租金。争议在于，此类行动在贸易政策下是合法的，但在竞争政策下是非法的。被认为存在的另一个冲突源于

designed to protect domestic producers and sellers of goods, whereas competition laws are meant to protect consumers and importers. It really comes down to the question of what anti-dumping laws are meant to achieve. Some of the early anti-dumping laws, such as the ***Anti-Dumping Act of 1916***, were intended to deal with ***predatory pricing***, an anti-competitive practice banned by many competition laws. But current anti-dumping laws do no longer seem to have this motivation. They are seen rather as a means of promoting fairer trade, often in the sense of the ***level playing field***. This apparent contradiction remains to be resolved. Countries and industries disadvantaged by anti-dumping measures tend to argue that such measures should be replaced by competition laws to the extent that they are actionable in this way. This has already happened in trade between Australia and New Zealand under ***ANZCERTA***, between the members of the ***European Union*** and within the ***European Economic Area***. These are special cases where the ground was carefully prepared over many years. There is widespread agreement among analysts that a measure of convergence in competition laws and their adequate enforcement will be necessary to achieve this goal more widely.

Competitive advantage: a contentious theory of industrial development popularized by Michael Porter and others in the *Competitive Advantage of Nations*. The origins of the theory itself appear to go back to the economist Alfred Marshall (1842–1924). It states that the success of a firm or an industry is based on cost advantages in the production of a relatively standardized product or product-based advantages related to the development of differentiated products. Firms with a competitive advantage are often concentrated geographically, which in turn assists the development of a workforce with the relevant skills. Critics of this theory have noted that through its emphasis on high-technology firms in advanced countries, and its devaluation of the importance of comparative costs, it appears to give legitimacy to public expenditure and protection policies designed to promote the premature development of high-technology industries. *See also* ***comparative advantage*** and ***strategic trade theory***. [Porter 1990]

Competitive devaluation: a government-induced depreciation or ***devaluation*** of the ***exchange rate*** aimed at undercutting the competition from other countries. The risk in doing so is that one's competitors may retaliate with their own devaluations and leave everyone worse off. *See also* ***beggar-thy-neighbour policies***.

Competitive hub-and-spoke bilateralism: describes a situation in which some countries in a given region try to conclude as many bilateral ***free-trade agreements*** as possible in an attempt to make themselves a regional economic hub.

Competitive liberalization: the idea, as described by Bergsten, that competing successfully in the global marketplace forces countries to liberalize their trade and investment regimes in response to liberalization by others. The term was adopted in 2002 by the United States to describe its policy of pursuing concurrently bilateral, regional and multilateral trade negotiations in the expectation

这样一个基本原则，即反倾销法旨在保护国内生产商和货物销售商，而竞争法意在保护消费者和进口商。这实际上就回到反倾销法意在实现什么的问题。早期的一些反倾销法，如《1916年反倾销法》，旨在处理掠夺性定价，这是一种被许多竞争法禁止的反竞争做法。但现行反倾销法似乎不再具有这种动机。它们反而被看作是促进更公平贸易的一种手段，通常是在公平竞争环境的意义上。这种明显的矛盾仍有待解决。因反倾销措施而处于不利地位的国家和产业倾向于认为，此类措施应被竞争法取代，只要这些措施在竞争法下是可诉的。这一点已经出现在澳大利亚和新西兰之间在《澳大利亚与新西兰更紧密经济关系贸易协定》(ANZCERTA)项下的贸易中，及欧盟成员国之间在欧洲经济区内的贸易中。这些都是经过多年积累形成的具有足够说服力的特特殊案例。分析人士普遍认同的是，为更广泛地实现这一目标，有必要在竞争法及其充分执行方面采取趋同的措施。

Competitive advantage

竞争优势

迈克尔·波特等人在《国家竞争优势》一书中提出的一种颇具争议的产业发展理论。该理论本身的起源似乎可以追溯到经济学家阿尔弗雷德·马歇尔(1842—1924)。该理论指出，一公司或一行业的成功有赖于生产相对标准化的产品所带来的成本优势或与开发差异化产品相关的基于产品的优势。具有竞争优势的企业在地理位置上较为集中，这反过来又有助于形成具有相关技能的劳动力队伍。这一理论的批评者指出，该理论强调先进国家的高技术公司，低估了比较成本的重要性，似乎使旨在促进高技术产业过早发展的公共开支和保护政策合法化了。*另见比较优势(comparative advantage)、战略性贸易理论(strategic trade theory)*。

Competitive devaluation

竞争性贬值

一种由政府引起的汇率的低估或贬值，旨在削弱来自其他国家的竞争。这样作的风险在于，该国的竞争对手可能会以自身货币贬值进行报复，使所有国家的境况都变得更糟。*另见以邻为壑政策(beggar-thy-neighbour policies)*。

Competitive hub-and-spoke bilateralism

竞争性轮轴-辐条式双边主义

描述这样一种情形，即一指定区域的一些国家试图使自己成为一个区域经济中心而缔结尽可能多的双边自由贸易协定。

Competitive liberalization

竞争性自由化

伯格斯滕指出，这一理念为，为能够在全球市场上成功竞争，迫使各国实行贸易和投资体制自由化，以应对其他国家的自由化。美国在2002年采用这一词语，用于描述其同时进行双边、区域和多边贸易谈判的政策，期望其中一个谈

that achievements in one of them would lead to further progress in another. [Bergsten 1996]

Competitive-need limitation: an aspect of the administration of the United States ***GSP*** scheme. If in any calendar year imports of a given product from a beneficiary country account for more than 50 per cent of United States imports of that product, the exporting country's eligibility for benefits for that product is terminated. Similarly, once a country's share of exports to the United States of a given product exceeds a specified value, benefits will also be terminated. The specified value varies from year to year. The competitive-need limitation may be waived in certain circumstances, especially if the exporting country gives reasonable access to United States goods and services, and if it offers proper protection for United States-owned ***intellectual property rights***. Most ***least-developed countries*** enjoy automatic waivers from the limitation. *See also* ***a priori limitation*** and ***graduation***.

Competitiveness: the ability of a firm, a production sector or even a country to hold its own in terms of economic efficiency against other firms, sectors or countries. Governments sometimes try to improve the competitiveness of a sector through the use of ***export targeting***, ***subsidies***, ***protection***, creation of ***national champions*** or other measures. This can only be done at the expense of the remainder of the economy, and the longer-term effect of such practices is to reduce the economy's competitiveness overall.

Competitive neutrality: a concept relevant to the examination and administration of the nature of competition between private-sector firms and deregulated government monopolies. The need for competitive neutrality arises from the fact that removing barriers to market entry and ending government monopolies may not be enough to achieve genuine competition in that sector. In such a situation, the advantage may still lie with the enterprise that previously was a government monopoly or part of one. The remedy usually is some form of pro-competitive regulation. *See also* ***deregulation*** and ***re-regulation***.

Compliance: observance of one's obligations under international agreements. *See also* ***enforceability*** and ***implementation***.

Compliance panel: a ***panel*** established under Article 21.5 of the ***Dispute Settlement Understanding***. A WTO member may ask for the establishment of such a panel when a party to previous dispute settlement proceedings does not comply with the decision then made. *See also* ***sequencing***.

Composite tariff: *see* ***compound tariff***.

Composition of trade: usually a statistical analysis of a country's trade in terms of product groups which shows what kinds of goods and services it imports from and exports to a given country.

Compound tariff: a rate of duty on a product which consists of two components. The first is an *ad valorem* rate, expressed as a percentage of the value of the product. The second component is a specific rate, expressed as a monetary value per article regardless of the value of the product. A hypothetical example

判取得成功即会使其他谈判取得更多进展。

Competitive-need limitation

竞争性需求限制

美国管理普惠制(GSP)的一个方面。如在任何一日历年中，从受益国进口的一指定产品占美国该产品进口总额的 50%以上，则该出口国在该产品上享受优惠的资格即终止。同样，一旦一国出口至美国的一指定产品的份额超过一规定价值，则优惠即终止。规定价值每年变化。在某些情况下，竞争性需求限制可以豁免，特别是如果出口国能够给予美国货物和服务合理的市场准入，且如果出口国对美国拥有的知识产权提供适当保护。大多数最不发达国家享受该限制的自动豁免。另见*预定限额(a priori limitation)*、*毕业(graduation)*。

Competitiveness

竞争力

一公司、一生产部门或甚至一国相对于其他公司、部门或国家保持自己经济效率的能力。政府有时试图通过使用出口目标、补贴、保护、创建国家冠军企业或其他措施，以提高一部门的竞争力。这样作只能以牺牲经济体的其余部分为代价，而且这种做法的长期影响是削弱经济体的整体竞争力。

Competitive neutrality

竞争中立

与审查和管理私营部门公司与放松管制的政府垄断公司之间竞争性质相关的概念。竞争中立的需要源于这样一个事实，即取消市场进入壁垒和结束政府垄断可能不足以在该部门实现真正竞争。在此种情况下，以往由政府垄断或部分垄断的企业可能仍有优势。补救措施通常是某种形式的有利于竞争的监管。另见*取消管制(deregulation)*、*重新管制(re-regulation)*。

Compliance

遵守

遵守国际协定项下的义务。另见*可执行性(enforceability)*、*实施(implementation)*。

Compliance panel

执行之诉专家组

根据《争端解决谅解》第 21.5 条设立的专家组。如前一争端解决程序的一方不遵守当时所作裁决，WTO 成员可以要求建立执行之诉专家组。另见*适用顺序问题(sequencing)*。

Composite tariff

复合关税

见*混合关税(compound tariff)*。

Composition of trade

贸易构成

通常为按产品类别对一国贸易进行的统计分析，显示该国从一指定国家进口和出口的货物和服务种类。

Compound tariff

混合关税

由两部分组成的对一产品的关税税率：第一部分是从价税率，以产品价值百分比表示。第二部分是从量税率，以每件物品的货币价值表示，不考虑该产

would be one where each compact disc incurs a ***specific tariff*** of one dollar plus an ***ad valorem tariff*** set at 10 per cent.

Comprehensive and Economic Cooperation Agreement: CECA. A name apparently preferred by India for its free-trade agreements, such as the India–Singapore CECA and the proposed Australia–India CECA.

Comprehensive and Progressive Agreement for Trans-Pacific Partnership: CPTPP. The renegotiated ***Trans-Pacific Partnership Agreement*** (TPP) following the announcement by the United States in January 2017 that it would not join it. This is actually a free-standing agreement to incorporate nearly all of the text of the TPP of 4 February 2016. The TPP itself remains unchanged, but for the time being unwanted. The Agreement was signed in March 2018. It entered into force on 30 December 2018 with an initial membership of Australia, Canada, Japan, Mexico, New Zealand and Singapore. Viet Nam joined on 14 January 2019. The Agreement will enter into force for Brunei Darussalam, Chile, Malaysia and Peru once they have completed their ratification process. The way has been left open for the United States to join. The following summarizes the contents of the Agreement. Chapter 1 contains the initial provisions and general definitions. It establishes a ***free-trade area*** consistent with Article XXIV of the ***GATT*** (Customs Unions and Free Trade Areas) and Article V of the ***General Agreement on Trade in Services*** (Economic Integration). Chapter 2 covers national treatment and market access for goods. Parties have to eliminate progressively their customs duties on ***originating goods***. No import or export restrictions may be maintained apart from those in accordance with GATT Article XI (General Elimination of Quantitative Restrictions). Each party has to be a participant in the WTO ***Information Technology Agreement***. Article 3 deals with ***rules of origin***. The agreement uses three methods to calculate the ***regional value content***: ***focused value method***, ***build-down method*** and ***build-up method*** or net-cost method (for automotive products only). Chapter 4 covers textiles and apparel, including ***product-specific rules*** for textiles. Customs administration and trade facilitation are covered in Chapter 5. Customs procedures must be applied in a manner that is predictable, consistent and transparent. Chapter 6 deals with ***trade remedies***. The parties may use ***global safeguards*** in accordance with GATT Article XIX (Emergency Action on Imports of Particular Products), and they may use ***transitional safeguards***. The parties retain their rights and obligations under the WTO ***Anti-Dumping Agreement*** and the WTO ***Agreement on Subsidies and Countervailing Measures***. Chapter 7 covers ***sanitary and phytosanitary measures***. Chapter 8 deals with ***technical barriers to trade***. Chapter 9 covers investment. It offers the other parties the usual national treatment and most-favoured-nation treatment. Non-conforming measures are in a negative list. It contains a provision on investor-state dispute settlement. Disputing parties are required to solve matters through consultation and conciliation, but they may go to arbitration if the dispute remains unresolved after six months. Chapter 10 covers ***cross-border trade in services***. It uses a negative list for non-conforming measures.

品价值。例如，每张光盘征收 1 美元从量关税，另加 10%从价关税。

Comprehensive and Economic Cooperation Agreement
全面经济合作协定

CECA。印度显然偏爱对其自由贸易协定按此称呼，例如《印度—新加坡全面经济合作协定》和拟议的《澳大利亚—印度全面经济合作协定》。

Comprehensive and Progressive Agreement for Trans-Pacific Partnership
全面与进步跨太平洋伙伴关系协定

CPTPP。美国于 2017 年 1 月宣布不加入《跨太平洋伙伴关系协定》(TPP)后重新谈判的协定。实际上是一个几乎纳入 2016 年 2 月 4 日 TPP 全部文本的单独协定。TPP 本身保持不变，但目前不再具有实际价值。协定于 2018 年 3 月签署，2018 年 12 月 30 日生效，最初成员包括澳大利亚、加拿大、日本、墨西哥、新西兰和新加坡。越南于 2019 年 1 月 14 日加入。该协定将待文莱、智利、马来西亚和秘鲁完成批准程序后对其生效。美国加入的通道仍然保持开放。以下总结了协定内容。第 1 章包含初始条款和一般定义，协定建立一个符合 GATT 第 24 条(关税同盟和自由贸易区)和《服务贸易总协定》第 5 条(经济一体化)的自由贸易区。第 2 章涵盖货物的国民待遇和市场准入，缔约方必须逐步取消它们对原产货物的关税，除依照 GATT 第 11 条(普遍取消数量限制)实施的措施外，不得维持进出口限制，每一方必须参加 WTO《信息技术协定》。第 3 章处理原产地规则，协定使用三种方法计算区域价值成分：价格法、扣减法和增值法或净成本法(仅适用于汽车产品)。第 4 章涵盖纺织品和服装，包括纺织品的特定产品规则。第 5 章涵盖海关管理和贸易便利化，海关程序必须以可预测、一致和透明的方式实施。第 6 章处理贸易救济，各方可依照 GATT 第 19 条(对某些产品进口的紧急措施)采取全球保障措施，并可使用过渡性保障措施，各方保留其在 WTO《反倾销协定》和《补贴与反补贴措施协定》项下的权利和义务。第 7 章涵盖卫生与植物卫生措施。第 8 章处理技术性贸易壁垒。第 9 章涵盖投资，向其他各方提供通常的国民待遇和最惠国待遇，不符措施以负面清单形式列出，包含关于投资者—国家争端解决的条款，争端各方被要求通过磋商和调解解决问题，但如果争端在 6 个月后仍未解决，可以诉诸仲裁。第 10 章涵盖跨境服务贸易，对不符措施采用负面清

Annex 10-A has more specific provisions for professional services, Annex 10-B for express delivery services and Annex 10-C on a ***ratchet mechanism for non-conforming measures***. Chapter 11 deals with financial services and Chapter 12 with the temporary entry of business persons. Chapters 13 and 14 cover telecommunications and electronic commerce, respectively. Chapter 15 deals with ***government procurement***. The parties afford each other national treatment and non-discrimination in respect of measures covered by the Agreement. Chapters 16 and 17 cover ***competition*** and ***state-owned enterprises***, respectively. Chapter 18 deals with all aspects of ***intellectual property rights***. The term of protection for ***copyright*** and related rights is seventy years. Chapter 19 deals with labour. Each party adopts and maintains in its statutes and regulations the rights stated in the ILO ***Declaration on Fundamental Principles and Rights at Work and its follow-up***. The objectives of Chapter 20 on environment are to promote mutually supportive trade and environment policies, high levels of environmental protection and enforcement of environmental laws. Chapter 21 outlines the processes and areas for ***capacity-building*** between the parties. Chapter 22 covers competitiveness and business facilitation. In Chapter 23 (Development) the parties commit to promote and strengthen an open trade and investment environment that seeks to improve welfare, reduce poverty, raise living standards and create new employment opportunities. Chapter 24 covers small and medium-sized enterprises, Chapter 25 deals with regulatory coherence and Chapter 26 with ***transparency*** and anti-corruption. Chapter 27 (Administrative and Institutional Provisions) establishes a Trans-Pacific Partnership Commission to administer the Agreement. Chapter 28 deals with ***dispute settlement***. Chapter 29 covers exceptions and general provisions. Chapter 30 (Final Provisions) deals with amendments, accession to the Agreement and its entry into force.

Comprehensive Economic and Trade Agreement: CETA. An agreement for a ***free-trade area*** agreed in 2016 between Canada and the European Union. It is not yet in force, but parts of it have been provisionally applied since 21 September 2017. Chapter One contains general definitions and initial provisions. These establish a free-trade area in conformity with Article XXIV of ***GATT*** (Customs Unions and Free Trade Areas) and Article V of the ***General Agreement on Trade in Services*** (Economic Integration). Chapter Two deals with national treatment and market access for goods. Tariffs are reduced or eliminated in accordance with annexed schedules. Customs duties may not be increased. No import or export restrictions may be maintained except those permitted by Article XI of the GATT (General Elimination of Quantitative Restrictions). Chapter Three covers ***trade remedies***. The parties reaffirm their rights and obligations under Article VI of the GATT (Anti-Dumping and Countervailing Duties) as well as the WTO ***Anti-Dumping Agreement*** and the ***Agreement on Subsidies and Countervailing Measures***. Global safeguards measures may also be taken within the WTO rules. Chapter Four deals with ***technical barriers to trade***. It incorporates several of the provisions of the WTO ***Agreement on***

单。附件 10-A 对专业服务作出更具体的规定，附件 10-B 对快递服务作出更具体的规定，附件 10-C 为不符措施棘轮机制。第 11 章处理金融服务。第 12 章处理商务人员临时入境。第 13 章和第 14 章分别涵盖电信和电子商务。第 15 章处理政府采购，双方在协定所涵盖的措施方面相互给予国民待遇和非歧视待遇。第 16 章和第 17 章分别涵盖竞争和国有企业。第 18 章处理知识产权的各个方面，版权及相关权利的保护期为 70 年。第 19 章处理劳工，各方在其法律法规中采用并维护国际劳工组织(ILO)《关于工作中基本原则和权利宣言及其后续措施》中规定的权利。关于环境的第 20 章的目标是促进贸易和环境相互支持的政策，高水平的环境保护和环境法律执法。第 21 章概述各方能力建设的程序和领域。第 22 章涵盖竞争力和商业便利化。在第 23 章(发展)中，各方承诺促进和加强开放的贸易和投资环境，力求改善福利、减少贫困、提高生活水平和创造新的就业机会。第 24 章涵盖中小企业。第 25 章处理监管一致性。第 26 章处理透明度和反腐败。第 27 章(管理和机构条款)设立跨太平洋伙伴关系委员会以管理协定。第 28 章处理争端解决。第 29 章涵盖例外和总则。第 30 章(最后条款)处理修正、协定加入及协定生效问题。

Comprehensive Economic and Trade Agreement
全面经济贸易协定

CETA。2016 年加拿大与欧盟达成的自由贸易区协定。该协定尚未生效，但部分内容自 2017 年 9 月 21 日起临时适用。第 1 章包含一般定义和最初条款，协定建立一个符合 GATT 第 24 条(关税同盟和自由贸易区)和《服务贸易总协定》第 5 条(经济一体化)的自由贸易区。第 2 章处理货物的国民待遇和市场准入。关税依照所附减让表削减或取消，关税不得提高。除 GATT 第 11 条(普遍取消数量限制)所允许的限制外，不得维持进口或出口限制。第 3 章涵盖贸易救济，双方重申在 GATT 第 6 条(反倾销税和反补贴税)以及 WTO《反倾销协定》和《补贴与反补贴措施协定》项下的权利和义务，全球保障措施也可以在 WTO 规则范围内采取。第 4 章处理技术性贸易壁垒，纳入了 WTO《技术

Technical Barriers to Trade. Chapter Five covers ***sanitary and phytosanitary measures***. The rights and obligations of the WTO ***Agreement on the Application of Sanitary and Phytosanitary Measures*** apply, supplemented by additional provisions. Chapter Six deals with customs and ***trade facilitation***. Chapter Seven covers ***subsidies***. The parties will conduct consultations as required on subsidies related to agricultural goods and fisheries products. Chapter Eight covers investment. The parties maintain negative lists for non-conforming measures. This chapter also sets out the investor-state dispute settlement provisions. Chapter Nine deals with cross-border trade in services. Existing non-conforming measures are contained in a negative list. Chapter Ten covers temporary entry and stay of natural persons for business purposes. It does not apply to employment, citizenship or residence. This is followed by Chapter Eleven on mutual recognition of professional qualifications. It applies to professions that are regulated in the parties. Professional bodies are encouraged to negotiate mutual recognition arrangements. Chapter Twelve deals with domestic regulations. It covers matters such as licensing and qualification requirements and procedures. Chapter thirteen covers financial services. Again, negative lists apply to non-conforming measures. Chapter Fourteen deals with international transport maritime services and Chapter Fifteen with telecommunications. Chapter Sixteen covers electronic commerce and Chapter Seventeen competition policy. Chapter Eighteen deals with state enterprises, monopolies and enterprises granted special rights or privileges. Chapter Nineteen deals with ***government procurement***. A general non-discrimination principle applies. Applicable procedures are outlined in detail. Chapter Twenty covers ***intellectual property***. It complements the rights and obligations of the parties under the ***Agreement on Trade-Related Aspects of Intellectual Property Rights***. In Chapter Twenty-One the parties agree to regulatory cooperation in a wide range of areas. In Chapters Twenty-Two (Trade and Sustainable Development), Twenty-Three (Trade and Labour) and Twenty-Four (Trade and Environment) the parties reaffirm their commitment to developing international trade in such a way as to contribute to sustainable development. Chapter Twenty-Five outlines the range of bilateral dialogues and cooperation, and Chapter Twenty-Six contains the administrative and institutional provisions. Chapter Twenty-Seven contains the rules on ***transparency*** and Chapter Twenty-Eight the applicable exceptions. Chapter Twenty-Nine outlines the procedures for dispute settlement. Chapter Thirty contains the final provisions. If a country requests to accede to the European Union, the concerns expressed by Canada about any matter regarding the agreement will be taken into account by the European Union.

Comprehensiveness: a principle agreed by ***APEC*** leaders to signify that the commitment to free and open trade and investment by 2010/2020 will apply within the target dates and across all sectors and impediments. The principle allows for some flexibility on the timing of liberalizing across or within the different areas of an economy. *See also* ***Bogor Declaration*** and ***Osaka Action Agenda***.

性贸易壁垒协定》的一些条款。第 5 章涵盖卫生与植物卫生措施，适用 WTO《实施卫生与植物卫生措施协定》的权利和义务，并辅之以额外规定。第 6 章处理海关和贸易便利化。第 7 章涵盖补贴，双方将按要求就与农产品和渔业产品有关的补贴进行磋商。第 8 章涵盖投资，双方保留不符措施负面清单，本章还列出了投资者—国家争端解决条款。第 9 章处理跨境服务贸易，现有不符措施包含在负面清单中。第 10 章涵盖为商业目的的自然人临时入境和停留，不适用于就业、公民身份或居住。第 11 章关于相互承认专业资格，适用于双方监管的职业，鼓励专业团体就相互承认安排进行谈判。第 12 章处理国内规制，涵盖许可、资格要求和程序等事项。第 13 章涵盖金融服务，同样，负面清单适用于不符措施。第 14 章处理国际海运服务。第 15 章处理电信。第 16 章涵盖电子商务。第 17 章涵盖竞争政策。第 18 章处理国有企业、垄断和被授予特殊权利或特权的企业。第 19 章处理政府采购，适用普遍的非歧视原则，适用程序详细列出。第 20 章涵盖知识产权，补充了双方在《与贸易有关的知识产权协定》项下的权利和义务。在第 21 章中，双方同意在广泛的领域进行监管合作。在第 22 章(贸易和可持续发展)、第 23 章(贸易和劳工)和第 24 章(贸易和环境)中，双方重申致力于以促进可持续发展的方式发展国际贸易。第 25 章概述了双边对话和合作的范围，第 26 章包含管理和机制规定。第 27 章包含透明度规则。第 28 章包含适用的例外。第 29 章概述了争端解决程序。第 30 章包含最后条款。如一国要求加入欧盟，欧盟将考虑加拿大就有关协定的任何事项所表达的关切。

Comprehensiveness

全面性

APEC 领导人议定的一项原则，指到 2010 年/2020 年实现贸易和投资自由和开放的承诺将在目标日期内适用于所有部门和障碍。该原则允许一经济体不同领域之间/之内在自由化时间上有一定灵活性。*另见茂物宣言(Bogor Deceleration)、大阪行动议程(Osaka Action Agenda)*。

Compulsory licensing: a procedure for authorities to license companies or individuals other than the ***patent*** owner to use the rights of the patent – to make, use, sell or import a product under patent (i.e. a patented product or a product made by a patented process) – without the permission of the patent owner. Article 31 of the ***Agreement on Trade-Related Aspects of Intellectual Property Rights*** sets out the framework under which this may be done. Compulsory licensing may only be pursued if efforts to obtain the right to use the intellectual property on reasonable commercial terms have not been successful. *See also* ***access to medicines***, ***Declaration on the TRIPS Agreement and Public Health***, ***exhaustion doctrine***, ***forced technology transfer*** and ***Paragraph 6 system***.

Computed value: one of the methods for ***customs valuation*** permitted by the WTO ***Agreement on Customs Valuation*** if no reliable price information is available. A computed value consists of the sum of (a) the cost or value of the materials and their processing, (b) a normal amount for profit and general expenses, and (c) the cost or value of all expenses necessary, such as transport, port handling charges and insurance.

COMTRADE database: its full name is United Nations Commodity Trade Statistics Database. This is a statistical database for the trade in goods of more than 170 countries and areas. Goods are classified according to ***SITC*** and the ***Harmonized Commodity Description and Coding System***. Data for many countries are available from 1962 to the present. The data can be interrogated on the COMTRADE website. [comtrade.un.org]

Concealed dumping: *see* ***hidden dumping***.

Concentric circles: a system of small and large, informal and formal, meetings handled by the chairman who is at the centre. The "outer circle" is the formal meeting of the full membership, where decisions are taken and statements are recorded in official minutes or notes. Inside, the circles represent informal meetings of the full membership or smaller groups of members, down to bilateral consultations with the chair. Members accept the process as long as they all have input and information is shared. *See also* ***inclusive*** and ***transparent***.

Concerted liberalization action: sometimes also called concerted unilateralism. One of mechanisms devised by ***APEC*** economies to achieve the goal of free and open trade and investment by 2010/2020 as envisaged in the ***Bogor Declaration***. Economies aim at roughly equal progress through the observance of ***comparability***, and they seek to ensure that all sectors are included in the liberalization, as envisaged in the ***comprehensiveness*** principle. *See also* ***APEC***, ***APEC individual action plans***, ***collective action*** and ***Osaka Action Agenda***.

Concerted unilateralism: *see* ***concerted liberalization action***.

Concertina approach: describes a staged approach to ***tariff*** reductions. The highest rates are reduced first, then the second-highest, and so on until the target levels have been achieved across the board.

Compulsory licensing

强制许可

指未经专利所有人许可，主管机关向专利所有人以外的公司或个人许可使用专利权的程序，包括制造、使用、销售或进口专利产品(即专利产品或经专利工艺生产的产品)。《与贸易有关的知识产权协定》第 31 条规定了强制许可的程序框架。只有在按合理商业条款获得使用知识产权权利的努力未获成功的情况下，方可进行强制许可。另见*获得药品(access to medicines)*、*关于与贸易有关的知识产权协定与公共健康的宣言(Declaration on the TRIPS Agreement and Public Health)*、*权利用尽原则(exhaustion doctrine)*、*强制技术转让(forced technology transfer)*、*第 6 段制度(Paragraph 6 system)*。

Computed value

计算价值

WTO《海关估价协定》所允许的、在无法获得可靠价格信息的情况下进行海关估价的方法之一。计算价值包括：(a)材料和加工的成本或价值；(b)利润和一般费用的金额；以及(c)所有必要费用，例如运输、港口装卸和保险。

COMTRADE database

商品贸易统计数据库

全名为联合国商品贸易统计数据库，一个涵盖超过 170 个国家和地区的商品贸易的统计数据库。货物根据国际贸易标准分类(SITC)和商品名称及编码协调制度进行分类。包含许多国家 1962 年至今的数据。这些数据可在 COMTRADE 网站上查询。

Concealed dumping

隐蔽倾销

见*隐蔽倾销(hidden dumping)*。

Concentric circles

同心圆

一个以会议主席为中心召集大大小小、非正式和正式会议的系统。“外圈”是全体成员参加的正式会议，会上作出决定，发言记入官方会议纪要或记录。在内部，圆圈可以代表全体成员或成员组的非正式会议，甚至与主席进行双边磋商。如果成员可以发表意见且信息共享，他们愿意接受这一过程。另见*包容(inclusive)*、*透明(transparent)*。

Concerted liberalization action

协调的自由化行动

有时也称协调的单边主义。APEC 经济体为实现《茂物宣言》中所设想的到 2010/2020 年实行贸易和投资的自由开放目标所设计的机制之一。各经济体的目标是通过遵守可比性来实现大致均等的进展，努力保证如全面性原则所设想的，将所有部门纳入自由化。另见*亚太经济合作组织(APEC)*、*APEC 单边行动计划(APEC individual action plans)*、*集体行动(collective action)*、*大阪行动议程(Osaka Action Agenda)*。

Concerted unilateralism

协调的单边主义

见*协调的自由化行动(concerted liberalization action)*。

Concertina approach

手风琴方式

指一种分阶段关税削减的方式。首先削减最高税率，然后是次高税率，依此类推，直至全面达到目标水平。

Concertina theorem: the theorem concerning ***piecemeal tariff reform***, i.e. reductions on selected items only, postulated by James Meade that "[t]here is more likely to be a gain in economic welfare if the rate of duty is high on the primary imports which will come in increased volume and is low on the secondary imports which will come in reduced volume". The validity of the theorem was demonstrated by Bertrand and Vanek to the effect, as expressed by López and Panagaryia, that "in a small open economy, if the highest tariff is reduced to the next highest one, welfare will rise provided the import demand for the good with the highest tariff exhibits gross substitutability with respect to all other goods". [Bertrand and Vanek 1971, López and Panagaryia 1992, Meade 1955]

Concession: in the WTO, the lowering of a ***tariff*** or the removal of an impediment to ***trade in services***, generally at the request of another party. In its narrowest sense, it may only cover the ***binding*** of a tariff item. Some commentators have suggested that this term should be replaced by ***commitment*** to remove the false impression that countries make a sacrifice by lowering tariff rates, and that ***trade liberalization*** is a cost on the economy. The ***General Agreement on Trade in Services*** already refers to commitments. *See also* ***requests and offers***, ***schedule of concessions*** and ***schedules of specific commitments on services***.

Conditional most-favoured-nation treatment: the granting of ***most-favoured-nation treatment*** (MFN) subject to conditions being met by the country receiving it. Membership of an agreement may be such a condition. In the case of the WTO ***Agreement on Government Procurement***, for example, MFN on government purchases only has to be extended to the other members of the Agreement. This is also called ***code-conditioned MFN treatment***. There are also cases where a country decides to grant MFN to another country only if some conditions unrelated to trade are met. Such a situation arose when the United States Congress adopted the ***Jackson-Vanik amendment*** to the 1974 Trade Act which limited the granting of MFN to countries having a liberal emigration policy.

Conditional national treatment: the imposition of conditions on foreign-owned companies as part of giving them ***national treatment*** in other respects. For example, foreign-owned companies may have to comply with performance requirements, ***reciprocity*** conditions or ***local content requirements*** not applying to others.

Conditional offers: offers made in trade negotiations either in the expectation that others will make offers of equivalent value or on the assumption that one's own offer will be seen as matching those already on the table. Conditional offers may be withdrawn or modified at any time until a general settlement has been reached. *See also* ***ad referendum agreement*** and ***without prejudice***.

Conduct: in ***competition policy***, the behaviour of a firm in the marketplace, particularly in terms of the applicable ***competition laws*** or ***antitrust laws***. Sometimes also called ***behaviour***.

Conference on International Economic Cooperation: CIEC. A meeting of developed and developing countries convened by the French Government

Concertina theorem

手风琴定理

詹姆斯·米德假设的关于零敲碎打的关税改革的定理，即"如果进口将会增加的初级商品的关税高而进口将会减少的次级商品的关税低，仅对有限税目进行削减，就更有可能获得经济福利"。伯特兰德和瓦内克证明了这一定理的有效性，其大意如洛佩兹和潘娜加利亚所表示的那样，即"在一个小型开放经济体中，如果最高关税削减至次高关税水平，福利将增加，前提是对关税最高商品的进口需求相对于所有其他商品具有总的可替代性"。

Concession

减让

在 WTO 中指降低关税或取消服务贸易障碍，通常应另一方请求。按最狭义的理解，减让可能仅涵盖关税约束。一些评论家建议，应以承诺代替减让一词，以消除一些错误印象，即国家降低关税税率是作出牺牲，贸易自由化是对经济的代价。《服务贸易总协定》中指承诺。另见*要价和出价(requests and offers)*、*减让表(schedule of concessions)*、*服务贸易具体承诺减让表(schedules of specific commitment on services)*。

Conditional most-favoured-nation treatment

有条件最惠国待遇

给予最惠国待遇(MFN)需要获得待遇的国家满足条件。一协定的成员资格可能就是这样一种条件。例如，就 WTO《政府采购协定》而言，关于政府采购的最惠国待遇只需给予该协定的其他成员。这也被称为以守则为条件的最惠国待遇。还有一些情况是，一国决定给予另一国最惠国待遇，前提是满足一些与贸易无关的条件。例如，美国国会通过《1974 年贸易法》的《杰克逊-瓦尼克修正案》，将最惠国待遇的给予仅限于实行自由移民政策的国家。

Conditional national treatment

附条件的国民待遇

对外资分企业附加条件，作为在其他方面给予其国民待遇的一部分。例如，外资企业可能必须符合实绩要求、互惠条件或当地含量要求等不适用于其他企业的要求。

Conditional offers

附条件出价

在贸易谈判中作出的出价，要么是期望其他方作出同等价值的出价，要么是假定自己的出价将被视为与已经摆在桌面上的出价相匹配。附条件出价可以在达成总体解决方案前随时撤回或修改。另见*待核准协定(ad referendum agreement)*、*不损害(without prejudice)*。

Conduct

行为

在竞争政策中，公司在市场中的行为，特别是在适用的竞争法或反垄断法方面。有时也称行为。

Conference on International Economic Cooperation

国际经济合作会议

CIEC。法国政府在 1975 年 12 月至 1977 年 6 月期间召集的发达国家和发展

between December 1975 and June 1977 to discuss international economic issues, including energy, raw material prices, development, and finance. Some say that this was the true start of the ***North–South dialogue***. France received much-deserved praise for this initiative, but it is not possible to point to any concrete results from the conference.

Conflict diamonds: also known as "blood diamonds". Defined in the ***Kimberley Process Certification Scheme*** as "rough diamonds used by rebel movements or their allies to finance conflict aimed at undermining legitimate governments, as described in relevant ***United Nations Security Council*** (UNSC) resolutions, insofar as they remain in effect . . .".

Conflict of laws: *see* ***private international law***.

Conformity assessment: includes, among other things, procedures for sampling, testing and inspection; evaluation, verification and assurance of conformity; and registration, accreditation and approval. The WTO ***Agreement on Technical Barriers to Trade*** sets out a ***Code of Good Practice for the Preparation, Adoption and Application of Standards*** which should be used by government and non-government bodies for framing and using technical regulations. It requires that procedures for determining conformity of products with national standards are fair and equitable, particularly where domestic and comparable imported products are involved. *See also* ***International Electrotechnical Commission*** and ***International Organization for Standardization***.

Connectivity: the ease and extent to which individual electronic devices can connect with others. *See also* ***Internet of Things***.

Conscious parallelism: a form of ***cartel*** in which the competitors observe each other's behaviour and make decisions on output, prices, etc., accordingly. One difference with a normal cartel is that there is no express agreement between the firms to act in this way. [Pierce 2000]

Consensus: the usual method for taking decisions in the WTO. The ***WTO Agreement*** states in Article IX:1 that the "WTO shall continue the practice of decision-making by consensus followed under ***GATT 1947***". It adds in a footnote that the "body concerned shall be deemed to have decided by consensus on a matter submitted for its consideration, if no member, present at the meeting when the decision is taken, formally objects to the proposed decision". Provision exists for formal voting, but such votes are rare or taken only when consensus has already been achieved. Consensus decisions reduce the scope for disputes arising from differing understandings of the rules. The search for consensus can, however, add to the negotiating period, and it can give rise to delays because of ***foot draggers***. The Doha Ministerial Declaration refers several times to decisions having to be made by explicit consensus. It is not yet clear whether this will affect the way consensus is reached. *See also* ***convoy problem***, ***decision-making in the WTO*** and ***reverse consensus***.

Conservative social welfare function: one of the factors governing the actions of governments in their consideration of trade-liberalizing policies. It was first identified by Max Corden in *Trade Policy and Economic Welfare*. He says that,

中国家共同讨论国际经济问题的会议，包括能源、原材料价格、发展以及金融。有人认为这是南北对话的真正开始。尽管法国因该倡议得到了应有的赞扬，但却不可能从会议中取得任何具体结果。

Conflict diamonds

冲突钻石

又称“血钻”。金伯利进程证书制度将其定义为“如联合国安全理事会(UNSC)相关决议中所述的(只要仍然有效)……反叛运动或其盟友用以资助旨在破坏合法政府的冲突的毛坯钻石”。

Conflict of laws

法律冲突

见*国际私法(private international law)*。

Conformity assessment

合格评定

包括抽样、检验和检查的程序；评估、验证和合格保证；以及注册、认可和批准。WTO《技术性贸易壁垒协定》规定了《关于制定、采用和实施标准的良好行为规范》，政府和非政府机构在制定和使用技术法规时应使用这一规范。要求确定产品是否符合国家标准的程序应公平和公正，特别是在涉及国产品和可比进口产品的情况下。另见*国际电工委员会(International Electrotechnical Commission)*、*国际标准化组织(International Organization for Standardization)*。

Connectivity

连通性

单个电子设备与其他设备连接的便利程度和范围。另见*物联网(Internet of Things)*。

Conscious parallelism

有意识的对应行为说

一种卡特尔形式，竞争者互相观察对方的行为，并相应对产量、价格等作出决定。与普通卡特尔的一个不同之处在于，企业之间没有明确的协议规定以这种方式行事。

Consensus

协商一致

WTO中作出决定的通常方法。《WTO协定》第9条第1款规定“WTO应继续实行 GATT 1947 项下所遵循的经协商一致作出决定的做法”。脚注中补充规定“如在作出决定时，出席会议的成员均未正式反对拟议的决定，则有关机构应被视为已经协商一致对提交其审议的事项作出决定”。有关于正式投票的条款，但是此类投票很少见或是在已经协商一致的情况下进行的。协商一致作出的决定减少了由于对规则的理解不同而引发的争议范围。然而，寻求协商一致会增加谈判时间，且会因为拖后腿者而导致延误。《多哈部长宣言》多处指出必须通过明确一致作出决定。目前还不清楚这是否会影响达成协商一致的方式。另见*舰队问题(convoy problem)*、*WTO决策机制(decision-making in the WTO)*、*反向协商一致(reverse consensus)*。

Conservative social welfare function

保守社会福利函数

在政府考虑贸易自由化政策时管辖其行动的因素之一。最早是由马克斯·科登在《贸易政策与经济福利》一书中提出的。他指出，简而言之，政府认为在

put in its simplest way, it means that governments feel that in an income distribution target any significant absolute reductions in real incomes should be avoided. In other words, he says, increases in incomes are given relatively low weights and decreases very high weights. The conservative social welfare function would therefore partly explain why governments sometimes are cautious about reducing tariffs or removing other trade measures which may affect adversely the operations of industries. [Corden 1974]

Consolidated Tariff Schedules: CTS. A database maintained by the WTO Secretariat. It contains the final bound tariffs of all members, as well as information on implementation periods, ***initial negotiating rights*** and other material relevant to a member's commitments. It is therefore an essential tool for tariff negotiations. *See also* ***Integrated Data Base***.

Constructed value: a method available under the WTO ***Anti-Dumping Agreement*** to calculate the production cost of a product in the exporting country. This method may only be used if there is no export price or if the export price is considered to be unreliable because of doubts about the existence of ***arm's-length pricing***. It is not normally used for ***market economies***. *See also* ***analogue country***, ***anti-dumping measures*** and ***normal value***.

Consular formalities: the requirement that firms exporting goods to some countries obtain an endorsement by the consular representations of the importing country of invoices, ***certificates of origin***, shipping manifests and other documents. Endorsement was subject to the payment of a fee often related to the value of the consignment. Fee structures and bureaucratic delays and procedures frequently became irritating factors in international trade relations. Most countries have now abolished consular formalities. *See also* ***preshipment inspection*** and ***trade facilitation***.

Consultation: the first stage in the WTO ***dispute settlement*** procedure, aimed at resolving issues cooperatively, sometimes through the ***good offices*** or ***mediation*** of a disinterested party. The fact-finding nature of consultation between parties often leads to a solution. If the consultations fail to settle a dispute within sixty days after a request has been made, the complaining party may request the ***Dispute Settlement Body*** to establish a dispute settlement ***panel***. The parties may go to a panel earlier if they conclude that the consultations will not settle the dispute. WTO members receiving a request for such consultations must therefore treat them seriously. They cannot use them to gain extended breathing space. *See also* ***Understanding on Rules and Procedures Governing the Settlement of Disputes***.

Consultative Group of Eighteen: an informal mechanism within the GATT, established on 11 July 1975 with a membership of eighteen, broadly representing developed and developing countries. The CG18 fell into disuse during the ***Uruguay Round***. *See also* ***Invisibles Group*** for a more recent consultative mechanism in the WTO.

Consultative Group on International Agricultural Research: CGIAR. An informal network of public and private bodies that supports sixteen

收入分配目标中，应避免实际收入的大幅绝对减少。换言之，他指出，收入增长所赋予的权重相对较低，而收入减少的权重则相对较高。因此，保守社会福利函数可以部分地解释为什么政府有时对削减关税或取消其他贸易措施可能对产业运行产生不利影响的行动持谨慎态度。

Consolidated Tariff Schedules

合并关税减让表

CTS。由 WTO 秘书处维护的数据库。包含所有成员的最终约束关税，以及关于实施期、最初谈判权及与成员承诺相关的其他资料的信息。因此是关税谈判的重要工具。另见*综合数据库(Integrated Data Base)*。

Constructed value

推定价格

WTO《反倾销协定》项下可用于计算产品在出口国中的生产成本的方法。只有在没有出口价格或因怀疑是否存在公平定价而使出口价格被认为不可靠的情况下，方可使用这种方法。通常不适用于市场经济体。另见*类比国(analogue country)*、*反倾销措施(anti-dumping measures)*、*正常价值(normal value)*。

Consular formalities

领事手续

一些国家要求货物出口公司必须获得进口国领事代表机构对发票、原产地证书、船运舱单和其他单证的背书。背书须缴付与交运货物价值相关联的费用。费用结构、官僚拖延和程序成为国际贸易关系中令人恼火的因素。大多数国家现在已经废除了领事手续。另见*装运前检验(preshipment inspection)*、*贸易便利化(trade facilitations)*。

Consultation

磋商

WTO 争端解决程序的第一阶段，旨在以合作方式解决问题，有时是通过一个无利害关系方的斡旋或调停。双方之间事实调查性质的磋商通常促成解决方案的达成。如在提出磋商请求后 60 天内未能解决争端，起诉方可请求争端解决机构设立争端解决专家组。如果双方认为磋商不能解决争端，可以提前请求设立专家组。因此，收到此类磋商请求的 WTO 成员必须认真对待。不能利用磋商获得更多喘息时间。另见*关于争端解决规则与程序的谅解(Understanding on Rules and Procedures Governing the Settlement of Disputes)*。

Consultative Group of Eighteen

18 国咨询小组

GATT 中的非正式机制，1975 年 7 月 11 日成立，有 18 个成员，广泛代表发达国家和发展中国家。18 国咨询小组在乌拉圭回合谈判中被弃用。另见 WTO 中最近形成的一个磋商机制——*无形小组(Invisibles Group)*。

Consultative Group on International Agricultural Research

国际农业研究磋商组织

CGIAR。由公共和私营机构组成的非正式网络，支持 16 个国际农业研究中心。

international agricultural research centres. CGIAR aims to further agriculture in developing countries to promote food security, to alleviate poverty and to preserve natural resources. Its secretariat is located within the ***World Bank***.

Consumer subsidy equivalent: usually abbreviated to CSE. For an agricultural commodity, the CSE is defined as the amount that consumers would need to be paid to compensate them for the effect of removing agricultural support programmes. Expressed as a percentage, it is the ratio of the total value of transfers received by consumers to total consumer expenditure on the product. When the consumer receives net assistance, CSEs are positive. When they are negative, the consumer is being taxed. *See also* ***producer subsidy equivalent***.

Consumption abroad: one of the ***modes of services delivery*** defined in the ***General Agreement on Trade in Services***. The consumer goes to the country of the producer to obtain the service, as is the case, for example, when one takes a holiday in another country.

Consumption tax: an ***ad valorem*** tax on goods and services, but not necessarily all of them, levied at the point where the consumer makes the purchase. For imported goods, this is after any customs duties have been paid on them. Common names for consumption taxes include value-added tax, goods and services tax, general sales tax, turnover tax, etc.

Contact points: *see* ***enquiry points***.

Container Security Initiative: CSI. Launched by the United States Customs Service on 17 January 2002. CSI consists of three core elements: (a) identify high-risk containers by using automated targeting tools to identify containers that pose a potential risk of terrorism, based on advance information and strategic intelligence, (b) pre-screen and evaluate containers before they are shipped, and screening them as early as possible, and (c) use technology to pre-screen high-risk containers to ensure that screening can be done rapidly without slowing down the movement of trade. This technology includes large-scale X-ray and gamma ray machines and redirection detection devices. Many of the world's largest ports now participate in this scheme. *See also* ***SAFE Framework of Standards to Secure and Facilitate Global Trade.***

Contestability of markets: *see* ***international contestability of markets***.

Continental Free Trade Area: *see* ***African Continental Free Trade Area.***

Contingent multilateralism: an American term to mean that multilateral action should be taken whenever possible to improve ***market access***, but sometimes preferential liberalization in the form of ***free-trade agreements*** and unilateral action would be better. *See also* ***unilateralism***.

Contingent protection: protective mechanisms, also called commercial defence mechanisms, that are legal under the WTO agreements. They may be triggered to counter the effects of ***dumping***, ***subsidies*** and unexpected import surges causing ***injury*** to domestic industry. Such mechanisms include ***anti-dumping measures***, countervailing duties and ***safeguards***.

Continuation clause: a provision contained in Article 20 of the WTO ***Agreement on Agriculture*** which calls for the resumption of multilateral negotiations on

CGIAR 旨在促进发展中国家的农业，以促进粮食安全、减轻贫困和保护自然资源。秘书处设在世界银行内。

Consumer subsidy equivalent
消费者补贴等值

CSE。对于农产品，CSE 被定义为补偿农业支持计划的取消而需对消费者支付的金额，以百分比表示，CSE 为消费者获得的转移的总价值与消费者对该产品总支出之比。当消费者获得净援助时，CSE 为正值。当结果为负值时，表明在对消费者征税。另见***生产者补贴等值****(producer subsidy equivalent)*。

Consumption abroad
国外消费

《服务贸易总协定》定义的服务提供模式之一。消费者前往服务提供者的国家获得服务，例如一个人去他国度假时的情况。

Consumption tax
消费税

在消费者进行购买时对货物和服务征收的从价税，但不一定对所有货物和服务征收。对于进口货物，是在缴纳关税之后征收。消费税的常见名称包括增值税、货物和服务税、一般销售税、营业税等。

Contact points
联络点

见***咨询点****(enquiry point)*。

Container Security Initiative
集装箱安全倡议

CSI。美国海关于 2002 年 1 月 17 日启动。CSI 包括三项核心要素：(a)识别高风险集装箱，根据事先获得的信息和战略情报，利用自动定向工具识别可能存在恐怖主义风险的集装箱；(b)在集装箱装运前进行预先筛选和评估，并尽早对其进行筛选；以及(c)利用技术对高风险集装箱进行预先筛选，以保证能够在不减缓贸易流动的情况下迅速进行筛选。此项技术包括大型 X 射线和伽马射线机和重定向探测设备。许多世界级大港现在参与此项计划。另见***全球贸易安全与便利标准框架****(SAFE Framework of Standards to Secure and Facilitate Global Trade)*。

Contestability of markets
市场的可竞争性

见***市场的国际竞争性****(international contestability of markets)*。

Continental Free Trade Area
大陆自由贸易区

见***非洲大陆自由贸易区****(African Continental Free Trade Area)*。

Contingent multilateralism
有条件的多边主义

美国使用的词语，意思是应尽可能通过多边行动改善市场准入，但有时以自由贸易协定和单边行动形式实行优惠自由化则会更好。另见***单边主义****(unilateralism)*。

Contingent protection
紧急保护

在《WTO 协定》项下合法的保护机制，也称为商业防御机制。可被启动用以应对倾销、补贴和意外进口激增对国内产业所造成的损害。此类机制包括反倾销措施、反补贴税和保障措施。

Continuation clause
继续谈判条款

WTO《农业协定》第 20 条所含规定，呼吁在议定实施期结束的前一年恢复多

agriculture one year before the end of the agreed implementation period, i.e. by 1 January 2000. The long-term objective of the continuation clause is substantial progressive reductions in support and protection. The resumed negotiations, which became part of the ***Doha Development Agenda***, also take into account (a) the experience up to then from implementing the reduction commitments, (b) the effects of the reduction commitments on world trade in agriculture, ***non-trade concerns***, and ***special and differential treatment*** on developing countries, (c) the objective to establish a fair and market-oriented agricultural trading system, and (d) other objectives needed to achieve the long-term objectives. *See also* ***built-in agenda***.

Continued Dumping and Subsidy Offset Act of 2000: *see* ***Byrd Amendment***.

Contraband: refers to neutral cargo in times of war capable of being used to assist the military operations of an enemy. Rules concerning contraband have always been flexible and subject to interpretation on the spot, but in principle, upon interception goods found to be peacetime commodities would be allowed to continue. War material could be stopped. The elaboration and administration of rules on contraband has always been difficult because many goods and commodities are capable of either civilian or military use. In popular parlance, contraband is often used where ***smuggling*** or smuggled goods would be the more appropriate term. *See also* ***dual-purpose exports***.

Contracting party: the formal term for members of the ***GATT 1947***. When the contracting parties acted jointly to adopt a decision, GATT documents denote this by the use of capital letters (the CONTRACTING PARTIES). GATT contracting parties are now WTO members.

Contractual non-reciprocal rules of origin: refers to ***rules of origin*** used under instruments such as the ***ACP-EU Partnership Agreement*** or ***SPARTECA***. Agreements of this kind give defined developing countries preferential access to the developed partners. The reverse does not apply. All the parties to these agreements participate in negotiating the applicable rules of origin, but the developing country members are under no obligation to apply them to goods imported from the developed-country members. [Inama 2000]

Contractual reciprocal rules of origin: refers to ***rules of origin*** applied to goods traded under preferential conditions, such as a ***free-trade agreement***. These rules are equally binding on all parties. [Inama 2000]

Contrary to honest commercial practice: *see* ***in a manner contrary to honest commercial practices***.

Conventional international law: internationally applicable rights and obligations created through conventions, treaties, covenants, international agreements and other binding instruments. Brownlie says that "Law-making treaties create *general* norms for the future conduct of the parties in terms of legal propositions, and the obligations are basically the same for all parties." Strictly speaking, treaties are only binding on the parties. However, as pointed out by Shaw, "where treaties reflect customary law then non-parties are bound, not because it is a treaty provision, but because it reaffirms a rule or rules of

边农业谈判，即2000年1月1日。继续谈判条款的长期目标是实质性逐步削减支持和保护。恢复的谈判已成为多哈发展议程一部分，还应考虑(a)届时从实施削减承诺中获得的经验；(b)削减承诺对世界农产品贸易、非贸易关注以及对发展中国家特殊和差别待遇的影响；(c)建立公平的、以市场为导向的农产品贸易体系的目标；以及(d)实现长期目标所需的其他目标。另见*既定议程(built-in agenda)*。

Continued Dumping and Subsidy Offset Act of 2000

2000年持续倾销与补贴抵消法

见*伯德修正案(Byrd Amendment)*。

Contraband

禁运品

指在战时能够用以协助敌军军事行动的中立货物。关于禁运品的规则一直以来是灵活的，并视当时的情况加以解释，但原则上，被截获后被认定属和平时期商品的货物将被允许继续进行交易，属战争物资则不得继续交易。详述和实施有关禁运品的规则一向很困难，因为许多货物和商品既可属民用也可属军用。平常所说的禁运品将其称为走私或走私货物更合适。另见*两用物品出口(dual-purpose exports)*。

Contracting party

缔约方

GATT 1947成员的正式称谓。当缔约方采取联合行动通过一项决定时，GATT文件用大写字母表示(the CONTRACTING PARTIES，中文译为“缔约方全体”—译注)。GATT缔约方现为WTO成员。

Contractual non-reciprocal rules of origin

契约性非互惠原产地规则

指在《非加太地区国家与欧盟伙伴关系协定》或《南太平洋区域贸易与经济合作协定》(SPARTECA)等文件中使用的原产地规则。此类协定给予特定发展中国家对发达国家的优惠准入。反向则不适用。这些协定的所有参加方参与适用的原产地规则的谈判，但发展中国家成员无义务将这些规则适用于自发达国家成员进口的货物。

Contractual reciprocal rules of origin

契约性互惠原产地规则

指适用于在优惠条件下交易货物的原产地规则，例如自由贸易协定。这些规则对所有参加方具有同等约束力。

Contrary to honest commercial practice

违反诚实商业行为

见*以违反诚实商业惯例的方式(in a manner contrary to honest commercial practices)*。

Conventional international law

协定国际法

通过公约、条约、盟约、国际协定和其他约束性文件创设的国际适用的权利和义务。布朗利指出“立法型条约就立法主张而言为缔约方未来行为创造了一般规范，而且义务基本上对所有缔约方均相同”。严格来说，条约只对缔约方具有约束力。然而，正如肖所指出的“如果条约反映习惯法，那么非缔约方就受到约束，并非因为是条约规定，而是因为重申了国际习惯法的一项或多项规

customary international law". *See also* ***customary international law***. [Brownlie 2019; Shaw 2014; Starke 1989]

Conventional tariff: a tariff in which most or all duty rates are the result of negotiations under international conventions or treaties. This term is now largely forgotten. *See also* ***maximum-minimum tariff***.

Conventional wisdom: words used by J. K. Galbraith in *The Affluent Society* to describe "beliefs that are at any time assiduously, solemnly and mindlessly traded between the pretentiously wise". He assesses the phrase as being nicely balanced between approval and ridicule. A description of the origin of this expression may be found in *A Life in our Times*, by the same author. *See also* ***QWERTY principle*** and ***vestigial thought***. [Galbraith 1958, Galbraith 1981]

Convention Concerning the Prohibition and Immediate Action for the Elimination of the Worst Forms of Child Labour: ILO Convention No. 182, adopted on 17 June 1999. It seeks to prohibit and eliminate the ***worst forms of child labour*** as a matter of urgency. *See also* ***Declaration on Fundamental Principles and Rights at Work and its follow-up***.

Convention for the Protection of Producers of Phonograms Against Unauthorized Duplication of their Phonograms: *see* ***Geneva Convention***.

Convention of Stockholm: *see* ***EFTA***.

Convention on a Code of Conduct for Liner Conferences: sometimes known as the ***UNCTAD*** Liner Code. An intergovernmental agreement which entered into force on 6 October 1983. It seeks to develop the share of commodities and goods carried in developing country ships to improve their ***balance of payments***. The Code's underlying principle is the 40-40-20 ratio which, although not specified in the Convention, allocates informally 40 per cent of trade to shipping lines of the importing country, 40 per cent to those of exporting country and 20 per cent to third-country shipping lines. Liner code member countries have had difficulties achieving these figures in the face of commercial reality and changing directions of trade. *See also* ***MFN exemption***.

Convention on Biological Diversity: CBD. Entered into force on 29 December 1993. Its objectives are the conservation of biological diversity, the sustainable use of its components and the fair and equitable sharing of the benefits arising out of the utilization of genetic resources. It contains provisions concerning appropriate access to genetic resources and transfer of relevant technologies. The CBD's secretariat is in Montreal. *See also* ***Cartagena Protocol on Biosafety***, ***multilateral environment agreements*** and ***trade and environment***.

Convention on Combating Bribery of Foreign Public Officials in International Business Transactions: entered into force on 15 February 1999. All thirty-six ***OECD*** countries plus Argentina, Brazil, Bulgaria, Colombia, Costa Rica, Peru, Russia and South Africa have acceded to it. The Convention makes it a crime to offer, promise or give a bribe to a foreign public official to secure a business transaction. Separately, OECD members also agreed to end the tax deductibility of bribery payments. *See also* ***Draft International Agreement on Illicit Payments***, ***Recommendation for Further Combating Bribery***

则。”另见*习惯国际法(customary international law)*。

Conventional tariff
协定关税

一种关税，其中大部分或全部税率为根据国际公约确定或条约谈判的结果。这一词语现在在很大程度上已被遗忘。另见*最高-最低关税(maximum-minimum tariff)*。

Conventional wisdom
传统智慧

J. K. 加尔布雷斯在《富裕社会》中的用词，描述“在自命不凡的智者之间一刻不停地、庄严地和无意识地交换的信念”。他认为这一词语在赞同和嘲笑之间取得了很好的平衡。这一表述的起源可在该作者的另一著作《我们时代的生活》中找到。另见 *QWERTY 键盘原则(QWERTY principle)*、*残余思想(vestigial thought)*。

Convention Concerning the Prohibition and Immediate Action for the Elimination of the Worst Forms of Child Labour
禁止和立即行动消除最恶劣形式的童工劳动公约

国际劳工组织(ILO)第 182 号公约，1999 年 6 月 17 日通过。公约旨在紧急禁止和消除最恶劣形式的童工劳动。另见*关于工作中基本原则和权利宣言及其后续措施(Declaration on Fundamental Principles and Rights at Work and its follow-up)*。

Convention for the Protection of Producers of Phonograms Against Unauthorized Duplication of their Phonograms
保护录音制品制作者防止未经许可复制其录音制品公约

见*日内瓦公约(Geneva Convention)*。

Convention of Stockholm
斯德哥尔摩公约

见*欧洲自由贸易联盟(EFTA)*。

Convention on a Code of Conduct for Liner Conferences
班轮公会行动守则公约

有时称为联合国贸易与发展会议(UNCTAD)班轮守则。1983 年 10 月 6 日生效的政府间协定。公约试图提高发展中国家轮船中所装运商品和货物的份额，以改善其国际收支。守则基本原则是 40-40-20 比例，尽管没有在公约中明确规定，非正式地将 40%的贸易分配给进口国航运公司，40%分配给出口国航运公司，20%分配给第三国航运公司。面对商业现实和贸易流向的变化，班轮守则成员国在实现这些数字目标方面遇到困难。另见*最惠国待遇豁免(MFN exemption)*。

Convention on Biological Diversity
生物多样性公约

CBD。1993 年 12 月 29 日生效，目标为保护生物多样性、生物多样性组成部分的可持续利用以及以公平公正方式共享遗传资源的利用。包含有关适当获取遗传资源和相关技术转让的规定。CBD 秘书处设在蒙特利尔。另见*卡塔赫纳生物安全议定书(Cartagena Protocol on Biosafety)*、*多边环境协定(multilateral environment agreements)*、*贸易与环境(trade and environment)*。

Convention on Combating Bribery of Foreign Public Officials in International Business Transactions
关于打击国际商业交易中行贿外国公职人员行为的公约

1999 年 2 月 15 日生效。所有 36 个经济合作与发展组织(OECD)国家及阿根廷、巴西、保加利亚、哥伦比亚、哥斯达黎加、秘鲁、俄罗斯和南非加入该公约。公约将向外国公职人员提供、承诺或行贿以获得商业交易定为犯罪行为。此外，OECD 成员国还同意停止贿赂付款的税收减免。另见*关于违法付款的国际协定草案(Draft International Agreement on Illicit Payments)*、*关于进一步*

of Foreign Public Officials in International Business Transactions, ***trade and illicit payments*** and ***United Nations Convention Against Corruption***.

Convention on Facilitation of International Maritime Traffic: FAL. Entered into force in 1967. It is administered by the ***International Maritime Organization***. Its main objectives are to prevent unnecessary delays in maritime traffic, to aid cooperation between governments and to secure the highest practicable degree of uniformity in formalities and other procedures. *See also* ***trade facilitation***. [www.imo.org]

Convention on International Civil Aviation: *see* ***Chicago Convention***.

Convention on International Trade in Endangered Species of Wild Fauna and Flora: *see* ***CITES***.

Convention on Persistent Organic Pollutants: a treaty to protect human health and the environment from chemicals that remain intact in the environment for long periods, become widely distributed geographically, accumulate in the fatty tissue of humans and wildlife and have harmful effects on human health and the environment. Entered into force on 17 May 2004. The Convention (a) prohibits and/or eliminates the production and use, as well as the import and export, of intentionally produced ***persistent organic pollutants*** (POPs) listed in Annex A, (b) restricts the production and use as well as the import and export of intentionally produced POPs listed in Annex B, and (c) reduces or eliminates releases from intentionally produced POPs listed in Annex C. The secretariat for the Convention is located in Geneva. *See also* ***multilateral environment agreements***. [chm.pops.int]

Convention on the Grant of European Patents: *see* ***European Patent Convention***.

Convention on the Law of the Sea: *see* ***United Nations Convention on the Law of the Sea***.

Convention on the Means of Prohibiting and Preventing the Illicit Import, Export and Transfer of Ownership of Cultural Property: a convention adopted by the ***United Nations Educational, Scientific and Cultural Organization*** (UNESCO) in 1970 in Nairobi. The parties designate the types of property, religious or secular, that are important for archaeology, prehistory, history, literature, art or science. They agree to oppose the illicit import, export or transfer of ownership of cultural property. Licit exports of cultural property are made under a system of certification. *See also* ***UNIDROIT Convention on Stolen or Illegally Exported Cultural Objects***.

Convention on the Organisation for Economic Co-operation and Development: *see* ***OECD***.

Convention on the Prior Informed Consent Procedure for Certain Hazardous Chemicals and Pesticides in International Trade: This Convention assists governments in preventing imports of chemicals that they cannot manage safely. If governments allow imports of a hazardous chemical or pesticide, exporters are obliged to provide extensive information on the chemical's possible health and environmental dangers. The Convention covers twenty-two

打击国际商业交易中行贿外国公职人员行为的建议(Recommendation for Further Combating Bribery of Foreign Public Officials in International Business Transaction)、*贸易与违法付款(trade and illicit payments)*、*联合国反腐败公约(United Nations Convention Against Corruption)*。

Convention on Facilitation of International Maritime Traffic
便利国际海上运输公约

FAL。1967 年生效，由国际海事组织管理。主要目标是防止海上交通出现不必要延误，协助政府之间的合作，并保证在手续和其他程序方面达到尽可能高的一致程度。另见*贸易便利化(trade facilitation)*。

Convention on International Civil Aviation
国际民用航空公约

见*芝加哥公约(Chicago Convention)*。

Convention on International Trade in Endangered Species of Wild Fauna and Flora
濒危野生动植物种国际贸易公约

见*濒危野生动植物种国际贸易公约(CITES)*。

Convention on Persistent Organic Pollutants
关于持久性有机污染物的公约

一项旨在保护人类健康和环境免受化学品危害的条约，这些化学品长期完整存在于环境中，在地理上广泛分布，在人类和野生动物的脂肪组织中积累，并对人类健康和环境产生有害影响。该公约于 2004 年 5 月 17 日生效。公约(a)禁止和/或消除有意生产出的附件 A 中所列持久性有机污染物(POPs)的生产、使用和进出口；(b)限制有意生产出的附件 B 中所列 POPs 的生产和使用以及进出口；以及(c)减少或消除有意生产出的附件 C 中所列 POPs 的排放。公约秘书处设在日内瓦。另见*多边环境协定(multilateral environment agreements)*。

Convention on the Grant of European Patents
欧洲专利授予公约

见*欧洲专利公约(European Patent Convention)*。

Convention on the Law of the Sea
海洋法公约

见*联合国海洋法公约(United Nations Convention on the Law of the Sea)*。

Convention on the Means of Prohibiting and Preventing the Illicit Import, Export and Transfer of Ownership of Cultural Property
关于禁止和防止非法进出口文化财产和非法转让其所有权的方法的公约

联合国教科文组织(UNESCO)于 1970 年在内罗毕通过的一项公约。缔约方根据宗教的或世俗的理由，指定具有重要意义的考古、史前学、历史、文学、艺术或科学价值的财产类型。缔约方同意反对文化财产非法进口、出口或所有权转让。文化财产的合法出口需要在一个证件体系下进行。另见*国际统一私法协会关于被盗或者非法出口文物的公约(UNIDROIT Convention on Stolen or Illegally Exported Cultural Objects)*。

Convention on the Organisation for Economic Co-operation and Development
经济合作与发展组织公约

见*经济合作与发展组织(OECD)*。

Convention on the Prior Informed Consent Procedure for Certain Hazardous Chemicals and Pesticides in International Trade
关于在国际贸易中对某些危险化学品和农药采用事先知情同意程序的公约

该公约协助各国政府防止进口那些它们无法安全管理的化学品。如果政府允许进口危险化学品或农药，出口商有义务提供关于该化学品可能对健康和环

pesticides and five industrial chemicals. This list can be extended through further negotiations. The Convention entered into force on 24 February 2004. It is administered jointly by the ***Food and Agriculture Organization*** and ***UN Environment Programme*** (UNEP). *See also* ***multilateral environment agreements*** and ***prior informed consent***.

Convention on the Settlement of Investment Disputes between States and Nationals of Other States: *see* ***ICSID***.

Convention Relating to the Distribution of Programme-Carrying Signals Transmitted by Satellite: concluded at Brussels on 21 May 1974. It requires its members to make sure that any programme (pictures, sound, or both) emitted by satellite is only distributed by those who are authorized to do so. The Convention is administered by ***WIPO***.

Convoy problem: this problem arises in ***multilateral trade negotiations*** when participants ready to move forward have to wait for the party least prepared or least willing to proceed. The slowest party, like the slowest ship in a convoy, then determines the pace of progress. *See also* **consensus** and ***foot dragger***.

Cooperation Council of the Arab States of the Gulf: *see* ***Gulf Cooperation Council***.

COP: Conference of the Parties. Refers, for example, to meetings, numbered, under the ***United Nations Framework Convention on Climate Change*** (UNFCC). [unfccc.int]

Copenhagen criteria: the standards, adopted in 1993, a ***candidate country*** must meet to qualify for membership of the ***European Union***. They are (a) stability of institutions guaranteeing democracy, the rule of law, human rights and respect for and, protection of minorities, (b) existence of a functioning ***market economy***, as well as the capacity to cope with competitive pressure and market forces within the Union, and (c) an ability to take on the obligations of membership, including adherence to the aims of political, economic and monetary union. *See also* ***enlargement***.

Copenhagen Declaration and Programme of Action: a set of non-binding undertakings by the 117 countries that attended the World Summit for Social Development in March 1995 in Copenhagen. Some of its provisions draw attention to the role of trade and investment in promoting social development and have relevance to the debate on ***trade and labour standards***.

Copyright: the exclusive right to do certain things with an original work, including the right to reproduce, publish, perform the work in public and to make adaptations of it. Copyright does not protect ideas themselves, but only the original expression of ideas. In literary, dramatic, musical or artistic works, it generally lasts for the lifetime of the author plus fifty years. The ***Comprehensive and Progressive Agreement for Trans-Pacific Partnership*** extends this to seventy years, as does the ***United States–Mexico–Canada Agreement***. *See also* ***Agreement on Trade-Related Aspects of Intellectual Property Rights***, ***Berne Convention***, ***fair-use doctrine***, ***intellectual property rights***, ***neighbouring rights*** and ***Universal Copyright Convention***.

境造成危害的广泛信息。公约涵盖 22 种农药和 5 种工业用化学品。此份清单可以通过进一步谈判加以扩大。公约于 2004 年 2 月 24 日生效。由粮农组织(FAO)和联合国环境规划署(UNEP)共同管理。另见*多边环境协定(multilateral environment agreements)*、*事先知情同意(prior informed consent)*。

Convention on the Settlement of Investment Disputes between States and Nationals of Other States

关于解决国家与其他国家国民之间投资争端公约

见*国际投资争端解决中心(ICSID)*。

Convention Relating to the Distribution of Programme-Carrying Signals Transmitted by Satellite

关于播送人造卫星传输节目信号公约

1974 年 5 月 21 日在布鲁塞尔缔结。要求其成员保证任何由卫星发射的节目(图片、声音或两者兼有)只能由获得授权者传输。公约由世界知识产权组织(WIPO)管理。

Convoy problem

舰队问题

这一问题产生于多边贸易谈判中，当参加方准备向前推进时，不得不等待准备最少或最不愿意推进的一方。最慢的一方，就如同舰队中最慢的那只船一样，决定了进展的速度。另见*协商一致(consensus)*、*拖后腿者(foot dragger)*。

Cooperation Council of the Arab States of the Gulf

海湾阿拉伯国家合作委员会

见*海湾合作委员会(Gulf Cooperation Council)*。

COP

缔约方会议

例如联合国气候变化框架公约(UNFCC)项下进行编号的会议。

Copenhagen criteria

哥本哈根标准

1993 年通过的关于候选国是否能达到欧盟成员国资格的标准，包括(a)保证民主、法治、人权以及尊重和保护少数群体的机制的稳定性；(b)存在运行良好的市场经济，及应对联盟内部竞争压力和市场力量的能力；以及(c)承担成员义务的能力，包括遵守政治、经济和货币联盟的目标。另见*扩盟(enlargement)*。

Copenhagen Declaration and Programme of Action

哥本哈根宣言和行动纲领

1995 年 3 月出席在哥本哈根举行的社会发展问题世界首脑会议的 117 个国家作出的一系列非约束承诺。其中某些条款提请人们注意贸易和投资在促进社会发展中的作用，且与贸易与劳工标准的争论有关。

Copyright

版权

使用原创作品作某些事情的专有权，包括复制、出版、公开表演作品和改编作品的权利。版权并不保护思想本身，而仅保护思想的原始表达。在文学、戏剧、音乐或艺术作品中，版权保护期一般为作者生前加死后50年。《全面与进步跨太平洋伙伴关系协定》和《美国—墨西哥—加拿大协定》将保护期延长至70年。另见*与贸易有关的知识产权协定(Agreement on Trade-Related Aspects of Intellectual Property Rights)*、*伯尔尼公约(Berne Convention)*、*合理使用原则(fair-use doctrine)*、*知识产权(intellectual property rights)*、*邻接权(neighbouring rights)*、*世界版权公约(Universal Copyright Convention)*。

Copyright Treaty: *see **WIPO Copyright Treaty***.

Core labour standards: minimum human rights standards applied to working conditions, but not defined as such in a single international instrument. The ILO ***Declaration on Fundamental Principles and Rights at Work***, adopted by the ***International Labour Organization*** in 1998, states that all ILO members are obligated to promote, respect and realize the following principles: (a) freedom of association and the effective recognition of the right to collective bargaining, (b) the elimination of all forms of forced or compulsory labour, (c) the effective abolition of child labour, and (d) the elimination of discrimination in respect of employment and occupation. This list is now accepted by many as representative of core labour standards. The United States ***Trade Promotion Authority*** lists five core labour standards: (a) the right of association, (b) the right to organize and bargain collectively, (c) a prohibition on the use of any form of forced or compulsory labour, (d) a minimum age for the employment of children, and (e) acceptable conditions of work with respect to minimum wages, hours of work, and occupational safety and health. Proponents of multilateral rules on ***trade and labour standards*** tend to take core labour standards as their starting point. The ***GSP*** scheme of the ***European Union*** contains a special incentive arrangement for countries whose national legislation incorporates the conventions of the International Labour Organization covering core labour standards. *See also **pauper-labour argument**, **race-to-the-bottom argument**, **social clause**, **social dumping**, **social labelling**, **social subsidies*** and ***wage-differential argument***. [International Labour Office 2003, OECD 2000, World Commission on the Social Dimension of Globalization 2004]

Coreper: an abbreviation of Comité des Représentants Permanents or Committee of Permanent Representatives. This is a ***European Union*** mechanism, established under Article 240 of the ***Treaty on the Functioning of the European Union***, responsible for preparing meetings of the ***Council of the European Union*** (the Council of Ministers). Coreper I, which deals with social and economic issues, is made up of the Deputy Permanent Representatives. Coreper II, consisting of the Permanent Representatives (ambassadors) of the member states, deals with political, financial and foreign policy matters. Coreper often deals with contentious issues, but it has no power to make decisions. Although it became very early on one of the administrative mechanisms, it was only established formally by the ***Treaty of Maastricht***.

Core–periphery thesis: a theory of ***international economic relations*** flourishing from about the 1950s to the 1980s. It postulates that the international economic system consists of an economically advanced core (the developed countries) and a less advanced periphery (the developing countries). It also assumes that the periphery is dependent on the core as markets for its products, especially primary commodities, and as a source of know-how. The theory is dynamic in that it assumes that in the long term the periphery itself may form new cores. Some have observed that the initial advantage of the core over the periphery may be whittled away. This process then creates new opportunities in the

Copyright Treaty
版权条约

见 *WIPO 版权条约(WIPO Copyright Treaty)*。

Core labour standards
核心劳工标准

适用于工作条件的最低人权标准，但并没有在一份单一的国际文件中如此定义。国际劳工组织(ILO)于 1998 年通过的《国际劳工组织关于工作中基本原则和权利的宣言》规定，所有国际劳工组织成员均有义务促进、尊重以及实现下列原则：(a)结社自由和有效承认集体谈判权利；(b)消除一切形式的强迫或强制劳动；(c)有效废除童工劳动；以及(d)消除就业与职业歧视。这一清单现在被许多国家作为有代表性的核心劳工标准加以接受。美国贸易促进授权列出 5 条核心劳工标准：(a)结社权；(b)集会和集体谈判权；(c)禁止使用各种形式的强迫或强制劳动；(d)雇佣儿童的最低年龄限制；以及(e)在最低工资、工作时间、职业安全及健康方面可接受的工作条件。贸易与劳工标准多边规则的支持者倾向于将核心劳工标准作为出发点。欧盟普惠制(GSP)方案包含了一项特殊激励安排，适用于那些国家立法已经纳入涵盖核心劳工标准的国际劳工组织公约的国家。另见*贫穷劳工论(pauper-labour)*、*底线竞赛论(race-to-bottom argument)*、*社会条款(social clause)*、*社会倾销(social dumping)*、*社会标签(social labelling)*、*社会补贴(social subsidies)*、*工资差别理论(wage-differential argument)*。

Coreper
常驻代表委员会

常驻代表委员会的缩写。根据《欧洲联盟运行条约》第 240 条设立的欧盟机制，负责筹备欧盟理事会(部长理事会)会议。Coreper I 处理社会与经济问题，由常驻副代表组成。Coreper II 由成员国的常驻代表(大使)组成，处理政治、金融和外交政策事务。Coreper 经常处理存在争议的问题，但其没有决策权。尽管很早即成为行政机制之一，但直到签订《马斯特里赫特条约》后才正式设立。

Core–periphery thesis
核心-外围理论

20 世纪 50 年代至 80 年代流行的国际经济关系理论。该理论假设国际经济体系由经济发达的核心(发达国家)和较不发达的外围(发展中国家)组成。还假设外围依赖核心作为其产品的市场，特别是初级商品，并作为专门知识的来源。这一理论是动态的，因为它假设从长远来看，外围本身可能会形成新的核心。一些人认为，核心相对于外围的最初优势可能会逐渐削弱。这一进程将在已

periphery which has become relatively more competitive. *See also* ***dependence theory***, ***North–South dialogue*** and ***Singer-Prebisch thesis***. [Prebisch 1963]

Corn laws: a set of laws first enacted in England in the twelfth century to protect agricultural production. These laws were repealed in 1846. Their repeal, together with that of the equally protectionist Navigation Acts in 1849, marked the victory of the free-traders and the beginning of the liberal regime characterizing England's trade policy for the next fifty years or so. It also meant the final acceptance of economic "science" as an instrument of policymaking. *See also* ***Cobden-Chevalier Treaty***.

Corporate dumping: refers to the alleged practice of companies to export to more accommodating markets products that may be out of date or no longer permitted to be sold in its usual markets. This is not a recognized trade policy concept.

Corporate Social Responsibility: CSR. The concept that corporations have a degree of responsibility not only for the economic consequences of their activities, but also for the social and environmental implications.

Corruption: the abuse of power or influence to obtain a benefit through offering or accepting an inducement. A common form of corruption is ***bribery***, but many other forms exist. Following are definitions in abbreviated form drawn from two conventions. The *Inter-American Convention Against Corruption* of 1996 lists (a) solicitation or acceptance, directly or indirectly, of any article of monetary value, or other benefit, such as gift, favour, promise or advantage, in exchange for performing a public function, (b) offering or granting, directly or indirectly, of any article of monetary value, etc., in exchange for performance of a public function, (c) any act or omission in the performance of one's duties to obtain a benefit illicitly, (d) fraudulent use of property, and (e) participation as a principal, co-principal, instigator, accessory, etc., after the fact. The ***African Union Convention on Preventing and Combating Corruption*** of 2003 lists in addition to these (a) diversion of any state property to anyone who is not the intended recipient, (b) offering or giving to, promising, soliciting or accepting from anyone in the private sector any undue advantage, (c) offering or soliciting, etc., an undue advantage to anyone claiming to be able to exert improper influence over another person, and (d) illicit enrichment. The ***World Bank*** attempts to say much of this with the phrase "abuse of public power for private benefit". *See also* ***Arusha Declaration, Convention on Combating Bribery of Foreign Public Officials in International Business Transactions***, ***Draft International Agreement on Illicit Payments***, ***Recommendation for Further Combating Bribery of Foreign Public Officials in International Business Transactions***, ***trade and illicit payments*** and ***United Nations Convention Against Corruption***.

Cotonou Agreement: *see* ***ACP-EU Partnership Agreement***.

Cotton: *see* ***International Cotton Advisory Committee*** and ***Sectoral Initiative in Favour of Cotton***.

Cotton Four: C4. A group in the WTO consisting of Benin, Burkina Faso, Chad and Mali which first introduced the ***Sectoral Initiative in Favour of Cotton*** in 2003. Côte d'Ivoire was admitted as an observer in November 2018. *See also*

变得相对更具竞争力的外围中创造新的机会。另见*依附理论(dependence theory)*、*南北对话(North-South dialogue)*、*辛格-普雷维什命题(Singer- Prebisch thesis)*。

Corn laws
玉米法

12 世纪英国首次颁布的一套保护农业生产的法律。这些法律于 1846 年废除。这些法律的废除与同样具有保护主义色彩的1849年《航海法案》的废除一起，标志着自由贸易者的胜利，并开启了随后 50 多年以自由制度为特征的英国贸易政策，也意味着最终接受经济“科学”作为一种政策制定工具。另见*科布登-舍瓦利埃条约(Cobden-Chevalier Treaty)*。

Corporate dumping
企业倾销

指所谓公司向更适合的市场出口可能过时或在其正常市场中不再允许销售的产品的做法。并非公认的贸易政策概念。

Corporate Social Responsibility
企业社会责任

CSR。企业不仅对其活动的经济后果负有一定责任，且对社会和环境影响也负有一定责任的概念。

Corruption
腐败

通过提供或接受诱惑而滥用权力或影响力以获取利益。一种常见的腐败形式是贿赂，但也存在许多其他形式。以下是源自两项公约的简要定义。1996 年《美洲反腐败公约》列举了(a)直接或间接索取或接受具有货币价值的任何物品或其他利益，例如礼物、优惠、许诺或好处，作为执行公务时的条件；(b)直接或间接提供或给予具有货币价值的任何物品等，作为执行公务时的条件；(c)在执行公务时以作为或不作为的方式非法获利；(d)欺诈性使用财产；以及(e)事后以主犯、共同主犯、教唆犯和从犯的身份参与。2003 年《非洲联盟预防和惩治腐败公约》列出了以下其他行为：(a)将任何国家财产转移至任何非指定接收人；(b)提供或给予、许诺、教唆或收受任何私营机构的不正当利益；(c)以提供或教唆等方式，向任何人宣称能够对另一人施加影响以获取不正当利益；以及(d)非法获利。世界银行尝试用“为私利滥用公权”的表述来解释这一概念。另见*阿鲁沙宣言(Arusha Declaration)*、*关于打击国际商业交易中行贿外国公职人员行为的公约(Convention on Combating Bribery of Foreign Public Officials in International Business Transactions)*、*关于违法付款的国际协定草案(Draft International Agreement on Illicit Payments)*、*关于进一步打击国际商业交易中行贿外国公职人员的建议(Recommendation for Further Combating Bribery of Foreign Public Officials in International Business Transactions)*、*贸易与违法付款(trade and illicit payments)*、*联合国反腐败公约(United Nations Convention Against Corruption)*。

Cotonou Agreement
科托努协定

见*非加太地区国家与欧盟伙伴关系协定(ACP-EU Partnership Agreement)*。

Cotton
棉花

见*国际棉花咨询委员会(International Cotton Advisory Committee)*、*棉花部门倡议(Sectoral Initiative in Favour of Cotton)*。

Cotton Four
棉花四国

C4。WTO 中贝宁、布基纳法索、乍得和马里组成的集团，2003 年首次提出

International Cotton Advisory Committee and ***Sectoral Initiative in Favour of Cotton***.

Council for Mutual Economic Assistance: usually known as Comecon. Established in January 1949 with Bulgaria, Czechoslovakia, Hungary, Poland, Romania and the Soviet Union as members. They were joined later by Cuba, the German Democratic Republic, Mongolia and Viet Nam. Albania was a member between 1949 and 1961. Yugoslavia was an associate member. The purpose of the Comecon was to facilitate the planned economic development of member country economies, acceleration of economic and technical progress, a rise in the level of industrialization in countries with less developed industries, uninterrupted growth of labour productivity, and a steady advance in the welfare of each member's people. The Comecon was dissolved in February 1991. *See also* ***economies in transition***.

Council for Trade in Goods: the body supervising the operation of the WTO multilateral agreements governing trade in goods included in Annex 1 to the ***WTO Agreement***. The most important of these is the GATT. All WTO members are automatically members of this Council.

Council for Trade in Services: the body administering the ***General Agreement on Trade in Services*** (GATS). All members of the WTO are automatically members of the Council.

Council for TRIPS: the body administering the ***Agreement on Trade-Related Aspects of Intellectual Property Rights*** (TRIPS). Its role is to supervise the operation of the Agreement and members' compliance with it. All WTO members are automatically Council members.

Council of Arab Economic Unity: established in 1957 to promote regional economic integration through a framework of economic and social development. Members are Egypt, Iraq, Jordan, Kuwait, Libya, Mauritania, Palestine, Somalia, Sudan, Syria, United Arab Emirates and Yemen. Its secretariat is located in Cairo.

Council of Europe: established in 1949. It aims to strengthen democracy, human rights and the rule of law in member countries. It now has forty-six members. Its secretariat is located in Strasbourg. The Council of Europe is not related to the ***European Council*** or the ***Council of the European Union***, both of which are organs of the ***European Union***.

Council of the European Union: a decision-making body, usually known as the Council of Ministers, which consists of representatives at ministerial level of all twenty-seven members of the ***European Union***. The presidency of the Council rotates every six months among the member states. Meetings are held frequently. There are no fixed members. Participation depends on the subjects to be discussed. Foreign Ministers meet as the ***General Affairs Council***. Decisions usually require a qualified majority (55 per cent of member states, representing at least 65 per cent of the European Union population), currently sixteen countries. Decisions can be blocked by at least four countries, representing at least 35 per cent of the total European Union population. Topics such

《棉花部门倡议》。科特迪瓦于 2018 年 11 月成为观察员。另见*国际棉花咨询委员会(International Cotton Advisory Committee)*、*棉花部门倡议(Sectoral Initiative in Favour of Cotton)*。

Council for Mutual Economic Assistance
经济互助委员会

通常简称为"经互会"(Comecon)。1949 年 1 月成立，成员包括保加利亚、捷克斯洛伐克、匈牙利、波兰、罗马尼亚和苏联。此后古巴、德意志民主共和国、蒙古和越南加入。阿尔巴尼亚在 1949 年至 1961 年期间为成员。南斯拉夫是联系成员。经互会的宗旨为促进成员国经济的有计划发展，加快经济和技术进步，提高工业不发达国家的工业化水平，不断提高劳动生产率，以及稳步提高每个成员国人民的福利。经互会于 1991 年 2 月解散。另见*转型经济体(economies in transition)*。

Council for Trade in Goods
货物贸易理事会

监督《WTO 协定》附件 1 所包括的 WTO 管辖货物贸易的多边协定运用的机构，其中最重要的是 GATT。所有 WTO 成员自动成为理事会成员。

Council for Trade in Services
服务贸易理事会

管理《服务贸易总协定》(GATS)的机构。所有 WTO 成员自动成为该理事会成员。

Council for TRIPS
与贸易有关的知识产权理事会

管理《与贸易有关的知识产权协定》(TRIPS)的机构，作用是监督协定运用和成员遵守情况。所有 WTO 成员自动成为理事会成员。

Council of Arab Economic Unity
阿拉伯经济统一理事会

1957 年成立，旨在通过经济和社会发展框架促进区域经济一体化。成员包括埃及、伊拉克、约旦、科威特、利比亚、毛里塔尼亚、巴勒斯坦、索马里、苏丹、叙利亚、阿拉伯联合酋长国和也门。秘书处设在开罗。

Council of Europe
欧洲委员会

1949 年成立。旨在加强成员国的民主、人权和法治。现有 46 个成员。秘书处设在斯特拉斯堡。欧洲委员会与欧洲理事会或欧盟理事会无关系，后两者均为欧盟机构。

Council of the European Union
欧盟理事会

决策机构，通常被称为部长理事会，由欧盟全部 27 个成员国的部长级代表组成。理事会主席每 6 个月由成员国轮流担任。会议经常举行。没有固定成员。参与成员取决于所要讨论的议题。外交部长以总务理事会名义召开会议。决策通常要求特定多数(代表欧盟总人口至少 65%的 55%的成员国)，目前是 16 个国家。至少 4 个国家并至少代表欧盟总人口 35%的成员国方可阻止决定通过。外交政策或税收等议题需要全体一致通过。程序和行政问题需要简单多

as foreign policy or taxation require a unanimous vote. A simple majority (15 out of the original 28 member states) is required for procedural and administrative issues. *See also* ***European Commission***.

Counterfeiting: unauthorized representation of a registered trademark carried on goods identical or similar to goods for which the trademark is registered, with a view to deceiving the purchaser that he or she is buying the original goods. *See also* ***Agreement on Trade-Related Aspects of Intellectual Property Rights***, ***Anti-Counterfeiting Trade Agreement***, ***intellectual property*** and ***intellectual property right infringements***.

Countermeasures: the means available to WTO members for dealing with exceptional circumstances and alleged breaches of the rules fall into two main categories. The first is made up of ***trade remedies***, also known as trade defence mechanisms and contingent protection. They include ***safeguards***, ***anti-dumping measures*** and countervailing duties. This group of measures can be initiated by any WTO member as long as it follows the relevant rules. The second group of countermeasures, i.e. the ***suspension of concessions or other obligations***, can only be taken with the authorization of the ***Dispute Settlement Body***. In other words, to obtain redress for an alleged breach of the rules by another member one has to launch a case. As the ***Appellate Body*** observed in *Canada – measures affecting the export of civil aircraft* "... no member is free to determine whether a *prima facie* case or defence has been established by the other party. That competence is necessarily vested in the panel under the DSU, and not in the Members that are parties to the dispute".

Counter-notification: *see* ***reverse notification***.

Countertrade: a more sophisticated and sometimes highly complex form of ***barter trade***. For example, a country may export coal and accept mining equipment in payment. No money changes hands in this transaction. The buyer of the coal then seeks to place it in a third market in exchange for payment or some other product. Goods to be traded in this way are usually valued in a third-country currency, e.g. Swiss Francs, for accounting purposes. Countertrade is an inefficient way to trade, but it has sometimes been attractive to countries experiencing severe foreign exchange shortages. *See also* ***compensation trade***.

Countervailable subsidy: refers to a ***subsidy*** against which, after an appropriate examination, ***countervailing measures*** may be taken.

Countervailing measures: action taken by the importing country, usually in the form of increased duties, to offset ***subsidies*** given to producers or exporters in the exporting country. GATT Article VI and the WTO ***Agreement on Subsidies and Countervailing Measures*** set out the rules for imposing such duties. Countervailing duties can be applied under certain restrictive conditions and subject to material ***injury*** being caused to a domestic industry. *See also* ***anti-dumping measures*** which are aimed at the actions of private firms rather than governments and ***de minimis subsidies***.

Country-hopping: an informal name for the practice by importers currently subject to ***anti-dumping measures*** of changing their sources of supply of

数(原 28 个成员国中的 15 个成员国)。另见*欧盟委员会(European Commission)*。

Counterfeiting

假冒

在与注册商标的货物相同或相似的货物上未经授权使用注册商标，意在欺骗购买者误以为他或她所购买的产品为正品。另见*与贸易有关的知识产权协定(Agreement on Trade-Related Aspects of Intellectual Property Rights)*、*反假冒贸易协定(Anti-Counterfeiting Trade Agreement)*、*知识产权(intellectual property)*、*侵犯知识产权(intellectual property right infringements)*。

Countermeasures

反措施

WTO 成员可使用的处理特殊情况和涉嫌违反两大类规则的手段。第一类由贸易救济组成，也称为贸易防御机制和紧急保护。包括保障措施、反倾销措施和反补贴税。这组措施可由任何 WTO 成员发起，只要其遵循相关规则。第二类反措施，即中止减让或其他义务，只能经争端解决机构授权采取。换言之，为纠正另一成员涉嫌违反规则，该成员必须提起诉讼。正如上诉机构在“加拿大-影响民用航空器出口措施案”中所评论的：“……任何成员无权决定另一方的初步证据或抗辩理由是否成立。该权限必须归属于《争端解决谅解》(DSU)下的专家组，而非作为争端方的成员。”

Counter-notification

反向通报

见*反向通报(reverse notification)*。

Countertrade

对销贸易

易货贸易的一种更为高级、有时极为复杂的形式。例如，一国可以出口煤，并接受采矿设备作为付款。在这笔交易中无货币易手。煤的买家随后寻求将其投放至第三方市场，以换取款项或其他产品。为记账目的，按这种方式交易的货物通常以第三国货币计价，例如瑞士法郎。对销贸易是一种效率低下的贸易方式，但有时对经历严重外汇短缺的国家具有吸引力。另见*补偿贸易(compensation trade)*。

Countervailable subsidy

可抵消补贴

指经过适当审查后可以采取反补贴措施的补贴。

Countervailing measures

反补贴措施

进口国采取的行动，通常以加税的形式，以抵消在出口国中给予生产者或出口商的补贴。GATT 第 6 条和 WTO《补贴与反补贴措施协定》规定了征收此类税的规则。反补贴税可以在某些限制条件下适用，且前提是对一国内产业造成实质损害。另见针对私营企业而非政府行为的*反倾销措施(anti-dompting measures)*、*微量补贴(de minimis subsidies)*。

Country-hopping

国别挑换

正在受反倾销措施影响的进口商将倾销产品的供应来源改为未接受调查的一

dumped products to a country or a company not under investigation. *See also* ***carousel effect***, ***circumvention*** and ***Persistent Dumping Clause***.

Country of origin: the country where a good or a service was produced or where, under applicable ***rules of origin***, its last ***substantial transformation*** took place. In ***intellectual property*** "country of origin" can mean an ***indication of source***, a ***geographical indication*** or an ***appellation of origin***. In Article 2(2) of the ***Lisbon Agreement*** it is defined as "the country, or the country in which is situated the region or locality whose name, constitutes the appellation of origin which has given the product its reputation". In other words, in this sense the country of origin is more than simply the place where the product has been made. Here it has given the product some essential characteristic that would be absent from a similar product made in another country. *See also* ***preferential rules of origin***. [Lisbon Agreement on the Protection of Appellations of Origin and their International Registration; WIPO SCT/5/3]

Country of origin marking: an inscription on a product or the packaging material of a product that tells the end-user in what country the product was made.

Country of origin principle: the basis for the establishment, for example, of the ***European Single Market***. It holds that European Union member countries may not impose conditions or obligations on a provider of goods and services that go beyond those by the provider's home country. *See also* ***Audiovisual Media Services Directive***.

Country risk: the odds that a country will not be able to meet its financial commitments. The odds are established through a risk assessment which takes into account economic, political and financial factors.

Court of International Trade: a United States tribunal established in 1980, but with functions dating back much earlier under different names, including the immediately preceding United States Customs Court. The Court has exclusive jurisdictional authority to decide any civil action against the United States, its officers, or its agencies arising out of any law pertaining to international trade. Its jurisdiction covers all of the United States, and it is authorized to hold hearings in other countries.

Court of Justice of the European Union: the judicial organ charged with ensuring that the law is observed in the interpretation and application of the treaties establishing the ***European Union*** as well as the provisions laid down by the various European Union institutions. The Court of Justice is the pre-eminent legal body in the European Union, but the courts of the member states retain a role in the application of laws within the European Union, especially where the member states are charged with carrying out certain functions and where European Union instruments confer directly individual rights on nationals of member states. The European Court of Justice is located in Strasbourg.

Covered agreements: the legal term for the agreements to which the WTO ***Dispute Settlement Understanding*** applies. These are (a) the Marrakesh Agreement Establishing the World Trade Organization, (b) the multilateral agreements on trade in goods consisting of the ***GATT 1994***, the ***Agreement on***

国家或一公司的做法的非正式名称。另见*旋转木马效应(carousel effect)*、*规避(circumvention)*、*持续性倾销条款(Persistent Dumping Clause)*。

Country of origin

原产国/原属国

生产一货物或一服务的国家，或根据适用的原产地规则发生最后一次实质性改变的国家。在知识产权领域，“原属国”可指产地标志、地理标志或原产地名称。《里斯本协定》第 2(2)条定义为“其名称构成原产地名称而赋予产品以声誉的国家或者地区或地方所在的国家”。换言之，从此意义上讲，原产地不仅是产品的制造地。在此赋予了一产品在其他国家生产的类似产品所不具备的一些基本特征。另见*优惠原产地规则(preferential rules of origin)*。

Country of origin marking

原产地标记

一产品上或包装材料上的文字，告知最终用户产品在哪一国生产。

Country of origin principle

原属国原则

建立欧洲单一市场的基础，此为一例。这一原则主张，欧盟成员国不得对货物和服务提供者施加超出提供者本国范围的条件或义务。另见*视听媒体服务指令(Audiovisual Media Services Directive)*。

Country risk

国家风险

一国不能履行其财务承诺的可能性。这一可能性通过考虑经济、政治和金融因素的风险评估加以确定。

Court of International Trade

国际贸易法院

成立于 1980 年的美国法院，但其职能可追溯到更早以前而名称不同，包括之前的美国海关法院。法院拥有专属管辖权，可对与国际贸易有关的任何法律所引发的针对美国、美国官员或美国机构的民事诉讼作出裁决。管辖范围覆盖美国全境，并授权在其他国家举行听证会。

Court of Justice of the European Union

欧洲法院

负责保证在解释和适用建立欧盟的各项条约以及欧盟各机构的规定时法律得到遵守的司法机关。法院是欧盟最重要的法律机构，但成员国法院在欧盟内部适用法律方面保留其作用，特别是在成员国负责履行某些职能以及欧盟法律直接赋予成员国国民个人权利的情况下。欧洲法院设在卢森堡(英文误为 Strasbourg，应为 Luxembourg—译注)。

Covered agreements

适用协定

WTO《争端解决谅解》所涵盖协定的法律术语。这些协定为：(a)《马拉喀什建立世界贸易组织协定》；(b)货物贸易协定，包括 GATT 1994、《农业协定》、

Agriculture, the ***Agreement on the Application of Sanitary and Phytosanitary Measures***, the ***Agreement on Textiles and Clothing*** (now expired), the ***Agreement on Technical Barriers to Trade***, the ***Agreement on Trade-Related Investment Measures***, the *Agreement on Implementation of Article VI of the General Agreement on Tariffs and Trade 1994* (the ***Anti-Dumping Agreement***), the *Agreement on Implementation of Article VII of the General Agreement on Tariffs and Trade 1994* (the ***Customs Valuation Agreement***), the ***Agreement on Preshipment Inspection***, the ***Agreement on Rules of Origin***, the ***Agreement on Import Licensing Procedures,*** the ***Agreement on Subsidies and Countervailing Measures***, the ***Agreement on Trade Facilitation*** and the ***Agreement on Safeguards***, (c) the ***General Agreement on Trade in Services***, (d) the ***Agreement on Trade-Related Aspects of Intellectual Property Rights***, (e) the ***Understanding on Rules and Procedures Governing the Settlement of Disputes***, and (f) the plurilateral trade agreements consisting of the ***Agreement on Trade in Civil Aircraft***, the ***Agreement on Government Procurement***, the ***International Dairy Agreement*** (now terminated) and the ***International Bovine Meat Agreement*** (also terminated).

Cradle-to-grave assessment: *see **life cycle assessment***.

Crawling peg system: a way to devalue or revalue a currency in stages in response to rapidly changing economic conditions. Each time the ***exchange rate*** is adjusted by the central bank, it remains fixed until the bank initiates the next change.

Creative ambiguity: used in the WTO, and probably elsewhere, to skirt around a difficult issue by leaving some aspect of it undefined. It normally leads to a compromise that leaves all more or less satisfied, at least at the time when the deal was made. The longer-term consequences can never be predicted.

Creative economy: defined in the 2018 UNCTAD report on the creative economy as including art crafts, audiovisuals, design, digital fabrication, new media, performing arts, publishing and visual arts.

Creative industries: describes occupations and industries deemed to entail a considerable degree of creativity or originality. Creative industries overlap to some extent with ***cultural industries***, but they are much less rooted in tradition, much closer to commercial and marketing activities and probably less nationalistic. Some may be at the forefront of information technology. *See also **knowledge-based economy***.

Creative minilateralism: a trade strategy for the opening of markets by the United States proposed by Thomas O. Bayard and Kimberley Ann Elliott in *Reciprocity and Retaliation in U.S. Trade Policy*. It involves (a) bilateral talks, if necessary with the support of ***Section 301*** or the threat of antitrust action, (b) a much stronger analytical capacity for assessing structural and access impediments, and(c) the use of favourable constituencies in target markets. This would be combined with publicity campaigns and technical assistance to developing countries to allow them to design and implement more effective regulatory frameworks. *See also* ***minilateralism***. [Bayard and Elliott 1994]

《实施卫生与植物卫生措施协定》、《纺织品与服装协定》(现已终止)、《技术性贸易壁垒协定》、《与贸易有关的投资措施协定》、《关于实施 1994 年关税与贸易总协定第 6 条的协定》(《反倾销协定》)、《关于实施 1994 年关税与贸易总协定第 7 条的协定》(《海关估价协定》)、《装运前检验协定》、《原产地规则协定》、《进口许可程序协定》、《补贴与反补贴措施协定》、《贸易便利化协定》、《保障措施协定》;(c)《服务贸易总协定》;(d)《与贸易有关的知识产权协定》;(e)《关于争端解决规则与程序的谅解》;以及(f)诸边贸易协定,包括《民用航空器贸易协定》、《政府采购协定》、《国际奶制品协定》(现已终止)、《国际牛肉协定》(现已终止)。

Cradle-to-grave assessment

从摇篮到坟墓评估

见*生命周期评价(life cycle assessment)*。

Crawling peg system

爬行盯住汇率制

根据快速变化的经济条件而逐步对货币进行贬值或重新估值的一种方法。中央银行每次调整汇率后,该汇率保持不变直至中央银行启动下一次调整。

Creative ambiguity

创造性模糊

用于 WTO 中,也可能用于其他场合,指不对一棘手问题的某些方面进行界定以绕开该问题。通常会形成一种使所有人或多或少满意的妥协,至少是在达成交易之时。而长期后果无法预测。

Creative economy

创意经济

联合国贸易与发展会议(UNCTAD)2018 年关于创意经济的报告中定义为,包括工艺品、视听、设计、数字制作、新媒体、表演艺术、出版和视觉艺术。

Creative industries

创意产业

描述被认为具有相当程度的创造力或原创性的职业和产业。创意产业在某种程度上与文化产业重叠,但植根于传统的程度要差很多,更接近于商业和营销活动,且可能不那么民族主义。有些创意产业可能处于信息技术的前沿。另见*知识型经济(knowledge-based economy)*。

Creative minilateralism

创造性小多边主义

美国开放市场的一种贸易策略,由托马斯·O. 贝亚德和金伯莉·安·艾略特在《美国贸易政策中的对等与报复》中提出。包括:(a)双边对话,必要时辅以 301 条款的支持或反垄断行动的威胁;(b)更加强大的分析能力,以评估结构性和准入障碍;以及(c)在目标市场中利用有利支持者。同时结合宣传活动和给予发展中国家的技术援助,使其能够制定并实施更有效监管框架。另见*小多边主义(minilateralism)*。

Credit for liberalization: *see **negotiating credits**.*

Creeping protectionism: developing a protectionist environment in small steps. *See also **protectionism**.*

Crisis cartel: also known as emergency cartel, rationalization cartel, depression cartel and similar names. This is a form of industry cooperation available in abnormal circumstances under some ***antitrust laws***. Conditions for its use tend to include factors such as a permanent and severe decline of an industry, the promise of efficiency gains which are in the public interest and the assumption that the improvements would not be attainable through other means. *See also **cartel*** and ***failing-firm doctrine***.

Critical mass: jargon probably borrowed inappropriately from nuclear physics. Its achievement is every trade negotiator's dream. It is the point at which support for a negotiating proposition becomes so strong that indifference or opposition by others no longer matters much.

Cross-border alliances: *see **strategic business alliances**.*

Cross-border investment: *see **foreign direct investment**.*

Cross-border paperless trade: *see **electronic commerce**.*

Cross-border supply of services: *see **cross-border trade in services*** and ***modes of services delivery***.

Cross-border trade: the movement of goods from one ***customs territory*** into another. *See also **frontier traffic**.*

Cross-border trade in services: buying or selling services across borders without the need for the buyer or the seller to establish a ***commercial presence*** in the exporting or importing country. This can be done through, for example, conducting trade over the Internet where the buyer and the seller do not have to meet. In the language of the ***General Agreement on Trade in Services*** this would be mode 1. A second possibility is that of the consumer going abroad to purchase the service, as is the case in international tourism (mode 2). A third method is that of a person going abroad to sell services, for example an engineer providing on-site advice on a construction project (mode 4). *See also **modes of services delivery**.*

Cross-compensation: this can occur as part of ***dispute settlement*** when, for example, the WTO member found to be in breach of an undertaking does not withdraw the offending measure or practice, but offers ***compensation*** in some other area of trade instead. *See also **suspension of concessions or other obligations**.*

Cross-cumulation: the practice of considering concurrently the effects of ***dumping*** and ***subsidies*** to ascertain whether ***injury*** has occurred. *See also **cumulative assessment of dumping**.*

Cross-retaliation: an avenue open in certain circumstances to a WTO member whose rights under one agreement administered by the WTO have been infringed, to retaliate against the offending member under another agreement also administered by the WTO. The ***Dispute Settlement Understanding*** makes this possible.

Crow-bar theory of trade policy: *see **aggressive reciprocity**.*

Credit for liberalization
自由化奖励
见*谈判奖励(negotiating credits)*。

Creeping protectionism
日益严重的保护主义
小步发展形成贸易保护主义环境。另见*保护主义(protectionism)*。

Crisis cartel
危机卡特尔
也称紧急卡特尔、合理化卡特尔、萧条卡特尔及类似名称。根据一些反垄断法在非正常环境下存在的一种产业合作形式。使用条件往往包括诸如一产业的永久严重衰退、符合公共利益的效率收益许诺以及推定无其他方法可实现改进等因素。另见*卡特尔(cartel)*、*破产公司原则(failing-firm doctrine)*。

Critical mass
临界数量
可能不恰当地借用的核物理学的术语。达到临界数量是每个贸易谈判者的梦想。指对谈判立场的支持变得如此强大而使其他人的冷漠或反对变得无关紧要的一个点。（指支持一自由化倡议的参加方达到足够多的数量，例如《信息技术协定》规定，代表全球信息技术产品贸易约 90%的参加方接受协定后即实施降税—译注。）

Cross-border alliances
跨境联盟
见*战略性商业联盟(strategic business alliances)*。

Cross-border investment
跨境投资
见*外国直接投资(foreign direct investment)*。

Cross-border paperless trade
跨境无纸贸易
见*电子商务(electronic commerce)*。

Cross-border supply of services
跨境服务提供
见*跨境服务贸易(cross-border trade in services)*、*服务提供模式(modes of services delivery)*。

Cross-border trade
跨境贸易
货物自一关税领土进入另一关税领土的流动。另见*边境贸易(frontier traffic)*。

Cross-border trade in services
跨境服务贸易
跨越边境购买或销售服务而无需买方或卖方在出口国或进口国中设立商业存在。例如，可以通过互联网开展贸易而无需买卖双方见面。在《服务贸易总协定》中，这是模式 1。第 2 种可能性是消费者出国购买服务，例如国际旅游(模式 2)。模式 3 是一人出国销售服务，模式 4 例如一工程师提供建筑项目的现场咨询。另见*服务提供模式(modes of services delivery)*。

Cross-compensation
交叉补偿
此点可能作为争端解决的一部分发生，例如，被认定违反一承诺的 WTO 成员没有撤销违法措施或做法，但作为替代在一些其他贸易领域提供补偿。另见*中止减让或其他义务(suspension of concessions or other obligation)*。

Cross-cumulation
交叉累积评估
同时考虑倾销和补贴的影响以确定损害是否已经发生的做法。另见*倾销累积评估(cumulative assessment of dumping)*。

Cross-retaliation
交叉报复
在某些情况下在 WTO 管理的一项协定项下的权利受到侵犯的 WTO 成员可以使用的途径，该成员可以根据 WTO 管理的另一项协定对违规成员进行报复。《争端解决谅解》使之成为可能。

Crow-bar theory of trade policy
贸易政策撬杆理论
见*主动互惠(aggressive reciprocity)*。

CRTA: Committee on Regional Trade Agreements. The WTO body that examines ***regional trade agreements*** for their consistency with the WTO rules.

Cryptocurrency: a currency that only exists in a virtual or digital state. It differs from other currencies in that it does not circulate in the form of metal or paper, and that it is not backed by a central bank. Cryptocurrencies can be used as a medium of exchange or as store of wealth, but their acceptance can be quite limited and their value subject to considerable fluctuation. In some countries their use is entirely forbidden. The production and circulation of such currencies is guaranteed by the use of ***blockchain*** technology. Bitcoin is probably the best known of them, but many others exist.

CTD: *see* ***Committee on Trade and Development***.

CTDSS: the WTO ***Committee on Trade and Development*** in special sessions, i.e. negotiating meetings.

CTE: *see* ***Committee on Trade and Environment***.

CTESS: the WTO ***Committee on Trade and Environment*** in special sessions, i.e. negotiating meetings.

CTG: ***Council for Trade in Goods***. Oversees WTO agreements on goods.

Cuban Liberty and Democratic Solidarity (LIBERTAD) Act: *see* ***Helms-Burton legislation***.

Cultural identity: the idea that countries have cultural characteristics that set them apart from other countries. There is nothing controversial about this, but it can become contentious in ***trade policy*** when countries seek trade rules to preserve or enhance their cultural traits. Many suspect that such rules would give countries the right to impose ***import restrictions***, ostensibly for cultural reasons, but in reality to achieve other aims. For example, some may wish to protect a traditional production process and the workforce employed in this way even though more modern technology may produce an identical product more competitively. *See also* ***Canadian periodicals***, ***cultural industries***, ***local content rules in broadcasting*** and ***trade and culture***.

Cultural industries: not an exact term. In the ***United Nations Educational, Scientific and Cultural Organization*** (UNESCO) it is taken to mean industries combining the creation, production and commercialization of contents that are cultural and intangible. These include printing, publishing and multimedia, audiovisual, phonographic and cinematographic productions as well as crafts and designs. This description is widely accepted. UNESCO notes, however, that in some countries architecture, visual and performing arts, sports, the manufacture of musical instruments, advertising and cultural tourism are also regarded as cultural industries. Article 2107 of ***NAFTA*** defines "cultural industries" as persons engaged in any of the following activities: (a) the publication, distribution, or sale of books, magazines, periodicals or newspapers in print or machine-readable form, but not including the sole activity of printing or typesetting any of the foregoing, (b) the production, distribution, sale or exhibition of film or video recordings, (c) the production, distribution, sale or exhibition of audio or video recordings, (d) the publication, distribution or sale of

CRTA
区域贸易协定委员会

WTO 审查区域贸易协定是否符合 WTO 规则的机构。

Cryptocurrency
加密货币

仅存在于虚拟或数字状态的货币。不同于其他货币，因为它不以金属或纸张形式流通，也没有中央银行的支持。加密货币可用作交换媒介或储存财富，但它们的接受程度可能相当有限，且其价值波动相当大。在一些国家，它们的使用完全禁止。此类货币的生产和流通得到区块链技术使用的保证。比特币可能是其中最著名的，但还存在许多其他加密货币。

CTD
贸易与发展委员会

见*贸易与发展委员会(Committee on Trade and Development)*。

CTDSS
贸易与发展委员会特别会议

以特别会议形式召开的 WTO 贸易与发展委员会，即谈判会议。

CTE
贸易与环境委员会

见*贸易与环境委员会(Committee on Trade and Environment)*。

CTESS
贸易与环境委员会特别会议

以特别会议形式召开的 WTO 贸易与环境委员会，即谈判会议。

CTG
货物贸易理事会

管理 WTO 有关货物的协定。

Cuban Liberty and Democratic Solidarity (LIBERTAD) Act
古巴自由与民主声援法

见*赫尔姆斯-伯顿法(Helms-Burton legislation)*。

Cultural identity
文化特性

一国拥有可将其与其他国家相区别的文化特征的理念。对此本无争议，但当各国寻求贸易规则来保护或增强其文化特征时，就会在贸易政策中引发争议。许多人怀疑，此类规则将给予各国实施进口限制的权利，表面上出于文化原因，而实际上是要实现其他目标。例如，一些国家可能希望保护传统生产工序和以这种方式雇佣的劳动力，尽管更为现代的科技可以更具竞争力的方式生产同样的产品。另见*加拿大期刊案(Canadian periodicals)*、*文化产业(cultural industries)*、*广播中的本地内容规则(local content rules in broadcasting)*、*贸易与文化(trade and culture)*。

Cultural industries
文化产业

并非一个准确词语。在联合国教科文组织(UNESCO)中，指融合了文化的和无形内容的创造、生产和商业化的产业。这些产业包括印刷、出版和多媒体、视听、唱片和电影制作以及工艺品和设计。此描述被广泛接受。但 UNESCO 也注意到在一些国家中建筑、视觉和表演艺术、体育、乐器制造、广告和文化旅游也被视为文化产业。《北美自由贸易协定》(NAFTA)第 2107 条将“文化产业”定义为从事下列任何活动的人：(a)出版、发行或销售纸质或机器可读形式的图书、杂志、期刊或报纸，但不包括上述各项单独的印刷、排版活动；(b)生

music in print or machine-readable form, or (e) radio-communications in which the transmissions are intended for direct reception by the general public, and all radio, television and broadcasting undertakings and all satellite programming and broadcast network services. *See also* ***creative economy*** and ***creative industries***. [en.unesco.org]

Cumulation: a provision allowing producers in one country to obtain parts and inputs from other countries without losing the ***originating status*** of that input. Under cumulation, foreign parts and input are not considered as imported (or ***non-originating goods***) for the purpose of the ***substantial transformation*** requirements. *See also* ***diagonal cumulation***.

Cumulation zone: under some ***preferential rules of origin*** it is possible to combine, or cumulate, the contributions of several countries to the production of a good. This makes it easier for the exporting country to reach the ***regional value content***. The countries from which inputs may be obtained in this way are known as the cumulation zone. *See also* ***diagonal cumulation***.

Cumulative assessment of dumping: the investigation by the importing country of alleged concurrent ***dumping*** by several countries of the same product. Under the WTO rules such an assessment is allowed only if (a) the ***margin of dumping*** for each country is more than *de minimis* and the imports from each are not negligible, and (b) the assessment would be appropriate in the light of competitive conditions between imported and domestic products. *See also* ***anti-dumping measures***, ***de-cumulation***, ***de minimis dumping margins*** and ***negligible imports***.

Cumulative rules of origin: a system of ***rules of origin*** which permits the production or transformation of a product in two or more specified countries in order to satisfy the access rules of the importing country. This method is sometimes used under the ***GSP*** regimes to allow preferential treatment for developing countries that might not by themselves qualify for it because they have insufficient processing capacity. *See also* ***diagonal cumulation*** and ***substantial transformation***.

Cumulative subsidies: the WTO ***Agreement on Subsidies and Countervailing Measures*** provides that if imports of a product from more than one country are concurrently the subject of a countervailing duty investigation, authorities may assess the cumulative effect of these subsidies. However, they may only do this if (a) amounts greater than ***de minimis subsidies*** are involved and (b) if such an assessment is appropriate in the light of the competitive conditions in the import market.

Currency board: pegging the value of a currency to that of another or a basket of currencies. This is usually done to stabilize a volatile currency and to give the government time to devise and institute macroeconomic reforms. Argument continues among economists as to whether stabilization of a currency should come before or after the establishment of a currency board, or whether a currency board is needed at all.

Current access tariff quotas: access opportunities to be opened for agricultural products where ***non-tariff measures*** have been converted into ***tariffs***.

产、发行、销售或展览电影或录像；(c)生产、发行、销售或展览音频或录像；(d)出版、发行或销售纸质或机器可读形式的音乐；或(e)传输直接供公众接收的无线电通信，所有收音机、电视和广播事业，以及所有卫星节目和广播网络服务。另见*创意经济(creative economy)*、*创意产业(creative industries)*。

Cumulation

累积

允许一国的生产者自其他国家获得零件和投入物而不失去该投入物原产地位的规定。根据累积规则，就实质性改变要求而言，外国零件和投入物不被视为进口(或非原产货物)。另见*对角累积(diagonal cumulation)*。

Cumulation zone

累积区

根据一些优惠原产地规则，可以合并或累积计算几个国家在一货物的生产过程中所占份额。这样可使出口国更容易达到区域价值成分。以这种方式成为投入物来源地的国家被称为累积区。另见*对角累积(diagonal cumulation)*。

Cumulative assessment of dumping

倾销累积评估

进口国对几个国家同时倾销同一产品的指控进行的调查。根据WTO规则，这种评估只有在下列情况下方被允许：(a)每一国家的倾销幅度超过微量倾销幅度，且自每一国家的进口并非可忽略不计；及(b)按照进口产品与国产品之间的竞争条件，此评估是适当的。另见*反倾销措施(anti-dumping measures)*、*去累积(de-cumulation)*、*微量倾销幅度 (de minimis dumping margin)*、*可忽略不计的进口量(negligible imports)*。

Cumulative rules of origin

原产地累积规则

允许一产品在两个或两个以上特定国家进行生产或改变以满足进口国准入规则的一种原产地规则制度。这种方法有时在普惠制(GSP)下使用，以使因加工能力不足而无资格获得优惠待遇的发展中国家享受这种待遇。另见*对角累积(diagonal cumulation)*、*实质性改变(substantial transformation)*。

Cumulative subsidies

累积补贴

WTO《补贴与反补贴措施协定》规定，如果来自一个以上国家的一产品同时接受反补贴调查，主管机关可以评估这些补贴的累积影响。然而，只有在下列情况下才这样作，即(a)涉及的金额大于微量补贴；及(b)按照进口市场上的竞争条件，此评估是适当的。

Currency board

货币局制度

将一种货币的价值盯住另一种货币或一篮子货币的价值。这样作通常为了稳定波动的货币，给政府留出时间设计和实施宏观经济改革。经济学家们围绕货币稳定应在货币局制度建立前还是建立后，或是否有必要建立货币局制度而争论不休。

Current access tariff quotas

关税配额现行准入

在非关税措施已经转为关税的情况下，对农产品开放的准入机会。乌拉圭回

A formula was devised during the ***Uruguay Round*** negotiations whereby the level of access to be opened for a given product was determined through a comparison of the level of imports with consumption during the ***base period***. Current access levels were adopted to ensure that imports represented at least 5 per cent of domestic consumption applying in the Uruguay Round base period of 1986–88. *See also* ***Agreement on Agriculture*** and ***minimum access tariff quotas***.

Current account: *see* ***balance of payments***.

Current domestic value: a method for valuing goods to be imported for the assessment of ***customs duties***. The value of the goods for duty purposes is the price at which goods comparable with those imported are sold under fully competitive conditions on the domestic markets of the country from which the goods were exported. This method has been superseded by the procedures contained in the WTO ***Customs Valuation Agreement*** (formally the *Agreement on Implementation of Article VII of the General Agreement on Tariffs and Trade 1994*). *See also* **customs valuation**.

Customary international law: internationally accepted rules of conduct or obligations that derive their authority from the fact that (a) they are customary among nations and (b) there is an expectation by nations that in a given situation they will be obliged to follow a certain course of action (the *opinio juris* principle). Custom may be based on long traditions, or it may have arisen quite recently. What matters is that these two criteria must be satisfied in a claim invoking customary international law. Starke notes that custom is not the same as usage: "Usage may be conflicting, custom must be unified and self-consistent". *See also* ***conventional international law***. [Aust 2000; Shaw 2014; Starke 1989]

Customs administration: these chapters in free-trade agreements typically cover topics such as those listed here, but not necessarily all of them: ***advance rulings***, automation of customs procedures, communication with traders on procedures, cooperation between the parties, ***enquiry points***, establishment of a committee on customs administration, express shipments, goods in transit, handling of confidential information, inspections at the border, penalties for breaches of customs laws, post-clearance audit, publication of customs laws and regulations, including online publication, release of goods, review and appeal against customs determinations, risk management, simplification of customs procedures, ***Single Window***, temporary admission of goods, ***trade facilitation***, transparency and predictability in customs procedures, use of ***authorized economic operators***, use of customs brokers and use of information technology.

Customs Convention on Temporary Admission: *see* ***Istanbul Convention***.

Customs Convention on the ATA Carnet for the Temporary Admission of Goods: adopted by the Customs Cooperation Council, now the ***World Customs Organization***, in 1961. It established the ATA Carnet, an international customs clearance document, which allows the temporary import of goods required for fairs and exhibitions, commercial samples, professional equipment, and sporting and musical equipment without the need to pay customs duties or

合谈判中设计了一个公式，一指定产品开放的准入水平通过比较基期的进口和消费水平加以确定。采用现行准入水平是为保证进口至少占 1986—1988 年乌拉圭回合基期适用的国内消费的 5%。另见*农业协定(Agreement on Agricultural)*、*关税配额最低准入(minimum access tariff quotas)*。

Current account

经常账户

见*国际收支(balance of payments)*。

Current domestic value

现行国内价格

为评估关税而对进口货物进行估价的一种方法。货物完税价格指可与进口货物相比较的货物在完全竞争条件下在货物出口国国内市场上销售的价格。这种方法已经被 WTO《海关估价协定》(正式名称为《关于实施 1994 年关税与贸易总协定第 7 条的协定》)规定的程序所取代。另见*海关估价(customs valuation)*。

Customary international law

习惯国际法

国际公认的行为准则或义务，其权威源自以下事实：(a)属各国之间的习惯；及(b)各国期望在某一指定情况下，它们有义务遵循某种特定做法(法律确信原则)。习惯可能基于悠久的传统，也可能在近期兴起。重要的是，这两条标准必须在援引习惯国际法的主张中得到满足。斯塔克指出，习惯和惯例是不一样的："惯例可以是相互矛盾的，而习惯则应是统一和自身一致的"。另见*协定国际法(conventional international law)*。

Customs administration

海关管理

自由贸易协定中的此类章节通常涵盖此处所列主题，但不一定全部包括：预裁定、海关程序自动化、就程序问题与贸易商沟通、各方合作、咨询点、设立海关管理委员会、快运货物、过境货物、机密信息处理、边境检查、违反海关法律的处罚、结关后审计、海关法律法规公布(包括在线公布)、货物放行、对海关裁定的审查和上诉、风险管理、简化海关程序、单一窗口、货物暂准进口、贸易便利化、海关程序的透明度和可预测性、经认证的经营者的使用、报关行的使用和信息技术的使用。

Customs Convention on Temporary Admission

货物暂准进口公约

见*伊斯坦布尔公约(Istanbul Convention)*。

Customs Convention on the ATA Carnet for the Temporary Admission of Goods

关于货物暂准进口的 ATA 报关单证册海关公约

海关合作理事会(现世界海关组织) 于 1961 年通过。建立了 ATA 报关单证册，这是一种国际海关清关单证，允许临时进口用于展会和展览的货物、商业样品、专业设备、运动和音响设备，而无需支付关税或交保证金。报关单证册的

the posting of a bond. The Carnet is normally valid for one year, and goods have to be re-exported within that time. The Convention was updated by the ***Istanbul Convention*** which entered into force in 1993.

Customs cooperation: cooperative activities between customs authorities, either bilaterally, regionally or through the ***World Customs Organization***, to improve, *inter alia*, the efficiency of their operations and to make them easier to use by clients. Cooperation can include exchange of information and views on improvements of working methods such as risk management, exchange of officers, promotion of ***paperless trading***, technical assistance programmes and many other similar activities.

Customs Cooperation Council: the predecessor of the ***World Customs Organization***.

Customs duties: charges levied at the border on goods entering or, much less often, leaving the country. These charges are specified in the national ***tariff schedule***. They are usually based on the value of the goods, known as ***ad valorem tariff*** and sometimes as a cost per unit in the form of a ***specific tariff***. *See also* ***compound tariff***, ***customs valuation***, ***multi-column tariff*** and ***single-column tariff***.

Customs risk assessments: estimates made by the customs authorities of the extent to which consignments may contravene customs laws and regulations. Contravention may take many forms, such as duty evasion, ***smuggling***, ***trafficking*** in prohibited substances and other articles, etc. Customs officers then pay extra attention to high-risk consignments.

Customs surcharge: a fee or a charge levied by customs authorities in addition to ***customs duties***. Sometimes it simply means a charge for the handling of a consignment roughly equivalent to the cost of providing the service. At other times it can mean an ***ad valorem*** addition to the duty payable. *See also* ***customs user fee***.

Customs territory: any state or territory with a ***tariff*** of its own and autonomy in the conduct of its international trade relations. Article XII of the ***WTO Agreement*** allows any state or separate customs territory to apply for membership of the WTO.

Customs union: an area consisting of two or more individual economies or ***customs territories*** which remove all tariffs and sometimes broader trade impediments between them. The members making up the area then apply a ***common external tariff***. They also need to develop a ***common commercial policy***. The ***European Union*** is a well-known example of a customs union. *See also* ***common market*** and ***free-trade area***.

Customs user fee: an administrative charge levied by a customs authority to clear the import or export of goods. This fee should be based on the cost of providing the service. It should not be used to protect domestic products or as a source of revenue for the government.

Customs valuation: methods used by customs authorities to allocate a value to imported goods for the purpose of striking the correct import duty. The WTO ***Customs Valuation Agreement*** (formally the *Agreement on Implementation of*

有效期通常为 1 年，货物必须在该期限内复出口。公约已为 1993 年生效的《伊斯坦布尔公约》所更新。

Customs cooperation

海关合作

海关之间通过双边、区域或世界海关组织开展的合作活动，以提高运转效率，易于客户使用。合作包括交流改进工作方法的信息和意见，例如风险管理、官员交流、促进无纸贸易、技术援助方案和其他许多类似活动。

Customs Cooperation Council

海关合作理事会

世界海关组织的前身。

Customs duties

关税

在边境对进入或离开(相对较少)一国的货物征收的费用。这些费用在一国关税税则中予以列明。通常基于货物的价值征收，即从价关税，有时也按单位征收，即从量关税。另见*混合关税(compound tariff)*、*海关估价(customs valuation)*、*多栏关税(mutil-column tariff)*、*单栏关税(single-column tariff)*。

Customs risk assessments

海关风险评估

海关对货物可能违反海关法律法规的程度所作评估。违规可有多种形式，例如逃税、走私、非法交易违禁物品及其他物品等。海关官员因此对高风险货物给予特别关注。

Customs surcharge

海关附加费

海关在征收关税之外所征收的费用。有时仅指与提供服务的成本大体相当的处理装运货物的费用。其他一些时候，可指应付税款之外的从价费用。另见*海关使用费(customs user fee)*。

Customs territory

关税领土

拥有自己的关税及在处理国际贸易关系方面享有自主权的任何国家或地区。《WTO 协定》第 12 条允许任何国家或单独关税区申请成为 WTO 成员。

Customs union

关税同盟

由两个或两个以上单个经济体或关税领土组成的区域，相互取消所有关税，且有时取消更广泛的贸易障碍。组成同盟的成员随后实施共同对外关税。还需要制定共同商业政策。欧盟是众所周知的关税同盟的例子。另见*共同市场(common market)*、*自由贸易区(free-trade area)*。

Customs user fee

海关使用费

海关为进口或出口货物结关而征收的行政费用。此项费用应基于提供服务的成本。不应当被用于保护本国产品或作为政府收入来源。

Customs valuation

海关估价

海关为确定准确的进口关税而用于确定进口货物价格的方法。WTO《海关估

Article VII of the General Agreement on Tariffs and Trade 1994) aims to set out a fair, uniform and neutral system for the valuation of goods that precludes the use of arbitrary or fictitious customs values. The basic rule is that the customs value of imported goods in the case of unrelated parties is the ***transaction value***, i.e. the price actually paid or payable for the goods when sold for export to the importing country. The buyer must be free to dispose of the goods as desired apart from legal restrictions imposed by the government, any limits on the geographical area in which the goods may be sold and any other restrictions that do not substantially affect the value of the goods. Additionally, the sale must not be subject to conditions for which a value cannot be determined, the buyer will not benefit directly or indirectly from a later resale, and the buyer and the seller must not be related. If they are related, the transaction value must be acceptable to the customs authorities. Freight, packaging, commissions, goods and services supplied to the buyer free of charge and some other costs may be added to the customs value. If there are suspicions that the transaction value is false, customs authorities may determine the value by going sequentially through five options: (a) the value of identical goods, (b) the value of ***similar goods***, (c) the imported price of ***identical goods*** or similar goods minus applicable deductions for costs, (d) ***computed value***, and (e) if none of these methods work, other reasonable means may be used. Additional considerations apply where the importer and exporter are related entities. The Agreement also sets out the measures that may not be used to establish a value. These include, for example, ***minimum customs values***, the price of goods on the domestic market of the exporting country, the selling price of goods produced in the importing country, a system which provides for the higher of two values, etc. *See also* ***arm's-length pricing***.

Customs Valuation Agreement: formally the *Agreement on Implementation of Article VII of the General Agreement on Tariffs and Trade 1994*. It sets out a framework of procedures for the valuation of goods by customs authorities for the purpose of levying the correct ***customs duty***. For most imports the basis for the valuation is the ***transaction value***. That is the price actually paid or payable for the goods when sold for export to the importing country. In most cases the assumption is that the buyer and seller are not related. Moreover, apart from certain defined conditions, the importers must be free to dispose of the goods without restriction. If the transaction value cannot be determined properly, other methods may be chosen. *See* the entry on ***customs valuation*** for an outline of these methods.

Customs value: the value of a good as assessed by a customs administration. The term is sometimes defined legally as the value of a good determined in accordance with the WTO ***Agreement on Customs Valuation***.

Cybersecurity: protection of internet-connected systems, networks and programs from external attack.

Cyclical dumping: *see* ***dumping***.

价协定》(正式名称为《关于实施 1994 年关税与贸易总协定第 7 条的协定》)旨在规定一个公平、统一和中立的货物估价制度，以防止使用任意的或虚构的完税价格。基本规则是，对于无关联方，进口货物的完税价格为成交价格，即货物出口销售至进口国时的实付或应付价格。除了政府施加的法律限制、货物销售地理区域的任何限制以及不会对货物价值产生实质影响的任何其他限制外，买方必须有权按意愿处置货物。此外，销售不得受限于导致价值无法确定的条件，买方不得直接或间接从此后的转售中获益，买方和卖方不得有任何关联。如果他们存在关联，交易价格必须是海关可以接受的。运费、包装、佣金和免费提供给买方的货物和服务以及其他一些费用可以被记入完税价格。如果怀疑成交价格不真实，海关可以依次使用以下 5 种方法确定价值：(a)相同货物的价格；(b)类似货物的价格；(c)相同货物或类似货物的进口价格减去适用的费用；(d)计算价格；以及(e)如果这些方法均未奏效，可以使用其他合理方法。如果进口商与出口商是关联实体，必须进行额外考虑。该协定还列出了不可用于确定价格的措施。例如，海关最低限价、出口国国内市场的货物价格、进口国中所生产货物的销售价格、规定选取两价格中较高者的制度等。另见*公平定价(arm's-length pricing)*。

Customs Valuation Agreement

海关估价协定

正式名称为《关于实施 1994 年关税与贸易总协定第 7 条的协定》。规定了海关为征收准确的关税目的而对货物进行估价的程序框架。对于大多数进口而言，估价基础为成交价格。这是货物出口销售至进口国时的实付或应付价格。大多数情况下的假设是买卖双方没有关联。此外，除了某些特定的条件，进口商必须有权处置货物而不受限制。如果成交价格无法正确确定，可以选择其他方法。这些方法的概要见*海关估价(customs valuation)*词条。

Customs value

完税价格

由海关管理机构评估的货物价值。这一术语有时在法律上定义为根据 WTO《海关估价协定》确定的商品价值。

Cybersecurity

网络安全

保护连接互联网的系统、网络和程序免受外部攻击。

Cyclical dumping

周期性倾销

见*倾销(dumping)*。

DAC: *see* ***Development Assistance Committee***.

DAC principles for developing the capacity for trade: *see* ***capacity-building***.

Dairy Export Incentive Program: DEIP. A United States subsidy programme first authorized by the 1985 Farm Act. Through this programme, the United States Department of Agriculture paid a cash bonus to exporters of some dairy products to allow them to sell these products on world markets for less than they bought them. It was repealed in 2014.

Damage: *see* ***injury*** and ***serious damage***.

D'Amato legislation: *see* ***Iran and Libya Sanctions Act***.

Data protection in trade in services: the ***General Agreement on Trade in Services*** contains several provisions to ensure confidentiality of records and data. Article IIIbis suspends the ***transparency*** requirement if disclosure of information would impede law enforcement, otherwise contravene the public interest or prejudice the legitimate commercial interests of private or public enterprises. Article IX (Business Practices) only requires the supply of publicly available non-confidential information concerning anti-competitive business practices. Other information may be made available if the requesting member undertakes to safeguard its confidentiality. Article XIV (General Exceptions) permits the suspension of obligations under the Agreement to protect the privacy of individuals in relation to personal data and the confidentiality of individual records and accounts.

Davignon Plan: a plan adopted in 1978 by the ***European Economic Community*** to revitalize its steel industry. The plan was aimed mainly at putting a cap on production capacity. It also had a longer-term segment for restructuring and rationalizing the steel industry. ***State aids*** and ***import restrictions*** were an important factor in achieving the planned targets. The plan was named after Viscount Etienne Davignon, the then European Commissioner for Internal Market and Industrial Affairs.

Deceptive indications of source: *see* ***indications of source***.

Decision: one of the means available to the ***European Union*** to enforce its mandate. A decision is binding only on those to whom it is addressed. This may be a member state, a single company or an individual. *See also* ***European Union legislation***.

Decision in Favour of Least-Developed Countries: *see* ***least-developed countries***.

Decision-making in the WTO: WTO members nearly always make their decisions by ***consensus***, but they may vote if a consensus is not possible.

DAC
发展援助委员会

见*发展援助委员会(Development Assistance Committee)*。

DAC principles for developing the capacity for trade
发展援助委员会贸易能力开发原则

见*能力建设(capacity-building)*。

Dairy Export Incentive Program
奶制品出口激励计划

DEIP。美国补贴计划，经《1985年农业法案》首次通过。通过该计划，美国农业部给予某些奶制品出口商现金奖金，使其能够以低于收购价的价格在世界市场上销售这些产品。该计划于2014年废除。

Damage
损害

见*损害(injury)*、*严重损害(serious damage)*。

D'Amato legislation
达托马法

见*伊朗与利比亚制裁法(Iran and Libya Sanctions Act)*。

Data protection in trade in services
服务贸易中的数据保护

《服务贸易总协定》包含了若干保证记录和数据机密性的条款。第3条之二规定，如果信息披露妨碍执法、违背公共利益或损害特定公私企业合法商业利益，即中止透明度要求。第9条(商业惯例)仅要求提供有关反竞争商业惯例的可公开获得的非机密信息。如果提出请求的成员保障其机密性，可提供其他信息。第14条(一般例外)允许中止协定项下的义务，以保护与个人信息有关的个人隐私及个人记录和账户的机密性。

Davignon Plan
达维央计划

欧洲经济共同体于1978年通过的重振其钢铁产业的计划。主要目标为限制产能。还有一个长期的内容是重组钢铁产业并使其合理化。国家援助和进口限制是实现计划目标的重要因素。该计划以当时的欧盟内部市场和产业事务专员艾蒂安·达维央子爵命名。

Deceptive indications of source
欺骗性产地标志

见*产地标志(indications of source)*。

Decision
决定

欧盟可用于行使其授权的方式之一。一项决定只对该决定的对象具有约束力。可以是一成员国、一单一公司或一人。另见*欧洲联盟立法(European Union legislation)*。

Decision in Favour of Least-Developed Countries
有利于最不发达国家措施的决定

见*最不发达国家(least-developed countries)*。

Decision-making in the WTO
WTO决策机制

WTO成员几乎总是以协商一致方式作出决定，但如果协商一致不可能，也可

The majority required for adoption of a measure varies with the subject. An interpretation of the agreements administered by the WTO, excepting the ***plurilateral agreements***, requires a three-fourths majority of the ***WTO Ministerial Conference*** or the ***General Council***, as does agreement to a ***waiver***. Amendments to the most-favoured-nation articles in the ***GATT***, the ***General Agreement on Trade in Services*** and the ***Agreement on Trade-Related Aspects of Intellectual Property Rights*** may only be made through unanimity. Each WTO member has one vote. The ***European Union*** is entitled to a number of votes equalling the number of its member states. Interpretation of the plurilateral agreements is done according to the provisions contained in these agreements. *See also* ***amendments to WTO agreements***. The Doha Ministerial Declaration has introduced the term "explicit consensus". It is not yet known what this means for achieving consensus.

Decision on Conflicting Requirements: taken by the ***OECD*** Ministerial Council in May 1984 to give effect to the *General Considerations and Practical Approaches Concerning Conflicting Requirements Imposed on Multinational Enterprises*. Revised in 2011. This instrument asks OECD members that may be contemplating legislative action which may conflict with the legal requirements of another member to endeavour to avoid or minimize such conflicts through moderation and restraint and respecting the interests of others. It asks members, *inter alia*, to be prepared to (a) develop mutually beneficial bilateral arrangements for notifying and consulting other members, (b) give prompt and sympathetic consideration to requests for notification and bilateral consultations, (c) inform other members as soon as practicable of new legislation or regulations, and (d) give full consideration to proposals made by others that would lessen or eliminate conflicts.

Decision on International Incentives and Disincentives: adopted by ***OECD*** members in 1984. Revised in 2011. It paves the way for consultations if a member country considers that its interests may be adversely affected by the impact on international investment flows of significant official incentives and disincentives to international direct investment by another member.

Declaration giving effect to the provisions of Article XVI:4: adopted in 1960. GATT members who acceded to the Declaration (all developed countries) agreed that from 1 January 1958 they would cease to grant, either directly or indirectly, any form of subsidy on the export of a product which would result in the sale of the exported product at a lower price than comparable prices charged for similar products in the domestic market. ***Primary products*** were exempted from this Declaration.

Declaration on Fundamental Principles and Rights at Work and its follow-up: adopted by the ***International Labour Organization*** (ILO) in June 1998. It holds that all members of the ILO have an obligation to promote and realize the following rights: (a) freedom of association and the effective recognition of the right to collective bargaining, (b) the elimination of all forms of forced or compulsory labour, (c) the effective abolition of child labour, and (d) the

以进行投票。通过一措施所需的多数票因主题不同而不同。对 WTO 所管理协定的解释，除诸边协定外，需要 WTO 部长级会议或总理事会四分之三多数通过。达成一项豁免的一致意见与此要求相同。对 GATT、《服务贸易总协定》和《与贸易有关的知识产权协定》中最惠国条款的修正只能经协商一致作出。每一 WTO 成员拥有一票。欧盟拥有的票数与其成员国数相等。对诸边协定的解释根据这些协定所含规定进行。另见 *WTO 协定的修正(amendments to WTO agreements)*。《多哈部长宣言》引入了"明确一致"一词。现在尚不知这对达成协商一致意味着什么。

Decision on Conflicting Requirements

关于相互抵触的要求的决定

经济合作与发展组织(OECD)部长理事会于 1984 年 5 月作出，以实施《关于对跨国企业提出相互抵触的要求的总体考虑和实践方法》，2011 年修订。文件要求如 OECD 成员国在考虑采取可能与另一成员国的法律要求相互抵触的立法行动时，应努力通过缓和、克制以及尊重其他成员国利益的方式，尽量避免或减少此类相互抵触。要求各成员国特别作好如下准备：(a)制定关于通报和与其他成员磋商的互惠双边安排；(b)对通报和双边磋商请求给予迅速同情考虑；(c)在可行时将新法律或新法规尽快告知其他成员国；以及(d)充分考虑其他成员提出的减少或消除相互抵触的建议。

Decision on International Incentives and Disincentives

关于国际鼓励和抑制的决定

经济合作与发展组织(OECD)成员国于 1984 年通过，2011 年修订。决定规定，如果一成员国认为，由于另一成员国对国际直接投资采取重大官方鼓励或抑制措施而对国际投资流动产生影响，使其利益可能受到不利影响，该成员可以进行磋商。

Declaration giving effect to the provisions of Article XVI:4

关于实施第 16 条第 4 款规定的宣言

于 1960 年通过。加入此宣言的 GATT 缔约方(全部为发达缔约方)同意，自 1958 年 1 月 1 日起，停止对任何产品的出口直接或间接给予任何形式的补贴，此种补贴可使供出口的此种产品的销售价格低于对国内市场中同类产品收取的可比价格。初级产品不受宣言约束。

Declaration on Fundamental Principles and Rights at Work and its follow-up

关于工作中基本原则和权利宣言及其后续措施

国际劳工组织(ILO)于 1998 年 6 月通过。宣言认为，国际劳工组织的所有成员国有义务促进和实现下列权利：(a)结社自由和有效承认集体谈判权利；(b)消除一切形式的强迫或强制劳动；(c)有效废除童工劳动；以及(d)消除就业与

elimination of discrimination in respect of employment and occupation. Most of these are listed in the ***Universal Declaration of Human Rights***. The Declaration offers a programme of technical cooperation and advisory services to help countries to achieve these aims. It also stresses that labour standards should not be used for protectionist trade purposes. The annex (revised in 2010) contains the work programme for a Follow-up to the Declaration. It includes an annual follow-up concerning non-ratified fundamental conventions and preparation of a global report on fundamental principles and rights at work. That report was issued in November 2011 with the title *Equality at work: the continuing challenge – Global Report under the follow-up to the ILO Declaration on Fundamental Principles and Rights at Work. See also* ***Convention Concerning the Prohibition and Immediate Action for the Elimination of the Worst Forms of Child Labour***, ***core labour standards*** and ***trade and labour standards***. [www.ilo.org]

Declaration on Global Economic Commerce: adopted at the Second ***WTO Ministerial Conference*** in 1998. It enjoins the ***General Council*** to establish a comprehensive work programme to examine all trade-related issues relating to global ***electronic commerce***.

Declaration on Implementation-Related Issues and Concerns: one of the documents adopted on 14 November 2001 at the ***Doha Ministerial Conference***. It identifies issues of concern to developing countries arising from the various agreements under the WTO and suggests how they should be dealt with in the negotiations. It also establishes a work programme for the ***Committee on Trade and Development*** on cross-cutting issues.

Declaration on International Investment and Multinational Enterprises: an OECD policy document first adopted in 1976 and revised several times, most recently in 2011. It consists of four parts. Part I states that members recommend the use of the ***OECD Guidelines for Multinational Enterprises*** to companies operating in their territories. Part II states that governments should accord, as far as possible, ***national treatment*** to foreign-owned or foreign-controlled enterprises in their territories. Part III requires governments to avoid or minimize conflicting requirements on multinational enterprises. Part IV requires governments to make international investment incentives and disincentives as transparent as possible. *See also* ***national treatment instrument***. [www.oecd.org]

Declaration on the Contribution of the World Trade Organization to Achieving Greater Coherence in Global Economic Policymaking: one of the outcomes of the Marrakesh Ministerial Meeting in April 1994 which formally ended the ***Uruguay Round***. The Declaration says that the positive outcome of the Uruguay Round is to be seen as a major contribution towards more coherent international economic policies. It notes that difficulties originating outside the trade field cannot be redressed through trade measures alone. The Declaration accordingly invites the Director-General of the WTO to discuss further with the ***IMF*** and the ***World Bank*** the possible forms of cooperation between the three with a view to achieving greater coherence in global economic policymaking.

职业歧视。上述大部分内容已列入《世界人权宣言》。宣言提供了技术合作与咨询服务以帮助成员国实现这些目标。宣言还强调，劳工标准不应用于贸易保护主义目的。宣言附件(2010 年修改)包含后续工作计划，包括一个关于未批准的基本公约的年度后续行动，以及编写一份关于工作中基本原则和权利的全球报告。该报告于 2011 年 11 月发表，题为《工作中的平等：持续的挑战——国际劳工组织工作中基本原则和权利宣言后续行动全球报告》。另见*禁止和立即行动消除最恶劣形式的童工劳动公约(Convention Concerning the Prohibition and Immediate Action for the Elimination of the Worst Forms of Child Labour)*、*核心劳工标准(core labour standards)*、*贸易与劳工标准(trade and labour standards)*。

Declaration on Global Economic Commerce
全球电子商务宣言

1998 年在第 2 届 WTO 部长级会议上通过。要求总理事会建立一项全面工作计划以审议所有与全球电子商务相关的贸易问题。

Declaration on Implementation-Related Issues and Concerns
关于与实施有关的问题和关注的决定

2001 年 11 月 14 日在多哈部长级会议上通过的文件。确定了发展中国家在 WTO 各项协定中所产生的关注问题，建议在谈判中如何处理这些问题。还为贸易与发展委员会建立了一项跨领域问题工作计划。

Declaration on International Investment and Multinational Enterprises
关于国际投资与跨国企业的宣言

经济合作与发展组织(OECD)政策文件，1976 年首次通过并几经修改，最近一次修改是在 2011 年。由 4 部分组成。第一部分指出，成员国建议在其领土内经营的公司使用 OECD《跨国企业行为准则》。第二部分指出，政府应尽可能对在其领土内的外资企业或外国控制企业给予国民待遇。第三部分要求政府避免或减少对跨国企业提出相互抵触的要求。第四部分要求政府使国际投资鼓励和抑制措施尽可能透明。另见*国民待遇文件(national treatment instrument)*。

Declaration on the Contribution of the World Trade Organization to Achieving Greater Coherence in Global Economic Policymaking
关于 WTO 对实现全球经济决策更大一致性所作贡献的宣言

1994 年 4 月正式结束乌拉圭回合的马拉喀什部长级会议的成果。宣言称，乌拉圭回合的积极成果被视为对更具一致性的国际经济政策的一项主要贡献。宣言指出，贸易领域之外的困难不能仅通过贸易措施解决。因此，宣言提请 WTO 总干事与国际货币基金组织(IMF)和世界银行进一步讨论三者之间可能的合作形式，以期实现全球经济决策的更大一致性。

Declaration on the Establishment of a New International Economic Order: *see* ***New International Economic Order***.

Declaration on the Expansion of Trade in Information Technology Products: *see* ***Information Technology Agreement***.

Declaration on the Right to Development: *see* ***Right to Development***.

Declaration on the TRIPS Agreement and Public Health: adopted at the ***Doha Ministerial Conference*** on 14 November 2001. The Declaration affirms that the TRIPS agreement can and should be interpreted flexibly to promote access to medicines for all. Key elements of the Declaration are that each member has the right to grant compulsory licences, to determine what constitutes a national emergency or extreme urgency in public health, and to establish its own regime handling ***exhaustion*** of ***intellectual property rights***. *See also* ***access to medicines*** and ***Paragraph 6 system***.

Decompilation: the analysis of a computer program to discover the ideas or principles on which it operates. This normally involves a substantial recreation or reproduction of the program. National jurisdictions have differing views on its legality under ***copyright*** acts. The practice is accordingly controversial. A United States court held that ***reverse engineering***, including decompilation of a program, to uncover its unprotected ideas and concepts was permissible under the relevant laws as "fair use", but in Australia decompilation may involve an infringement of the copyright owner's reproduction rights. *See also* ***fair-use doctrine***.

Découpage: a procedure adopted during the ***Kennedy Round*** in the negotiations on tariff reductions on chemicals. It arose from the need to separate the concessions made under the existing United States negotiating authority (the *Trade Expansion Act* of 1962) from those that required additional congressional approval. The latter group was centred around the proposed abolition of the ***American Selling Price*** system, a method of valuing some chemicals at the border for the purpose of ***customs duties***.

Decoupled income support: payments to farmers not related to prices, factors of production, type of production or the amount produced. *See also* ***Basic Payment Scheme***.

Decoupling: the separation of two or more actions, approaches or options that had previously been treated as a whole. For example, countries may decide to abolish the link between the amount of agricultural subsidies paid and the size of the planted acreage or the amount produced.

Decreed customs valuation: a practice of determining the value of a good through a decree. It is meant to prevent fraud or protection of domestic industry. The decreed value changes an ad valorem duty into a specific duty.

De-cumulation: when a petition for the imposition of ***anti-dumping measures*** against imports from several countries has been launched, the investigating authorities may decide to consider the combined impact of these products on the domestic market. This is called ***cumulation***. When they decide to look at one or more supplier countries separately, possibly because their circumstances are quite different, it is called de-cumulation. [Vermulst 1990]

Declaration on the Establishment of a New International Economic Order
建立国际经济新秩序宣言
见*国际经济新秩序(New International Economic Order)*。

Declaration on the Expansion of Trade in Information Technology Products
关于扩大信息技术产品贸易的宣言
见*信息技术协定(Information Technology Agreement)*。

Declaration on the Right to Development
发展权利宣言
见*发展权利(Right to Development)*。

Declaration on the TRIPS Agreement and Public Health
关于与贸易有关的知识产权协定与公共健康的宣言
2001 年 11 月 14 日，在多哈部长级会议上通过。宣言确认了《与贸易有关的知识产权协定》能够且应该加以灵活解释，以促进所有人获得药品。宣言的关键要素是，每一成员均有权发放强制许可，确定何种情况构成公共健康方面的国家紧急状态或极端紧急情况，并建立自己的处理知识产权用尽的制度。另见*获得药品(access to medicines)*、*第 6 段制度(Paragraph 6 system)*。

Decompilation
反向编译
对计算机程序的分析，以发现其运行的构思或原理。通常涉及对程序的实质性再造或复制。各国管辖范围对其在版权法下的合法性有不同看法。此种做法因此是有争议的。美国一法院认为，允许包括程序反向编译在内的逆向工程，以发现其未受保护的构思和概念，属于相关法律所允许的"合理使用"。但在澳大利亚，反向编译可能涉及侵犯版权所有者的复制权。另见*合理使用原则(fair-use doctrine)*。

Découpage
剪纸程序
肯尼迪回合期间化工品关税削减谈判所采用的程序。这样作需要将根据美国现有谈判授权(《1962 年贸易扩展法》)所作减让与需要国会额外批准的减让分开处理。后者主要围绕拟议废除美国销售价格制度，一种为征收关税目的而在边境对化工品进行估价的方法。

Decoupled income support
不挂钩的收入支持
对农民的支付不与价格、生产要素、生产类型或产量相关联。另见*基本支付方案(Basic Payment Scheme)*。

Decoupling
不挂钩
将两个或两个以上原被视为一体的行动、方式或观点分开。例如，国家可以决定取消所支付的农业补贴金额与种植面积或产量之间的关联。

Decreed customs valuation
法定海关估价
通过法令确定货物价值的一种做法。意在防止欺诈或保护国内产业。法定价值将从价税转变为从量关税。

De-cumulation
去累积
当要求对来自若干国家的进口产品实施反倾销措施的申请已经提出时，调查主管机关可以考虑这些产品对国内市场的合并影响，这就称为累积。而当主管机关决定分开调查一个或多个供应国，可能由于它们各自的情况十分不同，这就称为去累积。

Deep free-trade agreement: a ***free-trade agreement*** ostensibly going beyond the rules already available under the ***multilateral trading system***. It includes liberalization of trade in goods, trade in services and investment flows, but it goes beyond them into other areas promoting international economic relations. *See also* ***shallow free-trade agreement***.

Deep integration: the integration by two or more countries of national policy frameworks that usually are the preserve of national governments. These include ***competition policy***, technical standards, ***subsidies***, monetary and fiscal policies, regulation and supervision of financial institutions, environmental issues, ***government procurement*** and more. The ***European Union*** has moved ahead farthest in deep integration, but ***ANZCERTA*** and ***NAFTA*** (to be succeeded by the ***United States–Mexico–Canada Agreement***) are also examples of deep integration. A contrast is usually drawn with shallow integration which may range from a preferential trade area to a ***customs union*** or ***free-trade area***, but where each member retains a completely free hand concerning all other policies. Shallow integration also promotes a degree of harmonization of policies as has happened in the ***multilateral trading system***. *See also* ***European Single Market***, ***negative integration*** and ***positive integration***.

De facto*:** existing, whether legally or not. *See also* ***de jure.

De facto* discrimination:** a term first used in the report by the WTO ***Appellate Body on the 1996 banana panel decision. The Appellate Body contrasts *de facto* discrimination with *de jure*, or formal, discrimination. Its meaning appears to be close to that of ***implicit discrimination*** in that it is based on practice rather than a legislative requirement. *See also* ***banana cases***. [WT/DS27/AB/R]

***De facto* GATT membership:** former colonies used to be able, upon independence, to participate in the GATT as *de facto* members if they agreed to administer their trade regimes in accordance with the GATT rules. This could only be done if the parent countries had been GATT members. *De facto* membership is not possible in the WTO for any reason.

Deficiency payment: a type of agricultural domestic support, paid by governments to producers of certain commodities and based on the difference between a target price and the domestic market price.

Definitive anti-dumping duties: the anti-dumping duties imposed once all the investigations have been completed. They have to be ended after five years unless a review initiated beforehand indicates that ***dumping*** would continue or recur. *See also* ***anti-dumping measures*** and ***provisional anti-dumping duties***.

Definitive safeguard measures: refers to safeguard measures imposed after an investigation has shown a causal link between the difficulties experienced by domestic producers of a given good and an increase in imports of that good. *See also* ***provisional safeguard measures***.

Degressivity: generally the principle that ***protection*** should be reduced over time. It has been an issue particularly in the administration of ***safeguards*** where governments were supposed to initiate ***structural adjustment*** policies resulting

Deep free-trade agreement
深度自由贸易协定

表面上超越多边贸易体制已有规则的自由贸易协定。包括货物贸易、服务贸易和投资流动自由化，并超越了这些领域，涉及促进国际经济关系的其他领域。另见*浅层自由贸易协定(shallow free-trade agreement)*。

Deep integration
深度一体化

两个或两个以上国家的国家政策框架的一体化，这些框架通常是各国政府的专属领域。包括竞争政策、技术标准、补贴、货币和财政政策、金融机构的监管和监督、环境问题、政府采购等。欧盟在深度一体化方面取得的进展最大，但《澳大利亚与新西兰更紧密经济关系贸易协定》(ANZCERTA)和《北美自贸协定》(NAFTA)(《美国—墨西哥—加拿大协定》替代)也是深度一体化的例子。深度一体化通常与浅层一体化进行对比，浅层一体化可能从优惠贸易区发展到关税同盟或自由贸易区，但其中每一成员在所有其他政策方面保持完全自主。浅层一体化也促进了一定程度的政策协调，正如在多边贸易体制中所发生的那样。另见*欧洲单一市场(European Single Market)*、*消极一体化(negative integration)*、*积极一体化(positive integration)*。

De facto
事实上

存在，无论合法与否。另见*法律上(de jure)*。

***De facto* discrimination**
事实上的歧视

WTO 上诉机构关于 1996 年“香蕉案”专家组裁决的报告中首次使用的词语。上诉机构将事实上的歧视与法律上或正式的歧视进行了对比。其含义似乎接近于隐性歧视，因为是基于实践而非立法要求。另见*香蕉案(banana cases)*。

***De facto* GATT membership**
事实上的 GATT 成员资格

如果前殖民地同意依照 GATT 规则管理其贸易制度，它们可以在获得独立时作为事实上的成员加入 GATT。只有在母国已经成为 GATT 缔约方时方可如此。在 WTO 中事实上的成员资格无论如何是不可能的。

Deficiency payment
差价补贴

一种农业国内支持，由政府根据目标价格与国内市场价格之间的差价向某些商品的生产者支付。

Definitive anti-dumping duties
最终反倾销税

在所有调查完成后征收的反倾销税。反倾销税必须在 5 年后终止，除非此前开始的审议表明倾销将继续或再度发生。另见*反倾销措施(anti-dumping measures)*、*临时反倾销税(provisional anti-dumping duties)*。

Definitive safeguard measures
最终保障措施

指经调查显示一指定产品的国内生产商所遇困难与该产品的进口增加之间存在因果关系后所实施的保障措施。另见*临时保障措施(provisional safeguard measures)*。

Degressivity
递减性

一般指保护应随着时间的推移而逐渐减少的原则。特别是在保障措施的管理

in lower protection in the sectors given safeguard protection. Often they preferred to continue ***import restrictions*** at the same level.

Deindustrialization: a phenomenon associated by many with ***globalization*** and seen as a negative development. Sometimes also called "hollowing-out". It is defined generally as the long-term decline in the share of manufacturing employment in the advanced or industrialized economies. In the view of many, the most important factor accounting for deindustrialization is the systematic tendency for productivity in manufacturing to grow faster than in services. In many countries, perceived deindustrialization is one of the important forces driving the formulation of ***trade policy***, and governments often seek to stem its tide through imposing ***protection*** for ***sensitive sectors***. *See also* ***delocalization***, ***internationalization*** and ***structural adjustment***.

DEIP: *see* ***Dairy Export Incentive Program***.

De jure*:** existing in law. *See also* ***de facto.

De jure* discrimination:** discrimination among trading partners formally embodied in legislation or regulations. *See also* ***de facto discrimination.

Délocalisant: a ***semi-generic geographical indication***.

Delocalization: a term used by advocates of negotiations concerning ***trade and labour standards***. It means that a company may decide to relocate its production facilities from a high-cost location to a low-cost country because it expects to save on expenses for the support of social conditions for the workforce. This claim is disputed. With the shift towards advanced, flexible production systems and the need to assure quality and reliability, increasing importance is attached to such factors as infrastructures, educational standards and skill levels. Relative wage levels then are a factor, but not the only important one, in the choice of location. *See also* ***deindustrialization***, ***globalization***, ***internationalization***, ***race-to-the-bottom argument*** and ***worker rights***.

***De minimis*:** a legal term describing that something is of little or no importance in the matter concerned.

De minimis* dumping margins:** ***dumping margins of less than 2 per cent expressed as a percentage of the export price in the country of origin. In the case of such margins, a country may not take ***anti-dumping measures***. *See also* ***negligible imports***.

De minimis* imports:** the provisions of the WTO ***Agreement on Trade-Related Aspects of Intellectual Property Rights do not apply to small quantities of goods of a non-commercial nature contained in personal luggage or sent in small consignments.

De minimis* in rules of origin:** a provision sometimes included in the ***rules of origin of ***free-trade agreements***. It states that although a good may not have undergone a ***change in tariff classification*** sufficiently large in the partner country to enable it to qualify as an ***originating good***, the importing country may accept it as such if the value of all ***non-originating materials*** is less than a stipulated percentage. A *de minimis* limit of 10 per cent appears to be common.

中已经成为一个问题，各国政府被认为应该实行结构性调整政策，以降低被给予保障措施保护部门的保护。各国政府通常更愿意继续在同一水平实行进口限制。

Deindustrialization

去工业化

一种许多人与全球化相联系的现象，视为一种消极发展。有时也被称为“空心化”。通常被定义为发达或工业化经济体制造业就业比例的长期下降。在许多人看来，去工业化的最重要因素是制造业生产率增长快于服务业的系统性趋势。在许多国家，人们认为去工业化是推动贸易政策制定的重要力量之一，政府往往寻求通过对敏感部门进行保护以控制此种趋势。另见*去本地化(delocalization)*、*国际化(internationalization)*、*结构性调整(structural adjustment)*。

DEIP

奶制品出口激励计划

见*奶制品出口激励计划(Dairy Export Incentive Program)*。

De jure

法律上

存在于法律中。另见*事实上(de facto)*。

***De jure* discrimination**

法律上的歧视

正式包含在立法或法规中的贸易伙伴之间的歧视。另见*事实上的歧视(de facto discrimination)*。

Délocalisant

离岸外包

见*半通用地理标志(semi-generic geographical indication)*。

Delocalization

去本地化

有关贸易与劳工标准谈判的倡导者使用的词语。指一公司可以决定将其生产设施从高成本的地点迁移至低成本的地点，因为该公司期望节省用于支持与劳动力有关的社会条件的开支。这种主张是有争议的。因为随着向先进、灵活的生产系统的转移，以及保证质量和可靠性的需要，人们日益重视基础设施、教育标准和技术水平等因素。相关的薪酬水平在选择地点时是一个考虑因素，但不是惟一的重要因素。另见*去工业化(deindustrialization)*、*全球化(globalization)*、*国际化(internationalization)*、*竞次论(race-to-the-bottom argument)*、*劳工权利(worker rights)*。

De minimis

微量

法律名词，用于描述某种事物对有关问题的重要性很小或无重要性。

***De minimis* dumping margins**

微量倾销幅度

低于2%的倾销幅度，以产品原产地出口价格的百分比表示。如果属于此种倾销幅度，一国可以不采取反倾销措施。另见*可忽略不计的进口量(negligible imports)*。

***De minimis* imports**

微量进口

WTO《与贸易有关的知识产权协定》的条款不适用于个人行李中夹带的或小件托运中运送的少量非商业性货物。

***De minimis* in rules of origin**

原产地规则中的微量

在自由贸易协定的原产地规则中有时包括的一项条款。该条款规定，尽管一货物在伙伴国中所发生的税则归类改变不够大因而不符合原产货物条件，但如果全部非原产材料的价值低于一规定百分比，进口国仍可按原产货物予以接受。10%的微量限制似为常见。

De minimis* safeguards rule:** safeguards action may not be taken against a developing country if its share of the imports of the product concerned is less than 3 per cent. This rule only applies if the collective share of developing countries accounting for less than 3 per cent each of imports of the product concerned is no more than 9 per cent. *See also* ***Agreement on Safeguards, ***safeguards*** and ***selectivity***.

De minimis* subsidies:** the WTO ***Agreement on Subsidies and Countervailing Measures defines these as subsidies amounting to less than 1 per cent. Authorities investigating the effect of an alleged subsidy are required to terminate their enquiries immediately if the volume of the subsidy falls into this category. If developing countries are involved, the *de minimis* level is set at 2 per cent in the case of individual countries. This provision also applies if the volume of subsidized imports of the same product from developing countries does not exceed 4 per cent, unless imports from developing countries with a share of less than 4 per cent of imports exceed 9 per cent of total imports of the same product by the country making the investigation.

***De minimis* support in agriculture:** the WTO Agreement on Agriculture defines this as support to farmers amounting to up to 5 per cent of the value of production of a product or overall agriculture production in the case of developed country members and up to 10 per cent in the case of developing country members (with some exceptions). The support remaining below the *de minimis* level, while considered as trade distorting, does not have to be included in the calculation of Current Total AMS (i.e. the level of support actually provided during any given year).

***De minimis* threshold for customs shipments:** a value of a consignment below which no customs duties apply.

Democracy clause: a provision in trade laws or international trade and investment treaties which promotes the observance of democratic freedoms. One example is the ***ACP-EU Partnership Agreement***. Its members agree that respect for democratic principles and the rule of law is one of the essential elements of the Agreement. The ***Mediterranean Agreements*** concluded by the ***European Union*** also contain provisions requiring respect for human rights and democracy. *See also* ***human rights clause*** and ***social clause***.

Denial of benefits: members of the ***General Agreement on Trade in Services*** (GATS) may deny the benefits of the Agreement to another member if they can show that a service does not originate in the territory of a GATS member or if a company supplying the service is not a national of a GATS member. *See also* ***non-application***.

Denomination: *see* ***appellations of origin***, ***Geneva Act of the Lisbon Agreement on Appellations of Origin and Geographical Indications***, ***geographical indications, geographical names*** and ***Stresa Convention***.

Dependence theory: a theory much in vogue in the 1960s and 1970s holding that developing countries are economically, socially and politically dependent on power groups in developed countries, especially ***transnational corporations***.

***De minimis* safeguards rule**

保障措施微量规则

如一发展中国家在有关产品进口中所占份额低于 3%，则不得对其采取保障措施。这项规则只适用于有关产品进口份额低于 3%的发展中国家的集体份额不超过 9%的情况。另见*保障措施协定(Agreement on Safeguards)*、*保障措施(safeguards)*、*选择性(selectivity)*。

***De minimis* subsidies**

微量补贴

WTO《补贴与反补贴措施协定》将此类补贴定义为低于 1%的补贴。如果补贴金额属此范畴，调查被指控的补贴影响的主管机关应立即停止调查。如果涉及发展中国家，对单个国家的微量水平定为 2%。如果来自发展中国家的同类补贴进口产品的数量不超过 4%，该条款也适用，除非低于 4%进口份额的发展中国家的进口超过进行调查的成员总进口的 9%。

***De minimis* support in agriculture**

农业微量支持

WTO《农业协定》将其定义为对农民的支持，发达国家最高可达一产品产值的 5%或农业总产值的 5%，发展中国家最高可达 10%(有一些例外)。保持在微量允许水平以下的支持，虽然被视为扭曲贸易，但不需包括在现行综合支持总量(即任何一年实际提供的支持水平)的计算中。

***De minimis* threshold for customs shipments**

装运货物海关最低免税额

一票货物的价值，低于此值即免征关税。

Democracy clause

民主条款

贸易法或国际贸易和投资条约中促进尊重民主自由的条款。《非加太地区国家与欧盟伙伴关系协定》即属此例。成员同意，尊重民主原则和法治是协定基本要素之一。欧盟缔约的《地中海协定》也包含了要求尊重人权和民主的条款。另见*人权条款(human rights clause)*、*社会条款(social clause)*。

Denial of benefits

拒予利益

《服务贸易总协定》(GATS)成员如能证明一项服务并非源自 GATS 成员领土内或提供该项服务的公司并非 GATS 成员的国民，则该成员可拒绝给予另一成员该协定的利益。另见*互不适用(non-application)*。

Denomination

命名

见*原产地名称(appellations of origin)*、*原产地名称和地理标志里斯本协定日内瓦文本(Geneva Act of the Lisbon Agreement on Appellations of Origin and Geographical Indications)*、*地理标志(geographical indications)*、*地理名称(geographical names)*、*斯特雷萨公约(Stresa Convention)*。

Dependence theory

依附理论

20 世纪 60 年代和 70 年代非常流行的一种理论，认为发展中国家在经济、社会和政治上依赖发达国家中的实力集团，特别是跨国公司。该理论目前被认

The theory is now not considered to give a satisfactory account of the causes of development and underdevelopment and hence the policy choices available to developing countries. *See also* ***core–periphery thesis*** and ***Singer-Prebisch thesis***.

Derbez text: the draft ministerial statement prepared for the WTO ***Cancún Ministerial Conference*** by Luis Ernesto Derbez, then Foreign Minister of Mexico. It outlined a plan for making progress in the negotiations under the ***Doha Development Agenda***.

Deregulation: the process by which governments dismantle the regulatory structure of industries or professions to promote competition and hence improve the efficiency with which goods and services are delivered. It sometimes results in unintended consequences. *See also* ***privatization***, ***re-regulation*** and ***wider competition policy***.

Designated monopoly: a term found in some ***free-trade agreements***. It can mean an entity, whether private or government-owned, designated as a sole provider or purchaser of a good or service in a relevant market. It can also mean a privately owned monopoly that a party has so designated or will designate after the entry into force of the agreement. *See also* ***competition policy***.

Designation of origin: *see* ***protected designation of origin***.

Determination of dumping: the process described in the WTO ***Anti-Dumping Agreement*** which leads to an assessment of whether ***dumping*** has occurred. This means determining whether the ***export price*** of the product concerned is lower than its ***normal value***. Although an investigation may show that dumping has occurred, this does not necessarily mean that ***anti-dumping measures*** may be imposed. It still has to be shown that the dumped product caused, or threatened to cause, material ***injury*** to an established industry or that it may have materially retarded the establishment of a domestic industry. This is known as ***causality***.

Determination of origin: ascertaining where a good has come from, for example, for statistical purposes or to make sure that it qualifies for preferential tariff treatment under a ***free-trade agreement***. This is an aspect of the administration of ***rules of origin***.

Devaluation: a change in a country's ***exchange rate***, sometimes through a government decision, but more often through movements on foreign exchange markets, with the result that more units of that country's currency are needed to buy the same amount of the foreign currency.

Developed country: a term usually applied to ***OECD*** member countries, though some of the more recent members might not consider themselves wholly so. The term "developed country" tends to convey a picture of an economically and socially advanced country, but the differences between the poorest and the wealthiest members of this group are noticeable. Sometimes, developed countries are collectively referred to as the North because most of them are located in the northern hemisphere.

Developing countries and the multilateral trading system: when the text of the ***GATT*** was negotiated in 1947, there was an assumption among developed

为并不能满意地解释发展和欠发展的原因，以及发展中国家可获得的政策选择。另见*核心-外围理论(core–periphery thesis)*、*辛格-普雷维什命题(Singer-Prebisch thesis)*。

Derbez text

德贝斯文本

墨西哥时任外长路易斯・欧内斯托・德贝斯为 WTO 坎昆部长级会议准备的部长声明草案。声明描述了在多哈发展议程谈判中取得进展的计划。

Deregulation

取消管制

政府取消产业或行业监管构架以促进竞争的过程，从而提高提供产品和服务的效率。有时会导致意外后果。另见*私有化(privatization)*、*重新管制(re-regulation)*、*广义竞争政策(wider competition policy)*。

Designated monopoly

指定垄断

一些自由贸易协定中的用语。可以指一实体，无论私营或政府所有，被指定为在一相关市场上一货物或服务的惟一提供者或购买者。也可以指一方已经指定或将在协定生效后指定的私人垄断。另见*竞争政策(competition policy)*。

Designation of origin

原产地命名

见*原产地命名保护(protected designation of origin)*。

Determination of dumping

倾销的确定

WTO《反倾销协定》中描述的过程，对是否发生倾销进行评估。这意味着要确定有关产品的出口价格是否低于其正常价值。尽管调查可能表明倾销已经发生，但这并不一定意味着可以采取反倾销措施。调查还要证明倾销产品对建立的产业已经造成或威胁造成实质损害，或可能实质阻碍一国内产业的建立。此即因果关系。

Determination of origin

原产地的确定

确定一货物来自何处，例如为统计目的或为保证该货物有资格享受一自由贸易协定项下的优惠关税待遇。这是原产地规则管理的一个方面。

Devaluation

贬值

一国汇率的变化，有时是通过政府决定，但更多时候是通过外汇市场的波动，结果是需要更多单位的该国本币用以购买相同数量的外币。

Developed country

发达国家

通常适用于经济合作与发展组织(OECD)成员国的词语，尽管一些新成员国并不认为自己完全属发达国家。“发达国家”一词往往表达的是经济和社会先进国家的景象，但在这一集团最穷和最富成员之间的差距明显。有时，发达国家被集体称为“北方”，因为它们大多数位于北半球。

Developing countries and the multilateral trading system

发展中国家与多边贸易体制

在 1947 年谈判 GATT 文本时，发达国家认为，协定总体上应平等适用于处于

countries that on the whole it should apply equally to countries at different stages of development. At the same time, there was a strong developing-country view that they should not have to accord full ***reciprocity*** in ***trade liberalization*** to others, and that they should have preferential access to developed-country markets. In the end, provision was made in Article XVIII (Government Assistance to Economic Development) to facilitate the progressive development of developing country economies, especially the ones that could only support low standards of living and that were in the early stages of development. An interpretative note to the Article adds that the phrase "low standards of living" is to be taken to mean normal economic circumstances and not exceptionally favourable temporary conditions resulting from good export markets for primary commodities. The phrase "in the early stages of economic development" may apply not only to countries at the initial stages of economic development, but also to those which are undergoing a process of industrialization to correct an excessive dependence on primary production. Article XVIII permits developing countries to maintain tariff structures permitting the promotion of infant industries and to apply ***quantitative restrictions*** for ***balance-of-payments*** purposes. The administration of this provision has always been difficult because the criteria it uses are rather flexible. First, it assumes that countries will know when they are to be considered developing economies, and it does not contain a mechanism for them to graduate to developed-economy status. Second, the provisions relating to the development of infant industries can be quite complex in practice. Third, the criteria for ***import restrictions*** under the balance-of-payments provisions are not all that well defined. Restrictions may not be more severe than necessary (a) to forestall the threat of, or to stop, a serious decline in monetary reserves and (b) in the case of a member with inadequate monetary reserves, to achieve a reasonable rate of increase in its reserves. As the ***Korean beef*** case showed, however, the temptation exists to maintain balance-of-payments restrictions much longer than would objectively be necessary. In practice, developing countries have not found Article XVIII as useful to them as they had expected. Nor have developed countries viewed it as having great merit. A fundamental difficulty with the Article is in the eyes of some that it is based on the ***import substitution*** theory, the antithesis of the policies adopted by outward-looking, export-oriented economies. As economists have pointed out, the capital goods imports required by import substitution policies will invariably ensure a shortage of foreign exchange without an adequate balancing by export income. GATT articles are difficult to change, and the ***GATT review session*** of 1955 left this situation largely intact. Indeed, until the advent of the ***Kennedy Round***, the developing countries as a whole played a minor role in major GATT negotiations. The years between 1948 and 1963 were dominated by tariff negotiations rather than the consideration of systemic issues. Some of the primary commodities developing countries produced and in which they were important traders faced few entry barriers to developed-country markets. Agricultural products, textiles and ***tropical products*** were, of course, a different

不同发展阶段的国家。同时，发展中国家强烈认为，它们不必在贸易自由化中给予其他国家完全互惠，且它们应该获得对发达国家市场的优惠准入。最终，在第 18 条(政府对经济发展的援助)中作出规定，以促进发展中国家的逐步发展，特别是那些只能维持低生活水平且处于发展初期的发展中国家。对该条的注释补充道："低生活水平"指经济的正常状况，而不是初级产品暂时存在特别有利条件所产生的特殊情况。"处于发展初期"指不仅适用于刚开始经济发展的国家，而且适用于为纠正过分依赖初级产品而经济正处在工业化进程中的国家。第 18 条允许发展中国家保持能够促进幼稚产业的关税结构，并为国际收支目的而实施数量限制。这一规定的管理始终非常困难，因为其使用的标准相当灵活。第一，该条假定各国知道它们何时被视为发展中经济体，而该条并无使其毕业获得发达经济体地位的机制。第二，有关幼稚产业发展的规定在实践中十分复杂。第三，根据国际收支条款实施进口限制标准的定义根本不明确。采取的限制措施不得超过下列必要限度：(a)为防止货币储备严重下降的威胁或制止货币储备的严重下降；及(b)对于货币储备不足的缔约方，为实现其储备的合理增长率。但是，正如"韩国牛肉案"中所表明的，维持国际收支限制措施大大超过客观必要的诱惑是存在的。在实践中，发展中国家发现，第 18 条并不如它们所期望的那么有用。发达国家也不认为该条具有很大价值。在一些人看来，该条的根本性困难在于其基于进口替代理论，是与外向型、出口导向型经济体所采取的政策相对立的。正如经济学家们所指出的，进口替代政策所需要的资本品进口因缺乏出口收入的充分平衡而必将造成外汇短缺。改变 GATT 条文很困难，且 1955 年的 GATT 审议会议基本未改变上述状况。确实，直到肯尼迪回合之前，发展中国家作为一个整体，在 GATT 主要谈判中的作用很小。1948 年至 1963 年关税谈判占主要地位，而非考虑系统性问题。发展中国家生产且为重要贸易商的一些初级产品在进入发达国家市场时的准入壁垒很少。当然，农产品、纺织品和热带产品是另一种情况。另

matter. On the other hand, the system of ***requests and offers***, used to bring down many of the high tariffs for manufactured articles, and the associated rule of ***principal supplier rights***, meant that developing countries with their small market shares in most countries effectively were excluded from playing any role in the early tariff negotiating rounds. Despite their persistent efforts to show that they were not being drawn into the post-war trading system as had been expected, it was not until late 1957 that the GATT membership as a whole decided to study this problem more carefully. The result was the ***Haberler Report***, issued in 1958, which concluded that there was some justification in developing country views that current rules and conventions on ***commercial policy*** were relatively unfavourable to them. A committee was then established to look at the matter further, and to this can be traced in part the inclusion of specific developing-country issues in the Kennedy Round. In the meantime, decolonization led to the accession to the GATT of more developing countries. Some of them, and others outside it, began to view the ***United Nations*** system as a better potential mechanism for improvements in issues of interest to them. This eventually led to the convening of ***UNCTAD*** (United Nations Conference on Trade and Development) in 1964 and its establishment in the same year as a permanent body. Later, this was followed by calls for a ***New International Economic Order*** and a ***Charter of Economic Rights and Duties of States***, both to be negotiated under United Nations auspices. In the GATT, the big breakthrough for developing countries came with the launch of the Kennedy Round in 1963. For the first time, the negotiating mandate for a round referred specifically to developing countries. According to the Ministerial Declaration launching the Round, one objective was the adoption of measures for the expansion of trade of developing countries as a means of furthering their economic development. Results of the Round for developing countries were mixed. They benefited from tariff cuts particularly in non-agricultural items of interest to them. They also obtained ***Part IV of the GATT*** which freed them from the requirement to accord reciprocity to developed countries in trade negotiations. This, however, could be no more than a symbolic gesture, and its value to developing countries has been debated ever since. On the other hand, the ***Long-Term Arrangement Regarding International Trade in Cotton Textiles***, which put severe restrictions on their ability to expand their exports of cotton textiles, was extended for another three years and was well on its way to becoming a feature of the ***multilateral trading system*** in the form of the ***Multi-Fibre Arrangement*** until its replacement by the WTO ***Agreement on Textiles and Clothing*** more than thirty years later. In 1968, UNCTAD II adopted a resolution calling for the establishment of a ***GSP*** (Generalized System of Preferences) which would give developing countries preferential access to developed-country markets. The idea had been around for some years. In 1963, the ***European Economic Community*** had signed the ***Yaoundé Convention*** which gave special benefits to some African countries. The GATT faced up to the new reality in 1971 when it adopted a ten-year waiver for such schemes.

一方面，用于降低许多制成品高关税的要价和出价制度，以及相关的主要供应方权利规则，意味着在大多数国家占有很小市场份额的发展中国家在早期关税谈判中无法发挥任何作用。尽管发展中国家作出不懈努力，以表明它们未能如愿被纳入战后贸易体制，但直到1957年末，GATT缔约方才决定更认真地研究这一问题。结果就是1958年发布的《哈伯勒报告》。报告得出结论，发展中国家的观点有一些合理性，这种观点认为关于商业政策的现有规则和协定对其相对不利。随后设立了一个委员会以进一步研究该问题，此点可从肯尼迪回合纳入发展中国家特定问题的事实中找到痕迹。同时，去殖民化导致了更多发展中国家加入GATT。其中一些发展中国家，以及其他未加入的发展中国家，都开始将联合国体系视为改善其利益关注问题的一种更好的潜在机制。这最终促成了联合国贸易与发展会议(UNCTAD)在1964年召开，并在同年成为常设机构。随后产生了在联合国主持下谈判国际经济新秩序和《各国经济权利与义务宪章》的呼声。在GATT中，对于发展中国家的重大突破随着肯尼迪回合在1963年启动而到来。回合谈判授权中第一次专门提到发展中国家。根据启动该回合的部长宣言，其中一项目标是采取扩大发展中国家贸易的措施，作为促进它们经济发展的手段。对于发展中国家而言，回合的结果喜忧参半。发展中国家特别是在对其有利的非农产品关税削减方面获得利益。还达成了GATT第四部分，其中不再要求发展中国家在贸易谈判中对发达国家给予互惠。然而，这只不过是象征性姿态，其对发展中国家的价值始终存在争论。另一方面，严格限制发展中国家提高棉纺织品出口能力的《国际棉纺织品贸易长期安排》又被延长了3年，并且开启了以《多种纤维协定》形式成为多边贸易体制特点的发展轨迹，直至30多年后被WTO《纺织品与服装协定》所取代。1968年，UNCTAD第2届大会通过了一项决议，呼吁建立普惠制(GSP)，给予发展中国家对发达国家市场的优惠准入。该想法已经提出多年。1963年，欧洲经济共同体签署了《雅温得协定》，给予一些非洲国家特殊利益。GATT直到1971年才面对新现实，通过了针对普惠制方案的为期10年的豁免。发展中国家因此正式同时实现了非互惠和优惠市场准入的主要目

The developing countries had therefore achieved formally both of their main aims of non-reciprocity and preferential market access. They succeeded in buttressing their gains in the ***Tokyo Round*** through the adoption of the ***Enabling Clause*** which put ***special and differential treatment*** on a firmer footing. It also was seen as providing a permanent waiver for the GSP. However, neither of these achievements seemed to take the developing countries much further in the direction of achieving fuller participation in the multilateral trading system. Some of them certainly did very well as exporters of manufactures and as destinations for investment, but they had effectively given away their influence over the rules of the game. As far as many developed countries were concerned, there was little point in agreeing on rules with players who were not obliged to play by them. The years following the conclusion of the Tokyo Round therefore led to many calls for new GATT rules for developed countries, the so-called ***GATT plus*** proposals. Their adoption would have formalized the outsider role of developing countries further. The opposite was true of the ***Leutwiler Report*** of 1985 which called for greater emphasis on encouraging developing countries to take advantage of their competitive strength and to integrate them more fully into the trading system. In other words, they should look towards adopting more of the GATT's obligations in order to benefit more from its rights. This view gained some support from the more outward-looking developing countries. The ***Uruguay Round*** outcome reversed the trend. Developing countries then appeared to be accepting the fact that they would only have bargaining power if they were bound by all the results of negotiations. Some indications of this can be gained from the negotiations under the ***General Agreement on Trade in Services*** (GATS) where the obligations of developing countries are nearly equal to those of developed countries, the main difference being the relative number of listings to be made in the schedules of commitments. The multilateral trade negotiations launched in November 2001 are formally known as the ***Doha Development Agenda***. Developing countries achieved some gains in the implementation of the ***Agreement on Trade Facilitation***. Least-developed countries in particular also will benefit from the ***Paragraph 6 system*** and the ***LDC services waiver***. More recently a debate has been initiated in the WTO on the meaning of the term "developing country" and whether the current approach meets the needs of the organization. At present, developing-country status is self-declared. This leads to what some consider misalignments. For example, some countries listed in the WTO system as developing countries have accepted developing-country status in the ***OECD***. They have also pointed out that the ***World Bank*** classifies developing countries into four tiers, depending on their per-capita GNP. *See also* **graduation** and ***infant-industry argument***.

Developing country: an imprecise term based as much on economic and social foundations as on political and historical perceptions and aspirations. It is usually applied to a country that does not consider itself, or is not considered by others, in some or many respects as matching the characteristics of a

标。在东京回合中通过了授权条款，使特殊和差别待遇有了更坚实的基础，发展中国家巩固了它们的成果。这一条款被视为对普惠制给予了永久豁免。然而，这些成就似乎都未能使发展中国家在实现更充分参与多边贸易体制方面取得更多进展。一些发展中国家在作为制成品出口国和投资目的地方面作得很好，但它们实际上失去了对游戏规则的影响力。对于很多发达国家而言，与无义务遵守规则的国家就规则达成一致并无太大意义。在东京回合结束后的数年里，出现了为发达国家制定新的 GATT 规则的呼声，也就是所谓的超GATT 规则提案。如提案被采纳，将使发展中国家的局外人角色正式化。与此提案相反的是 1985 年的《路特威勒报告》，报告呼吁进一步强调鼓励发展中国家利用它们的竞争力更充分融入多边贸易体制。换言之，它们应该承担更多 GATT 义务，以从其权利中获益更多。这种观点得到了更外向型发展中国家的一些支持。乌拉圭回合的成果扭转了这种趋势。发展中国家似乎接受了这样的事实，即只有它们受所有谈判结果的约束，才能拥有讨价还价的能力。可以从《服务贸易总协定》(GATS)的谈判中发现某种迹象，其中发展中国家的义务几乎与发达国家相同，主要差别在于承诺减让表中所列条目的相对数量。2001 年 11 月启动的多边贸易谈判正式称为多哈发展议程。发展中国家在实施《贸易便利化协定》方面有所收获。特别是最不发达国家也将从第 6 段制度和最不发达国家服务豁免中获益。最近，WTO 中就“发展中国家”一词的含义以及现行方式是否符合该组织需要而展开了辩论。目前，发展中国家地位是自称的，导致一些人认为的存在错位。例如，一些在 WTO 中被列为发展中国家的国家接受了经济合作与发展组织(OECD)发达国家地位(英文误为发展中国家地位—译注)。它们还指出，世界银行按人均国内生产总值，将发展中国家分为四组。另见*毕业(graduation)*、*幼稚产业论(infant-industry argument)*。

Developing country
发展中国家

既基于经济和社会基础又基于政治和历史观念和愿望的不确切词语。通常适用于自认为或被其他国家认为在一些或许多方面不符合发达国家特征的国家。对于其他国家而言，发展中国家地位等同于 77 国集团成员身份。在发展中国

developed country. To others, developing-country status is the same as membership of the ***Group of 77***. Considerable differences exist in the make-up of developing countries. Some are very poor. Others could be considered quite wealthy. The ***World Bank*** takes account of this. It classifies its members into four tiers (***low-income economies***, ***lower-middle-income economies***, ***upper middle-income economies*** and ***high-income economies***). In the WTO developing-country status is self-declared. This leads to what some consider misalignments in that some countries that claim developing-country status in the WTO have accepted the obligations of developed countries in the ***OECD***. A debate on this issue is now under way in the WTO. Standards are available for classifying ***least-developed countries*** through the criteria set by ***ECOSOC***. *See also* ***developing countries and the multilateral trading system***, ***graduation*** and ***special and differential treatment***.

Development agenda: *see* ***Doha Development Agenda***.

Development assistance: aid given to developing countries in the form of loans, grants, credits or in kind, regardless of whether this is done by non-governmental organizations or as ***official development assistance***. *See also* ***capacity-building*** and ***trade-related technical assistance***.

Development Assistance Committee: DAC. A body established within the ***OECD*** as a forum for the consideration of bilateral and multilateral ***development assistance*** activities of member countries. *See also* ***capacity-building*** and ***official development assistance***.

Development box: additional flexibilities available for developing countries under Article 6.2 of the ***Agreement on Agriculture***. These include measures of assistance, direct or indirect, to encourage agricultural and rural development that are an integral part of development programmes of developing countries. Agricultural input subsidies generally available to low-income or resource-poor producers in developing countries, investment subsidies generally available and domestic support to producers to encourage diversification from growing illicit narcotic crops fit into this category.

Development Round: a name for the multilateral trade negotiations launched at Doha, Qatar, on 14 November 2001. The work programme for this round reflects the concerns of developing countries more than any previous round. *See also* ***developing countries and the multilateral trading system*** and ***Doha Development Agenda***.

Diagonal cumulation: permissible under the system of ***preferential rules of origin*** administered by the ***European Union***. The production of eligible goods must involve at least three partners. It is available to partner countries belonging to a network of ***free-trade agreements*** which have the same rules of origin and which allow this type of accumulation. *See also* ***pan-Euro-Mediterranean cumulation*** and ***pan-European cumulation system***. [ec.europa.eu]

Dialogue partners: these are countries that are not members of any given ***intergovernmental organization***, but that have more than ***observer status*** in its work. Dialogue partners often can attend the formal sessions of a meeting,

家的组成上存在很大差异。一些国家非常贫穷。其他国家则被认为十分富有。世界银行考虑到了这一点，而将其成员分为四个等级(低收入经济体、中等偏下收入经济体、中等偏上收入经济体和高收入经济体)。在 WTO 中，发展中国家地位是自称的。这导致了一些人认为的存在错位，因为一些国家在 WTO 中要求发展中国家地位而在经济合作与发展组织(OECD)中已经接受发达国家义务。WTO 正在就这一问题展开辩论。根据联合国经社理事会(ECOSOC)制定的标准，对最不发达国家有分类标准。另见*发展中国家与多边贸易体制(developing countries and the multilateral trading system)*、*毕业(graduation)*、*特殊和差别待遇(special and differential treatment)*。

Development agenda

发展议程

见*多哈发展议程(Doha Development Agenda)*。

Development assistance

发展援助

给予发展中国家的以贷款、赠款、信贷或实物为形式的援助，无论由非政府组织提供还是作为官方发展援助提供。另见*能力建设(capacity-building)*、*与贸易有关的技术援助(trade-related technical assistance)*。

Development Assistance Committee

发展援助委员会

DAC。经济合作与发展组织(OECD)中设立的机构，作为审议成员国双边和多边发展援助活动的场所。另见*能力建设(capacity-building)*、*官方发展援助(official development assistance)*。

Development box

发展箱

发展中国家根据《农业协定》第 6.2 条可以获得的额外灵活性。包括鼓励农业和农村发展援助措施，无论直接或间接，属发展中国家发展计划的组成部分；发展中国家中低收入或资源贫乏生产者可普遍获得的农业投入补贴；鼓励对以生产多样化为途径停止种植非法麻醉作物而向生产者提供国内支持。

Development Round

发展回合

2001 年 11 月 14 日在卡塔尔多哈启动的多边贸易谈判的名称。这一轮谈判的工作计划比以往任何一轮都更能反映发展中国家的关注。另见*发展中国家与多边贸易体制(developing countries and the multilateral trading system)*、*多哈发展议程(Doha Development Agenda)*。

Diagonal cumulation

对角累积

在欧盟管理的优惠原产地规则体制中所允许的做法。适格商品的生产必须涉及至少三个伙伴。属于适用相同原产地规则且允许此种累积的一自由贸易协定网络的伙伴国家可以使用此种方法。另见*泛欧—地中海累积(pan-Euro-Mediterranean cumulation)*、*泛欧累积制度(pan-European cumulation system)*。

Dialogue partners

对话伙伴

指不属任何指定政府间组织成员的国家，但在其工作中地位超过观察员地位。对话伙伴通常可以参加正式会议，并收到官方文件。通常是在会议接近结束

and they receive the official documents. They also have the opportunity, usually towards the end of the session, to have a separate meeting with the member states of the organization.

Dictum: *see* ***obiter dictum***.

Differential and More Favourable Treatment, Reciprocity and Fuller Participation of Developing Countries: *see* ***Enabling Clause***.

Differential export tax: the reverse of ***tariff escalation*** in the case of imports. Raw materials for export are taxed heavily, but processed materials made from the same raw material are taxed lightly. The purpose of this practice is to ensure that raw materials are processed before export.

Differential pricing: putting a price on a good or service that differs according to the market. In some cases this may contravene a country's ***competition laws***.

Diffuse reciprocity: *see* ***reciprocity at the margin***.

Digital divide: the gap between developed and developing countries in the use of, and access to, information and communications technology products and services.

Digital economy: describes the broad range of economic and social activities that are made possible by information and communications networks in the context of an economy generally. Its effects on global commerce are analysed in the *World Trade Report 2018*. *See also* ***G20 digital economy ministerial declaration***.

Digital Economy Report: an ***UNCTAD*** publication, previously known as the *Information Economy Report*, which analyses the implications of the rapid spread of digital technology from the perspective of developing countries. First published in 2019.

Digital Free Trade Zone: DFTZ. A Malaysian initiative, launched in November 2017, to enable Malaysian small and medium-sized enterprises to expand their exports globally through an e-commerce platform. [mydtfz.com]

Digitalization: the process of converting material or information into digital form. This was made possible by developments in the computer and telecommunications sector. The *World Trade Report 2018* contains a detailed analysis of this topic.

Digital product: a term frequently used in ***free-trade agreements*** concluded in recent years, particularly the more comprehensive ones. Some United States agreements define digital products as "computer programs, text, video, images, sound recordings and other products that are digitally encoded, regardless of whether they are fixed on a carrier medium or transmitted electronically". An example of a digital product would be a recorded piece of music which could be made available through a compact disc, a tape or through downloading from the Internet.

Digital Single Market: a set of initiatives issued in 2015 by the ***European Union*** to reduce regulatory barriers and assist the formation of the single market. The Digital Single Market has three pillars: (1) better access for consumers and businesses to digital goods and services across Europe, (2) creating the right conditions and a level playing field for digital networks and innovative services

时，还有机会与该组织成员国举行单独会见。

Dictum
附带判词
见*判决附带意见(obiter dictum)*。

Differential and More Favourable Treatment, Reciprocity and Fuller Participation of Developing Countries
发展中国家差别和更优惠待遇、互惠和更充分参与
见*授权条款(Enabling Clause)*。

Differential export tax
差别出口税
将进口方面的关税升级反向实施。供出口的原材料从高征税，但由相同原材料制成的加工产品则从低征税。这种做法的目的在于保证原材料在出口前得到加工。

Differential pricing
差别定价
根据市场对货物或服务制定不同价格。在一些情况下，这可能会违反一国的竞争法。

Diffuse reciprocity
分散互惠
见*边际互惠(reciprocity at the margin)*。

Digital divide
数字鸿沟
发达国家和发展中国家在使用和获取信息和通信技术产品及服务方面的差距。

Digital economy
数字经济
描述了在总体经济背景下，通过信息和通信网络实现的广泛的经济和社会活动。《世界贸易报告 2018》分析了数字经济对全球商业的影响。另见 *20 国集团数字经济部长宣言(G20 digital economy ministerial declaration)*。

Digital Economy Report
数字经济报告
联合国贸易与发展会议(UNCTAD)出版物，以前称为《信息经济报告》。该报告从发展中国家的角度分析了数字技术迅速传播的影响。首次发布于2019年。

Digital Free Trade Zone
数字自由贸易区
DFTZ。马来西亚于 2017 年 11 月启动的一项倡议，旨在使马来西亚中小企业能够通过电子商务平台在全球范围内扩大出口。

Digitalization
数字化
将材料或信息转换成数字形式的过程。计算机和电信部门的发展使之成为可能。《世界贸易报告 2018》包含了对该主题的详细分析。

Digital product
数字产品
在近年来缔结的自由贸易协定中经常使用的一个词语，特别是更全面的协定。一些美国缔结的协定将数字产品定义为“计算机程序、文本、视频、图像、声音记录及其他数字编码产品，无论这些产品是固定在载体介质上还是以电子方式传输”。数字产品的例子之一是可通过光盘、磁带或通过互联网下载而获得的音乐录音。

Digital Single Market
数字单一市场
欧盟在 2015 年发布的一系列倡议，以减少监管障碍，促进单一市场的形成。

to flourish, and (3) maximizing the growth potential of the digital economy. [ec.europa.eu]

Digital trade: in many ways quite similar to ***electronic commerce***. It involves the use of the Internet to conduct business electronically to the maximum extent and the promotion wherever possible of paperless trading. This applies also to the requirement of documents in the pursuit of international trade. Critical aspects of digital trade are electronic authentication and electronic signatures, online consumer protection and the protection of personal information. See the *World Trade Report 2018* for a detailed analysis of the emergence of digital trade; *see also* ***Digital Economy Report***, ***G20 priorities on digital trade*** and ***moratorium on customs duties on electronic transmissions***.

Digits, digit-level (tariffs): a reference to the codes used to identify products. Categories of products are subdivided by adding digits. *See* ***Harmonized Commodity Description and Coding System***.

Dillon Round: the fifth round of ***multilateral trade negotiations***, held in Geneva from 1960–61. It was named after Douglas C. Dillon, the then United States Under-Secretary of State. Much of the Dillon Round was concerned with tariff renegotiations resulting from the establishment of the ***European Economic Community*** and its ***common external tariff***, but more general tariff negotiations were conducted also. Despite the use of the term "round", it really was the last of the old-style tariff negotiating conferences. Its results were modest. About 4,400 tariff ***concessions*** were exchanged, compared to about 45,000 during the ***Geneva Tariff Conference, 1947***.

Dilution doctrine: an aspect of the law concerning ***trademarks***. It gives owners of ***famous marks*** protection against the use of the mark in a way that makes it unlikely that confusion occurs. For example, if someone were to use the name of an expensive car to describe cheap running shoes, few consumers would be misled to think that by buying the shoes they were buying something produced by or associated with the car factory. The owner of the car brand might, however, consider that using the mark in this way would be taking away something the reputation the brand has in the market. In other words, the owner might feel that the use of the brand in this way would dilute the reputation of the mark. Nevertheless, allowing the use of a famous mark for apparently unrelated purposes may be part of a sales strategy by the owners of the mark. Dilution is different to ***passing off***, where there is a clear intention to deceive the buyers that they are buying the genuine product.

Diplomatic protection: protection of an investment in a foreign country through the diplomatic mission of the investor's home country located in that country.

Direction of trade: a term describing the set of a country's trading partners, and how important its trade with single or groups of countries is. The principal statistical work containing this information is the *IMF Direction of Trade Statistics Yearbook*, published annually.

Directive: an official ***European Union*** act which is binding on the member states to which it is addressed. Member states are then free to implement the directive

数字单一市场有三个支柱：(1)在欧洲范围内使消费者和企业更好获得数字产品和服务；(2)为数字网络和创新服务繁荣创造适宜条件和公平竞争环境；以及(3)最大限度发挥数字经济增长潜力。

Digital trade

数字贸易

在许多方面与电子商务十分相似。涉及最大限度地利用互联网以电子方式开展业务，并尽可能推行无纸贸易。还适用于在开展国际贸易中对单证的要求。数字贸易的关键方面是电子认证和电子签名、在线消费者保护和个人信息保护。关于数字贸易兴起的详细分析见《世界贸易报告 2018》；另见*数字经济报告(Digital Economy Report)*、*20 国集团数字贸易优先事项(G20 priorities on digital trade)*、*电子传输暂免关税(moratorium on customs duties on electronic transmissions)*。

Digits, digit-level (tariffs)

编码、编码位数(关税)

指用于识别产品的编码。通过增加编码对产品类别进行细分。另见*商品名称及编码协调制度(Harmonized Commodity Description and Coding System)*。

Dillon Round

狄龙回合

第 5 轮多边贸易谈判，1960 年至 1961 年在日内瓦举行。以时任美国副国务卿道格拉斯・狄龙命名。狄龙回合的大部分内容是关于欧洲经济共同体的建立及其共同对外关税所导致的关税重新谈判，但也进行了更为一般性的关税谈判。尽管使用了“回合”一词，但它实际上是最后一次老式关税谈判会议。谈判结果有限，大约交换了 4400 项关税减让，而在 1947 年日内瓦关税会议中则交换了约 45000 项关税减让。

Dilution doctrine

淡化理论

商标法的一个方面。保护著名商标所有权人减少在商标使用中出现混淆的可能性。例如，如有人使用豪车车名描述廉价跑鞋，很少有消费者会被误导认为买鞋是在购买汽车厂生产的或与之相关联的某种物品。然而，汽车品牌所有权人会认为商标的这种使用方法有损该品牌的市场声誉。换言之，所有权人会觉得按此使用品牌会淡化商标声誉。尽管如此，允许将著名商标用于明显不相关的目的可能是该商标所有权人销售策略的一部分。淡化与假冒商品不同，后者有欺骗购买者的明显意图，使其认为自己购买的产品是正品。

Diplomatic protection

外交保护

通过一投资者的母国驻外国的外交使团对该投资者在该外国的投资进行保护。

Direction of trade

贸易地理方向

描述一国的贸易伙伴及其与单个或一组国家开展贸易的重要性的词语。包含这一信息的主要统计工作是每年出版的《IMF 贸易地理方向统计年鉴》。

Directive

指令

对所涉成员国具有约束力的欧盟正式法案。成员国即有权按它们喜欢的方式

in their preferred manner, provided that they give complete effect to its content. *See also* ***European Union legislation***.

Directly competitive or substitutable product: a phrase used in Article III (National Treatment) of the GATT where, however, it is not further defined. In *Korea – Taxes on Alcoholic Beverages* the ***Appellate Body*** held that "products are competitive or substitutable when they are interchangeable, or if they offer, as the ***Panel*** [on the same case] noted 'alternative ways of satisfying a particular need or taste'". *See also* ***like product***. [WT/DS75/AB/R, WT/DS84/AB/R]

Directly competitive products: a term used in Article XIX of the GATT (Emergency Action on Imports of Particular Products) and the ***Agreement on Safeguards***. *See* ***like or directly competitive products***.

Direct payments: payments to agricultural producers that can fall under all boxes, depending whether they are independent or not on type of production, volume of production, prices and/or factors of production. *See also* ***decoupling***.

Dirty Dozen: a group of developed countries first established during the ***Uruguay Round*** when it had twelve members. It was apparently named after an American motion picture popular at the time. Its core participants included Australia, Canada, European Community, Iceland, Japan, Norway, New Zealand, Switzerland and the United States.

Dirty quotification: excessive discretion used in setting and administering ***tariff rate quotas*** for trade in agricultural products.

Dirty tariffication: *see* ***water in the tariff***.

Discretionary/mandatory distinction: *see* ***GATT-consistency of national legislation***.

Discrimination: making a distinction between trading partners and treating some of them differently. Examples of allowable discrimination are according tariff-free entry to a ***free-trade agreement*** partner and giving preferential tariff treatment to a developing country under a ***GSP*** scheme. *See also* ***arbitrary or unjustifiable discrimination*** and ***non-discrimination***.

Disguised restriction on international trade: several of the agreements administered by the WTO require members to ensure that certain measures taken under them are not in fact "disguised restrictions on international trade". Among these are Article XX of the GATT (General Exceptions), Article VII (Recognition) and Article XIV of the ***General Agreement on Trade in Services***, Article 3 (National Treatment) of the ***Agreement on Trade-Related Aspects of Intellectual Property Rights*** and Article 3 (Assessment of Risk and Determination of the Appropriate Level of Sanitary and Phytosanitary Protection) of the ***Agreement on the Application of Sanitary and Phytosanitary Measures***. The phrase has no clear definition. In *European Communities – Measures Affecting Asbestos and Asbestos-Containing Products* the ***panel*** noted that the key to understanding this phrase lay not so much in the word "restriction" as in the word "disguised". One can therefore assume that a "disguised restriction on international trade" is a measure that has been framed, sometimes inadvertently

执行指令，只要它们全面实施指令内容。另见*欧洲联盟立法(European Union legislation)*。

Directly competitive or substitutable product
直接竞争产品或可替代产品

GATT 第 3 条(国民待遇)中使用的词语，但该条对此并无进一步定义。在“韩国-酒税案”中，上诉机构认为，“如产品可通用，则具有竞争性或可替代性，或如按专家组[同一案件]所述，这些产品可提供‘满足一特定需求或口味的替代方式’”。另见*同类产品(like product)*。

Directly competitive products
直接竞争产品

GATT 第 19 条(针对特定产品进口的紧急措施)和《保障措施协定》中使用的词语。另见*同类产品或直接竞争产品(like or directly competitive products)*。

Direct payments
直接支付

对农业生产者的支持，可归入各箱，取决于农业生产者是否与生产类型、产量、价格和/或生产要素挂钩。另见*不挂钩(decoupling)*。

Dirty Dozen
12国集团

最初于乌拉圭回合中成立的发达国家集团，当时有12个成员。该集团显然得名于当时流行的一部美国电影(电影中译名为“十二金刚”—译注)。核心参加方包括澳大利亚、加拿大、欧共体、冰岛、日本、挪威、新西兰、瑞士和美国。

Dirty quotification
肮脏的配额化

在设定和管理农产品贸易关税配额时过度使用自由裁量权。

Dirty tariffication
肮脏的关税化

见*关税水分(water in the tariff)*。

Discretionary/mandatory distinction
酌情/强制性区分

见*国家立法与 GATT 一致性(GATT-consistency of national legislation)*。

Discrimination
歧视

对贸易伙伴作出区分并区别对待部分贸易伙伴。允许实行的歧视，例如给予自由贸易协定伙伴零关税待遇，根据普惠制(GSP)方案给予一发展中国家优惠关税待遇。另见*任意或不合理的歧视(arbitrary or unjustifiable discrimination)*、*非歧视(non-discrimination)*。

Disguised restriction on international trade
对国际贸易的变相限制

WTO 所管理的多个协定要求成员保证根据协定采取的某些措施不得事实上构成“对国际贸易的变相限制”。包括 GATT 第 20 条(一般例外)、《服务贸易总协定》第 7 条(承认)和第 14 条(一般例外)、《与贸易有关的知识产权协定》第 3 条(国民待遇)以及《实施卫生与植物卫生措施协定》第 5 条(风险评估和适当的卫生和植物卫生保护水平的确定)(英文误为第 3 条—译注)。该词无明确定义。专家组在“欧洲共同体-影响石棉和含石棉产品措施案”中指出，理解该词的关键不在“限制”，而在“变相”。因此，可以认为“对国际贸易的变相限制”，有

and sometimes intentionally, to serve one purpose (e.g. promotion of public health), but which in fact has a protectionist aim or effect. Whether the measure has been announced publicly or whether it is, on the surface at any rate, not related to trade, is in the opinion of the panel of no great moment. What matters is whether the measure has a trade effect. [WT/DS135/R]

Disguised trade barriers: measures taken by governments ostensibly to achieve a goal unrelated to trade, but which can have a direct impact on imports. Among the measures sometimes so used are consumer protection laws, product standards and quarantine rules. *See also* ***sanitary and phytosanitary measures***, ***shelf-life restrictions*** and ***technical barriers to trade***.

Dispersed tariff rates: a ***tariff schedule*** in which there is a wide discrepancy between low rates and high rates. Also, relatively few concentrations of similar tariff rates appear in such a schedule. *See also* ***flat-tariff structure*** and ***peak tariffs***.

Dispute settlement: resolution of conflict arising between governments over the interpretation of trade or other rules, often through a compromise between opposing claims, sometimes through an intermediary. Dispute settlement can acquire a strongly adversarial or rules-based. Dispute settlement in the WTO usually starts after ***consultation*** has failed. The basic rules for consultation and dispute resolution are set out in Articles XXII and XXIII of the ***GATT*** for goods, Articles XXII and XXIII of the ***General Agreement on Trade in Services*** for services and Article 64 of the ***Agreement on Trade-Related Aspects of Intellectual Property Rights*** for intellectual property. The detailed rules to be followed in all cases are those contained in the ***Dispute Settlement Understanding***. *See also* ***Appellate Body***, ***Dispute Settlement Body*** and ***request for consultations***.

Dispute Settlement Body: DSB. The WTO ***General Council***, when it convenes to settle disputes arising between members. The DSB has the sole authority to establish ***panels***, adopt panel and appellate reports, maintain surveillance of implementation of rulings and recommendations, and authorize ***retaliation*** in cases where its recommendations are ignored. The WTO secretariat says that a case should normally take about one year to complete, and fifteen months if it goes to the ***Appellate Body***. *See also* ***dispute settlement*** and ***Dispute Settlement Understanding***.

Dispute Settlement Mechanism: *see* ***dispute settlement***, ***Dispute Settlement Body*** and ***Dispute Settlement Understanding***.

Dispute Settlement Panel: *see* ***panel*** and ***Dispute Settlement Understanding***.

Dispute Settlement Understanding: DSU. Formally the WTO *Understanding on Rules and Procedures Governing the Settlement of Disputes*. This is one of the ***Uruguay Round*** outcomes. Its underlying theme is that prompt settlement of disputes is essential for the proper functioning of the WTO. The understanding therefore sets out in some detail the procedures and timetable to be followed in resolving disputes. There is little scope for delaying tactics. The first stage in the resolution of a dispute consists of ***consultation*** between the parties who may call on the WTO Director-General to mediate. If consultation is unsuccessful, the formation of a ***panel*** is almost automatic. If the parties disagree with the panel's findings, they may appeal to the ***Appellate Body***, but the grounds for such appeals must be confined to legal issues. *See also* ***request for consultations***.

时无意而有时故意，是为服务于某种目的(例如促进公共健康)而制定的措施，但事实上具有保护主义目的或效果。该措施是否已经公开宣布或是否表面上在多大程度上与贸易无关，在专家组看来并不重要，重要的是措施是否对贸易产生影响。

Disguised trade barriers
变相贸易壁垒

政府所采取的表面上为实现与贸易无关的目标而可对进口产生直接影响的措施。以此方式使用的措施中包括消费者保护法、产品标准和检疫规定。另见*卫生与植物卫生措施(sanitary and phytosanitary measures)*、*保质期限制(shelf-life restrictions)*、*技术性贸易壁垒(technical barriers to trade)*。

Dispersed tariff rates
分散型税率

低税率与高税率之间存在较大差异的关税税则。同样，在此种关税税则中，相似税率的集中度相对较小。另见*单一关税结构(flat-tariff structure)*、*关税高峰(peak tariffs)*。

Dispute settlement
争端解决

解决政府之间因贸易或其他规则的解释而产生的冲突，通常是在对立主张之间达成妥协，有时会通过中间方实现。争端解决具有强烈对抗性或以规则为基础。WTO 中的争端解决通常在磋商失败后开始。磋商和争端解决的基本规则为 GATT 第 22 条和第 23 条(对于货物贸易争端)、《服务贸易总协定》第 22 条和第 23 条(对于服务贸易争端)以及《与贸易有关的知识产权协定》第 64 条(对于知识产权争端)。所有案件应遵循的详细规则包含在《争端解决谅解》中。另见*上诉机构(Appellate Body)*、*争端解决机构(Dispute Settlement Body)*、*磋商请求(request for consultations)*。

Dispute Settlement Body
争端解决机构

DSB。即为解决成员争端而召开会议的 WTO 总理事会。DSB 具有设立专家组、通过专家组和上诉机构报告、监督裁决和建议执行以及在其建议被忽视情况下授权报复的惟一权力。WTO 秘书处表示，一案件通常应在 1 年内完成，如提交上诉机构，则应在 15 个月内完成。见*争端解决(dispute settlement)*、*争端解决谅解(Dispute Settlement Understanding)*。

Dispute Settlement Mechanism
争端解决机制

见*争端解决(dispute settlement)*、*争端解决机构(Dispute Settlement Body)*、*争端解决谅解(Dispute Settlement Understanding)*。

Dispute Settlement Panel
争端解决专家组

见*专家组(panel)*、*争端解决谅解(Dispute Settlement Understanding)*。

Dispute Settlement Understanding
争端解决谅解

DSU。正式名称为 WTO《关于争端解决规则与程序的谅解》，为乌拉圭回合成果。基本思想为迅速解决争端对 WTO 正常运作极为重要。因此，谅解详细规定了解决争端应遵循的程序和时间表，几乎没有使用拖延战术的余地。争端解决第一阶段为争端各方之间的磋商，争端各方可以要求 WTO 总干事进行调停。如磋商不成功，基本上将自动组成专家组。争端各方如不同意专家组的裁决，可向上诉机构提起上诉，但上诉理由必须仅限法律问题。另见*磋商请求(request for consultations)*。

Distortion: a measure, policy or practice that shifts the market price of a product above or below what it would be if the product were traded in a competitive market. Measures causing distortions include ***subsidies***, ***import restrictions*** and ***restrictive business practices***.

Distribution foreign direct investment: this refers to ***foreign direct investment*** by a firm with the aim of finding outlets for its products. This happens, for example, when an oil company invests in a chain of service stations.

Diversionary dumping: the export of a product at dumped prices to an intermediate country from where it is exported to its true destination. The purpose of diversionary dumping may be to take advantage of the pricing structure of the intermediate country to avert ***anti-dumping measures***. *See also* **circumvention** and ***dumping***.

Docking and merging: possible mechanisms for combining existing ***free-trade areas*** which would avoid the problems of ***hubs and spokes***. The rapid increase in the number of free-trade areas raises the question whether at some stage it might be feasible or desirable to combine some of them to reduce the complexity of the trade landscape. Docking is seen as a way for a small free-trade area to join a bigger one. Many of the necessary textual adjustments probably would fall on the smaller partner. It is possible that the name of the resulting free-trade area would be the one of the bigger partner. In other words, docking would be similar to an ***accession***. A merger would apply where two free-trade areas are roughly equivalent in size. The two existing free-trade areas would lose their individual existence and create a new one. Regardless of the method chosen, some intensive negotiations might be necessary to achieve the aim of unification. So far, however, the preference has been to negotiate free-trade agreements from scratch with ever more members and ever greater inclusion of subject matter. *See also* ***multilateralization of free-trade agreements***.

Doctrine of Dilution: *see* ***dilution doctrine***.

Doctrine of reasonable expectations: the assumption that once countries have made commitments or pursued practices under their international trade regimes, these commitments will be honoured for the foreseeable future. An example frequently quoted to illustrate this doctrine is ***Australian subsidy on ammonium sulphate*** where a ***GATT*** working party found that Australia had not acted illegally in removing a subsidy on sodium nitrate imported from Chile while maintaining it on ammonium sulphate. However, in the view of the working party, Chile could have reasonably assumed that the subsidy would be maintained on both products as long as there was a domestic shortage of them in Australia. *See also* ***non-violation***.

Doha Development Agenda: DDA. The round of WTO ***multilateral trade negotiations*** launched on 14 November 2001 at the ***Doha Ministerial Conference.*** The Doha Ministerial Declaration contains prominent development objectives. Finding common ground on the framework for negotiations proved quite challenging from the start but, in any set of talks this broad and complex, arriving at a common understanding of the path forward inevitably takes time to develop. The following concentrates on progress as marked by successive ***WTO Ministerial Conferences***.

Distortion

扭曲

使一产品的市场价格高于或低于在竞争性市场中的交易价格的措施、政策或做法。造成扭曲的措施包括补贴、进口限制和限制性商业惯例。

Distribution foreign direct investment

分销型外国直接投资

指企业为其产品寻找经销店而进行的外国直接投资。例如，一石油公司投资连锁加油站即为此种情况。

Diversionary dumping

转移性倾销

将一产品以倾销价格出口至一中间国，再自该国出口至其真正目的地。转移性倾销的目的可能为利用中间国的定价结构以规避反倾销措施。另见*规避(circumvention)*、*倾销(dumping)*。

Docking and merging

接驳与合并

合并现有自由贸易区的可能机制，从而避免轮轴-辐条问题。自由贸易区数量迅速增加引发如下疑问，即在某阶段将其中一些合并以减少贸易格局的复杂性是否可行或可取。接驳是小型自由贸易区加入大型自由贸易区的一种方式，较小参加方可能需要进行许多必要的文本调整，且合并后形成的自由贸易区的名称可能使用较大参加方的自由贸易区的名称。换言之，接驳类似加入。合并适用于两个自由贸易区规模大致相当的情况，现有的两个自由贸易区将不复存在而创立一个新的自由贸易区。无论选择哪种方法，都需要进行一些密集谈判，以实现统一目标。然而迄今为止，人们更倾向于从零起步谈判自由贸易协定，接纳更多成员，并纳入更多议题。另见*自由贸易协定多边化(multilateralization of free-trade agreements)*。

Doctrine of Dilution

淡化理论

见*淡化理论(dilution doctrine)*。

Doctrine of reasonable expectations

合理预期学说

关于一旦一国在其国际贸易制度下已经作出承诺或开展实践，这些承诺在可预见的未来将得到履行的假说。"澳大利亚对硫酸铵补贴案"常被引用以说明这一学说，GATT工作组认为，澳大利亚取消对自智利进口的硝酸钠的补贴，同时保留对硫酸铵的补贴，这种做法并不违法。但工作组认为，智利可以合理地认为，只要澳大利亚国内出现这两种产品的短缺，对这两种产品的补贴就会保留。另见*非违反(non-violation)*。

Doha Development Agenda

多哈发展议程

DDA。WTO 新一轮多边贸易谈判于 2001 年 11 月 14 日在多哈部长级会议上启动。《多哈部长宣言》包含突出的发展目标。在谈判框架方面找到共同点从一开始即被证明具有很大挑战性，对于任何一系列如此广泛而复杂的谈判，就前进道路达成共识不可避免地需要花费时间。以下主要介绍历届 WTO 部

Each Ministerial Conference was preceded by long hours of negotiations across a range of formats that commence almost as soon as the previous conference has concluded. A mid-term review in Cancun in 2003 proved to be inconclusive. However, the WTO ***General Council*** meeting on 1 August 2004 adopted several framework decisions which appeared to give impetus to the negotiations. The Hong Kong Ministerial Conference in 2005 made further progress in some areas, and things appeared to be under way, albeit at a slow pace, until a series of events, notably the financial crisis, brought the Doha Round to a grinding halt. The Geneva ministerial gathering of July 2008 (the mini-ministerial) represented a further determined effort to make progress particularly in the agriculture and non-agricultural market access (NAMA) negotiations. The forty or so ministers attending the meeting made progress on many aspects of the DDA, but they were unable to prevent deadlock on the proposed special safeguard mechanism and the scope of "sectoral" negotiations aimed at achieving greater tariff reductions for specific industrial products. The Bali Ministerial Conference of 2014 set the WTO on a more productive negotiating course. A highlight of the meeting was the provisional adoption of the ***Agreement on Trade Facilitation***, subject to a legal review of the text. In 2017 the TFA entered into force. The 2015 Ministerial Conference in Nairobi turned out to be a high point with several agreements struck. In the Nairobi Package ministers agreed, *inter alia*, that developed countries would immediately end their remaining scheduled export subsidies in agriculture, and developing countries would do so by 2018. A range of other decisions of interest to developing countries was also adopted, including a start to negotiations of a special safeguard mechanism for developing countries and ***preferential rules of origin for least-developed countries***. Ministers from 53 WTO members also agreed to eliminate duties on 201 information technology products with an export value of USD 1.3 trillion. The Buenos Aires Ministerial Conference in December 2017 again was unable to make progress in many areas of the negotiations, but it adopted a work programme on ***fisheries subsidies*** with a view to concluding negotiations at the 2020 Ministerial Conference. It also extended the ***moratorium on customs duties on electronic transmissions*** as well as the ***moratorium on non-violation cases in intellectual property rights*** until then. Three ***joint initiatives*** were also adopted at the Buenos Aires conference. Seventy-one members announced that they would start exploratory work towards future WTO negotiations on trade-related aspects of electronic commerce. Seventy members announced plans to pursue structured discussions aimed at developing a multilateral framework for ***investment facilitation***. Eighty-seven members declared their intention to create, multilaterally, an Informal Working Group on MSMEs (micro, small and medium-sized enterprises) to address obstacles to foreign trade faced by such enterprises. Two other declarations were announced in Buenos Aires, one on domestic regulation in services and another on women's economic empowerment. Domestic regulation in services has subsequently come to be considered a joint initiative and proponents have made significant progress towards agreement.

Doha Development Agenda Global Trust Fund: a fund established in March 2002 by WTO members to provide technical assistance to developing countries

长级会议所取得的进展。每一届部长级会议之前都要进行长时间谈判，谈判有多种形式，几乎在上届会议结束后即开始。2003 年在坎昆举行的中期审议被证明无果。然而，2004 年 8 月 1 日的 WTO 总理事会会议通过了若干框架决定，似为谈判提供了动力。2005 年香港部长级会议在一些领域取得了进一步进展，尽管进展缓慢，但仍似在进行中，直到一系列事件发生，最引人瞩目的是金融危机，使多哈回合戛然而止。2008 年 7 月在日内瓦举行的部长级会议(小型部长级会议)是各方为取得进展所作的进一步艰难尝试，特别是在农业和非农产品市场准入谈判方面。出席会议的 40 多位部长在多哈发展议程的许多方面取得进展，但未能避免在拟议的特殊保障机制和部门减让谈判上出现僵局，后者旨在实现特定工业品的更大幅度关税削减。2013 年巴厘岛部长级会议使 WTO 走上更富有成效的谈判之路(英文误为 2014 年—译注)。会议的一个亮点是临时通过《贸易便利化协定》，文本有待法律审核。《贸易便利化协定》后于 2017 年生效。2015 年在内罗毕举行的部长级会议是一个高潮，达成多项协议。在内罗毕一揽子谈判结果中，部长们同意发达国家立即终止它们减让表中剩余的农产品出口补贴，发展中国家在 2018 年取消。还通过一系列有利于发展中国家的其他决定，包括开始谈判发展中国家特殊保障机制和最不发达国家优惠原产地规则。来自 53 个 WTO 成员的部长们还同意取消 201 种信息技术产品的关税，这些产品的出口额达 1.3 万亿美元。2017 年 12 月的布宜诺斯艾利斯部长级会议再度未能在许多谈判领域取得进展，但通过了渔业补贴工作计划，以期在 2020 年部长级会议上结束谈判。会议还延长了电子传输暂免关税以及知识产权非违反案件暂停起诉。布宜诺斯艾利斯会议还通过三项联合倡议。71 个成员宣布，将就未来 WTO 与贸易有关的电子商务谈判开展探索性工作。70 个成员国宣布开展系统谈判的计划，旨在制定投资便利化多边框架。87 个成员宣布计划设立多边中小微型企业(微型、小型和中型企业)非正式工作组，以处理此类企业在对外贸易方面所面临的障碍。在布宜诺斯艾利斯还宣布了两项声明：一项关于服务贸易国内规制，另一项是关于妇女经济赋权。服务贸易国内规制随后被视为一项联合倡议，支持者在达成协议方面取得重大进展。

Doha Development Agenda Global Trust Fund
多哈发展议程全球信托基金

WTO 成员于 2002 年 3 月设立的向发展中国家提供技术援助的基金，以协助其进行能力建设努力。另见*针对最不发达国家的与贸易有关的技术援助综合*

and to assist them with capacity-building efforts. *See also* ***Integrated Framework for Trade-Related Assistance to Least-Developed Countries***.

Doha Ministerial Conference: the ***WTO Ministerial Conference*** held in Doha, Qatar, from 9 to 13 November 2001. It resulted in the Doha Ministerial Declaration, adopted on 14 November, which launched the first round of multilateral trade negotiations under the auspices of the WTO. This is now known as the ***Doha Development Agenda***. Main areas for negotiations are ***implementation*** issues, agriculture, services, market access for non-agricultural products, WTO rules on anti-dumping and subsidies, and the creation of a multilateral system of ***geographical indications***. The mandate also entailed exploratory work on ***trade and investment***, trade and competition policy, ***transparency*** in ***government procurement***, ***trade facilitation*** and ***trade and environment***, especially the relationship between existing WTO rules and specific trade obligations set out in ***multilateral environment agreements***. Trade facilitation became part of the negotiations in 2004 through the ***July 2004 package***. Other subjects listed for examination or review and possible future negotiations are electronic commerce, small economies, trade, debt and finance, trade and transfer of technology, technical cooperation and ***capacity-building***, ***least-developed countries*** and ***special and differential treatment***. The Doha conference also issued a ***Declaration on Implementation-Related Issues and Concerns*** and a ***Declaration on the TRIPS Agreement and Public Health***.

Doha Ministerial Declaration: *see* ***Doha Ministerial Conference***.

Doha Round: an unofficial name for the multilateral trade negotiations launched at Doha, Qatar, on 14 November 2001. *See* ***Doha Development Agenda*** and ***Doha Ministerial Conference***.

Domestically prohibited goods: *see* ***export of domestically prohibited goods***.

Domestic content requirements: *see* ***local content requirements***.

Domestic exports: goods for export that are wholly or mainly of domestic origin, either because they have been grown or manufactured there, or because that is where they have undergone ***substantial transformation***. *See also* ***re-exports***.

Domestic international sales corporation: a corporate structure used in the United States until 1984, generally known as DISC. The principal benefit conferred by it was permission to defer payment of federal taxes on income from export profits until these had been distributed to their shareholders. DISCs covered mainly goods trade. In services, they were more or less confined to activities related to construction. In 1973, the ***European Economic Community*** notified the GATT of a dispute over the alleged subsidies DISCs enjoyed in steel exports. The ***panel*** found against the United States which then launched a retaliatory action on certain types of tax treatment available in the European Economic Community. The dispute was finally settled in 1982. In 1984, the DISC legislation was replaced by the ***Foreign Sales Corporation*** (FSC) programme, thought to be more in keeping with the GATT rules. A WTO panel later found that some aspects of it too were against the WTO rules.

框架(Integrated Framework for Trade-Related Assistance to Least-Developed Countries)。

Doha Ministerial Conference

多哈部长级会议

WTO部长级会议，2001年11月9日至13日在卡塔尔多哈举行。会议于11月14日通过《多哈部长宣言》，启动WTO主持下的首轮多边贸易谈判。现在称为多哈发展议程。谈判主要领域包括实施问题、农业、服务、非农产品市场准入、WTO关于反倾销和补贴的规则以及建立地理标志多边制度。谈判授权还包含贸易与投资、贸易与竞争政策、政府采购透明度、贸易便利化以及贸易与环境方面的探索性工作，特别是现行WTO规则与多边环境协定中规定的具体贸易义务之间的关系。根据2004年7月工作计划，贸易便利化在2004年被纳入谈判。列入审查或审议范围及今后可能谈判的其他议题包括电子商务、小经济体、贸易、债务与金融、贸易与技术转让、技术合作与能力建设、最不发达国家以及特殊和差别待遇。多哈会议还发表了《关于与实施有关的问题和关注的宣言》和《关于<与贸易有关的知识产权协定>与公共健康的宣言》。

Doha Ministerial Declaration

多哈部长宣言

见*多哈部长级会议(Doha Ministerial Conference)*。

Doha Round

多哈回合

2001年11月14日在卡塔尔多哈启动的多边贸易谈判的非正式名称。另见*多哈发展议程(Doha Development Agenda)*、*多哈部长级会议(Doha Ministerial Conference)*。

Domestically prohibited goods

国内禁止货物

见*国内禁止货物的出口(export of domestically prohibited goods)*。

Domestic content requirements

国内含量要求

见*当地含量要求(local content requirements)*。

Domestic exports

本国原产货物出口

供出口的货物全部或主要为本国原产，因其在本国种植或制造，或因其在本国经过实质性改变。另见*复出口(re-exports)*。

Domestic international sales corporation

本国国际销售公司

1984年前在美国使用的一种公司结构，一般称为DISC。该结构所带来的主要好处是，允许公司在将出口利润收入分配给股东之前推迟缴纳联邦税。DISC主要从事货物贸易。在服务方面，此类公司或多或少限于与建筑相关的活动。1973年，欧洲经济共同体通报GATT以DISC在钢铁出口中享受补贴为由发起争端。专家组裁决结果对美国不利，美国随即对欧共体内提供的某些类型的税收待遇采取报复行动。该争端最终于1982年解决。1984年，DISC立法被外国销售公司(FSC)计划取代，后者被认为更符合GATT规则。后来，WTO专家组判定，外国销售公司计划某些方面也违反WTO规则。

Domestic regulation: Article VI of the ***General Agreement on Trade in Services*** requires that, in areas where ***specific commitments*** are undertaken, members shall ensure that all measures of general application affecting trade in services are administered in a reasonable, objective and impartial manner. It also has a broad provision requiring that an applicant who has applied to provide a service should be informed within a reasonable period of the decision concerning the application. In sectors where members have undertaken specific commitments, they should not apply licensing and qualification requirements and technical standards that would nullify such commitments. Article VI.4 requires the ***Council for Trade in Services*** to develop necessary disciplines to ensure that measures relating to qualification requirements and procedures, technical standards and licensing requirements do not constitute unnecessary barriers to trade in services. The disciplines so developed should be based, *inter alia*, (a) on objective and transparent criteria, such as competence and the ability to supply the service, (b) be not more burdensome than necessary to ensure the quality of the service, and (c) in the case of licensing procedures, not in themselves a restriction on the supply of the service. To this end, a Working Party on Domestic Regulation was established in 1999 with a mandate to develop generally applicable disciplines meeting the requirements of Article VI.4. It may also develop disciplines as appropriate for individual sectors or groups thereof. This work is continuing. *See also* ***APEC Non-Binding Principles for Domestic Regulation of the Services Sector***.

Domestic support: another term for ***assistance***, ***internal support*** or ***subsidy***. In agriculture, any domestic subsidy or other measure designed to support agricultural producers. It includes market price support, but also refers to ***direct payments*** to producers, including ***deficiency payments***, and input and marketing cost reduction measures available only for agricultural production. Domestic support is one of the three pillars of the Agreement on Agriculture along with ***market access*** and ***export competition***. *See also* ***Agreement on Agriculture***, ***Agreement on Subsidies and Countervailing Measures*** and three pillars of agriculture.

Dominant supplier provision: a provision in the United States *Trade Expansion Act* of 1962 which permitted a reduction to zero in the tariff of any category of products in which the United States and the ***European Economic Community*** together had 80 per cent or more of the global market. *See also* ***zero-for-zero tariff reductions***.

Domino theory of regionalism: proposed by Richard Baldwin. He said that the growing interest in the early 1990s in a United States–Mexico ***free-trade agreement*** and the ***European Community***'s Single Market was not due to dissatisfaction with the slow progress in the ***Uruguay Round*** as some claimed. Rather, in his view, it was due to fears by countries outside these arrangements that they would be disadvantaged once the arrangements were in force. These fears would then prompt them to seek membership also. Baldwin says that in any country the political equilibrium determines the country's stance on regional liberalization. If enough exporters feel they are threatened by an emerging free-trade arrangement,

Domestic regulation

国内规制

《服务贸易总协定》第6条规定，在已作出具体承诺的部门中，成员应保证所有影响服务贸易的普遍适用的措施以合理、客观和公正的方式实施。其中还包含一项总的规定，要求在一合理时间内告知申请提供服务的申请人有关申请的决定。在成员已作出具体承诺的部门，不得实施使此类具体承诺失效的许可要求、资格要求和技术标准。第6.4条要求服务贸易理事会制定必要的纪律，以保证与资格要求和程序、技术标准和许可证要求相关的措施不对服务贸易构成不必要的壁垒。制定的此类纪律应特别根据(a)客观的和透明的标准，例如提供服务的资格和能力；(b)不得比保证服务质量所必需的限度更难以负担；以及(c)如为许可程序，则这些程序本身不成为对服务提供的限制。为此，国内规制工作组于1999年设立，任务为制定符合第6.4条要求的普遍适用的纪律。还可制定适合于单个部门或一组部门的纪律。此项工作正在进行中。另见*APEC服务业国内规制非约束性原则(APEC Non-Binding Principles for Domestic Regulation of the Services Sector)*。

Domestic support

国内支持

援助、内部支持或补贴的另一种称谓，即农业领域旨在支持农业生产者的任何国内补贴或其他措施。包括市场价格支持，也可指提供给生产者的直接支付，包括差价补贴，以及仅适用于农业生产的投入和销售成本削减措施。国内支持与市场准入和出口竞争一起是《农业协定》的三大支柱。另见*农业协定(Agreement on Agriculture)*、*补贴与反补贴措施协定(Agreement on Subsidies and Countervailing Measures)*、*农业三大支柱(three pillars of agriculture)*。

Dominant supplier provision

占主导地位的供应商条款

美国《1962 年贸易扩展法》中的条款，允许将美国和欧洲经济共同体合并占全球市场 80%或 80%以上的任何类别产品的关税削减至零。另见*零对零关税削减(zero-for-zero tariff reductions)*。

Domino theory of regionalism

地区主义的多米诺骨牌理论

由理查德·鲍德温提出。他指出，在20世纪90年代初期人们对美国—墨西哥自由贸易协定和欧洲共同体单一市场日益增加的兴趣，并非如一些人所认为的是因对乌拉圭回合进展缓慢感到不满所引发。相反，在他看来，是因为这些安排之外的国家担心，一旦这些安排生效，它们将处于不利地位。这些恐惧促使它们也寻求加入。鲍德温认为，任何国家中的政治平衡度决定了其在地区自由化问题上的立场。如足够多的出口商感受到来自一个新出现的自由贸易

they can bring about a change in the country's policy towards that arrangement. The expanding membership of the arrangement so prompted would then induce yet others to seek membership also because they in turn might now be harmed or at least feel disadvantaged as non-members. [Baldwin 1993]

Donor countries: a term used to describe the countries maintaining a ***GSP*** scheme. *See also* ***beneficiary countries***.

Double écart **formula:** a formula for linear tariff negotiations proposed by the ***European Economic Community*** (EEC) during the ***Kennedy Round***. It was based on the identification of significant disparities in the tariff rates of the major participants, particularly the EEC, Japan, the United Kingdom and the United States. Under this formula, tariff rates would have been considered disparate if there was a ratio greater than 2:1 between the rates compared. It would only have applied if the difference was at least 10 percentage points *ad valorem*. *See also* ***ad valorem tariff***, ***écrêtement***, ***tariff negotiations*** and ***thirty:ten formula***.

Double pricing: the practice of ensuring that domestic processors and manufacturers can purchase raw materials at a lower price than they are sold in export markets. This aim may be achieved through ***export quotas***, ***export tariffs*** and other measures with a similar aim.

Double transformation: occurs when a good undergoes two ***substantial transformations*** in succession. Examples would be the transformation of bauxite into alumina, followed by the transformation of alumina into aluminium, or the spinning of raw fibres into yarn, followed by weaving yarn into a fabric. *See also* ***triple transformation***.

Double-zero reductions: the same as ***zero-for-zero tariff reductions***.

Downpayment: an initial conditional offer of tariff reductions, an undertaking to follow an agreed negotiating plan or another stratagem demonstrating a serious interest in the outcome of proposed negotiations. In ***APEC***, an initial instalment on the longer-term commitment to free and open trade and investment as shown in an ***APEC individual action plan***. This was agreed as part of the November 1995 ***Osaka Action Agenda***.

Downstream dumping: a name given to the practice of selling a component of a product at less than full cost to a home country producer. This producer then transforms the component or incorporates it in another product, thereby gaining a price advantage on export markets. *See also* ***anti-dumping measures*** and ***dumping***.

Downstream flexibility: a provision in the WTO ***Agreement on Agriculture*** which permitted WTO members to exceed their commitments on ***export subsidies*** in any of the second to fifth year of the ***implementation period*** provided, *inter alia*, that the excess in any year was no greater than 3 per cent of the annual outlay and that the cumulative outlay over the implementation period was no greater than under conditions with full compliance.

Dracula effect: explained by Jagdish Bhagwati as "exposing evil to sunlight helps to destroy it". *See also* ***notification***, ***surveillance*** and ***transparency***. [Bhagwati 1988]

安排的威胁，他们即可以针对这些安排而改变本国的政策。由此促成的这些安排成员数量的增加，随即引发其他国家寻求成员资格，因为这些国家也相应地担心可能受到损害或至少认为自已作为非成员国将处于不利地位。

Donor countries

捐助国

对设立普惠制(GSP)方案国家的称谓。另见*受益国(beneficiary countries)*。

***Double écart* formula**

双差公式

欧洲经济共同体(EEC)在肯尼迪回合中提出的线性关税谈判公式。公式基于对主要参加方在税率方面的显著差异而确定，特别是欧共体、日本、英国和美国。根据该公式，如相比较的税率之比大于2:1，则被认为差异大。该公式仅适用于差距为至少为从价10个百分点的情况。另见*从价关税(ad valorem tariff)*、*关税削平(écrêtement)*、*关税谈判(tariff negotiations)*、*30:10 公式(thirty:ten formula)*。

Double pricing

双重定价

保证国内加工者和制造商能够以低于在出口市场中销售价格的价格购买原材料的做法。该目标可通过出口配额、出口关税和具有类似目标的其他措施实现。

Double transformation

双重改变

发生在一货物连续两次进行实质性改变之后。例如，将铝土矿转化成氧化铝，然后从氧化铝转化成铝，又如将原纤维纺成纱线，然后将纱线编织成织物。另见*三重改变(triple transformation)*。

Double-zero reductions

双零削减

与零对零关税削减相同。

Downpayment

入门费

关税削减的最初有条件出价、按照议定谈判计划的承诺或对拟议谈判的结果表示极为感兴趣的一种谋略。在APEC中，指APEC单边行动计划中所表明的贸易投资自由开放长期承诺的最初履行。是1995年11月《大阪行动议程》的部分议定内容。

Downstream dumping

下游倾销

低于全部成本的价格向本国生产商出售产品部件的做法。生产商随后对部件进行改造或将其组装入另一产品中，从而在出口市场上获得价格优势。另见*反倾销措施(anti-dumping measures)*、*倾销(dumping)*。

Downstream flexibility

后期灵活性

WTO《农业协定》条款，允许 WTO 成员在实施期第 2 年至第 5 年的任何一年中超出其出口补贴承诺，条件是任何一年的超出水平不超过年度支出水平的3%且实施期内累计支出总和不超过完全符合承诺水平时的总和。

Dracula effect

吸血鬼效应

贾格迪什·巴格瓦蒂将其解释为“让邪恶暴露于阳光之下有助于消灭它”。另见*通报(notification)*、*监督(surveillance)*、*透明度(transparency)*。

Draft International Agreement on Illicit Payments: an instrument produced under ***ECOSOC*** auspices in 1979, but not adopted by the ***United Nations General Assembly***. It would have made punishable by criminal penalties under national laws (a) the bribing of any public official to influence his or her actions in connection with an international commercial transaction, and (b) asking for a bribe by any public official for the same purpose. The Agreement would have required each party to it to establish a system of appropriate criminal penalties. *See also* ***Convention on Combating Bribery of Foreign Public Officials in International Business Transactions***, ***trade and illicit payments*** and ***United Nations Convention Against Corruption***.

Draft International Antitrust Code: produced in 1993 by the International Antitrust Code Working Group, also called the Munich Group, consisting of twelve scholars. Four principles governed the approach of the Working Group: (a) national laws should be used to deal with international competition issues, (b) national treatment should be accorded to any party, (c) there should be recognized minimum standards for national antitrust rules, and (d) an International Antitrust Authority should be established. The Working Group also proposed that the Draft Code should be developed into a ***plurilateral agreement*** under the WTO. The Draft Code has not attracted sufficient international support for any kind of intergovernmental consideration. *See also* ***antitrust laws***, ***competition policy*** and ***trade and competition***. [Fikentscher and Immenga 1995]

Draft International Code of Conduct on the Transfer of Technology: an instrument under negotiation in ***UNCTAD*** between 1976 and 1985. The aim of the Draft Code is to establish general and equitable standards for the conduct of parties engaged in the ***transfer of technology***. Substantial differences remained when negotiations were suspended. There are no current plans to resume discussions. *See also* ***Working Group on Transfer of Technology***.

Draft United Nations Code of Conduct on Transnational Corporations: a proposed multilateral instrument aimed at guiding the behaviour of ***transnational corporations*** in countries other than their home country. Work on it began in the late 1970s. The latest version of the Draft Code is that of 1990. Much detailed drafting has been done, but substantial differences remain among negotiators, including the extent to which the Draft Code should be mandatory.

Drawback: the practice of refunding customs, sales and excise duties on goods imported and then re-exported either in processed form or after having been incorporated in other products. *See also* ***border tax adjustments***, ***duty deferral programme*** and ***maquiladora industries***.

Droit de suite*:** an inalienable right, expressed in Article 14ter of the ***Berne Convention, of the author of a work of fine art to a royalty on the resale of the work after its first sale by the author. It is an aspect of the rules governing ***copyright***. In the ***European Union***, for example, the resale right applies to sales involving market professionals such as art dealers, art galleries and showrooms.

Draft International Agreement on Illicit Payments
关于违法付款的国际协定草案

1979 年由联合国经社理事会(ECOSOC)主持制定的一份文件，但未获联合国大会通过。该文件拟规定下列行为应根据国内法进行刑事处罚：(a)行贿任何公职人员以影响其与国际商业交易有关的行为；及(b)任何公职人员为相同目的索取贿赂。该协定拟要求每一参加方建立适当的刑事处罚制度。另见*关于打击国际商业交易中行贿外国公职人员行为的公约(Combating Bribery of Foreign Public Officials in International Business Transactions)*、*贸易与违法付款(trade and illicit payments)*、*联合国反腐败公约(United Nations Convention Against Corruption)*。

Draft International Antitrust Code
国际反垄断法典草案

国际反垄断法典工作组于1993年制定。该工作组也称慕尼黑集团，由12名学者组成。工作组的工作方法遵循四项原则：(a)应使用国内法处理国际竞争问题；(b)应给予任何一方国民待遇；(c)应有公认的国家反垄断规则的最低标准；以及(d)应设立一个国际反垄断机构。工作组还建议将法典草案发展成为WTO框架下的一项诸边协定。法典草案并未获得成为任何形式的政府间审议议题所应该获得的足够国际支持。另见*反垄断法(antitrust laws)*、*竞争政策(competition policy)*、*贸易与竞争(trade and competition)*。

Draft International Code of Conduct on the Transfer of Technology
国际技术转让行动守则草案

1976 年至 1985 年在联合国贸易与发展会议(UNCTAD)谈判的一份文件，行动守则旨在为从事技术转让的各方制定普遍公平的标准。谈判中止之时实质分歧依然存在。目前无恢复谈判的计划。另见*技术转让工作组(Working Group on Transfer of Technology)*。

Draft United Nations Code of Conduct on Transnational Corporations
联合国跨国公司行为守则草案

拟议的一份多边文件，旨在指导跨国公司在其母国以外国家中的行为。有关工作始于 20 世纪 70 年代末。守则草案的最新版本为 1990 年版本。已完成很多细节的起草，但谈判方之间存在实质性分歧，包括守则草案在多大程度上应为强制性。

Drawback
退还

对进口后以加工形式或组装入其他产品的形式复出口的货物退还关税、销售税和消费税的做法。另见*边境税调节(border tax adjustments)*、*递延纳税计划(duty deferral programme)*、*保税加工出口产业(maquiladora industries)*。

Droit de suite
追续权

如《伯尔尼公约》第14条之三所述，艺术作品的作者享有从第一次转让作品之后对作品的任何出售中分享版税的不可剥夺的权利。这是版权规则的一个方面。例如，在欧盟，转售权适用于涉及艺术品经销商、美术馆和展厅等市场专业人员的销售。涵盖图形艺术或造型艺术，但不包括作者或作曲家的原稿。版

It covers works of graphic or plastic art, but not original manuscripts of writers or composers. The royalty is paid by the seller according to a fixed scale. Other jurisdictions also have laws concerning *droit de suite*. *See also* ***moral rights***.

DSB: the ***Dispute Settlement Body***, i.e. the WTO ***General Council*** meeting to settle trade disputes.

DSU: Dispute Settlement Understanding or the WTO agreement that covers dispute settlement between the parties. Formally the ***Understanding on Rules and Procedures Governing the Settlement of Disputes***.

Dual pricing: the practice by countries of maintaining different prices for a product, depending on whether it is sold on domestic or export markets. It is also called ***double pricing***.

Dual-purpose exports: trade in goods, services and technologies suitable for civilian and military use. There can be disagreements over the extent to which products clearly made for civilian mass markets, such as advanced personal computers, can be applied to military purposes. Much depends on one's perception of the strategic balance at the time of the proposed sale. *See also* ***COCOM***, ***strategic exports*** and ***Wassenaar Arrangement on Export Controls for Conventional Arms and Dual-Use Goods and Technologies***.

Dual-use products: goods or services which may be applied to more than one purpose. An example from the negotiations towards the ***Information Technology Agreement*** may illustrate the point. Some said that a certain type of glue was only used in the production of motherboards, etc., and should be considered a relevant product, but others said glue was a chemical substance and therefore not an information technology product. The question of dual-use products often arises in ***sectoral trade negotiations***.

Due restraint provision: *see* ***peace clause***.

Dumped imports: in its strict meaning this refers to imported goods meeting the conditions for a finding of ***dumping*** as set out in Article VI of the ***GATT*** and the ***Anti-Dumping Agreement***. The expression is often used loosely, however, to describe imported goods exerting downward pressure on the prices of similar goods produced locally, even if there is no indication of dumping.

Dumping: occurs when goods are exported at a price less than their normal value, generally meaning they are exported for less than they are sold in the domestic market or third-country markets, or at less than production cost. GATT Article VI, which deals with anti-dumping and countervailing duties, does not prohibit dumping. It merely says that GATT ***contracting parties*** recognize that dumping is to be condemned if it causes or threatens ***material injury*** to an established industry or retards the establishment of a domestic industry in the territory of another member. If enquiries in the importing country show that dumping is taking place and causing material injury to an industry, governments may take ***anti-dumping measures***. The basis of comparison is usually the ex-factory price in the exporting country and the transaction price of the goods at the border of the importing country, less transport and other costs incurred after the good has left the factory. It appears, however, that some

税由卖家根据固定比例支付。其他管辖范围也有关于追续权的法律。另见*精神权利(moral rights)*。

DSB

争端解决机构

即为解决贸易争端而召开会议的 WTO 总理事会。

DSU

争端解决谅解

WTO 涵盖成员之间争端解决的协定。正式名称为《关于争端解决规则与程序的谅解》。

Dual pricing

双重定价

国家对一产品维持不同价格的做法，取决于该产品是在国内销售还是在出口市场销售。也被称为双重定价。

Dual-purpose exports

两用物品出口

适合于民用和军用的货物、服务和技术贸易。对于明确为民用大众市场制造的产品，例如先进个人计算机，在何种程度上可用于军事目的存在分歧。这在很大程度上取决于在拟议交易时对战略性平衡的看法。另见*多边出口管制协调委员会(COCOM)*、*战略性出口(strategic exports)*、*关于常规武器和两用物品及技术出口管制的瓦森纳安排(Wassenaar Arrangement on Export Controls for Conventional Arms and Dual-Use Goods and Technologies)*。

Dual-use products

两用产品

可用于一种以上目的的货物或服务。《信息技术协定》谈判中的一个例子可以说明此点。一些人认为某种胶水只用于生产主板等产品，应被视为相关产品，但其他人认为胶水是一种化学物质，而非一种信息技术产品。两用产品问题经常出现在部门贸易谈判中。

Due restraint provision

适当克制条款

见*和平条款(peace clause)*。

Dumped imports

倾销进口产品

严格意义上讲，指符合GATT第6条和《反倾销协定》中所规定的确定倾销条件的进口商品。但是这一表述经常不精准地用于描述对本地生产的类似货物的价格施加下行压力的进口货物，即使其无倾销迹象。

Dumping

倾销

发生在货物以低于其正常价值的价格出口之时，一般意味着货物以低于在本国市场或第三国市场中销售价格出口，或低于生产成本出口。GATT第6条处理反倾销税和反补贴税，并不禁止倾销。只规定，GATT缔约方认识到，如倾销对另一缔约方领土内一已建立的产业造成或威胁造成实质损害或实质阻碍一国内产业的建立，则应予以谴责。如一进口国的调查显示，倾销正在发生且

equate sales below the domestic price with sales below cost. This interpretation is strictly speaking incorrect. Dumping has on occasion been confused with the import of products benefiting from the payment of ***subsidies***. In ***trade policy***, dumping refers to the conduct of individual firms that see some advantage in discriminatory pricing arrangements and that finance these from their own resources. Subsidies, on the other hand, are paid, directly or indirectly, to industries by governments. The effect of subsidized and dumped products on the importing market can of course be the same. Commentators are wont to point out that the apparently simple concept of dumping has led to innumerable disputes over its occurrence and the appropriate remedy. A demonstration that dumping has occurred often depends on very detailed cost calculations. It may be difficult to allocate costs accurately even in cases where the accounting is exceedingly precise. Often, assumptions have to be made on how a cost is to be treated. A simple comparison between the two prices may be impossible when the pricing and accounting mechanism of a firm is so opaque as to prevent any meaningful insight into its cost structure. At other times, comparisons may be inappropriate because the exported product is not sold on the home market at all or only in small quantities. Dumping as a perceived trade problem has been around for a long time, but it only turned into a major trade policy issue after the First World War and particularly during the Great Depression of the 1930s. In the United States anti-dumping laws and ***antitrust laws*** appear to have originated in a perception that certain commercial practices were directly opposed to the public interest. Antitrust laws were enacted to deal with anti-competitive practices of domestic firms. Anti-dumping laws, on the other hand, were aimed at perceived anti-competitive practices of foreign firms which manifested themselves through sales that undercut domestic firms. In time, perceptions of the causes of dumping and its effect on domestic markets, as well as the correct remedies, diverged markedly from the antitrust policies. Much effort has gone into investigations of the reasons for dumping. Three examples of motivational classifications will suffice. In 1923 Jacob Viner devised a classification according to motive and to continuity in his *Dumping: A Problem in International Trade*. First, *sporadic dumping* disposes of surplus stocks and is unintentional. At any rate, most businesses would use it at some time. Second, *short-run or intermittent dumping* arises when a firm is meeting temporary low prices in existing markets, is attempting to develop new markets, forestalls competition and retaliates against dumping in the reverse direction. Third, *long-run or continuous dumping* occurs when firms maintain full production without cutting domestic prices, when they wish to obtain economies of larger-scale production without cutting domestic prices, and when they do it for purely mercantilist reasons. Greg Mastel divides motivations for dumping into *overcapacity dumping* (prevalent in industries that face longer-term reduced (firms are able to take advantage of below-cost inputs supported by governments), *tactical dumping and discriminatory pricing* (selling the same product in different markets at different prices, partly in order to meet the competition)

正在对一产业造成实质损害，政府可以采取反倾销措施。进行比较的基础通常是出口国中的出厂前价格和货物在进口国边境的交易价格，减去货物离开工厂后发生的运输和其他费用。然而，似乎有人将低于国内价格的销售与低于成本的销售等同起来。这一解释严格地讲并不正确。倾销有时会与从补贴中获益的进口产品混在一起。在贸易政策中，倾销指单个企业的行为，这些企业在歧视性定价安排中发现某些优势，并利用自己的资源资助这些安排。而另一方面，补贴是由政府直接或间接向企业支付的。补贴产品和倾销产品对进口市场的影响当然是相同的。评论者通常指出，倾销这一表面简单的概念已经导致无数关于其发生和适当救济的争论。证实倾销已经发生往往取决于非常详细的成本计算。即使在记账极其精确的情况下，也难以准确分配成本。通常，要对如何处理成本作出假设。如果一公司的定价和会计机制不透明，而无法有意义地解析其成本结构，对两种价格进行简单比较可能不可行。在其他情况下，比较可能不恰当，因为出口产品根本不在国内市场上销售或只少量销售。倾销被视为贸易方面的难题时日已久，但直至第一次世界大战后、特别是在20世纪30年代大萧条时期，才成为一个主要贸易政策问题。在美国，反倾销法和反垄断法似乎源于某些商业惯例直接违背公共利益的看法。制定反垄断法旨在处理国内企业的反竞争行为。另一方面，反倾销法针对外国公司所谓的反竞争行为，这些公司以低于本国公司的价格进行销售。随着时间推移，对倾销的原因及其对国内市场的影响，以及正确的救济措施的认识，与反垄断政策发生明显差别。对于倾销原因的调查进行了很多努力。用三个案例就可以解释动机分类。1923年瓦伊纳在其《倾销：国际贸易中的一个问题》中根据动机和持续性进行了分类。第一类，零星倾销。处置过剩库存且属非故意的。无论如何，大多数企业有时会使用此种倾销。第二类，短期或间歇倾销，发生在一公司在现有市场遇到暂时低价而试图开发新市场、防范竞争及反向报复倾销之时。第三类，长期或持续倾销，发生在企业在不降低国内价格的情况下维持满负荷生产、企业希望在不降低国内价格的情况下获得规模经济生产以及企业纯粹出于重商主义原因之时。格雷格·马斯特尔将倾销动机分为“产能过剩倾销”——面临长期减少的行业普遍存在(企业能够利用政府支持的低成本投入)；“战术性倾销和歧视性定价”——在不同市场以不同价格销售

and *predatory dumping* (undercutting the competition in order to drive it out of business). Robert Willig has devised one of the most useful approaches to the analysis of dumping, particularly because it provides some useful insights into the motivations for dumping, though his approach does not enjoy wholehearted support from the trade policy community. He divides the activity into non-monopolizing and monopolizing dumping. Non-monopolizing dumping includes *market-expansion dumping* (higher net prices in the home market support lower prices in the export market), *cyclical dumping* (aimed at eliminating substantial excess production to a down-turn in demand) and *state-trading dumping* (practised particularly by economies in which exchange rates may be fixed at levels unrelated to the market, the dominant aim is to obtain hard currency, or price signals do not matter). Monopolizing dumping includes *strategic dumping* (injury caused in the importing market through an overall strategy or general anti-competitive circumstances prevailing in the exporting country) and *predatory-pricing dumping* (exporting at low prices aimed at driving rivals out of business to achieve monopoly power in the importing country). At the time of the negotiations leading to the ***Havana Charter***, participants identified four categories of dumping: (a) ***price dumping*** for which the rules ultimately appearing in GATT Article VI were made; (b) ***service dumping***, where a price advantage for a product comes about because dumping occurs in the provision of shipping services; (c) ***exchange dumping***, based on manipulation of the exchange rate to achieve a competitive edge; and (d) ***social dumping***, caused by the import at low prices of goods made by prison or sweated labour. No rules were made for the latter three categories. For the trade policy community today, the main sub-categories of dumping are (a) ***hidden dumping***, defined in an ***ad note*** to GATT Article VI as the sale by an importer at a price below that corresponding to the price invoiced by an exporter with whom the importer is associated, and also below the price in the exporting country, i.e. dumping is achieved through transfer pricing; (b) ***indirect dumping***, where a product is imported via a third country where it would not be considered as having been dumped; and (c) ***secondary dumping*** which is the export of a product containing components imported at what would normally be considered dumped prices. Sometimes, a firm may be able to sell at a higher price abroad, a condition called *reverse dumping*. Few other trade policy topics are surrounded as much by emotion as they are by rational analysis. The literature on this subject is accordingly voluminous. A few examples of thoughtful analysis must suffice. K. W. Dam has drawn attention to an apparent contradiction in the dumping concept. He says that according to the rules, local firms suffer injury whenever the import price is the same or lower than the price they charge. Yet, he says, the injury is no greater when dumping is present than when the import price merely reflects the comparative advantage of the exporter. Professor Deardorff has pointed to the close connection between dumping and the degree of competition in the home market. He notes that if both the market and the firm are protected, they will almost certainly have to

同一产品，部分原因是为应对竞争；以及“掠夺性倾销”——通过削弱竞争迫其退出市场。罗伯特·维林设计了一种分析倾销最有用的方式，特别是这一方式对倾销动机提供了一些有益见解，尽管他的方式并未得到贸易政策界的全心支持。他将倾销活动分为非垄断性倾销和垄断性倾销。非垄断性倾销包括“市场扩张倾销”——国内市场的较高净价支持出口市场的较低价格、“周期性倾销”——旨在消除大量过剩生产导致需求下降以及“国家贸易倾销”——特别是由那些汇率可能固定在与市场无关水平的经济体，其主要目的为获得硬通货，或价格信号无关紧要。垄断性倾销包括“战略性倾销”——通过出口国中普遍存在的总体战略或反竞争总体情况在进口市场中造成损害和“掠夺性定价倾销”——以低价格出口，旨在挤垮竞争对手，以便在进口国获得垄断权。在谈判《哈瓦那宪章》时，参加方确定了4类倾销：(a)价格倾销，最终制定了出现在GATT第6条中的规则；(b)服务倾销，一产品的价格优势源于在提供航运服务时发生倾销；(c)外汇倾销，基于操纵汇率以获得竞争优势；以及(d)社会倾销，因低价进口由监狱劳役或血汗劳工制造的货物而引发。对于后三类未制定规则。对于今天的贸易政策界，主要的倾销分类为：(a)隐蔽倾销，GATT第6条补充注释中将其定义为一进口商以低于与联号的出口商所开发票上对应的价格、且低于出口国国内价格的价格进行销售，即通过转让定价实现倾销；(b)间接倾销，即一产品通过不视其为倾销的第三国进口；(c)二级倾销，即一出口产品所包含的组件是以通常被视为倾销的价格进口的。有时，一公司能够在国外以更高价格销售，此种情况被称为反向倾销。鲜有其他贸易政策议题被如此多的理性分析和情感所包围，关于这一议题的文献繁多。引述以下几个深思熟虑的分析就足以证明。K. W. 丹已经引起人们对倾销概念中一个明显矛盾的关注。他认为，根据规则，只要进口价格等于或低于当地企业收取的价格，当地企业就会受到损害。但是，他认为，当倾销存在时，损害并不比进口价格仅反映出口商比较优势时更大。迪尔多夫教授指出了倾销和本国市场竞争程度之间存在的密切联系。他指出，如果市场和企业都受到保

resort to selling at less than the domestic price if they are to make any export sales at all. Gabrielle Marceau sums it up well when she says that the origin of dumping remains the existence of different national economic and legal policies between two national markets. She adds that national differences are normal and reasonable unless internationally agreed standards exist. *See also* ***anti-circumvention***, ***Anti-Dumping Agreement***, ***circumvention***, ***competition policy and anti-dumping measures***, ***de minimis dumping margins*** and ***Persistent Dumping Clause***. [Dam 1970, Deardorff 1990, Marceau 1994, Mastel 1996, Russell 1999, Viner 1921, Willig 1998]

Dunkel Draft: the Draft Final Act embodying the results of the ***Uruguay Round*** negotiations which was issued by Arthur Dunkel, then Director-General of the ***GATT***, in December 1991. As it happened, negotiations continued for another two years, especially over agriculture, but much of the Dunkel Draft was eventually adopted with minor revisions only.

Dutiable goods: goods subject to ***customs duties*** on entering or leaving a ***customs territory***.

Duties and other regulations of commerce: an expression occurring in Article XXIV of the ***GATT*** which governs the formation of ***free-trade areas*** and ***customs unions***. The expression is not defined further. Article XXIV requires in both cases that duties and other regulations of commerce applicable to third parties must not be higher after the formation of the arrangement than they were before.

Duties and other restrictive regulations of commerce: an expression occurring in Article XXIV of the ***GATT*** which governs the formation of ***free-trade areas*** and ***customs unions***. Parties to such arrangements must eliminate duties and restrictive regulations of commerce on substantially all the trade between them. The expression is not defined further, except that, where necessary, measures permitted under Article XI (General Elimination of Quantitative Restrictions), Article XII (Restrictions to Safeguard the Balance of Payments), Article XIII (Non-discriminatory Administration of Quantitative Restrictions), Article XIV (Exceptions to the Rule of Non-discrimination), Article XV (Exchange Arrangements) and Article XX (General Exceptions) may still be maintained. *See also* ***substantially-all-trade criterion***.

Duty: a levy, tax or impost charged by governments within their entire jurisdiction on production, transactions and, less frequently, the ownership of an asset. The amount of duty levied is usually related to the value of the transaction. ***Customs duties***, consisting of import and export tariffs, are such charges. They are levied at the border. A WTO requirement is that duties must not be used to discriminate against imported products once they have passed legally through the border. Whatever clear distinction there may have been once between a duty and a tax has now become blurred in day-to-day use. To the economist, their impact is the same, but for the lawyer and the tax administrator the distinction may be important. *See also* ***Lerner's symmetry theorem***.

Duty absorption: occurs when a producer or exporter who is faced with ***anti-dumping duties***, decides to adjust the price of the good so as to make sure that

护，要想进行任何出口销售，几乎肯定要以低于国内价格的价格进行销售。加布里埃尔·马尔索作了很好总结，她表示倾销的起源仍然是两个国家市场之间存在的不同的国家经济和法律政策。她补充表示，除非存在国际议定标准，否则国家之间的差异正常且合理。另见*反规避(anti-circumvention)*、*反倾销协定(Anti-Dumping Agreement)*、*规避(circumvention)*、*竞争政策与反倾销措施(competition policy and anti-dumping measures)*、*微量倾销幅度(de minimis dumping margins)*、*持续性倾销条款(Persistent Dumping Clause)*。

Dunkel Draft

邓克尔案文

1991年12月由时任GATT总干事阿瑟·邓克尔散发的包含乌拉圭回合谈判结果的最后文件草案。此后谈判又进行了2年，特别是就农业议题，但邓克尔案文大部分内容最终被采纳，仅有少量修改。

Dutiable goods

应税货物

在进入或离开一关税领土时应缴纳关税的货物。

Duties and other regulations of commerce

关税和其他贸易法规

出现在GATT第24条中的表述，该条管辖自由贸易区和关税同盟的建立。这一表述无进一步定义。第24条规定，对于自由贸易区和关税同盟，在安排形成后适用于第三方的关税和其他贸易法规的水平不得高于以往的水平。

Duties and other restrictive regulations of commerce

关税和其他限制性贸易法规

出现在GATT第24条中的表述，该条管辖自由贸易区和关税同盟的建立。参加此类安排的参加方之间必须对实质上取消关税和限制性贸易法规。这一表述无进一步定义，但规定在必要时可保留根据下列条款采取的措施：第11条(普遍取消数量限制)、第12条(为保障国际收支而实施的限制)、第13条(数量限制的非歧视性管理)、第14条(非歧视规则的例外)、第15条(外汇安排)和第20条(一般例外)。另见*实质上所有贸易的标准(substantially-all-trade criterion)*。

Duty

税

政府在其整个管辖范围内对生产、交易及在较少情况下对财产所有权征收的税款、关税或进口税。所征税额通常与交易金额相关联。关税即为此种税费，包括进口关税和出口关税，在边境征收。WTO的要求是，一旦进口产品已经合法通过边境，即不得使用关税对其进行歧视。关税和国内税之间的差别无论以往多么清晰，现在在日常使用中已模糊不清。对于经济学家，二者影响相同，但对于律师和税务管理者，差别可能很重要。另见*勒纳对称定理(Lerner's symmetry theorem)*。

Duty absorption

关税吸收

此种情况发生在面临反倾销税的一生产商或进口商决定调整货物的价格从而

its cost in the importing market changes little. *See also* ***absorption*** and ***anti-absorption***.

Duty deferral programme: a mechanism which exempts an importer from paying customs duties on products that are re-exported or used in the production of an article to be re-exported as was the case, for example, under the *maquiladora* system. *See also* ***drawback***.

Duty drawback: *see* ***border tax adjustments***.

Duty evasion: the attempt to avoid paying the due duty to the customs authorities. Common means for this are ***under-invoicing*** and ***smuggling*** as well as seeking to import a good under a tariff classification mandating a lower tariff.

Dynamic comparative advantage: *see* ***comparative advantage***.

使其在进口市场中的成本变化不大之时。另见*吸收(absorption)*、*反吸收(anti-absorption)*。

Duty deferral programme

递延纳税计划

对于进口供复出口的产品或进口用于生产复出口物品的产品免征进口关税的机制，例如保税加工出口制度下的免税。另见*退还(drawback)*。

Duty drawback

退税

见*边境税调节(border tax adjustments)*。

Duty evasion

逃税

逃避向海关支付应缴税款的企图。常见手段有低开发票、走私以及试图按关税较低的税目进口货物。

Dynamic comparative advantage

动态比较优势

见*比较优势(comparative advantage)*。

E

EALAF: East Asia-Latin America Forum. Now replaced by the Forum for East Asia-Latin America Cooperation.

E-APEC strategy: a framework aimed at creating a digital society adopted in 2001 at the Shanghai ***APEC Economic Leaders' Meeting***. Its three pillars are: (a) to create an environment for strengthening market structures and institutions, (b) to facilitate an environment for infrastructure investment, and (c) to enhance human capacity-building and promote entrepreneurship.

Early harvest: agreement among negotiating partners that some of their targets could or should be reached and implemented without waiting for the formal end to the negotiations. The Doha Ministerial Declaration, for example, states that "... agreements reached at an early stage [of the negotiations launched by the Declaration] may be implemented on a provisional or a definitive basis". An example of an early harvest in the ***Uruguay Round*** was the creation of the ***Trade Policy Review Mechanism***. Maybe the ***Agreement on Trade Facilitation*** is an example of an early harvest in the ***Doha Development Agenda***. *See also* ***single undertaking***.

Early Voluntary Sectoral Liberalization: EVSL. A programme for tariff liberalization initiated at the November 1996 ***APEC Economic Leaders' Meeting***. Nine sectors were selected for implementation in 1999: environmental goods and services, energy sector, fish and fish products, toys, forest products, gems and jewellery, medical equipment and instruments, chemicals and a telecommunications mutual recognition arrangement. More preparatory work was to be done on the remaining six sectors: environmental goods and services, natural and synthetic rubber, fertilizers, automotive, oilseeds and oilseed products, and civil aircraft. The programme covered tariff and non-tariff measures as well as elements of trade facilitation and economic and technical cooperation. In November 1998 the initiative was converted into ***accelerated tariff liberalization*** and forwarded to the WTO for further work in the context of the ***Doha Development Agenda*** negotiations. *See also* ***APEC individual action plans***.

Earth Summit: the United Nations Conference on Environment and Development. *See* ***UNCED***.

East African Community: EAC. Established on 15 January 2001 as the successor to the East African Cooperation. It consists of Burundi, Kenya, Rwanda, South Sudan, Tanzania and Uganda. EAC's objectives are to widen and deepen cooperation among its member states in political, economic, social and cultural fields, research and technology, defence, security, and legal and judicial affairs.

E

EALAF
东亚—拉丁美洲论坛

现被东亚—拉丁美洲合作论坛所取代。

E-APEC strategy
数字APEC战略

2001年上海APEC经济领导人会议通过的旨在创建数字社会的框架。三大支柱为：(a)营造有益于强化市场结构与制度的环境；(b)推动有益于基础设施投资的环境；以及(c)加强人才能力建设和促进创业。

Early harvest
早期收获

谈判方之间同意部分目标可以或应该实现并实施而不必等待谈判正式结束。例如，《多哈部长宣言》指出，"……[本宣言所启动的谈判的]早期达成的协议可在临时或最终基础上实施"。乌拉圭回合早期收获的例子是贸易政策审议机制的建立。《贸易便利化协定》可视为多哈发展议程早期收获的一例。另见*一揽子承诺(single undertaking)*。

Early Voluntary Sectoral Liberalization
部门提前自愿自由化

EVSL。1996年11月APEC经济领导人会议上提出的关税自由化计划。选定9个部门在1999年实施：环境产品和服务、能源、鱼类和鱼类产品、玩具、林产品、宝石和珠宝、医疗设备和仪器、化工品以及电信互认安排。对于其他6个部门仍需进行进一步准备工作：环境产品和服务、天然橡胶和合成橡胶、化肥、汽车、油籽和油籽产品以及民用航空器。该计划涵盖关税和非关税措施以及贸易便利化和经济技术合作要素。1998年11月，该倡议转为加速关税自由化，并提交WTO，供在多哈发展议程谈判中开展进一步工作。另见*APEC单边行动计划(APEC individual action plans)*。

Earth Summit
地球峰会

联合国环境与发展会议。见*联合国环境与发展会议(UNCED)*。

East African Community
东非共同体

EAC。2001年1月15日建立，作为东非合作组织的后继组织。成员国包括布隆迪、肯尼亚、卢旺达、南苏丹、坦桑尼亚和乌干达。EAC的目标为扩大和深化成员国在政治、经济、社会和文化领域、研究和技术、国防、安全、法律以及司法事务方面的合作。成员国于2004年2月16日建立关税同盟，随后于2010年建立共同市场。货币联盟将于2023年建立。最终为建立东非政治联

Members established a ***customs union*** on 16 February 2004. This was followed by a ***common market*** in 2010. A monetary union is to be established by 2023. The ultimate stage is to be the East African Political Federation. Its secretariat is in Arusha, Tanzania. *See also* ***African regional economic integration***.

East African Cooperation: *see* ***East African Community***.

East African Development Bank: a regional development bank located in Kampala. It was established in 1967. Its members are Kenya, Tanzania and Uganda.

East ASEAN Growth Area: *see* ***BIMP-EAGA***.

East Asia Free Trade Agreement: EAFTA. At this stage mainly an overall term for a ***free-trade agreement*** including the countries of a broadly defined East Asian area. One suggestion is that it should include ***ASEAN***, possibly as the core of such an agreement. *See also* ***East Asian Economic Community***, ***Free Trade Area of the Asia-Pacific*** and ***Regional Comprehensive Economic Partnership***.

East Asian Community: also East Asia Community. This refers to various proposals, such as that of the ***East Asia Vision Group*** in 2001, for the creation of a regional grouping with political, economic, social and cultural aims. Both the coverage and the membership of the proposed Community remain to be defined.

East Asian Economic Community: EAEC. Proposed by the second ***East Asia Vision Group*** in 2012 for establishment by 2020. The proposed EAEC would be developed though ***ASEAN+3*** (ASEAN countries plus China, Japan and the Republic of Korea). It would have four main elements: (a) single market and production base, (b) financial stability, food and energy security, (c) equitable and sustainable development, and (d) a constructive contribution to the global economy. The proposal remains a key ASEAN+3 plank, but it is not currently on any negotiating agenda.

East Asia Summit: EAS. An annual meeting of heads of government first held in Kuala Lumpur on 14 December 2005. It includes the ten members of ***ASEAN*** plus Australia, China, Japan, India, New Zealand, Republic of Korea, Russia and the United States. EAS is always chaired by an ASEAN country.

East Asia Vision Group: EAVG. A group established in 1999 which consists of two academics nominated by each of the members of the ***ASEAN+3*** countries. Its mandate was to examine ways to promote regional cooperation. In 2010 it was reconstituted as East Asia Vision Group II. In a report published in 2012 it proposed the establishment of an ***East Asian Economic Community*** by 2020.

East Caribbean Common Market: *see* ***Organization of Eastern Caribbean States***.

East–South trade: described trade between the Comecon members and developing countries. The term is now obsolete in that meaning.

East–West trade: described trade between the ***OECD*** countries and the Comecon countries. Such trading posed special problems arising largely from the non-convertibility of the currencies of Comecon countries and the ***transfer of***

盟。秘书处设在坦桑尼亚阿鲁沙。另见*非洲区域经济一体化(African regional economic integration)*。

East African Cooperation

东非合作组织

见*东非共同体(East African Community)*。

East African Development Bank

东非开发银行

设在坎帕拉的一家地区开发银行，1967 年设立，成员包括肯尼亚、坦桑尼亚和乌干达。

East ASEAN Growth Area

东盟东部增长区

见*东盟东部增长区(BIMP-EAGA)*。

East Asia Free Trade Agreement

东亚自由贸易协定

EAFTA。目前阶段主要指包括定义广泛的东亚地区国家的自由贸易协定的总括词语。一项建议提出，应包括东盟，或许可以作为此种协定的核心。另见*东亚经济共同体(East Asian Economic Community)*、*亚太自由贸易区(Free Trade Area of the Asia-Pacific)*、*区域全面经济伙伴关系协定(Regional Comprehensive Economic Partnership)*。

East Asian Community

东亚共同体

指建立具有政治、经济、社会和文化目标的区域集团的各种建议，例如东亚展望小组在2001年提出的建议。拟议共同体的覆盖范围和成员仍有待确定。

East Asian Economic Community

东亚经济共同体

EAEC。第二期东亚展望小组于2012年提议到2020年前建立。拟议的EAEC将通过东盟+3(东盟国家加中国、日本和韩国)发展形成。将具备4个要素：(a)单一市场和生产基地；(b)金融稳定、粮食和能源安全；(c)公正和可持续发展；以及(d)对全球经济的建设性贡献。该提议仍为东盟+3峰会的关键议题，但目前并未列入任何谈判议程。

East Asia Summit

东亚峰会

EAS。政府首脑年度会议，首届会议于2005年12月14日在吉隆坡举办。参加方包括东盟10个成员国加澳大利亚、中国、日本、印度、新西兰、韩国、俄罗斯和美国。东亚峰会一直由一东盟国家主办。

East Asia Vision Group

东亚展望小组

EAVG。成立于 1999 年的小组，由东盟+3 成员国中每一成员提名的 2 名学者组成，任务为审查促进区域合作的途径。2010 年，经重组成为第二期东亚展望小组。在 2012 年发布的报告中，小组提议到 2020 年前建立东亚经济共同体。

East Caribbean Common Market

东加勒比共同市场

见*东加勒比国家组织(Organization of Eastern Caribbean)*。

East–South trade

东南贸易

形容经互会 (Comecon)国家与发展中国家之间的贸易。这一词语的此种含义已过时。

East–West trade

东西方贸易

描述经济合作与发展组织(OECD)国家与经互会(Comecon)国家之间的贸易。此种贸易带来特殊问题，主要产生于经互会国家货币的不可兑换性质和技术

technology. The term is now obsolete in its original meaning, but some continue to use it for trade between Eastern and Western Europe. *See also* ***dual-purpose exports***.

EBA: ***Everything But Arms***. The ***European Union*** initiative giving tariff-free access to all products from ***least-developed countries*** except arms.

EC: European Communities. Until 30 November 2009 the official name of the ***European Union*** in the WTO. *See also* ***common commercial policy***.

EC-92 programme: *see* ***European Single Market***.

ECAFE: Economic Commission for Asia and the Far East. One of the original ***United Nations regional commissions***. It was succeeded in 1974 by ***ESCAP*** (Economic and Social Commission for the Asia-Pacific).

ECDC: Economic Cooperation between Developing Countries. A mechanism operating mainly within the United Nations system designed to promote the economic advancement of developing countries through cooperative activities. *See also* ***Buenos Aires Plan of Action for Promoting and Implementing Technical Co-operation among Developing Countries***, ***Committee on Trade and Development***, ***GSTP*** and ***Second High-Level United Nations Conference on South–South Cooperation***.

ECLA: Economic Commission for Latin America, superseded in 1985 by the ***Economic Commission for Latin America and the Caribbean***.

ECLAC: *see* ***Economic Commission for Latin America and the Caribbean***.

Eclectic theory of international investment: a theory of ***foreign direct investment*** that assumes that investment decisions are driven by the identification of ownership, location and internalization advantages, and these three components are viewed as interacting. First, direct investment gives the investor control over the asset. Second, it allows the investor to choose the location of a production facility that fits in best with the company's aims. Third, foreign direct investment allows the investor company to utilize its existing intellectual capital in the best way.

Eco-dumping: used in common parlance for the production of goods for export under lax environmental conditions. The term does not have proper standing in trade policy formulation. The practice is assumed to give producers a cost advantage in export markets where more stringent conditions apply. It appears, however, that production costs that can be ascribed to environmental regulations are a much smaller factor in total costs than other production costs. Generally, it is likely that they account for no more than 2 per cent of total production cost. *See also* ***eco-duties*** and ***trade and environment***.

Eco-duties: proposed levies on imported products to compensate for a perceived unfair competitive advantage arising to producers operating under less stringent, and therefore less expensive, environmental standards for industry. This is a contentious concept which, if implemented, could be misused as a protectionist device. *See also* ***eco-dumping*** and ***trade and environment***.

Eco-labelling: a voluntary market mechanism designed to encourage industry to produce goods which have a reduced environmental impact and to encourage

转让。这一词语的原有含义已过时，但一些人仍用来指代东欧与西欧之间的贸易。另见*两用物品出口(dual-purpose exports)*。

EBA
除武器外的所有产品
欧盟关于给予来自最不发达国家的除武器外的所有产品免关税准入的倡议。

EC
欧洲共同体
欧盟2009年11月30日前在WTO中的正式名称。另见*共同商业政策(common commercial policy)*。

EC-92 programme
EC-92计划
见*欧洲单一市场(European Single Market)*。

ECAFE
亚洲及远东经济委员会
最早的联合国区域委员会。1974年被联合国亚洲及太平洋经济社会理事会(ESCAP)所取代。

ECDC
发展中国家间经济合作
主要在联合国系统内运作的机制，旨在通过合作活动促进发展中国家的经济进步。另见*促进和实施发展中国家间技术合作的布宜诺斯艾利斯行动计划(Buenos Aires Plan of Action for Promoting and Implementing Technical Co-operation among Developing Countries)*、*贸易与发展委员会(Committee on Trade and Development)*、*全球贸易优惠制(GSTP)*、*第二届联合国南南合作高级别会议(Second High-Level United Nations Conference on South–South Cooperation)*。

ECLA
拉丁美洲经济委员会
1985年被拉丁美洲和加勒比经济委员会所取代。

ECLAC
拉丁美洲和加勒比经济委员会
见*拉丁美洲和加勒比经济委员会(Economic Commission for Latin America and the Caribbean)*。

Eclectic theory of international investment
国际投资折中论
外国直接投资的一种理论，假设投资决定由所有权、区位和内部化优势的确定所驱动，且三个组成部分被视为相互作用。首先，直接投资给予投资者对资产的控制权；其次，允许投资者选择最符合公司目标的生产设施的位置；最后，外国直接投资允许投资公司以最佳方式利用其现有智力资本。

Eco-dumping
生态倾销
对在宽松环境条件下生产供出口货物的通俗说法。该词在贸易政策制定中并无恰当定位。此种做法被认为是在适用更严格条件的出口市场中给予生产者成本优势。但是，与其他生产成本相比，可归于环境法规的生产成本在总成本中所占比重要小得多。一般而言，此种成本可能不会超过总生产成本的2%。另见*环境税(eco-duties)*、*贸易与环境(trade and environment)*。

Eco-duties
环境税
拟对进口产品征收的税款，用以弥补生产者在较不严格因而成本较低的工业环境标准下经营所产生的被视为不公平的竞争优势。这是一个有争议的概念，如果实施，可能会被滥用成为一种保护主义手段。另见*生态倾销(eco-dumping)*、*贸易与环境(trade and environment)*。

Eco-labelling
生态标签
一种自愿市场机制，旨在鼓励产业生产对环境影响较小的货物，并鼓励消费

consumers to buy them in preference to others. A trade concern about eco-labelling schemes is that they can include production-related criteria discriminating against imports which only reflect the environmental preferences of the importing country. *See also* ***eco-duties***, ***genetic labelling***, ***social labelling*** and ***trade and environment***.

E-commerce and Development Report: *see* ***Digital Economy Report***.

Economic and Social Commission for the Asia-Pacific: *see* ***ESCAP***.

Economic and Social Commission for Western Asia: ESCWA. Originally established in 1973 as the Economic Commission for Western Asia (ECWA) and given its present name in 1985. It is one of the ***United Nations regional commissions***. It seeks to improve the economic well-being of its member states and their economic relations with each other. Its secretariat is located in Amman.

Economic and Social Council: a body established under the Charter of the ***United Nations***. It is widely known as ***ECOSOC***. It oversees broadly the trade and economic work of the various United Nations bodies, but it has no rule-making function.

Economic Commission for Africa: ECA. One of the ***United Nations regional commissions***. Established in 1958. It seeks to promote economic advances in African countries. Its secretariat is located in Addis Ababa.

Economic Commission for Europe: UN-ECE. One of the ***United Nations regional commissions***. Established in 1947. It has done much useful work particularly in the area of standards affecting international trade and in ***trade facilitation*** more generally. Its secretariat is located in Geneva. *See also* ***EDIFACT***.

Economic Commission for Latin America and the Caribbean: ECLAC. One of the ***United Nations regional commissions***. It was established in 1948 as the Economic Commission for Latin America (ECLA) and given its current name in 1985. It aims to promote economic progress in Latin American countries. Its secretariat is located in Rio de Janeiro.

Economic Commission for Western Asia: *see* ***Economic and Social Commission for Western Asia***.

Economic Community of Central African States: ECCAS. Established in October 1983. Its members are Angola, Burundi, Cameroon, Central African Republic, Chad, Congo, Gabon, Democratic Republic of Congo, Equatorial Guinea, Rwanda, and Sao Tome and Principe. It was inactive from 1992 to 1998. The aims of ECCAS are: to promote and reinforce harmonious cooperation and balanced and self-supporting development in the economic and social domains, especially in the areas of industry, transport and communications, agriculture, natural resources, commerce, customs, monetary and financial questions, human resources, tourism, education, culture, science and technology and the movement of people with a view to raising standards of living and growth and economic stability. The longer-term aim is to create by 2025 a zone of peace, solidarity, balanced development and the free movement of people, goods and services. *See also* ***African regional economic integration***.

者优先购买此类货物。对生态标签计划的贸易关注是，这些计划可能包括仅反映进口国环境偏好的对进口造成歧视的生产相关标准。另见*环境税(eco-duties)*、*基因标签(genetic labelling)*、*社会标签(social labelling)*、*贸易与环境(trade and environment)*。

E-commerce and Development Report
电子商务与发展报告

见*数字经济报告(Digital Economy Report)*。

Economic and Social Commission for the Asia-Pacific
亚洲及太平洋经济社会理事会

见*亚洲及太平洋经济社会理事会(ESCAP)*。

Economic and Social Commission for Western Asia
西亚经济社会委员会

ESCWA。最初以西亚经济委员会(ECWA)名义于1973年设立，1985年改为现名。联合国区域委员会。寻求改善成员国的经济福祉和相互间经济关系。秘书处设在安曼。

Economic and Social Council
经济及社会理事会

根据《联合国宪章》设立的机构。以联合国经社理事会(ECOSOC)之名广为人知。广泛监督联合国各机构的贸易和经济工作，但无规则制定职能。

Economic Commission for Africa
非洲经济委员会

ECA。联合国区域委员会，于1958年设立。旨在促进非洲国家的经济进步。秘书处设在亚的斯亚贝巴。

Economic Commission for Europe
欧洲经济委员会

UN-ECE。联合国区域委员会，于1947年设立。开展了很多有益工作，特别是在影响国际贸易的标准和更广泛的贸易便利化领域。秘书处设在日内瓦。另见*行政、商业和运输用电子数据交换(EDIFACT)*。

Economic Commission for Latin America and the Caribbean
拉丁美洲和加勒比经济委员会

ECLAC。联合国区域委员会，于1948年以拉丁美洲经济委员会名义(ECLA)设立，1985年改为现名。旨在促进拉丁美洲国家的经济发展。秘书处设在里约热内卢。

Economic Commission for Western Asia
西亚经济委员会

见*西亚经济社会委员会(Economic and Social Commission for Western Asia)*。

Economic Community of Central African States
中部非洲国家经济共同体

ECCAS。于1983年10月建立，成员有安哥拉、布隆迪、喀麦隆、中非共和国、乍得、刚果(布)、加蓬、刚果(金)、赤道几内亚、卢旺达及圣多美和普林西比。1992年至1998年期间处于非活跃状态。ECCAS的宗旨为：促进和加强经济和社会领域的协调合作及平衡和自给自足发展，特别是在产业、运输和通信、农业、自然资源、商业、海关、货币和金融问题、人力资源、旅游、教育、文化、科学和技术以及人员流动领域，以期提高生活水平、促进增长及经济稳定。较长期目标为到2025年建成和平、团结、均衡发展以及人员、货物和服务自由流动的区域。另见*非洲区域经济一体化(African regional economic integration)*。

Economic Community of the Great Lakes: *see* ***Communauté Économique des Pays des Grands Lacs***.

Economic Community of West African States: ECOWAS. Originally established in 1975 and relaunched in 1993. Its members are Benin, Burkina Faso, Cape Verde, Côte d'Ivoire, Gambia, Ghana, Guinea, Guinea-Bissau, Liberia, Mali, Niger, Nigeria, Senegal, Sierra Leone and Togo. ECOWAS is in the process of establishing a ***customs union*** under its Trade Liberalization Programme. It is also working towards the implementation of ECOWAS Vision 2020 which envisions, by 2020, a single unified regional market with a common currency supported by an integrated financial market and payment system. Its secretariat is in Lagos. *See also* ***African regional economic integration***.

Economic-complementarity agreements: another name for ***partial-scope trade agreements*** and ***sectoral free-trade areas*** sometimes negotiated by developing countries under the ***Enabling Clause***.

Economic cooperation agreement: a bilateral or plurilateral agreement to promote deeper economic cooperation between the partners. Such agreements do not follow a set pattern, but usually they do not contain ***market access*** provisions. Other names used for this type of instrument include ***economic framework agreement***, ***trade and economic agreement***, ***trade and investment facilitation agreement*** and ***trade and investment framework agreement***.

Economic Cooperation Area of Black Sea Countries: *see* ***Black Sea Economic Cooperation Organization***.

Economic Cooperation between Developing Countries: *see* ***ECDC***.

Economic Cooperation Organization: ECO. Established in 1985 to promote the economic development of its members, at that time Iran, Pakistan and Turkey. Since 1992 the members of ECO have been Afghanistan, Azerbaijan, Iran, Kazakhstan, Kyrgyz Republic, Pakistan, Tajikistan, Turkey, Turkmenistan and Uzbekistan. ECO's broad objectives were redefined in the Treaty of Izmir of 14 September 1996. The ECO Vision 2025 statement says that "ECO will pave the way to a territory of integrated and sustainable economies as well as a free-trade area achieved by highly advanced societies and improved governance through enhanced cooperation". This includes expanding the ***Economic Cooperation Organization Trade Agreement*** (ECOTA, concluded in 2003) to all member states by 2025. The ECO secretariat is located in Teheran. [www.ecosecretariat.org]

Economic Cooperation Organization Trade Agreement: ECOTA. A preferential trade agreement confined to trade in goods concluded in 2003. Its members are Afghanistan, Iran, Pakistan, Tajikistan and Turkey. ECO Vision 2025 envisages that all members of the ***Economic Cooperation Organization*** will become members of ECOTA by 2025. The agreement also is to be renegotiated as a ***free-trade agreement***.

Economic framework agreement: a treaty between two or more parties setting out basic rules for the conduct of economic relations between them. Provisions included in such agreements do not follow set patterns. At a minimum, they

Economic Community of the Great Lakes
大湖国家经济共同体

见*大湖国家经济共同体(Communauté Économique des Pays des Grands Lacs)*。

Economic Community of West African States
西非国家经济共同体

ECOWAS。最早于1975年建立，1993年重启。成员包括贝宁、布基纳法索、佛得角、科特迪瓦、冈比亚、加纳、几内亚、几内亚比绍、利比里亚、马里、尼日尔、尼日利亚、塞内加尔、塞拉利昂和多哥。ECOWAS正在根据其贸易自由化计划建立关税同盟。还致力于实施ECOWAS 2020年愿景，设想到2020年时在一体化金融市场和支付系统支持下建立拥有共同货币的单一一体化地区市场。秘书处设在拉加斯。另见*非洲区域经济一体化(African regional economic integration)*。

Economic-complementarity agreements
经济互补协定

发展中国家有时根据授权条款谈判达成的局部贸易协定和部门自由贸易区的另一名称。

Economic cooperation agreement
经济合作协定

旨在促进参加方之间更深层次经济合作的双边或诸边协定。此类协定不遵循固定模式，但通常不包含市场准入条款。此类文件的其他名称包括经济框架协定、贸易经济协定、贸易投资便利化协定以及贸易投资框架协定。

Economic Cooperation Area of Black Sea Countries
黑海国家经济合作区

见*黑海经济合作组织(Black Sea Economic Cooperation Organization)*。

Economic Cooperation between Developing Countries
发展中国家间经济合作

见*发展中国家间经济合作(ECDC)*。

Economic Cooperation Organization
经济合作组织

ECO。1985年建立，旨在促进其成员的经济发展，当时包括伊朗、巴基斯坦和土耳其。自1992年起，成员为阿富汗、阿塞拜疆、伊朗、哈萨克斯坦、吉尔吉斯斯坦、巴基斯坦、塔吉克斯坦、土耳其、土库曼斯坦和乌兹别克斯坦。1996年9月14日的《伊兹密尔条约》重新定义了ECO的广泛目标。经济合作组织2025年愿景声明中提到，“ECO将通过高度发达的社会和合作改善治理，为建立整个地区的一体化和可持续经济体及自由贸易区铺平道路”，包括到2025年将《经济合作组织贸易协定》(ECOTA，2003年缔结)扩展至所有成员国。秘书处设在德黑兰。

Economic Cooperation Organization Trade Agreement
经济合作组织贸易协定

ECOTA。2003年缔结的一项限于货物贸易的优惠贸易协定。成员为阿富汗、伊朗、巴基斯坦、塔吉克斯坦和土耳其。经济合作组织2025年愿景中设想，到2025年，经济合作组织所有成员国都将成为《经济合作组织贸易协定》成员。该协定也将作为一项自由贸易协定进行重新谈判。

Economic framework agreement
经济框架协定

两个或两上以上参加方签署的条约，规定参加方之间处理经济关系的基本规

usually contain elements of ***trade facilitation***. They also provide for ***non-discrimination*** between the parties. Depending on the level of obligations, there may also be a mechanism for consultation and dispute settlement. Among other names for this type of agreement are ***economic partnership agreement***, ***trade and economic agreement***, ***trade and investment framework agreement*** and ***trade and investment facilitation agreement***.

Economic impact criterion: a test sometimes suggested for use in the ***GATT*** to assess whether a domestic measure is impairing ***national treatment***. Under this criterion, the proof for a finding that the national treatment obligation had been breached would have to be found in changing trade flows. Finding the proof might pose many practical difficulties because there may be other reasons why a country's imports of a product might have changed. GATT dispute settlement panels have rejected the use of this criterion in favour of a test assessing whether there is ***equality of competitive opportunity***.

Economic integration: all economies, even those given to practising ***autarky***, are to some extent integrated with others, but the term is usually reserved for groups of economies that are manifestly combining their activities more quickly among themselves than with others. It is usual to distinguish between ***market-led integration*** (spontaneous integration without the formal involvement of governments) and ***policy-led integration*** (integration through intergovernmental frameworks). Another distinction is that between ***shallow integration*** and ***deep integration***. The former is confined, for example, to the formation of a ***free-trade area*** in which each member retains autonomy in economic policies. The latter implies cooperation or harmonization of matters such as ***competition laws***, monetary and financial policies, standards and other regulations, etc., as would be the case in a ***common market***. *See also* ***globalization*** and ***internationalization***.

Economic integration agreements: used in Article V of the ***General Agreement on Trade in Services*** to cover free-trade arrangements in services. This term was chosen because free trade in services requires the possibility of ***commercial presence*** in the importing country as well as the free movement of consumers and producers of services. This is seen as involving a greater degree of economic integration than might occur under conditions of free trade in goods. Economic integration agreements must have ***substantial sectoral coverage*** and provide for the absence or elimination of substantially all discrimination between its members to conform to WTO rules. *See also* ***free-trade areas*** and ***trade in services***.

Economic international commodity agreements: these are ***international commodity agreements*** that seek to influence the price of the commodity through ***buffer stocks***, ***export quotas*** and other measures manipulating the amounts reaching the market. *See also* ***administrative international commodity agreements***.

Economic nationalism: the view that economic advances can only be achieved at the expense of other participants in the international economy. *See also* ***autarky***, ***beggar-thy-neighbour policies***, ***mercantilism*** and ***zero-sum nationalism***.

则。此类协定所含条款不遵循固定模式。至少通常包括贸易便利化内容。还规定参加方之间给予非歧视待遇。根据义务水平，可能还包含磋商和争端解决机制。此类协定的其他名称包括经济伙伴关系协定、贸易经济协定、贸易投资框架协定以及贸易投资便利化协定。

Economic impact criterion

经济影响标准

在GATT中有时建议使用的测试，用以评估一项国内措施是否损害国民待遇。根据这一标准，违反国民待遇义务认定的证据应在变化中的贸易流中找到。寻找证据可能会带来许多实际困难，因为一国进口一产品的变化可能由于其他原因，GATT争端解决专家组已经拒绝使用该标准，而采用评估是否存在竞争机会均等的测试。

Economic integration

经济一体化

所有经济体，即使那些习惯经济闭关自守的经济体，在某种程度上与其他经济体是一体的，但这一词语专门留给那些与其他经济体相比，能够将各自活动更快结合在一起的经济体。通常分为市场主导一体化(无政府正式参与的自发式一体化)和政策主导一体化(通过政府间框架实现的一体化)。另一种区分方法是浅层一体化和深层一体化。前者是限于自由贸易区的形成，其中每一成员保留经济政策自主权；后者意味着就竞争法、货币和金融政策、标准和其他法规等事项进行合作或协调，共同市场即是此种情况。另见*全球化(globalization)*、*国际化(internationalization)*。

Economic integration agreements

经济一体化协定

在《服务贸易总协定》第 5 条中用于涵盖服务领域的自由贸易安排。之所以选择该词语，是因服务领域的自由贸易要求进口国中有设立商业存在及服务消费者和生产者的自由流动的可能性。此点被认为与货物自由贸易条件下的经济一体化相比较，服务贸易涉及的经济一体化程度更大。经济一体化协定必须涵盖众多部门，并规定其成员间不存在或实质性消除所有歧视，以符合WTO规则。另见*自由贸易区(free-trade areas)*、*服务贸易(trade in services)*。

Economic international commodity agreements

国际商品经济协定

旨在寻求通过缓冲储存、出口配额及操控流入市场数量的其他措施影响商品价格的国际商品协定。另见*国际商品管理协定(administrative international commodity agreements)*。

Economic nationalism

经济民族主义

认为经济进步只能以国际经济中其他参加方为代价才能实现的观点。另见*经济闭关自守(autarky)*、*以邻为壑政策(beggar-thy-neighbour policies)*、*重商主义(mercantilism)*、*零和民族主义(zero-sum nationalism)*。

Economic needs test: a mechanism controlled by government, industry or professional associations to decide whether the entry into the market of new foreign, and sometimes domestic, firms is warranted on economic grounds. Such mechanisms are often opaque. They may be discretionary and protectionist. Sometimes economic needs tests purport to protect the interests of consumers, but these are not always asked for their views on additional competition in the market. Article XVI of the ***General Agreement on Trade in Services*** setting out ***market access*** rules proscribes the use of economic needs tests.

Economic operator: a natural or legal person in the European Union that is engaged, for example, in the export and import of goods. *See also* ***authorized economic operator*** and ***authorized operators***.

Economic partnership agreement: EPA. A bilateral or plurilateral agreement. The content of such agreements varies greatly. Some merely promote voluntary economic cooperation between the partners. Others are proper ***free-trade agreements***. Japan, for example, tends to refer to its free-trade agreements as EPAs. The ***ACP-EU Partnership Agreement***, an ***asymmetrical trade agreement***, provides for the negotiation of economic partnership agreements with ACP regions compatible with the WTO rules. These were expected to enter into force by 1 January 2008 at the latest. *See also* ***economic cooperation agreement*** and ***trade and economic agreement*** for other instruments of this type.

Economic regulation: *see* ***regulation***.

Economic sanctions: economic and commercial measures sometimes taken by governments to achieve their foreign policy objectives. These measures include ***trade embargoes***, investment restrictions or prohibitions, travel restrictions, etc. Most commonly such measures are taken in the pursuit of ***United Nations economic sanctions***. In their analysis of economic sanctions imposed over a long period, Hufbauer and his colleagues have concluded that is not true to say that sanctions "never work" (*Economic Sanctions Reconsidered: History and Current Policy*). Rather, they consider that sanctions are of limited utility in achieving foreign policy goals that depend on compelling the target country to take actions it is determined to resist. Nevertheless, they consider that in the case of small target countries and comparatively modest policy goals, sanctions have brought about changes in behaviour. *See also* ***retaliation*** and ***security exceptions***. [Hufbauer, Schott and Elliott 1990]

Economic summits: *see* ***G7***.

Economic union: any group of countries with a ***common market*** for goods and services, free movement capital and labour amongst themselves and operating a mechanism for harmonizing financial and monetary policies.

Economic unity theory: an element of the ***competition policy*** of the ***European Union***. It holds that for the purposes of an antitrust action under Union law against a subsidiary of a company located within the Union, the two are considered a single economic unity. In other words, the parent company is deemed itself to be involved.

Economic needs test
经济需求测试

由政府、行业或专业协会控制的机制，用以决定新的外国企业、有时是本国企业进入市场是否具有经济理由。此类机制往往不透明，可能是任意的且具有保护主义性质。有时，经济需求测试声称保护消费者利益，但消费者并不总是被问及他们对市场中额外竞争的意见。《服务贸易总协定》第16条中的市场准入规则禁止使用经济需求测试。

Economic operator
经济运营者

在欧盟内从事货物进出口的自然人或法人。另见*经认证的经营者(authorized economic operator)*、*经认证经营者(authorized operators)*。

Economic partnership agreement
经济伙伴关系协定

EPA。双边或诸边协定。此类协定的内容差别很大。有些仅为促进伙伴之间的自愿经济合作，其他则是真正的自由贸易协定。例如，日本倾向于偏爱EPA 形式的自由贸易协定。作为一个非对称贸易协定，《非加太地区国家与欧盟伙伴关系协定》规定了以符合 WTO 规则的方式谈判非加太地区国家经济伙伴关系协定，期望最迟于 2008 年 1 月 1 日生效。此类其他机制另见*经济合作协定(economic cooperation agreement)*、*贸易经济协定(trade and economic agreement)*。

Economic regulation
经济管制

见*管制(regulation)*。

Economic sanctions
经济制裁

政府为实现其外交政策目标有时采取的经济和商业措施。此类措施包括贸易禁运、投资限制或禁止、旅行限制等。大多数情况下此类措施以联合国经济制裁的形式采取。在对长期实施的经济制裁进行分析后，霍夫鲍尔及其同事得出结论指出，如果说制裁“从来不起作用”是不对的(《经济制裁再思考：历史与当前政策》)。相反，他们认为制裁在实现迫使目标国采取其决意抵制的行动此种外交政策目标方面作用有限。尽管如此，他们认为对于较小目标国和相对温和的政策目标，制裁带来了行为的改变。另见*报复(retaliation)*、*安全例外(security exceptions)*。

Economic summits
经济峰会

见*7 国集团*(G7)。

Economic union
经济联盟

拥有货物和服务共同市场、资本和劳动力在相互之间自由流动以及运行金融和货币政策协调机制的任何国家集团。

Economic unity theory
单一主体原则

欧盟竞争政策的组成部分。该理论认为，就根据欧盟法律对设在欧盟内的一公司的子公司所采取的反垄断行动而言，两个公司被视为一个单一主体。换言之，母公司本身被视为参与其中。

Economies in transition: economies making the transformation from ***centrally-planned economies*** to ***market economies***. Sometimes, the expression is used also for developing countries that have embarked upon substantial economic ***deregulation***. The *Transition Report*, published annually by the European Bank for Reconstruction and Development (EBRD), contains detailed information on the economic performance of transition economies.

Economy: the formal name of the members of ***APEC***.

Eco-packaging: the use of packaging materials that have the smallest impact on the environment, either because their production is environmentally friendly or because they can easily be reused or recycled. Insistence on certain types of non-standard eco-packaging could result in protectionist effects if the supplying country cannot meet the required standards. *See also* ***trade and environment***.

Eco-protectionism: measures aimed protecting local industries under the guise of protecting the environment. *See also* ***trade and environment*** and ***trade and labour standards***.

ECOSOC: United Nations Economic and Social Council. It has fifty-four members of the United Nations who are elected by the United Nations General Assembly for a three-year term. Representation on ECOSOC is based on an agreed geographical distribution. Its annual high-level sessions of WTO, ***World Bank*** and ***IMF*** heads are considered to be helpful in promoting coherence of economic policy between countries. *See also* ***Commission on Science and Technology for Development***, ***Draft International Agreement on Illicit Payments*** and ***ECOSOC and the GATT***.

ECOSOC and the GATT: the Charter of the ***United Nations*** gave ***ECOSOC*** a range of responsibilities in international economic and social cooperation, including the ability to call international conferences on matters falling within its competence. The United States, the main power in the immediate post-war years promoting multilateral trade agreements, accordingly proposed that ECOSOC should convene what became the ***United Nations Conference on Trade and Employment***. The United States distinguished, however, between the aims of establishing an international trade organization and the negotiation of a multilateral tariff agreement. This was because it derived its mandate for negotiating the tariff agreement from the *Reciprocal Trade Agreements Act* of 1934 which did not envisage the establishment of any permanent institution to oversee international trade. Once ECOSOC had passed the resolution calling for a conference, it effectively was given no further role in the negotiations. From its inception, the GATT therefore was virtually independent of the United Nations system. This principle has been carried forward into the WTO. Of course, the WTO has a close working relationship with many United Nations bodies. *See also* ***United States Reciprocal Trade Agreements Program***.

Eco-standards: product, production or consumption standards imposed to reduce or eliminate damage to the environment. *See also* ***technical barriers to trade*** and ***trade and environment***.

Economies in transition

转型经济体

从中央计划经济体向市场经济体转型的经济体。有时，该表述也用于已开始实质性取消经济管制的发展中国家。欧洲复兴开发银行(EBRD)每年发布的《转型报告》包含转型经济体经济表现的详细信息。

Economy

经济体

APEC成员的正式名称。

Eco-packaging

环保包装

使用对环境影响最小的包装材料，因其生产对环境友好，或因其易于重复使用或循环。如供应国不能满足所需标准，坚持要求使用某些类型的非标准化环保包装，即可能导致保护主义影响。另见*贸易与环境(trade and environment)*。

Eco-protectionism

环境贸易保护主义

以保护环境为幌子行保护本地产业之实的措施。另见*贸易与环境(trade and environment)*、*贸易与劳工标准(trade and labour standards)*。

ECOSOC

联合国经济及社会理事会

包括由联合国大会选举产生的54个联合国成员，任期3年。经社理事会的代表权基于议定的地域分配。经社理事会与WTO、世界银行和国际货币基金组织(IMF)负责人的年度高级别会议被视为有助于促进各国间经济政策的一致性。另见*科学技术促进发展委员会(Commission on Science and Technology for Development)*、*关于违法付款的国际协定草案(Draft International Agreement on Illicit Payments)*、*经社理事会与GATT (ECOSOC and the GATT)*。

ECOSOC and the GATT

经社理事会与GATT

《联合国宪章》赋予联合国经社理事会(ECOSOC)在国际经济和社会合作方面一系列职责，包括就其职权范围内的事项召开国际会议的权利。美国作为战后推动多边贸易协定的主要力量，因此建议经社理事会召开后来的联合国贸易与就业会议。然而，美国将建立一个国际贸易组织的目标与谈判多边关税协定的目标区分开来。原因是美国自《1934年互惠贸易协定法》中获得的谈判关税协定的授权，而该法未设想建立监督国际贸易的任何常设机构。一旦经社理事会通过关于召开会议的决议，它实际上在谈判中就不会再发挥进一步作用。从一开始，GATT实际上就独立于联合国系统。WTO沿袭了这一原则。当然，WTO与许多联合国机构有着密切的工作关系。另见*美国互惠贸易协定计划(United States Reciprocal Trade Agreements Program)*。

Eco-standards

生态标准

为减少或消除对环境的损害而实施的产品、生产或消费标准。另见*技术性贸易壁垒(technical barriers to trade)*、*贸易与环境(trade and environment)*。

ECOTECH: economic and technical cooperation among ***APEC*** members. The ECOTECH goals, as agreed in 1996, are (a) attain sustainable growth and equitable development in the Asia-Pacific region, (b) reduce economic disparities among APEC economies, (c) improve the economic and social well-being of the people, and (d) deepen the spirit of community in the Asia-Pacific.

ECOWAS Vision 2020: *see* ***Economic Community of West African States***.

Ecrêtement**:** *Fr.* removing the peaks. A proposal for tariff harmonization through targeted reductions made early in the ***Kennedy Round*** (1963–67) by the ***European Economic Community*** (EEC). The proposal stemmed from an EEC view that its own tariffs were mostly in the 10 to 20 per cent range, whereas the United States tariffs in many cases ranged from 30 per cent to 50 per cent, with some going up to 100 per cent. The EEC therefore proposed lowering tariffs by half to target levels of 10 per cent for manufactures, 5 per cent for semi-manufactures and zero for raw materials. The proposal was not acceptable to the United States because it would have forced it to accept much larger tariff cuts in the face of an EEC unwillingness to do something on agriculture. *See also* ***double écart formula*** and ***thirty:ten formula***.

EDI: Electronic Data Interchange. The transfer of data in a standardized electronic form between companies through the use of networks such as the Internet.

EDIFACT: Electronic Data Interchange for Administration, Commerce and Transport. Developed under the auspices of the United Nations ***Economic Commission for Europe*** (UN-ECE). It is defined officially as a "set of internationally agreed standards, directories and guidelines for the electronic interchange of structured data, and in particular that related to trade in goods and services between independent, computerized information systems". *See also* ***trade facilitation***.

EEP: the United States ***Export Enhancement Program***. It gave American farmers export subsidies mainly to enable them to compete with subsidized agricultural exports from the ***European Community*** on certain export markets. The programme was repealed in 2008.

Effective market access: defined by some as the absence of domestic regulatory policies and other ***structural impediments*** that unintentionally limit competition or transparency. Tariff and non-tariff measures such as ***subsidies*** and ***voluntary restraint arrangements*** would be assessed separately.

Effective market presence: defined by some as the ability of foreign firms to compete in the market through investing, i.e. through enjoyment of the ***right of establishment***. *See also* ***trade and investment***.

Effective rate of assistance: ERA. Sometimes also called effective rate of protection. It is a framework for making clear the difference between the hypothetical situation of no domestic assistance to industry and the situation actually obtaining. The ERA concept is useful because it can measure government interventions such as subsidies or purchasing preferences that may influence trade flows without actually restricting flows at the border, including ***tariffs*** and ***non-tariff measures***. It also shows the additional costs borne by consumers

ECOTECH
经济技术合作

APEC成员间经济和技术合作。1996年议定的ECOTECH目标为：(a)实现亚太地区可持续增长和公正发展；(b)减少APEC经济体之间的经济差距；(c)改善人民的经济和社会福祉；以及(d)深化亚太大家庭精神。

ECOWAS Vision 2020
西非经共体 2020 年愿景

见*西非国家经济共同体(Economic Community of West African States)*。

Ecrêtement
关税削平

法语，移除高峰之义。欧洲经济共同体(EEC)在肯尼迪回合(1963—1967年)初期提出的通过有针对性削减以协调关税的提案。提案源于欧共体的一种观点，即其自身关税大多在10%至20%之间，而美国的关税许多在30%至50%之间，有些甚至高达100%。因此，欧共体建议将关税削减一半以达到目标水平，即制成品关税为10%，半制成品关税为5%，原材料关税为零。美国不接受该提案，因为面对欧共体不愿在农业方面作出让步的情况，该提案会迫使美国接受更大幅度的关税削减。另见*双差公式(double écart formula)*、*30:10公式(thirty:ten formula)*。

EDI
电子数据交换

通过互联网等网络在公司间以标准化电子形式传输数据。

EDIFACT
行政、商业和运输用电子数据交换

用于行政、商业和运输的电子数据交换。在联合国欧洲经济委员会(UN-ECE)主持下开发。正式定义为“一套用于独立的、计算机化的信息系统之间以电子方式交换结构化数据的国际议定标准、目录和准则，特别是与货物贸易和服务贸易相关的数据”。另见*贸易便利化(trade facilitation)*。

EEP
美国出口促进计划

向美国农民提供出口补贴，主要使他们能够在某些出口市场上与欧洲共同体的补贴出口农产品进行竞争。该计划于2008年被废除。

Effective market access
有效市场准入

一些人将此定义为不存在国内监管政策和无意限制竞争或透明度的结构性障碍的情况。关税及补贴和自愿限制安排等非关税措施分别评估。

Effective market presence
有效市场存在

一些人将此定义为外国公司通过投资，即通过享受设立权，在市场中竞争的能力。另见*贸易与投资(trade and investment)*。

Effective rate of assistance
有效援助率

ERA。有时也被称为有效保护率。是一个用于厘清产业无国内援助的假定情况与产业实际获得国内援助的情况之间的差别的框架。ERA 是有用的，因其可以衡量政府干预程度，例如补贴或购买偏好可以影响贸易流动但实际上并

because of domestic assistance. The ERA does not distinguish between measures that may be considered legal or illegal under the WTO agreements. *See also* ***nominal rate of protection*** and ***tariff escalation***.

Effective rate of protection: *see* ***effective rate of assistance***.

Effects doctrine: the principle that a state may have ***antitrust laws*** covering ***conduct*** outside of its territory if such conduct has an actual or potential effect on commerce within its territory. The effects doctrine is subject to a test of reasonableness. *See also* ***competition policy***, ***extraterritoriality*** and ***implementation doctrine***.

Efficiency-seeking investment: a term for ***foreign direct investment*** undertaken to supply other markets in the most competitive manner. *See also* ***market-seeking investment***.

EFTA: European Free Trade Association. Entered into force on 3 May 1960 through the Convention of Stockholm. Founding members were Austria, Denmark, Norway, Portugal, Sweden, Switzerland and the United Kingdom. Iceland joined in 1970. Finland became a full member in 1986 after having been an associate member. Denmark and the United Kingdom left on 31 December 1972 to join the ***European Economic Community***. They were followed by Portugal in 1985 and Austria, Finland and Sweden on 1 January 1995. EFTA now comprises Iceland, Liechtenstein, Norway and Switzerland. The ***EFTA Convention 2001*** revised the Stockholm Convention in major ways. *See also* ***European Economic Area***.

EFTA Convention 2001: the revised *Convention Establishing the European Free Trade Association*, or ***EFTA***, concluded on 21 June 2001 at Vaduz, Liechtenstein. Members are Iceland, Liechtenstein, Norway and Switzerland. It reflects progress in European economic integration since the formation of EFTA in 1960 and removes the anomalies arising from the fact that, alone of the EFTA members, Switzerland is not a member of the ***European Economic Area***. Among the main changes in the EFTA framework are expanded mutual recognition of conformity assessments and broader rules on ***intellectual property rights***. The Convention now contains comprehensive provisions liberalizing investment, ***trade in services*** and the movement of persons. Transport services remain restricted. EFTA members have opened their ***government procurement*** further to each other. Some slight improvements have been made to trade in agricultural goods, but this remains by far the least liberal part of the Convention.

Egregious: literally "standing out from the crowd", but its current meaning is defined in the *Concise Oxford Dictionary* as "shocking" or "gross". An adjective which, but for the efforts of United States legislators, might well be unknown among ***trade policy*** makers. *See* ***Special 301*** and ***Super 301***.

E-IAP: the electronic version of the ***APEC individual action plans*** prepared periodically by ***APEC*** members.

Ejusdem generis; sometimes *eiusdem*. Of the same kind, sort or nature. A rule for the interpretation of laws which says that if general words follow particular

不在边境限制贸易流动，包括关税和非关税措施。还可显示消费者因国内援助所承担的额外成本。ERA 不区分相关措施根据《WTO 协定》属合法或非法。另见*名义保护率(nominal rate of protection)*、*关税升级(tariff escalation)*。

Effective rate of protection

有效保护率

见*有效援助率(effective rate of assistance)*。

Effects doctrine

效果原则

一国对于实际或潜在影响其领土内商业的其领土外的行为适用反垄断法的原则。效果原则的合理性有待检验。另见*竞争政策(competition policy)*、*治外法权(extraterritoriality)*、*履行地原则(implementation doctrine)*。

Efficiency-seeking investment

追求效率型投资

用于描述以最具竞争力的方式供应其他市场的外国直接投资的词语。另见*寻求市场型投资(market-seeking investment)*。

EFTA

欧洲自由贸易联盟

通过《斯德哥尔摩公约》于1960年5月3日生效。创始成员包括奥地利、丹麦、挪威、葡萄牙、瑞典、瑞士和英国。冰岛于1970年加入。芬兰在成为联系成员后于1986年成为正式成员。丹麦和英国在1972年12月31日退出后加入欧洲经济共同体。随后葡萄牙于1985年、奥地利、芬兰和瑞典于1995年1月1日退出。EFTA由冰岛、列支敦士登、挪威和瑞士组成。《2001年欧洲自由贸易联盟公约》对《斯德哥尔摩公约》作出重大修订。另见*欧洲经济区(European Economic Area)*。

EFTA Convention 2001

2001年欧洲自由贸易联盟公约

《建立欧洲自由贸易联盟公约》(EFTA)的修订版本，2001年6月21日在列支敦士登瓦杜兹缔结。成员包括冰岛、列支敦士登、挪威和瑞士。公约反映了自1960年EFTA形成以来欧洲经济一体化的进展情况，消除了瑞士为EFTA成员国而非欧洲经济区成员国的异常情况。EFTA框架的主要变化为，扩盟的一致性评定互认和更广泛的知识产权规则。公约现包含全面的自由投资、服务贸易和人员流动条款。运输服务仍受限制。EFTA成员国间已进一步开放政府采购。农产品贸易方面已取得一些微小进步，但仍为公约中迄今开放程度最少的部分。

Egregious

恶劣的

字面义为“脱颖而出”，《简明牛津词典》现在将其定义为“令人震惊的”或“恶心的”。要不是美国立法者的努力，这个形容词很可能并不为贸易政策制定者所熟知。另见*特别 301 条款(Special 301)*、*超级 301 条款(Super 301)*。

E-IAP

电子版单边行动计划

APEC 成员定期准备的 APEC 单边行动计划电子版。

Ejusdem generis

同类

有时写作*eiusdem*，意为属同种、同类或同质。解释法律的规则，即如一般词

words, the general words will be considered as being limited to the same kind as the particular words.

Electronic commerce: work on electronic commerce, or e-commerce, is under way in many organizations, both governmental and non-governmental. This item is concerned mainly with that of the WTO. The WTO work programme, established in 1998 following the ***Declaration on Global Economic Commerce***, used the following definition: "exclusively for the purpose of the work programme, and without prejudice to its outcome, the term 'electronic commerce' is understood to mean the production, distribution, marketing, sale or delivery of goods and services by electronic means". The Declaration also initiated the ***moratorium on customs duties on electronic transmissions***. Work on electronic commerce mainly takes place in the WTO from the perspectives of trade in services, trade in goods, intellectual property, and trade and development. At the 2017 ***WTO Ministerial Conference*** in Buenos Aires, seventy-one WTO members launched a ***joint initiative*** to start exploratory work towards future WTO negotiations on trade-related aspects of electronic commerce. Any WTO member may participate in this work. See the *World Trade Report 2018*, *see also* ***digital economy***, ***Digital Economy Report***, ***Digital Single Market***, ***digital trade***, ***EDIFACT***, ***trade-related aspects of electronic commerce***, ***UNCITRAL model law on electronic commerce***, ***United Nations Convention on the Use of Electronic Communications in International Contracts*** and ***World Trade Point Federation***.

Electronic Data Interchange: *see* ***EDI***.

Electronic Single Window: *see* ***Single Window***.

Embedded liberalism: a term coined by John Ruggie to describe the post-war economic liberalism which resulted in the GATT and the ***Bretton Woods agreements***. The essence of economic liberalism is a multilateral economic framework subject to domestic interventionism. This would safeguard domestic stability and at the same time end discriminatory trade and exchange practices. [Ruggie 1982]

Embodied services: services embodied in a physical product, such as the intellectual component of computer software sold in the form of floppy disks or CD-ROMs. Some say that the estimated share of services in global trade statistics would double if embodied services were included in service trade statistics. This proposition may well be true, but a demonstration of it could only be achieved with great additional reporting burdens. Reporting embodied services separately would mean, for example, that iron ore exports would consist at least of a commodity component and services components involving at least prospecting, transport, marketing and management. It of course makes sense for a manufacturing firm to know what the services components of its products are worth, but it cannot sell its products separately from these. The customer therefore is charged a single unit price. *See also* ***trade in services statistics***.

Emergency protection: *see* ***escape clause***.

Emergency safeguard mechanism: ESM. Article X of the ***General Agreement on Trade in Services*** requires negotiations on the question of emergency

语跟随特定词语，则一般词语将被视为限于与特定词语属同一类别。

Electronic commerce

电子商务

许多政府组织和非政府组织中正在开展关于电子商务或电商的工作。本词条主要与WTO电子商务工作相关。在《全球电子商务宣言》(英文误为Economic，应为Electronic—译注)发布后，WTO工作计划于1998年设立，使用了如下定义："仅就本工作方案而言且在不损害其结果的情况下，'电子商务'一词被理解指通过电子方式生产、分销、销售或交付货物和服务"。宣言还提出对电子传输暂免关税。WTO中关于电子商务的工作主要从服务贸易、货物贸易、知识产权以及贸易与发展角度开展。2017年在布宜诺斯艾利斯举行的WTO部长级会议上，71个WTO成员发起一项联合倡议，开始就未来WTO与贸易有关的电子商务谈判开展探索性工作。任何WTO成员可参与此项工作。见《世界贸易报告2018》，另见*数字经济(digital economy)*、*数字经济报告(Digital Economy Report)*、*数字单一市场(Digital Single Market)*、*数字贸易(digital trade)*、*行政、商业和运输用电子数据交换(EDIFACT)*、*与贸易有关的电子商务(trade-related aspects of electronic commerce)*、*联合国国际贸易法委员会电子商务示范法(UNCITRAL model law on electronic commerce)*、*联合国国际合同使用电子通信公约(United Nations Convention on the Use of Electronic Communications in International Contracts)*、*世界贸易网点联盟(World Trade Point Federation)*。

Electronic Data Interchange

电子数据交换

见*电子数据交换*(EDI)。

Electronic Single Window

电子单一窗口

见*单一窗口(Single Window)*。

Embedded liberalism

内嵌自由主义

由约翰·鲁格创造的词语，用于描述导致GATT和布雷顿森林协定的战后经济自由主义。经济自由主义本质为受国内干涉主义影响的多边经济框架。可以保障国内稳定，同时终结歧视性贸易和交易惯例。

Embodied services

物化服务

将服务具体化到一有形产品中，例如以软盘或光盘形式销售的计算机软件智能组件。一些人认为，如将具体化服务包括在服务贸易统计中，全球贸易统计中服务的估计份额将翻倍。这一说法很可能是正确的，但是要证明其正确性就要增加巨大报告负担才能实现。将具体化服务单独报告意味着，对于铁矿石出口而言，至少包括商品部分和至少涉及勘探、运输、销售和管理等的服务部分。当然知道其产品服务部分的价值对于制造企业而言是有意义的，但并不能将其产品与这些服务分开销售，消费者因而被收取一个单一单价。另见*服务贸易统计(trade in services statistics)*。

Emergency protection

紧急保护

见*免责条款(escape clause)*。

Emergency safeguard mechanism

紧急保障机制

ESM。《服务贸易总协定》第10条要求就非歧视原则基础上的紧急保障措施

safeguard measures based on the principle of non-discrimination. The results of these negotiations were to enter into effect by 1 January 1998, but so far it has not been possible to find much common ground either on (a) the necessity or desirability of an ESM or (b) its feasibility. Both proponents and opponents of an ESM appear to have taken as their starting point Article XIX of the ***GATT*** which permits the use of ***safeguards*** in the goods trade. Issues raised have accordingly included (a) how an import surge in a service sector would manifest itself, (b) how, in the absence of detailed ***trade in services statistics***, an investigation could produce a reliable picture, and (c) what the remedy would be, bearing in mind the different ***modes of services delivery*** and in particular how ***commercial presence*** (mode 3) would be dealt with. The permitted duration of a safeguard, compensation for the affected party and possible ***structural adjustment*** in the relevant sector would also need to be considered. Developing countries have argued a need for an ESM for services as a political requirement for making liberalization of services more acceptable in their economies. This of course was precisely the reason for the inclusion of the ***escape clause*** in agreements negotiated under the ***United States Reciprocal Trade Agreements Program*** and later the GATT. Developed countries have tended to view the proposed ESM as a mechanism inviting ***protectionism*** because its use would necessarily depend to an even greater extent on perception than is the case for trade in goods.

Empire preferences: *see* ***imperial preferences arrangement***.

Empowerment Programme for National Trade Facilitation Bodies: a professional development programme run by ***UNCTAD*** for ***National Trade Facilitation Committees***. It aims to help them to implement trade facilitation reforms, including the provisions of the WTO ***Agreement on Trade Facilitation***. *See also* ***National Committee on Trade Facilitation***. [www.unctad.org]

Enabling Clause: the *Decision on Differential and More Favourable Treatment, Reciprocity and Fuller Participation of Developing Countries*, one of the outcomes of the ***Tokyo Round***. It allows developed WTO members to take action favouring developing countries without according the same treatment to other members. Main measures covered by it include the ***GSP***, ***non-tariff measures*** covered by the GATT, regional and global trading arrangements between developing countries and special treatment for the ***least-developed countries***. The Enabling Clause was intended to promote greater participation of developing countries in the world trading system, but there is doubt that it achieved its purpose. *See also* ***developing countries and the multilateral trading system***, ***GSTP***, ***Part IV of the GATT***, ***regional trade agreement*** and ***special and differential treatment***.

Energy Charter Treaty: concluded in December 1994 with the signature of the Final Act of the European Energy Charter Conference. Fifty-three countries have signed it. Membership includes most ***OECD*** countries, Central and East European countries and members of the ***Commonwealth of Independent States***. The purpose of the Treaty is to establish "a legal framework in order

问题进行谈判。谈判结果定于1998年1月1日生效，但迄今还不可能就(a)紧急保障机制的必要性或可取性或(b)其可行性找到更多共识。紧急保障措施的支持者和反对者似乎均以GATT第19条作为各自出发点，该条允许在货物贸易中使用保障措施。进而提出的问题包括：(a)服务部门的进口激增如何体现；(b)在无详细服务贸易统计的情况下，调查如何产生可靠的结果；以及(c)考虑到不同的服务提供模式、特别是如何处理商业存在(模式3)的问题，提供何种救济。保障措施的准许期限、对受影响方的补偿以及相关行业可能的结构性调整均需要考虑。发展中国家认为，需要服务紧急保障机制，以此作为使服务自由化在其经济中更易被接受的政治要求。这当然正是根据美国互惠贸易协定计划开展的谈判中及后来的GATT中免责条款的原因。发达国家倾向于将拟议的紧急保障机制视为一种引发保护主义的机制，原因是与货物贸易相比，这一机制的使用在更大程度上取决于感知。

Empire preferences

帝国特惠制

见*帝国特惠安排(imperial preferences arrangement)*。

Empowerment Programme for National Trade Facilitation Bodies

国家贸易便利化机构赋权计划

由联合国贸易与发展会议(UNCTAD)为国家贸易便利化委员会运营的专业发展计划，旨在帮助委员会实施贸易便利化改革，包括 WTO《贸易便利化协定》条款。另见*国家贸易便利化委员会(National Committee on Trade Facilitation)*。

Enabling Clause

授权条款

《关于发展中国家差别和更优惠待遇、互惠和更充分参与的决定》，东京回合成果。允许 WTO 发达国家成员采取有利于发展中国家的行动而不给予其他成员相同待遇。所涵盖的主要措施包括普惠制(GSP)、GATT 所涵盖的非关税措施、发展中国家之间的区域和全球贸易安排以及给予最不发达国家的特殊待遇。授权条款旨在促进发展中国家更多参与世界贸易体制，但对于是否能够实现目标存疑。另见*发展中国家与多边贸易体制(developing countries and the multilateral trading system)*、*全球贸易优惠制(GSTP)*、*GATT 第四部分(Part IV of the GATT)*、*区域贸易协定(regional trade agreement)*、*特殊和差别待遇(special and differential treatment)*。

Energy Charter Treaty

能源宪章条约

《欧洲能源宪章会议最终文件》，于1994年12月缔结，53国已经签署。成员包括大部分经济合作与发展组织(OECD)国家、中东欧国家以及独立国家联合体成员国。条约旨在“依照《欧洲能源宪章》的目标和原则，在互补和互利

to promote long-term co-operation in the energy field, based on complementarities and mutual benefit in accordance with the objectives and principles of the European Energy Charter". It covers broadly trade, investment promotion and protection and other matters relevant to energy. In 1998 the Treaty was amended to bring it into line with the ***WTO Agreement***. At the same time its rules were extended to cover energy-related equipment. These amendments entered into force on 21 January 2010. In 2015 members adopted the ***International Energy Charter***.

Enforceability: refers, for example, to the question of the extent to which provisions in ***free-trade agreements*** can be enforced if a party appears to depart from its commitments. This is relatively easy where the agreement simply incorporates ***WTO*** provisions and thereby provides access to the ***Dispute Settlement Understanding***. It is harder in cases where a party seeks to do it in a bilateral setting.

Enforcement: actions taken by governments through regulatory agencies and the courts to ensure that laws, regulations, rulings, etc., are observed by those to whom they are addressed. *See also* ***compliance***, ***compliance panel***, ***consultation***, ***cross-retaliation***, ***dispute settlement*** and ***retaliation***.

Enhanced Integrated Framework: EIF. The successor to the ***Integrated Framework for Trade-Related Technical Assistance to Least-Developed Countries***. The aims of the EIF are (a) to make trade a main part of national development strategies, (b) to set up structures needed to coordinate the delivery of trade-related technical assistance, and (c) to build capacity to trade which includes addressing critical supply-side constraints. The EIF is supported by a Trust Fund. Apart from the ***WTO***, core partners in EIF are the ***IMF***, ***International Trade Centre*** (ITC), ***UNCTAD***, the ***United Nations Development Programme*** and the ***World Bank***. The ***United Nations Industrial Development Organization*** (UNIDO) is an observer agency. The secretariat is in Geneva.

Enlargement: used especially for the ***accession*** of new member states to the ***European Union***. In 1958 the original six members of the ***European Economic Community*** were Belgium, Federal Republic of Germany, France, Italy, Luxembourg and the Netherlands. The first enlargement came on 1 January 1973 when Denmark, Ireland and the United Kingdom brought its membership to nine. The United Kingdom left the European Union on 31 January 2020. Greece joined in 1981. The enlargement to twelve came in 1986 when Portugal and Spain acceded. The accession of Austria, Finland and Sweden on 1 January 1995 brought its membership to fifteen. On 1 May 2004 Cyprus, Czech Republic, Estonia, Hungary, Latvia, Lithuania, Malta, Poland, Slovak Republic and Slovenia became members. Bulgaria and Romania joined on 1 January 2007, followed by Croatia on 1 July 2013. Membership criteria used to be informal, but in June 1993 the European Council adopted the Copenhagen criteria to judge the readiness for membership of new applicants. These are (a) stability of institutions guaranteeing democracy, the rule of law, human rights and respect for and, protection of minorities, (b) existence of a functioning

基础上，建立促进能源领域长期合作的法律框架”。广泛涵盖贸易、投资促进和保护以及其他与能源相关事项。1998年对条约进行修正使之符合《WTO协定》。同时，其规则扩大到能源相关设备。修正于2010年1月21日生效。成员于2015年通过《国际能源宪章》。

Enforceability

可执行性

举例而言，指如一参加方似乎背离其承诺，自由贸易协定中的条款在多大程度上能被执行的问题。如果简单将WTO条款纳入协定，即可以援引《争端解决谅解》，问题就相对容易。如果一参加方寻求在双边背景下解决，难度就会更大。

Enforcement

执行

政府为保证法律、法规、裁决等得到所针对方遵守而通过监管机构和法院采取的行动。*另见遵守(compliance)、执行之诉专家组(compliance panel)、磋商(consultation)、交叉报复(cross-retaliation)、争端解决(dispute settlement)、报复(retaliation)*。

Enhanced Integrated Framework

增强综合框架

EIF。针对最不发达国家的与贸易有关的技术援助综合框架的后继安排。该框架目标为：(a)使贸易成为国家发展战略的主要部分；(b)建立协调提供与贸易有关技术援助所需结构；以及(c)贸易能力建设，包括处理供给侧重大制约因素。EIF 由一个信托基金提供支持。除 WTO 外，EIF 核心伙伴包括国际货币基金组织(IMF)、国际贸易中心(ITC)、联合国贸易与发展会议(UNCTAD)、联合国开发计划署和世界银行。联合国工业发展组织(UNIDO)为观察机构。秘书处设在日内瓦。

Enlargement

扩盟

特别用于新成员国加入欧盟。1958 年，欧洲经济共同体 6 个创始成员国为比利时、德意志联邦共和国、法国、意大利、卢森堡和荷兰。首次扩盟是在 1973 年 1 月 1 日，丹麦、爱尔兰和英国加入，成员国增至 9 个。2020 年 1 月 31 日，英国脱欧。1981 年，希腊加入。1986 年，葡萄牙和西班牙加入，成员国增至 12 个。1995 年 1 月 1 日，奥地利、芬兰和瑞典加入，成员国达到 15 个。2004 年 5 月 1 日，塞浦路斯、捷克、爱沙尼亚、匈牙利、拉脱维亚、立陶宛、马耳他、波兰、斯洛伐克和斯洛文尼亚加入。2007 年 1 月 1 日，保加利亚和罗马尼亚于加入。2013 年 7 月 1 日，克罗地亚加入。成员资格标准过去并无正式规定，直至欧洲理事会于 1993 年 6 月通过哥本哈根标准，用以判断新申请成员国资格准备情况，包括：(a)保障民主、法治、人权和尊重及保护少数族裔的机构稳定性；(b)具备正常运作的市场经济及应对欧盟内部竞

market economy, as well as the capacity to cope with competitive pressure and market forces within the Union, and (c) an ability to take on the obligations of membership, including adherence to the aims of political, economic and monetary union. The European Union also needs to be able to integrate new members. *See also* ***Agenda 2000***, ***Brexit***, ***Treaty of Nice*** and ***Treaty on European Union***.

Enlightened mercantilism: *see* ***GATT-Think***.

Enquiry points: some WTO agreements as well as some ***free-trade agreements*** require members to establish points in their trade administrations where other members can obtain information on the sector covered by the agreement. Sometimes they are called contact points. The exchange of information is at the governmental level. Examples of such agreements are the ***General Agreement on Trade in Services*** (GATS), the ***Agreement on Trade-Related Aspects of Intellectual Property Rights*** and the ***Agreement on Technical Barriers to Trade***. The GATS also requires developed-country members to establish contact points where private firms from developing countries can find out about trade opportunities.

Enterprise-based definition of investment: *see* ***investment***.

Enterprise for the Americas Initiative: EAI. A United States programme launched in June 1990 to strengthen Latin American and Caribbean economies. The main components of the initiative are trade, investment and debt reduction programmes. The proposed ***FTAA*** had its origin under this initiative. *See also* ***Alliance for Progress***, ***Andean Trade Preference Act***, ***Andean Trade Promotion and Drug Eradication Act*** and ***Caribbean Basin Initiative***. [Green 2003]

Entities: a term used in the WTO ***Agreement on Government Procurement*** to describe any organization or body covered by the Agreement. Typical listings include central and provincial government ministries and offices and enterprises and service providers under their control. These can include water and electricity utilities, port and airport authorities, research organizations, medical services providers, transport enterprises, and so on.

Entrepôt trade: shipping goods through a port in one economy for re-export to another economy. Goods entering and leaving as entrepôt trade are not subject to tariffs. Apparent discrepancies in bilateral trade statistics may arise because goods may be recorded first as entering the intermediate country and then as re-exports to the final destination without any indication of the true country of origin. *See also* ***rules of origin*** and ***transshipment***.

Environmental Database: EDB. *See* ***WTO Environmental Database***.

Environmental dumping: *see* ***eco-dumping*** and ***eco-duties***.

Environmental Goods Agreement: EGA. A proposal for a plurilateral ***WTO*** agreement to liberalize trade in environmental goods. Negotiations were launched in 2014, but they have not yet led to a result. Goods under negotiation include air pollution control, solid and hazardous waste management, environmental remediation and clean-up, cleaner and renewable energy, energy and

争压力和市场力量的能力；以及(c)承担成员国义务的能力，包括遵守政治、经济和货币联盟目标。欧盟也需要能够融入新的成员。另见 *2000 年议程(Agenda 2000)*、*英国脱欧(Brexit)*、*尼斯条约(Treaty of Nice)*、*欧洲联盟条约(Treaty on European Union)*。

Enlightened mercantilism
开明重商主义

见 *GATT 思维(GATT-Think)*。

Enquiry points
咨询点

一些 WTO 协定以及一些自由贸易协定要求成员在其贸易管理部门设立专门的点，以便其他成员能够获得关于协定所涵盖部门的信息。有时也被称为联络点。信息交流是在政府一级进行。此类协定如《服务贸易总协定》(GATS)、《与贸易有关的知识产权协定》和《技术性贸易壁垒协定》。《服务贸易总协定》还要求发达国家成员设立联络点，以便利发展中国家的私营企业获得贸易机会。

Enterprise-based definition of investment
基于企业的投资定义

见*投资(investment)*。

Enterprise for the Americas Initiative
美洲企业倡议

EAI。美国于 1990 年 6 月启动的一项计划，旨在加强拉丁美洲和加勒比地区经济体。该倡议的主要内容是贸易、投资和债务削减计划。拟议中的美洲自由贸易区(FTAA)源于该倡议。另见*进步联盟(Alliance for Progress)*、*安第斯贸易优惠法(Andean Trade Preference Act)*、*安第斯贸易促进与毒品根除法(Andean Trade Promotion and Drug Eradication Act)*、*加勒比盆地倡议(Caribbean Basin Initiative)*。

Entities
实体

WTO《政府采购协定》中用于描述协定所涵盖的任何组织或机构的词语。典型的清单包括中央和省级政府部门、办公室以及在其控制下的企业和服务提供者。可以包括水电等公用事业、港口和机场、研究机构、医疗服务提供者、运输企业等。

Entrepôt trade
转口贸易

运输货物通过一经济体的港口复出口至另一经济体。作为转口贸易进出境的货物不征收关税。双边贸易统计中可能产生明显差异，因为货物可能首先在进入中转国时进行记录，随后在复出口至最终目的地时进行记录而不标明真正原产地。另见*原产地规则(rules of origin)*、*转运(transshipment)*。

Environmental Database
环境数据库

EDB。见 *WTO 环境数据库(WTO Environmental Database)*。

Environmental dumping
环境倾销

见*生态倾销(eco-dumping)*、*环境税(eco-duties)*。

Environmental Goods Agreement
环境产品协定

EGA。WTO诸边协定提案，旨在实现环境产品贸易自由化。谈判于2014年

resource efficiency, wastewater management and water treatment, noise and vibration abatement, environmental monitoring, analysis and assessment, and "environmentally preferable" goods. Members of the negotiating group include Australia, Canada, China, Costa Rica, European Union, Hong Kong (China), Iceland, Israel, Japan, Korea, New Zealand, Norway, Switzerland, Singapore, Chinese Taipei, United States and Turkey. *See also* ***APEC List of Environmental Goods***.

Environmental goods and services: many definitions of this sector are available. A representative one is that produced jointly by the ***OECD*** and Eurostat in 1999. It divides the environmental industry into three sectors: products, systems and services for pollution management, cleaner technologies and products, and resources management. Each of these is divided further as follows: (a) pollution management includes air pollution control, wastewater treatment, waste management, remediation and clean-up of contaminated land and water, noise and vibration control, environmental analysis and assessment, environmental research and development, general administration (public sector) and environmental management (private sector), (b) cleaner technologies and products which includes cleaner/resource-efficient technologies and processes and cleaner/resource-efficient products, and (c) resources management which includes portable water treatment and distribution, recycled materials, renewable energy plant and nature protection. Some WTO members have attempted to resolve the problem by listing products of interest to them. These have generally fallen into six categories: (a) air pollution control, (b) renewable energy, (c) waste management and water treatment, (d) environmental technologies (i.e. emission reductions, heat and energy management, environmental monitoring equipment), (e) carbon capture and storage, and (f) other areas that may deal with disposal, natural resource protection, etc. *See also* ***Environmental Goods Agreement***.

Environmentally preferable products: products or services that affect the environment less than other products having the same purpose. Such products typically contain recycled materials, save energy and water in their production, reduce waste and minimize toxic by-products. *See also* ***life cycle assessment***.

Environmentally preferable purchasing: policies that result in the purchase of products and services affecting the environment less than other products having the same purpose. Some governments have programmes to promote such policies. The United States Environmental Protection Agency, for example, has developed a framework of five principles for this purpose: (a) include environmental considerations as part of the normal purchasing process, (b) emphasize pollution prevention early in the purchasing process, (c) examine multiple environmental attributes throughout a product's or service's life cycle, (d) compare relevant environmental impacts when selecting products and services, and (e) collect and base purchasing decisions on accurate and meaningful information about environmental performance. *See also* ***life cycle assessment***. [www.epa.gov]

启动，但尚未产生结果。谈判产品包括空气污染控制、固体和危险废物管理、环境修复和清理、清洁和可再生能源、能源和资源效率、废水管理和水处理、噪音以及减振、环境监测、分析和评估以及“环境友好型”产品。谈判组成员包括澳大利亚、加拿大、中国、哥斯达黎加、欧盟、中国香港、冰岛、以色列、日本、韩国、新西兰、挪威、瑞士、新加坡、中国台北、美国和土耳其。*另见APEC环境产品清单(APEC List of Environmental Goods)*。

Environmental goods and services

环境产品和服务

这一部门有多种定义。具有代表性的定义是1999年由经济合作与发展组织(OECD)与欧盟统计局联合制定的。该定义将环境产业划分为3个部门：用于污染管理的产品、系统和服务、清洁技术和产品以及资源管理。每一部门细分如下：(a)污染管理，包括大气污染控制、废水管理、废物管理、受污染土地和水的修复和清洁、噪声与振动控制、环境分析和评价、环境研究与开发、行政管理(公共部门)和环境管理(私营部门)；(b)清洁技术和产品，包括清洁/节能技术和工艺及清洁/节能产品；以及(c)资源管理，包括饮用水处理和配送、再生材料、可再生能源工厂和自然保护。一些WTO成员试图通过列出感兴趣的产品解决问题。这些产品一般分为6类：(a)大气污染控制；(b)可再生能源；(c)废物管理和废水处理；(d)环境技术(即减少排放、热量和能源管理、环境监测设备)；(e)碳捕捉和储存；以及(f)废物处置、自然资源保护等的其他领域。*另见环境产品协定(Environmental Goods Agreement)*。

Environmentally preferable products

环境无害产品

与具有相同用途的其他产品相比较，对环境的影响更小的产品或服务。此类产品通常含有再生材料，在生产过程中节能节水，减少废物，并尽量减少有毒副产品。*另见生命周期评估(life cycle assessment)*。

Environmentally preferable purchasing

环保采购

与具有相同用途的其他产品相比较，所产生的货物和服务采购对环境的影响更小的政策。一些政府制定了促进此类政策的计划。例如，美国环境保护署为此制定了具有五项原则的框架：(a)将环境因素作为正常采购过程的一部分；(b)在采购过程较早环节强调污染防治；(c)在产品或服务的生命周期审查多种环境属性；(d)在选择产品和服务时比较相关环境影响；以及(e)收集并根据准确且有意义的环境绩效信息作出采购决定。*另见生命周期评估(life cycle assessment)*。

Environmentally sound technologies: these are technologies capable of reducing environmental damage through processes that create fewer potentially damaging substances.

Environmental rules under the WTO: the WTO does not have a system of rules specifically dealing with environmental matters, but that does not mean that it is indifferent to environmental concerns. The basic WTO tenet is that governments are free to set and enforce their own environmental standards in their territories if they do it without discriminating against other members, such as contravening the most-favoured-nation rule or the ***national treatment*** principle. ***GATT*** Article XX (General Exceptions), which permits the suspension of obligations under the Agreement to the extent necessary in narrowly defined circumstances, can be used to enforce some environmental objectives. Article XX(b) can be invoked to adopt or enforce measures necessary to protect human, animal or plant life or health. Article XX(d) can be used to ensure compliance with laws and regulations otherwise consistent with the GATT. Article XX(g) enables adoption or enforcement of measures relating to the conservation of exhaustible natural resources if such measures are made effective in conjunction with restrictions on domestic production or consumption. Some have argued that Article XX should be supplemented by a provision permitting the suspension of GATT obligations to promote environmental protection, but this proposition remains contentious. Article XIV of the ***General Agreement on Trade in Services*** permits in some cases suspension of the Agreement's provisions to protect human, animal or plant life or health. The WTO forum for the consideration of environmental matters is the ***Committee on Trade and Environment***. The ***Doha Ministerial Conference*** launched negotiations on the relationship between existing WTO rules and specific trade obligations set out in ***multilateral environment agreements***. It also extended the WTO work programme on ***trade and environment*** by establishing a work programme to examine (a) the effect of environmental measures on market access, (b) the environmental provisions of the ***Agreement on Trade-Related Aspects of Intellectual Property Rights*** and (c) labelling requirements for environmental purposes. Some prominent GATT and WTO disputes with an environmental component were ***Superfund***, ***Tuna I*** and ***Tuna II***. *See also* ***Agreement on the Application of Sanitary and Phytosanitary Measures***, ***eco-labelling***, ***fisheries subsidies***, ***general exceptions***, ***race-to-the-bottom argument*** and ***sanitary and phytosanitary measures***.

Environment and trade: *see* ***trade and environment***.

Environment and Trade Hub: launched by the United Nations Environment Programme (***UNEP***) in 2015. Its aim is to assist countries to use sustainable trade for achieving the ***Sustainable Development Goals***. [www.unenvironment.org]

ePing SPS and TBT notification alert system: a collaboration between the ***WTO***, the ***International Trade Centre*** and the United Nations Department of Economic and Social Affairs (DESA) resulting in an online alert system for

Environmentally sound technologies
环境友好型技术
能够通过使用产生更少潜在有害物质的工艺而减少环境损害的技术。

Environmental rules under the WTO
WTO 环境规则
WTO 中没有专门处理环境事务的规则系统，但这并不意味着它对环境问题不感兴趣。WTO 的基本信条是，各国政府有权在其领土内制定和执行各自的环境标准，只要这样作不歧视其他成员，例如违反最惠国待遇原则或国民待遇原则。GATT 第 20 条(一般例外)允许在严格定义的情况下在必要限度内中止履行协定项下义务，此条可以用以实施一些环境目标。可援引第 20 条(b)款采取或实施保护人类、动物或植物的生命或健康所必需的措施。第 20 条(d)款可用于保证遵守与 GATT 不相抵触的法律法规的实施。第 20 条(g)款允许采取或实施与保护可用尽的自然资源相关的措施，如此类措施与限制国内生产或消费一同实施。一些人认为，第 20 条应补充允许中止履行 GATT 义务以促进环境保护的条款，但这一主张存在争议。《服务贸易总协定》第 14 条允许在一些情况下中止该协定条款以保护人类、动物或植物的生命或健康。WTO 中审议环境问题的场所是贸易与环境委员会。多哈部长级会议启动了关于现行 WTO 规则与多边环境协定中具体贸易义务之间关系的谈判。同时通过建立一项工作计划，扩展了 WTO 关于贸易与环境的工作计划，以审查(a)环境措施对市场准入的影响；(b)《与贸易有关的知识产权协定》中的环境条款；以及(c)有关环境目标的标签要求。GATT 和 WTO 中与环境有关的著名争端案件包括“超级基金案”、“第一个金枪鱼案”和“第二个金枪鱼案”。另见*实施卫生与植物卫生措施协定(Agreement on the Application of Sanitary and Phytosanitary Measures)*、*生态标签(eco-labelling)*、*渔业补贴(fisheries subsidies)*、*一般例外(general exceptions)*、*竞次论(race-to-the-bottom argument)*、*卫生与植物卫生措施(sanitary and phytosanitary measures)*。

Environment and trade
环境与贸易
见*贸易与环境(trade and environment)*。

Environment and Trade Hub
环境与贸易中心
联合国环境规划署(UNEP)于 2015 年启动，目的是帮助各国利用可持续贸易实现可持续发展目标。

ePing SPS and TBT notification alert system
TBT/SPS ePing 通报提醒系统
WTO、国际贸易中心以及联合国经济和社会事务部(DESA)合作所产生的 WTO 成员根据《实施卫生与植物卫生措施协定》和《技术性贸易壁垒协定》

notifications submitted by WTO members under the ***Agreement on the Application of Sanitary and Phytosanitary Measures*** and the ***Agreement on Technical Barriers to Trade***. The alert system is searchable. [epingalert.org]

Equality of competitive opportunity: the principle underlying the ***national treatment*** obligation contained in Article III of the ***GATT***. It means that national laws and regulations have to be drafted so that imported products are able to compete effectively with domestic products. Normally, this means that regulations for imported and domestic products are identical, but there may be formally different rules for imports if this is the only way to achieve equal opportunity. *See also* ***competitive neutrality***, ***economic impact criterion*** and ***implicit discrimination***.

Equitable competition: a concept based on the assumption that there ought to be some degree of international harmonization of labour, environmental and other standards seen to affect the cost of production to achieve a framework in which firms compete on more equal terms. The wisdom underlying this concept is that countries permitting inadequate standards give their firms a cost advantage which translates into enhanced international competitiveness for them. *See also* ***fair competition***, ***level playing field***, ***social clause***, ***trade and environment*** and ***trade and labour standards***.

Equitable share of the market: an elusive concept enshrined in GATT Article XVI:3 (Subsidies) concerning allowable subsidies for ***primary products***. GATT members have held the view at least since 1955 that it was desirable to satisfy world requirements of primary commodities in the most effective and economic manner, and that account should be taken of any special factors regarding the exporting country's share of world trade in the product concerned during a representative period. The ***panel*** in the ***French wheat and wheat flour case*** in 1958 made useful observations on the concept of "equitable share", but these have not been developed and refined by later panels. Article 9 of the *Tokyo Round Agreement on Interpretation and Application of Articles VI, XVI and XXIII of the General Agreement on Tariffs and Trade* (the Subsidies Code) notes that with regard to new markets, traditional patterns of supply of the product to the region in which the new market is located must be taken into account in determining "equitable share of world export trade". GATT Article XIII (Non-discriminatory Administration of Quantitative Restrictions) also seeks to ensure the principle of fair market share. It requires the distribution of trade in a product subject to ***quantitative restrictions*** to approach as closely as possible the shares exporting countries might obtain in the absence of restrictions, and it sets out ways of how this might be done.

Equivalence: a principle set out in the WTO ***Agreement on the Application of Sanitary and Phytosanitary Measures***. It says that if an exporting country demonstrates objectively to an importing country that its sanitary and phytosanitary measures achieve the levels set by the importing country, the levels should be considered equivalent. The measures taken by the two countries need not be identical.

所提交通报的在线提醒系统。提醒系统具有查询功能。

Equality of competitive opportunity

竞争机会均等

GATT 第 3 条所含国民待遇义务的基本原理。意味着一国国内法律法规的制定应使进口产品能够与本国产品进行有效竞争。通常情况下，这意味着进口产品和本国产品的法规应相同，但针对进口产品的法规可能会在形式上有所不同，如果这是实现机会均等的惟一途径。另见*竞争中立(competitive neutrality)*、*经济影响标准(economic impact criterion)*、*隐性歧视(implicit discrimination)*。

Equitable competition

公平竞争

这一概念基于这样的假设，即劳工、环境及其他被认为影响生产成本的标准应进行一定程度的国际协调，以形成企业可在更平等条件下进行竞争的框架。这一概念所蕴含的智慧是，允许存在不完善标准的国家给予本国企业一种成本优势，这一优势转化为这些企业增强的国际竞争力。另见*公平竞争(fair competition)*、*公平竞争环境(level playing field)*、*社会条款(social clause)*、*贸易与环境(trade and environment)*、*贸易与劳工标准(trade and labour standards)*。

Equitable share of the market

公正市场份额

GATT第16条(补贴)第3款中包含的一个难以解释的概念，该款有关对初级产品允许使用的补贴。至少自1955年以来，GATT缔约方一直认为，宜采取最有效和最经济的方式满足世界对初级商品的要求，也应考虑在一代表期内该出口国的相关产品在世界贸易中所占份额等任何特殊因素。“法国小麦和小麦面粉案”专家组在1958年对“公正份额”的概念提出了有益的评论，但后来的专家组没有对此进行发展和完善。东京回合《关于解释和适用关税与贸易总协定第6条、16条和23条的协定》(《补贴守则》)第9条指出，就新市场而言，在确定“世界出口贸易的公正份额”时，必须考虑该产品对新市场所在区域的传统供应模式。GATT第13条(数量限制的非歧视管理)也寻求保证公正市场份额。该条要求受数量限制管理产品的贸易分配尽可能接近在无限制情况下出口国可以获得的份额，并就此规定了如何实现的途径。

Equivalence

等效

WTO《实施卫生与植物卫生措施协定》中规定的一项原则。指出如果一出口国客观地向一进口国证明其卫生与植物卫生措施达到进口国规定的水平，该水平应被视为等效。两国采取的措施不必相同。

Equivalence of advantages: achieved through the granting of a benefit to another party in return for a benefit of about the same size. *See also* ***reciprocity***.

Equivalent measure of support: EMS. A term used in the WTO ***Agreement on Agriculture***. It describes an annual level of support to agricultural producers, expressed in monetary terms, which cannot be calculated in accordance with the methods used for determining the aggregate measure of support.

Erga omnes**:** *Lat.* "against all" or "in relation to all". It is a term sometimes used in trade agreements, as in "If a party lowers its tariffs *erga omnes* . . .".

Erga omnes* obligations:** obligations to the international community as a whole, regardless of consent. Crawford says that "one can infer that the core cases of obligations *erga omnes* are the non-derogable obligations of a general character which arise either directly under general international law or under generally accepted multilateral treaties (e.g. in the field of human rights)". He continues that such obligations are "virtually coextensive with peremptory obligations (arising under norms of ***jus cogens)". Where the parties to an international regime have a common legal interest, i.e. where it is necessary to join a multilateral treaty for the legal interest to arise, the obligation is known as *erga omnes partes*. [Crawford 2000, Pauwelyn 2002]

ESCAP: the Economic and Social Commission for the Asia-Pacific. One of the ***United Nations regional commissions***. It was established in 1947 as the Economic Commission for Asia and the Far East (ECAFE) and given its present name in 1974. It has major work programmes on regional economic cooperation, environment and sustainable development, poverty alleviation, transport and communications, statistics and issues concerning least-developed, landlocked and island developing countries. ESCAP's secretariat is located in Bangkok. *See also* ***Asia-Pacific Trade Agreement***, ***Asia-Pacific Trade Facilitation Forum*** and ***Framework Agreement on Facilitation of Cross-border Paperless Trade in Asia and the Pacific***.

Escape clause: a provision in trade agreements which permits a party to suspend its obligations when imports cause or threaten to cause ***serious injury*** to the domestic producers of similar goods. GATT Article XIX contains the escape clause for trade in goods used by WTO members. It allows a member to suspend its obligations or to modify liberalizing commitments if there are ***unforeseen developments*** and if any product is imported in such increased quantities likely to cause or causing harm to domestic producers. The Article is supplemented by the detailed rules of the ***Agreement on Safeguards***. One clarification it makes is that ***customs unions*** may choose between imposing a safeguard measure on behalf of the entire union or on behalf of one member only. The decision has to be made at the time of the investigation. The ***General Agreement on Trade in Services*** does not yet have an escape clause, though Article X establishes the mandate for this. Two main reasons are usually given for the inclusion of safeguard provisions in agreements. First, they encourage greater liberalization since countries making liberalizing commitments will have the opportunity to step back from them if they have unwittingly provoked

Equivalence of advantages

利益对等

通过给予另一方一项利益换取大小几近相同的一项利益。另见***互惠*** *(reciprocity)*。

Equivalent measure of support

支持等值

EMS。WTO《农业协定》中使用的词语。描述了以货币形式表示的、向农业生产者提供的年度支持水平，此种支持无法按照确定综合支持量的方法进行计算。

Erga omnes

普遍

拉丁语。意为"对一切"或"与一切有关"。贸易协定中有时使用的词语，例如"如一方降低其全部关税……"。

***Erga omnes* obligations**

普遍义务

对整个国际社会的义务，无论是否同意。克劳福德指出："人们可以推断，普遍义务的核心案例是具有普遍特征的不可克减的义务，或是直接源自一般国际法或是源自普遍接受的多边条约(例如在人权领域) 。"他指出，这些义务"实际上与强制性义务(根据强制法的规范产生)同时存在。"如果一项国际制度的参加方具有共同法律利益，即必须加入一多边条约方可产生法律利益，那么该义务即为普遍义务。

ESCAP

亚洲及太平洋经济社会理事会

联合国区域委员会。于1947年设立，原名为亚洲及远东经济委员会(ECAFE)，1974 年改为现名。主要工作计划为区域经济合作、环境和可持续发展、减贫、运输和通信以及有关最不发达国家、内陆和小岛屿发展中国家的数据统计和事务。ESCAP 秘书处设在曼谷。另见***亚太贸易协定****(Asia-Pacific Trade Agreement)*、***亚太贸易便利化论坛****(Asia-Pacific Trade Facilitation Forum)*、***亚洲及太平洋跨境无纸贸易便利化框架协定****(Framework Agreement on Facilitation of Cross-border Paperless Trade in Asia and the Pacific)*。

Escape clause

免责条款

贸易协定中的一项条款，允许一参加方在进口产品对国内同类产品生产商造成或威胁造成严重损害时中止履行其义务。GATT 第 19 条包含 WTO 成员可使用的货物贸易免责条款。允许一成员在出未预见的情况和任何产品的进口数量如此之大可能对国内生产者造成或正在造成损害时，中止履行其义务或修改自由化承诺。《保障措施协定》的详细规则对第 19 条进行了补充。其中所作一项澄清为，关税同盟可以选择代表整个同盟或仅代表一成员实施保障措施。这一决定必须在调查时作出。《服务贸易总协定》目前尚无免责条款，但第10条为此制定了授权。在协定中包含保障措施条款通常有两个主要原因：一是这一条款鼓励更大程度的自由化，因为如果自由化承诺意外导致明显损害国内产业的进口激增，作出这些承诺的国家即有机会时退出承诺。二是通

a surge in imports clearly harming domestic industry. Second, they increase the flexibility of the ***multilateral trading system*** by promoting its longer-term stability. The immediate reason for including an escape clause in the GATT was United States Executive Order 9832 of February 1947 which made it mandatory for American trade negotiators to include in all future trade agreements an escape clause similar to that contained in the United States–Mexico Trade Agreement of December 1942. *See also* ***emergency safeguard mechanism***, ***parallelism in safeguards***, ***safeguards*** and ***Section 201***.

ESM: *see* ***emergency safeguard mechanism***.

Essential facilities doctrine: an antitrust term meaning broadly that the owner of an "essential", "bottleneck" or "gate-keeper" facility, such as a public electricity or water utility, a telecommunications network or a railway, must give access to competitors at a reasonable price so that they in turn can conduct their own businesses. The interpretation of this doctrine varies from country to country.

Essential products: WTO members may in defined circumstances impose restrictions on imports under GATT Article XII to safeguard their balance of payments. Developing-country members may also use Article XVIII. In doing so, they may give priority to the import of products deemed more essential than others. The ***Understanding on the Balance-of-Payments Provisions of the GATT***, concluded during the ***Uruguay Round***, defines "essential products" as those which meet basic consumption needs or those which contribute to an improvement of the balance-of-payments situation, such as capital goods or other inputs into production.

EST: environmentally-sound technology.

EST&P: environmentally-sound technology and products.

Establishment: *see* ***investment***, ***post-establishment***, ***pre-establishment, right of establishment*** and ***right of non-establishment***.

Estoppel: a rule in the law of evidence that a party in legal proceedings cannot deny or assert something when that would be inconsistent with its own statements or conduct. M. N. Shaw puts it this way: "states deemed to have consented to a state of affairs cannot afterwards alter their position". [Shaw 2014]

Eswatini: the official name since 19 May 2018 for what used to be Swaziland.

e-TRIPS Notifications Submission System: NSS. A system launched in early 2019 by the WTO to enable members to submit electronically notifications, review materials and reports. It can also be used for responding to questionnaires issued by the ***Council for TRIPS*** as well as regular reports on technical assistance and measures for technology transfer filed by members or intergovernmental organizations.

Eurasian Economic Community: EURASEC. It was first established in 1995 and given its present name on 30 May 2001. It consisted of Belarus, Kazakhstan, Kyrghyz Republic, Russia and Tajikistan. Moldova and Ukraine were observers. Abolished in 2014 and succeeded by the ***Eurasian Economic Union***.

过促进多边贸易体制的长期稳定，以增强这一体制的灵活性。在 GATT 中包括免责条款的直接原因是 1947 年 2 月美国《第 9832 号行政命令》，该行政命令要求美国贸易谈判代表必须在今后的所有贸易协定中包括类似于 1942 年 12 月《美国—墨西哥贸易协定》中所含免责条款。另见*紧急保障机制(emergency safeguard mechanism)*、*保障措施的平行性(parallelism in safeguards)*、*保障措施(safeguards)*、*201 条款(Section 201)*。

ESM

见*紧急保障机制(emergency safeguard mechanism)*。

Essential facilities doctrine

必要设施原则

反垄断用语，指“必要”、“瓶颈”或“关键”设施所有者，如公共供电或供水设施、电信网络或铁路，必须以合理价格允许竞争对手进入，从而使他们能够开展自己的业务。对原则的解释各国不尽相同。

Essential products

必需品

WTO成员可以在特定情况下根据GATT第12条对进口实施限制，以保障其国际收支。发展中国家成员还可以使用第18条。在这样作时，成员可以对与其他产品相比较更为必需的产品的进口给予优先考虑。乌拉圭回合期间达成的《关于1994年关税与贸易总协定国际收支条款的谅解》将“必需品”定义为满足基本消费需要或有助于改善国际收支状况的产品，例如资本货物或其他生产所需投入物。

EST

环境友好型技术

EST&P

环境友好型技术和产品

Establishment

设立

见*投资(investment)*、*准入后(post-establishment)*、*准入前(pre-establishment)*、*设立权(right of establishment)*、*无需设立商业实体权(right of non-establishment)*。

Estoppel

禁止反言

证据法中的一项规则，在法律诉讼中当事方不能否认或主张与其自身陈述或行为不一致之事。马尔科姆·N. 肖指出：“被视为同意某一事态的国家不能事后改变其立场。”

Eswatini

斯威士兰王国

斯威士兰自2018年5月19日起的正式国名，旧称Swaziland。

e-TRIPS Notifications Submission System

e-TRIPS 通报提交系统

NSS。WTO在2019年初推出的系统，可使成员以电子方式提交通报、审议材料和报告。还可用于答复与贸易有关的知识产权理事会散发的问题单，以及成员或政府间组织提交的关于技术援助和技术转让措施的定期报告。

Eurasian Economic Community

欧亚经济共同体

EURASEC。最初于1995年建立，2001年5月30日改为现名。由白俄罗斯、哈萨克斯坦、吉尔吉斯斯坦、俄罗斯和塔吉克斯坦组成。摩尔多瓦和乌克兰曾为观察员。2014年废止，由欧亚经济联盟取代。

Eurasian Economic Union: EAEU. Established on 20 January 2015. It consists of Armenia, Belarus, Kazakhstan, Kyrgyzstan and Russia. At present it is primarily a ***customs union***, but it has aspirations for higher levels of economic integration. Its secretariat is in Moscow.

Euro: €. The ***European Union*** common currency introduced on 1 January 1999. User countries make up the ***Eurozone***.

Euro-Mediterranean Association Agreements: the ***preferential trade arrangements***, often known informally as ***Mediterranean Agreements***, between the ***European Community*** and some countries located on the rim of the Mediterranean Sea. They are divided into first-generation cooperation agreements concluded in the 1960s and 1970s (now superseded by other agreements) and those concluded in the late 1990s. The modern Association Agreements include provisions concerning many trade and economic matters, including the establishment of a WTO-consistent ***free-trade area*** over twelve years. Other provisions deal with cooperation in social affairs and migration. They also include a ***democracy clause*** and a ***human rights clause***. *See also* **Barcelona process**.

Euro-Mediterranean Free Trade Area: EMFTA. A proposed ***free-trade area*** aimed at removing barriers to trade and investment between the ***European Union*** and Southern Mediterranean countries as well as between the Southern Mediterranean countries themselves. Originally it was intended to be concluded by 2020, but for various reasons the process has experienced significant delays.

Europe Agreements: a type of ***Association Agreement*** used by the ***European Union*** for its political and economic relations under preferential conditions with the countries of Central and Eastern Europe. They were concluded in the first half of the 1990s. The agreements covered trade-related issues, political dialogue and legal aspects. Under these agreements, Central and East European countries undertook to align their laws to those of the European Union in areas such as capital movement, ***competition laws***, ***intellectual property rights*** and ***government procurement***. Europe Agreements allowed for the possibility of eventual full membership of the Union, but they did not guarantee it. Most have now been superseded because the parties have joined the European Union. *See also* ***enlargement*** and ***Mediterranean Agreements***.

European Agricultural Fund for Rural Development: EAFRD. One of the two pillars for financing the ***common agricultural policy*** of the ***European Union***. It finances the rural development programmes of member states.

European Agricultural Guarantee Fund: EAGF. One of the two pillars financing the ***common agricultural policy*** of the ***European Union***. It finances direct payments to farmers and measures to regulate agricultural markets, such as ***intervention*** and export refunds. Other measures covered include promotion of fruit in schools, certain veterinary, animal and plant health programmes, promotion of farm produce and setting up and running farm accounting information systems.

European Agricultural Guidance and Guarantee Fund: the mechanism until the end of 2006 through which the ***European Union*** financed the ***common***

Eurasian Economic Union

欧亚经济联盟

EAEU。2015年1月20日建立。由亚美尼亚、白俄罗斯、哈萨克斯坦、吉尔吉斯斯坦和俄罗斯组成。目前主要是关税同盟，但希望实现更高水平的经济一体化。秘书处设在莫斯科。

Euro

欧元

€。1999 年 1 月 1 日起采用的欧盟共同货币。使用国构成欧元区。

Euro-Mediterranean Association Agreements

欧洲与地中海联系协定

欧洲共同体与位于地中海沿岸一些国家之间的优惠贸易安排，通常非正式地称为《地中海协定》。这些协定分为 20 世纪 60 年代和 70 年代缔结的第一代合作协定(现已被其他协定所取代)和 90 年代末缔结的协定。现代联系协定包括关于众多贸易和经济事务的条款，包括在 12 年内建立一个符合 WTO 规则的自由贸易区。其他条款处理社会事务和移民方面的合作，另外还包括一项民主条款和一项人权条款。另见*巴塞罗那进程(Barcelona process)*。

Euro-Mediterranean Free Trade Area

欧洲—地中海自由贸易区

EMFTA。拟议的自由贸易区，旨在消除欧盟与南地中海国家之间以及南地中海各国之间的贸易和投资壁垒。原拟2020年完成，但由于各种原因，进程明显延迟。

Europe Agreements

欧洲协定

欧盟使用的一种联系协定，用以处理与中东欧国家之间在优惠条件下的政治和经济关系。缔结于20世纪90年代上半叶。这些协定涵盖与贸易有关的问题、政治对话和法律问题。根据协定，中东欧国家承诺在使资本流动、竞争法、知识产权和政府采购等领域的法律与欧盟法律保持一致。欧洲协定考虑到了最终成为欧盟正式成员国的可能性，但并不作出保证。这些协定中的大多数已被取代，原因是参加方已经加入欧盟。另见*扩盟(enlargement)*、*地中海协定(Mediterranean Agreements)*。

European Agricultural Fund for Rural Development

欧洲农村农业发展基金

EAFRD。资助欧盟共同农业政策的两大支柱之一。为成员国的农村发展计划提供资金。

European Agricultural Guarantee Fund

欧洲农业担保基金

EAGF。资助欧盟共同农业政策的两大支柱之一。资助对农民的直接支付和规范农产品市场的措施，例如干预和出口退税。其他措施涵盖在学校推广水果、特定兽医、动物和植物健康计划、农产品推广以及建立和运行农场会计信息系统。

European Agricultural Guidance and Guarantee Fund

欧洲农业指导和担保基金

2006 年年底前运行的机制，欧盟通过基金为共同农业政策提供资金。基金分

agricultural policy. The Fund was in two parts: (a) the Guidance part which funded structural policy, and (b) the Guarantee part which supported markets and prices. It was replaced by the ***European Agricultural Guarantee Fund***.

European Coal and Steel Community: ECSC. Established in 1951 by the Treaty of Paris. It created a single market for coal and steel among member countries. Members delegated their powers in this regard to a newly created High Authority, a supra-national authority. The successful working of the ECSC was one of the factors leading to the negotiation of the ***Treaty of Rome*** which created the ***European Economic Community***. In 1965, the *Treaty establishing a Single Council of the European Communities* (the Merger Treaty) unified the High Authority with the Commission of the European Economic Community. The Treaty establishing the ECSC expired on 23 July 2002. *See also* ***European Communities*** and ***European Union***.

European Commission: one of the ***European Union*** institutions in which political authority resides. According to Article 17 of the ***Treaty on European Union*** the Commission's task is to promote the general interest of the European Union and to take appropriate initiatives to that end. It also must ensure the application of the Treaties (i.e. the *Treaty on European Union* and the ***Treaty on the Functioning of the European Union***) and measures adopted under them. It exercises a wide range of functions, but it should be clearly understood that even in areas where the Commission has sole responsibility for policies and activities, it operates in a finely balanced situation where the member states and the European Parliament, for example, ensure that their interests are duly considered. The Commission consists of twenty-seven members who are known, internally anyway, as the "college". They are appointed for five years. The Commission is headed by the President. The Commission is divided into policy departments known as Directorates-General, such as Agriculture and Rural Development, Competition, Economic and Financial Affairs, Environment, Maritime Affairs and Fisheries, and Trade. *See also* ***common commercial policy***.

European Communities: a term created with the adoption of the Merger Treaty (*Treaty establishing a Single Council of the European Communities*) in 1965 which created, among other institutional changes, a single Commission of the European Communities. The Commission unified the bodies administering the European Atomic Energy Community, the ***European Coal and Steel Community*** (ECSC) and the ***European Economic Community***. Article XI of the ***WTO Agreement*** refers to the European Communities as a member of the WTO. This is because there were doubts at that time whether the ***European Community*** had ***competence*** over matters falling within the ambit of the ECSC and the Atomic Energy Community. These doubts proved unjustified. In any case, the matter was laid to rest when the ***European Union*** acquired legal personality through the ***Treaty of Lisbon***. *See also* ***European Commission***. [Schroeder 2003, Wessel 2003]

European Community: created as a legal entity by the ***Treaty of Maastricht*** as the successor of the ***European Economic Community*** (EEC or the Common

为两部分：(a)指导部分，为结构性政策提供资金；及(b)担保部分，用于支持市场和价格。被欧洲农业担保基金所取代。

European Coal and Steel Community
欧洲煤钢共同体

ECSC。1951 年《巴黎条约》所建立。为成员国之间建立了一个煤炭和钢铁的单一市场。成员们将其在这方面的权力授予了新创设的一个超国家的权力机构——高级机构。ECSC 的成功运行是促成《罗马条约》谈判的因素之一，《罗马条约》创建了欧洲经济共同体。1965 年，《建立欧洲经济共同体单一理事会条约》(《合并条约》)将高级机构与欧洲经济共同体委员会合并。《建立欧洲煤钢共同体条约》于 2002 年 7 月 23 日失效。另见*欧洲共同体(European Communities)*、*欧洲联盟(European Union)*。

European Commission
欧盟委员会

拥有政治权力的欧盟机构。根据《欧洲联盟条约》第17条，委员会的任务是促进欧盟的普遍利益，并为此采取适当措施，还应保证条约的适用(例如《欧洲联盟条约》和《欧洲联盟运行条约》)及根据条约采取的措施的实施。委员会行使广泛职能，但是应该清楚地认识到，即使在委员会负有政策和行动惟一责任的领域，也是在一种微妙平衡的情况下运作，例如成员国和欧洲议会需要保证它们的利益得到适当考虑。委员会由27名委员组成，内部称为“委员团”，任期5年。委员会由主席领导，下设被称为“总司”的政策部门，例如农业和农村发展总司、竞争政策总司、经济和财政事务总司、环境总司、海事和渔业总司以及贸易总司等。另见*共同商业政策(common commercial policy)*。

European Communities
欧洲共同体

1965 年《合并条约》(即《建立欧洲经济共同体单一理事会条约》)通过后创造的词语。该条约创建了诸多机构变革，其中之一是欧洲共同体单一委员会。委员会统一了欧洲原子能共同体、欧洲煤钢共同体(ECSC)和欧洲经济共同体的管理机构。《WTO 协定》第 11 条将欧洲共同体视为一个 WTO 成员，这是由于当时对欧洲共同体是否有权处理属于欧洲煤钢共同体和原子能共同体职权范围内事务的权限存在疑问。这些怀疑被证明是不必要的。无论如何，在欧盟通过《里斯本条约》获得法律人格后，此问题不再被提及。另见*欧盟委员会(European Commission)*。

European Community
欧洲共同体

《马斯特里赫特条约》创设的法律实体，作为欧洲经济共同体(EEC 或共同

Market). Often shortened to EC. The term "European Community" was often used before the entry into force of the Treaty of Maastricht to mean the EEC. The exact meaning is usually clear from the context. *See also* ***enlargement***, ***European Union***, ***Treaty of Maastricht***, ***Treaty on European Union*** and ***Treaty on the Functioning of the European Union***.

European Council: consists of heads of state or governments of the member states of the ***European Union***, together with its president, the president of the ***European Commission*** and the High Representative for Foreign Affairs and Security Policy. It meets twice every six months. *See also* ***Council of the European Union*** and ***Treaty on European Union***.

European Court of Justice: *see* ***Court of Justice of the European Union***.

European Economic Area: EEA. Entered into force on 1 January 1994. It comprises the twenty-seven members of the ***European Union*** (EU) and three of the four members of ***EFTA*** (Iceland, Liechtenstein and Norway) in a single market. Switzerland decided in December 1992 not to join the EEA. For the EFTA countries membership of the EEA represents an intermediate step between a separate EFTA and full EU membership. The agreement establishing the EEA covers the ***four freedoms*** (free movement of goods, persons, services and capital). The EEA does not cover the ***common agricultural policy***, the ***common fisheries policy*** and the ***common commercial policy***, common foreign and security policy, justice and home affairs, direct and indirect taxation or economic and monetary union. Members of the EEA must adopt the ***acquis communautaire*** dealing with competition. EFTA states are also bound by the European Union rules on social policy, consumer protection, environment, company law and statistics.

European Economic Community: EEC. Established by the ***Treaty of Rome*** which was signed on 25 March 1957. It entered into force on 1 January 1958. The Treaty was intended to "lay the foundations of an ever closer union among the peoples of Europe". Among its principal aims were the elimination of tariff and non-tariff barriers among member states and the formation of a ***common market*** entailing also the free movement of persons, services and capital. Among the elements making up the EEC were the ***common agricultural policy***, the ***common commercial policy*** and a common transport policy. *See also* ***enlargement***, ***European Union***, ***four freedoms*** and ***Treaty on the Functioning of the European Union***.

European Free Trade Association: *see* ***EFTA***.

European Neighbourhood Policy: ENP. Launched in 2003 with the objective of avoiding the emergence of new dividing lines between the enlarged ***European Union*** and its neighbours and to strengthen the prosperity, stability and security of all. In 2015 ENP was revised to put the stabilization of the region in political, economic and security-related terms at its centre.

European Patent Convention: the *Convention on the Grant of European Patents* concluded on 5 October 1973. It establishes a common system of law for the grant of patents in member states. These European patents have the effect of national patents granted by member states.

市场)的后继组织，通常缩写为 EC。"欧洲共同体"一词在《马斯特里赫特条约》生效之前经常用于指"欧洲经济共同体(EEC)"。确切含义通常在上下文中是明确的。另见*扩盟(enlargement)*、*欧洲联盟(European Union)*、*马斯特里赫特条约(Treaty of Maastricht)*、*欧洲联盟条约(Treaty on European Union)*、*欧洲联盟运行条约(Treaty on the Functioning of the European Union)*。

European Council
欧洲理事会

由欧盟成员国的国家元首或政府首脑与欧洲理事会主席、欧盟委员会主席以及外交事务和安全政策高级代表组成。每 6 个月举行 2 次会议。另见*欧盟理事会(Council of the European Union)*、*欧洲联盟条约(Treaty on European Union)*。

European Court of Justice
欧洲法院

见*欧洲法院(Court of Justice of the European Union)*

European Economic Area
欧洲经济区

EEA。1994年1月1日生效。由欧盟(EU)27个成员国和欧洲自由贸易区(EFTA)4个成员国中的3个成员国(冰岛、列支敦士登和挪威)组成的单一市场。瑞士于1992年12月决定不加入欧洲经济区。对于欧洲自由贸易区国家而言，EEA成员资格是介于单独EFTA和正式欧盟成员资格之间的一个中间环节。建立欧洲经济区的协定包括四大自由(货物、人员、服务和资本的自由流动)。欧洲经济区不涵盖共同农业政策、共同渔业政策、共同商业政策、共同外交和安全政策、司法和内政、直接和间接税收或经济和货币联盟。欧洲经济区成员国必须采用欧盟现行法处理竞争问题。EFTA成员国也受欧盟关于社会政策、消费者保护、环境、公司法和统计的规则所约束。

European Economic Community
欧洲经济共同体

EEC。根据 1957 年 3 月 25 日签署的《罗马条约》建立，条约于 1958 年 1 月 1 日生效。条约旨在"为欧洲人民之间建立一个更加紧密的联盟奠定基础"。主要目标包括取消成员国之间的关税和非关税壁垒，建立共同市场并实现人员、服务和资本自由流动。欧洲经济共同体的主要要素为共同农业政策、共同商业政策和共同运输政策。另见*扩盟(enlargement)*、*欧洲联盟(European Union)*、*四大自由(four freedoms)*、*欧洲联盟运行条约(Treaty on the Functioning of the European Union)*。

European Free Trade Association
欧洲自由贸易联盟

见*欧洲自由贸易联盟(EFTA)*。

European Neighbourhood Policy
欧洲睦邻政策

ENP。2003年实施，目标是避免扩大后的欧盟与其邻国之间出现新的分界线，并加强所有国家的繁荣、稳定和安全。2015年，对这一政策进行了修订，将该地区的政治、经济和安全稳定性作为其工作中心。

European Patent Convention
欧洲专利公约

1973年10月5日缔结的《欧洲专利授予公约》。该公约为成员国授予专利建立了一个共同的法律体系。欧洲专利具有成员国国家专利的效力。

European Recovery Program: *see* ***Marshall Plan***.

European Single Market: launched in 1987 through the ***Single European Act***, an amendment to the ***Treaty of Rome***, and achieved in 1992. It entailed the elimination of the remaining physical (customs), technical (standards and licensing) and fiscal barriers between the then twelve members of the ***European Community***. This not only meant that goods and services produced in one member state had unhindered access to the other member states if they were wanted there, but also that foreign goods and services, once they were lawfully imported by one member state, could then be transferred to any other member state. Even then, there was a view at the time of its creation that it would not lead to a single market, and that without further reforms the European Community market would remain a collection of twelve national markets. *See also* ***European Union legislation***, ***four freedoms*** and ***Treaty on the Functioning of the European Union***.

European Social Charter: a ***Council of Europe*** treaty. The last revision entered into force in 1999. It guarantees rights and freedoms which concern all individuals in the ***European Union*** in their daily existence. It describes basic rights concerning health, education, employment, legal and social protection, movement of persons and non-discrimination. [www.coe.int]

European Union: EU. Created by the ***Treaty of Maastricht*** and given legal personality by the ***Treaty of Lisbon*** which entered into force on 1 December 2009. The EU replaced the European Community. Article 2 of the ***Treaty on European Union*** sets out the aims and objectives of the EU. These are, in much abbreviated form: (a) promotion of peace, the EU's values and the well-being of its peoples, (b) an area of freedom, security and justice without internal frontiers, (c) an internal market, (d) combat social exclusion and discrimination, (e) promote economic, social and territorial cohesion, (f) respect for cultural and linguistic diversity, (g) establish an economic and monetary union whose currency is the ***euro***, and (h) in the wider world, contribute to peace, security and sustainable development, free and fair trade, eradication of poverty and the protection of human rights, particularly the rights of the child and strict observance of international law, including respect for the United Nations Charter. Until 2009 the European Union was known officially in the WTO as the ***European Communities***. Applicants for membership of the European Union go through a lengthy accession procedure that requires them, among other matters, to satisfy the ***Copenhagen criteria***. The twenty-seven members of the European Union (as of 1 February 2020) are Austria, Belgium, Bulgaria, Croatia, Cyprus, Czechia, Denmark, Estonia, Finland, France, Germany, Greece, Hungary, Ireland, Italy, Latvia, Lithuania, Luxembourg, Malta, Netherlands, Poland, Portugal, Romania, Slovakia, Slovenia, Spain and Sweden. The United Kingdom was a member from 1 January 1973 to 31 January 2020. *See also* ***Brexit*** and ***Treaty on the Functioning of the European Union***.

European Union institutions: this item describes briefly some of the main institutions maintained by the ***European Union***. At the highest level political power

European Recovery Program

欧洲复兴计划

见*马歇尔计划(Marshall Plan)*。

European Single Market

欧洲单一市场

1987年通过《单一欧洲法》启动谈判，该法案是《罗马条约》的一项修正案，1992年达成。法案要求取消当时欧洲共同体12个成员国之间剩余的有形壁垒(海关)、技术壁垒(标准和许可程序)和财政壁垒。这不仅意味着在一成员国生产的货物和服务可以不受阻碍地进入其他成员国(如果其他成员国需要)，而且意味着外国货物和服务一旦由一成员国合法进口，就可以随后转运至任何其他成员国。即便如此，在创立之初有一种观点认为，法案不会引导形成单一市场，且如果不进行进一步改革，欧洲共同体市场仍将是12个国家市场的集合。另见*欧洲联盟立法(European Union legislation)*、*四大自由(four freedoms)*、*欧洲联盟运行条约(Treaty on the Functioning of the European Union)*。

European Social Charter

欧洲社会宪章

欧洲理事会的一项条约。最近一次修订于1999年生效。宪章旨在保证事关欧盟所有个人的日常生活中的权利和自由，描述了关于健康、教育、就业、法律和社会保护、人员流动以及非歧视的基本权利。

European Union

欧洲联盟

EU。《马斯特里赫特条约》创设，2009年12月1日生效的《里斯本条约》赋予其法律人格。欧盟取代欧洲共同体。《欧洲联盟条约》第2条规定了欧盟的目标和宗旨，归纳为：(a)促进和平、欧盟价值观及其人民的福祉；(b)没有内部边界的自由、安全、公正区域；(c)内部市场；(d)打击社会排斥和歧视；(e)促进经济、社会和领土凝聚力；(f)尊重文化和语言多样性；(g)建立以欧元为货币的经济和货币联盟；以及(h)在全球范围促进世界和平、安全和可持续发展；自由和公平贸易；消除贫穷和保护人权，特别是儿童权利；严格遵守包括《联合国宪章》在内的国际法。在2009年之前，欧盟在WTO中一直被正式称为欧洲共同体。欧盟成员资格的申请国需要经历漫长的加入程序，需要满足哥本哈根标准，还有其他事项方面的要求。欧盟27个成员国(截至2020年2月1日)为奥地利、比利时、保加利亚、克罗地亚、塞浦路斯、捷克、丹麦、爱沙尼亚、芬兰、法国、德国、希腊、匈牙利、爱尔兰、意大利、拉脱维亚、立陶宛、卢森堡、马耳他、荷兰、波兰、葡萄牙、罗马尼亚、斯洛伐克、斯洛文尼亚、西班牙和瑞典。英国在1973年1月1日至2020年1月31日期间曾为欧盟成员国。另见*英国脱欧(Brexit)*、*欧洲联盟运行条约(Treaty on the Functioning of the European Union)*。

European Union institutions

欧盟机构

本词条简要描述欧盟设立的一些主要机构。在最高层面，政治权力由4个机

is shared by four bodies. The ***European Council*** consisting of the heads of state government of the member states sets the broad priorities for the European Union. European citizens are represented in policymaking through the members of the European Parliament (MEPs) they elect directly. The ***European Commission*** promotes the interests of the European Union as a whole. Its members are appointed by national governments. Finally, the governments of the member states look after their countries' interests in the ***Council of the European Union***. The European Parliament, the European Commission and the Council of the European Union together develop policies and laws that apply throughout the European Union. The ***Court of Justice of the European Union*** ensures that the laws are observed. Many other bodies have specialized roles. [Europa.eu]

European Union–Japan Economic Partnership Agreement: a free-trade agreement that entered into force on 1 February 2019. It has a wide scope. Chapter 1 contains general provisions (objectives, definitions, etc.), Chapter 2 trade in goods, Chapter 3 rules of origin and origin procedures, Chapter 4 customs matters and trade facilitation, Chapter 5 trade remedies, Chapter 6 sanitary and phytosanitary measures, Chapter 7 technical barriers to trade, Chapter 8 trade in services, investment liberalization and electronic commerce, Chapter 9 capital movements, payments and transfers and temporary safeguard measures, Chapter 10 government procurement, Chapter 11 competition policy, Chapter 12 subsidies, Chapter 13 state-owned enterprises, enterprises granted special rights or privileges and designated monopolies, Chapter 14 intellectual property, Chapter 15 corporate governance, Chapter 16 trade and sustainable development, Chapter 17 transparency, Chapter 18 good regulatory practices and regulatory cooperation, Chapter 19 cooperation in the field of agriculture, Chapter 20 small and medium-sized enterprises, Chapter 21 dispute settlement, Chapter 22 institutional provisions and Chapter 23 final provisions. [trade.ec.europa.eu]

European Union legislation: the ***European Union*** has five legislative avenues to carry out its mandate. *Regulations* are official European Community acts which are binding in their entirety and which apply directly in all member states. Regulations therefore promote legislative harmonization, since community law prevails over national law where there is a conflict. *Directives* are official European Community acts which are binding on the member states to which they are addressed as far as their objectives are concerned, but member states are free to decide how to give effect to directives. This approach can make the implementation of controversial measures more acceptable. *Decisions* are binding in their entirety on those to whom they are addressed. *Recommendations* and *opinions* have no binding force, but they can be as effective as other measures.

European Union–Mercosur Association Agreement: a trade agreement under negotiation between the ***European Union*** and Argentina, Brazil, Paraguay and Uruguay.

构分享。欧洲理事会，由成员国政府首脑组成，为欧盟确定总体优先事项。欧洲公民通过其直接选举产生的欧洲议会成员参与决策。欧盟委员会，负责促进欧盟的整体利益，委员会成员由各国政府任命。各成员国政府在欧盟理事会中维护本国利益。欧洲议会、欧盟委员会和欧盟理事会共同制定适用于整个欧盟的政策和法律。欧洲法院负责保证法律得以遵守。许多其他机构发挥专门作用。

European Union–Japan Economic Partnership Agreement

欧盟—日本经济伙伴关系协定

2019年2月1日生效的自由贸易协定。范围广泛。第1章包含一般条款(目标、定义等)，第2章货物贸易，第3章原产地规则和原产地程序，第4章海关事务和贸易便利化，第5章贸易救济，第6章卫生与植物卫生措施，第7章技术性贸易壁垒，第8章服务贸易、投资自由化和电子商务，第9章资本流动、支付和转账及临时保障措施，第10章政府采购，第11章竞争政策，第12章补贴，第13章国有企业、授予特殊权利或特权的企业及指定垄断企业，第14章知识产权，第15章公司治理，第16章贸易和可持续发展，第17章透明度，第18章良好监管实践和监管合作，第19章农业合作，第20章中小企业，第21章争端解决，第22章机构安排，第23章最后条款。

European Union legislation

欧洲联盟立法

欧盟有5个立法途径来执行授权。条例，欧共体官方法案，具有整体约束力，直接适用于所有成员国。条例促进了立法协调性，因为在存在冲突的情况下，共同体法律优先于国家法律。指令，欧共体官方法案，就其目标而言，对所涉及的成员国具有约束力，但成员国可权决定如何实施指令，此种方式可使实施有争议的措施更易于接受。决定，对所涉及的成员具有完全约束力。建议和意见，无约束力，但可与其他措施同样有效。

European Union–Mercosur Association Agreement

欧盟与南方共同市场联系协定

欧盟与阿根廷、巴西、巴拉圭和乌拉圭正在谈判的贸易协定。

European Union–Mercosur Cooperation Agreement: *see* ***Interregional Framework Cooperation Agreement between the European Community and Mercosur***.

European Union trade agreements: the ***European Union*** has three main types of trade agreements: (a) ***customs union*** with a ***common external tariff***, (b) Association Agreements, free-trade agreements and economic partnership agreements, all of which reduce or eliminate tariffs in bilateral trade, and (c) ***partnership and cooperation agreements*** which provide a general framework for bilateral economic relations without eliminating customs tariffs. [ec.europa.eu]

European Union treaties: this entry outlines the main treaties underlying what became the ***European Union***. The ***European Economic Community*** (EEC) was established on 1 January 1958 through the ***Treaty of Rome***, signed on 25 March 1957. This Treaty, now much amended and enlarged, remains the instrument describing how the European Union works. At that time the EEC existed alongside the ***European Coal and Steel Community***, established in 1951, and the European Atomic Energy Community (EAEC), usually known as Euratom, also established on 1 January 1958. Early European integration therefore consisted of three separate communities governed by different institutions, but cooperating closely. The ***Merger Treaty*** (*Treaty establishing the European Community* or EC), signed on 8 April 1965 and entering into force on 1 July 1967, created a single governing council (the Council of the European Communities) for the three communities, as well as a Commission of the European Communities, usually known as the ***European Commission***. The next major step was the ***Single European Act*** (signed on 28 February 1986 and entry into force on 1 July 1987). This Act created the single internal market through the progressive elimination of many remaining restrictions. It gave the EC a range of new powers, improved the decision-making capacity of the Council of Ministers and strengthened the powers of the European Parliament. The ***Treaty of Maastricht*** established the European Union. It was signed on 7 February 1992 and entered into force on 1 November 1993. Article A notes that "This Treaty marks a new stage in the process of an ever closer union among the peoples of Europe, in which decisions are taken as closely as possible to the citizen". This Treaty was amended by the ***Treaty of Amsterdam***, signed on 2 October 1997, entered into force on 1 May 1999. It clarified some of the provisions and gave the Union some increased powers. Next, the ***Treaty of Nice*** amended the ***Treaty on European Union*** and the Treaties establishing the European Communities. It reformed the institutional structure of the European Union in light of an expected ***enlargement***. The Treaty was signed on 26 February 2001 and entered into force on 1 February 2003. The most recent major treaty action was the adoption of the ***Treaty of Lisbon***, signed on 13 December 2007 and entered into force on 1 December 2009. Among other changes, this Treaty gave legal status to the European Union, and it gave the European Parliament powers equal to those of the ***European Council***.

European Union–Mercosur Cooperation Agreement
欧盟与南方共同市场合作协定

见*欧洲共同体与南方共同市场区域间合作框架协定(Interregional Framework Cooperation Agreement between the European Community and Mercosur)*。

European Union trade agreements
欧盟贸易协定

欧盟主要有 3 类贸易协定：(a)具有共同对外关税的关税同盟；(b)联系协定、自由贸易协定和经济伙伴关系协定，所有这些协定旨在降低或取消双边贸易中的关税；以及(c)伙伴关系与合作协定，为双边经济关系提供总体框架，无需取消关税。

European Union treaties
欧洲联盟主要条约

本词条列出成立欧盟所依据的主要条约。根据1958年1月1日签署的《罗马条约》，欧洲经济共同体(EEC)于1957年3月25日成立。这一条约已经进行多次修正和扩充，但仍为描述欧盟如何运行的文件。当时，欧洲经济共同体与1951年建立的欧洲煤钢共同体和1958年1月1日建立的欧洲原子能共同体(EAEC)同时存在。早期欧洲一体化因此由三个共同体组成，分由不同机构管辖，但相互密切合作。1965年4月8日签署并于1967年7月1日生效的《合并条约》(《建立欧洲共同体条约》)为这三个共同体创设了一个单一的理事会，即欧洲共同体理事会，同时设立了一个欧洲共同体委员会，通常称为欧盟委员会。下一步是《单一欧洲法》(于1986年2月28日签署，1987年7月1日生效)。该法案通过逐步消除许多剩余限制，创设了单一内部市场。同时赋予了欧共体一系列新权力，提高了部长理事会的决策能力，加强了欧洲议会的权力。《马斯特里赫特条约》建立了欧盟。该条约于1992年2月7日签署，1993年11月1日生效。A条指出，"本条约标志着欧洲各国人民之间日益紧密的联盟进程进入一个新阶段，在这一进程中，各项决策的作出均尽可能与公民密切相关"。1997年10月2日签署的《阿姆斯特丹条约》对该条约进行了修正，于1999年5月1日生效。该条约澄清了一些条款，并赋予联盟一些新增的权力。接下来，《尼斯条约》修正了《欧洲联盟条约》和建立欧洲共同体的各项条约。《尼斯条约》根据扩盟的预期，改革了欧盟的体制结构。该条约于2001年2月26日签署，于2003年2月1日生效。最近的修约行动是通过了《里斯本条约》，于2007年12月13日签署，2009年12月1日生效。其中一项改变是赋予欧盟法律地位，并赋予欧洲议会与欧洲理事会相同的权力。由此产生《欧

It resulted in the current versions of the ***Treaty on European Union*** and the ***Treaty on the Functioning of the European Union***.

Eurozone: the nineteen countries in the ***European Union*** that have adopted the ***euro*** (€) as their common currency and sole legal tender. They are Austria, Belgium, Cyprus, Estonia, Finland, France, Germany, Greece, Ireland, Italy, Latvia, Lithuania, Luxembourg, Malta, Netherlands, Portugal, Slovakia, Slovenia and Spain. The remaining European Union members, except Denmark, will be required to join the zone once they meet certain conditions. The United Kingdom also was exempt from joining during its time as a member of the European Union. *See also* ***Brexit***.

EU–US aircraft agreement: formally the *Agreement Between the European Community and the Government of the United States Concerning the Application of the GATT Agreement on Trade in Civil Aircraft on Trade in Large Aircraft* which took effect on 17 July 1992. Terminated in 2006. The Agreement (a) prohibited government funding for the production of large civil aircraft (i.e. aircraft with more than 100 seats), (b) limited the level of government funding for the development of new aircraft, (c) limited the amount of "indirect" government support for developing new aircraft, (d) restricted government intervention in competition for sales, and (e) provided for the exchange of information concerning government support. *See also* ***Agreement on Trade in Civil Aircraft*** and ***Large Aircraft Sector Understanding***.

EU–US Privacy Shield: provides companies in the United States, the European Union, and through a separate agreement Switzerland, with a mechanism to comply with data protection requirements when transferring personal data between them. Companies must register to receive the benefits. *See also* ***General Data Protection Regulation***. [privacyshield.gov]

Evasion of customs duties: *see* ***smuggling***, ***trafficking*** and ***under-invoicing***.

Everything But Arms: EBA. A ***European Union*** initiative for duty-free and quota-free access to all products except arms and armaments originating in ***least-developed countries***. It took effect on 5 March 2001 for most products.

EVSL: ***Early Voluntary Sectoral Liberalization***. An ***APEC*** initiative for ***sectoral trade negotiations***.

***Ex aequo et bono*:** *Lat.* according to what is just and good.

***Ex ante*:** *Lat.* before a measure is applied.

Exchange controls: conditions or limits imposed by governments on the extent to which residents may have access to foreign exchange reserves. WTO members may use exchange controls imposed in accordance with the Articles of Association of the ***IMF***, but they may not use them to frustrate the intent of the GATT. For ***trade in services***, they may not apply restrictions on international transfers and payments for current transactions where they have made specific commitments. In both cases, exchange controls may be possible to safeguard the balance of payments under strictly defined conditions. *See also* ***balance-of-payments consultations, currency board*** and ***trade and foreign exchange***.

洲联盟条约》和《欧洲联盟运行条约》的现行版本。

Eurozone

欧元区

采用欧元(€)作为共同货币和惟一法定货币的19个欧盟国家，这些国家是奥地利、比利时、塞浦路斯、爱沙尼亚、芬兰、法国、德国、希腊、爱尔兰、意大利、拉脱维亚、立陶宛、卢森堡、马耳他、荷兰、葡萄牙、斯洛伐克、斯洛文尼亚和西班牙。除了丹麦之外的其他欧盟成员国，一旦满足某些条件，将被要求加入欧元区。英国在作为欧盟成员国期间也未加入欧元区。另见*英国脱欧(Brexit)*。

EU–US aircraft agreement

欧美航空器协定

正式称为《欧洲共同体与美国政府关于大型航空器适用 GATT 民用航空器贸易协定的协定》，1992 年 7 月 17 日生效，2006 年废止。协定规定(a)禁止政府资助大型民用航空器生产(即 100 座以上的航空器)；(b)限制政府开发新型航空器的资助水平；(c)限制政府对开发新型航空器的"间接"支持金额；(d)限制政府干预销售竞争；以及(e)规定交流有关政府支持的信息。另见*民用航空器贸易协定(Agreement on Trade in Civil Aircraft)*、*民用航空器行业谅解(Large Aircraft Sector Understanding)*。

EU–US Privacy Shield

欧盟—美国隐私护盾

对设在美国、欧盟以及通过单独协定对于设在瑞士的公司提供一种机制，在它们之间传输个人数据时符合数据保护要求。公司必须注册方可获得利益。另见*通用数据保护条例(General Data Protection Regulation)*。

Evasion of customs duties

逃避关税

见*走私(smuggling)*、*非法交易(trafficking)*、*低开发票(under-invoicing)*。

Everything But Arms

除武器外的所有产品

EBA。欧盟倡议，对源自最不发达国家的除武器和军火外的所有产品实行免关税和免配额准入。倡议于 2001 年 3 月 5 日对大多数产品生效。

EVSL

部门自愿提前自由化

APEC 关于部门贸易谈判的倡议。

Ex aequo et bono

公允和善良

拉丁语。意为根据公正和友好原则。

Ex ante

事先

拉丁语。意为在采取一项措施前。

Exchange controls

外汇管制

政府对居民获得外汇储备的程度所施加的条件或限制。WTO成员可依照《国际货币基金组织协定》实施外汇管制，但不得通过外汇管制使GATT的意图无效。对于服务贸易，成员不得对已作出具体承诺部门的国际转帐和支付施加限制。在以上两种情况下，外汇管理在严格限定的条件下可以用以保障国际收支。另见*国际收支磋商(balance-of-payments consultations)*、*货币局制度(currency board)*、*贸易与外汇(trade and foreign exchange)*。

Exchange dumping: suggested in the past by some as a category of ***dumping***. This was assumed to occur through manipulation of the ***exchange rate*** to give exporters an advantage in the importing market. So-called exchange dumping was discussed at the time of the ***Havana Charter*** negotiations, but no rules were established to deal with this practice. Some of the calls for negotiations on ***trade and foreign exchange*** appear to be based on the view that some forms of exchange dumping still persist.

Exchange of concessions: agreed bilateral outcomes arrived at as the result of ***requests and offers*** in ***multilateral trade negotiations***. A ***concession*** is in its narrow sense a ***binding***, but it is also used for tariff reductions more generally.

Exchange rate: the cost of a currency in terms of another currency. Some exchange rates are fixed. This is done through a government decision, usually against a currency showing moderate fluctuations in value. Floating exchange rates are determined by free markets in response to supply and demand. *See also* ***currency board*** and ***devaluation***.

Excise duty: a ***duty*** sometimes levied by governments on the production, purchase, sale or use of a commodity. A typical example is the duty levied on the distilling and sale of alcohol. Foreign and domestic products have to be given the same level of excise duty under the WTO rules on ***national treatment***.

Exclusive Economic Zone: EEZ. Part of the ***United Nations Convention on the Law of the Sea*** (UNCLOS). The EEZ is defined as an area beyond and adjacent to the territorial sea of a coastal state not exceeding 200 nautical miles. Within the EEZ the coastal state has sovereign rights for the purpose of exploring and exploiting, conserving and managing natural living and non-living resources and jurisdiction over the establishment and use of artificial islands, maritime scientific research and the protection and preservation of the maritime environment. One of the unresolved issues in the WTO negotiation on ***fisheries subsidies*** is whether proposed disciplines would depend on whether the subsidized fishing activity takes place within or beyond a member's EEZ. *See also* ***territorial waters***. [un.org]

Exclusive export rights: the right given to governmental and non-governmental enterprises to be the sole exporter of, usually, an agricultural commodity. *See also* ***single-desk selling***.

Exclusive import rights: the practice of giving holders of ***patents***, ***copyright*** and other ***intellectual property rights*** the ability to stop ***parallel imports*** of products embodying the same intellectual property rights. Some countries assign exclusive importing rights in particular products to ***state trading*** operations. *See also* ***trading rights***.

Exclusive marketing rights: EMRs. A concept used in the ***Agreement on Trade-Related Aspects of Intellectual Property Rights*** relating to ***patent*** protection for pharmaceuticals and agricultural chemical products. EMRs were be available for five years in cases where defined transitional arrangements were used to bring the provisions of the Agreement into effect.

Exchange dumping

外汇倾销

一些人过去建议将其作为一类倾销行为。通常认为是通过操纵汇率使出口商在进口市场上获得优势。所谓外汇倾销在《哈瓦那宪章》谈判时讨论过，但是没有制定任何规则处理这一做法。关于就贸易与外汇进行谈判的一些呼声似乎是基于某种形式的外汇倾销仍然存在的情况。

Exchange of concessions

交换减让

多边贸易谈判中要价和出价所产生的议定双边结果。狭义上讲减让是一种约束，但它也常用于指关税削减。

Exchange rate

汇率

一种货币相对于另一种货币的成本。一些汇率是固定的，通过政府决定实现，通常是针对币值适度波动的货币。浮动汇率由自由市场根据供给和需求决定。另见*货币局制度(currency board)*、*货币贬值(devaluation)*。

Excise duty

消费税

政府有时对一商品的生产、购买、销售或使用征收的税。典型的例子是对酒的蒸馏和销售征税。根据WTO国民待遇原则，需对外国产品和本国产品征收同等水平的消费税。

Exclusive Economic Zone

专属经济区

EEZ。《联合国海洋法公约》(UNCLOS)的一部分。专属经济区定义为一沿海国领海以外并邻接领海不超过200海里的区域。在专属经济区内，沿海国对探索和开发、养护和管理自然生物和非生物资源拥有主权权利，并对人工岛的建设和使用、海洋科学研究以及海洋环境保护和养护拥有管辖权。WTO渔业补贴谈判中尚未解决的问题之一是，拟议纪律是否取决于享受补贴的渔业活动是在成员专属经济区内还是在之外进行。另见*领水(territorial waters)*。

Exclusive export rights

专属出口权

赋予政府企业和非政府企业作为通常是农产品的惟一出口商的权利。另见*专责销售(single-desk selling)*。

Exclusive import rights

专属进口权

赋予专利、版权和其他知识产权持有人阻止拥有包含相同知识产权的产品平行进口的能力的做法。一些国家将特定产品的专属进口权指定为国营贸易业务。另见*贸易权(trading rights)*。

Exclusive marketing rights

专有销售权

EMRs。《与贸易有关的知识产权协定》中使用的一个概念，与药品和农药的专利保护相关。对于使用规定的过渡安排使协定条款生效的情况，独家营销权可使用 5 年。

Exclusive service suppliers: a small number of service suppliers established or authorized by the government. They usually operate in an environment of little or no competition.

Exemption: a dispensation from conforming with a certain measure, such as having the right to apply an ***MFN exemption*** under the ***General Agreement on Trade in Services***.

Ex-factory cost method: in ***rules of origin*** a method for calculating the value added to a good by the exporter, which includes the producer's expenditure on labour, overheads and materials within the ***free-trade area***. This amount is then compared with the cost that can be ascribed to producers outside the area.

Exhaustion doctrine: also called first-sale doctrine. This is the proposition that once a product embodying ***intellectual property rights*** (IPRs) has been placed on the market lawfully (i.e. with the consent of the owner of the rights), the owner of the rights cannot prevent or prohibit the resale or transfer of the product in that market. In other words, the owner's rights over the product are held to have been "exhausted". In reality, the situation is not quite as simple as this. Laws vary as to whether the right continues to be exhausted if the product is imported from one market to another, which affects the owner's rights over the trade in the protected product. A debate among WTO member governments is whether exhaustion applies to products put on the market under compulsory licences. Some intellectual property laws and conventions do set some limits on the resale or transfer of a product, depending on the IPR in question. Works of art, for example, may be subject to a ***droit de suite***. ***Moral rights*** may apply in matters of ***copyright***. Aside from these and other limitations, nobody disputes that the doctrine applies to products sold and resold on the same market. Its application to products traded internationally is, however, contentious. Some jurisdictions recognize the concept of "international exhaustion". This is the proposition that once a product has been placed on the market anywhere, it can be resold or transferred to any other market without the consent of the owner of any IPRs it may embody. The application of this proposition then permits ***parallel imports***. The ***Agreement on Trade-Related Aspects of Intellectual Property Rights*** does not establish any rule on exhaustion. *See also* ***Community exhaustion***, ***international exhaustion***, ***national exhaustion*** and ***regional exhaustion***.

Ex officio**:** a responsibility or entitlement one obtains through holding another office or another position.

Exon-Florio amendment: Section 5021 of the ***Omnibus Trade and Competitiveness Act*** of 1988 which authorizes the President to block on national security grounds mergers, acquisitions and joint ventures involving foreign investment. It has been revised, most recently in the Foreign Investment Risk Review Modernization Act of 2018. *See also* ***foreign investment screening***, ***national interest*** and ***security exceptions***.

Ex parte **communications:** the WTO ***Dispute Settlement Understanding*** expressly prohibits *ex parte* communications (communications with one party

Exclusive service suppliers
独家服务提供者

政府设立或授权的少数服务提供者。他们通常在一个竞争很少或没有竞争的环境中运营。

Exemption
豁免

免于遵守某项措施，例如根据《服务贸易总协定》适用最惠国待遇豁免的权利。

Ex-factory cost method
出厂成本法

在原产地规则中计算出口商对一货物所增加价值的方法，包括生产商在自由贸易区内的劳动力、间接费用和材料支出。随后将这一数额与可归因于该地区以外的生产商的成本进行比较。

Exhaustion doctrine
权利用尽原则

也称首次销售原则。该原则主张一旦包含知识产权的一产品合法投放市场(即经所有权人同意)，所有权人不能阻止或禁止该产品在该市场中进行转售或转让。换言之，所有权人对该产品的权利被认为已经“用尽”。事实上，情况并非如此简单。如果产品从一市场进口至另一市场权利是否仍然维持“用尽”的问题，法律规定各不相同，此点影响所有权人对受保护产品贸易的权利。WTO成员之间的一项争论是，用尽是否适用于根据强制许可投放市场的产品。一些知识产权法律和公约根据所涉知识产权，确实对一产品的转售或转让设定了一些限制。例如，艺术作品可以受到追续权的约束，道德权可能适用于版权问题。除此上述和其他限制，没有人对该原则适用于在同一市场中销售和转售产品提出质疑。但是，该原则对于进行国际贸易的产品的适用存在争议。一些管辖范围承认“国际用尽”的概念，指一产品一旦投放到任何地方的市场中，即可未经所含任何知识产权所有权人同意而转售或转移到任何其他市场。这一观点的适用因此允许平行进口。《与贸易有关的知识产权协定》没有就权利用尽制定任何规则。另见*共同体内权利用尽(Community exhaustion)*、*国际用尽(international exhaustion)*、*一国用尽(national exhaustion)*、*区域用尽(regional exhaustion)*。

Ex officio
依职权

一人通过担任另一职务或职位而获得的责任或权利。

Exon-Florio amendment
埃克森-弗罗里奥修正案

1988 年《综合贸易与竞争法》第 5021 条，授权总统以国家安全为由阻止涉及外国投资的合并、收购和合资。最近一次修订是在2018年的《外国投资风险评估现代化法案》中。另见*外国投资审查(foreign investment screening)*、*国家利益(national interest)*、*安全例外(security exceptions)*。

***Ex parte* communications**
单方面联系

WTO《争端解决谅解》明确禁止专家组或上诉机构就其考虑中的事项进行单

only to a dispute) with a ***panel*** or the ***Appellate Body*** concerning a matter they may be considering. Written submissions to a panel or the Appellate Body are treated as confidential, but they must be available to the parties to the dispute.

Explicit consensus: *see* ***consensus*** and ***decision-making in the WTO***.

Explicit harmonization: a form of cooperation between governments to achieve defined and legally binding uniform bilateral, regional or global standards. It entails some movement away from complete national autonomy for the making of standards towards decision-making in an international framework or within international institutions. *See also* ***zero-margin harmonization***.

Export: a good or a service sold by residents of one country to residents of another in return, usually, for foreign exchange. *See also* ***barter*** and ***countertrade***.

Exportation: the same as ***export***.

Export ban: a prohibition on the export of a good.

Export cartel: *see* ***cartel***.

Export competition: the practice of competing internationally in markets for agricultural commodities through, for example, ***export subsidies***, subsidized ***export credits***, ***state-trading enterprises***, ***differential pricing***, abuse of food aid and non-transparent market support systems. Export competition is one of the three pillars of the ***Agreement on Agriculture***, along with ***domestic support*** and **market access**, as a result of the Uruguay Round negotiations on agriculture. WTO members adopted at the 2015 Nairobi ***WTO Ministerial Conference*** a Decision on Export Competition to eliminate agricultural export subsidies and to set disciplines on export measures with equivalent effect, namely export finance for agricultural products, international food aid and agricultural exporting State Trading Enterprises. Under this decision, export subsidies will be eliminated by developed countries immediately, except for a handful of agriculture products, while developing countries have longer periods to do so. *See also* ***Agreement on Agriculture***, ***Nairobi WTO Ministerial Conference*** and ***three pillars of agriculture***.

Export controls: measures instituted by exporting countries to supervise export flows. Reasons for them include compliance with ***United Nations economic sanctions***, adherence to ***voluntary restraint arrangements***, observance of ***export quotas*** under ***international commodity agreements***, management of ***strategic exports*** and administration of rules concerning ***dual-purpose exports***, as well as a policy of preserving some raw materials and other articles for domestic production or consumption. *See also* ***grey-area measures*** and ***Wassenaar Arrangement on Export Controls for Conventional Arms and Dual-Use Goods and Technologies***.

Export credits: the granting to the importer (purchaser) of goods and services an extended term to pay for them. ***OECD*** members handle their government-supported export credits according to the ***OECD Arrangement on Officially Supported Export Credits***. The accepted practice today is to consider repayment terms of less than two years as short-term, between two and five years as

方面联系(仅与争端一方联系)。向专家组或上诉机构提交的书面陈述应按保密信息处理，但必须使争端各方可获得。

Explicit consensus

明确一致

见*协商一致(consensus)*、*WTO决策机制(decision-making in the WTO)*。

Explicit harmonization

明示协调

政府间合作的一种形式，以实现明确的、具有法律约束力且统一的双边、区域或全球标准。意味着从国家自主制定标准向在国际框架下或在国际机构中决策的转变。另见*零差别协调(zero-margin harmonization)*。

Export

出口

一国居民向另一国居民出售货物或服务，通常为获得外汇。另见*易货贸易(barter trade)*、*对销贸易(countertrade)*。

Exportation

出口

与出口同义。

Export ban

出口禁令

禁止出口某商品。

Export cartel

出口卡特尔

见*卡特尔(cartel)*。

Export competition

出口竞争

通过出口补贴、补贴出口信贷、国营贸易企业、差别定价、滥用粮食援助和不透明的市场支持体系等方式在国际农产品市场上竞争的做法。作为乌拉圭回合农业谈判成果，出口竞争成为《农业协定》三大支柱之一，另外两大支柱是国内支持和市场准入。WTO成员在2015年内罗毕WTO部长级会议上通过了《关于出口竞争的决定》，旨在取消农产品出口补贴，并制定具有同等效果的出口措施纪律，即农产品出口融资、国际粮食援助和出口农产品的国营贸易企业。根据这一决定，发达国家应立即取消出口补贴，除少数农产品外，发展中国家在更长时间内取消出口补贴。另见*农业协定(Agreement on Agriculture)*、*WTO内罗毕部长级会议(Nairobi WTO Ministerial Conference)*、*农业三大支柱(three pillars of agriculture)*。

Export controls

出口管制

出口国为监督出口流量而采取的措施。采取出口管制的原因包括：执行联合国经济制裁、遵守自愿限制安排、遵守国际商品协定项下的出口配额、管理战略性出口和执行两用物品出口规则以及保留一些原材料和其他物品供国内生产或消费。另见*灰色区域措施(grey-area measures)*、*关于常规武器和两用物品及技术出口管制的瓦森纳安排(Wassenaar Arrangement on Export Controls for Conventional Arms and Dual-Use Goods and Technologies)*。

Export credits

出口信贷

给予货物和服务的进口商(购买者)付款延长期。经济合作与发展组织(OECD)成员国根据OECD《官方支持出口信贷的安排》处理其政府支持的出口信贷。

medium-term and above five years as long-term. Many exporting countries have mechanisms to manage, support or guarantee export credits since, especially in the case of large contracts like power stations or port facilities, favourable terms of credit can influence considerably the competitiveness of a bid. The WTO ***Agreement on Subsidies and Countervailing Measures*** declares export credits prohibited if they are made at less than commercial rates. Export credits extended by OECD members in accordance with the OECD Arrangement are exempt from this prohibition. The December 2015 Nairobi Decision on Export Competition includes specific disciplines for export credits for agricultural products.

Export culture: a recognition among individuals, firms and governments that competitive exports contribute significantly to national economic welfare, and that participation in international markets must be a high priority. Promoting and sustaining an export culture requires a consistent effort to abolish domestic structural impediments to exporting and to ensure the availability of non-discriminatory ***market access*** in other countries.

Export duties: a tariff levied at the time a good is exported. *See* ***export tariffs***.

Export earnings guarantee schemes: mechanisms usually aimed at ensuring that individual commodity producers or countries mainly dependent on export earnings from commodities are not exposed fully to sharp drops in their incomes. They are also known as ***compensatory financing arrangements***.

Export Enhancement Program: EEP. A United States subsidy programme introduced in 1985. Its objective was to help American exporters compete against subsidized prices in specific markets. Commodities able to benefit from this programme were wheat, wheat flour, rice, frozen poultry, barley, barley malt, table eggs and vegetable oil. The EEP was repealed in 2008.

Export Expansion and Reciprocal Trade Agreements Act: the ***fast-track*** proposal tabled by President Clinton in September 1997. It was not adopted. *See also* ***Trade Promotion Authority*** and ***United States trade agreements legislation***.

Export incentives: Measures adopted by governments to promote the expansion of exports by domestic companies. Such measures can include direct subsidies, bounties, reduced import tariffs for components where they are incorporated into products to be re-exported, taxation concessions, etc. The ***Agreement on Subsidies and Countervailing Measures*** makes some types of export incentives illegal, including subsidies related to the export of products. *See also* ***bounty*** and ***export subsidies***.

Export inflation insurance schemes: schemes operated by governments particularly in the high-inflation environment of the 1970s. They were designed to minimize or eliminate the effects of monetary inflation on the cost of export contracts. Countries not maintaining such schemes held that they conferred a competitive advantage to exporters benefiting from them. These exporters could bid more aggressively in international markets, since they were secure in the knowledge that they would not have to bear the cost of inflation alone.

目前公认的做法是将少于2年的偿还期限视为短期，2年至5年的偿还期限视为中短期，5年以上视为长期。许多出口国设有管理、支持或担保出口信贷的机制，特别是在如发电站或港口设施的大型合同中，优惠的信贷条件可显著影响投标的竞争力。WTO《补贴与反补贴措施协定》规定，如出口信贷利率低于商业利率即应禁止。OECD成员国依照OECD安排提供的出口信贷免受此项禁止限制。2015年12月关于出口竞争的内罗毕决定包括农产品出口信贷的具体纪律。

Export culture

出口文化

个人、企业和政府的如下认知：竞争性出口对国家经济福利可以作出重要贡献，因此参与国际市场必须是一项高度优先事项。促进和维持出口文化需要作出一致努力，以消除出口的国内结构性障碍，并保证其他国家可提供非歧视市场准入。

Export duties

出口税

在一货物出口时征收的关税。另见*出口关税(export tariffs)*。

Export earnings guarantee schemes

出口收入保障计划

通常旨在保证单个商品生产者或主要依赖商品出口收入的国家避免面临收入急剧下降局面的机制。也被称为补偿性融资安排。

Export Enhancement Program

出口增强计划

EEP。美国于1985年采用的补贴计划。目的是帮助美国出口商在特定市场中与补贴价格进行竞争。可以自该计划受益的商品为小麦、面粉、大米、冷冻家禽、大麦、大麦麦芽、食用鸡蛋和植物油。EEP于2008年废除。

Export Expansion and Reciprocal Trade Agreements Act

出口扩张和互惠贸易协定法案

1997 年 9 月克林顿总统提出的快轨授权建议，未予采纳。另见*贸易促进授权(Trade Promotion Authority)*、*美国贸易协定立法(United States trade agreements legislation)*。

Export incentives

出口鼓励措施

政府为促进国内公司扩大出口所采取的措施。此类措施可包括直接补贴、津贴、对复出口产品所含组件降低进口关税、税收优惠等。《补贴与反补贴措施协定》规定一些类型的出口鼓励措施为非法，包括与产品出口相关的补贴。另见*津贴(bounty)*、*出口补贴(export subsidies)*。

Export inflation insurance schemes

出口通胀保险计划

政府运行的计划，特别是在20世纪70年代高通胀的环境下，旨在缩小或消除货币通胀对出口合同成本的影响。未维持此类计划的国家认为，计划给受益的出口商提供了竞争优势。这些出口商可以在国际市场上更积极地竞价，因

A ***panel*** established by the GATT in 1978 to examine whether such schemes amounted to a ***subsidy*** concluded that this would be true if the premium rates were "manifestly inadequate to cover long-term operating costs and losses". It also noted that the meaning of "long-term" still would have to be defined. In the current environment of low inflation any schemes of this nature which might still exist appear to be unused.

Exporting unemployment: the woolly idea that domestic economic activity can be raised, and employment thereby increased, if the flow of imports is stemmed in some way. In other words, proponents of this idea hold that it is possible to transfer the unemployment burden to some other country and protect and increase employment at home through keeping imports at bay. Generally, the more acceptable term of ***import substitution*** is used for this practice. Such policies may work in the short term, but only at the expense of lower ***competitiveness*** of the domestic industry. Factors to consider in the imposition of import substitution policies are that many imported products are inputs into the production process. Raising their prices raises the costs of domestic producers. Increased costs are a disincentive to purchasers, and this may lead to a dampening of economic activity. The aim of exporting unemployment can therefore lead to increased unemployment at home. *See also* ***beggar-thy-neighbour policies***, ***local content requirements*** and ***optimal-tariff argument***.

Export of domestically prohibited goods: allowing the manufacture of goods for export, but not for domestic consumption. Said to be done for reasons of health, safety, etc. Practical examples are hard to find. Views differ on the extent to which importing countries should agree to open their markets to these exporters. Some say that if a country does not allow such products in its domestic market, it should ban their export also. Others say that importing countries have no obligation to accept such products. At their worst, the arguments therefore amount to blatant ***protectionism*** on the part of those who dispute the right of countries to engage in such exports, but in many cases the reality is not so simple. This difficult issue has been on the GATT work programme since 1982. A solution is not readily apparent.

Export of jobs: the erroneous view expressed sometimes by trade unions and manufacturers in ***sensitive sectors*** that the import of products means the export of jobs because any order placed abroad means that someone in a foreign country now has a job. The remedy usually suggested is higher tariffs to promote ***import substitution***. However, such policies lead to higher costs for the economy overall, and they therefore make it less competitive with resulting higher unemployment. *See also* ***exporting unemployment*** and ***outsourcing***.

Export participation rate: a measurement indicating how many firms in a given industry in an economy are engaged in exporting or attempting to export goods and services. The export participation rate is a useful device for assessing the extent to which a country has acquired an ***export culture***.

Export performance measure: a requirement that a certain quantity of production must be exported. *See also* ***export performance requirements***.

为在知道自己不必单独承担通货膨胀的成本后他们是安全的。GATT于1978年成立的专家组负责审查此类计划是否构成补贴，得出的结论是，如果保险费率“明显不足以支付长期经营成本和损失”，则确实如此。专家组还指出，“长期”的含义仍有待确定。在当前低通胀的环境下，即使存在任何此类计划，也似乎未使用过。

Exporting unemployment
输出失业

较为模糊的概念，即如果以某种方式遏制进口流量，那么国内经济活动可以增加，因而增加就业。换言之，这种观点的支持者认为，可以通过控制进口，将失业负担转移到一些其他国家，以保护和增加国内就业。一般而言，对于此种做法使用更易被接受的进口替代一词。此类政策在短期内可能有效，但以降低国内产业竞争力为代价。在实施进口替代政策时需要考虑的因素是，许多进口产品是生产过程中的投入物。提高这些产品的价格即提高国内生产者的成本。增加的成本对购买者是抑制因素，且可能会抑制经济活动。因此，输出失业的目标可能导致国内失业率上升。另见*以邻为壑政策(beggar-thy-neighbour policies)*、*当地含量要求(local content requirements)*、*最优关税论(optimal-tariff argument)*。

Export of domestically prohibited goods
国内禁止货物的出口

允许生产货物供出口，但不允许用于国内消费。一般是出于健康、安全等原因，但实际的例子很难找到。对于进口国应该在何种程度上同意向此类出口国开放其市场，观点不同。一些人认为，如一国不允许此类产品进入其国内市场，即应该禁止此类产品的出口。另一些人认为，进口国无义务接受此类产品。最糟糕的是，认为对从事此类出口的国家的权利提出质疑相当于公然的保护主义，但在许多情况下，事实并非如此简单。自1982年以来，这一棘手问题一直在GATT的工作计划中，但并无明确解决方案。

Export of jobs
输出就业岗位

敏感部门的工会和制造商有时表达的一种错误观点，认为进口产品意味着输出就业岗位，理由是任何国外订单都意味着在外国的某人现在有了工作。通常建议的补救措施为提高关税以促进进口替代。但是，此类政策会导致整体经济的成本升高，由此导致竞争力下降，产生更高的失业率。另见*输出失业(exporting unemployment)*、*外包(outsourcing)*。

Export participation rate
出口参与率

衡量一经济体中的指定行业有多少企业从事或试图从事货物和服务出口的指标。出口参与率是评估一个国家已经具有出口文化程度的有用工具。

Export performance measure
出口实绩措施

关于一定产量必须出口的要求。另见*出口实绩要求(export performance requirements)*。

Export performance requirements: conditions imposed by the country authorizing foreign investment within its territory that are aimed at expanding that country's exports. At its simplest, the enterprise established with foreign investment has to export a certain percentage of its output, expressed either in value or quantity. Wholesale and retail traders may have to balance their imports with exports. The ***Agreement on Trade-Related Investment Measures*** bans most of these requirements.

Export pessimism: a view prevalent particularly in the 1950s in the heyday of ***import substitution*** policies by developing countries in the Latin American region. It was based on the assumption that the smallness of their exports would not be able to promote economic development, and that international integration would undermine whatever competitiveness an economy might have achieved. The conclusion was that import substitution was the only realistic policy. *See also* ***dependence theory***.

Export price: the price at which a good is exported from a country. It has a special significance if ***anti-dumping measures*** are considered against the good. If the export price is lower than ***normal value*** (the comparable price for the ***like product*** when it is intended for consumption in the exporting country), ***dumping*** may have occurred.

Export processing zones: *see* ***free-trade zones***.

Export propensity: the share of domestic production of goods and services that is exported. *See also* ***export participation rate***.

Export quotas: restrictions or ceilings imposed on the total value or volume of certain exports. They are designed to protect domestic producers and consumers from temporary shortages of these products or to improve the prices of specific products on world markets by shortening their supply. The latter is only possible where a country, or a group of countries, is the dominant exporter of a product. ***International commodity agreements*** with economic provisions can underpin their aim of price stabilization through export quotas, sometimes together with a ***buffer stock***, but such agreements are rather out of fashion. Article XX(h) (General Exceptions) of the GATT allows members to adopt measures in support of obligations they have accepted under any intergovernmental commodity agreements conforming to the 1947 ***ECOSOC*** principles. This is also reflected Chapter VI of the ***Havana Charter***. GATT Article XX(i) permits WTO members to maintain "restrictions on exports of domestic materials necessary to ensure essential quantities of such materials to a domestic processing industry during periods when the domestic price of such materials is held below the world price as part of a governmental stabilization plan", but such restrictions must not be used to increase exports of the commodity concerned or to give it greater protection. Reasons adduced at one time or another against export quotas include (a) their tendency to discriminate against low-cost producers and new entrants into the market, (b) their inability to alleviate shortages, (c) they may lead to unreasonable expectations of defensible price levels among producers, (d) they may work against the aim of putting

Export performance requirements

出口实绩要求

允许在其领土内进行外国投资的国家旨在扩大其出口而设置的条件。最简单的情况是，使用外国投资建立的企业需要出口一定比例的产出，以价值或数量表示。批发和零售贸易商可能需要平衡其进口和出口。《与贸易有关的投资措施协定》禁止了大部分此类要求。

Export pessimism

出口悲观主义

这种观点在20世纪50年代拉美地区发展中国家进口替代政策鼎盛时期尤为盛行。观点所依据的假设是，它们的出口规模很小无法促进经济发展，而国际一体化会破坏一经济体可能取得的任何竞争力。结论是，进口替代是惟一现实的政策。另见*依附理论(dependence theory)*。

Export price

出口价格

自一国出口的一货物的价格。如果针对该货物采取反倾销措施，出口价格即具有特殊意义。如果出口价格低于正常价值(出口国中供消费的同类产品的可比价格)，则可能发生倾销。

Export processing zones

出口加工区

见*自由贸易园区(free-trade zones)*。

Export propensity

出口倾向

出口的本国生产货物和服务的份额。另见*出口参与率(export participation rate)*。

Export quotas

出口配额

对某些出口产品的总值或总量施加的限制或上限，目的在于保护国内生产者和消费者免受这些产品暂时短缺的影响，或通过减少供应提高特定产品的国际市场价格。后者仅在一国或一组国家是一产品主要出口方的情况下方可实现。订有经济条款的国际商品协定强调通过出口配额稳定物价的目标，有时还辅以缓冲储存等措施，但此类协定已经过时。GATT第20条(一般例外) (h)款允许成员采取措施，以支持其在符合1947年联合国经社理事会(ECOSOC)原则的任何政府间商品协定项下所接受的义务。此点也反映在《哈瓦那宪章》第六章中。GATT第20条(i)款允许WTO成员“在作为政府稳定计划的一部分将国内原材料价格压至低于国际价格的时期内，为保证此类原料给予国内加工产业所必需的数量而限制此类原料出口的措施”，但此类限制不得用于增加有关商品的出口或增加对其提供的保护。不时提出的反对出口配额的理由包括：(a)存在歧视低成本生产者和新进入市场者的倾向；(b)无法缓解短缺；(c)可能导致生产者对合理价格水平的不合理预期；(d)不利于通过保证效率较

less on the market by guaranteeing less efficient producers a minimum price, (e) artificially high prices encourage consumers to use substitutes, synthetics or new technologies reducing the need for that commodity, (f) the general difficulty of negotiating and policing quotas, especially when there are structural changes in the market brought about, for example, by a shift in consumer preferences or the entry of new producer-based technologies, (g) ensuring that all significant producers are members of an agreement with export quotas is always difficult, and (h) in times of even minor oversupply a small additional exporter can have a disproportionate effect. Some argue that the ***Integrated Programme for Commodities*** would offer a defence against most of these perceived difficulties because of the universality of its membership. Others believe that the history of commodity negotiations since 1976, when the integrated programme was negotiated, does not support this claim adequately. *See also* ***commodity policy***.

Export restitution: occurs when world prices for an agricultural commodity are lower than domestic prices, and the government makes up the difference once the export has been made. It is in effect a variable ***export subsidy***.

Export restraint arrangement: *see* ***voluntary restraint arrangement***.

Export subsidies: government payments or other financial contributions by governments provided to domestic producers or exporters if they export their goods or services. They are illegal for manufactured products under the ***Agreement on Subsidies and Countervailing Measures***. *See also* ***agricultural export subsidies*** and ***export incentives***.

Export support: any form of governmental action that (a) reduces the cost of the exported product to the importer to less than its true market price or (b) reduces the cost of exporting or marketing for export to less than the cost actually incurred. Either of these actions is held, at any rate by those benefiting from them, as making the exporting country more competitive. However, the difference between the true cost and the actual return must be met somehow, and the taxpayer usually fills that role. *See also* ***export competition*** and ***export subsidies***.

Export targeting: the practice by an exporting country of selecting some countries as particularly promising markets for its products. The practice becomes reprehensible in the eyes of producers in importing countries when ***unfair trading practices*** are used. *See also* ***voluntary import expansion***.

Export tariffs: a levy on goods or commodities at the time they leave a ***customs territory***. Reasons for imposing export tariffs include raising revenue, the desire to promote further processing of commodities within the country and a policy of ensuring that commodities perceived as scarce and necessary for domestic production are reserved as much as possible for local industry. *See also* ***differential export tax***, ***double pricing***, ***export quotas***, ***Lerner's symmetry theorem*** and ***short-supply products***.

***Ex post*:** after a measure is applied.

Expressions of folklore: *see* ***folklore*** and ***traditional cultural expressions***.

低的生产者最低价格以减少市场投入的目标；(e)人为高价鼓励消费者使用替代品、合成材料或新技术，从而减少对该商品的需求；(f)谈判和监督配额的总体困难，特别是在市场发生结构性变化时，例如由于消费者喜好的变化或新的基于生产者的技术的引进；(g)保证所有重要生产者均为出口配额协定的成员通常是困难的；以及(h)即使在略微供应过剩时，少量增加出口即可能产生不成比例的影响。一些人认为，商品综合方案能为大多数这些困难问题提供保护作用，因其成员资格具有普遍性。其他人认为，自1976年谈判一体化方案以来的商品谈判历史未能充分支持这一主张。另见*商品政策(commodity policy)*。

Export restitution

出口补偿

在一种农产品的世界价格低于国内价格时，政府在该产品完成出口后弥补差额的做法。实际上是一种可变的出口补贴。

Export restraint arrangement

出口限制安排

见*自愿限制安排(voluntary restraint arrangement)*。

Export subsidies

出口补贴

政府向国内生产者或出口商提供的政府支付或其他财政资助，如果这些国内生产者或出口商出口其货物或服务。对制成品提供此类补贴在《补贴与反补贴措施协定》项下属非法。另见*农产品出口补贴(agricultural export subsidies)*、*出口鼓励措施(export incentives)*。

Export support

出口支持

任何形式的政府行动，旨在(a)将出口产品对进口商的成本降至低于其真实市场价格或(b)使出口成本或出口营销成本低于实际发生成本。这两种行动中的任一种，无论受益者受益程度如何，均使出口国更具竞争力。但是，真实成本与实际回报之间的差距必须以某种方式支付，而纳税人通常扮演这一角色。另见*出口竞争(export competition)*、*出口补贴(export subsidies)*。

Export targeting

出口目标

一出口国选择一些国家作为其产品有特别前景市场的做法。在进口国中的生产者看来，当使用不公平贸易做法时，此种做法应受到谴责。另见*自愿扩大进口(voluntary import expansion)*。

Export tariffs

出口关税

货物或商品离开一关税领土时征收的税。征收出口关税的理由包括：增加收入、意在促进商品在本国的进一步加工以及保证被认为稀缺的商品和国内生产所需商品尽可能留给本地产业。另见*差别出口税(differential export tax)*、*双重定价(double pricing)*、*出口配额(export quotas)*、*勒纳对称定理(Lerner's symmetry theorem)*、*短缺产品(short-supply products)*。

Ex post

事后

在实施一项措施之后。

Expressions of folklore

民间文学艺术表达

见*民间文学艺术(folklore)*、*传统文化表现形式(traditional cultural expressions)*。

Expropriation: confiscation by the host country of property owned by foreign nationals or taking action to nullify the value of property, usually under the guise of some public policy goal. Article III of the United States model bilateral investment treaty, for example, says that parties may only expropriate an investment for a public purpose, in a non-discriminatory manner, upon payment of prompt, adequate and effective compensation, and in accordance with due process of law. ***Bilateral investment treaties*** and ***investment promotion and protection agreements*** seek to establish procedures for just compensation of former owners *See also* ***Hull formula***. [Brownlie 2019, Shaw 2014]

Extended Balance of Payments Services Classification: EBOPS. A product-based classification of traded services developed in response to the new statistical information needs arising from the ***General Agreement on Trade in Services***. It supplements the fifth edition of the ***IMF Balance of Payments Manual***. *See also* ***trade in services statistics***.

Extended Credit Facility: ECF. An ***IMF*** facility under the ***Poverty Reduction and Growth Trust*** aimed at supporting low-income countries' economic programmes to move towards a stable and sustainable macroeconomic position consistent with strong and durable poverty reduction and growth.

Extended moratorium on customs duties on electronic transmissions: *see* **moratorium on customs duties on electronic transmissions**.

Extension of protection for geographical indications: the WTO ***Doha Ministerial Conference*** agreed to examine the question of extending protection of ***geographical indications*** to products other than wines and spirit and that this examination would be handled by the ***Council for TRIPS***. Few dispute that an extension of protection of geographical indications to other products is feasible in principle. The ***Paris Convention***, the observance of which is a requirement under the ***Agreement on Trade-Related Aspects of Intellectual Property Rights***, requires its members in Article 1 to protect indications of source or appellations of origin as a form of ***industrial property***. It defines "industrial property" as not only including industry and commerce proper, but also "agricultural and extractive industries and all manufactured or natural products, for example, wines, grain, tobacco leaf, fruit, cattle, minerals, mineral waters, beer, flowers and flour". Most countries already protect these forms of industrial property, not only as geographical indications but also as ***trademarks***, ***certification marks***, etc. Some say that the proposal for extending protection is impracticable, and they doubt that the cost of doing extending protection to other products would balance the likely benefits. This group also argues that, as far as extension is feasible, the same ends can be achieved through simpler means, such as protection of trademarks. Proponents of extension say that there are no economic or systemic reasons for protecting geographical indications for certain products differently from others, and that the administrative costs of doing so would negligible. *See also* ***multilateral system of notification and registration of geographical indications***.

Expropriation
征收

东道国没收外国侨民拥有的财产或采取行动使财产价值无效，通常以某种公共政策目标为幌子。例如，《美国双边投资条约文本》第3条规定，缔约方应仅为公共目的、以非歧视方式没收一投资，且应支付迅速、充足且有效赔偿且依照正当法律程序。双边投资条约和投资促进与保护协定寻求建立对前所有权人公正的赔偿程序。另见*赫尔公式(Hull formula)*。

Extended Balance of Payments Services Classification
国际收支服务扩展分类

EBOPS。根据《服务贸易总协定》所产生的新统计信息需求制定的基于产品的服务贸易分类。对国际货币基金组织(IMF)《国际收支手册》第5版进行了补充。另见*服务贸易统计(trade in services statistics)*。

Extended Credit Facility
中期贷款

ECF。国际货币基金组织(IMF)在减贫和成长信托基金下设立的融资机制，旨在支持低收入国家的经济计划，朝着稳定和可持续的宏观经济地位迈进，与强有力和持久的减贫和增长保持一致。

Extended moratorium on customs duties on electronic transmissions
延长电子传输暂免关税

见*电子传输暂免关税(moratorium on customs duties on electronic transmissions)*。

Extension of protection for geographical indications
地理标志保护扩大

WTO多哈部长级会议同意审查将地理标志保护扩大到葡萄酒和烈酒以外产品的问题，这项审查将由与贸易有关的知识产权理事会处理。将地理标志的保护扩大到其他产品原则上可行这一点并无争议。《与贸易有关的知识产权协定》要求遵守《巴黎公约》，该公约第1条要求其成员将产地标志或原产地名称作为一种工业产权形式加以保护。公约对“工业产权”的定义不仅包括工业和商业本身，还包括“农业和采掘工业以及一切制成品或天然产品，例如酒类、谷物、烟叶、水果、牲畜、矿产品、矿泉水、啤酒、花卉和面粉等”。大多数国家已经保护这些形式的工业产权，不仅作为地理标志，而且作为商标、认证标志等。一些人认为扩大保护范围的提议不切实际，他们怀疑将保护范围扩大到其他产品的成本会抵消可能的利益，他们还认为，即使扩大是可行的，但是同样的目的可以通过更简单的方法实现，例如商标保护。扩大范围的支持者认为，以不同于其他产品的方式保护某些产品的地理标志缺乏经济或制度理由，且这样作的行政成本可以忽略不计。另见*地理标志多边通报和注册制度(multilateral system of notification and registration of geographical indications)*。

External trade: this can mean the same as foreign trade generally. It can also refer to the foreign trade conducted by members of a ***preferential trade arrangement*** with non-members. The trade between the partners to such an arrangement is then called internal trade.

Extraordinary challenge: a procedure available under ***NAFTA*** Article 1904.13 concerning the settlement of disputes about anti-dumping or countervailing duty matters. The provision allows parties to challenge a panel decision on the claim that (a) a panel member was guilty of gross misconduct, bias, a serious conflict of interest or violating the rules of conduct in other ways, (b) the panel seriously departed from a fundamental rule of procedure, or (c) the panel manifestly exceeded its powers, and that any of these conditions materially affected the panel's decision and threatened the integrity of the panel review process.

Extraterritoriality: the enforcement of the laws of a country outside its territory. This is much disliked except by those economically powerful enough to benefit from it. *See also* ***antitrust laws***, ***effects doctrine***, ***Helms-Burton legislation*** and ***Iran and Libya Sanctions Act***.

Ex-works price: a concept used in the administration of some ***preferential rules of origin***. It is the value of a good when it leaves the factory. One major component is the value of all materials used in its manufacture. The other major component is all costs incurred in the manufacture of the good, such as wages, electricity, licences for ***intellectual property***, etc. In most cases, highly complex and probably irritating calculation methods have been developed under ***free-trade agreements*** using this method.

External trade

外部贸易

一般与对外贸易同义。也可指一优惠贸易安排的成员与非成员开展对外贸易。该优惠贸易安排的伙伴之间的贸易因此称为内部贸易。

Extraordinary challenge

特别质疑

《北美自由贸易协定》(NAFTA)第1904.13条规定的程序，涉及反倾销或反补贴税问题争端的解决。该规定允许当事方根据以下主张对一专家组的裁决提出质疑：(a)专家组成员犯有严重不当行为、偏见、严重利益冲突或以其他方式违反行为准则；(b)专家组严重偏离基本程序规则；或(c)专家组明显越权，且以上各条中的任一条实质影响专家组的决定和威胁专家组审查程序的完整性。

Extraterritoriality

治外法权

在一国领土之外执行该国法律。此种做法令人厌恶，而那些经济实力强大到足以从中获益的国家除外。另见*反垄断法(antitrust laws)*、*效果原则(effects doctrine)*、*赫尔姆斯-伯顿法(Helms-Burton legislation)*、*伊朗与利比亚制裁法(Iran and Libya Sanctions Act)*。

Ex-works price

出厂价格

一些优惠原产地规则管理中使用的概念。指一货物离开工厂时的价值。其中一个主要组成部分是制造过程中所使用的全部材料的价值，另一个主要组成部分是货物制造过程中产生的全部成本，如工资、电力、知识产权许可等。在大多数情况下，在自由贸易协定项下使用这一方法制定有极为复杂且可能令人恼火的计算方法。

F

Fabric formation rule: *see* ***fabric-forward rule***.

Fabric-forward rule: a ***rule of origin*** much favoured by the United States. The rule says that some specified fabrics and made-up non-apparel articles (e.g. ***flat goods***) are deemed to originate in the country where the fabric is woven, knitted or otherwise formed, regardless of any further finishing which may have been performed on the fabrics afterwards. The reasoning behind this rule is the assumption that fabric formation is the most important step in the production of such goods. *See also* ***yarn forward rule***.

Facilitation payments: another name for bribes. *See also* ***bribery***, ***corruption*** and ***trade and illicit payments***.

Facility for Investment Climate Advisory Services: FIAS. An advisory service operated by the ***World Bank Group*** which seeks to help developing countries develop a robust and responsible private sector that contributes to inclusive growth and poverty reduction, jobs, service delivery, food security, climate change mitigation and environmental sustainability. Its activities are based on three pillars: (1) improve the business environment, (2) expand market opportunities and (3) strengthen firm competitiveness. [worldbank.org]

Factor proportion theory: *see* ***Heckscher-Ohlin theorem***.

Failing-firm doctrine: a doctrine established under United States and some other ***antitrust laws***. It permits mergers that might otherwise be illegal, if some conditions are met. These usually are (a) a grave possibility of a business failure, (b) a lack of any other prospective buyer, and (c) a small chance for a successful reorganization of the firm. *See also* ***crisis cartel***.

Fair and equitable treatment: an obligation found in Article XVII (State Trading Enterprises) of the GATT concerning the conduct of ***state trading*** in relation to government import purchases. This obligation does not have the same force as ***most-favoured-nation treatment***, but it was originally meant to give non-discriminatory treatment to the maximum extent possible. The expression is common in ***bilateral investment treaties*** and other treaties concerned with investment, though it is not usually defined exactly. Some say that the phrase should be understood in its plain meaning, i.e. treatment has to be "fair" and "equitable". Others say that it is the same as the ***minimum standard of treatment***.

Fair competition: in ***trade policy*** the proposition that international trade should be conducted within the non-discriminatory rules of the ***multilateral trading system***. Sometimes this is also known as the ***level playing field***. One element of fair competition in trade is that competition is kept within certain bounds.

F

Fabric formation rule
织物成型规则

见*自织物开始规则(fabric-forward rule)*。

Fabric-forward rule
自织物开始规则

备受美国青睐的一种原产地规则。该规则规定，一些指定织物和非服装制品(例如平幅针织物)的原产地视为织物进行机织、针织或以其他方式成型的国家，不考虑此后对织物可能进行的任何进一步精加工。这一规则背后的原因是，假设织物成型是生产此类货物过程中最重要的工序。另见*自纱线开始规则(yarn forward rule)*。

Facilitation payments
通融费

贿赂的另一名称。另见*贿赂(bribery)*、*腐败(corruption)*、*贸易与违法付款(trade and illicit payments)*。

Facility for Investment Climate Advisory Services
外国投资咨询服务中心

FIAS。由世界银行集团运行的一项咨询服务，寻求帮助发展中国家发展强有力且负责任的私营部门，以促进包容性增长、减贫、就业、服务提供、粮食安全、减缓气候变化和环境可持续性。活动基于三大支柱：(1)改善商业环境；(2)拓展市场机会；以及(3)增强企业竞争力。

Factor proportion theory
要素比例理论

见*赫克舍尔-奥林定理(Heckscher-Ohlin theorem)*。

Failing-firm doctrine
破产公司原则

美国和其他国家反垄断法项下建立的原则。如果满足一些条件，允许进行原本属非法的并购，通常包括：(a)极有可能倒闭；(b)缺乏任何其他潜在买家；以及(c)公司成功重组的机会很小。另见*危机卡特尔(crisis cartel)*。

Fair and equitable treatment
公平和公正的待遇

GATT第17条(国营贸易企业)中的一项义务，涉及与政府进口采购有关的国营贸易行为。此项义务不具有与最惠国待遇相同的效力，但最初的目的是尽最大可能给予非歧视待遇。这一表述常见于双边投资条约及其他涉及投资的条约中，尽管通常没有确切定义。有些人说，这一短语应从字面意思理解，即待遇应是“公平的”和“公正的”。另一些人则认为该表述与最低待遇标准同义。

Fair competition
公平竞争

贸易政策中的一项主张，认为国际贸易应在多边贸易体制的非歧视原则内进

Otherwise, ***anti-dumping measures***, countervailing duties, etc., may apply. *See also* ***equitable competition*** and ***fair trade***.

Fair labour standards: a term with much the same meaning as ***core labour standards***. *See also* ***international labour standards*** and ***social clause***.

Fair trade: this has several meanings. It can be a trading system in which rights and obligations are balanced and observed by participants in the system. To others it means trade without reliance on ***dumping*** or ***subsidies***. In the 1980s, fair trade came to be defined by some as meaning something more akin to ***managed trade***, such as the effort to achieve forced bilateral ***balance of trade***. In ***competition policy***, fair trade refers to the conduct of commercial activities without resort to anti-competitive practices as described by a country's ***competition laws***. Fair trade also refers to a movement to give, *inter alia*, farmers stable and remunerative returns, decent working conditions, empowering farmers and workers and promoting gender equality by buying and selling products produced under these general conditions. The context usually makes clear the intended meaning.

Fair-use doctrine: the proposition that works under ***copyright*** may be drawn on to a limited extent through quotation of excerpts, particularly for scholarly purposes, without leading to claims of ***piracy***. Whether use would be considered fair in a particular instance would depend on the circumstances of the case. *See also* ***intellectual property rights*** and ***intellectual property right infringements***.

FAL Convention: *see* ***Convention on Facilitation of International Maritime Traffic.***

Fallacy of composition: the dilemma, as explained for example in the 2002 UNCTAD ***Trade and Development Report***, that "on its own a small developing country can substantially expand its exports without flooding the market and seriously reducing the prices of the products concerned, but this may not be true for developing countries as a whole". Proponents of this view often use the analogy of spectators in a football stadium. If the people in the front rows stand up to see better, those in the seats behind also have to stand up. The result is that hardly anybody is better off. The fallacy lies in assuming that if something works for one economy, it could or should work for lots of others also. *See also* ***Prisoner's Dilemma***. [Mayer 2002]

False indications of source: *see* ***indications of source***.

Famous mark: a ***trademark*** which is obviously known to many, but the meaning of the term does not appear to be defined further. Courts of law, in deciding whether a mark is famous, make use of criteria such as the geographical extent of the area where the mark is used or known, what distribution channels are used for the goods bearing the mark, the degree of recognition of the mark among those that buy and sell the good, and so forth. *See also* ***dilution doctrine*** and ***well-known mark***.

FAO: *see* ***Food and Agriculture Organization***.

Farmer's privilege: the right of farmers to make use of seeds produced from stock protected under the United States *Plant Variety Protection Act* of 1970 without

行，有时也称为公平竞争环境。贸易中公平竞争的一个要素是将竞争限制在一定范围内，否则即有可能适用反倾销措施、反补贴税等。另见*公平竞争(equitable competition)*、*公平贸易(fair trade)*。

Fair labour standards

公平劳工标准

该词的含义与核心劳工标准大致相同。另见*国际劳工标准(international labour standards)*、*社会条款(social clause)*。

Fair trade

公平贸易

该词有多种含义。可以是一个权利与义务平衡并得到参加方遵守的贸易体制。对于其他人而言，意味着不依赖倾销或补贴的贸易。20世纪80年代，一些人将公平贸易定义为更接近受管制的贸易，例如努力实现强制双边贸易平衡。在竞争政策中，公平贸易指开展商业活动而不援用一国竞争法所描述的反竞争行为。公平贸易还指通过购买和销售在一般条件下生产的产品，给予农民稳定的有偿报酬、体面的工作条件、赋予农民和工人权力以及促进性别平等。一般通过上下文能够明确想要表达的含义。

Fair-use doctrine

合理使用原则

版权作品可以通过摘录引文在有限程度上加以使用，特别是用于学术目的，而免于引致盗版索赔。使用在特定情况下是否被认为属合理取决于具体情况。另见*知识产权(intellectual property rights)*、*侵犯知识产权(intellectual property right infringements)*。

FAL Convention

国际便利海上运输公约

见*国际便利海上运输公约(Convention on Facilitation of International Maritime)*

Fallacy of composition

合成谬误

联合国贸易与发展会议(UNCTAD) 2002年《贸易与发展报告》举例说明的一个困境，即“一个小发展中国家本身可以大幅扩大其出口，而不会充斥市场和严重降低有关产品的价格，但对于发展中国家整体而言，情况可能并非如此”。这种观点的支持者经常使用足球场上的观众进行类比，如果坐在前排的人为了看清楚而站起来，坐在后排的人也不得不站起来。结果是，几乎没有人的生活会变得更好。谬误在于，认为对一个经济体有效的东西，对于其他许多经济体也能够或应该有效。另见*囚徒困境(Prisoner's Dilemma)*。

False indications of source

虚假产地标志

见*产地标志(indications of source)*。

Famous mark

著名商标

为许多人所知的商标，但这一词语的含义似乎并无进一步定义。法院在决定一商标是否属著名商标时使用的标准包括：该商标被使用或知晓的地理范围、带有该商标的货物的分销渠道、货物买家和卖家对该商标的认识程度等。另见*淡化理论(dilution doctrine)*、*驰名商标(well-known mark)*。

FAO

粮食及农业组织

见*粮食及农业组织(Food and Agriculture Organization)*。

Farmer's privilege

农民特权

农民有权使用根据美国1970年《植物品种保护法》受到保护的植物的种子，

infringing the ***intellectual property rights*** of the owner of the protected stock. [Abbott et al. 1999]

Farmers' rights: a concept developed by the ***Food and Agriculture Organization*** (FAO) through the ***International Undertaking on Plant Genetic Resources***, adopted in 1983. An interpretative resolution to the Undertaking passed in 1989 defines farmers' rights as "rights arising from the past, present and future contribution of farmers in conserving, improving and making available plant genetic resources, particularly those in the centres of origin/diversity". The FAO says that farmers' rights are not assigned to specific varieties, types of plants, or to specific farmers as, for example, ***intellectual property rights*** are. The purpose of farmers' rights is to encourage farmers and farming communities to nurture, conserve, utilize and improve plant genetic resources. Farmers' rights are therefore seen as a way to compensate farmers for improvements they have made over a long time, and for which they may not be able to benefit from protection through intellectual property rights. *See also* ***traditional knowledge***.

Fast-track: a mechanism, now renamed ***Trade Promotion Authority***, available since the passage of the 1974 United States Trade Act under which Congress can only approve or disapprove in its entirety a regional or multilateral trade package negotiated by ***USTR***. The main conditions are (a) that Congress is informed of the likely outcome of negotiations well before they are concluded to allow for consultations with the Administration, (b) that committees would report on the bill within a short time, and (c) that debate over the bill in both houses would be limited. Some WTO members think that the United States cannot negotiate seriously in ***multilateral trade negotiations*** until it has received fast-track authorization. There is much truth in this view, but Congress tends to take in any case a strong interest in all phases of the negotiations and make its views known to the Administration. Others see the main benefit of fast-track authority as giving other countries the signal that the United States is ready to negotiate and what its broad negotiating objectives are. *See also* ***reverse fast-track***.

Favourable-balance-of-trade objective: *see* ***mercantilism***.

FCN treaties: *see* ***Treaties of friendship, commerce and navigation***.

FDI Regulatory Restrictiveness Index: maintained by the ***OECD***. It measures statutory restrictions on ***foreign direct investment*** in sixty-eight countries and twenty-two sectors. It focuses on four types of measures: (a) equity restrictions, (b) screening and approval requirements, (c) restrictions on foreign key personnel, and (d) other operational restrictions such as limits on purchase of land and repatriation of profits and capital. *See also* ***Overall Trade Restrictiveness Index***. [www.oecd.org]

Federal Trade Commission: FTC. A United States agency with a mandate to protect consumers and to promote competition. It enforces United States ***antitrust laws*** including, among others, the ***Clayton Act***, the Hart-Scott-Rodino Antitrust Improvement Act, the International Antitrust Enforcement Act and the

而不损害受保护植物所有权人的知识产权。

Farmers' rights

农民权利

粮农组织(FAO)在1983年通过《植物遗传资源国际承诺》后形成的一个概念。1989年通过的对该条约的解释性决议将农民权利定义为"由于农民过去、现在和未来在保护、改进和提供植物遗传资源方面作出贡献所产生的权利，特别是在原产地/多样性中心的农民"。粮农组织表示，农民权利不像知识产权那样分配给特定品种、类型的植物或特定的农民。农民权利的目的是鼓励农民和农业社区培育、保护、利用和改善植物遗传资源。农民权利因此被视为对农民长期以来所作贡献的一种补偿，也是对农民可能无法通过知识产权得到保护的一种补偿。另见*传统知识(traditional knowledge)*。

Fast-track

快轨授权

自美国《1974年贸易法》通过以来设立的一种机制，现更名为贸易促进授权，根据美国《1974年贸易法》，国会只能要么全部批准或要么全部否决美国贸易代表办公室(USTR)谈判达成的区域或多边贸易谈判一揽子结果。主要条件为：(a)国会在谈判结束前的较早阶段即已被告知可能的谈判结果，国会从而可以与政府进行协商；(b)委员会在短期内就议案作出报告；以及(c)参众两院对议案进行有限的辩论。一些WTO成员认为，在获得快轨授权之前，美国无法在多边贸易谈判中进行认真谈判。此种观点很有道理，但国会倾向于在任何情况下对谈判所有阶段均有浓厚兴趣，并使政府了解其观点。另一些人认为，快轨授权的主要好处是向其他国家发出信号，表明美国已准备好进行谈判，并表明其谈判主要目标。另见*反向快轨授权(reverse fast-track)*。

Favourable-balance-of-trade objective

贸易顺差目标

见*重商主义(mercantilism)*。

FCN treaties

友好通商航海条约

见*友好通商航海条约(Treaties of friendship, commerce and navigation)*。

FDI Regulatory Restrictiveness Index

外国直接投资监管限制指数

由经济合作与发展组织(OECD)编制，衡量 68 个国家和 22 个行业对外国直接投资的法定限制。聚焦 4 类措施：(a)股权限制；(b)审查和批准要求；(c)对外国关键人员的限制；以及(d)其他业务限制，例如购买土地限制及利润和资本汇回限制。另见*总体贸易限制指数(Overall Trade Restrictiveness Index)*。

Federal Trade Commission

联邦贸易委员会

FTC。美国拥有保护消费者和促进竞争授权的机构。负责执行美国反垄断法，其中包括《克莱顿法》、《哈特-斯科特-罗迪诺反垄断改进法》、《国际反垄断

Webb-Pomerene Act. *See also* ***antitrust guidelines for international enforcement and cooperation***.

Fibre-forward rule: a ***rule of origin*** favoured especially by the United States. It requires that fibres must be made in the territories of the partners to these trade agreements and subsequent processing must also occur there if the product is to receive preferential treatment. *See also* ***fabric-forward rule*** and ***yarn forward rule***.

Fifth Protocol to the General Agreement on Trade in Services: gives effect to the commitments on trade in ***financial services*** following negotiations in 1996 and 1997. It entered into force on 1 March 1999.

Final determination of dumping: once all aspects of a petition for ***anti-dumping measures*** have been examined, the investigating authority will give the reasons for its decision in a final determination. This may have been preceded by a ***preliminary determination of dumping***. The final determination can either be negative (i.e. the requirements for imposing anti-dumping measures have not been met) or positive (i.e. the requirements have been met). Investigations leading to a final determination normally will be concluded within twelve months of the initiation, but in exceptional cases it may last up to eighteen months. All determinations have to be published. *See also* ***dumping***.

Final goods and services: goods and services bought by end-users. They are not used in any further production process. This distinguishes them from intermediate goods and services. The distinction depends entirely on who buys them. A teapot bought for use at home is a final product, but teapots bought by hotels for the provision of breakfast tea are clearly an intermediate good for the provision of a final service.

Final rate: in a programme of phased or staged tariff reductions the rate reached when the last reduction has been made.

Financial services: banking, general insurance, life insurance, funds management, securities trading and advisory services related to these activities. *See also* ***Understanding on Commitments in Financial Services***.

Financial Stability Board: FSB. Established in 2009 as the successor to the Financial Stability Forum. Its members are central banks and finance ministries or treasuries of the ***G20*** members as well as international financial institutions and international standard-setting bodies. The FSB's mandate is to promote international financial stability. It does this by coordinating national financial authorities and international standard-setting bodies working on regulatory and supervisory policies. Its decisions are not legally binding on members. [fsb.org]

First Account: the programme under the ***Common Fund for Commodities*** which finances international ***buffer stocks*** and internationally coordinated national stocks, but only if they are operated in the framework of the ***Integrated Programme for Commodities***. This programme is inactive. *See also* ***Second Account***.

First Agreement on Trade Negotiation Among Developing Countries of ESCAP: *see* ***Asia-Pacific Trade Agreement***.

法》和《韦布-波默林法》。另见*国际执法与合作反垄断指导原则(antitrust guidelines for international enforcement and cooperation)*。

Fibre-forward rule
自纤维开始规则

备受美国青睐的一种原产地规则。规则要求纤维必须在贸易协定伙伴的领土内生产，如果产品要获得到优惠待遇，后续加工也必须在该国进行。另见*自织物开始规则(fabric-forward rule)*、*自纱线开始规则(yarn forward rule)*。

Fifth Protocol to the General Agreement on Trade in Services
服务贸易总协定第五议定书

经过 1996 年和 1997 年的谈判，该议定书使金融服务领域承诺得以生效。议定书于 1999 年 3 月 1 日生效。

Final determination of dumping
倾销最终裁定

一旦对反倾销措施请求的所有方面已经进行审查，调查机关将在最终裁定中说明其作出决定的理由。此前可能作出倾销初步裁定。最终裁定可以是否定的(即未满足实施反倾销措施的条件)，也可以是肯定的(即已满足条件)。产生最终裁定的调查通常会在启动后12个月内完成，但在特殊情况下，调查可能会持续达18个月。所有裁定必须公布。另见*倾销(dumping)*。

Final goods and services
最终产品和服务

最终用户购买的产品和服务，不用于任何进一步生产过程，这是它们与中间产品和服务的区别。这种区别完全取决于购买者。购买的家用茶壶是最终产品，但酒店为提供早餐茶而购买的茶壶显然是提供最终服务的中间产品。

Final rate
最终税率

在分期或分阶段关税削减方案中，完成最后一次削减后达到的税率。

Financial services
金融服务

银行、普通保险、人寿保险、基金管理、证券交易以及与此类活动相关的咨询服务。另见*关于金融服务承诺的谅解(Understanding on Commitments in Financial Services)*。

Financial Stability Board
金融稳定委员会

FSB。2009年作为金融稳定论坛的后继组织设立。成员包括20国集团成员国的中央银行和财政部，以及国际金融机构和国际标准制定机构。金融稳定委员会的任务是促进国际金融稳定，通过协调各国金融监管部门和国际标准制定机构的监管和监督政策来实现这一目标，其决定对成员无法律约束力。

First Account
第一账户

商品共同基金项下的计划，为国际缓冲储存和国际协调下的国家储存提供资金，但必须在商品综合方案框架内运行。该计划处于非活动状态。另见*第二账户(Second Account)*。

First Agreement on Trade Negotiation Among Developing Countries of ESCAP
亚太经社会发展中成员之间国贸易谈判第一协定

见*亚太贸易协定(Asia-Pacific Trade Agreement)*。

First-difference negotiations: another name for the technique of bilateral ***requests and offers*** followed in the WTO system for trade in goods and services.

First-difference reciprocity: a term used by Bhagwati to describe bargaining for tariff cuts based on perceived advantages at the margin. He contrasts this with negotiations that would lead to perceived equality of market access and reverse market access. *See also* ***first-difference negotiations***. [Bhagwati 1988]

First-in, first-out: a method of inventory management which uses the cost of the oldest goods in stock as the valuation basis. Its main relevance to trade policy stems from the need to calculate a ***regional value content*** under the ***rules of origin*** adopted in some ***free-trade agreements***. *See also* ***averaging*** and ***last-in, first-out***.

First in time, first in right: the principle that the first person acquiring an ***intellectual property right***, such as a ***trademark*** or a ***geographical indication***, is the person who has the right to use it.

First-mover advantage: the benefits said to be available to a firm because it is the first in the market with a new technology or a new process.

First-order protectionism: the trade-restrictive measures falling broadly into the category of ***voluntary restraint arrangements***. This term is based on the incontrovertible intention that any such measures should be protectionist. *See also* ***protectionism***.

First regionalism: a term used by Bhagwati to describe the wave of ***preferential trade arrangements*** concluded during the 1950s and 1960s. The two main surviving arrangements from that time are the ***European Union*** and ***EFTA***, both of them following several transformations. [Bhagwati 1993]

First-sale doctrine: *see* ***exhaustion doctrine***.

First-to-file: a procedure to determine priority of ***patent*** rights. Most countries accord priority of invention to the person registering first regardless of when the invention took place. Until March 2013 the United States used the "first-to-invent" principle to accord priority. It has now changed to a "first-inventor-to-file" system. The main advantage of the first-to-file method is that, if a dispute arises about the precedence of claims, it establishes a clear starting point for any determination of which inventor may have priority rights. Under the first-to-invent method, the applicable date may have to be established laboriously through the use of notebooks and other records. *See also* ***intellectual property rights***.

First-to-invent: *see* ***first-to-file***.

Fisheries: *see* ***Blue BioTrade***, ***common fisheries policy***, ***Exclusive Economic Zone***, ***fisheries subsidies***, ***Friends of Fish***, ***German imports of sardines***, ***Herring and salmon***, ***IUU fishing***, ***overcapacity (fishing)***, ***Sustainable Development Goals***, ***territorial waters***, ***Tuna (Canada–United States, 1982)***, ***Tuna I*** and ***Tuna II***.

Fisheries subsidies: a set of negotiations originally launched in 2001 as part of the ***Doha Development Agenda*** negotiations on subsidies. The Hong Kong

First-difference negotiations
一级差分谈判
WTO体系中货物贸易和服务贸易适用的双边要价和出价技巧的另一名称。

First-difference reciprocity
一级差分互惠
巴格瓦蒂用于描述基于感知边际优势而进行的关税削减谈判的词语。他将此与那些可能导致市场准入与反向市场准入的感知平等的谈判进行对比。另见*一级差分谈判(first-difference negotiations)*。

First-in, first-out
先进先出法
一种使用存储时间最久货物的价值作为估价基础的存货管理方法。与贸易政策最主要的关联源于根据一些自由贸易协定采用的原产地规则计算区域价值成分的需求。另见*平均法(averaging)*、*后进先出法(last-in, first-out)*。

First in time, first in right
先在权利优先
指第一个获得商标或地理标志等知识产权的人即为有权使用该权利的人的原则。

First-mover advantage
先发优势
一企业因其率先在市场中拥有新技术或新工艺而获得的利益。

First-order protectionism
一阶保护主义
大体属于自愿限制安排类别的贸易限制措施。这一词语基于任何此类措施均应属保护主义性质这一无可争议的意图。另见*保护主义(protectionism)*。

First regionalism
第一次区域主义浪潮
巴格瓦蒂用于描述20世纪50年代和60年代缔结的优惠贸易安排浪潮的词语。当时达成且目前仍然存在的两个主要安排是欧盟和欧洲自由贸易联盟(EFTA)，两者均经历了几次转型。

First-sale doctrine
首次销售原则
见*权利用尽原则(exhaustion doctrine)*。

First-to-file
注册在先
确定专利优先权的程序。大多数国家将发明的优先权授予最先注册的人，而不考虑该发明的发生时间。直至2013年3月，美国采用“发明在先”原则授予优先权。现已改为“发明者注册在先”制度。注册在先的主要优势在于，如果对索赔优先权产生争议，此种方法即确定哪位发明人可能拥有优先权设定了一个明确的起点。根据发明在先方法，适用日期可能需要通过使用笔记本和其他记录进行艰难确定。另见*知识产权(intellectual property rights)*。

First-to-invent
发明在先
见*注册在先(first-to-file)*。

Fisheries
渔业
见*蓝色生物贸易(Blue BioTrade)*、*共同渔业政策(common fisheries policy)*、*专属经济区(Exclusive Economic Zone)*、*渔业补贴(fisheries subsidies)*、*渔业之友(Friends of Fish)*、*德国沙丁鱼进口案(German imports of sardines)*、*鲱鱼和鲑鱼案(Herring and salmon)*、*非法、未报告和无管制捕捞(IUU fishing)*、*产能过剩(捕捞)(overcapacity (fishing))*、*可持续发展目标(Sustainable Development Goals)*、*领水(territorial waters)*、*1982年加拿大-美国金枪鱼案(Tuna (Canada–United States, 1982))*、*第一个金枪鱼案(Tuna I)*、*第二个金枪鱼案(Tuna II)*。

Fisheries subsidies
渔业补贴
最初于2001年作为多哈发展议程中补贴谈判一部分启动的谈判。2005年香港WTO部长级会议同意，应加强渔业部门的补贴纪律，包括可能禁止某些

WTO Ministerial Conference in 2005 agreed that disciplines on subsidies in the fisheries sector should be strengthened, including the possibility of a prohibition on some subsidies that contribute to overcapacity and overfishing. At the Buenos Aires WTO Ministerial Conference in 2017 members agreed to continue negotiations with a view to concluding them by the next Ministerial Conference. Members also agreed that appropriate and effective ***special and differential treatment*** for developing country members and least-developed country members should be an integral part of the negotiations. A successful outcome would support Goal 14 of the United Nations ***Sustainable Development Goals***: conserve and sustainably use the oceans, seas and marine resources for sustainable development. *See also* ***overcapacity (fishing)***.

Fixed exchange rate: *see* ***exchange rate***.

Fixed quota: a quota set for the volume of import of goods that may not be exceeded in a set period. *See also* ***tariff rate quota***.

Flag of convenience: a nationality of a ship, indicated by the flag it flies, different to the nationality of the ship's owner. Flag-of-convenience registries offer the shipowner a choice of the least onerous conditions in terms of registration costs, mandatory manning requirements, wages and, possibly, safety requirements.

Flat goods: in the textiles trade items such as bed linen, quilts, blankets, table linen, wall hangings, curtains, interior blinds, towels, etc.

Flat-tariff structure: a ***tariff schedule*** in which all tariff rates are equal or nearly equal. The famous example is that of Chile which has an ***applied MFN tariff rate*** of 6 per cent for nearly all imports. The bound rate for most of these tariffs is much higher. *See also* ***dispersed tariff***.

Flexibility in geometry: *see* ***variable geometry***.

Flexibility provisions: these relate to the reductions to be made in agricultural export subsidies as a result of the ***Uruguay Round*** negotiations. If a country's export subsidies increased since the 1986–90 ***base period*** on which the negotiations were based, it had the option of using 1991–92 as the base period. However, the end-points for achieving the reductions remained the same. Flexibility provisions were also part of the ***Agreement on Textiles and Clothing***. They permitted swing (transfer of part of an export quota for one product to another product), carryover (the use in the current year of an unused export quota from the previous year) and carry forward (the use of part of next year's quota during the current year). The flexibility provisions listed in the Agreement on Textiles and Clothing had their origin in the ***Multi-Fibre Arrangement***. *See also* ***Agreement on Textiles and Clothing***.

Floating exchange rate: *see* ***exchange rate***.

Floating initial negotiating rights: *see* ***initial negotiating right***.

Floor price: a guaranteed price level for commodity producers. It may be higher or lower than the world market price for that commodity. In ***international commodity agreements*** the floor price may be the level at which the ***buffer stock*** manager must buy in an effort to reduce supply to the market and in this

助长产能过剩和过度捕捞的补贴。在2017年布宜诺斯艾利斯WTO部长级会议上，成员同意继续谈判，以期在下一届部长级会议结束谈判。成员还同意，对发展中国家成员和最不发达国家成员适当和有效的特殊和差别待遇应成为谈判的组成部分。成功的谈判结果将支持联合国可持续发展目标中的第14目标：为促进可持续发展而养护和可持续利用海洋和海洋资源。另见*产能过剩(捕捞)(overcapacity (fishing))*。

Fixed exchange rate
固定汇率

见*汇率(exchange rate)*。

Fixed quota
固定配额

对货物进口量设定的配额，在规定期限内不得超过该配额量。另见*关税配额(tariff rate quota)*。

Flag of convenience
方便旗

由所悬挂旗帜表明的船舶国籍，不同于船东的国籍。方便旗注册处为船东在注册费用、强制性人员配备要求、工资以及可能的安全要求方面提供最不苛刻的条件选择。

Flat goods
平幅针织物

纺织品贸易中的物品，例如床上用品、被子、毯子、桌布、壁挂、窗帘、室内卷帘、毛巾等。

Flat-tariff structure
单一关税结构

所有关税税率相同或接近相同的关税税则。著名的例子是智利，该国对几乎所有进口产品均实行 6%的最惠国实施税率。其中大部分关税的约束税率要高得多。另见*分散型税率(dispersed tariff rates)*。

Flexibility in geometry
灵活几何

见*可变几何(variable geometry)*。

Flexibility provisions
灵活性条款

与作为乌拉圭回合谈判结果的对农产品出口补贴的削减有关。如果一国的出口补贴自谈判所依据的 1986—1990 年基期以来有所增加，即可以选择使用1991—1992年作为基期。但是，完成削减的终点不变。灵活性条款也是《纺织品与服装协定》的一部分。允许调用(将一种产品的部分出口配额转移至另一种产品)、留用(当年使用上一年未使用的出口配额)和借用(当年使用下一年部分配额)。《纺织品与服装协定》所列的灵活性条款源自《多种纤维协定》。另见*纺织品与服装协定(Agreement on Textiles and Clothing)*。

Floating exchange rate
浮动汇率

见*汇率(exchange rate)*。

Floating initial negotiating rights
浮动最初谈判权

见*最初谈判权(initial negotiating right)*。

Floor price
最低价格

给予商品生产商的保证价格水平。可能高于或低于该商品的世界市场价格。在国际商品协定中，最低价格可能是缓冲储存经理人为努力减少市场供应而

way support the price. *See also* ***common agricultural policy***, ***loan rate*** and ***trigger price***.

Florence Agreement: *Agreement on the Importation of Educational, Scientific and Cultural Materials*. Adopted under ***United Nations Educational, Scientific and Cultural Organization*** (UNESCO) auspices in 1950. Parties to the Agreement undertake not to levy import duties on books, publications, documents and educational, scientific and cultural materials listed in the annexes. A protocol to the Agreement adopted in 1977 modernized the lists of materials covered.

Flying-geese paradigm: the proposition that economic development in a given region can be led by a major economy, with others following behind, similar to the V-pattern adopted by flying geese. It apparently was originally proposed by the Japanese economist Kaname Akamatsu in the 1930s. [Kasahara 2004]

FOB: free on board. The producer, seller or exporter of a good meets all costs and charges for the handling of a good until it has been loaded on a ship in the agreed port. For example, an exporter might quote the price of a good as "FOB Antwerp". The buyer would then be responsible for the cost of freight and insurance from the point it has been put aboard the ship in Antwerp. *See also* ***CIF***.

FOB value method: one of the methods used to establish whether a good imported from another party to a ***free-trade agreement*** qualifies for the ***preferential tariff***. In the free-trade agreement between Japan and Singapore the formula is:

$$\text{QVC} = \frac{\text{FOB} - \text{NQM}}{\text{FOB}} \times 100$$

where QVC is the qualifying value content (in other agreements often described as the ***regional value content***) of a good, expressed as a percentage, FOB is the free-on-board value of a good payable by the buyer to the seller regardless of the mode of shipment, and NQM is the non-qualifying value of the materials used in the production of the good. This method is the same as the ***build-down method*** and the ***transaction value method***.

Focused value method: used in the ***Trans-Pacific Partnership Agreement*** to calculate whether a good satisfies the ***regional value content*** (RVC) as follows:

$$\text{RVC} = \frac{\text{Value of the good} - \text{FVNM}}{\text{Value of the good}} \times 100$$

FVNM is the value of the ***non-originating materials***, including materials of undetermined origin, as specified in the applicable ***product-specific rule***. The meaning of focused net value is that only non-originating materials from a specific ***chapter***, ***heading*** or ***sub-heading*** have to be considered. This appears to be an attempt to lessen the impact on the producer or exporter.

Folklore: an aspect of ***traditional knowledge***. The protection of folkloric expressions against illicit exploitation has been discussed in the ***United Nations***

必须购买的价格，并以此种方式支持该价格。另见*共同农业政策(common agricultural policy)*、*基准贷款价格(loan rate)*、*触发价格(trigger price)*。

Florence Agreement

佛罗伦萨协定

《关于教育、科学和文化物品的进口的协定》。1950 年在联合国教科文组织(UNESCO)主持下通过。协定参加方承诺不对附录中所列书籍、出版物、文件以及教育、科学和文化物品征收进口关税。1977 年通过的协定议定书对所涵盖的产品清单进行了更新。

Flying-geese paradigm

雁型模式

一特定区域的经济发展可由一主要经济体引领、其他经济体紧随其后的主张，类似于飞行大雁所采用的 V 字型编队。显然这最初是由日本经济学家赤松要于 20 世纪 30 年代提出的。

FOB

离岸价格

货物的生产商、销售商或出口商承担一货物装卸的所有成本和费用，直至货物在约定港口装船。例如，出口商可能会将一货物的价格报为“离岸价格安特卫普”。买方因此将负责自货物在安特卫普装船起的运费和保险费。另见*到岸价格(CIF)*。

FOB value method

离岸价格法

用于确定一自自由贸易协定另一参加方进口的货物是否有资格享受优惠关税的方法。日本与新加坡自由贸易协定中的公式如下：

$$QVC=\frac{FOB-NQM}{FOB}\times 100$$

QVC 指货物的合格价值成分(在其他协定中通常称为区域价值成分)，以百分比表示；FOB 指买方向卖方支付的货物离岸价格，不考虑运输方式；NQM 指生产货物时使用的非合格材料价格。此种方法与扣减法和成交价格法相同。

Focused value method

价格法

《跨太平洋伙伴关系协定》中用于计算一产品是否符合区域价值成分(RVC)的方法，公式如下：

$$RVC=\frac{\text{货物价格}-FVNM}{\text{货物价格}}\times 100$$

FVNM 指非原产材料价格，包括在适用的特定产品规则中列明的未确定原产地的材料。净值的含义是仅需考虑来自特定章、税目或子目的非原产材料。这似乎是试图减轻对生产商或出口商的影响。

Folklore

民间文学艺术

传统知识的一方面。保护民间文学艺术表达方式免受非法利用的问题在联合

Educational, Scientific and Cultural Organization and ***WIPO*** for many years. Some have suggested that it should also become part of the WTO agenda. *See also* ***traditional cultural expressions***.

Food Aid: donation of food commodities for human consumption, including through grants and loans for the purchase of food, to address hunger, food insecurity and under-nutrition. Three categories of food aid have traditionally been recognized: emergency, project and programme food aid.

Food Aid Convention: replaced on 1 January 2013 by the Food Assistance Convention. *See* ***International Grains Agreement***.

Food and Agricultural Organization: FAO. Established in 1945 as one of the ***United Nations specialized agencies***. Its aims, as set out in the preamble to its constitution, are (a) raising levels of nutrition and standards of living of the peoples of member states, (b) securing improvements in the efficiency of the production of all food and agricultural products, (c) bettering the condition of rural populations, and (d) in this way contributing towards an expanding world economy and ensuring humanity's freedom from hunger. The FAO has, among others, committees on commodity problems, agriculture, and world ***food security***. The FAO is active in land and water development, plant and animal production, forestry and fisheries. Together with the World Health Organization, the FAO administers the ***Codex Alimentarius Commission***, intended to promote the harmonization of requirements for food and thereby facilitate international trade. The FAO is located in Rome. *See also* ***International Treaty on Plant Genetic Resources for Food and Agriculture***, ***International Undertaking on Plant Genetic Resources*** and ***World Food Programme***.

Food Assistance: the provision of assistance to address hunger, food insecurity and under nutrition. This can include ensuring food availability, access to nutritious food, proper nutrition awareness, and appropriate feeding practices. Food assistance may involve the direct provision of food, but may utilize a wider range of tools, including the transfer or provision of relevant services, inputs or commodities, cash or vouchers, skills or knowledge.

Food for Peace Program: originally established through the United States Agriculture and Trade Development Assistance Act often known as ***PL 480***. The current reauthorization is valid until the end of the 2023 financial year.

Food for Progress Program: a United States programme established under the *Food Security Act* of 1985. It encourages agricultural policy reform in developing countries through food donations and sales at concessional prices. Commodities are provided under this programme to developing countries and emerging democracies that have committed themselves to some elements of free enterprise in their agricultural economies.

Food security: when the nutritional needs of a country or population are met consistently. This is commonly described as people or populations having "at all times physical and economic access to sufficient, safe and nutritious food to meet their dietary needs for a healthy life". "Food security" and "self-sufficiency" are not the same, and a key debate is whether policies aiming for

国教科文组织(UNESCO)和世界知识产权组织(WIPO)中讨论了多年。一些人建议这一问题也应成为 WTO 议程的一部分。另见*传统文化表现形式(traditional cultural expressions)*。

Food Aid

粮食援助

捐赠食品供人类消费，包括通过用于购买粮食的赠款和贷款，以解决饥饿、粮食短缺和营养缺乏。传统意义上被认可的三类粮食援助包括：紧急粮食援助、计划粮食援助和项目粮食援助。

Food Aid Convention

粮食援助公约

2013 年 1 月 1 日被《粮食援助公约》所取代。见*国际谷物协定(International Grains Agreement)*。

Food and Agricultural Organization

粮食及农业组织

FAO。1945 年作为联合国专门机构设立。章程的前言中指出其目标为：(a)提高成员国人民的营养水平和生活水平；(b)保证所有粮食和农产品生产效率的提升；(c)改善农村人口的条件；以及(d)以此方式促进扩大世界经济和保证人类免于饥饿。FAO 设有商品问题委员会、农业委员会和世界粮食安全委员会。FAO 积极参与土地和水资源开发、动植物生产、林业和渔业。FAO 与世界卫生组织一起管理食品法典委员会，旨在促进食品要求的协调，从而便利国际贸易。FAO 设在罗马。另见*粮食与农业植物遗传资源国际条约(International Treaty on Plant Genetic Resources for Food and Agriculture)*、*植物遗传资源国际条约(International Undertaking on Plant Genetic Resources)*、*世界粮食计划署(World Food Programme)*。

Food Assistance

粮食援助

提供援助以处理饥饿、粮食短缺和营养缺乏。可包括保证粮食可获性、获得营养食物、正确营养意识和适当喂养方式。粮食援助可涉及直接提供粮食，但可能利用更广泛的工具，包括转让或提供相关服务、投入物或商品、现金或票券、技能或知识。

Food for Peace Program

粮食换和平计划

最初通过《美国农产品贸易发展与援助法》设立，通常称为《480 号公法》。目前的重新授权有效期至 2023 财政年度结束。

Food for Progress Program

粮食促进步计划

根据《1985 年粮食安全法》设立的美国计划。该计划鼓励通过粮食捐赠和折扣价销售推动发展中国家中的农业政策改革。在本计划项下商品提供给那些已经承诺在其农业经济中采用一些自由企业要素的发展中国家和新兴民主国家。

Food security

粮食安全

当一国或人口的营养需求得到持续满足之时。通常被描述为人民或人口“在

self-sufficiency would help or hinder food security. *See also* ***Food and Agriculture Organization*** and ***World Food Programme***.

Foot dragger: a party to ***multilateral trade negotiations*** which uses the ***consensus*** rule to prevent a decision or to water down the force of a provision to suit its own purposes. *See also* ***convoy problem***.

Footloose industries: a term used for industries for which the location is relatively unimportant for production and sales because they do not depend on an elaborate physical infrastructure or large fixed investment. They can easily move elsewhere in search of a cheaper and better operating environment. Sometimes they have to do this in order to satisfy new ***rules of origin***. Some service activities, such as information processing, are thought to fall into the category of footloose industries. ***Globalization***, which can spread the production process over many countries, is thought to give some impetus to the emergence of such industries. Remember, though, that in the long run all industries are footloose. *See also* ***delocalization***.

Forced technology transfer: a ***transfer of technology*** made under threat or coercion. It describes an involuntary transfer that would not have occurred if the owner had been able to make a free choice, or it would have occurred in a different form. It is difficult to say how widespread this practice is. Firms seeking to establish a joint venture in a market may find that the prospective joint venture partner expects the transaction to involve a degree of technology transfer. As such transactions are voluntary, it would not necessarily be easy to establish that coercion has occurred, but it is quite possible that the owner of the technology has to put more of it into play than expected simply to make the joint venture work. Forced technology transfer would also occur if permission to invest were given only on condition that a certain technology is made available to another party. A forced transfer of technology is not the same as theft of technology. The former is more or less overt, but not more palatable for that reason. Theft, on the other hand, is covert and only discovered after the fact. It is also subject to laws available to remedy, for example, ***intellectual property right infringements***. *See also* ***compulsory licensing***.

Foreign Corrupt Practices Act: FCPA. A United States law adopted in 1977 which imposes criminal liability on its corporations and individuals who are involved in offering inducements to officers of foreign governments to obtain or retain business. The FCPA is therefore directly relevant to rules and practices governing ***government procurement***. *See also* ***bribery in international transactions*** and ***trade and illicit payments***.

Foreign direct investment: defined by the ***IMF*** as "direct ***investment*** that is made to acquire a lasting interest in an enterprise operating in an economy other than that of the investor, the investor's purpose being to have an effective voice in the management of the enterprise". Much thought has been given to the meaning of "lasting interest". The ***OECD*** has recommended that 10 per cent or greater ownership should satisfy this requirement. The OECD also defines direct investment flows as (i) the direct investor's net purchases of the

任何时候都能从物质和经济上获得充足的、安全的和有营养的食物，来满足其健康生活的膳食需要”。“粮食安全”和“自给自足”是不同的，一个关键的争论点是旨在实现自给自足的政策是否有助于或有碍于粮食安全。另见*粮食及农业组织(Food and Agriculture Organization)*、*世界粮食计划署(World Food Programme)*。

Foot dragger
拖后腿者

采用协商一致原则的多边贸易谈判的一方，为满足其自身目的而阻止一决定或降低一条款的效力。另见*舰队问题(convoy problem)*。

Footloose industries
自由布局型产业

该词用于指对生产和销售地点相对不重要的产业，因为这些产业不依赖于复杂的有形基础设施或大规模固定投资。它们可以很容易地转移到其他地方以寻找更便宜和更好的经营环境。有时，它们为满足新的原产地规则而不得不如此。一些服务活动，例如信息处理，被认为属于自由布局型产业类别。能将生产过程遍布许多国家的全球化被认为对此类产业的出现注入了某种动力。然而，需要记住的是，从长远看，所有的产业都是自由布局的。另见*去本地化(delocalization)*。

Forced technology transfer
强制技术转让

在威胁或胁迫下进行的技术转让。它描述了一种非自愿转让，如果所有者能够自由选择，此种转让不会发生，或者会以不同形式发生。很难说此种做法有多么普遍。寻求在市场中建立合资企业的公司可能会发现潜在的合资企业伙伴期望交易包含一定程度的技术转让。由于此种交易是自愿的，因此不一定能轻易确定发生胁迫，但技术所有者很可能为使合资企业运作，就需要投入比预期更多的技术。如果投资许可的授予仅以向另一方提供某种技术为条件，也会发生强制技术转让。强制技术转让不同于窃取技术。前者或多或少是公开的，但并非因此可以接受。另一方面，窃取是隐蔽的，只有在事后才能被发现。它还受到补救法律的约束，例如知识产权侵权行为。另见*强制许可(compulsory licensing)*。

Foreign Corrupt Practices Act
反海外腐败法

FCPA。1977 年通过的美国法律，对参与向外国政府官员提供利诱以获得或保留业务的美国公司和个人规定了刑事责任。FCPA 因此与管辖政府采购的相关规则和做法直接相关。另见*国际交易中的行贿行为(bribery in international transactions)*、*贸易与违法付款(trade and illicit payments)*。

Foreign direct investment
外国直接投资

国际货币基金组织(IMF)将其定义为“为获得在投资者所在经济体以外的一经济体中经营的一企业的持续利益而进行的直接投资，投资者的目的在于对该企业的管理拥有有效发言权”。人们对“持续利益”的含义进行了大量思考。经济合作与发展组织(OECD)建议，10% 或更高的股权份额应可满足这一要求。OECD 还将直接投资流量定义为：(1)直接投资者购买公司股本和净贷款、

company's share capital and net loans, trade and other credits advanced, and (ii) the direct investor's share of reinvested earnings. *See also **APEC Non-Binding Investment Principles**, **non-equity-based investment**, **portfolio investment*** and ***World Bank Guidelines on the Treatment of Foreign Direct Investment***.

Foreign exports: *see **re-exports*** and, for comparison, ***domestic exports***.

Foreign investment protection agreements: *see **bilateral investment treaties*** and ***investment promotion and protection agreements***.

Foreign investment screening: a mechanism operated by many countries to ensure that projects financed with foreign investment meet national development objectives and ***economic needs tests***, and that foreign equity in specific sectors or companies does not exceed legal limits. Screening also aims to promote *bona fide* investment proposals. The importance of foreign investment screening for ***trade policy*** stems from the fact that some see it as capable of being a trade impediment in cases where foreign investment is essential for effective ***market access***. The screening process may result in the refusal of an application to invest and therefore to a denial of market access. *See also **Exon-Florio amendment*** and ***pre-establishment***.

Foreign parity: *see **most-favoured-nation treatment***.

Foreign sales corporation: FSC. A corporation established and maintained in a foreign country responsible for the export, sale and lease of goods and services produced in the United States. In this way, it may benefit from some tax exemptions and special administrative pricing rules. An FSC need not be affiliated with or controlled by a United States corporation to qualify for the benefits, but the benefits are greatest if such a relationship exists. Accordingly, most FSCs are subsidiaries of United States corporations. The FSC scheme was introduced in the early 1980s as the successor to the ***domestic international sales corporation*** (DISC) after a GATT panel ruled in 1976 that DISC was inconsistent with GATT rules. In 1998 the ***European Communities*** requested the establishment of a WTO ***panel*** because in its view the United States provisions for FSCs constituted a subsidy and that, therefore, the United States had violated its obligations under the ***Agreement on Subsidies and Countervailing Measures***. The panel found against the United States. Following an appeal by the United States, the ***Appellate Body*** ruled that the FSC constituted a prohibited subsidy under this Agreement on Subsidies and Countervailing Duties and under the ***Agreement on Agriculture***.

Formal/informal: formal meetings are recorded in minutes, decisions can be taken, and formal procedures apply. Informal meetings are for exchanging views or information, with no official record.

Formula cuts: tariff reductions across whole sectors done through the use of a formula, such as the ***Swiss Formula***.

Formula-plus tariff reductions: the use of ***linear tariff cuts***, accompanied by other methods to achieve tariff reductions.

Formula tariff reductions: *see **linear tariff cuts***.

贸易和其他预付信贷；及(2)直接投资者的再投资收益份额。另见*APEC 投资非约束性原则(APEC Non-Binding Investment Principles)*、*非股权投资(non-equity-based investment)*、*证券投资(portfolio investment)*、*世界银行外国直接投资待遇指南(World Bank Guidelines on the Treatment of Foreign Direct Investment)*。

Foreign exports

外国产品出口

见*复出口(re-exports)*、*本国原产货物出口(domestic exports)*以作比较。

Foreign investment protection agreements

外国投资保护协定

见*双边投资条约(bilateral investment treaties)*、*投资促进与保护协定(investment promotion and protection agreements)*。

Foreign investment screening

外国投资审查

许多国家运行的一种机制，目的在于保证由外国投资资助的项目符合国家发展目标和经济需求测试，在特定部门或公司的外国股本不超过法定限额。审查还旨在促进善意的投资提议。外国投资审查对于贸易政策的重要性源自以下事实，即一些人认为，在外国投资对于有效市场准入至关重要时，此种审查会成为贸易障碍。审查过程可能导致拒绝投资申请，从而导致拒绝市场准入。另见*埃克森-弗罗里奥修正案(Exon-Florio amendment)*、*准入前(pre-establishment)*。

Foreign parity

对外同等

见*最惠国待遇(most-favoured-nation treatment)*。

Foreign sales corporation

外国销售公司

FSC。在外国设立并维持的公司，负责在美国生产的货物和服务的出口、销售和租赁。通过此种方式，可以从一些免税和特殊行政定价规则中获益。外国销售公司不必附属于或受控于美国公司才有资格享受优惠，但如果存在此种关系，优惠是最大的。因此，大多数外国销售公司都是美国公司的子公司。在 GATT 专家组于 1976 年裁定本国国际销售公司(DISC)不符合 GATT 规则后，外国销售公司计划于 20 世纪 80 年代初作为本国国际销售公司的后继安排引入。1998 年，欧洲共同体要求成立 WTO 专家组，因为它认为美国关于金融服务公司的规定构成补贴，美国因此违反《补贴与反补贴措施协定》项下的义务。专家组判定美国败诉。在美国提出上诉后，上诉机构裁定外国销售公司构成《补贴与反补贴措施协定》和《农业协定》项下所禁止的补贴。

Formal/informal

正式/非正式

正式会议有会议记录，可以作出决定，并适用正式程序。非正式会议为交流观点或信息而召开，无正式记录。

Formula cuts

公式削减

通过使用公式对整个部门进行关税削减，例如瑞士公式。

Formula-plus tariff reductions

公式加其他方法关税削减

使用线性关税削减，辅以其他方法，以实现关税削减。

Formula tariff reductions

公式关税削减

见*线性关税削减(linear tariff cuts)*。

Fortress effect: this refers to the possibility that ***regional integration arrangements*** may lead to more protectionist attitudes by member countries towards non-members. Much careful analysis of this problem has not led to conclusive evidence either way.

Fortress Europe: a term expressing the fear by some that the formation of the ***European Single Market*** would turn the ***European Community*** into an inward-looking market more difficult to penetrate. Such fears have not been justified.

Forum-shopping: the practice of introducing a proposal or pursuing a dispute in one forum after another until a favourable outcome has been achieved. Sometimes also called forum-hopping. Many free-trade agreements have a provision forcing the initiator of a case to make an unalterable choice at the outset.

Four freedoms: in the ***European Union*** the free movement of goods, capital, labour and ***services***. First set out in the ***Treaty of Rome***. *See also* ***deep integration*** and ***European Economic Area***.

Four pillars of trade liberalization: described by Curzon in *Multilateral Commercial Diplomacy* as ***most-favoured-nation treatment***, reliance on the ***customs tariff*** rather than ***non-tariff measures***, ***tariff negotiations*** leading to reduction of tariffs and tariff stabilization through rules enabling the binding of tariffs. [Curzon 1965]

Fourth Protocol to the General Agreement on Trade in Services: gives effect to the commitments on ***basic telecommunications services*** negotiated after the conclusion of the ***Uruguay Round***. It entered into force on 5 February 1998. *See also* ***Agreement on Basic Telecommunications Services***.

Framework Agreement on Facilitation of Cross-border Paperless Trade in Asia and the Pacific: a treaty concluded by ***ESCAP*** members in 2016. Not yet in force. Its objective, set out in Article 1, is to promote cross-border paperless trade by enabling the exchange and mutual recognition of trade-related data and documents in electronic form and facilitating interoperability among national and subregional single windows and/or other paperless trade systems, for the purpose of making international trade transactions more efficient and transparent while improving regulatory compliance. Its general principles, set out in Article 5, are (a) functional equivalence, (b) non-discrimination of the use of electronic communications, (c) technological neutrality, (d) promotion of interoperability, (e) improved trade facilitation and regulatory compliance, (f) cooperation between public and private actors, and (g) improving transboundary trust environment. The ESCAP Secretariat provides the secretariat for the Framework Agreement. *See also* ***trade facilitation***.

Framework Agreement on the BIMSTEC Free Trade Area: *see* ***Bay of Bengal Initiative for Multi-Sectoral Technical and Economic Cooperation***.

Framework agreements: the name given to four outcomes of the ***Tokyo Round*** negotiations dealing particularly with developing-country issues. The four instruments are (i) the ***Enabling Clause***, (ii) the Declaration on Trade Measures Taken for Balance-of-Payments Purposes, (iii) the Decision on Safeguard

Fortress effect
堡垒效应

指区域一体化安排导致成员对非成员采取更具保护主义态度的可能性。对这一问题的仔细分析并未得出正反两方面的结论性证据。

Fortress Europe
欧洲堡垒

表达一些人对形成欧洲单一市场会导致欧洲共同体变为更难以进入的内向型市场担忧的词语。此类担忧并未证明属合理。

Forum-shopping
挑选法院

在一个又一个场所提出建议或解决争端直至获得有利结果的做法。有时也被称为更换法院。许多自由贸易协定都包含关于要求案件发起人在一开始即作出不可改变的选择的条款。

Four freedoms
四大自由

在欧盟内货物、资本、人员和服务的自由流动。首次在《罗马条约》中规定。另见*深度一体化(deep integration)*、*欧洲经济区(European Economic Area)*。

Four pillars of trade liberalization
贸易自由化四大支柱

寇松在《多边商业外交》中将其描述为最惠国待遇、依赖关税而不是非关税措施、通过关税谈判削减关税、通过约束性关税规则稳定关税。

Fourth Protocol to the General Agreement on Trade in Services
服务贸易总协定第四议定书

该议定书使乌拉圭回合结束后谈判达成的关于基础电信服务的承诺得以生效。该议定书本身于1998年2月5日生效。另见*基础电信协定(Agreement on Basic Telecommunications Services)*。

Framework Agreement on Facilitation of Cross-border Paperless Trade in Asia and the Pacific
亚洲及太平洋跨境无纸贸易便利化框架协定

亚太经社会(ESCAP)成员于2016年签署的一项条约。尚未生效。协定第1条所列目标为，通过交换和互认电子形式的与贸易有关数据和单证，便利国家和次区域单一窗口和/或其他无纸贸易系统之间的互操作性，以便利跨境无纸贸易，从而使国际贸易交易更高效和透明，同时改善监管合规。第5条所列一般原则为：(a)功能等同；(b)电子通信的非歧视使用；(c)技术中立；(d)促进互操作性；(e)改善贸易便利化和监管合规；(f)公共部门和私营部门之间合作；以及(g)改善跨界信任环境。亚太经社会秘书处为该框架协定提供秘书服务。另见*贸易便利化(trade facilitation)*。

Framework Agreement on the BIMSTEC Free Trade Area
环孟加拉湾多领域经济技术合作倡议自贸区框架协定

见*环孟加拉湾多领域经济技术合作倡议(Bay of Bengal Initiative for Multi-Sectoral Technical and Economic Cooperation)*。

Framework agreements
框架协定

东京回合谈判专门处理发展中国家问题的4项成果的名称。这4个文件为：(1)授权条款；(2)《关于为国际收支目的而采取贸易措施的声明》；(3)《关于

Action for Development Purposes, and (iv) the Understanding Regarding Notification, Consultation, Dispute Settlement and Surveillance. The term "framework agreements" was taken from paragraph 2 of the ***Tokyo Declaration*** which sought, among other matters, an "improvement of the international framework for the conduct of world trade" in response to developing-country concerns that the trading system did not meet fully their needs. *See also* ***developing countries and the multilateral trading system*** and ***Tokyo Round agreements***.

Framework Convention on Climate Change: *see* ***United Nations Framework Convention on Climate Change***.

Framework for Comprehensive Partnership between Japan and the Association of South-East Asian Nations: *see* ***ASEAN–Japan Comprehensive Economic Partnership***.

Framework for Pacific Regionalism: adopted by the ***Pacific Islands Forum*** in July 2014. Its principal objectives are (a) sustainable development that combines economic, social and cultural development in ways that improve livelihoods and wellbeing and use the environment sustainably, (b) economic growth that is inclusive and equitable, (c) strengthened governance, legal, financial and administrative systems, and (d) security that ensures stable and safe human, environmental and political conditions for all.

Free and fair trade: the idea, enunciated particularly well in United States tariff and trade policy, that from the perspective of economic development and global welfare ***free trade*** is a highly desirable objective, but only if one's trading partners also play fairly under the rules they have accepted. If they adhere to unfair practices, they should not be entitled to the benefits of open market access. There is a well-documented view, for example, that the thinking underpinning the emergence of ***Section 301*** is aimed not at protecting the United States market, but to ensure that other economies similarly open their markets. *See also* ***level playing field***.

Freedom-of-emigration provision: *see* ***Jackson-Vanik amendment***.

Freedom of transit: the right, available to members of the WTO under Article V of the GATT, to transport goods unhindered across the territory of another member for them to be able to reach their final destination. The right includes the use of vessels and other means of transport for the purpose. Members may not discriminate between goods and means of transport from other members, and they may not levy ***customs duties*** on goods in transit. They are, however, entitled to recover administrative expenses based on the actual cost of any services provided in connection with the transit.

Freedoms of the air: aviation experts divide the right of airlines to fly through or over their domestic territories into eight categories called freedoms of the air, though only the first six are in common use. The eight are (i) the right to fly over a country, (ii) the right to land in a country to refuel or similar purposes, but not to pick up or set down passengers or cargo, (iii) the right to set down passengers or cargo in another country, (iv) the right to pick up passengers or

为发展目的而采取保障措施的决定》；以及(4)《关于通报、磋商、争端解决及监督的谅解》。"框架协定"一词源自《东京宣言》第2段，该段除其他事项外，寻求"改进开展世界贸易的国际框架"，以回应发展中国家对贸易体制没有充分满足其需要的关切。另见*发展中国家与多边贸易体制(developing countries and the multilateral trading system)*、*东京回合协定(Tokyo Round agreements)*。

Framework Convention on Climate Change

气候变化框架公约

见*联合国气候变化框架公约(United Nations Framework Convention on Climate Change)*。

Framework for Comprehensive Partnership between Japan and the Association of South-East Asian Nations

东南亚国家联盟与日本全面伙伴关系框架

见*东盟—日本全面经济伙伴关系协定(ASEAN–Japan Comprehensive Economic Partnership)*。

Framework for Pacific Regionalism

太平洋区域主义框架

太平洋岛国论坛于2014年7月通过。主要目标为：(a)将经济、社会和文化发展以改善生计和福祉及可持续利用环境的方式加以结合的可持续发展；(b)具有包容性和公正性的经济增长；(c)增强的治理、法律、金融和行政系统；以及(d)保证人人享有稳定平安的人文、环境和政治条件的安全。

Free and fair trade

自由和公平贸易

在美国的关税和贸易政策中特别阐明的观点，即从经济发展和全球福利的角度看，自由贸易是一个非常理想的目标，但只有在一方的贸易伙伴也根据其已经接受的规则进行公平竞争的前提下。如果它们坚持采取不公平做法，就不应享有开放市场准入的利益。例如，有一种有据可查的观点认为，支持301 条款产生的想法不是为了保护美国市场，而是为了保证其他经济体同样开放其市场。另见*公平竞争环境(level playing field)*。

Freedom-of-emigration provision

自由移民条款

见*杰克逊-瓦尼克修正案(Jackson-Vanik amendment)*。

Freedom of transit

过境自由

WTO成员可以根据GATT第5条获得的权利，运输货物途经另一成员领土时不受阻碍，使货物能够到达最终目的地。此项权利包括为此目的而使用船舶和其他运输工具。成员不得对来自其他成员的货物和运输工具加以区别对待，也不得对过境货物征收关税。但是，它们有权根据与过境相关而提供的任何服务的实际成本收取管理费用。

Freedoms of the air

航空自由

航空专家将航班飞经或飞越其国内领土的权利分为 8 类，称为航权，但只有前6类是常用的。这8类权利为：(1)领空飞越权；(2)技术经停权，在一个国

cargo in another country and set them down in the airline's home country, (v) the right to carry passengers or cargo between third countries using one's own country as a hub, (vi) the ability to combine rights acquired under the third and fourth freedoms, (vii) the right to operate air services between third countries entirely outside one's home country, and (viii) the right to provide air services within a country, often called ***cabotage***. These freedoms are usually negotiated between governments on behalf of domestic airlines. *See also* ***bilateral air services agreements***, ***Chicago Convention***, ***Multilateral Agreement on the Liberalization of International Air Transportation*** and ***open-skies arrangements***.

Free imports: goods that can be imported without the payment of any ***customs duties***. *See also* ***free list*** and ***zero rating***.

Free list: a listing of products that can be imported free of customs duties or that are not subject to ***import licensing*** requirements.

Free riders: casual term used to imply that a country which does not make any trade concessions, profits, nonetheless, from tariff cuts and concessions made by other countries under the most-favoured-nation principle. From an economic perspective, free riders do themselves harm because they deny themselves the benefits of trade liberalization. *See also* ***most-favoured-nation treatment***.

Free trade: in principle, the free movement across borders of goods, services, capital and people. In practice, national policy and regulatory objectives put greater or lesser constraints on the movement of each. The meaning of "free trade" itself has changed over the years. Observers have noted that in the case of American policy free trade meant a tariff under 20 per cent in the early nineteenth century. By the late nineteenth century free-traders advocated tariff levels below 40 per cent. By the middle of the twentieth century free trade meant a tariff of less than 5 per cent. In the case of ***AFTA***, free trade was understood to be a tariff ranging from 0 per cent to 5 per cent. Under Article XXIV of the GATT, ***customs unions*** and ***free-trade areas*** have to eliminate duties and other restrictive regulations of commerce on substantially all the trade between the parties to meet the free-trade criterion. The norm there is the abolition of all tariffs between the partners either immediately or over several years. *See also* ***Bogor Declaration***, ***economic integration agreements***, ***four freedoms*** and ***free and fair trade***.

Free-trade agreement: a contractual arrangement between two or more countries under which they give each other ***preferential market access***, usually called ***free trade***. In practice, free-trade agreements tend to allow for all sorts of exceptions, many of them temporary, to cover ***sensitive products***. In some cases, free trade is no more than a longer-term aim. In other cases the agreement creates a form of managed trade liberalization. Observers have noted that many recent free-trade agreements have run to several hundred pages, whereas a true free-trade agreement would require only a few lines. ***Preferential rules of origin***, an essential part of any free-trade agreement, can be too strict for the Agreement to be of much benefit to exporters. Indeed, some recent analytical

家着陆加油或类似目的的权利，但不包括接载乘客或货物：(3)目的地下客权，在另一国下客或卸货的权利；(4)目的地上客权，在另一国载客或载货，并在航班东道国下客或卸货的权利；(5)中间点权或延远权，以东道国为中心，在第三国之间运送乘客或货物的权利；(6)桥梁权，前述第3项和第4项自由权利结合起来的权利；(7)完全第三国运输权，在航班东道国之外完全在第三国间提供航空服务的权利；以及(8)国内运输权，在一国之内提供航空服务的权利，通常被称为国内交通运输权。这些自由权通常由代表本国航班的政府间谈判取得。另见*双边航空服务协定(bilateral air services agreements)*、*芝加哥公约(Chicago Convention)*、*国际航空运输自由化多边协定(Multilateral Agreement on the Liberalization of International Air Transportation)*、*开放天空安排(open-skies arrangements)*。

Free imports

自由进口

货物可以在无需支付任何关税的情况下进口。另见*免税清单(free list)*、*零税率(zero rating)*。

Free list

免税清单

可免关税进口或不受进口许可要求限制的产品清单。

Free riders

搭便车者

非正式用语，用于指未作出任何贸易减让的一国，却从其他国家根据最惠国待遇原则作出的关税削减和减让中获益。从经济角度看，搭便车者会对自己造成损害，因为它们拒绝享受贸易自由化的好处。另见*最惠国待遇(most-favoured-nation treatment)*。

Free trade

自由贸易

原则上指货物、服务、资本和人员的跨境自由流动。在实践中，国家政策和监管目标对每一种要素的流动均或多或少设有限制。“自由贸易”本身的含义多年来已经发生改变。观察家注意到，就美国政策而言，在19世纪初自由贸易意味着关税低于20%。到19世纪末，自由贸易者主张关税低于40%。到了20世纪中期，自由贸易意味着关税低于5%。对于《东盟自由贸易区协定》(AFTA)，自由贸易被理解为关税在0至5%之间。根据GATT第24条，关税同盟和自由贸易区必须对于参加方之间实质上所有贸易取消关税和其他限制性贸易法规，以满足自由贸易标准。此处的标准是伙伴之间的所有关税立即取消或在几年内取消。另见*茂物宣言(Bogor Declaration)*、*经济一体化协议(economic integration agreements)*、*四大自由(four freedoms)*、*自由和公平贸易(free and fair trade)*。

Free-trade agreement

自由贸易协定

两个或多个国家之间的契约安排，这些国家据此相互给予优惠市场准入，通常称为自由贸易。在实践中，自由贸易协定往往允许涵盖敏感产品的各种形式的例外，其中许多是临时的。在一些情况下，自由贸易不过是一个长期目标。在其他情况下，协定创造了一种有管理的贸易自由化形式。观察家注意

evidence strongly suggests that many free-trade agreements do not make a worthwhile contribution to trade expansion between the parties. *See also* ***best practice for RTAs/FTAs in APEC***, ***customs union***, ***free-trade area***, ***regional integration arrangement*** and ***regional trade agreement***.

Free-trade area: a group of two or more countries or economies, ***customs territories*** in technical language, that have eliminated ***tariffs*** and all or most ***non-tariff measures*** affecting trade among themselves. Participating countries usually continue to apply their existing tariffs on external goods. Free-trade areas are called reciprocal when all partners eliminate their tariffs and other barriers towards each other. There are cases where developing country partners are exempt from making equivalent reductions, as is the case with ***SPARTECA*** and the ***ACP-EU Partnership Agreement***, even though they get free access to developed-country markets. These are called non-reciprocal free-trade areas. *See also* ***customs union***, ***trade creation***, ***trade deviation*** and ***trade diversion***.

Free Trade Area of the Americas: *see* ***FTAA***.

Free Trade Area of the Asia-Pacific: FTAAP. In 2006 APEC members agreed to examine the long-term prospect of an FTAAP at the suggestion of ABAC. The following year's meeting initiated a process of analytical work, though it is hard to judge what level of commitment to the idea of an FTAAP actually existed within APEC. Some members were willing to take the next step to investigate what the content of such an agreement might be. Few were willing to express views on membership, except that the core membership would consist of APEC members. This situation became slightly clearer in 2010 when it was agreed that the FTAAP would build on regional undertakings, such as the ***Regional Comprehensive Economic Partnership*** (RCEP) and the ***Trans-Pacific Partnership Agreement*** (TPP). Further analytical work followed. The 2014 ***Beijing Roadmap for APEC's Contribution to the Realization of the FTAAP*** established the principles, among others, that the FTAAP should be comprehensive, high quality and address "next-generation" trade issues, and that it would be realized outside of APEC, but parallel with the APEC process. At the same time a comprehensive study was launched to identify the various issues involved, to be completed by the end of 2016. APEC considered this study and in the ***Lima Declaration on FTAAP*** of that year asked for an examination of the contribution of current pathways to the realization of FTAAP, together with a continuation of analytical work on other issues. This work will be completed no later than 2020. The prospects for an eventual FTAAP remain unclear. In particular, its place in the company of RCEP and TPP will require a careful assessment. The scope for overlap would appear to be considerable, but in itself that would not necessarily be considered an insurmountable obstacle.

Free Trade Delusion: a topic addressed in the ***UNCTAD*** 2018 ***Trade and Development Report***. It questions whether trade policy can by itself solve a multitude of global problems and whether the idea of a "***level playing field***, governed through a mixture of formal rules, tacit norms and greater competition will guarantee prosperity for all" is appropriate.

到，许多最近达成的自由贸易协定已经长达几百页，而真正的自由贸易协定仅需几行字。优惠原产地规则是任何自由贸易协定的重要组成部分，可能过于严格，使协定对出口商没有多大好处。的确，最近的一些分析证据有力地证明许多自由贸易协定并没有对参加方之间的贸易扩大作出有价值的贡献。*另见 APEC 区域贸易协定/自由贸易协定最佳实践(best practice for RTAs/FTAs in APEC)*、*关税同盟(customs union)*、*自由贸易区(free-trade area)*、*区域一体化安排(regional integration arrangement)*、*区域贸易协定(regional trade agreement)*。

Free-trade area

自由贸易区

由两个或两个以上国家或经济体组成的集团，用技术语言表述为关税领土，取消影响相互之间贸易的关税和全部或大部分非关税措施。参加国通常继续对外部货物适用现行关税。自由贸易区在所有伙伴相互之间取消关税和其他壁垒时被称为互惠。有些情况是发展中国家伙伴免于作出同等削减，尽管它们获得对发达国家市场的免税准入，例如《南太平洋区域贸易经济合作协定》(SPARTECA)和《非加太地区国家与欧盟伙伴关系协定》。这些被称为非互惠自由贸易区。*另见关税同盟(customs union)*、*贸易创造(trade creation)*、*贸易偏移(trade deviation)*、*贸易转移(trade diversion)*。

Free Trade Area of the Americas

美洲自由贸易区

见美洲自由贸易区(FTAA)。

Free Trade Area of the Asia-Pacific

亚太自由贸易区

FTAAP。2006 年，APEC 成员同意审查 APEC 工商咨询理事会(ABAB)建议的亚太自由贸易区的长期前景。次年的会议启动了分析工作进程，尽管很难判断 APEC 内实际存在的对 FTAAP 想法的承诺水平。一些成员愿意采取下一步行动，探究此种协定可能包括的内容。除组成 APEC 的核心成员外，鲜有国家愿就成员资格发表意见。情况在 2010 年变得略微清晰，各方同意 FTAAP 将建立在区域承诺基础之上，例如《区域全面经济伙伴关系协定》(RCEP)和《跨太平洋伙伴关系协定》(TPP)。随后开展了进一步分析工作。2014 年《APEC 推动实现亚太自由贸易区北京路线图》确立了原则，即 FTAAP 应全面、高质量并可解决下一代贸易议题，将在 APEC 之外实现，但与 APEC 进程并行。与此同时，启动全面研究以确定所涉众多议题，定于 2016 年年底完成。APEC 审议了此项研究，并在当年的《亚太自由贸易区利马宣言》中要求对实现 FTAAP 的当前路径所作贡献进行审查，同时继续开展其他问题的分析工作。此项工作将不迟于 2020 年完成。建立最终 FTAAP 的前景仍不明朗。特别是 FTAAP 相对于 RCEP 和 TPP 的地位需要认真评估。重叠的范围似乎相当大，但对其本身而言不一定被认为是无法克服的障碍。

Free Trade Delusion

自由贸易错觉

联合国贸易与发展会议(UNCTAD)2018 年《贸易与发展报告》中讨论的一个主题。质疑贸易政策本身是否能够解决众多全球问题，及“正式规则、默认规范和更大竞争相结合管辖的公平竞争环境将保证所有人的繁荣”的想法是否适当。

Free-trade zones: these are defined areas, also called export processing zones, normally located near transport nodal points and designated by governments for the duty-free import of raw materials or manufacturing components intended for further processing or final assembly and their re-export afterwards. Such products are exported to markets in other countries. Successful free-trade zones tend to have a plentiful supply of relatively cheap and adequately skilled labour. Countries establishing free-trade zones usually are characterized by non-competitive domestic industries and regulatory frameworks, and this is one way in which they gain access to foreign investment and markets. Such zones sometimes lead to technology transfers to host countries, but often that is not an objective of companies establishing operations in them.

French plan: *see **Pflimlin plan***.

French wheat and wheat flour* case:** in 1958 Australia lodged a complaint in the ***GATT that because of subsidies granted by the French Government on exports of wheat and wheat flour, French exports of these products had displaced Australian exports to its traditional wheat flour markets in Ceylon (now Sri Lanka), Indonesia and Malaya (now Malaysia). Australia maintained that France was acting inconsistently with its obligations under GATT Article XVI:3. This Article states that members should seek to avoid the use of export subsidies on the export of ***primary products***, and that if they were using them, it should not be done in such a manner as to result in them obtaining a more than equitable share of world trade in that primary product. The case therefore centred on the meaning of "equitable share". French exports of wheat and wheat flour in the previous twenty-five years had fluctuated widely, but there was a sudden increase in wheat, and especially wheat flour, exports beginning in 1954. Prices charged for French wheat flour exports had on the whole been lower than those of other exporters. The ***panel*** found that the French practices resulted in the payment of subsidies on the export of wheat and wheat flour and therefore fell within the ambit of Article XVI:3. The panel then turned to the question of whether France had in this way obtained more than an equitable share of the world market for wheat and wheat flour. It noted that GATT Article XVI did not offer a definition of "equitable share". There was, however, implicit agreement among GATT members in the light of their negotiations of the negotiations of the ***Havana Charter*** and the ***GATT review session*** of 1955 that "equitable share" applied to the global market and not to exports to an individual market. It was understood also, the panel said, that the need for the efficient and economic supply of world markets should not be ignored. The panel recalled that French exports of wheat and wheat flour had risen substantially from 1954 above the levels achieved in the previous twenty years, and that they also represented an increase in France's share of world exports in these products. It concluded on the basis of the evidence on tonnages and price levels that France's subsidy arrangements had contributed to a large extent to a share of world exports that had to be considered more than equitable. The panel recommended that France consider measures to avoid creating adverse effects

Free-trade zones

自由贸易园区

指规定区域，也称出口加工区，通常设在临近运输节点，由政府指定用于随后复出口的进一步加工产品或最后组装产品的原材料或制造部件的免税进口。此类产品出口至其他国家市场。成功的自由贸易园区往往有大量相对廉价和技术熟练的劳动力供应。建立自由贸易园区的国家通常以非竞争性国内产业和监管框架为特征，这是它们获得外国投资和市场的一种方式。此类自由贸易园区有时会导致技术转让到东道国，但这通常不是在这些国家开展业务的公司的目标。

French plan

法国计划

见*普夫里姆林计划(Pflimlin plan)*。

***French wheat and wheat flour* case**

法国小麦和小麦面粉案

1958年，澳大利亚向GATT提出起诉，称由于法国政府对出口小麦和小麦面粉给予补贴，法国的这些出口产品取代了澳大利亚对锡兰(现斯里兰卡)、印度尼西亚和马来亚(现马来西亚)等其传统小麦面粉市场的出口。澳大利亚认为，法国的行为不符合其在GATT第16条第3款下的义务。该条规定，成员应寻求避免对初级产品出口使用出口补贴，如果使用出口补贴，其方式不应导致它们在该初级产品的世界贸易中占有不公正份额。该案因此聚焦“公正份额”的含义。法国的小麦和小麦面粉出口在以往的25年中波动很大，但自1954年起，小麦、特别是小麦面粉的出口突然增加。对法国小麦面粉出口收取的价格总体低于其他出口国。专家组认为法国的做法导致对小麦和小麦面粉出口提供补贴，因而属于第16条第3款的范围。专家组随后转向法国是否以此种方式获得超过小麦和小麦面粉世界市场公正份额的问题。专家组指出，GATT第16条并未提供“公正份额”的定义。但是，考虑到关于《哈瓦那宪章》的谈判和1955年GATT审议会议，GATT缔约方达成了默认的协议，即“公正份额”适用于全球市场，而非对一单个市场的出口。专家组指出，各方理解，不应忽视世界市场有效和经济供应的需要。专家组回想到，法国的小麦和小麦面粉出口自1954年起大幅增加，超过前20年达到的水平，而且这也显示法国在这些产品的世界出口中份额增加。根据关于吨位和价格水平的证据，专家组得出结论，法国的补贴安排在很大程度上促成了其在世界出口中的份额，这种份额必须被认为是超过了公正份额。专家组建议法国考虑采取

on Australian exports of flour to South-East Asian markets. This might be done through changing its payments system or entering into consultations with Australia before new contracts were concluded by French exporters of flour to these markets.

Friends of Fish: an informal coalition of around eleven WTO members which seeks to reduce ***fisheries subsidies*** significantly.

Friends of Investment Facilitation for Development: FIFD. An informal group of developing and least-developed country WTO members. It discusses issues such as linkages between trade and investment, member country activities to facilitate investment and what role the WTO might have to further ***investment facilitation***. *See also* ***joint initiatives***.

Friends of Multifunctionality: an informal group active at one time formed to promote acceptance of the concept of ***multifunctionality*** of agriculture in the WTO and elsewhere. Core members are the European Community, Japan, Mauritius, Norway, Republic of Korea and Switzerland.

Friends of Special Products: *see* ***G-33***.

Frontier traffic: usually refers to trade across a frontier by local inhabitants in a clearly defined geographical area who have well-developed kinship ties or a long-standing economic association. Under Article XXIV of the GATT countries may decide not to apply all of the usual customs formalities to border trade. Goods traded in this way are not expected to find their way into the broader economy on either side of the border. The GATT does not specify what distance each side of the frontier is to be considered to lie within the frontier zone, but many pre-war trade agreements settled on a limit of fifteen kilometres on either side of the border. The ***General Agreement on Trade in Services*** states that ***most-favoured-nation treatment*** need not apply in the case of exchanges of services in contiguous frontier zones if they are produced and consumed locally.

Frontloading: refers to the practice of ensuring that liberalization commitments under an agreement or arrangement are proportionately heavier at the beginning of the implementing period. *See also* ***Agreement on Textiles and Clothing*** and ***backloading***.

FTAA: Free Trade Area of the Americas. Also called Western Hemisphere Free Trade Agreement. Agreed as an objective at the Miami Summit of the Americas in December 1994 to cover all the Americas, except Cuba. Negotiations were launched at the Summit of the Americas held in March 1998 in Santiago de Chile with 2005 is the target date for its entry into force. However, negotiations were abandoned in 2004.

FTAAP: *see* ***Free Trade Area of the Asia-Pacific***.

Full balance-of-payments consultations: consultations in the WTO following the invocation by a member of the WTO provisions permitting measures to safeguard its external financial position. Full consultations are distinguished from the simplified consultations used mainly for ***least-developed countries***. Consultations are done using documentation prepared by the member itself, a

措施，避免对澳大利亚出口到东南亚市场的面粉造成不利影响。法国可以通过改变其支付系统或与对这些市场的面粉出口商订立新合同前与澳大利亚进行磋商加以实现。

Friends of Fish

渔业之友

由约 11 个 WTO 成员组成的非正式联盟，寻求大幅削减渔业补贴。

Friends of Investment Facilitation for Development

投资便利化之友

FIFD。由发展中国家和最不发达国家组成的 WTO 非正式集团。讨论诸如贸易与投资关系、成员国便利投资的活动以及 WTO 在促进投资便利化方面可以发挥的作用等问题。另见*联合倡议(joint initiatives)*。

Friends of Multifunctionality

多功能性之友

一个一度活跃的、致力于促进在 WTO 中和其他处接受农业多功能性概念的非正式集团。核心成员为欧洲共同体、日本、毛里求斯、挪威、韩国和瑞士。

Friends of Special Products

特殊产品之友

见 *33 国协调组(G-33)*。

Frontier traffic

边境贸易

通常指明确界定的地理区域内的当地居民跨越边境进行贸易，这些居民具有广泛的亲属关系或长期经济关联。根据 GATT 第 24 条，各国可决定不对边境贸易适用全部正常海关手续。以此种方式交易的货物预计不会进入边境两侧更广泛的经济领域。GATT 未规定边境两侧属于边境地区的距离，但许多战前贸易协定规定边界两侧 15 公里的限制。《服务贸易总协定》规定，对于毗邻边境地区的在当地生产和消费的服务，不需要适用最惠国待遇。

Frontloading

前期实施

指保证一协定或安排项下的自由化承诺在实施期开始时相对较多实施的做法。另见*纺织品与服装协定(Agreement on Textiles and Clothing)*、*后期实施(backloading)*。

FTAA

美洲自由贸易区

又称《西半球自由贸易协定》。1994 年 12 月在迈阿密美洲国家首脑会议上的一项议定目标，涵盖除古巴外的所有美洲国家。在 1998 年 3 月智利圣地亚哥举行的美洲国家首脑会议上启动谈判，2005 年是生效的目标日期。但是，2004 年放弃谈判。

FTAAP

亚太自由贸易区

见*亚太自由贸易区(Free Trade Area of the Asia-Pacific)*。

Full balance-of-payments consultations

国际收支全面磋商

在 WTO 中一成员援引允许采取措施以保护其外部财务状况的条款而启动的

factual background paper drafted by the WTO Secretariat and an analysis prepared by the ***IMF*** on recent economic developments. The consultations cover the member's ***balance of payments*** and prospects, alternative methods to restore equilibrium, system and methods of restrictions and the effects of restrictions. *See also* ***balance-of-payments consultations***.

Full cumulation: used in the administration of ***preferential rules of origin***. Any processing of a good within the area covered by a preferential trade agreement is counted as ***qualifying value content*** regardless of whether the process is sufficient to turn it into an ***originating good***. In this case, the whole preferential area is considered a single territory, and any processing within it is counted towards the determination of origin. *See also* ***diagonal cumulation***.

Full parallelism: *see* ***parallelism in export support***.

Full preferential trade agreement: describes a preferential trade agreement under which all of the parties accord each other free trade in all or nearly all products. *See also* ***partial preferential trade agreement***.

Functional trade agreement: a form of trade agreement now seldom used. It seeks to deal with a particular type of form of trade, measure or occurrence. Examples are ***government procurement***, measures to restrict or manage trade and the imposition of countervailing duties.

Functioning of the GATT System: FOGS. One of the negotiating groups established at the start of the ***Uruguay Round***. Its negotiating mandate was defined as enhancing the surveillance in the GATT of national trade policies, improving the overall effectiveness and decision-making of the GATT as an institution and increasing the contribution of the GATT to greater coherence in global economic policymaking. One of its achievements was the establishment of the ***Trade Policy Review Mechanism***.

Fundamental principles and rights at work: *see* ***Declaration on Fundamental Principles and Rights at Work and its follow-up***.

Fungible goods: also called fungibles or fungible materials. It is a term used in the administration of ***rules of origin***. In ***NAFTA***, for example, fungible goods are described as goods or materials that are virtually the same and that can be used interchangeably. *See also* ***identical goods*** and ***similar goods***.

磋商。全面磋商区别于主要用于最不发达国家的简化磋商。磋商使用成员自己准备的文件、WTO 秘书处起草的事实背景文件和国际货币基金组织(IMF)准备的关于近期经济发展的分析报告。磋商内容涵盖该成员的国际收支和前景、恢复平衡的替代方法、限制的制度和方法以及限制的影响。另见*国际收支磋商(balance-of-payments consultations)*。

Full cumulation

完全累积

用于优惠原产地规则的管理。在一优惠贸易协定所涵盖区域内对一货物的任何加工均计为合格价值成分，不考虑该加工是否足以使其成为原产货物。在此种情况下，整个优惠区被视为一单一领土，在其中进行的任何加工均被计入原产地的确定之中。另见*对角累积(diagonal cumulation)*。

Full parallelism

完全平行性

见*出口支持的平行性(parallelism in export support)*。

Full preferential trade agreement

全面优惠贸易协定

指所有参加方针对所有或几乎所有产品相互给予自由贸易的优惠贸易协定。另见*部分优惠贸易协定(partial preferential trade agreement)*。

Functional trade agreement

功能性贸易协定

贸易协定的一种形式，现在很少使用。旨在处理一种特殊形式的贸易、措施或事件。例如政府采购、限制或管理贸易的措施以及征收反补贴税。

Functioning of the GATT System

GATT 体制运行谈判组

FOGS。乌拉圭回合开始时设立的谈判组。其谈判授权被确定为加强 GATT 中对国家贸易政策的监督，改善 GATT 作为一个机构的总体效率和决策，以及加强 GATT 对全球经济决策更大一致性所作贡献。谈判组的成就之一是设立贸易政策审议机制。

Fundamental principles and rights at work

工作中基本原则和权利

见*关于工作中基本原则和权利宣言及其后续措施(Declaration on Fundamental Principles and Rights at Work and its follow-up)*。

Fungible goods

可替代产品

也称可替代品或可替代材料。原产地规则管理中使用的词语。例如，在《北美自由贸易协定》(NAFTA)中，将可替代产品描述为实际上相同且可以互换使用的产品或材料。另见*相同货物(identical goods)*、*类似货物(similar goods)*。

G

G7: the group of seven leading industrial countries. They are Canada, France, Germany, Italy, Japan, United Kingdom and the United States. The ***European Union*** also attends the annual summits. The G7 meets annually to discuss issues such as global economic governance, international security, gender equality, climate change and environmental questions. The member country holding the presidency is responsible for arranging and hosting that year's summit. The persons from the G7 responsible for preparing the summits are called sherpas. They are the personal representatives of heads of state or government.

G8: an informal group of countries from 1997 to 2014. It consisted of the members of the ***G7*** and Russia. In 2014 Russia's membership was suspended for an indefinite period following its annexation of the Crimea. In 2018 Russia announced that it would permanently withdraw from the G8.

G8 African Action Plan: adopted by the ***G8*** summit at Kananaskis, Canada, on 27 June 2002. It sought to support the implementation of the ***New Partnership for Africa's Development***.

G-10: in the WTO a coalition of countries lobbying for agriculture to be treated as diverse and special because of non-trade concerns.

G-15: a group originally of fifteen developing countries acting as the main political organ for the Non-Aligned Movement. It was established in 1989. Its members now are: Algeria, Argentina, Brazil, Chile, Egypt, India, Indonesia, Iran, Jamaica, Kenya, Malaysia, Mexico, Nigeria, Peru, Senegal, Sri Lanka, Venezuela and Zimbabwe. The G-15's main objectives are to harness the potential for greater cooperation among developing countries, to review the impact of the world economic situation and the state of international relations on developing countries, to serve as forum for consultations among developing countries with a view to coordinating policies and actions, to identify and implement new schemes for ***South–South cooperation*** and to pursue a more productive ***North–South dialogue***. Its secretariat is in Geneva.

G20: a forum for international economic cooperation and decision-making established in 1999. It conducts annual discussions on ways to strengthen the global economy, reform of international financial institutions, improving financial regulation and implementation of economic reforms. It achieved prominence during the ***global financial crisis***. Its members are Australia, Brazil, Canada, China, France, Germany, India, Indonesia, Italy, Japan, Republic of Korea, Mexico, Russia, Saudi Arabia, South Africa, Turkey, United Kingdom, United

G

G7

7 国集团

由 7 个主要工业国家组成的集团，即加拿大、法国、德国、意大利、日本、英国和美国。欧盟也出席年度峰会。7 国集团每年举行会议，讨论全球经济治理、国际安全、性别平等、气候变化和环境问题等议题。担任主席国的成员国负责安排和主办当年峰会。7 国集团负责筹备峰会的人员被称为“协调人”(sherpas，夏尔巴人)。他们是国家元首或政府首脑的个人代表。

G8

8 国集团

1997 年至 2014 年的一个非正式国家集团。由 7 国集团和俄罗斯组成。2014 年，克里米亚并入俄罗斯后，俄成员资格被无限期中止。2018 年，俄罗斯宣布永久退出 8 国集团。

G8 African Action Plan

8 国集团非洲行动计划

2002 年 6 月 27 日在加拿大卡纳纳斯基斯举行的 8 国集团首脑会议上通过。旨在支持实施非洲发展新伙伴关系计划。

G-10

10 国协调组

WTO 中以非贸易关注为由游说对农业进行多样化和特殊处理的国家联盟。

G-15

15 国集团

最初由 15 个发展中国家组成的集团，作为不结盟运动的主要政治机构。1989 年成立。成员目前包括：阿尔及利亚、阿根廷、巴西、智利、埃及、印度、印度尼西亚、伊朗、牙买加、肯尼亚、马来西亚、墨西哥、尼日利亚、秘鲁、塞内加尔、斯里兰卡、委内瑞拉和津巴布韦。15 国集团的主要目标是利用发展中国家之间更大的合作潜力，审议世界经济形势和国际关系状况对发展中国家的影响，作为发展中国家之间协调政策和行动的协商场所，确定和实施南南合作新计划，并致力于开展更有成效的南北对话。秘书处设在日内瓦。

G20

20 国集团

国际经济合作和决策的论坛，1999 年成立。就加强全球经济、改革国际金融机构、改善金融监管和实施经济改革开展年度讨论。该集团在全球金融危机期间发挥重大作用。成员包括澳大利亚、巴西、加拿大、中国、法国、德国、印度、印度尼西亚、意大利、日本、韩国、墨西哥、俄罗斯、沙特阿拉伯、南

States and the European Union. It does not have a permanent secretariat. That task is taken on by the country in line for hosting the next series of meetings.

G20 Anti-Corruption Action Plan: first established in 2010 and updated regularly since. Topics to be addressed in to 2019–2021 Action Plan include (a) strengthening integrity and transparency in the public and private sectors, (b) tackle financial crime related to corruption, including money laundering and recovering stolen assets, (c) enhance practical anti-corruption cooperation, (d) address topics such as foreign bribery and corruption related to infrastructure, sports and other vulnerable sectors, and (e) consider possible actions on emerging issues, such as the measurement of corruption and linkages between gender and corruption.

G-20 Developing Nations: a group of developing countries established in 2003 to achieve better market access in the ***Doha Development Agenda*** negotiations for the agricultural products of developing countries. Its membership varied, but among its core members were Argentina, Bolivia, Brazil, Chile, China, Cuba, Egypt, India, Indonesia, Mexico, Nigeria, Pakistan, Paraguay, Philippines, South Africa, Tanzania, Thailand, Venezuela and Zimbabwe.

G20 digital economy ministerial declaration: adopted in April 2017. It recognizes that the digital economy is an increasingly important driver of global inclusive growth and that it plays a significant role in accelerating economic development. It calls for harnessing the potential of global digitalization for inclusive growth and employment and seeks to strengthen trust in the digital world. An annex provides a roadmap for digitalization. *See also* ***digital economy***, ***digital trade*** and ***G20 priorities on digital trade***. [bmwi.de]

G20 Guiding Principles for Global Investment Policymaking: adopted at the ***G20*** Ministerial Meeting in 2016 in Shanghai. The Guiding Principles have three objectives: (1) fostering an open, transparent and conducive policy environment for investment, (2) promoting coherence in national and international policymaking, and (3) promoting inclusive economic growth and sustainable development. The principles are, in abbreviated form, (I) governments should avoid protectionism in relation to cross-border investment, (II) investment policies should establish open, non-discriminatory, transparent and predictable conditions for investment, (III) investment policies should provide legal certainty and strong protection to investors and investments, and dispute settlement procedures should be fair, open and transparent, (IV) investment regulation should be developed in a transparent manner and embedded in an institutional framework based on the rule of law, (V) investment policies should be coherent at both the national and international levels and aimed at fostering investment consistent with the objective of sustainable development and inclusive growth, (VI) governments reaffirm the right to regulate investment for legitimate public policy purposes, (VII) policies for investment promotion should be aimed at attracting and retaining investment and matched by facilitation efforts that promote transparency and are conducive for investors to establish, conduct and expand their businesses, (VIII) investment policies

非、土耳其、英国、美国和欧盟。无常设秘书处。此项任务依次由主办下一届系列会议的国家承担。

G20 Anti-Corruption Action Plan

20 国集团反腐败行动计划

最初于 2010 年制定，此后定期更新。2019—2021 年行动计划所解决的问题包括:(a)加强公共和私营部门的廉洁和透明度;(b)解决与腐败有关的金融犯罪，包括洗钱和追回被盗资产；(c)加强反腐败务实合作；(d)处理与基础设施、体育和其他脆弱部门有关的外国行贿和腐败等问题；以及(e)考虑针对新出现的问题采取可能的行动，例如腐败的衡量方法及性别与腐败之间的联系。

G-20 Developing Nations

发展中国家 20 国协调组

2003 年成立的发展中国家协调组，旨在在多哈发展议程谈判中为发展中国家的农产品争取更好的市场准入。成员时有变化，但核心成员包括阿根廷、玻利维亚、巴西、智利、中国、古巴、埃及、印度、印度尼西亚、墨西哥、尼日利亚、巴基斯坦、巴拉圭、菲律宾、南非、坦桑尼亚、泰国、委内瑞拉以及津巴布韦。

G20 digital economy ministerial declaration

20 国集团数字经济部长宣言

2017 年 4 月通过。宣言认识到数字经济是全球包容性增长的日益重要的驱动力，在加快经济发展方面发挥着重要作用。呼吁利用全球数字化的潜力促进包容性增长和就业，并寻求加强对数字世界的信任。附件提供了一份数字化路线图。另见*数字经济(digital economy)*、*数字贸易(digital trade)*、*20 国集团数字贸易优先事项(G20 priorities on digital trade)*。

G20 Guiding Principles for Global Investment Policymaking

20 国集团全球投资决策指导原则

2016 年在上海举行的 20 国集团部长会议上通过。指导原则包含三项目标：(1)促进开放、透明和有利的投资政策环境；(2)促进国家和国际政策制定的一致性；以及(3)促进包容性经济增长和可持续发展。这些原则简述如下：(1)政府应避免在跨境投资方面的保护主义；(2)投资政策应设立开放、非歧视、透明和可预测的投资条件；(3)投资政策应向投资者和投资提供法律确定性和有力保护，争端解决程序应公平、公开和透明；(4)应以透明方式制定投资法规，并将其纳入基于法治的制度框架；(5)投资政策应在国家和国际层面上保持一致，并旨在促进符合可持续发展和包容性增长目标的投资；(6)政府重申为合法公共政策目的监管投资的权利；(7)投资促进政策应旨在吸引和保留投资，并辅以促进透明度和有利于投资者设立、开展和扩大其业务的便利化努力；(8)投资政策应促进和推动负责任的商业行为和公司治理的国际最佳实践和适

should promote and facilitate international best practice and applicable instruments of responsible business conduct and corporate governance, and (IX) the international community should continue to cooperate and engage in dialogue. *See also* ***Investment Policy Review*** and ***Policy Framework for Investment***.

G20 Investment Facilitation Package: proposed by some ***G20*** members for discussion at the 2017 G20 meetings, but it has not yet received consideration. Objectives include (a) reaffirming and complementing the ***G20 Guiding Principles for Global Policymaking***, (b) fostering open and transparent business climates that are conducive to investment, and (c) promoting inclusive economic growth, sustainable development and a level playing field for all investors. The objectives would be supported by four actions: transparency, predictability and consistency, efficiency, and stakeholder relations. *See also* ***investment facilitation***.

G20 priorities on digital trade: an annex to the ***G20 digital economy ministerial declaration***. The priorities are: (a) better measurement of digital trade, (b) strengthening international frameworks on digital trade, and (c) recognizing the development dimension of digital trade. *See also* ***trade-related aspects of electronic commerce***. [www.bmwi.de]

G-24: Intergovernmental Group of Twenty-Four on International Monetary Affairs, established in 1971. Its objective is to coordinate positions of developing countries on monetary and development finance issues. Its members are Algeria, Argentina, Brazil, China (attends as a special invitee), Colombia, Congo, Côte d'Ivoire, Ecuador, Egypt, Ethiopia, Gabon, Ghana, Guatemala, Haiti, India, Iran, Kenya, Lebanon, Mexico, Morocco, Nigeria, Pakistan, Peru, Philippines, South Africa, Sri Lanka, Syria, Trinidad and Tobago, and Venezuela. Indonesia, United Arab Emirates and Saudi Arabia are observers. Its secretariat is in Washington DC.

G-33: a coalition of developing countries consisting of rather more of them than the name suggests, pressing for flexibility for developing countries to undertake limited market opening in agriculture. *See also* ***Alliance for Strategic Products and Special Safeguard Mechanism***.

G-77: *see* ***Group of 77***.

G-90: in the WTO consists of the ***African Group***, the ***ACP states*** and ***least-developed countries***. Seventy-two of them are WTO members, ten are WTO observers and nine are neither members nor observers.

Gaiatsu: a Japanese expression meaning pressure from outside. It is used to describe, both in Japanese and in foreign-language texts, the pressure sometimes brought to bear on Japan by other countries to reform this or that policy.

Gains-from-trade theory: that part of the theory of ***international economic relations*** which demonstrates that two countries with different price structures are maximizing their economic returns if they trade with each other rather than pursuing ***autarky***. The gain lies in the ability of either country to buy more at a lower cost from the other than it would be if it attempted to be self-sufficient. The consequence is specialization in production. *See also* ***absolute advantage***,

用准则；以及(9)国际社会应继续合作和参与对话。另见*投资政策审议(Investment Policy Review)*、*投资政策框架(Policy Framework for Investment)*。

G20 Investment Facilitation Package

20 国集团投资便利化一揽子计划

由部分 20 国集团成员提出供 2017 年 20 国集团会议讨论，但尚未审议。目标包括：(a)重申和补充 20 国集团全球投资决策指导原则；(b)促进有利于投资的开放和透明的商业环境；以及(c)促进包容性经济增长、可持续发展和为所有投资者提供公平竞争环境。这些目标得到四项行动的支持：透明度、可预见性和一致性、高效和利益相关方关系。另见*投资便利化(investment facilitation)*。

G20 priorities on digital trade

20 国集团数字贸易优先事项

20 国集团数字经济部长宣言的附件。优先事项为：(a)更好地衡量数字贸易；(b)加强数字贸易国际框架；以及(c)认识数字贸易的发展问题。另见*与贸易有关的电子商务(trade-related aspects of electronic commerce.)*。

G-24

24 国集团

1971 年成立的由 24 国组成的协调国际货币事务的政府间组织。目标是协调发展中国家在货币和发展融资问题上的立场。成员为阿尔及利亚、阿根廷、巴西、中国(作为特别邀请方出席)、哥伦比亚、刚果(布)、科特迪瓦、厄瓜多尔、埃及、埃塞俄比亚、加蓬、加纳、危地马拉、海地、印度、伊朗、肯尼亚、黎巴嫩、墨西哥、摩洛哥、尼日利亚、巴基斯坦、秘鲁、菲律宾、南非、斯里兰卡、叙利亚、特立尼达和多巴哥以及委内瑞拉。印度尼西亚、阿拉伯联合酋长国和沙特阿拉伯为观察员。秘书处设在华盛顿特区。

G-33

33 国协调组

发展中国家联盟，组成国家数量多于其名称所示数量，强调给予发展中国家灵活性，承担有限的农产品市场开放。另见*战略产品与特殊保障机制联盟(Alliance for Strategic Products and Special Safeguard Mechanism)*。

G-77

77 国集团

见 *77 国集团(Group of 77)*。

G-90

90 国协调组

WTO 中由非洲集团、非加太地区国家和最不发达国家组成的协调组。其中 72 个成员为 WTO 成员，10 个为 WTO 观察员，9 个既非成员也非观察员。

Gaiatsu

外部压力

日语表述，指来自外部的压力。在日语和外语文本中，用于描述有时其他国家对日本施加要求其改革这种或那种政策的压力。

Gains-from-trade theory

贸易利得理论

国际经济关系理论的一部分，表明如果两个拥有不同价格结构的国家相互开展贸易而非追求经济闭关自守，即会使其经济收益最大化。收益在于任何一国均能以低于其自给自足时的成本自另一国购买更多的商品。其结果是生产专业化。另见*绝对优势(absolute advantage)*、*比较优势(comparative advantage)*、

comparative advantage, ***globalization***, ***Heckscher-Ohlin theorem***, ***international division of labour***, ***internationalization***, ***self-reliance*** and ***self-sufficiency***.

Gate-keeper effect: control by a company of an infrastructure facility that is essential for others to develop their businesses. *See also* ***essential facilities doctrine***.

GATS: *see* ***General Agreement on Trade in Services***.

GATS 2000: refers to the new round of negotiations on ***trade in services*** mandated by Article XIX of the ***General Agreement on Trade in Services*** which began in 2000 and which has been subsumed in the ***Doha Development Agenda***.

GATT: *General Agreement on Tariffs and Trade*. This has two meanings. The first is the international organization and the secretariat that administered the Agreement. This has been superseded by the WTO. The second meaning is the text of the Agreement itself. The GATT entered into force on 1 January 1948 as a provisional agreement and remained so until it was superseded by the WTO framework on 1 January 1995. It consists of four parts. Parts I to III are, with minor changes, the original GATT adopted in 1947. Part IV was added in 1966. Part I, in Article I, contains the obligation to extend ***most-favoured-nation treatment*** to all other members of the Agreement. Article II requires each member (called *contracting party* in the Agreement) to maintain a schedule which sets out the terms and conditions under which a good may be imported. This is usually known as the tariff schedule. Part II contains most of the provisions applicable to trade in goods. Article III requires members to apply internal taxes and other charges to imported goods only to the extent that the same charges are applied to goods made locally. This is the ***national treatment*** obligation. Article IV contains some special provisions relating to films. Screen quotas must conform to certain conditions. Article V guarantees ***freedom of transit*** through the territory of each member. Goods in transit are exempt from customs duties. Article VI sets out the conditions under which ***anti-dumping measures*** and countervailing duties may be imposed. The ***Anti-Dumping Agreement*** (formally *Agreement on Implementation of Article VI of the General Agreement on Tariffs and Trade 1994*) now contains much more detailed provisions for the use of anti-dumping measures. Similarly, the ***Agreement on Subsidies and Countervailing Measures*** sets out the procedures to be followed when countervailing duties are considered. Article VII states that the value of imported goods for customs purposes should be based on the actual value of the goods. Assessments must not be based on national origin or on fictitious values. The *Agreement on Implementation of Article VII of the General Agreement on Tariffs and Trade 1994*, usually known as the ***Customs Valuation Agreement***, now contains much more detailed provisions on ***customs valuation*** procedures. Article VIII says that all fees connected with the import or export of goods must be limited to the approximate cost of the services rendered. Under Article IX ***marks of origin*** must not be used to disadvantage the products of other members or to discriminate between them. Article X requires each member to publish promptly all laws, regulations,

全球化(globalization)、*赫克歇尔-俄林定理(Heckscher-Ohlin theorem)*、*国际分工(international division of labour)*、*国际化(internationalization)*、*自力更生(self-reliance)*、*自给自足(self-sufficiency)*。

Gate-keeper effect

守门人效应

由一家公司控制对其他公司发展业务至关重要的基础设施。另见*必要设施原则(essential facilities doctrine)*。

GATS

服务贸易总协定

见*服务贸易总协定(General Agreement on Trade in Services)*。

GATS 2000

2000 年服务贸易总协定

指《服务贸易总协定》第 19 条授权的新一轮服务贸易谈判，谈判始于 2000 年，已纳入多哈发展议程。

GATT

关税与贸易总协定

包含两层含义：第一层含义是管理总协定的国际组织和秘书处，已被 WTO 所取代。第二层含义是总协定文本本身，GATT 作为临时协定于 1948 年 1 月 1 日生效，并作为临时协定直至 1995 年 1 月 1 日被 WTO 框架所取代。总协定由四部分组成：第一部分至第三部分是 1947 年通过的原 GATT，略经修改。第四部分于 1966 年增加。第一部分第 1 条包含将最惠国待遇扩大到总协定所有其他缔约方的义务。第 2 条要求每一成员(在总协定中称为缔约方)维持一份列明货物据以进口的条款和条件的减让表。通常称为关税减让表。第二部分包含适用于货物贸易的大部分条款。第 3 条要求缔约方只有在对本国制造货物适用相同费用的情况下方可对进口产品适用国内税和其他费用，此即国民待遇义务。第 4 条包含与电影相关的一些特殊条款，放映配额必须符合特定条件。第 5 条保证通过每一缔约方领土的过境自由，过境货物免关税。第 6 条规定据以实施反倾销措施和反补贴税的条件，《反倾销协定》(正式名称为《关于实施 1994 年关税与贸易总协定第 6 条的协定》)现在包含关于使用反倾销措施的更为具体的条款。同样，《补贴与反补贴措施协定》规定在考虑征收反补贴税时应遵循的程序。第 7 条规定，进口货物的完税价格应基于货物的实际价值，估价不应根据本国产品的价格或虚构的价格。《关于实施 1994 年关税与贸易总协定第 7 条的协定》，通常称为《海关估价协定》，现在包含关于海关估价程序的更为具体的条款。第 8 条规定，与进口或出口货物有关的所有费用必须限于提供服务所需的近似成本。根据第 9 条，原产地标记不得用于使其他缔约方的产品处于不利地位或对它们进行歧视。第 10 条要求每一缔约方迅速公布有关其进出口贸易的所有法律、法规、司法裁决和普遍适用的

judicial decisions and ***administrative rulings of general application*** concerning its import and export trade to enable other governments to become familiar with them. Measures must be published officially before they can be applied. This is the ***transparency*** obligation. Article XI requires the general elimination of ***quantitative restrictions***. Quotas, import or export licences are banned except for some closely defined circumstances. The ***Agreement on Import Licensing Procedures*** now contains rules for the non-discriminatory administration of import licensing. Under Article XII members may resort to import restrictions to safeguard their external financial position, but no more than is necessary to prevent the imminent threat of a serious decline in monetary reserves or to achieve a reasonable increase in monetary reserves if these are low. The Understanding on Balance-of-Payments Provisions of ***GATT 1994*** is also relevant for the use of this Article. Members may not, under Article XIII, discriminate between other members when they apply quantitative restrictions. The *Agreement on Import Licensing Procedures* contains rules for the administration of such restrictions. Article XIV states that discrimination in the use of restrictions may be permitted under defined conditions if the benefits to the parties concerned outweigh substantially any injuries to the trade of other members. Article XV sets out the basis of the relationship between the GATT and the ***IMF*** (International Monetary Fund). This is aimed to coordinate the relationship between ***exchange rate*** policy and quantitative restrictions. Article XVI requires members to notify all ***subsidies*** and to seek to avoid the use of subsidies in the export of ***primary products***. The ***Agreement on Subsidies and Countervailing Measures*** sets out more detailed rules concerning the use of subsidies in non-agricultural trade. Under Article XVII ***state-trading enterprises*** must act in a manner consistent with the principle of ***non-discrimination*** prescribed for private traders. The *Understanding on the Interpretation of Article XVII of the General Agreement on Tariffs and Trade 1994* is also relevant. Article XVIII sets out the conditions under which developing countries may deviate from other provisions of the GATT if they have to support lower standards of living or are in the early stages of development. Action open to them may include balance-of-payments measures or measures for the promotion of infant industries. The *Understanding on Balance-of-Payments Provisions of the General Agreement on Tariffs and Trade 1994* is also relevant for the use of this Article. Article XIX allows members to impose temporary import restrictions if, as a result of ***tariff concessions***, an import surge threatens to cause or causes ***serious injury*** to domestic producers. This is the ***safeguards*** article. All safeguard measures must be applied in a non-discriminatory manner. The ***Agreement on Safeguards*** now contains detailed procedures concerning the impositions of such measures. Article XX contains the ***general exceptions*** and Article XXI the ***security exceptions***. Article XXII requires each member to respond sympathetically to requests for ***consultations*** on matters covered by the GATT. Article XXIII forms the legal basis for initiation of ***dispute settlement*** and sets out the basic procedures to be followed. The

行政裁定，以使其他国家政府能够知晓，措施在实施前必须正式公布。此即透明度义务。第 11 条要求普遍取消数量限制，禁止使用配额、进口或出口许可证，一些严格规定的情况除外。《进口许可程序协定》现在包含对进口许可进行非歧视管理的规定。根据第 12 条，缔约方可以使用进口限制以保障其对外金融地位，但不得超过防止货币储备严重下降的迫近威胁或在货币储备很低的情况下实现货币储备合理增长的必要限度。《关于 1994 年关税与贸易总协定国际收支条款的谅解》也与该条款的使用相关。根据第 13 条，缔约方在实施数量限制时，不得在其他缔约方之间造成歧视。《进口许可程序协定》包含管理此类限制的规则。第 14 条规定，如果有关方的利益大大超过对其他缔约方贸易的任何损害，允许在特定条件下在使用限制措施时进行歧视。第 15 条规定 GATT 与国际货币基金组织(IMF)关系的基础，旨在协调汇率政策与数量限制的关系。第 16 条要求缔约方通报所有补贴，并设法避免在初级产品出口中使用补贴。《补贴与反补贴措施协定》列出关于非农产品贸易中使用补贴的更为具体的规定。根据第 17 条，国营贸易企业的行为必须符合适用于私营贸易商的非歧视原则。《关于解释 1994 年关税与贸易总协定第 17 条的谅解》也与此相关。第 18 条规定发展中国家在必须维持较低生活水平或处于发展初期阶段时可以偏离 GATT 其他条款所依据的条件。它们可以采取的行动包括国际收支措施或促进幼稚产业措施。《关于 1994 年关税与贸易总协定国际收支条款的谅解》也与该条款的适用相关。第 19 条允许缔约方如因关税减让造成进口激增而对国内生产者造成或威胁造成严重损害可以实施临时进口限制，此即保障措施条款，所有保障措施必须以非歧视方式实施。《保障措施协定》现在包含有关实施此类措施的具体程序。第 20 条包含一般例外。第 21 条包含安全例外。第 22 条要求每一缔约方对就 GATT 所涵盖事项的磋商请求给予积极考虑。第 23 条构成启动争端解决的法律基础，并规定应遵循的基本程序。

Dispute Settlement Understanding now contains far more detailed procedures to be followed in the case of consultations and dispute settlement. Part III of the GATT begins with Article XXIV which governs conditions concerning the formation of ***free-trade areas*** and ***customs unions***. It exempts ***frontier traffic*** from the GATT provisions, and it obliges members to take reasonable measures to ensure observance of the Agreement by regional and local government authorities. Article XXV authorizes members to take ***joint action***, now overtaken by the provisions of the ***WTO Agreement***, and to adopt ***waivers***. The *Understanding in Respect of Waivers of Obligations under the General Agreement on Tariffs and Trade 1994* terminated all waivers in existence at the time of the establishment of the WTO unless they had been reauthorized under WTO rules. Article XXVI, now also superseded by the WTO Agreement, describes the conditions under which governments could have become GATT members, and when the Agreement would enter into force. Article XXVII has also been superseded by the WTO Agreement. It states that members do not have to observe the results of tariff negotiations with countries that did not in the end join the GATT or that terminated their membership. Article XXVIII sets out the conditions under which members may modify or withdraw tariff concessions. These used to be valid for three years and were then open to negotiated changes. Rights to ***compensation*** are also defined. The *Understanding on the Interpretation of Article XXVIII of the General Agreement on Tariffs and Trade 1994* now sets out the conditions applying to principal supplying rights which may be used to initiate ***tariff negotiations***. Under Article XXVIIIbis members may launch multilateral tariff negotiations from time to time. Article XXIX describes how the GATT was to be treated if the ***Havana Charter*** had entered into force. Article XXX deals with amendments to the GATT. Any amendments would now have to be done under the WTO Agreement. Article XXXI authorized members to withdraw by giving six months' notice. Withdrawals from the GATT are now only possible as part of withdrawal from the WTO Agreement. Article XXXII deals with membership matters and Article XXXIII with accessions. Both of these articles have been superseded by the WTO Agreement. The only way to adopt the GATT obligations is by joining the WTO. Article XXXIV states that the annexes are an integral part of the Agreement. Eight of these annexes are mainly of historical interest. The ninth, Annex I, contains notes and supplementary provisions important for the interpretation of many of the articles. These are the ***ad notes***. Article XXXV describes the conditions under which a member does not have to apply its obligations towards another member. This provision has been superseded by the ***non-application*** article of the WTO Agreement. ***Part IV of the GATT*** is concerned with trade and development. In Article XXXVI members agree that measures are needed to ensure more favourable market access for products of interest to developing countries. Developed countries agree that they do not expect ***reciprocity*** when they act in favour of developing countries. In Article XXXVII developed members undertake to give high priority to

《争端解决谅解》现在包含在磋商和争端解决过程中应遵循的更为具体的程序。GATT 第三部分自第 24 条开始，管辖自由贸易区和关税同盟形成的条件。该条规定边境贸易免于适用 GATT 条款，并要求缔约方采取合理措施以保证地区和地方政府遵守总协定。第 25 条授权缔约方采取联合行动(现已被《WTO 协定》条款所取代)并通过豁免。《关于豁免 1994 年关税与贸易总协定义务的谅解》终止了在 WTO 成立时存在的所有豁免，除非根据 WTO 规则获得重新授权。第 26 条规定各国政府成为 GATT 缔约方的条件及总协定何时生效，现在已被《WTO 协定》所取代。第 27 条也已被《WTO 协定》所取代。该条规定，缔约方不必遵守与最终未加入 GATT 或与终止缔约方资格的国家所进行的关税谈判的结果。第 28 条规定缔约方可以修改或撤销关税减让的条件。这些减让以往在 3 年内有效，随后可以通过谈判改变。同时规定补偿权利。《关于解释 1994 年关税与贸易总协定第 28 条的谅解》现在规定适用于可以发起关税谈判的主要供应方权力的条件。根据第 28 条之二，缔约方可不时启动多边关税谈判。第 29 条规定，如《哈瓦那宪章》生效后如何处理 GATT 的问题。第 30 条处理修正 GATT 的问题。现在任何修正必须根据《WTO 协定》进行。第 31 条授权缔约方可在提前 6 个月作出通知后退出。现在退出 GATT 只有作为退出《WTO 协定》才有可能。第 32 条处理缔约方资格事务。第 33 条处理加入问题。这两条已被《WTO 协定》所取代。接受 GATT 义务的惟一途径是加入 WTO。第 34 条规定附件为总协定组成部分，其中 8 个附件仅有历史意义。第 9 个附件，即附件 I，包含对解释许多条款很重要的注释和补充规定，这些属于补充注释。第 35 条规定一缔约方不必对另一缔约方适用其义务的条件。这一条款已被《WTO 协定》的互不适用条款所取代。GATT 第四部分关于贸易与发展问题。在第 36 条中，缔约方同意需要采取措施，保证给予对发展中国家具有利益的产品更有利的市场准入。发达国家同意，在采取有利于发展中国家的行动时，不期望获得互惠。在第 37 条中，发达缔约方承诺最优

reducing and eliminating trade barriers to products of interest to developing countries. Developing countries undertake to open their markets to other developing countries to the extent that their circumstances permit. In Article XXXVIII GATT members agree to collaborate to further these objectives. Some of the articles have ***ad notes***. These are later additions to the articles. *See also* ***GATT 1947*** and ***GATT 1994***. [Hoekman and Kostecki 1995, Jackson 1969, Jackson 1997]

GATT 1947: *General Agreement on Tariffs and Trade 1947*. The old (pre-1994) version of the GATT, adopted at the conclusion in 1947 of the Second Session of the Preparatory Committee of the ***United Nations Conference on Trade and Employment***, and as subsequently rectified, amended or modified. It was in force from 1 January 1948 until the conclusion of the ***Uruguay Round*** when it was replaced by the ***GATT 1994***. The two basic texts are virtually identical, but legally distinct, in that the GATT 1947 was an international treaty, provisionally applied, whereas the GATT 1994 is only one of the components of the ***WTO Agreement***.

GATT 1994: *General Agreement on Tariffs and Trade 1994*. The new version of the ***GATT***, which governs trade in goods. It is the formal name for the ***GATT 1947*** and the collected amendments, interpretations, additions, etc. to it made since its entry into force. It is a part of the agreement establishing the WTO, and it has no independent legal status. It consists, in addition to the provisions contained in the GATT 1947 (not the GATT 1947 agreement itself), of protocols and certifications relating to tariff concessions, protocols of accession, decisions on waivers still in force and other decisions taken by the GATT contracting parties, but not the ***grandfather clause***. It also includes six understandings interpreting several GATT articles and the Marrakesh Protocol to GATT 1994 which covers tariff concessions made by members. Countries joining the WTO accept all the rights and obligations contained in the GATT 1994, but they cannot accede separately to it. *See also* ***WTO Agreement*** and ***single undertaking***.

GATT à la carte: a derisory term used by some commentators to describe the situation prevailing up to the end of the ***Uruguay Round*** whereby GATT members could to a large extent decide themselves which of the ***Tokyo Round agreements*** they should join. *See also* ***single undertaking***.

GATT Analytical Index: a two-volume guide to the interpretation and application of the *GATT* (*General Agreement on Tariffs and Trade*) prepared by the Legal Division of the then GATT Secretariat. The *Analytical Index* contains at a highly detailed level the interpretations of the GATT articles made by its membership, dispute settlement panels, etc. up to 1994. It is now superseded by the ***WTO Analytical Index***. *See also* ***GATT Basic Instruments and Selected Documents***.

GATT Basic Instruments and Selected Documents: BISD. Reports published annually by the GATT Secretariat between 1952 and 1994 which contain decisions, conclusions and reports adopted in the reporting period. The BISD

先考虑削减和消除对发展中国家具有利益的产品的贸易壁垒。发展中国家承诺在其条件允许的限度内向其他发展中国家开放其市场。在第 38 条中，GATT 缔约方同意为推进这些目标而进行合作。一些条款有补充注释。这些是后来补充到条款中的。另见 *1947 年关税与贸易总协定(GATT 1947)*、*1994 年关税与贸易总协定(GATT 1994)*。

GATT 1947

1947 年关税与贸易总协定

指旧版(1994 年以前的)GATT，在 1947 年联合国贸易与就业会议筹备委员会第二次会议结束时获得通过，后经更正、修正或修改。自 1948 年 1 月 1 日起生效，直至乌拉圭回合结束时被 GATT1994 所取代。这两个基本文本实际上是相同的，但法律上是不同的，因为 GATT 1947 是一项临时适用的国际条约，而 GATT 1994 仅为《WTO 协定》的组成部分之一。

GATT 1994

1994 年关税与贸易总协定

指新版 GATT，管辖货物贸易。是 GATT 1947 及自其生效以来对其所作修正、解释、补充等的正式名称，是《建立世界贸易组织协定》的一部分，无独立法律地位。除包括 GATT 1947 所含条款外(不是 GATT 1947 年本身)，还包括与关税减让有关的议定书和核证、加入议定书、仍然有效的关于豁免的决定以及 GATT 缔约方所作其他决定，但不包括祖父条款。还包括解释 GATT 若干条款的 6 项谅解和涵盖成员所作关税减让的《1994 年关税与贸易总协定马拉喀什议定书》。加入 WTO 的国家接受 GATT 1994 所含所有权利和义务，但它们不能单独加入。另见 *WTO 协定(WTO Agreement)*、*一揽子承诺(single undertaking)*。

GATT à la carte

GATT 选择性承诺

一些评论家使用的调侃性词语，用于描述直至乌拉圭回合结束时的一种普遍情况，即 GATT 缔约方在很大程度上可以自行决定它们应该加入哪一个东京回合协定。另见 *一揽子承诺(single undertaking)*。

GATT Analytical Index

GATT 分析索引

由当时的 GATT 秘书处法律司编写的两卷本解释和适用 GATT 条款的指南。分析索引包含截至 1994 年由缔约方、争端解决专家组等对 GATT 条款的详细解释。现已被《WTO 分析索引》所取代。另见 *GATT 基本文件资料选编(GATT Basic Instruments and Selected Documents)*。

GATT Basic Instruments and Selected Documents

GATT 基本文件资料选编

BISD。GATT 秘书处在 1952 年至 1994 年间每年出版的报告，包含报告期内

is indispensable for the administration and study of the GATT and related agreements and codes. It has now been succeeded by the ***WTO Basic Instruments and Selected Documents.***

GATT-consistency of national legislation: under the Protocol of Provisional Accession national legislation in effect before 1 January 1948 was allowed to remain in force even if it was inconsistent with the provisions of the GATT through the ***grandfather clause***. Laws passed after that date had to be in conformity with the GATT, though certain exceptions, for example in the form of strictly circumscribed ***waivers***, were still possible. In the ***Manufacturing Clause*** case, the panel found that amendments to grandfathered legislation may be possible if they do not make it more inconsistent with the GATT, or if they do not cancel rightful expectations of other members. Another panel ruling, this time in the ***Superfund*** case, held that the mere existence of national legislation permitting discretionary action inconsistent with the GATT did not constitute a violation of obligations under the GATT. The approach to this question was that outlined in *United States – Measures Affecting the Importation, Internal Use and Use of Tobacco* that "[p]anels had consistently ruled that legislation which mandated action inconsistent with the General Agreement could be challenged as such, whereas legislation which merely gave the discretion to the executive authority of a contracting party to act inconsistently with the General Agreement could not be challenged as such; only the actual application of such legislation inconsistent with the General Agreement could be subject to challenge".

GATT Council of Representatives: established on 4 June 1960 to administer the GATT more effectively in view of its expanding work programme. Until then, an intersessional committee composed of seventeen members had provided continuity between the annual sessions of the ***contracting parties***. The Council's main functions were to consider matters requiring urgent attention between the annual sessions of the contracting parties and to supervise the work of committees, working parties and other subsidiary bodies. All GATT members automatically became members of the Council which met about once a month. In the WTO, the body most nearly performing the functions of the GATT Council is the ***General Council***.

GATT plus: an expression implying imposition or acceptance of international trade disciplines more stringent than those prescribed by the GATT or extending the GATT rules to areas beyond trade in goods. One of the most ambitious examples of "GATT plus" was the proposal in 1976 by the Atlantic Council of the United States that there should be a code of ***trade liberalization*** within the GATT framework with stronger rules for the conduct of trade relations between industrialized countries willing to accept them. According to its proponents, the benefits would have been extended to all GATT members according to the most-favoured-nation clause. The code would also have been open to new members willing to accept its obligations, but only code members would have been able to initiate ***tariff negotiations*** with another code member.

通过的决定、结论和报告。BISD 对于管理和研究 GATT 及其相关协定和守则是不可或缺的。现已被《WTO 基本文件资料选编》所取代。

GATT-consistency of national legislation

国家立法与 GATT 一致性

根据《临时适用议定书》，在 1948 年 1 月 1 日之前生效的国家立法，即使与 GATT 条款不一致，而通过祖父条款仍允许继续有效。在该日期之后通过的法律必须符合 GATT，尽管存在某些例外情况，例如以严格限定的豁免形式仍有可能。在“制造条款案”中，专家组认为，如果不使祖父条款立法与 GATT 更加不一致或如果此类立法不消除其他成员的合法预期，对祖父条款立法进行修正是可能的。在另一项专家组裁决中，即“超级基金案”中，专家组认为仅存在允许与 GATT 不一致的自由裁量行为的国家立法并不构成对 GATT 项下义务的违反。对这一问题的处理方式在“美国-影响烟草进口、国内使用和使用措施案”中有所描述，即“专家组一致裁决，可以质疑授权采取与总协定不一致的立法本身，而不能质疑仅赋予一缔约方行政当局以不符合总协定的方式行事的自由裁量权的立法本身；仅当该立法的实际适用情况不符合总协定时方可对其提出质疑。”

GATT Council of Representatives

GATT 理事会

1960 年 6 月 4 日设立，以便在 GATT 工作计划不断扩大的情况下更有效管理 GATT。直到那时，一个由 17 名成员组成的闭会期间委员会在两届缔约方年度会议之间保证连续性。理事会的主要职能是审议需要在两届缔约方年度会议之间采取紧急行动的事项，并监督各委员会、工作组和其他附属机构的工作。所有缔约方自动成为该理事会成员，大致每月举行一次会议。在 WTO 中，职能最接近 GATT 理事会的机构是总理事会。

GATT plus

超 GATT 规则

该表述含义为施加或接受严于 GATT 所规定纪律的国际贸易纪律或将 GATT 规则扩大到货物贸易以外的领域。最具雄心水平的一个例子是美国大西洋理事会在 1976 年提出的建议，即应在 GATT 框架内制定一项贸易自由化守则，对愿意接受的工业化国家之间的贸易关系制定更严格的规则。据其支持者称，相关利益本应根据最惠国待遇条款扩大至所有 GATT 缔约方。守则还将对愿意接受其义务的新成员开放，但只有守则成员能够与另一守则成员启动关税

The proposal did not find favour with GATT members as a whole. *See also* ***most-favoured-nation treatment*** and ***WTO-plus***. [Atlantic Council of the United States 1976]

GATT review session: usually refers to the ninth session of the contracting parties (members) of the GATT, held from October 1954 to March 1955. It reviewed all aspects of the operations of the GATT. Several articles were amended as a consequence, most notably Article XVIII dealing with economic development issues and the rights and obligations of developing countries. Most other changes were minor. *See also* ***developing countries and the multilateral trading system***.

GATT-Think: characterized by Paul Krugman as three simple rules about the objectives of negotiating countries in the GATT: (1) exports are good, (2), imports are bad, (3) other things equal, an equal increase in imports and exports is good. He says that GATT-Think is enlightened ***mercantilism*** and economic nonsense. Despite all this, Krugman concedes that the GATT has after all played a useful role in liberalizing the world trading system. [Krugman 1991]

General Affairs Council: a body consisting of the Ministers for Foreign Affairs of the members of the ***European Union***. It covers topics spanning many policy areas, such as ***enlargement*** and the preparations of institutional and administrative matters. It also prepares the meetings of the ***European Council***.

General Agreement on Tariffs and Trade: *see* ***GATT***.

General Agreement on Trade in Services: frequently known as GATS. One of the ***Uruguay Round*** outcomes. Parts I, II, IV, V and VI apply to all services. Part III applies to the extent that a member has made specific commitments on services activities. Part I deals with scope and definitions. Article I states that the GATS covers all trade in services except bilateral air traffic rights. It also describes the four modes of delivery for services: (1) cross-border supply (seller and customer do not meet), (2) consumption abroad (customer goes abroad to buy the services), (3) commercial presence (seller establishes an office in the export market), and (4) through the presence of natural persons. Part II covers general obligations and disciplines. Article II prescribes ***most-favoured-nation treatment*** for services and services suppliers. It is possible, but not all that easy, to obtain exemptions from this obligation for individual traded services under defined conditions. These are the ***MFN exemptions***. Article III deals with ***transparency***. This is the obligation to publish domestic regulations on trade in services as well as major changes to them, and to notify international agreements on trade in services to the WTO. Members also must establish enquiry points where information on regulations may be obtained. Article IV seeks to promote greater participation by developing countries in international services trade. Articles V and Vbis describe, respectively, the conditions under which members may conclude ***economic integration arrangements*** and ***labour markets integration agreements***. Free-trade agreements for services fall under these two articles. Article VI requires members to ensure that all general domestic regulations affecting trade in services are

谈判。此项建议没有得到 GATT 缔约方全体的支持。另见*最惠国待遇(most-favoured-nation treatment)*、*超 WTO 规则(WTO-plus)*。

GATT review session

GATT 审议会议

通常指 1954 年 10 月至 1955 年 3 月举行的 GATT 缔约方(成员)第 9 届会议。会议审议了 GATT 运用的所有方面。作为结果，对若干条款进行了修正，最引人注目的是处理经济发展问题和发展中国家权利与义务的第 18 条。其他大部分条款的修正较小。另见*发展中国家与多边贸易体制(developing countries and the multilateral trading system)*。

GATT-Think

GATT 思维

保罗·克鲁格曼将之总结为 GATT 中谈判国目标的三条简单规则：(1)出口是好的；(2)进口是坏的；(3)在其他条件相同的情况下，进口和出口同样增长是好的。他指出，GATT 思维是开明的重商主义和经济上的谬论。尽管如此，克鲁格曼承认，GATT 毕竟在世界贸易体制自由化方面发挥了有益作用。

General Affairs Council

总务理事会

由欧盟成员国外交部长组成的机构。涵盖分布在许多政策领域的主题，如扩盟和筹备机构和行政事务。还负责筹备欧洲理事会的会议。

General Agreement on Tariffs and Trade

关税与贸易总协定

见*关税与贸易总协定(GATT)*。

General Agreement on Trade in Services

服务贸易总协定

通常称为 GATS。乌拉圭回合成果。第一部分、第二部分、第四部分、第五和第六部分适用于所有服务。第三部分适用于对服务活动作出具体承诺的一成员。第一部分处理范围和定义。第 1 条规定，GATS 涵盖所有服务贸易，双边航权除外。该条还描述了服务的 4 种提供模式：(1)跨境交付(卖方和客户不见面)；(2)境外消费(客户到国外购买服务)；(3)商业存在(卖方在出口市场中建立办公室)；以及(4)自然人移动。第二部分涵盖一般义务和纪律。第 2 条规定对服务和服务提供者的最惠国待遇，单个交易的服务在规定的条件下有可能获得这一义务的豁免，但并非易事，这些是最惠国待遇豁免。第 3 条处理透明度问题，即公布国内服务贸易法规及对其的重大变更的义务，并向 WTO 通报关于服务贸易的国际协定的义务，成员还必须建立咨询点，在咨询点可以获得有关法规的信息。第 4 条寻求促进发展中国家更多参与国际服务贸易。第 5 条和第 5 条之二分别描述成员可以缔结经济一体化安排和劳动力市场一体化协定的条件，服务自由贸易协定属于这两条。第 6 条要求成员保证所有影响服务贸易的普遍适用的国内法规以合理和公正的方式实施，必须制定核实

administered reasonably and impartially. Adequate procedures must be in place for verifying professional qualifications. Under Article VII members may not use recognition of qualifications and experience as a disguised barrier to trade. Members may recognize the qualifications of another country and enter into ***mutual recognition arrangements*** without the need to extend the same conditions to third countries. Article VIII requires members to ensure that monopolies and exclusive service suppliers behave in accordance with the most-favoured-nation principle and the specific commitments they have made. Article IX recognizes that some business practices may restrain competition and restrict trade in services. Members therefore have the right to ask for consultations with a view to eliminating such practices. Article X authorizes negotiations on an article covering emergency ***safeguard*** measures. Under Article XI members may not impose restrictions on payments and transfers for current transaction in sectors where they have made a specific commitment other than as set out in Article XII (restrictions to safeguard the balance the payments). Any restrictions so imposed must be non-discriminatory. Article XIII exempts ***government procurement*** from the most-favoured-nation, market access and national treatment provisions. Articles XIV and XIVbis contain the ***general exceptions*** and ***security exceptions***. Article XV recognizes that subsidies may distort trade in services. It also requires members to enter into negotiations on rules concerning subsidies. Part III of the Agreement contains the rules applying to specific commitments. Article XVI covers ***market access for services*** and Article XVII guarantees ***national treatment***. Formally different treatment of foreign firms is possible if formally identical treatment were found to be disadvantaging them. Article XVIII permits members to make ***additional commitments*** going beyond market access and national treatment. These may include matters concerning qualifications, standards or licensing. Part IV establishes the framework for progressive liberalization of trade in services. Article XIX mandates new rounds of negotiations and outlines the conditions under which these negotiations will be conducted. Article XX describes the contents of the schedules of specific commitments. Entries on market access and national treatment are obligatory. Article XXI requires that, as a rule, a commitment cannot be reduced or withdrawn inside three years. If such a change is made, ***compensation*** may be necessary. Unilateral improvements may be made at any time. Part V deals with institutional matters. Article XXII contains the right to ***consultations***. Article XXIII states that if a member considers that the outcome of consultations has not been satisfactory, it may seek a solution through ***dispute settlement***. In this case, the unified WTO procedures will apply. These are set out in the ***Dispute Settlement Understanding***. Article XXIV establishes the ***Council for Trade in Services*** which in turn may establish subsidiary bodies. Article XXV makes technical cooperation available to developing countries through the Council for Trade in Services. Article XXVI authorizes the WTO ***General Council*** to make arrangements for cooperation with United Nations bodies and other ***intergovernmental organizations*** concerned with

专业资格的适当程序。根据第 7 条，成员不得将承认资格和经验作为变相贸易限制，成员可以承认另一国的资格，并达成相互承认安排，而无需将同样的条件扩大至第三国。第 8 条要求成员保证垄断企业和独家服务供应者依照最惠国待遇原则和他们所作具体承诺行事。第 9 条认识到，一些商业惯例可能限制竞争和限制服务贸易，成员们因此有权要求进行磋商，以期消除此类惯例。第 10 条授权就一项涵盖紧急保障措施的条款进行谈判。根据第 11 条，成员不得对其已作出具体承诺的部门的经常项目交易的支付和转移施加限制，第 12 条(保障国际收支的限制)所规定的除外。如此施加的任何限制必须是非歧视的。第 13 条将政府采购例外于最惠国待遇、市场准入和国民待遇条款。第 14 条和第 14 条之二包含一般例外和安全例外。第 15 条认识到补贴可能扭曲服务贸易，还要求成员就有关补贴的规则进行谈判。协定第三部分包含适用于具体承诺的规则。第 16 条涵盖服务市场准入。第 17 条保证提供国民待遇，如果发现形式上相同的待遇对外国公司不利，可以对其进行形式上的区别对待。第 18 条允许成员作出超出市场准入和国民待遇的附加承诺，这些承诺可能包括有关资格、标准或许可事项。第四部分建立服务贸易逐步自由化的框架。第 19 条授权进行新一轮谈判，并规定开展这些谈判的条件。第 20 条描述具体承诺减让表的内容，关于市场准入和国民待遇的栏目是强制性的。第 21 条要求作为一项规则，一项承诺在 3 年内不得削减或撤销，如果进行修改，可能需要作出补偿，可以随时作出单方面修改。第五部分处理机构事项。第 22 条规定磋商权利。第 23 条规定，如果一成员认为磋商结果不满意，可以通过争端解决寻求解决办法，在此种情况下，将适用 WTO 统一程序，这些程序列在《争端解决谅解》中。第 24 条规定设立服务贸易理事会，理事会可随后设立附属机构。第 25 条规定通过服务贸易理事会向发展中国家提供技术合作。第 26 条授权 WTO 总理事会作出安排，与联合国机构和其他与服务有

services. Part VI contains the final provisions. Under Article XXVII it is possible to deny the benefits of the Agreement to a service supplier under closely defined conditions. Article XXVIII contains more definitions. Article XXIX contains eight annexes. *Annex on Article II exemptions*: Article II of the GATS contains the obligation to extend MFN treatment to the other members of the agreement. Exceptions to this rule are possible under the conditions prescribed in the annex. MFN exemptions must have a specific aim, and they should not last longer than ten years. *Annex on movement of natural persons supplying services under the Agreement*: this annex states that the GATS does not apply to measures regarding citizenship, residence or employment on a permanent basis. GATS members may regulate entry to their territories, but they must not use this right to negate their specific commitments. The ***Third Protocol to the General Agreement on Trade in Services*** contains new commitments in this area. *Annex on air transport services*: the GATS does not apply to bilateral air traffic rights or services directly related to them. This exception is to be reviewed after five years. *Annex on financial services*: this annex describes in greater detail how the GATS rules apply to trade in financial services. *Second annex on financial services*: this annex is the basis for the negotiations on trade in financial services which concluded on 28 July 1995. The results of these negotiations are contained in the ***Second Protocol to the General Agreement on Trade in Services***. The outcome of further negotiations on financial services is contained in the ***Fifth Protocol to the General Agreement on Trade in Services***. *Annex on negotiations in maritime transport services*: MFN treatment and MFN exemptions in maritime services will only enter into force once the negotiations on maritime transport services have concluded. *Annex on telecommunications*: members must ensure that foreign service suppliers have access to public telecommunications networks on reasonable and non-discriminatory terms. The annex specifies how this should be done. *Annex on negotiations on basic telecommunications*: MFN treatment and MFN exemptions in basic telecommunications will only enter into force once the negotiations have concluded. The ***Fourth Protocol to the General Agreement on Trade in Services*** contains the outcome of the negotiations. The negotiations mandated in Article XIX began in 2000. They are now part of the ***Doha Development Agenda***. *See also* ***LDC services waiver***.

General Considerations and Practical Approaches Concerning Conflicting Requirements Imposed on Multinational Enterprises: *see* ***Decision on Conflicting Requirements***.

General Council: this is a body composed of all WTO members. It has general authority to supervise the various agreements under the jurisdiction of the WTO. It exercises authority between the biennial ***WTO Ministerial Conferences*** and on behalf of them. It meets about once a month. *See also* ***Dispute Settlement Body*** and ***Trade Policy Review Mechanism***.

General Data Protection Regulation: GDPR. The ***European Union***'s ***Regulation*** (EU) 2016/679 which regulates the processing by an individual, a

关的政府间组织进行合作。第六部分包含最后条款。根据第 27 条，在严格规定的条件下可以拒绝向一服务提供者给予 GATS 的利益。第 28 条包含更多定义。第 29 条包含 8 个附件。《关于第 2 条豁免的附件》：GATS 第 2 条包含成员向其他成员提供最惠国待遇的义务。根据该附件规定的条件，这一规则可以例外。最惠国待遇豁免必须有特定目的且不超过 10 年。《关于本协定项下提供服务的自然人移动的附件》：该附件规定，GATS 不适用于有关永久性公民身份、居住或就业的措施。成员可管理对其领土的进入，但不得利用这一权利使其具体承诺无效。《服务贸易总协定第三议定书》包含这一领域的新承诺。《关于空运服务的附件》：GATS 不适用于双边航权或与之直接相关的服务。这一例外将在 5 年后进行审议。《关于金融服务的附件》：该附件更为详细地描述 GATS 规则如何适用于金融服务贸易。《关于金融服务的第二附件》：该附件是 1995 年 7 月 28 日达成的有关金融服务贸易谈判的基础，谈判结果包含在《服务贸易总协定第二议定书》之中，关于金融服务的进一步谈判的结果包含在《服务贸易总协定第五议定书》之中。《关于海运服务谈判的附件》：规定海运服务的最惠国待遇和最惠国豁免只有在海运服务谈判结束后方可生效。《关于电信服务的附件》：成员必须保证外国服务提供者以合理和非歧视性的条件接入公共电信网络。该附件具体规定如何作到这一点。《关于基础电信谈判的附件》：基础电信的最惠国待遇和最惠国豁免只有在谈判结束后方可生效。《服务贸易总协定第四议定书》包含有关谈判结果。第 19 条授权的谈判于 2000 年开始，现在是多哈发展议程的一部分。另见*最不发达国家服务豁免(LDC services waiver)*。

General Considerations and Practical Approaches Concerning Conflicting Requirements Imposed on Multinational Enterprises

关于对跨国企业提出相互抵触的要求的总体考虑和实践做法

见*关于相互抵触的要求的决定(Decision on Conflicting Requirements)*。

General Council

总理事会

由 WTO 所有成员组成的机构。拥有监督 WTO 管辖范围内各项协定的总体职能。在每 2 年一届的 WTO 部长级会议闭会期间代表部长级会议行使职能。大致每月举行一次会议。另见*争端解决机构(Dispute Settlement Body)*、*贸易政策审议机制(Trade Policy Review Mechanism)*。

General Data Protection Regulation

通用数据保护条例

GDPR。欧盟第 2016/679 号条例，规范个人、公司或组织对与欧盟境内个人有

company or organization of personal data relating to individuals in the European Union. It entered into force in May 2018 and provides one set of data protection rules for all companies operating in the European Union. The Regulation applies to the processing of personal data wholly or partly by automated means and the processing other than by automated means of personal data which form part of a filing system or are intended to form part of a filing system. Basic principles relating to the processing of personal data are (a) lawfulness, fairness and transparency, (b) a limitation on purpose, (c) data minimization, (d) accuracy, (e) storage for no longer than is necessary, (f) appropriate security of storage, and (g) accountability of the holder of the personal data. *See also* ***EU–US Privacy Shield***. [eur-lex.europa.eu]

General exceptions: the ***General Agreement on Trade in Services*** (GATS) in Article XIV and the ***GATT*** in Article XX give WTO members the right not to apply the provisions of these agreements in specified circumstances. But these articles may not be invoked to discriminate between countries or as a ***disguised restriction on international trade***. Under the GATT this right may be used, to the extent that it is necessary to do so, (a) to protect public morals, (b) to protect human, animal or plant life or health, (c) to cover trade in gold and silver, (d) to ensure compliance with laws and regulations otherwise consistent with the GATT, customs enforcement, enforcement of monopolies, the protection of intellectual property rights and prevention of deceptive practices, (e) to deal with products made by ***prison labour***, (f) to protect national treasures of artistic, historic or archaeological value, (g) to conserve exhaustible natural resources, but only in combination with domestic restrictions on production and consumption, (h) to pursue obligations under international commodity agreements, (i) to restrict exports of domestic materials under strictly defined conditions, and (j) to adopt measures essential for the acquisition or distribution of products in general or local short supply. The GATS, apart from identical provisions on public morals and human, animal and plant life, also mentions public order in cases of genuine and sufficiently serious threat to one of the fundamental interests of society. Its other exceptions cover compliance with laws and regulations not inconsistent with GATS rules, collection of direct taxes and double taxation agreements. *See also* ***security exceptions***.

Generalized System of Preferences: *see* ***GSP***.

Generally Accepted Accounting Principles: GAAP. These are accounting rules that have achieved the status of widely-used principles to measure and report financial data. They vary between industries and between countries. Their purpose is to present credible financial data to investors, creditors and regulatory authorities. The calculation of the ***regional value content*** under ***preferential rules of origin*** sometimes depends on these rules. In the ***free-trade agreement*** between Canada and Chile GAAP is described as "recognized consensus or substantial authoritative support in the territory of a party with respect to the recording of revenues, expenses, costs, assets and liabilities, disclosure of information and preparation of financial statements. These

关的个人数据的处理。2018 年 5 月生效，为在欧盟经营的所有公司提供一套数据保护规则。该条例适用于全部或部分以自动方式对个人数据的处理，及以自动方式以外的方式对构成文件系统一部分或意在构成文件系统一部分的个人数据的处理。与个人数据处理有关的基本原则为：(a)合法、公平和透明；(b)目的限制；(c)数据最少化；(d)准确性；(e)存储时间不超过必要时间；(f)存储的适当安全性；以及(g)个人数据持有人的责任。*另见欧盟—美国隐私护盾(EU–US Privacy Shield)*。

General exceptions

一般例外

《服务贸易总协定》(GATS)第 14 条和 GATT 第 20 条规定，WTO 成员有权在特定情况下不适用这些协定的条款。但是不得援引这些条款以区别对待各国或作为对国际贸易的变相限制。根据 GATT，可以在必要时使用这一权利：(a)保护公共道德；(b)保护人类、动物或植物的生命或健康；(c)涉及黄金和白银的贸易；(d)保证遵守在其他方面符合 GATT 的法律法规，包括海关执法、实行垄断、保护知识产权和防止欺诈行为；(e)处理监狱劳役产品；(f)保护具有艺术、历史或考古价值的国宝；(g)保护可用尽的自然资源，但只能与限制国内生产和消费一同实施；(h)履行国际商品协定规定的义务；(i)在严格限定的条件下限制国内材料的出口；以及(j)在普遍或局部供应短缺的情况下，为获取或分配产品所必须的措施。GATS 除关于公共道德及人类、动物和植物生命的相同规定外，还提到在真正和足够严重威胁到社会基本利益之一的情况下的公共秩序。其他例外包括遵守与 GATS 规则不相抵触的法律法规、征收直接税和双重征税协定。*另见安全例外(security exceptions)*。

Generalized System of Preferences

普遍优惠制

见普惠制(GSP)。

Generally Accepted Accounting Principles

公认会计原则

GAAP。指已经获得用于衡量和报告财务数据的广泛使用原则地位的会计准则。这些原则因行业和国家不同而不同。目的是向投资者、债权人和监管机构提交可信的财务数据。优惠原产地规则下区域价值成分的计算有时根据这些准则。在加拿大与智利的自由贸易协定中，公认会计原则被描述为“在一参加方领土内记录关于收入、支出、成本、资产和负债的记录、信息披露和财务报表编制的公认共识或实质性权威支持。这些标准可以是普遍适用的概括性的准

standards may be broad guidelines of general application as well as detailed standards, practices and procedures". *See also* ***international accounting standards***.

General most-favoured-nation treatment: *see* ***most-favoured-nation treatment***.

General obligations: obligations which should be applied to all services sectors at the entry into force of the ***General Agreement on Trade in Services***.

General Preferential Tariff: GPT. Canada's scheme for giving preferential market access to eligible developing countries. *See also* ***GSP***.

General services in agriculture: under the WTO ***Agreement on Agriculture*** an open-ended list of domestic support measures that have no, or at most minimal, trade-distorting effects or on production. They include in abbreviated form (a) research programmes, (b) pest and disease control, (c) training services, (d) extension and advisory services, (e) inspection services, (f) marketing and promotion services, (g) infrastructural services such as electricity and water supply, roads and other means of transport, etc. At the Bali ***WTO Ministerial Conference*** in 2013 the following were added as ways to promote rural development and poverty alleviation: (i) land rehabilitation, (ii) soil conservation and resource management, (iii) drought management and flood control, (iv) rural employment programmes, (v) issuance of property titles, and (vi) farmer settlement programmes.

General tariff: this term nowadays is often used instead of ***most-favoured-nation tariff*** in that it applies to the bulk of one's trading partners. Before the emergence of general ***most-favoured-nation treatment*** with the entry into force of the GATT in 1948, the general tariff often referred to the tariff applied to countries not receiving ***preferences*** of one kind or another. In some cases, countries still distinguish between a general tariff and a most-favoured-nation tariff, and the rates contained in the former are usually higher. *See also* ***normal trade relations***.

General trade: goods traded under the rates contained in the ***general tariff***. In modern usage it often means goods receiving ***most-favoured-nation treatment***.

Generic: in pharmaceutical products refers to copies of a patented drug or of a drug whose patent has expired (sometimes also related to trademarks).

Generic geographical indications: refers to ***geographical indications*** which once had meaning in describing a product as having special characteristics because it came from a defined area, but which now has become a common name for a product of that kind. *Moutarde de Dijon* or *Dijon Mustard* and *Swiss Cheese* are the standard examples of generic indications. Once a geographical indication has become generic, it no longer enjoys protection under the relevant laws or treaties. Difficulties can arise when a name is considered a geographical indication in its home country, but a generic name in others. *See also* ***semi-generic geographical indications***. [Audier 2000; Council Regulation (EEC) 2081/92; WIPO SCT/8/4]

Generic springboarding: this is the contentious process by which a firm starts to prepare for the commercial production and sale as a generic product of an item

则，也可以是详细的标准、惯例和程序”。另见*国际会计标准(international accounting standards)*。

General most-favoured-nation treatment

普遍最惠国待遇

见*最惠国待遇(most-favoured-nation treatment)*。

General obligations

一般义务

在《服务贸易总协定》生效时应适用于所有服务部门的义务。

General Preferential Tariff

普遍优惠关税

GPT。加拿大给予符合条件的发展中国家的优惠市场准入方案。另见*普惠制(GSP)*。

General services in agriculture

农业一般服务

根据 WTO《农业协定》，对贸易没有扭曲作用或此类作用非常小的国内支持措施开放式清单。措施概括而言包括：(a)研究计划；(b)病虫害控制；(c)培训服务；(d)推广和咨询服务；(e)检验服务；(f)营销和促销服务；(g)基础设施服务，如电力和水力供应、道路和其他运输方式等。在 2013 年巴厘岛 WTO 部长级会议上，增加下列内容作为促进农村发展和脱贫的途径：(1)土地复垦；(2)土壤保持和资源管理；(3)干旱管理和洪水控制；(4)农村就业计划；(5)产权证发放；以及(6)农民安置计划。

General tariff

普通关税

该词现在通常用以替代最惠国关税，因为其适用于一国大部分贸易伙伴。在普遍最惠国待遇随着 GATT 于 1948 年生效而出现之前，普通关税通常指适用于没有享受某种优惠的国家的关税。在一些情况下，各国仍然区分普通关税和最惠国关税，前者所含税率通常较高。另见*正常贸易关系(normal trade relations)*。

General trade

一般贸易

以普通关税所含税率交易的商品。在现代使用中，通常指享受最惠国待遇的货物。

Generic

仿制药

在医药产品中，指专利药品或专利过期药品的复制品(有时也与商标有关)。

Generic geographical indications

通用地理标志

指地理标志，该词曾指因来自特定地区而具有特殊特征的产品，而现在已成为此类产品的通用名称。Moutarde de Dijon Dijon Mustard(第戎芥末酱)和 Swiss Cheese(瑞士奶酪)是通用标志的典型例子。一旦地理标志成为通用标志，即不再受到相关法律或条约的保护。当一名称在其母国被视为地理标志而在其他国家被视为通用标志时就产生了困难。另见*半通用地理标志(semi-generic geographical indications)*。

Generic springboarding

仿制药跳板

指一企业开始准备将仍受专利保护的产品作为非专利产品进行商业生产和销售的有争议的程序。跳板的目的是保证一旦专利期到期，非专利产品的生产

which is still under ***patent*** protection. The aim of springboarding is to ensure that producers of generic products can enter the market as early as possible once the patent term expires. In the case of pharmaceuticals, where several years may be required to develop a generic drug, springboarding enables firms to manufacture an item still under patent protection for the purpose of meeting pre-regulatory requirements. But commercial activity is not permitted at this stage, and doing so would involve an ***intellectual property right infringement***. *See also* ***Bolar exception***, ***decompilation***, ***intellectual property*** and ***reverse engineering***.

Genetically modified micro-organism: GMM. A micro-organism in which the genetic material has been altered in a way that would not occur in the natural world.

Genetically modified organism: GMO. An organism in which the genetic material has been altered in a way that would not occur in the natural world.

Genetic labelling: a system of product labelling advocated by some to indicate whether the product or its components have been modified genetically. Proponents argue that doing so is in the interest of consumers and users. Opponents say that this is yet another unnecessary ***technical barrier to trade*** because, for reasons of cost, many producers would prefer not to keep genetically modified crops separate from others. All ***European Union*** members were required to enact genetic-labelling legislation by 31 July 1997 to ensure that firms located in member states use the labels when necessary. *See also* ***eco-labelling*** and ***social labelling***.

Geneva Act of the Lisbon Agreement on Appellations of Origin and Geographical Indications: adopted in ***WIPO*** in 2015. It allows the international registration of ***geographical indications***, in addition to ***appellations of origin***, under the ***Lisbon Agreement***. The Act also allows the accession of intergovernmental organizations under certain conditions.

Geneva Agreement on Trade in Bananas: *see* ***banana cases***.

Geneva Convention: *Convention for the Protection of Producers of Phonograms Against Unauthorized Duplication of their Phonograms*. It protects a producer of phonograms of another member state against the making of duplicates without consent. "Phonogram" means an exclusively aural fixation, i.e. a recording (record, compact disc, tape, etc.). The term does not include sound films or videocassettes.

Geneva mini-ministerial meeting: *see* ***Doha Development Agenda***.

Geneva Tariff Conference, 1947: consisted of tariff negotiations between the participants in the Preparatory Committee of the ***United Nations Conference on Trade and Employment***. About 45,000 ***concessions*** were exchanged. This was the first occasion when tariff negotiations were conducted multilaterally. Negotiations were conducted under the ***principal supplier rule***. In other words, the granting of a concession only had to be considered if the country supplying the largest part of the product made a request for a tariff reduction. The Geneva Tariff Conference is deemed to have been the first round of ***multilateral trade negotiations***. *See also* ***principal supplier right***.

商可以尽早进入市场。就药品而言，开发一种仿制药可能需要多年时间，跳板使企业能够生产仍受专利保护的产品，以满足预先监管要求。但在这一阶段不允许进行商业活动，而且这样作会涉及知识产权侵权。另见*博拉例外(Bolar exception)*、*反向编译(decompilation)*、*知识产权(intellectual property)*、*逆向工程(reverse engineering)*。

Genetically modified micro-organism
转基因微生物

GMM。遗传物质被以在自然界不会发生的方式加以改变的微生物。

Genetically modified organism
转基因生物

GMO。遗传物质被以在自然界不会发生的方式加以改变的生物。

Genetic labelling
基因标签

被一些人提倡的一种产品标签制度，用以表明产品或其组成部分是否经过基因改造。支持者认为这样作符合消费者和使用者的利益。反对者认为这仍是一个不必要的技术性贸易壁垒，因为由于成本原因，许多生产者不愿将转基因谷物与其他谷物加以区分。所有欧盟成员国均被要求在 1997 年 7 月 31 日前颁布基因标签立法，以保证设在成员国中的公司可在必要时使用标签。另见*生态标签(eco-labelling)*、*社会标签(social labelling)*。

Geneva Act of the Lisbon Agreement on Appellations of Origin and Geographical Indications
原产地名称和地理标志里斯本协定日内瓦文本

2015 年在世界知识产权组织(WIPO)中获得通过。除原产地名称外，文本还允许根据《里斯本协定》对地理标志进行国际注册，允许政府间组织在特定条件下加入。

Geneva Agreement on Trade in Bananas
关于香蕉贸易的日内瓦协定

见*香蕉案(banana cases)*。

Geneva Convention
日内瓦公约

《保护录音制品制作者防止未经许可复制其录音制品公约》。公约保护另一成员国的录音制品制造者避免未经许可的复制。“录音制品”指仅听觉可感知的对声音的固定，即录音(唱片、光盘、磁带等)。该词不包括有声电影或录像带。

Geneva mini-ministerial meeting
日内瓦小型部长级会议

见*多哈发展议程(Doha Development Agenda)*。

Geneva Tariff Conference, 1947
1947 年日内瓦关税会议

由联合国贸易与就业会议筹备委员会参加方之间的关税谈判组成。交换了约 45,000 项减让。这是关税谈判首次以多边形式进行。谈判根据主要供应方规则开展。换言之，只有在供应一产品大部分份额的国家提出关税削减请求时，才必须考虑给予减让。日内瓦关税会议被视为是首轮多边贸易谈判。另见*主要供应方权利(principal supplier right)*。

Geneva Tariff Conference, 1955–56: a minor round of multilateral tariff negotiations, largely because the United States Congress had limited the negotiating authority of its delegation. It was the last of the formal ***Tariff Conferences***, and it is deemed the fourth round of ***multilateral trade negotiations***. *See also* ***Dillon Round***.

Geographical indications: GIs. A category of ***indications of source*** enjoying protection under ***intellectual property*** laws or treaties. A geographical indication on a product denotes a close connection between it and the place where it was harvested, processed or produced which gives it a special quality, reputation or characteristic. Some use the term interchangeably with ***appellation of origin***. A ***WIPO*** committee of experts considered in 1990 whether to replace the concepts of "appellations of origin" and "indication of source" with the single term "geographical indication", but it was not able to reach agreement. There seems to be agreement, however, that "appellation of origin" is a narrower term than "geographical indication". Geographical indications are protected by laws or treaties against imitation or misuse. In this way, the good name of a region (e.g. a wine-growing region) built up over a long time cannot be exploited by a company or producers located in another part of the country or abroad. Depending on a country's legal system and the product in question, this can be done through laws concerning ***geographical indications***, ***trademarks*** or under laws governing ***unfair competition*** or ***passing off***. Broadly speaking, the systems of geographical indications for wines and spirits are most developed, partly because it is in this sector that the protection of geographical indications was first implemented in many countries. The protection of geographical indications is sometimes linked with verification of production processes. One cannot assume that all of the wine taken from a bottle bearing a certain geographical indication is necessarily from that area. Mixing regulations often permit the addition of wines brought in from elsewhere. However, the ***European Union*** rules on wine permit member states to make use of a geographical indication conditional on the wine being produced exclusively in the territory whose name it bears. Efforts to protect geographical indications for cheeses through, for example, the ***Stresa Convention***, have been less successful. There is little dispute that geographical indications should be protected unless they have become generic, but opinions on how best to do this vary considerably. Here we can only give an outline of the issues. Intellectual property experts broadly divide the rules for protecting geographical indications into the Lisbon model and the TRIPS model. The Lisbon model is named after the ***Lisbon Agreement*** which did not, until 2015, use the term "geographical indication". Instead it referred to "appellation of origin". In Article 2(1) the Agreement defines appellation of origin as "the geographical name of a country, region, or locality, which serves to designate a product originating therein, the quality and characteristics of which are due exclusively or essentially to the geographical environment, including natural and human factors". Article 2(2) continues that the "country of origin is the country whose

Geneva Tariff Conference, 1955–56

1955—1956 年日内瓦关税会议

小规模多边关税谈判，主要原因是美国国会限制了其代表团的谈判权力。这是最后一次正式的关税会议，也被认为是第 4 轮多边贸易谈判。另见*狄龙回合(Dillon Round)*。

Geographical indications

地理标志

GIs。根据知识产权法律或条约享受保护的一类产地标志。产品的地理标志体现该产品与赋予其特殊质量、声誉或特征的收获、加工或生产地点之间的密切联系。一些人将该词与原产地名称互换使用。世界知识产权组织(WIPO)的一个专家委员会在1990年审议了是否用“地理标志”一词取代“原产地名称”和“产地标志”的概念，但未能达成一致。但是，人们似乎一致认为，“原产地名称”相较于“地理标志”范围更窄。地理标志受到法律或条约的保护免于被模仿或滥用。这样，长期建立起来的一地区(例如葡萄酒产区)的良好声誉就无法被设在该国其他地区或国外的公司或生产商利用。取决于一国法律制度和所涉产品，此点可以通过有关地理标志、商标的法律或根据不正当竞争或假冒商品的法律实现。总体而言，葡萄酒和烈酒的地理标志制度最为成熟，部分由于许多国家在这一部门率先实施了地理标志保护。地理标志保护有时与生产工艺认证相关联。人们不能假设取自带有特定地理标志的一个瓶子里的全部葡萄酒都一定来自该地区。混合规则通常允许添加来自其他地区的葡萄酒。但是，欧盟关于葡萄酒的规定允许成员国使用地理标志的条件是，葡萄酒必须全部产自其名称所在的地区。但是对于奶酪地理标志保护的努力则不太成功，如《斯特雷萨公约》。地理标志应予以保护，除非已经通用化，此点几无争议，但是对于最佳实施方法分歧巨大。在此仅对有关问题作一概述。知识产权专家大体上将保护地理标志的规则分为里斯本模式和TRIPS模式。里斯本模式以《里斯本协定》命名，该协定直至2015年才使用“地理标志”一词，此前使用“原产地名称”一词。该协定第2条第1款将原产地名称定义为“指一个国家、地区或地方的地理名称，用于指示一项产品来源于该地，其质量或特征完全或主要取决于地理环境，包括自然和人为因素”。第2条第2款继续指出，“原属国系指

name, or the country in which is situated the region or locality whose name constitutes the appellation of origin which has given the product its reputation". In 2015 WIPO adopted the ***Geneva Act of the Lisbon Agreement on Appellations of Origin and Geographical Indications*** which extended the coverage of the ***Lisbon Agreement*** to geographical indications. *See also* ***Organization for an International Geographical Indications Network***. The TRIPS model is named after the WTO ***Agreement on Trade-Related Aspects of Intellectual Property Rights*** (TRIPS) which contains two levels of protections. First, Article 22.1 defines geographical indications as "indications which identify a good as originating in the territory of a Member, or a region or locality in that territory, where a given quality or other characteristic is essentially attributable to its geographical origin". Second, a higher level of protection obligations applies for geographical indications for wines and spirits. In Article 23.1 it requires WTO members to afford the legal means to interested parties to prevent the use of geographical indications for wines and spirits not originating in the place indicated by the geographical indication, even where the true origin of the goods is indicated or the geographical indication is translated or accompanied by expressions such as "kind, "type, "style", "imitation", etc. This is close to the language on appellations of origin in the Lisbon Agreement. For geographical indications identifying products other than wines and spirits, the TRIPS Agreement requires its members to have in place the legal means for interested parties to prevent the use of a designation that indicates or suggests that the good in question originates in an area other than the true place of origin or any use constituting an act of ***unfair competition***. Making provision for interested parties to protect their geographical indications does not necessarily mean that WTO members have to pass new laws, but sometimes legislative action may be necessary. One difference between the two models is that under the Lisbon Agreement the quality and characteristics of a product must be due exclusively or essentially to the geographical environment, including natural and human factors. In the TRIPS model the quality, reputation or other characteristic of a product must be attributable essentially to its geographical origin. The Lisbon model therefore would appear to be more strict or more narrow than the TRIPS model in that the latter's definition of geographical indications would seem to capture a greater number of them. Some see the relationship between the Lisbon provisions and the TRIPS provisions as contentious. They say that the TRIPS provisions should supersede the Lisbon disciplines to the extent that there is an inconsistency between them. The TRIPS Agreement provides some exceptions to the protection of geographical indications, such as the possibility in Article 24 to continue to use a geographical indication of another country identifying wines or spirits if this use had lasted for at least the ten years preceding the conclusion of the TRIPS Agreement. Members of this Agreement are not obliged to afford protection to a geographical indication of another country if it is not protected in its country of origin. The administration of systems for the protection of geographical indications has always required a

其名称构成原产地名称而赋予产品以声誉的国家或者地区或地方所在的国家”。2015年，WIPO通过了《原产地名称和地理标志里斯本协定日内瓦文本》，将《里斯本协定》的涵盖范围扩大到地理标志。另见*国际地理标志网络组织(Organization for an International Geographical Indications Network)*。TRIPS模式以WTO《与贸易有关的知识产权协定》(TRIPS)命名，该协定包含两层保护：一是第22条第1款将地理标志定义为“识别一货物源自一成员领土内或该领土内一地区或地方的标志”。二是更高水平的保护义务适用于葡萄酒和烈酒的地理标志。第23条第1款要求WTO成员向利害关系方提供法律手段，以防止将地理标志用于并非源自所涉地理标志所标明地方的葡萄酒和烈酒，即使已标明货物的真实原产地或该地理标志用于翻译中或附有“种类”、“类型”、“特色”、“仿制”等词语。这与《里斯本协定》中关于原产地名称的措辞非常接近。对于识别葡萄酒和烈酒以外产品的地理标志，《TRIPS协定》要求成员向利害关系方提供法律手段，以防止使用标明或暗示所涉货物源自真实原产地之外的一地理区域的名称或构成不正当竞争行为的任何使用。对保护利害关系方的地理标志作出规定并不一定意味着WTO成员必须通过新的法律，但有时可能需要采取立法行动。这两种模式之间的一点不同是，根据《里斯本协定》，产品的质量和特征必须完全或基本取决于地理环境，包括自然和人为因素。在TRIPS模式中，产品的质量、声誉或其他特征必须主要取决于其地理来源。因此，里斯本模式似乎比TRIPS模式更严格或更有限，因为后者对地理标志的定义似乎涵盖了更多地理标志。一些人认为里斯本条款和TRIPS条款之间的关系存在争议。他们认为在两者之间存在不一致之处，TRIPS条款应该取代里斯本条款。《TRIPS协定》在保护地理标志方面规定了一些例外，例如第24条规定，如果在缔结《TRIPS协定》之前至少10年一直使用另一个国家识别葡萄酒或烈酒的标志，则可以继续使用该地理标志。如果另一国的产品地理标志在其原属国中未受到保护，本协定成员无义务为其提供保护。地理标志保护体系的

degree of flexibility. One reason for this is the occurrence of ***homonymous geographical indications*** (the same name occurring in more than one country). In some cases geographical indications can turn into ***semi-generic geographical indications*** or ***generic geographical indications***. Once this happens, only a most determined effort can turn the situation around, but in most cases it will be a lost cause. A complicated situation arises when a name of a product is deemed to be the equivalent of a geographical indication even though it is not a place name. This is the case, for example, with *Liebfraumilch* or *Liebfrauenmilch* (Milk of Our Lady), a German white wine of varying quality. Originally the name was used for wines coming from the vineyards of the Liebfrauenkirche (Church of Our Lady) in Worms. German law now requires that wine carrying this name must come from the Rheinhessen, Rheinpfalz, Rheingau or Nahe regions. At issue here is not whether the owners of the name *Liebfraumilch* should enjoy protection against its unlawful use, but whether a name that is clearly no longer a geographical indication should be treated as one because the product bearing it must always come from a defined area. In other words, it is a proxy for a geographical indication. One may contrast this with, for example, the name *Château Giscours*, a French wine. In this case it is possible, through reliance on title registers, maps and local knowledge, to define exactly the locations that are entitled to use this name. At the ***Doha Ministerial Conference*** WTO members agreed to negotiate "the establishment of a multilateral system of notification and registration of geographical indications for wines and spirits" by the time of the fifth ministerial conference. They also agreed that issues related to the ***extension of protection for geographical indications*** provided for in Article 23 to products other than wines and spirits will be addressed as an implementation issue. Negotiations are now under way. [Lisbon Agreement for the Protection of Appellations of Origin and their International Registration; WIPO SCT/5/3, SCT/8/4, SCT/9/4; Abbott et al. 1999, Addor and Grazioli 2002, Audier 2000, Rangnekar 2003]

Geographical names: many goods traded internationally have displayed on them or their packaging their geographical origin. Audier notes that "a geographical name applied to a product can mean three different things: an ***indication of source***, with no special implications in terms of the product's characteristics, and a ***geographical indication*** or ***appellation of origin***, which implies that the product will have a quality or characteristic attributable to its place of origin". The broadest of these names, according to ***WIPO*** usage, are indications of source. More narrow are geographical indications. Narrower still are appellations of origin. The use of "denomination" in the ***Stresa Convention*** seems to be roughly equal to geographical indication. In the ***European Community*** the term ***protected designation of origin*** is evidently more narrow than a ***protected geographical indication***. The definition of geographical names can overlap in laws and treaties. Geographical names themselves are used in different ways. Consider an example given by the International Trademark Association: Swiss cheese, Napa Valley chardonnay and Philadelphia cream cheese. The word

管理往往需要一定程度的灵活性。其中一个原因是同音异义地理标志的出现(在一个以上国家使用的相同地理标志)。在一些情况下，地理标志会转变为半通用地理标志或通用地理标志。一旦此种情况发生，只有最坚定的努力才能扭转局面，但在大多数情况下都不会成功。当一产品的名称被认为等同于一地理标志时，即使它不是一个地名，也会出现复杂情况。例如，Liebfraumilch或Liebfrauenmilch(圣母之奶)是一种具有不同品质的德国白葡萄酒。最初，这一名字用以形容来自Liebfrauenkirche (圣母教堂)葡萄园的葡萄酒。德国法律现在要求，带有这一名称的葡萄酒必须来自莱茵黑森、莱茵法尔茨、莱茵高或纳厄河地区。争议的问题不是Liebfraumilch这一名称的所有者是否应得到保护免于非法使用，而是一个显然不再是地理标志的名称是否应被视为地理标志，因为带有这一名称的产品必须始终来自一特定地区。换言之，它是地理标志的替代物。人们可以将其与法国葡萄酒名称Château Giscours(斯基古酒堡)进行对比。在此种情况下，可以通过产权登记、地图和当地知识，准确定义有权使用这一名称的地点。在WTO多哈部长级会议上，WTO成员同意在第5届部长级会议之前就“建立葡萄酒和烈酒地理标志通报和注册的多边制度”进行谈判。成员还同意，将第23条中所规定的地理标志保护扩大至葡萄酒和烈酒以外的产品作为一个实施问题加以处理。该谈判还在进行中。

Geographical names
地理名称

许多在国际间交易的货物自身或包装上标明其地理来源。奥迪尔指出：“适用于一产品的地理名称可以表明三种不同涵义：对产品的特征没有特别含义的产地标志，表明产品的质量或特征取决于其原产地的地理标志或原产地名称。”根据世界知识产权组织(WIPO)的用法，这些名称中涵盖范围最广的是产地标志。含义相对较窄的是地理标志，含义更窄的是原产地名称。在《斯特雷萨公约》中“命名”一词的使用大致等同于地理标志。在欧洲共同体，原产地命名保护一词的含义显然比地理标志保护更窄。地理名称的定义在法律和条约中可能出现重叠。地理名称本身的使用有不同方式。国际商标协会提出的一个例

"Swiss" is used as a generic expression, "Napa Valley" is a geographical indication and "Philadelphia" is used as a ***trademark***. The commercial implications flowing from the three categories are considerable. Any dairy factory can choose to make a cheese loosely resembling the original *Emmental* cheese, though the characteristic large holes are often missing, and sell it as "Swiss cheese". The "Philadelphia cheese" trademark may only be used by its rightful owner who can use it to produce the cheese wherever this is commercially attractive. The owner can also insist that licensed producers make the product in accordance with his standards. "Napa Valley wine", however, may only originate in the territory described as Napa Valley, and this results in a theoretical production ceiling. Many wineries are able to use this geographical indication, and this means that the quality and characteristics of the wines produced in the area show marked variations. *See also* ***extension of protection for geographical indications***, ***generic geographical indications***, ***Geneva Act of the Lisbon Agreement on Appellations of Origin and Geographical Indications***, ***homonymous geographical indications***, ***multilateral system of notification and registration of geographical indications*** and ***semi-generic geographical indications***. [Audier 2000; International Trademark Association 2000; WIPO SCT/8/4]

Georgetown Agreement: adopted on 6 June 1975 in Georgetown, Guyana. It established the group of ***ACP states***. It was revised on 26 November 1992 with the objective of promoting the aims of the ***Lomé Convention***. Membership is open to all states that are members of the Convention, now the ***ACP-EU Partnership Agreement***. Cuba is a member of the Georgetown Agreement, but not the ACP-EU Partnership Agreement. The Convention's secretariat is in Brussels.

German imports of sardines: in 1952 Norway brought a complaint to the GATT concerning the alleged discrimination by Germany on imports of *clupea pilchardus* (sardines), *clupea sprattus* (sprats) and *clupea harengus* (herring). In the course of its economic liberalization programme, Germany had decided to place sardines on a list allowing unrestricted imports, but sprats and herring remained subject to ***quantitative restrictions***. This led to a substantial decrease of Norwegian exports of sprats and herring to Germany. The ***panel*** was asked by Norway to find that the German measures were in conflict with GATT Articles I:1 (General Most-Favoured-Nation Treatment) and XIII:1 (Nondiscriminatory Administration of Quantitative Restrictions) which require imports of ***like products*** from different countries to receive similar treatment. It considered whether sardines, sprats and herrings should be considered like products, and it noted that Germany in its accession negotiations had always thought the three to be separate products. The panel decided that insufficient evidence had been presented to permit a judgement of discriminatory treatment. *See also* ***Brazilian unroasted coffee***. [GATT BISD 1S]

Glass-Steagall Act: the United States Bank Act of 1933, largely repealed in 1999. It separated commercial and investment banking. Banks, including foreign bank branches and subsidiaries, could not underwrite or deal in securities of non-governmental issuers. *See also* ***financial services***.

子是瑞士奶酪、纳帕谷霞多丽和费城奶油奶酪。“瑞士”一词用作通用表述，“纳帕谷”是地理标志，“费城”用作商标。这三个类别所带来的商业影响相当可观。任何一家奶制品厂都可以选择生产一种与最原始的埃门塔尔奶酪大致相似、但经常缺少标志性大洞的奶酪，并将其以“瑞士奶酪”出售。“费城奶酪”商标只能被其合法所有者使用，他们可以在这种奶酪具有商业吸引力的任何地点生产奶酪。商标所有者还可以要求授权生产者按照其标准进行生产。但是，“纳帕谷葡萄酒”只能源自名为纳帕谷的地区，这就形成了理论上的生产上限。许多酿酒厂能够使用这一地理标志，这即意味着该地区生产的葡萄酒的质量和特征显示明显差异。另见***地理标志保护扩大****(extension of protection for geographical indications)*、***通用地理标志****(generic geographical indications)*、***原产地名称和地理标志里斯本协定日内瓦文本****(Geneva Act of the Lisbon Agreement on Appellations of Origin and Geographical Indications)*、***同音异义地理标志****(homonymous geographical indications)*、***地理标志通报和注册多边制度****(multilateral system of notification and registration of geographical indications)*、***半通用地理标志****(semi-generic geographical indications)*。

Georgetown Agreement
乔治敦协定

1975年6月6日在圭亚那乔治敦通过。该协定建立了非加太地区国家。后于1992年11月26日修订，目的是促进《洛美公约》的目标。成员资格对属《洛美公约》成员的所有国家开放，即现在的《非加太地区国家与欧盟伙伴关系协定》。古巴是《乔治敦协定》成员，但不是《非加太地区国家与欧盟伙伴关系协定》成员。协定秘书处设在布鲁塞尔。

German imports of sardines
德国沙丁鱼进口案

1952年挪威向GATT提出起诉，指控德国歧视进口沙丁鱼、小鲱鱼和鲱鱼。在德国经济自由化计划进程中，决定将沙丁鱼列入允许无限制进口的产品清单，但小鲱鱼和鲱鱼仍然受到数量限制。这导致挪威对德国出口的小鲱鱼和鲱鱼大幅减少。挪威要求专家组认定，德国的措施违反GATT第1条第1款(普遍最惠国待遇)和第13条第1款(数量限制的非歧视管理)，以上两项条款要求同等对待来自不同国家进口的同类产品。专家组审议了是否应将沙丁鱼、小鲱鱼和鲱鱼视为同类产品的问题，指出德国在其加入谈判中始终将这三种鱼视为不同产品。专家组认为没有足够证据作出存在歧视性待遇的判断。另见***巴西未焙炒咖啡案****(Brazilian unroasted coffee)*。

Glass-Steagall Act
格拉斯-斯蒂格尔法

美国《1933年银行法》，1999年基本废除。该法将商业银行与投资银行区别对待。包括外国银行分行及附属公司在内的银行不能承销或交易非政府发行人的证券。另见***金融服务****(financial services)*。

Global Action Menu for Investment Facilitation: *see* ***UNCTAD Global Action Menu for Investment Facilitation***.

Global Alliance for Sugar Trade Reform and Liberalization: *see* ***Global Sugar Alliance***.

Global Alliance for Trade Facilitation: a collaboration of international organizations, governments and business to enhance ***trade facilitation*** implementation by bringing together the public and private sectors as equal partners and to address delays and unnecessary red tape at borders. It seeks to assist developing and ***least-developed countries***. *See also* ***Agreement on Trade Facilitation***. [tradefacilitation.org]

Global commons: defined by the ***World Commission on Environment and Development*** as the oceans, outer space and Antarctica, i.e. those parts of the planet that fall outside national jurisdictions. *See also* ***trade and environment***.

Global Compact: proposed by the Secretary-General of the United Nations to business leaders at the ***World Economic Forum*** on 31 January 1999. It consists of ten principles: (1) support and respect the protection of international human rights within the sphere of influence of business, (2) make sure corporations are not complicit in human rights abuses, (3) freedom of association and effective recognition of the right to collective bargaining, (4) elimination of all forms of forced and compulsory labour, (5) effective abolition of ***child labour***, (6) elimination of discrimination in respect of employment and occupation, (7) support a precautionary approach to environmental challenges, (8) undertake initiatives to promote greater environmental responsibility, (9) encourage the development and diffusion of environmentally-friendly technologies, and (10) business should work against corruption in all its forms, including extortion and bribery. *See also* ***trade and environment***, ***trade and human rights*** and ***trade and labour standards***.

Global Environment Facility: GEF. A mechanism for the provision of grants and concessional funding for programmes protecting the global environment and promoting sustainable economic growth. It concentrates on climate change, biological diversity, international waters and stratospheric ozone. GEF projects and programmes and funds for them are awarded and supervised by the ***World Bank***, the ***United Nations Development Programme*** (UNDP) and ***UN Environment Programme*** (UNEP). *See also* ***trade and environment***.

Global financial crisis: GFC. A period of extreme stress in global financial markets and banking systems between the middle of 2007 and early 2009. Some date the start of the GFC to the collapse of Lehman Brothers, a financial services firm, on 15 September 2008, but obviously events had been set in train much earlier. Some economists consider the GFC to have been the worst financial crisis since the Great Depression of the late 1920s and the early 1930s. The GFC had a range of causes, but excessive risk-taking in a favourable macroeconomic environment, increased borrowings by banks and investors and policy errors seem to have been the main causes. *See also* ***Basel III***.

Global Action Menu for Investment Facilitation
全球投资便利化行动清单

见*UNCTAD全球投资便利化行动清单(UNCTAD Global Action Menu for Investment Facilitation)*。

Global Alliance for Sugar Trade Reform and Liberalization
全球糖业贸易改革和自由化联盟

见*全球糖业联盟(Global Sugar Alliance)*。

Global Alliance for Trade Facilitation
全球贸易便利化联盟

国际组织、政府和企业之间的合作，通过将公共部门和私营部门作为平等伙伴聚集在一起以加强贸易便利化的实施，并处理边境上的延误和不必要的繁文缛节。联盟寻求帮助发展中国家和最不发达国家。另见*贸易便利化协定(Agreement on Trade Facilitation)*。

Global commons
全球公域

世界环境与发展委员会将其定义为海洋、外太空和南极洲，即地球上不属于国家管辖范围的部分。另见*贸易与环境(trade and environment)*。

Global Compact
全球契约

联合国秘书长1999年1月31日在世界经济论坛上向商界领袖提出。包括10项原则：(1)在企业的影响范围内支持和尊重对国际人权的保护；(2)保证公司不参与侵犯人权；(3)结社自由和有效承认集体谈判的权利；(4)消除一切形式的强迫和强制劳动；(5)有效废除童工；(6)消除就业和职业歧视；(7)支持对环境挑战采取预防性措施；(8)采取主动行动，承担更大的环境责任；(9)鼓励开发和传播环境友好型技术；以及(10)企业应反对各种形式的腐败，包括敲诈和贿赂。另见*贸易与环境(trade and environment)*、*贸易与人权(trade and human rights)*、*贸易与劳工标准(trade and labour standards)*。

Global Environment Facility
全球环境基金

GEF。为保护全球环境和促进可持续经济增长项目提供赠款和优惠资金的机制。关注气候变化、生物多样性、国际水域和臭氧层。GEF项目和计划及用于项目和计划的基金由世界银行、联合国开发计划署(UNDP)和联合国环境规划署(UNEP)授予和监督。另见*贸易与环境(trade and environment)*。

Global financial crisis
全球金融危机

GFC。2007年年中至2009年年初全球金融市场和银行系统面临极度压力的时期。一些人将全球金融危机的发生日期定为2008年9月15日金融服务公司雷曼兄弟的倒闭，但显然事件发生的时间要早得多。一些经济学家认为，此次全球金融危机是自20世纪20年代末、30年代初的大萧条以来最严重的金融危机。全球金融危机有一系列原因，但是在有利的宏观经济环境中过度冒险、银行和投资者借款增加以及政策失误似乎是主要原因。另见*第三版巴塞尔协议(Basel III)*。

Global Food Market Information Group: consists of technical representatives from countries participating in the ***Agricultural Market Information System***. It provides data regarding the supply and demand as well as probable short-term positions for wheat, rice and soybeans. It is supported by a secretariat located in the ***Food and Agriculture Organization*** in Rome.

Global Forum on Steel Excess Capacity: GFSEC. A group of thirty-three countries and regions, drawn from ***OECD*** and ***G20*** members, established in 2016 to address overcapacity in the steel industry. The GFSEC is facilitated by the OECD, and it reports annually to G20 ministers.

Global Green New Deal: a proposal discussed in the 2019 UNCTAD ***Trade and Development Report*** (TDR). It postulates that a successful response to climate change would result in many environmental benefits. Achieving such aims would require a massive new wave of investment in renewing and creating new technologies on a global scale. The TDR notes that this wave of green investment would be a major source of income and employment growth which would contribute to global macroeconomic recovery. Funding such a policy would be a major challenge requiring the mobilization of multilateral funding, governmental initiatives and private foreign capital. Similar aims and mechanisms were proposed in *A Global Green New Deal*, a report issued in 2009 by the United Nations Environment Programme (UNEP). *See also* ***global new deal***.

Global Information Infrastructure: GII. A proposal formulated by the United States in 1994 for international cooperation in the development of a more efficient and more versatile global telecommunications and information network. Five basic principles would have governed the establishment of the GII: encouraging private sector investment, promoting competition, providing open access, creating a flexible regulatory environment, and ensuring universal service. *See also* ***Okinawa Charter on Global Information Society***.

Globality: sometimes used to refer to one of the general negotiating principles that form part of the ***Punta del Este Declaration*** that launched the ***Uruguay Round***. The principle held that the launching, conduct and implementation of the negotiations were to be treated as parts of a ***single undertaking***. This principle was often expressed in the phrase "nothing is agreed until everything is agreed".

Globalization: from an economist's point of view, at its simplest, a decline in costs of doing business across space. The term describes the increasing integration of national economic systems through growth in international trade, investment and capital flows. Definitions of globalization, both benevolent and malevolent, are too numerous to list here. The ***World Commission on the Social Dimension of Globalization*** says in its report that "the term 'globalization' has acquired many emotive connotations ... At one extreme, [it] is seen as an irresistible and benign force for delivering economic prosperity to people throughout the world. At the other, it is blamed as a source of all contemporary ills". Many analysts distinguish globalization from ***internationalization*** which they tend to see as more benign. In reality, globalization and

Global Food Market Information Group
全球食品市场信息组

由参与农产品市场信息系统国家的技术代表组成。提供有关小麦、大米和大豆供应、需求以及可能的短期仓位数据。由设在罗马的粮农组织(FAO)内的一个秘书处提供支持。

Global Forum on Steel Excess Capacity
钢铁产能过剩全球论坛

GFSEC。由来自经济合作与发展组织(OECD)和20国集团的33个国家和地区组成的集团，2016年成立，旨在处理钢铁行业产能过剩问题。GFSEC由OECD推动，每年向20国集团部长汇报工作。

Global Green New Deal
全球绿色新政

联合国贸易与发展会议(UNCTAD) 2019年《贸易与发展报告》中所讨论的提案。提案假定成功应对气候变化将带来许多环境效益。要实现这些目标，就需要在全球范围内进行更新和创新技术的新一轮大规模投资。报告指出，此轮绿色投资将是收入和就业增长的主要来源，将有助于全球宏观经济复苏。资助这一政策将是一个重大挑战，需要动员多边资金、政府倡议和私人外国资本。联合国环境规划署(UNEP)在2009年发布的一份报告《全球绿色新政》中提出了类似的目标和机制。*另见全球新政(global new deal)*。

Global Information Infrastructure
全球信息基础设施

GII。美国1994年制定的一项提案，旨在开展国际合作，建立一个更高效和更灵活的全球电信和信息网络。建立全球信息基础设施应遵循五项基本原则：鼓励私营部门投资、促进竞争、提供开放准入、创造灵活的监管环境和保证普遍服务。*另见全球信息社会冲绳宪章(Okinawa Charter on Global Information Society)*。

Globality
全球性

有时用于指构成发起乌拉圭回合的《埃斯特角城宣言》一部分的普遍谈判原则之一。该原则认为，谈判的发起、开展和实施应被视为一揽子承诺的一部分。这一原则经常被表述为"所有内容达成一致才能达成协议"。

Globalization
全球化

从经济学家的角度看，最简单的讲，就是跨越空间作生意的成本降低。该词描述了各国经济体制通过国际贸易、投资和资本流动的增长而日益融合。关于全球化的定义，无论褒义还是贬义，数量众多难以全部列出。全球化社会问题世界委员会在其报告中指出，"'全球化'一词产生许多情感内涵……在一个极端，[它]被视为为全世界人民带来经济繁荣的一种不可抗拒的良性力量。在另一个极端，它被指责为当代所有弊病的根源。"许多分析家将全球化与国际化区分开来，他们倾向于认为国际化更为温和。而实际上，全球化和国际化并

internationalization exist side by side. Globalization is promoted by rapid improvements in international transport and communications and the lowering of barriers to trade and investment. But many do not see globalization simply as an economic matter. This is because one of its effects is the relocation and integration of production processes among countries, reflecting the most appropriate technology and the best production cost. Globalization implies therefore a degree of reciprocal action and interdependence and a greater exposure to global economic developments, described by some as a loss of independence by national governments. Greater participation in the international economy has social and political implications. Inflows of foreign investment into developing countries cause changes in employment and national income. Opponents of globalization claim that it increases the gap not only between rich and poor countries, but also among the peoples especially of developing countries. Some claim that globalization simply means corporations chasing ever cheaper labour and raw materials, and governments willing to ignore consumer, labour and environmental laws. To holders of this view, globalization is an insidious result of market forces, the economic power of ***multinational corporations*** and the growth of world trade. This is the ***race-to-the-bottom argument***. Holders of this view sometimes also tend to look to restricted trade and investment flows as the preferred remedy. Defenders of globalization say poverty has many causes, including weak and corrupt governmental. They claim that developing countries that have opened their economies have seen the greatest reductions in poverty, and they cast doubt on the notion of rising global inequality. David Dollar points out that since 1980 the growth rates of developing countries have accelerated, that the number of poor people in the world has declined significantly, that global inequality among citizens of the world has seen a modest decline, that there is no general trend towards higher inequality within countries, and that wage inequality is rising worldwide. He says that solutions may depend partly on improved economic development strategies of developing countries and better access by them to the markets of developed countries. In other words, the solution to the problems caused by globalism, assuming that one accepts this proposition, lies in fact in greater global integration and more globalization. *See also* ***anti-globalization***, ***autarky***, ***borderless world***, ***deindustrialization***, ***delocalization***, ***hyperglobalization***, ***trade and poverty*** and ***Washington Consensus***. [Dollar 2002, Kohl 2003, Stiglitz 2002, Wolf 2004, World Commission on the Social Dimension of Globalization 2004]

Globally Harmonized System of Classification and Labelling of Chemicals: GHS. First adopted in 2002 and revised several times since. It aims to provide all countries with a structure to classify and label hazardous chemicals with the objectives (a) to enhance to enhance the protection of human health and environment by providing an internationally comprehensible system for hazard communication, (b) to provide a recognized framework for those countries without an existing system, (c) to reduce the need for testing and evaluation of chemicals, and (d) to facilitate international trade in chemicals whose hazards

存。国际运输和通信的快速发展及贸易和投资壁垒的降低促进了全球化的发展。但是很多人并不把全球化简单地视为经济问题。这是因为其效果之一是生产过程在各国之间重新布局和整合，反映出最适合的技术和最佳生产成本。全球化因此意味着一定程度的相互作用和相互依存，并更多地受到全球经济发展的影响，被一些人认为是国家政府独立性的丧失。更多参与国际经济产生了社会和政治影响。流入发展中国家的外国投资带来了就业和国民收入的变化。全球化的反对者声称，全球化不仅增加了富国与穷国之间的差距，而且特别加大了发展中国家人民内部的差距。一些人声称，全球化仅仅意味着大公司追逐更廉价的劳动力和原材料，而政府会忽视消费者、劳工和环境法律。持这种观点的人认为，全球化是市场力量、跨国公司的经济实力和世界贸易增长带来的潜在结果。这就是竞次论。持有这种观点的人有时也倾向于把限制贸易和投资流动作为首选的救济措施。全球化的捍卫者认为贫困有多种原因，包括政府的软弱和腐败。他们认为，经济已经开放的发展中国家的贫困得到最大幅度削减，他们对全球不平等加剧的概念表示怀疑。大卫·多拉尔指出，自 1980 年以来，发展中国家的增长速度加快，世界贫困人口数量大幅下降，世界人口之间的全球不平等程度有所下降，各国国内并未出现更加不平等的总体趋势，而世界范围内的工资不平等正在加剧。他认为，问题的解决办法可能部分取决于发展中国家改善经济发展战略及发展中国家对发达国家市场的更好准入。换言之，全球主义所引发问题的解决办法在于更广泛的全球一体化和全球化，假设有人接受这一命题的话。另见*反全球化(anti-globalization)*、*经济闭关自守(autarky)*、*无国界世界(borderless world)*、*去工业化(deindustrialization)*、*去本地化(delocalization)*、*超全球化(hyperglobalization)*、*贸易与贫困(trade and poverty)*、*华盛顿共识(Washington Consensus)*。

Globally Harmonized System of Classification and Labelling of Chemicals
全球化学品统一分类和标签制度

GHS。2002 年首次通过，此后多次修订。旨在为所有国家提供一个危险化学品分类和标签体系，目标为：(a)通过提供国际通用的危险通报系统，加强对人类健康和环境的保护；(b)为没有现行系统的国家提供公认的框架；(c)减少对化学品进行测试和评估的需求；以及(d)为已在国际上进行危害正确评估与

have been properly assessed and identified on an international basis. The GHS is based on harmonized criteria for classifying substances and mixtures according to their health, environmental and physical hazards, and harmonized hazard communication elements, including requirements for labelling and safety data sheets. It covers all hazardous chemicals, but it does not include establishment of uniform test methods or promotion of further testing. The GHS is administered by a secretariat located within the United Nations ***Economic Commission for Europe***. [unece.org]

Global Negotiations: full name *Global Negotiations Relating to International Cooperation for Development*. The plan for global negotiations grew out of the proposals for a ***New International Economic Order***. The negotiations were expected to be launched by the ***United Nations General Assembly*** in 1980 after more than three years of consultations on a possible agenda, procedures and timeframes, but in the end this did not happen. *See also* ***Charter of Economic Rights and Duties of States*** and ***North–South dialogue***.

Global new deal: a proposal raised in the 2017 UNCTAD ***Trade and Development Report*** (TDR). The Report attempts to develop a programmatic understanding from the perspective of developing countries on how the ***Sustainable Development Goals*** are to be achieved. It notes that recovery, regulation and redistribution "remain at the heart of any attempt to forge more inclusive and sustainable growth and development paths". The main elements of a global new deal would include (a) an end to austerity and recognition of the significance of increased public spending, (b) expansion of fiscal space since higher public spending would need to be financed somehow, and (c) regulating rentier capitalism to increase capital formation in productive investment. The TDR recognizes that all of this would be challenging. [www.unctad.org]

Global Plan of Action for the Conservation and Sustainable Utilization of Plant Genetic Resources for Food and Agriculture: adopted in Leipzig on 23 June 1996 under the auspices of the ***Food and Agriculture Organization***. The Global Plan is based on the view that countries are interdependent in respect of plant genetic resources for food and agriculture. Its main aims are (a) to ensure the conservation of plant genetic resources for food and agriculture as a basis for ***food security***, (b) to promote sustainable utilization of plant genetic resources for food and agriculture, (c) to promote a fair and equitable sharing of the benefits arising from the use of plant genetic resources, (d) to assist countries and institutions responsible for conserving and using plant genetic resources to identify priorities for action, and (e) to strengthen national, regional and international programmes for the conservation and utilization of plant genetic resources for food and agriculture. *See also* ***International Treaty on Plant Genetic Resources for Food and Agriculture*** and ***International Undertaking on Plant Genetic Resources***.

Global quota: a limit set by a country on the total quantity of a product that may be imported or exported within a specified period, usually one year. *See also* ***tariff quota***.

识别的化学品的国际贸易提供便利。GHS 基于根据健康、环境和物理危害对物质和混合物进行分类的统一标准，包括标签和安全数据单要求的统一危害通报要素。涵盖所有危险化学品，但不包括制定统一测试方法或促进进一步测试。GHS 由联合国欧洲经济委员会中的一个秘书处进行管理。

Global Negotiations

全球谈判

全称为“关于国际发展合作的全球谈判”。全球谈判计划源自国际经济新秩序建议。在就可能的议程、程序和时间表进行 3 年多磋商后，原计划由联合国大会于 1980 年发起谈判，但最终未能实现。另见*各国经济权利与义务宪章(Charter of Economic Rights and Duties of States)*、*南北对话(North–South dialogue)*。

Global new deal

全球新政

联合国贸易与发展会议(UNCTAD) 2017 年《贸易与发展报告》中提出的一项建议。报告试图从发展中国家的角度，对如何实现可持续发展目标形成程序性理解。报告指出，恢复、监管和再分配“仍然是任何旨在形成更具包容性和可持续增长和发展途径尝试的核心”。全球新政的主要要素包括：(a)结束紧缩政策，承认增加公共开支的重要性；(b)扩大财政空间，因为增加公共开支需要以某种方式融资；以及(c)规范寻租资本主义，以增加生产性投资的资本形成。报告指出以上所有内容都具有挑战性。

Global Plan of Action for the Conservation and Sustainable Utilization of Plant Genetic Resources for Food and Agriculture

全球粮食和农业植物遗传资源保存及可持续利用行动计划

在粮农组织(FAO)主持下于 1996 年 6 月 23 日在莱比锡通过。全球计划基于以下观点，即各国在粮食和农业植物遗传资源方面是相互依存的。主要目标为：(a)保证粮食和农业植物遗传资源的保护，以此作为粮食安全的基础；(b)促进粮食和农业植物遗传资源的可持续利用；(c)促进公平和公正地分享利用植物遗传资源所产生的效益；(d)帮助国家和负责保护利用植物遗传资源的机构确定行动优先事项；以及(e)加强关于粮食和农业植物遗传资源的保护和利用的国家、区域和国际计划。另见*粮食与农业植物遗传资源国际条约(International Treaty on Plant Genetic Resources for Food and Agriculture)*、*植物遗传资源国际承诺(International Undertaking on Plant Genetic Resources)*。

Global quota

全球配额

一国对一产品在规定期限内(通常为 1 年)进口或出口总量设定的限额。另见*关税配额(tariff quota)*。

Global reciprocity: *see* ***multilateralism***.

Global safeguards: the safeguard measures available through GATT Article XIX. *See* ***safeguards***.

Global Sugar Alliance: formally Global Alliance for Sugar Trade Reform and Liberalization. A group of sugar producers which aims to reform international trade in sugar. It was formed in 1999. Its members include producers in Australia, Brazil, Canada, Chile, Colombia, Guatemala and Thailand.

Global System of Trade Preferences: *see* ***GSTP***.

Global Trade Alert: GTA. A policy-oriented and research initiative of the Centre for Economic Policy Research in London. It provides comprehensive information on state interventions affecting trade in goods and services, foreign investment and labour force migration. [globaltradealert.org]

Global Trade Helpdesk: a multi-year development project managed jointly by the ***International Trade Centre***, ***UNCTAD*** and the ***WTO*** to build a global platform with up-to-date market information facilitating trade and investment decisions of MSMEs (micro-, small and medium-sized enterprises). The project's objectives are (a) to provide a unique entry point to existing trade-related information, (b) to translate trade-related information into trade intelligence, and (c) to raise awareness and assist MSMEs in the use of trade information and intelligence. [helpmetrade.org]

Global Trade Point Network: *see* ***World Trade Point Federation***.

Global value chain: GVC. Describes the range of value-added activities as across the world required to bring a good or a service from design to production and marketing. Each stage and each location adds further value to the product. Hence a GVC is a part of the process of ***globalization***. *See also* ***value-added***.

Good faith: also referred to as *bona fides*. Malcolm N. Shaw calls it "perhaps the most important general principle underpinning many international legal rules". He adds that "[i]n the absence of a certain minimum belief that states will perform their treaty obligations in good faith, there is no reason for countries to enter into such obligations with each other". The principle is defined in the ***Vienna Convention on the Law of Treaties*** to the effect that a state is "obliged to refrain from acts which would defeat the object and purpose of a treaty". The WTO ***Dispute Settlement Understanding*** exhorts members to enter and engage in ***consultation***, ***dispute settlement*** and ***arbitration*** procedures in good faith. The Understanding does not describe the meaning of "good faith". One panel report (*United States – Section 310*) thought it was "notoriously difficult, or at least delicate, to construe the requirement that a treaty shall be interpreted in good faith . . . not least because of the possible imputation of bad faith to one of the parties". The ***Appellate Body*** observed in *United States – Continued Dumping and Subsidy Act Offset Act of 2000* that "[n]othing, however, in the covered agreements supports the conclusion that simply because a WTO member is found to have violated a substantive treaty provision, it has therefore not acted in good faith. In our view, it would be necessary to prove more than

Global reciprocity

全球互惠

见*多边主义(multilateralism)*。

Global safeguards

全球保障措施

根据 GATT 第 19 条可采取的保障措施。另见*保障措施(safeguards)*。

Global Sugar Alliance

全球糖业联盟

正式名称为"全球糖业贸易改革和自由化联盟"。旨在改革国际食糖贸易的糖生产者组织，1999 年成立，成员包括澳大利亚、巴西、加拿大、智利、哥伦比亚、危地马拉和泰国的生产商。

Global System of Trade Preferences

全球贸易优惠制

见*全球贸易优惠制(GSTP)*。

Global Trade Alert

全球贸易预警

GTA。伦敦经济政策研究中心提出的政策导向和研究倡议。提供影响货物贸易和服务贸易、外国投资和劳动力迁移的国家干预的全面信息。

Global Trade Helpdesk

全球贸易服务台

由国际贸易中心、联合国贸易与发展会议(UNCTAD)和 WTO 联合管理的多年发展项目，目的是建立一个全球平台，提供最新市场信息，促进中小微企业的贸易和投资决策。该项目的目标为：(a)为现有与贸易有关的信息提供独特的接入点；(b)将与贸易有关的信息转化为贸易情报；以及(c)提高认识并协助中小微企业使用贸易信息和情报。

Global Trade Point Network

全球贸易点网络

见*世界贸易网点联盟(World Trade Point Federation)*。

Global value chain

全球价值链

GVC。描述将一货物或一服务自设计、生产至销售的跨越世界的一系列增值活动。产品价值在每一阶段和每一地点均增加。因此，全球价值链是全球化进程的组成部分。另见*增值(value-added)*。

Good faith

善意/真诚

马尔科姆·N. 肖称之为"也许是支撑许多国际法律规则最重要的总体原则"。他补充称，"如果缺乏关于各国善意履行其条约义务的最低信念，各国就没有理由相互承担此类义务"。《维也纳条约法公约》将这一原则定义为，一国"有义务避免采取有损条约目标和宗旨的行动"。WTO《争端解决谅解》鼓励成员真诚参与磋商、争端解决和仲裁程序。该谅解没有描述"真诚"的含义。"美国-310 条款案"专家组报告认为，"理解条约应以善意原则加以解释的要求相当困难，或至少十分棘手……特别是因为其中一方可能受到恶意指控"。上诉机构在"美国-2000 年持续倾销与补贴补偿法"案中指出，"然而，在适用协定中，

mere violation to support such a conclusion". The ***Dispute Settlement Understanding*** gives some helpful pointers on the meaning of "good faith". Article 3.7 asks members to exercise their judgement whether an action would be fruitful. It stresses that the aim of the dispute settlement mechanism is to secure a positive solution to a dispute, and that a solution acceptable to both parties and consistent with the WTO rules is clearly preferable. Article 3.10 says that requests for conciliation and the use of the dispute settlement procedures should not be intended or considered as contentious acts, and hence that all members would engage in the procedures in good faith to resolve the dispute. It continues that complaints and counter-complaints in regard to distinct matters should not be linked. At the very least we can therefore say that the WTO setting for the settlement of disputes should not be considered a suitable venue for vexatious behaviour, and that members should do nothing to undermine the intent of the rules. But ***panel*** proceedings always are adversarial. Industries asking for the initiation of consultations and their political backers expect results. The heat is therefore easily turned up. Against this background it is surprising how few disputes brought before the WTO have led to bad blood. Equally impressive is the extent to which most parties so far have participated in dispute settlement and implemented panel decisions in good faith. *See also* ***legitimate expectation***. [Jung and Lee 2003, Shaw 2014]

Good governance: highly desirable attributes of decision-making and decision-implementing processes. The main attributes are participation by all who may be affected, respect for the rule of law, transparency, responsiveness to the views of participants, consensus, equity and inclusiveness, and effectiveness and efficiency. Most importantly, those making and implementing decisions must be accountable to those affected by them.

Good offices: a form of ***mediation*** between parties to a dispute. It describes an offer by a disinterested third party, often a person of distinction in the field, to examine what can be done to settle a difficult dispute. The offer to assist may be made spontaneously, or it may be part of a framework for settling disputes. Good offices and mediation always consist of giving advice. They never have the binding force of ***arbitration***. Article 5 of the WTO ***Dispute Settlement Understanding*** says that the parties may use the good-offices procedure, assuming they agree among themselves to do so. Either party may call for its introduction. It may begin or be terminated at any time. The procedure may run parallel to a panel process. Also, the Director-General of the WTO may offer his or her good offices in an ***ex officio*** capacity. *See also* ***arbitration***.

Good Practice Guide on Implementing Specific Articles of the Convention on Combating Bribery of Foreign Public Officials in International Business Transactions: *see* ***Recommendation for Further Combating Bribery of Foreign Public Officials in International Business Transactions***.

Goods Trade Barometer: a WTO indicator that combines several trade-related indices into a single composite index. It highlights turning points in world merchandise trade and provides an indication of its likely trajectory in the near

任没有何内容支持这样的结论，即仅仅因为一 WTO 成员被认定违反一项实质性条约规定，即因此未能善意地采取行动。在我们看来，要支持这样的结论，就必须证明不仅仅是违反了规定”。《争端解决谅解》对理解“真诚”的含义有所帮助。第 3.7 条要求成员就措施是否有效作出判断。强调，争端解决机制的目的是保证争端得到积极解决，双方共同接受且符合 WTO 规则的解决办法无疑是首选办法。第 3.10 条规定，请求调停和使用争端解决程序不应用作或被视为引起争议的行为，因此所有成员将真诚参与争端解决程序。该条继续指出，有关不同事项的起诉和应诉不应联系在一起。我们因此至少可以认为，WTO 争端解决机制的设置不应被认为是滋生无理行为的合适场所，且成员不应作出任何有损规则意图的行为。但是专家组的程序总是对抗性的。寻求启动磋商的产业及其政治支持者期望获得结果。因此热度很容易升高。在此背景下，令人惊讶的是很少有诉诸 WTO 的争端引发敌对情绪。同样令人印象深刻的是迄今为止大部分争端方均真诚参与争端解决和执行专家组裁决。另见*合理预期(legitimate expectation)*。

Good governance
良治

决策和决策执行过程的非常理想的属性。主要属性是可能受到影响的各方均参与、尊重法治、透明度、对参加方意见的响应、协商一致、公平和包容性以及有效和高效。最重要的是，决定的制定者和执行者必须对受决定影响的人负责。

Good offices
斡旋

争端各方之间进行调停的一种形式。指与案件无利害关系的一第三方，通常是有关领域有名望之人，主动提出审查一项棘手争端的解决办法。提供协助可以是自愿的，也可以是争端解决框架的一部分。斡旋和调解通常涉及建议的提出，都缺少仲裁所具有的约束力。WTO《争端解决谅解》第 5 条规定，争端各方可以使用斡旋程序，假设双方同意这样作。任何一方均可以请求采用斡旋程序。该程序可以随时开始或终止，可与专家组程序同时进行。此外，WTO 总干事可以依职权进行斡旋。另见*仲裁(arbitration)*。

Good Practice Guide on Implementing Specific Articles of the Convention on Combating Bribery of Foreign Public Officials in International Business Transactions
关于实施关于打击国际商业交易中行贿外国公职人员行为公约特定条款的良好实践指南

见*关于进一步打击国际商业交易中行贿外国公职人员行为的建议(Recommendation for Further Combating Bribery of Foreign Public Officials in International Business Transactions)*。

Goods Trade Barometer
货物贸易晴雨表

WTO 的一项指标，将多个与贸易有关的指数合并为一项单一综合指数。突出显示世界货物贸易的转折点，并标示世界货物贸易在不久的将来可能的轨迹。

future. The Goods Trade Barometer replaces the World Trade Outlook Indicator. *See also* ***Services Trade Barometer***.

Government procurement: also called public procurement. It covers purchases of goods and services by governments and governmental authorities for their own use. The ***GATT*** and the ***General Agreement on Trade in Services*** exempt government procurement from the application of their rules. *See also* ***Agreement on Government Procurement***, ***APEC Non-Binding Principles on Government Procurement***, ***Revised Agreement on Government Procurement***, ***UNCITRAL model law on procurement of goods, construction and services*** and ***Working Group on Transparency in Government Procurement***.

Government trading monopolies: the exclusive allocation by a country to one firm, often state-owned, of the right to trade internationally in certain products. *See also* ***single-desk selling*** and ***state trading***.

Government use: for ***patents***, when the government itself uses or authorizes other persons to use rights over a patented product or process for government purposes, without the permission of the patent owner. *See also* ***compulsory licensing***.

Graduation: the removal of tariff preferences accorded to developing countries under ***GSP*** (Generalized System of Preferences) programmes because a country has exceeded a certain level of per capita GDP. Many countries also have graduating mechanisms allowing the removal of GSP concessions for particular products once a supplier country captures more than a defined share of the import market for that product. *See also* ***a priori limitation*** and ***competitive-need limitation***.

Graduation clause: paragraph 7 of the ***Enabling Clause*** notes that less-developed GATT members expect that their capacity to make contributions under the GATT provisions would improve with the progressive development of their economies and trade. Accordingly, they would expect to participate more fully in the framework of rights and obligations under the GATT. *See also* ***developing countries and the multilateral trading system*** and ***graduation***.

Grains Trade Convention: *see* ***International Grains Agreement***.

Grandfather clause: refers to a provision in the ***Protocol of Provisional Application*** adopted by the original members of the GATT in 1947 which states that Part II of the GATT would be applied "to the fullest extent not inconsistent with existing legislation". This was a device which permitted the continuing existence of national legislation in violation of the GATT articles. It was based on the view that the entry into force of the GATT would be delayed indefinitely if members first had to bring their legislation into conformity with it. This provision became known as the "grandfather clause" because it accepted as a *fait accompli* legislation predating the agreement. The grandfather clause has not been carried forward into the ***GATT 1994***. *See also* ***GATT-consistency of national legislation***.

Greater Arab Free Trade Area: GAFTA. Also known as Pan-Arab Free Trade Area. Launched on 1 January 1998 for establishment within ten years. The

货物贸易晴雨表取代了世界贸易展望指标。另见*服务贸易晴雨表(Services Trade Barometer)*。

Government procurement

政府采购

又称公共采购。涵盖政府和政府部门购买供自用的货物和服务。GATT和《服务贸易总协定》将政府采购例外于规则适用范围。另见*政府采购协定(Agreement on Government Procurement)*、*APEC政府采购非约束性原则(APEC Non-Binding Principles on Government Procurement)*、*政府采购协定修正版(Revised Agreement on Government Procurement)*、*联合国国际贸易法委员会货物、工程和服务采购示范法(UNCITRAL model law on procurement of goods, construction and services)*、*政府采购透明度工作组(Working Group on Transparency in Government Procurement)*。

Government trading monopolies

政府贸易垄断

一国将某些产品的国际贸易权专门分配给一公司的行为，通常为国有公司。另见*专责销售(single-desk selling)*、*国营贸易(state trading)*。

Government use

政府使用制度

对于专利，指政府在未经专利所有人许可的情况下，为政府自用或授权其他人为政府目的使用专利产品或专利工艺。另见*强制许可(compulsory licensing)*。

Graduation

毕业

因一发展中国家人均国内生产总值超过某一水平而取消其在普惠制(GSP)项下的关税优惠。许多国家还建立了毕业机制，允许在一供应国的一特定产品在进口市场上占有超过规定份额时可以取消对该产品的普惠制减让。另见*预定限额(a priori limitation)*、*竞争性需求限制(competitive-need limitation)*。

Graduation clause

毕业条款

授权条款第7段指出，GATT欠发达缔约方希望，随着其经济和贸易的逐步发展，其根据GATT条款作出贡献的能力将会提高。因此，它们期望更充分参与GATT项下的权利和义务框架。另见*发展中国家与多边贸易体制(developing countries and the multilateral trading system)*、*毕业(graduation)*。

Grains Trade Convention

谷物贸易公约

见*国际谷物协定(International Grains Agreement)*。

Grandfather clause

祖父条款

指GATT创始缔约方于1947年通过的《临时适用议定书》中的一项条款，规定GATT第二部分将“在与已存在的立法不相抵触的最大限度内”适用。这是一种允许违反GATT条款的国家立法继续存在的手段。其依据的观点是，如果缔约方首先必须使其立法符合GATT，那么GATT的生效将被无限期延迟。这一条款之所以称为“祖父条款”，是因为它接受了协定达成之前的既成事实立法。祖父条款未纳入GATT 1994。另见*国家立法与GATT一致性(GATT-consistency of national legislation)*。

Greater Arab Free Trade Area

大阿拉伯自由贸易区

GAFTA。也称为“泛阿拉伯自由贸易区”。1998年1月1日启动，计划在10年

mandated tariff reductions were achieved early, and GAFTA entered into force in 2005. It now has eighteen members: Algeria, Bahrain, Egypt, Iraq, Jordan, Kuwait, Lebanon, Libya, Morocco, Oman, Palestine, Qatar, Saudi Arabia, Sudan, Syria, Tunisia, United Arab Emirates and Yemen. A customs union is intended to supersede GAFTA, followed by the formation of an Arab Common Market.

Greater Horn of Africa: consists of Burundi, Djibouti, Eritrea, Ethiopia, Kenya, Rwanda, Somalia, South Sudan, Sudan and Uganda but descriptions vary. *See also* ***Horn of Africa***.

Green box: domestic support policies for agricultural products exempt from the ***Uruguay Round*** reduction commitments and permitted without limits. Green box policies include relief to farmers through a wide range of assistance measures which have no or a minimal impact on trade, such as disaster relief, research, disease control, infrastructure and environmental protection. *See also* ***Agreement on Agriculture***, ***amber box***, ***blue box*** and ***general services in agriculture***.

Green economy: defined by ***UN Environment Programme*** as an economy that is low-carbon, resource-efficient and socially inclusive. The organization says that in a green economy growth in employment and income are driven by public and private investment into such economic activities, infrastructure and assets that allow reduced carbon emissions and pollution, enhanced energy and resource efficiency, and the prevention of loss of ***biodiversity*** and ecosystem services. [unenvironment.org]

Green growth: achieving economic growth and development in a manner that uses natural resources in a sustainable way.

Greenhouse gases: listed in Annex A to the ***Kyoto Protocol*** as carbon dioxide (CO_2), methane (CH_4), nitrous oxide (N_2O), surface ozone (O_3), hydrofluorocarbons (HFCs), perfluorocarbons (PFCs) and sulphur hexafluoride (SF_6). Some add water vapour (H_2O) as a natural greenhouse gas. *See also* ***Paris Agreement*** and ***United Nations Framework Convention on Climate Change***.

Greening the GATT: a term popularized by Daniel Esty in a book of the same title, published in 1994. It expresses the hopes of those who would like the WTO to be more responsive to their particular environmental concerns and who see it as necessary for the GATT to reflect clearly the aims of environmental protection. *See also* ***environmental rules under the WTO***, ***Global Green New Deal*** and ***trade and environment***. [Esty 1994]

Green labelling: *see* ***eco-labelling***.

Green Paper: a report originally bearing a green cover issued by a government as part of a consultation process to stimulate public discussion of policy issues. Although governments do not usually consider themselves bound to adopt any particular proposal examined in a Green Paper, the ideas explored by them often turn into policy proposals. *See also* ***White Paper***. [www.europa.eu.int]

Green procurement: purchasing policies and practices that favour environmentally-friendly parts and materials.

Green protectionism: *see* ***eco-protectionism*** and ***trade and environment***.

内建成。由于授权的关税削减提前实现，GAFTA 于 2005 年生效。目前有 18 个成员：阿尔及利亚、巴林、埃及、伊拉克、约旦、科威特、黎巴嫩、利比亚、摩洛哥、阿曼、巴勒斯坦、卡塔尔、沙特阿拉伯、苏丹、叙利亚、突尼斯、阿拉伯联合酋长国和也门。计划以关税同盟取代 GAFTA，随后形成阿拉伯共同市场。

Greater Horn of Africa
大非洲之角

由布隆迪、吉布提、厄立特里亚、埃塞俄比亚、肯尼亚、卢旺达、索马里、南苏丹、苏丹和乌干达组成，但表述各不相同。另见*非洲之角(Horn of Africa)*。

Green box
绿箱

免于乌拉圭回合削减承诺的无限制的农产品国内支持政策。绿箱政策包括通过范围广泛的援助措施向农民提供救济，这些措施对贸易没有影响或影响很小，例如救灾、研究、疾病控制、基础设施和环境保护。另见*农业协定(Agreement on Agriculture)*、*黄箱(amber box)*、*蓝箱(blue box)*、*农业一般服务(general services in agriculture)*。

Green economy
绿色经济

联合国环境规划署将其定义为低碳、资源节约型和社会包容性的经济。该组织认为，在绿色经济中，就业和收入的增长由对此类经济活动、基础设施和资产的公共和私人投资所驱动，可以减少碳排放和污染、提高能源和资源效率，并防止生物多样性和生态系统服务的损失。

Green growth
绿色增长

以可持续的方式利用自然资源实现经济增长和发展。

Greenhouse gases
温室气体

列在《京都议定书》附件 A 中的二氧化碳(CO_2)、甲烷(CH_4)、氧化亚氮(N_2O)、地表臭氧(O_3)、氢氟碳化物(HFCs)、全氟化碳(PFCs)和六氟化硫(SF_6)。一些人增加水蒸气(H_2O)作为天然温室气体。另见*巴黎协定(Paris Agreement)*、*联合国气候变化框架公约(United Nations Framework Convention on Climate Change)*。

Greening the GATT
绿化 GATT

丹尼尔·艾斯提在 1994 年出版的同名书中推广的词语。表达了一些人希望 WTO 能对其特定环境关切作出更多反应且认为 GATT 有必要明确反映环境保护的目标。另见 *WTO 环境规则(environmental rules under the WTO)*、*全球绿色新政(Global Green New Deal)*、*贸易与环境(trade and environment)*。

Green labelling
绿色标签

见*生态标签(eco-labelling)*。

Green Paper
绿皮书

政府发布的作为其协商进程一部分意在鼓励对政策问题进行公开讨论的报告，最初为绿色封面。虽然政府通常不认为其有义务采纳绿皮书中所审议的任何具体建议，但其探讨的想法通常会变为政策建议。另见*白皮书(White Paper)*。

Green procurement
绿色采购

优选环境友好型零部件和材料的采购政策和做法。

Green protectionism
绿色保护主义

见*环境贸易保护主义(eco-protectionism)*、*贸易与环境(trade and environment)*。

Green Room: the informal name of the WTO Director-General's conference room. It is used to refer to meetings of twenty to forty delegations, usually at the level of heads of delegation. These meetings can take place elsewhere such as at ***WTO Ministerial Conferences***, and they can be called by the minister chairing the conference as well as the Director-General.

Green supply chain: a supply chain that minimizes or eliminates wastage at all levels of production. This includes, for example, hazardous chemical emissions, waste management, material selection, manufacturing process, delivery of the product and end-of-life management of the product. *See also* ***APEC Cooperation Network on Green Supply Chain*** and ***life cycle assessment***.

Green tariff: *see* ***carbon tariff***.

Grexit: an abbreviation for a potential exit by Greece from the ***European Union*** and the ***Eurozone***. In use particularly from about 2012 to 2015 in connection with Greece's budgetary problems at the time. *See also* ***Brexit***.

Grey-area measures: discriminatory export and import restraints agreed between governments which are usually contrary to the principles governing the ***multilateral trading system***, but which were not clearly illegal under the multilateral rules until the end of the ***Uruguay Round***. Examples of grey-area measures are ***orderly marketing arrangements*** and voluntary export arrangements. These are now illegal under the WTO ***Agreement on Safeguards***. Existing grey-area measures had to be eliminated by 1999. Emerging grey-area measures may be ***cartel*** arrangements between private firms implicitly sanctioned by governments and ***voluntary import expansion*** agreements between governments.

Grey marketing: a North American expression denoting the practice of ***parallel imports***. Goods so imported are known as "grey market goods" or as "grey market imports".

Group: an organizational feature of many international negotiations, particularly where the number of participants is large. Members of a given group usually have broad common negotiating aims which they seek to strengthen by alliances. Examples are the ***Cairns Group*** for agriculture, the ***Cotton Four*** for cotton and the ***G-15*** for greater South–South cooperation. Membership may be more or less informal, sometimes by invitation and other times through self-selection. Some groups have a short life, while others have become a permanent feature of the negotiating landscape, such as the ***Group of 77***.

Group of 15: *see* ***G-15***.

Group of 20: *see* ***G20*** or ***G-20 Developing Nations***.

Group of 24: *see* ***G-24***.

Group of 77: G77. A loosely organized group of developing countries, originally numbering 77, which was formed at the first meeting of ***UNCTAD*** in 1964. The G77 quickly became the main force in setting the agenda for the UNCTAD work programme. It now has over 130 members. The group's aim is to help developing countries to articulate and promote their collective interests, and to enhance their joint negotiating capacity in all major economic areas of the United Nations system. Existing members use broad economic

Green Room
绿屋

WTO 总干事会议室的非正式名称。指 20 至 40 个代表团的会议，通常为代表团团长级别。这些会议可以在其他场所举行，例如 WTO 部长级会议期间，并可由主持会议的部长和总干事召集。(因 GATT 总干事邓克尔在其办公室召集非正式磋商以推动发起乌拉圭回合谈判而得名—译注。)

Green supply chain
绿色供应链

在所有生产环节上使浪费最小化或消除浪费的供应链。例如包括危险化学品排放、废物管理、材料选择、制造过程、产品交付和产品报废管理。另见 *APEC 绿色供应链合作网络(APEC Cooperation Network on Green Supply Chain)*、*生命周期评估(life cycle assessment)*。

Green tariff
绿色关税

见*碳关税(carbon tariff)*。

Grexit
希腊脱欧

希腊可能退出欧盟和欧元区的缩写。特别是在 2012 年至 2015 年期间与希腊预算问题相关时使用。另见*英国脱欧(Brexit)*。

Grey-area measures
灰色区域措施

政府间议定的歧视性出口和进口限制，这些限制通常违反管辖多边贸易体制的原则，但直到乌拉圭回合结束之前，这些限制根据多边规则是否合法并未明确。灰色区域措施的例子包括有序销售安排和自愿出口安排。根据 WTO《保障措施协定》，这些措施现在属非法。当时存在的灰色区域措施必须在 1999 年前取消。新出现的灰色区域措施包括政府默许的私营企业之间的卡特尔安排和政府之间的自愿扩大进口协议。

Grey marketing
灰色营销

北美地区形容平行进口做法的表述。平行进口的货物被称为“灰色市场货物”或“灰色市场进口产品”。

Group
集团/协调组

许多国际谈判的组织特征，特别是在参加方数量众多的情况下。特定集团/协调组的成员通常持有广泛的共同谈判目标，它们寻求通过联盟加强这一目标。例如，农业凯恩斯集团、棉花四国与关于加强南南合作 15 国协调组。成员资格可能或多或少属非正式的，有时通过邀请，有时通过自行决定。一些集团/协调组的寿命很短，而其他已经成为谈判领域的永久特征，如 77 国集团。

Group of 15
15 国协调组

见 *15 国集团(G-15)*。

Group of 20
20 国协调组

见 *20 国集团(G20)*或*发展中国家 20 国协调组(G-20 Developing Nations)*。

Group of 24
24 国集团

见 *24 国集团(G-24)*。

Group of 77
77 国集团

G77。一个松散组织起来的发展中国家集团，最初的成员数量为 77 个，成立于 1964 年首届联合国贸易与发展会议(UNCTAD)召开之时。77 国集团迅速成

and political criteria to decide whether a country should be admitted to membership. The G77 chairmanship rotates at fixed intervals among the groups representing the African, Latin American and Asian countries. The G77 also functions in other parts of the United Nations system, but it does not operate in the WTO. China is not a formal member of the G77, but it cooperates with it through the arrangement known as ***Group of 77 and China***. *See also* ***group system***.

Group of 77 and China: an informal association between the ***Group of 77*** and China, begun in 1991. China contributes to the funding of the Group of 77 and can participate in all of its proceedings.

Group of Article XII: a group of members that joined the WTO after 1995. Excludes ***least-developed countries*** and ***EU*** members that joined after 1995. Refers to Article XII of the ***WTO Agreement*** covering accessions to the WTO. The Group's aim is to close what they see as the gap between the commitments of the original members and the greater level of commitments undertaken by members of the Group as part of their WTO accessions. Members are Albania, Armenia, Cabo Verde, China, Ecuador, Georgia, Jordan, Kazakhstan, Kyrgyz Republic, Moldova, Mongolia, North Macedonia, Oman, Panama, Russian Federation, Saudi Arabia, Seychelles, Chinese Taipei, Tajikistan, Tonga, Ukraine and Viet Nam.

Group of Latin American and Caribbean Countries: *see* ***GRULAC***.

Group of Negotiations on Goods: GNG. A group established to manage all negotiating issues relating to the GATT and trade in goods in the ***Uruguay Round***, including trade-related aspects of intellectual property rights and trade-related investment measures.

Group of Negotiations on Services: GNS. A group established to handle all issues relating to ***trade in services*** in the ***Uruguay Round***.

Group of Three: a free-trade arrangement between Colombia, Mexico and Venezuela. It entered into force on 1 January 1995. Venezuela withdrew in 2006. In August 2011 it became the Colombia–Mexico Free Trade Agreement. *See also* ***free-trade area***.

Group system: the system on which negotiations in ***UNCTAD*** in particular were based for a long time. The UNCTAD membership was divided formally into four groups: Asian and African countries (Group A), OECD countries (Group B), Latin American and Caribbean countries (Group C) and the socialist countries of Eastern Europe and Russia (Group D). Positions of responsibility in the various UNCTAD committees rotated among the groups according to agreed guidelines. At UNCTAD I in 1964, Groups A and C decided to meet jointly, creating the ***Group of 77***. In legal terms, Groups A and C continued to exist, but they only met sporadically. Negotiations were carried out through group coordinators upon whom it fell to arrive at a common group position. Often, this left them little leeway for flexibility because they always had to negotiate with other groups on the basis of delicately balanced compromises within their own groups. Successive

为制定UNCTAD工作计划议程的主要力量。目前有超过130个成员。该集团的目的是帮助发展中国家阐明和促进它们的集体利益，并加强其在联合国系统内所有主要经济领域的联合谈判能力。现有成员使用宽泛的经济和政治标准来决定一国是否能被接纳为成员。77国集团主席国在由代表非洲、拉丁美洲和亚洲国家的集团之间定期轮换。77国集团也在联合国系统的其他领域发挥作用，但不在WTO内运作。中国不是77国集团的正式成员，但通过称为"77国集团与中国"的安排开展合作。另见*集团制度(group system)*。

Group of 77 and China

77国集团与中国

77国集团与中国之间的非正式联盟，始于1991年。中国为77国集团提供资金，并可参与其所有程序。

Group of Article XII

第12条协调组

由1995年后加入WTO的成员组成的协调组。不包括1995年后加入的最不发达国家和欧盟成员国。第12条指涵盖加入WTO规定的《WTO协定》第12条。协调组的目的是缩小创始成员的承诺与协调组成员作为其加入WTO一部分所作更高水平承诺之间的差距。成员包括阿尔巴尼亚、亚美尼亚、佛得角、中国、厄瓜多尔、格鲁吉亚、约旦、哈萨克斯坦、吉尔吉斯斯坦、摩尔多瓦、蒙古、北马其顿、阿曼、巴拿马、俄罗斯、沙特阿拉伯、塞舌尔、中国台北、塔吉克斯坦、汤加、乌克兰和越南。

Group of Latin American and Caribbean Countries

拉丁美洲与加勒比国家集团

见*拉丁美洲与加勒比国家集团(GRULAC)*。

Group of Negotiations on Goods

货物谈判组

GNG。在乌拉圭回合中设立的管理与GATT和货物贸易有关的所有谈判问题的谈判组，包括与贸易有关的知识产权问题和与贸易有关的投资措施。

Group of Negotiations on Services

服务谈判组

GNS。在乌拉圭回合中设立的处理与服务贸易有关的所有问题的谈判组。

Group of Three

3国集团

哥伦比亚、墨西哥和委内瑞拉之间的自由贸易安排。协定于1995年1月1日生效。委内瑞拉于2006年退出。2011年8月转为《哥伦比亚—墨西哥自由贸易协定》。另见*自由贸易区(free-trade area)*。

Group system

集团制度

联合国贸易与发展会议(UNCTAD)长期以来作为谈判基础的制度。UNCTAD成员正式分为4个集团：亚洲和非洲国家(A组)、经济合作与发展组织(OECD)国家(B组)、拉丁美洲和加勒比国家(C组)以及东欧社会主义国家和俄罗斯(D组)。UNCTAD各委员会所负职责根据议定方针在各集团之间轮换。在1964年的UNCTAD第1届大会上，A组和C组决定举行联合会议，创建了77国集团。在法律上，A组和C组继续存在，但双方只是偶尔召开会议。谈判通

enlargements of the ***European Union*** led to a situation where the majority of Group B members was part of an influential internal bloc. Group D ceased functioning after the changes in Central and Eastern Europe of 1989. Adopting common positions through groups that barely functioned became very difficult. The group system could be seen as one of the factors preventing UNCTAD from reaching its full potential because it forestalled the emergence of subject-oriented coalitions where some developed and developing countries had shared interests.

Growth triangles: sub-regional economic zones identified by governments as holding particular promise for rapid economic development by virtue of their location or factor endowment. On a map, they sometimes look like triangles, but other Euclidean shapes may be found. They are often conceived in the form of ***free-trade zones***. Growth triangles in most cases include territory of two or three states that cooperate in their development, but they may be contained within a single country. *See also* ***BIMP-EAGA***.

GRULAC: the Group of Latin American and Caribbean Countries which operates informally within the WTO.

GSP: Generalized System of Preferences. First proposed at UNCTAD II in 1968. Entered into force in 1971. It gives developing countries a ***margin of preference*** in the tariff rates their goods face in the markets of developed countries and in this way increases their competitiveness. Countries maintaining GSP schemes are usually called *donor countries*. Those using them are called *beneficiary countries*. The massive tariff reductions since 1971 as a result of ***multilateral trade negotiations*** and unilateral actions, as well as changes in productivity, have reduced the importance of the GSP to many developing-country exporters, but it remains an important plank in the trade policies of many developing countries. ***UNCTAD*** is the main forum for a discussion of GSP issues. *See also* ***GSP+***.

GSP+: a component of the ***GSP*** scheme of the ***European Union*** that offers additional benefits to countries that fulfil standard GSP conditions if they also meet vulnerability criteria and sustainable development criteria. The latter entail ratification and effective implementation of fifteen core human and labour rights UN/ILO conventions and twelve conventions related to the environment and to governance principles. They include the ***Convention Concerning the Prohibition and Immediate Action for the Elimination of the Worst Forms of Child Labour***, ***CITES***, ***United Nations Framework Convention on Climate Change***, ***Convention on Persistent Organic Pollutants***, ***Kyoto Protocol*** and the ***United Nations Convention Against Corruption***. The scheme is valid until 2023. [Regulation (EU) No 978/2012]

GSTP: Global System of Trade Preferences Among Developing Countries. It entered into force in 1989. It aims to promote the development of economic cooperation among developing countries through the exchange of ***tariff preferences***. ***Non-tariff preferences*** may also be exchanged. ***Least-developed countries*** do not have to offer reciprocal concessions. Membership of the GSTP is

过集团协调员进行，最终达成集团共同立场。通常，这使得协调员没有多少灵活性的余地，因为他们常常不得不在集团内部微妙平衡的妥协基础上与其他集团进行谈判。欧盟的持续扩员导致 B 组的大多数成员成为一个有影响力的内部集团的一部分。D 组在 1989 年中东欧发生变化后停止运行。通过几乎不起作用的集团采取共同立场变得非常困难。集团制度可被视为妨碍 UNCTAD 充分发挥潜力的因素之一，因为这一制度阻止了以议题为导向的联盟的出现，而在这类联盟中，一些发达国家和发展中国家拥有共同利益。

Growth triangles

增长三角

政府根据地理位置或要素禀赋确定的特别有望实现经济快速发展的次区域经济区。在地图上，这一经济区有时看似三角形，但有时也会是其他几何形状。它们通常被规划为自由贸易园区。增长三角在大多数情况下包括两个或三个进行发展合作的国家的领土，但也可能位于一国之内。*另见**东盟东部增长区**(BIMP-EAGA)*。

GRULAC

拉丁美洲与加勒比国家集团

在 WTO 中非正式运行的拉丁美洲和加勒比国家集团。

GSP

普惠制

全称为普遍优惠制。1968 年联合国贸易与发展会议(UNCTAD)第 2 届大会上首次提出，于 1971 年生效。该制度给予发展中国家在其货物进入发达国家市场所面临的关税税率方面一定优惠幅度，以此增加发展中国家的竞争力。维持普惠制方案的国家通常称为援助国，使用该制度的国家称为受益国。自 1971 年以来，作为多边贸易谈判、单边行动以及生产率变化的结果，普惠制对许多发展中国家出口商的重要性大大降低，但这一制度仍然是许多发展中国家贸易政策的一个重要方面。UNCTAD 是讨论普惠制问题的主要场所。*另见**普惠制附加**(GSP+)*。

GSP+

普惠制附加

欧盟普惠制(GSP)方案的组成部分，对符合标准普惠制条件且符合脆弱性标准和可持续发展标准的国家提供额外优惠。后者包括批准和有效实施 15 项核心人权和劳工权利的联合国/国际劳工组织(ILO)公约和 12 项与环境和治理原则有关的公约。其中包括《禁止和立即行动消除最恶劣形式的童工劳动公约》、《濒危野生动植物种国际贸易公约》(CITES)、《联合国气候变化框架公约》、《关于持久性有机污染物的公约》、《京都议定书》和《联合国反腐败公约》。方案有效期至 2023 年。

GSTP

全球贸易优惠制

发展中国家间全球贸易优惠制。该制度于 1989 年生效，旨在通过交换关税优惠促进发展中国家间的经济合作发展。非关税优惠也可以交换。最不发达国

open to members of the ***Group of 77***. Negotiations are conducted under ***UNCTAD*** auspices. Forty-three countries participate in the GSTP. *See also* ***ECDC*** and ***trade negotiations between developing countries***.

Guarantee mark: *see* ***certification mark***.

Guidelines for Multinational Enterprises: *see* ***OECD Guidelines for Multinational Enterprises***.

Guidelines for Mutual Recognition Agreements or Arrangements in the Accountancy Sector: a set of non-binding principles adopted by the WTO on 29 May 1997 aimed at making it easier for governments to negotiate the mutual recognition of professional qualifications. Part A of the Guidelines deals with the conduct of negotiations and the relevant obligations governments have under the ***General Agreement on Trade in Services***. Part B sets out various issues that may have to be addressed in negotiations, such as the intended participants, the purpose and scope of the arrangement, the conditions under which mutual recognition will be accorded, the mechanism for implementation, and other related matters. *See also* ***mutual recognition arrangements*** and ***Working Party on Professional Services***.

Guidelines for Recipient Country Investment Policies Relating to National Security: an ***OECD*** Recommendation adopted in 2009. It recommends that, if governments consider or introduce investment policies designed to safeguard national security, they should be guided the following principles: (1) non-discrimination, (2) transparency/predictability including codification and publication, prior notification, consultation, procedural fairness and predictability and disclosure of investment policy actions, (3) regulatory proportionality: restrictions on investment should not be greater than needed to protect national security; each country has a right to determine what is necessary to protect its national security; restrictions should have a narrow focus, be designed with appropriate expertise and be used as a last resort, and (4) accountability procedures for internal government oversight, judicial review, periodic regulatory impact assessments and requirements that important decisions should be taken at high government levels to ensure accountability of the implementing authorities. *See also* ***investment***. [www.oecd.org]

Guiding Principles Concerning Environmental Policies: an ***OECD*** recommendation adopted on 26 May 1972. The five principles it contains deal mainly with the international economic and trade implications of environmental policies. First, costs of public measures to reduce pollution and to allocate resources better should be met through the ***polluter-pays principle***. Second, it encourages harmonization of environmental standards, though it allows that this may be difficult to achieve. In any case, it deems striving towards more stringent standards as desirable. Measures to protect the environment should avoid the creation of non-tariff barriers to trade. Third, measures to protect the environment should be applied in accordance with the principles of ***national treatment*** and ***non-discrimination***, described as identical treatment for imported products regardless of their national origin. Fourth, procedures should

家不需要提供互惠减让。GSTP 成员资格对 77 国集团成员开放。GSTP 谈判在联合国贸易与发展会议(UNCTAD)主持下进行。43 个国家参与 GSTP。另见*发展中国家间经济合作(ECDC)*、*发展中国家间贸易谈判(trade negotiations between developing countries)*。

Guarantee mark

保证标志

见*认证标志(certification mark)*。

Guidelines for Multinational Enterprises

跨国企业行为准则

见 *OECD 跨国企业行为准则(OECD Guidelines for Multinational Enterprises)*。

Guidelines for Mutual Recognition Agreements or Arrangements in the Accountancy Sector

关于会计部门相互承认协定或安排的指导原则

WTO 于 1997 年 5 月 29 日通过的一套不具约束力的原则，旨在使各国政府更易于就相互承认专业资格进行谈判。该指南的 A 部分处理谈判的开展及政府在《服务贸易总协定》项下的相关义务。B 部分列出谈判中可能需要处理的各种问题，例如有意参加者、安排的目的和范围、给予相互承认的条件、执行机制和其他有关事项。另见*相互承认安排(mutual recognition arrangements)*、*专业服务工作组(Working Party on Professional Services)*。

Guidelines for Recipient Country Investment Policies Relating to National Security

与国家安全有关的接受国投资政策指导原则

经济合作与发展组织(OECD) 2009 年通过的建议。建议如果政府考虑或采用旨在维护国家安全的投资政策，应遵循以下原则：(1)非歧视；(2)透明度/可预见性，包括编纂和公布、事先通知、磋商、程序公正性和可预测性以及投资政策行动的披露；(3)监管相称性：对投资的限制不应高于保护国家安全所需的程度；每一国家均有权确定保护其国家安全的必要条件；限制措施应足够聚焦，设计时应具备适当的专业知识，并作为最后手段使用；以及(4)政府内部监督问责程序、司法审查、监管影响的定期评估以及重要决定应由政府高层作出以保证对执行部门问责的要求。另见*投资(investment)*。

Guiding Principles Concerning Environmental Policies

关于环境政策的指导原则

经济合作与发展组织(OECD)1972 年 5 月 26 日通过的建议。包含五项原则，主要处理环境政策对国际经济和贸易的影响。第一，因采取旨在减少污染和更合理资源配置的公共措施的成本应通过污染者赔付原则解决。第二，鼓励环境标准的协调，尽管可能难以实现。无论如何，这一原则认为努力达到更严格的标准是可取的。保护环境的措施应避免造成非关税贸易壁垒。第三，应依照国民待遇和非歧视原则实施保护环境的措施，无论进口产品原产地如何均

be established for checking conformity to product standards. The fifth principle is that differences in environmental policies should not lead to the introduction of compensating import levies or export rebates. *See also* ***trade and environment***.

Gulf Cooperation Council: GCC. Formal name *Cooperation Council of the Arab States of the Gulf.* Established in 1981. It consists of Saudi Arabia, Kuwait, Bahrain, Qatar, the United Arab Emirates and Oman. Among its major political and economic aims is that of drawing up similar regulations in the economic and financial fields, trade, customs and transport, information and tourism. Its secretariat is located at Riyadh.

GVCS Blueprint: *see* ***APEC Strategic Blueprint for Promoting Global Value Chains Development and Cooperation***.

应给予相同待遇。第四，应建立产品标准一致性的检查程序。第五，环境政策的差异不应导致采用补偿性进口税或出口退税。另见*贸易与环境(trade and environment)*。

Gulf Cooperation Council

海湾合作委员会

GCC。正式名称为"海湾阿拉伯国家合作委员会"。1981 年成立。由沙特阿拉伯、科威特、巴林、卡塔尔、阿拉伯联合酋长国和阿曼组成。主要政治和经济目标是在经济和金融领域、贸易、海关和运输、信息和旅游业制定类似的规定。委员会秘书处设在利雅得。

GVCS Blueprint

全球价值链发展与合作战略蓝图

见 *APEC 促进全球价值链发展与合作战略蓝图(APEC Strategic Blueprint for Promoting Global Value Chains Development and Cooperation)*。

H

Haberler Report: in late 1957 GATT members decided to commission an examination of past and current international trade trends and their implications. It was to enquire particularly into (a) the failure of the trade of less developed countries to develop as rapidly as that of industrialized countries, (b) excessive short-term fluctuations in the prices of primary products, and (c) widespread resort to agricultural protection. This was the first such examination in the GATT looking particularly at issues facing developing countries. A panel of distinguished economists was assembled, led by Gottfried Haberler of Harvard University. The panel report, titled *Trends in International Trade*, was issued in October 1958. It became known immediately as the Haberler Report. The report contained sixty conclusions. The first fifteen are factual accounts of short-term fluctuations and long-term trends in commodities and manufactures trade prevailing at the time. The next eight conclusions deal with the interpretation of past trends, future import requirements and prospects for exports. The report was unable to conclude whether there had been an increase in agricultural protection in industrial countries in recent years, but it also cautioned against counting on any improvement in the ***terms of trade*** of the non-industrialized countries to raise their ability to purchase imports. The next thirty-three conclusions were the most important ones. They called for the stabilization of particular commodity markets, but not in a too ambitious way. They also argued for a moderation of agricultural ***protectionism*** in North America and Western Europe. One prediction was concerned with the diversion of trade in raw materials and foodstuffs away from outside sources to European sources as real incomes in Europe rose. In the final four conclusions, the experts agreed that although the issues covered in the report would affect primarily the policies of the highly industrialized countries, they too would gain from the proposed changes. The experts concluded in any case that there was some justification in developing-country views that current rules and conventions on commercial policies were relatively unfavourable to them. The Haberler Report had a small immediate impact on rule-making in the GATT, although it furnished some ideas for the Programme for the Expansion of Trade, adopted in November 1958, which ultimately led to the ***Dillon Round***. *See also* ***commodity policy*** and ***developing countries and the multilateral trading system***.

Hague System for the International Deposit of Industrial Designs: a system for the protection of ***industrial designs*** in more than one country through its registration with the International Bureau of ***WIPO***. A design must be new or

H

Haberler Report
哈伯勒报告

1957 年稍晚时，GATT 缔约方决定对过去和当前国际贸易趋势及其影响开展审查。特别探究以下问题：(a)欠发达国家的贸易未能像工业化国家的贸易那样迅速发展；(b)初级产品价格的短期过度波动；以及(c)农业保护政策广泛采用。这是 GATT 首次专门审查发展中国家所面临的问题。由杰出经济学家组成了专家组，由哈佛大学的戈特弗里德·哈伯勒领导。名为《国际贸易趋势》的专家组报告于 1958 年 10 月发布。这份报告随即被称为《哈伯勒报告》。报告包含 60 条结论。前 15 条是对当时商品和制成品贸易的短期波动和长期趋势的如实描述。接下来的 8 条结论是关于对过去趋势、未来进口要求和出口前景的说明。报告无法断定近年来工业化国家的农业保护是否有所增加，但也提醒不能依靠非工业国家改善贸易条件以提高其购买进口产品的能力。接下来的 33 条结论是最为重要的。他们呼吁稳定特定商品市场，但不能以过于雄心勃勃的方式。他们还主张北美和西欧克制使用农业保护主义。一项预测提出，随着欧洲实际收入的提高，原材料和食品贸易会从外部来源转向欧洲来源。在最后的 4 条结论中，专家们认为，虽然报告所涵盖问题会主要影响高度工业化国家的政策，但这些国家也会从建议的改变中获益。专家们总结指出，无论如何，发展中国家认为现行商业政策规则和公约对它们相对不利的观点是有一定道理的。《哈伯勒报告》对 GATT 中的规则制定产生的即时影响很小，但是对 1958 年 11 月通过的“贸易扩大计划”提供了一些想法，这一计划最终促成狄龙回合。另见*商品政策(commodity policy)*、*发展中国家与多边贸易体制(developing countries and the multilateral trading system)*。

Hague System for the International Deposit of Industrial Designs
工业品外观设计国际注册海牙体系

通过在世界知识产权组织(WIPO)国际局注册，在一个以上国家保护工业品外观设计的制度。外观设计必须是新的或原创的才有资格注册。保护的一般期

original to be eligible for registration. The normal term of protection is five years, and it can be renewed for up to fifteen years. The instrument under which this is done is *The Hague Agreement Concerning the International Deposit of Industrial Designs*, made on 2 June 1935 and revised several times since, most recently through the *Geneva Act* of July 1999.

Hard core cartel: a type of ***cartel*** defined in the OECD ***hard core cartel recommendation*** as an "anti-competitive agreement, anti-competitive concerted practice, or anti-competitive arrangement by competitors to fix prices, make rigged bids (collusive tenders), establish output restrictions or quotas, or share or divide markets by allocating customers, suppliers, territories, or lines of commerce". It does not include agreements aimed at lawful cost-reduction, agreements excluded by a member country's competition law, or those authorized in accordance with those laws. [OECD C(98)35/FINAL]

Hard core cartel recommendation: an OECD recommendation adopted in 1998 which asks member countries to "provide for (a) effective sanctions, of a kind and at a level adequate to deter firms and individuals from participating in such cartels; and (b) enforcement procedures and institutions with powers adequate to detect and remedy hard core cartels, including powers to obtain documents and information and to impose penalties for non-compliance". OECD members are asked to cooperate with each other in enforcing their laws against such cartels. [OECD C(98)35/FINAL]

Hard-core waiver: a decision taken in the GATT in 1955 to allow members in certain cases to retain ***quantitative restrictions*** that had been maintained over several years because of persistent balance-of-payments difficulties. The ***waiver*** was subject to some conditions. For example, members had to demonstrate that a sudden removal of a quantitative restriction would result in serious ***injury*** to a domestic industry, and they had to carry out a policy of progressive liberalization. *See also* ***residual quantitative restrictions***.

Hard law: in ***trade policy*** usage, international arrangements that entail legally enforceable rights and obligations on their members. Examples of hard law are the WTO obligations as embodied in the ***GATT*** (General Agreement on Tariffs and Trade) and the GATS (***General Agreement on Trade in Services***) both of them part of the ***WTO Agreement***. Such arrangements are usually in the form of treaties, or they have the status of a treaty. *See also* ***soft law***.

Harmonization of standards and qualifications: the adoption of a single standard or qualification requirement by two or more countries where previously each might have had its own set of requirements. Harmonization may involve the creation of an entirely new standard, the adoption of the standard of the most influential participant in the arrangement, the adoption of the most reasonable standard or a mixture of them. Achieving harmonization often entails laborious negotiations. *See also* ***Agreement on Technical Barriers to Trade***, ***explicit harmonization***, ***International Electrotechnical Commission***, ***International Organization for Standardization***, ***managed mutual recognition*** and ***mutual recognition arrangements***.

限是 5 年，可以延长最多至 15 年。所依据的法律文件是 1935 年 6 月 2 日订立的《工业品外观设计国际注册海牙协定》，此后多次修订，最近一次是根据 1999 年 7 月的《日内瓦文本》进行的修订。

Hard core cartel

核心卡特尔

经济合作与发展组织(OECD)"核心卡特尔建议"中定义的一种卡特尔，即"竞争者之间签订的限制竞争的协议、共谋做法或安排，进行固定价格、操纵投标(串通投标)、建立产量限制或配额或通过分配顾客、供应商、商业、领域或界限的方式分享或瓜分市场"。不包括旨在合法降低成本的协议、成员国竞争法排除的协议或依照这些竞争法授权的协议。

Hard core cartel recommendation

核心卡特尔建议

经济合作与发展组织(OECD)于 1998 年通过的一项建议，请成员国规定"(a)有效制裁措施，制裁的种类和程度应足以威慑公司和个人参与此类卡特尔；(b)执法程序及拥有足够权力以核查核心卡特尔并提出纠正建议的机构，包括获取文件和信息以及惩戒不服从行为的权力"。请求 OECD 成员国在执行针对此类卡特尔时开展相互合作。

Hard-core waiver

核心义务豁免

1955 年在 GATT 中作出的一项决定，允许缔约方在某些情况下，保留由于持续存在国际收支困难而维持多年的数量限制。该豁免需符合一些条件。例如，缔约方必须证明突然取消一项数量限制会对一国内产业造成严重损害，且它们必须执行循序渐进的自由化政策。另见*剩余数量限制(residual quantitative restrictions)*。

Hard law

硬法

贸易政策用语，指对其成员规定法律上可强制执行的权利和义务的国际协定。硬法的例子包括 GATT 和《服务贸易总协定》(GATS)中所包含的 WTO 义务，两者均为《WTO 协定》一部分。此类安排通常以条约的形式出现，或具有条约的地位。另见*软法(soft law)*。

Harmonization of standards and qualifications

标准和资格的协调

指原有各自标准或资格要求的两个或两个以上国家采用单一标准或资格要求。协调可能涉及创设一个全新的标准、采用该安排中最具影响力参加者的标准、采用最合理的标准或者以上方式的结合。实现协调通常需要经过艰苦谈判。另见*技术性贸易壁垒协定(Agreement on Technical Barriers to Trade)*、*明示协调(explicit harmonization)*、*国际电工委员会(International Electrotechnical Commission)*、*国际标准化组织(International Organization for Standardization)*、*托管互认(managed mutual recognition)*、*相互承认安排(mutual recognition arrangements)*。

Harmonized Commodity Description and Coding System: an international nomenclature developed by the ***World Customs Organization***, often called the Harmonized System. Its aims are (a) to achieve international uniformity in the classification of goods for customs purposes, (b) to facilitate the collection, analysis and comparison of world trade statistics, (c) to provide a common international system for coding, describing and classifying goods for commercial purposes, and (d) to provide an updated nomenclature to take account of technological developments and changes in international trade patterns. Products are arranged in ninety-seven chapters. Chapter 97 has not yet been allocated to any product group, hence the reference to ninety-six chapters in some descriptions. In addition, Chapters 98 and 99 are reserved for special use by individual countries. Chapters are at the two-digit level. They are broken down into headings at the four-digit level. The most detailed breakdown is the six-digit level. Beyond the six-digit level countries are free to break product groups down further.

Harmonized rules of origin: *see* ***rules of origin***.

Harmonized System: *see* ***Harmonized Commodity Description and Coding System***.

Harmonized tariff reductions: one of the ways to reduce tariff levels explored in the ***Tokyo Round*** negotiations. It was aimed at bringing tariffs of the participants for the same products to roughly similar levels. Harmonization is as difficult now as it was at the time of the Tokyo Round because of its impact on ***sensitive products***. *See also* ***linear tariff cuts*** and ***tariff negotiations***.

Harmonizing formula: used in tariff negotiations for much steeper reductions in higher tariffs than in lower tariffs to bring them closer together, i.e. to harmonize them.

Harries Report: a report commissioned by the Australian Government in 1978 to examine the nature of Australia's relationship with the ***Third World*** and to make proposals for the development of that relationship. The report was published in 1979 under the title *Australia and the Third World*. It contributed to a better understanding of the issues subsumed in the ***North–South dialogue*** and the ***New International Economic Order***.

Hatters' fur*:** a dispute in 1950 between the United States and Czechoslovakia about the interpretation of "unforeseen developments***". This is one of the conditions set out in GATT Article XIX (Emergency Action on Imports of Particular Products) which have to be satisfied before emergency action to cut imports can be taken. The United States argued that a change in hat fashions was an unforeseen development and therefore justification for action against the import of hatters' fur from Czechoslovakia. Czechoslovakia argued that changes in fashions were normal and should be expected. The United States won. John Jackson said of this case in *World Trade and the Law of the GATT* that one could almost conclude that an increase in imports could itself be an unforeseen development. The WTO ***Agreement on Safeguards*** now permits the use of safeguards action only if it has been properly determined that a

Harmonized Commodity Description and Coding System

商品名称及编码协调制度

由世界海关组织制定的国际命名规则，通常称为协调制度。旨在：(a)实现海关货物分类的国际统一；(b)为收集、分析和比较世界贸易统计数字提供便利；(c)为商业用途货物的编码、描述和分类提供一个共同的国际制度；以及(d)提供一个考虑到技术发展和国际贸易格局变化的最新命名规则。产品分列在 97 章之中。第 97 章尚未被分配任何产品组，因此在一些著述中称为 96 章。此外，第 98 章和第 99 章专门为个别国家的特殊用途保留。章为 2 位编码，再细分为 4 位编码，最详细的划分为 6 位编码，6 位编码之下各国有权对产品组进一步细分。

Harmonized rules of origin

经协调的原产地规则

见*原产地规则(rules of origin)*。

Harmonized System

协调制度

见*商品名称及编码协调制度(Harmonized Commodity Description and Coding System)*。

Harmonized tariff reductions

协调关税削减

东京回合谈判中探讨的削减关税水平的方法之一。目的在于将参加方相同产品的关税降至大致相同的水平。由于对敏感产品的影响，现在进行协调与在东京回合谈判时进行协调同样困难。另见*线性关税削减(linear tariff cuts)*、*关税谈判(tariff negotiations)*。

Harmonizing formula

协调公式

用于关税谈判中，对高关税进行比低关税更大幅度的削减，从而使两者水平更为接近，即对高关税和低关税进行协调。

Harries Report

哈里斯报告

澳大利亚政府于 1978 年委托编写的一份报告，旨在审查澳大利亚与第三世界关系的性质，并为发展此种关系提出建议。报告于 1979 年以《澳大利亚与第三世界》的题目发布，有助于更好地理解南北对话和国际经济新秩序所包含的问题。

Hatters' fur

裘皮女帽案

1950 年美国与捷克斯洛伐克关于"未预见的情况"的解释的争端。这是 GATT 第 19 条(对某些产品进口的紧急措施)规定的条件之一，在采取紧急措施减少进口前必须满足。美国认为，帽饰时尚的变化是未预见的情况，因此有理由对自捷克斯洛伐克进口的裘皮女帽采取行动。捷克斯洛伐克认为，时尚的变化是正常的和可预见的。美国胜诉。约翰·杰克逊在《世界贸易与 GATT 法》中谈到这一案件时指出，人们几乎可以得出结论，进口增加本身可被视为未预见的情况。WTO《保障措施协定》现在只有在已适当确定进口产品数量增

product is being imported in such increased quantities as to cause or threaten to cause serious ***injury*** to domestic industry that produces like or directly competitive products. [GATT/CP/106, Jackson 1969, Mueller 2003]

Havana Charter: the final draft of the *Charter for an International Trade Organization* (***ITO***), adopted at Havana in 1948. The breadth of its provisions can be gauged from its chapter headings: employment and economic activity, economic development and reconstruction, investment, restrictive business practices, intergovernmental commodity agreements, and commercial policy. The Charter never became part of international trade law for quite complex reasons. It was meant to be a binding set of articles, but successive rounds of negotiations on its contents gradually turned more and more of them into best-endeavours obligations. Developing countries opposed an open investment regime. Ultimately, the aims of the Charter became entangled in United States domestic politics and concerns that it would constrain domestic sovereignty. The Executive therefore delayed bringing the Charter before Congress, but in 1950 it decided that it would no longer seek to have the Charter adopted by Congress. This served as a signal to other countries not to pursue further any ratification proceedings. Much of the contents of the chapter on commercial policy survived as the General Agreement on Tariffs and Trade. This had been negotiated separately in 1947, and it entered provisionally into force on 1 January 1948. *See also* ***Protocol of Provisional Application***. [Brown 1950]

Hawley-Smoot tariff: *see* ***Smoot-Hawley Tariff Act***.

Hazard Analysis and Critical Control Points: HACCP. A system for assuring the safe manufacture of food products. It consists of seven steps: (1) analysis of hazards, (2) identification of critical control points, (3) establishing critical limits for each control point, (4) monitoring of the control points, (5) establishing a system of corrective action, (6) effective record-keeping, and (7) establishing procedures to verify that the system is working properly. HACCP had its origin in the food safety requirements developed by NASA for the United States space programme.

Hazardous wastes: *see* ***Basel Convention***.

Heading: a four-digit entry in the ***Harmonized Commodity Description and Coding System***. Examples are 1701 (cane or beet sugar and chemically pure sucrose, in solid form), 5001 (silk-worm cocoons suitable for reeling) and 9108 (watch movements, complete and assembled). *See also* ***chapter*** and ***sub-heading***.

Heavily Indebted Poor Countries (HIPC) Initiative: launched in 1996 by the ***IMF*** and the ***World Bank*** with the aim of ensuring that no poor country faces a debt burden it cannot manage. To benefit from the Initiative countries must meet certain criteria, commit to poverty reduction through policy change and demonstrate a good track record over time.

Heckscher-Ohlin theorem: states that countries will export those goods whose production is relatively intensive in the factors with which they are well endowed. The basic assumption underlying the theorem is that demand patterns

加如此之大，以至于对生产同类或直接竞争产品的国内产业造成或威胁造成严重损害的情况下，才允许使用保障措施。

Havana Charter

哈瓦那宪章

1948 年在哈瓦那通过的《国际贸易组织宪章》(ITO)最后草案。宪章条款的广度可以从其各章标题中看出：就业和商业活动、经济发展和重建、投资、限制性商业惯例、政府间商品协定及商业政策。由于十分复杂的原因，宪章从未成为国际贸易法的一部分。宪章原本应成为一套具有约束力的条款，但是就其内容开展的连续几轮谈判，逐渐将越来越多的条款变为最佳努力义务。发展中国家反对开放投资体制。最终，宪章的目标同美国国内政治及宪章将限制国家主权的担忧纠缠在一起。美国行政当局因此推迟将宪章提交国会，但在 1950 年决定不再寻求国会批准宪章。这成为向其他国家发出的不再寻求任何进一步核准程序的信号。宪章关于商业政策一章的大部分内容以 GATT 的形式保留了下来。GATT 于 1947 年单独谈判，并于 1948 年 1 月 1 日临时生效。另见*临时适用议定书(Protocol of Provisional Application)*。

Hawley-Smoot tariff

霍利-斯穆特关税

见*斯穆特-霍利关税法(Smoot-Hawley Tariff Act)*。

Hazard Analysis and Critical Control Points

危害性分析与关键控制点

HACCP。保证食品安全生产的制度，由 7 个步骤组成：(1)危害分析；(2)识别关键控制点；(3)建立每一控制点的关键限值；(4)监测控制点；(5)建立一套修正系统；(6)进行有效记录；以及(7)建立程序以验证系统运转正常。HACCP 起源于美国航空航天局为美国太空计划制定的食品安全要求。

Hazardous wastes

危险废物

见*巴塞尔公约(Basel Convention)*。

Heading

品目

商品名称及编码协调制度中的 4 位编码条目。例如 1701(固体甘蔗糖、甜菜糖及化学纯蔗糖)、5001(适于缫丝的蚕茧)和 9108(已组装的完整表芯)。另见*章(chapter)*、*子目(sub-heading)*。

Heavily Indebted Poor Countries (HIPC) Initiative

重债穷国倡议

国际货币基金组织(IMF)和世界银行于 1996 年发起的倡议，旨在避免穷国面临无法应对的债务负担。为从该倡议中获益，有关国家必须满足某些标准、承诺通过政策改革减少贫困，并随着时间推移表现出良好的业绩记录。

Heckscher-Ohlin theorem

赫克舍尔-奥林定理

该定理指出，一国将出口那些生产要素禀赋相对集中的货物。该定理的基本

do not differ much between countries. The theorem was first formulated by Eli Filip Heckscher in 1919 and publicized by Bertil Gotthard Ohlin in 1933, both eminent Swedish economists. It has been refined considerably over the years as a result of a patient statistical analysis. Essentially, the theorem is a restatement of the theory of ***comparative advantage***. *See also* ***new trade theory*** and ***Stolper-Samuelson theorem***.

Helms-Burton legislation: The United States *Cuban Liberty and Democratic Solidarity (Libertad) Act* of 1996. Its stated aims are "to seek international sanctions against the Government of Cuba headed by Fidel Castro" and "to plan for support of a transition government leading to a democratically elected government in Cuba". The Act contains several economic provisions. Section 108 requires the President to submit to Congress an annual report detailing (1) a description of all bilateral assistance given to Cuba by all other foreign countries, (2) a description of Cuba's commerce with other countries, (3) a description of all joint ventures entered into by foreign nationals with Cuba, (4) a determination of whether the facilities described under (3) are subject of a claim by a United States national against Cuba, (5) a determination of Cuba's foreign debt, (6) a description of the steps taken to ensure that no Cuban goods enter the United States, and (7) an identification of countries purchasing arms from Cuba. Section 110 prohibits the import into the United States of any merchandise wholly or partly made in Cuba or transported from or through Cuba. Title III contains the most contentious economic provisions. It deals with the protection of property rights of United States nationals and sets out in some detail the proposed remedies. The precepts of this Title are that (a) the Government of Cuba has confiscated the property of many United States nationals, (b) it is now making some of this property available to foreign investors, (c) this "trafficking" in property undermines the foreign policy of the United States, (d) the international judicial system lacks fully effective remedies for this type of problem, (e) international law recognizes that a law may be applied extraterritorially if it is intended to have effect substantially within its home territory, and (f) United States nationals whose property was confiscated should be able to have recourse through the United States courts. Section 306 states that damages may be sought against anyone engaged in trafficking after 1 November 1996. The law has since been amended to allow some United States export to Cuba if certain conditions are met. *See also* ***effects doctrine*** and ***extraterritoriality***.

***Herring and salmon*:** a case brought before the GATT by the United States against Canada in 1987 concerning Canadian regulations prohibiting the export or sale for export of unprocessed herring and pink and sockeye salmon. The facts were that Canada had proclaimed a regulation under the authority of the *Fisheries Act* of 1970 that "no person shall export from Canada any sockeye or pink salmon unless it is canned, salted, smoked, dried or frozen and has been inspected in accordance with the *Fish Inspection Act*". A similar provision applied to the export from the Province of British Columbia of food herring, roe

假设是，各国的需求模式无太大区别。该定理最早由伊莱·菲利普·赫克舍尔于 1919 年提出，并于 1933 年由贝蒂尔·圣哥达·奥林发表，两人都是瑞典著名经济学家。这一理论多年来经过细心统计分析得到了很大改进。从本质上讲，这一定理是对比较优势理论的重新阐述。另见*新贸易理论(new trade theory)*、*斯托尔帕-萨缪尔森定理(Stolper-Samuelson theorem)*。

Helms-Burton legislation

赫尔姆斯-伯顿法

即美国 1996 年《古巴自由与民主声援法》。该法声称的目的为“寻求对菲德尔·卡斯特罗领导的古巴政府实行国际制裁”并“计划支持一个过渡政府，使古巴形成民选政府”。法案包含了若干经济条款。第 108 条要求总统向国会提交一份年度报告，详细包括：(1)所有其他国家给予古巴的全部双边援助的说明；(2)古巴与其他国家商业往来的说明；(3)其他外国国民与古巴设立的所有合资企业的说明；(4)确定第(3)条所述设施是否是美国国民对古巴主张的权利的客体；(5)确定古巴的外债；(6)为保证无古巴货物进入美国而采取步骤的说明；以及(7)确定自古巴购买武器的国家。第 110 条禁止美国进口任何全部或部分在古巴制造、自古巴运输或经古巴运输的制成品。第三章包含最具争议的经济条款，处理对美国国民财产权的保护，并详细规定建议的救济措施。制定该章的原因为：(a)古巴政府没收了许多美国国民的财产；(b)古巴政府现在使外国投资者可以获得其中一些财产；(c)此种“非法交易”的财产破坏了美国的对外政策；(d)国际司法制度对此种问题缺乏充分有效的救济措施；(e)国际法承认，如果一项法律意在其本国领土内产生实质性影响，则可在域外适用；以及(f)被没收财产的美国国民应能够通过美国法院追索赔偿。第306条规定，在 1996 年 11 月 1 日后，可向任何从事非法交易者要求损害赔偿。这项法律后来进行了修正，允许在满足某些条件的情况下一些美国产品可以向古巴出口。另见*效果原则(effects doctrine)*、*治外法权(extraterritoriality)*。

Herring and salmon

鲱鱼和鲑鱼案

1987 年美国向 GATT 起诉加拿大的案件，涉及加拿大禁止出口或出口销售未经加工的鲱鱼、粉红鲑鱼和红鲑鱼的法规。实际情况是加拿大根据 1970 年《渔业法》的授权颁布了一项法规，规定“除非经罐装、腌制、熏制、干燥或冷冻，且依照《鱼类检验法》进行检验，否则任何人不得自加拿大出口任何红鲑鱼和粉红鲑鱼”。一个类似规定适用于自不列颠哥伦比亚省出口的食用鲱鱼、卵鲱

herring, herring roe or herring spawn. Canada had also maintained since the early decades of the twentieth century governmental measures for the conservation, management and development of salmon and herring stocks in the waters off British Columbia. These measures included intergovernmental agreements and conventions. At the time of this dispute, sockeye and pink and herring fisheries dominated commercial fishing of the Canadian West Coast. They gave employment to almost five-sixths of the workers in the British Columbia fish processing industry. Canada stated that the measures concerned were an integral and long-standing component of its West Coast fisheries conservation and management regime. They were therefore completely justified under GATT Article XX(g) which gives members the right not to apply the provisions of the Agreement if this necessary to conserve exhaustible natural resources, but only in conjunction with domestic restrictions on production and consumption. Canada also said that its strict quality and marketing regulations for the three species were necessary to maintain its reputation for safe, high-quality fish products. In making its findings, the ***panel*** noted that Canada prohibited the export of fish not meeting its standards, but that it banned the export of certain unprocessed herring and salmon even if they met Canadian export standards. The panel therefore found that the export prohibitions were not necessary to maintain standards. The panel agreed that salmon and herring stocks were "exhaustible natural resources" and that harvest limitations were "restrictions on domestic production" as intended by Article XX(g). It considered, however, that while a trade measure did not have to be essential to the conservation of an exhaustible natural resource, it had to be aimed primarily at conservation. The panel concluded finally that Canada's export prohibitions could not be considered as aimed primarily at the conservation of salmon and herring stock because they only related to the export of these species in their unprocessed form. Canada only limited the purchases of unprocessed herring and salmon stocks by foreign processors and consumers, but not those by domestic processors and consumers. The panel therefore decided that the export prohibitions were not justified by Article XX(g) also. *See also* ***general exceptions*** and ***trade and environment***. [GATT BISD 35S]

Hidden dumping: a form of ***dumping*** said to occur when a firm exports goods at ostensibly market prices to a related firm, but in reality at a lower cost. The second firm then sells the goods in the importing country at about that price, but the transaction has all the time been below market price. *See also* ***anti-dumping measures***.

High-income economies: a group of eighty economies classified by the ***World Bank*** as having had as of July 2018 a per capita GNI (gross national income) of more than $12,376. *See also* ***low-income economies***, ***lower-middle-income economies*** and ***upper-middle-income economies***.

High-Level United Nations Conference on South–South Cooperation: held in Nairobi in 2009. *See also* ***Second High-Level United Nations Conference on South–South Cooperation***, held in Buenos Aires in March 2019.

鱼、鲱鱼卵和鲱鱼幼鱼。自20世纪初期起，加拿大还一直维持保护、管理和发展不列颠哥伦比亚省水域的鲑鱼和鲱鱼种群的政府措施。这些措施包括政府间协议和公约。在这一争端发生时，红鲑鱼、粉红鲑鱼和鲱鱼占加拿大西海岸商业捕捞的主体，为不列颠哥伦比亚省鱼类加工业提供近六分之五工人的就业。加拿大表示，有关措施是其西海岸渔业保护和管理制度中长期存在的组成部分。因此根据GATT第20条(g)款是完全合理的。该款规定缔约方如为保护可用尽自然资源所必需，可以不适用总协定条款，但必须与限制国内生产和消费的措施一同实施。加拿大还表示，对这三种鱼类实行的严格质量和销售规定是维护自身安全、高质量鱼产品声誉所必需的。在调查结果中，专家组指出加拿大禁止出口不符合其标准的鱼类，但禁止某些未加工鲱鱼和鲑鱼的出口，即使符合加拿大出口标准。专家组因此认为，出口禁止并不是维持标准所必需的。专家组一致认为，鲑鱼和鲱鱼种群是"可用尽自然资源"，捕捞限制属于第20条(g)款所指的"对国内生产的限制措施"。但专家组认为，虽然贸易措施不一定对保护可用尽的自然资源至关重要，但必须主要以保护为目的。专家组最终认定，加拿大的出口禁止只涉及属未经加工形式的鲑鱼和鲱鱼种群出口，所以不能被视为主要目的是保护两个鱼种。加拿大只限制外国加工商和消费者购买未加工的鲱鱼和鲑鱼，而不限制本国加工商和消费者购买。专家组因此决定，出口禁止也不能根据第20条(g)款认定属合理。另见*一般例外(general exceptions)*、*贸易与环境(trade and environment)*。

Hidden dumping
隐蔽倾销

一种倾销形式，指在一公司表面上以市场价格向一关联公司出口商品，而实际以更低价格出口。第二家公司随后在进口国以该价格出售商品，而交易始终低于市场价格。另见*反倾销措施(anti-dumping measures)*。

High-income economies
高收入经济体

世界银行列出的截至2018年7月人均国民总收入(GNI)超过12,376美元的80个经济体。另见*低收入经济体(low-income economies)*、*中等偏下收入经济体(lower-middle-income economies)*、*中等偏上收入经济体(upper-middle-income economies)*。

High-Level United Nations Conference on South–South Cooperation
联合国南南合作高级别会议

2009年在内罗毕举行。另见2019年3月在布宜诺斯艾利斯举行的*第二届联合国南南合作高级别会议(Second High-Level United Nations Conference on South–South Cooperation)*。

Historical preferences: in the WTO framework this refers to benefits under ***preferential trade arrangements*** in existence before the GATT entered into force on 1 January 1948. Such arrangements were allowed to continue even though they contravened ***most-favoured-nation treatment***, but under Article I of the GATT (General Most-Favoured-Nation Treatment) the maximum ***margin of preference*** could not be increased. The ***imperial preferences arrangement*** is one example of historical preferences. The value of historical preferences decreased steadily as ***most-favoured-nation tariffs*** came down. Most have now disappeared.

Hit-and-run dumping: *see* ***sporadic dumping***.

HLM: usually refers to the WTO High-Level Meeting for Least-Developed Countries, held in October 1997 in Geneva.

HODs: heads of delegations, usually ambassadors or ministers.

Hollowing-out: *see* ***deindustrialization*** and ***delocalization***.

Home market visibility test: finding out how prominent a product is in its home market. This is important in investigations of whether ***anti-dumping measures*** can be imposed. Part of the investigation will establish the ***normal value*** of the product. The ***Anti-Dumping Agreement*** requires that at least 5 per cent of the sales of the product in question should occur in its home market (called "exporting market" in the Agreement) to give a reliable indication of its normal value in that market. If the home market is smaller, it may be necessary to determine normal value through the use, for example, of an ***analogue country*** or a ***constructed value***.

Homestyle exemption: refers to Section 110(5) of the United States Copyright Act, as amended by the *Fairness in Music Licensing Act* of 1998. It permits some shops and food service or drinking establishments of a defined size to broadcast radio and television programmes using a limited number of loudspeakers or television sets without leading to an infringement of ***copyright***. Main assumptions are that this would be the kind of equipment normally used at home, and that the establishment using it would be too small to subscribe to a commercial background music service. Section 110(5) does not apply to the playing of recorded music, such as compact discs or cassettes. In 1999 the ***European Communities*** sought the establishment of a ***panel*** on the grounds that this Section violated the obligations of the United States under the ***Agreement on Trade-Related Aspects of Intellectual Property Rights***, especially those relating to the ***Berne Convention***. The panel found in favour of the European Communities. [WT/DS160/R]

Homonymous geographical indications: identical ***geographical indications*** in use in more than one country. These can occur whenever countries share a language, but especially when emigrants take the place names of their home country with them.

Hong Kong, China: the formal name of Hong Kong in the WTO, ***APEC*** and some other international organizations.

Hong Kong Ministerial Conference: the sixth ***WTO Ministerial Conference***, held from 13 to 18 December 2005.

Historical preferences
历史性优惠

WTO 框架内，指 1948 年 1 月 1 日 GATT 生效之前存在的优惠贸易安排项下的优惠。此类安排允许继续存在，尽管违反最惠国待遇，但根据 GATT 第 1 条(普遍最惠国待遇)，最高优惠幅度不得增加。帝国特惠安排是历史性优惠的一例。随着最惠国关税的降低，历史性优惠的价值逐步降低，大多数已消失。

Hit-and-run dumping
打了就跑的倾销

见*偶然性倾销(sporadic dumping)*。

HLM
高级别会议

通常指 1997 年 10 月在日内瓦举行的 WTO 最不发达国家高级别会议。

HODs
代表团团长

通常为担任代表团长的大使或部长。

Hollowing-out
产业空心化

见*去工业化(deindustrialization)*、*去本地化(delocalization)*。

Home market visibility test
国内市场能见度测试

了解一产品在其国内市场的重要程度。这在决定是否实施反倾销措施的调查中很重要。调查的一部分将确定产品的正常价值。《反倾销协定》要求，所涉产品至少 5%的销售应发生在其本国市场(协定中称为“出口国市场”)，以可靠地表明其在该市场中的正常价值。如果国内市场较小，则可能有必要通过使用替代国或推定价格确定正常价值。

Homestyle exemption
家庭型例外

指经《1998 年音乐公平许可法》修正的《美国版权法》第 110(5)条。允许一些商店和规定规模的餐饮营业场所使用有限数量的扬声器或电视机播放广播和电视节目，而不会导致侵犯版权。主要假设为，这通常是家用设备类型，且使用的营业场所规模太小而不能订阅商业背景音乐服务。第 110(5)条不适用于播放录制音乐，如光盘或盒式磁带。1999 年，欧洲共同体以该条违反美国在《与贸易有关的知识产权协定》项下义务为由要求成立专家组，特别是与《伯尔尼公约》相关的内容。专家组裁决支持欧共体。

Homonymous geographical indications
同音异义地理标志

在一个以上国家使用的相同地理标志。此种情况在不同国家使用同一种语言时可能会发生，特别是在移民带来母国的地名时。

Hong Kong, China
中国香港

香港在 WTO、APEC 及其他国际组织中的正式名称。

Hong Kong Ministerial Conference
香港部长级会议

第 6 届 WTO 部长级会议，2005 年 12 月 13 日至 18 日举行。

Horizontal: cutting across or common to several issues.

Horizontal arrangements: *see* ***competition policy***.

Horizontal commitments: a component of the schedules of commitments attached by WTO member countries to the ***General Agreement on Trade in Services***. Horizontal commitments apply to all services trade covered in a schedule of commitments. Generally, they relate to investment, formation of corporate structures, land acquisition, the movement of personnel, etc. *See also* ***commitment***.

Horizontal foreign direct investment: this refers to ***foreign direct investment*** by a firm in the area of activities it already pursues at home. For example, a car manufacturer in country A invests in a car plant in country B. *See also* ***tariff-jumping investment***.

Horizontal *keiretsu*: *see* ***keiretsu relationships***.

Hormone growth promotants: chemical substances which accelerate the growth of animals through increasing the efficiency of feed conversion. Proponents of their use say that they permit the animal to produce more muscle and less fat without adverse effects if they are administered properly. The use of hormone growth promotants is legal in the United States and other major beef-producing countries. In 1989 the ***European Community*** banned the import of beef and beef products produced with the addition of hormone growth promotants on the grounds that their use led to dangerous levels of residues. United States producers claim that their beef products are safe, and that the European Community action was motivated above all by the need to deal with a mounting beef surplus. Accusations and counter-accusations led nowhere, and in 1996 the United States brought the dispute before the WTO. Australia, Canada and New Zealand supported the United States action. The ***panel*** handed down its decision in mid-1997, and it found against the European Community. *See also* ***sanitary and phytosanitary measures***.

Horn of Africa: consists of Djibouti, Eritrea, Ethiopia and Somalia. *See also* ***Greater Horn of Africa***.

Host country operational measures: HCOMs. An ***UNCTAD*** contribution to the analysis of ***international investment agreements***. It describes "the vast array of [investment] measures implemented by host countries concerning the operation of foreign affiliates once inside their jurisdictions". UNCTAD divides HCOMs into three groups. The first, so-called "red light" HCOMs, contains measures explicitly prohibited by multilateral agreements, such as the ***Agreement on Trade-Related Investment Measures***. The second group, the "yellow light" HCOMs, is made up of measures additionally prohibited, conditioned or discouraged by inter-regional, regional or bilateral agreements. The third group, the "green light" HCOMs, are not generally prohibited through international investment rules. *See also* ***traffic light approach***.

Hub and spokes: a concept used in the analysis of ***free-trade areas***. It postulates that a large country could be a member of several free-trade arrangements, but that smaller countries might only belong to one of these arrangements each.

Horizontal
水平

对若干问题属于水平的或共同的问题。

Horizontal arrangements
水平安排

见*竞争政策(competition policy)*。

Horizontal commitments
水平承诺

WTO 成员在《服务贸易总协定》所附承诺减让表的组成部分。水平承诺适用于减让表中涵盖的所有服务贸易。通常涉及投资、企业结构的组成、土地收购、人员流动等。另见*承诺(commitment)*。

Horizontal foreign direct investment
横向外国直接投资

指一企业对其已在本国开展经营活动的领域进行的外国直接投资。例如，A 国的一家汽车制造商在 B 国投资一家汽车工厂。另见*跳越关税投资(tariff-jumping investment)*。

Horizontal *keiretsu*
水平经连

见*经连关系(keiretsu relationships)*。

Hormone growth promotants
激素生长促进剂案

激素生长促进剂是通过提高饲料转化效率加速动物生长的化学物质。使用支持者认为，如果管理得当，可以使动物生长更多的肌肉和更少的脂肪，而不会产生不良影响。在美国和其他主要牛肉生产国，使用激素生长促进剂属合法。1989 年，欧洲共同体禁止进口添加激素生长促进剂的牛肉和牛肉制品，理由是这些产品的使用会导致残留物达到危险水平。美国牛肉生产商称，他们的牛肉产品是安全的，欧共体采取行动的首要动机是为了解决不断增加的牛肉过剩。双方的指控和抗辩无任何结果，1996 年，美国将争端提交 WTO。澳大利亚、加拿大和新西兰支持美国的行动。专家组在 1997 年年中作出了不利于欧共体的裁决。另见*卫生与植物卫生措施(sanitary and phytosanitary measures)*。

Horn of Africa
非洲之角

由吉布提、厄立特里亚、埃塞俄比亚和索马里组成。另见*大非洲之角(Greater Horn of Africa)*。

Host country operational measures
东道国执行措施

HCOMs。联合国贸易与发展会议(UNCTAD)对国际投资协定分析的一项内容。指"东道国针对进入其管辖范围内的外国子公司的运营实施的大量(投资)措施"。UNCTAD 将 HCOMs 分为三组：第一组即所谓的红灯措施，包含多边协定明确禁止的措施，例如《与贸易有关的投资措施协定》。第二组为黄灯措施，由区域间、区域内或双边协定额外禁止、制约或阻止的措施组成。第三组为绿灯措施，通常不为国际投资规则所禁止。另见*交通灯法(traffic light approach)*。

Hub and spokes
轮轴-辐条

分析自由贸易区时使用的概念。假定一个大国可以是若干自由贸易安排的成员，但较小国家只可能是其中一个自由贸易安排的成员。大国因此将作为轮

The large country would then be the hub, and the others would form the spokes in a series of discriminatory bilateral trade arrangements. Unlike in the case of a free-trade area, where all parties negotiate as equals, under a hub-and-spokes arrangement the larger country generally sets the terms and conditions for membership. Some, however, argue that hub-and-spoke arrangements may be stepping stones to larger free-trade areas. Others maintain that the country forming the hub would have no incentive to extend such arrangements and trade preferences to others. This argument remains unresolved. However, as the 1995 WTO study on *Regionalism and the World Trading System* notes, in the case of a hub-and-spoke system, the essence is always the same: goods and services (and perhaps capital and labour) flow more freely between the hub and each spoke than they do between the spokes.

Hub and Spokes Programme: a joint programme of the ***European Union***, ***Commonwealth*** Secretariat, the ***ACP states*** and the Organisation Internationale de la Francophonie. Its aim is to help participating countries to develop and implement trade policies and agreements that reflect national priorities and are effective in a global trading system. It does this by helping countries to train key stakeholders and policy makers in trade policy issues, negotiating and implementing trade agreements and establishing national and regional trade networks. *See also* ***capacity-building***. [thecommonwealth.org/hubandspokes]

Hull formula: sometimes Hull rule. The view expressed in 1938 by Cordell Hull, then United States Secretary of State, in response to Mexican agrarian nationalization measures that there should be "prompt, adequate and effective" compensation in cases of ***expropriation***. [Seid 2002]

Human Development Report: a report published by the ***United Nations Development Programme*** (UNDP). Its focus usually is on progress made by UNDP towards achieving one or more of its main goals. For example, the 2015 report dealt with work for human development, the 2016 report with human development for everyone and the 2019 report with inequality. Separately UNDP publishes National Human Development Reports dealing with individual countries.

Human rights: many definitions are available for this term. All share the idea that human rights belong to all humans and cannot be taken away from them, i.e. that they are "inalienable". The starting point for post-war human rights actions is the ***Universal Declaration of Human Rights***, adopted by the ***United Nations General Assembly*** on 10 December 1948. Entries in this dictionary concerned with human rights include ***core labour standards***, ***Declaration on Fundamental Principles and Rights at Work and its fullow-up***, ***International Covenant on Economic, Social and Cultural Rights***, ***Millennium Declaration***, ***Millennium Development Goals***, ***Right to Development***, ***trade and gender***, ***trade and human rights*** and ***trade and poverty***.

Human rights clause: a provision in national trade laws or international treaties which promotes the observance of human rights. The ***ACP-EU Partnership Agreement***, for example, requires from its members respect for all human rights

轴，而其他国家在一系列具有歧视性的双边贸易安排中将成为辐条。与所有参加方平等谈判自贸区的情况不同，在轮轴-辐条安排下，大国通常规定成员资格的条款和条件。但是，一些人认为轮轴-辐条安排可以是更大自贸区的垫脚石。其他人则认为构成轮轴的国家没有向其他国家推广此类安排和贸易优惠的动力。这一争论没有结果。但是，如 1995 年 WTO 关于《区域主义与世界贸易体制》的研究报告所指出的，轮轴-辐条系统的实质总是相同的，即货物和服务(可能还有资本和劳动力)在轮轴和辐条之间的流动要比辐条之间的流动更为自由。

Hub and Spokes Programme

轮轴-辐条计划

欧盟、英联邦秘书处、非加太地区国家和法语国家及地区国际组织的联合项目。旨在帮助参加国发展和实施反映国家优先事项和在全球贸易体制中发挥作用的贸易政策和协定。通过在贸易政策问题、贸易协定谈判和实施、建立国家和地区贸易网络等方面帮助各国培训关键利益相关方和决策者以实现上述目标。另见*能力建设(capacity-building)*。

Hull formula

赫尔公式

有时称为赫尔准则。1938 年由时任美国国务卿科德尔 · 赫尔提出的观点，以回应墨西哥的土地国有化措施，即在征收情况下应给予"及时、充分和有效的"补偿。

Human Development Report

人类发展报告

由联合国开发计划署(UNDP)发布的报告。该报告通常聚焦 UNDP 达成的一个或多个主要目标的进展情况。例如，2015 年报告涉及人类发展工作，2016 年报告涉及人人享有人类发展，2019 年报告则关于不平等问题。此外，UNDP 还出版处理个别国家的国家人类发展报告。

Human rights

人权

该词有多种定义。所有定义都包含人权属于所有人而不能剥夺的思想，即人权是"不可分割的"。战后人权行动的起点是联合国大会于 1948 年 12 月 10 日通过的《世界人权宣言》。本辞典中有关人权的词条包括：*核心劳工标准(core labour standards)*、*关于工作中基本原则和权利宣言及其后续措施(Declaration on Fundamental Principles and Rights at Work and its follow-up)*、*经济、社会和文化权利国际公约(International Covenant on Economic, Social and Cultural Rights)*、*联合国千年宣言(Millennium Declaration)*、*联合国千年发展目标(Millennium Development Goals)*、*发展权利(Right to Development)*、*贸易与性别(trade and gender)*、*贸易与人权(trade and human rights)*、*贸易与贫穷(trade and poverty)*。

Human rights clause

人权条款

在国家贸易法或国际条约中用以促进遵守人权的条款。例如，《非加太地区国家与欧盟伙伴关系协定》要求成员尊重全部人权和基本自由，作为该协定的

and fundamental freedoms as an essential element of the Agreement. The ***Mediterranean Agreements*** concluded by the ***European Union*** also require respect for human rights and democracy. Some have suggested that Article XX (General Exceptions) of the ***GATT*** should be supplemented by a reference to human rights, but this has not yet attracted widespread support. Chapter 19 of the ***Comprehensive and Progressive Agreement for Trans-Pacific Partnership*** requires the parties to adopt and maintain in their statutes and regulations the rights stated in the ILO ***Declaration on Fundamental Principles and Rights at Work and its follow-up***. Not so long ago this would have been unthinkable in a trade agreement involving such a diverse range of parties. *See also* ***democracy clause***, ***GSP+***, ***social clause*** and ***trade and human rights***. [Bal 2001, Petersmann 2001]

Hyperglobalization: used to describe the rapid changes in globalization in the late twentieth and early twenty-first centuries. Due to Rodrik (2012).

基本要素。欧盟缔结的《地中海协定》也要求尊重人权和民主。有人建议 GATT 第 20 条(一般例外)应增加对有关人权的内容，但还未得到广泛的支持。《全面与进步跨太平洋伙伴关系协定》第 19 章要求缔约方在其法律法规中采纳并维持国际劳工组织(ILO)《关于工作中基本原则和权利宣言及其后续措施》所表述的权利。不久前在包含如此多样参加方的贸易协定中这一点还是无法想象的。另见*民主条款(democracy clause)*、*普惠制附加(GSP+)*、*社会条款(social clause)*、*贸易与人权(trade and human rights)*。

Hyperglobalization
超全球化

用于描述 20 世纪晚期和 21 世纪早期全球化中发生的快速变化。

I

IBRD: International Bank for Reconstruction and Development. *See* ***World Bank*** and ***World Bank Group***.

ICC Guidelines for International Investment: *see* ***International Chamber of Commerce (ICC) Guidelines for International Investment***.

ICC-WTO Small Business Champions initiative: launched jointly by the ***International Chamber of Commerce*** and the ***WTO*** in 2017 to facilitate participation by smaller companies in international trade.

ICITO: Interim Commission for the International Trade Organization. Established in 1948 to prepare the administrative arrangements for entry into force of the ***ITO***. At the same time, it was agreed that ICITO would supply the secretariat services for GATT. As the ITO did not enter into force, ICITO's only reason for existence was the latter arrangement.

ICSID: International Centre for Settlement of Investment Disputes, located in Washington, DC, chaired *ex officio* by the president of the ***World Bank***. It was established by the *Convention on the Settlement of Investment Disputes between States and Nationals of Other States* which entered into force on 14 October 1966. ICSID provides facilities for conciliation and arbitration of disputes. It describes its main objective as the promotion of a climate of mutual confidence between states and foreign investors conducive to an increasing flow of resources to developing countries. It publishes the *ICSID Review: Foreign Investment Law Journal* which is a source of commentary and analysis of the legal treatment of foreign investment, including investment treaties. *See also* ***foreign direct investment***.

ICT: information and communication(s) technology. *See* ***digital divide***, ***Digital Economy Report*** and ***Okinawa Charter on Global Information Society***.

Identical goods: defined in the ***Customs Valuation Agreement*** as "goods that are the same in all respects, including physical characteristics, quality and reputation. Minor differences in appearance would not preclude goods otherwise conforming to the definition from being regarded as identical". Among other conditions, goods are not regarded as "identical goods" unless they were produced in the same country as the goods being valued. *See also* ***accordion of likeness***, ***fungible goods***, ***like product*** and ***similar goods***.

Illicit trade: international trade in goods and services, including illicit financial flows, in contravention of international and national laws. *See also* ***Arusha Declaration***, ***CITES***, ***contraband***, ***corruption***, ***counterfeiting***, ***Draft International Agreement on Illicit Payments***, ***smuggling*** and ***trafficking***.

I

IBRD
国际复兴开发银行
见*世界银行(World Bank)*、*世界银行集团(World Bank Group)*。

ICC Guidelines for International Investment
国际商会国际投资准则
见*国际商会国际投资指南(International Chamber of Commerce (ICC) Guidelines for International Investment)*。

ICC-WTO Small Business Champions initiative
国际商会-WTO 小企业冠军赛倡议
国际商会与WTO在2017年共同发起的倡议，以便利较小企业参与国际贸易。

ICITO
国际贸易组织临时委员会
1948 年设立，为国际贸易组织(ITO)生效作出行政安排。同时，各方议定 ICITO 为 GATT 提供秘书服务。由于国际贸易组织没有生效，ICITO 存在的惟一原因是后一种安排。

ICSID
国际投资争端解决中心
中心设在美国华盛顿特区，世界银行行长依职权担任主席。依据 1966 年 10 月 14 日生效的《解决国家与他国国民间投资争议公约》设立。ICSID 提供争议调解和仲裁的场所。主要目标是在国家和外国投资者之间促进形成相互信任的氛围，以有助于增加向发展中国家的资源流动。中心发布《国际投资争端解决中心评论：外国投资法学刊》，包含对外国投资的法律待遇的评论和分析，包括投资条约。另见*外国直接投资(foreign direct investment)*。

ICT
信息通信技术
见*数字鸿沟(digital divide)*、*数字经济报告(Digital Economy Report)*、*全球信息社会冲绳宪章(Okinawa Charter on Global Information Society)*。

Identical goods
相同货物
《海关估价协定》中的定义为“在所有方面均相同的货物，包括物理特性、质量和信誉。外观上的微小差别并不妨碍在其他方面符合定义的货物被视为相同货物”。在其他情形下，除非货物与被估价货物在同一国生产，否则不被视为“相同货物”。另见*符合同类性(accordion of likeness)*、*可替代产品(fungible goods)*、*同类产品(like product)*、*类似货物(similar goods)*。

Illicit trade
非法贸易
违反国际和国家法律的国际货物贸易和服务贸易，包括非法资金流动。另见*阿鲁沙宣言(Arusha Declaration)*、*濒危野生动植物种国际贸易公约(CITES)*、*禁运品(contraband)*、*腐败(corruption)*、*假冒(counterfeiting)*、*关于违法付款的国际协定草案(Draft International Agreement on Illicit Payments)*、*走私(smuggling)*、*非法交易(trafficking)*。

ILO: *see* ***International Labour Organization***.

ILO Convention No. 138: *see* ***child labour***.

ILO Convention No. 182: the ***Convention Concerning the Prohibition and Immediate Action for the Elimination of the Worst Forms of Child Labour***.

ILO Declaration on Fundamental Principles and Rights at Work: *see* ***Declaration on Fundamental Principles and Rights at Work and its follow-up***.

ILO Tripartite Declaration of Principles Concerning Multinational Enterprises and Social Policy: a non-binding set of principles adopted by the ***International Labour Organization***. It became effective in 1978 and has been amended several times since. The Declaration recognizes the importance of the role played by multinational enterprises in the economies of most countries and in international economic relations. The Declaration does not provide a definition of multinational enterprises, but it states that it applies to parent companies and/or local entities. The Declaration aims to encourage the positive contribution multinational enterprises can make to economic and social progress and the realization of decent work for all. It recognizes that this aim will be furthered by appropriate laws and policies, measures and actions adopted by governments. The Declaration is meant to guide governments in taking appropriate measures and social policies. It does not aim at introducing or maintaining inequalities of treatment between multinational and national enterprises. Finally, it sets out principles in the fields of employment, training, conditions of work and life and industrial relations. The Declaration is therefore relevant to the consideration of ***trade and labour standards***.

IMF: International Monetary Fund. One of the organizations established at the 1944 United Nations Monetary and Financial Conference held at Bretton Woods. It oversees the international monetary system through (a) encouraging international monetary cooperation, (b) facilitating the expansion of balanced growth of international trade, (c) assisting member countries in correcting balance of payments deficits through short- to medium-term credits, and (d) promoting foreign exchange stability and orderly exchange relations among its members. ***GATT*** Article XV provides for consultation and coordination between the two organizations on matters concerning monetary reserves, balances of payment or foreign exchange arrangements. GATT members either had to join the IMF or enter into a special exchange arrangement with the other GATT members to ensure that the provisions of the Agreement were not frustrated by foreign exchange measures. The relationship of the WTO with the IMF is based on the provisions that have governed the GATT's relationship with it. The IMF participates in ***balance-of-payments consultations*** conducted under Articles XII and XVIII:B of the GATT. *See also* ***Bretton Woods Agreements*** and ***Trade Integration Mechanism***.

IMF Balance of Payments Manual: currently in its sixth edition, published in 2010 and updated in 2013. It provides detailed guidance to statistical offices on

ILO
国际劳工组织
见国际劳工组织(International Labour Organization)。

ILO Convention No. 138
国际劳工组织公约第 138 号
见*童工(child labour)*。

ILO Convention No. 182
国际劳工组织公约第 182 号
《禁止和立即行动消除最恶劣形式的童工劳动公约》。

ILO Declaration on Fundamental Principles and Rights at Work
国际劳工组织关于工作中基本原则和权利的宣言
见*关于工作中基本原则和权利宣言及其后续措施(Declaration on Fundamental Principles and Rights at Work and its follow-up)*。

ILO Tripartite Declaration of Principles Concerning Multinational Enterprises and Social Policy
国际劳工组织关于多国企业和社会政策的三方原则宣言
国际劳工组织(ILO)采用的一套非约束性原则。宣言于 1978 年生效，此后经过多次修正。宣言认识到跨国企业在大多数国家的经济和国际经济关系中所发挥的重要作用。宣言未对跨国企业作出定义，但指出宣言适用于母公司和/或本地实体。宣言旨在鼓励跨国企业对经济和社会进步和实现人人享有体面工作作出积极贡献，认识到这一目标将通过各国政府采取适当的法律和政策、措施和行动加以促进。宣言旨在指导各国政府采取适当措施和社会政策，而非引入或维持跨国企业和国家企业之间的不平等待遇。最后，宣言列出在就业、培训、工作、生活和产业关系领域的原则。宣言因此与贸易与劳工标准的审议相关。

IMF
国际货币基金组织
1944 年在布雷顿森林举行的联合国货币与金融会议所建立的组织，通过下列途径监督国际货币体系：(a)鼓励国际货币合作；(b)促进国际贸易平衡增长的扩大；(c)通过中短期信贷帮助成员国纠正国际收支赤字；以及(d)促进成员国之间的外汇稳定和有序汇率关系。GATT 第 15 条规定，两组织就有关货币储备、国际收支或外汇安排的事项进行磋商和协调。GATT 缔约方要么必须加入 IMF，要么与 GATT 其他缔约方签订特殊外汇安排，以保证 GATT 条款不因外汇行动而无效。WTO 与 IMF 的关系建立在管辖 GATT 与 IMF 关系的条款之上。IMF 参加根据 GATT 第 12 条和第 18 条 B 节进行的国际收支磋商。另见*布雷顿森林协定(Bretton Woods Agreements)*、*贸易一体化机制(Trade Integration Mechanism)*。

IMF Balance of Payments Manual
国际货币基金组织国际收支手册
现已到第 6 版，2010 年出版，2013 年更新。手册为统计部门根据一套国际议

the recording of cross-border transactions according to a set of international agreed guidelines. [www.imf.org]

IMF Buffer Stock Financing Facility: abolished in 2000. *See **buffer stocks**.*

IMF financing facilities: the ***IMF*** has a wide range of lending instruments tailored to address different types of balance of payments problems that member countries may have encountered. When this happens, the IMF and the member country applying for funds usually negotiate to arrive on a programme of economic policies before it releases any funds. Such agreements usually require the country concerned to address the roots of the problem. The ***Poverty Reduction and Growth Trust*** is aimed specifically at low-income countries. It consists of the Extended Credit Facility for countries experiencing serious payments imbalances because of structural impediments, the Standby Credit Facility to address short-term problems and the Rapid Credit Facility with an urgent balance of payments need, including those caused by commodity price shocks, natural disasters and domestic fragilities. All three of these lend funds on concessional terms.

Impairment: a negative effect on a WTO member's rights under one or more of the agreements administered by the WTO. *See also **non-violation** and **nullification or impairment**.*

Impediments to trade: *see **barriers to trade**.*

Imperial preferences arrangement: established formally at the 1932 Ottawa Imperial Conference. The basic feature of the arrangement was that pairs of countries making up the British Empire at the time exchanged reciprocal trade preferences. The United Kingdom was a party to the agreements in most cases. The arrangement became a target of United States ***commercial policy*** at the time of the drafting of the ***Atlantic Charter*** in 1941, and again in Article 7 of the ***mutual aid agreement*** between the United Kingdom and the United States of 1942. The Article sought "the elimination of all forms of discriminatory treatment in international commerce". When the GATT entered into force in 1948, it prohibited an increase in all ***margins of preference***. This ceiling, combined with negotiated tariff reductions under the GATT, ensured that preference margins were soon eroded. Most have disappeared. The increasing use of the term "British Commonwealth of Nations" in the inter-war years also led to the more widespread use of Commonwealth preferences instead of Imperial preferences. The modern ***Commonwealth*** has not had any role in the arrangement. *See also **historical preferences** and **preferential trade arrangements**.*

Implementation: putting into effect the undertakings made in trade negotiations. This is usually considered much less exciting by trade policy people than negotiating new things. In the WTO, implementation sometimes refers to a set of issues argued for by ***developing countries***. The first is that some of their ***Uruguay Round*** obligations were too heavy for them. The second is that there should be negotiations to redress the unfair balance carried by developing countries. Third, that they could only meet some of their other obligations

定准则记录跨境交易提供详细指导。

IMF Buffer Stock Financing Facility

国际货币基金组织缓冲储存融资机制

2000 年废止。见*缓冲储存(buffer stocks)*。

IMF financing facilities

国际货币基金组织融资机制

国际货币基金组织(IMF)拥有多种借贷工具，专门用以处理成员国可能已经遇到的不同类型的国际收支问题。当出现国际收支问题时，IMF 和申请资金的成员国通常在 IMF 发放资金前进行磋商以达成一项经济政策计划。此类协定通常需要有关国家解决问题根源。"减贫与增长信托基金"专门针对低收入国家。包括为因结构性障碍而出现严重国际收支失衡的国家提供的"中期信贷安排"，解决短期问题的"备用信贷安排"，以及紧急国际收支需要的"快速信贷安排"，包括由商品价格冲击、自然灾害和国内脆弱性造成的问题。全部三项均以优惠条件提供资金。

Impairment

减损

对一成员在 WTO 所管理的一项或多项协定项下的权利造成消极影响。另见*非违反(non-violation)*、*丧失或减损(nullification or impairment)*。

Impediments to trade

贸易障碍

见*贸易壁垒(barriers to trade)*。

Imperial preferences arrangement

帝国特惠安排

1932 年在渥太华帝国会议上正式订立。安排的基本特点是当时构成大英帝国的国家之间交换互惠贸易优惠。大多数情况下，英国是这些协定的参加方。这一安排在 1941 年起草《大西洋宪章》时成为美国商业政策的目标，并在 1942 年英国和美国之间的相互援助协定第 7 条中再次成为目标。该条寻求"消除国际贸易中所有形式的歧视性待遇"。当 GATT 在 1948 年生效时，禁止增加所有优惠幅度。这一上限，加上在 GATT 项下议定的关税削减，使优惠幅度很快受到侵蚀。大多数已经消失。在两次世界大战期间，"英联邦国家"一词得到越来越多地使用，因而更广泛地使用英联邦特惠安排而非帝国特惠安排。现代英联邦在这一安排中不发挥任何作用。另见*历史性优惠(historical preferences)*、*优惠贸易安排(preferential trade arrangements)*。

Implementation

实施

执行贸易谈判中所作承诺。贸易政策人士通常认为，这远不如谈判新事物更令人兴奋。在 WTO 中，实施有时指发展中国家争论的一组问题：一是其部分乌拉圭回合义务对发展中国家而言过重。二是应通过谈判解决发展中国家遭受的不公平。三是发展中国家只有通过延长最后期限和增加技术援助才能履

through extended deadlines and increased technical assistance. The ***Doha Ministerial Conference*** adopted a ***Declaration on Implementation-Related Issues and Concerns*** which seeks to find solutions to some of these problems. *See also* ***capacity-building***.

Implementation doctrine: the principle in ***competition law*** that ***conduct*** by firms may be actionable in the country or group of countries where it occurs, even though it may have been decided on elsewhere. *See also* ***antitrust laws***, ***competition policy*** and ***effects doctrine***.

Implementation periods: *see* ***staging***.

Implicit discrimination: a legislative, tax or other measure applicable to domestic and imported goods and services that may indirectly or unintentionally discriminate against the imported product or service. Having to conform with certain domestic measures maintained by the importing country may cause them to lose their competitive advantage. *See* ***wine gallon assessment*** for a practical example of this concept.

Implicit tariff equivalent: an ***import quota*** on a good normally restricts its availability on the market. Such an induced scarcity may push the good's price up, much in the same way as a ***tariff*** increases the price of a good on the import market. The *implicit tariff equivalent*, denoted as a percentage, expresses the difference between the cost of the good under quotas and what it would have been without quotas.

Import: a good or a service bought by residents of one country from residents in another in return, normally, for foreign exchange. *See also* ***barter*** and ***countertrade***.

Importation: the same as ***import***.

Import cartel: *see* ***cartel***.

Import deposit schemes: mechanisms administered by governments or on behalf of governments which require the lodging of a monetary deposit at the time an import order is placed. Such schemes are often part of ***import licensing*** systems. Their purpose is to ensure that import orders are actually executed or that a minimum import price is met.

Import discipline hypothesis: the proposition that a liberal trading regime has a beneficial effect on the efficiency of domestic firms and the welfare of the consumer through preventing the formation of economic rents.

Import licensing: the need to obtain a permit for importing a product. It is defined in the WTO ***Agreement on Import Licensing Procedures*** as "administrative procedures used for the operation of import licensing regimes requiring the submission of an application or other documentation to the relevant administrative body as a condition for importing". Import licensing is considered automatic when applications are approved in all cases. *See also* ***import deposit schemes***.

Import licensing agreement: *see* ***Agreement on Import Licensing Procedures***.

Import market value: a system for the valuation of goods to be imported for the purpose of levying ***customs duties*** which is based on the value of the

行其义务。多哈部长级会议通过了《关于与实施有关的问题和关注的决定》(英文误为 Declaration，应为 Decision—译注)，以寻求解决其中一些问题。另见*能力建设(capacity-building)*。

Implementation doctrine
履行地原则

竞争法中的原则，即公司的行为在其发生的国家或国家集团可以被起诉，即使这一行为可能是在其他地点作出的决策。另见*反垄断法(antitrust laws)*、*竞争政策(competition policy)*、*效果原则(effects doctrine)*。

Implementation periods
实施期

见*降税期(staging)*。

Implicit discrimination
隐性歧视

适用于国产和进口货物和服务的可能间接或非故意歧视进口产品或服务的立法、税收或其他措施。必须遵守进口国维持的某些国内措施可能会使进口产品或服务失去竞争优势。该概念的实例见*葡萄酒加仑评估法(wine gallon assessment)*。

Implicit tariff equivalent
隐性关税等值

对一货物实施进口配额通常会限制该货物在市场上的可获性。由此引发的稀缺性可能会抬高该货物的价格，很大程度上与关税抬高一货物在进口市场上价格的方式相同。隐性关税等值以百分比表示，显示实施配额的货物的成本与无配额情况下的成本之间的差异。

Import
进口

一国居民自另一国居民处购买货物或服务，另一国居民则通常为换取外汇。另见*易货贸易(barter trade)*、*对销贸易(countertrade)*。

Importation
进口

与进口同义。

Import cartel
进口卡特尔

见*卡特尔(cartel)*。

Import deposit schemes
进口保证金制

政府管理或代表政府管理的机制，要求在进口订货时提交货币保证金。此类机制通常是进口许可制度的一部分。目的是保证进口订单得到实际执行或符合最低进口价格。

Import discipline hypothesis
进口纪律假说

自由贸易制度通过防止形成经济租金而对国内企业的效率和消费者福利产生有利影响的提法。

Import licensing
进口许可

进口产品需要获得许可证。WTO《进口许可程序协定》将其定义为：“用以实施进口许可制度的行政程序，该制度要求向相关行政机关提交申请或其他单证”。在所有申请均获批准的情况下，进口许可被视为自动许可。另见*进口保证金制(import deposit schemes)*。

Import licensing agreement
进口许可协定

见*进口许可程序协定(Agreement on Import Licensing Procedures)*。

Import market value
进口市场价格

为征收关税目的而根据进口国国内市场目前在售货物的价格对拟进口货物进

same goods currently sold in the internal markets of the importing country. This system never was common. It has been superseded by the ***transaction value*** method described in the WTO ***Customs Valuation Agreement***. *See also* ***customs valuation***.

Import quotas: restrictions or ceilings imposed by an importing country on the value or volume of certain products that may be bought from abroad. They are designed to protect domestic producers from the effects of lower-priced imported products. Import quotas are a form of ***quantitative restrictions***.

Import relief: protection of domestic producers against competition from imports, mainly through the use of ***safeguards***. *See also* ***anti-dumping measures***.

Import restriction: any governmental ***measure*** that makes import flows smaller than they would be in the absence of the measure. Examples are foreign exchange restrictions, ***import licensing*** and ***import quotas***. Import ***cartels*** may have the same effect.

Import risk assessment: *see* ***risk assessment***.

Import substitution: a policy for the development of a domestic productive capacity in goods and services to reduce or displace imports, often with the expectation of increases in employment and reductions in the current account deficit. Import substitution also seems to be a natural policy to follow when countries seek to deal with the phenomenon described by the ***Singer-Prebisch thesis***. This thesis postulates that the ***terms of trade*** of commodity-producing developing countries in their trade with developed countries will deteriorate over time. The suggested remedy for this was often seen in policies promoting industrialization. Countries practising import substitution often find that their foreign exchange reserves do not show any improvement at all, partly because they still have to import capital goods. To the extent that this policy involves restrictions on imports or domestic subsidies, it raises domestic costs and limits a country's exports.

Import substitution subsidy: a ***subsidy*** payable only if local materials or components are used in the production of a good, regardless of whether this is the sole condition for its availability. All such subsidies are prohibited under the WTO ***Agreement on Subsidies and Countervailing Measures***.

Import surcharge: a levy added to the normal ***customs duties***. Countries sometimes apply a surcharge to improve a current account deficit, usually with limited success because persistent ***trade deficits*** tend to reflect a particular type of economic structure or, sometimes, more deep-seated economic problems. Import surcharges also raise the cost of domestic producers and cause them to become less competitive against international standards. The imposition of a surcharge may be legal under the WTO rules if it does not exceed the margin between the ***applied tariff rates*** and the bound rates. *See also* ***primage***.

Import target: *see* ***voluntary import expansion***.

Import tariffs: these are ***customs duties*** levied at the border on products imported from other economies. *See also* ***customs territory***, ***export tariffs***, ***multi-column tariff*** and ***single-column tariff***.

行估价的制度。这一制度并不常见。已被 WTO《海关估价协定》中的成交价格法所取代。另见*海关估价(customs valuation)*。

Import quotas
进口配额

进口国对可能自海外购买的某些产品实施的价格和数量限制或上限，旨在保护国内生产者免受低价进口产品的影响。进口配额是数量限制的一种形式。

Import relief
进口救济

保护国内生产者免受进口竞争影响，主要通过使用保障措施。另见*反倾销措施(anti-dumping measures)*。

Import restriction
进口限制

使进口流量小于无措施情况的任何政府措施。例如外汇限制、进口许可和进口配额。进口卡特尔可能具有相同效果。

Import risk assessment
进口风险评估

见*风险评估(risk assessment)*。

Import substitution
进口替代

旨在发展货物和服务的国内产能以减少或替代进口的政策，通常伴随增加就业和削减经常项目赤字的预期。当国家寻求解决辛格-普雷维什命题中所述的现象时，进口替代也似乎成为一种自然而然的政策。这一命题假设生产商品的发展中国家在与发达国家开展的贸易中，贸易条件将随着时间的推移而恶化。建议的补救措施往往是促进工业化的政策。实行进口替代的国家经常发现，它们的外汇储备根本没有任何改善，部分原因是它们仍然必须进口资本货物。只要这一政策涉及进口限制或国内补贴，即会抬高国内成本并限制一国出口。

Import substitution subsidy
进口替代补贴

只有在生产一货物中使用当地材料或成分才支付的一种补贴，无论这是否是可获得补贴的惟一条件。所有此类补贴在 WTO《补贴与反补贴措施协定》项下均属禁止性补贴。

Import surcharge
进口附加税

指在正常关税外征收的税款。国家有时为改善经常项目赤字而征收附加税，通常作用有限，因为持久的贸易赤字往往反映经济结构的特定类型，或有时是更为深层的经济问题。进口附加税还会提高国内生产者的成本，降低他们在国际标准方面的竞争力。如果附加税不超过实施税率与约束税率之间的差额，征收附加税在 WTO 规则下是合法的。另见*关税附加税(primage)*。

Import target
进口目标

见*自愿扩大进口(voluntary import expansion)*。

Import tariffs
进口关税

指对自其他经济体进口的产品在边境征收的关税。另见*关税领土(customs territory)*、*出口关税(export tariffs)*、*多栏关税(multi-column tariff)*、*单栏关税(single-column tariff)*。

In a manner contrary to honest commercial practices: the ***Agreement on Trade-Related Aspects of Intellectual Property Rights*** gives natural and legal persons the right to have ***undisclosed information*** protected by governments and governmental agencies against disclosure, acquisition or use by others in a manner contrary to honest commercial practices. Such practices are defined as at least a breach of contract, breach of confidence and inducement to breach. They include the acquisition of undisclosed information by third parties who knew, or were grossly negligent in failing to know, that such practices were involved in the acquisition. An identical provision can be found in Article 1721 of ***NAFTA***. *See also* ***trade secrets***.

Inappropriate patenting: the practice of applying for a ***patent*** for an invention that is not new or does not involve an ***inventive step***. This practice is sometimes used to affect the business plans of a possible competitor, but at other times it is entirely inadvertent. *See also* ***intellectual property rights***.

In-bond manufacturing: the production of goods within a ***free-trade zone***, or a facility recognized for the purpose by the customs authorities, where no duties have to be paid on the import of components or raw materials as long as they are exported to another customs territory.

Inclusive: ensuring all members have input into a process even when meetings involve only some of them. In ***WTO*** negotiations, and other decision-making, ideas are tested and issues are discussed in a variety of meetings, many of them with only some members present. Members approve of this process so long as information is shared and they have an input either by being present or being represented by a group coordinator. The final decision can only be taken by a formal meeting of the full membership. *See also* ***concentric circles*** and ***transparent***.

Inclusive economy: broadly an economy that allows people to participate fully in economic life and that offers opportunities to more people in a sustainable environment and to benefit from economic growth and in a stable setting.

Income equalization: *see* ***agricultural subsidies***.

Incoterms: standard definitions of trade terms used in international sales contracts. Examples are FAS (free alongside ship), FOB (free on board) and CIF (cost, insurance and freight). The Incoterms are administered by the ***International Chamber of Commerce***.

Incremental progress: when little or no progress has been made, more likely the latter, but something positive has to be said anyway about the event.

Independence of protection: an ***intellectual property*** concept enshrined in the ***Paris Convention***. It means, for example, that any Australian patent granted under the Paris Convention enjoys protection in Australia quite independently of any protection it may enjoy in respect of the same invention under patents granted in other countries, whether or not these are signatories of the Paris Convention.

Independent Commission on International Development Issues: *see* ***Brandt Report***.

In a manner contrary to honest commercial practices
以违反诚实商业惯例的方式

《与贸易有关的知识产权协定》给予自然人和法人要求政府和政府机关对未披露信息予以保护的权利，防止被他人以违反诚实商业惯例的方式进行披露、取得或使用。此类惯例定义为，至少包括违反合同、泄密和违约诱导，并包括第三方取得未披露信息，而该第三方知道或因严重疏忽未能知道未披露信息的取得涉及此类做法。可在《北美自由贸易协定》(NAFTA)第1721条中找到相同规定。另见*商业秘密(trade secrets)*。

Inappropriate patenting
不适专利

为一项不属新的或不涉及创造性的发明申请专利的做法。此种做法有时用以影响可能的竞争者的商业计划，而有时又是完全无意的。另见*知识产权(intellectual property rights)*。

In-bond manufacturing
保税仓库内生产

在自由贸易园区内或在由海关认可的为此目的的一设施内生产货物，进口组件或原材料无需缴纳关税，只要货物出口至另一关税领土。

Inclusive
包容

保证所有成员在一进程中均有所投入，即使会议只涉及部分成员。在WTO谈判及其他决策中，在各种会议中测试想法，讨论问题，其中很多会议只有部分成员出席。只要信息得到共享且成员们通过出席或由一协调组的协调员代为出席，他们就会支持这一进程。最终决定只能由全体成员出席的正式会议作出。另见*同心圆(concentric circles)*、*透明(transparent)*。

Inclusive economy
包容性经济

泛指可以使人们充分参与经济生活、为更多人在可持续的环境中提供机会、从经济增长和稳定环境中获益的经济。

Income equalization
收入均衡

见*农业补贴(agricultural subsidies)*。

Incoterms
国际贸易术语解释通则

国际销售合同中使用的贸易术语的标准定义，例如FAS(船边交货)、FOB(离岸价格)、CIF(到岸价格)。通则由国际商会管理。

Incremental progress
渐进式进展

取得很少进展或没有进展，更可能是后者，但总要对一事件说些积极的话。

Independence of protection
独立保护原则

《巴黎公约》包含的知识产权概念。意味着，例如，根据《巴黎公约》授予的一项澳大利亚专利在澳大利亚享有的保护完全独立于该专利在其他国家就同一发明授予的专利下可享有的任何保护，无论这些国家是否属《巴黎公约》签署方。

Independent Commission on International Development Issues
国际发展问题独立委员会

见*勃兰特报告(Brandt Report)*。

Independent entity: an entity constituted jointly by the ***International Federation of Inspection Agencies*** (IFIA), representing preshipment inspecting agencies, and the ***International Chamber of Commerce*** (ICC), representing exporters. The entity administers an independent review procedure for the purposes of the ***Agreement on Preshipment Inspection*** to resolve disputes between an exporter and a preshipment inspection provider.

Indian Ocean Rim Association: IORA. The successor since 2014 to the Indian Ocean Association for Regional Cooperation (IOR-ARC) established in 1997. Its objectives are (a) promotion of sustained growth and balanced development of the region, (b) a focus on areas of cooperation that provide maximum opportunities to develop shared interests and reap mutual benefits, (c) give impetus to priority agenda areas, (d) explore all possibilities and avenues for trade liberalization and remove impediments to the flow of goods, services, investment and technology in the region, (e) encourage close interaction of trade and industry, academic institutions and people in the region, (f) encourage dialogue among member states in international fora on global economic issues, and (g) promote cooperation in the development of human resources. Members are Australia, Bangladesh, Comoros, India, Indonesia, Iran, Kenya, Madagascar, Malaysia, Mauritius, Mozambique, Oman, Seychelles, Singapore, Somalia, South Africa, Sri Lanka, Tanzania, Thailand, United Arab Emirates, and Yemen. IORA's secretariat is in Mauritius.

Indian Ocean Rim Association for Regional Cooperation: *see* ***Indian Ocean Rim Association***.

Indications of geographical origin: *see* ***geographical indications***.

Indications of source: names on a good itself or on its packaging material of the country, and sometimes also the region, where it has been produced or made. The ***Paris Convention*** requires its members to seize goods with a false indication of source both in the country where the unlawful use occurred or the country into which the good was imported. The ***Madrid Agreement for the Repression of False or Deceptive Indications of Source on Goods*** requires its members additionally, as the name of the agreement implies, to seize all goods bearing a false or deceptive indication of source on import or in the country where the unlawful use occurred. Article 4 leaves it to national courts to decide what generic products should not be protected by the Agreement, except for "regional appellations concerning the source of products of the vine". In other words, the Agreement discriminates in favour of such products. Neither the Paris Convention nor the Madrid Agreement defines the meaning of "indication of source". Addor and Grazioli offer this definition: "any expression or sign used to indicate that a product or a service originates in a country, region or a specific place, without any element of quality or reputation". The ***Lisbon Agreement*** offers additional protection for ***appellations of origin***, a subcategory of indications of source, which are protected "as such" in the country of origin and registered with the ***International Bureau of Intellectual Property*** within ***WIPO***. *See also* ***Geneva Act of the Lisbon Agreement on Appellations***

Independent entity

独立实体

指由代表装运前检验机构的国际检验机构联盟(IFIA)和代表出口商的国际商会(ICC)联合组成的实体。该实体管理就《装运前检验协定》而言的独立审查程序，以解决出口商与装运前检验提供商之间的争端。

Indian Ocean Rim Association

环印度洋联盟

IORA。自 2014 年起成为 1997 年成立的环印度洋地区合作联盟(IOR-ARC)的后继组织。目标为：(a)促进本地区的可持续增长和均衡发展；(b)聚焦可以提供最大机会以形成共同利益和互惠互利的合作领域；(c)推动优先议程领域；(d)探索贸易自由化和消除本地区货物、服务、投资和技术流动阻碍的所有可能性和途径；(e)鼓励本地区内贸易、产业、学术机构和人员的紧密联系；(f)鼓励成员国之间在讨论全球经济问题的国际场合进行对话；以及(g)推动人力资源开发合作。成员为：澳大利亚、孟加拉国、科摩罗、印度、印度尼西亚、伊朗、肯尼亚、马达加斯加、马来西亚、毛里求斯、莫桑比克、阿曼、塞舌尔、新加坡、索马里、南非、斯里兰卡、坦桑尼亚、泰国、阿拉伯联合酋长国和也门。秘书处设在毛里求斯。

Indian Ocean Rim Association for Regional Cooperation

环印度洋地区合作联盟

见*环印度洋联盟(Indian Ocean Rim Association)*。

Indications of geographical origin

原产地地理标志

见*地理标志(geographical indications)*。

Indications of source

产地标志

商品自身或者包装物上加贴的其生产或制造国的名称，有时是地区的名称。《巴黎公约》要求其成员在非法使用发生的国家或在货物进口的国家扣押带有虚假产地标志的货物。《制止商品来源虚假或欺骗性标记马德里协定》还要求成员，如协定名称所示，在进口时或在非法使用发生的国家，扣押所有带有虚假或欺骗性产地标志的货物。第 4 条规定由各国法院确定何种通用性质产品不应受到协定保护，“葡萄产品的地区性产地名称”除外。换言之，协定对此类产品给予特殊待遇。无论《巴黎公约》还是《马德里协定》均未对“产地标志”进行定义。阿多尔和格拉齐奥利提出了有关定义：“用于表明一产品或一服务源于一国、一地区或一特定地点的任何表述或标志，不包含质量或声誉的任何要素。”《里斯本协定》将原产地名称作为产地标志的一个子类提供额外保护，在原属国中按原产地名称得到保护并在世界知识产权组织(WIPO)知识产权国际局进行注册。另见*原产地名称和地理标志里斯本协定日内瓦文本(Geneva Act of the Lisbon Agreement on Appellations of Origin and Geographical*

of Origin and Geographical Indications, ***geographical indications***, ***geographical names***, ***marks of origin*** and ***rules of origin***. [Addor and Grazioli 2002]

Indicators of market openness: conceptual frameworks for the measurement of the extent to which markets can be contested by new entrants, particularly those located in other countries. There are three basic approaches to constructing such indicators. The first assesses levels of ***tariff*** barriers, ***non-tariff barriers*** and ***tariff equivalents***. The second looks at the results of liberalization through examining its effect on trade flows, extent and growth of ***intra-industry trade***, etc. This is done through modelling work. The third approach is aimed at the interaction between barriers and the competitive process in a given market. In other words, it looks at the structural openness of markets to competition. There is considerable agreement on the most appropriate methods for the first two approaches, but they can differ rather more for the third class of indicators. *See also* ***international contestability of markets***, ***Overall Trade Restrictiveness Index***, ***trade and competition*** and ***Trade Restrictiveness Index***.

Indigenous knowledge: distinctive knowledge held by indigenous peoples and transmitted to future generations. It is a sub-category of ***traditional knowledge***. [WIPO/IPTK/MCT/02/INF.4]

Indirect dumping: the usual definition of ***dumping*** is the sale of a product abroad for less than it is sold on the home market. This definition assumes that only two countries are involved, i.e. the product is exported from country A to country B. An allegation of indirect dumping would claim that the article causing injury was first exported from country A to country B where it would not be considered as having been dumped, then from country B to country C. *See also* ***anti-dumping measures***, ***dumping*** and ***hidden dumping***.

Indirect material: this is either a good used in the production, testing or inspection of a good, but not physically incorporated into the good, or it is a good used in the maintenance of buildings or the operation of equipment associated with the production of a good. Examples of indirect materials are fuel and energy, tools, spare parts, safety equipment, lubricants and greases. *See also* ***rules of origin***.

Individual action plans: *see* ***APEC individual action plans***.

Industrial designs: the shape, configuration, pattern or ornamentation of a useful article, but not a method or principle of construction. *See also* ***Hague System for the International Deposit of Industrial Designs***, ***intellectual property*** and ***Locarno Agreement Establishing an International Classification for Industrial Designs***.

Industrial property: mainly deals with ***inventions***, ***trademarks*** and ***industrial designs***, but also the repression of ***unfair competition***. *See also* ***intellectual property***.

Industrial research: defined in the WTO ***Agreement on Subsidies and Countervailing Measures*** as planned search or critical investigation aimed at discovery of new knowledge, with the objective that such knowledge may be useful in developing new products, processes or services, or in bringing about a

Indications)、*地理标志(geographical indications)*、*地理名称(geographical names)*、*原产地标记(marks of origin)*、*原产地规则(rules of origin)*。

Indicators of market openness

市场开放度指标

衡量新进入者对市场竞争程度的概念框架，特别是位于其他国家的新进入者。构建此种指标有三种基本方式：第一种是评估关税壁垒、非关税壁垒和关税等值的水平。第二种是通过审查自由化对贸易流、产业内部贸易的程度和增长等的影响，评定自由化的结果。需要通过建模工作。第三种方式专注于一给定市场中的壁垒与竞争过程之间的相互作用。换言之，此种方式关注市场对竞争的结构性开放程度。对于前两种方式，人们已就最适当的方法达成很大程度上的一致，但对第三类指标分歧很大。另见*市场的国际竞争性(international contestability of markets)*、*总体贸易限制指数(Overall Trade Restrictiveness Index)*、*贸易与竞争(trade and competition)*、*贸易限制指数(Trade Restrictiveness Index)*。

Indigenous knowledge

本地知识

原住民拥有并传给后代的独特知识。为传统知识的子类。

Indirect dumping

间接倾销

倾销通常的定义是以低于本国市场的价格在国外销售产品。这一定义假设只涉及两个国家，即产品自A国出口至B国。对间接倾销的指控认为，造成损害的物品首先从A国出口至B国，在B国不会被认为属倾销，随后自B国出口至C国。另见*反倾销措施(anti-dumping measures)*、*倾销(dumping)*、*隐蔽倾销(hidden dumping)*。

Indirect material

间接材料

指在一货物生产、测试或检验时使用的一货物，而前一货物并未实际包含后一货物，或指在与一货物生产有关的建筑物维护中或设备运行中使用的一货物。间接材料的例子如燃料和能源、工具、配件、安全设备、润滑剂和润滑油。另见*原产地规则(rules of origin)*。

Individual action plans

单边行动计划

见*APEC 单边行动计划(APEC individual action plans)*。

Industrial designs

工业品外观设计

指一有用物品的形状、结构、图案或装饰，但不是构造方法或原理。另见*工业品外观设计国际注册海牙体系(Hague System for the International Deposit of Industrial Designs)*、*知识产权(intellectual property)*、*建立工业品外观设计国际分类洛迦诺协定(Locarno Agreement Establishing an International Classification for Industrial Designs)*。

Industrial property

工业产权

主要处理发明、商标和工业品外观设计，但也处理制止不正当竞争。另见*知识产权(intellectual property)*。

Industrial research

工业研究

在WTO《补贴与反补贴措施协定》中的定义为，旨在发现新知识的有计划探

significant improvement to existing products, processes or services. ***Assistance*** qualifying as ***non-actionable subsidies*** for up to 75 per cent of the cost of such industrial research may be allowable under the Agreement if it is limited to costs of personnel, instruments, equipment, land and buildings, consultancy, additional overhead costs directly related to research and other running costs incurred directly as result of the research activity. *See also* ***pre-competitive development activity***.

Industrial tariffs: in strict terms, ***tariffs*** levied on manufactures and semi-manufactures to distinguish them from tariffs on primary agricultural and mineral commodities. Sometimes used, however, to refer to tariffs on non-agricultural products generally. *See also* ***non-agricultural market access***.

Industry policy: in its wide meaning, this term refers to policies adopted by governments towards all industries or industrial development generally. In its narrow meaning, it covers governmental policy towards selected industrial sectors to ensure their development or restructuring. This can be done in many ways, and one of them is ***protection***. Sometimes, calls for an active industry policy reflect no more than a desire to pursue ***mercantilism***, freer availability of ***subsidies***, preference for domestic manufacturers in ***government procurement*** and ***local content requirements***. *See also* ***infant-industry argument***, ***learning-by-doing argument***, ***national champions***, ***picking winners***, ***strategic trade theory*** and ***structural adjustment***.

Industry-to-industry understandings: a euphemistic name given to ***voluntary restraint arrangements***. They are understandings between industries only because governments insist on them, though in some cases industries are quite happy to accept them because of the opportunity for windfall profits they offer to importers and exporters alike.

Inertial policy determinism: adherence to policies long after they have outlived their ostensible utility. *See also* ***conventional wisdom***, ***QWERTY principle*** and ***vestigial thought***.

Infant-industry argument: this argument holds that if a given industry with a potential ***comparative advantage*** was accorded ***protection***, usually in the form of ***tariffs***, ***subsidies***, ***local content requirements***, ***bounties***, ***import quotas***, etc., to allow it to establish itself, it would be able in the long run to succeed in the market without the need for special protection. One of the flaws in the argument is that if the cost of current protection is to be repaid in the future, above-average returns will be needed after the industry is established, and that is at best problematical. In practice, few infant industries grow up of their own volition. Instead, they tend to seek to perpetuate their protection. *See also* ***learning-by-doing argument***, ***picking winners*** and ***strategic trade theory***.

Infant-industry provision: Article XVIII of the GATT (Governmental Assistance to Economic Development) allows developing countries under certain conditions to impose measures aimed at fostering the development of infant industries. *See also* ***developing countries and the multilateral trading system*** and ***infant-industry argument***.

求或关键性调查，目的在于此类知识有益于新产品、新工序或新服务的开发，或有益于对现有产品、工序或服务带来重大改进。根据协定，援助满足作为不可诉补贴的条件是，不超过产业研究费用的 75%，且此种援助仅限于人员费用、仪器、设备、土地和建筑物的费用、因研究活动而直接发生的额外管理费以及因研究活动而直接发生的其他日常费用。另见*竞争前开发活动(pre-competitive development activity)*。

Industrial tariffs
工业品关税

严格地讲，指对制成品和半制成品征收的关税，与对初级农产品和矿产品征收的关税相区别。但是，有时也泛指非农产品关税。另见*非农产品市场准入(non-agricultural market access)*。

Industry policy
产业政策

广义而言，指政府针对所有产业或产业总体发展所采取的政策。狭义而言，指针对部分工业部门采取的政府政策，以保证其发展或重构。此点可通过多种方式实现，其中之一是保护。有时呼吁采取积极的产业政策不过是反映一种追求重商主义的、更易获得补贴、在政府采购和当地含量要求方面优先考虑国内制造商的期望。另见*幼稚产业论(infant-industry argument)*、*干中学理论(learning-by-doing argument)*、*国家冠军(national champions)*、*挑选赢家(picking winners)*、*战略性贸易理论(strategic trade theory)*、*结构性调整(structural adjustment)*。

Industry-to-industry understandings
产业间谅解

对自愿限制安排的一种委婉的称呼。之所以是产业间的谅解，只是因为政府强调这样作，尽管在有些时候产业乐于接受这些安排，因为它们有机会给进口商和出口商均带来暴利。

Inertial policy determinism
惯性政策决定论

遵循已经失效很久的政策。另见*传统智慧(conventional wisdom)*、*QWERTY 键盘原则(QWERTY principle)*、*残余思想(vestigial thought)*。

Infant-industry argument
幼稚产业论

该理论认为，如果以关税、补贴、当地含量要求、津贴、进口配额的形式对某一具有潜在比较优势的给定产业进行保护，使其站稳脚跟，该产业长期而言无需特殊保护即可在市场上获得成功。这一理论的错误之一在于，如果未来要对现行保护作出回馈，在该产业建立后即需要获得高于平均值的回报，而这正是问题所在。实际上，没有几个幼稚产业能如愿以偿地得到发展，而往往寻求长期保护。另见*干中学理论(learning-by-doing argument)*、*挑选赢家(picking winners)*、*战略性贸易理论(strategic trade theory)*。

Infant-industry provision
幼稚产业条款

GATT 第 18 条(政府对经济发展的援助)允许发展中国家在某些条件下实行旨在培育幼稚产业发展的措施。另见*发展中国家与多边贸易体制(developing countries and the multilateral trading system)*、*幼稚产业论(infant-industry argument)*。

Informal trade: describes trade in goods, usually between neighbouring countries, which does not pass formally through customs controls. Informal trade seems to range from legitimate border trade to ***smuggling***. *See also* ***unrecorded trade***.

Informal Working Group on MSMEs: *see* ***joint initiatives***.

Information Economy Report: *see* ***Digital Economy Report***.

Information Technology Agreement: ITA. Originally adopted by twenty-nine WTO members at the 1996 ***Singapore WTO Ministerial Conference***. The parties agreed to eliminate ***customs duties*** on a wide range of information technology products through equal reductions beginning in 1997 and ending in 2000. They also bound the zero tariff. Non-members also benefit from the zero tariff on an MFN basis. The product range included computers, telecommunication equipment, semiconductors, semiconductor manufacturing equipment, software, scientific instruments and most parts and accessories of these products. Consumer electronic goods are excluded. At the 2015 ***WTO Ministerial Conference*** in Nairobi members adopted a *Declaration on the Expansion of Trade in Information Technology Products* to expand the product list adding a further 201 products. The ITA now has eighty-two members representing about 97 per cent of world trade in information technology products.

InforMEA initiative: a harmonized and interoperable information system which brings together ***multilateral environment agreements***. It is managed by ***UNEP*** (United Nations Environment Programme) and supported financially by the ***European Union***. [www.informea.org]

Initial commitments: trade-liberalizing commitments in services which WTO members are prepared to make early in negotiations.

Initial negotiating right: INR. The right of a WTO member to ask for tariff ***concessions*** by another member in a WTO negotiating round even though it is not the principal supplier. INRs remain negotiating tools for countries with important trade interests in a product or commodity, though these rights no longer hold the importance they once had in trade negotiations. The question of who has initial negotiating rights does not arise in the case of ***linear tariff cuts*** because all participants agree to cut tariffs on specified product categories by the same percentage rate, regardless of their importance to any given trading partner. It may, however, come up in subsequent bilateral negotiations. WTO members have therefore agreed to create so-called floating initial negotiating rights. These are initial negotiating rights that would be enjoyed by members having ***principal supplier rights*** at the time of the renegotiation of a tariff item that had earlier been subject to linear cuts. Such initial negotiating rights are called "floating" because they remain hypothetical until a concrete case arises. *See also* ***principal supplying interest*** and ***principal supplier rule***.

Initiative for ASEAN Integration: a programme launched in November 2000 by the ***ASEAN*** countries with the twin aims of integrating ASEAN as a whole better into the world economy and to integrate the four newer ASEAN members (Cambodia, Laos, Myanmar and Viet Nam) better into the ASEAN framework.

Informal trade

非正式贸易

指通常在邻国之间开展的未正式通过海关监管的货物贸易。非正式贸易似乎从合法边境贸易到走私均涵盖。另见*未记录贸易(unrecorded trade)*。

Informal Working Group on MSMEs

中小微企业非正式工作组

见*联合倡议(joint initiatives)*。

Information Economy Report

信息经济报告

见*数字经济报告(Digital Economy Report)*。

Information Technology Agreement

信息技术协定

ITA。最初由 29 个 WTO 成员在 1996 年新加坡 WTO 部长级会议上通过。参加方同意自 1997 年至 2000 年通过均等降税，取消一系列信息技术产品的关税。同时对零关税进行约束。非参加方也可在最惠国待遇基础上自零关税中获益。产品包括计算机、通信设备、半导体、半导体生产设备、软件和科学仪器及这些产品的大部分零部件。不包括消费电子产品。2015 年内罗毕 WTO 部长级会议通过《关于扩大信息技术产品贸易的宣言》，产品清单增加 201 项。ITA 现在有 82 个成员参加，代表世界信息技术产品贸易的 97%。

InforMEA initiative

关于多边环境协定信息的倡议

一个经协调和可互操作的汇集多边环境协定的信息系统。由联合国环境规划署(UNEP)管理，并由欧盟提供财政支持。

Initial commitments

初始承诺

WTO 成员准备在谈判初期作出的服务贸易自由化承诺。

Initial negotiating right

最初谈判权

INR。在 WTO 谈判回合中，一 WTO 成员要求另一成员进行关税减让的权利，即使前者不是主要供应方。最初谈判权对于在一产品或商品上具有重要贸易利益的国家而言仍然是一个谈判工具，尽管这些权利的重要性已不如以往。对于线性关税削减，不产生最初谈判权的问题，因为所有参加方均同意按相同比例削减规定产品类别的关税，而不考虑这些产品对任何给定贸易伙伴的重要性。但是最初谈判权有可能在随后的双边谈判中出现。因此，WTO 成员同意创设所谓“浮动最初谈判权”，指在较早时进行线性削减的一关税税目在重新谈判时具有主要供应方权利的成员的最初谈判权，之所以称其为“浮动”，是因为出现具体事例前只是一种假设。另见*主要供应方利益(principal supplying interest)*、*主要供应方规则(principal supplier rule)*。

Initiative for ASEAN Integration

东盟一体化倡议

东盟国家 2000 年 11 月发起的倡议，旨在使东盟作为整体更好地融入世界经济并使 4 个东盟新成员(柬埔寨、老挝、缅甸和越南)更好地融入东盟框架的双重目标。

Injury: an adverse effect on domestic industry assumed to be caused by the actions of exporters from other countries, for example, through ***dumping***, ***subsidies*** or import surges. In the case of dumping, action can be taken if there is ***material injury***. In ***safeguards***, ***serious injury*** must be threatening or have occurred. Both terms allow for a subjective assessment, but serious injury is deemed to be more grave than material injury. The WTO has a highly developed framework for the assessment of injury and any remedial action in the case of injury or threat of injury. The ***Agreement on Textiles and Clothing*** permits members to impose ***transitional safeguards*** under certain conditions in cases of ***serious damage***, or the threat of serious damage, to domestic industry as a result of increased imports. *See also* ***Agreement on Safeguards*** and ***anti-dumping measures***.

Inland parity: *see* ***national treatment***.

Inorganic integration: described by some as the process resulting from formal and politically oriented trade agreements forged among countries to reduce or eliminate tariff and non-tariff barriers and harmonize trade-relevant domestic economic policies. *See also* ***economic integration***.

Input dumping: said to be done of products that are not in themselves dumped, but which are claimed to contain components acquired at dumped prices. *See also* ***secondary dumping***.

In-quota rate: the ***tariff*** applicable to a product imported within the limits of a ***tariff quota***.

In-quota trade: the trade that occurs within a given ***tariff rate quota***.

Insufficient operations: also called insufficient processing or non-qualifying operations. This is a term used in the administration of ***preferential rules of origin*** to signify that a product imported from one party to a ***free-trade agreement*** does not qualify for the preferential tariff rate because it has not undergone ***substantial transformation*** in that party. The free-trade agreement between Japan and Singapore, a typical example, describes as insufficient operations: (a) preservation of products in good condition during transport and storage, (b) changes of packaging, (c) affixing marks or labels on the products or their packaging, (d) disassembly, (e) placing in bottles, cases or boxes, and other simple packaging operations, (f) simple cutting, (g) simple mixing, (h) simple assembly of parts to form a complete product, (i) simple making up of sets of articles, and (j) any combination of these operations. *See also* ***minimum operations***.

Insufficient processing: *see* ***insufficient operations***.

Integrated Data Base: IDB. Maintained by the WTO Secretariat. It contains information supplied by members concerning ***applied MFN tariff rates***, import statistics, etc. Tariff and trade data are matched at the tariff line level. *See also* ***Consolidated Tariff Schedules***. [WTO TN/MA/S/2]

Integrated Framework for Trade-Related Technical Assistance to Least-Developed Countries: adopted in 1998 to improve the trade-related benefits available to ***least-developed countries*** from the WTO and five other multilateral

Injury
损害

假定因其他国家出口商的行动而对国内产业造成的不利影响，例如通过倾销、补贴或进口激增。对于倾销，如存在实质损害，可采取行动。对于保障措施，必须出现严重损害威胁或已经发生严重损害。两词语均允许客观评估，严重损害被认为比实质损害更严重。对于损害或损害威胁，WTO 对评估损害和任何补救行动规定了详细的机制。《纺织品与服装协定》允许成员因进口增加而对本国产业造成严重损害或严重损害威胁时，在某些条件下采取过渡性保障措施。另见*保障措施协定(Agreement on Safeguards)*、*反倾销措施(anti-dumping measures)*。

Inland parity
对内同等

见*国民待遇(national treatment)*。

Inorganic integration
无机一体化

一些人将其描述为国家间为削减或消除关税和非关税壁垒及协调与贸易有关的国内经济政策而达成的正式的以政治为导向的贸易协定的过程。另见*经济一体化(economic integration)*。

Input dumping
原材料倾销

指产品本身并未倾销，但产品包含以倾销价格获得的部件。另见*二级倾销(secondary dumping)*。

In-quota rate
配额内税率

在关税配额限定数量内进口的产品所适用的关税。

In-quota trade
配额内贸易

在给定关税配额内发生的贸易。

Insufficient operations
不充分操作

也称为不充分加工或不符操作。优惠原产地规则管理中使用的词语，指从自由贸易协定一参加方进口的一产品因未在该参加方进行实质性改变而无资格享受优惠关税税率。典型例子如，日本与新加坡自由贸易协定将不充分操作描述为：(a)运输和储存期间产品保持良好状态；(b)改换包装；(c)产品或其包装加贴标记或标签；(e)拆卸；(5)装瓶、装盒或装箱及其他简单包装加工；(f)简单切割；(g)简单混合；(h)将零件简单组装成完整产品；(i)简单组装成套物品；以及(j)以上操作的任何组合。另见*最小操作(minimum operations)*。

Insufficient processing
不充分加工

见*不充分操作(insufficient operations)*。

Integrated Data Base
综合数据库

IDB。由 WTO 秘书处负责维护，包含成员提供的有关最惠国实施税率、进口数据等信息。关税和贸易数据对应各税目。另见*合并关税减让表(Consolidated Tariff Schedules)*。

Integrated Framework for Trade-Related Technical Assistance to Least Developed Countries
针对最不发达国家的与贸易有关的技术援助综合框架

1998 年获得通过，旨在改善最不发达国家自 WTO 和 5 个其他多边机构(即国

agencies (***IMF***, ***International Trade Centre***, ***WTO***, ***UNCTAD*** and the ***United Nations Development Programme***). This has now been succeeded by the ***Enhanced Integrated Framework***. *See also* ***Doha Development Agenda Global Trust Fund***.

Integrated Programme for Commodities: IPC. A programme adopted at UNCTAD IV in 1976 which envisaged the negotiation of international agreements or arrangements for eighteen specified commodities. These were bananas, bauxite, cocoa, coffee, copper, cotton and cotton yarns, hard fibres and products, iron ore, jute and products, manganese, meat, phosphates, rubber, sugar, tea, tropical timber, tin, vegetable oils, including olive oils and oilseeds. Other products may at any time be added to this list. The IPC has several objectives, including avoiding excessive price fluctuations, the achievement of price levels which would be remunerative to producers and equitable to customers, increased export earnings for developing countries, improvements in market access and reliability of supply. The ***Common Fund for Commodities***, a financing facility for the IPC, was created at the same time. *See also* ***buffer stocks***, ***international commodity agreements***, ***international commodity bodies*** and ***UNCTAD***.

Integrated Tariff of the European Union: TARIC. A multilingual database integrating all measures relating to the ***European Union*** customs tariff, commercial and agricultural legislation. Its main categories are tariff measures, including third-country duty, agricultural measures, trade defence instruments (anti-dumping and countervailing duties), prohibitions and restrictions to import and export, and surveillance of movements of goods at import and export. [ec.europa.en]

Integration: *see* ***deep integration***, ***economic integration***, ***inorganic integration***, ***market-led integration***, ***organic integration*** and ***policy-led integration***.

Integration programme: the phasing out of ***Multi-Fibre Arrangement*** (MFA) restrictions in four stages starting on 1 January 1995 and ending on 1 January 2005. *See also* ***Agreement on Textiles and Clothing***.

Integrity: *see* ***African Union Convention on Preventing and Combating Corruption***, ***anti-corruption***, ***bribery***, ***Convention on Combating Bribery of Foreign Public Officials in International Business Transactions***, ***OECD Recommendation on Public Integrity*** and ***United Nations Convention Against Corruption***.

Integrity in customs: *see* ***Arusha Declaration***.

Intellectual property: generally includes ***patents***, ***trademarks***, ***industrial designs***, ***layout-designs of integrated circuits***, ***copyright***, ***geographical indications*** and ***trade secrets*** (confidential business information). *See also* ***Agreement on Trade-Related Aspects of Intellectual Property Rights***, ***traditional knowledge***, ***United Nations Educational, Scientific and Cultural Organization*** and ***WIPO***.

Intellectual property protection: the safeguarding of an owner's ***intellectual property rights*** through national legislation and international agreements especially concerning ***copyright***, ***patents*** and ***trademarks***. Many commentators

际货币基金组织、国际贸易中心、联合国贸易与发展会议和联合国开发计划署)可获得的与贸易有关的利益。现已为"增强综合框架"所替代。另见*多哈发展议程全球信托基金(Doha Development Agenda Global Trust Fund)*。

Integrated Programme for Commodities
商品综合方案

IPC。1976 年联合国贸易与发展会议(UNCTAD)第 4 届大会通过的一项计划，设想就 18 种特定商品谈判达成国际协定或安排。具体为香蕉、铝土矿、可可、咖啡、铜、棉花及棉纱、硬纤维及制品、铁矿砂、黄麻及制品、锰、肉类、磷酸盐、橡胶、食糖、茶叶、热带木材、锡、包括橄榄油和油籽在内的植物油。其他产品可随时加入清单。商品综合方案有多项目标，包括避免价格过度波动、实现对生产商有利且对客户公平的价格水平、增加发展中国家的出口收入、改善市场准入和供应可靠性。同时成立了商品综合方案的融资机构——商品共同基金。另见*缓冲储存(buffer stocks)*、*国际商品协定(international commodity agreements)*、*国际商品机构(international commodity bodies)*、*联合国贸易与发展会议(UNCTAD)*。

Integrated Tariff of the European Union
欧盟关税数据库

TARIC。包含与欧盟关税、商业和农业立法相关的所有措施的多语言数据库。主要分类为关税措施(包括第三国关税)、农业措施、贸易防御工具(反倾销税和反补贴税)、进出口禁止和限制、进出口货物流动监测。

Integration
一体化

见*深度一体化(deep integration)*、*经济一体化(economic integration)*、*无机一体化(inorganic integration)*、*市场主导一体化(market-led integration)*、*有机一体化(organic integration)*、*政策主导一体化(policy-led integration)*。

Integration programme
一体化方案

自 1995 年 1 月 1 日起至 2005 年 1 月 1 日分四阶段逐步取消《多种纤维协定》(MFA)限制的计划。另见*纺织品与服装协定(Agreement on Textiles and Clothing)*。

Integrity
廉洁

见*非洲联盟预防和惩治腐败公约(African Union Convention on Preventing and Combating Corruption)*、*反腐败(anti-corruption)*、*贿赂(bribery)*、*关于打击国际商业交易中行贿外国公职人员行为的公约(Convention on Combating Bribery of Foreign Public Officials in International Business Transactions)*、*OECD 关于公共廉洁的建议(OECD Recommendation on Public Integrity)*、*联合国反腐败公约(United Nations Convention Against Corruption)*。

Integrity in customs
海关廉政建设

见*阿鲁沙宣言(Arusha Declaration)*。

Intellectual property
知识产权

通常包括专利、商标、工业品外观设计、集成电路布图设计、版权、地理标志和商业秘密(机密商业信息)。另见*与贸易有关的知识产权协定(Agreement on Trade-Related Aspects of Intellectual Property Rights)*、*世界知识产权组织(WIPO)*、*传统知识(traditional knowledge)*、*联合国教育、科学及文化组织(United Nations Educational, Scientific and Cultural Organization)*。

Intellectual property protection
知识产权保护

通过专门关于版权、专利和商标的国家立法和国际协定保护知识产权所有人

insist that the strength or weakness of a country's system of intellectual property protection seems to have a substantial effect on the kinds of technology firms transfer to another country. *See also* ***intellectual property right infringements***, ***sui generis right*** and ***transfer of technology***.

Intellectual property right infringements: such infringements on a commercial scale are classified as ***piracy*** if they involve the unauthorized reproduction of copyright materials, or as ***counterfeiting*** where there is copying of ***trademarks*** with the intention of passing the goods off as those of the authentic producer. Trademarks can be infringed through the unauthorized use of a mark that is identical or so similar to an existing mark that it may lead to confusion among consumers. ***Patents*** can be infringed through unauthorized manufacture, use or sale in the country of registration of the invention claimed in the patent. *See also* ***Agreement on Trade-Related Aspects of Intellectual Property Rights***, ***dilution doctrine*** and ***forced technology transfer***.

Intellectual property rights: ownership of expressions of ideas, including literary and artistic works protected by ***copyright***, ***inventions*** protected by ***patents***, signs for distinguishing goods of an enterprise protected by ***trademarks*** and other elements of ***industrial property***. Intellectual property rights give the innovator an exclusive legal right, i.e. a monopoly, to exploit the innovation for a certain time. This serves as a reward and encourages others to innovate. Thus intellectual property rights can be in conflict with ***competition policy*** which seeks to remove impediments to the efficient functioning of the markets through, for example, minimizing the power of monopolies. The challenge in the drafting of intellectual property laws therefore is to ensure that innovators receive sufficient encouragement to be creative and, at the same time, that owners of intellectual property rights are not in a position to abuse these rights. *See also* ***Agreement on Trade-Related Aspects of Intellectual Property Rights*** and ***competition law***. [Gervais 2003]

Intellectual property theft: *see* ***forced technology transfer*** and ***intellectual property right infringements***.

Inter-Agency Task Force on International Trade Statistics: consists of Eurostat, ***Food and Agriculture Organization***, ***IMF***, ***OECD***, ***UNCTAD***, ***United Nations Industrial Development Organization***, ***United Nations regional commissions***, the ***World Customs Organization*** and the ***WTO***. Its aims include the development of international standards, international cooperation in the collection, processing and dissemination of trade statistics and the development of national statistical systems that include the provision of the best-quality estimates of trade in value added. *See also* ***OECD-WTO Trade in Value Added Initiative***. [unstats.un.org]

Inter-Agency Task Force on Statistics of International Trade in Services: created in 1994. Consists of the United Nations Statistics Division, European Union Eurostat, IMF, OECD (convenor), UNCTAD, World Tourism Organization and WTO representatives. Its objectives are to satisfy the statistical requirements of the ***General Agreement on Trade in Services***. In 2010 it

的权利。许多评论家坚持认为，一国知识产权保护体制的强弱似乎会对公司将技术转让另一国家的类型产生实质影响。另见*知识产权侵权(intellectual property right infringements)*、*特殊权利(sui generis right)*、*技术转让(transfer of technology)*。

Intellectual property right infringements
侵犯知识产权

达到商业规模的此类侵权，如涉及版权产品未经授权的复制即属盗版，如仿冒商标意在将商品冒充为正品生产者的产品则属假冒。未经授权使用与现有商标相同或相似的商标，导致消费者混淆，可构成商标侵权。在专利中所要求的发明进行注册的国家未经授权制造、使用或销售专利产品，可构成专利侵权。另见*与贸易有关的知识产权协定(Agreement on Trade-Related Aspects of Intellectual Property Rights)*、*淡化理论(dilution doctrine)*、*强制技术转让(forced technology transfer)*。

Intellectual property rights
知识产权

指思想表达的所有权，包括版权保护的文学和艺术作品、专利保护的发明、商标保护的企业特色产品的标记，以及工业产权的其他要素。知识产权给予创新者在一定时间内利用此项发明的专有法律权利，即垄断权。起到奖励和鼓励他人创新的作用。但知识产权可能会与竞争政策发生冲突，后者寻求通过尽量缩小垄断权力消除妨碍市场有效运行的障碍。因此，起草知识产权法的挑战在于，既要确保创新者获得充分鼓励从而保持创造力，同时又要保证知识产权所有人不滥用这些权利。另见*与贸易有关的知识产权协定(Agreement on Trade-Related Aspects of Intellectual Property Rights)*、*竞争法(competition law)*。

Intellectual property theft
知识产权盗窃

见*强制技术转让(forced technology transfer)*、*侵犯知识产权(intellectual property right infringements)*。

Inter-Agency Task Force on International Trade Statistics
国际贸易统计机构间特别工作组

由欧盟统计局、粮农组织、国际货币基金组织、经济合作与发展组织、联合国贸易与发展会议、联合国工业发展组织、联合国区域委员会、世界海关组织和WTO组成。目标包括制定国际标准、在收集、处理和传播贸易统计数据和开发国家统计系统方面开展国际合作，包括提供增加值贸易的最佳估算。另见*OECD-WTO增加值贸易倡议(OECD-WTO Trade in Value Added Initiative)*。

Inter-Agency Task Force on Statistics of International Trade in Services
国际服务贸易统计机构间特别工作组

创建于1994年。由联合国统计司、欧洲统计局、国际货币基金组织、经济合作与发展组织(召集人)、联合国贸易与发展会议、世界旅游组织和世界贸易组织的代表组成。目标是满足《服务贸易总协定》的统计要求。2010年出版了

published a revised version of the ***Manual on Statistics of International Trade in Services***. *See also* ***trade in services statistics***.

Inter-American Convention Against Corruption: *see* ***corruption***.

Inter-American Convention on International Commercial Arbitration: adopted by the member states of the ***Organization of American States*** on 30 January 1975. The parties agree in Article I that "an agreement in which the parties undertake to submit to arbitral decision any differences that may arise between them with respect to a commercial transaction is valid". Article 4 states that any arbitral decision or award that cannot be appealed against under the applicable law has the force of a final judicial judgement. *See also* ***arbitration*** and ***New York Convention***.

Interconnection: *see* ***telecommunications termination services***.

Interconnection charge: a charge levied by telecommunications network operators to cover the cost of connecting calls originating from or destined for another network.

Interested parties: persons who may have rights when an enquiry or investigation leading to possible ***anti-dumping measures***, ***safeguards*** or ***countervailing measures*** is undertaken. They must be notified of the information required by the authorities, they must be given ample time to make their case, and they must have a full opportunity for a defence of their interest. The WTO ***Anti-Dumping Agreement***, which sets out the rules applicable for the handling of anti-dumping cases, defines interested parties as (a) an exporter or foreign producer or the importer of a product subject to investigation, or a trade or business association which has a majority of producers, exporters or importers of such products as members, (b) the government of the exporting member, and (c) a producer of the ***like product*** in the importing member or a trade and business association with a majority of members who produce the like product in the territory of the importing member. The WTO ***Agreement on Subsidies and Countervailing Measures*** has the same definition, but it does not mention the government of the exporting member. The WTO ***Agreement on Safeguards*** also requires members about to impose a ***safeguards*** action to give an opportunity for consultations to those members with a substantial interest in the product concerned, but it does not define how the term "substantial interest" is to be understood.

Interested third parties: the WTO ***Dispute Settlement Understanding*** allows for the consideration of the interests of member countries in a dispute in which they are not directly involved. Such members have the right to be heard by a ***panel*** and to make submissions to it, but to do so they must be able to show through trade figures that they have a substantial interest in the matter. As the panel in *Korea – Definitive Safeguard Measures on Imports of Certain Dairy Products*, held, this does not necessarily mean an economic interest. In *European Communities – Regime for the Importation, Sale and Distribution of Bananas* the ***Appellate Body*** ruled "substantial interest" could not be interpreted either as meaning a "legal interest" only. [WT/DS27/AB/R, WT/DS98/R]

《国际服务贸易统计手册》修订版。另见*服务贸易统计(trade in services statistics)*。

Inter-American Convention Against Corruption

美洲国家反腐败公约

见*腐败(corruption)*。

Inter-American Convention on International Commercial Arbitration

美洲国家国际商事仲裁公约

美洲国家组织成员国1975年1月30日通过。参加方在第1条中同意，“当事方将他们之间在商务活动方面可能发生的任何争议交付仲裁裁决的协议是有效的”。第4条指出，根据适用法律不可上诉的任何仲裁或裁决与最终司法裁决具有同等效力。另见*仲裁(arbitration)*、*纽约公约(New York Convention)*。

Interconnection

互连

见*电信终端服务(telecommunications termination services)*。

Interconnection charge

互连收费

电信网络运营商收取的费用，用于支付连接自另一网络呼入电话或向另一网络呼出电话的成本。

Interested parties

利害关系方

在可能导致反倾销措施、保障措施或反补贴措施的问询或调查中具有利益的人。必须将主管机关所要求提供的信息向利害关系人进行通报，必须给予他们足够的时间陈述理由，他们必须有维护其利益的充分机会。WTO《反倾销协定》规定了处理反倾销案件的适用规则，协定将利害关系方定义为：(a)被调查产品的出口商或外国生产者或进口商，或大多数成员为该产品的生产者、出口商或进口商的行业协会或商会；(b)出口成员的政府；以及(c)进口成员中同类产品的生产者，或大多数成员在进口成员领土内生产同类产品的行业协会或商会。WTO《补贴与反补贴措施协定》有相同定义，但未提及出口成员的政府。WTO《保障措施协定》也要求即将实施保障措施的成员，为对有关产品具有实质利益的成员提供磋商机会，但未界定如何理解“实质利益”一词。

Interested third parties

利害关系第三方

WTO《争端解决谅解》允许考虑争端未直接涉及的成员的利益。此类成员有权获得专家组的听证机会并提交意见，但想要这样作，它们就必须能够通过贸易数据证明对有关事项具有实质利益。正如“韩国-奶制品进口最终保障措施案”专家组所认为的，此点并不一定是一种经济利益。在“欧共体-香蕉进口、销售和分销体制案”中，上诉机构裁定，“实质利益”也不能仅被解释为“法律利益”的意思。

Intergovernmental Authority on Development: IGAD. Established in 1986 and revitalized in 1996. Consists of Djibouti, Eritrea, Ethiopia, Kenya, Somalia, South Sudan, Sudan and Uganda. IGAD's mission is to promote regional cooperation and to add value to the efforts of member states in achieving peace, security and prosperity. Among its objectives is the promotion of the ***Common Market for Eastern and Southern Africa*** (COMESA) and the ***African Economic Community***. Its secretariat is in Djibouti. *See also* ***African regional economic integration***. [igad.int]

Intergovernmental conference: a mechanism available to the ***European Union*** to consider revisions of and amendments to the framework of treaties constituting it. Intergovernmental conferences can stretch over months and even years, but they usually lead to substantial steps forward.

Intergovernmental control agreements: *see* ***commodity policy***.

Intergovernmental Group of Twenty-Four on International Monetary Affairs: *see* ***G-24***.

Intergovernmental organizations: IGs. These are organizations usually established through a ***treaty*** bringing together governments regionally or multilaterally for the pursuit of a common purpose. IGs usually are administered by a secretariat which supports the organization's governing body, consisting of representatives of member states, as well as subsidiary bodies established by the governing body. IGs and their staffs often enjoy full or partial diplomatic privileges in the country hosting them.

Interim agreement necessary for the formation of a customs union or a free-trade area: an instrument mentioned in GATT ***Article XXIV*** which deals with ***customs unions*** and ***free-trade areas***. Such agreements have to be notified to the WTO, together with a timetable for their implementation. Few interim agreements appear to have been notified to the GATT or the WTO. Nor have working parties, in examining notified agreements, always been able to agree whether they were dealing with an interim agreement or a final agreement. However, in a sense nearly all notified free-trade agreements have been interim agreements even though the parties may have regarded them as final agreements. This is because many free-trade agreements intended to conform immediately to Article XXIV contain phase-in provisions for the elimination of trade restrictions in ***sensitive products***.

Interim Commission on Phytosanitary Measures: *see* ***Commission on Phytosanitary Measures***.

Interim Co-ordinating Committee for International Commodity Arrangements: *see* ***commodity policy***.

Interlaken Declaration on the Kimberley Process Certification Scheme for Rough Diamonds: *see* ***Kimberley Process Certification Scheme***.

Intermediate agricultural products: these are agricultural products that have been processed to some extent, but not generally enough to be sold to consumers. Examples are hides and skins, animal fats, raw sugar and wheat flour.

Intermediate goods and services: *see* ***final goods and services***.

Intergovernmental Authority on Development
东非政府间发展机构

IGAD。1986 年成立，1996 年恢复活动。由吉布提、厄立特里亚、埃塞俄比亚、肯尼亚、索马里、南苏丹、苏丹和乌干达组成。IGAD 的任务是促进区域合作，为成员国实现和平、安全与繁荣的努力增加价值。目标之一是促成东部和南部非洲共同市场(COMESA)和非洲经济共同体。秘书处设在吉布提。另见*非洲区域经济一体化(African regional economic integration)*。

Intergovernmental conference
政府间会议

欧盟考虑修改和修正其构成条约框架的机制。政府间会议可以持续召开数月甚至数年，但会议通常可带来实质性进展。

Intergovernmental control agreements
政府间控制协定

见*商品政策(commodity policy)*。

Intergovernmental Group of Twenty-Four on International Monetary Affairs
国际货币事务 24 国政府间集团

见 *24 国集团(G-24)*。

Intergovernmental organizations
政府间组织

IGs。这些组织通常通过一条约建立，在区域或多边将各国政府聚集在一起以追求一共同目标。政府间组织通常由秘书处管理，为由成员国代表组成的该组织的管理机构提供支持，并为由管理机构设立的附属机构提供支持。政府间组织及其工作人员在驻在国通常享受完全或部分的外交特权。

Interim agreement necessary for the formation of a customs union or a free trade area
形成关税同盟或自由贸易区所需临时协定

GATT 第 24 条中提及的处理关税同盟和自由贸易区的一种法律文件。此类协定及其实施时间表需要通报 WTO。但似乎很少有临时协定向 GATT 或 WTO 通报。工作组在审查通报的协定时，对于它们所处理的是临时协定还是最终协定往往不能达成一致。然而，在一定程度上，几乎所有通报的自由贸易协定都曾经是临时协定，即使参加方可能视其为最终协定。这是因为，许多旨在立即符合第24条的自由贸易协定中包含旨在取消敏感产品的贸易限制的过渡性条款。

Interim Commission on Phytosanitary Measures
植物卫生措施临时委员会

见*植物卫生措施委员会(Commission on Phytosanitary Measures)*。

Interim Co-ordinating Committee for International Commodity Arrangements
国际商品安排临时协调委员会

见*商品政策(commodity policy)*。

Interlaken Declaration on the Kimberley Process Certification Scheme for Rough Diamonds
关于金伯利进程未加工钻石证书制度的因特拉肯宣言

见*金伯利进程证书制度(Kimberley Process Certification Scheme)*。

Intermediate agricultural products
中间农产品

已经进行一定程度加工的农产品，但总体上还未达到向消费者出售的程度，例如皮革和毛皮、动物脂肪、原糖和面粉。

Intermediate goods and services
中间产品和服务

见*最终产品和服务(final goods and services)*。

Intermediate material: a term used in the ***rules of origin*** of ***free-trade agreements***. It means a material produced by the producer of a good and used in the production of that good. Such goods may be included in the calculation of the value of a product to make it qualify for preferential customs treatment under the Agreement.

Internal market: used both for a market lying within a single jurisdiction and the market made up through the formation of a ***customs union***, a ***free-trade area*** or a ***common market***, such as the ***European Union***.

Internal support: the same as ***domestic support***. It encompasses any measure which acts to maintain producer prices at levels above those prevailing in international markets. This is done through direct payments to producers, such as ***subsidies*** and ***deficiency payments***, and input and marketing cost reduction measures available only for agricultural production.

Internal taxes: government charges applied to sale of goods and services inside a ***customs territory***. Article III (National Treatment on Internal Taxation and Regulation) of the GATT requires that such charges are levied at the same rate for domestic products as for imported products. In other words, ***national treatment*** is a fundamental obligation in this regard. *See also* ***behind-the-border issues***.

Internal trade: usually the trade between the partners to a ***preferential trade arrangement***. Their trade with third countries is known as external trade. Sometimes internal trade is used to describe commercial activity within a single economy, but the use of ***commerce*** for this is sometimes preferred.

International accounting standards: accounting standards being developed by the International Accounting Standards Committee (IASC) with the aim of enhancing the comparability of financial information, improving disclosure, reducing compliance cost and encouraging uniform financial reporting by multinational companies. These standards are therefore seen as a means for a better and more efficient allocation of financial resources. *See also* ***Generally Accepted Accounting Principles***, ***Guidelines for Mutual Recognition Agreements or Arrangements in the Accountancy Sector*** and ***harmonization of standards and qualifications***.

International Agreement on Jute and Jute Products: entered into force in 1984 under the ***Integrated Programme for Commodities***. It was renegotiated in 1989 with entry into force in 1991. It expired on 11 April 2000 and was replaced by the ***International Jute Study Group*** which in turn does no longer seem active. This Agreement was confined to the aims of achieving better markets for jute and jute products, transparency in international trade and improved production and processing techniques. It was administered by the International Jute Organization, located in Dhaka.

International Agreement on Olive Oil and Table Olives: first established in 1956 and known as the International Olive Oil Agreement until 1996. The current agreement entered into force on 1 January 2017 and is valid until 31 December 2026. The objectives of the Agreement broadly are (a)

Intermediate material

中间材料

自由贸易协定的原产地规则中使用的词语，指一货物的生产者所生产的、在该货物生产中使用的材料。此类货物可以包括在一产品价值的计算中，使该产品能够满足获得协定项下优惠海关待遇的资格。

Internal market

内部市场

用于指位于单一管辖范围内的市场和通过形成关税同盟、自由贸易区或共同市场而形成的市场，例如欧盟。

Internal support

内部支持

义同国内支持。包括将生产者价格维持在高于国际市场现行价格的水平的任何措施。可通过向生产者提供补贴或差价补贴等直接支付实施及提供仅农业生产可获得的投入和营销成本削减措施实施。

Internal taxes

国内税

适用于关税领土内货物和服务销售的政府收费。GATT 第 3 条(国内税和国内法规的国民待遇)要求，对进口产品征收的此类费用应与国产品的费率相同。换言之，国民待遇在这方面属一项基本义务。另见*边境后问题(behind-the-border issues)*。

Internal trade

内部贸易

通常指优惠贸易安排伙伴之间的贸易。它们与第三国的贸易称为外部贸易。有时，内部贸易用于形容一单个经济体内部的商业活动，但有时更倾向于使用“商业”一词。

International accounting standards

国际会计标准

由国际会计标准委员会(IASC)制定的会计标准，目的在于增强金融信息的可比性、提高披露程度、减少合规成本以及鼓励跨国公司采用统一财务报表。这些标准因此被视为更好和更有效分配财政资源的一种手段。另见*公认会计原则(Generally Accepted Accounting Principles)*、*关于会计部门相互承认协定或安排的指导原则(Guidelines for Mutual Recognition Agreements or Arrangements in the Accountancy Sector)*、*标准和资格的协调(harmonization of standards and qualifications)*。

International Agreement on Jute and Jute Products

国际黄麻和黄麻制品协定

根据商品综合方案于 1984 年生效。1989 年重新谈判后于 1991 年生效。协定于 2000 年 4 月 11 日到期后被国际黄麻研究小组所取代,后者似乎不再活跃。协定的目标仅限于为黄麻及黄麻制品营造更好的市场、增加国际贸易透明度以及提高生产及加工技术。协定由设在达卡的国际黄麻组织管理。

International Agreement on Olive Oil and Table Olives

国际橄榄油和食用橄榄协定

最初于 1956 年达成，1996 年之前称为《国际橄榄油协定》。现行协定于 2017 年 1 月 1 日生效，有效期至 2026 年 12 月 31 日。协定目标大体上为：(a)橄榄

standardization and research in the production and trade of olive oils and table olives, (b) fostering technical cooperation and promoting olive oil products, and (c) information sharing. The agreement is open to producers and consumers. It is administered by the International Olive Council in Madrid.

International Bank for Reconstruction and Development: *see* ***World Bank*** and ***World Bank Group***.

International Bovine Meat Agreement: one of the ***WTO plurilateral trade agreements***, originally negotiated in the ***Tokyo Round*** as the *Arrangement Regarding Bovine Meat*. Its objectives were (a) expanding, liberalizing and stabilizing trade in meat and livestock, (b) encouraging greater international cooperation in all aspects of trade in bovine meat and livestock, (c) to secure additional benefits for developing countries, and (d) to expand trade further on a competitive basis, taking into account the traditional position of efficient producers. Until it was terminated at the end of 1997, it was administered by the International Meat Council.

International Bureau of Intellectual Property: this is the secretariat administering the governing bodies of ***WIPO*** and its Unions. A Union consists of the states that have acceded to one of the ***intellectual property*** conventions. The International Bureau also maintains international registration services in the fields of ***patents***, ***trademarks***, ***industrial designs*** and ***appellations of origin***. It is located in Geneva.

International Centre for Settlement of Investment Disputes: *see* ***ICSID***.

International Centre for Trade and Sustainable Development: ICTSD. A ***non-governmental organization*** established in 1996 to promote better understanding of the relationship between international trade, ***sustainable development*** and environmental issues more generally. It is located in Geneva.

International Chamber of Commerce: ICC. A business organization represented in more than 130 countries. The ICC promotes an open international trade and investment system and the market economy. Among the services it provides to its members is the ***International Court of Arbitration***. Its headquarters are in Paris. *See also* ***Incoterms***, ***independent entity*** and ***International Chamber of Commerce (ICC) Guidelines for International Investment***.

International Chamber of Commerce (ICC) Guidelines for International Investment: adopted in 1972, revised in 2012 and relaunched in 2016. The guidelines are grouped into three categories: (1) business confidence regarding sovereign debt policies, macroeconomic imbalances, taxation, and regulatory uncertainty, (2) reregulation of foreign investment, and (3) state-owned enterprises and sovereign wealth funds. They address both investors and host governments. [iccwbo.org]

International Civil Aviation Organization: *see* ***Chicago Convention***.

International Cocoa Agreement: first concluded in 1972 and renegotiated several times. The current agreement entered into force on 1 January 2011 and is valid for ten years. Its objectives include, among others, (a) promote international cooperation in the world cocoa economy, (b) strive towards obtaining

油和食用橄榄的生产和贸易方面的标准化和研究；(b)促进技术合作和推广橄榄油产品；以及(c)信息分享。协定对生产者和消费者开放。由设在马德里的国际橄榄油理事会管理。

International Bank for Reconstruction and Development
国际复兴开发银行

见*世界银行(World Bank)*、*世界银行集团(World Bank Group)*。

International Bovine Meat Agreement
国际牛肉协定

WTO 诸边贸易协定，最初作为《关于牛肉的安排》在东京回合中进行谈判。目标为：(a)扩大、放宽、稳定肉类和牲畜贸易；(b)在牛肉和牲畜贸易的所有方面鼓励更广泛的国际合作；(c)保证发展中国家获得额外利益；以及(d)在竞争基础上进一步扩大贸易，同时考虑高效生产者的传统地位。协定原由国际肉类理事会管理，直至 1997 年底终止。

International Bureau of Intellectual Property
知识产权国际局

世界知识产权组织(WIPO)的管理机构及其联盟的秘书处。联盟由已经加入一项知识产权公约的国家组成。国际局还在专利、商标、工业品外观设计和原产地名称方面提供国际注册服务。设在日内瓦。

International Centre for Settlement of Investment Disputes
国际投资争端解决中心

见*国际投资争端解决中心(ICSID)*。

International Centre for Trade and Sustainable Development
国际贸易与可持续发展中心

ICTSD。成立于 1996 年的非政府组织，旨在促进更好地理解国际贸易、可持续发展以及与更广泛的环境问题之间的关系。设在日内瓦。

International Chamber of Commerce
国际商会

ICC。商业组织，在 130 多个国家有其代表。国际商会进行开放的国际贸易和投资体制及市场经济。向其成员提供的服务之一是国际仲裁法院。国际商会总部设在巴黎。另见*国际贸易术语解释通则(Incoterms)*、*独立实体(independent entity)*、*国际商会国际投资指南(International Chamber of Commerce (ICC) Guidelines for International Investment)*。

International Chamber of Commerce (ICC) Guidelines for International Investment
国际商会国际投资指南

于 1972 年通过，2012 年修订，2016 年重新发布，指南分为三类：(1)对于主权债务政策、宏观经济失衡、税收和监管不确定性的商业信心；(2)外国投资重新管制；以及(3)国有企业和主权财富基金。同时针对投资者和东道国政府。

International Civil Aviation Organization
国际民用航空组织

见*芝加哥公约(Chicago Convention)*。

International Cocoa Agreement
国际可可协定

最初于 1972 年达成，后经多次重新谈判。现行协定于 2011 年 1 月 1 日生效，

fair prices leading to equitable economic returns to both producers and consumers in the cocoa value chain, (c) promote a sustainable cocoa economy in economic, social and environmental terms, (d) encourage research, (e) promote transparency in the world cocoa economy, and in particular the cocoa trade, (f) promote and encourage consumption of chocolate and cocoa-based products, and (g) promote cocoa quality and appropriate safety procedures in the cocoa sector. The Agreement's administrative body, the International Cocoa Council, is in London.

International Code of Conduct on the Transfer of Technology: *see* ***Draft International Code of Conduct on the Transfer of Technology***.

International Coffee Agreement: first concluded in 1962 and renegotiated several times since. The current Agreement entered into force on 2 February 2011. It is valid for ten years. Its objectives include, among others, (a) promote international cooperation on coffee matters, (b) provide a forum for consultation on coffee matters among governments, and with the private sector, (c) encourage members to develop a sustainable coffee sector in economic, social and environmental terms, (d) facilitate the expansion and transparency of international trade in all types and forms of coffee and promote the elimination of trade barriers, (e) collect, disseminate and publish economic, technical and scientific information, statistics and studies, and (f) promote the development of consumption and markets for all types and all forms of coffee. The Agreement is administered by the International Coffee Organization in London.

International commercial dispute resolution: resolution of disputes between private parties in different countries outside the framework of courts. This can be done through negotiation, mediation and conciliation, expert determination and expert appraisal, ***arbitration*** and a combination of such processes. The method selected depends on the views of the parties. *See also* ***ICSID*** and ***International Court of Arbitration***.

International commodity agreements: ICAs. These are intergovernmental agreements intended to improve the functioning of global commodity markets by balancing the interests of producers and consumers. They are of two types: (a) administrative agreements aimed at increasing consumption of the commodity, promoting transparency in production and market conditions through, for example, statistical work, and (b) economic agreements which seek to influence the market price of the commodity. The agreement establishing the ***Common Fund for Commodities***, negotiated under ***UNCTAD*** auspices, which aims at the conclusion of economic agreements, sets out four elements it deems necessary for an ICA: (a) agreements and arrangements must be concluded between governments, (b) agreements should promote international cooperation in that commodity, (c) producers and consumers must be included, and (d) the agreement should cover the bulk of world trade in the commodity concerned. Some of them are made up of producers only. Most ICAs are negotiated for periods normally ranging from three to ten years, when their operations are reviewed. ICAs with economic provisions typically contain obligations aimed at

有效期10年。目标包括：(a)促进世界可可经济的国际合作；(b)努力达成为可可价值链中的生产者和消费者带来公平经济回报的价格；(c)促进可可经济在经济、社会和环境方面的可持续性；(d)鼓励研究；(e)促进世界可可经济的透明度，特别是在可可贸易方面；(f)促进和鼓励巧克力和可可制品的消费；以及(g)促进可可质量和可可部门的适当安全程序。协定由设在伦敦的国际可可理事会管理。

International Code of Conduct on the Transfer of Technology

国际技术转让行动守则

见*国际技术转让行动守则草案(Draft International Code of Conduct on the Transfer of Technology)*。

International Coffee Agreement

国际咖啡协定

最初于1962年达成，后经多次重新谈判。现行协定于2011年2月2日生效，有效期10年。目标包括：(a)促进有关咖啡的国际合作；(b)为政府间和与私营部门就咖啡进行磋商提供场所；(c)鼓励成员在经济、社会和环境各方面发展可持续的咖啡部门；(d)便利所有种类和形式咖啡国际贸易的扩大和透明，促进贸易壁垒的取消；(e)收集、传播并公布经济、技术和科学信息、数据及研究；以及(f)促进各种类和各形式咖啡消费和市场的开发。协定由设在伦敦的国际咖啡组织管理。

International commercial dispute resolution

国际商事纠纷解决

在法庭框架外解决不同国家私营团体间的争端。可以通过谈判、调停和调解、专家裁定和专家评估、仲裁以及此类方法的组合进行。所选择的方法取决于当事人的意见。另见*国际投资争端解决中心(ICSID)*、*国际仲裁法院(International Court of Arbitration)*。

International commodity agreements

国际商品协定

ICAs。旨在通过平衡生产者和消费者利益，改善全球商品市场运行的政府间协定。协定有两种：(a)管理协定，旨在通过统计工作，增加商品消费、提高生产和市场条件的透明度；及(b)经济协定，旨在寻求影响商品的市场价格。在联合国贸易与发展会议(UNCTAD)主持下谈判的建立商品共同基金协定，旨在缔结经济协定，列出了其认为国际商品协定所需的4个要素：(a)协定和安排必须在政府间缔结；(b)协定应促进有关商品的国际合作；(c)必须包括生产者和消费者；以及(d)协定应涵盖有关商品的大部分国际贸易。一些协定仅由生产者组成。大部分国际商品协定通常需要经过3年至10年的谈判，届时对其运用情况进行审议。订有经济条款的国际商品协定通常包含旨在稳定价格、

stabilizing prices, financing a ***buffer stock*** (none of these seems to exist currently), disposal of non-commercial stockpiles, commitments to improve market access and to promote consumption. Some agreements also seek to encourage further processing in producing countries, and they contain provisions for the exchange of information on production, trade and consumption. Most also include consultation and dispute settlement provisions. The 1954 sugar and tin agreements carried a "fair labour standards" clause which stipulated that labour engaged in the production of the relevant commodity should receive fair remuneration, adequate social security protection and other satisfactory employment conditions. The ***International Coffee Agreement*** which entered into force in 2011 requires members to give consideration to standard of living and working conditions of the populations engaged in the coffee sector. At the same time, members agreed that they would not use this provision for protectionist purposes. Most ICAs are administered by a body established for the purpose. Members are divided into producers and consumers, with the two categories having an equal number of total votes. Producer countries often also import the same commodity, and consumer countries also export. The definition of producer and consumer therefore can hinge on whether a country is a net exporter or importer. Voting is usually based on the share of international trade a member has in that commodity. ICAs commonly operate autonomously, but their negotiation or renegotiation usually takes place under UNCTAD auspices which, upon its establishment in 1964, acquired responsibility for commodity matters within the ***United Nations*** system. Two agreements have, however, been negotiated in the ***GATT***, and they were part of the WTO plurilateral agreements until the end of 1997. The two are the ***International Dairy Agreement*** and the ***International Bovine Meat Agreement***. Both were ostensibly aimed at expanding, liberalizing and stabilizing trade in the commodities under their purview. *See also* ***commodity policy***, ***Integrated Programme for Commodities*** and ***international commodity bodies***.

International commodity bodies: ICBs. These are organizations that either administer ***international commodity agreements*** or are constituted as commodity study groups. The ***Common Fund for Commodities*** established through ***UNCTAD*** has designated twenty-three organizations which represent more than thirty commodities as ICBs. The first group consists of the International Cocoa Organization, International Coffee Organization, International Copper Study Group, International Cotton Advisory Committee, International Grains Council, International Lead and Zinc Study Group, International Network for Bamboo and Rattan, International Nickel Study Group, International Olive Council, International Rubber Study Group, International Sugar Organization and the International Tropical Timber Organization. The second group consists of bodies located within the ***Food and Agriculture Organization***, Intergovernmental Sub-Group on Bananas, Intergovernmental Group on Citrus Fruit, Intergovernmental Sub-Committee on Fish Trade, Intergovernmental Group on Grains, Intergovernmental Group on Hard Fibres, Intergovernmental

为缓冲储存(目前似乎已不存在)融资、处理非商业库存、改善市场准入和促进消费的承诺。一些协定还寻求鼓励在生产国进行进一步加工，并包含交换生产、贸易和消费信息的条款。大部分还包含磋商和争端解决条款。1954 年的糖和锡协定包含"公平劳工标准"条款，规定从事相关商品生产的劳动力应得到公平报酬、充足社会安全保障以及其他令人满意的就业条件。2011 年生效的《国际咖啡协定》要求成员考虑咖啡部门从业人员的生活和工作条件的标准。同时，成员同意不将此条款用于保护主义目的。大部分国际商品协定由一个专门设立的机构管理。成员分为生产者和消费者，两类成员拥有相同投票数。生产国通常进口相同商品，而消费国通常出口相同商品。因此，对生产国和消费国的定义取决于一国是否属净出口国还是净进口国。投票一般根据一成员占该商品国际贸易的份额而定。国际商品协定通常自主运行，但协定的谈判或重新谈判自 UNCTAD 于 1964 年成立起即通常在该组织主持下进行，UNCTAD 在联合国系统内负责处理商品事务。但是，有两个协定是在 GATT 中谈判的，这两个协定在 1997 年底之前属于 WTO 诸边协定，即《国际奶制品协定》和《国际牛肉协定》。两协定显然旨在扩大、放宽和稳定其所辖范围的商品贸易。另见*商品政策(commodity policy)*、*商品综合方案(Integrated Programme for Commodities)*、*国际商品机构(international commodity bodies)*。

International commodity bodies

国际商品机构

ICBs。管理国际商品协定的组织或由商品研究小组组成的组织。通过联合国贸易与发展会议(UNCTAD)建立的商品共同基金指定代表 30 多种商品的 23 个组织为国际商品机构。第一组包括国际可可组织、国际咖啡组织、国际铜研究小组、国际棉花咨询委员会、国际谷物理事会、国际铅锌研究小组、国际竹藤组织、国际镍研究小组、国际橄榄油理事会、国际橡胶研究小组、国际糖组织和国际热带木材组织。第二组包括粮农组织(FAO)内的机构、政府间香蕉小组、政府间柑橘类水果小组、政府间鱼类贸易分委会、政府间谷物小组、政府间硬纤维小组、政府间皮革小组、政府间肉类和奶制品小组、政府间油、油籽

Sub-Group on Hides and Skins, Intergovernmental Group on Meat and Dairy Products, Intergovernmental Group on Oils, Oilseeds and Fats, Intergovernmental Group on Rice, Intergovernmental Group on Tea and Intergovernmental Sub-Group on Tropical Fruits. All these bodies are eligible to sponsor projects for financial support by the Common Fund. *See also* separate entries for some of the agreements administered by these bodies.

International commodity-related environment agreement: ICREA. A type of voluntary intergovernmental instrument suggested at one time by ***UNCTAD*** as conducive to the promotion of environmental objectives in commodity production and to facilitate cooperation among producers and consumers in this regard. ICREAs could either be concerned with the setting of standards, or they could be aimed at funding the transition to more sustainable production methods. *See also* ***commodity policy*** and ***trade and environment***.

International Competition Network: ICN. This is an international body concerned with issues in the enforcement of competition law. It does not make rules. Membership is open to any national or multinational competition authority. [www.internationalcompetitionnetwork.org]

International Conference on Financing and Development: *see* ***Monterrey Consensus***.

International contestability of markets: used for assessing from the perspective of exporters in other countries the extent to which markets are free of distortion caused by regulation and anti-competitive governmental or private action. International contestability is determined by such factors as tariff and non-tariff measures, regulatory conditions affecting the import of services, ***structural impediments*** in the form of, for example, distribution systems, internal regulation of investment and competition, and private anti-competitive practices. A fully contestable market would be one in which firms can compete purely on the basis of price and ability to deliver the product or service wanted by the market. *See also* ***indicators of market openness*** and ***trade and competition***.

International Convention for the Protection of New Varieties of Plants: concluded in 1961 in Paris and revised in 1978 in Geneva. It provides for the grant of ***patents*** or special titles of protection to breeders of new plant varieties. It is administered by the International Union for the Protection of New Varieties of Plants (UPOV), rather than by ***WIPO***. *See also* ***intellectual property rights***.

International Convention for the Protection of Performers, Producers of Phonograms and Broadcasting Organizations: *see* ***Rome Convention***.

International Convention for the Use of Appellations of Origin and Denomination of Cheeses: *see* ***Stresa Convention***.

International Convention on Mutual Administrative Assistance for the Prevention, Investigation and Repression of Customs Offences: adopted in Nairobi on 9 June 1977 under the auspices of the ***World Customs Organization*** (WCO). Parties to this Convention undertake to give each other assistance aimed at preventing, investigating and repressing customs offences. Its provisions do not cover requests for the arrest of persons or the recovery of duties.

和脂肪小组、政府间大米小组、政府间茶叶小组和政府间热带水果小组。所有这些机构有资格资助商品共同基金提供财政支持的项目。另见关于这些机构所管理的部分协定的词条。

International commodity-related environment agreement
与商品有关的国际环境协定

ICREA。由联合国贸易与发展会议(UNCTAD)曾经建议达成的一种自愿政府间文件，有助于促进商品生产过程中的环境目标，便利生产者和消费者在此方面的合作。此类协定可能关注标准的制定，或旨在为过渡到更可持续性的生产方法提供资金。另见*商品政策(commodity policy)*、*贸易与环境(trade and environment)*。

International Competition Network
国际竞争网络

ICN。关注竞争法执行问题的国际机构，本身不制定规则。成员资格向任何国家或国际竞争主管机关开放。

International Conference on Financing and Development
发展筹资问题国际会议

见*蒙特雷共识(Monterrey Consensus)*。

International contestability of markets
市场的国际竞争性

用以从其他国家出口商角度评估市场免受管制及政府或私营部门反竞争行为扭曲的程度。确定国际竞争性的因素包括关税、非关税措施、影响服务进口的管制条件、分配制度、投资和竞争的国内管制等结构性障碍以及私营部门反竞争做法等。充分竞争的市场应为，企业可以仅根据价格和提供市场所需产品或服务的能力进行竞争。另见*市场开放度指标(indicators of market openness)*、*贸易与竞争(trade and competition)*。

International Convention for the Protection of New Varieties of Plants
国际植物新品种保护公约

1961年在巴黎达成，1978年在日内瓦修订。公约规定对植物新品种育种者授予专利，或给予专门保护权。公约由国际植物新品种保护联盟(UPOV)管理，而不是由世界知识产权组织(WIPO)管理。另见*知识产权(intellectual property rights)*。

International Convention for the Protection of Performers, Producers of Phonograms and Broadcasting Organizations
保护表演者、录音制品制作者和广播组织的国际公约

见*罗马公约(Rome Convention)*。

International Convention for the Use of Appellations of Origin and Denomination of Cheeses
乳制品产地俗称使用和命名国际公约

见*斯特雷萨公约(Stresa Convention)*。

International Convention on Mutual Administrative Assistance for the Prevention, Investigation and Repression of Customs Offences
关于防止、调查和惩处违犯海关法罪实行行政互助的国际公约

1977年6月9日在世界海关组织(WCO)主持下在内罗毕通过。公约缔约方承

The Convention was supplemented by a Model Bilateral Agreement on Mutual Assistance in Customs Matters, last revised in 2004, which WCO members can use when negotiating such agreements with other customs services. [www.wcoomd.org]

International Convention on the Harmonized Commodity Description and Coding System: *see* ***Harmonized Commodity Description and Coding System***.

International Convention on the Simplification and Harmonization of Customs Procedures: *see* ***Kyoto Convention***.

International Copper Study Group: ICSG. An international organization established in 1992 under ***UNCTAD*** auspices to promote international cooperation on matters concerning copper. Its objectives are (a) promoting international cooperation on matters related to copper, such as health, environment, research, technology transfer, regulations and trade, (b) providing a global forum where industry and governments can meet and discuss common problems and objectives, and (c) increasing market transparency and promoting an exchange of information on production, consumption, stocks, trade and prices of copper. Its secretariat is in Lisbon. *See also* ***international commodity bodies***.

International Cotton Advisory Committee: ICAC. Established in 1939 as an association of cotton producers and restructured in 1945 to admit consumers also. It collects and disseminates statistics on cotton production and trade. Also serves as a clearing house for technical information about cotton and cotton textiles and as a forum for discussion of cotton matters of international significance. Its secretariat is located in Washington, DC. *See also* ***international commodity bodies*** and ***Sectoral Initiative in Favour of Cotton***.

International Court of Arbitration: established in 1923 as the ***arbitration*** body of the ***International Chamber of Commerce***. It offers resolution of commercial disputes without litigation in national court systems. *See also* ***alternative dispute resolution***.

International Court of Justice: the principal judicial organ of the ***United Nations***. Its two functions are to settle legal disputes between states and to give advisory opinions on legal questions submitted by authorized international organizations and agencies, all of them being United Nations agencies. The sources of law used by the Court include international treaties and conventions, international custom, general principles of law, judicial decisions and academic work. The Court was established in 1946 as the successor to the Permanent Court of International Justice. It is located at The Hague.

International Covenant on Economic, Social and Cultural Rights: entered into force on 3 January 1976. This Covenant, especially aspects of Part III, is relevant to the discussion of ***trade and labour standards*** and ***trade and human rights***. In Article 6 the parties recognize the right to work, including access to technical and vocational guidance and training programmes. Article 7 recognizes the right to fair wages and equal remuneration for work of equal value, safe and healthy working conditions, equal opportunity to be promoted, and

诺进行互助，旨在防止、调查和惩处违犯海关法罪。公约条款未涵盖逮捕人员或追回税款的要求。公约由一份海关事务双边互助协定范本补充，范本最近一次修订是在 2004 年，WCO 成员可以在与其他海关部门谈判此类协定时使用该范本。

International Convention on the Harmonized Commodity Description and Coding System

商品名称及编码协调制度国际公约

见*商品名称及编码协调制度(Harmonized Commodity Description and Coding System)*。

International Convention on the Simplification and Harmonization of Customs Procedures

关于简化和协调海关业务制度的国际公约

见*京都公约(Kyoto Convention)*。

International Copper Study Group

国际铜研究小组

ICSG。为促进与铜有关事务的国际合作，在联合国贸易与发展会议(UNCTAD)主持下于 1992 年成立的国际组织。目标为：(a)促进与铜相关事务的国际合作，例如健康、环境、研究、技术转让、法规和贸易；(b)为产业和政府提供见面和讨论共同问题和目标的全球平台；以及(c)增强市场透明度，并促进关于铜的生产、消费、库存、贸易和价格的信息交流。秘书处设在里斯本。另见*国际商品机构(international commodity bodies)*。

International Cotton Advisory Committee

国际棉花咨询委员会

ICAC。1939 年作为棉花生产商协会成立，并于 1945 年重组，以接纳消费者。委员会收集和传播关于棉花生产和贸易的统计数据，同时作为棉花和棉纺织品的技术信息交换机构及讨论具有国际意义的棉花问题的场所。秘书处设在华盛顿特区。另见*国际商品机构(international commodity bodies)*、*棉花部门倡议(Sectoral Initiative in Favour of Cotton)*。

International Court of Arbitration

国际仲裁法院

作为国际商会的仲裁机构于 1923 年成立。法院为未在国内法院系统提起诉讼的商业纠纷提供解决方案。另见*非诉讼争端解决 (alternative dispute resolution)*。

International Court of Justice

国际法院

联合国主要司法机构。法院的两个职能是，解决国家间的法律争端和对属联合国机构授权的国际组织和机构提交的法律问题提供咨询意见。国际法院的法律依据包括国际条约和公约、国际惯例、法律通则、法院判决以及学术著作。国际法院成立于 1946 年，前身为国际常设法院，设在海牙。

International Covenant on Economic, Social and Cultural Rights

经济、社会和文化权利国际公约

1976 年 1 月 3 日生效。公约、特别是第三部分内容，与贸易与劳工标准和贸易与人权的讨论相关。在第 6 条中，缔约方承认工作权，包括获得技术和职业指导及培训项目。第 7 条承认公平的工资和同工同酬、安全和卫生的工作

rest, leisure and reasonable limitation of working hours. In Article 8 the Parties undertake to ensure the right of everyone to form and join trade unions, the right of trade unions to establish national federations and to form or join international trade union organizations, the right of trade unions to function freely, and the right to strike in accordance with the law. Article 9 recognizes the right of everyone to social security, including social insurance. *See also* ***Universal Declaration of Human Rights***. [ohchr.rg]

International Dairy Agreement: one of the WTO plurilateral agreements, negotiated during the ***Tokyo Round*** as the *International Dairy Arrangement*, but terminated in 1997. Its objectives were (a) to achieve the expansion and ever greater liberalization of world trade in dairy products under market conditions as stable as possible on the basis of mutual benefit to exporting and importing countries, and (b) to further the economic and social development of developing countries. The Agreement covered trade in fresh and preserved milk and cream, butter, cheese and curd, and casein. It was administered by the International Dairy Council.

International Dairy Arrangement: *see* ***International Dairy Agreement***.

International Dairy Council: *see* ***International Dairy Agreement***.

International Development Association: IDA. This is an agency of the ***World Bank*** which makes concessional loans to the poorest of developing countries. Its aim is to reduce disparities between and within countries, and it concentrates on primary education, basic health, water supply and sanitation. IDA mainly lends to countries that do not have the financial ability to borrow from the World Bank on commercial terms. In 2018 most of the countries eligible for IDA funds had an annual per capita income of less than $1,165. In some cases, countries are eligible for combined IDA/World Bank loans. The IDA is funded mainly through contributions from the wealthier member countries, rather than by borrowing on financial markets as is the case for the World Bank itself. *See also* ***International Finance Corporation*** and ***Multilateral Investment Guarantee Agency***.

International division of labour: the arranging of production processes to promote ever greater specialization of labour, economies of scale and standardized products. Its aim is to enable firms to compete through the price mechanism. The international division of labour was originally based on the analogy of dividing the manufacture of a product in such a way that the greatest possible part of it could be produced by cheaper unskilled and semi-skilled labour, but the complexity of many products now produced and traded internationally has greatly undermined this rationale. *See also* ***delocalization***, ***globalization***, ***new international division of labour*** and ***product cycle theory***.

International economic relations: includes directly, in addition to international trade, international monetary and financial cooperation and activities, such as capital movements and foreign investment. More indirectly, almost any international activity can have an economic aspect or effect.

International Electrotechnical Commission: IEC. The main international body for cooperation on ***standards*** and ***conformity assessment*** in the fields of

条件、提级的同等机会以及休息、闲暇和工作时间的合理限制的权利。在第8条中，缔约方承诺人人有权组织和参加工会，工会有权建立全国性联合会，有权组织或参加国际工会组织，工会有权自由地进行工作，有权在符合法律规定下提出罢工。第 9 条承认人人有权享受社会保障，包括社会保险。另见*世界人权宣言(Universal Declaration of Human Rights)*。

International Dairy Agreement
国际奶制品协定

WTO 诸边协定，在东京回合中以《国际奶制品安排》名义进行谈判，1997 年终止。目标为：(a)在出口国和进口国互利基础上，在尽可能稳定的市场条件下，实现世界奶制品贸易的扩大和更大自由化；及(b)促进发展中国家经济和社会发展。协定涵盖鲜奶和保鲜奶、奶油、黄油、奶酪和凝乳以及酪蛋白的贸易。由国际奶制品理事会管理。

International Dairy Arrangement
国际奶制品安排

见*国际奶制品协定(International Dairy Agreement)*。

International Dairy Council
国际奶制品理事会

见*国际奶制品协定(International Dairy Agreement)*。

International Development Association
国际开发协会

IDA。世界银行机构，为最贫穷的发展中国家发放优惠贷款。旨在缩小国与国之间和国家内部的差距，集中在基础教育、基本健康、供水和卫生方面。IDA 主要向没有财政能力以商业条款自世界银行借款的国家提供贷款。2018 年大多数有资格申请 IDA 资金的国家的人均年收入低于 1,165 美元。在一些情况下，国家有资格获得 IDA/世界银行合并贷款。IDA 资金主要来源于更富裕成员国的捐助，而不是像世界银行那样从金融市场借款。另见*国际金融公司(International Finance Corporation)*、*多边投资担保机构(Multilateral Investment Guarantee Agency)*。

International division of labour
国际分工

对生产过程进行安排以促进劳动力更大程度专业化、规模经济和标准化产品。旨在使企业能够通过价格机制进行竞争。国际分工最初根据这样一种类比，即将产品的制造过程划分为将尽可能多的部分交由廉价的、不熟练和半熟练劳动力生产，但现在所生产的和进行国际贸易的许多产品的复杂程度大大削弱了这一理论。另见*去本地化(delocalization)*、*全球化(globalization)*、*新国际分工(new international division of labour)*、*产品周期理论(product cycle theory)*。

International economic relations
国际经济关系

直接而言，除国际贸易外，还包括国际货币和金融合作及活动，例如资本流动和外国投资。更间接地讲，几乎任何国际活动都包含经济方面或有经济影响。

International Electrotechnical Commission
国际电工委员会

IEC。在电力、电子及相关技术领域就标准和合格评定开展合作的主要国际机

electricity, electronics and related technologies. It provides a forum for the preparation and implementation of consensus-based voluntary international standards. The IEC is associated with the WTO through the ***Agreement on Technical Barriers to Trade***. Its secretariat is located in Geneva. *See also* ***International Organization for Standardization***.

International Energy Agency: IEA. An intergovernmental organization established in 1974 after the first oil shock. It consists of ***OECD*** member countries. Its main concerns are increased energy efficiency, energy conservation and the development of new sources of energy. The IEA's secretariat is in Paris.

International Energy Charter: adopted on 20 May 2015. Its signatories favour sustainable energy development, improving energy security and maximizing the efficiency of production, conversion, transport, distribution and use of energy, to enhance safety in a manner which would be socially acceptable, economically viable and environmentally sound. Signatories will take action in three fields: (a) development of trade in energy consistent with major relevant multilateral agreements, such as the ***WTO Agreement*** and related instruments and nuclear non-proliferation obligations and undertakings, (b) cooperation in many areas of the energy field, and (c) creating mechanisms and conditions to promote energy efficiency and environmental protection. *See also* ***Energy Charter Treaty***. [www.energycharter.org]

International exhaustion: the proposition that once a product embodying ***intellectual property rights*** (IPRs) has been lawfully placed on the market anywhere (i.e. with the consent of the owner of the IPRs), it can be resold or transferred to any other market without the further consent of the owner of these IPRs. *See also* ***exhaustion doctrine***, ***parallel imports*** and ***regional exhaustion***. [Maskus 2000]

International Federation of Inspection Agencies: IFIA. An organization of international testing, inspection and certification companies based in Brussels. IFIA, together with the ***International Chamber of Commerce***, form an ***independent entity*** when this is required to solve a dispute about preshipment inspection. *See also* ***Agreement on Preshipment Inspection***.

International Finance Corporation: IFC. The part of the ***World Bank*** charged with providing finance for private enterprise in developing countries to promote their economic development. The IFC coordinates its activities closely with the World Bank, but it operates essentially as an independent agency. *See also* ***International Development Association***, ***Multilateral Investment Guarantee Agency*** and ***World Bank Group***.

International financial institutions: IFIs. A term used for intergovernmental organizations, such as the ***IMF***, the ***World Bank*** or the ***Asian Development Bank***. They are concerned mainly with the promotion of sound economic management by member states or the provision of financial support to member states for defined purposes. Developing countries often can obtain financial assistance for the development of their economies under concessional conditions, such as extended repayment periods and interest below market

构。为制定和实施以协商一致为基础的自愿国际标准提供场所。IEC 通过《技术性贸易壁垒协定》与 WTO 相关联。秘书处设在日内瓦。另见*国家标准化组织(International Organization for Standardization)*。

International Energy Agency

国际能源机构

IEA。第一次石油危机后于 1974 年成立的政府间组织。由经济合作与发展组织(OECD)成员国组成。主要关注提高能源效率、节约能源和开发新能源。秘书处设在巴黎。

International Energy Charter

国际能源宪章

2015 年 5 月 20 日通过。签署国支持可持续能源发展、改善能源安全以及实现能源生产、转化、运输、配送和使用过程中效率的最大化，以社会可接受、经济上可行、适应环境要求的方式提高安全性。签署国将在三个领域采取行动：(a)按照主要相关多边协定发展能源贸易，例如《WTO 协定》和有关文书以及核不扩散义务和承诺；(b)在能源领域的许多方面开展合作；以及(c)创设机制和条件以促进能源效率和环境保护。另见*能源宪章条约(Energy Charter Treaty)*。

International exhaustion

国际用尽

该原则认为，一旦包含知识产权的一产品已在任何地方合法投放市场(即已经过知识产权所有人同意)，该产品即可无需知识产权所有人进一步同意而在任何其他市场上转售或转让知识产权。另见*权利用尽原则(exhaustion doctrine)*、*平行进口(parallel imports)*、*区域用尽(regional exhaustion)*。

International Federation of Inspection Agencies

国际检验机构联盟

IFIA。设在布鲁塞尔的由国际检测、检验和认证公司组成的组织。在需要解决装运前检验纠纷时，IFIA 与国际商会一起组成独立实体。另见*装运前检验协定(Agreement on Preshipment Inspection)*。

International Finance Corporation

国际金融公司

IFC。属世界银行一部分，负责向发展中国家中的私营企业提供资金，以促进其经济发展。IFC 的活动紧密配合世界银行，但基本上作为独立机构运营。另见*国际开发协会(International Development Association)*、*多边投资担保机构(Multilateral Investment Guarantee Agency)*、*世界银行集团(World Bank Group)*。

International financial institutions

国际金融机构

IFIs。用于指国际货币基金组织、世界银行或亚洲开发银行等政府间机构的词语。这些机构主要关注促进其成员国的良好经济管理，或为特定目标向成员国提供财政支持。发展中国家经常能以优惠条件获得促进其经济发展的财政

rates. *See also* ***Asian Infrastructure Investment Bank***, ***multilateral development banks***, ***New Development Bank*** and ***structural adjustment***.

International Fund for Agricultural Development: IFAD. One of the ***United Nations specialized agencies***. It began operations in 1977 with a mandate to finance agricultural development projects leading to improved food supplies and ***food security*** in developing countries. The bulk of its loans are made available to low-income countries, usually on highly concessional terms. *See also* ***Food and Agricultural Organization*** and ***World Food Programme***.

International Grains Agreement: IGA. The successor to the ***International Wheat Agreement***. It entered into force on 1 July 1995 for three years, with provision for renewal every two years. The IGA consists of two instruments: the Grains Trade Convention and the Food Assistance Convention. The objectives of the Grains Trade Convention are (a) to further international cooperation in all aspects of trade in grains, particularly as they affect food grain, (b) to promote the expansion of international trade in grain, and to secure the freest possible flow of trade, (c) to contribute to fullest extent possible to the stability of international grain markets, to enhance world food security and to contribute to the development of countries that are heavily dependent on commercial sales of grains, and (d) to provide a forum for exchange of information regarding trade in grains. The Convention covers wheat, maize, soybeans, rice and oilseeds. The objectives of the *Food Assistance Convention* are to save lives, reduce hunger, improve food security and improve the nutritional status of the most vulnerable populations by (a) providing food assistance that improves access to, and consumption of, adequate, safe and nutritious food, (b) through appropriate, timely, effective and efficient assistance, and (c) through facilitating information sharing, cooperation and coordination. Food assistance may be provided to any country listed as a recipient by the OECD ***Development Assistance Committee***. The IGA is administered by the International Grains Council located in London. *See also* ***Food and Agriculture Organization*** and ***food security***.

International Group of Twenty-Four on International Monetary Affairs and Development: *see* ***G-24***.

International investment agreement: IIA. This is an agreement between two or more parties for the treatment of investment flows between them. Most of these agreements aim to protect and promote investment, but more recent ones also liberalize conditions for investment. ***Treaties of friendship, commerce and navigation*** are among the oldest such instruments. Current forms are ***investment promotion and protection agreements*** and ***bilateral investment treaties***. ***UNCTAD's Reform Package for the International Investment Regime*** estimates that more than 2,300 such treaties have been concluded, mostly before 2010. The ***Energy Charter Treaty*** is an example of a regional investment agreement. An ambitious attempt to establish common rules for international investment was the OECD ***Multilateral Agreement on Investment***, but negotiations towards it were abandoned in 1999. IIAs typically have provisions

援助，例如延长还款期或低于市场标准的利率。另见*亚洲基础设施投资银行(Asian Infrastructure Investment Bank)*、*多边开发银行(multilateral development banks)*、*新开发银行(New Development Bank)*、*结构性调整(structural adjustment)*。

International Fund for Agricultural Development
国际农业发展基金

IFAD。联合国专门机构，自 1977 年起运营，负责为农业发展项目提供资金，以改善发展中国家粮食供应和粮食安全。大部分贷款通常以非常优惠的条件向低收入国家提供。另见*粮食及农业组织(Food and Agricultural Organization)*、*世界粮食计划署(World Food Programme)*。

International Grains Agreement
国际谷物协定

IGA。《国际小麦协定》的后继协定。1995 年 7 月 1 日生效，为期 3 年，规定每 2 年展期一次。IGA 由 2 份文书组成，即《谷物贸易公约》和《粮食援助公约》。《谷物贸易公约》的目标为：(a)全面推进谷物贸易国际合作，特别是影响食用谷物的国际合作；(b)推动谷物国际贸易的扩大，保证尽可能自由的贸易流动；(c)尽最大可能为国际谷物市场稳定作出贡献，加强世界粮食安全，并为严重依赖谷物商业销售国家的发展作出贡献；以及(d)为谷物贸易信息交流提供场所。公约涵盖小麦、玉米、大豆、大米和油籽。《粮食援助公约》的目标是拯救生命、减少饥饿、提高粮食安全和改善最脆弱人群的营养状况，通过(a)提供粮食援助，改善充足、安全和有营养食物的获得和消费；(b)通过适当、及时、有效且高效的援助；以及(c)通过便利信息分享、合作和协作。粮食援助可以向经济合作与发展组织(OECD)发展援助委员会列为受援国的任何国家提供。IGA 由设在伦敦的国际谷物理事会管理。另见*粮食及农业组织(Food and Agriculture Organization)*、*粮食安全(food security)*。

International Group of Twenty-Four on International Monetary Affairs and Development
国际货币事务与发展问题 24 国集团

见 *24 国集团(G-24)*

International investment agreement
国际投资协定

IIA。两个或多个参加方之间关于投资流动待遇的协定。大多数此类协定旨在保护和促进投资，但最近的协定也涉及放宽投资条件。友好通商航海条约是最古老的此类文件之一。现行的形式为投资促进与保护协定和双边投资协定。据联合国贸易与发展会议(UNCTAD)《关于国际投资制度的一揽子改革方案》估计，已达成超过 2300 个类似条约，大部分是在 2010 年之前。《能源宪章条约》是区域投资协定的例子。经济合作与发展组织(OECD)的《多边投资协定》是试图为国际投资建立共同规则的一次雄心勃勃的尝试，但谈判在 1999 年停

concerning the ***standard of treatment*** to be accorded to foreign investors and their investments. These standards include ***most-favoured-nation treatment***, ***national treatment***, ***minimum standard of treatment*** and ***fair and equitable treatment***. The former two are found in virtually every agreement, the latter only in some. Other main provisions include rules on ***establishment*** (i.e. act of investing), entry of personnel to manage the investment, ***expropriation*** and compensation, dispute settlement between the parties and ***investor-state disputes***. Beginning with the entry into force of ***NAFTA*** in 1994 many ***free-trade agreements*** have included comprehensive investment chapters, such as ***NAFTA Chapter 11***. Some of these investment chapters perform the concurrent functions of promoting, protecting, liberalizing and facilitating investment, a development already anticipated by some bilateral investment treaties. Such agreements proscribe, for example, performance requirements. Others emphasize liberalization and leave promotion and protection to separate instruments. UNCTAD has suggested a significant programme of reform of such agreements by addressing what it describes as the development dimension of these agreements, the balance between rights and obligations of investors and states and the systemic complexity of the applicable regime. *See also* ***investment facilitation***.

Internationalization: the extension of economic activity across national borders to harness the benefits of lower costs in other economies, with countries specializing in a particular stage of production. It is one of the results of decreasing costs of transport and communications which promotes the integration of markets for goods, services, technology, ideas, capital and human resources. Analysts tend to distinguish internationalization from ***globalization***. Some see the former as allowing countries to retain their economic independence and the latter as weakening national sovereignty.

International Jute Study Group: established on 13 March 2001 as the successor to the ***International Agreement on Jute and Jute Products***. Now defunct.

International Labour Organization: ILO. Established in 1919 as part of the Treaty of Versailles. It became a ***United Nations specialized agency*** in 1946. Its objectives are to improve working and living conditions through the adoption of international conventions and recommendations setting minimum standards for wages, hours of work, conditions of employment, social security, etc. It is located in Geneva. *See also* ***child labour***, ***core labour standards*** and ***trade and labour standards***.

International labour standards: expressions of international agreement in the form of conventions and recommendations arrived at in the ***International Labour Organization***. They cover labour conditions, social policy, human rights and civil rights matters. Among them are freedom of association, the right to organize, collective bargaining, abolition of forced labour, and equality of opportunity and treatment. *See also* ***core labour standards*** and ***trade and labour standards***.

International Lead and Zinc Study Group: ILZSG. Established in 1959 as the successor to the Lead and Zinc Study Committee. It is a forum for consultation between producers and consumers on issues related to the production of and

止。国际投资协定通常包括给予外国投资者及其投资待遇标准的条款。这些标准包括最惠国待遇、国民待遇、最低待遇标准以及公平和公正的待遇。前两种待遇几乎每一协定中均包含，后者仅部分协定包含。其他主要条款包括关于设立(即投资行为)、管理投资人员进入、征收和补偿、当事方争议解决和投资者—国家间争端的规定。随着 1994 年《北美自由贸易协定》(NAFTA)生效，许多自由贸易协定包括全面的投资章节，例如 NAFTA 第 11 章。这些投资章节中的部分章节同时发挥促进、保护、放宽和便利投资的作用，这是一些双边投资条约已经预见的发展情况。例如此类协定禁止实绩要求。其他章节则强调放宽投资，而将促进和保护交由单独文件处理。UNCTAD 提出了对此类协定进行改革的重要方案，通过处理 UNCTAD 所称的这些协定的发展问题，投资者—国家间的权利与义务的平衡问题以及适用制度的体制复杂性问题。另见*投资便利化(investment facilitation)*。

Internationalization

国际化

将经济活动扩展至国境之外以获取其他经济体更低成本的利益，是各国专门从事生产的特定阶段。这是运输和通信成本降低的结果之一，促进了货物、服务、技术、想法、资本和人力资源的市场一体化。分析人士倾向于区分国际化和全球化。有人认为，国际化允许各国保持经济独立性，而全球化削弱国家主权。

International Jute Study Group

国际黄麻研究小组

2001 年 3 月 13 日成立，作为《国际黄麻和黄麻制品协定》的后继机构。现已不复存在。

International Labour Organization

国际劳工组织

ILO。作为《凡尔赛条约》的一部分于 1919 年成立，1946 年成为联合国专门机构。目标是通过采用规定最低工资标准、工作时间、就业条件、社会保障的国际公约和建议，改善工作和生活条件。该组织设在日内瓦。另见*童工(child labour)*、*核心劳工标准(core labour standards)*、*贸易与劳工标准(trade and labour standards)*。

International labour standards

国际劳工标准

以在国际劳工组织(ILO)中达成的公约和建议形式表达的国际协定。涵盖劳动标准、社会政策、人权和民权事务。其中包括结社自由、组织权利、集体谈判、废除强迫劳动以及机会和待遇平等。另见*核心劳工标准(core labour standards)*、*贸易与劳工标准(trade and labour standards)*。

International Lead and Zinc Study Group

国际铅锌研究小组

ILZSG。作为铅锌研究委员会的后继组织于 1959 年成立。是生产者和消费者之间就与铅锌生产和贸易有关的问题进行磋商的场所，包括统计数据汇编。ILZSG 设在伦敦，但其会议由联合国贸易与发展会议(UNCTAD)主持。另见*国*

trade in lead and zinc, including the compilation of statistics. The ILZSG is located in London, but its meetings are conducted under the auspices of ***UNCTAD***. *See also* ***international commodity bodies***.

Internationally recognized labour standards: *see* ***core labour standards*** and ***international labour standards***.

International Maritime Organization: IMO. One of the ***United Nations specialized agencies***. It was established in 1959 as the Inter-Governmental Maritime Consultative Organization and given its present name in 1982. The IMO provides a forum for intergovernmental cooperation on matters such as facilitation of international maritime traffic, maritime safety standards, liability and compensation issues and measures to prevent pollution from ships. It is located in London. *See also* ***Convention on Facilitation of International Maritime Traffic*** and ***maritime transport services***.

International Meat Council: the body which administered the ***International Bovine Meat Agreement***, one of the WTO plurilateral agreements, until its termination at the end of 1997.

International Monetary Fund: *see* ***IMF***.

International Natural Rubber Agreement: first concluded in 1979, renewed in 1987 and terminated in 1999. It was administered by the International Natural Rubber Organization, located in Kuala Lumpur. *See also* ***International Rubber Study Group***.

International Network on Bamboo and Rattan: INBAR. A multilateral development organization established in 1997 which promotes sustainable development using bamboo and rattan. Its secretariat is in Beijing. One of the ***international commodity bodies***.

International Nickel Study Group: INSG. Established under ***UNCTAD*** auspices. Entered into force on 23 May 1990. It promotes international cooperation on issues concerning nickel, especially by improving statistics and other information on the nickel market, and it provides a forum for discussing nickel issues of common interest and concern. Its secretariat is located in Lisbon.

International non-governmental organizations: *see* ***non-governmental organizations***.

International Observatory on Creative Industries for Development: at one time proposed for establishment by ***UNCTAD*** to analyse policies in developing countries on ***creative industries*** and to collect statistics on them.

International Office of Epizootics: *see* ***World Organisation for Animal Health***.

International Olive Oil Agreement: *see* ***International Agreement on Olive Oil and Table Olives***.

International Organisation of Vine and Wine: OIV. Established as the successor to the International Vine and Wine Office through the *Agreement Establishing the International Organisation of Vine and Wine*, done at Paris on 3 April 2001, which became effective on 1 January 2004. It is located in Paris. Article 1 of Agreement the states that it "is an ***intergovernmental organisation*** of a scientific and technical nature of recognised competence for its work

际商品机构(international commodity bodies)。

Internationally recognized labour standards

国际公认劳工标准

见*核心劳工标准(core labour standards)*、*国际劳工标准(international labour standards)*。

International Maritime Organization

国际海事组织

IMO。联合国专门机构。于 1959 年成立，原名为政府间海事协商组织，1982 年改为现名。国际海事组织为就便利国际海上交通、海上安全标准、责任和赔偿事宜及防止船舶污染措施开展政府间合作提供场所。该组织设在伦敦。另见*便利国际海上运输公约(Convention on Facilitation of International Maritime Traffic)*、*海运服务(maritime transport services)*。

International Meat Council

国际肉类理事会

管理 WTO 诸边协定《国际牛肉协定》的机构，直至 1997 年底该协定终止。

International Monetary Fund

国际货币基金组织

见*国际货币基金组织(IMF)*。

International Natural Rubber Agreement

国际天然橡胶协定

最初于 1979 年缔结，1987 年展期，1999 年终止。协定由设在吉隆坡的国际天然橡胶组织管理。另见*国际橡胶研究小组(International Rubber Study Group)*。

International Network on Bamboo and Rattan

国际竹藤组织

INBAR。1997 年成立的多边发展组织，旨在通过使用竹藤促进可持续发展。秘书处设在北京。属国际商品机构。

International Nickel Study Group

国际镍研究小组

INSG。在联合国贸易与发展会议(UNCTAD)主持下成立，1990 年 5 月 23 日生效。研究小组促进有关镍问题的国际合作，特别是通过改进关于镍市场的统计和其他信息，并为讨论具有共同利益和关切的镍问题提供场所。秘书处设在里斯本。

International non-governmental organizations

国际非政府组织

见*非政府组织(non-governmental organizations)*。

International Observatory on Creative Industries for Development

国际发展创意产业瞭望台

联合国贸易与发展会议(UNCTAD)曾经提议建立，旨在分析发展中国家中关于创意产业的政策，并收集有关数据。

International Office of Epizootics

国际兽疫局

见*世界动物卫生组织(World Organisation for Animal Health)*。

International Olive Oil Agreement

国际橄榄油协定

见*国际橄榄油和食用橄榄协定(International Agreement on Olive Oil and Table Olives)*。

International Organisation of Vine and Wine

国际葡萄与葡萄酒组织

OIV。作为国际葡萄与葡萄酒局的后继机构，通过 2001 年 4 月 3 日在巴黎签

concerning vines, wine, wine-based beverages, table grapes, raisins and other vine-based products". It has forty-seven member states. Its main activities are (a) to promote and guide scientific and technical research and experimentation, (b) to draw up and implement recommendations concerning conditions for grape production, oenological practices, definition and/or description of products, labelling and marketing conditions, methods for analysing and assessing vine products, and (c) to examine proposals relating to guaranteeing the authenticity of vine products, protecting ***geographical indications***, especially vine- and wine-growing areas and the related ***appellations of origin*** and improving scientific and technical criteria for recognizing and protecting new grape plant varieties. [oiv.int]

International Organization for Standardization: ISO. A worldwide federation of national standards bodies established in 1947 to promote the development of standardization and related activities with a view to facilitating the international exchange of goods and services. Each country is represented by one organization only. The ISO also promotes the development of cooperation in intellectual, scientific, technological and economic activities. It is associated with the WTO especially through work concerning the ***Agreement on Technical Barriers to Trade*** which seeks to ensure that standards are not used as disguised barriers to trade. *See also* ***International Electrotechnical Commission***, ***ISO 9000*** and ***ISO 14000***.

International Organization of Securities Commissions: *see* ***IOSCO***.

International Patent Classification: IPC. *See* ***Strasbourg Agreement Concerning the International Patent Classification***.

International Plan of Action to Prevent, Deter and Eliminate IUU Fishing: *see* ***IUU fishing***.

International Plant Protection Convention: entered into force on 3 April 1952 and revised in 1979. It is administered by the ***Food and Agriculture Organization***. Its objective is securing common and effective international action to prevent the introduction and the spread of pests of plants and plant products and to promote measures for their control. The Convention was amended in 1997 partly to meet the standard-setting requirements of the WTO ***Agreement on the Application of Sanitary and Phytosanitary Measures***. The revised convention entered into force on 2 October 2005.

International political economy: broadly defined as the academic discipline concerned with the relationship between the political and economic domains in contemporary international society. ***Trade policy*** is one aspect of this relationship.

International Programme on the Elimination of Child Labour: IPEC. A programme initiated in 1992 by the ***International Labour Organization*** to assist member countries in their efforts to eliminate child labour. Activities under IPEC include the development of national action programmes, establishing demonstration projects and awareness programmes for government, non-government organizations, workers and employers. Some twenty countries are now participating in

订并于2004年1月1日生效的《建立国际葡萄与葡萄酒组织协定》设立。该组织设在巴黎。协定第1条规定："该组织是一个关于葡萄、葡萄酒、葡萄酒饮料、鲜食葡萄、葡萄干和其他葡萄制品方面具有公认的科学和技术能力的政府间组织"。该组织有47个成员。主要活动为：(a)促进和指导科学技术研究和试验；(b)拟订和执行关于葡萄生产条件、酿酒方法、产品定义和/或描述、标签和营销条件、葡萄产品分析和评估方法的建议；以及(c)审查有关下列内容的提案：保证葡萄产品真伪，保护地理标志，特别是葡萄和葡萄酒产区及有关原产地名称，以及改进识别和保护葡萄树新品种的科学和技术标准。

International Organization for Standardization

国际标准化组织

ISO。1947年成立的世界范围的国家标准机构联合会，旨在促进标准的制定及相关活动，以便利国际货物和服务的交换。每一国家仅由一个组织作为代表。ISO还促进知识、科学、技术和经济活动合作的发展。特别通过有关《技术性贸易壁垒协定》的工作与WTO相关联，该协定寻求保证标准不被用作变相贸易壁垒。另见*国际电工委员会(International Electrotechnical Commission)*、*ISO9000质量管理体系(ISO9000)*、*ISO14000环境管理体系(ISO14000)*。

International Organization of Securities Commissions

国际证监会组织

见*国际证监会组织(IOSCO)*。

International Patent Classification

国际专利分类

见*国际专利分类斯特拉斯堡协定(Strasbourg Agreement Concerning the International Patent Classification)*。

International Plan of Action to Prevent, Deter and Eliminate IUU Fishing

防止、阻止和消除非法、未报告和无管制捕捞的国际行动计划

见*非法、未报告和无管制捕捞(IUU fishing)*。

International Plant Protection Convention

国际植物保护公约

1952年4月3日生效，于1979年修订。由粮农组织(FAO)管理。目标是保证采取共同和有效的国际行动，以防止植物和植物产品害虫的传入和传播，并促进控制这些害虫的措施。公约于1997年进行了部分修正，以满足WTO《实施卫生与植物卫生措施协定》的标准制定要求。修订后的公约于2005年10月2日生效。

International political economy

国际政治经济学

广泛定义为有关当代国际社会中政治和经济领域之间关系的学科。贸易政策是这一关系的一个方面。

International Programme on the Elimination of Child Labour

消除童工现象国际方案

IPEC。国际劳工组织(ILO)于1992年启动的一项方案，旨在协助成员国努力消除童工现象。IPEC下的活动包括制定国家行动方案，为政府、非政府组织、工人和雇主制定示范项目和提高认识方案。大约20个国家现在正在参与IPEC。

IPEC. *See also* ***child labour***, ***core labour standards***, ***social clause***, ***trade and labour standards*** and ***worst forms of child labour***. [www.ilo.org]

International regulatory cooperation mechanisms: formal (such as treaties) and informal (such as dialogues) ways used by governments to reduce the cost of doing business internationally and to make it more predictable.

International Rubber Study Group: IRSG. A body consisting of producer and consumer countries established in 1944. Its purpose is to act as a forum for the discussion of matters related to the production, consumption and trade in natural and synthetic rubber. It also publishes an extensive range of statistical material. Its secretariat is located in London. *See also* ***International Natural Rubber Agreement*** and ***International Tripartite Rubber Organization***.

International Standard Classification of Occupations: ISCO. A four-level classification maintained by the ***International Labour Organization*** as (a) a basis for the international reporting, comparison and exchange of statistical and administrative data about occupations, (b) a model for the development of national and regional classifications and occupations, and (c) a system that can be used directly in countries that have not developed their own national classification. The current version is ISCO-8, adopted in December 2007. [www.ilo.org]

International Standard Industrial Classification of All Economic Activities: ISIC. This is a classification of the entire range of economic activities regardless of ownership. It allows entities to be classified according to the activity they carry out. ISIC is maintained by the United Nations Statistical Office. [unstats.un.org]

International Standards for Phytosanitary Measures: ISPM. These are plant quarantine standards established under the ***International Plant Protection Convention*** which have been endorsed by the ***Food and Agriculture Organization***, the Interim Commission on Phytosanitary Measures or the ***Commission on Phytosanitary Measures***. These standards are part of the international standards, guidelines and recommendations recognized under the WTO ***Agreement on the Application of Sanitary and Phytosanitary Measures***.

International standards for sanitary and phytosanitary measures: the ***Agreement on the Application of Sanitary and Phytosanitary Measures*** requires WTO members to base their sanitary and phytosanitary measures on international standards, guidelines or recommendations where these exist. Among these are (a) the standards for food safety established by the ***Codex Alimentarius Commission*** relating to food additives, veterinary drug and pesticide residues, contaminants, methods of analysis and sampling, and codes and guidelines of hygienic practice, (b) for animal health the standards developed by the International Office of Epizootics, (c) for plant health the standards established under the ***International Plant Protection Convention***, and (d) any other international standards set by international organizations open for membership to all.

International steel cartel: at one time or another a ***cartel*** allegedly dividing the world steel market into two hemispheres, with the dividing line running through

另见*童工(child labour)*、*核心劳工标准(core labour standards)*、*社会条款(social clause)*、*贸易与劳工标准(trade and labour standards)*、*最恶劣形式的童工劳动(worst forms of child labour)*。

International regulatory cooperation mechanisms

国际监管合作机制

政府为降低国际商业成本及使其更具预测性而采用的正式(例如条约)和非正式(例如对话)方式。

International Rubber Study Group

国际橡胶研究小组

IRSG。1944 年成立，由生产国和消费国组成。目的是作为讨论与天然橡胶和合成橡胶生产、消费和贸易有关问题的场所。研究小组还发布内容广泛的统计资料。秘书处设在伦敦。另见*国际天然橡胶协定(International Natural Rubber Agreement)*、*国际三国橡胶联盟(International Tripartite Rubber Organization)*。

International Standard Classification of Occupations

国际标准职业分类

ISCO。国际劳工组织(ILO)制定的四级分类作为：(a)关于职业统计和管理数据的国际报告、比较和交换的基础；(b)制定国家和区域分类和职业的模式；以及(c)可在尚未制定本国分类的国家直接使用的系统。目前的版本 ISCO-8 于 2007 年 12 月采用。

International Standard Industrial Classification of All Economic Activities

全部经济活动国际标准行业分类

ISIC。对整个经济活动范围的分类而不考虑所有权。允许根据实体所从事的活动对其进行分类。ISIC 由联合国统计司制定。

International Standards for Phytosanitary Measures

国际植物卫生措施标准

ISPM。根据《国际植物保护公约》制定的植物检疫标准，已获得粮农组织(FAO)、植物卫生措施临时委员会或植物卫生措施委员会的认可。这些标准是 WTO《实施卫生与植物卫生措施协定》所认可的国际标准、准则和建议的一部分。

International standards for sanitary and phytosanitary measures

卫生与植物卫生措施国际标准

《实施卫生与植物卫生措施协定》要求 WTO 成员根据现有国际标准、准则或建议制定卫生与植物卫生措施。其中包括：(a)食品法典委员会制定的与食品添加剂、兽药和除虫剂残留物、污染物、分析和抽样方法相关的标准、指南和建议，以及卫生惯例的守则和指南；(b)国际兽疫局主持下制定的标准；(c)根据《国际植物保护公约》制定的植物卫生标准；以及(d)成员资格向所有国家开放的国际组织制定的任何其他国际标准。

International steel cartel

国际钢铁卡特尔

曾经据称将世界钢铁市场划分为两个半球的卡特尔，分界线穿过缅甸。据那

Burma. According to those claiming knowledge of the existence of this cartel, steel mills on either side of the line did or do not export to markets on the other side. *See also* ***Multilateral Steel Agreement***.

International Sugar Agreement: the first sugar agreements were negotiated in the 1860s. A new agreement was concluded in 1931 between producer associations whose governments then had to give effect to its provisions. At the same time, a permanent secretariat was established at The Hague. The agreement aimed to liquidate surplus stocks through ***export quotas***, but it failed in this because non-members raised their production. A second agreement was negotiated in 1937. It provided for representation of consumers and producers. The first post-war sugar agreement was concluded in 1954 and renegotiated several times. The agreement ran a ***buffer stock*** until 1977. The 1984 agreement did not contain economic provisions, but set itself the task of negotiating a new agreement of this type. A successor administrative agreement entered into force in 1993 for five years, with no limit on the number of possible extensions. Its objectives are (a) to ensure enhanced international cooperation in connection with world sugar matters and related issues, (b) to provide a forum for intergovernmental consultations on sugar and on ways to improve the world sugar economy, (c) to facilitate trade by collecting and providing information on the world sugar market and other sweeteners, and (d) to encourage increased demand for sugar, particularly for non-traditional uses. The administering body, the International Sugar Organization, is located in London.

International Tea Agreement: first entered into force in 1933 as a producer-only arrangement and expired long ago. Tea is one of the commodities included in the ***Integrated Programme for Commodities***, but efforts to negotiate a new tea agreement have not been successful.

International Telecommunication Union: ITU. Established in 1865 and restructured in 1947 as one of the ***United Nations specialized agencies***. Its responsibilities are (a) to maintain and extend international cooperation for the improvement and rational use of telecommunications of all kinds, (b) to promote the development of technical facilities and their most efficient operation with a view to improving the efficiency of telecommunications services, increasing their usefulness and making them, so far as possible, generally available to the public, and (c) to harmonize the actions of members in the attainment of those ends. The ITU secretariat is in Geneva. *See also* ***Agreement on Basic Telecommunications Services***.

International Textiles and Clothing Bureau: a body established in 1985 and located in Geneva whose objectives were (a) to achieve the elimination of discrimination and protectionism directed against members' exports of textiles and clothing and (b) to promote the full application of GATT principles to trade in these products. Members were Argentina, Bangladesh, Brazil, China, Colombia, Costa Rica, Democratic People's Republic of Korea, Egypt, El Salvador, Guatemala, Honduras, Hong Kong (China), India, Indonesia, Macau-China, Maldives, Pakistan, Paraguay, Peru, Republic of Korea,

些声称了解这一卡特尔存在的人称，分界线两侧的钢铁厂未曾或不会出口至另一侧的市场。另见*多边钢铁协定(Multilateral Steel Agreement)*。

International Sugar Agreement
国际糖协定

早期的糖协定于19世纪60年代进行谈判。1931年，生产者协会之间达成了一项新的协定，这些生产者协会的政府随即需要执行协定条款。同期在海牙设立了常设秘书处。协定旨在通过出口配额清理剩余库存，但由于非成员国提高了产量，此点未能实现。第二个协定于1937年进行谈判。规定要有消费者和生产者代表参加。战后第一个糖协定于1954年缔结，并多次重新谈判。在1977年之前，该协定一直管理缓冲储存。1984年协定未包含经济条款，但是规定了谈判此种类型新协定的任务。后继管理协定于1993年生效，为期5年，对可能的展期次数没有作出限制。协定目标为：(a)保证在世界糖事务和有关问题方面加强国际合作；(b)提供就糖及改善世界糖经济的途径进行政府间协商的场所；(c)通过收集和提供关于世界糖市场和其他甜味剂的信息以便利贸易；以及(d)鼓励增加对糖的需求，特别是用于非传统用途的需求。协定管理机构国际糖组织设在伦敦。

International Tea Agreement
国际茶叶协定

最初于1933年仅作为生产者安排生效，现早已失效。茶叶是商品综合方案中所含商品之一，但谈判新的茶叶协定的努力并未获得成功。

International Telecommunication Union
国际电信联盟

ITU。于1865年建立，1947年重组为联合国专门机构。责任为：(a)维持和扩大国际合作，以改善和合理使用各种类型的电信；(b)促进技术设施的发展及其最有效运作，以期提高电信服务的效率，增加其实用性，并尽可能使公众可普遍获得这些服务；以及(c)协调成员为实现这些目标而采取的行动。ITU秘书处设在日内瓦。另见*基础电信协定(Agreement on Basic Telecommunications Services)*。

International Textiles and Clothing Bureau
国际纺织服装局

1985年设立的机构，设在日内瓦，目标为：(a)实现针对成员纺织品和服装出口的歧视和保护主义的取消；及(b)促进GATT原则完成适用于这些产品的贸易。成员包括阿根廷、孟加拉国、巴西、中国、哥伦比亚、哥斯达黎加、朝鲜、埃及、萨尔瓦多、危地马拉、洪都拉斯、中国香港、印度、印度尼西亚、中国澳门、马尔代夫、巴基斯坦、巴拉圭、秘鲁、韩国、斯里兰卡、泰国、乌拉圭

Sri Lanka, Thailand, Uruguay and Viet Nam. Cuba, Mauritius and Singapore were observers.

International Tin Agreement: first concluded in 1931 and renewed in 1934. These early agreements did not allow for consumer representation. The third Agreement, concluded in 1937, invited the two largest consumer countries to attend its meetings. The Agreement was renegotiated to include producers and consumers in 1954, then 1961, 1966, 1971, 1975 and in 1980 for a duration of five years. All versions of the Agreement established a ***buffer stock*** and ran a system of ***export quotas***. This, in the end, became one of the reasons for the undoing of the Agreement in 1985. It appears that the buffer stock manager's forward dealings on the London Metals Exchange resulted in a funds shortage. Another reason was that some major producers and consumers were not members, and they therefore were not bound by the Agreement's provisions. Views differ on the causes of the Agreement's demise. *See also* ***International Tin Study Group***.

International Tin Study Group: established in 1989 as a result of the United Nations Tin Conference, but not yet operational because too few participants have notified their acceptance. The aims of the group are to ensure enhanced international cooperation on tin, improve statistical information and exchange information on production and trade. *See also* ***International Tin Agreement***.

International Trade Centre: ITC. Established in 1964 as the focal point in the United Nations system for technical cooperation with developing countries in ***trade promotion***. The ITC is a joint agency of the WTO and the United Nations. Its work programme now covers product and market development, development of trade support services, trade information, human resource development, international purchasing and supply management and trade promotion needs. The centre is located in Geneva. *See also* ***trade facilitation***.

International Trade Commission: ITC. A United States governmental agency charged with reporting on the effects of ***tariffs*** and ***non-tariff measures*** maintained by other countries on United States exports. Originally established in 1916 as the United States Tariff Commission. Its mandate also covers the determination of ***dumping***, action concerning the effects of ***export subsidies*** by other countries and ***safeguard*** action. It also advises the President whether agricultural imports interfere with agricultural price support programmes. The ITC does not make ***trade policy***, but its findings are among the basic determinants of United States trade policy.

International trade law: the body of multilateral, regional and bilateral trade agreements and other international agreements having a bearing on the way international trade is conducted. For many countries, the WTO agreements are the most important of these instruments for trade relations with countries that are also WTO members. In the remaining cases, bilateral agreements and other instruments form the body of applicable international trade law. Another stream of international trade law is concerned with the activities of private firms. *See also* ***private international law***, ***public international law*** and ***UNCITRAL***.

和越南。古巴、毛里求斯和新加坡为观察员。

International Tin Agreement

国际锡协定

最初于 1931 年缔结，1934 年展期。这些早期协定不允许消费者代表参加。1937 年缔结的第 3 个协定邀请两个最大消费国参加会议。协定在 1954 年重新谈判，将生产者和消费者包括在内，并于 1961 年、1966 年、1971 年、1975 年和 1980 年重新谈判，有效期均为 5 年。协定的所有版本均建立缓冲储存，并实行出口配额制度。此点最终成为 1985 年协定失效的原因之一。似乎是缓冲储存经理在伦敦金属交易所的远期交易导致了资金短缺。另一个原因是一些主要生产商和消费者不是会员，他们因此不受协定条款约束。对于协定失败的原因观点各有不同。*另见国际锡研究小组(International Tin Study Group)*。

International Tin Study Group

国际锡研究小组

作为联合国锡会议成果于 1989 年设立，但尚未投入运营，原因是通报接受的缔约方过少。该小组的目标是保证加强关于锡的国际合作，改善统计信息，交换生产和贸易信息。*另见国际锡协定(International Tin Agreement)*。

International Trade Centre

国际贸易中心

ITC。1964 年设立，作为联合国系统内与发展中国家在贸易促进方面技术合作的协调中心。ITC 是 WTO 和联合国的联合机构。工作计划目前包括产品和市场开发、贸易支持服务的开发、贸易信息、人力资源开发、国际采购和供应管理以及贸易促进需要。中心设在日内瓦。*另见贸易便利化(trade facilitation)*。

International Trade Commission

国际贸易委员会

ITC。美国政府机构，负责报告其他国家维持的关税和非关税措施对美国出口的影响。最初作为美国关税委员会于 1916 年设立。授权还涵盖倾销的确定、就其他国家出口补贴的影响采取行动以及保障措施。委员会还就农产品进口是否会干扰农产品价格支持计划而向总统提出建议。ITC 不制定贸易政策，但其调查结果是美国贸易政策的基本决定因素之一。

International trade law

国际贸易法

多边、区域和双边贸易协定以及影响国际贸易开展方式的其他国际协定的汇编。对于许多国家，《WTO 协定》是与同属 WTO 成员的国家之间贸易关系的最重要文件。在其他情况下，双边协定和其他文件构成适用国际贸易法的主体。国际贸易法的另一分支涉及私营企业的活动。*另见国际私法(private international law)、国际公法(public international law)、联合国国际贸易法委员会(UNCITRAL)*。

International Trade Organization: *see **ITO***.

International trade writ large: a term used by Ernest Preeg to describe the international exchange of goods, services and the factors of production. Many now see this overall approach as more relevant than simply looking at import and export trade. *See also **four freedoms***. [Preeg 1970]

International Treaty on Plant Genetic Resources for Food and Agriculture: adopted by the ***Food and Agriculture Organization*** on 3 November 2001. Entered into force on 29 June 2004. The objectives of the Treaty are the conservation and sustainable use of plant genetic resources for food and agriculture and the fair and equitable sharing of the benefits arising out of their use, in harmony with the ***Convention on Biological Diversity***, for sustainable agriculture and ***food security***. The Treaty recognizes ***farmers' rights***, establishes a multilateral system of access and benefit-sharing for plant genetic resources listed in Annex I to the Treaty, and it enjoins the parties to implement the rolling ***Global Plan of Action for the Conservation and Sustainable Utilization of Plant Genetic Resources for Food and Agriculture***. *See also **International Undertaking on Plant Genetic Resources***.

International Tripartite Rubber Council: ITRC. Formed in 2014 by the countries that made up the ***International Tripartite Rubber Organization*** (Indonesia, Malaysia and Thailand). In September 2017 Viet Nam agreed to join as strategic partner.

International Tripartite Rubber Organization: established in 2001 after the collapse of the International Natural Rubber Organization. It consisted of Indonesia, Malaysia and Thailand. Now defunct.

International Tropical Timber Agreement: ITTA. Concluded in 1983 under the auspices of the ***Integrated Programme for Commodities*** and succeeded in 1994 by a new agreement lasting for four years with the option of two three-year extensions. A successor agreement was concluded on 27 January 2006. It entered into force on 7 December 2011 and is valid for ten years from that date. The ITTA does not contain economic provisions. Its main objective is to provide an effective framework for consultation, international cooperation and policy development among all members with regard to all relevant aspects of the world timber economy. Other trade-related aims include (a) to provide a forum for consultation to promote non-discriminatory timber trade practices, (b) to enhance the capacity of members to form sustainable export strategies, (c) to promote the expansion and diversification of international trade in tropical timber from sustainable sources, (d) to improve market intelligence, (e) to promote increased and further processing in producer member countries, (f) to improve marketing and distribution, and (g) to encourage information-sharing on the international timber market. The administering body, the International Tropical Timber Organization, is in Yokohama. *See also **trade and environment***.

International Undertaking on Plant Genetic Resources: resolution 8/83 adopted by the ***Food and Agriculture Organization*** (FAO) in 1983. The

International Trade Organization
国际贸易组织

见*国际贸易组织(ITO)*。

International trade writ large
大国际贸易

欧内斯特·普里格用于描述货物、服务和生产要素的国际交换的词语。许多人现在认为这种整体方式要比简单看待进出口贸易更具相关性。另见*四大自由(four freedoms)*。

International Treaty on Plant Genetic Resources for Food and Agriculture
粮食与农业植物遗传资源国际条约

粮农组织(FAO)于2001年11月3日通过，2004年6月29日生效。条约的目标是保存和可持续利用粮食和农业植物遗传资源，并按照《生物多样性公约》，公平合理分享利用这些资源所产生的利益，以促进可持续农业和粮食安全。条约承认农民权利，建立了条约附件1所列植物遗传资源的获取和利益分享的多边系统，并责成缔约方执行滚动式《全球粮食和农业植物遗传资源保存及可持续利用行动计划》。另见*植物遗传资源国际承诺(International Undertaking on Plant Genetic Resources)*。

International Tripartite Rubber Council
国际三国橡胶联盟理事会

ITRC。2014年由组成国际三国橡胶联盟的国家(印度尼西亚、马来西亚和泰国)设立。2017年9月，越南同意作为战略伙伴加入。

International Tripartite Rubber Organization
国际三国橡胶联盟

在国际天然橡胶组织解体后于2001年成立。由印度尼西亚、马来西亚和泰国组成。现已停止运营。

International Tropical Timber Agreement
国际热带木材协定

ITTA。在商品综合方案主持下于1983年缔结，1994年由一个为期4年的新协定所取代，新协定可展期2次，每次3年。后继协定于2006年1月27日缔结，2011年12月7日生效，有效期为自该日期起的10年。ITTA不包含经济条款。主要目标是为所有成员间就世界木材经济的所有相关方面开展磋商、国际合作和制定政策提供有效框架。其他与贸易有关的目标包括：(a)提供就促进非歧视性木材贸易做法进行磋商的场所；(b)增强成员形成可持续出口战略的能力；(c)促进可持续来源的热带木材国际贸易的扩大和多样化；(d)改进市场情报；(e)促进生产成员国提高加工程度和进一步加工；(f)改进销售和分销；以及(g)鼓励分享国际木材市场信息。协定管理机构为国际热带木材组织，设在横滨。另见*贸易与环境(trade and environment)*。

International Undertaking on Plant Genetic Resources
植物遗传资源国际承诺

粮农组织(FAO)于1983年通过的第8/83号决议。承诺的目的是保证具有经济

objective of the Undertaking is to ensure that plant genetic resources of economic and/or social interest, particularly for agriculture, will be explored, preserved, evaluated and made available for plant breeding and scientific purposes. In the view of the FAO, the Undertaking is at the cross-roads where agriculture, environment and trade meet. A revised and expanded Undertaking was adopted on 3 November 2001 in the form of the ***International Treaty on Plant Genetic Resources for Food and Agriculture***. *See also* ***farmers' rights***.

International Union for the Conservation of Nature and Natural Resources: *see* ***CITES***.

International Union for the Protection of New Varieties of Plants: UPOV. *See* ***International Convention for the Protection of New Varieties of Plants***.

International Vine and Wine Office: *see* ***International Organisation of Vine and Wine***.

International Wheat Agreement: in its final version this consisted of two instruments: (a) the *Wheat Trade Convention* of 1986 which was a consultative forum with a programme for the collection and dissemination of statistics and (b) the *Food Aid Convention* concluded at the same time. On 1 July 1995 the Agreement was succeeded by the *Grains Trade Convention* under the ***International Grains Agreement***. All parties to the Agreement were members of the International Wheat Council, now the International Grains Council, located in London.

Internet of Things: IoT. The concept of being able to connect anything that can be switched on or off to the Internet or to each other. This includes mobile phones, coffee machines, washing machines, lamps, heaters and lots of other objects and devices. All of this is meant to result in greater efficiency and economic benefits.

Internet Treaties: *see* ***WIPO Copyright Treaty*** and ***WIPO Performances and Phonograms Treaty***.

Interoperability: the ability of two or more electronic communications systems or parts of them to exchange information and use the information that has been exchanged.

Interregional Framework Cooperation Agreement between the European Union and Mercosur: entered into force in 1999. This is the framework for trade relations between the ***European Union*** and ***Mercosur*** (Brazil, Paraguay, Uruguay and Argentina). It specifies the following as main areas of cooperation: (a) market access liberalization of trade and trade disciplines, (b) trade relations with non-member countries, (c) compatibility of trade with WTO rules, (d) identification of sensitive and priority products, and (e) cooperation and exchanges of information on services. Other areas of cooperation include agricultural and industrial products, customs administration, transport and economic integration. *See also* ***European Union–Mercosur Association Agreement***.

Intervention: in the context of international trade any action by a government to stop, slow down, interrupt, promote or otherwise influence a trade flow.

及/或社会利益的植物遗传资源，特别是用于农业的植物遗传资源，得到研究、保存、评估并可用于培育和科学目的。在 FAO 看来，承诺处于农业、环境和贸易交汇的十字路口。2001 年 11 月 3 日，经修订和扩大的承诺以《粮食与农业植物遗传资源国际条约》的形式获得通过。另见*农民权利(farmers' rights)*。

International Union for the Conservation of Nature and Natural Resources
保护自然和自然资源国际联盟

见*濒危野生动植物种国际贸易公约(CITES)*。

International Union for the Protection of New Varieties of Plants
国际植物新品种保护联盟

UPOV。见*国际植物新品种保护公约(International Convention for the Protection of New Varieties of Plants)*。

International Vine and Wine Office
国际葡萄与葡萄酒局

见*国际葡萄与葡萄酒组织(International Organisation of Vine and Wine)*。

International Wheat Agreement
国际小麦协定

协定最终文本包括两个文件：(a)《1986 年小麦贸易公约》，属磋商场所，有一项收集和传播统计数据的方案；及(b)同时缔结的《食品援助公约》。1995 年 7 月 1 日，该协定被《国际谷物协定》项下的《谷物贸易公约》所取代。该协定的所有缔约方均为设在伦敦的国际小麦理事会的成员，即现在的国际谷物理事会。

Internet of Things
物联网

IoT。能够将可以打开或关闭的任何物品与互联网连接或相互连接的概念。包括移动电话、咖啡机、洗衣机、灯、加热器和其他许多物品和设备。所有这些均意味着更高效率和经济利益。

Internet Treaties
互联网条约

见 *WIPO 版权条约(WIPO Copyright Treaty)*、*WIPO 表演和录音制品条约(WIPO Performances and Phonograms Treaty)*。

Interoperability
互操作性

两个或多个电子通信系统或其部分系统交换信息和使用已交换信息的能力。

Interregional Framework Cooperation Agreement between the European Union and Mercosur
欧盟与南方共同市场区域间合作框架协定

1999 年生效。欧盟与南方共同市场(Mercosur)(巴西、巴拉圭、乌拉圭和阿根廷)之间的贸易关系框架。规定了下列主要合作领域：(a)贸易市场准入自由化和贸易纪律；(b)与非成员国的贸易关系；(c)贸易与 WTO 规则的兼容性；(d)确定敏感和优先产品；以及(e)关于服务的合作和信息交流。其他合作领域包括农产品和工业品、海关管理、运输和经济一体化。另见*欧盟与南方共同市场联系协定(European Union–Mercosur Association Agreement)*。

Intervention
干预

在国际贸易背景下，政府为阻止、减缓、中断、促进或在其他方面影响贸易流动而采取的任何行动。

Intervention price: a mechanism whereby a government buys an agricultural commodity at a certain price. The intervention price expresses the intention to support the current income levels of farmers even when output is above requirements. *See also* ***floor price***.

Intra-firm trade: international trade conducted between units of the same company. The bulk of this type of trade is conducted between units of multinational enterprises. Estimates of the size of intra-firm trade differ, but studies suggest that it may account for about one-third of total trade. Some commentators see intra-firm trade as a form of ***managed trade*** on the assumption that a multinational enterprise would rather purchase from its own units, even if a cost difference is involved, than using the open market. Opinion on this proposition remains divided. *See also* ***globalization***.

Intra-industry trade: the concurrent export and import by an industry of essentially the same product. For example, an automotive industry in one economy may both import and export automotive parts. Intra-industry trade has been debated intensively by economists since the 1970s, with some holding that it is a special case of international trade. There is no disagreement, however, on the importance of intra-industry trade in terms of international trade flows. *See also* ***globalization***.

Invention: the creation of something new which may turn into ***industrial property***. To benefit from ***intellectual property protection*** in the form of a ***patent***, an invention has to be new (i.e. not already described or used somewhere), it must be non-obvious (in ***WIPO*** terms, it would not have occurred to a specialist asked to provide a solution to the particular problem) and it must be capable of industrial use.

Inventive step: one of the criteria for the granting of a ***patent***. The European Patent Office, for example, says that an "invention is an inventive step if, having regard to the state of the art, it is not obvious to a person skilled in the Art". *See also* ***intellectual property rights***. [epo.org]

Investigation: an examination to ascertain whether, for example, a case has been made for the imposition of ***anti-dumping measures***, ***countervailing measures*** or ***safeguards***. If a petition has been received for the imposition of any of these ***trade remedies***, the authority making the investigation must follow the rules set out in the ***Anti-Dumping Agreement***, the ***Agreement on Safeguards*** or the ***Agreement on Subsidies and Countervailing Measures***, as the case may be.

Investigation effect: refers to the possibility that an investigation into alleged ***dumping*** or an examination of the desirability of ***safeguards*** may itself have the effect of lowering imports of the products being examined. *See also* ***trade harassment***.

Investment: a stake in a business, a company or an enterprise. Many definitions exist. The *World Investment Report 2003* divides the definitions used in ***international investment agreements*** into asset-based, transaction-based and enterprise-based. An example of an asset-based definition is that used in the ***Energy Charter Treaty***, concluded in December 1994, which defines

Intervention price
干预价格

政府以特定价格购买农产品的机制。干预价格表达了支持农民当前收入水平的意图，即使产出高于需求。另见*最低价格(floor price)*。

Intra-firm trade
公司内部贸易

同一公司的各部门之间进行的国际贸易。此类贸易的大部分是在跨国企业的各部门之间进行的。对企业内部贸易规模的估计各有不同，但研究表明，可能占全部贸易的约三分之一。一些评论人士将公司内部贸易视为受管制的贸易的一种形式，他们的假设是，即使涉及成本差异，跨国企业宁愿从自己的部门购买，也不愿使用公开市场。对于这一命题意见不一。另见*全球化(globalization)*。

Intra-industry trade
产业内部贸易

一产业同时进口和出口基本相同的产品。例如，一经济体中的汽车产业可能同时进口和出口汽车零部件。自 20 世纪 70 年代以来，经济学家对产业内部贸易进行了激烈辩论，一些人认为这是国际贸易的一个特例。但是，关于产业内部贸易对国际贸易流动的重要性并无分歧。另见*全球化(globalization)*。

Invention
发明

创造可以转变为工业产权的新东西。如想以专利形式获得知识产权保护，一项发明必须是新的(即尚未在某处描述或使用)，必须是非显而易见的(对于WIPO 而言，被要求对特定问题提供解决方案的专家所未曾想到的)，且必须具有工业用途。

Inventive step
创造性

授予专利的标准之一。例如，欧洲专利局表示，“如果考虑到现有技术，一项发明对于本领域技术人员而言不属显而易见，那么它即具有创造性”。另见*知识产权(intellectual property rights)*。

Investigation
调查

为确定实施反倾销措施、反补贴措施或保障措施的理由而进行的审查。如收到实施任何此类贸易救济措施的申请，进行调查的主管部门必须遵守《反倾销协定》、《保障措施协定》或《补贴与反补贴措施协定》(视情况而定)中规定的规则。

Investigation effect
调查影响

指一项针对所谓倾销的或针对是否需要保障措施的审查本身可能产生减少被审查产品的进口的影响。另见*贸易干扰(trade harassment)*。

Investment
投资

一商业、一公司或一企业的投机股本。有多种定义。《2003 年世界投资报告》将国际投资协定中使用的定义分为基于资产、基于交易和基于企业三类。基

investment as every kind of asset, owned or controlled directly or indirectly by an investor. It includes: (a) tangible and intangible, and movable and immovable, property, and any property rights such as leases, mortgages, liens and pledges, (b) a company or business enterprise, or shares, stock, or other forms of equity participation in a company or business enterprise, (c) claims to money and claims to performance pursuant to contract having an economic value and associated with an investment, (d) intellectual property, (e) returns, and (f) any right conferred by law or contract or by virtue of any licences and permits granted pursuant to law to undertake an economic activity in the energy sector. The working definition used by the participants in the negotiations for the ***Multilateral Agreement on Investment***, which were abandoned in early 1999, was also asset-based. It states that investment means every kind of asset owned or controlled directly by an investor, including: (a) an enterprise (a legal person, whether or not for profit, private or government-owned or -controlled, including a corporation, trust, partnership, sole proprietorship, branch, joint venture, association or organization), (b) shares, stocks or other forms of equity participation in an enterprise, and rights reserved therefrom, (c) bonds, debentures, loans and other forms of debt, and rights derived therefrom, (d) rights under contracts, including turnkey, construction, management, production or revenue-sharing contracts, (e) claims to money and claims to performance, (f) intellectual property rights, (g) rights conferred pursuant to law or contract or concessions, licences, authorizations and permits, and (h) any other tangible and intangible, movable and immovable property, and any related property rights, such as leases, mortgages, liens and pledges. The transaction-based method is used in the 1961 *OECD Code of Liberalisation of Capital Movements*. It defines direct investment as "investment for the purpose of establishing lasting economic relations with an undertaking such as, in particular, investments which give the possibility of exercising an effective influence on the management thereof by means of (1) creation or extension of a wholly owned enterprise, subsidiary or branch, acquisition of full ownership of an existing enterprise, (2) participation in a new or existing enterprise, and (3) a loan of five years or longer". ***NAFTA***, which entered into force on 1 January 1994, uses the enterprise-based approach. It defines investment as (a) an enterprise, (b) an equity security of an enterprise, (c) a debt security of an enterprise where the enterprise is an affiliate of the investor and the original maturity of the debt security is at least three years, (d) a loan to an enterprise which is an affiliate of the investor and where the original maturity of the loan is at least three years, (e) an interest in an enterprise that entitles the owner to share in income or profits, (f) an interest in an enterprise that entitles the owner to share in the assets of that enterprise on dissolution, (g) real estate or other property, tangible or intangible, acquired in the expectation or used for the purpose of economic benefit or other business purposes, and (h) interests arising from the commitment of capital or other resources in the territory of a party to NAFTA. *See also* ***APEC Non-Binding Investment Principles***, ***Facility***

于资产的定义的例子如 1994 年 12 月缔结的《能源宪章条约》，其中将投资定义为一投资者直接或间接拥有或控制的各种资产。包括：(a)有形和无形的动产和不动产，以及任何产权，例如租赁、抵押、留置和质押；(b)一公司或商业企业，或对一公司或商业企业中的股份、股票及其他形式的参股；(c)根据具有经济价值且与投资相关的合同提出的资金要求和履约要求；(d)知识产权；(e)收益；以及(f)法律或合同所授予的任何权利或凭借依法授予的在能源部门开展经济活动的执照或许可所拥有的任何权利。1999 年初放弃的《多边投资协定》的谈判参加方所使用的工作定义也是基于资产的定义。协定指出，投资指一投资者直接拥有或控制的各种资产，包括：(a)一企业(一法人，无论是否营利，私人或政府所有或控制，包括公司、信托公司、合伙企业、独资企业、分支机构、合资企业、协会或组织)；(b)一企业的股份、股票或其他形式的股权参与，及由此保留的权利；(c)债券、公司债券、贷款及其他形式的债务，及由此产生的权利；(d)合同项下的权利，包括统包合同、施工合同、管理合同、生产合同或收入分配合同；(e)对货币报酬的主张和对业绩的主张；(f)知识产权；(g)根据法律或合同或特许权、执照、授权和许可所赋予的权利；以及(h)任何其他有形和无形的动产和不动产，以及任何相关财产权，如租赁、抵押、留置和质押。以交易为基础的定义用于 1961 年经济合作与发展组织(OECD)《资本流动自由化通则》中。通则将直接投资定义为“旨在与一项事业建立长久经济关系的投资，例如特别通过下列方式对经营管理施加有效影响的投资：(1)设立或扩大全资企业、子公司或分支机构，收购现有企业的全部所有权；(2)参与新的或现有企业；以及(3)提供 5 年或 5 年以上贷款”。1994 年 1 月 1 日生效的《北美自由贸易协定》(NAFTA)使用基于企业的定义。协定将投资定义为：(a)一企业；(b)一企业的股权证券；(c)属投资者附属公司的一企业的债权证券，且债权证券原始期限至少为 3 年；(d)对属投资者附属公司的一企业的贷款，且贷款的原始期限至少为 3 年；(e)使所有者有资格分享收益或利润的一企业的权益；(f)使所有者在企业解散时有资格分享资产的一企业的权益；(g)预期为获得或用于经济利益或其他商业目的而购置或使用房地产或其他有形或无形财产；以及(h)在 NAFTA 一缔约方领土内投入资本或其他资源所产生的权益。另见 *APEC 投资非约束性原则(APEC Non-Binding Investment Prin-*

for Investment Climate Advisory Services, ***foreign direct investment***, ***International Chamber of Commerce (ICC) Guidelines for International Investment*** and ***World Association of Investment Promotion Agencies***.

Investment facilitation: an emerging subject for multilateral consideration, such as at the ***WTO***, but it has been part of the work programme of ***UNCTAD***, the ***World Bank***, ***OECD*** and other international organizations for a long time. UNCTAD defines investment facilitation as "the set of policies and actions aimed at making it easier for investors to establish and expand their investments, as well as to conduct their day-to-day business in host countries". In the OECD it briefly means to "provide investors with a transparent, predictable and efficient regulatory and administrative framework" and to "reduce or eliminate obstacles faced by investors in the host economy when investing or reinvesting". The ***APEC Investment Facilitation Action Plan*** (IFAP) lists a large number of actions governments could take to be more welcoming of investment. In all of these approaches it becomes clear that investment facilitation may occur at any of the stages of investment from pre-establishment to final disposal, and that its form largely depends on the regulatory and administrative conditions in the host country. The OECD offers some principles to inform investment facilitation, such as (a) provide investors with a transparent, predictable and easily accessible regulatory and administrative framework for investment, (b) provide investors with efficient and streamlined rules and procedures to minimize potential obstacles when investing or expanding, and (c) maximize the benefits of investment to society through a sound policy framework that promotes and enables sustainable development and responsible business conduct. Much thought is now being given to the options for strengthening investment facilitation in a multilateral context, possibly through the development of an investment facilitation framework. It is clear from the practical and analytical work of the World Bank, UNCTAD and OECD that many developing countries in particular are not attracting the level of investment they could absorb. The reasons are varied. Among them are inadequate regulatory frameworks, non-transparent administration, inappropriate taxation regimes, less than optimal infrastructure, and so on. The ***World Bank Doing Business Report*** offers many examples of such obstacles and how they can be reduced or eliminated. Problems of this kind are perhaps best addressed through mechanisms such as the World Bank's investment facilitation work, the ***UNCTAD Global Action Menu for Investment Facilitation*** or the OECD's ***Policy Framework for Investment***. In any case, the experience with the ***Multilateral Agreement on Investment*** shows how difficult it can be to negotiate on ***behind-the-border issues*** in a multilateral setting. The Joint Ministerial Statement on Investment Facilitation for Development issued at the WTO's 11th Ministerial Conference in Buenos Aires in December 2017 stresses that the signatories to the document see market access, investment promotion and investor-state dispute settlement as excluded from any multilateral action. On the other hand, they would include issues such as transparency, streamlining of

ciples)、*外国投资咨询服务中心(Facility for Investment Climate Advisory Services)*、*外国直接投资(foreign direct investment)*、*国际商会国际投资指南(International Chamber of Commerce (ICC) Guidelines for International Investment)*、*世界投资促进机构协会(World Association of Investment Promotion Agencies)*。

Investment facilitation

投资便利化

新出现的多边审议议题，例如在 WTO 中所讨论的议题，但长期以来是联合国贸易与发展会议(UNCTAD)、世界银行、经济合作与发展组织(OECD)和其他国际组织工作计划的一部分。UNCTAD 将投资便利化定义为“旨在使投资者更容易建立和扩大投资以及在东道国开展日常业务的一套政策和行动”。在 OECD 中，简单的意思为“向投资者提供透明、可预测和有效的监管和行政框架”及“减少或消除投资者在投资或再投资时在东道国经济中面临的障碍”。APEC 投资便利化行动计划(IFAP)列出了政府可采取的使投资更受欢迎的行动。在所有这些方式中，显而易见的是，投资便利化可以在从设立前到最后处置的任何投资阶段出现，其形式在很大程度上取决于东道国中的监管和管理条件。OECD 提出了可以体现投资便利化的几项原则，例如：(a)为投资者提供一个透明、可预测和容易获得的投资监管和行政框架；(b)为投资者提供有效和简化的规则和程序，以尽量减少投资或扩大投资时的潜在障碍；以及(c)通过促进和实现可持续发展和负责任商业行为的健全政策框架，最大限度地扩大投资对社会的利益。目前人们正在考虑在多边领域加强投资便利化的选项，可能通过发展投资便利化框架。世界银行、UNCTAD 和 OECD 的实践和分析工作中清楚地表明，特别是许多发展中国家没有吸收它们可以吸收的投资水平，原因各有不同，其中包括不充分的监管框架、不透明的管理、不适当的税收制度、不完善的基础设施等等。世界银行《营商环境报告》提供了此类障碍的许多例子及如何减少或消除这些障碍的建议。这一类型的问题可能最好通过世界银行的投资便利化工作、UNCTAD 全球投资便利化行动清单或 OECD 投资政策框架等机制加以解决。无论如何，《多边投资协定》的经验表明，在多边环境下就边境后问题进行谈判有多么困难。2017 年 12 月在布宜诺斯艾利斯举行的第 11 届 WTO 部长级会议发表的《关于投资便利化的部长联合声明》强调，该文件的签署方认为，市场准入、投资促进和投资者—国家间争端解决排除在任何多边行动之外。另一方面，包括诸如透明度、简化程序、

procedures, exchange of information on best practices and relations with stakeholders on a range of issues, including dispute prevention, as feasible. *See also* ***Friends of Investment Facilitation for Development*** and ***G20 Investment Facilitation Package***.

Investment Policy Framework for Sustainable Development: launched by ***UNCTAD*** in 2015. It consists of an overarching objective and ten principles. The overarching objective is to promote investment for inclusive growth and sustainable development. The ten principles are: (1) policy coherence: investment policies to be promoted within a country's overall development strategy, (2) public governance and institutions: involve all stakeholders, institutional framework based on rule of law, high standards of public governance and transparency, (3) dynamic policymaking: regular reviews, (4) balanced rights and obligations, (5) right to regulate, (6) openness to investment, (7) investment protection and treatment: adequate protection of established investors and non-discriminatory treatment, (8) investment promotion and facilitation: align with sustainable development goals and minimize risk of harmful competition for investment, (9) corporate governance and responsibility: adopt best international practices of corporate social responsibility, and (10) international cooperation. *See also* ***Sustainable Development Goals***. [investmentpolicy.unctad.org]

Investment Policy Review: IPR. In ***UNCTAD*** an objective evaluation of a country's legal, regulatory and institutional framework for ***foreign direct investment*** (FDI) aimed at allowing it to attract increased foreign and direct investment and to maximize the benefits from it. Topics reviewed include FDI entry and establishment, treatment and protection of investment, taxation, the business environment and sectoral regulation. A large number of developed and developing countries have been reviewed. In the ***OECD*** reviews are done under the ***Policy Framework for Investment***. Topics include investment policy, investment promotion and facilitation, competition, trade, taxation, corporate governance, finance, infrastructure, developing human resources, policy to promote responsible business conduct and investment in support of ***green growth***. *See also* ***investment facilitation***.

Investment Promotion Action Plan: IPAP. An ***ASEM*** mechanism established in 1997 to generate greater two-way investment flows between Asia and Europe through enhancing the investment climate between and within Asia and Europe. *See also* ***investment promotion and protection agreements*** and ***World Association of Investment Promotion Agencies***.

Investment promotion and protection agreements: IPPAs. Agreements concluded bilaterally by many countries aimed at promoting the flow of capital for economic activity and development. Such agreements typically contain provisions entailing the application of ***most-favoured-nation treatment***, and setting out conditions concerning entry of personnel, ***expropriation*** and nationalization, transfers of funds, ***dispute settlement*** between the parties, etc. *See also* ***bilateral investment treaties***, ***international investment agreement*** and ***World Association of Investment Promotion Agencies***.

就最佳实践交换信息以及在一系列问题上与利益攸关方建立关系，在可行的情况包括争端预防。另见*投资便利化之友(Friends of Investment Facilitation for Development)*、*20 国集团投资便利化一揽子计划(G20 Investment Facilitation Package)*。

Investment Policy Framework for Sustainable Development
可持续发展投资政策框架

联合国贸易与发展会议(UNCTAD)2015 年启动。包括一个总体目标和 10 项原则。总体目标是促进包容性增长和可持续发展的投资。10 项原则为：(1)政策一致性：在国家总体发展战略内促进投资政策；(2)公共治理和体制：所有利益攸关方参与、基于法治的体制框架、高标准的公共治理和透明度；(3)动态决策：定期审议；(4)权利和义务的平衡；(5)监管权；(6)投资开放；(7)投资保护和待遇：对既有投资者的充分保护和非歧视待遇；(8)投资促进和便利：符合可持续发展目标和尽量减少有害的投资竞争风险；(9)公司治理和责任：采用公司社会责任方面的最佳国际实践；以及(10)国际合作。另见*可持续发展目标(Sustainable Development Goals)*。

Investment Policy Review
投资政策审议

IPR。在联合国贸易与发展会议(UNCTAD)中对一国外国直接投资的法律、监管和体制框架进行的客观评价，旨在使其能够吸引更多外国投资和直接投资，并最大程度地从中获益。审议的主题包括外国直接投资的进入和建立、投资待遇和保护、税收、商业环境和部门监管。许多发达国家和发展中国家已经审议。在经济合作与发展组织(OECD)中，审议在投资政策框架下进行。主题包括投资政策、投资促进和便利化、竞争、贸易、税收、公司治理、金融、基础设施、人力资源开发、促进负责任商业行为的政策和支持绿色增长的投资。另见*投资便利化(investment facilitation)*。

Investment Promotion Action Plan
投资促进行动计划

IPAP。1997 年建立的亚欧会议机制，旨在通过增强亚洲和欧洲之间及其内部的投资环境，在亚欧之间创造更大的双向投资流动。另见*投资促进与保护协定(investment promotion and protection agreements)*、*世界投资促进机构协会(World Association of Investment Promotion Agencies)*。

Investment promotion and protection agreements
投资促进与保护协定

IPPAs。许多国家在双边缔结的协定，旨在为经济活动和发展目的促进资本流动。此类协定通常包含适用最惠国待遇的条款，并规定有关人员入境、征收和国有化、资金转让、当事方之间争端解决等方面的条件。另见*双边投资条约(bilateral investment treaties)*、*国际投资协定(international investment agreement)*、*世界投资促进机构协会(World Association of Investment Promotion Agencies)*。

Investment-related trade measures: governmental measures aimed at promoting investment by foreign firms in one's economy. Sometimes these measures include high tariff barriers aimed at giving these firms a captive market. *See also* ***Agreement on Trade-Related Investment Measures*** and ***tariff-jumping investment***.

Investment substitution: a term used by some to describe the replacement of GATT-restricted measures with other, sometimes more distorting practices, including domestic policy instruments. *See also* ***Agreement on Trade-Related Investment Measures***.

Investor-state disputes: treaties, whether bilateral, regional or multilateral, are between states, and they convey rights and obligations on the states (parties) to them. If a natural or judicial person residing in one of the member states wishes to have its concerns over another party's operation of the treaty addressed under the consultation or dispute settlement provisions of the treaty, it must first convince its own government to take up the case. There are exceptions. ***NAFTA***, for example, allows investors in some circumstances to submit to ***arbitration*** claims that another party has breached an obligation in relation to investment obligations in the agreement and in matters concerning monopolies and/or state enterprises. A claim may only be made if an investor has incurred loss or damage because of the alleged breach, and it must be made no more than three years after the investor first acquired, or should have first acquired, knowledge of the alleged breach and loss of damage. The ***free-trade agreement*** between Australia and Thailand also has a provision on investor-state disputes. It states that an investor cannot pursue a claim against matters concerning conditions placed on the establishment, acquisition or expansion of an investment, or the enforcement of such conditions. *See also* ***NAFTA Chapter 11***. [UNCTAD 2005]

Invisible barriers to trade: *see* ***non-tariff measures***.

Invisible earnings: income derived from the sales of services in other countries, as well as profits, dividends, royalties, etc., resulting from investments abroad.

Invisible hand: an expression used by Adam Smith in *An Inquiry into the Nature and Causes of the Wealth of Nations* when he deals with the motivation of those investing capital in industry. He rejects the view that a trader or investor intends to promote the public interest, or that he even knows how much he might be promoting it. Smith claims that the trader or investor "by directing [domestic] industry in such a manner as its produce may be of the greatest value, he intends only his own gain, and he is in this, as in many other cases, led by an invisible hand to promote an end which was not of his intention".

Invisibles Group: an informal group of capital-based senior officials from WTO member countries, both developed and developing, which met irregularly, usually in Geneva. It concerned itself with an exploration of major issues of common concern on the WTO work programme. It had no decision-making powers. *See also* ***Consultative Group of Eighteen***.

Invisibles trade: *see* ***trade in services***.

Investment-related trade measures
与投资有关的贸易措施

旨在促进外国公司在一经济体中投资的政府措施。有时这些措施包括高关税壁垒，目的在于给予这些公司一个垄断市场。另见*与贸易有关的投资措施协定(Agreement on Trade-Related Investment Measures)*、*跳越关税投资(tariff-jumping investment)*。

Investment substitution
投资替代

一些人用于描述以其他的、有时更具扭曲性的做法替代 GATT 限制措施的词语，包括国内政策工具。另见*与贸易有关的投资措施协定(Agreement on Trade-Related Investment Measures)*。

Investor-state disputes
投资者—国家间争端

无论双边、区域还是多边条约均为国家之间签订的，这些条约对条约参加国(缔约方)规定了权利与义务。如居住在一成员国的自然人或法人希望根据条约的磋商或争端解决条款处理其对另一缔约方条约运用的关注，则必须首先说服本国政府受理此案。但有例外。例如，《北美自由贸易协定》(NAFTA)允许投资者在一些情况下提出仲裁要求，声称另一方违反协定中与投资有关的义务及与垄断和/或国有企业有关的事项。只有在投资者因指称的违反行为而遭受损失或损害的情况下方可提出索赔，且索赔必须在投资者首次知晓或应当知晓关于指称的违约行为和损失或损害的 3 年内提出。澳大利亚和泰国之间的自由贸易协定也包含投资者—国家间争端的条款。规定投资者不能针对有关对设立、收购或扩大投资设置的条件或此类条件执行的事项提出索赔。另见*北美自由贸易协定第 11 章(NAFTA Chapter 11)*。

Invisible barriers to trade
无形贸易壁垒

见*非关税措施(non-tariff measures)*。

Invisible earnings
无形收入

在其他国家销售服务所产生的收入，以及在国外投资所产生的利润、股息、特许权使用费等。

Invisible hand
看不见的手

亚当·斯密在《国富论》一书中探讨那些对产业进行投资之人的动机时使用的词语。他拒绝接受这样的观点，即贸易商或投资者企图增进公共福利，或他清楚增进的公共福利有多少。斯密声称，贸易商或投资者"指导这种工业去使其产品能具有最大的价值，他这样做只是为了他自己的利益，也像在许多其他场合一样，他这样做只是被一只看不见的手引导着，去促进一个并不是出自他本心的目的"。

Invisibles Group
无形集团

由来自 WTO 成员的首都高级官员组成的非正式协调组，包括发达成员和发展中成员，不定期召开会议，通常在日内瓦。该协调组关注探讨 WTO 工作计划中共同关心的主要问题，无决策权。另见*18 国咨询小组(Consultative Group of Eighteen)*。

Invisibles trade
无形贸易

见*服务贸易(trade in services)*。

Invisible tariffs: an older expression for what is now broadly subsumed under the category of non-tariff barriers, ***non-tariff measures***, trade-restrictive use of ***customs valuation*** procedures and ***trade remedies***.

IOR-ARC: succeeded in 2014 by the ***Indian Ocean Rim Association***.

IOSCO: International Organization of Securities Commissions. Brings together the world securities regulators. Its objectives are (a) to cooperate in developing, implementing and promoting adherence to internationally recognized and consistent standards of regulation, oversight and enforcement to protect investors, maintain fair, efficient and transparent markets, and to seek to address systemic risks, (b) to enhance investor protection and promote investor confidence in the integrity of securities markets, and (c) to exchange information at both local and regional levels on their respective experiences to assist the development of markets, strengthen market infrastructure and implement appropriate regulation. IOSCO's secretariat is in Madrid. [www.iosco.org]

IPRs: *see* ***intellectual property rights***.

Iran and Libya Sanctions Act: ILSA. A United States law adopted on 5 August 1996 for five years, then extended in 2001 for another five years. On 30 September 2006 it was renamed the ***Iran Sanctions Act*** as its provisions no longer applied to Libya. The aim of ILSA was to impose sanctions on persons making certain investments directly and significantly contributing to the enhancement of the ability of Iran or Libya to develop their petroleum resources. It also imposed sanctions on persons exporting goods that enhanced Libya's weapons or aviation capabilities or its ability to develop its petroleum resources.

Iran Sanctions Act: ISA. Until 30 September 2006 the provisions of this Act were part of the ***Iran and Libya Sanctions Act*** of 1996 as amended. The ISA gives effect to "the policy of the United States to deny Iran the ability to support acts of international terrorism and to fund the development and acquisition of weapons of mass destruction and the means to deliver them by limiting the development of Iran's ability to explore for, extract, refine or transport by pipeline petroleum resources of Iran". ISA was extended by ten years on 1 December 2016.

Iron law of subsidies: the proposition that ***subsidies*** delay reforms and depress productivity by keeping inefficient producers in business, unless the granting of the subsidy is accompanied by strict and enforced rules for reform. *See also* ***law of constant protection***.

ISIC: *see* ***International Standard Industrial Classification of All Economic Activities***.

ISO 9000: a series of quality systems standards developed by the ***International Organization for Standardization*** (ISO). These are standards for evaluating the way a firm does its work. They should not be confused with product standards. Quality systems standards enable firms to identify the means of meeting consistently the requirements of its customers.

ISO 14000: a series of environmental management standards prepared by the ***International Organization for Standardization*** (ISO) covering six areas: environmental managing systems; environmental auditing; environmental labelling;

Invisible tariffs

无形关税

旧时表述，现已大部分广泛包含在非关税壁垒、非关税措施、海关估价程序的限制贸易使用和贸易救济类别中。

IOR-ARC

环印度洋地区合作联盟

2014 年被环印度洋联盟取代。

IOSCO

国际证监会组织

汇集世界范围内的证券监管机构。目标为：(a)在制定、实施和促进遵守国际公认和一致的监管、监督和执行标准方面开展合作，以保护投资者，维持公平、高效和透明的市场，并设法应对系统性风险；(b)加强投资者保护，促进投资者对证券市场完整性的信心；以及(c)在地方和区域两级交流各自经验，以协助市场发展，加强市场基础设施和执行适当监管。国际证监会组织秘书处设在马德里。

IPRs

知识产权

见*知识产权(intellectual property rights)*。

Iran and Libya Sanctions Act

伊朗与利比亚制裁法

ILSA。美国于 1996 年 8 月 5 日通过的法律，为期 5 年，随后在 2001 年延长 5 年。2006 年 9 月 30 日，该法更名为《伊朗制裁法》，因其条款不再适用于利比亚。ILSA 旨在对直接进行某些投资且明显有助于增强伊朗或利比亚开发其石油资源能力的人实施制裁。还对那些出口能够增强利比亚武器或航空能力或开发石油资源能力的货物的人实施制裁。

Iran Sanctions Act

伊朗制裁法

ISA。该法的条款直至 2006 年 9 月 30 日是经修正的 1996 年《伊朗与利比亚制裁法》的一部分。ISA 实施了“通过限制伊朗勘探、开采、提炼或管道运输石油资源的能力，剥夺伊朗支持国际恐怖主义行为和资助发展和获取大规模杀伤性武器及其交付手段的美国政策”。ISA 在 2016 年 12 月 1 日延长 10 年。

Iron law of subsidies

补贴铁律

关于补贴使低效率生产者继续经营而延迟改革和压制生产率的观点，除非给予补贴的同时辅以严格和强制的改革规定。另见*恒定保护定律(law of constant protection)*。

ISIC

全部经济活动国际标准行业分类

见*全部经济活动国际标准行业分类(International Standard Industrial Classification of All Economic Activities)*。

ISO 9000

ISO 9000 质量管理体系

由国际标准化组织(ISO)制定的一系列质量体系标准。这些标准用于评估一企业的工作方式。不应与产品标准相混淆。质量体系标准使企业能够确定始终如一满足客户要求的途径。

ISO 14000

ISO 14000 环境管理体系

由国际标准化组织(ISO)制定的一系列环境管理标准，涵盖 6 个领域：环境管

environmental performance evaluation; life cycle assessment; terms and definitions. Most of the standards are intended as guidance documents on environmental tools and systems to help companies and other organizations integrate environmental considerations into their normal business processes. Only one of the standards, ISO 14001 on environmental management systems, contains specifications for certification or registration purposes. ISO 14000 does not create production or pollution control requirements. *See also* ***trade and environment***.

Istanbul Convention: the *Customs Convention on Temporary Admission* which entered into force on 27 November 1993. This Convention updates the ***Customs Convention on the ATA Carnet for the Temporary Admission of Goods***. It created a single instrument to simplify and harmonize temporary admission formalities. Goods admitted temporarily must be re-exported to the country of origin. They must not undergo any transformation while they are under temporary admission. The Convention is administered by the ***World Customs Organization***.

Istanbul Programme of Action: *see* ***Programme of Action for the Least-Developed Countries for the Decade 2011–2020***.

ITA: the ***Information Technology Agreement***, or formally the *Ministerial Declaration on Trade in Information Technology Products*, under which participants removed tariffs on IT products by 2000. At the 2015 ***WTO Ministerial Conference*** they added a further 201 products to the list.

ITC: the International Trade Centre, originally established by the old GATT. It is now operated jointly by the WTO and the ***United Nations***, the latter acting through ***UNCTAD***. The ITC is a focal point for technical cooperation on trade promotion of developing countries.

ITCB: *see* ***International Textiles and Clothing Bureau***.

ITC Trade Map: a database maintained by the ***International Trade Centre*** (ITC) which gives indicators on export performance, international demand and competitive markets. Information is provided in the form of tables, graphs and maps. Trade Map covers 220 countries and territories. [www.trademap.org]

Item: in the administration of ***rules of origin*** and other customs procedure this sometimes refers to a ***tariff line*** of seven or more digits.

Item-by-item tariff negotiations: tariff negotiations in which each item is looked at separately. The method is more laborious than ***formula cuts***, linear tariff reductions or ***sectoral trade negotiations***, but it may be the only possible method for achieving results, especially if ***sensitive products*** are involved.

I-TIP services: a set of linked databases that provides information on ***commitments*** made by WTO members under the ***General Agreement on Trade in Services***, ***regional trade agreements***, applied measures in services and services statistics. The database is a joint initiative of the WTO and the ***World Bank***. *See also* ***trade in services statistics***.

ITO: International Trade Organization. The proposal for the establishment of an ITO was one of the outcomes of the 1944 Bretton Woods conference. The ITO

理系统、环境审计、环境标签、环境绩效评价、生命周期评价、条件和定义。大部分标准旨在作为环境工具和系统的指导文件，以帮助公司和其他组织将环境考虑因素纳入其正常业务流程。这些标准中，只有关于环境管理体系的ISO14001包含认证或注册目的的规范。ISO14000并不产生生产或污染控制要求。另见*贸易与环境(trade and environment)*。

Istanbul Convention

伊斯坦布尔公约

1993年11月27日生效的《货物暂准进口公约》。该公约对《关于货物暂准进口的ATA报关单证册海关公约》进行了更新。创建了简化和协调暂准入境手续的单一文件。暂准入境货物必须复出口至原产国。在暂准入境期间，货物不得进行任何变更。公约由世界海关组织(WCO)管理。

Istanbul Programme of Action

伊斯坦布尔行动计划

见*2011—2020年十年期支援最不发达国家行动纲领(Programme of Action for the Least-Developed Countries for the Decade 2011–2020)*。

ITA

信息技术协定

正式名称为《关于信息技术产品贸易的部长宣言》，参加方据此在2000年前取消信息技术产品关税。在2015年WTO部长级会议上，参加方增加了201项产品。

ITC

国际贸易中心

最初由原GATT设立。现由WTO和联合国联合运营，后者通过联合国贸易与发展会议(UNCTAD)发挥作用。ITC是发展中国家贸易促进技术合作的联络点。

ITCB

国际纺织服装局

见*国际纺织服装局(International Textiles and Clothing Bureau)*。

ITC Trade Map

国际贸易中心贸易地图

国际贸易中心(ITC)维护的数据库，提供关于出口实绩、国际需求和竞争市场的指标。相信息以表格、图表和地图形式提供。贸易地图覆盖220个国家和地区。

Item

条目

在原产地规则和其他海关程序的管理中，有时指7位或更多位编码的税目。

Item-by-item tariff negotiations

逐税目关税谈判

每一税目单独考虑的关税谈判。此种方法比公式削减、线性关税削减或部门贸易谈判更费力，但可能是取得结果的惟一可能方法，特别是在涉及敏感产品的情况下。

I-TIP services

I-TIP服务

一套链接数据库，提供WTO成员在《服务贸易总协定》项下所作承诺、区域贸易协定、服务贸易实施措施和服务统计的信息。该数据库由WTO和世界银行的联合倡议建立。另见*服务贸易统计(trade in services statistics)*。

ITO

国际贸易组织

建立国际贸易组织的提议是1944年布雷顿森林会议的成果之一。ITO意在涵

was meant to cover a wide range of economic issues, including ***investment***, ***restrictive business practices***, ***commodity arrangements***, rules for international trade and trade issues related to economic development. All these topics were subject to intensive negotiations at Havana in 1947 and 1948. A compromise of sorts was reached in the end, but at the expense of an agreement with fewer teeth than its early main proponents would have liked. The only surviving part was the set of trade rules and tariff commitments now known as the GATT which was based on the chapter on ***commercial policy***, but which had been negotiated on a parallel track. The ITO accordingly was never established. *See also* ***Bretton Woods agreements***, ***Havana Charter***, ***Organization for Trade Cooperation*** and ***WTO***.

IUU fishing: illegal, unreported and unregulated fishing. A subject of the United Nations ***Food and Agriculture Organization*** (FAO) International Plan of Action to Prevent, Deter and Eliminate IUU Fishing. It refers *inter alia* to fishing and fishing-related activities conducted in contravention of national, regional or international laws; non-reporting, misreporting or under-reporting of information on fishing operations and their catches; fishing by "stateless" vessels; fishing in areas under the mandate of Regional Fisheries Management Organizations (REMOs); and fishing activities which are not regulated by states and cannot easily be monitored and accounted for. In the ***WTO*** negotiations members are debating which IUU determinations, by which entities, and under which conditions they could be used as the basis for prohibiting subsidies that contribute to IUU fishing.

盖广泛的经济问题，包括投资、限制性商业惯例、商品安排、国际贸易规则和与经济发展有关的贸易问题。所有这些议题均为 1947 年和 1948 年在哈瓦那进行的密集谈判的主题。最终达成了某种程度上的妥协，但代价是达成的协议没有最初主要支持者所希望的那么有力。惟一幸存的部分是一套贸易规则和关税承诺，现称《关税与贸易总协定》(GATT)，以商业政策一章为基础，而谈判是平行进行的。ITO 因此从未建立。另见*布雷顿森林协定(Bretton Woods agreements)*、*哈瓦那宪章(Havana Charter)*、*贸易合作组织(Organization for Trade Cooperation)*、*世界贸易组织(WTO)*。

IUU fishing

非法、未报告和无管制捕捞

粮农组织(FAO)《防止、阻止和消除非法、未报告和无管制捕捞的国际行动计划》的一个主题。特别指违反国家、区域或国际法而进行的捕捞和与捕捞有关的活动；未报告、误报或少报有关捕捞作业及其渔获量的资料；“无国籍”船只捕捞；在区域渔业管理组织主管水域开展的捕捞；以及不受国家管制、不易监测和不易追究责任的捕捞。在 WTO 谈判中，成员正在辩论哪些属于 IUU 捕捞、哪些实体以及在什么条件下可用来作为禁止助长 IUU 捕捞的补贴的依据。

J

Jackson-Vanik amendment: an amendment to the 1974 United States Trade Act proposed by Senator Henry Jackson (D) and Representative Charles Vanik (D) and enacted as Section 402. It denied the granting of ***most-favoured-nation treatment*** (MFN) to ***non-market economies*** if they (a) denied their citizens the right to emigrate, (b) imposed more than a nominal tax on emigration and (c) imposed more than a nominal charge on citizens if they wished to emigrate. The President could waive the requirement for full compliance with Section 402 if he determined that this would substantially promote the freedom-of-emigration provisions, and if he had received assurances that the emigration practices of the country would lead substantially to the achievement of this objective. The Jackson-Vanik amendment was aimed originally at the USSR, but it was also used against other countries. Withdrawal of MFN meant that the high tariff rates contained in the ***Smoot-Hawley Tariff Act*** (the *Tariff Act* of 1930) applied. These would make an exporter quite uncompetitive in the United States market. The Act was repealed in 2012. *See also* ***conditional most-favoured-nation treatment*** and ***normal trade relations***.

Japanese measures on leather**:** a case launched under the GATT in 1983 by the United States. It concerned ***import restrictions*** maintained by Japan on bovine, equine, sheep, lamb, goat and kid leather. Japan explained that its restrictions reflected the historical, cultural and socio-economic background of the "Dowa problem". The Dowa are a national minority traditionally performing jobs considered less desirable, such as tanning. Japan noted that they were a product of its feudal society before the Meiji Reformation (1868). The people of Dowa districts had been, as an established social institution, classified as being outside and below the hierarchy of samurais, peasants, artisans and merchants. They had been subjected to severe institutional discrimination in all aspects of social life. Since 1871, the Japanese Government had initiated various measures to emancipate them, although the elimination of poverty still had a long way to go. Likewise, Japan submitted, psychological discrimination in Japanese society at large still existed, though this was now reduced to a large extent. The Japanese tanning industry, traditionally an occupation of Dowa people, employed about 12,000 people in small, backward enterprises. Its low technological level made it uncompetitive. Japan claimed that if the import restrictions on leather were eliminated immediately, the industry would collapse with "unmeasurable social, regional-economic and political problems". The ***panel*** noted that Japan's case rested almost entirely on considerations resulting from the particular

J

Jackson-Vanik amendment

杰克逊-瓦尼克修正案

民主党参议员亨利 · 杰克逊和民主党众议员查尔斯 · 瓦尼克提出的对美国《1974 年贸易法》的修正案，成为第 402 条。该条拒绝给予非市场经济体最惠国待遇(MFN)，如果它们：(a)拒绝给予其公民移民的权利；(b)对移民征收超过名义税水平的税费；以及(c)对希望移民的公民征收超过名义收费水平的费用。总统如果确定可以实质性促进移民自由条款，且确信有关国家的移民做法将实质性实现这一目标，他可以豁免第 402 条的要求适用于该国。《杰克逊-瓦尼克修正案》最初针对苏联，但也用以针对其他国家。撤销最惠国待遇意味着需要适用《斯穆特-霍利关税法》(《1930 年关税法》)所含的高税率，这会使出口商在美国市场上失去竞争力。该法在 2012 年废除。另见*有条件最惠国待遇(conditional most-favoured-nation treatment)*、*正常贸易关系(normal trade relations)*。

Japanese measures on leather

日本皮革措施案

1983 年美国根据 GATT 规则发起的争端案。该案涉及日本对牛皮、马皮、绵羊皮、羔羊皮、山羊皮和小山羊皮维持的进口限制。日本解释称，限制反映了“部落民问题”的历史、文化和社会经济背景。部落民是日本少数民族，传统上从事较为低下的工作，例如鞣革。日本指出，他们是明治维新(1868 年)前封建社会的产物。作为既定的社会制度，部落民区的人被划分在武士、农民、工匠和商人等级之外和之下。他们在社会生活的各个方面都受到严重的制度性歧视。自 1871 年以来，日本政府采取了各种措施来解放他们，尽管消除贫困还有很长的路要走。同样，日本提出，在整个日本社会的心理歧视仍然存在，尽管这种歧视现在已经在很大程度上减少了。日本制革业传统上属于部落民从事的行业，在落后的小企业中雇佣了大约 12000 人。这些小企业的低技术水平使其没有竞争力。日本声称，如果立即取消对皮革的进口限制，该行业将因“无法衡量的社会、地区经济和政治问题”而崩溃。专家组注意到，日本的案件几乎完全基于被称为部落民的人口群体有关的特殊问题所产生的考虑因素。

problems connected with the population group known as the Dowa people. It continued that it could not take into account the special circumstances mentioned by Japan since its terms of reference were to examine the matter "in the light of the relevant GATT provisions". These provisions did not allow such a justification for import restrictions. Accordingly, it found that the Japanese import restrictions on leather contravened GATT Article XI (General Elimination of Quantitative Restrictions). The fact that the restrictions had existed for a long time could not alter this finding. *See also* ***Belgian family allowances*** for another case dealing with social issues. [GATT BISD 27S]

JI: Joint Implementation. *See* ***Kyoto Protocol***.

JITAP: *see* ***Joint Integrated Technical Assistance Programme***.

Johannesburg Declaration on Sustainable Development: *see* ***World Summit on Sustainable Development***.

Johannesburg Plan of Implementation: *see* ***World Summit on Sustainable Development***

Joint action: action taken by all the ***contracting parties*** (members) of the GATT concerning administration of the provisions of the Agreement or with a view to furthering its objectives. Joint action was necessary, for example, for granting a ***waiver***. Whenever you see CONTRACTING PARTIES written in this way, you know that joint action had been taken by the contracting parties (members).

Joint Declaration on Trade and Women's Economic Empowerment: issued at the ***WTO Ministerial Conference*** in Buenos Aires in 2017. It expresses agreement to make trade and development policies more gender-responsive by (1) sharing experiences relating to policies and programmes on women's participation in national and international economies, (2) sharing best practices for conducting gender-based analysis of trade policies and for monitoring their effects, (3) sharing methods and procedures for collecting gender-disaggregated data and their use, (4) working together in the WTO to remove barriers to women's economic empowerment and increase their participation in trade, and (5) ensuring that ***Aid for Trade*** supports tools and know-how for analysing, designing and implementing more gender-responsive trade policies. A work programme to support these aims was established at the same time. *See also* ***trade and gender***.

Joint Implementation: *see* ***Kyoto Protocol***.

Joint initiatives: refers to initiatives by a significant number of WTO members at the ***Buenos Aires WTO Ministerial Conference*** in December 2017. First, a group of seventy-one WTO members announced that they would initiate exploratory work together towards future WTO negotiations on trade-related aspects of ***electronic commerce***. Participation in the group would be open to all WTO members. Second, seventy members called for a start to structured discussions with the aim of developing a multilateral framework on ***investment facilitation***. Aims of such discussions would be (a) improve the transparency and predictability of investment measures, (b) streamline and speed up administrative procedures and requirements, and (c) enhance international cooperation,

专家组接下来指出，不能考虑日本提到的特殊情况，因为专家组的职权范围是“根据 GATT 相关条款”审查这一问题。这些条款不允许以这样的理由实施进口限制。因此，专家组认定日本对皮革的进口限制违反了 GATT 第 11 条(普遍取消数量限制)。这些限制长期存在的事实并不能改变这一调查结果。另见涉及社会问题的案件——*比利时家庭津贴案(Belgian family allowances)*。

JI

联合履约

见*京都议定书(Kyoto Protocol)*。

JITAP

技术援助共同综合方案

见*技术援助共同综合方案(Joint Integrated Technical Assistance Programme)*。

Johannesburg Declaration on Sustainable Development

约翰内斯堡可持续发展宣言

见*可持续发展问题世界首脑会议(World Summit on Sustainable Development)*。

Johannesburg Plan of Implementation

约翰内斯堡实施计划

见*可持续发展问题世界首脑会议(World Summit on Sustainable Development)*。

Joint action

联合行动

所有 GATT 缔约方(成员)为实施总协定条款或为促进其目标实现而采取的行动。联合行动十分必要，例如授予豁免就需要联合行动。每当你看到英文大写字母的“缔约方”字样时，就知道缔约方(成员)已经采取联合行动(CONTRACTING PARTIES 中文译为“缔约方全体”—译注)。

Joint Declaration on Trade and Women's Economic Empowerment

贸易与妇女经济赋权联合宣言

2017 年在布宜诺斯艾利斯举行的 WTO 部长级会议上通过，同意通过以下方式使贸易和发展政策更能促进两性平等：(1)分享有关妇女参与国家和国际经济政策和方案的经验；(2)分享对贸易政策进行基于性别的分析和监测其影响的最佳实践；(3)分享收集按性别分列的数据及其使用的方法和程序；(4)在 WTO 中共同努力，消除增强妇女经济赋权的障碍，增加她们对贸易的参与；以及(5)保证促贸援助支持分析、设计和实施更能促进两性平等的贸易政策的工具和专门知识。同时制定了支持这些目标的工作计划。另见*贸易与性别(trade and gender)*。

Joint Implementation

联合履约

见*京都议定书(Kyoto Protocol)*。

Joint initiatives

联合倡议

指 WTO 多个成员在 2017 年 12 月布宜诺斯艾利斯 WTO 部长级会议上提出的倡议。首先，71 个 WTO 成员组成的小组宣布，它们将就未来 WTO 与贸易有关的电子商务谈判共同开展探索性工作。该小组开放供所有 WTO 成员参加。其次，70 个成员呼吁开始结构化讨论，以期制定一个投资便利化的多边框架。此类讨论的目的为：(a)提高投资措施的透明度和可预测性；(b)简化和加快行

information sharing, exchange of best practices, and relations with relevant stakeholders, including dispute prevention. The discussions would not address market access, investment protection and investor-state dispute settlement. The group would be open to all WTO members. Third, eighty-seven members announced that they had decided to create an Informal Working Group on MSMEs (micro-, small and medium-sized enterprises) with the aim of establishing a formal work programme at the 2020 Ministerial Conference. The group also would be open to all members. Another declaration announced in Buenos Aires on domestic regulation in services has subsequently come to be considered a joint initiative and proponents have made significant progress towards agreement. The initiative is open to all WTO members. The 59 signatories to the Joint Statement on Services Domestic Regulation reaffirmed their commitment to advancing negotiations on domestic regulation in services and to intensifying work towards concluding the negotiations of disciplines in advance of the next Ministerial Conference. The objective is to develop any necessary disciplines to ensure that domestic regulation measures relating to qualification requirements and procedures, technical standards and licensing requirements do not constitute unnecessary barriers to trade in services.

Joint Integrated Technical Assistance Programme: JITAP. Established in 1998 by the ***WTO***, ***UNCTAD*** and the ***International Trade Centre*** with three objectives: (a) build national capacity to understand the evolving ***multilateral trading system*** (MTS) and its implications for international trade, (b) adapt the national trading system to the obligations and disciplines of the new MTS, and (c) seek maximum advantage from the new MTS by enhancing the readiness of exporters to recognize new opportunities. In 2003 a second phase, JITAP II, was launched with the objectives of strengthening capacity in (a) trade negotiations, implementation of WTO agreements and related policy formulation, (b) national knowledge base on MTS, and (c) supply capacity and market knowledge of exporting and export-ready enterprises to benefit from liberalization under the emerging MTS. JITAP was funded through a trust fund. It ceased operations in 2007.

Joint Ministerial Statement – Declaration on the Establishment of a WTO Work Programme for MSMEs: *see **joint initiatives***.

Joint Ministerial Statement on Investment Facilitation for Development: *see **joint initiatives***.

Joint Recommendation Concerning Provisions on the Production of Well-Known Marks: adopted by ***WIPO*** on 29 September 1999. It establishes criteria for determining whether a mark is well known. These are (a) the degree of knowledge or recognition the mark enjoys, (b) duration, extent and geographical area of use of the mark, (c) duration, extent and geographical area of any promotion of the mark, (d) duration and geographical area of any registration or application for registration of the mark, (e) the record of successful enforcement of rights in the mark, and (f) the value associated with the mark. The Recommendation also contains detailed provisions for dealing

政程序和要求；以及(c)加强国际合作、信息共享、最佳实践交流以及与有关利益相关方的关系，包括争端预防。讨论不涉及市场准入、投资保护和投资者—国家间争端解决。该小组将对所有WTO成员开放。第三，87个成员宣布，它们已决定设立一个中小微企业(MSMEs)非正式工作组，目的是在2020年部长级会议上制定一项正式工作计划。该小组也将对所有成员开放。在布宜诺斯艾利斯宣布的另一项关于服务贸易国内规制的声明随后被视为一项联合倡议，支持者在达成协议方面取得了重大进展。该倡议对所有WTO成员开放。《关于服务贸易国内规制的联合声明》的59个签署方重申，致力于推进关于服务贸易国内规制的谈判，并加紧努力，争取在下一届部长级会议之前完成关于纪律的谈判。目的是制定任何必要纪律，以保证与资格要求和程序、技术标准和许可要求有关的国内规制措施不会对服务贸易构成不必要的障碍。

Joint Integrated Technical Assistance Programme
技术援助共同综合方案

JITAP。1998年由WTO、联合国贸易与发展会议(UNCTAD)和国际贸易中心共同制定，有三项目标：(a)建设理解不断演变的多边贸易体制(MTS)及其对国际贸易影响的国家能力；(b)使国家贸易体制与新的多边贸易体制的义务和纪律相适应；以及(c)通过提高出口商认识新机会的准备程度，从新的多边贸易体制中寻求最大利益。2003年启动第二阶段技术援助共同综合方案，目的是增强下列能力：(a)贸易谈判、WTO协定实施和有关政策制定；(b)关于多边贸易体制的国家知识库；以及(c)出口企业和准备从事出口的企业的供应能力和市场知识，以便从正在形成的多边贸易体制的自由化中获益。JITAP由一个信托基金提供资金。2007年停止运营。

Joint Ministerial Statement – Declaration on the Establishment of a WTO Work Programme for MSMEs
联合部长声明—关于建立中小微企业WTO工作计划的宣言

见***联合倡议****(joint initiatives)*。

Joint Ministerial Statement on Investment Facilitation for Development
关于投资便利化的联合部长声明

见***联合倡议****(joint initiatives)*。

Joint Recommendation Concerning Provisions on the Production of Well-Known Marks
关于驰名商标保护规定的联合建议

世界知识产权组织(WIPO)于1999年9月29日通过。联合建议建立了确定商标是否为驰名商标的评价体系。这些指标包括：(a)商标享有的理解或认知程度；(b)商标使用的期限、程度和地域范围；(c)商标任何宣传的持续时间、程度和地理范围；(d)商标的注册或注册申请的期限和地域范围；(e)成功实施商标权的记录；以及(f)商标的相关价值。联合建议还包含处理发生冲突标记的

with conflicting marks (reproduction, imitation, translation or transliteration of a mark liable to create confusion with the well-known mark).

Joint Statement on Electronic Commerce: *see* ***joint initiatives***.

Joint Statement on Services Domestic Regulation: *see* ***joint initiatives***.

Joint trade committee: a mechanism normally instituted under ***bilateral trade agreements*** for periodic meetings reviewing bilateral trade flows and issues arising from them. Meetings may be held at ministerial or officials level, and their location normally alternates between the two countries involved. *See also* ***mixed commission***.

Joint venture: a cooperative association between two or more firms or individuals to carry out a specific activity. Joint ventures may be dissolved when a task, such as the construction of a bridge or a research and development project, has been completed. In the case of a production facility, there may be agreement to dissolve the joint venture after a fixed number of years, usually along previously agreed guidelines. The main reasons for the formation of joint ventures include the pooling of financial, technical or intellectual resources, sharing risks or developing new markets. Sometimes, forming a joint venture with a local company is the only realistic way to enter a new market. *See also* ***ASEAN Industrial Cooperation Scheme***, ***intellectual property protection*** and ***transfer of technology***.

Jones Act: the United States *Merchant Marine Act* of 1920. Section 27 of the Act requires that all goods transported by water between United States ports must be carried in vessels built and registered in the United States, owned by United States citizens and fully crewed by United States citizens and permanent residents. *See also* ***cabotage***.

Judicial activism: a term of no fixed meaning, but it embodies the idea that judges may be assuming functions properly belonging to the legislative or executive branches. As the judicial, legislative and executive branches together represent the idea of government and they operate within the same system, the boundaries are not necessarily always clear. Views tend to be strongly held for or against judicial activism. Some say that it is necessary in some cases to overturn legal injustices. Others say that it merely reflects the personal views of the judges and should not be condoned. Some ***WTO*** members have argued that the ***Appellate Body*** has erred in some cases in the direction of judicial activism. *See also* ***advisory opinion*** and ***Dispute Settlement Understanding***.

Judicial economy: a term apparently embodying several principles. Among these are that the time of courts should not be wasted, that legitimate cases should be dealt with speedily, that frivolous cases should be dismissed, and that judges should hear and decide all related parts of a case at the same time.

Judicial review: the review by a tribunal of a decision made by a government authority or agency, usually following an appeal by a person affected by the decision. Such tribunals are normally independent of the body that made the decision. Grounds for review vary, but a common thread tends to be at a

详细规定(复制、模仿、翻译或音译容易造成与驰名商标相混淆的标记)。

Joint Statement on Electronic Commerce

关于电子商务的联合声明

见*联合倡议(joint initiatives)*。

Joint Statement on Services Domestic Regulation

服务贸易国内规制联合声明

见*联合倡议(joint initiatives)*。

Joint trade committee

联合贸易委员会

通常根据双边贸易协定建立的机制，定期举行会议以审议双边贸易流动及由此产生的问题。会议可以在部长级或官员级别举行，会议地点通常在所涉两国之间轮换。另见*混合委员会(mixed commission)*。

Joint venture

合资企业

两个或两个以上公司或个人之间开展特定活动的合作组织。合资企业可以在一项任务完成后终止，例如桥梁建设或研发项目。对于生产性设施，可能会制定在一固定年限后合资企业终止的协议，通常按照事先议定的准则。成立合资企业的主要原因包括筹集资金、技术或智力资源、分担风险或开发新市场。有时，与当地公司成立合资企业是进入新市场的惟一现实途径。另见*东盟产业合作计划(ASEAN Industrial Cooperation Scheme)*、*知识产权保护与技术转让(intellectual property protection and transfer of technology)*。

Jones Act

琼斯法案

《1920 年美国海商法》。该法第 27 条要求，在美国港口之间经水路运输的所有货物必须由在美国制造、在美国注册、由美国公民拥有且船员全部是美国公民和永久居民的船舶运输。另见*国内交通运输权(cabotage)*。

Judicial activism

司法能动主义

无固定含义的词语，但包含这样一种观念，即法官可以适当承担属于立法或行政部门的职能。由于司法部门、立法部门和执法部门共同代表着政府的理念，它们在同一个系统中运作，因此界限并不一定总是清晰的。人们要么强列支持、要么强烈反对司法能动主义。一些人认为，在一些情况下有必要推翻法律上的不公正。另一些人则认为，这仅反映了法官的个人观点，不应纵容。一些 WTO 成员认为，上诉机构在一些情况下在司法能动主义方面犯了错误。另见*咨询意见(advisory opinion)*、*争端解决谅解(Dispute Settlement Understanding)*。

Judicial economy

司法经济

明显包含若干原则的词语。其中包括不应浪费开庭时间，应迅速处理合法案件，应驳回轻率的案件，法官应同时审理和裁决案件的所有相关部分。

Judicial review

司法审查

法庭对政府主管部门或机构所作决定的审查，通常在受该决定影响的人提起

minimum the launch of an enquiry as to whether the process leading to the decision followed the prescribed administrative steps. *See also* ***administrative ruling of general application***.

July 2004 package: the WTO ***General Council*** decision of 1 August 2004 which sets out a work programme leading to what then was thought to be the conclusion of negotiations under the ***Doha Development Agenda***. It takes its name from the intensive negotiations during July 2004 leading up to the decision. [WT/L/579]

Juridical person: a term used in the ***General Agreement on Trade in Services***. A legal entity, such as a corporation, trust, partnership, joint venture, sole proprietorship, association, etc., formed for the purpose of supplying ***services***.

Jus cogens**:** peremptory forms of international law from which it is not possible to depart. Article 53 of the ***Vienna Convention on the Law of Treaties*** states that "A treaty is void if, at the time of its conclusion, it conflicts with a peremptory norm of general international law. For the purposes of the present Convention, a peremptory norm of general international law is a norm accepted and recognized by the international community of States as a whole as a norm from which no derogation is permitted and which can be modified only by a subsequent norm of general international law having the same character". Article 64 of the same Convention states that "If a new peremptory norm of international law emerges, any existing treaty which is in conflict with that norm becomes void and terminates". [Brownlie 2019, Starke 1989]

上诉后进行。此类法庭通常独立于作出决定的机构。审查的理由各不相同，但一个共同的主线往往是至少应对导致作出决定的程序是否遵循规定的行政步骤展开调查。另见*普遍适用的行政裁定(administrative ruling of general application)*。

July 2004 package

2004 年 7 月工作计划

WTO 总理事会 2004 年 8 月 1 日的决定，其中列出达成多哈发展议程项下当时认为的谈判结果的工作计划。得名于为达成决定而在 2004 年 7 月进行的密集谈判。

Juridical person

企业法人

《服务贸易总协定》中使用的词语。指为提供服务而成立的法人实体，例如公司、信托、合伙企业、合资企业、独资企业、协会等。

Jus cogens

强制法

国际法中不可能背离的强制性形式。《维也纳条约法公约》第 53 条规定，“条约在缔结时与一般国际法强制规律抵触者无效。就适用本公约而言，一般国际法强制规律指国家之国际社会全体接受并公认为不许损抑且仅有以后具有同等性质之一般国际法规律始得更改之规律”。公约第 64 条规定，“遇有新一般国际法强制规律产生时，任何现有条约之与该项规律抵触者即成为无效而终止”。

K

Kaleidoscopic comparative advantage: a term suggested by Jagdish Bhagwati to describe situations of industries in which many countries concurrently have a fragile ***comparative advantage***. In other words, the comparative advantage may change very quickly like the image seen through a kaleidoscope. Slight changes in the domestic environment might in these circumstances bring about a shift of industries across countries as they seek to maintain their competitive edge. This then may result in ***footloose industries*** or ***screwdriver operations***. *See also* ***delocalization*** and ***globalization***. [Bhagwati 1995]

Keiretsu **relationships:** a term denoting complex traditional Japanese distribution systems and industrial conglomerate arrangements seen to make it difficult for newcomers to compete on price. Historically, *keiretsu* relationships appear to have been based on a desire by firms for continuity of supplies and orders. Today *keiretsu* relationships are sometimes seen by foreign exporters in particular as major non-tariff barriers or ***restrictive business practices***. Japanese commentators tend to argue that the power of *keiretsus* is overrated, and that the relationships generally are not strong enough to negate price signals. Some distinguish between horizontal *keiretsus* (arrangements between firms in several sectors) and vertical *keiretsus* (arrangements between firms at different production and distribution stages in the same sector). *See also* ***Market-Oriented Sector-Specific talks*** and ***Structural Impediments Initiative***.

Kennedy Round: the sixth round of GATT ***multilateral trade negotiations***, held from 1963 to 1967. It was named after President John F. Kennedy in recognition of his support for the reformulation of the United States trade agenda which resulted in the *Trade Expansion Act* of 1962. This Act gave the President the widest-ever negotiating authority (see ***United States trade agreements legislation*** for a brief description of how this is done). As the ***Dillon Round*** went through the laborious process of ***item-by-item tariff negotiations***, it became clear, long before the Round ended, that a more comprehensive approach was needed to deal with the emerging challenges resulting from the formation of the ***European Economic Community*** (EEC) and ***EFTA***, as well as Europe's re-emergence as a significant international trader more generally. Japan's high economic growth rate portended the major role it would play later as an exporter, but the focal point of the Kennedy Round always was the United States–EEC relationship. Indeed, there was an influential American view that saw what became the Kennedy Round as the start of a transatlantic partnership that might ultimately lead to a transatlantic economic community. To an extent,

K

Kaleidoscopic comparative advantage
万花筒式比较优势

贾格迪什·巴格瓦蒂提出的词语，描述许多国家同时具有一种脆弱的比较优势的产业情况。换言之，比较优势可能会像万花筒中的图像一样迅速变化。国内环境的轻微变化在此种情况下可能会带来产业的跨国转移，因其寻求保持自己的竞争优势。这就可能导致自由布局型产业或螺丝刀式经营。另见*去本地化(delocalization)*、*全球化(globalization)*。

***Keiretsu* relationships**
经连关系

指复杂的传统日本分销系统与产业企业集团安排，被视为使新来者难以在价格上进行竞争。从历史上看，经连关系似乎建立在企业对供应和订单连续性的渴望之上。而今天，经连关系有时被外国出口商视为主要的非关税壁垒或限制性商业惯例。日本评论家倾向于认为，经连关系的力量被高估了，这种关系通常没有强大到足以使价格信号无效。一些人区分横向经连(若干部门中公司之间的安排)和纵向经连(属同一部门不同生产和分销阶段的公司之间的安排)。另见*市场导向型的多领域谈判方案(Market-Oriented Sector-Specific talks)*、*日美结构协议会(Structural Impediments Initiative)*。

Kennedy Round
肯尼迪回合

1963 年至 1967 年举行的第 6 轮 GATT 多边贸易谈判。以肯尼迪总统的名字命名，以认可他对重新制定美国贸易议程的支持，该议程产生了《1962 年贸易扩展法》。该法案赋予总统有史以来最广泛的谈判权力，此点如何实现见*美国贸易协定立法(United States trade agreements legislation)*词条对此的简要描述。由于狄龙回合经历了逐税目关税谈判的艰苦进程，在该回合远未结束时就已经清楚地表明，需要采取更全面的方式处理欧洲经济共同体(EEC)和欧洲自由贸易联盟(EFTA)的成立以及欧洲再次作为一个重要的国际贸易方所出现的挑战。日本的高经济增长率预示着日后它将作为出口国所发挥的主要作用，但肯尼迪回合的焦点一直都是美国与欧共体的关系。事实上，有一种颇具影响力的美国观点，即认为肯尼迪回合是跨大西洋伙伴关系的开端，最终可能促成跨大西洋经济共同体的形成。在某种程度上，欧洲也持有这一观点，但欧

this view was shared in Europe, but the process of European unification created its own stresses under which the Kennedy Round at times became a secondary focus for the EEC. An example of this was the French veto in January 1963, before the round had even started, on membership by the United Kingdom. Another was the internal crisis of 1965 which ended in the ***Luxembourg Compromise***. Preparations for the new round were immediately overshadowed by the ***Chicken War***, an early sign of the impact ***variable levies*** under the ***common agricultural policy*** would eventually have. Some participants in the Round had been concerned that the convening of ***UNCTAD***, scheduled for 1964, would result in further complications, but its impact on the actual negotiations was minimal. In May 1963 Ministers reached agreement on three negotiating objectives for the round: (a) measures for the expansion of trade of developing countries as a means of furthering their economic development, (b) reduction or elimination of tariffs and other barriers to trade, and (c) measures for access to markets for agricultural and other primary products. The working hypothesis for the tariff negotiations was a linear tariff cut of 50 per cent with the smallest number of exceptions. A drawn-out argument developed about the trade effects a uniform linear cut would have on the dispersed rates (low and high tariffs quite far apart) of the United States as compared to the much more concentrated rates of the EEC which also tended to be in the lower half of United States tariff rates. The EEC accordingly argued for an evening-out or harmonization of peaks and troughs through its ***écrêtement***, ***double écart*** and ***thirty:ten proposals***. Once negotiations had been joined, this lofty working hypothesis was soon undermined. The ***special-structure countries*** (Australia, Canada, New Zealand and South Africa), so called because their exports were dominated by raw materials and other primary commodities, negotiated their tariff reductions entirely through the item-by-item method. In the end, the result was an average 35 per cent reduction in tariffs, except for textiles, chemicals, steel and other sensitive products; plus a 15–18 per cent reduction in tariffs for agricultural and food products. In addition, the negotiations on chemicals led to a provisional agreement on the abolition of the ***American Selling Price*** (ASP). This was a method of valuing some chemicals used by the United States for the imposition of import duties which gave domestic manufacturers a much higher level of protection than the tariff schedule indicated. However, this part of the outcome was disallowed by Congress, and the American Selling Price was not abolished until Congress adopted the results of the ***Tokyo Round***. The results of the Kennedy Round in agriculture overall were poor. The most notable achievement was agreement on a *Memorandum of Agreement on Basic Elements for the Negotiation of a World Grains Arrangement* which eventually was rolled into a new International Grains Arrangement. The EEC claimed that for it the main result of the negotiations on agriculture was that they "greatly helped to define its own common policy". The developing countries, who played a minor role throughout the negotiations in this Round, benefited nonetheless from substantial tariff cuts particularly in non-agricultural items of interest to them.

洲统一进程产生了自身的压力，在这种压力下，肯尼迪回合有时成为欧共体的次要焦点。这方面的一个例子是在此轮回合还未开始的 1963 年 1 月，法国否决了英国的成员国资格。另一个例子是 1965 年的内部危机，最终导致达成《卢森堡妥协方案》。新一轮的准备工作随即被“鸡肉战”蒙上阴影，这是共同农业政策项下差价税最终产生影响的一个早期迹象。此轮回合的一些参加方担心，定于 1964 年召开的联合国贸易与发展会议(UNCTAD)会带来更多的复杂性，但它对实际谈判的影响微乎其微。1963 年 5 月，部长们就回合的三个谈判目标达成一致：(a)扩大发展中国家贸易的措施，以此作为促进其经济发展的手段；(b)减少或取消关税和其他贸易壁垒；以及(c)农产品和其他初级产品市场准入措施。关税谈判的工作假设是 50%的线性关税削减，只允许最小数量的例外。这引发了一场冗长的争论，即统一线性削减对美国分散型税率(高低关税相差较大)的贸易影响与对欧共体相对集中税率的贸易影响相比较，且欧共体的税率比美国的税率低一半还多。欧共体因此主张通过其提出的关税削平、双差公式和 30:10 公式以削平或协调高关税和低关税。一旦开始谈判，这一崇高工作假设即遭到破坏。特殊结构国家(澳大利亚、加拿大、新西兰和南非)——之所以如此称呼，是因为它们的出口主要为原材料和其他初级商品——它们完全通过逐税目法谈判关税削减。最终，结果是关税平均削减 35%，纺织品、化工品、钢铁和其他敏感产品除外；农产品和食品的关税削减 15%至 18%。此外，关于化工品的谈判达成了废除美国销售价格(ASP)的临时协议。这是美国为征收进口关税而用以对某些化工品进行估价的方法，给予国内制造商远高于美国税则所列水平的保护水平。但是，这部分结果被国会否决了，美国的销售价格直到国会通过东京回合结果时才被废除。肯尼迪回合在农业方面的结果总体上少得可怜。最引人注目的成果是就《世界谷物安排谈判基本要素的协议备忘录》达成一致，最后演变成为新的《国际谷物协定》。欧共体声称，农业谈判的主要结果是“极大地帮助确定了自已的共同政策”。发展中国家在此轮回合中发挥了次要作用，但是仍然得益于实质性关税削减，特别是对它们具有利益的非农产品。但是，它们当时的主要成就被认为

Their main achievement at the time, however, was seen to be the adoption of ***Part IV of the GATT*** which absolved them from according ***reciprocity*** to developed countries in trade negotiations. In the view of many developing countries, this was a direct result of the call at UNCTAD I for a better trade deal for them. There has been argument ever since whether this symbolic gesture was a victory for them, or whether it ensured their exclusion in the future from meaningful participation in the ***multilateral trading system***. On the other hand, there was no doubt that the extension of the ***Long-Term Arrangement Regarding International Trade in Cotton Textiles***, which later became the ***Multi-Fibre Arrangement***, for three years until 1970 led to the longer-term impairment of export opportunities for developing countries. Another outcome of the Kennedy Round was the adoption of an Anti-dumping Code which gave more precise guidance on the implementation of Article VI of the GATT. In particular, it sought to ensure speedy and fair investigations, and it imposed limits on the retrospective application of anti-dumping duties. The Code, however, also ran into difficulties with the United States Congress which precluded it from operating as had been intended. The United States nevertheless claimed that it was complying fully with the new code. *See also* ***anti-dumping measures*** and ***developing countries and the multilateral trading system***. [Preeg 1970]

Kimberley Process Certification Scheme: KPCS. Entered into force on 1 January 2003. It aims to eliminate trade in conflict diamonds, defined as "rough diamonds used by rebel movements or their allies to finance conflict aimed at undermining legitimate governments". Sometimes they are also called "blood diamonds". The KPCS requires its member countries to ensure that a Kimberley Process Certificate accompanies each shipment of rough diamonds exported from it. It bans trade in rough diamonds with countries not participating in the scheme. Participants also are exhorted to establish a system of internal controls and to share information on the functioning of the scheme and to encourage closer cooperation between law enforcement and customs agencies of member countries. More than eighty countries and customs territories now participate in the KPCS.

Knowledge-based economy: defined in APEC as "an economy in which the production, distribution and use of knowledge is the main driver of growth, wealth creation and employment across all industries". Features of a knowledge-based economy are held to be an openness to trade, new ideas and new enterprises; sound macroeconomic policy; the importance attached to education and lifelong learning; and the enabling role of information and telecommunications infrastructure. *See also* ***creative industries***. [APEC 2000]

Knowledge-based industry: an industry thought to rely more than others on the creation of new ideas and new expressions of ideas. Accordingly, knowledge-based industries rely heavily on ***intellectual property protection***.

Kodak–Fuji case: proceedings in the WTO launched in 1997 by the United States against Japan. The case takes its name from the principal companies thought to

是通过了 GATT 第四部分，使它们在贸易谈判中免于给予发达国家互惠。在许多发展中国家看来，这是首届联合国贸易与发展大会呼吁为发展中国家达成更好的贸易协议的直接结果。自此人们一直在争论这一象征性姿态是它们的胜利，还是保证它们被排除在有意义参与多边贸易体制的进程之外。另一方面，毫无疑问的是，将《国际棉纺织品贸易长期安排》(后成为《多种纤维协定》)延长 3 年至 1970 年，导致发展中国家出口机会的长期损害。肯尼迪回合的另一项成果是通过了一项反倾销守则，该守则对 GATT 第 6 条的实施提供了更精确的指导。特别是，守则寻求保证进行迅速和公正的调查，并对追溯适用反倾销税设置限制。但是，该守则也在美国国会遇到困难，使其无法按计划加以运用。尽管如此，美国仍然声称完全遵守了新守则。另见*反倾销措施(anti-dumping measures)*、*发展中国家与多边贸易体制(developing countries and the multilateral trading system)*。

Kimberley Process Certification Scheme

金伯利进程证书制度

KPCS。2003 年 1 月 1 日生效。旨在消除冲突钻石贸易，冲突钻石即"反叛运动或其盟友用于资助旨在破坏合法政府的冲突的毛坯钻石"。有时它们也被称为"血钻"。金伯利进程证书制度要求其成员国保证自其出口的每批毛坯钻石需附金伯利进程证书。禁止与未参加该计划的国家进行毛坯钻石贸易。还敦促参加方建立内部控制制度，以分享关于该计划运作情况的信息，并鼓励与成员国执法机构和海关部门之间开展更密切合作。目前 80 多个国家和关税领土参与金伯利进程证书制度。

Knowledge-based economy

知识型经济

在 APEC 中的定义为"知识的生产、分配和使用是所有行业增长、创造财富和就业的主要驱动力的经济"。知识型经济的特点被认为包括：对贸易、新思想和新企业的开放、健全的宏观经济政策、重视教育和终身学习以及信息和电信基础设施的促进作用。另见*创意产业(creative industries)*。

Knowledge-based industry

知识型产业

比其他产业更依赖于新思想创造和新思想表达的产业。因此，知识型产业严重依赖知识产权保护。

Kodak–Fuji case

柯达-富士案

1997 年美国针对日本在 WTO 中提起的诉讼。该案得名于被认为处于最底层

have been at the bottom of it. The United States alleged that Japanese governmental measures denied fair and equitable market opportunities to its suppliers of consumer photographic film and paper. The United States also claimed that the Japanese measures of particular concern were (a) vertical distribution channels handling Japanese products only, (b) a law restricting the growth of large department stores, and (c) measures restricting the use of sales promotions. The United States case consisted of three elements: (a) a ***non-violation*** claim, (b) an infringement of GATT Article III (national treatment), and (c) an infringement of GATT Article X (transparency). The ***panel*** held that the United States had not been able to show under any of the three elements that Japan had contravened its WTO obligations. [WT/DS44/R]

Korean beef*:** three separate cases launched against the Republic of Korea by Australia, New Zealand and the United States in 1988 concerning its beef ***import restrictions. Korea claimed that the restrictions had been imposed for ***balance-of-payments*** reasons. The ***panel*** found that the restrictions contravened GATT Article XI (General Elimination of Quantitative Restrictions). Nor were they needed to shore up Korea's rapidly improving balance of payments. The matter eventually went to the ***Appellate Body*** which largely upheld the panel findings. In 2001 the parties agreed on the implementation of the recommendations and ruling of the Appellate Body. *See also* ***balance-of-payments consultations***. [GATT BISD 36S, WT IDS 161]

Kyoto Convention: *International Convention on the Simplification and Harmonization of Customs Procedures*. Originally entered into force in 1974. The revised convention entered into force on 3 February 2006. Administered by the ***World Customs Organization***. Its main principles are (a) transparency and predictability of customs actions, (b) standardization and simplification of goods declarations and supporting documents, (c) simplified procedures for authorized persons, (d) maximum use of information technology, (e) minimum necessary customs control to ensure compliance with regulations, (f) use of risk management and audit-based controls, (g) coordinated interventions with other agencies, and (h) partnership with the traders. An extensive list of annexes deals with more detailed aspects of customs administration. *See also* ***Harmonized Commodity Description and Coding System***, ***Istanbul Convention*** and ***trade facilitation***.

Kyoto Protocol: a protocol to the ***United Nations Framework Convention on Climate Change*** (UNFCC), adopted on 11 December 1997 in Kyoto and entered into force on 16 February 2005. It aims to reduce greenhouse gas emissions by the ***Annex I countries*** to agreed targets in the commitment period (2008 to 2012). Several paths are available to countries to meet their obligations. First, they can reduce their actual emissions through domestic measures. Second, they can buy emission credits from countries that are below their targets through emissions trading. Third, a country can earn emission reduction credits through Joint Implementation (JI). It would do this through funding a project in another country which would result in lower emissions there. Fourth,

的主要公司。美国声称日本的政府措施拒绝给予美国消费照相胶卷和相纸供应商公平和公正的市场机会。美国还声称，特别令人关注的日本措施为：(a)只处理日本产品的垂直分销渠道；(b)限制大型百货公司增长的法律；以及(c)限制使用促销活动的措施。美国的案件包括 3 个要素：(a)非违反之诉；(b)违反 GATT 第 3 条(国民待遇)；以及(c)违反 GATT 第 10 条(透明度)。专家组认为，美国未能根据这 3 个要素中的任何一个证明日本违反其 WTO 义务。

Korean beef
韩国牛肉案

1988 年澳大利亚、新西兰和美国针对韩国牛肉进口限制提起的三起单独诉讼。韩国声称这些限制是出于国际收支原因。专家组认为，这些限制违反了 GATT 第 11 条(普遍取消数量限制)。韩国正在迅速改善的国际收支也不需要这些限制的支持。该问题最终提交上诉机构，上诉机构在很大程度上支持专家组的调查结果。2001 年，双方同意执行上诉机构的建议和裁决。另见*国际收支磋商(balance-of-payments consultations)*。

Kyoto Convention
京都公约

《关于简化和协调海关业务制度的国际公约》。最初于 1974 年生效。修订后的公约于 2006 年 2 月 3 日生效。由世界海关组织管理。主要原则为：(a)海关行动的透明度和可预测性；(b)货物申报和证明文件的标准化和简化；(c)授权人员的简化程序；(d)最大限度利用信息技术；(e)保证遵守法规的最少必要海关管控；(f)使用风险管理和基于审计的管控；(g)与其他机构协调干预；以及(h)与贸易商建立伙伴关系。一份详尽的附件清单处理海关管理的更为详细的方面。另见*商品名称及编码协调制度(Harmonized Commodity Description and Coding System)*、*伊斯坦布尔公约(Istanbul Convention)*、*贸易便利化(trade facilitation)*。

Kyoto Protocol
京都议定书

《联合国气候变化框架公约》(UNFCC)的议定书，1997 年 12 月 11 日在京都通过，2005 年 2 月 16 日生效。旨在使附件 1 国家的温室气体排放在承诺期(2008 年至 2012 年)内减少至议定目标。这些国家可通过若干路径履行其义务。一是可通过国内措施减少实际排放。二是可通过排放交易从低于目标的国家购买排放信用。三是一国可通过联合履约(JI)获得减排信用。该国可通过资助

the Clean Development Mechanism (CDM) allows developed countries to earn credits by financing projects resulting in reduced emissions in developing countries. Countries are not allowed to rely solely on either emissions trading, Joint Implementation or the Clean Development Mechanism to achieve their emission targets. *See also* ***climate change***, ***greenhouse gases*** and ***Paris Agreement***.

另一国的产生更低排放的项目实现此点。四是清洁发展机制(CDM)允许发达国家通过资助发展中国家中的减排项目来获得信用。各国不能仅依靠排放交易、联合履约或清洁发展机制实现其排放目标。另见*气候变化(climate change)*、*温室气体(greenhouse gases)*、*巴黎协定(Paris Agreement)*。

L

Labelling: *see* ***eco-labelling***, ***genetic labelling***, ***marks of origin*** and ***social labelling***.

Labour markets integration agreements: listed in the ***General Agreement on Trade in Services*** as a subset of ***economic integration agreements***. WTO members may join an agreement establishing full integration of the labour market between the parties if (a) citizens of the parties to the agreement do not have to obtain residency and work permits and (b) if the agreement is notified to the ***Council for Trade in Services***. Full integration of labour markets is described as citizens of the parties concerned having the right of free entry to the employment markets of the other parties. Integration should also cover measures such as conditions of pay, other conditions of employment and social benefits.

Labour market testing: the practice of ascertaining whether qualified local people might be available when assessing whether to support an application for the employment of foreign nationals. Article XVI of the ***General Agreement on Trade in Services*** states, among other things, that in sectors where market access ***commitments*** have been made, limitations or numerical quotas may not be maintained or adopted on the total number of persons employed.

Labour standards in international trade: *see* ***core labour standards***, ***human rights***, ***international labour standards***, ***social clause***, ***trade and human rights*** and ***trade and labour standards***.

Labour value content: LVC. The value of wages paid to the workforce as part of the determination of the ***regional value content***. The ***United States–Mexico–Canada Agreement*** (USMCA) has detailed provisions for the calculation of the LVC in the automotive industry. Automotive plants must have a production wage rate of at least US$16 an hour. *See also* ***USMCA rules of origin for automotive products***.

LAFTA: Latin American Free Trade Association. An intergovernmental organization created by the Treaty of Montevideo in February 1960, designed to establish gradually a ***free-trade area*** which would provide the basis for a Latin American Common Market. By 1980, only 14 per cent of the trade of member countries was covered by the LAFTA rules. Following LAFTA's perceived inability to produce concrete results, ***ALADI*** (Latin American Integration Association) was formed in that year.

Lagos Plan of Action: formally the Lagos Plan of Action for the Economic Development of Africa, 1980–2000. Adopted by the ***Organization of African***

L

Labelling
标签

见*生态标签(eco-labelling)*、*基因标签(genetic labelling)*、*原产地标记(marks of origin)*、*社会标签(social labelling)*。

Labour markets integration agreements
劳动力市场一体化协定

列在《服务贸易总协定》中作为经济一体化协定的一个子集。WTO成员在下列情况下可以加入在参加方之间建立劳动力市场完全一体化的协定：(a)协定参加方的公民无需获得居留和工作许可；及(b)协定向服务贸易理事会作出通报。劳动力市场完全一体化被描述为参加方的公民有权自由进入其他参加方的就业市场。一体化还应涵盖诸如工资条件、其他就业条件和社会福利等措施。

Labour market testing
劳动力市场测试

在评估是否支持外国国民的就业申请时，确定是否存在可雇佣的合格当地人的做法。《服务贸易总协定》第16条规定，除其他事项外，在已作出市场准入承诺的部门，不得维持或采取对就业总人数的限制或数量配额。

Labour standards in international trade
国际贸易中的劳工标准

见*核心劳工标准(core labour standards)*、*人权(human rights)*、*国际劳工标准(international labour standards)*、*社会条款(social clause)*、*贸易与人权(trade and human rights)*、*贸易与劳工标准(trade and labour standards)*。

Labour value content
劳动价值含量

LVC。作为确定区域价值成分的一部分，支付给劳动力的工资价值。《美国—墨西哥—加拿大协定》(USMCA)对汽车工业的 LVC 计算有详细的规定。汽车厂的生产工资标准必须至少达到每小时 16 美元。另见 *USMCA 汽车产品原产地规则(USMCA rules of origin for automotive products)* 。

LAFTA
拉丁美洲自由贸易协会

根据《蒙得维的亚条约》于1960年2月设立的政府间组织，旨在逐步建立一个自由贸易区，为拉丁美洲共同市场奠定基础。到1980年，成员国的贸易中只有14%为LAFTA规则所涵盖。在LAFTA被认为无法产生实际成果后，拉丁美洲一体化协会(ALADI)于当年成立。

Lagos Plan of Action
拉各斯行动计划

正式名称为《1980—2000 年非洲经济发展拉各斯行动计划》。由非洲统一组织于 1980 年在拉各斯通过。附件 1 呼吁加强现有区域经济共同体(RECs)，建立

Unity in Lagos in 1980. Annex I calls for the strengthening of existing ***Regional Economic Communities*** (RECs) and for the establishment of other economic groupings and the creation of an eventual ***African Economic Community***. *See also* ***African regional economic integration***.

LAIA: Latin American Integration Association. *See* ***ALADI*** (Asociación Latinoamericana de Integración).

Laissez-faire policies: economic policies based on minimum governmental intervention to allow the market to produce the best outcomes. *See also* ***invisible hand***.

Land-locked developing countries: LLDC. Thirty-two countries are recognized as land-locked developing countries. They are Afghanistan, Armenia, Azerbaijan, Bhutan, Bolivia, Botswana, Burkina Faso, Burundi, Central African Republic, Chad, Eswatini, Ethiopia, Kazakhstan, Kyrgyzstan, Laos, Lesotho, North Macedonia, Malawi, Mali, Mongolia, Nepal, Niger, Paraguay, Moldova, Rwanda, South Sudan, Tajikistan, Turkmenistan, Uganda, Uzbekistan, Zambia and Zimbabwe. *See also* ***Almaty Programme of Action*** and ***Vienna Programme of Action for Landlocked Developing Countries for the Decade 2014–2024***.

Large Aircraft Sector Understanding: LASU. Refers to Annex III of the ***OECD Arrangement on Officially Supported Export Credits***. Its purpose is to "provide a framework for the predictable, consistent and transparent use of officially supported export credits for the sale or lease of aircraft and other goods and services". LASU applies to (a) new and used civil aircraft, (b) spare engines, (c) spare parts, (d) maintenance and service contracts for civil aircraft and engines, (e) conversion, major modifications and refurbishment of civil aircraft, and (f) engine kits. It does not apply to new and used military aircraft. LASU seeks to encourage competition among exporters based on quality and price of goods and services, rather than the best officially supported terms and conditions. *See also* ***Agreement on Trade in Civil Aircraft***.

Last-in, first-out: a method of inventory management which uses the cost of the newest goods in stock as the valuation basis. Its main relevance to trade policy stems from the need to calculate a ***regional value content*** under the ***rules of origin*** adopted in some ***free-trade agreements***. *See also* ***averaging*** and ***first-in, first-out***.

Lasting interest: *see* ***foreign direct investment***.

Last substantial transformation: a concept used in the administration of ***rules of origin*** to decide whether a good will be eligible for the ***preferential tariff***. It means that the good has to have undergone sufficient processing or re-working to meet, for example, the ***change-in-tariff-classification*** criterion or a ***value-added criterion***. The last substantial transformation has to occur in one of the parties to the preferential trade agreement in question, and it has to be done immediately before the good is exported. *See also* ***substantial transformation***.

Latin American Economic System: *see* ***SELA***.

Latin American Integration Association: *see* ***ALADI***.

Latin American MFN suppliers of bananas: *see* ***banana cases***.

其他经济集团，并建立最终的非洲经济共同体。另见*非洲区域经济一体化(African regional economic integration)*。

LAIA
拉丁美洲一体化协会
见*ALADI(拉丁美洲一体化协会)*。

Laissez-faire policies
自由放任政策
基于最小政府干预使市场产生最佳结果的经济政策。另见*无形之手(invisible hand)*。

Land-locked developing countries
内陆发展中国家
LLDC。32 个国家被认定为属内陆发展中国家，即阿富汗、亚美尼亚、阿塞拜疆、不丹、玻利维亚、博茨瓦纳、布基纳法索、布隆迪、中非共和国、乍得、斯威士兰、埃塞俄比亚、哈萨克斯坦、吉尔吉斯斯坦、老挝、莱索托、北马其顿、马拉维、马里、蒙古、尼泊尔、尼日尔、巴拉圭、摩尔多瓦、卢旺达、南苏丹、塔吉克斯坦、土库曼斯坦、乌干达、乌兹别克斯坦、赞比亚和津巴布韦。另见*阿拉木图行动纲领(Almaty Programme of Action)*、*内陆发展中国家 2014—2024 年十年维也纳行动纲领(Vienna Programme of Action for Landlocked Developing Countries for the Decade 2014–2024)*。

Large Aircraft Sector Understanding
民用航空器行业谅解
LASU。指OECD《官方支持出口信贷的安排》附件三。目的是“为出售或租赁航空器及其他货物和服务提供一个可预测、持续的和透明的官方支持出口信贷使用框架”。LASU 适用于：(a)新造和二手的民用航空器；(b)备用引擎；(c)备件；(d)民用航空器及引擎的维修和服务合同；(e)民用航空器的改造、大修和翻新；以及(f)引擎设备。不适用于新的和二手的军用航空器。LASU 寻求在鼓励出口商之间基于商品和服务的质量和价格的竞争，而不是最佳的官方支持条款和条件。另见*民用航空器贸易协定(Agreement on Trade in Civil Aircraft)*。

Last-in, first-out
后进先出法
使用库存中最新货物的成本作为估价基础的库存管理方法。与贸易政策的主要相关性源自需要根据一些自由贸易协定中的原产地规则计算区域价值成分。另见*平均法(averaging)*、*先入先出法(first-in, first-out)*。

Lasting interest
持久利益
见*外国直接投资(foreign direct investment)*。

Last substantial transformation
最后实质性改变
在原产地规则管理中使用的概念，用以决定一货物是否有资格享受优惠关税。这意味着货物必须经过足够的加工或再加工，以满足税则归类改变标准或增值标准。最后实质性改变必须发生在所涉优惠贸易协定一参加方领土内，而且必须在紧接货物出口前完成。另见*实质性改变(substantial transformation)*。

Latin American Economic System
拉丁美洲经济体系
见*拉丁美洲经济体系(SELA)*。

Latin American Integration Association
拉丁美洲一体化协会
见*拉丁美洲一体化协会(ALADI)*。

Latin American MFN suppliers of bananas
拉丁美洲最惠国香蕉供应商
见*香蕉案(banana cases)*。

Latin American regional integration arrangements: this entry summarizes the main ***regional integration arrangements*** concluded or proposed by Latin American countries since the 1960s. It only lists arrangements with at least three members. Two arrangements dominate Central America. One began with the ***Central American Common Market*** in 1961. The original members were Costa Rica, El Salvador, Guatemala, Honduras and Nicaragua. It was revitalized in 1993 through the ***Central American Integration System*** (Sistema de la Integración Centroamericana or SICA). Its mandate is very wide, well beyond trade and economics. Its members are Belize, Costa Rica, Dominican Republic, El Salvador, Guatemala, Honduras, Nicaragua and Panama. The second is the ***Secretariat of Central American Economic Integration*** (Secretaría de Integración Centroamericana or SIECA). It is charged with the economic aspects of Central American Integration. Its members are Costa Rica, El Salvador, Guatemala, Honduras, Nicaragua and Panama. ***LAFTA*** (Latin American Free Trade Association) was formed in 1960 by Argentina, Brazil, Chile, Mexico, Paraguay, Peru and Uruguay. In 1980 it was replaced by ***ALADI*** (Asociación Latino Americana de Integración or Latin American Integration Association) with Bolivia, Colombia, Ecuador and Venezuela as additional members. The Andean Pact was established in 1969 as a sub-group of LAFTA. In 1997 it became the ***Andean Community***. Its members are Bolivia, Colombia, Ecuador, Peru and Venezuela. The ***Pacific Alliance***, created in 2011, which consists of Chile, Colombia, Mexico and Peru, will abolish tariffs between the parties by 2020. ***Mercosur***, consisting of Argentina, Brazil, Paraguay and Uruguay, was formed in 1991. The ***Community of Latin American and Caribbean States***, the successor to the Rio Group, looks at broader regional political and security issues, but it is not a regional integration arrangement as such. The proposed ***FTAA***, launched in 1994, and consisting of all American hemisphere countries except Cuba, would have dwarfed all the other arrangements, but negotiations for it were abandoned in 2004. The ***South American Community of Nations***, which was launched in 2004, and would have led to a convergence between Mercosur, the Andean Community as well as Chile, Surname and Guyana, has made very slow progress. The ***Economic Commission for Latin America and the Caribbean*** (ECLAC) has the overall mandate for promoting economic progress, but it is not directly involved in individual arrangements.

Lattice regionalism: describes the view that an interlacing framework of bilateral ***free-trade agreements*** among regional economies could be the forerunner of broader regional economic integration. *See also* ***docking and merging***. [Dent 2006]

Law of constant protection: a term proposed by Jagdish Bhagwati to mean that if ***protectionism*** is stopped in some form or other, it will arise in some other guise elsewhere. *See also* ***iron law of subsidies***. [Bhagwati 1988]

Law of Similars: a Brazilian law, now rarely used, which permits the authorities to impose a high tariff on an imported product if a similar domestic product is available. The law was meant to support an ***import substitution*** policy.

Latin American regional integration arrangements

拉丁美洲区域一体化安排

本词条总结了自20世纪60年代以来拉丁美洲国家缔结或提出的主要区域一体化安排。仅列出与至少包含3个成员的安排。两项安排在中美洲占主导地位。一项是1961年的中美洲共同市场。最初成员为哥斯达黎加、萨尔瓦多、危地马拉、洪都拉斯和尼加拉瓜。这一安排在1993年通过中美洲一体化体系(SICA)得以重振。授权非常广泛，远超贸易和经济范围。成员为伯利兹、哥斯达黎加、多米尼加、萨尔瓦多、危地马拉、洪都拉斯、尼加拉瓜和巴拿马。第二项是中美洲经济一体化秘书处(SIECA)，负责中美洲一体化的经济方面的事务。成员为哥斯达黎加、萨尔瓦多、危地马拉、洪都拉斯、尼加拉瓜和巴拿马。拉丁美洲自由贸易协会(LAFTA)于1960年由阿根廷、巴西、智利、墨西哥、巴拉圭、秘鲁和乌拉圭建立。1980年被拉丁美洲一体化协会(ALADI)所取代，玻利维亚、哥伦比亚、厄瓜多尔和委内瑞拉成为新成员。安第斯条约组织于1969年建立，作为 LAFTA的一个分组，1997年成为安第斯共同体，成员为玻利维亚、哥伦比亚、厄瓜多尔、秘鲁和委内瑞拉。太平洋联盟于2011年成立，由智利、哥伦比亚、墨西哥和秘鲁组成，将在2020年前取消各参加方之间的关税。南方共同市场(Mercosur)成立于1991年，由阿根廷、巴西、巴拉圭和乌拉圭组成。作为里约集团的后继组织，拉丁美洲和加勒比国家共同体着眼于更广泛的区域政治和安全问题，但它本身并不是一项区域一体化安排。拟议的美洲自由贸易区(FTAA)于1994年启动，由除古巴外的所有美洲半球国家组成，本该会使所有其他安排相形见绌，但有关该安排的谈判于2004年被放弃。2004年启动的南美洲国家共同体本来可以促成南方共同市场、安第斯共同体以及智利、苏里南和圭亚那之间的融合，但进展非常缓慢。拉丁美洲和加勒比经济委员会(ECLAC)有促进经济进步的总体授权，但不直接参与单个安排。

Lattice regionalism

格子区域主义

描述这样一种观点，即区域经济体之间相互交织的双边自由贸易协定框架可成为更广泛区域经济一体化的前身。另见*接驳与合并(docking and merging)*。

Law of constant protection

恒定保护定律

贾格迪什·巴格瓦蒂提出的词语，指如果以某种形式停止实施保护主义，保护主义会在其他地方以某种其他形式出现。另见*补贴铁律(iron law of subsidies)*。

Law of Similars

相似法

巴西的一项法律，现在很少使用，该法允许在有相似国产品的情况下，主管机关可对进口产品征收高额关税。该法旨在支持进口替代政策。

Layout-designs of integrated circuits: one of the forms of ***intellectual property*** enjoying protection under the ***Agreement on Trade-Related Aspects of Intellectual Property Rights***. Protection is often afforded through a ***sui generis right***, a method applying in this case specifically to layout-designs (or topography) of integrated circuits. It prohibits the unauthorized reproduction or distribution of such designs. ***Reverse engineering*** is allowed under the laws of many countries.

LCA: *see **life cycle assessment***, also called life cycle analysis. A method to assess whether a good or service is environmentally friendly by taking into account, among other factors, how it will be disposed of.

LDCs: *see **least-developed countries***.

LDC services waiver: adopted at the Geneva ***WTO Ministerial Conference*** in 2011 to enable developing country and least-developed country members to accord preferences to services and service suppliers of least-developed country members. The ***waiver*** is valid for fifteen years from its adoption. The preferential treatment may be utilized by ***least-developed countries*** so designated by the United Nations. *See also **General Agreement on Trade in Services.***

Lead economy: in ***APEC*** and some other international groupings the member economy which has been given the task of coordinating or managing a project or activity.

Leaders' Agenda to Implement Structural Reform: LAISR. An ***APEC*** work programme adopted in 2004 to promote structural reform in the APEC region. Its priority areas are regulatory reform, strengthening economic legal infrastructure, competition policy and public sector management. The methods to promote structural reform include (a) identify an institutional mechanism to address structural reform, (b) stimulate policy-oriented discussions on structural reform, (c) foster an understanding of the benefits of structural reform, (d) promote further capacity-building, and (e) strengthen cooperation and collaboration with relevant international fora. *See also **APEC New Strategy for Structural Reform*** and ***Renewed APEC Agenda for Structural Reform***. [www.apec.org]

Leaders' Statement to Implement APEC Transparency Standards: *see **APEC principles on transparency standards***.

League of Arab States: founded in 1945. A loose confederation of twenty-two Arab countries to improve coordination among its members on matters of common interest. Its secretariat is in Cairo. *See **Arab Common Market*** and ***Arab Customs Union***.

League of Nations: the forerunner of the United Nations, established in 1919 as part of the Treaty of Versailles. The League's main aims were collective security, arbitration of international disputes, reductions in armaments and open diplomacy. By the 1930s there were serious doubts about its efficacy, though it continued to have a legal existence until its abolition. The League had a work programme on international trade, but the onset of the Great Depression in the late 1920s and the deteriorating international political situation eliminated any

Layout-designs of integrated circuits
集成电路布图设计

享受《与贸易有关的知识产权协定》项下保护的一种形式的知识产权。保护通常通过一种特殊权利提供，在此种情况下此种方法专门适用于集成电路布图设计(或拓扑图)。禁止未经授权复制或传播此类设计。许多国家的法律允许逆向工程。

LCA
生命周期评估

见*生命周期评估(life cycle assessment)*，也称生命周期分析。通过考虑如何处置该货物或服务等因素，评估一货物或服务是否属环境友好的方法。

LDCs
最不发达国家

见*最不发达国家(least-developed countries)*。

LDC services waiver
最不发达国家服务豁免

在 2011 年日内瓦 WTO 部长级会议上获得通过(《关于给予最不发达国家服务和服务提供者优惠待遇的决定》—译注)，使发展中国家和最不发达国家成员能够对最不发达国家成员的服务和服务提供者给予优惠。该豁免在通过后的 15 年内有效。联合国指定的最不发达国家可以使用此种优惠待遇。另见*服务贸易总协定(General Agreement on Trade in Services)*。

Lead economy
领头经济体

在APEC和其他一些国际组织中，被赋予协调或管理一项目或活动任务的成员经济体。

Leaders' Agenda to Implement Structural Reform
领导人实施结构性改革议程

APEC于2004年通过的一项工作计划，以促进APEC区域的结构改革。优先领域为监管改革、加强经济法律基础、竞争政策和公共部门管理。促进结构改革的方法包括：(a)确定处理结构改革的体制机制；(b)鼓励就结构改革进行政策性讨论；(c)促进对结构改革利益的理解；(d)促进进一步能力建设；以及(e)加强与有关国际论坛的合作和协作。另见*APEC 结构性改革新战略(APEC New Strategy for Structural Reform)*、*APEC结构性改革新议程(Renewed APEC Agenda for Structural Reform)*。

Leaders' Statement to Implement APEC Transparency Standards
关于实施 APEC 透明度标准的领导人声明

见 *APEC 透明度标准原则(APEC principles on transparency standards)*。

League of Arab States
阿拉伯国家联盟

1945 年成立，由 22 个阿拉伯国家组成的松散联盟，旨在改善成员国在共同关心问题上的协调。秘书处设在开罗。另见*阿拉伯共同市场(Arab Common Market)*、*阿拉伯关税同盟(Arab Customs Union)*。

League of Nations
国际联盟

联合国的前身，作为《凡尔赛条约》的一部分于1919年成立。国联的主要目标是集体安全、国际争端仲裁、削减军备和开放外交。到20世纪30年代，人们对国联的效力产生严重怀疑，尽管它在被废除之前一直合法存在。国联有关于国际贸易的工作计划，但是在20世纪20年代末期大萧条的发生和日益恶化的

great enthusiasm to engage in joint action for the revival of international trade. The League dissolved itself on 18 April 1946.

Learning-by-doing argument: a variation of the ***infant-industry argument***. It proposes that government protection of an industry is warranted if the industry can in this way learn to be competitive. *See also* ***import substitution***.

Least-developed countries: LDCs. A group of forty-seven developing countries so designated by ***ECOSOC*** on the basis of the following indicators: per capita GNP, life expectancy at birth, per capita calorie supplies, combined primary and secondary enrolment ratio, adult literacy rate, share of manufacturing in GDP, share of employment in industry, per capita electricity consumption, and export concentration ratio. These indicators and the list of countries designated as LDCs are reviewed by ECOSOC every three years. The list currently comprises Afghanistan, Angola, Bangladesh, Benin, Bhutan, Burkina Faso, Burundi, Cambodia, Central African Republic, Chad, Comoros, Democratic Republic of the Congo, Djibouti, Eritrea, Ethiopia, Gambia, Guinea, Guinea-Bissau, Haiti, Kiribati, Lao People's Democratic Republic, Lesotho, Liberia, Madagascar, Malawi, Mali, Mauritania, Mozambique, Myanmar, Nepal, Niger, Rwanda, Sao Tome and Principe, Senegal, Sierra Leone, Solomon Islands, Somalia, South Sudan, Sudan, Timor-Leste, Togo, Tuvalu, Uganda, United Republic of Tanzania, Vanuatu, Yemen and Zambia. Some of the WTO provisions recognize the special difficulties and needs of LDCs in several ways. First, LDCs can avail themselves of ***Part IV of the GATT*** and the ***Enabling Clause*** which allow developed countries to take measures in their favour without expecting reciprocal treatment. In addition, the ministerial Decision in Favour of Least-Developed Countries taken at Marrakesh in April 1994 allows them to undertake ***commitments*** and ***concessions*** to the extent consistent with their individual development, financial and trade needs. The decision also seeks a quick implementation of tariff and non-tariff measures of interest to LDCs and improvements to the ***GSP***. LDCs also receive increased technical assistance to enable them to expand their trade. Several of the agreements administered by the WTO contain provisions concerning LDCs. For example, the ***Agreement on Trade-Related Aspects of Intellectual Property Rights*** allows LDCs ten years before they have to apply its provisions. The ***General Agreement on Trade in Services*** requires its members to take measures enabling LDCs to participate more actively in global ***services*** trade. This was supplemented in 2011 by the ***LDC services waiver***. ***UNCTAD*** publishes annually the *Least-Developed Countries Report* which deals with key developmental issues facing LDCs, their short-term outlook and prospects for growth. *See also* ***Everything But Arms***, ***food security***, ***HLM***, ***Integrated Framework for Trade-Related Technical Assistance to Least-Developed Countries***, ***Programme of Action for the Least-Developed Countries for the Decade 2011-2020*** and ***SNPA***.

Least-Developed Countries Report: published annually by ***UNCTAD***. *See* ***least-developed countries***.

国际政治形势消弭了参与复兴国际贸易联合行动的任何大的热情。国联于1946年4月18日解散。

Learning-by-doing argument

干中学理论

幼稚产业论的变体。该理论提出，政府对一行业的保护是有根据的，如果该行业能够通过此种方式学会竞争。另见*进口替代(import substitution)*。

Least-developed countries

最不发达国家

LDCs。联合国经社理事会(ECOSOC)根据以下指标指定的47个发展中国家：人均国民生产总值、出生时预期寿命、人均卡路里供应量、小学和中学综合入学率、成人识字率、制造业在国内生产总值中所占份额、工业领域就业占比、人均电力消耗量和出口集中度。ECOSOC每3年对这些指标和指定为最不发达国家的国家进行一次审议。目前名单包括阿富汗、安哥拉、孟加拉国、贝宁、不丹、布基纳法索、布隆迪、柬埔寨、中非共和国、乍得、科摩罗、刚果(金)、吉布提、厄立特里亚、埃塞俄比亚、冈比亚、几内亚、几内亚比绍、海地、基里巴斯、老挝、莱索托、利比里亚、马达加斯加、马拉维、马里、毛里塔尼亚、莫桑比克、缅甸、尼泊尔、尼日尔、卢旺达、圣多美和普林西比、塞内加尔、塞拉利昂、所罗门群岛、索马里、南苏丹、苏丹、东帝汶、多哥、图瓦卢、乌干达、坦桑尼亚、瓦努阿图、也门和赞比亚。WTO中的一些规定通过几种方式承认最不发达国家的特殊困难和需要。第一，最不发达国家可以利用GATT第四部分和授权条款，上述规定允许发达国家采取有利于最不发达国家的措施，而不期望获得互惠。此外，1994年4月在马拉喀什作出的《关于有利于最不发达国家措施的决定》使它们能够在与其各自发展、财政和贸易需要的范围内作出承诺和减让。该决定还寻求快速实施对最不发达国家具有利益的关税和非关税措施，并改善普惠制(GSP)。最不发达国家还获得了增加的技术援助，使它们能够扩大贸易。WTO管理的几项协定包含有关最不发达国家的条款。例如，《与贸易有关的知识产权协定》允许最不发达国家在10年过渡期后再实施协定条款。《服务贸易总协定》要求其成员采取措施，使最不发达国家能够更积极参与全球服务贸易。此项规定得到2011年通过的最不发达国家服务豁免的补充。联合国贸易与发展会议(UNCTAD)每年发布《最不发达国家报告》，涉及最不发达国家面临的主要发展问题、短期前景和增长前景。另见*除武器外的所有产品(Everything But Arms)*、*粮食安全(food security)*、*高级别会议(HLM)*、*针对最不发达国家的与贸易有关的技术援助综合框架(Integrated Framework for Trade-Related Technical Assistance to Least-Developed Countries)*、*2011—2020年十年期支援最不发达国家行动纲领(Programme of Action for the Least-Developed Countries for the Decade 2011-2020)*、*20世纪80年代支援最不发达国家新的实质性行动纲领(SNPA)*。

Least-Developed Countries Report

最不发达国家报告

每年由联合国贸易与发展会议(UNCTAD)发布。见*最不发达国家(Least-developed countries)*。

Least-trade-restrictive-alternative test: when a ***panel*** is set up to adjudicate in a dispute over the legality of a *trade measure,* its finding may be that the aim of the measure was legitimate. The panel may then have to consider whether the measure used was appropriate in the circumstances. A yardstick it can use is an examination of what kind of measure achieving the same aim would have the least impact on trade flows. If it finds that such a measure would have been reasonably available, it may rule against the defendant. This test differs from the ***necessity test*** which asks whether the measure was needed in the first place.

Leather: *see* ***Japanese measures on leather***.

Left-over tariffs: *see* ***residual tariffs***.

Legal persons: incorporated companies, as opposed to ***natural persons***, i.e. people. *See also* ***juridical person***.

Legitimate expectation: a doctrine used in the WTO, not defined precisely, which holds that a country should have reasonable grounds to expect that a ***market access*** commitment, once made, would not be undermined or negated through a later action. The doctrine is therefore an aspect of ***good faith***. It refers to changes in conditions which could not have been reasonably foreseen. For example, an exporting country might have a legitimate expectation that there would be no sudden change in a product standard in the importing country, but such a change was for some reason made anyway. This may result in a disruption of trade. The doctrine does not apply to changes caused by the use of ***trade remedies***. The assumption in these cases is, for example, that if ***dumping*** has been identified, the importing country may be entitled to impose ***anti-dumping measures***, and the exporting country should be aware of this. *See also* ***non-violation***. [Jung and Lee 2003]

Leontief Paradox: *see* ***new trade theory***.

Lerner's symmetry theorem: named after the economist Abba Lerner who demonstrated in 1936 that a tax on exports has the same effect on the economy as a tax on imports. [Lerner 1936]

Less-advantaged countries: a term used for countries that traditionally have not been active in international trade negotiations. It includes the ***least-developed countries***, some other developing countries and some ***economies in transition***.

Less-developed countries: a term in common use until the 1970s for what we now call ***developing countries***.

Lesser-duty principle: the principle in the administration of ***anti-dumping measures*** that additional duties imposed on products found dumped should be less than the ***margin of dumping*** if a duty less than that is enough to eliminate the ***injury***.

Less than fair value: under United States anti-dumping laws, broadly a lower export price of a product than its value on the exporter's home market. If the export price is less than the domestic price, less than fair value is deemed to exist. The difference, the ***margin of dumping***, together with material ***injury***, if that has been established, then forms part of the assessment for possible ***anti-dumping measures***.

Least-trade-restrictive-alternative test
最小贸易限制替代措施测试

当设立一专家组以裁决针对一贸易措施合法性的争端时，专家组的调查结果可能是该措施的目的是合法的，随后专家组可能必须考虑所使用的措施在当时的情况下是否适当。专家组可以使用的一项标准是审查能够实现同一目的措施中哪一种对贸易流动的影响最小。如果发现此种措施可以合理获得，就可能作出不利于被告的裁决。这一测试不同于必要性测试，后者首先要问的是该措施是否属必要。

Leather
皮革

见*日本皮革措施案(Japanese measures on leather)*。

Left-over tariffs
剩余关税

见*剩余关税(residual tariffs)*。

Legal persons
法人

法人公司，与自然人，即人相对应。另见*企业法人(juridical person)*。

Legitimate expectation
合理预期

WTO中使用的一种原则，并无明确定义，认为一国应有合理期望，即一旦作出市场准入承诺，则不会因后来的行动而受到损害或否定。因此，该原则是善意的一个方面。指无法合理预见的条件变化。例如，一出口国可能有一个合理预期，即进口国中的产品标准不会突然改变，但出于某种原因这种改变还是发生了，这可能就会导致贸易的中断。该原则不适用于因使用贸易救济而引发的变化。例如，在这些情况下的假设是，如果确定存在倾销，进口国即有权实施反倾销措施，而出口国应当意识到这一点。另见*非违反(non-violation)*。

Leontief Paradox
列昂惕夫悖论

见*新贸易理论(new trade theory)*。

Lerner's symmetry theorem
勒纳对称定理

以经济学家阿巴·勒纳命名，他在1936年证明了出口税对经济的影响与进口税对经济的影响相同。

Less-advantaged countries
弱势国家

用于指传统上在国际贸易谈判中不活跃的国家。包括最不发达国家、其他一些发展中国家和一些转型经济体。

Less-developed countries
欠发达国家

在20世纪70年代之前的常用词语，指我们现在所称的发展中国家。

Lesser-duty principle
低税原则

反倾销措施管理中的原则，即如果低于倾销幅度的关税足以消除损害，则对被认定倾销的产品所征收的额外关税应低于该幅度。

Less than fair value
低于公允价值

根据美国反倾销法，大致指一产品的出口价格低于其在出口商国内市场的价值。如果出口价格低于国内价格，则被认为存在低于公平价值的情况。该差额，即倾销幅度，连同实质损害，如已确定，则构成可能的反倾销措施的评估的一部分。

Leutwiler Report: in late 1983, about one year after the inconclusive 1982 GATT Ministerial Meeting which was seen by many as the low point in the GATT history, the Director-General of the GATT assembled a group of seven eminent people from business, government and academia, led by Dr Fritz Leutwiler, then chairman of the Swiss National Bank. The Group's task was to look at the state of the international trading system, the fundamental reasons for the difficulties it faced and to make proposals for action. The resulting report, *Trade Policies for a Better Future*, appeared in March 1985. Its fifteen recommendations influenced considerably the impetus for a new round of trade negotiations and the mandate for it. Most of them can be seen reflected in the ***Uruguay Round*** outcome, though not necessarily with the same degree of ambition. In summary, the recommendations were that (i) the making of ***trade policy*** should be brought into the open in each country, (ii) agricultural trade should be based on clearer and fairer rules, (iii) a timetable should be established to bring ***grey-area measures*** within GATT rules, (iv) trade in textiles and clothing should be fully subject to GATT rules, (v) rules on subsidies should be made more effective, (vi) the GATT codes on ***non-tariff distortions*** should be improved, (vii) the rules permitting ***free-trade areas*** and ***customs unions*** needed to be clarified and tightened up, (viii) there should be more international ***surveillance*** of trade policies and actions, (ix) emergency ***safeguard*** protection should be provided only in accordance with the rules, (x) greater emphasis should be placed on encouraging developing countries to take advantage of their competitive strength and to integrate them more fully into the trading system, (xi) the possibility of multilateral rules for ***trade in services*** should be explored, (xii) ***dispute settlement*** procedures and implementation of ***panel*** recommendations should be improved, (xiii) a new round of GATT negotiations should be launched, (xiv) a permanent Ministerial-level body should be established to encourage prompt negotiations on problems, and (xv) efforts towards satisfactory resolution of the world debt problem, adequate flows of development finance, better international coordination of macroeconomic policies and greater consistency between trade and financial policies.

Level playing field: a term used to describe ***fair trade***, with all adherents playing by the rules. There are differing views on what is meant by a level playing field. Some concede that the available trade rules do not favour one party over another in a strictly legal sense, but they are of the view that there is a tilted playing field, often said to consist of otherwise unidentified ***non-tariff measures*** and ***subsidies***. Hence, in their view, some of the players will always face an inherent up-hill struggle if they agree to play by the rules. The level playing field has therefore been used increasingly by those who favour various forms of ***protection*** to suggest that for trade to be "fair", all distortions must be removed. If that cannot be done, as is obviously the case, at least in the near future, then government intervention against imports is justified. Failing that, no further domestic ***trade liberalization*** should be undertaken until the others have mended their ways. As many commentators have pointed out, it is possible to

Leutwiler Report

路特威勒报告

1983年年末，即大约在1982年GATT部长级会议无果而终的一年后，此次会议被许多人视为是GATT历史上的低谷，GATT总干事召集了一个由来自商界、政府和学术界的7位知名人士组成的小组，由当时瑞士国家银行主席弗里茨·路特威勒博士领导。小组的任务是研究国际贸易体制的状况、所面临困难的根本原因，并提出行动建议。由此产生的报告《促进更美好未来的贸易政策》于1985年3月出台。报告中的15项建议极大地影响了新一轮贸易谈判的动力和授权。可以看到其中大多数已经反映在乌拉圭回合结果之中，尽管不一定具有相同的雄心水平。简而言之，这些建议为：(1)贸易政策制定应在每一国家中进行公开；(2)农产品贸易应基于更明确和更公平的规则；(3)应制定将灰色区域措施纳入GATT规则的时间表；(4)纺织品和服装贸易应完全遵守GATT规则；(5)补贴规则应更加有效；(6)GATT关于非关税扭曲的守则应进行改进；(7)关于自由贸易区和关税同盟的规则应予以澄清和加严；(8)应对贸易政策和行动增加国际监督；(9)紧急保障措施保护应仅依照规则提供；(10)应更加强调鼓励发展中国家利用其竞争优势和更充分纳入贸易体制；(11)应探讨制定服务贸易多边规则的可能性；(12)应改进争端解决程序和专家组建议执行；(13)应启动新一轮GATT回合谈判；(14)设立常设部长级机构以鼓励就有关问题进行迅速谈判；以及(15)努力满意地解决世界债务问题，提供充足的发展资金，更好地协调宏观经济政策以及实现贸易和金融政策的更大一致性。

Level playing field

公平竞争环境

用于描述公平贸易的词语，即所有拥护者均遵守规则。对于公平竞争环境的含义观点各有不同。有些人承认，现有贸易规则从严格法律意义上讲并未偏袒一方胜过另一方，但他们认为，存在着一个倾斜的竞争环境，通常被认为是由其他未明确的非关税措施和补贴组成。因此，在他们看来，如果一些参与者同意按规则行事，他们将常常面临一种固有的艰苦斗争。公平竞争环境越来越多地被那些偏爱各种形式保护的人所使用，以表明要使贸易“公平”，就必须消除所有扭曲。如果此点作不到，情况显然如此，那么至少在不久的将来，政府对进口的干预是合理的。如果作不到，就不应该再实施国内贸易自由化，直至其他人改过自新。正如许多评论人士所指出的，在一个经济体中有可能建

have a level playing field within an economy because everyone plays by the same rules. It is rather more difficult to achieve it when the rules of many players are involved. Apart from this, the level-playing-field concept is so loaded with individual assumptions that it is of no use as an analytical concept.

Lex posterior (derogat priori)**:** *Lat.* later law prevails over an earlier law. A rule used in the interpretation of international treaties which holds that if a country becomes a party to two treaties which have conflicting provisions, the obligations it assumes in the later accession are the ones applicable.

Lex specialis (derogat legi generali)**:** *Lat.* specific law prevails over general law. This principle applies to situations that could be dealt with under two different laws. In such cases, the courts will apply the specific law because the situation is one of many that might fall under the general law.

LIBOR: London Interbank Offered Rate. The benchmark interest rate at which major global banks lend to each other on the interbank market for short-term loans.

Life cycle assessment: LCA. A way of ascertaining the environmental effects of a product, process or service over its entire life. This includes the ultimate disposal of the product. A life cycle assessment covers the entirety of the resources consumed in the production of a good or a service, as well as the impact on the environment caused by the existence of these products. Sometimes, a life cycle assessment is also called a cradle-to-grave assessment. *See also* ***trade and environment***.

Like domestic product: *see* ***like product***.

Like or directly competitive products: a term used in Article XIX of the GATT (Emergency Action on Imports of Particular Products) and the ***Agreement on Safeguards***. Both of them permit the imposition of ***safeguards*** under defined conditions. One of these is that a product is imported in such increased quantities as to cause or threaten ***serious injury*** to domestic producers of like or directly competitive products. In WTO usage "like" is deemed to equate to "same", but "directly competitive" is much harder to define. A luxury car and a basic car are broadly speaking like products, but they are hardly directly competitive. This is one of the reasons why the ***Appellate Body*** has referred to an ***accordion of likeness***. *See also* ***directly competitive or substitutable product***.

Like product: this expression occurs in several of the agreements administered by the WTO. It is one of the standards that can be used to examine whether discrimination against the imported product has occurred. In disputes concerning the meaning of "like products", ***panels*** have been inclined to look at criteria such as international usage and accepted customs classifications. The tendency has been, however, to equate "like" with "same". This approach has been formalized in the case of ***anti-dumping measures*** where action may only be taken if the industry producing the like product has suffered material ***injury***. Under the relevant WTO rules, the term "like product" means a product which is identical, i.e. alike in all respects to the product under consideration. If such a product is not available, another product may be used which, although not alike in all respects,

立公平竞争环境，因为每个人按规则行事。当涉及许多参与者的规则时，要实现这一点就比较困难了。除此以外，公平竞争环境的概念充满了个人假设，因而作为一个分析性概念毫无用处。

Lex posterior (derogat priori)
后法原则

拉丁语。意为后法优于前法。解释国际条约时使用的一条规则，认为如果一国成为两个条约的参加方，而两个条约包含相互冲突的条款，那么该国后加入条约中的义务为适用义务。

Lex specialis (derogat legi generali)
特殊法优先原则

拉丁语。意为特殊法优先于一般法。这一原则适用于可以根据两个不同法律处理的情况。在此类情况下，法院将适用特殊法，因为此种情况是可能属于一般法的众多情况之一。

LIBOR
伦敦银行同业拆借利率

全球主要银行在同业拆借市场上相互借贷的基准利率。

Life cycle assessment
生命周期评估

LCA。一种确定产品、工序或服务在整个生命周期对环境影响的方法。包括对产品的最终处置。生命周期评估涵盖一货物或一服务的生产过程所消耗的全部资源，以及这些产品的存在对环境的影响。有时，生命周期评估也被称为从摇篮到坟墓评估。另见*贸易与环境(trade and environment)*。

Like domestic product
国内同类产品

见*同类产品(like product)*。

Like or directly competitive products
同类产品或直接竞争产品

GATT 第 19 条(对某些产品进口的紧急措施)和《保障措施协定》中使用的词语。两者均允许在规定条件下实施保障措施。其中一个条件是，一产品的进口数量如此之大以至于对同类产品或直接竞争产品的国内生产者造成或威胁造成严重损害。在 WTO 中，“同类”被视为与“相同”一词同义，而“直接竞争”则难以定义。一辆豪华轿车和一辆普通轿车从广义而言属同类产品，但它们几乎不会直接竞争。这就是上诉机构提到符合同类性的原因之一。另见*直接竞争产品或可替代产品(directly competitive or substitutable product)*。

Like product
同类产品

这一表述出现在WTO管理的若干协定中。用以审查是否发生针对进口产品的歧视的标准之一。在有关“同类产品”含义的争端中，专家组倾向于考虑诸如国际使用和公认海关分类等标准。但是，专家组倾向于将“同类”视为与“相同”同义。在反倾销措施案件中，这一方式已经正式化，只有在生产同类产品的行业遭受实质损害的情况下方可采取行动。根据WTO相关规则，“同类产品”一词指相同产品，即在各方面均相同的产品。如无此种产品，则为尽管并非在各方面均相同，但具有与考虑中的产品极为相似特点的另一产品。“巴西未焙炒咖

has characteristics closely resembling those of the product under consideration. ***Brazilian unroasted coffee*** and ***German imports of sardines*** are disputes based on the meaning of "like product". *See also* ***accordion of likeness***.

Lima Declaration on FTAAP: adopted by ***APEC*** in 2016. It dealt with the results of the comprehensive study of issues related to the proposed ***Free Trade Area of the Asia-Pacific*** which was undertaken in the wake of the ***Beijing Roadmap for APEC's Contribution to the Realization of the FTAAP***. It commissioned an examination of the contribution of current pathways to the realization of the FTAAP, among which are the ***Regional Comprehensive Economic Partnership*** and the ***Trans-Pacific Partnership Agreement***. It also asked for further analytical work on other relevant issues.

Linear country: a term used particularly during the ***Kennedy Round*** for countries disposed to make ***linear tariff cuts***.

Linear tariff cuts: also known as formula approach. These are tariff cuts of equal magnitude, usually expressed in percentage points, across whole classes of products. They were first introduced formally into ***multilateral trade negotiations*** during the ***Kennedy Round*** (1963–67), but the EEC's initial offer in the ***Dillon Round*** (1960) had already envisaged them. The main reason this method was not adopted before the Kennedy Round was the lack of United States negotiating authority for doing so. The United States rejected linear tariff cuts for the ***Uruguay Round***. *See also* ***Swiss formula*** which was used in the ***Tokyo Round*** tariff negotiations.

Lisbon Agreement: *Agreement for the Protection of Appellations of Origin and their International Registration.* Concluded in Lisbon in 1958 and revised in 1967. It provides for the protection of ***appellations of origin***. Such names are registered by ***WIPO*** upon request of the interested state. All members must protect the internationally registered name as long as it continues to be protected in the country of origin, except in the case where a member declares within one year that it cannot ensure the protection of a registered name. In 2011 this agreement was supplemented by the ***Geneva Act of the Lisbon Agreement on Appellations of Origin and Geographical Indications*** which now also allows the registration of geographical indications. *See also* ***intellectual property***.

Living agreement: an agreement that is meant to be updated periodically to keep pace with developments in trade policy and relevant technology.

Living modified organism: LMO. Defined in the Cartagena Protocol as any living organism that possesses a novel combination of genetic material obtained through the use of modern biotechnology.

LLDC: *see* ***land-locked developing countries***.

Loan rate: part of the agricultural support framework administered by the United States ***Commodity Credit Corporation***. The loan rate is the price at which the Corporation is prepared to purchase crops against which it has issued loans. It therefore acts a ***floor price***.

Local content requirements: sometimes also called mixing requirements. Governmental measures setting out certain minimum levels of locally made

啡案”和“德国沙丁鱼进口案”是基于“同类产品”含义的争端。另见*符合同类性(accordion of likeness)*。

Lima Declaration on FTAAP
亚太自由贸易区利马宣言

APEC 于 2016 年通过。宣言针对与拟议的亚太自由贸易区相关问题全面研究所产生的结果，该研究是在紧随《APEC 推动实现亚太自由贸易区北京路线图》制定之后开展的。宣言授权对实现亚太自由贸易区的当前途径的作用进行审查，其中包括《区域全面经济伙伴关系协定》和《跨太平洋伙伴关系协定》。宣言还要求对其他相关问题进行进一步分析。

Linear country
线性削减国家

特别用于肯尼迪回合期间的词语，指更倾向于进行线性关税削减的国家。

Linear tariff cuts
线性关税削减

也称公式方式。这是一种同等幅度的关税削减，通常以百分点表示，涵盖整个产品类别。最初在肯尼迪回合(1963 年至 1967 年)期间正式引入多边贸易谈判，但欧洲经济共同体在狄龙回合(1960 年)中的最初出价已经设想了此种方法。此种方法在肯尼迪回合之前未予采用的主要原因是美国缺乏这样作的谈判授权。美国在乌拉圭回合中拒绝了线性关税削减。另见东京回合关税谈判中使用的*瑞士公式(Swiss formula)*。

Lisbon Agreement
里斯本协定

《保护原产地名称及其国际注册协定》。于 1958 年在里斯本缔结，1967 年修订。规定对原产地名称进行保护。此类名称由世界知识产权组织(WIPO)应利害关系国家请求进行注册。只要国际注册的名称在原属国继续受到保护，所有成员即必须保护该名称，除非一成员在一年内宣布无法保证对已注册名称进行保护。2011 年，《原产地名称和地理标志里斯本协定日内瓦文本》对该协定进行了补充，现在还允许对地理标志予以注册。另见*知识产权(intellectual property)*。

Living agreement
活协定

规定定期更新从而与贸易政策和相关技术同步发展的协定。

Living modified organism
改性活生物体

LMO。在《卡塔赫纳议定书》中定义为任何具有凭借现代生物技术获得的遗传材料新异组合的活生物体。

LLDC
内陆发展中国家

见*内陆发展中国家(land-locked developing countries)*。

Loan rate
基准贷款价格

由美国商品信贷公司管理的农业支持框架的一部分。基准贷款价格是该公司准备购买已发放贷款的农作物的价格，因此是最低价格。

Local content requirements
当地含量要求

有时也称混合要求。规定本国生产的货物或服务之中需要包含某种最低水平

components to be incorporated in goods or services produced domestically. Minimum levels of local content may be set in the form of weight, volume, value, etc. The aims of such programmes include, among others, encouraging the development of local industry, finding an assured market for an uncompetitive industry and the promotion of regional development. All local content schemes entail a degree of ***protection*** for the suppliers of the component in question and therefore a higher cost for consumers. This is self-evident, since competitive industries have no need to search for captive markets. However, governments sometimes consider that these costs are outweighed by the prospective benefits of the programme. GATT Article III:5 (National Treatment on Internal Taxation and Regulation) prohibits internal quantitative regulations relating to the mixture, processing or use of products in specified amounts or the mandatory use of domestic products. *See also* ***Agreement on Trade-Related Investment Measures***.

Local content rules in broadcasting: such rules generally require radio and television broadcasters to use at least defined minimum amounts of locally produced materials during certain time slots. The definition of a local product may be based on any combination of the nature of the content of the material, the nationality of the production house, the producer, director and the main actors, funding sources, etc. *See also* ***audiovisual services***, ***cultural identity*** and ***trade and culture***.

Local presence: the requirement to maintain a branch office, representative office or to station people in the territory of the importing country for the purpose of selling goods and services. *See also* ***commercial presence*** and ***right of establishment***.

Locarno Agreement Establishing an International Classification for Industrial Designs: concluded in Locarno on 8 October 1968 and amended on 28 September 1979. It establishes a single classification for ***industrial designs*** which consists as of 1 January 2019 of a list of 32 classes and 237 sub-classes. It also contains an alphabetical list of goods in which industrial designs are incorporated, with an indication of the classes and sub-classes into which theses goods fall. The Agreement is administered by ***WIPO***. *See also* ***Hague System for the International Deposit of Industrial Designs***.

Locomotive effect: the impetus given by economic growth in large economies to economic development in smaller economies.

Log-rolling: an American expression for helping each other out in the political arena, with the implication that this may be done at the expense of someone else. Also known as trading of votes. [Dam 2001 and many others]

Lomé Convention: the umbrella agreement, first signed in 1975 as the successor to the ***Yaoundé Convention*** and last renegotiated in 1990 for ten years (Lomé-IV), for a type of association by seventy-one African, Caribbean and Pacific (ACP) states with the ***European Economic Community*** (EEC), now the ***European Union***. Associated countries receive tariff-free access to the EEC for nearly all products, and significant aid flows. They also had access to two ***export earnings guarantee schemes*** offering concessional loans if their export

的当地成分的政府措施。当地含量的最低水平可以按重量、体积、价值等形式设定。此类计划的目的包括鼓励当地产业发展，为缺乏竞争力的产业找到有保障的市场以及促进区域发展。所有当地含量计划均意味着对所涉部件供应商一定程度的保护，因此意味着消费者要付出更高成本。这是不言而喻的，因为有竞争力的产业没有必要寻找垄断市场。但是，政府有时认为有关计划的预期利益超过了这些成本。GATT第3条第5款(国内税收和国内法规的国民待遇)禁止实行与特定数量产品的混合、加工或使用有关的国内数量法规或强制使用国产品。*另见与贸易有关的投资措施协定(Agreement on Trade-Related Investment Measures)*。

Local content rules in broadcasting

广播中的本地内容规则

此类规则通常要求广播和电视广播公司在特定时段内至少使用规定最低数量的本地制作的节目。本地产品的定义可以基于节目内容的性质、制作公司、制片人、导演及主要演员的国籍以及资金来源等的任何组合。*另见视听服务(audiovisual services)*、*文化特性(cultural identity)*、*贸易与文化(trade and culture)*。

Local presence

当地存在

关于为销售货物和服务而在进口国领土内设立分支机构、代表处或派驻人员的要求。*另见商业存在(commercial presence)*、*设立权(right of establishment)*。

Locarno Agreement Establishing an International Classification for Industrial Designs

建立工业品外观设计国际分类洛迦诺协定

1968年10月8日在洛迦诺缔结，1979年9月28日修正。协定为工业品外观设计建立了一个单一分类，截至2019年1月1日，该分类包含32个大类和237个小类。还包含一个按字母顺序排列的包含工业品外观设计货物的清单，同时注明这些货物所属大类和小类。协定由世界知识产权组织(WIPO)管理。*另见工业品外观设计国际注册海牙体系(Hague System for the International Deposit of Industrial Designs)*。

Locomotive effect

火车头效应

大经济体的经济增长对较小经济体经济发展的推动作用。

Log-rolling

滚木

美国对于在政治舞台上互相帮助的表述，暗示这样作可能要以牺牲他人为代价。也称选票交易。

Lomé Convention

洛美公约

伞状协定，最初作为《雅温得公约》的后继协定于 1975 年签署，最后一次重新谈判是在 1990 年，为期 10 年(第四个《洛美协定》)，作为由 71 个非洲、加勒比和太平洋国家与欧洲经济共同体(EEC，现欧盟)之间建立的一种联盟。联系国获得几乎所有产品对欧共体免关税准入及大量援助。如果它们的出口收入遭受严重突然下降，还可以使用两个出口收入担保方案，方案提供优惠

earnings suffered a serious and sudden decline. These were ***STABEX*** and ***SYSMIN***. The EEC did not have tariff-free access to the ***ACP states***. The Lomé Convention has been superseded by the ***ACP-EU Partnership Agreement***.

London Guidelines for the Exchange of Information on Chemicals in International Trade: adopted on 25 May 1989 under ***UN Environment Programme*** (UNEP). The guidelines aim to enhance the sound management of chemicals through the exchange of scientific, technical, economic and legal information, including the use of the ***prior-informed-consent*** principle. There are special provisions for banned or severely restricted chemicals in international trade. *See also* ***trade and environment***.

London Interbank Offered Rate: *see* ***LIBOR***.

Long-Term Arrangement Regarding International Trade in Cotton Textiles: LTA. An arrangement in the GATT for ***managed trade*** in cotton textiles and clothing which entered into force in 1962 for five years as the successor to the ***Short-Term Arrangement Regarding International Trade in Cotton Textiles***. It was extended for another three years as part of the ***Kennedy Round*** outcome. After a further extension in 1970, the arrangement was replaced in 1973 by the ***Multi-Fibre Arrangement***. *See also* ***Agreement on Textiles and Clothing*** which brought trade in textiles and clothing again under the normal multilateral trade rules on 1 January 2005.

Lower-middle-income economies: a group of forty-seven economies classified as such by the ***World Bank*** as having had in July 2018 a per capita GNI (gross national income) ranging from $1,026 to $3,995. *See also* ***high-income economies***, ***low-income economies*** and ***upper-middle-income economies***.

Low-income economies: a group of thirty-one economies so classified by the ***World Bank*** as having had in 2018 a per capita GNI (gross national income) of $1,025 or less. The group includes many of the ***least-developed countries***. *See also* ***high-income economies***, ***lower-middle-income economies*** and ***upper-middle-income economies***.

Low-income economies in transition: in the WTO negotiations this group consists of Armenia, Kyrgyz Republic and Moldova, but in agriculture Georgia is also part of it. The group seeks to achieve the treatment accorded to ***least-developed countries***.

Luxembourg Compromise: the resolution in January 1966 of a crisis within the ***European Economic Community*** which had held up negotiations in the ***Kennedy Round*** for about six months. It had as its immediate cause the failure of France and Germany to agree on how the ***common agricultural policy*** should be financed. The larger issue, however, appears to have been France's intention to seek a change in the envisaged transition from unanimous decisions to majority voting which would have undermined its ability to use its veto power. The compromise consisted of agreement to disagree on the voting question and to agree that agricultural pricing would be looked at again in the context of the Kennedy Round agricultural negotiations.

贷款。这两个计划是出口收入稳定机制(STABEX)和矿产生产及出口促进制度(SYSMIN)。欧共体没有获得对非加太地区国家的免关税准入。《洛美协定》已被《非加太地区国家与欧盟伙伴关系协定》所取代。

London Guidelines for the Exchange of Information on Chemicals in International Trade

关于化学品国际贸易资料交换的伦敦准则

1989 年 5 月 25 日在联合国环境规划署(UNEP)下通过。准则旨在通过科学、技术、经济和法律信息交流，加强对化学品的健全管理，包括使用事先知情同意原则。对于国际贸易中被禁止或严格限制的化学品有特殊规定。另见*贸易与环境(trade and environment)*。

London Interbank Offered Rate

伦敦银行同业拆借利率

见*伦敦银行同业拆借利率(LIBOR)*。

Long-Term Arrangement Regarding International Trade in Cotton Textiles

国际棉纺织品贸易长期安排

LTA。GATT 中关于棉纺织品和服装受管制的贸易的安排，作为《国际棉纺织品贸易短期安排》的后继安排，于 1962 年生效，为期 5 年。作为肯尼迪回合成果的一部分，该安排又延长 3 年。在 1970 年进一步延长后，该安排于 1973 年被《多种纤维协定》所取代。另见*纺织品与服装协定(Agreement on Textiles and Clothing)*，该协定于 2005 年 1 月 1 日将纺织品和服装贸易重新纳入正常多边贸易规则。

Lower-middle-income economies

中等偏下收入经济体

由世界银行如此分类的 47 个经济体组成的国家组，分类标准为 2018 年 7 月的人均国民总收入(GNI)在 1,026 美元至 3,995 美元之间。另见*高收入经济体(high-income economies)*、*低收入经济体(low-income economies)*、*中等偏上收入经济体(upper-middle-income economies)*。

Low-income economies

低收入经济体

由世界银行如此分类的 31 个经济体组成的国家组，分类标准为 2018 年的人均国民总收入(GNI)为 1,025 美元或以下。该国家组中包括许多最不发达国家。另见*高收入经济体(high-income economies)*、*中等偏下收入经济体(lower-middle-income economies)*、*中等偏上收入经济体(upper-middle-income economies)*。

Low-income economies in transition

低收入转型经济体

在 WTO 谈判中，这一成员组包括亚美尼亚、吉尔吉斯斯坦和摩尔多瓦，但在农业方面，格鲁吉亚也是其中一员。该成员组寻求实现给予最不发达国家的待遇。

Luxembourg Compromise

卢森堡妥协方案

1966年1月对欧洲经济共同体内部危机的解决方案，这场危机使肯尼迪回合谈判停顿了大约6个月。危机的直接原因是法国和德国未能就共同农业政策的融资方式达成一致。但是更大的问题似乎是法国有意寻求改变从一致决定向多数表决过渡的设想，因为这将削弱法国使用否决权的能力。妥协的结果是同意在表决问题上可以存在分歧、同意对于农产品定价问题在肯尼迪回合农业谈判背景下进行再次审视。

Made in China 2025: a plan issued by China in 2015 intended to increase the domestic market share of Chinese suppliers for "basic core components and important basic materials" to 70 per cent by 2025. Key sectors are next-generation information technology, high-end numerical control tools and robotics, aerospace equipment, ocean engineering equipment and high-end ships, advanced railway equipment, agricultural machinery, new materials, and biomedicine and high-performance medical devices.

Made-to-measure tariffs: describes ***tariffs*** that are just high enough to allow domestic producers to cover their costs plus normal profits. Because industries have differing cost structures, this results in a complicated tariff structure as each industry receives tariff support apparently made to measure. Some call them tailor-made tariffs.

Madrid Agreement Concerning the International Registration of Marks: concluded on 14 April 1891 and last revised in Stockholm on 14 July 1967. The Agreement was supplemented in 1989 by the *Protocol Relating the Madrid Agreement* which entered into force on 1 April 1996. Together they constitute the Madrid Union. The Agreement and the Protocol are separate treaties, and membership of one is possible independent of the other. The Agreement enables nationals of member countries to secure international protection for their marks applicable to goods and services registered in the country of origin by filing them with the ***International Bureau of Intellectual Property*** of ***WIPO***. This saves them the expense and the effort of registering in each market separately. The Protocol aims to make this system acceptable to more countries.

Madrid Agreement for the Repression of False or Deceptive Indications of Source on Goods: concluded in Madrid on 14 April 1891 and revised several times, the last in 1967. It is administered by ***WIPO***. The Agreement provides for the cases and the manner in which seizure may be requested and effected for goods bearing a false or deceptive indication of source. It prohibits the use of all publicity indications capable of deceiving the public as to the source of the goods. Each member state may decide what appellations, because of their generic character, are not covered by the Agreement, except for "regional appellations concerning the source of products of the vine". *See also* ***appellations of origin***, ***Geneva Act of the Lisbon Agreement on Appellations of Origin and Geographical Indications***, ***geographical indications***, ***indications of source*** and ***Lisbon Agreement***.

M

Made in China 2025
中国制造2025

中国在2015年发布的一项计划，旨在到2025年将“核心基础零部件和关键基础材料”的中国供应商在国内市场的份额提高到70%。主要领域包括新一代信息技术、高档数控机床和机器人、航空航天装备、海洋工程装备及高技术船舶、先进轨道交通装备、农机装备、新材料、生物医药及高性能医疗器械。

Made-to-measure tariffs
定制关税

指关税刚好高到足以使国内生产商涵盖其成本加正常利润。由于产业成本结构各有不同，由此导致复杂的关税结构，因为每一产业都明显得到了定制关税的支持。有些人称之为特制关税。

Madrid Agreement Concerning the International Registration of Marks
商标国际注册马德里协定

1891年4月14日缔结，1967年7月14日在斯德哥尔摩进行最近一次修订。1989年协定得到1996年4月1日生效的《马德里协定有关议定书》的补充，共同组成了马德里联盟。协定和议定书是独立的条约，其中一个协定或议定书的成员资格可以独立于另一个。协定使成员国的国民能够通过向世界知识产权组织(WIPO)知识产权国际局提交申请，获得对其适用于在原属国注册的商品和服务商标的国际保护，省去了在每一市场单独注册的费用和精力。议定书旨在使这一制度为更多国家所接受。

Madrid Agreement for the Repression of False or Deceptive Indications of Source on Goods
制止商品来源虚假或欺骗性标记马德里协定

1891 年 4 月 14 日在马德里缔结，经多次修订，最近一次是在 1967 年。协定由世界知识产权组织(WIPO)管理。协定规定了可以要求对带有虚假或欺骗性来源标记的货物予以没收的情况和方式。协定禁止使用可能欺骗公众的有关货物来源的所有宣传标志。每一成员国可以决定哪些名称因其通用性质而不适用协定条款，但“关于葡萄产品地区性产品名称”除外。另见*原产地名称(appellations of origin)*、*原产地名称和地理标志里斯本协定日内瓦文本(Geneva Act of the Lisbon Agreement on Appellations of Origin and Geographical Indications)*、*里斯本协定(Lisbon Agreement)*。

Madrid Protocol: *see* ***Madrid Agreement Concerning the International Registration of Marks***.

Madrid Union: *see* ***Madrid Agreement Concerning the International Registration of Marks***.

Maghreb region: this usually refers to Algeria, Libya, Mauritania, Morocco, Tunisia and the Western Sahara. *See also* ***Arab Maghreb Union***.

Mailbox: refers to a requirement of the ***Agreement on Trade-Related Aspects of Intellectual Property Rights*** applying to WTO members which do not yet provide product patent production for pharmaceuticals and for agricultural chemicals. Since 1 January 1995, when the WTO agreements entered into force, these countries have had to establish a means by which applications of patents for these products can be filed. They must also put in place a system for granting ***exclusive marketing rights*** for the products whose patent applications have been filed.

Mala fides**:** *Lat.* bad faith, often met as *mala fide* (in bad faith). Taking on an obligation without meaning to keep it. More or less the opposite of ***good faith***.

Malevolent mercantilism: *see* ***mercantilism***.

Managed liberalism: used by some to describe the practice by existing members of ***free-trade agreements*** of exempting particular sectors from the operations of the agreement, particularly when new members accede to it. *See also* ***block exemptions***.

Managed mutual recognition: postulated by Kalypso Nicolaïdis as the process adopted by the ***European Community*** to achieve mutual recognition of qualification, licensing and certification requirements. The proposition is that managed mutual recognition does not require extensive prior harmonization of qualifications across borders. Rather, it accepts that there are differences in the way professions are regulated, and it deals with these differences flexibly. *See also* ***harmonization of standards and qualifications***. [Nicolaïdis 1997]

Managed trade: international trade in which some sectors or products are not traded according to the demands of market forces. Means for this include ***voluntary restraint arrangements***, ***orderly marketing arrangements***, ***quantitative restrictions*** and other ***non-tariff measures***. The aim of managed trade in these cases always is to protect domestic industry. More modern versions of managed trade seek not to restrict access, but to increase exports through numerical targets, usually at the expense of third-country exporters. *See also* ***fair trade***, ***grey-area measures***, ***Multi-Fibre Arrangement*** and ***voluntary import expansion***.

Managed trade liberalization: *see* ***managed liberalism***.

Mandatory but not compulsory: a description of the status of retaliatory action under ***Super 301***, used during congressional hearings in 1988 on the ***Omnibus Trade and Competitiveness Act***. Its meaning was clear to those involved.

Mandatory/discretionary distinction: *see* ***GATT-consistency of national legislation***.

Manila Action Plan for APEC: the work programme adopted at the November 1996 ***APEC*** leaders' meeting in Manila. It integrates the ***APEC individual***

Madrid Protocol
马德里议定书
见*商标国际注册马德里协定(Madrid Agreement Concerning the International Registration of Marks)*。

Madrid Union
马德里联盟
见*商标国际注册马德里协定(Madrid Agreement Concerning the International Registration of Marks)*。

Maghreb region
马格里布地区
通常指阿尔及利亚、利比亚、毛里塔尼亚、摩洛哥、突尼斯和西撒哈拉。另见*阿拉伯马格里布联盟(Arab Maghreb Union)*。

Mailbox
邮箱
指《与贸易有关的知识产权协定》的一项要求，适用于尚未为药品和农用化学品提供产品专利生产的WTO成员。自1995年1月1日《WTO协定》生效以来，这些国家必须设立一种手段，据此可以提出这些产品的专利申请。它们还必须建立授予已提交专利申请产品专有销售权的制度。

Mala fides
恶意
拉丁语。意为背信弃义，经常被认为是恶意的(背信弃义)。承担义务而无意遵守义务。或多或少与善意的意思相反。

Malevolent mercantilism
恶意重商主义
见*重商主义(mercantilism)*。

Managed liberalism
有管理的自由主义
一些人用于描述自由贸易协定的现有成员对特定部门免于运用协定的做法，特别是在新成员加入协定的情况下。另见*集体豁免(block exemptions)*。

Managed mutual recognition
托管互认
由卡利普索·尼古拉迪斯假设的欧洲共同体采用的实现相互承认资格认可、许可和认证要求的程序。建议为，托管互认并不要求对资格进行跨越国界的广泛事先协调，而是接受职业规范方面存在的差异，且灵活处理这些差异。另见*标准和资格的协调(harmonization of standards and qualifications)*。

Managed trade
受管制的贸易
一些部门或产品的国际贸易不按照市场力量的要求进行交易。这方面的手段包括自愿限制安排、有序销售安排、数量限制和其他非关税措施。在这些情况下，受管制的贸易的目的总是保护国内产业。受管制的贸易的更现代版本不是限制准入，而是通过数字目标增加出口，通常是以第三国出口商为代价。另见*公平贸易(fair trade)*、*灰色区域措施(grey-area measures)*、*多种纤维协定(Multi-Fibre Arrangement)*、*自愿扩大进口(voluntary import expansion)*。

Managed trade liberalization
有管理的贸易自由化
见*有管理的自由主义(managed liberalism)*。

Mandatory but not compulsory
法定但非强制
对超级301条款项下报复行动地位的描述，在关于1988年《综合贸易与竞争法》的国会听证会上中使用。其含义对所涉及人员是清楚的。

Mandatory/discretionary distinction
强制/自由裁量区别
见*国家立法与GATT一致性(GATT-consistency of national legislation)*。

Manila Action Plan for APEC
APEC马尼拉行动计划
1996年11月在马尼拉举行的APEC领导人会议上通过的工作方案。工作方

action plans, ***Collective Action Plans*** and the work programmes prepared by the various bodies established within APEC.

Mano River Union: a preferential trade area established in 1973. It consists of Côte d'Ivoire, Guinea, Liberia and Sierra Leone. Its secretariat is in Freetown, Sierra Leone. *See also* ***Economic Community of West African States***.

Mansholt proposals: two proposals named after Sicco Mansholt, ***European Economic Community*** Commissioner for Agriculture during the ***Kennedy Round***. The first was concerned with establishing a common EEC pricing regime for cereals. Member states whose prices were lowered through the proposed harmonization were to be compensated by direct EEC payments. The second proposal formed the outline of the EEC offer on agriculture for the Round. In essence, it offered to bind the ***montant de soutien*** (level of internal support) for three years on the basis of reciprocity. The EEC was able to reach internal agreement on the first proposal, but its negotiating partners in the Round remained unconvinced of the merits of the second. *See also* ***agriculture and the multilateral trading system***.

Manual on Statistics of International Trade in Services: published in 2010 by the ***Inter-Agency Taskforce on Statistics of International Trade in Services***. It arose from a need to provide better statistics on trade in services following the entry into force of the ***General Agreement on Trade in Services***, but it also meets many other needs, for example, by building on the sixth edition of the ***IMF Balance of Payments Manual***. *See* ***trade in services statistics***. [unstats.un.org]

Manufacturer's Certificate of Origin: MCO. A certificate or statement specifying the ***country of origin*** of a product. It may be required for the assessment of a tariff at the border, but other governmental agencies may also wish to see for one purpose or another. *See also* ***certificate of origin.***

Manufacturer's Statement of Origin: MSO. *See* ***Manufacturer's Certificate of Origin***.

Manufacturing Clause**:** a dispute brought before the GATT in 1983 by the ***European Communities***. The facts were that Section 601 (the *Manufacturing Clause*) of United States Public Law 97–215 of 1982 prohibited, with certain exceptions, the import into the United States or public distribution there of a work under ***copyright*** consisting mainly of non-dramatic material unless the material had been manufactured in the United States or Canada. The definition of "manufacture" included typesetting, printing and binding. The *Manufacturing Clause* had originally been enacted in 1891 and amended several times. The 1976 amendment included a ***sunset clause*** applicable before 1 July 1982. The Act expired and was re-enacted on 13 July 1982 with 1986 as the new expiry date. The main interest in this case was in whether the amended Act was covered by the Protocol of Provisional Accession. This protocol allowed GATT members to retain legislation not fully consistent with GATT rules if it was in force on 30 October 1947. The ***panel*** held that legislative changes to the *Manufacturing Clause* did not necessarily disqualify it as "existing legislation".

案整合了APEC单边行动计划、集体行动计划和APEC内设立的各机构制定的工作方案。

Mano River Union

马诺河联盟

1973年建立的优惠贸易区。由科特迪瓦、几内亚、利比里亚和塞拉利昂组成。秘书处设在塞拉利昂弗里敦。另见*西非国家经济共同体(Economic Community of West African States)*。

Mansholt proposals

曼索托建议

以肯尼迪回合期间欧洲经济共同体农业委员西科·曼索托命名的两个提案。第一个提案关于建立欧共体谷物共同定价制度。价格因拟议的协调被降低的成员国将得到欧共体直接支付的补偿。第二个提案构成了欧共体在该轮回合中农业出价的概要。实质上，提案提出在互惠基础上将支持幅度约束3年。欧共体能够就第一个提案达成内部协议，但是欧共体在该回合的谈判伙伴不相信第二个提案的好处。另见*农业与多边贸易体制(agriculture and the multilateral trading system)*。

Manual on Statistics of International Trade in Services

国际服务贸易统计手册

由国际服务贸易统计机构间特别工作组于2010年出版。因《服务贸易总协定》生效后提供更好服务贸易统计数据的需要而产生，但是也满足了其他许多需要，例如，用于编写国际货币基金组织(IMF)《国际收支手册》第6版。另见*服务贸易统计(trade in services statistics)*。

Manufacturer's Certificate of Origin

制造商原产地证书

MCO。列出一产品原产地的证书或声明。在边境评估关税时可能需要这一证书，但其他政府机构也可能出于这样或那样的目的而想看到这一证书。另见*原产地证书(certificate of origin)*。

Manufacturer's Statement of Origin

制造商原产地声明

MSO。见*制造商原产地证书(Manufacturer's Certificate of Origin)*。

Manufacturing Clause

制造条款案

欧洲共同体1983年向GATT提起的争端。实际情况是，1982年美国97-215公法第601节(制造条款)，除某些例外情况，禁止将主要由非戏剧节目构成的版权作品进口至美国或在美国公开发行，除非节目是在美国或加拿大制造的。“制造”的定义包括排版、印刷和装订。制造条款最初是在1891年颁布的，并经多次修正。1976年的修正包括1982年7月1日之前适用的日落条款。该法到期后，于1982年7月13日重新颁布，1986年为新的到期日。这一案件中的主要关注点是修正后的法案是否为《临时适用议定书》所涵盖。该议定书允许GATT缔约方保留与GATT规则不完全一致的立法，如果这些立法在1947年10月30日已生效。专家组认为，对制造条款立法的修改并不一定使其失去“已存在的立法”的

It considered, however, that the insertion of the sunset clause in the 1976 Act constituted a policy change representing a move towards greater GATT conformity. The re-enactment in 1982 postponing the expiry date was a reversal of the move towards greater conformity and therefore an increase in the degree of inconsistency with the GATT. The panel accordingly found in favour of the European Communities on this point. [GATT BISD 31S]

Manufacturing Related Services Action Plan: MASP. A plan adopted by ***APEC*** in 2015 to increase availability and accessibility of services through progressive liberalization and facilitation of manufacturing-related services. The plan includes pre-manufacturing services, such as research, consulting and design, and post-manufacturing services, such as advertising, marketing and repair.

Maputo Declaration: *see* ***Arusha Declaration***.

Maquiladora* industries:** Mexican production facilities engaged in processing or secondary assembly of imported components for re-export, primarily to the United States. The *maquiladora* programme was created in the late 1960s by Mexico to alleviate economic and social problems. Materials could be imported free of tariffs if they were re-exported. Article 303 of ***NAFTA has changed the *maquiladora* programme substantially. This article prohibits the refunding, waiving or reducing the amount of customs duties on goods imported into the territory of a party, if a condition is that the product is exported to another party or used in the production of a good to be exported to another party.

Marginalization: putting people on the sidelines where they don't matter or can't influence things. It is an expression favoured by ***UNCTAD***, among others, to describe what it considers a complex phenomenon existing on two levels. First, it can be seen as a social condition referring to disadvantaged groups within individual societies. Second, it can be an economic phenomenon affecting entire countries and jeopardizing their economic and development prospects. Countries affected in this way may find it difficult to reap the benefits of increasing integration. Marginalization is often regarded as a process occurring alongside ***globalization***. *See also* ***core–periphery thesis***.

Margin of dumping: a key concept in ***dumping*** enquiries which determines the extent to which ***anti-dumping measures*** may be imposed. The margin of dumping is the difference between the assessment by the relevant authority of what should be considered ***normal value*** and the export price of the product exported from one country to another. Procedures to be followed in ascertaining the margin of dumping are set out in the WTO ***Anti-Dumping Agreement***. The authorities may only impose anti-dumping measures to the extent necessary to cover the margin of dumping. *See also* ***de minimis dumping margins*** and ***lesser-duty principle***.

Margin of preference: the difference between the duty that would be paid under some kind of ***preferential trade arrangement*** and the duty payable on a most-favoured-nation (MFN) basis.

Maritime transport services: in 1995 the ***Council for Trade in Services*** established a Negotiating Group on Maritime Transport Services (NGMTS) with the

资格。但是，专家组认为，在1976年法案中加入日落条款构成了一项政策变化，代表着朝更符合GATT的方向迈出了一步。1982年重新颁布推迟到期日的法律，是朝着更符合GATT的方向的逆转，因此增加了与GATT不一致的程度。因此，专家组在这一点上支持欧共体。

Manufacturing Related Services Action Plan

制造业相关服务行动计划

MASP。APEC2015年通过的计划，旨在通过逐步开放和便利与制造业相关的服务，增加服务的可获性和可及性。该计划包括制造前服务，例如研究、咨询和设计，以及制造后服务，例如广告、营销和修理。

Maputo Declaration

马普托宣言

见*阿鲁沙宣言(Arusha Declaration)*。

***Maquiladora* industries**

保税加工出口产业

墨西哥生产设施，从事供复出口的进口零部件的加工或二次组装，主要出口至美国。保税加工出口计划是墨西哥在20世纪60年代末为缓解经济和社会问题而设立的。如果材料用于复出口即可免关税进口。《北美自由贸易协定》(NAFTA)第303条对这一计划进行了实质修改。该条禁止退还、免除或减少进口至一参加方领土内的货物的关税，如进口条件是该产品出口至另一参加方或用于将出口至另一参加方的货物的生产过程中。

Marginalization

边缘化

将人们置于无关紧要或无法影响事情的边线。是联合国贸易与发展会议(UNCTAD)等机构偏爱的表述，用于描述其认为存在于两个层面上的复杂现象：一是可以被视为一种社会状况，指个体社会中的弱势群体。二是可以是影响整个国家和危及其经济和发展前景的经济现象。以此方式受到影响的国家可能会发现很难获得日益一体化的好处。边缘化通常被认为是伴随全球化发生的一个过程。另见*核心-外围理论(core–periphery thesis)*。

Margin of dumping

倾销幅度

倾销调查中的关键概念，决定可能实施反倾销措施的程度。倾销幅度是相关主管机关对应被视为正常价值的判定与产品自一国出口至另一国的出口价格之间的差额。WTO《反倾销协定》规定了确定倾销幅度应遵循的程序。主管机关只能在涵盖倾销幅度的必要限度内实施反倾销措施。另见*微量倾销幅度(de minimis dumping margins)*、*低税原则(lesser-duty principle)*。

Margin of preference

优惠幅度

根据某种优惠贸易安排支付的关税与根据最惠国待遇应付的关税之间的差额。

Maritime transport services

海运服务

服务贸易理事会在 1995 年设立海运服务谈判组(NGMTS)，目的在于增加《服

aim of increasing commitments under the ***General Agreement on Trade in Services*** (GATS) in international shipping, auxiliary services and access to, and use of, ports. The NGMTS was intended to conclude its negotiations by 30 June 1996, but it proved impossible to arrive at an agreed result. Negotiations on maritime transport services resumed in 2000 as part of the new round of services negotiations mandated by Article XIX of the GATS. *See also* ***cabotage***, ***Doha Development Agenda***, ***Jones Act*** and ***progressive liberalization***.

Market access: one of the basic concepts in international trade. It describes the extent to which an imported good or service can compete in another market with goods or services made there. In the WTO framework it is a legalistic term outlining the government-imposed conditions under which a product may enter a country under non-discriminatory conditions. Market access in the WTO sense is expressed through border measures, i.e. ***tariffs*** and ***non-tariff measures***, in the case of goods, and regulations inside the market in the case of ***services***. Traditionally, multilateral ***trade policy*** has sought to make market access predictable and, preferably, more liberal. This is done through the reduction of tariffs and "binding" them at the lower level. A ***binding*** is a contractual obligation not to raise the tariff above the levels specified in the ***schedules of concessions***. The removal of market access impediments in the form of non-tariff measures is more complex since some of them may escape precise legal definition. The rapid growth of ***trade in services*** and the process of ***globalization*** have drawn attention to market access impediments inside the border. Of the WTO agreements, the ***General Agreement on Trade in Services*** has gone furthest in seeking to deal with trade-restrictive regulatory measures, but other instruments, such as the ***Agreement on Subsidies and Countervailing Measures*** have also extended the reach of trade rules into the domestic domain. The coverage of these rules is, however, patchy, and there have been calls for the insertion of ***competition policy*** into the WTO system. In competition frameworks, market access is described as the ability to compete effectively in a market. Its aim is the regulation or removal of anti-competitive private ***conduct*** and ***regulation***. A merging of these two market access concepts, if it turned out to be feasible, could make a powerful contribution to the furthering of the ***international contestability of markets***. Access for ***foreign direct investment*** can also influence market access. One school of thought holds that market access is too limiting a concept, and that it should be replaced by the more embracing concept of ***market presence***. *See also* ***equality of competitive opportunity***, ***market access for agriculture***, ***market access for services***, ***most-favoured-nation treatment*** and ***national treatment***.

Market access for agriculture: an omnibus term covering the ***tariffs***, ***tariff quotas*** and various non-tariff measures impacting imports of agricultural goods. Market access is one of the three key pillars of the Agreement on Agriculture along with ***domestic support*** and ***export competition***, as a result of the Uruguay Round negotiations on agriculture. The Uruguay Round outcome restricted the expansion of trade-distorting measures and maintained or

务贸易总协定》项下关于国际航运、附属服务以及港口设施的进入和使用的承诺。NGMTS 原计划在 1996 年 6 月 30 日前完成谈判，但事实证明不可能达成议定结果。关于海运服务的谈判于 2000 年恢复，作为《服务贸易总协定》第 19 条授权的新一轮服务贸易谈判的一部分。另见*国内交通运输权(cabotage)*、*多哈发展议程(Doha Development Agenda)*、*琼斯法案(Jones Act)*、*逐步自由化(progressive liberalization)*。

Market access

市场准入

国际贸易的基本概念。描述一进口货物或服务在另一市场上与当地生产的货物或服务竞争的程度。在 WTO 框架内，是一个法律术语，概述政府规定的一产品在非歧视条件下进入一国的条件。WTO 意义上的市场准入是通过边境措施表示的，即对于货物为关税和非关税措施，对于服务为市场内部的规制。传统上，多边贸易政策寻求使市场准入可预测，且最好是更自由。此点通过降低关税并将其约束在较低水平上加以实现。约束是不得将关税提高至超过减让表中规定水平的一种契约义务。消除非关税措施形式的市场准入障碍则更为复杂，因为其中一些可能无法进行精确的法律定义。服务贸易的快速增长和全球化进程引起了人们对边境内市场准入障碍的关注。在 WTO 协定中，《服务贸易总协定》在寻求处理限制贸易的管制措施方面走得最远，但《补贴与反补贴措施协定》等其他文件也将贸易规则的范围扩大到国内领域。但是，这些规则的覆盖范围并不完整，有人呼吁将竞争政策纳入 WTO 体系。在竞争框架中，市场准入被描述为在市场中有效竞争的能力，其目的是规范或消除反竞争的私人行为和管制。这两个市场准入概念的合并，如果证明是可行的，可以对促进市场的国际竞争性作出有力贡献。外国直接投资准入也会影响市场准入。有一种观点认为，市场准入是一个过于狭隘的概念，应该被更具包容性的市场存在的概念所取代。另见*竞争机会平等(equality of competitive opportunity)*、*农产品市场准入(market access for agriculture)*、*服务市场准入(market access for services)*、*最惠国待遇(most-favoured-nation treatment)*、*国民待遇(national treatment)*。

Market access for agriculture

农产品市场准入

涵盖关税、关税配额和影响农产品进口的各种非关税措施的综合词语。作为乌拉圭回合农业谈判的结果，市场准入与国内支持和出口竞争一起成为《农业协定》的三大支柱。乌拉圭回合的结果限制了贸易扭曲措施的扩大，并维持

opened new access to markets for agricultural products. *See also* ***agriculture and the multilateral trading system*** and ***three pillars of agriculture***.

Market access for services: the ***General Agreement on Trade in Services*** promotes the goal of open and non-discriminatory market access for services and their suppliers. It does not define market access, but in Article XVI it lists six types of measures which must not be maintained or adopted for sectors listed in a country's ***schedule of specific commitments on services***. Broadly, they are (i) limitations on the number of service suppliers, (ii) limitations on the total value of service transactions, (iii) limitations on the total number of service operations, (iv) limitations on the number of persons that may be employed, (v) entity restrictions or joint-venture requirements, and (vi) limitations on the level of foreign equity. ***Economics needs tests*** governing market access are to be eliminated.

Market disruption: one of the justifications used for the imposition of ***safeguards*** measures. Such situations are said to occur when an increasing flow of imports puts serious strain on the ability of domestic producers to stay in business. In the textile trade, market disruption emerged as a key concept in the ***Long-Term Arrangement Regarding International Trade in Cotton Textiles*** where it referred to any sudden large flow of very low-priced imports from one or more trading partners. This concept was carried forward into the ***Multi-Fibre Arrangement***. *See also* ***Transitional Product-Specific Safeguard Mechanism***.

Market dominance: the rationale in many countries for creating the need for ***competition policy***. Market dominance is the ability of a firm to influence the behaviour of other firms, either upstream or downstream. In most cases, competition policy accepts the existence of market dominance, but is concerned with eliminating its abuse. *See also* ***antitrust laws*** and ***market power***.

Market economy: an economy in which the price mechanism determines what is produced and traded, though too often price signals are distorted by ***subsidies***, ***industry policy*** and other types of government intervention. *See also* ***centrally-planned economies*** and ***non-market economies***.

Market-expansion dumping: *see* ***dumping***.

Market failure: an economist's term for imperfectly functioning markets. It does not mean that the market has collapsed. Market failure can occur when participants in the market are insufficiently informed, when there are few buyers or few sellers (***monopoly*** or ***monopsony*** conditions) or when the costs and benefits of producing a product are of relevance to some market participants only.

Marketing boards: private or public bodies sometimes established by producer countries to promote, market and export agricultural commodities. Their functions may include the funding of research for more efficient production and storage, processing and identifying new uses. Marketing boards sometimes have a statutory monopoly on exports. Their administration is often funded through levies on producers. *See also* ***single-desk selling*** and ***state trading***.

Market-led integration: regional economic integration occurring through or promoted by business activities. This may happen without an intergovernmental framework for integration. *See also* ***policy-led integration***.

或开放新的农产品市场准入。另见*农业与多边贸易体制(agriculture and the multilateral trading system)*、*农业三大支柱(three pillars of agriculture)*。

Market access for services
服务市场准入

《服务贸易总协定》促进服务及其提供者的开放和非歧视性市场准入目标的实现。协定未定义市场准入，但在第16条中列出了6类措施，这些措施不得在一国的服务贸易具体承诺减让表所列部门中维持或采用。概括地讲包括：(1)对服务提供者数量的限制；(2)对服务交易总值的限制；(3)对服务业务总数的限制；(4)对可雇用人数的限制；(5)对实体的限制或合资企业的要求；以及(6)对外国股权水平的限制。要求取消管辖市场准入的经济需求测试。

Market disruption
市场扰乱

用于实施保障措施的一种理由。此类情况据说发生在不断增长的进口流量对国内生产商的经营能力带来严重压力之时。在纺织品贸易中，市场扰乱作为《国际棉纺织品贸易长期安排》中的一个关键概念出现，指来自一个或多个贸易伙伴的极低价格进口的任何突然大量流入。这一概念被借用到了《多种纤维协定》之中。另见*特定产品过渡性保障机制(Transitional Product-Specific Safeguard Mechanism)*。

Market dominance
市场支配地位

许多国家产生竞争政策必要性的理由。市场支配地位是一公司影响其他公司行为的能力，无论是上游公司还是下游公司。在大多数情况下，竞争政策接受市场支配地位的存在，但关注于消除其滥用。另见*反垄断法(antitrust laws)*、*市场支配力(market power)*。

Market economy
市场经济

由价格机制决定生产什么和交易什么的经济，尽管价格信号经常被补贴、产业政策和其他类型的政府干预所扭曲。另见*中央计划经济体(centrally-planned economies)*、*非市场经济体(non-market economies)*。

Market-expansion dumping
市场扩张型倾销

见*倾销(dumping)*。

Market failure
市场失灵

经济学家对运转不完善市场的用词。并不意味着市场已经崩溃。市场失灵可能发生在市场参与者知情不足、买方少或卖方少(垄断或买方垄断条件)或生产一种产品的成本和收益仅与某些市场参与者有关的情况下。

Marketing boards
销售局

有时由生产国建立的私营或公共机构，以促进、营销和出口农产品。职能可以包括资助关于更有效生产和储存、加工和确定新用途的研究。销售局有时对出口实施法定垄断。通常由来自对生产者的征税提供管理所需的资金。另见*专责销售(single-desk selling)*、*国营贸易(state trading)*。

Market-led integration
市场主导一体化

通过商业活动产生或促进的区域经济一体化。可以在无政府间一体化框架的情况下发生。另见*政策主导一体化(policy-led integration)*。

Market-opening initiatives: a term used especially by the United States to describe its activities aimed at eliminating alleged persistent trade barriers against its exports. Typical examples are the ***Market-Oriented Sector-Specific talks*** of 1985 and the ***Structural Impediments Initiative*** of 1989, both directed against Japan. Market-opening initiatives are often managed under ***Section 301***.

Market-Oriented Sector-Specific talks: the MOSS talks. A 1985 United States initiative to open up the Japanese market for forest products, pharmaceuticals and medical equipment, electronics, telecommunications equipment, auto parts and transportation machinery. *See also* ***Structural Impediments Initiative*** and ***United States–Japan Framework for a New Economic Partnership***.

Market power: the fundamental assumption underlying ***antitrust laws***. It is based on the view that firms may have the ability to increase their prices without suffering a decrease in their sales. Antitrust laws are aimed at ensuring the existence of price competition in the market. *See also* ***competition policy*** and ***market dominance***.

Market presence: a term thought to reflect better than ***market access*** the fact that firms may need to establish some kind of operation in the importing country if they are to succeed. Market presence includes the notion that firms may wish to invest, and that they need adequate opportunities to compete. *See also* ***commercial presence*** and ***right of establishment***.

Market-seeking investment: a term used for ***foreign direct investment*** undertaken with the dominant aim of supplying one or more markets. *See also* ***tariff-jumping investment***.

Market-sharing arrangements: schemes supported or instituted by governments to ensure that the share of local industry in a given activity does not fall below a certain level. They can apply to goods and services. In services, two important examples are the ***bilateral air services agreements*** and the United Nations ***Convention on a Code of Conduct for Liner Conferences***. There may be strong competition within each of the defined shares. ***Voluntary restraint arrangements*** are also a form of market-sharing.

Market transparency: the extent to which participants in a market are able to assess, on the basis of the information available to them, how the market is likely to behave. The information necessary to enable a good assessment is to a large extent statistical, including data on production, sales and pricing. Advance notice of major investment proposals may also be desirable. Many ***international commodity agreements*** have market transparency as their main aim. *See also* ***administrative international commodity agreements*** and ***APEC principles on transparency standards***.

Marks of origin: a mark on a product which signifies the country of its origin, usually beginning with "Made in . . ." or "Product of . . .". *See also* ***certificate of origin***, ***indications of source*** and ***rules of origin***.

Marrakesh Agreement Establishing the World Trade Organization: *see* ***WTO Agreement***.

Market-opening initiatives
市场开放倡议

美国专门用于描述其所开展的旨在消除据称针对其出口持续存在的贸易壁垒活动的词语。典型的例子是针对日本的 1985 年市场导向型的多领域谈判方案和 1989 年日美结构协议会。市场开放倡议通常根据 301 条款进行管理。

Market-Oriented Sector-Specific talks
市场导向型的多领域谈判方案

MOSS 谈判。1985 年美国提出的开放日本林产品、药品和医疗设备、电子产品、通信设备、汽车零部件和运输设备市场的倡议。另见*日美结构协议会(Structural Impediments Initiative)*、*美日新经济伙伴关系框架(United States–Japan Framework for a New Economic Partnership)*。

Market power
市场支配力

反垄断法的基本假设。基于这样一种观点，即企业可能有能力提高价格而不会遭受销售额下降。反垄断法旨在保证市场中存在价格竞争。另见*竞争政策(competition policy)*、*市场支配地位(market dominance)*。

Market presence
市场存在

被认为比市场准入一词更能反映公司要取得成功就可能需要在进口国中建立某种业务的事实的词语。市场存在包括企业可能希望投资的概念，以及它们需要足够的机会进行竞争。另见*商业存在(commercial presence)*、*设立权(right of establishment)*。

Market-seeking investment
寻求市场型投资

用于指以供应一个或多个市场为主要目的而进行的外国直接投资。另见*跳越关税投资(tariff-jumping investment)*。

Market-sharing arrangements
市场分享安排

政府支持或制定的方案，以保证本地产业在一特定活动中的份额不低于某一水平。可以适用于货物和服务。在服务业中，两个重要的例子是双边航空服务协定和《联合国班轮公会行动守则公约》。在每一个规定的份额内可能会有激烈的竞争。自愿限制安排也是市场分享的一种形式。

Market transparency
市场透明度

市场参与者能够根据他们所获得的信息评估市场可能如何运作的程度。作出好的评估所需信息在很大程度上是统计信息，包括关于生产、销售和定价的数据。重大投资建议的预先通知也是可取的。许多国际商品协定都以市场透明度为主要目标。另见*国际商品管理协定(administrative international commodity agreements)*、*APEC 透明度标准原则(APEC principles on transparency standards)*。

Marks of origin
原产地标记

产品上标明原产地的标志，通常以"…制造"开头或"…产品"。另见*原产地证书(certificate of origin)*、*产地标志(indications of source)*、*原产地规则(rules of origin)*。

Marrakesh Agreement Establishing the World Trade Organization
马拉喀什建立世界贸易组织协定

见 *WTO 协定(WTO Agreement)*。

Marshall Plan: a plan for the post-war economic rehabilitation of Europe first proposed by George C. Marshall, then United States Secretary of State, in a speech at Harvard University on 5 June 1947. It was put into effect on 3 April 1948 when President Truman signed the *Foreign Assistance Act*. The United States made available an estimated $13,000 million between 1948 and 1952 for this purpose. The Marshall Plan was administered through the ***Organisation for European Economic Co-operation*** (OEEC), the predecessor of the ***OECD***. Apart from its direct contribution to the reconstruction of the participating economies, the Plan also gave impetus to the later European economic integration through the ***European Economic Community*** and ***EFTA***.

Mashreq countries: Jordan, Lebanon, Syria, West Bank and Gaza. Egypt is sometimes included.

Massachusetts Burma Law: adopted by the Massachusetts state legislature in 1996 to promote improvements in human rights in Burma (Myanmar). The law gave companies avoiding doing business with Burma a 10 per cent preference margin in purchases by the Massachusetts state government. Following a challenge by the National Foreign Trade Council the Supreme Court held in 1998 that the law was an infringement of the exclusively federal constitutional right to regulate foreign trade.

Material injury: a condition that has to be satisfied before ***anti-dumping measures*** can be taken. The WTO ***Anti-Dumping Agreement*** does not define the term. It requires, however, that a determination of injury must be based on positive evidence and involve an objective examination of (a) the volume of the dumped imports and their effect on prices in the domestic market for ***like products*** and (b) the impact of such imports on domestic producers. *See also* ***injury***.

Material retardation of the establishment of an industry: a phrase occurring in both the ***Anti-Dumping Agreement*** and the ***Agreement on Subsidies and Countervailing Measures***. Neither agreement defines it. However, it seems that material retardation should be considered a less severe event than ***injury***, ***material injury***, threat of injury or threat of material injury.

Material transfer agreement: the legal instrument used to protect the transfer of genetic material from a provider/user to another user. Such an agreement is normally considered subject to ***trade secrets*** law.

Maximum-minimum tariff: a ***tariff schedule*** that gives for some tariff items the maximum and the minimum rate the customs authorities may apply to imported products. Such tariffs usually were developed autonomously by national legislatures. The intention was to reward those countries perceived as having relatively open markets with the lower rates and to impose the higher rates on countries considered relatively closed. General most-favoured-nation treatment rules out the use of a maximum-minimum tariff among WTO members in this way, though it would still be legal in the conduct of their trade relations with non-members. *See also* ***conventional tariff*** and ***negative reciprocity***.

Marshall Plan
马歇尔计划

欧洲战后经济复兴计划，1947年6月5日时任美国国务卿乔治·卡特利特·马歇尔在哈佛大学演讲时首次提出。杜鲁门总统于1948年4月3日签署《对外援助法》，开始实施该计划。在1948年至1952年期间，美国为此目的提供了约130亿美元。马歇尔计划通过欧洲经济合作组织(OEEC)管理，即经济合作与发展组织(OECD)前身。该计划除对参与经济体的重建作出直接捐款外，还通过欧洲经济共同体和欧洲自由贸易联盟(EFTA)推动后来的欧洲经济一体化。

Mashreq countries
马什雷克国家

约旦、黎巴嫩、叙利亚、约旦河西岸和加沙。埃及有时也包括在内。

Massachusetts Burma Law
马萨诸塞州缅甸法

马萨诸塞州立法机构1996年通过，目的在于促进缅甸人权的改善。该法规定，不与缅甸作生意的公司可在马萨诸塞的州政府采购中享受10%的优惠幅度。在美国对外贸易委员会提出质疑之后，最高法院于1998年裁定，该法侵犯了监管对外贸易的专属联邦宪法权。

Material injury
实质损害

在采取反倾销措施之前必须满足的条件。WTO《反倾销协定》并未定义这一词语。但是，协定要求损害的确定必须根据肯定性证据，并包括客观审查(a)倾销进口产品的数量及其对国内市场中同类产品价格的影响；及(b)此类进口品对国内生产者的影响。另见*损害(injury)*。

Material retardation of the establishment of an industry
实质阻碍一产业建立

在《反倾销协定》和《补贴与反补贴措施协定》中均出现的词语。两协定均未定义。但是，实质阻碍与损害、实质损害、损害威胁或实质损害威胁相比应被认为属不那么严重的事件。

Material transfer agreement
材料转让协定

用于保护遗传材料从提供者/使用者向另一使用者转让的法律文件。此种协定通常被认为受商业秘密法的约束。

Maximum-minimum tariff
最高-最低关税

给予海关可以在一些关税税目项下针对进口产品适用最高和最低税率的关税税则。此类关税通常由国家立法机关自主制定。意在用较低税率奖励那些被认为拥有相对开放市场的国家，而对那些被认为相对封闭的国家适用较高税率。普遍最惠国待遇排除了WTO成员之间使用这种最高-最低关税的方式，但WTO成员使用此种做法与非成员处理贸易关系仍然合法。另见*协定关税(conventional tariff)*、*消极互惠(negative reciprocity)*。

Means-and-ends test: an examination to ascertain (a) whether the objectives of a ***trade measure*** are in themselves defensible, and (b) whether the methods proposed for attaining the objectives are going to do that. *See also* ***least-trade-restrictive-alternative test*** and ***necessity test***.

MEAs: ***multilateral environment agreements*** concluded between three or more states, such as the Montreal Protocol on Substances that Deplete the Ozone Layer and the ***United Nations Framework Convention on Climate Change***.

Measure: normally any law, rule, regulation, policy, practice or action carried out by government or on behalf of a government.

Measurement of commercial policy: assigning a numerical value to the impact of a ***trade measure***. This is relatively straightforward in the case of ***ad valorem tariffs*** since they are normally expressed as a percentage of the ***transaction value*** of a good. ***Specific tariffs*** (e.g. a duty of $5 per 100 litres regardless of the value), are more complex to assess since their impact varies with the price of the good. Most difficult to assess is the impact of ***non-tariff measures***. Some of these are intended to control the flow of imports or even to stop them, but others ensure no more than that the imported good is of the same standard as the domestically produced good. *See* quantification of ***non-tariff measures*** for a brief discussion of the technical issues. *See also* ***Overall Trade Restrictiveness Index*** and ***Trade Restrictiveness Index***.

Media services: includes products and activities such as e-books, ***audiovisual services***, such as music, films and television streaming, online games, etc.

Mediation: now in most cases indistinguishable from ***good offices***. It used to have the meaning of direct negotiations between the parties under the guidance of a mediator. The WTO ***Dispute Settlement Understanding*** allows the parties to accept mediation, either by a third party or the WTO Director-General.

Mediterranean Agreements: the ***preferential trade arrangements***, formally known as ***Euro-Mediterranean Association Agreements***, between the ***European Community*** and some Mediterranean countries other than Turkey, Cyprus and Malta. *See also* ***Association Agreements*** and ***Europe Agreements***.

Meeting of APEC Ministers Related to Trade: the annual meeting of APEC trade ministers usually held in about June. *See also* ***APEC ministerial meetings*** and ***APEC sectoral ministerial meetings***.

Mega-regionals: used, for example, by Lejárraga (2014) for large-scale ***free-trade agreements***, such as the ***Trans-Pacific Partnership Agreement***, the ***Tripartite Free Trade Area*** or the proposed ***Free Trade Area of the Asia-Pacific***.

Mega-tariff: an imprecise term descriptive of an extremely high tariff. *See also* ***prohibitive tariff***.

Melanesian Free Trade Agreement: *see* ***Melanesian Spearhead Group Trade Agreement***.

Melanesian Spearhead Group Trade Agreement: a ***preferential trade arrangement*** between Fiji, Papua New Guinea, Solomon Islands and Vanuatu.

Means-and-ends test
手段与目的测试
一种审查，以确定(a)一贸易措施的目标本身是否站得住脚；及(b)为实现这些目标而提出的方法是否能够实现这些目标。另见*最小贸易限制替代措施测试(least-trade-restrictive-alternative test)*、*必要性测试(necessity test)*。

MEAs
多边环境协定
三个或三个以上国家缔结的多边环境协定，如《关于消耗臭氧层物质的蒙特利尔议定书》和《联合国气候变化框架公约》。

Measure
措施
通常由政府或代表政府执行的任何法律、规定、法规、政策、做法或行动。

Measurement of commercial policy
商业政策测算
对一项贸易措施的影响分配一个数值。对于从价关税，此点相对简单，因为从价关税通常以货物成交价格的百分比表示。从量关税(例如关税为每100升5美元，不考虑其价值)评估起来更为复杂，因为其影响随货物价格而变化。最难评估的是非关税措施的影响。其中一些措施旨在控制进口流量，甚至阻止进口，但其他措施只不过是要保证进口货物与国内生产货物的标准相同。关于技术问题的简要讨论见非关税措施量化词条。另见*总体贸易限制指数(Overall Trade Restrictiveness Index)*、*贸易限制指数(Trade Restrictiveness Index)*。

Media services
媒体服务
包括电子书等产品和活动、音乐、电影和电视流媒体等视听服务以及网络游戏等。

Mediation
调停
现在大多数情况下与斡旋无异。过去的含义为在调停人指导下的双方直接谈判。WTO《争端解决谅解》允许争端方接受第三方或 WTO 总干事的调停。

Mediterranean Agreements
地中海协定
欧洲共同体与除土耳其、塞浦路斯和马耳他外的一些地中海国家之间的优惠贸易安排，正式名称为《欧洲与地中海联系协定》。另见*联系协定(Association Agreements)*、*欧洲协定(Europe Agreements)*。

Meeting of APEC Ministers Related to Trade
APEC 贸易部长会议
APEC 贸易部长年会通常在 6 月左右举行。另见 *APEC 部长级会议(APEC ministerial meetings)*、*APEC 部门部长级会议(APEC sectoral ministerial meetings)*。

Mega-regionals
特大区域
用于指大规模自由贸易协定，如莱加拉加(2014年)所用，例如《跨太平洋伙伴关系协定》、三方自由贸易区或拟议的亚太自由贸易区。

Mega-tariff
超高关税
描述极高关税的一个不精确的词语。另见*禁止性关税(prohibitive tariff)*。

Melanesian Free Trade Agreement
美拉尼西亚自由贸易协定
见*美拉尼西亚先锋集团贸易协定(Melanesian Spearhead Group Trade Agreement)*。

Melanesian Spearhead Group Trade Agreement
美拉尼西亚先锋集团贸易协定
斐济、巴布亚新几内亚、所罗门群岛和瓦努阿图之间的优惠贸易安排。包含关

Contains a negative list for tariff liberalization. The Agreement is expected to lead to a Melanesian Free Trade Agreement.

Members: in the ***WTO*** these are the governments that constitute the organization. The first letter is capitalized (Member) in official WTO documents.

Memorandum of understanding: MOU. A non-binding agreement between two or more parties. It does not have the legal force of a ***treaty***, but it may be more than simply a statement of good intentions. That is, parts of an MOU may be enforceable. It is normally easier to conclude than a treaty, partly because it does not need to ratified, and it can be kept confidential. *See also* ***pacta sunt servanda***.

Mercado Comum do Sul: *see* ***Mercosur***.

Mercado Común del Sur: *see* ***Mercosur***.

Mercantilism: an enduring seventeenth-century set of views which holds that the aim of international trade should be the accumulation of an increased share of global wealth in the form of bullion. In the modern world the aim is to accumulate as much foreign exchange as possible. Mercantilism always seeks to maximize exports and minimize imports. Lars Magnusson points out in *Mercantilism: The Shaping of an Economic Language* that mercantilism in its traditional form was not a well-structured doctrine containing principles to describe economic behaviour or to prescribe policy measures. Rather, it was characterized by a strong emphasis on the means to achieve national wealth and power. Douglas Irwin notes in *Against the Tide: An Intellectual History of Free Trade* that virtually all mercantilists would have agreed with the following proposition: exports of manufactures were beneficial and exports of raw materials (for use by foreign manufacturers abroad) were harmful; imports of raw materials were advantageous and imports of manufactured goods were damaging. This proposition sounds quite familiar to the contemporary policy maker. A shorter way of expressing it is that trade is good, but imports are bad. Most mercantilists also were in favour of expanding trade to promote economic development. A. W. Coats distinguishes in *Mercantilism: Economic Ideas, History, Policy* between three levels of mercantilist ideas: (a) the ultimate ends or objectives of economic policy, e.g. the promotion of the wealth, power and security of the state, (b) the intermediate ends, e.g. adequate supply of precious metals, stable exchange rate, favourable balance of trade, protection of home industry, etc., and (c) the means to achieve the intermediate ends, e.g. bounties on exports, duties and prohibitions on imports of finished goods, prohibitions on the export of precious metals, etc. Robert Gilpin distinguishes in his *Political Economy of International Relations* between benign mercantilism (aimed at protecting the national economic interest as the minimum required for the security of the state) and malevolent mercantilism (aimed at imperialist expansion and national aggrandizement). Adherents of mercantilism implicitly assume that global wealth is fixed. They portray trade as a zero-sum activity in which one country can only prosper at the expense of another. Mercantilism is therefore a form of economic nationalism. The massive growth

税自由化的负面清单。协定有望促成《美拉尼西亚自由贸易协定》。

Members

成员

在WTO中为组成该组织的政府。在WTO正式文件中，首字母大写(Member)。

Memorandum of understanding

谅解备忘录

MOU。双方或多方之间不具约束力的协议。不具备条约的法律效力，但也可能不仅是一份善意的声明，即谅解备忘录的部分内容可以执行。通常要比缔约一项条约更容易，部分原因是MOU无需批准，且可保密。另见*条约必须遵守(pacta sunt servanda)*。

Mercado Comum do Sul

南方共同市场

见*南方共同市场(Mercosur)*。

Mercado Común del Sur

南方共同市场

见*南方共同市场(Mercosur)*。

Mercantilism

重商主义

源自17世纪的持续存在的一套观点，认为国际贸易的目标应是以金条形式积累更多的全球财富份额。在现代世界中，目标是积累尽可能多的外汇。重商主义总是寻求出口最大化和进口最小化。拉斯·马格努松在《重商主义：一套经济话语的形成》一书中指出，传统形式的重商主义并不是一种包含描述经济行为或规定政策措施的原则的结构良好的学说。相反，它的特点是强调实现国家财富和权力的手段。道格拉斯·欧文在《自由贸易思想史》一书中指出，实际上所有重商主义者都会同意以下主张：制成品出口是有益的，而原材料出口(供外国制造商在国外使用)是有害的；原材料进口是有利的，而制成品进口是有害的。这一命题听起来对于当代政策制定者相当熟悉。简而言之，即贸易是好的，而进口是坏的。大多数重商主义者也赞成扩大贸易以促进经济发展。科茨在《重商主义：经济思想、历史、政策》一书中区分了三个层次的重商主义思想：(a)经济政策的最终目的或目标，例如促进国家的财富、权力和安全；(b)中间目的，例如贵金属的充足供应、稳定的汇率、有利的贸易平衡、保护本国产业等；以及(c)实现中间目的的手段，例如出口奖励、对进口制成品的关税和禁令、禁止贵金属出口等。罗伯特·吉尔平在他的《国际关系政治经济学》一书中区分了善意重商主义(旨在将保护国家经济利益作为国家安全的最低要求)和恶意重商主义(旨在帝国主义扩张和国家强化)。重商主义的追随者隐含地认为，全球财富是固定的。他们将贸易描绘为一种零和活动，在其中一国只能以牺牲另一国为代价才能繁荣。重商主义因此是经济民族主义的一种形式。过去200多年间，世界贸易和财富的大规模增长表明，贸易实际上

of world trade and wealth over the past two hundred years or more demonstrates that trade is, in fact, a positive-sum activity. It also shows that all can prosper through efficient specialization. *See also* ***balance of trade*** and ***neo-mercantilism***. [Coats 1987, Gilpin 1987, Irwin 1996, Magnusson 1994]

Merchandise trade: the import and export of physical goods, i.e. raw materials, semi-manufactures and manufactures. *See also* ***balance on merchandise trade*** and ***trade in services***.

Merchant Marine Act of 1920: *see* ***Jones Act***.

Mercosul: Mercado Comum do Sul. Southern Common Market. The name in Portuguese of ***Mercosur***.

Mercosur: Mercado Común del Sur (Southern Common Market). Currently a ***customs union*** covering trade in goods except sugar and automobiles. Mercosur objectives include the free transit of all goods, services and the factors of production, and the lifting of non-tariff restrictions. It was established on 29 November 1991 through the Treaty of Asunción and amended on 17 December 1994 through the Protocol of Ouro Preto which covers mainly institutional issues. It includes Argentina, Brazil, Paraguay and Uruguay. Venezuela is also a member, but it has been suspended since 1 December 2016. Chile signed an association agreement on 1 October 1996. Bolivia did so on 1 March 1997. Membership is open to ***ALADI*** members. The Mercosur secretariat is located in Montevideo.

Merger Treaty: a treaty concluded in 1965 which created a single Commission of the ***European Communities*** to replace the bodies administering the European Atomic Energy Community, the ***European Coal and Steel Community*** and the ***European Economic Community***. *See also* ***European Commission***, ***European Union*** and ***European Union treaties***.

Merging of free-trade areas: *see* ***docking and merging***.

METI: the Japanese Ministry of Economy, Trade and Industry. Until 6 January 2001 it was known as MITI (Ministry of International Trade and Industry). Many see the *dirigiste* industrial and trade policies administered by MITI as a major reason for Japan's post-war economic success. Others have tried to emulate MITI, but without much success. METI itself has long been a market-oriented ministry.

MFA: the ***Multi-Fibre Arrangement*** under which countries whose markets are disrupted by increased imports of textiles and clothing were able to negotiate quota restrictions.

MFN: most-favoured-nation treatment, i.e. the principle of not discriminating between one's trading partners. It is required by Article I of the GATT, Article II of the ***General Agreement on Trade in Services*** and Article IV of the ***Agreement on Trade-Related Aspects of Intellectual Property Rights***.

MFN applied tariff: *see* ***applied MFN tariff rate***.

MFN exemption: under the ***General Agreement on Trade in Services*** (GATS), permission granted to a member country not to apply ***most-favoured-nation treatment*** in a given sector. In most cases, these are necessary because of earlier

是一种正和活动。还表明，通过有效专业化，所有国家都可以实现繁荣。另见*贸易平衡(balance of trade)*、*新重商主义(neo-mercantilism)*。

Merchandise trade

商品贸易

实体货物的进口和出口，即原材料、半制成品和制成品。另见*商品贸易平衡(balance on merchandise trade)*、*服务贸易(trade in services)*。

Merchant Marine Act of 1920

1920 年商船法

见*琼斯法案(Jones Act)*。

Mercosul

南方共同市场

南方共同市场(Mercosur)的葡萄牙语名称。

Mercosur

南方共同市场

目前涵盖除食糖和汽车外所有货物的关税同盟。南方共同市场的目标包括所有货物、服务和生产要素的自由运输，以及取消非关税限制。通过《亚松森条约》于1991年11月29日建立，并于1994年12月17日经《欧鲁普雷图议定书》修正，该议定书主要涵盖体制问题。包括阿根廷、巴西、巴拉圭和乌拉圭。委内瑞拉也是成员之一，但自2016年12月1日以来被暂停成员资格。智利于1996年10月1日签署联系协定。玻利维亚于1997年3月1日签署联系协定。成员资格对拉丁美洲一体化协会(ALADI)成员开放。南方共同市场秘书处设在蒙得维的亚。

Merger Treaty

合并条约

1965 年缔结的条约，条约设立了单一的欧洲共同体委员会，以取代管理欧洲原子能共同体、欧洲煤钢共同体和欧洲经济共同体的机构。另见*欧盟委员会(European Commission)*、*欧洲联盟(European Union)*、*欧洲联盟主要条约(European Union treaties)*。

Merging of free-trade areas

自由贸易区的合并

见*接驳与合并(docking and merging)*。

METI

日本经济产业省

在2001年1月6日之前称为 MITI(通商产业省)。许多人认为，日本战后经济成功的一个主要原因在于日本通产省实行的统制式的产业和贸易政策。其他国家试图效仿通产省，但没有取得多大成功。经产省自身长期以来是一个以市场为导向的部门。

MFA

多种纤维协定

根据这一安排，市场因纺织品和服装进口增加而受到干扰的国家能够谈判配额限制。

MFN

最惠国待遇

即不歧视一国贸易伙伴的原则。为 GATT 第 1 条、《服务贸易总协定》第 2 条和《与贸易有关的知识产权协定》第 4 条所要求。

MFN applied tariff

最惠国实施关税

见*最惠国实施税率(applied MFN tariff rate)*。

MFN exemption

最惠国待遇豁免

根据《服务贸易总协定》，给予一成员在一指定部门不实施最惠国待遇的许可。

treaty obligations, such as membership of a market-sharing agreement, a preferential arrangement or a cooperation agreement. MFN exemptions are for a maximum of ten years, and they have to be reviewed after five years. Many WTO members took out MFN exemptions when the GATS entered into force. Others have since been granted exemptions upon accession. It is possible for existing members to take out new MFN exemptions, but this can only be done with the agreement of 75 per cent of the WTO membership at a ***WTO Ministerial Conference***. *See also* ***waiver***.

MFN rules of origin: the ***rules of origin*** applied by a country to goods imported under its ***MFN tariff***. *See* ***non-preferential rules of origin***.

MFN tariff: the tariff rates applied to goods imported from countries enjoying ***most-favoured-nation treatment*** under one's trade laws.

Miami Summit: *see* ***FTAA***.

Middle East Free Trade Area Initiative: MEFTA. A proposal offering "a vision of openness, trade integration and economic development for the Middle east" launched by the United States in 2003. It has seven elements: (1) United States support for countries seeking WTO membership, (2) an expanded ***GSP*** scheme, (3) an offer to negotiate ***trade and investment framework agreements***, (4) an offer to negotiate ***bilateral investment treaties***, (5) comprehensive ***free-trade agreements***, (6) aid for ***capacity-building***, and (7) the eventual goal of a regional free-trade agreement.

Midrand Declaration: a non-binding statement adopted at ***UNCTAD*** IX (May 1996) which sets out broadly UNCTAD's task for the next four years. Its main themes are the impact of ***globalization*** and liberalization, partnerships for development through cooperation between developed and developing countries, the focal points for UNCTAD's future work, partnerships involving the private sector and institutional reform of UNCTAD.

Millennium Declaration: adopted by the United Nations on 8 September 2001, mainly concerned with political and security matters, but it has a bearing also on ***trade policy***. The Declaration stresses ***good governance*** at home and internationally as well as ***transparency*** in the financial, monetary and trading system. It contains a commitment to an open, equitable, rule-based, predictable and non-discriminatory multilateral trading and financial system. The Declaration calls on developed countries to give duty-free and quota-free access for essentially all exports from the ***least-developed countries***, and it encourages the pharmaceutical industry to make essential drugs more widely available and affordable for all who need them in developing countries. It also forms the basis of the ***Millennium Development Goals***.

Millennium Development Goals: the eight goals for human development adopted in 2000 and given a realization target of 2015 as part of the ***Millennium Declaration***. They are (1) eradicate extreme poverty and hunger, (2) achieve universal primary education, (3) promote gender equality and empower women, (4) reduce child mortality, (5) improve mental health, (6) combat HIV/AIDS, malaria and other diseases, (7) ensure environmental sustainability,

在大多数情况下，由于存在较早条约义务的原因，这是必要的，例如市场分享协定、优惠安排或合作协定的成员资格。最惠国待遇豁免时间最长为 10 年，5 年后需要重新审议。在《服务贸易总协定》生效时，许多 WTO 成员获得了最惠国待遇豁免。其他成员则在加入时被给予豁免。现有成员有可能获得新的最惠国待遇豁免，但只有在WTO 部长级会议上获得 75%的 WTO 成员同意方可作到。另见*豁免(waiver)*。

MFN rules of origin

最惠国原产地规则

一国对在最惠国关税项下进口的货物适用的原产地规则。另见*非优惠原产地规则(non-preferential rules of origin)*。

MFN tariff

最惠国关税

对自根据一国贸易法享受最惠国待遇的国家进口的货物适用的关税税率。

Miami Summit

迈阿密峰会

见*美洲自由贸易区(FTAA)*。

Middle East Free Trade Area Initiative

中东自由贸易区倡议

MEFTA。美国2003年提出的关于“中东开放、贸易一体化和经济发展愿景”的建议。包含7个要素：(1)美国支持各国寻求加入WTO；(2)扩大普惠制(GSP)方案；(3)提议谈判贸易投资框架协定；(4)提议谈判双边投资条约；(5)全面自由贸易协定；(6)能力建设援助；以及(7)形成区域自由贸易协定的最终目标。

Midrand Declaration

米德兰特宣言

联合国贸易与发展会议(UNCTAD)第9届大会1996年5月通过的一项非约束性声明，概述了UNCTAD未来4年的任务。主题是全球化和自由化的影响、通过发达国家与发展中国家之间的合作促进发展伙伴关系、UNCTAD未来工作的协调中心、涉及私营部门的伙伴关系以及UNCTAD机制改革。

Millennium Declaration

千年宣言

联合国2001年9月8日通过，主要涉及政治和安全事务，但也对贸易政策产生影响。宣言强调在国内和国际上的良好治理以及金融、货币和贸易体制的透明度。包含对一个开放的、公平的、有章可循的、可预测的和非歧视性的多边贸易和金融体制的承诺。呼吁发达国家给予源自最不发达国家基本上所有出口产品免关税和免配额准入，并鼓励制药行业让发展中国家所有有此需要的人更容易买到价格相宜的必要药品。宣言同时成为千年发展目标的基础。

Millennium Development Goals

千年发展目标

2000年通过的8项人类发展目标，作为《千年宣言》的一部分，规定2015年的实现目标。包括：(1)消灭极端贫穷和饥饿；(2)普及小学教育；(3)两性平等和女性赋权；(4)降低儿童死亡率；(5)改善产妇保健(英文误为mental，应为maternal—译注)；(6)对抗艾滋病毒/艾滋病、疟疾及其他疾病；(7)保证环境可持续性；以

and (8) develop a global partnership for development. The *Millennium Development Goals Report* of 2015 found that considerable progress had been made in all eight areas. It also notes that progress had been uneven across regions and countries, and that targeted efforts will be needed to reach the most vulnerable people. The ***Sustainable Development Goals*** are designed to continue this effort up to 2030. *See also* ***United Nations Development Programme***. [United Nations Development Programme 2003]

Millennium Round: a name suggested in 1997 by Sir Leon Brittan, then Vice-President of the ***European Commission***, for the new round of ***multilateral trade negotiations*** that he and others expected would get under way in about 2000 or 2001. The name did not take on. *See also* ***Seattle Ministerial Conference*** and ***Doha Ministerial Conference***.

Minilateralism: a preference for conducting ***trade policy*** in the company of a few countries. No exact definition exists for "minilateral". It definitely describes a relationship that is more than bilateral, but not involving many which, of course, is equally inexact. The ***Quadrilaterals***, however, would fit the bill well. *See also* ***creative minilateralism*** and ***plurilateralism***.

Minimal operations or processes: if goods are to qualify for ***preferential market access***, i.e. if they meet the ***preferential rules of origin***, the exporting country has to add value equalling or exceeding an agreed threshold. Minimal operations or processes are those that do not meet this threshold. Among these are preservation of goods in storage, packaging, cleaning, simple assembly of parts, etc. *See also* ***insufficient operations***.

Mini-ministerial meeting: a name often associated with the Geneva mini-ministerial meeting of 2008 which sought to revitalize the ***Doha Development Agenda***. Generally, this is an informal meeting to which a limited, but representative, number of ministers is invited. These meetings are normally used to seek ways to maintain impetus in negotiations or to discuss key issues in negotiations. Accordingly, the selection of ministers to be invited depends to some extent on the topics to be discussed.

Minimum access tariff quotas: a mechanism giving a minimum level of access opportunities for agricultural products where ***non-tariff measures*** have been converted into tariffs. The ***Uruguay Round*** negotiations led to a formula whereby the level of access to be opened for a certain product was based on the import/consumption ratio during the 1986–88 ***base period***. In countries where imports were less than 3 per cent of consumption during the base period, access was to be increased immediately to 3 per cent and expanded to 5 per cent by the end of the Uruguay Round implementation period for agriculture commitments. *See also* ***Agreement on Agriculture***, ***current access tariff quotas*** and ***tariffication***.

Minimum customs values: the arbitrary allocation by customs authorities of a value to an imported good, usually above the market value as the importer assesses it. *See* ***customs valuation***.

Minimum labour standards: *see* ***core labour standards*** and ***international labour standards***.

及(8)发展全球发展伙伴关系。《2015年千年发展目标报告》指出，在所有8个领域取得可观进展。报告还指出，各地区和各国家间的进展不平衡，且需要作出有针对性努力以帮助最脆弱人群。可持续发展目标旨在将这一努力持续至2030年。另见*联合国开发计划署(United Nations Development Programme)*。

Millennium Round
千年回合

时任欧盟委员会副主席的莱昂 · 布里坦爵士于 1997 年为新一轮多边贸易谈判提出的名称，他与其他人期望此轮谈判将在 2000 年或 2001 年左右开始。这一名称未被采纳。另见*西雅图部长级会议(Seattle Ministerial Conference)*、*多哈部长级会议(Doha Ministerial Conference)*。

Minilateralism
小多边主义

在少数国家的公司中执行贸易政策的偏好。对于“小多边”并无确切定义。确实描述了一种超越双边的关系，但又不涉及许多关系，具体多少同样不能精确定义。但是，“4 方”可以很好地满足这一要求。另见*创造性小多边主义(creative minilateralism)*、*诸边主义(plurilateralism)*。

Minimal operations or processes
微小操作或工序

如果货物想有资格获得优惠市场准入，即如果它们想要符合优惠原产地规则，出口国对货物所增加的价值必须等于或超过议定的最低标准。微小操作或工序即为不符合这一最低标准的操作或工序，包括储存、包装、清洁、零件的简单装配等。另见*不充分操作(insufficient operations)*。

Mini-ministerial meeting
小型部长级会议

通常与2008年日内瓦小型部长级会议联系在一起，会议寻求重振多哈发展议程。一般而言，小型部长级会议属非正式会议，邀请有限但具有代表性的部长参加。会议通常用于寻找保持谈判动力的途径或讨论谈判中的关键问题。因此，被邀请部长的选择在一定程度上取决于所讨论的话题。

Minimum access tariff quotas
关税配额最低准入

给予非关税措施已经转化为关税的农产品最低准入水平的机制。乌拉圭回合谈判产生了一个公式，即某一产品开放的准入水平根据 1986—1988 年基期的进口与消费比确定。基期进口占消费不足 3%的国家，准入将立即增至 3%，并在乌拉圭回合实施期结束时增至 5%。另见*农业协定(Agreement on Agriculture)*、*关税配额现行准入(current access tariff quotas)*、*关税化(tariffication)*。

Minimum customs values
海关最低限价

海关对一进口货物任意分配的价格，通常高于进口商评估的市场价格。另见*海关估价(customs valuation)*。

Minimum labour standards
最低劳工标准

见*核心劳工标准(core labour standards)*、*国际劳工标准(international labour standards)*。

Minimum operations: in the administration of ***preferential rules of origin*** this generally refers to work on a product deemed insufficient to make it qualify as a product of the exporting country. Hence the product would not benefit from any ***preferential tariff***. Such operations can include simple assembly, final quality testing or packaging. *See also* ***insufficient operations*** and ***substantial transformation***.

Minimum standard of treatment: some ***international investment agreements*** and investment chapters in ***free-trade agreements***, such as Article 1105 of ***NAFTA***, require the parties to accord to investments of investors of another party a minimum standard of treatment. This is generally held to be treatment in accordance with international law, including fair and equitable treatment and full protection and security. This provision has caused considerable comment and analysis, though, as many have pointed out, such provisions have been around for some time. One difference is that NAFTA has the judicial environment where this provision can be enforced. Views on the meaning and impact of this provision are still evolving. A judgment in a NAFTA dispute illustrates the issue. The judge in *The United Mexican States v. Metalclad Corporation* held that Article 1105 was framed in absolute terms, "intended to establish a minimum standard so that a party may not treat investments of another investor worse than this standard irrespective of the manner in which the Party treats other investors and their investments". He quoted with approval the tribunal's view on 13 January 2000 in *S. D. Myers, Inc. v. Government of Canada* (another NAFTA case) that the "minimum standard" was a floor below which treatment of foreign investors must not fall, even if a government were not acting in a discriminatory manner. He noted that the introductory phrase to Article 1105 referred to "treatment in accordance with international law". Hence, in order to qualify as a breach of Article 1105, the treatment in question must fail to accord with international law. So the judge. The significance therefore of the "minimum standard" is that it establishes an absolute standard for treatment of investors, in contrast to the relative standards implied by ***most-favoured-nation treatment*** (non-discrimination between foreign investors) and ***national treatment*** (non-discrimination between foreign and domestic investors). Neither of these two standards prescribes how well a party must treat foreign investors, except in terms of its own practices.

Ministerial Conference: *see* ***WTO Ministerial Conference***.

Ministerial Declaration on Trade in Information Technology Products: *see* ***Information Technology Agreement***.

Mini-trading area: used by some to describe a ***free-trade area***, but for others it is more like a ***growth triangle***. The context will make clear what is meant.

Minor exceptions doctrine: Article 13 of the ***Agreement on Trade-Related Aspects of Intellectual Property Rights*** requires WTO members to confine limitations or exceptions to exclusive rights in the area of ***copyright*** to "certain special cases which do not conflict with a normal exploitation of the work and do not unreasonably prejudice the legitimate interests of the right holder".

Minimum operations

最小操作

在优惠原产地规则管理中，通常指对一产品所作的被认为不足以使该产品符合出口国产品资格的操作。因此，该产品不会从任何优惠关税中获益。此类操作可以包括简单组装、最终质量检验或包装。另见*不充分操作(insufficient operations)*、*实质性改变(substantial transformation)*。

Minimum standard of treatment

最低待遇标准

一些国际投资协定和自由贸易协定的投资章节，例如《北美自由贸易协定》(NAFTA)第1105条，要求缔约方给予另一方投资者的投资最低待遇标准。这通常被认为属依照国际法获得的待遇，包括公平和公正的待遇以及充分保护和安全。这一条款引发了相当多的评论和分析，尽管正如许多人所指出的，此类条款已经存在一段时间。有一点不同之处在于，NAFTA拥有可以执行这一条款的司法环境。关于这一条款的含义和影响的观点仍在形成中。一项NAFTA项下争端的判决说明了这一问题。在"梅特克莱德公司诉墨西哥合众国案"中，法官认为，第1105条是绝对条款，"旨在建立一个最低标准，使一当事方对待另一投资者的投资不得比这一标准更差，不论该缔约方以何种方式对待其他投资者及其投资"。他赞同地引用了法庭2000年1月13日在"迈尔斯公司诉加拿大政府案"(NAFTA项下另一案)中的观点，即"最低标准"是下限，外国投资者的待遇不得低于此，即使政府并未以歧视性方式行事。他指出，第1105条的引言提到了"根据国际法的待遇"。因此，要构成对第1105条的违反，所涉待遇必须是不符合国际法的。法官如此认为。因此"最低标准"的重要意义在于，它确立了投资者待遇的绝对标准，而不是最惠国待遇(不在外国投资者之间造成歧视)和国民待遇(不在外国投资者与国内投资者之间造成歧视)所包含的相对标准。这两个标准均未规定一缔约方必须如何对待外国投资者，除非就其自身实践而言。

Ministerial Conference

部长级会议

见*WTO部长级会议(WTO Ministerial Conference)*。

Ministerial Declaration on Trade in Information Technology Products

关于信息技术产品贸易的部长宣言

见*信息技术协定(Information Technology Agreement)*。

Mini-trading area

小型贸易区

一些人用于描述一自由贸易区，但对于其他人，更像一个增长三角。通过上下文可明确其含义。

Minor exceptions doctrine

轻微例外原则

《与贸易有关的知识产权协定》第13条要求WTO成员将版权领域专有权的限制或例外仅限于"与作品的正常利用不相冲突且不得无理损害权利持有人的合法利益的某些特殊情况"。这些条件清楚地表明，符合这些标准的例外情

These conditions make clear that exceptions meeting these criteria would always have to be of a minor nature, especially since they have to be read in the context of Articles 11 and 11bis of the ***Berne Convention*** which give authors exclusive rights to authorize public performances, recordings and broadcasts of their works.

Mirror-image reciprocity: the expectation that trade benefits offered to another country will be matched exactly. *See also* ***reciprocity*** and ***reciprocity at the margin***.

Mirror retaliation: the suspension of the same obligations as have been breached by the country against which the ***retaliation*** is aimed. It is also known as reciprocal retaliation.

MITI: Ministry of International Trade and Industry. *See also* ***METI***.

Mixed commission: usually a body established under a ***bilateral trade agreement*** which consists of representatives of both parties. The task of a mixed commission is to review periodically the operation of the agreement. *See also* ***joint trade committee***.

Mixed credits: the provision by developed donor countries to developing countries of credits partly on commercial terms and partly at subsidized interest rates. The aim of such credits usually is to fund projects capable of making an important contribution to the economic development of the recipient country. The assumption is that these projects would not proceed if they had to rely entirely on commercial funding. *See also* ***official development assistance*** and ***trade and aid***.

Mixed export cartel: *see* ***cartel***.

Mixed tariff: *see* ***compound tariff***.

Mixed trade policies: the concurrent application of the mix deemed most appropriate of trade policies having different immediate aims, though they all are meant to expand a given country's exports. These might be (a) unilateral policies to improve the competitiveness of domestic industries through market-opening measures, (b) stronger emphasis on ***reciprocity*** in market access to other countries, accompanied by market-opening initiatives, and (c) the use of ***contingent protection*** (anti-dumping, countervailing and safeguard measures) and, sometimes, other, less transparent measures to protect domestic producers. *See also* ***competitive liberalization***.

Mixing requirements: *see* ***local content requirements***.

Mobility of business people: *see* ***business mobility***.

Modalities: ways or forms of organizing work in the WTO, including trade negotiations. They set broad outlines, such as formulas or approaches for tariff reductions, for final commitments.

Model Arbitration Clause: also called Separate Arbitration Agreement. It is contained in the ***UNCITRAL Arbitration Rules***. It reads as follows: "Any dispute, controversy or claim arising out of or relating to this contract, or the breach, termination or invalidity thereof, shall be settled by arbitration in accordance with the UNCITRAL Arbitration Rules as present in force. Parties

况必须是轻微性质的，特别是因为这些例外必须在《伯尔尼公约》第11条和第11条之二的范围内解读，这些条款给予作者授权公开表演、录音和广播其作品的专有权。

Mirror-image reciprocity
镜像互惠

期望给予另一国的贸易利益将得到完全匹配。另见*边际互惠(reciprocity at the margin)*、*互惠(reciprocity)*。

Mirror retaliation
镜像报复

中止与报复对象国已经违反的义务相同的义务。也称对等报复。

MITI
通商产业省

见*经济产业省(METI)*。

Mixed commission
混合委员会

通常根据双边贸易协定设立的由双方代表组成的机构。混合委员会的任务是定期审议协定执行情况。另见*联合贸易委员会(joint trade committee)*。

Mixed credits
混合信贷

发达捐助国向发展中国家提供部分按商业条件和部分按补贴利率的信贷。此类信贷的目的通常为资助能够为受援国经济发展作出重要贡献的项目。假设为如果全部依赖商业融资这些项目即无法推进。另见*官方发展援助(official development assistance)*、*贸易与援助(trade and aid)*。

Mixed export cartel
混合出口卡特尔

见*卡特尔(cartel)*。

Mixed tariff
混合关税

见*混合关税(compound tariff)*。

Mixed trade policies
混合贸易政策

同时实施被认为最适当的但具有不同近期目标的多种贸易措施组合，尽管这些政策的目的均为扩大一国出口。这些措施可以是：(a)通过市场开放措施提高国内产业竞争力的单边政策；(b)更加强调对其他国家市场准入的互惠，同时采取市场开放倡议；以及(c)采用紧急保护(反倾销、反补贴和保障措施)，有时采取其他不太透明的措施以保护国内生产者。另见*竞争性自由化(competitive liberalization)*。

Mixing requirements
混合要求

见*当地含量要求(local content requirements)*。

Mobility of business people
商业人员流动性

见*商业流动性(business mobility)*。

Modalities
模式

WTO中组织工作的方式或形式，包括贸易谈判。模式为最终承诺设定总的框架，例如关税削减的公式或方式。

Model Arbitration Clause
示范仲裁条款

也称独立仲裁协议。包含在《联合国国际贸易法委员会仲裁规则》中。内容如下：“合同中的示范仲裁条款任何争议、争执或请求，凡由于本合同而引起的

may wish to consider adding: (a) The appointing authority shall be (name of institution or person); (b) The number of arbitrators shall be (one or three); (c) The place of arbitration shall be (town or country); The language(s) to be used in the arbitral proceedings shall be (language)." *See also* ***arbitration***. [uncitral.org]

Model Bilateral Agreement on Mutual Administrative Assistance in Customs Matters: *see* ***International Convention on Mutual Administrative Assistance for the Prevention, Investigation and Repression of Customs Offences***.

Model measures for RTAs/FTAs: a set of indicative examples of provisions being developed in ***APEC*** that might be included in a ***free-trade agreement***. The model measures are not in legal language, and they are not binding. The chapters concluded so far are competition policy, environment, trade in goods, rules of origin and origin procedures, temporary entry of business persons, trade facilitation, technical barriers to trade, government procurement, transparency, dispute settlement and cooperation. *See also* ***Best practice for RTAs/FTAs in APEC***.

Modes of services delivery: in the ***Uruguay Round*** negotiations on the ***General Agreement on Trade in Services*** participants agreed to divide services trade into four modes: (1) *cross-border supply*, where the producer remains in one territory and the consumer in another; (2) *consumption abroad*, where the consumer travels from one country to the country of the service producer to obtain the service; (3) *commercial presence*, where services are provided through ***establishment*** of an operation in the other country; and (4) *presence of natural persons*, where the producer travels from one country to another to produce or deliver a service. This approach is useful for analytical purposes, but it does not necessarily reflect the way services are traded, and it has made the listing and interpretation of ***commitments*** more complex than need be the case. *See also* ***cross-border trade in services***, ***services*** and ***trade in services***.

Monetary assessments: refers to proposals arising from time to time for the use of fines instead of trade sanctions to secure compliance with dispute settlement panel decisions made under ***free-trade agreements***. Assessing the damage suffered by the winning party because of the losing party's failure to remedy its failings is of course possible. It is less certain that an adequate mechanism could be found to enforce a reasonably prompt payment of these assessments.

Monetary Compensation Amounts: MCAs. A system of border levies and subsidies in force in the ***European Economic Community*** until 31 December 1992. MCAs were abolished as part of achieving the ***European Single Market*** which did away with internal borders for economic activities.

Monetary union: the use by two or more economies of the same currency and the pursuit of a common monetary policy. *See also* ***Euro*** and ***Eurozone***.

Monopoly: a single provider or seller of goods and services who is often maintained through legislation permitting no others to perform the same activities. Monopolies can also occur through natural market development in the private

或与之有关的，或由于本合同的违反、终止或无效而引起的或与之有关的，均应按照《联合国国际贸易法委员会仲裁规则》仲裁解决。各当事方应当考虑增列：(a)指定机构应为(机构名称或人名)；(b)仲裁员人数应为(1名或3名)；(c)仲裁地应为(城市或国家)；(d)仲裁程序中使用的语言应为(语言)。”另见*仲裁(arbitration)*。

Model Bilateral Agreement on Mutual Administrative Assistance in Customs Matters

关于海关事务行政互助的双边示范协定

见*关于为防止、调查和惩处违犯海关法罪行为实行行政互助的国际公约(International Convention on Mutual Administrative Assistance for the Prevention, Investigation and Repression of Customs Offences)*。

Model measures for RTAs/FTAs

区域贸易协定/自由贸易协定示范措施

APEC制定的一套可纳入自由贸易协定的条款指示性示例。示范措施不使用法律语言，且不具约束力。目前已完成的章节为竞争政策、环境、货物贸易、原产地规则和原产地程序、商务人员临时入境、贸易便利化、技术性贸易壁垒、政府采购、透明度、争端解决及合作。另见*APEC区域贸易协定/自由贸易协定最佳实践(Best practice for RTAs/FTAs in APEC)*。

Modes of services delivery

服务提供模式

在乌拉圭回合关于《服务贸易总协定》的谈判中，参加方同意将服务贸易分为4种模式：(1)跨境提供，指生产者位于一领土中，消费者位于另一领土中；(2)境外消费，指消费者从一国旅行至服务生产者所在国家获得服务；(3)商业存在，指通过在另一国设立提供服务；以及(4)自然人流动，指生产者从一国旅行至另一国生产或交付服务。此种方式虽有助于进行分析，但不一定完全反映服务交易方式，且使承诺的列出和解释比实际需要更为复杂。另见*跨境服务贸易(cross-border trade in services)*、*服务(services)*、*服务贸易(trade in services)*。

Monetary assessments

货币评估

指不时提出的为保证根据自由贸易协定作出的争端解决专家组裁决得到遵守而使用罚款代替贸易制裁的建议。评估胜诉方因败诉方未能纠正其错误而遭受的损失是可能的，但不确定的是能否找到适当的机制合理及时强制支付评估得出的结果。

Monetary Compensation Amounts

货币补偿额

MCAs。1992年12月31日之前在欧洲经济共同体内实施的边境税和补贴制度。此种制度作为实现欧洲单一市场的一部分成果已被废除，单一市场取消了经济活动的内部边界。

Monetary union

货币联盟

指两个或两个以上经济体使用同一种货币，并推行共同货币政策。另见*欧元(Euro)*、*欧元区(Eurozone)*。

Monopoly

垄断

货物或服务的单一提供者或销售者，通常通过不允许其他人从事相同活动的立法得以维持。垄断还可以通过私营部门中的自然市场发展而产生，但此种

sector, but they tend to be under constant threat from prospective new entrants. *See also* ***deregulation***, ***essential facilities doctrine***, ***natural monopoly***, ***re-regulation*** and ***single-desk selling***.

Monopsony: the existence of a single buyer of certain goods or services, usually maintained through legislation.

Montant de soutien*:** *Fr.* margin of support. An element in the proposal by the ***European Economic Community for negotiations on agriculture during the ***Kennedy Round***. According to the definition offered by the EEC, "the margin of support for a given agricultural product is equal to the difference between the price of the product on the international market and the remuneration actually obtained by the national producer". Critics at the time noted that this definition had the advantage, from the EEC's perspective, of directing attention to the support mechanisms of others, but that it had serious flaws. The most important one was the absence of a competitive world price for major agricultural products since these prices were themselves influenced by domestic price support systems and subsidies.

Monterrey Consensus: adopted on 22 March 2002 in Monterrey, Mexico, as the outcome of the International Conference on Financing and Development, organized under the auspices of the ***United Nations***. It sought to achieve the goal of eradicating poverty, achieving sustained economic growth and promoting sustainable development through calls for (a) mobilizing domestic financial resources for development, (b) harnessing international trade as an engine for development and reaffirming the commitment of participants to trade liberalization, (c) increasing international financial and technical cooperation for development, and (d) appropriate strategies for dealing with external debt. Conference participants also committed themselves to keeping fully engaged to ensuring proper follow-up to implementation of conference commitments.

Montreal mid-term review: *see* ***Uruguay Round***.

Montreal Protocol: *Montreal Protocol on Substances that Deplete the Ozone Layer*. Adopted in 1987. The Protocol addresses concerns about the impact that uncontrolled production or consumption by non-parties would have on the effectiveness of controls agreed by the parties. It contains provisions designed to restrict the relocation of industries using or producing CFCs (chlorofluorocarbons) from signatory countries to countries that are not signatories. These provisions may be in conflict with the WTO most-favoured-nation principle. Developing countries may apply for funding from the Multilateral Fund for the Implementation of the Montreal Protocol to support the implementation of their commitments under the Protocol. *See also* ***multilateral environment agreements***.

Moral hazard: the risk that a policy or mechanism aimed at preventing a certain event makes it more likely that the event will occur. This term is mainly used in discussions of finance and insurance matters. For example, a borrower may become more profligate if he or she knows that emergency funds are available if a default seems possible.

垄断经常受到潜在新加入者的威胁。另见*取消管制(deregulation)*、*必要设施原则(essential facilities doctrine)*、*自然垄断(natural monopoly)*、*重新管制(re-regulation)*、*专责销售(single-desk selling)*。

Monopsony

买方垄断

存在某种货物或服务的单一买家，通常通过立法得以维持。

Montant de soutien

支持幅度

法语。在肯尼迪回合中，欧洲经济共同体农业谈判提案的一部分。根据欧共体提出的定义，指"对一指定农产品的支持幅度等于国际市场上该产品的价格与国内生产者实际获得的补偿之间的差额"。当时的批评者指出，从欧共体的角度出发，这一定义有利于将注意力转移到其他国家的支持机制上，但有严重的缺陷。最主要的缺陷是，缺乏主要农产品有竞争力的世界价格，因为这些价格本身受到国内价格支持和补贴的影响。

Monterrey Consensus

蒙特雷共识

2002年3月22日在墨西哥蒙特雷通过，作为联合国主持下召开的发展筹资问题国际会议的成果。共识旨在实现消除贫穷、实现持续性经济增长和促进可持续发展目标，通过呼吁：(a)筹集国内金融资源促进发展；(b)利用国际贸易作为发展动力，并重申参与者致力于实现贸易自由化；(c)加强国际金融和技术合作以促进发展；以及(d)处理外债的适当战略。与会者还承诺将继续全面参与，以保证适当跟进会议承诺的执行。

Montreal mid-term review

蒙特利尔中期审评

见*乌拉圭回合(Uruguay Round)*。

Montreal Protocol

蒙特利尔议定书

1987年通过的《关于消耗臭氧层物质的蒙特利尔议定书》。议定书关注非缔约方不受控制地生产或消费对缔约方议定的控制措施的有效性产生的影响。议定书包含旨在限制使用或生产氟氯碳化合物的产业从签署方转移到非签署方的条款。这些条款可能与WTO最惠国待遇原则相冲突。发展中国家可以向蒙特利尔多边基金申请资助以支持履行其在议定书项下的承诺。另见*多边环境协定(multilateral environment agreements)*。

Moral hazard

道德风险

指旨在防止某一事件发生的一项政策或机制反而使该事件更有可能发生的风险。该词主要用于金融和保险事务的讨论中。例如，如果借款人知道在可能发生违约的情况下可以获得应急资金，那么就可能会变得更加挥霍。

Moral rights: the idea expressed in Article 6bis of the ***Berne Convention*** that "independently of the author's economic rights, and even after the transfer of the said rights, the author shall have the right to claim authorship of the work and to object to any distortion, mutilation or other modification of, or derogatory action to, the said work, which would be prejudicial to his honour or reputation". Moral rights therefore pertain to the author's person, whereas ***copyright*** pertains to the work itself. Not all members of the Berne Convention recognize moral rights in their national copyright legislation. *See also* ***intellectual property*** and ***WIPO***.

Moratorium: in ***trade policy*** negotiations this is the same as a ***standstill***. It is usually is imposed before the start of negotiations to ensure the participants do not raise their ***tariffs*** or change their regulations with the sole aim of using them as ***negotiating coin***.

Moratorium on customs duties on electronic transmissions: adopted as part of the WTO *Ministerial* ***Declaration on Global Electronic Commerce*** in 1998. This was a non-binding undertaking not to impose customs duties on products ordered and delivered (transmitted) electronically. The moratorium has been extended several times. It is now valid until the 2020 Ministerial Conference. ***APEC*** adopted a similar moratorium in 2000 and converted it into a long-term action in 2002.

Moratorium on non-violation cases in intellectual property rights: Article 64 of the ***Agreement on Trade-Related Aspects of Intellectual Property Rights*** states that ***non-violation*** cases in intellectual property may not be launched for a period of five years after the entry into force of the Agreement, i.e. until 1 January 2000, and that WTO members must examine the scope and modalities for such complaints. The common ground has not yet been found, and the moratorium has been extended several times. It is now valid until the next ***WTO Ministerial Conference***.

More than an equitable share of the market: *see* ***equitable share of the market*** and ***Wheat flour***.

Most-favoured-nation tariff: MFN tariff. The ***tariff*** applied by WTO members to goods from other WTO members with which they have not concluded a ***preferential trade arrangement***. Strictly speaking, the MFN tariff also applies to ***non-originating goods*** imported from free-trade partners. In the case of WTO non-members, the application of these rates may be a requirement of a ***bilateral trade agreement***. *See also* ***general tariff*** and ***most-favoured nation treatment***.

Most-favoured-nation treatment: MFN. This is the rule, usually established through a trade agreement, that a country gives each of the trading partners with which it has concluded relevant agreements the best treatment it gives to any of them in a given product. MFN is not in itself an obligation to extend any favourable treatment to another party, nor is it an obligation to negotiate for better treatment. The fundamental point of MFN therefore is equality of treatment of other countries, and in some older treatises it is indeed called

Moral rights

精神权利

《伯尔尼公约》第6条之二所表达的观点，即"不受作者财产权的影响，甚至在上述财产权转让之后，作者仍保有主张对其作品的著作者身份的权利，并享有反对对上述作品进行任何歪曲或割裂或有损于作者声誉的其他损害的权利。"因此，精神权利属于作者本人，而版权属于作品本身。并非所有《伯尔尼公约》成员国都在其国家版权立法中纳入精神权利。另见*知识产权(intellectual property)*、*世界知识产权组织(WIPO)*。

Moratorium

暂停

在贸易政策谈判中，该词与维持现状同义。通常在谈判开始前实行，以保证参加方不会提高关税或修改法规，而其惟一目的是用作谈判筹码。

Moratorium on customs duties on electronic transmissions

电子传输暂免关税

1998 年 WTO 部长级会议通过的 WTO《全球电子商务宣言》的一部分。是关于通过电子方式订购和交付(传输)的产品免征关税的非约束承诺。暂免已经多次延长。目前有效期至 2020 年 WTO 部长级会议。APEC 在 2000 年通过了类似的暂免措施，并于 2002 年转为长期行动。

Moratorium on non-violation cases in intellectual property rights

知识产权非违反案件暂停起诉

《与贸易有关的知识产权协定》第 64 条规定，在协定生效之日起 5 年内，即 2000 年 1 月 1 日之前，不得提起知识产权非违反之诉，WTO 成员必须审查此类起诉的范围和模式。WTO 成员尚未形成共同立场，暂停已经多次延长。现在的有效期至下一届 WTO 部长级会议。

More than an equitable share of the market

不公正市场份额

另见*公正市场份额(equitable share of the market)*、*小麦面粉案(Wheat flour)*。

Most-favoured-nation tariff

最惠国关税

MFN 关税。WTO 成员对于源自未与其缔结优惠贸易安排的其他 WTO 成员的货物适用的关税。严格地讲，最惠国关税也适用于从自由贸易伙伴进口的非原产货物。对于非 WTO 成员而言，适用这些税率可能是双边贸易协定的一项要求。另见*普通关税(general tariff)*、*最惠国待遇(most-favoured nation treatment)*。

Most-favoured-nation treatment

最惠国待遇

MFN。通常通过贸易协定确立的规则，规定一国对与其签订相关协定的每一贸易伙伴所给予的待遇应为其给予任一贸易伙伴的一给定产品的最佳待遇。最惠国待遇本身并不是向另一方提供任何优惠待遇的一项义务，也不是谈判更好待遇的一项义务。因此，最惠国待遇的根本点是给予其他国家待遇的平

"foreign parity". Despite the apparently static nature of MFN, it has acted as a powerful motor for ***trade liberalization***. Together with ***national treatment***, MFN makes up the principle of ***non-discrimination***. The MFN rule, in one form or another, can be traced back at least to the sixteenth century. Typical of these older provisions is the formulation contained in the *Treaty of Peace and Friendship between Great Britain and Spain* of 1713, part of the instruments making up the *Treaty of Utrecht*. This says that "the subjects of each kingdom ... shall have the like favour in all things as the subjects of France, or any other foreign nation, the most favour'd, have, possess and enjoy, or at any time hereafter may have, possess or enjoy". An MFN clause was included in the ***Cobden-Chevalier Treat***y between England and France of 1860. This is thought to be the ancestor of its modern application. At any rate, the MFN rule was then copied into many other European trade agreements. In the years before the First World War, the MFN rule suffered a decline. The war years led to its virtual demise. In the third of his fourteen points, President Wilson called in January 1918 for the removal, as far as possible, of all economic barriers and the establishment of an equality of trade conditions among all the nations consenting to the peace and associating themselves for its maintenance. This is deemed by some to have been the equivalent of a call for MFN. The Versailles peace conference did not discuss trade barriers, but in the peace treaty Germany and the other central powers were required to extend unconditional MFN for three years to the trade of the allied powers. The Covenant of the ***League of Nations*** only referred to "equitable treatment" of commerce of other League members. This fell well short of an MFN clause. The Geneva World Economic Conference of May 1927 pronounced strongly in favour of the widest possible interpretation of the MFN clause, and it stressed that its use in commercial treaties ought to be normal. In 1933, the League of Nations published a 300-word model text of an MFN clause. By that time, economic conditions had been very difficult for several years, and the MFN principle was not able to attract broad support. The ***Atlantic Charter*** of 1941 revived the MFN principle and made it the cornerstone of the post-war ***multilateral trading system*** as exemplified by the ***GATT***. In the WTO, MFN is the binding general obligation that any ***concession*** made to another country must immediately be extended to all other members. All WTO members grant each other treatment for trade in goods as favourable as they give to any other country in the application and administration of customs regulations, tariffs and related charges. A similar provision applies to ***trade in services***. There are, however, exceptions to the MFN obligation. Here, we mention only some of the important ones. MFN members satisfying the conditions of GATT ***Article XXIV*** and ***Article V*** of the ***General Agreement for Trade in Services*** (GATS) for membership of preferential ***free-trade areas*** or ***customs unions*** are not obliged to give countries that are not members of the same preferential trading arrangement the same kind of access. ***Part IV of the GATT*** and the ***Enabling Clause*** allow discriminatory treatment in favour of developing countries. Developed

等性，在一些较早的条约中，最惠国待遇确实被称为“对外同等”。尽管最惠国待遇具有明显静态特征，但它发挥了实现贸易自由化的强大动力。最惠国待遇与国民待遇一起构成非歧视原则。这样或那样形式的最惠国规则至少可以追溯到16世纪。这些较早条款的一个典型例子是1713年的《大不列颠与西班牙和平友好条约》中所含表述方式，该条约构成《乌德勒支和约》法律文件的一部分。这一条款规定：“每一王国的臣民……在所有事务上都应与法国或享有最优厚待遇的任何别国臣民一样，在当下和今后，得到、拥有和享受同样的待遇。”1860年英格兰和法国之间签署的《科布登-舍瓦利埃尔条约》中包含了一项最惠国待遇条款。这被认为是现代适用的最惠国待遇的鼻祖。无论如何，最惠国待遇规则随后被复制到许多其他欧洲贸易协定中。在第一次世界大战前的几年里，最惠国待遇规则受到冷落。战争年代导致其事实上的消亡。威尔逊总统在1918年1月的十四点原则中的第三点呼吁，尽可能取消所有经济壁垒并在所有支持和平并联合起来维持和平的国家之间建立平等的贸易条件。此点被一些人认为相当于呼吁最惠国待遇。凡尔赛和平会议没有讨论贸易壁垒问题，但在和平公约中，德国和其他轴心国被要求在3年内将最惠国待遇无条件扩大到与协约国的贸易中。《国际联盟盟约》仅提到了“公正对待”与其他盟约成员的商业。这与最惠国条款相去甚远。1927年5月召开的日内瓦世界经济会议强有力地赞成尽可能最宽泛地解释最惠国待遇条款，并强调这一条款在商业条约中的使用应当是正常的。1933年，国际联盟发表了一份300字的最惠国待遇条款模板文本。那时经济状况已经多年出现困难，最惠国待遇原则未能得到广泛支持。1941年的《大西洋宪章》重新激活了最惠国待遇原则，并使之成为战后多边贸易体制的基石，GATT就是一例。在WTO中，最惠国待遇是具有约束力的普遍义务，即对另一成员作出的任何减让均必须立即给予所有其他成员。在海关规章、关税和有关费用的适用和管理方面，所有WTO成员相互给予货物贸易的待遇不得低于给予任何其他成员的待遇。类似规定也适用于服务贸易。但是，最惠国待遇义务也有例外。在此只提及其中一些重要的例外。例如满足GATT第24条和《服务贸易总协定》(GATS)第5条的条件的加入优惠自由贸易区或关税同盟的最惠国待遇成员，无义务给予不属同一优惠贸易安排的成员相同的准入。GATT第四部分和授权条款允许提供有利于发展中国家的差别待遇。发达国家可维持普惠制(GSP)方案，对来自发展中国家的进口产品给予优惠待遇。可以请求获得豁免，以此作为给予一些成员更优惠待遇的法律根据。还有互不适用的可能性，即现有WTO成员可以对一新加入

countries may maintain ***GSP*** schemes which give preferential treatment to developing country imports. It is possible to ask for a ***waiver*** which provides the legal basis for treating some members more favourably. There is also the possibility of ***non-application*** under which an existing WTO member can deny the benefits of the agreement to a newly acceding member. The GATS also permits the taking out of a time-bound ***MFN exemption***. A concern sometimes voiced about the MFN principle is that it allows ***free riders*** to take advantage of trade-liberalizing actions of others without making an equivalent effort. *See also* ***conditional most-favoured-nation treatment***, ***general tariff***, ***general trade***, ***Jackson-Vanik amendment***, ***LDC services waiver***, ***minimum standard of treatment***, ***normal trade relations*** and ***permanent normal trade relations***.

MOU: *see* ***memorandum of understanding***.

Moutarde de Dijon: *see* ***generic geographical indications***.

Movement of goods: another way to describe what happens when goods are trade internationally, i.e. when they are imported and exported.

Movement of natural persons: a term used in the ***General Agreement on Trade in Services*** to signify the temporary entry by service suppliers, i.e. people, into another jurisdiction for the purpose of selling or supplying a service. *See also* ***business mobility*** and ***modes of services delivery***.

MSMEs: micro-, small and medium-sized enterprises. *See* ***joint initiatives***.

Multi-column tariff: a ***tariff schedule*** that discriminates between the various trading partners. Tariff rates in the first column might be reserved for countries not receiving ***most-favoured-nation treatment*** (MFN) and the second column for countries accorded MFN. The third and additional columns would contain the rates applicable to various ***preferential trade arrangements***, such as ***free-trade area*** partners or those given to developing countries under the ***GSP*** (Generalized System of Preferences). *See also* ***single-column tariff***.

Multi-domestic corporation: a form of ***transnational corporation*** which adopts a strategy for its units centred in each case on individual countries. Typically, it sets up an operation in another country mainly to supply the market of that country.

Multi-Fibre Arrangement: MFA, formally *Agreement Regarding International Trade in Textiles*. This was an agreement between textile-producing and consuming countries concluded in 1973 and renegotiated periodically afterwards to manage trade in textile products through the concept of ***market disruption***. The MFA was replaced by the WTO ***Agreement on Textiles and Clothing*** under which restrictions had to be phased out over ten years starting on 1 January 1995. *See also* ***Long-Term Arrangement Regarding International Trade in Cotton Textiles*** and ***Short-Term Arrangement Regarding International Trade in Cotton Textiles***.

Multifunctionality: the idea that agriculture has many functions in addition to producing food and fibre. These functions may be environmental protection, landscape preservation, rural employment, etc. The term appears to have originated in a communiqué issued in March 1998 by agricultural ministers

成员拒绝给予协定利益。《服务贸易总协定》还允许采取有时限的最惠国待遇例外。有时对最惠国待遇原则提出的担心是，该原则允许搭便车者利用其他成员的贸易自由化行动而不必付出同样的努力。另见*有条件最惠国待遇(conditional most-favoured-nation treatment)*、*普通关税(general tariff)*、*一般贸易(general trade)*、*杰克逊-瓦尼克修正案(Jackson-Vanik amendment)*、*最不发达国家服务贸易豁免(LDC services waiver)*、*最低待遇标准(minimum standard of treatment)*、*正常贸易关系(normal trade relations)*、*永久正常贸易关系(permanent normal trade relations)*。

MOU
谅解备忘录
见*谅解备忘录(memorandum of understanding)*。

Moutarde de Dijon
第戎芥末
见*通用地理标志(generic geographical indications)*。

Movement of goods
货物流动
描述当货物在国际间进行贸易的状态的另一种方式，即当货物进口或出口时。

Movement of natural persons
自然人流动
《服务贸易总协定》中使用的词语，表示为销售或提供一服务，服务提供者，即人，临时进入另一管辖范围。另见*商业流动性(business mobility)*、*服务提供模式(modes of services delivery)*。

MSMEs
中小微企业
微型、小型和中型企业。另见*联合倡议(joint initiatives)*。

Multi-column tariff
多栏关税
区别对待不同贸易伙伴的关税税则。第一栏中的税率可能专门适用于不享受最惠国待遇(MFN)的国家，第二栏适用于享受最惠国待遇的国家，第三栏和其他栏可以包含适用于各优惠贸易安排的税率，例如自由贸易区伙伴或根据普惠制(GSP)给予发展中国家的税率。另见*单栏关税(single-column tariff)*。

Multi-domestic corporation
多国化公司
跨国公司的一种形式，采用其组成单位以所在单个国家为中心的战略。典型情况为，公司在另一国开展经营以供应该国市场为主。

Multi-Fibre Arrangement
多种纤维协定
正式名称为《国际纺织品贸易安排》(英文误为 agreement，应为 arrangement—译注)。纺织品生产国和消费国于 1973 年缔结的一项协定，此后定期重新谈判，目的在于以市场扰乱的概念管理纺织品贸易。《多种纤维协定》已被 WTO《纺织品与服装协定》所取代，后者规定限制措施在 1995 年 1 月 1 日开始的 10 年时间内逐步取消。另见*国际棉纺织品贸易长期安排(Long-Term Arrangement Regarding International Trade in Cotton Textiles)*、*国际棉纺织品贸易短期安排(Short-Term Arrangement Regarding International Trade in Cotton Textiles)*。

Multifunctionality
多功能性
农业除生产食品和纤维外还有许多功能的理念。这些功能可能是环境保护、

from ***OECD*** countries. The recognition of the various roles agriculture can play is hardly new, but multifunctionality has quickly become one of the dividing lines of agricultural ***trade policy***. Those who stress its importance are seen as leaning towards ***protectionism***. Those who oppose its use like to think of themselves as promoters of agricultural trade liberalization. *See also* ***Friends of Multifunctionality*** and ***non-trade concerns***. [OECD 2003]

Multilateral agreement on competition: a proposal at one time or another for future intergovernmental negotiations, but not yet on any negotiating agenda. Some see its prospective purpose as enabling cooperation between national antitrust or competition authorities on enforcement matters. ***Mutual assistance in antitrust matters*** tends to an area where governments tread carefully. Others would prefer an agreement for the international administration of ***antitrust laws*** which would entail common rights and obligations. This may be attempting more than is achievable. *See also* ***Draft International Antitrust Code*** and ***trade and competition***.

Multilateral Agreement on Investment: MAI. The ***OECD*** Ministerial Council Meeting of June 1995 decided to launch negotiations for an agreement on investment liberalization which would also be open to OECD non-members. Ministers hoped that the agreement would contain high standards for liberalizing national investment regimes and that it would have effective dispute settlement provisions. After a promising start the negotiations quickly got bogged down in nearly all areas as the complexities of the matter became clearer. Negotiators also were increasingly attacked by ***non-governmental organizations*** for their alleged secrecy and their purported aim to create an unhindered investment flow between member countries. Neither assessment was accurate, though negotiators were slow to make the negotiating text available publicly or to argue persuasively what the benefits of the proposed agreement would be. More probably, the negotiations collapsed because of irreconcilable differences between members on key provisions and, to outsiders at any rate, the increasingly incomprehensible language of the draft MAI as negotiators tried to reach compromises. Moreover, it appeared that very few non-member countries would seek to accede to the agreement. By 1998, when the negotiating deadline had been extended by one year, one sensed that some governments had decided that the political cost of the proposed agreement had become very high. Negotiations were abandoned in early 1999.

Multilateral Agreement on the Liberalization of International Air Transportation: MALIAT. This Agreement seeks to promote ***open-skies arrangements***. Members agree to open route schedules, open traffic rights (including ***seventh-freedom cargo services***), open capacity, multiple airline designation, third-country code-sharing and a minimal tariff-filing regime. Members also agree to maintain airline investment provisions based on effective control and principal place of business which at the same time protect against ***flag-of-convenience*** carriers. The Agreement entered into force on 21 December 2001. Its members are Brunei Darussalam, Chile, Cook Islands, Mongolia

景观保护、农村就业等。该词似乎源于1998年3月经济合作与发展组织(OECD)国家农业部长级会议发表的一份公报。认识到农业可以发挥多种作用并不新鲜，但多功能性已经迅速成为农业贸易政策的一个分界线。那些强调其重要性的人被认为是倾向于保护主义。那些反对其使用的人倾向于把自己看作是农业贸易自由化的推动者。另见*多功能性之友(Friends of Multifunctionality)*、*非贸易关注(non-trade concerns)*。

Multilateral agreement on competition
多边竞争协定

曾经提出的未来进行政府间谈判的提案，但未列入任何谈判议程。一些人认为，其预期目的是促进国家反垄断或竞争主管部门在执行事务上的合作。反垄断事务互助往往是政府小心对待的领域。其他人则主张制定包含共同权利和义务的反垄断法国际管理的协定。这可以是一种尝试，而实现不太可能。另见*国际反垄断法典草案(Draft International Antitrust Code)*、*贸易与竞争(trade and competition)*。

Multilateral Agreement on Investment
多边投资协定

MAI。经济合作与发展组织(OECD)部长理事会1995年6月会议决定启动投资自由化协定的谈判，该谈判也对非OECD成员国开放。部长们希望该协定包含国家投资体制自由化的高标准，且包含有效的争端解决条款。在充满希望的开端过后，随着问题的复杂性更加清晰，几乎所有领域都陷入停滞。由于谈判者声称的机密性及标榜的在成员国之间建立无障碍投资流动的目标，他们越来越多地受到非政府组织的攻击。这两种看法都不准确，尽管谈判者在公开谈判文本或在令人信服地说明拟议协定好处方面行动迟缓。更有可能的是，谈判破裂是由于成员之间在关键条款上存在着不可调和的分歧，且对于局外人而言，谈判者为努力达成妥协而使多边投资协定草案的文字愈发难以理解。此外，似乎很少有OECD非成员国寻求加入该协定。截至1998年，谈判的最后期限延长了1年，人们察觉到，一些成员政府已经认定，拟议协定的政治成本已经变得非常高。谈判在1999年初被放弃。

Multilateral Agreement on the Liberalization of International Air Transportation
国际航空运输自由化多边协定

MALIAT。协定寻求促进开放天空安排。成员同意开放航线时刻表、开放交通权(包括货运第 7 航权)、开放运力、多航线指定、第三国代码共享和最低关税申报制度。成员还同意维持基于有效管制和主要营业地点的航线投资条款，同时保证防止方便旗航空公司。协定于 2001 年 12 月 21 日生效效。成员包括

(for cargo only), New Zealand, Samoa, Singapore, Tonga and the United States. *See also* ***freedoms of the air***. [maliat.gov.nz]

Multilateral Agricultural Framework: an idea emerging in the later stages of the ***Tokyo Round*** for a mechanism which would oversee the negotiating results in agriculture, and which also would provide a forum for the exchange of information aimed at preventing problems in agricultural trade. In particular, it was thought that the framework would eliminate continuing political and commercial confrontations in this sector. The proposal also aimed to establish an International Agriculture Consultative Council under GATT auspices. When the Tokyo Round ended on 12 April 1979, participants were still far from an agreement on this proposal, and post-Round negotiations did not lead to a result.

Multilateral development banks: institutions established to provide financial support and advice to support the economic and social development of developing countries through long-term loans on commercial terms, credits on concessional terms and grants. Membership of these banks consists of developed and developing countries. The main ones are the African Development Bank (based in Abidjan, Côte d'Ivoire), the Asian Development Bank (Manila), the European Bank for Reconstruction and Development (London), the ***World Bank*** and the Inter-American Bank Group (both in Washington DC). More recent creations are the ***Asian Infrastructure Investment Bank*** and the ***New Development Bank***. *See also* ***international financial institutions***.

Multilateral environment agreements: agreements, conventions and protocols agreed multilaterally and aimed at eliminating or reducing damage to the environment. The United Nations ***InforMEA initiative*** lists thirty-four global treaties and protocols and fifty-three regional treaties and protocols classified into biodiversity, chemicals and waste, climate and atmosphere, and marine and freshwater categories. At least eighteen of them contain specific trade provisions. Among these are the ***Basel Convention***, ***Cartagena Protocol on Biosafety***, ***CITES***, ***Convention on Biological Diversity***, ***Convention on Persistent Organic Pollutants***, ***Convention on the Prior Informed Consent Procedure for Certain Hazardous Chemicals and Pesticides in International Trade***, ***Montreal Protocol***, ***United Nations Framework Convention on Climate Change*** and the ***Kyoto Protocol***. Some other agreements contain provisions which could have an effect on the formulation of trade policy, including ***Agenda 21*** and the ***Rio Declaration on Environment and Development***. [www.informea.org]

Multilateral Fund for the Implementation of the Montreal Protocol: *see* ***Montreal Protocol***.

Multilateral Investment Fund: established in 1993 by the Inter-American Development Bank to encourage growth in the private sector in Latin America and the Caribbean. It is located in Washington, DC.

Multilateral Investment Guarantee Agency: MIGA. Established on 12 April 1988 under the auspices of the ***World Bank***. Its purpose is to encourage increased levels of private direct investment in developing countries. It acts

文莱、智利、库克群岛、蒙古(仅限货物)、新西兰、萨摩亚、新加坡、汤加和美国。另见*航空自由(freedoms of the air)*。

Multilateral Agricultural Framework

多边农业框架

东京回合后期提出的设想，即建立一种机制，以监督农业谈判的结果，并提供交流信息的场所以避免农业贸易问题。特别是，人们认为该框架将消除这一部门持续存在的政治和商业冲突。提案还旨在建立在GATT主持下的国际农业咨询理事会。当东京回合于1979年4月12日结束时，参加方仍然远未就这一提案达成一致，且回合之后的谈判也没有产生结果。

Multilateral development banks

多边开发银行

通过提供基于商业条件的长期贷款、基于优惠条件的信贷和赠款为支持发展中国家经济和社会发展提供财政支持和咨询的机构。银行成员包括发达国家和发展中国家。主要机构包括非洲开发银行(设在科特迪瓦阿比让)、亚洲开发银行(设在马尼拉)、欧洲复兴开发银行(设在伦敦)、世界银行和美洲银行集团(均设在华盛顿)。最近创设的有亚洲基础设施投资银行和新开发银行。另见*国际金融机构(international financial institutions)*。

Multilateral environment agreements

多边环境协定

指多边议定的旨在消除或减少对环境破坏的协定、公约和议定书。联合国关于多边环境协定信息的倡议列出了 34 项全球条约和议定书及 53 项区域条约和议定书，分为生物多样性、化学品和废物、气候和大气以及海洋和淡水等类别。其中至少有 18 项包含具体贸易条款。其中包括：《巴塞尔公约》、《卡塔赫纳生物安全议定书》、《濒危野生动植物种国际贸易公约》、《生物多样性公约》、《关于持久性有机污染物的公约》、《关于在国际贸易中对某些危险化学品和农药采用事先知情同意程序的公约》、《蒙特利尔议定书》、《联合国气候变化框架公约》和《京都议定书》。其他一些协定包含可能对贸易政策制定产生影响的条款，包括《21 世纪议程》和《里约环境与发展宣言》。

Multilateral Fund for the Implementation of the Montreal Protocol

蒙特利尔多边基金

见*蒙特利尔议定书(Montreal Protocol)*。

Multilateral Investment Fund

多边投资基金

1993年由美洲开发银行设立，旨在鼓励拉丁美洲和加勒比地区私营部门的发展。该机构设在华盛顿。

Multilateral Investment Guarantee Agency

多边投资担保机构

MIGA。1988 年 4 月 12 日在世界银行主持下设立，旨在鼓励增加在发展中国家的私人直接投资。针对东道国的某些政治风险，起到投资保险公司的作用。

as an insurer of investment against certain political risks in the host country. It also offers technical assistance to help developing countries to improve their investment climates and to attract new investment. MIGA is located in Washington, DC. *See also* ***foreign direct investment*** and ***World Association of Investment Promotion Agencies***.

Multilateralism: an approach to the conduct of international trade based on cooperation, equal rights and obligations, ***non-discrimination*** and the participation as equals of many countries regardless of their size or share of international trade. This is the basis of the rules and principles embodied in treaties such as the ***WTO Agreement*** and its components.

Multilateralization of free-trade agreements: the spread of ***free-trade agreements*** and other ***preferential trade arrangements*** over the past two decades has led to the conduct of a large proportion of international trade under such agreements. Some countries are parties to several arrangements with the same parties. A simple example is that of Australia and Singapore. The Singapore–Australia Free Trade Agreement entered into force in 2003. Both of them are parties to the ASEAN–Australia–New Zealand Free Trade Agreement of 2010. They are also parties to the ***Comprehensive and Progressive Agreement for Trans-Pacific Partnership*** of 2018, and they are both negotiating partners in the ***Regional Comprehensive Economic Partnership***. The architecture of free-trade agreement also has shown convergence, but there are of course important differences in the operation and impact of these provisions in the various agreements. Overall, however, the rules of the ***multilateral trading system*** remain the framework for the conduct of international trade. It is clear that most free-trade agreements can only function because there is such a framework. Another aspect is that, while the pace of multilateral trade liberalization has slowed down, the negotiation of free-trade agreements is continuing apace. The question of how preferential agreements could contribute in a more systematic way to multilateral trade liberalization has occupied analysts and policy makers alike. One proposed way of proceeding is that regional trade agreements could be multilateralized. At first glance, this looks feasible, but there are important difficulties in its way. For example, a choice would have to be made of the provisions in free-trade agreements that could actually be multilateralized. Tariffs would be easy enough. They are the centre of the ***GATT***, and there is huge experience in tariff negotiations, both bilaterally and multilaterally. Much more difficult would be the question of ***preferential rules of origin***. These form the dense undergrowth of free-trade agreements, and ***product-specific rules*** would be hard to harmonize so that everyone would be satisfied. The ***General Agreement on Trade in Services*** (GATS) has detailed rules for trade in services, and the services rules in most free-trade agreements are based on them. The problem would be how to deal with the schedules of commitments appended to these agreements. There may be limited interest among the parties to bring them under the purview of the GATS. Investment and competition would be more difficult since neither of these is subject to a

该机构还提供技术援助，以帮助发展中国家改善投资环境，吸引新投资。该机构设在华盛顿。另见*外国直接投资(foreign direct investment)*、*世界投资促进机构协会(World Association of Investment Promotion Agencies)*。

Multilateralism

多边主义

众多国家在合作、权利与义务平等、非歧视以及平等参与基础上开展国际贸易的方式，不论国家大小或国际贸易份额多少。这是《WTO协定》及其组成协定等条约中规则和原则的基础。

Multilateralization of free-trade agreements

自由贸易协定多边化

自由贸易协定和其他优惠贸易安排在过去20年间的扩张使国际贸易中很大一部分在此类协定项下进行。一些国家与相同参加方签署了多项安排。简单的例子是澳大利亚和新加坡。《新加坡—澳大利亚自由贸易协定》于2003年生效。两国均为2010年《东盟—澳大利亚—新西兰自由贸易协定》参加方。两国还是2018年《全面与进步跨太平洋伙伴关系协定》缔约方，且均为《区域全面经济伙伴关系协定》的谈判伙伴。自由贸易协定的结构也表现出趋同性，当然不同协定中这些条款的运用和影响存在很大区别。但是总体而言，多边贸易体制的规则仍然是开展国际贸易的框架。很明显，大多数自由贸易协定是因为存在这样一个框架才能够发挥作用。另一个方面是，尽管多边贸易自由化的步伐已经放缓，但自由贸易协定的谈判仍在迅速开展。优惠协定如何以更系统的方式促进多边贸易自由化的问题一直困扰着分析家也困扰着决策者。一种建议的方式是区域贸易协定可以多边化。乍一看来，这似乎是可行的，但是此种方式存在重大困难。例如，必须在自由贸易协定中选择那些可以多边化的条款。关税会很简单，这是GATT的核心，在双边和多边关税谈判中积累了丰富的经验。更为困难的问题是优惠原产地规则。这类规则形成了自由贸易协定的密集规则，且特定产品规则难以协调一致而使每个人都满意。《服务贸易总协定》(GATS)规定了详细的服务贸易规则，大多数自由贸易协定的服务贸易规则均以这些规则为基础。问题在于如何处理这些协定所附承诺减让表。各方对将其纳入《服务贸易总协定》的范围兴趣不大。投资和竞争的多边

multilateral framework of rules. In the case of investment the difficulty would also be of how to deal with the lists of ***non-conforming measures***. Another question is how the multilateralization of free-trade agreements would be done. If a party to an agreement were minded to do so, it would want to be sure that the other party had no objections since its perceived benefits would lose some of their value. It would of course be possible for both of the parties, in the case of a bilateral agreement, to make a unilateral commitment to multilateralize the provisions of their agreement. Apart from the obvious question of why they had concluded a preferential agreement in the first place, it might not necessarily be seen as a good option by the producers and exporters covered by the agreement. It would also leave the problem of what to do with the provisions that could not easily be multilateralized because there is no ready access to multilateral rules. Competition is an example. Presumably these provisions had been seen as having value when they were negotiated. In the case of tariffs the long-term trend has been for the preferential rates (normally zero) and the ***applied tariff rates*** under the GATT to converge. A situation in which most of international trade is conducted free of tariffs under the multilateral rules is therefore not too difficult to envisage. It is less certain that this could be the case for services and investment. The progress of the negotiations under the ***Doha Development Agenda*** has shown the difficulties facing multilateral trade liberalization even when the objectives and issues are completely understood. It is hard to see how the objective of a multilateralization of free-trade agreements would fare better. *See also* ***next-generation trade issues***.

Multilateral procurement: the purchase of goods and services by multilateral bodies (e.g. ***United Nations***, ***IMF***, WTO, etc.) for their own use or for use on projects funded and managed by them. *See also* ***government procurement***.

Multilateral Specialty Steel Agreement: MSSA. A proposal for a sectoral agreement made in early 1996 by industry associations in Europe and the United States for an agreement that would (a) ban subsidies, (b) remove tariff and non-tariff barriers, and (c) eliminate trade-distorting anti-competitive practices in global specialty steel trade. It would also address the problem of surplus production capacity. The Specialty Steel Industry of North America, a private-sector organization, would in addition like such an agreement "to ensure the effectiveness of United States trade law and to make the ***Section 201*** injury standard compatible with the WTO ***injury*** standard". The proposed agreement is not on any negotiating agenda. *See also* ***Multilateral Steel Agreement***.

Multilateral Steel Agreement: MSA. In the second half of the ***Uruguay Round*** negotiations the United States proposed the conclusion of an MSA with coverage of subjects such as tariff reductions, the elimination of ***quantitative restrictions***, subsidies, the imposition of ***anti-dumping measures***, countervailing duties, etc., related specifically to trade in steel. Negotiations were conducted on a track separate to the Uruguay Round negotiations, and thirty-six countries took part in them. However, negotiations broke down in March 1992. There have been periodic suggestions since, especially by the American Iron

化将更为困难，因为这两者均不在多边规则框架中。对于投资而言，困难还在于如何处理不符措施清单。另一个问题是如何实现自由贸易协定的多边化。如果协定一参加方想这样作，它就需要确定另一参加方没有异议，因为另一参加方所认为的利益将会失去部分价值。对于双边协定而言，双方均有可能作出将双边协定条款多边化的单方面承诺。除为什么当初缔结优惠协定这一显而易见的问题外，协定所涵盖的生产商和出口商可能并不一定认为这是一个好的选择。还有一个问题是，如何处理那些由于没有现存多边规则而无法轻易实现多边化的条款。竞争规则就是一例。想必这些条款在谈判时被认为是有价值的。就关税而言，长期趋势是优惠税率(通常为零)与GATT项下的实施税率趋同。大部分国际贸易是在多边规则之下以零关税进行的情况就不难想象了。对于服务和投资而言就不那么确定了。多哈发展议程谈判的进展显示即使目标和问题已得到充分理解，多边贸易自由化仍然面临困难。很难想象自由贸易协定多边化的目标如何能更好实现。另见*下一代贸易议题(next-generation trade issues)*。

Multilateral procurement

多边采购

多边组织(即联合国、国际货币基金组织、世界贸易组织等)为自用或用于其所资助和管理的项目而购买货物和服务。另见*政府采购(government procurement)*。

Multilateral Specialty Steel Agreement

多边特种钢协定

MSSA。1996年初由欧洲和美国的行业协会提出的一项部门协定的建议，协定将(a)禁止补贴；(b)消除关税和非关税壁垒；以及(c)消除全球特种钢贸易中扭曲贸易的反竞争做法。协定还将处理产能过剩问题。北美特种钢行业协会是一个私营部门组织，还希望达成这样一项协定以“保证美国贸易法的有效性，并使201条款的损害标准与WTO损害标准相一致”。拟议协定未出现在任何谈判议程上。另见*多边钢铁协定(Multilateral Steel Agreement)*。

Multilateral Steel Agreement

多边钢铁协定

MSA。在乌拉圭回合谈判后半期，美国提议缔结一项与专门钢铁贸易有关的多边钢铁协定，涵盖关税削减、取消数量限制、补贴、反倾销措施实施、反补贴税征收等。谈判在独立于乌拉圭回合的轨道上进行，有36个国家参加。但是谈判在1992年3月破裂。自此定期有人提出建议，特别是美国钢铁协会，认为

and Steel Institute, that the MSA should remain a trade policy objective for the United States. Its proponents argue that it should contain a mechanism for ***alternative dispute resolution*** because it would be faster and cheaper than trade litigation, partly because it would not require proof of injury in cases where the MSA had been violated. *See also* ***Multilateral Specialty Steel Agreement*** and ***sectoral trade negotiations***.

Multilateral system of notification and registration of geographical indications: negotiations for such a system were mandated by Article 23.4 of the WTO ***Agreement on Trade-Related Aspects of Intellectual Property Rights*** and set in train by the ***Doha Ministerial Conference***. Negotiations were meant to conclude by the ***Cancún Ministerial Conference***, but agreement was not possible. Negotiations are continuing. *See also* ***geographical indications***.

Multilateral trade agreements: intergovernmental agreements aimed at expanding and liberalizing international trade under non-discriminatory, predictable and transparent conditions set out in an array of rights and obligations. The motivation for taking on these obligations is that all members will increase their welfare by adhering to a common standard of conduct in the management of their trade relations. Typically, such agreements have numerous members representing small, medium-sized and large trading nations. Membership of this kind of agreement is open-ended, but countries wishing to accede usually have to demonstrate that their trade regimes are in keeping with the aims of the agreement, and that the access conditions to their markets roughly match those of existing members. If necessary, they must make adjustments. Before the ***GATT***, entered into force in 1948, trade agreements were mostly bilateral, or they were preferential, such as the ***imperial preferences arrangement***. In the WTO, the term "Multilateral Trade Agreement" refers to the arrangements and associated legal instruments contained in Annexes 1, 2 and 3 to the ***WTO Agreement***. *See also* ***accession***, ***bilateral trade agreement***, ***plurilateral trade agreements*** and ***Prisoner's Dilemma***.

Multilateral trade negotiations: MTN. Also known as *rounds*. They aim to strengthen the rules that ensure orderly and fair conduct of international trade and to reach mutually beneficial agreements reducing barriers to world trade. Eight rounds have been held under GATT auspices since 1947. Each round has consisted of long bargaining sessions. The eight completed rounds and the names by which they are commonly known were: Geneva (1947), Annecy (1949), Torquay (1950), Geneva (1955–56), Dillon (1960–61), Kennedy (1963–67), Tokyo (1973–79) and Uruguay (1986–94). The ninth round, the ***Doha Development Agenda***, was launched by the ***Doha Ministerial Conference*** in November 2001 The content of the rounds up to the ***Kennedy Round*** was tariff reductions only. The early rounds essentially were made up of a series of bilateral negotiations, the results of which were then made available to other members on a most-favoured-nation (MFN) basis. From the Kennedy Round onwards, ***non-tariff measures*** and ***systemic issues*** were also on the agenda. The abbreviation "MTN" was in common use during the ***Tokyo Round***, and it is often used to refer

多边钢铁协定应该仍是美国贸易政策的目标。支持者认为，协定应该包含一个非诉讼争端解决机制，因为这会比贸易诉讼更快、费用更低，部分原因是在违反多边钢铁协定的案件中，不要求损害证明。另见*多边特种钢协定(Multilateral Specialty Steel Agreement)*、*部门贸易谈判(sectoral trade negotiations)*。

Multilateral system of notification and registration of geographical indications
地理标志通报和注册多边制度

WTO《与贸易有关的知识产权协定》第23条第4款授权发起关于这一制度的谈判，多哈部长级会议对此作出安排。谈判原计划到坎昆部长级会议完成，但未能达成一致。谈判仍在进行中。另见*地理标志(geographical indications)*。

Multilateral trade agreements
多边贸易协定

旨在通过规定一系列权利和义务在非歧视、可预测和透明条件下扩大和放宽国际贸易的政府间协定。承担这些义务的动力在于所有成员通过遵守管理其贸易关系的共同行为准则以增加福利。一般而言，此类协定拥有代表小型、中型、大型贸易国家的众多成员。此种协定的成员资格是开放的，但希望加入的国家通常需要证明其贸易制度符合协定宗旨，且其市场准入条件与现有成员的市场准入条件大致相同。如必要，它们还必须作出调整。在GATT于1948年生效之前，贸易协定大多为双边的，或为优惠性的，例如帝国特惠安排。在WTO中，“多边贸易协定”一词指《WTO协定》附件1、2和3所载的协定和有关法律文件。另见*加入(accession)*、*双边贸易协定(bilateral trade agreement)*、*诸边贸易协定(plurilateral trade agreements)*、*囚徒困境(Prisoner's Dilemma)*。

Multilateral trade negotiations
多边贸易谈判

MTN。也称回合。目的在于增强保证国际贸易有序公平进行的规则，并达成关于削减世界贸易壁垒的互利协定。自1947年以来，在GATT主持下举行了8轮回合谈判。每一回合谈判都包含长时间的讨价还价过程。已完成的8个回合及其广为人知的名称为：日内瓦回合(1947年)、安纳西回合(1949年)、托奎回合(1950年)、日内瓦回合(1955年至1956年)、狄龙回合(1960年至1961年)、肯尼迪回合(1963年至1967年)、东京回合(1973年至1979年)和乌拉圭回合(1986年至1994年)。第9轮回合，即多哈发展议程，于2001年11月由多哈部长级会议启动。在肯尼迪回合之前的回合谈判内容只有关税削减。早期回合谈判基本上是由一系列双边谈判组成的，谈判结果随后在最惠国待遇基础上使其他成员可以享受。自肯尼迪回合起，非关税措施和体制性问题也被提上议程。“MTN”的缩写在东京回合中广泛使用，且常用来特指东京回合。另见*安纳西关税会*

specifically to that Round. *See also* ***Annecy Tariff Conference***, ***Dillon Round***, ***Geneva Tariff Conference, 1947***, ***Geneva Tariff Conference, 1955–56***, ***Millennium Round***, ***Torquay Tariff Conference*** and ***Uruguay Round***.

Multilateral trading system: the non-discriminatory arrangement for international trade which came into existence with the ***GATT*** in 1947 and which is now represented by the WTO system.

Multi-modal: transport using more than one mode. In negotiations under the ***General Agreement on Trade in Services*** the term relates essentially to door-to-door services that include international shipping.

Multinational enterprises: *see* ***transnational corporations***.

Multiple transformations: *see* ***double transformation*** and ***triple transformation***.

Munich Group: *see* ***Draft International Antitrust Code***.

Mutatis mutandis**:** *Lat.* with the appropriate and/or necessary changes.

Mutual aid agreement: an agreement concluded on 23 February 1942 between the United Kingdom and the United States concerning the principles applying to mutual aid in the prosecution of the war against aggression. It builds on the ***Atlantic Charter*** and is one of the important steps which ultimately led to the convening of the ***United Nations Conference on Trade and Employment*** in 1947, the negotiation of the ***GATT*** in 1947 and the emergence of the ***Havana Charter*** in 1948. Article 7 of the Agreement dealt with international economic relations. It looked forward to agreed action between the two countries, which would be "open to participation by all other countries of like mind, directed to the expansion, by appropriate international and domestic measures, of production, employment, and the exchange and consumption of goods, which are the material foundations of the liberty and welfare of all peoples; to the elimination of all forms of discriminatory treatment in international commerce, and to the reduction of tariffs and other trade barriers".

Mutual assistance in antitrust matters: sometimes mutual assistance in competition matters. Usually a treaty or a ***memorandum of understanding*** in which the parties agree to help one another and to cooperate on a reciprocal basis in providing or obtaining antitrust evidence. That evidence may assist in determining whether a person has violated, or is about to violate, respective antitrust laws. These agreements usually describe in considerable detail what kind of assistance will be provided, in what form the assistance must be requested and under what conditions it will actually be provided.

Mutual recognition arrangements: agreements between two or more countries to recognize each other's standards, qualifications, licensing requirements or testing procedures and results. They can cover goods, services, education and professional qualifications. Mutual recognition can contribute to the expansion of trade through removing some technical obstacles. Achieving mutual recognition may require the parties to meet agreed minimum standards, and it can lead to laborious negotiations. Members of the ***General Agreement on Trade in Services*** who recognize each other's standards and qualifications do not have to extend recognition to others on a most-favoured-nation basis. If a third country

议(Annecy Tariff Conference)、*狄龙回合(Dillon Round)*、*1947年日内瓦关税会议(Geneva Tariff Conference, 1947)*、*1955—1956年日内瓦关税会议(Geneva Tariff Conference, 1955-56)*、*千年回合(Millennium Round)*、*托奎关税会议(Torquay Tariff Conference)*、*乌拉圭回合(Uruguay Round)*。

Multilateral trading system

多边贸易体制

国际贸易的非歧视性安排，与GATT一起在1947年出现，现由WTO体制代表。

Multi-modal

多式联运

使用一种以上方式的运输。在《服务贸易总协定》项下的谈判中，该词主要与包括国际运输的门到门服务有关。

Multinational enterprises

跨国企业

见*跨国公司(transnational corporations)*。

Multiple transformations

多重改变

见*双重改变(double transformation)*、*三重改变(triple transformation)*。

Munich Group

慕尼黑集团

见*国际反垄断法典草案(Draft International Antitrust Code)*。

Mutatis mutandis

在细节上作必要修改后

拉丁语。意为经过适当和/或必要修改。

Mutual aid agreement

相互援助协定

英国和美国在1942年2月23日达成的《关于在进行反侵略战争中相互援助所适用原则的协定》。协定以《大西洋宪章》为基础，是最终促成1947年召开联合国贸易与就业会议、1947年举行GATT谈判和1948年形成《哈瓦那宪章》的重要步骤之一。协定第7条处理国际经济关系。协定期待两国之间采取议定行动，并"开放供所有其他志同道合的国家参与这些行动，以便通过采取适当国际和国内措施扩大生产、就业以及货物交换和消费，此为全人类自由和福利的物质基础；消除国际贸易中各种形式的歧视性待遇，并降低关税和其他贸易壁垒"。

Mutual assistance in antitrust matters

反垄断事务互助

有时为竞争事务互助。通常是一项条约或谅解备忘录，其中各方同意相互帮助，并在提供或获得反垄断证据方面开展合作。证据可能有助于确定当事人是否违反或将要违反相关反垄断法。这些协定通常相当详细地说明将提供何种协助、必须以何种形式请求提供协助以及实际提供协助的条件。

Mutual recognition arrangements

相互承认安排

两个或两个以上国家之间达成的协定，承认各自的标准、资格、许可要求或测试程序及结果。可以涵盖货物、服务、教育和专业资格。相互承认可以通过消除一些技术障碍来扩大贸易。实现相互承认可能需要各方达到议定最低标准，并可能需要进行艰难谈判。相互承认各自的标准和资格的《服务贸易总协定》成员无需在最惠国待遇基础上承认其他成员的标准和资格。如果一第三方希

wishes to demonstrate that it, too, can meet the requirements for recognition of qualifications, it must be given an opportunity to do so. A 1979 ruling by the European Court of Justice in the *Cassis de Dijon* case established the principle of ***European Community*** mutual recognition of similar product standards, rather than identical standards. This made mutual recognition within the Community simpler, and it also removed standards from the category of very difficult issues. *See also* ***Guidelines for Mutual Recognition Agreements or Arrangements in the Accountancy Sector***, ***harmonization of standards and qualifications***, ***managed mutual recognition***, ***technical barriers to trade*** and ***zero-margin harmonization***.

望证明自己也能满足资格承认要求，即必须给予该第三方进行证明的机会。欧洲法院在1979年对“第戎黑加伦酒案”所作裁决确立了欧洲共同体相互承认类似产品标准的原则，而不是相同产品标准。这使共同体内部的相互承认变得更加简单，同时也将标准问题移出了非常棘手问题的类别。另见*关于会计部门相互承认协定或安排的指导原则(Guidelines for Mutual Recognition Agreements or Arrangements in the Accountancy Sector)*、*标准和资格的协调(harmonization of standards and qualifications)*、*托管互认(managed mutual recognition)*、*技术性贸易壁垒(technical barriers to trade)*、*零差别协调(zero-margin harmonization)*。

N

NAFTA: North American Free Trade Agreement. Entered into force on 1 January 1994. Its members are Canada, United States and Mexico. This agreement, though long and complex, has exerted a strong influence on the architecture of later ***free-trade agreements*** negotiated by countries other than the United States. Only a basic introduction to its structure can be given here. NAFTA's objectives, as set out in Chapter 1, are to eliminate barriers to trade in goods and services, promote fair competition, adequate and effective protection of ***intellectual property rights***, effective procedures for settlement of disputes and to provide a framework for further trilateral, regional and multilateral cooperation. Chapter 2 contains definitions. Chapter 3 provides for ***national treatment*** of goods. Most tariffs were eliminated over ten years. ***Anti-dumping rules*** are also part of this chapter. Chapter 4 sets out the ***rules of origin***. These use the ***change-in-tariff-classification*** method. Common customs procedures are listed in Chapter 5. Energy and trade in basic petrochemicals, dealt with in Chapter 6, are to be liberalized. Chapter 7 contains the rules for agriculture and ***sanitary and phytosanitary measures***. Chapters 8, 9 and 10, respectively, set out the ***safeguards***, ***technical barriers to trade*** and ***government procurement*** provisions. ***NAFTA Chapter 11*** is the investment chapter. ***National treatment*** and ***most-favoured-nation treatment*** apply to investment. This chapter also outlines the concept of a ***minimum standard of treatment***. Chapter 12 concerns ***cross-border trade in services***. The agreement covers all ***modes of services delivery***, but mode 3 (commercial presence) is covered by the investment rules. This is followed by more specific rules for telecommunications and financial services in Chapters 13 and 14, respectively. Chapter 15 covers ***competition policy***, monopolies and state enterprises. Chapter 16 deals with the temporary entry of business persons. ***Intellectual property*** provisions are contained in Chapter 17. Chapter 18 deals with the publication, notification and administration of laws, i.e. ***transparency***. Chapters 19 and 20 deal, respectively, with review and dispute settlement in anti-dumping and countervailing duty matters, and institutional arrangements and dispute settlement procedures. Chapter 21 covers exceptions. It has provisions on ***general exceptions***, national security, taxation, balance of payments, disclosure of information and ***cultural industries***. Chapter 22 covers matters such as entry into force, amendments and withdrawals. Side agreements were concluded in the form of the ***North American Agreement on Labor Cooperation*** and the North American Agreement on Environmental Cooperation. Some agricultural matters have also been dealt

N

NAFTA

北美自由贸易协定

1994年1月1日生效。缔约方为加拿大、美国和墨西哥。协定虽然长且复杂，但对后来美国之外的国家所谈判的自由贸易协定的结构产生了重要影响。在此仅对其结构作一基本介绍。如第1章所列，NAFTA的目标为消除货物贸易和服务贸易壁垒，促进公平竞争，充分和有效保护知识产权，提供争端解决的有效程序以及提供未来三边、区域和多边合作的框架。第2章包含定义。第3章规定了货物的国民待遇。大部分关税在10年内取消。反倾销规则也是本章一部分。第4章规定了原产地规则。这些规则使用税则归类改变方法。共同海关程序列在第5章中。第6章处理能源和基础石油化工产品贸易自由化问题。第7章包含农业规则和卫生与植物卫生措施。第8、9、10章分别规定了保障措施、技术性贸易壁垒及政府采购的条款。《北美自由贸易协定》第11章是投资章节。国民待遇和最惠国待遇适用于投资。该章还明确了最低待遇标准的概念。第12章涉及跨境服务贸易。协定涵盖所有服务提供模式，但模式3(商业存在)为投资规则所涵盖。随后的第13、14章分别对电信和金融服务作出了更为具体的规定。第15章涵盖竞争政策、垄断和国有企业。第16章处理商务人员临时入境。第17章包含知识产权条款。第18章处理法律的公布、通报和管理，即透明度。第19章和第20章分别处理反倾销和反补贴事项的审议和争端解决，以及机构安排和争端解决程序。第21章涵盖例外条款。该章对一般例外、国家安全、税收、国际收支、信息披露和文化产业作出了规定。第22章涵盖生效、修正和退出等事项。补充协定以《北美劳工合作协定》和《北美环境合作协定》的形式

with in separate agreements. A Cabinet-level Free Trade Commission supervises the implementation and operation of NAFTA. It is assisted by a secretariat consisting of national sections. Each party funds its own secretariat staff. The secretariat is responsible, among other things, for administering panels and committees established for the settlement of disputes. NAFTA will be superseded by the ***United States–Mexico–Canada Agreement*** two months after all members have completed their internal procedures. *See also* ***investor-state disputes***.

NAFTA Chapter 11: contains the ***NAFTA*** rules on investment. It provides for ***national treatment*** (Article 1102) and ***most-favoured-nation treatment*** (Article 1103). The better of the two treatments is to be applied to NAFTA member investors and their investments (Article 1104). Article 1105 provides for a ***minimum standard of treatment***. It requires each party "to accord to investments of investors in another party treatment in accordance with international law, including fair and equitable treatment and full protection and security". Article 1106 prohibits a broad range of performance requirements. No party may impose export requirements, domestic content rules, domestic purchase rules, a relationship between import and export flows, measures relating the sale of goods and services to foreign exchange earnings, requirements to transfer technology or exclusive supplier provisions to specific markets. Article 1110 permits ***expropriation*** under certain conditions. Under Article 1116 an investor of one party may file a claim of ***arbitration*** against another party on the grounds that it has breached an obligation under the investment chapter or against the behaviour of state enterprises, but only within three years of the alleged breach. That is, this chapter permits ***investor-state disputes***.

NAFTA rules of origin: under Article 401 of NAFTA (North American Free Trade Agreement), to be superseded in due course by the ***United States–Mexico–Canada Agreement***, an ***originating good*** is (a) one wholly obtained or produced entirely within the territory of one or more of the parties, (b) or each of the ***non-originating materials*** undergoes an applicable ***change in tariff classification***, or the good satisfies the applicable requirements where no change in tariff classification is required, or the good satisfies all other applicable requirements, or (c) the good is produced entirely in the territory of one or more of the parties exclusively from ***originating materials***, or (d) the good is produced entirely in the territory of one or more of the parties, but one or more of the non-originating materials does for a specific reason not undergo a change in tariff classification. In that case it must meet a specified ***regional value content***. The Annex to Article 401 of NAFTA sets out the specific origin requirements for goods.

Nagging rights: used by some to describe provisions in trade agreements which allow a party to exhort another party to adopt new measures or commitments. The party so addressed is not contractually obliged to respond, but it may decide to take some action anyway if the request is made often enough.

缔结。一些农业问题也在单独协定中加以处理。一个内阁级别的自由贸易委员会监督NAFTA的实施和运用。委员会得到由各国家部门组成的秘书处的协助。每一缔约方为其秘书处职员提供经费。秘书处还负责管理为解决争端而设立的专家组和委员会。NAFTA将在所有成员国完成内部程序2个月后被《美国—墨西哥—加拿大协定》所取代。另见*投资者—国家间争端(investor-state disputes)*。

NAFTA Chapter 11

北美自由贸易协定第11章

该章包含《北美自由贸易协定》(NAFTA)的投资规则。该章规定了国民待遇(第1102条)和最惠国待遇(第1103条)。两项待遇中的较高待遇将适用于协定缔约方的投资者及其投资(第1104条)。第1105条规定了最低待遇标准。要求每一缔约方"给予另一缔约方的投资者的投资与国际法相一致的待遇，包括公平和公正的待遇及全面的保护和安全"。第1106条禁止内容广泛的实绩要求。任何缔约方不得对特定市场强加出口要求、国内含量规则、国内采购规则、进出口流量关联、将货物和服务销售与外汇收入关联的措施、技术转让要求或特定市场独家供应条款。第1110条允许某些条件下的征收。根据第1116条，一缔约方的投资者可以针对另一缔约方以其已经违反投资章节下义务为由或针对国有企业的行为提出仲裁要求，但仅限于在被指称的违约行为发生后的3年内，即该章允许投资者—国家间争端。

NAFTA rules of origin

北美自由贸易协定原产地规则

根据《北美自由贸易协定》(NAFTA)第401条，适当时将被《美国—墨西哥—加拿大协定》所取代，原产货物指：(a)在一个或多个缔约方领土内完全获得或生产；或(b)每一种非原产材料均经过税则归类改变，或在不要求税则归类改变的情况下货物满足所有其他适用要求；或(c)货物在一个或多个缔约方领土内全部由原产材料生产；或(d)货物全部在一个或多个缔约方领土内生产，但一种或多种非原产材料由于特定原因而未发生税则归类改变。在此种情况下，必须满足规定的区域价值成分。NAFTA第401条的附件规定了货物的具体原产地要求。

Nagging rights

提醒权

一些人用于描述贸易协定中允许一方敦促另一方采取新措施或作出承诺的条款。被敦促的一方并无作出回应的契约义务，但如果请求频繁提出，另一方可能会决定采取一些行动。

Nairobi Convention: *see* ***Convention on the Means of Prohibiting and Preventing the Illicit Import, Export and Transfer of Cultural Property*** and ***International Convention on Mutual Administrative Assistance for the Prevention, Investigation and Repression of Customs Offences***.

Nairobi Package: *see* ***Doha Development Agenda*** and ***Nairobi WTO Ministerial Conference***.

Nairobi WTO Ministerial Conference: the tenth ***WTO Ministerial Conference*** held in Nairobi in December 2015. Its outcomes led to hopes that the ***Doha Development Agenda*** negotiations had regained momentum, but in hindsight this does not seem to have been the case. The following are among the highlights. The Conference agreed *inter alia* on the elimination of agricultural export subsidies and disciplines on export measures with equivalent effect, and on duty-free and quota-free access for cotton and cotton-related agricultural products from ***least-developed countries***. The ***moratorium on customs duties on electronic transmissions*** was extended for two years. A Declaration on the Expansion of Trade in Information Technology Products was also adopted. *See also* ***Information Technology Agreement***.

NAM: *see* ***Non-Aligned Movement***.

NAMA: non-agricultural market access. This refers to the tariff negotiations under the ***Doha Development Agenda*** for goods other than agricultural ones.

Narrow competition policy: this deals with the range of practices usually covered by ***antitrust laws*** or by laws aimed at controlling ***restrictive business practices***. The main targets of narrow competition policy are horizontal and vertical arrangements, misuse of ***market power*** and the control of anti-competitive conditions resulting from mergers and acquisitions. *See also* ***competition policy*** and ***wider competition policy***.

National champions: companies designated in some countries to act as promoters of new technologies, new processes or new management methods from whom other companies will be able to learn. Often, they already enjoy a pre-eminent position in their sector when they are nominated. National champions usually benefit from preferential tax treatment and other support measures. They may also be exempt from some ***competition laws***. The impact of such firms on the domestic markets can be considerable, but their role in international markets may be quite minor. There is no way of telling whether a national champion will fulfil the expectations of its proponents, or whether it will simply turn into a protected and uncompetitive entity. *See also* ***infant-industry argument***, ***learning-by-doing argument*** and ***picking winners***.

National Committee on Trade Facilitation: the WTO ***Agreement on Trade Facilitation*** requires members either to establish or maintain a National Committee for the purpose of domestic coordination and implementation of the Agreement.

National exhaustion: the doctrine that once a product embodying ***intellectual property rights*** has been sold in a national market with the consent of the owner of these rights, the product can be resold or transferred within that market

Nairobi Convention
内罗毕公约
见*关于禁止和防止非法进出口文化财产和非法转让其所有权的方法的公约(Convention on the Means of Prohibiting and Preventing the Illicit Import, Export and Transfer of Cultural Property)*、*关于防止、调查和惩处违犯海关法罪实行行政互助的国际公约(International Convention on Mutual Administrative Assistance for the Prevention, Investigation and Repression of Customs Offences)*。

Nairobi Package
内罗毕方案
见*多哈发展议程(Doha Development Agenda)*、*WTO 内罗毕部长级会议(Nairobi WTO Ministerial Conference)*。

Nairobi WTO Ministerial Conference
WTO 内罗毕部长级会议
2015 年 12 月在内罗毕举行的第 10 届 WTO 部长级会议。会议成果带来了多哈发展议程谈判重获动力的希望，但事后看来似乎并非如此。以下为会议一些亮点。除其他成果外，会议同意取消农产品出口补贴，议定了关于具有同等效果的出口措施的纪律，议定了对源自最不发达国家的棉花和棉花相关产品实行免关税和免配额市场准入。电子传输暂免关税延长 2 年。会议通过了《关于扩大信息技术产品贸易的宣言》。另见*信息技术协定(Information Technology Agreement)*。

NAM
不结盟运动
见*不结盟运动(Non-Aligned Movement)*。

NAMA
非农产品市场准入
指多哈发展议程框架下针对农产品以外的货物的关税谈判。

Narrow competition policy
狭义竞争政策
这一政策处理通常由反垄断法或旨在抑制限制性商业惯例的法律所涵盖的一系列做法。狭义竞争政策的主要规制对象是水平和垂直安排、滥用市场支配力以及控制因兼并和并购所产生的反竞争条件。另见*竞争政策(competition policy)*、*广义竞争政策(wider competition policy)*。

National champions
国家龙头企业
在一些国家被指定作为新技术、新工序或新管理方法推动者的企业，其他公司能够向这些企业学习。通常，这些企业在被指定时已属所在部门杰出企业。国家龙头企业一般享有税收优惠待遇和其他支持措施。这些企业也可能免于一些竞争法的规制。这些企业对国内市场的影响可能很大，但是它们在国际市场上的作用可能很小。无法判断一家国家龙头企业能否实现其支持者的期望，或是否会变成一个受到保护和缺乏竞争力的实体。另见*幼稚产业论(infant-industry argument)*、*干中学理论(learning-by-doing argument)*、*挑选赢家(picking winners)*。

National Committee on Trade Facilitation
国家贸易便利化委员会
WTO《贸易便利化协定》要求成员建立或设立一个旨在进行国内协调和执行协定的国家委员会。

National exhaustion
一国用尽
一旦含有知识产权的产品经知识产权所有人同意在国内市场销售，该产品即

without the further consent of the owner of these rights. *See also* ***exhaustion doctrine***, ***international exhaustion*** and ***parallel imports***. [Maskus 2000]

National interest: a term describing a range of criteria, seldom described exactly or even listed in writing, whose fulfilment is considered basic to the welfare of the state. Interest or lobby groups often equate the national interest with their own aims. In a strict sense, only national governments have the competence to judge and invoke the national interest by virtue of the responsibilities assigned to them by the constitution and the laws flowing from it. There are cases when the use of this discretionary power leads to vigorous debate about their appropriateness, especially when the specific criteria triggering the national-interest clause are not spelt out. Nevertheless, there is widespread agreement that the administration of some sectors of government requires the flexibility offered by national-interest provisions. *See also* ***Exon-Florio amendment***, ***foreign investment screening***, ***general exceptions***, ***rule of reason*** and ***security exceptions***.

National policy space: another way to say that governments need flexibility in their observance of their rights and obligations under international trade or investment agreements. Many treaty provisions are in fact drafted to allow this. *See also* ***national interest***. [World Investment Report 2003]

National schedules: the equivalent of ***tariff schedules*** in ***GATT***, laying down commitments accepted unilaterally or through negotiation by WTO members.

National Trade Estimate Report on Foreign Trade Barriers: an annual report to the President and Congress by ***USTR*** as required under Section 181 of the *Trade and Tariff Act* of 1974, as amended by the ***Omnibus Trade and Competitiveness Act*** of 1988, and Section 301 of the Uruguay Round Trade Agreements Act. The report covers (a) significant barriers to United States exports of goods, services, intellectual property and foreign direct investment, (b) the trade-distorting effects of these barriers and the value of lost trade and investment opportunities, (c) a listing of ***Section 301*** and other actions taken to remove these barriers, or an explanation why no action was taken, and (d) United States priorities to expand exports.

National Trade Facilitation Bodies: NTFB. Recommended for establishment in UN/CEFACT Recommendation No. 4 as a component of trade policy formulation. An NTFB is seen as embracing the views and opinions of all stakeholders and pursuing agreement, cooperation and collaboration. Its work would encompass trade facilitation issues including regulatory, operational, customs, multimodal transport, transit, logistics, banking and finance, agriculture, sanitary and phytosanitary, health and electronic business issues. *See also* ***Empowerment Programme for National Trade Facilitation Bodies*** and ***trade facilitation***. [www.unece.org]

National Trade Facilitation Committees: NTFCs. Some of these are established and maintained with the assistance of ***UNCTAD*** as a coordinating mechanism. Their purpose is to streamline trade procedures and implement ***trade facilitation*** measures at the national level. *See also* ***National Committee on Trade***

可无需权利所有人进一步同意而在该市场内再销售或转让的理论。另见*权利用尽原则(exhaustion doctrine)*、*国际用尽(international exhaustion)*、*平行进口(parallel imports)*。

National interest

国家利益

用于描述一系列标准的词语，这些标准很少准确描述甚至书面列出，而这些标准的实现被认为是国家福利的基础。利益集团或游说集团经常将国家利益等同于他们自己的目标。严格地讲，只有国家政府才有权根据宪法和根据宪法制定的法律赋予它们的责任判断和援引国家利益。在一些情况下，这种自由裁量权的使用会导致对其适当性的激烈辩论，特别是在触发国家利益条款的具体标准并未明确规定的情况下。尽管如此，普遍认为一些政府部门的管理需要使用国家利益条款提供的灵活性。另见*埃克森-弗罗里奥修正案(Exon-Florio amendment)*、*外国投资审查(foreign investment screening)*、*一般例外(general exceptions)*、*合理原则(rule of reason)*、*安全例外(security exceptions)*。

National policy space

国家政策空间

政府在遵守其在国际贸易或投资协定项下权利和义务方面需要灵活性的另一种说法。许多条约条款实际上允许此种灵活性。另见*国家利益(national interest)*。

National schedules

国别减让表

相当于 GATT 中的关税减让表，规定了 WTO 成员单方面或通过谈判接受的承诺。

National Trade Estimate Report on Foreign Trade Barriers

对外贸易壁垒国家贸易评估报告

美国贸易代表办公室(USTR)根据经 1988 年《综合贸易与竞争法》修正的《1974 年贸易法》(英文多出 and tariff 两词—译注)第 181 节和《乌拉圭回合贸易协定法》第 301 节的要求，向总统和国会提交的年度报告。报告包括：(a)美国货物、服务、知识产权和外国直接投资的主要壁垒；(b)这些壁垒对贸易的扭曲影响及损失的贸易价值和投资机会；(c)301 条款清单和为消除这些壁垒所采取的其他行动的清单，或关于为什么未采取行动的说明；以及(d)美国扩大出口的优先事项。

National Trade Facilitation Bodies

国家贸易便利化机构

NTFB。联合国贸易便利化与电子商务中心(UN/CEFACT)第4号建议中作为贸易政策制定组成部分而建议设立。NTFB 应采纳所有利益攸关方的观点和意见，并寻求达成协议和开展合作和协作。该机构的工作将涵盖贸易便利化问题，包括监管、运行、海关、多式联运、过境、物流、银行和金融、农业、卫生与植物卫生、健康和电子商务等。另见*国家贸易便利化机构赋权计划(Empowerment Programme for National Trade Facilitation Bodies)*、*贸易便利化(trade facilitation)*。

National Trade Facilitation Committees

国家贸易便利化委员会

NTFCs。一些委员会是在联合国贸易与发展会议(UNCTAD)协助下作为协调机制建立和设立的。目的在于在国家层面简化贸易程序和实施贸易便利化措施。

Facilitation, a requirement under the WTO ***Agreement on Trade Facilitation***. [www.unctad.org]

National treatment: the principle of giving other states and/or their products the same treatment as one accords to one's own nationals and/or products. In the older literature, this principle is sometimes called "inland parity". It is a simple proposition, but it has been the cause of many disputes, partly because a strict interpretation of national treatment may in fact disadvantage foreign suppliers. The classic example of this possibility is the ***wine gallon assessment***. For this reason, the national treatment principle has been refined over the years to allow for different or formally better treatment of foreign products if that is the only way to guarantee that foreign products are not disadvantaged. Sometimes countries deliberately give foreign investors better than national treatment to attract suitable firms. The basic principle underlying Article III of the ***GATT***, which deals with national treatment for goods, is that of ***equality of competitive opportunity***. The Article starts with the general statement that GATT members recognize that internal taxes and other charges, laws and regulations affecting the internal sale, transport and distribution, and internal quantitative regulations should not be applied to imported or domestic products to give protection to domestic production. It then says that imported products must not be subject to internal taxes or other internal charges above those applied to domestic products. The Article also requires that all laws, regulations, etc., must apply equally to imported and domestic products. Additionally, internal quantitative restrictions must be applied in a non-discriminatory way. In ***intellectual property***, under the ***Agreement on Trade-Related Aspects of Intellectual Property Rights*** a WTO member must, in terms of Article 3, accord to the nationals of other members treatment no less favourable than it accords to its own nationals. There may be some exceptions to this because of pre-existing rights under the ***Paris Convention***, the ***Berne Convention*** or the ***Rome Convention*** and the ***Treaty on Intellectual Property in Respect of Integrated Circuits***. For ***services***, national treatment, as described in Article XVII of the ***General Agreement on Trade in Services***, is the obligation to guarantee foreign service providers and their services equivalent treatment to that given to domestic service providers and the services they supply, but only for activities inscribed in the ***schedules of specific commitments on services***. Treatment for foreign suppliers may be formally different if that is required to achieve equality of opportunity. *See also* ***economic impact criterion***, ***implicit discrimination***, ***minimum standard of treatment***, ***most-favoured-nation treatment*** and ***non-discrimination***.

National treatment instrument: formally *National Treatment for Foreign-controlled Enterprises*. An OECD instrument first adopted in 1976 and revised several times, most recently in 2017. It requires OECD members to notify all their investment measures that are exceptions to ***national treatment***. These notifications are examined at least every three years with a view to eliminating the measures. Members may notify measures of any other member if they consider that it is acting contrary to its undertakings. The national treatment

另见WTO《贸易便利化协定》所要求设立的*国家贸易便利化委员会(National Committee on Trade Facilitation)*。

National treatment

国民待遇

给予其他国家和/或产品的待遇与给予本国国民和/或产品的待遇相同的原则。在较早的文献中，这一原则有时被称为“对内同等”。这一观点很简单，但却是许多争议的原因，部分原因是对国民待遇的严格解释可能实际上使外国供应商处于不利地位。这种可能性的典型例子是“葡萄酒加仑评估法”。正因为如此，多年来对国民待遇原则进行了完善，允许给予外国产品不同的或形式上更好的待遇，如果这是保证外国产品摆脱不利地位的惟一途径的话。有时为了吸引合适的公司，一些国家会专门给予外国投资者优于国民待遇的待遇。GATT第3条处理货物的国民待遇，所依据的基本原则是“竞争机会均等”。该条的总体陈述指出，GATT缔约方认识到，国内税和其他国内费用及影响产品的国内销售、运输和分销的法律、法规以及国内数量法规，不得以为国内生产提供保护的目的对进口产品或本国产品适用。该条要求，对进口产品征收的国内税或其他国内费用不得高于适用于本国产品的国内税或其他国内费用。该条还要求所有法律、法规必须对进口产品和本国产品同等适用。此外，国内数量限制必须以非歧视的方式实施。在知识产权方面，根据《与贸易有关的知识产权协定》第3条的规定，WTO成员给予其他成员国民的待遇不得低于给予本国国民的待遇。这方面可能有一些例外，因为在《巴黎公约》、《伯尔尼公约》或《罗马公约》和《集成电路知识产权条约》中规定了预先存在的权利。对于服务，根据《服务贸易总协定》第17条，国民待遇义务旨在保证外国服务提供者及其服务获得与国内服务提供者及其服务相同的待遇，仅限于服务贸易具体承诺减让表中所列活动。如果需要实现机会均等，对外国提供者的待遇可能在形式上会有所不同。另见*经济影响标准(economic impact criterion)*、*隐性歧视(implicit discrimination)*、*最低待遇标准(minimum standard of treatment)*、*最惠国待遇(most-favoured-nation treatment)*、*非歧视(non-discrimination)*。

National treatment instrument

国民待遇文件

正式名称为《外资控股企业的国民待遇》。经济合作与发展组织(OECD)1976年首次通过的文件，后经多次修订，最近一次修订是在2017年。该文件要求OECD成员国通报构成国民待遇例外的所有投资措施。这些通报至少每3年审议一次，旨在消除这些措施。成员如果认为任何其他成员国以违反其承诺的方式行事，可以通报该其他成员国的措施。国民待遇文件因此对在OECD成员

instrument is therefore a strong promoter of non-discriminatory foreign investment in OECD countries. *See also* ***Declaration on International Investment and Multinational Enterprises***. [www.oecd.org]

National Treatment Study: a study published by the United States Department of the Treasury every four years under the ***Omnibus Trade and Competitiveness Act*** of 1988. The final report was issued in 1998. *See also* ***National Trade Estimate Report on Foreign Trade Barriers***.

Natural monopoly: the supply, usually of a service, rarely a good, deemed to be most efficiently provided when there is only one supplier. Until quite recently gas, water, electricity, telecommunications and mail delivery services were thought to be natural monopolies. Few would argue so now. It is now not too difficult to supply these services under competitive conditions with considerable benefits to the consumer. *See also* ***competition*** and ***competition law***.

Natural persons: people, as distinct from ***juridical persons*** or ***legal persons***, such as companies. If they are service suppliers to other members of the ***General Agreement on Trade in Services***, they have rights under the Agreement.

Natural resource-based products: NRBPs. In the GATT environment these include minerals, ores, fish and fisheries products, forest products, timber and paper. They were the subject of a separate negotiating group in the ***Uruguay Round***.

Natural trading blocs: a term used by some economists for modelling purposes to describe countries which are close together, have low transport costs and that therefore trade with each other.

Natural trading partners fallacy: the view that the concept of natural trading partners, regardless of whether it is based on geographic proximity, complementary economies or whether the prospective participants already are major trading partners, has limited value in analysing whether a proposed ***free-trade area*** will lead to increasing trade between the prospective partners. The statistical evidence certainly appears to indicate that geographical proximity is no guide to the intensity of trade within the free-trade area. [Schiff and Winters 2003]

Natural trading partners hypothesis: the proposition that ***free-trade areas*** between countries already conducting the bulk of their trade with each other yield the greatest gain. *See also* ***natural trading partners fallacy***.

Necessity test: sometimes used to refer to the steps necessary to justify invoking the ***general exceptions*** of the ***GATT***. WTO members may adopt or enforce measures necessary to protect public morals (Article XX(a)), necessary to protect human, animal or plant life or health (XX(b)), necessary to secure compliance with laws or regulations not inconsistent with the provisions of the GATT (XX(d)), and restricting exports of domestic materials necessary to ensure the supply of essential quantities to domestic industry (XX(e)), provided that this does not constitute arbitrary or unjustifiable discrimination between countries or a disguised restriction on international trade. The GATT ***security exceptions*** (Article XXI) allow WTO members to take any action they consider

国中实施非歧视性外国投资政策起到有力推动作用。另见*关于国际投资与跨国企业的宣言(Declaration on International Investment and Multinational Enterprises)*。

National Treatment Study

国民待遇研究报告

美国财政部根据1988年《综合贸易与竞争法》每4年发布的研究报告。最后一份报告于1998年发布。另见*对外贸易壁垒国家贸易评估报告(National Trade Estimate Report on Foreign Trade Barriers)*。

Natural monopoly

自然垄断

当仅有一个提供者时能够获得最有效供应的情况，通常为服务，很少有货物。直至不久前，燃气、水、电、电信和邮递服务被认为属自然垄断。而现在很少有人这样认为。现在在竞争条件下提供这些服务并不困难，消费者可从中获得很多益处。另见*竞争(competition)*、*竞争法(competition law)*。

Natural persons

自然人

区别于企业法人和法人的人。如果自然人属《服务贸易总协定》的其他成员的服务提供者，他们在该协定项下享有权利。

Natural resource-based products

自然资源产品

NRBPs。在GATT语境下，这些产品包括矿物、矿石、鱼和水产品、林产品、木材和纸张。在乌拉圭回合中，这些产品为一单独谈判小组的议题。

Natural trading blocs

自然贸易集团

一些经济学家为建立模型而使用的词语，用于描述距离近、运输成本低而因此相互开展贸易的国家。

Natural trading partners fallacy

自然贸易伙伴谬误

一种观点，认为自然贸易伙伴的概念，无论是基于地理邻近性和经济互补性，还是基于潜在参加方已经为主要贸易伙伴，在分析拟议自由贸易区是否会带来潜在伙伴之间的贸易增加方面价值有限。统计证据确实表明，地理邻近性并不能说明自由贸易区内的贸易强度。

Natural trading partners hypothesis

自然贸易伙伴假说

一种主张，认为相互之间已经开展各自大部分贸易的国家之间的自由贸易区将产生最大收益。另见*自然贸易伙伴谬误(natural trading partners fallacy)*。

Necessity test

必要性测试

有时用于指证明援引GATT一般例外属正当而需要的必要步骤。在不构成国家间任意或不合理的歧视，或对国际贸易的变相限制的前提下，WTO成员可以采取或实施必要措施，以保护公共道德(第20条(a)款)，保护人类、动物或植物的生命或健康(第20条(b)款)，保证与GATT不相抵触的法律或法规得到遵守(第20条(d)款)，以及为保证国内产业必需数量的供应而限制国内资源的出口

necessary for the protection of their essential security interests. The ***General Agreement on Trade in Services*** contains similar necessity tests in Article XIV (General Exceptions) and Article XIVbis (Security Exceptions). *See also* ***least-trade-restrictive-alternative test*** and ***means-and-ends test***.

Negative comity: also called traditional comity. It is a term used, for example, in the administration of ***competition policy***. It means that, under the terms of relevant bilateral arrangements, a country has to take account of the interests of the other country when it initiates an action under its ***competition laws***. *See also* ***positive comity***.

Negative deindustrialization: occurs when labour no longer needed in industry cannot find productive employment in the services sector. This results in persistent unemployment. *See also* ***positive deindustrialization***. [Trade and Development Report 2003]

Negative integration: the removal of barriers to ***cross-border trade*** without the creation of new regulatory frameworks. *See also* ***positive integration***.

Negative listings: a method used in ***free-trade agreements*** to list commitments in services and investment. The starting point for this method is that an investment or a service supply is permitted unless it is restricted through an inscription in the schedules of commitments. The inscription specifies the reason for the restriction, usually a limitation on ***market access*** or ***national treatment***. Investment chapters often use a more elaborate form of negative listing called the ***two-annex method***. In this case, the first annex, the list of ***non-conforming measures***, lists all sectors and activities that are not in full conformity with the agreement. Again, it describes the reason for this. Non-conforming measures are expected to be brought into conformity with the agreement over time. The second annex, the ***reserved list***, lists sectors and activities for which the government wishes to retain flexibility of regulation. It reserves the right to alter the rules at any time and to make them more restrictive. Inclusion of a sector in the reserved list does not necessarily mean that foreign investment is prohibited in that area. Developed countries have used negative listing for their commitments on financial services under the ***General Agreement on Trade in Services***. *See also* ***positive listings***.

Negative margin of dumping: in ***dumping*** investigations, a finding that the ***export price*** is greater than the ***normal value***. In other words, no dumping has occurred. *See also* ***positive margin of dumping***.

Negative reciprocity: this term is now of historical interest only. It describes the practice followed by the United States and some others in the nineteenth and early twentieth centuries of raising tariffs against those countries that were seen as maintaining unreasonably high tariffs themselves. Negative reciprocity was, however, regarded mainly as a market-opening mechanism. Proponents of this practice took scant regard of the generally high level of their own tariff, and the basis of their thinking was always ***mercantilism***.

Negligible imports: defined in Article 5.8 of the ***Anti-Dumping Agreement*** as a volume of dumped imports from a particular country accounting for less than

(第20条(e)款)。GATT安全例外(第21条)允许WTO成员采取为保护其基本安全利益而必要的任何行动。《服务贸易总协定》第14条(一般例外)和第14条之二(安全例外)中包含类似的必要性测试。另见*最小贸易限制替代措施测试(least-trade-restrictive-alternative test)*、*手段与目的测试(means-and-ends test)*。

Negative comity

消极礼让

也称传统礼让。用于诸如竞争政策管理的词语。指根据相关双边安排的条款，一国在根据其竞争法采取行动时必须考虑另一国的利益。另见*积极礼让(positive comity)*。

Negative deindustrialization

消极去产业化

当产业不再需要的劳动力无法在服务部门找到生产性就业时即会发生此种情况。这会导致持续性失业。另见*积极去产业化(positive deindustrialization)*。

Negative integration

消极一体化

在不建立新的监管框架情况下消除跨境贸易壁垒。另见*积极一体化(positive integration)*。

Negative listings

负面清单

自由贸易协定中用于列举服务和投资承诺的一种方法。此种方法的出发点是，允许进行投资或提供服务，除非通过在减让承诺表中列明而加以限制。减让表所列内容列明限制理由，通常为市场准入或国民待遇限制。投资章节通常使用一种更为详细的负面清单形式，称为双附件法。在此种情况下，第一个附件为不符措施清单，列出不完全符合协定的所有部门和活动，同时列出理由。随着时间推移应使不符措施与协定相符合。第二个附件为保留清单，即政府希望保留监管灵活性的部门和活动。保留随时修改规则并使之更具限制性的权利。将一部门列入保留清单并不一定意味着该领域禁止外国投资。发达国家在《服务贸易总协定》项下的金融服务承诺中使用负面清单。另见*正面清单(positive listings)*。

Negative margin of dumping

负倾销幅度

在倾销调查中，出口价格高于正常价值的调查结果。换言之，没有发生倾销。另见*正倾销幅度(positive margin of dumping)*。

Negative reciprocity

消极互惠

这一词语现在只有历史意义。指美国等国家在19世纪和20世纪初针对那些被视为保留不合理高关税的国家提高关税的做法。但是消极互惠主要被视为一种打开市场的机制。此种做法的支持者很少考虑他们自己的关税也普遍很高，其思想基础始终是重商主义。

Negligible imports

可忽略不计的进口量

《反倾销协定》第5.8条中的定义为，来自一特定国家的倾销进口产品的数量

3 per cent of imports of the ***like product*** in the importing country. If this situation applies, an anti-dumping investigation will have to cease immediately in respect of such a country. The situation is different if the dumped imports of the like product from several countries combined exceed 7 per cent of imports. In this case, imports will no longer be considered negligible even though each country looked at separately accounts for less than 3 per cent of dumped imports of the like product. *See also* ***anti-dumping measures***, ***de minimis dumping margins*** and ***dumping***.

Negotiated protectionism: a term sometimes used to describe the growing acceptance in the early 1980s of negotiated instruments for restricting trade, such as ***orderly marketing arrangements*** and ***voluntary restraint arrangements***.

Negotiating coin: what one is willing to give away in negotiations in order to secure something one would like. Sometimes one's negotiating coin is imaginary, but it becomes important in questions such as the payment for ***autonomous liberalization***. *See also* ***bargaining tariff***.

Negotiating credits: the informal practice in WTO negotiations whereby countries take into account unilateral tariff reductions made by other participants before a fixed date, usually a date associated with the start of the negotiations. The practice is meant to ensure that participants do not have to lower their barriers without receiving adequate ***compensation*** in the form of lower barriers by others. In this way the practice encourages countries to liberalize their trade whenever the time is appropriate. The entire concept is based on the erroneous idea that trade liberalization is a cost to the liberalizing country.

Negotiating Group on Basic Telecommunications: (NGBT). Established by the ***Council for Trade in Services*** to achieve the progressive liberalization of trade in telecommunication transport networks. Its work resulted in the ***Agreement on Basic Telecommunications Services***. *See also* ***Fourth Protocol to the General Agreement on Trade in Services***.

Negotiating Group on Maritime Transport Services: *see* ***maritime transport services***.

Negotiating rights: one of the purposes of the WTO is to act as a forum for the reduction and elimination of trade barriers. This is done through negotiations, but the right to engage in them is subject to certain rules. The bulk of barrier reductions is now done through ***multilateral trade negotiations***, the so-called rounds, and sometimes ***sectoral trade negotiations***. All WTO members have the right to participate in them. In other circumstances, they may not have automatic negotiating rights. Whether they do may depend on the fulfilment of some conditions, including the ***principal supplier rule*** and the substantial supplier rule. The entry on ***renegotiation of tariffs*** contains instances where negotiating rights may arise. *See also* ***initial negotiating right***.

Neighbouring rights: exclusive rights, also called related rights, of performers, producers of phonograms and broadcasters. Such rights have historically been considered to "neighbour" on the traditional areas of copyright protection.

占进口国中同类产品进口的不足3%。如出现此种情况，针对该国的反倾销调查必须立即停止。而如果来自几个国家的同类产品的倾销进口合计超过进口的7%，情况即不同。在此种情况下，即使每一国占同类产品倾销进口不足3%，进口也不再被视为可忽略不计。另见*反倾销措施(anti-dumping measures)*、*微量倾销幅度(de minimis dumping margins)*、*倾销(dumping)*。

Negotiated protectionism

谈判达成的保护主义

有时用于描述在20世级80年代初日益被接受的通过谈判达成的限制贸易措施，例如有序销售安排和自愿限制安排等。

Negotiating coin

谈判筹码

一方在谈判中为得到自己想要的东西而愿意放弃的东西。有时一方的谈判筹码是虚构的，但在诸如自主自由化的代价等问题上就变得很重要。另见*互惠协定关税(bargaining tariff)*。

Negotiating credits

谈判奖励

WTO谈判中的一种非正式做法，即各国将其他参加方在一固定日期之前作出的单方面关税削减纳入考虑范围，这一日期通常与谈判开始日期相关联。此种做法旨在保证参加方在未获得其他参加方以降低壁垒为形式提供的足够补偿的情况下，不必降低自己的壁垒。通过此种方式，该做法鼓励各国在适当时开放贸易。整个概念基于一个错误的观念，即贸易自由化对自由化国家是一种代价。

Negotiating Group on Basic Telecommunications

基础电信谈判组

NGBT。服务贸易理事会设立，旨在实现电信运输网络贸易的逐步自由化。工作成果为《基础电信协定》。另见*服务贸易总协定第四议定书(Fourth Protocol to the General Agreement on Trade in Services)*。

Negotiating Group on Maritime Transport Services

海运服务谈判组

见*海运服务(maritime transport services)*。

Negotiating rights

谈判权

WTO的目的之一是作为削减和取消贸易壁垒的场所。此点通过谈判实现，但是参与谈判的权利受到某些规则的约束。目前大部分的壁垒削减通过多边贸易谈判实现，即所谓“回合”，有时通过部门贸易谈判。所有WTO成员有权参与。在其他情况下，成员可能并不拥有自动谈判权。是否拥有这一权利取决于是否满足一定条件，包括主要供应方规则和实质供应方规则。进行关税重新谈判即涉及产生谈判权的情况。另见*最初谈判权(initial negotiating right)*。

Neighbouring rights

邻接权

表演者、唱片制作者和广播公司拥有的排他性权利，也称相关权利。此类权利

Neighbouring rights are said to relate to derivative subject matter (e.g. a recording company recording a musical composition) where it may be relatively more difficult to identify the creative person deserving of reward. *See also* ***Berne Convention*** and ***copyright***.

Neo-mercantilism: a ***trade policy*** founded on the belief that governments need to control trade and industry to secure national prosperity. Specifically, neo-mercantilism seeks to promote enhanced domestic production accompanied by rising employment, to increase exports and to decrease imports. *See also* ***infant-industry argument***, ***mercantilism*** and ***pop mercantilism***.

NEPAD: *see* ***New Partnership for Africa's Development***.

NEPAD Agency: NEPAD Planning and Coordinating Agency. *See* ***New Partnership for Africa's Development***.

Net cost value method: one of the methods used to establish whether a good imported from another party to a ***free-trade agreement*** has undergone ***substantial transformation*** and qualifies for the ***preferential tariff***. In the free-trade agreement between Canada and Chile the formula is:

$$RVC = \frac{NC - VNM}{NC} \times 100$$

where RVC is the ***regional value content*** expressed as a percentage, NC is the net cost of the good and VNM is the value of ***non-originating materials*** used by the producer in the production of the good. The net cost is the total cost incurred in respect of all goods produced by a producer minus any costs related to sales promotion, marketing, after-sales service, royalties, shipping, packaging and non-allowable interest payments. The resulting net cost incurred in producing all goods is then "reasonably" allocated to the good in question.

New-age agreement: sometimes used to refer to ***free-trade agreements*** supplemented by extensive provisions for cooperation in related economic fields, such as those contained in the *Japan–Singapore Economic Partnership Agreement for a New Age*, concluded in 2001.

Newcomer provision: systems for the allocation of ***quotas*** under ***import licensing*** regimes sometimes are based on the ability of a quota holder to fill previous allocations. An arrangement purely based on historical performance would prevent prospective new entrants from obtaining a quota since they have no performance to point to. This problem can be remedied through a newcomer provision which ensures that part of the global quota is open to competition from new entrants. The ***Anti-Dumping Agreement*** also contains a newcomer provision. Here it means that an anti-dumping order against products from a certain country cannot be applied automatically against new exporters (i.e. exporters not in the market during the anti-dumping investigation) of the same product from that country. However, a review may be conducted to ascertain whether they should also be subject to anti-dumping duties. New exporters will then have to show that they are not related to any of the exporters from that already subject to anti-dumping duties.

历来被认为与版权保护的传统领域"相邻接"。邻接权被认为与衍生的客体(例如唱片公司录制的乐曲)相关，在此种情况下，可能较难确定需要保护的创意者。另见*伯尔尼公约(Berne Convention)*、*版权(copyright)*。

Neo-mercantilism

新重商主义

建立在认为政府需要控制贸易和产业以保证国家繁荣信念上的贸易政策。具体而言，新重商主义寻求国内生产的增强，同时提高就业率，以增加出口和减少进口。另见*幼稚产业论(infant-industry argument)*、*重商主义(mercantilism)*、*现代重商主义(pop mercantilism)*。

NEPAD

非洲发展新伙伴关系计划

见*非洲发展新伙伴关系计划(New Partnership for Africa's Development)*。

NEPAD Agency

非洲发展新伙伴关系计划机构

非洲发展新伙伴关系计划规划和协调机构。见*非洲发展新伙伴关系计划(New Partnership for Africa's Development)*。

Net cost value method

净成本法

用于确定从自由贸易协定另一参加方进口的一货物是否经过实质性改变并符合优惠关税条件的方法。加拿大与智利自由贸易协定中的公式如下：

$$\mathrm{RVC} = \frac{\mathrm{NC} - \mathrm{VNM}}{\mathrm{NC}} \times 100$$

其中RVC表示区域价值成分，以百分比表示，NC为货物净成本，VNM为生产者在生产该货物时使用的非原产材料的价值。净成本为一生产者所生产的全部商品的总成本减去与促销、销售、售后服务、特许权使用费、运输、包装和非免税利息支付相关的任何费用。由此产生的生产全部货物的净成本被"合理"分摊至所涉货物。

New-age agreement

新世纪协定

有时用于指辅以在相关经济领域开展合作的广泛规定的自由贸易协定，例如2001年缔结的《日本与新加坡新世纪经济伙伴关系协定》中所含规定。

Newcomer provision

新进入者条款

有时根据配额持有者完成先前分配量的能力在进口许可制度下分配配额的制度。完全根据历史实绩的安排将会阻止潜在的新进入者获得配额，因为他们没有明确的实绩。这一问题可以通过新进入者条款加以解决，该条款保证全球配额的一部分向新进入者开放竞争。《反倾销协定》也包含新进入者条款。在此意味着，针对某国产品的反倾销命令不能自动适用于该国相同产品的新出口商(即在反倾销调查期间未进入市场的出口商)。但是，可以进行审查，以确定是否也应对这些新出口商征收反倾销税。因此，新出口商不得不证明他们与任何已被征收反倾销税的出口商没有关联。

New commercial policy instrument: NCPI. A ***regulation*** first adopted by the ***European Community*** in 1984. Substantially revised in 1994 and issued as the ***Trade Barriers Regulation***, partly to bring it into line with the European Community's obligations under the WTO instruments. The objective of the regulation was to give European companies and European Community member states the means to request the European Commission to seek the elimination of trade barriers, described as obstacles to trade, maintained by third countries. [Regulation (EC) No 3286/94]

New Development Bank: NDB. A bank established by Brazil, Russia, India, China and South Africa, collectively known as ***BRICS***. It became operational in 2016. Its aim is to support infrastructure and sustainable development in BRICS and other emerging economies through innovation and cutting-edge technology. The NDB is located in Shanghai. *See also* ***Asian Infrastructure Investment Bank***.

New economy: the economic boom caused in the late 1990s by the perception that massive investment in information technology and extensive use of the Internet would give firms doing so a decisive commercial advantage. Its premise seems to have been that those engaged in the ***old economy*** would not be able to adapt to a rapidly changing environment where business would be conducted over the Internet. The boom's symbol was the *dot.com* company. Many who invested in this boom later wished they had never heard of it. *See also* ***first-mover advantage***.

Newer ASEAN members: Cambodia, Laos, Myanmar and Viet Nam. They are also known as the CLMV countries. *See* ***ASEAN***.

New industrial policies: NIPs. This is a term sometimes used for targeted industrial development policies that differ both from ***laissez-faire policies*** which allow the market to determine the broad lines of industrial development and simple protectionism which seeks to give industries a shield against competition from imports. NIPs include governmental measures to increase savings and capital investment, compulsory or guided sharing of technology among enterprises, forced mergers to promote efficiency, shared research and development facilities, possibly subsidized, etc. *See also* ***national champions***.

New international division of labour: an evolution of the concept of the ***international division of labour*** in which price competition is no longer the sole or dominant determinant of how a firm manufactures its products. The system in part reflects a recognition of the power of the consumers, but it also gives them many pseudo-choices. Analysts say that this system requires, among others, product flexibility, rapid innovation, a multiskilled workforce and closer integration of production schedules and product development of related production units. Corporations distribute their production units internationally in the way that best satisfies their competing requirements. *See also* ***globalization***, ***product cycle theory*** and ***transnational corporations***.

New International Economic Order: NIEO. A campaign launched in the early 1970s by developing countries to bring about radical changes in the international economic order. It was based on a perception that the economic and

New commercial policy instrument

新商业政策工具

NCPI。欧洲共同体于1984年首次采用的条例，1994年进行实质修改，并作为《贸易壁垒条例》发布，使之部分符合欧洲共同体在WTO文件中的义务。该条例的目的是，为欧洲公司和欧洲共同体成员提供手段，使其能够请求欧盟委员会设法消除第三国维持的、被视为贸易障碍的贸易壁垒。

New Development Bank

新开发银行

NDB。由合称"金砖国家(BRICS)"的巴西、俄罗斯、印度、中国和南非共同建立的银行。2016年开始运营。目标为通过创新和尖端技术支持金砖国家和其他新兴经济体的基础设施建设和可持续发展。新开发银行设在上海。另见*亚洲基础设施投资银行(Asian Infrastructure Investment Bank)*。

New economy

新经济

20世纪90年代末由如下认知所带来的经济繁荣：对信息技术的大规模投资和互联网的广泛应用将会给如此投资和应用的公司带来决定性商业优势。此种认知的前提似乎是，那些从事旧经济的公司将无法适应通过互联网开展贸易的迅速变化的环境。经济繁荣的象征是dot. com公司。许多投资于这一繁荣的公司后来希望自已从未听说过这一认知。另见*先发优势(first-mover advantage)*。

Newer ASEAN members

新东盟成员

指柬埔寨、老挝、缅甸和越南。也称 CLMV 国家。另见*东盟(ASEAN)*。

New industrial policies

新产业政策

NIPs。这一词语有时用于指预定产业发展政策，此种政策不同于允许市场决定产业发展总体思路的自由放任政策和寻求使产业免受进口竞争的简单保护主义。新产业政策包括增加储蓄和资本投资、强制或引导企业分享技术、为提高效率而强制合并、共享研发设施以及可能的补贴等政策措施。另见*国家龙头企业(national champions)*。

New international division of labour

新国际分工

由国际分工这一概念演变而来，其中价格竞争不再是企业如何制造其产品的惟一或主要决定因素。这一体制部分反映了对消费者权力的认同，但也给消费者提供了许多伪选择。分析人士表示，这一体制要求产品灵活性、快速创新、多技能劳动力以及更紧密融合生产计划和有关生产单元的产品开发。企业以最能满足其竞争要求的方式在国际上分配生产单元。另见*全球化(globalization)*、*产品周期理论(product cycle theory)*、*跨国公司(transnational corporations)*。

New International Economic Order

国际经济新秩序

NIEO。发展中国家在20世纪70年代初发起的旨在根本改变国际经济秩序的运动。这一运动基于这样一种认识，即自第二次世界大战结束以来的经济发展

technological progress since the end of the Second World War had not enriched the lives of people in developing countries in any meaningful way. Developing countries dependent on commodity exports in particular felt that they were caught by the early 1970s between the so-called revolution of rising expectations and falling commodity prices. A perception was also building up that development through concessional, but conditional, loans only increased the debt burden of developing countries and thus put them increasingly at the mercy of developed country policies and actions. Demands for the NIEO gained considerable impetus through the decision by the 1973 ***OPEC*** ministerial conference to raise oil prices fourfold. The evident success of this policy in increasing the revenues of OPEC member countries encouraged the view that other commodities would lend themselves to the furthering of developing country aspirations. The NIEO consisted of a *Declaration on the Establishment of a New International Economic Order* and a *Programme of Action on the Establishment of a New International Economic Order* in the form of General Assembly resolutions 3201 (S-VI) and 3202 (S-VI), respectively. The *Declaration* was concerned particularly with the problems of raw materials and development, noting that since 1970 the world economy had experienced a series of grave crises with severe repercussions on developing countries. It stressed the reality of interdependence of all countries and proposed a New International Economic Order based on the following principles, given here in abbreviated form: (a) sovereign equality of states and self-determination of all peoples, (b) broadest cooperation of all states to banish prevailing disparities and to secure prosperity, (c) full and effective participation on the basis of equality in the solving of world economic problems in the common interest of all countries, (d) the right of every country to adopt the economic and social system it deems the most appropriate for its own development, (e) full and permanent sovereignty of states over their natural resources and all economic activities, including the right to nationalization or transfer of ownership to its nationals, (f) the right of all states under foreign occupation to restitution and full compensation for the exploitation of natural resources, (g) regulation and supervision of the activities of transnational corporations by taking measures in the interest of the national economy, (h) the right of developing countries under colonial domination to achieve their liberation and regain effective control over their natural resources and economic activities, (i) extension of assistance to developing countries under foreign domination or subjected to other coercive measures, (j) just and equitable relationship between the prices of raw materials, primary commodities and manufactures exported by developing countries and their capital goods and other imports with the aim of improving their unsatisfactory ***terms of trade***, (k) active and unconditional assistance to developing countries by the whole international community, (l) a reformed international monetary system assisting the developing countries and ensuring an adequate flow of resources to them, (m) improved competitiveness of natural materials facing competition from synthetic materials, (n) preferential and non-reciprocal

和技术进步并未以任何有意义的方式提高发展中国家人民的生活水平。特别是依赖商品出口的发展中国家感到，它们在20世纪70年代初被卡在了期望值上升而商品价格下降的所谓变革之中。当时形成的另一种观点认为，通过优惠但附条件的贷款实现的发展，只会增加发展中国家的债务负担，因而使它们任由发达国家政策和行动的摆布。1973年石油输出国组织(OPEC)部长级会议将石油价格提高4倍的决定，使建立国际经济新秩序的要求获得了相当大的动力。这一政策在增加OPEC成员国收入方面取得显著成功，促进了这样一种观点的提出，即其他商品将有助于实现发展中国家的愿望。NIEO由《建立国际经济新秩序宣言》和《建立国际经济新秩序行动纲领》组成，分别为联合国大会第3201(S-VI)号决议和第3202(S-VI)号决议。《宣言》特别关注原材料和发展问题，指出自1970年以来，世界经济经历了一系列严重危机，对发展中国家产生了严重影响。强调所有国家相互依存的现实，并提议建立基于下列原则的国际经济新秩序，这些原则可以简单表述为：(a)各国主权平等和一切民族实行自决；(b)所有国家进行最广泛的合作，以消除普遍存在的差距，并保证实现繁荣；(c)为了一切国家的共同利益，在平等的基础上充分和有效地参加解决世界经济问题；(d)每一国家有权实行自己认为对自已发展最适合的经济和社会制度；(e)每一国家对其自然资源和一切经济活动拥有充分的永久主权，包括国有化或将所有权转移给自己国民的权利；(f)遭受外国占领的一切国家有权要求偿还自然资源的开采权并获得充分赔偿；(g)采取有利于国民经济的措施，限制和监督跨国公司的活动；(h)处于殖民统治下的发展中国家有权取得解放和恢复对它们自然资源和经济活动的有效控制；(i)援助遭受外来占领或其他胁迫的发展中国家；(j)在发展中国家出口的原材料、初级产品和制成品与它们进口的资本货物和其他进口产品的价格之间建立公平和公正的关系，以使它们改善不能令人满意的贸易条件；(k)整个国际大家庭向发展中国家提供积极和无条件援助；(l)改革的国际货币制度向发展中国家提供援助并保有足够的资源流入这些国家；(m)改善天然原料在面临合成材料情况下的竞争地位；(n)在国际经济合作的各个领域对发展中国家给予优惠的和非互惠待

treatment for developing countries in all fields of international economic cooperation, (o) securing favourable conditions for the transfer of financial resources to developing countries, (p) access for them to science and technology achievements, promotion of the ***transfer of technology*** and the creation of indigenous technology, (q) an end to the waste of natural resources, including food products, (r) developing countries to concentrate all their technical resources for development, (s) strengthened technical cooperation among developing countries as well as through economic, trade and financial activities, and (t) facilitating the role of producer associations in promoting sustained growth in the world economy and accelerated development. The *Programme of Action* was equally ambitious. It sought solutions to the fundamental problems of raw materials and primary commodities as related to trade and development, and the food crisis. It also proposed a long list of trade actions, including ***compensatory financing arrangements***, an improved ***GSP*** and the setting up of commodity ***buffer stocks***. Improvements were sought also in transport and insurance and the international monetary system. Many of these items were pursued in ***UNCTAD***, leading, for example, in 1976 to the proposal for the establishment of a ***Common Fund for Commodities*** and the ***Integrated Programme for Commodities***. Aspects of the NIEO ran into fierce opposition from developed countries, but some of the major developed-country commodity producers were seduced by the prospect of higher export returns if the commodity measures could be made to work. Other international organizations, including the GATT in the concurrent ***Tokyo Round***, also paid greater attention to developing country views, but the NIEO as a programme had run its course by the early 1980s. *See also* ***Charter of Economic Rights and Duties of States*** and ***North–South dialogue***.

Newly Independent States: this group of countries comprises Armenia, Azerbaijan, Belarus, Georgia, Kazakhstan, Kyrgyz Republic, Moldova, Tajikistan, Turkmenistan, Ukraine and Uzbekistan which were part of the USSR. Sometimes Russia is included in this list. *See also* ***Commonwealth of Independent States*** which in addition includes Russia.

Newly industrializing economies: also called newly industrializing countries. A term used particularly in the 1980s for developing economies which were transforming significant parts of their economies to a stage where they had many of the characteristics of industrialized economies. Examples of such economies include Hong Kong (China), Mexico, Malaysia, Republic of Korea, Singapore and Chinese Taipei.

Newly liberalizing countries: a term for the countries of Central and Eastern Europe, those making up the ***Commonwealth of Independent States***, and China which are transforming their previously ***centrally-planned economies*** into ***market economies***. At the same time, their centralized foreign trade regimes are being liberalized.

New Miyazawa Initiative: the finance package made available by Japan to countries affected by the 1997 Asian economic crisis. Main elements of the

遇；(o)为把财政资金转移到发展中国家创造有利条件；(p)使发展中国家具有获得科学和技术成果的途径，促进技术转让和建立本国技术；(q)制止浪费包括食品在内的自然资源；(r)发展中国家集中一切资源从事发展事业；(s)加强发展中国家之间的技术、经济、贸易和财政方面的相互合作；以及(t)发挥生产国联合组织在促进世界经济可持续增长和加速发展方面的作用。《行动纲领》同样雄心勃勃。寻求解决与贸易和发展有关的原材料和初级商品的根本问题以及粮食危机。还提出一系列贸易行动清单，包括补偿性融资安排、改善的普惠制(GSP)和建立商品缓冲储存。还寻求改善运输、保险以及国际货币体系。其中许多项目在联合国贸易与发展会议(UNCTAD)中进行探讨，例如，1976年提出设立商品共同基金和商品综合方案。NIEO的一些内容遭到发达国家的强烈反对，但一些主要发达国家的商品生产商认为如果商品措施奏效，出口回报可能会更高而受到诱惑。其他国际组织，包括GATT，在当时正在进行的东京回合中，也更加关注发展中国家的观点。但是，NIEO作为一项计划到20世纪80年代初已经走到尽头。另见*各国经济权利与义务宪章(Charter of Economic Rights and Duties of States)*、*南北对话(North–South dialogue)*。

Newly Independent States

新独立国家

这组国家包括曾属苏联的亚美尼亚、阿塞拜疆、白俄罗斯、格鲁吉亚、哈萨克斯坦、吉尔吉斯斯坦、摩尔多瓦、塔吉克斯坦、土库曼斯坦、乌克兰和乌兹别克斯坦。有时俄罗斯也在这一名单之中。另见包括俄罗斯在内的*独立国家联合体(Commonwealth of Independent States)*。

Newly industrializing economies

新兴工业化经济体

也称新兴工业化国家。这一词语特指20世纪80年代将其经济的重要部分向具有工业化经济体许多特征的阶段转变的发展中经济体。此类经济体例如中国香港、墨西哥、马来西亚、韩国、新加坡和中国台北。

Newly liberalizing countries

新自由化国家

用于称呼中东欧国家、组成独立国家联合体的国家以及中国的词语。这些国家正在将其以前的中央计划经济体转变为市场经济体。同时，它们的中央外贸体制正在实行自由化。

New Miyazawa Initiative

新宫泽喜一倡议

日本向受1997年亚洲金融危机影响的国家提供的一揽子金融措施。主要内容

initiative were $30 billion in short-term and long-term funds, purchase of bonds issued by Asian governments and provision of concessional yen loans. *See also* ***Chiang Mai Initiative***.

New Partnership for Africa's Development: NEPAD. Adopted by the ***Organization of African Unity*** (OAU) in July 2001. The ***African Union*** (AU), the successor to the OAU, adopted NEPAD as one of its programmes in 2002. The long-term objectives of NEPAD are (a) to eradicate poverty in Africa and to place African countries, both individually and collectively, on the path of sustainable development and thus halt the marginalization of Africa in the globalization process, and (b) to promote the role of women in all activities. In 2010 the NEPAD Planning and Coordination Agency (NEPAD Agency) was formed (a) to facilitate and coordinate the development of continent-wide programmes and projects and (b) to mobilize resources, engage global partners, regional communities and member states in the implementation of these programmes and projects. The NEPAD Agency is located at Midrand, South Africa. *See also* ***African Continental Free Trade Area*** and ***African regional economic integration***.

New protectionism: a term common in the 1980s. It was used to refer to measures such as ***quantitative restrictions***, ***voluntary restraint arrangements***, ***orderly marketing arrangements***, etc., in contrast to protective action expressed through high tariffs. *See* ***grey-area measures***. [Salvatore 1987]

New Silk Road: refers either to a proposal by China in 2011 for a rail transport route between Europe and Asia or the ***Belt and Road Initiative***.

New trade agenda: a term used by some to describe the ***market access*** issues still needing resolution. From this perspective, the traditional trade agenda is represented by efforts to reduce border measures consisting of ***tariffs*** and ***non-tariff measures***. The new trade agenda, on the other hand, is aimed more at impediments inside the market, such as standards, excessive reliance on ***sanitary and phytosanitary measures***, and private and public anti-competitive practices. To some extent, the new trade agenda overlaps with the ***new trade issues***, but in other respects it seeks to promote optimal results from existing multilateral trade agreements. *See also* ***technical barriers to trade***.

New trade issues: issues arising because of the emergence of new trading patterns, new products, new technologies or the confluence of ***trade policy*** and social policies. The term "new trade issues" often simply means that there is not yet a formal multilateral trade framework in existence for dealing with relevant matters or that they have only recently been taken up within the WTO. New trade issues include ***trade and competition***, ***trade and illicit payments***, ***trade and investment*** and ***trade and labour standards***. Some add ***trade and environment*** to this list, but the decision to establish a ***Committee on Trade and Environment*** in the WTO has persuaded many that this is now an established, if unresolved, issue. Intermittently there are suggestions that ***trade and culture***, ***trade and foreign exchange*** and ***trade and taxation*** should also be looked at. Since the ***Doha Ministerial Conference*** the WTO has had a

为，建立300亿美元的短期和长期基金、购买亚洲国家的政府债券以及提供优惠日元贷款等。另见*清迈倡议(Chiang Mai Initiative)*。

New Partnership for Africa's Development

非洲发展新伙伴关系计划

NEPAD。非洲统一组织(OAU)于2001年7月通过。非洲统一组织的继承者非洲联盟(AU)，在2002年将NEPAD作为其计划之一予以通过。NEPAD的长期目标为：(a)消除非洲的贫穷，使非洲国家单独和集体走上可持续发展道路，从而防止非洲在全球化进程中被边缘化；及(b)促进妇女在所有活动中的作用。2010年成立NEPAD规划和协调机构(NEPAD机构)，旨在(a)促进和协调整个大陆方案和项目的发展；及(b)调动资源，使全球伙伴、区域共同体和成员国参与执行这些方案和项目。NEPAD机构设在南非米德兰。另见*非洲大陆自由贸易区(African Continental Free Trade Area)*、*非洲区域经济一体化(African regional economic integration)*。

New protectionism

新保护主义

20 世纪 80 年代常见的词语。用于指诸如数量限制、自愿限制安排、有序销售安排等措施，与通过高关税表示的保护性措施形成对比。另见*灰色区域措施(grey-area measures)*。

New Silk Road

新丝绸之路

指中国在 2011 年提出的在欧洲和亚洲之间建立一条铁路运输线路的建议，或指"一带一路"倡议。

New trade agenda

新贸易议程

一些人用于描述仍需解决的市场准入问题。从这一角度看，传统的贸易议程以削减由关税和非关税措施组成的边境措施为代表。而另一方面，新贸易议程更多针对市场内部的障碍，例如标准、过度依赖卫生与植物卫生措施，以及私人和公共反竞争做法。在某种程度上，新贸易议程与新贸易议题重叠，但在其他方面，新贸易议程寻求促进在现有多边贸易协定项下取得最佳成果。另见*技术性贸易壁垒(technical barriers to trade)*。

New trade issues

新贸易议题

由于新贸易方式、新产品、新技术的出现或受贸易政策和社会政策的共同影响而产生的问题。"新贸易议题"通常仅指尚未建立处理相关问题的正式多边贸易框架或只在最近在 WTO 中提及的问题。新贸易议题包括贸易与竞争、贸易与违法付款、贸易与投资以及贸易与劳工标准。一些人将贸易与环境列入这一清单，但在 WTO 设立贸易与环境委员会的决定使许多人相信，这是一个已经设立的议题，即使还未解决。不时有人建议考虑贸易与文化、贸易与外汇以及贸易与税收等议题。自多哈部长级会议以来，WTO 已制定关于贸易与技

work programme on trade and the transfer of technology. *See also* ***Singapore issues***.

New trade order: in contemporary literature this term refers often to the global trading system that began with the establishment of the WTO, but it does not have a precise meaning. Some use it to describe what in their view would be a desirable trading system, if only certain instruments or rules could be negotiated.

New trade theory: an approach to the analysis of international trade that had its origin in the "Leontief Paradox". In 1953 the American economist Wassily Leontief found in his analysis of input-output statistics that the United States, a capital-rich country, exported labour-intensive products more successfully than capital-intensive products. This was contrary to what he had expected under the ***Heckscher-Ohlin theorem*** which is a restatement of the theory of ***comparative advantage***. Attempts by economists to explain this eventually led to the new trade theory which also takes into account the influence of factors such as technology and research and development. These factors can allow a country to acquire a comparative advantage where before it had none. An important medium-term result was the ***product cycle theory*** which appeared in 1967. The final stage was the ***strategic trade theory*** of which there are differing interpretations. The theory certainly has been used to defend ***targeting*** and ***picking winners***. That does not appear generally to be the aim of economists supporting it. *See also* ***competitive advantage***.

New Transatlantic Agenda: endorsed on 3 December 1995 at a ***European Union***–United States summit in Madrid. It enables the two sides to join forces on a wide range of international economic, social and political issues. Objective III of its four objectives deals with strengthening the world trading system and achieving closer economic cooperation. It aims at (a) moves to ensure that the WTO works as well as intended and cooperation on the ***new trade issues***, (b) efforts to achieve further bilateral reduction, or elimination, of tariffs in industrial products and to accelerate reductions due under the ***Uruguay Round***, and (c) concrete steps to remove regulatory and other obstacles to transatlantic trade through the creation of the ***New Transatlantic Marketplace***. The other three objectives are promoting peace, development and democracy around the world, responding to global challenges, and building bridges across the Atlantic. *See also* ***Positive Economic Agenda***, ***Transatlantic Business Dialogue***, and ***Transatlantic Investment Partnership***.

New Transatlantic Marketplace: one of the objectives of the ***New Transatlantic Agenda*** with a work programme covering a joint study to facilitate trade in goods and services and eliminating tariff and non-tariff barriers; confidence building through resolving bilateral trade issues; standards, certification and regulatory issues; veterinary and plant health issues; ***government procurement***; ***intellectual property rights***; expansion of the bilateral dialogue on ***financial services***; conclusion of a customs cooperation and mutual assistance agreement; expanding the bilateral Information Society Dialogue and cooperation on information

术转让的工作计划。另见*新加坡议题(Singapore issues)*。

New trade order

新贸易秩序

在现代文献中，该词语通常指自WTO建立以来形成的全球贸易体制，但并无准确含义。有些人用于描述在他们看来的理想贸易体制，如果只有某些文件或规则可以进行谈判的话。

New trade theory

新贸易理论

一种源于“列昂惕夫悖论”的国际贸易分析方法。1953年，美国经济学家瓦西里·列昂惕夫在投入产出统计数据的分析中发现，美国作为一个资本丰富的国家，出口劳动密集型产品比出口资本密集型产品更为成功。这与他在赫克歇尔-俄林定理下的预期相矛盾，该定理重申了比较优势理论。经济学家试图解释这一现象，最终带来了新贸易理论，该理论也考虑了诸如技术、研发等因素的影响。这些因素可使一国获得以前没有的比较优势。一个重要的中期成果是1967年出现的产品周期理论。最后阶段出现的战略贸易理论，对该理论的解释各不相同。这一理论已经被用来为目标策略和挑选赢家的做法提供辩护。但这似乎并非支持这一理论的经济学家的目标。另见*竞争优势(competitive advantage)*。

New Transatlantic Agenda

新跨大西洋议程

1995年12月3日在马德里举行的欧盟—美国峰会上获得通过。议程使双方在国际经济、社会和政治问题等一系列广泛领域方面开展合作。四项目标中的第三项目标处理加强世界贸易体制和实现更紧密经济合作问题。目标为：(a)采取行动以保证WTO发挥作用并按预期在新贸易议题上开展合作；(b)努力实现双边进一步削减或取消工业品关税，并加快进行乌拉圭回合中规定的削减；以及(c)通过建立“新跨大西洋市场”，采取具体步骤，消除跨大西洋贸易的监管障碍和其他障碍。另外3项目标为促进世界和平、发展和民主，应对全球性挑战以及建立跨大西洋桥梁。另见*积极经济议程(Positive Economic Agenda)*、*跨大西洋商业对话(Transatlantic Business Dialogue)*、*跨大西洋投资伙伴关系(Transatlantic Investment Partnership)*。

New Transatlantic Marketplace

新跨大西洋市场

新跨大西洋议程目标之一，工作计划包括：开展联合研究以便利货物和服务贸易，取消关税和非关税壁垒；通过解决双边贸易问题建立信任；标准、认证和监管问题；兽医和植物健康问题；政府采购；知识产权；扩大金融服务双边对话；缔结海关合作和互助协定；扩大双边信息社会对话以及信息和通信合

technology and telecommunications; deepening cooperation in competition matters; discussion of data protection issues; expanded cooperation on air and maritime transport matters; intensified cooperation on energy-related issues; biotechnology; and safety and health. *See also* ***Transatlantic Business Dialogue***.

New York Convention: the *United Nations Convention on the Recognition and Enforcement of Foreign Arbitral Awards*, adopted on 10 June 1958. Article II requires the contracting states to recognize an agreement in writing under which parties undertake to submit to ***arbitration*** differences which have arisen between them. Article III requires each contracting state to recognize arbitral awards as binding and enforce them under the conditions set out in subsequent articles of the Convention.

New Zealand Australia Free Trade Agreement: NAFTA. The trade agreement governing trade relations between Australia and New Zealand from 1966 to 1982. It achieved significantly liberalized trade between the two countries, but well short of free trade. It was replaced on 1 January 1983 by *ANZCERTA* (*Australia New Zealand Closer Economic Relations Trade Agreement*).

Next-generation free-trade agreements: sometimes new-generation free-trade agreements. An imprecise term for ***free-trade agreements*** that are, in the view of their proponents, rather comprehensive in their coverage. *See also* ***third-generation free-trade agreements***.

Next-generation trade issues: an indeterminate set of issues that might become the subject of future trade negotiations. Two possible criteria might be used to identify them. One is whether there is sufficient interest among countries to nominate a subject. The other is whether the subject can be negotiated productively. Even if both of these criteria lead to an affirmative answer, there is still the question of the forum in which such negotiations might be conducted. The ***Multilateral Agreement on Investment*** is an example where countries were in agreement that negotiations were desirable and feasible, but in the end several substantial issues were beyond resolution. The history of the ***Doha Development Agenda*** negotiations has shown that even extensions to familiar issues can become intractable. The ***European Union*** of course has come to grips with most of what could be considered next-generation trade issues. The ***United States–Mexico–Canada Agreement*** and the ***Trans-Pacific Partnership Agreement*** are examples that have made start on many such issues. It is quite possible that for the time being ***free-trade agreements*** will be a more fertile ground for negotiations than other negotiating environments. *See also* ***new trade issues***.

NGBT: *see* ***Negotiating Group on Basic Telecommunications***.

NGMTS: *see* ***maritime transport services***.

NGOs: *see* ***non-governmental organizations*** and ***civil society***.

Nice Agreement Concerning the International Classification of Goods and Services for the Purposes of the Registration of Marks: concluded in 1957 and last revised in 1979. It created a system of forty-two classes of goods and services which is used for the assessment and registration of trademarks. The Agreement is administered by ***WIPO***.

作；深化竞争问题合作；讨论数据保护问题；扩大航空和海运问题合作；加强能源相关问题合作；生物技术；以及安全与健康。另见*跨大西洋商业对话(Transatlantic Business Dialogue)*。

New York Convention

纽约公约

1958年6月10日通过的《联合国承认及执行外国仲裁裁决公约》。第2条要求各缔约国以书面协定承允彼此间所发生或可能发生之一切或任何争议提交仲裁。第3条要求各缔约国应承认仲裁裁决具有拘束力，并依援引裁决地之程序规则及公约各条所载条件执行之。

New Zealand Australia Free Trade Agreement

新西兰—澳大利亚自由贸易协定

NAFTA。1966年至1982年管辖澳大利亚与新西兰贸易关系的贸易协定。协定使两国贸易很大程度上实现了自由化，但并未实现自由贸易。协定在1983年1月1日被《澳大利亚与新西兰更紧密经济关系贸易协定》(ANZCERTA)所取代。

Next-generation free-trade agreements

下一代自由贸易协定

有时称新一代自由贸易协定。对于支持者而言，是对涵盖范围相当广泛的自由贸易协定的一个不精确词语。另见*第三代自由贸易协定(third-generation free-trade agreements)*。

Next-generation trade issues

下一代贸易议题

可能成为未来贸易谈判议题的一系列范围不确定的问题。两个可能的标准可用来确定这些问题。一个是各国是否有足够多的兴趣提出一项议题。另一个是该议题是否可以进行富有成效的谈判。即使这两个标准均能得出肯定答案，仍然存在开展此类谈判的场所问题。例如《多边投资协定》，各国一致认为谈判是可取和可行的，但最终若干实质问题无法解决。多哈发展议程谈判的历史表明，即使是对熟悉问题的延伸也可能变得棘手。当然，欧盟已经开始处理可被视为下一代贸易议题中的大部分问题。《美国—墨西哥—加拿大协定》和《跨太平洋经济伙伴关系协定》已经着手处理许多此类问题。可能的情况下，自由贸易协定将会成为较其他谈判环境更富有成果的谈判场所。另见*新贸易议题(new trade issues)*。

NGBT

见*基础电信谈判组(Negotiating Group on Basic Telecommunications)*。

NGMTS

见*海运服务(maritime transport services)*。

NGOs

非政府组织

见*非政府组织(non-governmental organizations)*、*公民社会(civil society)*。

Nice Agreement Concerning the International Classification of Goods and Services for the Purposes of the Registration of Marks

商标注册用商品和服务国际分类尼斯协定

1957年缔结，1979年进行最近一次修订。协定创立了由42类货物和服务组成的系统，用于商标评估和注册。协定由世界知识产权组织(WIPO)管理。

Noerr-Pennington doctrine: the principle in United States law that attempts to lobby a governmental or administrative body with the aim of influencing legislation or law enforcement cannot be prosecuted under the ***Sherman Act*** even if the lobbying has anti-competitive aims. *See also* ***antitrust laws***.

Nominal rate of assistance: defined by the Australian Productivity Commission as "the percentage change in gross returns per unit of output relative to the (hypothetical) situation of no assistance".

Nominal rate of protection: indicates the extent by which the domestic price of a product exceeds the price at the border (i.e. before the application of any customs duties). It is usually expressed as a percentage. *See also* ***effective rate of assistance*** and ***price wedge***.

Nominal tariff: the tariff rate appearing in a country's ***tariff schedule*** for a given product. It may differ from the ***applied tariff rates*** (the tariff rate actually levied by the customs administration when the product is imported). *See also* ***binding***.

Non-actionable subsidies: a class of subsidies identified in the WTO ***Agreement on Subsidies and Countervailing Measures***. It includes assistance to research and development, assistance to disadvantaged regions and assistance to promote the adaptation of existing facilities to new, more burdensome, environmental requirements. This was a time-bound provision which has not applied since 31 December 1999. *See also* ***actionable subsidies***, ***prohibited subsidies*** and ***subsidies***.

Non-agricultural market access: NAMA. Tariff negotiations on products other than those covered by the ***Agreement on Agriculture***. This term was created in the preparatory phase for the ***Seattle Ministerial Conference***.

Non-agricultural products: in the ***non-agricultural market access*** negotiations, products not covered by Annex 1 of the ***Agreement on Agriculture***. Fish and forestry products are therefore non-agricultural, along with industrial products in general.

Non-Aligned Movement: NAM. A group of about 115 members, mainly developing countries, which has its origin in the 1955 Asia-Africa Conference, held in Bandung, Indonesia. The first NAM summit was convened in Belgrade in 1961. Membership criteria include the requirement that the joining country should have adopted an independent policy based on the coexistence of states with different political and social systems and on non-alignment or should be showing a trend in favour of such a policy. NAM's early years were dominated by political issues, but since the early 1990s it has increasingly paid attention to global economic problems. *See also* ***Group of 77***.

Non-application: Article XIII of the ***WTO Agreement*** lays down that this Agreement and the other agreements administered by the WTO do not apply between two members if either of them does not consent to their application at the time either of them becomes a member. Non-application is therefore available only at the time a ***customs territory*** accedes to the WTO. *See also* ***denial of benefits***.

Noerr-Pennington doctrine
诺尔-彭宁顿学说

美国法律中的原则，即旨在影响立法或执法的针对立法或行政机构的游说活动不能根据《谢尔曼法》进行起诉，即使游说具有反竞争目标。另见*反垄断法(antitrust laws)*。

Nominal rate of assistance
名义援助率

澳大利亚生产力委员会将其定义为“与(假设)无援助情况相比较，每一单位产出的总回报百分比变化”。

Nominal rate of protection
名义保护率

表示产品国内价格超过边境价格(即未征收任何关税的价格)的程度。通常以百分比表示。另见*有效援助率(effective rate of assistance)*、*价格差额(price wedge)*。

Nominal tariff
名义关税

一国关税税则上显示的产品关税税率。可能不同于实施税率(即海关在产品进口时实际征收的关税税率)。另见*约束(binding)*。

Non-actionable subsidies
不可诉补贴

WTO《补贴与反补贴措施协定》确定的一类补贴。包括研发援助、落后地区援助以及使现有设施适应新的更严格的环境要求而提供的援助。这是一个有时间限制的条款，自1999年12月31日起不再适用。另见*可诉补贴(actionable subsidies)*、*禁止性补贴(prohibited subsidies)*、*补贴(subsidies)*。

Non-agricultural market access
非农产品市场准入

NAMA。对于《农业协定》未涵盖产品的关税谈判。该词创设于WTO西雅图部长级会议的筹备阶段。

Non-agricultural products
非农产品

非农产品市场准入谈判处理《农业协定》附件1未涵盖的产品。鱼和林产品与一般工业品因而属非农产品。

Non-Aligned Movement
不结盟运动

NAM。由大约115个国家组织的集团，其中主要为发展中国家，源于1955年在印度尼西亚万隆召开的亚非会议。第一届不结盟运动首脑会议于1961年在贝尔格莱德举行。成员资格标准包括要求加入国实行独立自主的政策，坚持不同政治和社会制度的国家和平共处且不结盟，或表示支持此种政策。不结盟运动早期主要以政治问题为主，但自20世纪90年代初以来，越来越关注全球经济问题。另见*77国集团(Group of 77)*。

Non-application
互不适用

《WTO协定》第13条规定，如一成员在另一成员成为成员时不同意在彼此之间适用本协定和WTO所管理的其他协定，则上述协定在该两成员之间互不适用。因此互不适用仅在一关税领土加入WTO时方可援引。另见*拒予利益(denial of benefits)*。

Non-automatic import licensing: an ***import licensing*** system under which it is necessary to obtain a permit each time a designated good is imported. *See also* ***automatic import licensing***.

Non-conforming measures: in a ***free-trade agreement*** using ***negative listings*** for scheduling commitments concerning services and investment laws, regulations, policies, etc., these are measures that do not comply fully with the provisions of the agreement when it enters into force. In the case of investment, the provisions usually cover ***national treatment***, ***most-favoured-nation treatment***, performance requirements and senior management and boards of directors. In the case of services, the applicable provisions usually are national treatment, most-favoured-nation treatment, ***market access*** and ***local presence***. Some agreements limit themselves to national treatment, market access and local presence. The listings explain why the measure is non-conforming. The parties usually agree that such measures will be brought into conformance with the agreement over time. *See also* ***positive listings***, ***ratchet mechanism***, ***reserved list*** and ***two-annex method***.

Non-conforming measures ratchet mechanism: *see* ***ratchet mechanism for non-conforming measures***.

Non-discrimination: treating all of one's trading partners in the same way. This is a fundamental concept in the multilateral trade framework. A country may not discriminate among foreign supplier countries, and it may not apply adverse discriminatory treatment to products once they have entered its territory legally. The WTO rules permit some exceptions to this concept under strictly defined conditions. For example, members of a ***free-trade area*** or a ***customs union*** may discriminate against non-members in the application of tariff rates. WTO members may also maintain preferential tariff schemes for developing countries. *See also* ***GSP***, ***most-favoured-nation treatment*** and ***national treatment***.

Non-dutiable goods: goods that are not subject to customs duties on entering or leaving a ***customs territory***. *See also* ***free list***.

Non-economic objectives: *see* ***non-trade concerns***.

Non-equity-based investment: investments in the form of licensing agreements, management contracts, production-sharing arrangements, risk-sharing contracts, international sub-contracting, licensing agreements, etc. *See also* ***foreign direct investment***, ***investment*** and ***portfolio investment***.

Non-establishment: *see* ***right of non-establishment***.

Non-governmental organizations: NGOs. A category of national or international organizations that are independent of governments. NGOs have a specific mandate (e.g. promotion of human rights, protection of the environment, advancement of women, the professional development of members, etc.). These are sometimes called "advocacy" NGOs because they seek to influence the behaviour of governments and ***intergovernmental organizations***. Others deliver services. These are classified as "operational" NGOs. Most NGOs do not seek to make a profit, but they usually charge a membership fee. Sometimes they ask for, and receive, business or government funding. In many cases, NGO

Non-automatic import licensing

非自动进口许可

一种进口许可制度，根据该制度，指定进口产品每次进口时必须获得许可。另见*自动进口许可(automatic import licensing)*。

Non-conforming measures

不符措施

在自由贸易协定中，使用负面清单列出有关服务和投资的法律、法规、政策等的承诺，这些措施在协定生效时并不完全符合协定条款。对于投资，条款通常涵盖国民待遇、最惠国待遇、实绩要求以及高级管理人员和董事的规定等。对于服务，适用条款通常为国民待遇、最惠国待遇、市场准入和当地存在。一些协定仅限于国民待遇、市场准入和当地存在。清单中说明措施不符的原因。参加方通常同意将随着时间的推移使此类措施符合协定。另见*正面清单(positive listings)*、*棘轮机制(ratchet mechanism)*、*保留清单(reserved list)*、*双附件法(two-annex method)*。

Non-conforming measures ratchet mechanism

不符措施棘轮机制

见*不符措施棘轮机制(ratchet mechanism for non-conforming measures)*。

Non-discrimination

非歧视

以相同方式对待一国的所有贸易伙伴。多边贸易框架中的一个基本概念。一国不可以在供应国之间实行歧视，且不可以在产品合法进入其领土后采取不利的歧视性待遇。WTO规则在严格限定的条件下允许这一概念存在一些例外。例如，自由贸易区或关税同盟的成员可以在实施税率方面对非成员实行歧视。WTO成员也可以对发展中国家保留优惠关税方案。另见*普惠制(GSP)*、*最惠国待遇(most-favoured-nation treatment)*、*国民待遇(national treatment)*。

Non-dutiable goods

不征税货物

在进入和离开关税领土时不征收关税的货物。另见*免税清单(free list)*。

Non-economic objectives

非经济目标

见*非贸易关注(non-trade concerns)*。

Non-equity-based investment

非股权投资

以许可协议、管理合同、生产分享安排、风险共担合同、国际转包合同等形式进行的投资。另见*外商直接投资(foreign direct investment)*、*投资(investment)*、*证券投资(portfolio investment)*。

Non-establishment

无需设立商业实体

见*无需设立商业实体权(right of non-establishment)*。

Non-governmental organizations

非政府组织

NGO。独立于政府的一类国家或国际组织。非政府组织具有特定授权(例如促进人权、保护环境、提高妇女地位、成员的职业发展等)。有时被称为“倡导型”

membership is available to anyone who agrees to support its aims. Professional bodies usually require a minimum standard of qualifications. *See also* ***civil society*** and ***intergovernmental organizations***.

Non-market economies: sometimes non-market country. Similar to ***centrally-planned economies***, but sometimes with the difference that some sectors of these economies may show all or most characteristics of a similar sector in a ***market economy***. Much of the discussion of non-market economies centres on China. The protocol formalizing China's accession to the WTO states that for the purpose of ***anti-dumping measures*** China could be treated as a non-market economy until December 2016 if Chinese firms could not prove that they operated under market conditions. China maintains that after that date it should have enjoyed ***market economy*** status, but others, including Canada, the European Union, India, Mexico and the United States, hold that China is still a non-market economy. A solution is not in sight. The ***United States–Mexico–Canada Agreement*** (USMCA, not yet in force), for example, requires a party to inform the other parties at least three months before the start of negotiations of its intention to start free-trade agreement negotiations with a non-market country. In this case a non-market country is defined as a "country that on the date of the signature of this Agreement at least one party has determined to be a non-market economy for the purposes of its trade remedy laws and is a country with which no Party has a free-trade agreement". If a party enters into a free-trade agreement with a non-market economy, the other parties can terminate USMCA and replace with a bilateral agreement.

Non-originating goods: in the administration of ***rules of origin*** for preferential trade agreements these are goods not receiving preferential treatment because they are deemed not to be the product of the country normally receiving preferential access. *See also* **originating goods**.

Non-originating materials: components of a good traded under a ***preferential trade arrangement*** which do not originate in the territory of a partner to the arrangement.

Non-paper: an informal proposal, usually on plain paper, issued by a country acting alone or in a group, aimed to test whether a new approach to a problem is worth pursuing. A non-paper is a useful way to deal with deadlock since its rejection is not seen as reflecting adversely on its sponsor.

Non-preferential rules of origin: refers to ***rules of origin*** applied by an importing country to all goods traded under most-favoured-nation conditions. These are also called ***MFN rules of origin***. A joint work programme is under way in the WTO and the ***World Customs Organization*** to harmonize non-preferential rules of origin.

Non-price predation: the action of seeking to drive efficient competitors out of business through abusive litigation and other means of imposing major costs on them. Abusive litigation would, for example, be aimed at ensuring that competitors could not use some crucial ***intellectual property rights***, rather than ensuring that these rights are protected. *See also* ***predatory pricing***.

非政府组织，因为这些组织寻求影响政府和政府间组织的行为。其他非政府组织则提供服务，称为"运作型"非政府组织。大多数非政府组织不以盈利为目的，但通常收取会员费。有时这些组织会请求和接受商业或政府资金。在许多情况下，同意支持其目标的任何人均可获得成员资格。专业机构通常要求最低资格标准。另见*公民社会(civil society)*、*政府间组织(intergovernmental organizations)*。

Non-market economies

非市场经济体

有时称非市场国家。与中央计划经济体类似，但有时存在差别，即这些经济体的一些部门可能表现出市场经济中类似部门的全部或大部分特征。关于非市场经济体的讨论大多集中于中国。中国加入WTO议定书规定，在2016年12月之前，如果中国企业不能证明其在市场条件下经营，那么就反倾销措施而言，中国可被视为非市场经济体。中国认为，在该日期之后，中国应该享有市场经济地位，但其他国家，包括加拿大、欧盟、印度、墨西哥和美国则认为中国仍然是非市场经济体。还未找到解决办法。例如，《美国—墨西哥—加拿大协定》(USMCA)要求一方应至少在谈判开始前3个月通知其他方其计划与非市场国家开展自由贸易协定谈判。在此种情况下，非市场国家定义为"在本协定签署之日，至少一方就其贸易救济法律而言确定属非市场经济体且无任何一方与之签署自由贸易协定的国家"。如果一方与非市场经济体订立自由贸易协定，其他方可以终止USMCA而代之以双边协定。

Non-originating goods

非原产货物

在管理优惠贸易协定的原产地规则时，这些货物因被视为不属通常接受优惠准入国家的产品而不享受优惠待遇。另见*原产货物(originating goods)*。

Non-originating materials

非原产材料

根据优惠贸易安排进行贸易的货物中所含不原产自有关安排的成员领土的组成部分。

Non-paper

非文件

一国单独或一组国家提出的非正式提案，通常使用普通文件形式，目的在于试探是否值得对一问题采取的新方式。非文件是处理僵局的有效方法，因为即使被拒绝也不会被认为会对其提出者产生不利影响。

Non-preferential rules of origin

非优惠原产地规则

指进口国对在最惠国待遇条件下进行交易的所有货物实施的原产地规则。也称最惠国原产地规则。WTO和世界海关组织(WCO)正在开展协调非优惠原产地规则的联合工作计划。

Non-price predation

非价格掠夺

寻求通过滥用诉讼和使有效竞争者大幅增加成本的其他手段，将竞争者逐出市场的行为。例如，滥用诉讼的目的是使竞争对手不能使用某些关键的知识产权，而不是使这些权利得到保护。另见*掠夺性定价(predatory pricing)*。

Non-product-related process and production: a way of looking at the production process which concentrates on the finished product and which, in a hypothetical extreme case, would pay no attention to how the product is made. What matters is the result of the production process. An example would be the production of a steel bar. Examined from this perspective, it would not matter whether the bar was made from recycled iron and steel, or whether it was made in a process beginning with iron ore and coking coal. Of course, the steelmaker would still have to meet, for example, health and safety standards, and the steel would have to meet the applicable technical specifications. *See also* ***process and production method***.

Non-qualifying operations: *see* ***insufficient operations***.

Non-qualifying value: in ***rules of origin*** the part of the value of a good that does not meet the requirements for preferential access.

Non-reciprocal free-trade area: *see* ***free-trade area***.

Non-reciprocity: in trade negotiations, acceptance of the principle that an offer or undertaking by a party to do something need not be matched, either wholly or partly, by the party standing to benefit from the offer. This principle is contained, for example, in ***Part IV of the GATT*** (Article XXXVI:8) which states that the "developed ***contracting parties*** do not expect ***reciprocity*** for commitments made by them in trade negotiations to reduce or remove tariffs and other barriers to the trade of the less-developed contracting parties". *See also* ***Enabling Clause***.

Non-tariff barriers: *see* ***non-tariff measures***.

Non-tariff distortions: adverse influences on trade flows caused by the existence of ***non-tariff measures***.

Non-tariff measures: NTMs. Measures other than ***tariffs*** applied by governments at the border that determine the extent to which a good has access to the import market. This term is used by many in preference to non-tariff barriers (NTBs) because it conveys more clearly the fact that many of these measures are not meant to be import barriers, and that they do not place the imported good at a disadvantage. An example of this reasoning is the case where an NTM would merely consist of applying the rules governing domestically produced goods to imported goods also. This would be the case with product standards agreed internationally. Assuming these standards were met, the good could be imported to whatever extent would make commercial sense. From this perspective, calling the measure an NTM would be appropriate. If, however, there was an element of putting the foreign good at a disadvantage, it would be better to refer to the measure as an NTB. Many commentators prefer to use NTM instead of NTB because the former is less likely to prejudge whether a given measure has a protectionist effect. In practice, though, the two terms are often used interchangeably. Laird and Vossenar have suggested the following classification of NTMs: (a) *measures to control the volume of imports*, including both quantitative restrictions and export restraint arrangements, (b) *measures to control the price of imported goods*, such as ***trigger price*** mechanisms, ***variable***

Non-product-related process and production
与产品无关的工序和生产

一种看待生产工序的方法，此种生产工序集中在成品上，在一种假设的极端情况下，此种生产工序不关注产品是如何生产的，而重要的是生产工序的结果。例如钢筋生产。从这一角度来看，无论棒材是用回收的钢铁制造的，还是用铁矿石和炼焦煤制造的，并不重要。当然，钢铁制造商仍然必须达到健康和安全标准，且钢铁必须满足适用的技术规格。另见*工序和生产方法(process and production method)*。

Non-qualifying operations
不符操作

见*不充分操作(insufficient operations)*。

Non-qualifying value
不符价值

在原产地规则中，货物价值中不符合优惠准入要求的部分。

Non-reciprocal free-trade area
非互惠自由贸易区

见*自由贸易区(free-trade area)*。

Non-reciprocity
非互惠

在贸易谈判中接受如下原则，即一方作某事的提议或承诺不必全部或部分得到接受或得益于该提议的另一方相匹配。例如，这一原则载于GATT第四部分(第36条第8款)，该条规定，"在削减或取消针对欠发达缔约方贸易的关税和其他壁垒的谈判中，发达缔约方不期望因其作出的承诺而获得互惠"。另见*授权条款(Enabling Clause)*。

Non-tariff barriers
非关税壁垒

见*非关税措施(non-tariff measures)*。

Non-tariff distortions
非关税扭曲

因非关税措施的存在而对贸易流动造成的不利影响。

Non-tariff measures
非关税措施

NTMs。政府在边境实施的决定货物对进口市场准入程度的除关税外的措施。许多人更愿意使用这一词语而不是非关税壁垒，因为这一词语更清楚地表明这样一个事实，即许多这些措施并不意味着属进口壁垒，而不会使进口货物处于不利地位。这方面的例子如，一项非关税措施仅包括将管辖本国产品的规定适用于进口货物。对于国际议定的产品标准即为此种情况。假设达到这些标准，货物可以在任何具有商业意义的程度上进口。从这一角度来看，称此种措施为"非关税措施"是合适的。但是，如果存在将外国商品置于不利地位的因素，那么最好将该措施称为非关税壁垒。许多评论家更喜欢使用"非关税措施"而不是"非关税壁垒"，因为前者不大可能预先判断一项指定措施是否具有保护主义效果。但是在实践中，两词经常互换使用。莱尔德和沃森纳建议将非

levies, ***anti-dumping measures***, countervailing duties, etc., (c) *monitoring measures including price and volume investigations and surveillance*, (d) *production and export measures*, mainly ***subsidies*** or taxation measures, and (e) *technical barriers*, such as various standards imposed for health and safety reasons. Deardorff and Stern have proposed a different classification. They suggest (a) *quantitative restrictions and similar specific limitations* such as ***import quotas***, export limitations, licensing, prohibition, etc., (b) *non-tariff charges and related policies affecting imports*, including variable levies, ***advance deposits***, anti-dumping duties, countervailing duties and ***border tax adjustments***, (c) *government participation in trade, restrictive practices, and more general government policies*, such as subsidies and other aids, government procurement policies, ***state trading***, ***competition policies***, etc., (d) *customs procedures and administrative practices*, and (e) *technical barriers to trade*, including safety and industrial standards, health and sanitary regulations, packaging and labelling regulations, and advertising and media regulations. Strictly speaking, anti-dumping duties and countervailing measures are non-tariff measures to the extent that investigations and related procedures may cause a ***trade-chill effect***. In a quantitative assessment of non-tariff measures, any duties imposed after an investigation would count as a ***tariff***. A report issued by UNCTAD and the World Bank in 2018 classifies import-related NTMs into technical measures and non-technical measures. Technical measures include ***sanitary and phytosanitary measures***, ***technical barriers to trade*** and ***preshipment inspections*** and other formalities. Non-technical measures included actions such as contingent trade protection; non-automatic licensing, quotas, prohibitions and quantity-control measures; price-control measures, including additional taxes and charges; finance measures affecting competition; trade-related investment measures; distribution restrictions; restrictions on post-sale services; subsidies (excluding export subsidies); government procurement restrictions; intellectual property; and rules of origin. *See also* ***Agreement on Safeguards***, ***APEC Cross-Cutting Principles on Non-Tariff Measures*** and ***tariffication***. [Deardorff and Stern 1997, Laird and Vossenar 1991]

Non-tariff preferences: discrimination in favour of some trading partners in the use of ***non-tariff measures***. This sometimes happens under ***free-trade agreements***.

Non-tradables: goods and services that are not, or only rarely, traded internationally because they are abundant and cheap everywhere or because the cost of support services needed for trading them would exceed the value of the product in the importing market. A list of non-tradables would change considerably over the years and probably become shorter. Two examples will suffice. Sand and gravel, at one time quarried locally and considered non-tradable, have become tradable for a range of reasons, including more stringent environmental measures governing their extraction. Haircuts remain among the non-tradable services even though a person living very close to a border may find it convenient to hop across the border for a haircut. *See also* ***semi-tradables*** and ***tradables***.

关税措施分类如下：(a)控制进口量的措施，包括数量限制和出口限制安排；(b)控制进口货物价格的措施，例如触发价格机制、差价税、反倾销措施、反补贴税等；(c)监控措施，包括价格和数量调查和监督；(d)生产和出口措施，主要为补贴或税收措施；以及(e)技术壁垒，例如因健康和安全原因而实施的各种标准。迪尔多夫和斯特恩提出了不同的分类方法。他们建议分为：(a)数量限制和类似具体限制，例如进口配额、出口限制、许可程序、禁止等；(b)影响进口的非关税费用和相关政策，包括差价税、保证金、反倾销税、反补贴税和边境税调节；(c)政府参与贸易、限制性惯例以及更一般的政府政策，例如补贴和其他援助、政府采购政策、国营贸易、竞争政策等；(d)海关程序和行政管理措施；以及(e)技术性贸易壁垒，包括安全和产业标准、健康和卫生法规、包装和标签法规以及广告和媒体法规。严格地讲，反倾销税和反补贴措施在调查和相关程序可能造成贸易冷却效应的范围内属于非关税措施。在对非关税措施进行量化评估时，在调查后加征的任何税均被视为关税。联合国贸易与发展会议(UNCTAD)和世界银行在2018年发布的报告将与进口相关的非关税措施分为技术性措施和非技术性措施。技术性措施包括卫生与植物卫生措施、技术性贸易壁垒和装运前检验及其他手续。非技术性措施包括紧急贸易保护；非自动许可程序、配额、禁止和数量控制措施；价格控制措施，包括额外征税和收费；影响竞争的金融措施；与贸易有关的投资措施；分销限制；售后服务限制；补贴(不包括出口补贴)；政府采购限制；知识产权；以及原产地规则。另见*保障措施协定(Agreement on Safeguards)*、*APEC非关税措施交叉原则(APEC Cross-Cutting Principles on Non-Tariff Measures)*、*关税化(tariffication)*。

Non-tariff preferences

非关税优惠

在使用非关税措施方面有利于一些贸易伙伴的差别待遇。此种情况有时发生在自由贸易协定项下。

Non-tradables

非贸易品

因各地均数量丰富且廉价或因贸易所需支持服务的费用在进口国中超过产品价值，而不在或仅少量在国际间进行交易的商品和服务。随着时间的推移，非贸易品的清单会发生很大变化，且可能会变短。举两例即可说明。沙子和砾石曾一度在当地开采而被视为非贸易品，由于对开采采取更严格的环境措施等一系列原因而已经成为贸易品。理发仍属非贸易服务之列，即使生活在非常接近边境的人可能发现越过边境去理个发很方便。另见*半贸易品(semi-tradables)*、*贸易品(tradables)*。

Non-trade concerns: used in the agricultural trade negotiations as a more neutral expression than, for example, ***multifunctionality***. The preamble of the ***Agreement on Agriculture*** specifies ***food security*** and environmental protection as examples. Also cited by WTO members are rural development and employment, and poverty alleviation. *See also* ***non-trade objectives in trade policy***.

Non-trade objectives in trade policy: this refers to the formulation of trade rules to achieve aims other than the traditional goals of freer, predictable and non-discriminatory trade. Such aims can include the protection of the environment, the promotion of ***core labour standards*** or ***human rights***, support for democratic values and social and political ideas more generally. Some also include rules concerning competition and investment in this category, but others dispute this because of the frequently complementary relationship between ***trade policy*** and investment or competition. Arguments about the validity of non-trade objectives are often fierce. A basic principle seems to be that my concerns are legitimate, but yours are suspect and probably protectionist. *See also* ***animal welfare***, ***democracy clause***, ***human rights clause***, ***multifunctionality***, ***trade and competition***, ***trade and environment***, ***trade and human rights***, ***trade and investment*** and ***trade and labour standards***.

Non-violation: action taken under the WTO dispute settlement rules falls into one of two categories. The first is violation cases. The plaintiff believes that the defendant has violated one or more of his obligations under the WTO rules. Most disputes are of this kind. The second category covers non-violation cases. Here the plaintiff does not argue that the defendant has acted contrary to the rules and, indeed, may agree that they were observed to the letter. The plaintiff will seek to show, however, that the defendant has altered some other conditions with the result that he was denied a benefit available him before the action was taken. In other words, the defendant may have had "nullified or impaired" what he considers his reasonable expectations by a measure either consistent with the rules or not subject to them. An example of this would be to cancel out the lowering of a tariff with some other measure either consistent with the rules or not covered by them. ***Australian subsidy on ammonium sulphate***, ***Kodak–Fuji case*** and ***Oilseeds*** are examples of non-violation cases. A debate is under way in the ***Doha Development Agenda*** negotiations on the feasibility or desirability of a non-violation clause in ***intellectual property***. The ***Agreement on Trade-Related Aspects of Intellectual Property Rights*** contains a moratorium for five years on bringing forward such cases. This has now been extended several times. *See also* ***nullification or impairment***. [Cho 1998, Mavroidis 2000]

Nordic countries: refers to Denmark, Finland, Iceland, Norway and Sweden and their autonomous territories associated with them. The latter are Åland (Finland), Faroe Islands and Greenland (both Denmark). They cooperate officially through the Nordic Council, a parliamentary cooperation body, and the Nordic Council of Ministers, a governmental cooperation body. The two bodies maintain separate secretariats in Copenhagen.

Non-trade concerns

非贸易关注

在农业贸易谈判中使用的比多功能性更为中立的表述。《农业协定》序言以粮食安全和环境保护为例。WTO成员还提到了农村发展和就业以及减贫等。另见*贸易政策中的非贸易目标(non-trade objectives in trade policy)*。

Non-trade objectives in trade policy

贸易政策中的非贸易目标

指制定贸易规则以实现更自由、可预测和非歧视贸易的传统目标以外的其他目标。此类目标可包括保护环境、促进核心劳工标准或人权、更普遍地支持民主价值观和社会政治思想。一些目标还将竞争和投资规则包括在这一类别中，但其他人对此提出质疑，因为贸易政策与投资或竞争之间经常存在互补关系。关于非贸易目标有效性的争论常常是激烈的。一个基本原则似乎是，我的关注是合理的，而你的关注是可疑的且可能具有保护主义性质。另见*动物福利(animal welfare)*、*民主条款(democracy clause)*、*人权条款(human rights clause)*、*多功能性(multifunctionality)*、*贸易与竞争(trade and competition)*、*贸易与环境(trade and environment)*、*贸易与人权(trade and human rights)*、*贸易与投资(trade and investment)*、*贸易与劳工标准(trade and labour standards)*。

Non-violation

非违反

根据WTO争端解决规则提起的诉讼可分为两类。第一类是违反案件。原告认为被告违反其在WTO规则下的一项或多项义务。大多数争端属于这一类。第二类是非违反案件。原告并不提出被告的行为违反规则，而事实上，原告可能同意被告遵守了规则。但是，原告试图证明，被告改变了其他一些条件，导致原告在提起诉讼之前被剥夺了其可获得的利益。换言之，被告通过符合规则或不受规则约束的措施使原告认为其合理预期应获得的利益受到“丧失或减损”。例如，采取符合规则或规则所不涵盖的其他一些措施而不降低关税。“澳大利亚对硫酸铵补贴案”、“柯达-富士案”和“油籽案”均为非违反案件。在多哈发展议程谈判中，正在就知识产权非违反条款的可行性或可取性开展辩论。《与贸易有关的知识产权协定》包含在5年内暂停起诉此类案件的规定。现在已延长多次。另见*丧失或减损(nullification or impairment)*。

Nordic countries

北欧国家

指丹麦、芬兰、冰岛、挪威和瑞典及与之相关的自治领土。后者指芬兰的奥兰群岛、丹麦的法罗群岛和格陵兰岛。这些领土通过议会合作机构——北欧理事会和政府合作机构——北欧部长理事会开展正式合作。两机构在哥本哈根分别设有秘书处。

Normal trade relations: the term now often used by the United States instead of ***most-favoured nation treatment***. *See also* ***permanent normal trade relations*** and ***temporary normal trade relations***.

Normal value: a key concept used in determining whether ***dumping*** has taken place. GATT Article VI condemns the introduction of products into the commerce of another member at less than normal value. Article 2 of the ***Anti-Dumping Agreement*** sets out the meaning of "normal value" and the procedures for its determination. A product is considered dumped, or introduced at less than normal value, if its price, when being exported in the ***ordinary course of trade***, is less than the comparable price for the like product when destined for consumption in the exporting country. If there are no sales in the domestic market of the exporting country or if these sales do not permit a proper comparison, the export price to an appropriate and representative third country may be used. A third method is using the cost of production in the country of origin plus a reasonable amount for administrative, selling and general costs and for profits. Precise rules are available if the product is found not to have been exported in the ordinary course of trade, or for trade that may have been short term only. If no export price is available, or if it appears that the export price is unreliable because of an association between the exporter and the importer or a third party, the export price may be constructed on the basis of the price at which the imported products are sold to an independent buyer. The comparison between export price and normal value must be made under similar conditions, with allowance for unavoidable differences. *See also* ***anti-dumping measures***.

North: *see* ***developed country*** and ***North–South dialogue***.

North American Agreement on Environmental Cooperation: *see* ***NAFTA***.

North American Agreement on Labor Cooperation: an agreement containing binding obligations signed by the Canada, Mexico and United States in September 1993 as part of their obligations under ***NAFTA*** with the main objective of improving working conditions and living standards in the territory of each party. The parties to the Agreement undertake to promote eleven labour principles which include, in addition to the ***core labour standards***, the right to strike, minimum employment standards, equal pay for women and men, prevention of occupational injuries and illnesses, compensation in cases of occupational injuries and illnesses and protection of migrant workers. The Agreement permits trade measures to enforce the observance of standards relating to occupational safety and health, ***child labour*** or minimum wage technical standards, but not the core labour standards such as freedom of association or the right to bargain collectively. The administration of the Agreement is supervised by a Commission for Labour Cooperation consisting of a ministerial council and a secretariat.

North American Free Trade Agreement: *see* ***NAFTA***.

North Atlantic Free Trade Area: a proposal for a ***free-trade area*** between the United States and the European Economic Community which appeared

Normal trade relations

正常贸易关系

美国现在经常使用的替代最惠国待遇的词语。另见*永久正常贸易关系(permanent normal trade relations)*、*临时正常贸易关系(temporary normal trade relations)*。

Normal value

正常价值

用于确定是否发生倾销的关键概念。GATT第6条谴责将产品以低于正常价值的价格引入另一成员的商业。《反倾销协定》第2条规定了"正常价值"的含义及其确定程序。如一产自一国出口至另一国的出口价格低于正常贸易过程中出口国中供消费的同类产品的可比价格，则该产品被视为倾销，即以低于其正常价值的方式进入另一国的商业。如出口国国内市场不存在销售，或对此类销售无法进行适当比较，则可使用对适当和具有代表性的第三国的出口价格。第三种方法是使用原产国中的生产成本加合理金额的管理、销售和一般费用及利润。如果发现产品不属在正常贸易过程中所出口的，或可能只是短期贸易，协定规定了明确的规则。如果无出口价格，或由于出口商与进口商或第三方之间的关联，出口价格似乎不可靠，则出口价格可在进口产品出售给独立购买者的价格基础上推定。出口价格和正常价值之间的比较必须在相似的条件下进行，并考虑不可避免的差异。另见*反倾销措施(anti-dumping measures)*。

North

北方

见*发达国家(developed country)*、*南北对话(North–South dialogue)*。

North American Agreement on Environmental Cooperation

北美环境合作协定

见*北美自由贸易协定(NAFTA)*。

North American Agreement on Labor Cooperation

北美劳工合作协定

加拿大、墨西哥和美国于1993年9月签署的协定，其中包含具有约束力的义务，作为三国在《北美自由贸易协定》(NAFTA)项下义务的一部分，主要目标为改善每一缔约方领土内的工作条件和生活水平。协定缔约方承诺促进11项劳工原则，其中除核心劳工标准外，还包括罢工权、最低就业标准、男女同工同酬、预防职业伤害和疾病、职业伤害和疾病赔偿以及保护流动工人。协定允许采取贸易措施以强制遵守与职业安全和健康、童工或最低工资技术标准有关的标准，但不包括结社自由或集体谈判权等核心劳工标准。协定的管理由劳工合作委员会监督，该委员会由部长级理事会和秘书处组成。

North American Free Trade Agreement

北美自由贸易协定

见*北美自由贸易协定(NAFTA)*。

North Atlantic Free Trade Area

北大西洋自由贸易区

20世纪60年代不时出现的建议，即在美国和欧洲经济共同体之间建立自由贸

sporadically in the 1960s. Irreconcilable differences concerning agricultural trade, the friction it was meant to resolve above all else, meant that it did not reach the negotiating table. *See also* ***TAFTA*** and ***Transatlantic Trade and Investment Partnership***.

North East Asia Free-Trade Area: NEAFTA. Proposed in 1999 by Prime Minister Obuchi of Japan as a long-term project for closer regional economic integration. Prospective members could include Japan, Republic of Korea, China, Hong Kong (China) and others. No timetable for negotiations exists. *See also* ***East Asia Free-Trade Agreement***.

North–South: A Programme for Survival**:** *see* ***Brandt Report***.

North–South dialogue: a process of discussions and negotiations, frequently acrimonious and fruitless, between the developed or industrialized countries (the North) and the developing countries (the South). Some see it as having begun in the early 1960s with, for example, the ***Alliance for Progress*** and the moves leading to the establishment of ***UNCTAD*** (United Nations Conference on Trade and Development) in 1964 and the concurrent formation of the ***Group of 77***. Others date the beginning of the North–South dialogue to the ***Conference on International Economic Cooperation*** (CIEC), convened by France in 1975, which itself concluded in 1977 without any concrete results. The more or less formal end of the dialogue came with the 1980 Special Session of the ***United Nations General Assembly***. There is little disagreement on this point. Whatever exact starting point one accepts for the North–South dialogue, it followed the arrival in the United Nations and its specialized agencies of a large number of newly-independent developing countries. Their numbers allowed them increasingly to define or influence the work programme of these bodies. This, coupled with the view advocated strongly by many developing countries that their legitimate concerns about development, economic growth and participation in the global trading system were not being taken seriously by the developed countries, led by the early 1970s to a realization by the North that something had to be done. The ***OPEC*** decision in 1973 to quadruple the price of oil provided an additional incentive for this. What followed was a range of political and economic initiatives, many of which did not endure. In outline, in 1974 the United Nations General Assembly passed a resolution on the ***New International Economic Order***, in effect a vast claim for the transfer of resources from the North to the South. The adoption of the ***Charter of Economic Rights and Duties of States***, an attempt to redefine aspects of international law, occurred in the same year. Early in 1975 followed the first ***Lomé Convention*** which, though producing advantages for developing countries, also showed that probably they did not have the power to force a rapid change. This became clearer at CIEC, mentioned above, held in the same year. There had been moves in the United Nations system since 1977 to start a programme of ***Global Negotiations*** in 1980. The launch of the ***Brandt Report*** in 1980 appeared to give promise of a new start. However, by that time the gap between the two sides had become unbridgeable, their positions largely incapable of

易区。由于建议首先需要解决农业贸易不可调和的分歧这一摩擦，即意味着这一建议未能提到谈判桌上来。另见*跨大西洋自由贸易协定(TAFTA)*、*跨大西洋贸易与投资伙伴协定(Transatlantic Trade and Investment Partnership)*。

North East Asia Free-Trade Area

东北亚自由贸易区

NEAFTA。日本首相小渊惠三于1999年作为一项长期计划提出，旨在促成更紧密区域经济一体化。潜在成员包括日本、韩国、中国、中国香港及其他国家。无谈判时间表。另见*东亚自由贸易协定(East Asia Free-Trade Agreement)*。

North–South: A Programme for Survival

北方和南方：争取生存的纲领

见*勃兰特报告(Brandt Report)*。

North–South dialogue

南北对话

发达国家或工业化国家(北方)与发展中国家(南方)之间的讨论和谈判进程，通常尖锐而无果。一些人认为，南北对话始于20世纪60年代初，例如，进步联盟和促成1964年成立联合国贸易与发展会议(UNCTAD)和同时成立77国集团的行动。其他一些人认为，南北对话始于法国于1975年召开的国际经济合作会议(CIEC)，会议于1977年结束，未形成任何实质性成果。对话的大致正式结束是在1980年联合国大会特别会议上。在这一点上没有什么分歧。无论人们所接受的南北对话的确切开始时间是什么，对话开始后联合国及其专门机构中加入了大批新独立的发展中国家。发展中国家的数量使其能够越来越多地决定或影响这些机构的工作计划。加上许多发展中国家强烈主张的观点，即发达国家没有认真对待发展中国家对发展、经济增长和参与全球贸易体系的合理关切，促成了北方(发达国家)在20世纪70年代初认识到必须采取一些行动。石油输出国组织(OPEC)在1973年决定将石油价格提高4倍为此增加了额外的刺激因素。随之而来的是一系列政治和经济倡议，其中许多并未持续下去。概括而言，1974年联合国大会通过了一项关于国际经济新秩序的决议，实际上是要求将资源从北方转移到南方的一项内容广泛的主张。同年通过的《各国经济权利与义务宪章》是重新界定国际法各方面的一种尝试。1975年初，达成第一个《洛美公约》，虽然公约为发展中国家带来了利益，但也表明可能这些国家没有权力促成迅速改变。在同年举行的CIEC会议上，这一点变得更加清晰。自1977年以来，联合国系统内一直在就1980年启动一项全球谈判计划开展工作。1980年《勃兰特报告》的发布似乎预示着一个新的开始。但是，那时

movement, and the dialogue petered out. There have been periodic calls for the revival of the North–South dialogue, but discussions on how to do it always got bogged down in the preliminaries. *See also* ***Harries Report***.

Nothing is agreed until everything is agreed: a frequent understanding between participants in trade negotiations at the start of proceedings. This principle preserves each party's bargaining power, and it ensures that the result is considered balanced by all. *See also* ***ad referendum agreement***, ***globality*** and ***single undertaking***.

Notification: an obligation to report to the relevant body of the WTO the adoption of trade measures that might have an effect on the members of the agreement it administers. Notifying promotes ***transparency*** and assists ***surveillance***. Notifying has no bearing on whether the measure itself will be judged to be in conformity with the rules. The *Decision on Notification Procedures* taken at Marrakesh in April 1994 contains an illustrative list of twenty types of notifiable measures as follows: tariffs, tariff quotas and surcharges, quantitative restrictions (including voluntary export restraints and orderly marketing arrangements), other non-tariff measures such as licensing and mixing requirements and variable levies, customs valuation, rules of origin, government procurement, technical barriers, safeguard actions, anti-dumping actions, countervailing actions, export taxes, export subsidies, export tax exemptions, concessionary export financing, free-trade zones (including in-bond manufacturing), export restrictions, any other government assistance, role of state-trading enterprises, foreign exchange controls related to imports and exports, government-mandated countertrade, etc. In drawing up the list, negotiators have cast a wide net, and few measures could in principle escape it. The WTO Secretariat maintains a list of all notified measures and reminds members when they have to put in a standard notification. *See also* ***ePing SPS and TBT notification alert system***, ***e-Trips Notification Submission System***, ***reverse notification***, ***surveillance*** and ***transparency***.

Not inconsistent with: an expression frequently used by ***panels*** in WTO ***dispute settlement*** reports. It means that, as far as the panel can establish, the measure being examined does not contravene any WTO rules. Accordingly, the party maintaining the measure is not required to change it. The use of this expression appears to stem partly from the fact that the ***GATT 1947*** was in force provisionally only, and partly from a desire by panels to shield themselves against the possibility of undiscovered facts. *See also* ***Protocol of Provisional Application***.

Not indispensable, but necessary: in *Korea – Various Measures Affecting Imports of Fresh, Chilled and Frozen Beef* the ***Appellate Body*** considered whether a measure might not be indispensable, but nevertheless necessary, to attain a certain objective. It noted that sometimes "indispensable" and "necessary" would have the same meaning, but on other occasions the meaning of "necessary" might be limited to "making a contribution to". The Appellate Body found that sometimes one would not get around considering "the relative

的双方差距已经无法弥合，双方立场已难以变化，对话逐渐减少。间或有重启南北对话的呼声，但是关于如何重启对话的讨论总是在一开始即陷入僵局。另见*哈里斯报告(Harries Report)*。

Nothing is agreed until everything is agreed

所有内容达成一致才能达成协议

贸易谈判的参加方之间在谈判开始时通常的理解。这一原则保留了每一方讨价还价的能力，并保证结果被各方视为平衡的。另见*待核准协定(ad referendum agreement)*、*全球化(globality)*、*一揽子承诺(single undertaking)*。

Notification

通报

向WTO相关机构报告采用可能对WTO所管理协定的成员产生影响的贸易措施的义务。通报可以提高透明度，并有助于监督。通报与对于判断措施本身是否符合规则并无影响。1994年4月在马拉喀什作出的《关于通报程序的决定》包含20种应通报措施的指示性清单，其中包括：关税、关税配额和附加税、数量限制(包括自愿出口限制和有序销售安排)、其他非关税措施(例如许可程序、掺配要求和差价税)、海关估价、原产地规则、政府采购、技术性壁垒、保障措施、反倾销措施、反补贴措施、出口税、出口补贴、免税、优惠性出口融资、自由贸易园区(包括保税仓库内生产)、出口限制、其他政府援助、国营贸易企业的作用、与进出口有关的外汇管制、政府授权的补偿贸易等。在起草该清单时，谈判者考虑范围很广，原则上几乎没有什么措施不在此列。WTO秘书处持有一份所有通报措施的清单，并提醒成员何时需要提交标准通报。另见*TBT/SPS ePing通报提醒系统(ePing SPS and TBT notification alert system)*、*e-Trips通报提交系统(e-Trips Notification Submission System)*、*反向通知(reverse notification)*、*监督(surveillance)*、*透明度(transparency)*。

Not inconsistent with

不相抵触

WTO争端解决报告中专家组经常使用的表述。指在专家组能够确定的范围内，被审查的措施并不违反任何WTO规则。因此，维持该措施的一方不需要改变该措施。这一表述的使用似乎部分因为GATT 1947只是临时适用，部分因为专家组希望保护自己不受可能未发现事实的影响。另见*临时适用议定书(Protocol of Provisional Application)*。

Not indispensable, but necessary

并非必不可少，但仍属必需

在"韩国-影响进口新鲜、冷藏和冷冻牛肉多项措施案"中，上诉机构审议了一项措施对于实现某一目标是否并非必不可少但仍属必需的问题。指出，有时"必不可少"和"必需"具有相同含义，但在其他情况下，"必需"的含义可能仅限于"作出某种贡献"。上诉机构认为，有时人们不会考虑"实施法律或法规旨在

importance of the common interests or values that the law or regulation to be enforced is intended to protect". Accordingly, "the more vital or important those common interests or values are, the easier it would be to accept as 'necessary' a measure designed as an enforcement instrument". The Appellate Body noted that this issue could be looked at from other angles. For example, the more important a measure was to realize an end, the more easily it might be deemed "necessary". Yet another angle would be that of the restrictive effect of the measure on imports. The less the impact was, the easier it might be considered "necessary". In other words, a measure might not be "indispensable", but it could still be "necessary". *See also **mandatory but not compulsory**.* [WT/DS161/AB/R, WT/DS169/AB/R]

Not-made-here syndrome: *see **techno-nationalism**.*

Not-on-the-whole-higher-or-more-restrictive criterion: one of the criteria used in the assessment of whether a ***customs union*** is in conformity with the rules of the ***GATT***. Article XXIV requires that the ***common external tariff*** of a new customs union must not on the whole be higher or more restrictive than the national tariffs of the members were before they joined the union. Much argument has arisen over the method to be used in ascertaining whether the criterion has been met, especially over the question of the use of the ***average tariff*** or a ***trade-weighted average tariff***. Outcomes clearly can be quite different depending on which calculation is used. The *Understanding on the Interpretation of Article XXIV* concluded as part of the ***Uruguay Round*** clarified the matter. It says that an evaluation of tariff levels must be based on an overall assessment of weighted average tariff rates and of ***customs duties*** collected.

Notoriety: a word used by ***intellectual property*** specialists to indicate whether something, e.g. a ***trademark***, is well known.

NTBs: non-tariff barriers. *See **non-tariff measures*** or ***NTMs***.

NTMs: ***non-tariff measures***, such as quotas, import licensing systems, sanitary regulations, prohibitions, etc.

Nuisance tariff: a ***tariff*** so low that it costs the government more to collect it than the revenue it generates. Sometimes also used to refer to any tariff without a protective effect. Some countries defend this as necessary to raise revenues. *See also **revenue tariff**.*

Nullification or impairment: damage to a country's benefits and expectations from its WTO membership through another country's change in its trade regime or failure to carry out its WTO obligations. If the matter cannot be solved through ***consultation***, it is then open to members to resort to formal ***dispute settlement*** procedures. Nullification and impairment can occur through a violation of the rules, but the same is possible through ***non-violation***.

保护的共同利益或价值观的相对重要性”。因此，“这些共同利益或价值观越关键或越重要，旨在作为一种实施工具的措施就越易于被接受为属‘必需’”。上诉机构指出，这一问题可以从其他角度看待。例如，措施对于实现一目标越重要，就越易于被认为属“必需”。但是，另一个角度可能是该措施对进口的限制作用影响越小，就越易于被认为属“必需”。换言之，一项措施可能并非“必不可少”，但仍属“必需”。另见*法定但非强制(mandatory but not compulsory)*。

Not-made-here syndrome

非本地制造综合症

见*技术民族主义(techno-nationalism)*。

Not-on-the-whole-higher-or-more-restrictive criterion

总体不高于或严于标准

用于评估关税同盟是否符合GATT规则的标准之一。第24条要求，新关税同盟的共同对外关税总体上不得高于或严于其成员在加入该同盟之前的国别关税。对于用于确定是否符合这一标准的方法，特别是对于使用平均关税或贸易加权平均关税的问题存在许多争论。结果显然大不相同，取决于使用哪种计算方法。作为乌拉圭回合一部分达成的《关于解释1994年关税与贸易总协定第24条的谅解》澄清了这一问题。谅解认为，对关税水平的评估应根据对加权平均关税税率和实征关税的全面评估作出。

Notoriety

驰名性

知识产权专家用于表示商标等是否著名的词语。

NTBs

非关税壁垒

见*非关税措施(non-tariff measures)*、*非关税措施(NTMs)*。

NTMs

非关税措施

例如配额、进口许可制度、卫生法规、禁令等。

Nuisance tariff

低率关税

关税非常低，政府收取关税的成本超过了关税所产生的收入。有时也用来指没有保护作用的任何关税。一些国家认为此种关税对于增加财政收入是必需的。另见*财政关税(revenue tariff)*。

Nullification or impairment

丧失或减损

一国作为WTO成员的利益或期望因另一国改变其贸易制度或未能履行其WTO义务而受到损害。如果这一问题不能通过磋商解决，那么成员可以诉诸正式的争端解决程序。丧失或减损可能由于违反规则而发生，但也可能由于非违反而发生。

Obiter dictum: a remark or observation by a court that is not essential for deciding a case. It is not binding on the lower courts nor later on the court that made it. *See also* ***stare decisis***.

Observer status: participation in a meeting to observe the formal proceedings, but without the right to intervene in the debate or take part in making decisions. Observers are not usually admitted to informal sessions or negotiating meetings. They have, however, the right in most cases to address formal meetings, usually after all of the ordinary participants have had their say. They also normally receive all of the formal documents. *See also* ***dialogue partners***.

OECD: Organisation for Economic Co-operation and Development. Established in 1961 as the successor to the ***Organisation for European Economic Co-operation*** (OEEC) through the *Convention on the Organisation for Economic Co-operation and Development*. Its objectives are (a) to achieve the highest sustainable economic growth and employment and a rising standard of living in member countries, while maintaining financial stability, and thus to contribute to the development of the world economy, (b) to contribute to sound economic expansion in member as well as in non-member countries in the process of economic development, and (c) to contribute to the expansion of world trade on a multilateral, non-discriminatory basis in accordance with international obligations. The OECD can point to considerable achievements in the trade and economic fields over the last forty years, assisted to some extent by the reasonably homogeneous nature of its membership. Membership consists of Australia, Austria, Belgium, Canada, Chile, Czech Republic, Denmark, Estonia, Finland, France, Germany, Greece, Hungary, Iceland, Ireland, Israel, Italy, Japan, Korea, Latvia, Lithuania, Luxembourg, Mexico, Netherlands, New Zealand, Norway, Poland, Portugal, Slovak Republic, Slovenia, Spain, Sweden, Switzerland, Turkey, United Kingdom and the United States. Colombia is in the process of accession. The ***European Commission*** takes part in proceedings, but it does not have the right to vote. The highest OECD body is the annual Ministerial Council Meeting, usually held in May or June. The OECD secretariat is located in Paris. *See also* ***Arrangement on Officially Supported Credits***, ***Convention on Combating Bribery of Foreign Public Officials in International Business Transactions***, ***Guiding Principles Concerning Environmental Policies***, ***Investment Policy Review***, ***Large Aircraft Sector Understanding***, ***Multilateral Agreement on Investment***, ***OECD***

O

Obiter dictum

判决附带意见

法院作出的对判决案件并非必要的评论或意见。对下级法院及随后对作出判决的法院无约束力。另见*遵循先例(stare decisis)*。

Observer status

观察员身份

参加会议以观察正式程序，但无权参加辩论或参与决定的作出。观察员通常不允许参加非正式会议或谈判会议。但是，他们在大多数情况下有权在正式会议上发言，通常是在所有普通参加方发言之后。他们通常会收到所有正式文件。另见*对话伙伴(dialogue partners)*。

OECD

经济合作与发展组织

1961年通过《经济合作与发展组织公约》建立，是欧洲经济合作组织(OEEC)的后继组织。目标为：(a)在保持财政稳定的同时，实现成员国最高的可持续经济增长、就业和不断提高的生活水平，从而为世界经济发展作出贡献；(b)在经济发展过程中促进成员国和非成员国经济的稳健扩张；以及(c)依照国际义务，在多边和非歧视基础上促进世界贸易的扩大。OECD可以指出的是，过去40年中在贸易和经济领域取得了相当大的成就，这在某种程度上得益于其成员资格的合理同质性。成员包括澳大利亚、奥地利、比利时、加拿大、智利、捷克、丹麦、爱沙尼亚、芬兰、法国、德国、希腊、匈牙利、冰岛、爱尔兰、以色列、意大利、日本、韩国、拉脱维亚、立陶宛、卢森堡、墨西哥、荷兰、新西兰、挪威、波兰、葡萄牙、斯洛伐克、斯洛文尼亚、西班牙、瑞典、瑞士、土耳其、英国和美国。哥伦比亚正在加入过程中。欧盟委员会参与进程，但无投票权。OECD的最高机构是年度部长级理事会会议，通常在5月或6月举行。OECD秘书处设在巴黎。另见*官方支持出口信贷的安排(Arrangement on Officially Supported Credits)*、*关于打击国际商业交易中行贿外国公职人员行为的公约(Convention on Combating Bribery of Foreign Public Officials in International Business Transactions)*、*关于环境政策的指导原则(Guiding Principles Concerning Environmental Policies)*、*投资政策审议(Investment Policy Review)*、*民用航空器行业谅解(Large Aircraft Sector Understanding)*、*多边投资协定(Multilateral Agreement on Investment)*、*OECD跨国企业行为准则(OECD*

Guidelines for Multinational Enterprises, ***OECD shipbuilding agreement***, ***trade and illicit payments*** and other entries beginning with OECD.

OECD Action Plan for Electronic Commerce: adopted on 9 October 1998. It contains four themes: (a) building trust for users and consumers through protection of privacy and personal data, secure infrastructure and technologies, authentication and certification, and consumer protection, (b) establishing transparent and predictable ground rules for the digital marketplace, (c) enhancing the information infrastructure for electronic commerce, including access to and use of the information infrastructure, and (d) maximizing the benefits of electronic commerce, paying attention to its economic and social impact. *See also* ***electronic commerce***. [OECD SG/EC(98)9/REV5]

OECD Arrangement on Officially Supported Export Credits: a non-binding OECD Arrangement concluded in 1978 and updated regularly, most recently in July 2018. The purpose of the Arrangement is to provide a framework for the orderly use of officially supported export credits. It seeks to encourage competition among exporters based on quality of goods and services exported, rather than the most favourable officially supported financial terms and conditions. The Arrangement applies to all official support provided by or on behalf of government which have a repayment term of two years or more. Sector understandings annexed to the Arrangement cover (a) ships, (b) nuclear power plants, (c) civil aircraft, (d) renewable energy, climate change adaptation and mitigation and water projects, (e) rail infrastructure, and (f) coal-fired electricity generation projects. Current participants are Australia, Canada, European Union, Japan, Korea, New Zealand, Norway, Switzerland and the United States.

OECD Guidelines for Multinational Enterprises: a set of voluntary guidelines in the form of recommendations for the behaviour of multinational enterprises (MNEs) first adopted by ***OECD*** member countries in 1976 and last revised in 2011. The guidelines are not intended to distinguish between MNEs and domestic enterprises. Rather, they are meant to reflect good practice for all. Chapter I states that the guidelines provide principles and standards for good practice consistent with applicable laws and internationally recognized standards. They are not legally enforceable. Chapter II contains a range of general policies (contribute to economic, social and environmental progress in host countries, respect for human rights, encouragement of local capacity-building, encourage human capital formation, support and uphold good corporate principles, etc.). Chapter III recommends that enterprises should ensure disclosure of timely, regular, reliable and relevant information regarding their activities, structure, financial situation and performance. Chapter IV covers human rights. It notes that states have the duty to protect human rights, and that enterprises should, within the framework of internationally recognized human rights, respect the international human rights in the countries in which they operate. Chapter V on employment and industrial relations asks enterprises, among other things, to respect the right of employees to be represented

Guidelines for Multinational Enterprises)、*OECD造船协定(OECD shipbuilding agreement)*、*贸易与违法付款(trade and illicit payments)*以及以OECD开头的其他词条。

OECD Action Plan for Electronic Commerce

OECD电子商务行动计划

1998年10月9日通过。包含四项主题：(a)通过隐私和个人数据保护、安全基础设施和技术、认证和证明以及消费者保护，为用户和消费者建立信任；(b)为数据市场制定透明和可预测的基本规则；(c)加强电子商务的信息基础设施，包括获得和使用信息基础设施；以及(d)最大限度地发挥电子商务的利益，同时注意其经济和社会影响。另见*电子商务(electronic commerce)*。

OECD Arrangement on Officially Supported Export Credits

OECD官方支持出口信贷的安排

1978年缔结的不具约束力的OECD安排，定期更新，最近一次是在2018年7月。安排的目的是为有序使用官方支持的出口信贷提供一个框架。旨在鼓励出口商之间基于出口商品和服务质量的竞争，而不是基于最有利的官方支持的融资条款和条件。安排适用于所有由政府提供或代表政府提供的、偿还期限为2年或2年以上的官方支持。安排所附的部门谅解涵盖：(a)船舶；(b)核电站；(c)民用航空器；(d)可再生能源、气候变化适应和缓解及供水项目；(e)铁路基础设施；以及(f)燃煤发电项目。目前的参加方包括澳大利亚、加拿大、欧盟、日本、韩国、新西兰、挪威、瑞士和美国。

OECD Guidelines for Multinational Enterprises

OECD跨国企业行为准则

关于跨国企业行为的自愿指导准则，采取建议的形式，最初于1976年由经济合作与发展组织(OECD)成员国通过，最近一次修订是在2011年。准则并不意在区分跨国企业和本国企业。而是旨在反映所有企业的良好实践。第1章指出，准则为良好实践提供与适用法律和国际公认标准相一致的原则和标准。原则和标准在法律上不具有强制执行性。第2章包含一系列一般政策(促进东道国的经济、社会和环境进步、尊重人权、鼓励本地能力建设、鼓励人力资本形成、支持和维护良好公司原则等)。第3章建议企业应保证披露关于其活动、结构、财务状况和业绩的及时、定期、可靠和相关的信息。第4章涵盖人权，指出国家有责任保护人权，企业应在国际公认的人权框架内，在其经营所在国尊重国际人权。第5章关于就业和劳资关系，要求企业尊重雇员由工会所代表的权

by trade unions, to contribute to the effective abolition of ***child labour*** and the elimination of all forms of forced or compulsory labour, not to discriminate among employees on grounds of race, colour, sex, religion, etc., and to provide employee representatives with assistance in developing effective collective agreements. Chapter VI asks enterprises to take due account of the need to protect the environment, public health and safety and to contribute to the wider goal of ***sustainable development***. Chapter VII asks companies neither to offer nor to accept bribes. Chapter VIII on consumer interests recommends taking all reasonable steps to ensure the safety and quality of goods and services. Chapter IX states that enterprises should (a) ensure that their activities are compatible with the science and technology plans and policies of host countries, (b) that they adopt practices permitting the rapid diffusion of technologies and know-how with due regard to the protection of ***intellectual property rights***, (c) when appropriate, employ host country personnel and encourage their training, (d) grant licences on reasonable terms and conditions, and (e) develop ties with local universities and public research institutions where this relevant to commercial objectives. Chapter X states that enterprises should carry out their activities in a manner consistent with all applicable competition laws and regulations, taking into account the competition laws of all jurisdictions in which the activities may have anti-competitive effects. Chapter XI stresses that enterprises contribute to the public finances of host countries by making timely payment of their tax liabilities. They should comply with both the letter and the spirit of the tax laws and regulations of the countries in which they operate. *See also* ***Draft United Nations Code of Conduct on Transnational Corporations*** and ***ILO Tripartite Declaration of Principles Concerning Multinational Enterprises and Social Policy***.

OECD legal instruments: these are created in five categories. *Directions*: binding on all members except those which abstain at the time of adoption. *Recommendations*: not legally binding, but carrying considerable force. *Declarations*: general principles or long-term goals. *International agreements*: legally binding on the parties. *Arrangements, understandings and others*: ad hoc instruments developed over time.

OECD Policy Framework for Investment: *see* ***Policy Framework for Investment***.

OECD Recommendation on Public Integrity: adopted in 2017. It recommends that OECD members and non-members (1) demonstrate commitment at the highest political and management levels within the public sector to enhance public integrity and reduce corruption, (2) clarify institutional responsibilities across the public sector to strengthen the effectiveness of the public integrity system, (3) develop a strategic approach for the public sector based on evidence and mitigating public security risks, (4) set high standards of conduct for public officials, (5) promote a whole-of-society culture of public integrity, (6) invest in integrity leadership to demonstrate a public sector organization's commitment

利，促进有效废除童工和消除一切形式的强迫或强制劳动，不基于种族、肤色、性别、宗教等原因歧视雇员，并协助雇员代表制定有效的集体协议。第6章要求企业适当考虑保护环境、公共健康和安全的需要，并为实现可持续发展的更广泛目标作出贡献。第7章要求公司既不行贿也不受贿。第8章关于消费者利益，建议采取一切合理措施保证货物和服务的安全和质量。第9章规定，企业应(a)保证其活动符合东道国的科学和技术计划和政策；(b)采取允许的迅速传播技术和专门知识的做法，同时适当注意保护知识产权；(c)适当时，雇用东道国人员并鼓励对其进行培训；(d)以合理的条款和条件发放许可；以及(e)在与商业目标相关的情况下，与本地大学和公共研究机构建立联系。第10章规定，企业开展活动的方式应符合所有适用的竞争法律法规，同时考虑可能产生反竞争影响的所有管辖范围的竞争法。第11章强调，企业应通过及时纳税，为东道国的公共财政作出贡献。企业应全面遵守经营所在国税收法律法规。另见*联合国跨国公司行为守则草案(Draft United Nations Code of Conduct on Transnational Corporations)*、*国际劳工组织关于多国企业和社会政策的三方原则宣言(ILO Tripartite Declaration of Principles Concerning Multinational Enterprises and Social Policy)*。

OECD legal instruments

OECD法律文件

这些文件分为5类。指示：对所有成员具有约束力，在通过时弃权的成员除外。建议：不具有法律约束力，但具有相当效力。宣言：一般原则或长期目标。国际协定：对参加方具有法律约束力。安排、谅解及其他：随着时间推移制定的临时文件。

OECD Policy Framework for Investment

OECD投资政策框架

见*投资政策框架(Policy Framework for Investment)*。

OECD Recommendation on Public Integrity

OECD关于公共廉洁的建议

2017年通过。建议经济合作与发展组织(OECD)成员国和非成员国：(1)在公共部门最高政治和管理层面展现加强公共廉洁和减少腐败的承诺；(2)澄清全部公共部门加强公共廉洁制度有效性的机构责任；(3)为公共部门制定一项基于证据和减轻公共安全风险的战略方针；(4)为公职人员制定高的行为标准；(5)促进形成全社会的公共廉洁文化；(6)投资于廉洁领导，以展现公共部门组织

to integrity, (7) promote a merit-based professional public sector dedicated to public-service values and good governance, (8) provide sufficient information, training and guidance and timely advice for public officials to apply integrity standards in the workplace, (9) support an open organizational culture within the public sector responsive to integrity concerns, (10) apply an internal control and risk management framework, (11) ensure that enforcement mechanisms provide appropriate responses, (12) reinforce the role of external oversight and control within the public integrity system, and (13) encourage transparency and stakeholders' engagement. *See also* ***anti-corruption***, ***bribery*** and ***corruption***.

OECD Services Trade Restrictiveness Index: a diagnostic tool developed by the OECD to provide a picture of trade barriers in twenty-two sectors across forty-five countries. It is aimed at policy makers and trade negotiators. *See also* ***World Bank Services Trade Restrictiveness Index***. [www.oecd.org]

OECD shipbuilding agreement: formal name *Agreement Respecting Normal Competitive Conditions in the Commercial Shipbuilding and Repair Industry*. It was concluded on 21 December 1994, but it is not yet in force. The Agreement seeks to eliminate the use of subsidies in the construction and repair of self-propelled seagoing vessels of more than 100 gross tons. It does not cover military vessels and fishing boats destined for own use by a party. Annex I contains a list of support measures that are inconsistent with the Agreement, including ***export credits*** or subsidies and, domestic support and some support measures for research and development. Parties to the agreement also will have access to a mechanism to deal with injurious pricing which is based on the ***anti-dumping measures*** available under the WTO agreements. There is also a dispute settlement mechanism. The Agreement is open for signature to countries outside the OECD.

OECD Trade Facilitation Indicators: TFIs. An interactive tool to help governments obtain greater benefits from ***trade facilitation***. It uses eleven indicators: information availability, involvement of the trade community, advance rulings, appeal procedures, fees and charges, formalities – documents, formalities – automation, formalities – procedures, internal cooperation, external cooperation, and governance and impartiality. [www.oecd.org.trade.aft]

OECD Transfer Pricing Guidelines for Multinational Enterprises and Tax Administration: last revised in 2017. Intended to serve the dual objectives of securing the appropriate tax base in each jurisdiction and avoiding double taxation. The guidelines are also intended to minimize conflict between tax administrations and to promote international trade and investment. *See also* ***transfer pricing***. [OECD 2017]

OECD–WTO Trade in Value Added Initiative: TiVA. A database containing estimates of the value being added in producing goods and services by country and industry. ***UNCTAD*** also is developing a TiVA database.

Offer: in a negotiation, a country's proposal for its own further liberalization, usually an offer to improve access to its markets.

的廉洁承诺；(7)促进形成致力于公共服务价值和良好治理的以业绩为基础的专业公共部门；(8)为公职人员在工作场所适用廉洁标准提供充分的信息、培训和指导以及及时的建议；(9)支持公共部门内部响应廉洁关注的开放式组织文化；(10)实施内部控制和风险管理框架；(11)保证执行机制提供适当应对措施；(12)加强在公共廉洁系统内的外部监督和控制的作用；以及(13)鼓励透明度和利益攸关方的参与。另见*反腐败(anti-corruption)*、*贿赂(bribery)*、*腐败(corruption)*。

OECD Services Trade Restrictiveness Index

OECD服务贸易限制指数

经济合作与发展组织(OECD)开发的诊断工具，提供45个国家的22个部门的贸易壁垒情况。针对决策者和贸易谈判人员。另见*世界银行服务贸易限制指数(World Bank Services Trade Restrictiveness Index)*。

OECD shipbuilding agreement

OECD造船协定

正式名称为《关于商船造修业正常竞争条件的协定》。协定于1994年12月21日缔结，但尚未生效。协定寻求取消对建造和维修大于100吨位的自航式海船的补贴，不涵盖参加方的军用船只和自用渔船。附件1包含不符合协定的支持措施清单，包括出口信贷或补贴、国内支持和一些研发支持措施。该协定参加方还可以利用一个基于WTO协定项下的反倾销措施的机制处理损害性定价问题。协定还包含一个争端解决机制。协定开放供经济合作与发展组织(OECD)以外的国家签署。

OECD Trade Facilitation Indicators

OECD贸易便利化指标

TFIs。帮助政府从贸易便利化中获得更大利益的互动工具。采用11项指标：信息可获性、贸易界的参与、预裁定、上诉程序、规费和费用、手续-单证、手续-自动化、手续-程序、内部合作、外部合作以及治理和公正性。

OECD Transfer Pricing Guidelines for Multinational Enterprises and Tax Administration

OECD跨国企业与税务机关转让定价指南

最近一次修订是在2017年。旨在服务于保证每一管辖范围的适当税基和避免双重征税两项目标。该指南还旨在尽量减少税务机关之间的冲突，并促进国际贸易和投资。另见*转让定价(transfer pricing)*。

OECD–WTO Trade in Value Added Initiative

OECD-WTO增加值贸易倡议

TiVA。包含国家和行业在生产货物和服务过程中增加值的估算值的数据库。联合国贸易与发展会议(UNCTAD)也在开发一个TiVA数据库。

Offer

出价

谈判中，一国对其自身进一步自由化的提议，通常为改善其市场准入的出价。

Office International des Epizooties: OIE. Until 2003 it was the International Office of Epizootics. It is now known as the ***World Organisation for Animal Health***.

Official development assistance: defined by the ***Development Assistance Committee*** of the ***OECD*** as grants or loans by its members to a defined list of developing countries. To qualify as official development assistance, activities must be (a) undertaken by the official sector of the donor country, (b) aimed mainly at the promotion of economic development and welfare, and (c) at concessional financial terms. Technical cooperation activities are included, but grants, loans and credits for military purposes do not qualify.

Official support: assistance by governments to exporters through export credit insurance and guarantees, interest-rate support, credits, etc.

Official tariff rate: the tariff rate listed in the government's tariff schedule. It is often higher than the ***applied tariff rate***.

Offsets: measures used to encourage the development of local industry or to improve the ***balance of trade*** by means of ***local content requirements***, licensing of technology, investment requirements, ***countertrade*** or similar requirements. Some of these measures are illegal under the ***Agreement on Trade-Related Investment Measures***. The ***Agreement on Government Procurement*** prohibits all such offset requirements for its members. Governments are normally attracted to offsets as a form of infant industry development. As with all forms of ***protection***, offsets may raise domestic costs and therefore harm a country's export efforts. *See also* ***infant-industry argument***.

Oilseeds*:** this was a long drawn-out dispute originally brought by the United States against the European Economic Community (EEC) in 1989. It is an example of the application of the ***GATT rule on ***non-violation***. The first ***panel*** report on this case, adopted in 1990, found that the EEC regulations authorizing payments to seed processors, on condition that the oilseeds originated in the EEC, were inconsistent with the GATT ***national treatment*** obligation. The panel also found that the ***subsidy*** scheme for oilseeds operated by the EEC isolated EEC producers completely from the movement of prices on international markets. Therefore, ***tariff concessions*** in the form of ***zero bindings*** made by the EEC could not have any impact on the competitiveness of imported oilseeds. In December 1991 the panel was reconvened at the request of the United States to determine whether the changes made by the EEC as a result of the earlier panel would eliminate the difficulties. The panel found that the revised support scheme still rendered the level of EEC production substantially insensitive to the movement of world market prices. It therefore continued to impair the benefits the United States could expect to accrue to it under the relevant tariff concessions. The panel then recalled that over two years had passed since the original report had been adopted, and it recommended that the EEC should act expeditiously to eliminate the impairment of tariff concessions. In other words, the EEC's right to institute subsidies on certain products and the level of these subsidies was not at issue and not inconsistent with GATT rules.

Office International des Epizooties

国际兽疫局

OIE。2003年之前称为国际兽疫局。现称"世界动物卫生组织"。

Official development assistance

官方发展援助

经济合作与发展组织(OECD)发展援助委员会将官方发展援助定义为，其成员向指定的发展中国家提供的赠款或贷款。符合官方发展援助资格的活动必须：(a)由捐助国的官方部门进行；(b)主要旨在促进经济发展和福利；以及(c)以优惠的融资条件提供。技术合作活动包括在内，但用于军事目的的赠款、贷款和信贷不具备资格。

Official support

官方支持

政府通过出口信用保险和担保、利率支持、信贷等方式向出口商提供的援助。

Official tariff rate

官方税率

政府关税税则中所列税率。通常高于实施税率。

Offsets

补偿

通过当地含量要求、技术许可程序、投资要求、对销贸易或类似要求，鼓励本地产业发展或改善贸易平衡的措施。其中一些措施在《与贸易有关的投资措施协定》项下属非法。《政府采购协定》禁止其参加方使用所有此类补偿要求。政府通常会因补偿作为幼稚产业发展的一种形式而被吸引。与所有形式的保护一样，补偿可能会增加国内成本，因而损害一国的出口努力。另见*幼稚产业论(infant-industry argument)*。

Oilseeds

油籽案

最初由美国在1989年起诉欧洲经济共同体(EEC)的旷日持久的争端案。关于适用GATT非违反规则的案例。1990年通过的关于本案的第一份专家组报告认为，欧共体准许以油籽原产于欧共体为条件向种子加工商进行支付的条例，不符合GATT国民待遇义务。专家组还认为，欧共体实施的油籽补贴计划使欧共体生产商不受国际市场价格波动的影响。因此，欧共体作出的以零关税约束为形式的关税减让不会对进口油籽的竞争力产生任何影响。1991年12月，应美国请求，专家组重新召集，以确定欧共体因先前专家组而作出的改变是否会消除这些困难。专家组认为，经修改的支持计划仍然使欧共体的生产水平实质上对世界市场价格波动不敏感，因而继续损害美国在相关关税减让下可以预期获得的利益。专家组随后提及，最初报告获得通过已过去2年多，专家组建议欧共体应迅速采取行动，消除对关税减让的减损。换言之，欧共体对某些产品实行补贴的权利及这些补贴的水平并不存在争议，也与GATT规则不相抵

However, the use of subsidies as they affected oilseed producers impaired and nullified the rights of other GATT members. This is the basis of the non-violation argument in this case. The panel decision was not the end of the matter. It remained an irritant in European Community–United States trade relations for the remainder of the ***Uruguay Round***. It was resolved as part of the ***Blair House Accord*** in November 1992 when the European Community agreed to set acreage limits for oilseeds production. [GATT BISD 37S]

Okinawa Charter on Global Information Society: adopted at the ***G8*** summit in Okinawa in July 2000. Participants agreed on several key principles, including (a) promoting competition and opening markets for information technology and telecommunications products and services, (b) protection of ***intellectual property rights***, (c) commitment to using software in full compliance with intellectual property rights, (d) importance of efficient telecommunications, transport, trade and customs procedures, (e) promoting cross-border ***electronic commerce***, (f) adopting consistent approaches to taxation, (g) desisting from imposing customs duties on electronic transmissions, (h) promoting market-driven standards, (i) promoting consumer trust in the electronic marketplace, (j) developing effective and meaningful privacy protection for consumers, and (k) developing electronic authentication, electronic signature, cryptography and other means to ensure the security of transactions. The G8 members also pledged themselves to making efforts to bridge the ***digital divide***.

Old economy: the economy as we knew it until talk in the late 1990s about the superiority of the ***new economy*** and the accompanying investment boom made it briefly unfashionable. It turned out that managers of the old economy were much more adaptable than the proponents of the new economy thought possible.

OMA: *see* ***orderly marketing arrangement***.

OMC: Organisation Mondiale du Commerce. *See* ***WTO***.

Omnibus Trade and Competitiveness Act: A comprehensive United States law of 1988. The word "omnibus" reflects the fact that the Act has several provisions not related to trade attached to it, and that its ambit therefore is rather wide-ranging. The Act declares that the overall United States negotiating objectives with respect to trade agreements are to obtain (1) more open and equitable market access, (2) the reduction or elimination of barriers and other trade-distorting practices, and (3) a more effective system of international trading procedures. Among many other provisions it gave duty-free entry to the United States to a wide range of audiovisual products. It also implemented the ***Harmonized Commodity Description and Coding System*** for the United States. Other provisions covered telecommunications, ***intellectual property rights*** and agriculture. It also gave the President ***fast-track*** negotiating authority until 1 June 1991 to participate in the ***Uruguay Round***. In the end this had be extended. *See also* ***market-opening initiatives***, ***National Treatment Study***, ***priority foreign country***, ***Section 1377 Review***, ***Special 301***, ***Super 301*** and ***Trade Promotion Authority***.

触。但是，由于补贴的使用影响到了油籽生产者，因此使其他GATT缔约方的权利造成减损和丧失。这是本案非违反观点的基础。专家组的裁决并不是这件事的终结。这件事在乌拉圭回合余下的时间里成为欧共体与美国贸易关系中的芥蒂。这一问题在1992年11月作为《布莱尔宫协议》的一部分得到解决，欧共体同意对油籽生产设定种植面积限制。

Okinawa Charter on Global Information Society

全球信息社会冲绳宪章

2000年7月在冲绳举行的8国集团首脑会议上通过。参加方就若干关键原则达成一致，包括：(a)促进竞争，并开放信息技术和电信产品及服务市场；(b)保护知识产权；(c)承诺以完全符合知识产权的方式使用软件；(d)高效电信、运输、贸易和海关程序的重要性；(e)促进跨境电子商务；(f)对税收采取一致方式；(g)停止对电子传输征收关税；(h)促进市场驱动的标准；(i)促进消费者对电子市场的信任；(j)为消费者制定有效和有意义的隐私保护；以及(k)发展电子认证、电子签名、加密及其他手段，以保证交易的安全。8国集团成员还承诺致力于弥合数字鸿沟。

Old economy

旧经济

直到20世纪90年代末谈论新经济的优越性时我们才知道的那种经济，随之而来的投资热潮使旧经济一度不再流行。事实证明，旧经济的管理者比新经济支持者所认为的更具适应性。

OMA

有序销售安排

见*有序销售安排(orderly marketing arrangement)*。

OMC

世界贸易组织

见*世界贸易组织(WTO)*。

Omnibus Trade and Competitiveness Act

综合贸易与竞争法

1988年美国的一项综合法。“综合”一词反映了如下事实：该法附有若干与贸易无关的条款，因此其范围相当广泛。该法宣称，美国关于贸易协定谈判的总体目标为：(1)获得更开放和公正的市场准入；(2)减少或消除壁垒和其他扭曲贸易的做法；以及(3)建立更有效的国际贸易程序体系。在许多其他条款中，该法给予内容广泛的视听产品免税进入美国的待遇。还包括美国实施商品名称及编码协调制度的规定。其他条款涵盖电信、知识产权和农业。该法还授予总统直到1991年6月1日参加乌拉圭回合的谈判快轨授权。后来这一授权得以延长。另见*市场开放倡议(market-opening initiatives)*、*国民待遇研究(National Treatment Study)*、*重点国家(priority foreign country)*、*1377审查(Section 1377 Review)*、*特别301条款(Special 301)*、*超级301条款(Super 301)*、*贸易促进授权(Trade Promotion Authority)*。

OMPI: Organisation Mondiale de la Propriété Intellectuelle. The World Intellectual Property Organization. *See **WIPO***.

One Belt and One Road Initiative: *see **Belt and Road Initiative***.

One-stop border post: OSBP. A concept originating in the process established by the ***Tokyo International Conference on African Development*** (TICAD). It aims to eliminate complex border crossing procedures between African countries by a system embracing all border procedures, such as customs, immigration and vehicular clearance, in one short step. *See also **Single Window*** and ***trade facilitation***.

One village, one product: a Japanese proposal made at the WTO ***Hong Kong Ministerial Conference***. It is intended to help developing countries to identify products capable of being exported and to find markets for them.

One-way free-trade area: *see **asymmetrical trade agreements***.

OPEC: Organization of Petroleum Exporting Countries. Established in 1960. Its members are Algeria, Angola, Congo, Ecuador, Equatorial Guinea, Gabon, Iran, Iraq, Kuwait, Libya, Nigeria, Saudi Arabia, United Arab Emirates and Venezuela. Membership is open to countries with a substantial net export of crude petroleum. OPEC aims to coordinate and unify the petrol prices of its member countries, ensure the stabilization of oil markets to secure an efficient, economic and regular supply of petroleum to consumers, a steady income to producers and a fair return on capital for those investing in the oil industry. Its secretariat is located in Vienna.

Open-accession clauses: provisions, for example, in ***free-trade agreements***, which invite or enable additional countries to join the agreement. *See also **accession*** and ***enlargement***.

Open-ended: in the ***WTO***, meetings, usually informal, open to all members.

Openness: the extent to which a country is open to competition from goods and services from other countries. *See also **international contestability of markets*** and ***Overall Trade Restrictiveness Index***.

Open regionalism: a term which implies that any regional arrangement should be outward-looking and lowering barriers to economies outside the arrangement as well as those within it. For some, open regionalism means that full ***most-favoured-nation treatment*** will apply to tariff reductions by members of an arrangement. For others it allows the possibility of a ***preferential trade arrangement***, coupled with easy access to membership.

Open-season negotiations: an opportunity available every three years to GATT members under Article XXVIII to conduct technical tariff negotiations when ***bindings*** expired. Bindings originally were made for three years. Such negotiations often led to modifications or withdrawals of ***concessions***. Resort to such negotiations is less common now that bindings are deemed to be permanent. *See also **renegotiation of tariffs***.

Open-skies arrangements: these are arrangements between governments to give each other unrestricted access to their airports for scheduled passenger and cargo flights. Most international air routes and service frequencies are still

OMPI
世界知识产权组织
见*世界知识产权组织(WIPO)*。

One Belt and One Road Initiative
“一带一路”倡议
见*“一带一路”倡议(Belt and Road Initiative)*。

One-stop border post
一站式边境口岸
OSBP。源自东京非洲发展国际会议(TICAD)所建立进程的概念。目标是通过一个包含海关、移民和车辆清关等所有边境程序的系统，取消非洲国家之间复杂的过境程序。另见*单一窗口(Single Window)*、*贸易便利化(trade facilitation)*。

One village, one product
一村一品
日本在WTO香港部长级会议上的提案。旨在帮助发展中国家确定能够出口的产品并找到市场。

One-way free-trade area
单向自由贸易区
见*非对称贸易协定(asymmetrical trade agreements)*。

OPEC
石油输出国组织
成立于1960年。成员为阿尔及利亚、安哥拉、刚果(布)、厄瓜多尔、赤道几内亚、加蓬、伊朗、伊拉克、科威特、利比亚、尼日利亚、沙特阿拉伯、阿拉伯联合酋长国和委内瑞拉。成员资格对拥有大量原油净出口的国家开放。OPEC旨在协调和统一其成员国的油价，保证石油市场稳定，从而保证向消费者提供高效、经济和正常的石油供应，使生产者获得稳定收入，并使投资于石油产业的人获得公平资本回报。OPEC秘书处设在维也纳。

Open-accession clauses
开放加入条款
例如，自由贸易协定中邀请或允许其他国家加入协定的条款。另见*加入(accession)*、*扩盟(enlargement)*。

Open-ended
不限成员名额
在WTO中对所有成员开放的会议，通常是非正式会议。

Openness
开放性
一国对来自其他国家的货物和服务竞争的开放程度。另见*市场的国际竞争性(international contestability of markets)*、*总体贸易限制指数(Overall Trade Restrictiveness Index)*。

Open regionalism
开放的区域主义
该词意味着任何区域安排均应为外向型的，并针对安排之外和之内的经济体降低壁垒。对于一些国家，开放的区域主义意味着对一安排的成员所进行的关税削减适用完全的最惠国待遇。对于其他国家，允许提供优惠贸易安排的可能性，并辅以容易获得的成员资格。

Open-season negotiations
开放期谈判
GATT缔约方每3年可获得一次在约束失效后根据第28条进行技术性关税谈判的机会。约束最初为期3年。此类谈判往往产生减让的修改或撤销。由于约束被认为属永久性的，因而现在诉诸此类谈判已不常见。另见*关税重新谈判(renegotiation of tariffs)*。

Open-skies arrangements
开放天空安排
政府间达成的允许彼此不受限制地进入各自机场进行定期客运和货运航班的

allocated on the basis of ***bilateral air services agreements***. These agreements usually specify the maximum number of passenger seats that may be offered and the airports that may be used. *See also* ***freedoms of the air*** and ***Multilateral Agreement on the Liberalization of International Air Transportation***.

Opinio juris (sive necessitatis)*:** the expectation by nations that in a given situation they will be obliged to follow a certain course of action. *See also* ***customary international law. [Shaw 2014, Starke 1989]

Opinion: one of the ways in which the ***European Union*** institutions are able to influence the actions of member states. An opinion is not binding, but it expresses a preference for a certain type of action. *See also* ***European Union legislation***.

OPTAD: Organization of Pacific Trade and Development. This was proposed in 1979 as an organization linking the countries of the Pacific Rim, but it never reached the negotiating stage. Its proponents thought that it would act as forum for the resolution of economic problems, to provide a stimulus for investment and trade flows into the region, to provide a forum for the longer-term economic transformation of the region, and to form the foundation for a more constructive approach to the expansion of relations with the Soviet Union, China and Viet Nam. Its prospective membership would have included most of the economies that are now the ***APEC*** members. *See also* ***Free Trade Area of the Asia-Pacific***.

Optimal-intervention principle: the use of the instrument that attains the policy goal with the least amount of undesired side-effect, usually the one that attacks the identified policy problem directly at its source.

Optimal-tariff argument: also called optimum-tariff argument. Its starting point is that the imposition of a tariff leads to a reduction in the volume of trade that would have occurred if there had been no tariff. The result is a change in the ***terms of trade*** of the importing and exporting country, but these effects cancel each other out. Both countries are now worse off. The optimal-tariff argument postulates that if a country is large enough, and if the tariff is not high, the effect of the tariff will lead to an improvement in that country's terms of trade which will exceed the loss of real income caused by the reduction in the volume of trade. The improvement in the terms of trade will only be beneficial for a reduced import volume. Small countries, however, would invariably maximize their welfare by not having the tariff. Harry G. Johnson noted that only the optimum-tariff argument provides an economic justification for tariffs, and that all other arguments for protection are arguments for subsidies. [Johnson 1968, Kjeldsen-Kragh 2001]

Orderly marketing arrangement: OMA. A bilateral arrangement whereby an exporting country (government or industry) agrees to reduce or restrict exports so as to shield the importing country from having to make use of quotas, tariffs or other import controls. OMAs fall in the same category of trade distortions as ***voluntary restraint arrangements*** and ***voluntary import expansion*** schemes. *See also* ***Agreement on Safeguards***.

安排。大多数国际航线和服务频率仍然根据双边航空服务协定进行分配。这些协定通常规定可以提供的最大乘客座位数量和可以使用的机场。另见*航空自由(freedoms of the air)*、*国际航空运输自由化多边协定(Multilateral Agreement on the Liberalization of International Air Transportation)*。

Opinio juris (sive necessitatis)

法律确信(法律必要确信)

指各国预期在一指定情况下它们有义务遵循某一行动方针。另见*习惯国际法(customary international law)*。

Opinion

意见

欧盟机构能够影响成员国行动的方式之一。意见并不具有约束力，但表示对某种行动的偏好。另见*欧洲联盟立法(European Union legislation)*。

OPTAD

太平洋贸易与发展组织

1979年提出，作为一个连接环太平洋国家的组织，但从未达到谈判阶段。支持者认为，该组织将成为解决经济问题的场所，刺激投资和贸易流入该区域，为该区域的长期经济转型提供场所，并为扩大与苏联、中国和越南的关系形成更具建设性的方式。潜在成员包括大部分现为APEC成员的经济体。另见*亚太自由贸易区(Free Trade Area of the Asia-Pacific)*。

Optimal-intervention principle

最优干预原则

使用产生最少不良副作用的手段实现政策目标，通常为直接从根源上解决所确定政策问题的手段。

Optimal-tariff argument

最优关税论

也称"最佳关税论"。出发点为征收关税会导致在无关税情况下的贸易量的减少。结果是进口国和出口国改变贸易条件，而这些影响相互抵消，两国都变得更差。最优关税论假定，如一国足够大，且如关税不高，关税的影响将促成该国贸易条件的改善，超过贸易量减少所造成的实际收入损失。贸易条件的改善只会在进口量减少的情况下才有利。但是，小国总是通过不征收关税而使其福利最大化。哈瑞·约翰逊指出，只有最优关税论才能为关税提供经济合理性，而其他所有保护论均为补贴论。

Orderly marketing arrangement

有序销售安排

OMA。出口国(政府或产业)同意减少或限制出口以保护进口国免于使用配额、关税或其他进口管制的双边安排。OMA与自愿限制安排和自愿扩大进口计划同属贸易扭曲措施类别。另见*保障措施协定(Agreement on Safeguards)*。

Ordinary course of trade: the WTO ***Anti-Dumping Agreement*** requires that the price comparison between the ***normal value*** of a product and its ***export price*** be based on the comparable price, in the ordinary course of trade, for the ***like product*** when it is intended to be sold in the exporting country. The Agreement does not say how the "ordinary course of trade" should be interpreted. The phrase does, however, point in the direction of established or customary behaviour by the importer and exporter in the trade of a particular product. The United States Department of Commerce, among others, has developed a definition of this phrase which says that "generally, sales are in the ordinary of course of trade if made under conditions and practices that, for a reasonable period of time prior to the date of sale of the subject merchandise, have been normal for the sales of the foreign like product". *See also* ***anti-dumping measures***. [Durling and Nicely 2002]

Organic integration: private cross-border flows of capital, goods and services, technology and information, driven in large part by multinational enterprises. *See also* ***economic integration***.

Organisation for European Economic Co-operation: OEEC. Established in 1948 as the body administering the ***Marshall Plan*** and superseded in 1961 by the ***OECD***.

Organisation internationale de la vigne et du vin: OIV. Established in 1924 to collect and disseminate scientific, technical, economic and legal information on matters related to wine. Its work is of relevance to international trade in wine because many important wine-growing countries adopt its standards for their wine industries. Its secretariat is located in Paris. On 1 January 2004 it became the Organisation internationale de la vigne et du vin (***International Organisation of Vine and Wine***). *See also* ***appellation contrôlée*** and ***geographical indications***. [oiv.int]

Organization for an International Geographical Indications Network: ORIGIN. A non-profit ***intergovernmental organization*** based in Geneva. It was established in 2003 with these aims: (a) campaign for the effective legal protection and enforcement of ***geographical indications*** at the national, regional and international level and (b) promote geographical indications as a sustainable development tool for producers and communities. Its members are drawn from forty countries. *See also* ***multilateral system of notification and registration of geographical indications***.

Organization for International Economic Cooperation: the successor organization to the ***Council for Mutual Economic Assistance***. Its mandate is to advise member states on trade and economic matters. It now is inactive.

Organization for Trade Cooperation: OTC. Proposed in 1955 through a GATT working party report as a permanent mechanism for administering the GATT. Its mandate would have been a limited version of what had been expected of the ***ITO***. All GATT members would automatically have become members of the organization. One interesting point raised in the report of the working party is that countries appointed to the Intersessional Committee, which at that time was

Ordinary course of trade
正常贸易过程

WTO《反倾销协定》要求，一产品的正常价值与其出口价格之间的价格比较应以正常贸易过程中在出口国供销售时的同类产品的可比价格为基础。协定未规定“正常贸易过程”应如何解释。但是，该措辞确实指向了进口商和出口商在一特定产品贸易中的既定或习惯性行为的方向。美国商务部对这一措辞作出定义，认为“一般而言，如果销售按照所涉商品销售日期之前的一段合理期限内按照销售外国同类产品属正常的条件或做法进行，则属正常贸易过程中的销售”。另见*反倾销措施(anti-dumping measures)*。

Organic integration
有机一体化

在很大程度上由跨国企业驱动的资本、货物和服务、技术和信息的私下跨境流动。另见*经济一体化(economic integration)*。

Organisation for European Economic Co-operation
欧洲经济合作组织

OEEC。作为管理马歇尔计划的机构于1948年成立，1961年被经济合作与发展组织(OECD)所取代。

Organisation internationale de la vigne et du vin
国际葡萄与葡萄酒组织

OIV。1924年成立，旨在收集和传播与葡萄酒相关的科学、技术、经济和法律信息。工作与国际葡萄酒贸易相关，因为许多重要的葡萄酒生产国都采用了其葡萄酒行业标准。秘书处设在巴黎。2004年1月1日，成为国际葡萄与葡萄酒组织。另见*原产地命名控制(appellation d'origine contrôlée)*、*地理标志(geographical indications)*。

Organization for an International Geographical Indications Network
国际地理标志网络组织

ORIGIN。非营利性政府间组织，总部设在日内瓦，于2003年成立，目的为：(a)在国家、区域和国际层面开展有效地理标志法律保护和执法行动；及(b)促进地理标志作为生产者和社区的可持续发展工具。成员来自40个国家。另见*地理标志通报和注册多边制度(multilateral system of notification and registration of geographical indications)*。

Organization for International Economic Cooperation
国际经济合作组织

经济互助委员会的后继组织。授权是就贸易和经济事项向成员国提出建议。但目前无活动。

Organization for Trade Cooperation
贸易合作组织

OTC。1955年通过一份GATT工作组报告提出，作为管理GATT的常设机制。其授权是期望国际贸易组织(ITO)所获授权的一个有限版本。所有GATT缔约方将自动成为该组织成员。工作组报告中提出的一个有趣观点是，被任命为

the only means of conducting business between the annual sessions, might consider appointing representatives of suitable calibre and the necessary authority to live in Geneva or nearby capitals so that they could contribute to its deliberations. Another of its recommendations was that the organization should be brought into a specialized agency relationship within the ***United Nations***. The proposal for an OTC failed to get United States congressional approval, and it lapsed. *See also* ***GATT Council of Representatives***, ***United Nations specialized agencies*** and ***WTO***.

Organization of African Unity: OAU. Established on 25 May 1963. Many of its aims were political, but one of them was economic cooperation, including transport and communications. All independent sovereign nations of Africa could become members. Its secretariat was located in Addis Ababa. Superseded in July 2001 by the ***African Union***. *See also* ***African Economic Community***.

Organization of American States: OAS. Established through the Bogotá Charter of 1948 which entered into force in 1951. Thirty-five sovereign states of the Americas participate in it. Cuba was excluded from membership in 1962. OAS seeks, among mainly political objectives, to solve economic problems that may arise among member states and to promote, by cooperative action, their economic, social and cultural development. The OAS secretariat is located in Washington.

Organization of Eastern Caribbean States: OECS. Originally established in 1981 through the Treaty of Basseterre to promote, among other objectives, economic cooperation among its members. At the same time it superseded the East Caribbean Common Market. In 2010 OECS created an economic union through the Revised Treaty of Basseterre. It established a single financial and economic space for the free movement of goods, people and capital, as well as harmonized fiscal policies. Its members are Antigua and Barbuda, Dominica, Grenada, Montserrat, Saint Kitts and Nevis, Saint Lucia, and Saint Vincent and the Grenadines. Anguilla and Martinique are associated members. Its secretariat is in Castries, Saint Lucia.

Organization of Islamic Cooperation: OIC. Previously the Organization of the Islamic Conference. It was founded in 1969 and has fifty-seven members. Priority areas in its ten-year programme 2016–25 include investment and finance, poverty alleviation, climate change and sustainability, and the empowerment of women. The OIC is located in Jeddah.

Origin: *see* ***rules of origin***.

Original membership of the WTO: deemed to have been attained by the members of the ***GATT 1947*** who had on 1 January 1995 (a) accepted the ***WTO Agreement***, (b) the multilateral trade agreements annexed to it, and (c) annexed schedules of ***concessions*** to the ***GATT 1994*** and schedules of specific commitments to the ***General Agreement on Trade in Services***. Countries meeting these requirements did not have to undergo the ***accession*** formalities, but original membership did not confer any other rights.

闭会期间委员会成员的国家，该委员会是当时年度会议之间开展工作的惟一手段，可以考虑任命具有合适才干和必要权力的代表居住在日内瓦或附近首都，以便有助于审议工作。另一项建议是，该组织应建立联合国内专门机构的关系。成立贸易合作组织的提议未能得到美国国会的批准，因而失效。另见*GATT理事会(GATT Council of Representatives)*、*联合国专门机构(United Nations specialized agencies)*、*世界贸易组织(WTO)*。

Organization of African Unity
非洲统一组织

OAU。1963年5月25日建立。很多目标为政治目标，但其中之一是包括运输和通信在内的经济合作。非洲所有独立的主权国家可以成为成员。秘书处设在亚的斯亚贝巴。2001年7月被非洲联盟所取代。另见*非洲经济共同体(African Economic Community)*。

Organization of American States
美洲国家组织

OAS。根据1948年《波哥大宪章》建立，该宪章于1951年生效。美洲的35个主权国家参加该组织。古巴在1962年被排除在成员资格之外。在主要政治目标中，该组织寻求解决成员国之间可能出现的经济问题，并通过合作行动促进其经济、社会和文化发展。秘书处设在华盛顿。

Organization of Eastern Caribbean States
东加勒比国家组织

OECS。最初通过《巴斯特尔条约》于1981年建立，除其他目标外，旨在促进其成员国之间的经济合作。同时取代了东加勒比共同市场。2010年，东加勒比国家组织通过《经修订的巴斯特尔条约》创建经济联盟，为货物、人员和资本的自由流动以及协调财政政策建立了单一金融和经济空间。成员为安提瓜和巴布达、多米尼加、格林纳达、蒙特塞拉特、圣基茨和尼维斯、圣卢西亚以及圣文森特和格林纳丁斯。安圭拉和马提尼克为联系成员。秘书处设在圣卢西亚卡斯特里。

Organization of Islamic Cooperation
伊斯兰合作组织

OIC。此前为伊斯兰会议组织。成立于1969年，有57个成员。2016年至2025年十年计划的优先领域包括投资和金融、减贫、气候变化和可持续性以及妇女赋权。伊斯兰合作组织设在吉达。

Origin
原产地

见*原产地规则(rules of origin)*。

Original membership of the WTO
WTO创始成员资格

在1995年1月1日(a)已接受《WTO协定》；(b)接受该协定所附多边贸易协定；以及(c)减让表附在GATT 1994之后和具体承诺减让表附在《服务贸易总协定》之后的GATT 1947缔约方。满足这些要求的国家不必经经过加入程序，但创始成员资格并不赋予任何其他权利。

Originating goods: in the administration of ***rules of origin*** for preferential trade agreements these are goods deemed to be a product of the party enjoying preferential access. *See also* ***non-originating goods***.

Originating materials: components of a good traded under a ***preferential trade arrangement*** which have been produced in the territory of a partner to the arrangement. *See also* ***non-originating materials***.

Originating status: given to a part or input that satisfies the ***regional value content*** prescribed under a given agreement.

Origin procedure: the process used by customs offices to determine whether a given good qualifies for preferential treatment under a given ***free-trade agreement***. The criteria for doing so are part of the ***rules of origin***. The process usually begins with a claim for preferential treatment by the importer. This is done through the presentation of a ***certificate of origin*** or a statement of origin completed by the exporter. This states that the good is an ***originating good***. When customs are satisfied that the criteria have been met, the good is admitted according to the applicable system of preferences. Sometimes this requirement is waived when the value of the consignment is small. Importers must maintain records that can be used to verify claims, sometimes through a periodic audit.

Osaka Action Agenda: the agenda for trade and investment liberalization and economic cooperation agreed by ***APEC*** leaders on 19 November 1995 at their meeting in Osaka. It was seen as a step towards realizing the aims of the 1994 ***Bogor Declaration***. The action agenda consists of three pillars: (a) trade and investment liberalization, (b) trade and investment facilitation, and (c) economic and technical cooperation. The aims of the action agenda are to be achieved through encouraging and converting the evolving efforts of voluntary liberalization in the region, taking collective actions to advance liberalization and facilitation objectives, and stimulating and contributing to further momentum for global liberalization. The Agenda's guiding principles are ***comprehensiveness***; ***transparency***; ***standstill***; ***non-discrimination***; simultaneous start, continuous process, differentiated timetables; and flexibility and cooperation. Individual action plans had to be submitted to the 1996 APEC Ministerial Meeting. Their overall implementation began in January 1997, followed by annual reviews. *See also* ***APEC individual action plan***, ***comparability*** and other entries beginning with ***APEC***.

OTDS: overall trade-distorting domestic support, a concept considered (but not yet defined) in agriculture negotiations.

Other regulations of commerce: *see* ***duties and other regulations of commerce*** and ***duties and other restrictive regulations of commerce***.

Other restrictive regulations of commerce: *see* ***duties and other restrictive regulations of commerce***.

Ottawa Imperial Conference: the conference held in 1932 which established the ***imperial preferences arrangement*** for the countries then making up the British ***Commonwealth***. The arrangement entered into force in October 1932.

Originating goods
原产货物

在优惠贸易协定的原产地规则管理中，这些货物被视为享受优惠准入的一参加方的产品。另见*非原产货物(non-originating goods)*。

Originating materials
原产材料

根据一优惠贸易安排进行交易的一货物的部件，这些部件在该安排的一合作伙伴领土内生产。另见*非原产材料(non-originating materials)*。

Originating status
原产地位

给予满足一指定协定项下所规定的区域价值成分的零件或投入物。

Origin procedure
原产地程序

海关用于确定一指定货物是否符合一指定自由贸易协定项下优惠待遇的过程。操作标准是原产地规则的一部分。这一过程通常始于进口商所提出的优惠待遇要求。通过提交原产地证书或出口商出具的原产地声明完成。证书或声明表明该货物属原产货物。在海关确信标准得到满足后，即准许该货物根据适用的优惠制度予以进口。如装运货物价值很小，有时会免除这一要求。进口商必须保持可用于核实其要求的记录，有时核实通过定期审计进行。

Osaka Action Agenda
大阪行动议程

1995年11月19日APEC领导人在大阪会议上议定的贸易和投资自由化及经济合作议程。被视为实现1994年《茂物宣言》目标的一个步骤。行动议程包括三个支柱：(a)贸易和投资自由化；(b)贸易和投资便利化；以及(c)经济和技术合作。行动议程目标的实现方式为：鼓励和转变本区域在自主自由化方面的不懈努力，采取集体行动推进自由化和便利化目标，以及刺激和促进全球自由化的更多动力。议程的指导原则为全面性、透明度、维持现状、非歧视、同步启动、持续进程、差别时间表以及灵活性和合作。单独行动计划应提交1996年的APEC部长级会议，1997年1月起全面实施，此后进行年度审议。另见*APEC单独行动计划(APEC individual action plan)*、*可比性(comparability)*及其他以APEC开头的词条。

OTDS
扭曲贸易的国内支持总量

农业谈判中考虑的一个概念(但尚未定义)。

Other regulations of commerce
其他贸易法规

见*关税和其他贸易法规(duties and other regulations of commerce)*、*关税和其他限制性贸易法规(duties and other restrictive regulations of commerce)*

Other restrictive regulations of commerce
其他限制性贸易法规

见*关税和其他限制性贸易法规(duties and other restrictive regulations of commerce)*。

Ottawa Imperial Conference
渥太华帝国会议

1932年举行的会议，为当时组成英联邦的国家建立了帝国特惠安排。该安排于1932年10月生效。

Our Common Future: *see* ***World Commission on Environment and Development***.

Out-of-cycle reviews: this is a mechanism created by ***USTR*** to administer ***Special 301***. Under the provisions of the ***Omnibus Trade and Competitiveness Act***, USTR must make an annual report on its monitoring and enforcement activities and the compliance of other countries with trade agreements of which the United States is a member. Where the matter is considered serious enough, USTR will start a review without waiting for the cycle of annual reports. That then is an "out-of-cycle review".

Out-of-quota rate: the ***tariff*** rate applicable to products imported in excess of a ***tariff quota***. This rate is meant to discourage imports above the quota limit. It is usually much higher than the one applied to imports within the quota. *See also* ***in-quota rate***.

Outsourcing: also known as business process outsourcing or BPO. This refers to the purchasing of goods and services, more often the latter, necessary for the running of an organization from outside that organization rather than relying on one's staff to provide them. Sometimes this is done because of cost advantages, but another reason is that specialist providers are much more likely to be familiar with changing technology and practices. In the environment of a corporation or a government department outsourcing could mean, for example, purchasing all information technology services from a suitable provider and having provider staff located permanently within the organization. More recently, the term has also been used for obtaining services from another country, mainly because the foreign country can supply the service at a lower cost. In some countries the practice has provoked strong adverse reactions. However, purchasing services from abroad because they can be made more cheaply elsewhere is really no different to importing manufactures. *See also* ***comparative advantage***.

Outward-oriented development: a strategy of economic development based on an expansion of exports and reliance on financing from global capital markets. [Moon 2000]

Outward processing: exporting a part-finished good for further processing and re-importing it for final manufacture. Outward processing may affect the status of the good under ***preferential rules of origin***. Many such systems have strict limits on the value that may be added to a good in this way.

Overall trade-distorting domestic support: *see* ***OTDS***.

Overall Trade Restrictiveness Index: OTRI. An analytical tool used by the ***World Bank***. The OTRI summarizes the trade policy of a country by calculating its weighted average tariff, with the weights reflecting the composition of import volume and import demand elasticities of each imported product. *See also* ***OECD Services Trade Restrictiveness Index***, ***Trade Restrictiveness Index*** and ***World Bank Services Trade Restrictiveness Index***. [datacatalog.worldbank.org]

Overcapacity (fishing): overcapacity generally refers to the ability of a fleet to fish at levels which exceed the sustainable catch level in a fishery (for example,

Our Common Future
我们共同的未来
见*世界环境与发展委员会(World Commission on Environment and Development)*。

Out-of-cycle reviews
周期外审议
美国贸易代表办公室(USTR)为管理特别301条款而设立的机制。根据《综合贸易与竞争法》条款，USTR必须就其监督和执行活动及其他国家遵守美国为成员的贸易协定的情况提交年度报告。如果认为问题足够严重，USTR将不等待年度报告周期即开始审查。此即“周期外审议”。

Out-of-quota rate
配额外税率
适用于超过关税配额的进口产品的关税税率。该税率旨在阻止超过配额限额的进口。通常大大高于对配额内进口适用的税率。另见*配额内税率(in-quota rate)*。

Outsourcing
外包
也称“业务流程外包”或“BPO”。指一组织自外部采购而不是依靠自己的工作人员提供该组织运行所必需的货物和服务，通常指后者。有时这样作是由于成本优势，但另一个原因是，专业提供者更有可能熟悉不断变化的技术和实践。对于一公司或一政府部门，外包可能意味着自一合适的供应商处购买所有信息技术服务，并使提供者的工作人员常驻组织内。最近，这一词语也被用于描述自另一国家获得服务，主要是因为外国可以较低成本提供服务。在一些国家，这种做法引起了强烈的不良反应。但是，从国外购买服务是因为这些服务可以在其他地方更便宜地生产，实际上与进口制成品并无不同。另见*比较优势(comparative advantage)*。

Outward-oriented development
外向型发展
基于扩大出口和依靠全球资本市场融资的经济发展战略。

Outward processing
外运加工
出口一件部分完成的货物以进行进一步加工，再复进口该货物进行最终制造。在优惠原产地规则下，外加工可能会影响货物的地位。许多此类制度对以此种方式对货物增加的价值设有严格限制。

Overall trade-distorting domestic support
扭曲贸易的国内支持总量
见*扭曲贸易的国内支持总量(OTDS)*。

Overall Trade Restrictiveness Index
总体贸易限制指数
OTRI。世界银行使用的分析工具。OTRI通过计算一国的加权平均关税以总结该国的贸易政策，权重反映每种进口产品的进口量和进口需求弹性的构成。另见*OECD服务贸易限制指数(OECD Services Trade Restrictiveness Index)*、*贸易限制指数(Trade Restrictiveness Index)*、*世界银行服务贸易限制指数(World Bank Services Trade Restrictiveness Index)*。

Overcapacity (fishing)
产能过剩(捕捞)
产能过剩通常指船队的捕鱼能力超过渔业可持续捕捞水平(例如由于过多的

because of too many vessels and/or too many fishers). There is no generally agreed method to measure capacity. The ***Food and Agriculture Organization*** has warned that overcapacity frequently leads to overfishing and ***IUU fishing***. In the ***WTO*** negotiations members are debating whether and how to discipline subsidies that contribute to overcapacity, and how such subsidies could be identified. *See also* ***Exclusive Economic Zone*** and ***territorial waters***.

Overfishing/overfished stocks: *see* ***overcapacity (fishing)***.

Over-invoicing: preparing or presenting an invoice giving a price for goods or services that is higher than the price actually paid. One reason for this practice is to transfer funds abroad in contravention of foreign exchange regulations. *See also* ***under-invoicing***.

Over-quota tariff rate: *see* ***out-of-quota rate***.

Over-quota trade: trade in a given product subject to a ***tariff rate quota*** which occurs outside that quota. Where over-quota trade is permitted, it always attracts a higher than that set for ***in-quota trade***.

船只和/或过多的渔民)。并无普遍认同衡量产能的方法。粮农组织(FAO)提出警告，产能过剩经常导致过度捕捞和非法、未报告和无管制捕捞。在WTO谈判中，成员正在辩论是否及如何约束导致产能过剩的补贴，以及如何确定此类补贴。另见*专属经济区(Exclusive Economic Zone)*、*领水(territorial waters)*。

Overfishing/overfished stocks
过度捕捞/过度捕捞种群

见*产能过剩(捕捞)*(overcapaci*ty (fishing))*。

Over-invoicing
高开发票

制备或出具显示货物或服务的价格高于实际支付价格的发票。这一做法的原因之一是违反外汇管理规定将资金转移到国外。另见*低开发票(under-invoicing)*。

Over-quota tariff rate
配额外税率

见*配额外税率(out-of-quota rate)*。

Over-quota trade
配额外贸易

在关税配额产品的配额限额外发生的贸易。如果允许进行配额外贸易，它总是会比配额内贸易更有吸引力。

P

P-4 Agreement: *see* ***Trans-Pacific Strategic Economic Partnership Agreement.***

P-5: short for Pacific-5. It includes Australia, Chile, New Zealand, Singapore and the United States. At the time of the Auckland ***APEC*** meetings (1999) Fred Bergsten suggested that the P-5 should consider forming a ***free-trade agreement*** among themselves.

Pacific Agreement on Closer Economic Relations: PACER. An agreement adopted in August 2001 by the ***Pacific Islands Forum*** which set out the framework for the development of trade relations between the Forum members. It was not a ***free-trade agreement***, but it allowed for the establishment of ***free-trade areas***. One of these is the ***Pacific Island Countries Trade Agreement.*** PACER entered into force on 3 October 2002. It will be superseded by the ***Pacific Agreement on Closer Economic Relations (PACER) Plus*** when it enters into force. *See also* ***SPARTECA***.

Pacific Agreement on Closer Economic Relations (PACER) Plus: a ***free-trade agreement*** covering goods, services and investment for countries in the Pacific region. A key objective is to support Pacific Island countries to become more active partners in, and benefit from, regional and global trade. Australia, Cook Islands, Kiribati, Nauru, New Zealand, Niue, Samoa, Solomon Islands, Tonga, Tuvalu and Vanuatu signed the Agreement on 14 June 2017. It is not yet in force.

Pacific Alliance: a regional integration initiative created in 2011 by Chile, Colombia, Mexico and Peru. Its stated aim is to move gradually towards the free movement of goods, services, capital and people. All tariffs between the parties are to be abolished by 2020.

Pacific Community: an organization to promote economic and social cooperation in the Pacific area. Its members are American Samoa, Australia, Cook Islands, Federated States of Micronesia, Fiji, France, French Polynesia, Guam, Kiribati, Marshall Islands, Nauru, New Caledonia, New Zealand, Niue, Northern Mariana Islands, Palau, Papua New Guinea, Pitcairn Islands, Samoa, Solomon Islands, Tokelau, Tonga, Tuvalu, United States, Vanuatu and Wallis and Futuna. It is administered by the ***Secretariat of the Pacific Community***, located at Noumea.

Pacific Free Trade Area: PAFTA. An idea for a regional preferential trade arrangement that has been around since the 1960s. Most of the various proposals brought forward over the years have included either the United States or Japan, often both, as the centre of any prospective arrangement. None of

P

P-4 Agreement

P-4协定

见*跨太平洋战略经济伙伴关系协定(Trans-Pacific Strategic Economic Partnership Agreement)*。

P-5

太平洋5国

包括澳大利亚、智利、新西兰、新加坡和美国。在1999年奥克兰APEC会议上，弗雷德·伯格斯滕建议太平洋5国应该考虑在它们之间形成自由贸易协定。

Pacific Agreement on Closer Economic Relations

太平洋更紧密经济关系协定

PACER。太平洋岛国论坛于2001年8月通过的协定，为论坛成员之间发展贸易关系规定了框架。不属自由贸易协定，但允许建立自由贸易区。其中之一为《太平洋岛国贸易协定》。PACER于2002年10月3日生效。待《太平洋更紧密经济关系协定》(PACER Plus)生效时将取代PACER。另见*南太平洋区域贸易经济合作协定(SPARTECA)*。

Pacific Agreement on Closer Economic Relations (PACER) Plus

太平洋更紧密经济关系协定(PACER Plus)

涵盖太平洋地区国家货物、服务和投资的自由贸易协定。关键目标之一是支持太平洋岛国成为区域和全球贸易中更积极的合作伙伴，并从中获益。澳大利亚、库克群岛、基里巴斯、瑙鲁、新西兰、纽埃、萨摩亚、所罗门群岛、汤加、图瓦卢和瓦努阿图于2017年6月14日签署协定。协定尚未生效。

Pacific Alliance

太平洋联盟

智利、哥伦比亚、墨西哥和秘鲁在2011年创建的区域一体化倡议。既定目标为逐步实现货物、服务、资本和人员的自由流动。各方之间所有关税将在2020年前取消。

Pacific Community

太平洋共同体

促进太平洋地区经济和社会合作的组织。成员包括美属萨摩亚、澳大利亚、库克群岛、密克罗尼西亚、斐济、法国、法属玻利尼西亚、关岛、基里巴斯、马绍尔群岛、瑙鲁、新喀里多尼亚、新西兰、纽埃、北马里亚纳群岛、帕劳、巴布亚新几内亚、皮特凯恩群岛、萨摩亚、所罗门群岛、托克劳、汤加、图瓦卢、美国、瓦努阿图、瓦利斯和富图纳。由设在努美阿的太平洋共同体秘书处负责管理。

Pacific Free Trade Area

太平洋自由贸易区

PAFTA。自20世纪60年代即提出的区域优惠贸易安排的设想。多年来提出的各项提案大部分均包括美国或日本，经常是两者均包括在内，作为任何未来安排的中心。但均未能到达谈判阶段。另见*亚太自由贸易区(Free Trade Area*

them have reached the negotiating stage. *See also* ***Free Trade Area of the Asia-Pacific***, ***OPTAD***, ***PBEC*** and ***PECC***.

Pacific Island Countries Free Trade Agreement: PICTA. A ***free-trade agreement*** adopted in August 2001 by the ***Pacific Islands Forum***. It entered into force on 13 April 2003. The Agreement calls for the establishment of a ***free-trade area*** over the next ten years. Members are Cook Islands, Federated States of Micronesia, Fiji, Kiribati, Marshall Islands, Nauru, Niue, Palau, Papua New Guinea, Samoa, Solomon Islands, Tonga, Tuvalu, and Vanuatu. Australia and New Zealand are eligible to join if they wish. *See also* ***Pacific Agreement on Closer Economic Relations (PACER) Plus*** and ***SPARTECA***.

Pacific Islands Forum: PIF. Founded in 1971 as the South Pacific Forum. Renamed in 2000. Its work is guided by the ***Framework for Pacific Regionalism*** and includes regional economic, social and cultural matters. The Forum conducts an annual meeting with its eighteen dialogue partners. PIF members are Australia, Cook Islands, Federated States of Micronesia, Fiji, French Polynesia, Kiribati, Marshall Islands, Nauru, New Caledonia, New Zealand, Niue, Palau, Papua New Guinea, Samoa, Solomon Islands, Tonga, Tuvalu and Vanuatu.

Pacific Rim: an imprecise term for the countries bordering the Pacific Ocean. Also known as Pacific Basin. *See* ***APEC***, ***PBEC*** and ***PECC***.

Packaging Directive: a ***directive*** issued by the ***European Union***. Its history began in 1985 with rules on the production, marketing, recycling and refilling of containers of liquids for human consumption. In 1994 the directive concerning the management of packaging and packaging waste was adopted. It aims at providing a high level of environmental protection and ensuring the function of the internal market by avoiding obstacles to trade and distortion of competition. The directive was revised in 2015 to address the use of lightweight plastic carrier bags. *See also* ***eco-packaging*** and ***environmentally preferable products***.

Pacta sunt servanda*:** the principle in international treaties law, as expressed in Article 26 of the ***Vienna Convention on the Law of Treaties, that "every treaty is binding upon the parties to it and must be performed by them in ***good faith***".

Pan-Arab Free Trade Area: *see* ***Greater Arab Free Trade Area***.

Panel: an independent group of three experts established by the ***Dispute Settlement Body*** to examine and issue recommendations on particular disputes in the light of WTO provisions. Sometimes used figuratively for the actual finding or decision made by a panel. Panels are not guided by extraneous factors or rules established outside the WTO framework. *See also* ***dispute settlement*** and ***Dispute Settlement Understanding***.

Pan-Euro-Mediterranean cumulation: permits the application of ***diagonal cumulation*** between the states of the ***European Union***, ***EFTA***, Turkey, the states that have signed the ***Barcelona Declaration***, the Western Balkans and the Faroe Islands. The various protocols covering ***rules of origin*** now in existence will over time be replaced by the rules contained in the ***Regional Convention on pan-Euro-Mediterranean preferential rules of origin*** (PEM convention). [ec.europa.eu]

of the Asia-Pacific)、*太平洋贸易与发展组织(OPTAD)*、*太平洋盆地经济理事会(PBEC)*、*太平洋经济合作会议(PECC)*。

Pacific Island Countries Free Trade Agreement
太平洋岛国自由贸易协定

PICFTA。太平洋岛国论坛于2001年8月通过的自由贸易协定。2003年4月13日生效。协定要求在未来10年内建立自由贸易区。成员包括库克群岛、密克罗尼西亚、斐济、基里巴斯、马绍尔群岛、瑙鲁、纽埃、巴布亚新几内亚、萨摩亚、所罗门群岛、汤加、图瓦鲁和瓦努阿图。澳大利亚和新西兰如愿意即有资格加入。另见*太平洋更紧密经济关系协定(PACER Plus)*、*南太平洋地区贸易经济合作协定(SPARTECA)*。

Pacific Islands Forum
太平洋岛国论坛

PIF。1971年成立，原名"南太平洋论坛"，2000年更名。工作以太平洋区域主义框架为指导，包括区域经济、社会和文化事务。论坛与其18个对话伙伴举行年度会议。太平洋岛国论坛成员包括澳大利亚、库克群岛、密克罗尼西亚、斐济、法属波利尼西亚、基里巴斯、马绍尔群岛、瑙鲁、新喀里多尼亚、新西兰、纽埃、帕劳、巴布亚新几内亚、萨摩亚、所罗门群岛、汤加、图瓦卢以及瓦努阿图。

Pacific Rim
环太平洋

对太平洋沿岸国家的一个不精确的词语。也称太平洋盆地。另见*亚太经济合作组织(APEC)*、*太平洋盆地经济理事会(PBEC)*、*太平洋经济合作会议(PECC)*。

Packaging Directive
包装指令

由欧盟发布的指令。始于1985年，最初是关于供人类消费的液体容器的生产、销售、回收和再灌装的规定。1994年，关于包装和包装废弃物管理的指令获得通过。旨在通过避免贸易障碍和竞争扭曲以提供高水平的环境保护和保证内部市场的功能。指令在2015年进行修订，以解决轻型塑料手提袋的使用问题。另见*环保包装(eco-packaging)*、*环境无害产品(environmentally preferable products)*。

Pacta sunt servanda
条约必须遵守

国际条约法中的原则，如《维也纳条约法公约》第26条所述，即"凡有效之条约对其各当事国拘束力，必须由各该国善意履行"。

Pan-Arab Free Trade Area
泛阿拉伯自由贸易区

见*大阿拉伯自由贸易区(Greater Arab Free Trade Area)*。

Panel
专家组

争端解决机构设立的由3名专家组成的独立小组，根据WTO条款审查特定争端并提出建议。有时用于比喻专家组的实际裁决或决定。专家组不受外部因素或WTO框架之外建立规则的指导。另见*争端解决(dispute settlement)*、*争端解决谅解(Dispute Settlement Understanding)*。

Pan-Euro-Mediterranean cumulation
泛欧—地中海累积

允许在欧盟、欧洲自由贸易联盟(EFTA)、土耳其、签署《巴塞罗那宣言》的国家、西巴尔干和法罗群岛之间适用对角累积。随着时间的推移，涵盖现有原产地规则的各种议定书将被《泛欧—地中海优惠原产地规则区域公约》(PEM公约)所含规则取代。

Pan-European cumulation system: a name commonly used for a scheme established on 1 January 1997 under which goods consisting of components made in more than one participating country are treated in the same way as domestically produced goods. The system consists of the ***European Union*** and most of its European trading partners. *See also* ***pan-Euro-Mediterranean cumulation*** and ***preferential rules of origin***.

Pan-Pacific Free Trade Area: one of several names for a proposed ***free-trade agreement*** for Asia and perhaps the Pacific also. *See also* ***Comprehensive and Progressive Agreement for Trans-Pacific Partnership***, ***East Asia Free-Trade Agreement*** and ***Free Trade Area of the Asia-Pacific***.

Paperless trading: eliminating the requirement for paper documents, such as customs declarations and freight manifestos, to be used in the conduct of international trade and using electronic documents instead. The successful introduction of paperless trading requires overcoming legal and authentication barriers (ensuring that the document transmitted electronically is genuine and has not been tampered with), harmonization of documentation requirements between participants and agreement on the technical standards to be used. *See also* ***APEC paperless trading initiative***, ***electronic commerce*** and ***Framework Agreement on Facilitation of Cross-border Paperless Trade in Asia and the Pacific***.

Paragraph 6 countries: a group of countries with less than 35 per cent of ***non-agricultural products*** (usually abbreviated to ***NAMA***) covered by legally bound tariff ceilings. They have agreed to increase their binding coverage substantially, but want to exempt some products. Named after paragraph 6 of the first NAMA negotiating text.

Paragraph 6 system: a process to allow particularly the least-developed countries to benefit from the production of generic pharmaceutical products made under ***compulsory licensing***. Article 31(f) of the ***Agreement on Trade-Related Aspects of Intellectual Property Rights*** (the TRIPS Agreement) limits the production of generic medicines under compulsory licensing predominantly to the supply of the domestic market. Paragraph 6 of the ***Declaration on the TRIPS Agreement and Public Health*** of 2001 recognizes that this could be a problem for countries with little or no manufacturing capacity in the pharmaceutical sector. This situation would force them to rely on other countries which, however, might be unable to export these products. In 2003 a ***waiver*** was adopted to exempt the least-developed countries from this limitation. In December 2005 WTO members adopted a protocol amending the TRIPS Agreement through a new Article 31bis which enables the production of a pharmaceutical product falling into this category and its export to an eligible importing member, primarily least-developed countries, under defined conditions. In January 2017 Article 31bis became part of the TRIPS Agreement following formal acceptance by two-thirds of the WTO membership.

Parallel imports: also called "grey-market imports. The term denotes the import outside the manufacturer's or distributor's authorized channel of a product with an ***intellectual property*** content from another country where the product has

Pan-European cumulation system

泛欧累积制度

对于1997年1月1日制定的方案使用的常用名称，根据该方案，由在一个以上参与国中生产的部件组成的货物与本国生产货物同等对待。该体系由欧盟及其大多数欧洲贸易伙伴组成。另见*泛欧—地中海累积(Pan-Euro-Mediterranean cumulation)*、*优惠原产地规则(preferential rules of origin)*。

Pan-Pacific Free Trade Area

泛太平洋自由贸易区

拟议的亚洲及可能包括太平洋的自由贸易协定的几个名称之一。另见*全面与进步跨太平洋伙伴关系协定(Comprehensive and Progressive Agreement for Trans-Pacific Partnership)*、*东亚自由贸易协定(East Asia Free-Trade Agreement)*、*亚太自由贸易区(Free Trade Area of the Asia-Pacific)*。

Paperless trading

无纸贸易

取消在开展国际贸易时使用纸质单证的要求，例如海关申报单和货运清单，转而使用电子单证。成功实行无纸交易必须克服法律和认证障碍(保证以电子方式传送的单证是真实的，未被篡改)，协调参与者之间的单证要求，并就所使用的技术标准达成协议。另见*APEC 无纸贸易倡议(APEC paperless trading initiative)*、*电子商务(electronic commerce)*、*亚洲及太平洋跨境无纸贸易便利化框架协定(Framework Agreement on Facilitation of Cross-border Paperless Trade in Asia and the Pacific)*。

Paragraph 6 countries

第6段国家

非农产品(通常缩写为NAMA)中法定约束关税上限涵盖范围不足35%的一组国家。这些国家已经同意实质性提高约束涵盖范围，但希望例外一些产品。以第一份非农产品市场准入谈判文本第6段命名。

Paragraph 6 system

第6段制度

允许特别是最不发达国家从根据强制许可进行的仿制药生产中获益的程序。《与贸易有关的知识产权协定》第31条(f)款限制强制许可下生产的仿制药主要供应国内市场。2001年《关于<与贸易有关的知识产权协定>与公共健康的宣言》第6段承认，这对于医药部门生产能力不足或缺乏的国家而言可能面临问题。此种情况将迫使它们依赖其他国家，而其他国家可能无法出口这些产品。2003年通过了一项豁免，使最不发达国家免于这一限制。2005年12月，WTO成员通过了一项议定书，通过新增第31条之二对《与贸易有关的知识产权协定》进行了修正，该条规定允许生产属于这一类别的药品，并将其出口至有资格的进口成员，主要是最不发达国家。2017年1月，第31条之二经WTO成员的三分之二正式接受而成为《TRIPS协定》一部分。

Parallel imports

平行进口

又称“灰市进口”。该词指自制造商或经销商授权渠道之外从另一国进口包含知识产权内容的产品，在该另一国中该产品已经由知识产权所有人或经所有

been lawfully placed on the market by the owner of the ***intellectual property right*** or with the owner's consent. Such imports compete with the same product produced or distributed, also with the authorization of the holder of the rights, in the domestic market. They are therefore said to be imported in parallel with the authorized channels. The motivation for doing so arises when the parallel import can be put on the market more cheaply. Some say that strictly speaking the same person should hold the intellectual property rights in both countries, but the term more generally now describes situations where ownership has been split by contract. Parallel importing remains a contentious practice, and its legality varies according to jurisdiction. Competition authorities tend to be in favour of this practice because the consumer clearly benefits from it. Others, however, hold that the practice undermines the system of ***intellectual property rights*** which is designed to foster innovation and creativity. Neither the WTO ***Agreement on Trade-Related Aspects of Intellectual Property Rights*** nor the ***WIPO Copyright Treaty*** concluded in December 1996 preclude governments from permitting parallel imports. *See also* **exhaustion doctrine**. [Maskus 2000]

Parallelism in export support: an expression used by the ***European Union*** (EU) in the ***Doha Development Agenda*** negotiations on agriculture. When the EU offered to enter into negotiations leading to the elimination of ***export subsidies*** for agricultural products, it did so on condition that all other forms of ***export support*** would also be put on the negotiating table. Sometimes this was also referred to as full parallelism.

Parallelism in safeguards: a concept that made its first appearance in the ***Appellate Body*** report concerning *Argentina – Safeguard Measures on Footwear*. The first of its two parts is that (a) a country may make a determination of ***serious injury*** under the conditions set out in Article 2.1 of the ***Agreement on Safeguards*** and (b) in its investigation whether serious injury has occurred, it has to take into account the factors listed in Article 4.2 of the Agreement. The second part is Article 2.2 which states that "safeguard measures shall be applied to a product being imported irrespective of its source". The Appellate Body held that "the imports included in the [injury] determination made under Articles 2.1 and 4.2 should correspond to the imports included in the application of the measure, under Article 2.2". The Appellate Body gave as its reason that the words "product . . . being imported" occurred in both Articles 2.1 and 2.2, and that they ought to have the same meaning. [Pauwelyn 2004, WT/DS121/AB/R]

Parallel trade: *see* ***parallel imports***.

Para-tariffs: a name sometimes used for charges levied on imports instead of, or in addition to, ***tariffs***. These can consist of service fees, additional import surcharges or other fees levied on imported products inside the market. Para-tariffs are illegal if they are levied on imports inside the market, but not at the same time on domestic products. Their imposition in such cases would be a denial of ***national treatment***.

Pareto optimum (or efficiency): the principle defined by Vilfredo Pareto that resources are allocated efficiently when no person can be made better off

人同意合法投放市场。此类进口产品在国内市场上与同样获得权利持有人授权生产或销售的相同产品进行竞争，也得到了权利持有人的授权。因此，它们被认为与授权渠道平行进口。当平行进口产品能够以更低价格投放到市场上时，这样作的动机就产生了。一些人称，严格地讲，同一人应在两国均拥有知识产权，但该词现在更普遍用于描述所有权被合同分割的情况。平行进口仍然是一个有争议的做法，其合法性因管辖范围不同而不同。竞争管理机关倾向于支持此种做法，因为消费者明显从中获益。但是，其他人认为，此种做法破坏了旨在促进创新和创造力的知识产权体系。无论是WTO《与贸易有关的知识产权协定》，还是1996年12月缔结的《世界知识产权组织版权条约》均未妨碍政府允许平行进口。另见*权利用尽原则(exhaustion doctrine)*。

Parallelism in export support

出口支持的平行性

欧盟在多哈发展议程农业谈判中使用的表述。当欧盟提出参与取消对农产品出口补贴的谈判时，其参与条件是应将其他所有形式的出口支持均放在谈判桌上。有时也称完全平行性。

Parallelism in safeguards

保障措施中的平行性

首次出现在上诉机构关于"阿根廷鞋类保障措施案"报告中的概念。这一概念由两部分组成，第一部分为：(a)一国可根据《保障措施协定》第 2.1 条中规定的条件作出严重损害的确定；及(b)在调查是否发生严重损害时，需要考虑《保障措施协定》第 4.2 条中所列因素。第二部分为：第 2.2 条规定"保障措施应针对一正在进口的产品实施，而不考虑其来源"。上诉机构认为，"根据第 2.1 条和第 4.2 条作出的[损害]确定所包括的进口应与根据第 2.2 条适用措施所包括的进口相对应"。上诉机构给出的理由为，第 2.1 条和第 2.2 条均出现"正在进口的……产品"的措辞，两措辞应具有相同含义。

Parallel trade

平行贸易

见*平行进口(parallel imports)*。

Para-tariffs

准关税

这一名称有时用于称呼对进口产品征收的替代关税的费用或在关税之上征收的费用。这些费用可以包括服务费、额外的进口附加费或对市场中进口产品征收的其他费用。对市场中的进口产品征收准关税而同时不对本国产品征收即属非法。在此种情况下，征收准关税即为拒绝给予国民待遇。

Pareto optimum (or efficiency)

帕雷托最优(或效率)

维尔弗雷多 · 帕雷托所定义的原则，即在没有人的境况能够变得更好且其他

without some other person being made worse off. Intermediate situations between the current stage and the optimum are called Pareto-superior.

Paris Agreement: adopted on 12 December 2015 at the 21st Conference of the Parties (COP) to the ***United Nations Framework Convention on Climate Change*** (UNFCC). The Paris Agreement builds on the UNFCC through its central aim of strengthening the global response to the threat of climate change by keeping a global temperature rise this century below 2 degrees Celsius above pre-industrial levels, and eventually to 1.5 degrees Celsius. Means to reach these goals include mobilization and provision of financial resources, a new technology framework and enhanced capacity-building. The Parties have to report regularly on their emissions and their implementation efforts. A stocktake is to be held every five years to assess collective progress. The Paris Agreement entered into force on 4 November 2016. *See also* ***Kyoto Protocol***. [unfccc.int]

Paris Club: a forum consisting mainly of ***OECD*** member countries which was established to bring together creditor and debtor countries in cases where there are difficulties in meeting loan repayments. It seeks to avoid defaults on loans through debt rescheduling and other mechanisms. The French Treasury provides a secretariat for the Paris Club. [www.clubdeparis.org]

Paris Convention: full name *Paris Convention for the Protection of Industrial Property* which established the Paris Union. It came into force in 1884, and it has been revised several times. The latest version is the 1967 Stockholm Revision. The Convention is administered by ***WIPO***. It provides protection for ***patents***, ***trademarks*** and ***industrial designs*** and applies broadly to ***industrial property***, including ***geographical indications*** and ***appellations of origin***. The main features of the Convention are ***national treatment***, ***right of priority*** (a person filing for a patent in one member country has a right of priority to file in another country within one year), and ***independence of protection*** (patents applied for in member countries by nationals of member countries are independent of patents obtained for the same invention in other countries). *See also* ***Agreement on Trade-Related Aspects of Intellectual Property Rights***.

Paris Union: *see* ***Paris Convention***.

Parliamentary Conference on the WTO: a conference held annually, organized jointly by the Interparliamentary Union (IPU) and the European Parliament. The conference gives parliamentarians the opportunity to examine developments in the WTO, obtain first-hand information on the state of multilateral negotiations and to consider how they might contribute to the process.

Part IV of the GATT: a protocol to the GATT which had its origin in the ***Kennedy Round*** and entered into force on 27 June 1966. It added Articles XXXVI to XXXVIII to the GATT. In these three articles developed countries agreed broadly that they would not expect ***reciprocity*** for tariff reductions and removal of trade barriers where the trade of developing countries is affected. Developed countries would also take measures to ensure that the trade of developing countries would not be disadvantaged by actions taken by developed countries and to work together with them to promote and expand

人的境况没有变得更糟的情况下，资源即得到有效分配。介于当前阶段和最优阶段之间的中间状态称为帕雷托更优。

Paris Agreement

巴黎协定

2015年12月12日《联合国气候变化框架公约》(UNFCC)第21次缔约方会议通过。《巴黎协定》以《联合国气候变化框架公约》为基础，核心目标是加强全球应对气候变化威胁的能力，将本世纪全球平均气温较前工业化时期上升幅度控制在2摄氏度以内，并最终限制在1.5摄氏度以内。实现这些目标的手段包括动员和提供财政资源，建立新的技术框架和加强能力建设。缔约方必须定期报告它们的排放量和实施努力。每5年进行一次回顾，以评估集体进展情况。《巴黎协定》于2016年11月4日生效。另见*京都议定书(Kyoto Protocol)*。

Paris Club

巴黎俱乐部

一个主要由经济合作与发展组织(OECD)成员国组成的论坛，目的在于在偿还贷款有困难的情况下将债权国和债务国聚集在一起。试图通过债务重组及其他机制避免贷款违约。法国财政部为巴黎俱乐部提供秘书处。

Paris Convention

巴黎公约

全称为《保护工业产权巴黎公约》，该公约建立了巴黎联盟。1884 年生效，并经多次修订。最新版本为 1967 年的斯德哥尔摩修订版。公约由世界知识产权组织(WIPO)管理。为专利、商标和工业品外观设计提供保护，并广泛适用于工业产权，包括地理标志和原产地名称。公约的主要特点为国民待遇、优先权(在一成员国申请专利的人有权在 1 年内在另一国优先申请)、独立保护原则(成员国国民在一成员国申请的专利与在其他国家为同一发明获得的专利无关)。另见*与贸易有关的知识产权协定(Agreement on Trade-Related Aspects of Intellectual Property Rights)*。

Paris Union

巴黎联盟

见*巴黎公约(Paris Convention)*。

Parliamentary Conference on the WTO

WTO议联大会

由各国议会联盟(IPU)和欧洲议会联合举办的年度会议。会议使议员们有机会审查WTO中的发展情况，获得关于多边谈判状况的第一手信息，并考虑它们如何能够对这一进程作出贡献。

Part IV of the GATT

GATT第四部分

GATT的一份议定书，起源于肯尼迪回合，于1966年6月27日生效。增加了GATT第36条至第38条。在这3个条款中，发达国家广泛同意，在发展中国家的贸易受到影响的情况下，不寻求在降低关税和消除贸易壁垒方面获得互惠。发达国家还将采取措施，以保证发展中国家的贸易不会因发达国家所采取的

their trade. Although these three articles impose few legal conditions on developed countries, they have shaped to a considerable extent the form of the trading system since 1965 through lessening expectations of what developing countries could or should be required to do. *See also* ***developing countries and the multilateral trading system***, ***Enabling Clause*** and ***special and differential treatment***.

Partial preferential trade agreement: a term used to describe either preferential trade agreements confined to trade in some sectors or an ***asymmetrical trade agreement*** under which only some of the participants grant free access to products from the other members. *See also* ***full preferential trade agreement***.

Partial-scope trade agreements: another name for ***sectoral free-trade areas*** sometimes negotiated by developing countries under the ***Enabling Clause***.

Partners for Progress: an ***APEC*** mechanism based on mutual assistance and voluntarism to promote economic and technical cooperation more efficiently within APEC. It was established by the November 1995 ***APEC*** Ministerial Meeting. The mechanism is aimed at activities that support directly the liberalization and facilitation of trade and investment. *See also* ***Bogor Declaration*** and ***Osaka Action Agenda***.

Partnership and cooperation agreement: PCA. A legally binding agreement between the ***European Union*** and third countries. The European Union uses PCAs to support the democratic and economic development of a country. The normal duration of a PCA is ten years. After that it is automatically extended if no objections are raised. PCAs are used mainly for countries included in the ***European Neighbourhood Policy***, such as the ***Newly Independent States*** and northern Africa, but the go further afield. A PCA with the Philippines entered into force on 1 March 2018. These agreements typically include provisions such as ***most-favoured-nation treatment*** (MFA) for trade in goods, cross-border supply of services, investment, ***intellectual property protection*** and other areas. There is no presumption of an automatic progression to a ***preferential trade arrangement***. [eur-lex.europa.eu]

Passing off: the use of someone else's reputation, ***trademark***, design or other distinctive characteristic in the manufacture or sale of a product and implying, overtly or implicitly, that the product is, or could be, the work of the rightful owner of these properties. Passing off always involves a degree of deception. *See also* ***piracy***.

Passive reciprocity: a concept introduced by William R. Cline which means that two countries may agree cooperatively that reciprocal trade liberalization offers benefits to both of them. Under WTO rules, such liberalization would have to be extended to all WTO members on a ***most-favoured-nation treatment*** basis. *See also* ***aggressive reciprocity*** and ***reciprocity***. [Cline 1983]

Pass-through operations: the process of first shipping goods into a ***free-trade area*** through the member country that has the lowest general tariff or which is known for a relatively lax administration of customs rules and then forwarding the goods to their intended market, another member of the free-trade area, in the

行动而处于不利地位，并与其共同努力促进和扩大贸易。虽然这3个条款对发达国家设置的法律条件很少，但自1965年以来，这些条款通过降低对发展中国家可以或应该被要求作什么的期望，在很大程度上影响了贸易体制的形式。另见*发展中国家与多边贸易体制(developing countries and the multilateral trading system)*、*授权条款(Enabling Clause)*、*特殊和差别待遇(special and differential treatment)*。

Partial preferential trade agreement
部分优惠贸易协定

用于指仅限于一些部门贸易的优惠贸易协定或只有一些参加方给予源自其他成员的产品免关税进口的非对称贸易协定的词语。另见*全面优惠贸易协定(full preferential trade agreement)*。

Partial-scope trade agreements
部分范围贸易协定

发展中国家有时根据授权条款谈判的部门自由贸易区的另一名称。

Partners for Progress
进步伙伴

基于互助和自愿原则以促进内部更有效的经济和技术合作的 APEC 机制。由 1995 年 11 月的 APEC 部长级会议建立。该机制针对直接支持贸易和投资自由化和便利化的活动。另见*茂物宣言(Bogor Declaration)*、*大阪行动议程(Osaka Action Agenda)*。

Partnership and cooperation agreement
伙伴关系与合作协定

PCA。欧盟与第三国之间具有法律约束力的协定。欧盟使用此类协定支持一国的民主和经济发展。一项 PCA 的正常期限为 10 年。此后如无异议即自动延长。PCA 主要用于欧洲睦邻政策所包括的国家，例如新独立国家和北非，但范围更广。与菲律宾的 PCA 于 2018 年 3 月 1 日生效。这些协定通常包括对货物贸易、跨境服务供应、投资、知识产权保护和其他领域的最惠国待遇(MFA)等条款。没有关于协定自动发展成为优惠贸易安排的推定。

Passing off
假冒商品

在制造或销售产品时使用他人的名誉、商标、设计或其他显著特征，并明示或暗示该产品是或可能是这些财产权的合法所有人的作品。假冒总是涉及一定程度的欺骗。另见*盗版(piracy)*。

Passive reciprocity
被动互惠

威廉 · 克莱恩提出的概念，意即两国通过合作方式同意，即互惠贸易自由化对双方均带来好处。根据 WTO 规则，此种自由化必须在最惠国待遇基础上给予所有 WTO 成员。另见*主动互惠(aggressive reciprocity)*、*互惠(reciprocity)*。

Pass-through operations
直通做法

首先将货物通过一普通关税最低或海关规则管理相对不严的成员运入一自由贸易区，随后将货物转运至其预定市场，即自由贸易区的另一成员，预期无需

expectation that no further duties will be payable. This practice is also known as ***transshipment***. Strictly enforced ***rules of origin*** are aimed at preventing this practice. *See also* ***preferential rules of origin***, ***preferential trade arrangements*** and ***substantial transformation***.

Pass-through subsidy: a ***subsidy*** given to producers of a good at a given stage, the benefits of which are deemed to flow on automatically to producers at a later stage of the production process. For example, a subsidy given to loggers might be assumed to benefit sawmills also. [WT/DS257/R]

Pasta*:** launched by the United States against the ***European Economic Community (EEC) in 1982 on the grounds that EEC export subsidies on pasta products (macaroni, spaghetti and similar products) manufactured from durum wheat were inconsistent with Article 9 of the ***Tokyo Round*** Subsidies Code. This Article states that signatories shall not grant export subsidies on products other than certain primary products. The EEC argued that pasta products were a type of ***primary product***. The facts were that the EEC operated a common system for the internal market in cereals and cereal-based products. It provided for a single system of internal prices for the whole Community and a common trading system with third countries which prevented price fluctuations of the world market from affecting internal cereal prices. The system also provided for export licensing and for application of export refunds in a prescribed manner. Export refunds could be granted to cover the difference between the internal prices and those on third markets for cereals exported in natural state or in the form of specified goods. Pasta products were included in this list of specified goods. The funding of the export refund on durum wheat in the form of pasta was made by a public contribution from the EEC budget which also paid the export refunds on cereals. In its findings, the ***panel*** was of the opinion that pasta was not a primary product, but a processed agricultural product. It also concluded that the EEC system of granting refunds had to be considered a form of subsidy in the sense of GATT Article XVI (Subsidies). The panel held that the terms of Article XVI, as interpreted in Articles 9 and 10 of the Subsidies Code, excluded the possibility of considering the export of a processed product on the same terms as the export of its constituent components. Accordingly, it concluded that the EEC export refunds were granted on the exports of pasta products and operated to increase these exports and that the EEC subsidies on exports of pasta products were granted in a manner inconsistent with Article 9 of the Subsidies Code. [GATT SCM/43]

Patent: the exclusive right given to an inventor through a certificate to prevent others for a specified period from making, using, selling or importing an ***invention***. To qualify for a patent an invention must be useful (capable of industrial application, novel (it must not already be in the public domain), and it must be non-obvious (it must involve some inventive step from the point of view of someone skilled in that area). Patents are available for products and processes. They can be bought, sold or licensed to others. Some countries issue

再支付任何关税。此种做法也被称为转运。严格执行的原产地规则旨在防止这种做法。另见*优惠原产地规则(preferential rules of origin)*、*优惠贸易安排(preferential trade arrangements)*、*实质性改变(substantial transformation)*。

Pass-through subsidy

直通补贴

在指定阶段给予一货物生产者的补贴，补贴的好处被认为自动流向生产过程后期阶段的生产者。例如给予伐木工人的补贴可能被认为也会使锯木厂受益。

Pasta

意大利面食案

美国于1982年针对欧洲经济共同体(EEC)提出此案，理由是欧共体对用硬粒小麦制作的意大利面食产品(通心粉、意大利面条和类似产品)的出口补贴不符合东京回合《补贴守则》第9条。该条规定，除某些初级产品外，签署国不得给予产品出口补贴。欧共体认为，意大利面食产品是一种初级产品。事实是，欧共体在内部市场中运行着一个谷物和谷物制品的共同系统，为整个共同体提供单一内部价格体系，并与第三国建立共同贸易体系，以防止世界市场价格波动影响内部谷物价格。该体系还规定了出口许可证和以规定方式申请出口退税。可以通过给予出口退税弥补以自然状态或特定货物形式出口谷物的国内价格与第三市场价格的差额。意大利面食产品包括在这一特定货物清单中。以意大利面食形式的硬粒小麦的出口退税由来自欧共体预算的公共捐款提供资金，该资金还支付谷物的出口退税。专家组在调查结果中认为，意大利面食不是一种初级产品，而是一种加工农产品。专家组还得出结论，欧共体的退税制度应被视为GATT第16条(补贴)意义上的一种补贴。专家组认为，经《补贴守则》第9条和第10条解释的GATT第16条排除了考虑将一加工产品的出口条件与其组成部分的出口条件相同的可能性。因此，专家组得出结论认为，欧共体对意大利面食产品给予出口退税，并增加这些产品出口，欧共体以与《补贴守则》第9条不符的方式对意大利面食产品出口给予补贴。

Patent

专利

通过证书赋予发明者的专有权，在一规定期限内防止他人制造、使用、销售或进口一项发明。一项发明获得专利资格，必须是有用的(可供工业应用)、新颖的(必须尚未进入公有领域)，且必须是非显而易见的(从该领域技术人员的角度来看，必须包含一些创造性)。产品和工序可以申请专利。专利可以被购买、出售或许可他人使用。一些国家发布小专利，对创造性的要求不那么严格，保

petty patents. These require a less strict test for inventiveness and the period of protection is shorter. *See also* ***Agreement on Trade-Related Aspects of Intellectual Property Rights***, ***intellectual property*** and ***Strasbourg Agreement Concerning the International Patent Classification***.

Patent Cooperation Treaty: provides for the filing of an international ***patent*** application in member states. Filing has to be done through the patent office of which the applicant is a national or resident, and it has the same effect in member states as filing an application with a national patent office of that state. The Treaty has more than 100 members. It is administered by ***WIPO***. *See also* ***intellectual property*** and ***intellectual property right infringements***.

Pathfinder Initiative for Self-Certification of Origin: an ***APEC*** initiative aimed at simplifying the administration of ***certificates of origin***. Participants agree to practise ***self-certification*** with ***free-trade agreement*** partners based on reciprocity and a set of common operating guidelines. The key provision is that a trader's declaration of a product's origin is accepted in good faith by the importing country. *See also* ***APEC Pathfinders***.

Pathfinder on facilitating trade in remanufactured goods: in 2011 a group of APEC economies agreed (a) not to apply import-related measures aimed at used goods to remanufactured goods, (b) to refrain from applying import prohibitions against remanufactured goods, (c) to give remanufactured goods the same tariff treatment as they would give new goods, and (d) to apply technical regulations, conformity assessments and import licensing requirements for new goods to remanufactured goods also. *See also* ***APEC Pathfinders***.

Pauper-labour argument: the argument that industry in countries paying high wages cannot withstand the competition from low-wage countries, and that some form of ***protection*** is therefore needed. *See also* ***core labour standards***, ***race-to-the-bottom argument***, ***social clause***, ***trade and labour standards*** and ***wage-differential argument***.

PBEC: Pacific Basin Economic Council. A non-governmental organization established in 1967 and consisting of more than 1,100 companies located in nineteen economies around the Pacific Rim. It seeks to promote a business environment conducive to open trade and investment and encouraging competitiveness. It also contributes to the development of policies in ***APEC***. PBEC has a secretariat based in Hong Kong.

Peace clause: a provision in Article 13 of the WTO ***Agreement on Agriculture*** which prevented challenges to agricultural subsidies until 31 December 2003 under other WTO agreements under this and other WTO agreements, especially the ***Agreement on Subsidies and Countervailing Measures*** and the ***GATT***.

Peak tariffs: if the ***tariff*** rates contained in a typical national tariff schedule were represented chapter by chapter as a continuous line in a graph, the result probably would be something like a series of plateaus interspersed with sudden peaks. Each peak would mean that that product, or group of products, is benefiting from higher ***protection*** than the products expressed by plateaus. Peak tariff rates are to a large extent a relative concept, though during the

护期较短。另见*与贸易有关的知识产权协定(Agreement on Trade-Related Aspects of Intellectual Property Rights)*、*知识产权(intellectual property)*、*国际专利分类斯特拉斯堡协定(Strasbourg Agreement Concerning the International Patent Classification)*。

Patent Cooperation Treaty

专利合作条约

条约对在成员国提交国际专利申请作出规定。申请需要通过申请人作为国民或居民的专利局完成，申请在成员国内与向一国家专利局提交的申请具有同等效力。条约有 100 多个成员。由世界知识产权组织(WIPO)管理。另见*知识产权(intellectual property)*、*侵犯知识产权(intellectual property right infringements)*。

Pathfinder Initiative for Self-Certification of Origin

原产地自我认证探路者倡议

APEC 旨在简化原产地证书管理的倡议。参与者同意与自由贸易协定伙伴在互惠和一套共同操作指南基础上实行自我认证。关键条款是贸易商对产品原产地的声明被进口国真诚接受。另见*APEC 探路者(APEC Pathfinders)*。

Pathfinder on facilitating trade in remanufactured goods

促进再制造货物贸易探路者

2011年，部分APEC经济体同意：(a)不对再制造货物适用与二手货物有关的进口措施；(b)不对再制造货物适用进口禁令；(c)给予再制造货物与新货物相同的关税待遇；以及(d)对再制造货物也适用新货物的技术法规、合格评定和进口许可要求。另见*APEC探路者(APEC Pathfinders)*。

Pauper-labour argument

贫民劳动论

关于支付高工资的国家的产业无法承受来自低工资国家的竞争，因此需要某种形式保护的论点。另见*核心劳工标准(core labour standards)*、*竞次论(race-to-the-bottom argument)*、*社会条款(social clause)*、*贸易与劳工标准(trade and labour standards)*、*工资差别理论(wage-differential argument)*。

PBEC

太平洋盆地经济理事会

1967年成立的非政府组织，由位于太平洋沿岸的19个经济体的1100多家公司组成。寻求促进有利于开放贸易和投资的商业环境，并鼓励竞争。还致力于APEC政策的发展。理事会秘书处设在香港。

Peace clause

和平条款

WTO《农业协定》第 13 条规定，在 2003 年 12 月 31 日前免于根据该协定和其他 WTO 协定对农业补贴提出质疑，特别是《补贴与反补贴措施协定》和GATT。

Peak tariffs

关税高峰

如果一典型的国别关税税则中所含关税税率以曲线图中的连线逐章显示，那么结果可能像是一系列由突兀高峰隔开的高原形状。每一峰值即意味着该产品或一组产品比高原形状所显示的产品享受更高的保护。关税高峰税率在很

Uruguay Round they were defined for negotiating purposes as above 15 per cent. That figure is also used in the ***OECD***. A rate of 10 per cent in a schedule averaging 4 per cent, as many of the developed-country rates for industrial products are as a result of the Uruguay Round, would represent a peak just as a rate of 40 per cent would in the environment of rates around 20 per cent. The presence of pronounced peak tariff rates may show only one aspect of the protection available to domestic producers. There are cases where their absence is masked by a range of ***non-tariff measures*** with the same or a greater impact. *See also* ***sensitive products***.

PECC: Pacific Economic Cooperation Conference. Established in 1980. It consists of business, academic and governmental representatives. PECC has twenty-three members (Australia, Brunei Darussalam, Canada, Chile, China, Colombia, Ecuador, Hong Kong (China), Indonesia, Japan, Korea, Malaysia, Mexico, Mongolia, New Zealand, Pacific Islands Forum, Peru, the Philippines, Singapore, Chinese Taipei, Thailand, United States and Viet Nam) and one associate member (France) who share their perspectives and expertise on of economic cooperation issues in the Asia-Pacific region. Its secretariat is in Singapore.

PECC competition principles: a non-binding set of fifteen principles and key requirements adopted by ***PECC*** in May 1999. Their aim is to promote competition throughout ***APEC***. The core first-level principles are (a) comprehensiveness (competition policy to apply to all goods and services), (b) transparency (principles, policies and processes to be clear to all), (c) accountability (those responsible for applying competition principles to be accountable for departures from them), and (d) non-discrimination (ensuring competitive neutrality in respect of different modes of domestic and international supply). *See also* ***APEC Principles to Enhance Competition and Regulatory Reform***.

Pelly Amendment: *see* ***Tuna I***.

PEM convention: *see* ***Regional Convention on pan-Euro-Mediterranean preferential rules of origin***.

Percentage criterion method: some ***free-trade agreements*** have ***rules of origin*** which require that qualifying for ***tariff preferences*** must have at least a minimum amount of value added to them by the exporting country. This is usually expressed as a percentage. The rule may apply either across the board, as in ***AFTA***, or to some goods only, sometimes together with a mandatory change in tariff heading. *See also* ***value-added criterion***.

Performance requirements: *see* ***export performance requirements***.

Performers and Phonogram Treaty: *see* ***WIPO Performances and Phonograms Treaty***.

Peril points: a provision first included in the United States *Trade Agreements Extension Act* of 1948, but deleted in 1949. It was reintroduced in the *Trade Agreements Extension Act* of 1955. The provision required the United States Tariff Commission to set, through a process involving public hearings, a floor tariff rate for each product which indicated that a reduction below that rate would cause or threaten to cause ***injury*** to domestic industry. The President

大程度上是一个相对概念，尽管在乌拉圭回合中为谈判目的而将其定义为15%以上，经济合作与发展组织(OECD)也采用了这一数字。在平均税率为4%的减让表中10%的税率所代表的高峰就如税率约为20%的情况下40%的税率所代表的高峰，作为乌拉圭回合的结果，许多发达国家的工业产品平均关税税率即为4%。显著关税高峰的存在可能仅表明国内生产者可获得保护的一个方面。在某些情况下，关税高峰的缺失被一系列具有相同或更大影响的非关税措施所掩盖。另见*敏感产品(sensitive products)*。

PECC

太平洋经济合作会议

1980年成立，由商业、学术和政府代表组成。太平洋经济合作有23个成员(澳大利亚、文莱、加拿大、智利、中国、哥伦比亚、厄瓜多尔、中国香港、印度尼西亚、日本、韩国、马来西亚、墨西哥、蒙古、新西兰、太平洋岛国论坛、秘鲁、菲律宾、新加坡、中国台北、泰国、美国和越南)和一个联系成员(法国)，这些国家分享它们在亚太地区经济合作问题方面的观点和专业知识。委员会秘书处设在新加坡。

PECC competition principles

太平洋经济合作会议竞争原则

太平洋经济合作会议(PECC)1999年5月采纳的15条非约束性原则和核心要求。目标是促进整个APEC的竞争。第一层次的核心原则为：(a)全面性(适用于所有货物和服务的竞争政策)；(b)透明度(所有人都清楚的原则、政策和程序)；(c)问责制(负责适用竞争原则的人对背离这些原则的行为负责)；以及(d)非歧视(保证不同国内和国际供应模式的竞争中立)。另见*APEC增强竞争和监管改革原则(APEC Principles to Enhance Competition and Regulatory Reform)*。

Pelly Amendment

贝利修正案

见*第一个金枪鱼案(Tuna I)*。

PEM convention

PEM 公约

见*泛欧—地中海优惠原产地规则区域公约(Regional Convention on pan-Euro-Mediterranean preferential rules of origin)*。

Percentage criterion method

百分比标准法

一些自由贸易协定规定的原产地规则，要求获得关税优惠资格的产品必须包含出口国对其增加的最低价值，通常以百分比表示。这一规定可能适用于所有货物，如东盟自由贸易协定(AFTA)，也可能仅适用于一些货物，有时还需要强制性的税目改变。另见*增值标准(value-added criterion)*。

Performance requirements

实绩要求

见*出口实绩要求(export performance requirements)*。

Performers and Phonogram Treaty

表演者和录音制品条约

见 *WIPO 表演和录音制品条约(WIPO Performances and Phonograms Treaty)*。

Peril points

危险点

该条款首次包括在美国《1948年贸易协定延长法》中，但在1949年删除，又在《1955年贸易协定延长法》中重新引入。该条要求美国关税委员会通过包括

could go below the peril point, but he had to explain his decision to Congress. This provision was not incorporated in the *Trade Expansion Act* of 1962. *See also* ***United States trade agreements legislation***.

Permanent Group of Experts: a body established under the WTO ***Agreement on Subsidies and Countervailing Measures***. It consists of five independent persons who are qualified in the fields of subsidies and trade relations. The function of the Group is to assist ***panels*** that may have been convened to adjudicate on the alleged existence of ***prohibited subsidies*** and to give advisory opinions on proposed or existing subsidies.

Permanent normal trade relations: PNTR. An American term since 1998 for ***most-favoured-nation treatment***, particularly in relation to countries that have been subject to annual renewals. *See also* ***normal trade relations*** and ***temporary normal trade relations***.

Per se **conduct:** used in the administration of ***antitrust*** laws for ***behaviour*** by a firm that is always against the rules. *Per se* rules have the advantage of setting a definite legal standard, and they are relatively cheap to enforce since it is only necessary to show that the ***conduct*** has occurred. *See also* ***competition policy*** and ***rule of reason***.

Persistent Dumping Clause: a provision in United States Tariff Act of 1930 which allows the Department of Commerce to initiate an anti-dumping investigation in the absence of a petition. This can be done if (a) more than one anti-dumping order is in effect with respect to imports of a class or kind of merchandise, (b) there is reason to believe that there is an extraordinary pattern of persistent dumping from one or more additional supplier countries, and (c) this extraordinary pattern is causing a serious commercial problem for the domestic industry. This clause therefore deals with an aspect of ***circumvention*** of ***anti-dumping measures***. *See also* ***recidivist dumping***.

Persistent organic pollutants: POPs. Carbon-based chemical substances listed for action in the ***Convention on Persistent Organic Pollutants***. The characteristics of POPs are that, once released into the environment, they (a) remain intact for an exceptionally long time, (b) become widely distributed throughout the environment as result of natural processes involving soil, water and air, (c) accumulate in the fatty tissue of living organisms, and (d) are toxic to both humans and wildlife. The Convention seeks to eliminate or reduce production of POPs. The initial list of pollutants under the Convention was twelve. Another sixteen have been added since, and several more are under review. [chm.pops.int]

Petty patent: *see* ***patent***.

Pflimlin plan: this was a proposal by France in 1951 for a 30 per cent average tariff reduction by all GATT members. The plan would have allowed for extensive waivers for developing countries which would have exempted them from similarly large cuts. It was discussed extensively, but in the end the limited United States negotiating authority, which did not permit anything but item-by-item tariff reductions, put paid to this plan. M. Pierre

公开听证在内的程序，为每种产品设定最低税率，表明低于这一税率将对或可能对国内产业造成损害。美国总统可以将关税降至危险点以下，但必须向国会对其决定作出解释。此条未纳入《1962年贸易扩展法》。另见*美国贸易协定立法(United States trade agreements legislation)*。

Permanent Group of Experts

常设专家小组

根据 WTO《补贴与反补贴措施协定》设立的机构。由 5 名在补贴和贸易关系领域的资深独立人士组成。小组的职能为向就是否存在禁止性补贴作出裁决而召集的专家组提供协助，并就拟议或现有补贴提出咨询意见。

Permanent normal trade relations

永久正常贸易关系

PNTR。美国自 1998 年以来对最惠国待遇的称谓，特别是相对于需要每年展期的国家而言。另见*正常贸易关系(normal trade relations)*、*临时正常贸易关系(temporary normal trade relations)*。

***Per se* conduct**

固有行为

用于反垄断法的管理中，指一公司总是违反规则的行为。固有规则所具有的好处是规定了一个明确的法律标准，且执行成本相对较低，因为只需要表明行为已经发生。另见*竞争政策(competition policy)*、*合理原则(rule of reason)*。

Persistent Dumping Clause

持续性倾销条款

美国《1930年关税法》中允许商务部在没有申请的情况下启动反倾销调查的条款。实施条件为：(a)对于一类或一种商品的进口实施一种以上的反倾销令；(b)有理由相信存在来自一个或多个额外供应国持续倾销的异常模式；以及(c)此种异常模式正在对国内产业造成严重商业问题。该条因此处理反倾销措施中规避问题的一个方面。另见*倾销累犯(recidivist dumping)*。

Persistent organic pollutants

持久性有机污染物

POPs。列入《关于持久性有机污染物的公约》行动的碳基化学物质。持久性有机污染物的特点为，一旦释放到环境中，它们(a)在特别长的时间内保持完整；(b)由于涉及土壤、水和空气的自然过程而在环境中广泛分布；(c)在活生物体的脂肪组织中积累；以及(d)对人类和野生动物均有毒。公约旨在消除或减少持久性有机污染物的产生。公约项下污染物最初清单含12种，后又增加16种，还有几种正在审议中。

Petty patent

小专利

见*专利(patent)*。

Pflimlin plan

普夫里姆林计划

法国在1951年提出的一项提案，要求所有GATT缔约方关税平均削减30%。提案允许发展中国家享有广泛豁免，不必进行类似的大幅削减。提案得到广泛讨论，但最终由于美国谈判授权有限，授权只允许进行逐税目关税削减，这一

Pflimlin was the French Minister for Foreign Economic Relations at the time. *See also* ***waiver***.

Phase-in for rules of origin: sometimes part of a system of ***preferential rules of origin*** under which the qualifying threshold for ***preferential market access*** is raised or lowered over some years. For example, the ***regional value content*** may move up or down, depending on what has been agreed.

Phase-in periods: the staged introduction of a new agreement or new ***commitments***, sometimes according to an agreed timetable. The end-point is fixed. For example, the tariff reductions agreed during the ***Uruguay Round*** could be phased in through five annual equal reductions, though faster action was of course possible. Most ***free-trade agreements*** have a phase-in mechanism for some of the tariffs to be eliminated. Other examples of phase-in periods are those applicable under the ***Agreement on Textiles and Clothing*** or the ***Information Technology Agreement***. *See also* ***implementation*** and ***staging***.

Phonogram: a recording of the sound of a performance on, for example, a tape or a compact disk. *See* ***Geneva Convention***, ***Rome Convention*** and ***WIPO Performances and Phonograms Treaty***.

Picking winners: the occasional inclination of governments to identify some industrial activities as having particular promise for the future, and to institute support frameworks to promote the development of these industries. High-technology industries are especially favoured. Successes globally have been at least balanced by failures, and in most cases industries so picked have performed no better than the average of industries or firms not favoured by special attention. It is worth recalling, too, Adam Smith's admonition that "[i]t is thus that every system which endeavours, either by extraordinary encouragements to draw towards a particular species of industry a greater share of the capital of the society than what would naturally go to it, or, by extraordinary restraints, force from a particular species of industry some share of the capital which would otherwise be employed in it, is really subversive of the great purpose which it means to promote. It retards, instead of accelerating, the progress of the society towards real wealth and greatness; and diminishes, instead of increasing, the real value of the annual produce of its land and labour." *See also* ***national champions*** and ***strategic trade theory***.

Piecemeal tariff reform: tariff reductions for certain groups of goods only. *See also* ***concertina approach*** and ***concertina theorem***.

Pillars: *see* ***three pillars*** and ***three pillars of agriculture***.

Pipeline protection: the practice of according protection of ***intellectual property rights*** to inventions before a ***patent*** has been granted formally. Products benefiting from this practice include particularly agricultural chemicals and pharmaceuticals.

Pipeline sanctions: an international problem in 1982 involving the application of United States ***extraterritoriality***. It was aimed at ensuring that American suppliers, their affiliates and foreign firms using American technology would be

计划以失败告终。M. 皮埃尔 · 普夫里姆林时任法国外交经济关系部长。另见*豁免(waiver)*。

Phase-in for rules of origin
原产地规则分阶段实施

有时是优惠原产地规则制度的一部分，在该制度下，优惠市场准入的资格最低标准在若干年内提高或降低。例如，区域价值成分可能会提高或降低，取决于议定情况。

Phase-in periods
分阶段实施期

指分阶段引入新协定或新承诺，有时按照议定时间表进行。终点是固定的。例如，乌拉圭回合期间议定的关税削减通过 5 次年度均等削减实施，尽管加快实施是可能的。大多数自由贸易协定对若干有待削减的关税均有分阶段实施机制。其他关于分阶段实施的例子为《纺织品与服装协定》或《信息技术协定》。另见*实施(implementation)*、*降税期(staging)*。

Phonogram
录音制品

对表演的声音的录制品，例如录制在磁带或光盘上。另见*日内瓦公约(Geneva Convention)*、*罗马公约(Rome Convention)*、*WIPO 表演和录音制品条约(WIPO Performances and Phonograms Treaty)*。

Picking winners
挑选赢家

政府有时倾向于认为某些产业活动在未来很有前途，从而建立了支持框架以促进这些产业的发展。高科技产业特别受到青睐。在全球范围内成功与失败至少同样多，而且在大多数情况下，如此选择的产业的表现并未比不受特别关注的产业或公司的平均表现更好。同样值得一提的是，亚当 · 斯密曾告诫说："因此每一种制度，实际上都是对其所要促进的伟大目标的破坏，不论是通过特别的激励使某一特定产业类别所吸纳的社会资本份额多于其本应吸纳的份额，还是通过特别的限制自某一特定类别的产业移走其本应使用的部分资本份额。这种制度阻碍而非加快社会走向真正的富裕和伟大的进程，减少而非增加土地和劳动每年产出的真正价值。"另见*国家龙头企业(national champions)*、*战略性贸易理论(strategic trade theory)*。

Piecemeal tariff reform
零敲碎打的关税改革

仅对某些类别的货物进行关税削减。另见*手风琴方式(concertina approach)*、*手风琴定理(concertina theorem)*。

Pillars
支柱

见*三大支柱(three pillars)*、*农业三大支柱(three pillars of agriculture)*。

Pipeline protection
管道保护

在正式授予专利前对发明进行知识产权保护的做法。受益于这种做法的产品特别包括农用化学品和药品。

Pipeline sanctions
管道制裁

1982年涉及美国治外法权适用的国际问题。旨在保证阻止美国供应商、关联公司和使用美国技术的外国公司参与俄罗斯管道建设。欧洲公司受到严重影

prevented from participating in the construction of Russian pipelines. European firms were affected heavily, and the United States action led to considerable tension in its relations with the ***European Community***. The matter was in due course settled amicably. *See also* ***Westinghouse Uranium***.

Piracy: unauthorized copying of materials protected by ***intellectual property rights*** (such as ***copyright***, ***trademarks***, ***patents***, ***geographical indications***, ***neighbouring rights***, etc.) for commercial purposes and unauthorized commercial dealing in copied materials. *See also* ***bootlegging*** and ***fair-use doctrine***.

PL 480: Public Law 480. The United States *Agricultural Trade and Development Assistance Act* of 1954 which established the **Food for Peace Program**. This Act has been superseded by the Food for Peace Act 2008.

Plant breeders' rights: a ***sui generis right*** of ***intellectual property protection*** available under the ***International Convention for the Protection of New Varieties of Plants***. To be eligible for protection, a plant variety must be (a) distinct (i.e. distinguishable from other commonly known varieties), (b) stable (i.e. repeated reproduction must not change its characteristics), (c) homogeneous as far as reproduction or propagation is concerned, and (d) novel in that it has not previously been offered for sale or marketed in the source country with the agreement of the holder of the right. Protection is normally accorded for fifteen to twenty years. *See also* ***International Plant Protection Convention***.

Ploughshares War: an expression used by Nicholas Butler to describe the trade friction in the agricultural area between the United States and the European Community since the establishment of the ***common agricultural policy***. *See also* ***Chicken War***. [Butler 1983]

Plurilateral free-trade agreement: a ***free-trade agreement*** with three or more parties.

Plurilateralism: doing things in small groups involving more than ***bilateralism*** (two participants), but less than ***multilateralism*** (many participants). *See also* ***minilateralism*** and ***WTO plurilateral trade agreements***.

Plurilateral trade agreements: usually refers to the agreements under the WTO accession to which is not a precondition for WTO membership. *See* ***WTO plurilateral trade agreements***.

Plus-three countries: also plus-3 and +3. Usually China, Japan and the Republic of Korea in the context of ***ASEAN+3***.

PNTR: *see* ***permanent normal trade relations***.

Policy competitiveness: the aim of governments to ensure that major firms establish new production facilities within their jurisdictions through offering better terms and conditions than other prospective sites. It is a consequence of the view that it is possible to benefit at the expense of others. Often the taxpayer is the unwitting underwriter of attempts to achieve policy competitiveness.

Policy Framework for Investment: PFI. A comprehensive ***OECD*** review programme to support economic growth. First developed in 2006. The current version was adopted in 2015. The PFI contains many core questions and principles as well as supplemental questions on many aspects of investment

响，美国的行动导致其与欧洲共同体的关系相当紧张。该问题在适当的时候得到了友好解决。另见*西屋铀案(Westinghouse Uranium)*。

Piracy
盗版

为商业目的未经授权复制受知识产权保护的材料(例如版权、商标、专利、地理标志、邻接权等) 及未经授权对复制材料进行商业交易。另见*非法制造(bootlegging)*、*合理使用原则(fair-use doctrine)*。

PL480
480 号公法

1954 年《美国农产品贸易发展与援助法》，该法设立了粮食换和平计划。该法已被 2008 年《粮食换和平法》所取代。

Plant breeders' rights
植物育种者权利

《国际植物新品种保护公约》项下可获得的知识产权保护的特殊权利。要获得保护资格，植物品种必须：(a)独特(即有别于其他常见品种)；(b)稳定(即重复繁殖不得改变其特征)；(c)就再生或繁殖而言具有同质性；以及(d)新颖，尚未经权利持有人同意在来源国销售。权利保护期一般为 15 至 20 年。另见*国际植物保护公约(International Plant Protection Convention)*。

Ploughshares War
犁铧战

尼古拉斯 · 巴特勒用于描述自建立共同农业政策以来，美国与欧共体之间在农业领域的贸易摩擦。另见*鸡肉战(Chicken War)*。

Plurilateral free-trade agreement
诸边自由贸易协定

3 个或 3 个以上参加方的自由贸易协定。

Plurilateralism
诸边主义

指在超过双边主义(两个参加方)，但少于多边主义(许多参加方)的小集团内进行活动。另见*小多边主义(minilateralism)*、*WTO 诸边贸易协定(WTO plurilateral trade agreements)*。

Plurilateral trade agreements
诸边贸易协定

通常指 WTO 框架下的协定，加入这些协定不是加入 WTO 的先决条件。另见*WTO 诸边贸易协定(WTO plurilateral trade agreements)*。

Plus-three countries
其他 3 国

也写作 plus-3 和+3。通常指在东盟+3 的背景下的中国、日本和韩国。

PNTR
永久正常贸易关系

见*永久正常贸易关系(permanent normal trade relations)*。

Policy competitiveness
政策竞争力

通过提供比其他潜在地点更好的条款和条件以保证主要企业在其管辖范围内建立新的生产设施的政府目标。这是这样一种观点的结果，即以牺牲他人为代价而获益是可能的。纳税人往往在不知情的情况下成为实现政策竞争力努力的承保人。

Policy Framework for Investment
投资政策框架

PFI。用于支持经济增长的经济合作与发展组织(OECD)全面审议计划。2006年

policy, defined as referring not only to laws, regulations and policies relating to the admission of investors, the rules once established and the protection of the property of investors, but also to the goals and expectations concerning the contribution of investment to sustainable development. The section on investment promotion and facilitation aims to set out key principles for both. The PFI emphasizes the close connection between ***trade policy*** and the investment climate. It notes that effective ***competition*** is essential for a dynamic business environment in which firms are willing to take risks and invest. Tax policy, corporate governance, policies for responsible business conduct, developing human resources for development, investment for infrastructure, financing investment, public governance, and an investment framework for ***green growth*** are all put in the context of a successful investment strategy. *See also* ***investment facilitation***. [www.oecd.org]

Policy-led integration: regional economic integration promoted through a formal arrangement, usually through a preferential ***regional trade agreement***. *See also* ***market-led integration***.

Politically optimal tariff: the proposition that a tariff would be optimal from a government's perspective if the tariff could be set without taking into account the views of other governments or any effect on the ***terms of trade***. [Godek 1986]

Political will: from the point of view of a trade negotiator, the trait missing among opponents who are unwilling to change their positions. Calls for a demonstration of political will usually are tantamount to a request for more flexibility by the other side. Thus it is by no means uncommon that all negotiators join in a call for a show of political will, no matter how stubbornly they defend their own positions.

Polluter-pays principle: a principle embodied in the OECD ***Guiding Principles Concerning Environmental Policies***. It states that the polluter should bear the expenses of carrying out measures decided by public authorities to reduce pollution and to reach a better allocation of resources. The cost of these measures should be reflected in the cost of goods and services which cause pollution in production and/or consumption. Such measures should not be accompanied by subsidies that would create significant distortions in international trade and investment. *See also* ***trade and environment***.

Pollution haven: a country intent, at least perceived by some to be so, on attracting trade and investment regardless of the consequences for the environment. The assumption that pollution havens exist, and the perceived need to contain their spread, is one of the motivations for the discussion of ***trade and environment***.

Pollution-haven hypothesis: the proposition that (a) countries with lax environmental standards will use their trade and investment regimes to attract all manner of industries with the intention of exporting goods made regardless of adverse environmental consequences, and (b) that countries with strict environmental production standards will import these goods and ignore the conditions

首次制定。目前版本于2015年通过。PFI包含许多核心问题和原则以及关于投资政策多个方面的补充问题，其定义不仅涉及与接纳投资者相关的法律、法规和政策、曾经制定的规则和投资者财产保护，而且涉及关于投资对可持续发展所作贡献的目标和期望。关于投资促进和便利化目标部分列出这两方面的关键原则。PFI 强调贸易政策和投资环境之间的密切联系。指出，有效竞争对于形成企业愿意承担风险和进行投资的具有活力的商业环境至关重要。税收政策、公司治理、负责任的企业行为政策、促进发展的人力资源开发、基础设施投资、融资投资、公共治理以及绿色增长投资框架均为成功投资战略的一部分。*另见投资便利化(investment facilitation)*。

Policy-led integration

政策主导一体化

通过正式安排，通常通过优惠区域贸易协定以促进区域经济一体化。*另见市场主导一体化(market-led integration)*。

Politically optimal tariff

政治最优关税

如果关税的设定可以不考虑其他政府的观点或对贸易条件的任何影响，那么这一关税在政府看来即为最优的。

Political will

政治意愿

从贸易谈判者的角度看，不愿改变立场的反对者所缺少的特质。呼吁显示政治意愿通常等同于另一方要求表现更多灵活性。因此，所有谈判者一致呼吁显示政治意愿并不足为奇，无论他们多么顽固地捍卫自己的立场。

Polluter-pays principle

污染者赔付原则

经济合作与发展组织(OECD)《关于环境政策的指导原则》中的一项原则。规定，为了减少污染和实现更好的资源分配，污染者应该承担公共权力机关为实现上述目的而决定采取措施所产生的费用。这些措施的成本应体现在生产和/或消费过程中引起污染的货物和服务的成本中。此类措施不应与补贴一起实施，因为后者将对国际贸易和投资造成明显扭曲。*另见贸易与环境(trade and environment)*。

Pollution haven

污染天堂

一国意在吸引贸易和投资，而不顾对环境造成的后果，这一意图至少被若干国家所察觉。认为污染天堂存在的假设，及意识到有必要控制其扩散，是讨论贸易与环境问题的原因之一。

Pollution-haven hypothesis

污染天堂假说

这种假说认为：(a)环境标准宽松的国家将利用其贸易和投资制度吸引所有形式的产业，意在出口制作过程中不考虑不利环境后果的货物；及(b)环境生产

under which they were made. The pollution-haven hypothesis differs from the ***race-to-the-bottom*** hypothesis. The latter predicts an equilibrium among all countries at low, possibly unsatisfactory, standards.

Pop mercantilism: not a serious ***trade policy*** term, but of interest all the same. According to Mark Harrison of the University of Warwick, it describes the popular view that (a) industries or activities can be classed as essential or inessential, or ranked in order of national priority, and (b) when competition occurs in international markets, some countries gain and others lose. *See also* ***mercantilism*** and ***neo-mercantilism***. [Harrison 2001]

Portfolio investment: minority holdings of shares, bonds and other securities as part of a diversified portfolio. The main difference between portfolio investment and ***foreign direct investment*** is generally seen in the amount of investment involved. Equity holdings of less than 10 per cent would normally be considered portfolio investment. *See also* ***investment*** and ***non-equity-based investment***.

Positive adjustment programmes: *see* ***structural adjustment***.

Positive comity: a term used in the administration of ***competition policy***. It means that a country may, under the rules of a relevant bilateral arrangement, request the other country to initiate an action under the ***competition laws*** of that country. This can result in action that may otherwise not have been taken by the authorities of the other country. Article IX (Business Practices) of the ***General Agreement on Trade in Services*** incorporates the principle of positive comity. *See also* ***negative comity***.

Positive deindustrialization: occurs when labour no longer needed in industrial production finds new employment opportunities in the services sector. *See also* ***negative deindustrialization***. [Trade and Development Report 2003]

Positive Economic Agenda: launched on 3 May 2002 as part of a framework for bilateral cooperation between the ***European Union*** and the United States. The indicative list of items to be pursued is (a) financial markets, (b) guidelines for regulatory cooperation and transparency, (c) sanitary and phytosanitary (SPS) issues, (d) insurance sector, (e) organic farming and products, (f) electronic tendering, and (g) electronic customs. *See also* ***New Transatlantic Agenda*** and ***Transatlantic Trade and Investment Partnership***.

Positive integration: economic integration achieved through the creation of new institutions and regulatory frameworks established for the purpose. *See also* ***negative integration***.

Positive intervention: often another way of referring to a ***subsidy***, especially by those who would like to get one.

Positive listings: when countries inscribe their commitments under the ***General Agreement on Trade in Services*** in the form of positive listings, they list the activities they wish to be covered. Only these activities are then covered by all GATS articles, importantly the ***market access*** and ***national treatment*** obligations. The disadvantage of this method is that all services have to be listed even if there are no market access or national treatment limitations in the sense of the

标准严格的国家将进口这些产品而无视其制造条件。污染天堂假说与竞次论不同。后者预测一种所有国家间按低的、可能不令人满意的标准达成的均衡。

Pop mercantilism

现代重商主义

不是严肃的贸易政策词语，但同样具有意义。据华威大学的马克·哈里森称，这一词语描述的流行观点为：(a)产业或活动可分为必要的或非必要的，或按国家重点排序；及(b)当国际市场上产生竞争时，一些国家获利而其他国家受损。另见*重商主义(mercantilism)*、*新重商主义(neo-mercantilism)*。

Portfolio investment

证券组合投资

作为多样化投资组合的一部分，持有少数股票、债券和其他证券。证券投资和外国直接投资的主要区别在于所涉投资额。持有少于 10% 的股权通常被认为是证券组合投资。另见*投资(investment)*、*非股权投资(non-equity-based investment)*。

Positive adjustment programmes

积极调整计划

见*结构性调整(structural adjustment)*。

Positive comity

积极礼让

在管理竞争政策时使用的词语。指一国可以按照一项相关双边安排的规定，要求另一国按照其竞争法采取行动。这可能导致该另一国主管机关采取本不会采取的行动。《服务贸易总协定》第 9 条(商业惯例)包含积极礼让的原则。另见*消极礼让(negative comity)*。

Positive deindustrialization

积极去工业化

此种情况发生在工业生产所不再需要的劳动力在服务部门找到新就业机会之时。另见*消极去工业化(negative deindustrialization)*。

Positive Economic Agenda

积极经济议程

作为欧盟与美国双边合作框架的一部分，于 2002 年 5 月 3 日启动。所追求项目的指示性清单为：(a)金融市场；(b)监管合作和透明度准则；(c)卫生与植物卫生问题；(d)保险部门；(e)有机农业和产品；(f)电子招标；以及(g)电子海关。另见*新跨大西洋议程(New Transatlantic Agenda)*、*跨大西洋贸易与投资伙伴关系协定(Transatlantic Trade and Investment Partnership)*。

Positive integration

积极一体化

通过建立新机构和监管框架实现的经济一体化。另见*消极一体化(negative integration)*。

Positive intervention

积极干预

通常为指代补贴的另外一种方式，特别是那些想得到补贴的人使用的词语。

Positive listings

正面清单

各国在将其承诺以正面清单形式纳入《服务贸易总协定》项下时，它们列出的是希望协定所涵盖的活动。只有这些活动因此才为《服务贸易总协定》所有条款涵盖，其中重要的是市场准入和国民待遇义务。此种方法的缺点是，必须列出所有服务，即使不存在协定意义上的市场准入或国民待遇限制。大多数国

Agreement. Most countries have made all of their listings in this form. Some ***free-trade agreements*** have positive lists for services and investment commitments. *See also* ***market access for services*** and ***negative listings***.

Positive margin of dumping: in ***dumping*** investigations, a finding that the ***export price*** is less than the ***normal value***. In other words, dumping has occurred. *See also* ***negative margin of dumping***.

Post-establishment: after an investment has been made. *See also* ***pre-establishment*** and ***right of establishment***.

Poverty: can be divided into *relative poverty* (being poorer, sometimes considerably so, or less affluent than other members of the same society) and *absolute poverty* (being poor in comparison to the amount of money necessary to meet the most basic needs, such as food, clothing and shelter). Discussions of poverty in multilateral development organizations usually are concerned with absolute poverty, also called extreme poverty or destitution and how the conditions of people in this category might be alleviated. In ***World Bank*** papers the income ceiling for absolute poverty is usually taken to be US$1.90 a day. Several measures are used to assess the incidence of poverty. Taken together, they offer a persuasive picture of poverty and being poor. The ***World Development Report*** 2000/2001 offers a summary of possible ways to measure poverty that remains relevant. The first is income poverty (using monetary income or consumption to identify and measure poverty). The second measure is the degree of deprivation experienced by people in health and education. The third measure is ***vulnerability***. This assesses the risk that a household or individual will experience an episode of income or health poverty over time. It also assesses the probability of being exposed to other risks, such as violence, crime, natural disasters or being pulled out of school. The fourth measure is voicelessness and powerlessness. Measuring income is easiest, but it may not be the best way of portraying the impact of poverty on people. As the United Nations explains in the ***Sustainable Development Goals***: poverty is more than a lack of income and resources to ensure a sustainable livelihood; it manifests itself in hunger and malnutrition, limited access to education and other basic services, social discrimination and exclusion as well as a lack of participation in decision-making. Views differ on the causes of poverty. Some poverty is doubtless due to inappropriate domestic policies made worse in some cases by a range of external factors. In other cases, awful government, endemic corruption or persistent civil strife should be included in the list of main causes. Some progress in poverty alleviation is being made. For example, the ***Millennium Development Goal*** of halving, between 1990 and 2015, the proportion of people whose income is less than US$1.25 a day was reached in 2010, but this can obviously only be an interim step. *See also* ***Sustainable Development Goals*** and ***trade and poverty***.

Poverty reduction: *see* ***trade and poverty***.

Poverty Reduction and Growth Trust: PRGT. An ***IMF*** mechanism to promote growth and poverty reduction in ***low-income countries***. The PRGT has three

家均按照此种形式列出其清单。一些自由贸易协定包含服务和投资承诺的正面清单。另见*服务市场准入(market access for services)*、*负面清单(negative listings)*。

Positive margin of dumping

肯定倾销幅度

在倾销调查中，关于出口价格低于正常价值的调查结果。换言之，倾销已经发生。另见*否定倾销幅度(negative margin of dumping)*。

Post-establishment

准入后

指一项投资完成后。另见*准入前(pre-establishment)*、*设立权(right of establishment)*。

Poverty

贫困

可以分为相对贫困(比同一社会中其他成员更贫困，有时非常贫困，或不太富裕)和绝对贫困(相对于满足食物、衣服和住房等大部分基本需求所必需的金钱数额而言是贫困的)。多边发展组织中关于贫困的讨论通常涉及绝对贫困，也称为赤贫或一无所有，以及如何改善这类人的条件。在世界银行文件中，绝对贫困的收入上限通常被认为是每天1.90美元。几个衡量标准被用来评估贫困发生率。综合起来构成了一幅关于贫困和贫穷的有说服力的画面。2000/2001年《世界发展报告》对相关的衡量贫困的可能方法进行了总结。第一个衡量标准是收入贫困(使用货币收入或消费以确定和衡量贫困)。第二个衡量标准是人们在健康和教育方面所经历的贫困程度。第三个衡量标准是脆弱性。评估一个家庭或一个人在一段时间内所经历的收入或健康贫困的风险。还评估暴露于其他风险的可能性，例如暴力、犯罪、自然灾害或辍学。第四个衡量标准是无话语权和无力感。衡量收入是最简单的方法，但可能不是描述贫困对人们影响的最佳方法。正如联合国在可持续发展目标中所说明的那样：贫困不仅是缺少保证可持续生计的收入和资源；自身表现为饥饿和营养不良、获得教育和其他基本服务的机会有限、社会歧视和排斥以及缺乏决策参与。人们对造成贫困原因的看法不同。一些贫困无疑是由于不恰当的国内政策造成的，又在一些情况下因一系列外部因素而变得更糟。在其他情况下，糟糕的政府、普遍的腐败或持续的内乱应该包括在主要原因列表中。在减少贫困方面取得了一些进展。例如，千年发展目标中关于在1990年至2015年期间将日收入低于1.25美元的人口比例减半的目标在2010年即实现，但这显然只是一个过渡阶段。另见*可持续发展目标(Sustainable Development Goals)*、*贸易与贫困(trade and poverty)*。

Poverty reduction

减贫

见*贸易与贫困(trade and poverty)*。

Poverty Reduction and Growth Trust

减贫与增长信托基金

PRGT。国际货币基金组织(IMF)促进低收入国家经济增长和减贫的机制。

concessional lending windows: (a) Extended Credit Facility for providing support in case of protracted balance of payments problems, (b) Standby Credit Facility to provide support in case of actual or potential short-term balance of payments and adjustment needs, and (c) Rapid Credit Facility which gives support in the form of single up-front payments for low-income countries facing urgent balance of payments needs. All of these provide funding on concessional terms. *See also* ***IMF financing facilities***. [www.imf.org]

PPM: *see* ***process and production method***.

PPM labelling: a label on a good which gives information on how it was produced. In other words, it indicates what processes and production methods were applied. *See* ***process and production method***.

Prebisch thesis: the proposition that the ***terms of trade*** of commodity-exporting developing countries will deteriorate in the long term. It is named after Raúl Prebisch, an Argentinian economist who was the first Secretary-General both of ***ECLA*** and of ***UNCTAD***. *See* ***Singer-Prebisch thesis***.

Precaution: *see* ***precautionary principle***.

Precautionary approach: *see* ***precautionary principle***.

Precautionary principle: this refers to Principle 15 of the ***Rio Declaration on Environment and Development***. In the ***Cartagena Protocol on Biosafety*** it is called the precautionary approach. Trade negotiators sometimes simply refer to "precaution". The principle states that where there are threats of serious or irreparable damage [to the environment], lack of full scientific certainty shall not be used as a reason for postponing cost-effective measures to prevent environmental degradation. The precautionary principle has been incorporated in Article 5.7 of the ***Agreement on the Application of Sanitary and Phytosanitary Measures***. This principle is one of the contentious issues in trade negotiations. Those who seek to enshrine it in trade rules are often accused by opponents of opening the way to protectionism. In fact, most countries use the precautionary principle when it suits them, though it may be more or less informal. The ***European Union*** has established formal conditions for the application of the precautionary principle. These are: (a) where the scientific data are insufficient, inconclusive or uncertain and (b) where a preliminary scientific evaluation shows that potentially dangerous effects for the environment and human, animal or plant health can reasonably be feared. Additionally, three rules must be obeyed: (1) a complete scientific evaluation carried out by an independent authority to determine the degree of scientific uncertainty, (2) an assessment of the potential risks and the consequences of inaction, and (3) the participation, under conditions of maximum transparency, of all the interested parties in the study of possible measures. *See also* ***rebuttable presumption*** and ***trade and environment***.

Pre-competitive development activity: a concept used in the WTO ***Agreement on Subsidies and Countervailing Measures***. Assistance, i.e. subsidies, for research activities conducted by firms or on their behalf is permitted if it does not cover more than 50 per cent of pre-competitive development activities.

PRGT 有三个优惠贷款窗口：(a)中期信贷安排，出现持久的国际收支问题时提供支持；(b)备用信贷安排，出现实际或潜在短期国际收支和调整需要时提供支持；以及(c)快速信贷安排，以一次性预付款的形式向面临紧急国际收支需求的低收入国家提供支持。所有这些贷款均以优惠条件提供资金。另见*国际货币基金组织融资机制(IMF financing facilities)*。

PPM

工序和生产方法

见*工序和生产方法(process and production method)*。

PPM labelling

工序和生产方法标签

货物的一种标签，显示关于生产方法的信息。换言之，显示所使用的工序和生产方法。另见*工序和生产方法(process and production method)*。

Prebisch thesis

普雷维什命题

该命题认为，商品出口发展中国家的贸易条件从长期来看会恶化。以阿根廷经济学家劳尔·普雷维什命名，曾先后任拉美经济委员会(ECLA)和联合国贸易与发展会议(UNCTAD)首任秘书长。见*辛格-普雷维什命题(Singer-Prebisch thesis)*。

Precaution

预防

见*预防原则(precautionary principle)*。

Precautionary approach

预防方式

见*预防原则(precautionary principle)*。

Precautionary principle

预防原则

指《里约环境与发展宣言》第15条原则。在《卡塔赫纳生物安全议定书》中，被称为“预防方式”。贸易谈判者有时将其简称为“预防”。该原则指出，如果存在(对环境)严重或不可恢复的破坏威胁，那么缺乏充分的科学确定性不能用作推迟采取具有成本效益的措施防止环境退化的理由。预防原则已纳入《实施卫生与植物卫生措施协定》第5.7条中。这一原则是贸易谈判中存在争议的问题之一。那些寻求将其写入贸易规则的人常常被反对者指责是为保护主义大开方便之门。事实上，大多数国家在条件符合时使用预防原则，尽管可能或多或少属非正式性质。欧盟已经为实施预防原则制定正式条件。条件为：(a)科学数据不充分、无定论或不确定；及(b)初步科学评估显示对环境和人类、动物或植物健康的潜在危险影响的担忧合乎逻辑。此外，还必须遵守三条规则：(1)由独立机构进行全面科学评估，以确定科学不确定性的程度；(2)对不作为的潜在风险和后果进行评估；以及(3)在最大透明度的条件下，所有利害关系方参与关于可能措施的研究。另见*可反驳的推定(rebuttable presumption)*、*贸易与环境(trade and environment)*。

Pre-competitive development activity

竞争前开发活动

WTO《补贴与反补贴措施协定》中使用的概念。对公司或代表公司进行研究

These are defined as the translation of industrial research findings into a plan, blueprint, or design for new, modified or improved products, processes or services whether intended for sale or use, including the creation of a first prototype which would not be capable of commercial use. It may also include the conceptual formulation and design of products, processes or services.

Predatory pricing: the setting of prices at aggressively low levels, also known as ruinous competition, below-cost pricing, etc. This is the concept thought to underlie the treatment in the GATT of ***dumping***, but it is not actually mentioned in its provisions. No single definition of predatory behaviour enjoys unanimous support, but there is agreement that to qualify as predatory pricing, an action should be aimed at driving efficient competitors out of the market. It has always been difficult to determine what the dividing line between competitive pricing and predatory pricing might be. Predation is a costly activity, and it would only be worth it to the predator if in the end all the costs incurred and the revenues foregone could be recovered. This is a doubtful proposition. *See also* ***Areeda-Turner test*** and ***non-price predation***.

Predatory-pricing dumping: *see* ***dumping***.

Pre-establishment: the phase in a foreign direct investment proposal between a decision by a company to invest and the receipt of approval from relevant authorities to proceed. In many cases, pre-establishment is simply a necessary planning stage, but it can be contentious if ***foreign investment screening*** is involved.

Pre-expiration testing: the analysis of patented products, often pharmaceutical products, shortly before the ***patent*** on them expires with a view to bringing a product with the same characteristics on the market shortly after the patent has expired. *See also* ***Bolar exception***, ***generic springboarding*** and ***reverse engineering***.

Preference erosion: disappearing ***margins of preference*** as countries reduce their ***MFN tariffs*** to levels at or below the margin of preference. *See also* ***historical preferences*** and ***relative preferential margin***.

Preferences: favours extended to some trading partners, usually in the form of lower tariffs or non-application of some ***non-tariff measures***. *See also* ***GSP***, ***GSTP***, ***historical preferences***, ***most-favoured-nation treatment*** and ***preferential trade arrangements***.

Preference utilization: the extent to which countries receiving trade preferences of one kind or another actually make use of them. This can be difficult to calculate because exporters may be able to choose from several schemes, such as ***free-trade agreements***, ***GSP*** and ***GSTP***.

Preferential investment arrangements: formal or informal arrangements which give better access terms to investment capital and investors from selected countries or groups of countries. This may include expedited consideration of investment proposals, permission to invest in activities closed to others, higher ceilings for foreign equity, etc. Investment chapters in ***free-trade agreements*** can fall in this category.

活动的援助，即补贴，如果不超过竞争前开发活动的 50%，即被允许。这些活动被定义为，将工业研究结果转化为新的、改型的或改进的产品、工序或服务的计划、蓝图或设计，无论是否旨在用于销售或使用，包括制造不能用于商业用途的第一个原型。还可以包括产品、工序或服务的概念表述和设计。

Predatory pricing
掠夺性定价

将价格设定在极低的水平上，也称为破坏性竞争、低于成本定价等。这一概念被认为是GATT中处理倾销问题的基础，但实际上未在GATT条款中提及。没有一个掠夺性行为的单独定义得到一致支持，但存在形成共识的是，构成掠夺性定价，一行动的目的必定是将有效率的竞争者逐出市场。竞争性定价和掠夺性定价之间的分界线一直难以确定。掠夺是有代价的活动，只有在最终能够收回所有产生的成本和损失的收入的情况下，对于掠夺者才是值得的。这是一个不确定的命题。另见*阿瑞达-特纳检验(Areeda-Turner test)*、*非价格掠夺(non-price predation)*。

Predatory-pricing dumping
掠夺性定价倾销

见*倾销(dumping)*。

Pre-establishment
准入前

一项外国直接投资建议中，自公司作出投资决定至获得有关主管机关批准推进的阶段。在许多情况下，准入前仅为一个必需的计划阶段，但如果涉及外国投资审查即会引起争议。

Pre-expiration testing
到期前测试

在专利即将到期前对专利产品(通常是药品)进行分析，以便在专利到期后不久即将具有相同特性的产品推向市场。另见*博拉例外(Bolar exception)*、*仿制药跳板(generic springboarding)*、*逆向工程(reverse engineering)*。

Preference erosion
优惠侵蚀

因各国将最惠国关税削减至优惠幅度水平甚至更低水平而使优惠幅度消失。另见*历史性优惠(historical preferences)*、*相对优惠幅度(relative preferential margin)*。

Preferences
优惠

给予一些贸易伙伴的优惠，通常是以更低关税或不适用一些非关税措施的形式。另见*普惠制(GSP)*、*全球贸易优惠制(GSTP)*、*历史性优惠(historical preferences)*、*最惠国待遇(most-favoured-nation treatment)*、*优惠贸易安排(preferential trade arrangements)*。

Preference utilization
优惠利用率

接受各种不同贸易优惠的国家实际使用这些优惠的程度。这可能难以计算，因为出口商可以从几个方案中选择，例如自由贸易协定、普惠制和全球贸易优惠制。

Preferential investment arrangements
优惠投资安排

规定为来自选定国家或国家集团的投资资本和投资者提供更好准入条件的正式或非正式安排。可以包括投资建议的迅速考虑、允许对禁止其他国家投资的活动进行投资、外资股权的更高上限等。自由贸易协定中的投资章节可归

Preferential market access: any ***market access*** conditions afforded to a trading partner that are more favourable than the non-discriminatory ***most-favoured-nation treatment***. Preferential access may be reciprocal or symmetrical as in ***customs unions***, ***free-trade areas***, or through the now residual imperial preferences. It can also be non-reciprocal or asymmetrical, as is the case with the ***ACP-EU Partnership Agreement***, the ***Caribbean Basin Initiative***, ***SPARTECA*** and other such agreements.

Preferential rules of origin: a system of ***rules of origin*** (ROOs) to determine whether a good exported under a preferential trading arrangement, such as a ***free-trade area***, will be admitted by another member of the arrangement under the applicable preferential rules. In most cases this would be free of ***customs duties***. Preferential rules of origin are therefore meant to ensure that preferences given to the other members of the arrangement do not leak to third countries. ***Wholly obtained goods*** always qualify. In the case of other goods these rules seek to determine whether a ***substantial transformation*** has occurred, i.e. whether the imported good has been given its present form in the exporting country. One yardstick commonly applied to determine whether a good originates in the other member is the ***regional value content*** (RVC), expressed as a percentage of the total value of the good. The RVC is the share of the value of the good that can be ascribed to the exporting member or, in the case of several countries, the other members combined. It is the ratio between ***originating materials***, which receive preferences, and ***non-originating materials***, which do not. Two main methods have been devised to determine the RVC. All can entail complicated cost calculations. First, the ***ex-factory cost method***, also known as the net cost method, takes into account all costs incurred by the producer up to the point where the good leaves the factory. Related to this is the ***build-up method*** which is based on a calculation of the value of originating materials. Second, the ***FOB value method***, also known as ***transaction value method*** or ***build-down method***, takes into account all costs, including a profit component, up to the point where the good has been loaded on the ship in the port of export. The calculation is based on ascertaining the value of non-originating material. A second yardstick used in the determination of the origin of a good is the change in tariff heading, also known as ***change in chapter heading***. The basis of this method is that if a good has entered the country under one chapter heading, usually specified as a ***chapter***, a ***heading*** or a ***sub-heading*** in the ***Harmonized Commodity Description and Coding System***, it will necessarily be classified as a different product when it is exported. A calculation of the value added in the producing country is not necessary. The third yardstick used is a system of specific processing operations that must be met. Many free-trade agreements use more than one of these yardsticks. Sometimes the exporter can choose the method best suited to his or her products, but in other cases the product exported determines what rule will be used. A country that is a member of several free-trade agreements will have a different system of ROOs for each. *See also* ***preferential rules of origin for least-developed countries***.

Preferential market access

优惠市场准入

向贸易伙伴提供的比非歧视最惠国待遇更优惠的市场准入条件。优惠准入可以像关税同盟、自由贸易区那样是互惠的或对称的，或通过现在余留的帝国特惠制。也可以是非互惠的或不对称的，例如《非加太地区国家与欧盟伙伴关系协定》、《加勒比盆地倡议》、《南太平洋区域贸易经济合作协定》(SPARTECA)以及其他此类协定。

Preferential rules of origin

优惠原产地规则

一种原产地规则(ROOs)制度，用于确定根据优惠贸易安排(例如自由贸易区)出口的货物是否会被该安排的另一成员根据适用优惠规则予以承认。在大多数情况下，货物是免关税的。优惠原产地规则因此是为保证给予该安排其他成员的优惠不会使第三国获得。完全获得的货物始终符合资格。就其他货物而言，这些规则用于确定是否发生实质性改变，即进口货物是否在出口国中被赋予目前的形态。第一个经常用来确定一货物是否源自另一成员的衡量标准是区域价值成分，以货物总价值的百分比表示。区域价值成分是货物中可归于出口成员的价值的份额，或如涉及若干国家，则为其他成员加总的份额。区域价值成分(RVC)是获得优惠的原产材料和不获得优惠的非原产材料的比例。目前已经设计两种确定区域价值成分的方法，均需要进行复杂的成本计算。第一种是出厂成本法，也称净成本法，考虑直到货物离开工厂之时生产商所产生的全部成本。与此相关的是基于确定的原产材料价格计算的增值法。第二种是离岸价格法，也称成交价格法或扣除法，考虑直到货物在出口港装船之时的所有成本，包括利润部分。此种计算基于对非原产材料价格的确定。用于确定货物原产地的第二个衡量标准是税目改变，也称章改变。此种方法的基础是，如果一货物进入一国时归入某一章，通常为商品名称及编码协调制度中的章、税目、子目，该货物出口时即必须按不同产品进行归类，无需计算在生产国中增加的价值。使用的第三种衡量标准是必须满足特定加工工序。许多自由贸易协定使用了一种以上的衡量标准。有时出口商可以选择最适合其产品的方法，但在其他情况下，所使用的规则取决于出口的产品。属多个自由贸易协定成员的国家需要为每一协定制定不同的原产地规则制度。另见*最不发达国家优惠原产地规则(preferential rules of origin for least-developed countries)*。

[Estevadeordal and Suominen 2003, Vermulst, Waer and Bourgeois 1994, WTO WT/REG/W/45]

Preferential rules of origin for least-developed countries: application of ***rules of origin*** designed to make it easier for exports from ***least-developed countries*** to gain preferential access to markets. The Bali ***WTO Ministerial Conference*** in 2013 set out the requirement that such rules of origin should be as transparent, simple and objective as possible, that ***cumulation*** should be part of them, and that documentary requirements should be simple and transparent. A decision adopted by the 2015 ***Nairobi WTO Ministerial Conference*** gave a further description of such rules. This includes detailed requirements for an assessment of sufficient or ***substantial transformation***, encourages the use of one of four options of cumulation, and it requires importing countries to refrain from using a ***certificate of non-manipulation*** unless there are grounds for suspecting, for example, fraud or ***transshipment***. Preference-granting WTO members were required to advise the WTO by the end of 2016 of the steps they intended to take in support of this decision.

Preferential tariff: a ***tariff schedule*** which shows the tariff rates applicable under ***preferential trade arrangements***. The applicable tariff is usually lower than ***general tariff*** or the ***most-favoured-nation tariff***. Preferential tariffs can be contractual as in a ***free-trade agreement*** or autonomous as under a ***GSP*** scheme.

Preferential Trade Area for Eastern and Southern African States: *see* ***Common Market for Eastern and Southern Africa***.

Preferential trade arrangements: these are trade arrangements under which a party agrees, either unilaterally or as a result of negotiations, to accord one or more other parties preferential treatment in trade in goods or services. The scope for establishing such arrangements is subject to reasonably precise WTO rules, though developing countries have more flexibility. They may give each other preferences in the form of reduced tariffs, their complete elimination or, in the case of services, partial or complete liberalization. Developed countries must establish either a ***free-trade area***, a ***customs union*** under ***Article XXIV*** of the ***GATT*** or, in the case of services, an ***economic integration agreement*** under ***Article V*** of the ***General Agreement on Trade in Services***. That is, they must remove substantially all barriers to trade among those receiving preferences. If, for example, they wanted to give each other a preference in some product lines only, they would have to offer the same access conditions to all of their trading partners under the rule of ***most-favoured-nation treatment***. Under the WTO rules, preferential trade arrangements are legal also in the form of ***GSP*** schemes set up by developed countries, and participation in the ***GSTP*** scheme by developing countries. For preferential arrangements other than these, it would be necessary to obtain a ***waiver***. Some classify ***treaties of friendship, commerce and navigation*** as preferential agreements because the parties to them might be guaranteeing certain standards of behaviour towards the other party without giving trade preferences. *See also* ***ACP-EU Partnership Agreement***,

Preferential rules of origin for least-developed countries

最不发达国家优惠原产地规则

适用旨在使最不发达国家的出口更易于获得优惠市场准入的原产地规则。2013 年巴厘岛 WTO 部长级会议规定了有关要求，此类原产地规则应尽可能透明、简单和客观，累积应成为其中一部分，此外单证要求应简单和透明。2015 年内罗毕 WTO 部长级会议通过的一项决定进一步描述了此类规则。包括判定充分或实质性改变的详细要求，鼓励使用 4 种累积方法中的一种，并要求进口国避免使用未再加工证明，除非有理由怀疑存在欺诈或转运等情况。要求 WTO 给惠成员在 2016 年底之前将它们为实施这一决定所采取的措施告知 WTO。

Preferential tariff

优惠关税

显示优惠贸易安排项下所适用的关税税率的关税税则。适用关税通常低于普通关税或最惠国关税。优惠关税可以如在自由贸易协定中的属契约性质，或如在普惠制(GSP)方案中属自主性质。

Preferential Trade Area for Eastern and Southern African States

东部和南部非洲国家优惠贸易区

见*东部和南部非洲共同市场(Common Market for Eastern and Southern Africa)*。

Preferential trade arrangements

优惠贸易安排

一参加方据以单方面或通过谈判同意在货物贸易或服务贸易中给予一参加方或多个参加方优惠待遇的贸易安排。建立此类安排需要遵守相当精确的WTO规则，尽管发展中国家有更多灵活性。它们相互给予优惠的形式包括削减关税、或全部取消关税，或部分或全部实行服务自由化。发达国家必须根据GATT第24条建立自由贸易区或关税同盟，或对于服务贸易，根据《服务贸易总协定》第5条达成经济一体化协定。即它们必须在接受优惠的成员之间取消实质上所有贸易壁垒。例如，如果它们只想对部分产品相互给予优惠，就必须根据最惠国待遇规则向所有贸易伙伴提供相同准入条件。根据WTO规则，优惠贸易安排属合法，包括发达国家制定的普惠制(GSP)方案及发展中国家参加的全球贸易优惠(GSTP)方案。对于除此之外的优惠安排，则需要获得豁免。有些人将友好通商航海条约归为优惠协定，因为条约签署方可能在不给予贸易优惠的情况下彼此保证某些行为标准。另见*非加太地区国家与欧盟伙伴关系协定(ACP-EU Partnership Agreement)*、*加勒比盆地倡议(Caribbean Basin initai-*

Caribbean Basin Initiative, ***imperial preferences arrangement***, ***preferential market access*** and ***SPARTECA***.

Preliminary affirmative determination of subsidization: no earlier than sixty days after the start of an investigation in the WTO whether countervailing duties can be imposed, an investigating authority may determine that enough evidence exists to do so. It may then decide to impose ***provisional countervailing duties***, but for a period not exceeding four months. It is at this stage that a ***price undertaking*** may be sought or accepted.

Preliminary determination of dumping: when an investigating authority examines a petition for the imposition of ***anti-dumping measures***, it may conclude that there is enough evidence of ***dumping*** before all aspects of the case have been examined. It can then issue a preliminary determination of dumping and impose ***provisional anti-dumping duties***. These may be imposed no earlier than sixty days after the start of the investigation. Their duration is limited to between four and six months. After that, a ***final determination of dumping*** is needed to maintain the additional duties. All determinations have to be published with the reasons for them.

Preparatory work: *see* ***travaux préparatoires***.

Presence of natural persons: one of the ***modes of services delivery***. The producer travels to another country to sell or deliver the service.

Preshipment inspection: PSI. Inspection of goods by specially appointed firms before they are shipped to other countries. PSI is defined in the WTO ***Agreement on Preshipment Inspection*** as "all activities imposed by a WTO member relating to the verification of the quality, quantity, price, including currency, exchange rates and financial terms, and/or the customs classification of goods to be exported to its territory". *See also* ***independent entity***.

Pressure valve actions: refers mainly to ***anti-dumping measures*** and ***safeguards***, but sometimes also to tariff renegotiations possible under GATT Article XXVIII.

Price bands systems: mechanisms for the management of commodity prices. Two main varieties occur. The first is a mechanism maintained by some countries to ensure that the price on internal markets of mainly agricultural commodities is kept in a certain relationship to the international market price through a moving floor price to afford domestic producers a measure of protection. The way this is done is that when the price of the imported product is high compared to the domestic price, the ***tariff*** is lowered. If the imported price is low compared to the domestic price, the tariff is raised. Some have therefore described this kind of price band system as a ***variable tariff***. The second variety of price band systems underpins the operations of ***buffer stocks***. The simplest system consists of three bands, related to the market price of the commodity. When the price is low, the manager may buy. When it is at a medium level, the manager may buy or sell. When the price is high, the manager usually sells.

Price collusion: a tacit or explicit agreement between firms to fix prices of certain goods in a market, usually with the aim of not undercutting each other. *See also* ***antitrust laws*** and ***competition policy***.

tive)、*帝国特惠安排(imperial preferences arrangement)*、*优惠市场准入(preferential market access)*、*南太平洋地区贸易经济合作协定(SPARTECA)*。

Preliminary affirmative determination of subsidization

补贴初步肯定裁定

WTO 中启动关于是否可以征收反补贴税的调查后不早于 60 天，调查机关可以裁定拥有征收反补贴税的充足证据。随后调查机关可以决定征收临时反补贴税，期限不超过 4 个月。在这一阶段可以寻求或接受价格承诺。

Preliminary determination of dumping

倾销初步裁定

调查机关在审查实施反倾销措施申请时，在对案件的所有方面进行审查之前可以确定拥有倾销的充分证据。随后调查机关可以发布倾销的初步裁定，并征收临时反倾销税。必须在启动调查后不早于60天征收。征收期限限于4至6个月。此后，需要作出倾销最终裁定，以维持额外征税。所有裁定均应公布并附说明。

Preparatory work

准备工作

见*准备工作文件(travaux préparatoires)*。

Presence of natural persons

自然人存在

服务提供模式。生产者前往另一国销售或提供服务。

Preshipment inspection

装运前检验

PSI。货物运往其他国家前，由专门指定的公司进行检验。WTO《装运前检验协定》将此定义为"一WTO成员采取的与核实将出口至用户成员领土的货物的质量、数量、价格，包括汇率和融资条件，和/或海关归类相关的所有活动。"另见*独立实体(independent entity)*。

Pressure valve actions

压力阀措施

主要指反倾销措施和保障措施，但有时也指根据GATT第28条下可能进行的关税重新谈判。

Price bands systems

价格幅度机制

一种商品价格管理机制。主要有两类。第一种是一些国家维持一种机制，即通过浮动最低价格保证主要农产品的国内市场价格与国际市场价格保持某种关联，从而为国内生产者提供一种保护措施。运作方式为，当进口产品的价格高于国内价格时，降低关税；当进口价格低于国内价格时，提高关税。因此，一些人将这种价格幅度机制描述为可变关税。第二种价格幅度机制是缓冲储存运作的基础。最简单的制度由与商品市场价格相关的三个幅度构成。当价格低时，经理人可以购买；当价格处于中等水平时，经理人可买可卖；当价格高时，经理人通常卖出。

Price collusion

价格合谋

企业之间默认或明确的协议，以固定市场上某些商品的价格，通常目的是不相互削弱。另见*反垄断法(antitrust laws)*、*竞争政策(competition policy)*。

Price-contingent subsidy: a subsidy that is only payable if the price for the good or the service in question moves outside a certain range. This is the case when the return to the producer is very low, or when the consumer would otherwise have to pay a very high price.

Price depression: a term used in the WTO ***Agreement on Subsidies and Countervailing Measures***, but not defined there. It is, however, generally taken to mean a price forced lower than would have been the case without state intervention, i.e. the payment of a ***subsidy***. It seems to have virtually the same meaning as ***price suppression***.

Price dumping: a category of ***dumping*** identified at the time of the ***Havana Charter*** negotiations which is now subject to Article VI of the GATT. It is based on the concept that the exporter sells goods abroad at a lower price than in the domestic market, and that this may have an injurious effect on industry in the importing country producing similar goods. *See also* ***anti-dumping measures*** and ***predatory pricing***.

Price equalization mechanism: a mechanism designed to ensure that market prices for commercially produced and traded commodities, and therefore returns to their producers, do not fluctuate excessively. This aim is seen as promoting the orderly development of the industry by assuring producers of more predictable remunerative returns. At the same time, it is thought to benefit consumers who can look forward to modest price changes at any one time. Such mechanisms operate in many different ways. The main challenge for all of them is to ensure that it does not turn into a more or less permanent ***subsidy***. This can be done if the producers are responsible for the funding of the mechanism. In this way, price signals will not be ignored. *See also* ***buffer stocks***, ***common agricultural policy***, ***floor price***, ***international commodity agreements***, ***price bands system*** and ***variable tariff***.

Price suppression: a term used in the WTO ***Agreement on Subsidies and Countervailing Measures***, but not defined there. It seems to have virtually the same meaning as ***price depression***.

Price taker: a firm or a country that is too small on its own to influence the price of a good.

Price undertaking: an undertaking by an exporter to raise the export price of the product to avoid the possibility of an anti-dumping or countervailing duty. In the case of the former, a price undertaking is not supposed to exceed the alleged ***margin of dumping***, and preferably it should be at the lowest possible level that would be adequate to remove the threat of ***injury*** from domestic industry. In the case of the latter, the price increases must not be higher than necessary to eliminate the amount of the subsidy. Authorities are not compelled in either case to agree to offers of price undertakings. *See also* ***anti-dumping measures***, ***lesser-duty principle*** and ***trade harassment***.

Price wedge: the difference between the price of a product in a protected market and its price under fully competitive conditions.

Price-contingent subsidy

视价格而定的补贴

仅在所涉货物或服务的价格超出特定范围时才给予的补贴。此种情况发生在生产者利润非常低或消费者需要支付非常高的价格之时。

Price depression

价格压低

WTO《补贴与反补贴措施协定》中使用的词语，协定中并未定义。但是通常指将价格强行压低至无国家干预的情况，即没有给予补贴的情况。看似实际上与价格抑制同义。

Price dumping

价格倾销

《哈瓦那宪章》谈判时确定的一种倾销类型，现在受 GATT 第 6 条约束。所根据的概念是，出口商以低于国内市场的价格向国外销售货物，可能对进口国中生产类似货物的产业产生有害影响。另见*反倾销措施(anti-dumping measures)*、*掠夺性定价(predatory pricing)*。

Price equalization mechanism

价格均衡机制

旨在保证商业生产和交易货物的市场价格及对生产者的回报不过度波动的机制。目的在于通过保证生产者获得更可预见的收益回报，促进产业有序发展。与此同时，目的在于使消费者在可预见未来的任何时候因商品价格变化不大而从中获益。此类机制以许多不同方式运作。这些机制所面临的主要挑战是保证不会或多或少成为一种永久补贴。如果生产者负责该机制的融资，可以解决上述问题。这样，价格信号就不会被忽视。另见*缓冲储存(buffer stocks)*、*共同农业政策(common agricultural policy)*、*最低价格(floor price)*、*国际商品协定(international commodity agreements)*、*价格幅度机制(price bands system)*、*可变关税(variable tariff)*。

Price suppression

价格抑制

WTO《补贴与反补贴措施协定》中使用的词语，但协定中未定义。似与价格压低实际同义。

Price taker

价格接受者

一企业或一国，因其规模太小而自身不能影响一货物的价格。

Price undertaking

价格承诺

出口商为避免反倾销税或反补贴税而提高产品出口价格的承诺。对于反倾销，价格承诺不应超过所谓的倾销幅度，最好是在足以消除国内产业损害威胁的最低水平。对于反补贴税，价格增加不得超过消除补贴所必要的金额。无论哪种情况，主管机关均不会被迫同意价格承诺。另见*反倾销措施(anti-dumping measures)*、*低税原则(lesser-duty principle)*、*贸易干扰(trade harassment)*。

Price wedge

价格差额

一产品在受保护市场中的价格与其在充分竞争条件下的价格之间的差额。

***Prima facie*:** *Lat.* variously rendered as on the face of it, at first sight, on first impression, etc.

Prima facie* case:** enough evidence to allow the plaintiff to win the case unless the defence presents additional evidence or legal argument to rebut it. The ***Appellate Body described such a situation in *Canada – Measures Affecting the Export of Civil Aircraft* as "a case which, in the absence of effective refutation by the defending party ... requires a panel, as matter of law, to rule in favour of the complaining party presenting a *prima facie* case".

Primage: a term denoting the temporary imposition of an ***import surcharge*** or a similar measure having the effect of increasing the normal ***customs duties***.

Primary dealers: in the United States banking system, these are firms that have established a trading relationship with the Federal Reserve Bank of New York. To qualify as a primary dealer, a firm must be willing to make markets in the full range of Treasury issues for a reasonably diverse group of customers, and it must satisfy minimum capital requirements. Some United States acts, such as the ***Iran Sanctions Act***, may lead to the cancellation of a primary dealer licence if the firm engages in activities declared illegal under the acts.

Primary products: defined in GATT Article XVI:4 for the purposes of the applicable subsidies regime as "any product of farm, forest or fishery, or any mineral, in its natural form or which has undergone such processing as is customarily required to prepare it for marketing in substantial volume in international trade". The reference to "minerals" was omitted when the *Agreement on Interpretation and Application of Articles VI, XVI and XXIII of the General Agreement on Tariff and Trade* (the Subsidies Code) was adopted in 1979 as part of the ***Tokyo Round*** outcome. In 1957, GATT members rejected a United States suggestion that subsidies should be permitted for the export of cotton textiles if the subsidy was essentially the payment that would have been made on raw cotton if the raw material had been exported in its natural form. In the ***pasta*** case the panel found that pasta was not a primary product, but a processed agricultural product. The European Economic Community had argued that the disputed exported refund in that case was granted in respect of the durum wheat that had been used, that the refund did not include any component by way of processing aid, and that durum wheat was undeniably a primary product. *See also* ***Agreement on Agriculture*** and ***basic agricultural products***.

Principal supplier right: the right, obtained by virtue of one's status as the largest supplier of a particular tariff line to another trading partner, to ask for tariff negotiations under the ***principal supplier rule***.

Principal supplier rule: a major feature of the system governing tariff negotiations in the GATT, particularly in the earlier negotiating rounds. Under this rule, requests for tariff concessions to a particular GATT member could only be made by the principal supplier of the product in question. The rule is based on the assumption that the country making the ***concession*** will only be able to get compensated for it once, and that the country invited to make the concession

Prima facie
初步证据

拉丁语。可译为表面上、第一眼、第一印象等。

***Prima facie* case**
初步证据确凿的案件

有足够证据可使原告赢得案件，除非被告提出额外证据或法律论据予以反驳。上诉机构在“加拿大-影响民用航空器出口措施案”中描述了此种情况，指“在被告方未能进行有效反驳的案件中……要求专家组，在法律问题上，作出有利于提交初步证据的起诉方的裁决”。

Primage
关税附加税

指暂时征收进口附加税或具有提高正常关税效果的类似措施的词语。

Primary dealers
一级交易商

指在美国银行系统中，与纽约联邦储备银行已经建立交易关系的公司。为获得一级交易商资格，一公司必须愿意为相当广泛的客户群体提供国债发行全过程业务，且必须满足最低资本要求。一些美国法规定，例如《伊朗制裁法》，如一公司从事根据该法属违法的活动，可能导致一级交易商执照被吊销。

Primary products
初级产品

在GATT第16条第4款中就适用的补贴制度而言将之定义为“自然形态或已经过供在国际贸易中大量销售所通常要求的加工过程的农产品、林产品或渔业产品，或任何矿物”。1979年，作为东京回合结果一部分而通过的《关于解释和实施关税与贸易总协定第6条、第16条和第23条的协定》（《补贴守则》）漏掉了“矿物”一词。1957年，GATT缔约方拒绝了美国的一项建议，即如果补贴基本上是在原材料以自然形态出口情况下对原棉的支付，则应允许对棉纺织品的出口提供补贴。在“意大利面食案”中，专家组认为意大利面食不是一种初级产品，而是一种加工农产品。欧共体辩称，该案中引发争议的出口退税是针对所使用的硬粒小麦给予的，退税不包括以加工助剂形式添加的部分，硬粒小麦无疑是一种初级产品。另见*农业协定(Agreement on Agriculture)*、*基本农产品(basic agricultural products)*。

Principal supplier right
主要供应方权利

指一方凭借其作为另一贸易伙伴一特定关税税目最大供应方地位而获得的根据主要供应方规则要求进行关税谈判的权利。

Principal supplier rule
主要供应方规则

管辖GATT中关税谈判制度的主要特征，特别是在早期谈判回合中。根据这一规则，对一特定GATT缔约方提出的关税减让要价只能由所涉商品的主要供应方提出。这一规则所依据的假设是，作出减让的国家仅能获得一次对减让的补偿，且被邀请作出减让的国家将通过与最大供应方作出交换而使其收益最

will be able to maximize its returns by dealing with the largest supplier. It is also meant to reduce the unintended benefits ***free riders*** may otherwise obtain. In practice, reliance on this system alone led to the effective exclusion of smaller and developing countries from the negotiating process. The method of linear tariff reductions in the ***Kennedy Round*** and the ***Tokyo Round***, as well as the practice of negotiations across broader product categories, such as the ***Information Technology Agreement***, have reduced the importance of the principal supplier rule. *See also* ***initial negotiating right***, ***principal supplying interest*** and ***sectoral trade negotiations***.

Principal supplying interest: a right to participate in WTO tariff negotiations for specified product items based on a ranking of export interest in a given product. It is held by the WTO member having the highest ratio of exports affected by the item. It is therefore a right based on the relative magnitude of trade flows. A principal supplying interest differs from ***principal supplier rights*** which are based on absolute magnitude of trade flows. It also is unlike ***initial negotiating rights*** which are accorded by one member to another through negotiations. In determining whether a country has a principal supplying interest, the WTO secretariat may only take into account products traded on a most-favoured-nation basis. One of the purposes of the concept of principal supplying interest is to allow smaller and medium-sized traders an opportunity to initiate tariff negotiations in products of major importance to them. *See also* ***substantial supplying interest***.

Prior art: a term used in ***patent*** examinations to describe all publicly available information relevant to the ***invention*** for which the patent has been sought.

Prior informed consent: PIC. One of the provisions of the ***Convention on the Prior Informed Consent Procedure for Certain Hazardous Chemicals and Pesticides in International Trade***. The procedure applies to all chemicals listed in Annex III to the Convention (currently thirty-four pesticides, fifteen industrial chemicals and one chemical in both of the categories). The PIC procedure entails a mechanism for formally obtaining and disseminating the decisions of importing countries as to whether they might wish to receive future shipments of chemicals listed in Annex III. The Convention also facilitates an international exchange among the parties for a broad range of potentially hazardous chemicals. The procedure itself is not a recommendation to ban or restrict the use of a chemical. The ***Food and Agriculture Organization*** and ***UN Environment Programme*** play a major role in the implementation of the Convention. *See also* ***multilateral environment agreements*** and ***trade and environment***.

Priority foreign country: this is a term used in sections 1302 and 1303 of the ***Omnibus Trade and Competitiveness Act*** of 1988. These two sections are usually known as ***Super 301*** and ***Special 301***, respectively. Super 301 requires ***USTR*** to inform Congress of priority foreign countries maintaining practices which, if eliminated, would have the greatest potential for increasing United States exports. Special 301 requires a similar list of countries, known as the priority watch list, that deny adequate and effective protection of ***intellectual***

大化。这也意味着减少搭便车者可能获得的意料之外的利益。实践中，只依赖这一制度导致较小国家和发展中国家被有效排除在谈判进程之外。肯尼迪回合和东京回合中的线性关税减让方法，以及《信息技术协定》等较大范围的产品类别谈判做法，降低了主要供应方规则的重要性。另见*最初谈判权(initial negotiating right)*、*主要供应利益(principal supplying interest)*、*部门贸易谈判(sectoral trade negotiations)*。

Principal supplying interest

主要供应利益

WTO中基于一指定产品出口利益的排序参与特定产品关税谈判的权利。出口份额受该产品类别影响最大的成员享有该权利。因此，这是一项基于贸易流的相对幅度的权利。主要供应利益不同于主要供应方权利，后者是基于贸易流的绝对幅度。也不同于一成员通过谈判给予另一成员的最初谈判权。在确定一国是否具有主要供应利益时，WTO秘书处只考虑在最惠国基础上交易的产品。主要供应利益这一概念的目的之一是使中小规模的贸易方有机会就对其具有重要意义的产品发起关税谈判。另见*实质供应利益(substantial supplying interest)*。

Prior art

先有技艺

专利审查中使用的词语，用于描述与申请专利的发明相关的所有公开可获得的信息。

Prior informed consent

事先知情同意

PIC。《关于在国际贸易中对某些危险化学品和农药采用事先知情同意程序的公约》的条款之一。该程序适用于公约附件 3 所列全部化学品(目前有 34 种农药、15 种工业用化学品和 1 种同属两类别的化学品)。事先知情同意程序包含一种机制用于正式获得和传播进口国关于它们是否希望未来接收附件 3 所列化学品运输的决定。公约还为缔约方之间就范围广泛的潜在危险化学品进行国际交流提供便利。该程序本身并非关于对一化学品使用进行禁止或限制的建议。粮农组织(FAO)和联合国环境规划署在公约实施中扮演重要角色。另见*多边环境协定(multilateral environment agreements)*、*贸易与环境(trade and environment)*。

Priority foreign country

重点国家

1988年《综合贸易与竞争法》第1302和1303节中使用的词语。两节通常分别称为超级301条款和特别301条款。超级301条款要求美国贸易代表办公室(USTR)向国会报告重点国家名单，这些国家所维持的一些做法如被取消将具有增加美国出口的最大潜力。特别301条款要求列出类似的国家名单，称为重点观察名单，这些国家拒绝充分和有效保护美国公司的知识产权。在此种情况下，重

property rights to United States firms. In this case, priority foreign countries are countries that have (a) the most onerous or ***egregious*** acts, policies or practices that deny adequate and effective intellectual property rights or deny fair and equitable ***market access*** to United States persons that rely upon ***intellectual property*** protection, and (b) that are not prepared to enter into bilateral or multilateral negotiations to find remedies. Once a country has been identified as a priority foreign country, USTR must start a ***Section 301*** investigation. Countries may be deleted from the list, but USTR must give reasons for doing so.

Priority foreign country practices: *see* ***Super 301***.

Priority watch list: *see* ***priority foreign country*** and ***Special 301***.

Prisoner's Dilemma: a device used to demonstrate that apparently rational micro-level decisions do not necessarily lead to rational macro-level outcomes. It is often used in game theory to explain the virtue of collective action as practised under the ***multilateral trading system***. The dilemma, which occurs in many variations, has in outline the following features. Several prisoners face separate interrogation. Each knows that if none of the others confess, it will result in freedom for all. Each also knows that if one of them confesses, but none of the others do, the one making the confession will get freedom. All of the others will receive severe sentences. If all confess, they will all be punished, but less severely than if only one confessed. The apparently rational decision by each individual prisoner therefore is to confess without bothering too much about the others. The moral is that they all are worse off by confessing than if they had been able to agree among themselves not to confess at all. This proposal was apparently first presented formally by A. W. Tucker in 1950, but it seems to have existed in some form or other long before that.

Prison labour: GATT Article XX(e) allows WTO members to adopt restrictions on the import of goods made by prison labour. Many countries have adopted laws enabling them to ban the import of such products, but the extent to which they enforce them varies. *See also* ***core labour standards*** and ***social dumping***.

Private cartel: *see* ***cartel***.

Private international cartel: a ***cartel*** with member firms in more than one economy or affecting markets in more than one jurisdiction.

Private international law: the field of law dealing with relations between individuals domiciled in different jurisdictions. As no two countries have the same legal system, the question arises as to which law should prevail. This area of the law is therefore also known as conflict of laws. *See also* ***public international law***.

Privatization: the process by which public assets, previously owned and managed by the state, are restructured as public entities with share capital being offered to the public. Governments sometimes retain a substantial share of the privatized enterprise. The expression is also sometimes used to describe the conversion of a publicly listed company into a private one. *See also* ***deregulation*** and ***re-regulation***.

点国家为：(a)采取最繁琐复杂或最恶劣的法律、政策或做法的国家，拒绝充分和有效的知识产权或拒绝对依靠知识产权保护的美国人给予公平和公正的市场准入；及(b)不准备通过双边或多边谈判寻求救济的国家。一旦一国被确定为重点国家，USTR即必须启动301条款调查。所列国家可以从名单上删除，但是USTR必须给出理由。

Priority foreign country practices
重点国家做法

见*超级 301 条款(Super 301)*。

Priority watch list
重点观察名单

见*重点国家(priority foreign country)*、*特别 301 条款(Special 301)*。

Prisoner's Dilemma
囚徒困境

用于证明看似理性的微观决策并不一定导致理性宏观层面结果的手段。在博弈论中经常用于解释如多边贸易体制下所采取的集体行动的优点。此种困境以多种形式出现，大致有下列特点：单独审讯几个囚犯，每个人都知道，如果其他人都不认罪，那么所有人都会获得自由；每个人也都知道，如果其中一人认罪，而其他人都不认罪，那么认罪的人就会获得自由，而其他人都会受到严厉惩罚。如果所有人认罪，他们都会受到惩罚，但惩罚比只有一人认罪的情形要轻。因此每一囚犯作出的看似理性的决策就是认罪，而不必过多考虑其他人。寓意在于，他们所有人认罪的后果都比他们之间达成一致不认罪的后果要差。这一理论显然是由A．W．塔克在1950年首次正式提出的，但似乎早在那之前就以某种形式存在。

Prison labour
监狱劳役

GATT第20条(e)款允许WTO成员对监狱劳役产品进口实行限制。许多国家通过法律禁止进口此类产品，但是法律执行的程度各不相同。另见*核心劳工标准(core labour standards)*、*社会倾销(social dumping)*。

Private cartel
私人卡特尔

见*卡特尔(cartel)*。

Private international cartel
国际私人卡特尔

指在一个以上经济体中拥有成员企业的卡特尔或影响一个以上司法管辖范围内的市场的卡特尔。

Private international law
国际私法

处理居住在不同管辖范围内的个人之间关系的法律领域。因为不存在两个国家拥有相同法律体系的情况，由此产生以哪种法律为准的问题。这一法律领域因此也被称为法律冲突。另见*国际公法(public international law)*。

Privatization
私有化

将以往由国家所有或管理的公共资产改组为向公众提供股本的公共实体的过程。政府有时会保留私有化企业的大部分股权。这一表述有时也用于指将一上市公司转为私营公司。另见*取消管制(deregulation)*、*重新管制(re-regulation)*。

Procedural protectionism: the abuse especially of ***anti-dumping measures***, countervailing duties or ***safeguards*** in a way that turns them into protectionist mechanisms.

Process and production method: PPM. A term used in discussions concerning ***trade and environment***. It deals with the environmental effects of processes by which goods and services are produced. A negative effect may occur in two main ways: (a) through the transformation of the product itself and (b) through a production process that does not affect the characteristics of the finished good. What is important is that the process and production resulting in the good is in itself deemed to determine how the finished good should be dealt with. Some have argued that a labelling system should be established to let the consumer know what processes have been used in the production of a good. This is the so-called PPM-labelling. *See also* ***non-product-related process and production***.

Process protectionism: a term used by I. M. Destler to describe a domestic system under which ***trade remedies*** can be invoked more easily than under the standard WTO rules. [Destler 1993]

Procès-verbal: the preparation of minutes, recording of agreed conclusions and other written descriptions of transactions occurring in a meeting.

PRO Committees: Established through ***UN/CEFACT*** recommendation No. 4. This recommendation, first adopted in 1974 and revised several times since, suggests that governments establish ***National Trade Facilitation Bodies*** (NTFB) as a component of trade policy formulation to improve their trade procedures. It also provides a non-exhaustive list of the interests that should be represented in an NTFB, such as importers, exporters, freight forwarders, carriers, customs, banks, insurance companies, etc. *See also* ***trade facilitation***. [tfig.unece.org]

Producer subsidy equivalent: PSE. A term used in agricultural negotiations. PSE is defined as the subsidy that would be necessary to compensate agricultural producers for removing government support. Expressed as a percentage, it is the ratio of the total value of transfers to producers as a result of government policies to total producer income. When this ratio is positive, the PSE indicates that the producer is receiving ***assistance***. When it is negative, the producer is taxed. *See also* ***consumer subsidy equivalent***.

Product-by-product negotiations: *see* ***item-by-item tariff negotiations***.

Product cycle theory: proposed by Raymond Vernon in 1966. It states that highly industrialized countries enjoy a ***comparative advantage*** in the research and development of new products because they have better access to capital and specialized human resources. The product cycle is assumed to consist of several stages, beginning with production in a small custom-oriented market, later becoming the domain of the multinational firm and reaching its apex with the manufacture of the product in lower-cost countries from where the product is re-exported to the market in which it had been developed originally. *See also* ***Heckscher-Ohlin theorem***. [Vernon 1966]

Product-mandating: a governmental requirement that a new investor export to certain countries or regions. *See also* ***export performance requirements***.

Procedural protectionism
程序性保护主义
特指滥用反倾销措施、反补贴税或保障措施，使上述措施成为保护主义机制。

Process and production method
工序和生产方法
PPM。在有关贸易与环境的讨论中使用的词语。指生产货物和服务的工序对环境的影响。消极影响主要以两种方式产生：(a)通过产品本身的转化；及(b)通过不影响制成品性质的生产工序。重要的是，制造产品的工序和生产本身被认为决定处理制成品的方式。一些人认为应该建立一种标签制度，使消费者知道货物生产过程中使用的工序。此即所谓的PPM标签。另见*与产品无关的工序和生产(non-product-related process and production)*。

Process protectionism
过程保护主义
I. M. 德斯勒用于描述相对于标准 WTO 规则更容易援引贸易救济的国内体制。

Procès-verbal
会议记录
起草纪要、记录议定结论及会议中所产生事项的其他书面说明。

PRO Committees
贸易便利化委员会
通过联合国贸易便利化与电子商务中心(UN/CEFACT)第4号建议设立。此项建议最初于1974年获得通过，此后多次修订，提议各国政府设立国家贸易便利化机构(NTFB)，作为贸易政策的组成部分，以改进贸易程序。建议还提供了一个NTFB中应代表的利害关系方的非详尽清单，例如进口商、出口商、货运代理、承运人、海关、银行、保险公司等。另见*贸易便利化(trade facilitation)*。

Producer subsidy equivalent
生产者补贴等值
PSE。农业谈判中使用的词语。PSE定义为因取消政府支持而对农业生产者进行补偿所需给予的补贴，以百分比表示，是根据政府政策对生产者转移的总价值与生产者总收入之比。当这一比率为正时，PSE表示生产者正在接受援助。当其为负值时，即表示对生产者进行征税。另见*消费者补贴等值(consumer subsidy equivalent)*。

Product-by-product negotiations
逐项产品谈判
见*逐税目关税谈判(item-by-item tariff negotiations)*。

Product cycle theory
产品周期理论
雷蒙德·弗农在1966年提出的理论。该理论指出，高度工业化的国家在新产品的研究和开发方面享有比较优势，因为这些国家可以更容易获得资本和专业化人力资源。产品周期假定包括若干阶段，始于小型的面向客户的市场中的生产，随后成为跨国公司的领域，在成本较低的国家中制造，并自这些国家向最初开发产品的市场复出口，从而达到周期顶点。另见*赫克舍尔-奥林定理(Heckscher-Ohlin theorem)*。

Product-mandating
产品强制要求
政府关于新投资者向特定国家或地区出口的要求。另见*出口实绩要求(export performance requirements)*。

Product-specific non-preferential rules of origin: refers to ***rules of origin*** applied by an importing country to goods traded under most-favoured-nation conditions. Such a system of rules prescribes product by product the conditions that have to be met for a product to be considered originating from a given country. An example of such rules is the requirement that chemical products may have to be the result of a chemical reaction in the exporting country. Mere mixing of components, such as adding a pigment, would not be enough.

Product-specific rule: a ***rule of origin*** that specifies how a particular product can meet the requirement for preferential treatment under the relevant ***preferential trade arrangement***. This is usually either a ***change in tariff classification*** (i.e. the extent to which the product must have changed from one state to another, such as wool turning into fabric), or a prescribed level of ***regional value content*** or a combination of the two. Many of the changes are straightforward in that they would be achieved in any case because of the required production process. Other changes are not so simple. Often they can only be understood in terms of the technical requirements by someone with deep experience in the production and trade of that product, and one suspects sometimes that they are not meant to bring about free trade too quickly.

Produit similaire: *see* ***like product***.

Professional services: a class of ***services*** usually provided by persons having specialist educational qualifications or training. Sometimes permission to offer such services also depends on membership of a professional body. Examples of professional services are those offered by accountants, architects, auditors, chemists, engineers, doctors, lawyers, librarians, pharmacists, physiotherapists, psychologists, surveyors and veterinarians. In ***NAFTA*** professional services are defined as services where the delivery requires specialized post-secondary education or equivalent training or experience, subject to a right to practice being granted by a party to the Agreement. Services provided by tradespersons or ship and aircrew members do not qualify as professional services.

Profit-shifting tariff: a concept in economic theory founded in ***mercantilism*** which proposes that it is possible to shift monopoly rents from a foreign country to one's own territory through the imposition of a tariff. The tariff would cream off the excess profit the foreign firm would otherwise be making. Economists have noted that the profit-shifting tariff is yet another mercantilist argument for restricting imports and promoting exports. *See also* ***balance of trade***.

Programme of Action for the Least-Developed Countries for the Decade 2011–2020: adopted in 2011 by the Fourth UN Conference on the Least-Developed Countries in Istanbul. It contains several principles, including that the ownership, leadership and primary responsibility for their development lies with the countries themselves. The objectives of the Programme are (a) achieve sustained, equitable and inclusive economic growth by strengthening the productive capacity of least-developed countries, (b) build human capacity by fostering sustained, equitable and inclusive human and social development, gender equality and the empowerment of women, (c) reduce the vulnerability of

Product-specific non-preferential rules of origin
特定产品非优惠原产地规则

指进口国对在最惠国条件下交易的货物所适用的原产地规则。此种规则体系规定了每一产品被视为原产于一指定国家所需满足的条件。例如，此类规则要求化工品应为在出口国中某种化学反应的结果，而组成部分的简单混合，例如添加颜料，不足以满足要求。

Product-specific rule
特定产品规则

规定一特定产品如何满足相关优惠贸易安排项下优惠待遇要求的原产地规则。通常为税则归类改变(即产品必须自一种形态转变为另一种形态，如羊毛变成织物)，或区域价值成分的规定水平，或两者的混合。许多改变是直接的，因其所需的生产过程无论如何要发生改变。其他的改变则没有那么简单。通常情况下，只有在该产品的生产和贸易方面具有丰富经验的人才能从技术要求角度理解这些改变，有观点怀疑有时这些改变并非意味着要使自由贸易过快实现。

Product similar
类似产品

见*同类产品(like product)*。

Professional services
专业服务

通常由具有专业学历或培训的人提供的一类服务。有时提供此类服务的许可还取决于一专业机构的成员资格。例如，会计师、建筑师、审计师、化学家、工程师、医生、律师、图书管理员、药剂师、理疗师、心理学家、测量师和兽医所提供的专业服务。在《北美自由贸易协定》(NAFTA)中，专业服务定义为受过专业高等教育或获得同等培训或经验的人所提供的服务，需由一协定参加方授予执业权利。由商人或船舶及机组人员提供的服务不符合专业服务的条件。

Profit-shifting tariff
利润转移关税

建立在重商主义基础上的经济理论概念，认为存在通过征收关税将外国的垄断租金转移至本国领土的可能。关税可以去除外国公司可以赚取的超额利润。经济学家指出，利润转移关税是重商主义限制进口和促进出口的又一理由。*另见贸易平衡(balance of trade)*。

Programme of Action for the Least-Developed Countries for the Decade 2011–2020
2011—2020年十年期支援最不发达国家行动纲领

2011年在伊斯坦布尔举行的第四次联合国最不发达国家问题会议上获得通过。包含若干原则，包括最不发达国家发展的自导权、领导权和基本责任由这些国家自身承担。行动纲领的目标为：(a)通过增强最不发达国家的生产能力以实现持续、公正和包容性经济增长；(b)通过促进持续、公正和有包容性人类和社会发展、性别平等和女性赋权以期建设人的能力；(c)通过增强最不发达

least-developed countries to economic, natural and environmental shocks and disasters through strengthening their resilience, (d) ensure enhanced financial resources, and (e) enhance good government at all levels by strengthening democratic processes, institutions and the rule of law. The Fifth UN Conference on the Least-Developed Countries will take place in March 2021 in Qatar. [unohrlls.org]

Programme of Action on the Establishment of a New International Economic Order: *see* ***New International Economic Order***.

Progressive liberalization: a principle enshrined in the ***General Agreement on Trade in Services***. It had its origin in the Punta del Este Declaration which launched the ***Uruguay Round***. There it was identified with ***transparency*** and economic growth as one of the aims for the forthcoming services negotiations. This principle was carried forward into Article XIX of the GATS which requires members to enter into successive rounds of negotiations at least every five years and no later than 1 January 2000. *See also* ***WTO built-in agenda***.

Progressivity and flexibility: virtually the same as ***special and differential treatment***. Its underlying principle is that developing countries should be able to take on new obligations selectively and in stages.

Prohibited subsidies: a concept used in the WTO ***Agreement on Subsidies and Countervailing Measures*** to denote subsidies contingent on export performance or subsidies contingent on the use of domestic rather than imported goods. WTO members are not allowed to maintain this type of subsidies. *See also* ***actionable subsidies***, ***Agreement on Trade-Related Investment Measures***, ***agricultural export subsidies***, ***local content requirements***, ***local content rules in broadcasting***, ***non-actionable subsidies*** and ***subsidies***.

Prohibitive tariff: a tariff rate set so high that it acts as a strong barrier to imports. *See also* ***protective tariff***.

Proportionality: a concept used to compare the trade costs of a measure with the benefits that the measure might have for other areas of governmental policy. The idea is that there should be some rational relationship between the cost impact of a measure and the benefits it is likely to produce. It is one measure that can be used for determining the necessity of a trade measure.

Proprietary information: *see* ***trade secrets***.

***Proprio motu*:** *Lat.* on one's own initiative. For example, Article 144.4 of the Japan–Singapore free-trade agreement states that the "arbitral tribunal may, at the request of a Party or *proprio motu*, select, in consultation with the parties, no fewer than two scientific or technical experts who shall assist the arbitral tribunal".

Pro-rating: used in a proposal in the ***Doha Development Agenda*** negotiations on agriculture to ensure that the triggering of the Special Safeguard Mechanism (SSM) should take into account an earlier use of the SSM, assuming that this was the case. The reason is that an earlier imposition of safeguards may have led to a lower trend in imports, and that this might exaggerate an import surge in a later year.

国家的韧性以减少其面对经济、自然和环境冲击和灾害的脆弱性；(d)保证增加财政资源；以及(e)通过强化民主进程、机构和法治，加强各级政府的良好治理。第五次联合国最不发达国家问题会议定于2021年3月在卡塔尔举行。

Programme of Action on the Establishment of a New International Economic Order
建立新的国际经济秩序行动纲领

见*国际经济新秩序(New International Economic Order)*。

Progressive liberalization
逐步自由化

《服务贸易总协定》中所包含的一项原则。源自发起乌拉圭回合的《埃斯特角城宣言》。与透明度和经济增长一同作为即将开展的服务贸易谈判的目标。该原则纳入《服务贸易总协定》第 19 条之中，该条要求成员至少每 5 年且不迟于 2000 年 1 月 1 日起进行连续回合的谈判。另见 *WTO 既定议程(WTO built-in agenda)*。

Progressivity and flexibility
渐进性和灵活性

实际上与特殊和差别待遇同义。基本原则是，发展中国家应能够有选择地分阶段承担新义务。

Prohibited subsidies
禁止性补贴

WTO《补贴与反补贴措施协定》中使用的概念，指视出口实绩，或视国内货物而非进口货物使用情况而给予的补贴。WTO 成员不允许维持此类补贴。另见*可诉补贴(actionable subsidies)*、*与贸易有关的投资措施协定(Agreement on Trade-Related Investment Measures)*、*农产品出口补贴(agricultural export subsidies)*、*当地含量要求(local content requirements)*、*广播中的本地内容规则(local content rules in broadcasting)*、*不可诉补贴(non-actionable subsidies)*、*补贴(subsidies)*。

Prohibitive tariff
禁止性关税

设定极高而对进口构成巨大障碍的关税。另见*保护性关税(protective tariff)*。

Proportionality
相称性

用于比较一项措施的贸易成本与该项措施对政府政策其他领域可能产生利益的概念。此种观点认为，一项措施的成本影响与其可能产生的利益之间应该存在某种合理关系。是用于确定贸易措施必要性的衡量标准。

Proprietary information
专有信息

见*商业秘密(trade secrets)*。

Proprio motu
自行

拉丁语。意为自行。例如，《日本—新加坡自由贸易协定》第144.4条规定，“仲裁庭经与当事方磋商，可应一缔约方请求或自行选择不少于2名科学或技术专家协助仲裁庭”。

Pro-rating
按比例分配

多哈发展议程农业谈判中的一项提案，以保证特殊保障机制的触发应考虑以往使用该机制的情况，假设存在此种情况。理由是，较早实施的保障措施可能导致进口的下降趋势，且可能夸大下一年的进口激增。

Prospect theory: the proposition, developed by D. Kahneman and A. Tversky in 1979, that in making decisions, people overemphasize small probabilities of success and underemphasize large probabilities of success. Or, as Kenneth Dam puts it, "groups work harder to avoid a loss than to gain a benefit". *See also* ***conservative social welfare function***. [Dam 2001, Kahneman and Tversky 1979]

Protected appellation of origin: an ***appellation of origin*** protected under the ***Lisbon Agreement***. This Agreement defines "appellation of origin" as "the geographical name of a country, region, or locality, which serves to designate a product originating therein, the quality and characteristics of which are due exclusively or essentially to the geographical environment, including natural and human factors". The Agreement gives protection against any usurpation or imitation, even if the true origin of the product is indicated, or if the appellation is in translated form, accompanied by terms such as "kind", "type", "imitation", or the like. Recognition of a protected appellation is usually done through a law, decree or other administrative act following an investigation of the claim for recognition. *See also* ***geographical indications*** and ***Lisbon Agreement***. [Audier 2000; WIPO SCT/8/4]

Protected designation of origin: PDO. A ***European Union*** system for protecting the name of a product originating in a specific region and following a particular traditional production process. Product names registered as PDO have very strong links to the place in which they are made. They include food, agricultural products and wine. Every part of the production, processing and preparation process must take place in the specific region. In the case of wines the grapes have to come exclusively from the geographical area where the wine is made. A label indicating PDO is mandatory for food and agricultural products, but optional for wine. *See also* ***appellations of origin***, ***geographical indications***, ***protected geographical indication*** and ***traditional speciality guaranteed***. [ec.europa.eu]

Protected geographical indication: PGI. A ***European Union*** system for protecting the name of a product originating in a specific region. A PGI emphasizes the relationship between the geographic region and the name of the product where a particular quality, reputation or characteristic can be attributed to its geographical origin. PGI can be given to food, agricultural products and wines. For most products at least one of the stages of production, processing or preparation takes place in the nominated region. For wine at least 85 per cent of the grapes have to come exclusively from the geographical area where the wine is made. A label indicating PGI is mandatory for food and agricultural products, but optional for wines. *See also* ***appellations of origin***, ***geographical indications***, ***protected designation of origin*** and ***traditional speciality guaranteed***. [ec.europa.eu]

Protection: the extent to which domestic producers and their products are shielded from the competition of the international market. The incidence or cost of protection can be measured or estimated with a high degree of accuracy. ***Tariffs*** are the starting point in the case of goods, but the matter becomes more

Prospect theory
前景理论

D．卡内曼和A．特沃斯基于1979年提出的命题，即在作出决定时，人们过分强调成功的小概率，而不重视成功的大概率。或如肯尼斯·达姆所说，“团队努力工作以避免损失而非获得利益。”另见*保守社会福利函数(conservative social welfare function)*。

Protected appellation of origin
受保护的原产地名称

根据《里斯本协定》保护的原产地名称。该协定将“原产地名称”定义为“指一个国家、地区或地方的地理名称，用于指示一项产品来源于该地，其质量或特征完全或主要取决于地理环境，包括自然和人为因素”。该协定旨在防止任何假冒和仿冒，即使标明了产品的真实来源或者使用名称的翻译形式或附加‘类’‘式’‘样’‘仿’字样或类似字样。对受保护原产地名称的承认通常需在对该承认主张进行调查后，通过法律、法令或其他行政行为完成。另见*地理标志(geographical indications)*、*里斯本协定(Lisbon Agreement)*。

Protected designation of origin
原产地命名保护

PDO。欧盟保护源自特定地区并遵循特定传统生产工序的产品名称的制度。进行PDO注册的产品名称与其产地密切关联，包括食品、农产品和葡萄酒。生产、加工和制备流程的每一部分都必须在特定地区进行。就葡萄酒而言，葡萄必须全部来自于酿造葡萄酒的地理区域。强制要求食品和农产品加贴PDO标签，葡萄酒则为选择性加贴。另见*原产地名称(appellations of origin)*、*地理标志(geographical indications)*、*地理标志保护(protected geographical indication)*、*注册传统特色产品(traditional specialty guaranteed)*。

Protected geographical indication
地理标志保护

PGI。欧盟保护源自一特定地区的产品名称的制度。PGI强调地理区域与产品名称之间的关系，特定质量、声誉或特点可归因于产品的地理来源。PGI可授予食品、农产品和葡萄酒。对于大多数产品，生产、加工或制备阶段中至少一个需要在指定地区进行。对于葡萄酒，至少85%的葡萄需全部来自酿造葡萄酒的地理区域。强制要求食品和农产品加贴PGI标签，葡萄酒则为选择性加贴。另见*原产地名称(appellations of origin)*、*地理标志(geographical indications)*、*原产地命名保护(protected designation of origin)*、*注册传统特色产品(traditional specialty guaranteed)*。

Protection
保护

国内生产者及其产品免受国际市场竞争影响的程度。保护的发生或成本可以进行高精度衡量或评估。对于货物，关税是起点，但如关税伴有非关税措施，

complicated where tariffs are accompanied by ***non-tariff measures***, or if protection consists entirely of non-tariff measures, or government regulation in the case of services. Methods are available also for estimating the cost of protection of service industries, but these are rather less accurate than the ones for goods. Protection differs considerably from ***protectionism***. *See also* ***assistance***, ***bounty***, ***effective rate of assistance***, ***international contestability of markets*** and ***subsidy***.

Protectionism: economic policies which prevent the exposure of domestic producers to the rigours of the international market, often under the guise of some other policy objective. The basic means for achieving this are ***tariffs***, ***subsidies***, ***voluntary restraint arrangements*** and other ***non-tariff measures***, with an emphasis on the less transparent measures. More complex cases can involve alleged cultural, ***sanitary and phytosanitary measures***, environmental and other considerations. Protectionism can also be promoted through the vigorous use of ***contingent protection***. In most cases, protectionism merely delays the inevitable adjustment of inefficient industries to the market. *See also* ***cultural identity***, ***structural adjustment*** and ***trade and environment***.

Protection of geographical names: *see* ***Agreement on Trade-Related Aspects of Intellectual Property Rights***, ***appellation d'origine contrôlée***, ***appellations of origin***, ***certification mark***, ***collective mark***, ***extension of protection for geographical indications***, ***Geneva Act of the Lisbon Agreement on Appellations of Origin and Geographical Indications***, ***geographical indications***, ***indications of source***, ***Lisbon Agreement***, ***Madrid Agreement for the Repression of False or Deceptive Indications of Source on Goods***, ***Organization for an International Geographical Indications Network***, ***Paris Convention***, ***protected appellation of origin***, ***protected designation of origin***, ***registered geographical indication***, ***semi-generic geographical indications***, ***Stresa Convention*** and ***traditional speciality guaranteed***.

Protective tariff: a ***tariff*** designed to shelter part of the national productive capacity from the full impact of foreign competition. *See also* ***protection***, ***protectionism*** and ***revenue tariff***.

Protocol: a protocol is a ***treaty*** drafted to supplement another treaty or convention. It contains all the elements found in other types of treaties (preamble, definitions, signature, ratification, entry into force, etc.), and it shares the same legally binding quality. A protocol must be consistent with its parent treaty. If a conflict arises, the parent treaty prevails over the protocol. A protocol is needed each time the results of multilateral negotiations have to be added to the WTO instruments, for example the additional agreements attached to the ***General Agreement on Trade in Services***. The Second Protocol deals with the 1995 commitments on financial services. The Third Protocol deals with movement of natural persons. The Fourth Protocol deals with telecommunications services, and the Fifth Protocol deals with financial services. Note, however, that some instruments designated as protocols are treaties in their own right.

或保护全部由非关税措施构成或服务领域的政府规章，则情形会变得复杂。同样有方法估算服务领域的保护成本，但准确度要低于对货物的估算。保护与保护主义有很大差别。另见*援助(assistance)*、*津贴(bounty)*、*有效援助率(effective rate of assistance)*、*市场的国际竞争性(international contestability of markets)*、*补贴(subsidy)*。

Protectionism

保护主义

防止国内生产者受到国际市场严峻影响的经济政策，经常以其他一些政策目标作为伪装。实现此目的的基本手段为关税、补贴、自愿限制安排和其他非关税措施，着重使用透明度较差的措施。更复杂的情况可能涉及所谓的文化措施、卫生与植物卫生措施、环境措施及其他考虑因素。保护主义也可以通过大量使用紧急保护加以实施。在大多数情况下，保护主义只是延缓了低效率产业所不可避免的对市场的调整。另见*文化特性(cultural identity)*、*结构性调整(structural adjustment)*、*贸易与环境(trade and environment)*。

Protection of geographical names

地理名称保护

见*与贸易有关的知识产权协定(Agreement on Trade-Related Aspects of Intellectual Property Rights)*、*原产地命名控制(appellation d'origine contrôlée)*、*原产地名称(appellations of origin)*、*认证标志(certification mark)*、*集体商标(collective mark)*、*地理标志保护扩大(extension of protection for geographical indications)*、*原产地名称和地理标志里斯本协定日内瓦文本(Geneva Act of the Lisbon Agreement on Appellations of Origin and Geographical Indications)*、*地理标志(geographical indications)*、*产地标志(indications of source)*、*里斯本协定(Lisbon Agreement)*、*制止商品来源虚假或欺骗性标记马德里协定(Madrid Agreement for the Repression of False or Deceptive Indications of Source on Goods)*、*国际地理标志网络组织(Organization for an International Geographical Indications Network)*、*巴黎公约(Paris Convention)*、*受保护的原产地名称(protected appellation of origin)*、*原产地命名保护(protected designation of origin)*、*注册地理标志(registered geographical indication)*、*半通用地理标志(semi-generic geographical indications)*、*斯特雷萨公约(Stresa Convention)*、*注册传统特色产品(traditional specialty guaranteed)*。

Protective tariff

保护性关税

旨在保护国家部分生产能力免受外国竞争全面影响的关税。另见*保护(protection)*、*保护主义(protectionism)*、*财政关税(revenue tariff)*。

Protocol

议定书

为补充另一条约或公约而起草的条约。包含其他类型条约所含全部要素(序言、定义、签署、批准、生效等)，并具有相同法律约束力。议定书必须与其母条约相一致。如产生冲突，母条约优先于议定书。每轮多边谈判的结果需要以议定书形式纳入WTO法律文书之中。例如《服务贸易总协定》所附的附加协定，第二议定书涉及1995年金融服务承诺，第三议定书涉及自然人流动，第四议定书涉及电信服务，第五议定书涉及金融服务。但需要注意的是，一些被称为议定书的文书本身即为条约。

Protocol of accession: the instrument which sets out the terms and conditions under which a country or customs territory becomes a member of the WTO, or for that matter, other international organizations. In the WTO, these protocols are largely standardized, but they sometimes reflect particular circumstances of the acceding member. *See also* ***accession***.

Protocol of Ouro Preto: *see* ***Mercosur***.

Protocol of Provisional Application: PPA. This was adopted by the original members of the ***GATT*** in 1947 to apply the Agreement provisionally pending a decision to do so permanently. That decision never was taken. The PPA is not part of the ***GATT 1994***.

Protocol of Tegucigalpa: *see* ***Central American Integration System***.

Provisional anti-dumping duties: duties or charges imposed once it becomes evident that there is a *prima facie* case of ***dumping***. The WTO rules on ***anti-dumping measures*** permit governments to impose provisional anti-dumping duties under three conditions. These are that (a) a proper investigation has been initiated, (b) a preliminary affirmative determination has been made of dumping and consequent ***injury*** to domestic industry, and (c) the authorities deem provisional duties necessary to prevent injury being caused during the investigation period. Provisional anti-dumping duties may not exceed the provisionally estimated ***margin of dumping***. The WTO rules stress, however, that asking for a cash or bond security would be preferable. In principle, provisional anti-dumping duties should be imposed for no longer than four months, though this may be extended to up to nine months in some circumstances.

Provisional countervailing duties: once a government has initiated an investigation concerning alleged subsidies applied by another WTO member, it may impose provisional countervailing measures. The three main conditions to be fulfilled are (a) that the investigation has been initiated according to the rules, (b) that a preliminary finding has been made that a ***subsidy*** exists and that it is causing ***injury*** to domestic industry, and (c) that there is a view that further injuries would occur if subsidization was maintained during the remainder of the investigation. Provisional countervailing measures may be in the form of cash deposits or bonds equal to the amount of subsidization. Provisional measures cannot be applied earlier than sixty days after the start of an investigation, and they must not remain in force for more than four months.

Provisional safeguard measures: may be applied under the WTO ***Agreement on Safeguards*** if a preliminary determination shows that increased imports have caused or are threatening to cause serious ***injury***. Provisional safeguard measures may be applied for no longer than 200 days. WTO members have to go through the full safeguards procedures if they want to continue the measures beyond that limit. Many ***free-trade agreements*** have a similar provision in the articles governing bilateral safeguards.

Prudence: *see* ***prudential regulation***.

Prudential regulation: in ***financial services***, terms used to describe an objective of market regulation by authorities to protect investors and depositors or to

Protocol of accession
加入议定书

规定一国或一关税领土成为WTO成员或成为其他国际组织成员的条款或条件的文书。在WTO中，这些议定书很大程度上是标准化的，但有时会反映加入成员的特殊情况。另见*加入(accession)*。

Protocol of Ouro Preto
欧鲁普雷图议定书

见*南方共同市场(Mercosur)*。

Protocol of Provisional Application
临时适用议定书

PPA。GATT创始缔约方在1947年为在适用GATT的永久性决定作出之前临时适用GATT而通过的议定书。永久性决定从未作出。PPA不属GATT 1994的一部分。

Protocol of Tegucigalpa
特古西加尔巴议定书

见*中美洲一体化体系(Central American Integration System)*。

Provisional anti-dumping duties
临时反倾销税

一旦表明存在倾销的初步证据即征收的关税或费用。WTO关于反倾销措施的规则允许政府在三个条件下征收临时反倾销税。即：(a)已启动适当调查；(b)已对倾销及由此对国内产业造成损害作出初步肯定裁定；以及(c)主管机关判断征收临时反倾销税对防止在调查期间造成损害是必要的。临时反倾销税不得超过临时估算的倾销幅度。但WTO规则强调，要求交纳现金保证金或保函更为可取。原则上临时反倾销税的实施不超过4个月，但某些情况下可延长至9个月。

Provisional countervailing duties
临时反补贴税

一旦一政府已经发起关于另一WTO成员实施的被指控补贴的调查，即可征收临时反补贴税。需要满足的三个主要条件为：(a)已依照规定发起调查；(b)已作出关于存在补贴和补贴进口产品对国内产业造成损害的初步肯定裁定；以及(c)认为如在调查的剩余期间内继续维持补贴，将会造成进一步损害。临时反补贴措施可采取等于补贴金额的现金保证金或保函的形式。采取临时措施不得早于发起调查后的60天，实施期限不得超过4个月。

Provisional safeguard measures
临时保障措施

如初步裁定表明，增加的进口已造成或威胁造成严重损害，则可根据WTO《保障措施协定》实施临时保障措施。临时保障措施的实施期限不得超过200天。如果WTO成员想在该期限后继续实施，即需要通过完整的保障措施程序。许多自由贸易协定在管辖双边保障措施的条款中有类似规定。

Prudence
审慎

见*审慎监管(prudential regulation)*。

Prudential regulation
审慎监管

在金融服务中，该词用于描述主管部门为保护投资者和储户或为避免不稳定

avoid instability or crises. Prudential measures require banks and insurance companies to maintain certain capital reserves and mandatory asset ratios. They have to meet strict reporting requirements. There is no agreement on what an optimal level of prudential control might be. Opinion is in favour of clear and enforceable prudential measures, but they have not prevented some spectacular exploits by financial services firms or company crashes. Prudential measures are not normally considered impediments to trade in financial services, and they do not have to be listed under the GATS as measures capable of affecting ***market access*** and ***national treatment***.

PSI: ***preshipment inspection***. The practice of employing specialized private companies to check shipment details of goods ordered overseas, i.e. price, quantity, quality, etc. *See also* ***Agreement on Preshipment Inspection***.

Public body: one of the definitions of a subsidy established by the ***Agreement on Subsidies and Countervailing Measures*** is that of a financial contribution by any public body in the territory of a member. The term "public body" is not further defined. There is little argument that statutory authorities and the like are public bodies. There is, however, a view that ***state-owned enterprises*** should also be considered public bodies. If this expansion of the definition were adopted, it would widen considerably the range of actions that could be subject to an investigation leading to possible countervailing duties. [Messenger 2017]

Public cartel: *see* ***cartel***.

Public interest test: the WTO ***Agreement on Safeguards*** requires countries starting an investigation whether ***safeguards*** are justified to consider, among other matters, whether the application of a safeguard measure would be in the public interest. The term is not defined further, but the agreement refers to importers, exporters and other interested parties. The public interest therefore goes beyond the interests of the industry petitioning for an investigation. Some have advocated that the public interest should be one of the factors to be considered before ***anti-dumping measures*** can be taken. This might include the impact of the measures on users of the product, the impact on consumers, effect on competition in the marketplace, efficient allocation of resources, etc. The public interest is not identical to the ***national interest***, but one assumes that an effective public interest provision would similarly permit the relevant authority to suspend all or part of a proposed anti-dumping measure. Some anti-dumping laws already allow for or require a public interest test. Such tests are also administered in other areas of public administration, such as ***competition policy***. *See also* ***Community interest clause***. [Leclerc 1999, Marceau 1994, Steele 1996]

Public international law: the law concerning relations between states or between states and international organizations. *See also* ***International Court of Justice*** and ***private international law***.

Public procurement: *see* ***government procurement***.

Public stockholding for food security: public reserves mostly of cereals for used in emergencies, to promote ***food security*** and to create an environment for price

或危机的市场监管目标。审慎措施要求银行和保险公司保持一定的资本准备金和强制性资产比率。对于最佳审慎控制水平并无一致意见。倾向于支持明确和可执行的审慎措施，而这些措施并未能防止金融服务企业巧取豪夺或公司破产。审慎措施通常不被视为金融服务贸易的障碍，也不必作为能够影响市场准入和国民待遇的措施而列在《服务贸易总协定》项下。

PSI

装运前检验

雇佣专业私营公司检查海外订购货物的装运细节，如价格、数量、质量等。另见*装运前检验协定(Agreement on Preshipment Inspection)*。

Public body

公共机构

《补贴与反补贴措施协定》中确定的补贴的一项定义是一成员领土内任何公共机构的财政资助。“公共机构”一词并未进一步定义。官方机构及类似部门属于公共机构并无太大争议，而有观点认为国有企业也应被视为公共机构。如果这一扩大的定义被采用，将大幅度扩大接受可能导致征收反补贴税调查行动的范围。

Public cartel

公共卡特尔

见*卡特尔(cartel)*。

Public interest test

公共利益测试

WTO《保障措施协定》要求发起关于保障措施是否合理的调查的国家，除其他事项外，考虑保障措施的实施是否符合公共利益。该词未进一步定义，但协定提及进口商、出口商和其他利害关系方。因此，公共利益超出了申请进行调查的行业的利益。一些人主张，在采取反倾销措施之前，应将公共利益作为考虑因素之一。可能包括该措施对产品用户的影响、对消费者的影响、对市场竞争的影响以及资源的有效分配等。公共利益不同于国家利益，但有人认为有效的公共利益条款同样允许有关部门中止全部或部分拟议的反倾销措施。一些反倾销法已经允许或要求进行公共利益测试。此类测试也在公共管理的其他领域实施，例如竞争政策。另见*共同体利益条款(Community interest clause)*。

Public international law

国际公法

关于国家之间关系或国家与国际组织之间关系的法律。另见*国际法院(International Court of Justice)*、*国际私法(private international law)*。

Public procurement

公共采购

见*政府采购(government procurement)*。

Public stockholding for food security

粮食安全公共储备

用于紧急情况的以谷物为主的公共储备，以促进粮食安全和创造价格稳定的

stabilization. Such stockholdings can be extensive to maintain, they have to be rotated regularly, and they therefore can have an influence on the local market. In the WTO system such stockholdings are considered to fall under ***amber box*** domestic support if they are above 10 per cent of the value of production (the *de minimis* level) for agriculture considered to distort trade. If this is the case, they are subject to reduction commitments. The ***Bali WTO Ministerial Conference*** of 2013 decided that, until a permanent solution could be worked out, developing countries could continue to operate such stockholdings provided that they supplied up-to-date information on what was happening. [www.wto.org]

Public telecommunications transport network: defined in the ***Annex on Telecommunications*** to the ***General Agreement on Trade in Services*** as "the public telecommunications infrastructure which permits telecommunications between and among defined termination points".

Public telecommunications transport services: defined in the ***Annex on Telecommunications*** to the ***General Agreement on Trade in Services*** as "any telecommunications transport service required, explicitly or in effect, by a Member to be offered to the public generally. Such services may include, *inter alia*, telegraph, telephone, telex, and data transmission typically involving the real-time transmission of customer-supplied information between two or more points without any end-to-end change in the form or content of the customer's information".

Punitive tariff: a tariff set so high, often as a form of ***retaliation***, that in most cases trade no longer occurs under it. It has the same effect as a ***prohibitive tariff***.

Punta del Este Declaration: the Ministerial Declaration formally launching the ***Uruguay Round*** on 25 September 1986.

Purchase abroad: the same as ***consumption abroad***, one of the ***modes of services delivery***.

Pure export cartel: *see* ***cartel***.

环境。维持此类储备可能需要很大体量，且需要定期轮换，因此可以对本地市场产生影响。在WTO体系中，如果此类储备超过农业产值的10%(微量允许水平)即被认为具有贸易扭曲作用，则被视为属黄箱国内支持。如属此种情况，即受到削减承诺的约束。2013年巴厘岛WTO部长级会议决定，在永久解决办法制定之前，发展中国家可以继续运营此类储备，只要它们提交最新情况的通报。

Public telecommunications transport network

公共电信传输网络

《服务贸易总协定》中的《关于电信服务的附件》中将其定义为“可在规定的两个或多个网络端接点之间进行通信的公共电信基础设施”。

Public telecommunications transport services

公共电信传输服务

《服务贸易总协定》中的《关于电信服务的附件》将其定义为“一成员明确要求或实际上要求向公众普遍提供的任何电信传输服务。此类服务可特别包括电报、电话、电传和数据传输，其典型特点是在两点或多点之间对客户提供的信息进行实时传输，而客户信息的形式或内容无任何端到端的变化”。

Punitive tariff

惩罚性关税

作为一种报复形式，将税率设置极高而导致大多数情况下无贸易发生的关税。与禁止性关税具有相同效果。

Punta del Este Declaration

埃斯特角城宣言

1986年9月25日正式发起乌拉圭回合谈判的部长宣言。

Purchase abroad

境外购买

与境外消费相同，一种服务提供模式。

Pure export cartel

纯出口卡特尔

见*卡特尔(cartel)*。

QRs: *see* ***quantitative restrictions***.

Quadrilaterals: established in 1981 as periodic ***trade policy*** talks between the United States, the ***European Community***, Japan and Canada. Now also applied to the four acting together. Sometimes also used for Australia, India, Japan and the United States. Often shortened to Quad. *See also* ***minilateralism***.

Qualifying area: one of the criteria used in the administration of ***rules of origin***. It is the territory within which a product must have been produced or from which it must have been exported to enjoy preferential treatment in the importing country. For ***free-trade areas*** this is usually the territory of the parties to the agreement. Under other schemes, such as the ***GSP***, the qualifying area may include other developing countries. This criterion may have to be met together with others, such as the ***regional value content*** or ***substantial transformation***. *See also* ***pan-Euro-Mediterranean cumulation*** and ***pan-European cumulation system***.

Qualifying value content: in the administration of ***rules of origin*** the same as ***regional value content***. It denotes the point at which a product is considered to be the product of another party because enough value has been added to it. The product is accordingly eligible for preferential customs treatment.

Quantitative easing: an expansionary monetary policy under which a central bank releases large amounts of money through the purchase of government securities and other assets to stimulate the economy. This step is usually taken when interest rates are at or near zero, and the option of stimulating the economy through lowering interest rates is no longer available or effective.

Quantitative export restrictions: *see* ***export quotas*** and ***voluntary restraint arrangement***.

Quantitative restrictions: specific limits on the quantity or value of goods that can be imported (or exported) during a given period. Article XI of the GATT proscribes the use of quantitative restrictions, subject to specified exceptions, including those listed in Article XX which covers ***general exceptions***. *See also* ***export quotas***, ***import quotas*** and ***tariff quota***.

Quantum leap: in physics an abrupt change of an electron from one energy level to another. These leaps are unimaginably small. In common parlance, however, a "quantum leap" is any abrupt or dramatic advance, usually in a positive sense.

Quarantine measures: *see* ***sanitary and phytosanitary measures***.

Quint: consisted of the agriculture ministers of Australia, Canada and Japan, the United States Secretary of Agriculture and the European Commissioner for Agriculture. The group met during the ***Uruguay Round***.

QRs
数量限制

见*数量限制(quantitative restrictions)*。

Quadrilaterals
4方

1981年成立，美国、欧洲共同体、日本和加拿大之间进行的定期贸易政策会谈。现在也适用于4方联合行动。有时也用于指澳大利亚、印度、日本和美国。通常缩写为Quad。另见*小多边主义(minilateralism)*。

Qualifying area
合格区域

原产地规则管理中使用的标准。指生产或出口可以享受进口国优惠待遇的产品的领土。对于自由贸易区，通常为协定参加方的领土。在其他制度下，例如普惠制(GSP)，合格区域可以包括其他发展中国家。这一标准可能需要与其他标准一同得到满足，例如区域价值成分或实质性改变。另见*泛欧—地中海累积(pan-Euro Mediterranean cumulation)*、*泛欧累积制度(pan-European cumulation system)*。

Qualifying value content
合格价值成分

在原产地规则管理中与区域价值成分同义。指一产品在增加足够多的价值后可被视为另一参加方的产品的点。该产品因此有资格享受海关优惠待遇。

Quantitative easing
量化宽松

一种扩张型货币政策，据此中央银行通过购买政府债券和其他资产以释放大量货币从而刺激经济。这一步骤通常在利率为零或接近于零且通过降低利率以刺激经济的选择不再可行或不再有效的情况下采取。

Quantitative export restrictions
出口数量限制

见*出口配额(export quotas)*、*自愿限制安排(voluntary restraint arrangement)*。

Quantitative restrictions
数量限制

在一指定期限内可以进口(或出口)货物的数量或价值的特定限制。GATT第11条禁止使用数量限制，但规定了特定例外，包括第20条一般例外中所列情况。另见*出口配额(export quotas)*、*进口配额(import quotas)*、*关税配额(tariff quota)*。

Quantum leap
量子飞跃

物理学中电子从一个能级突然变化到另一个能级的情况，这种飞跃小到难以想象。但是通常“量子飞跃”指任何突然或戏剧性的进步，通常具有积极意义。

Quarantine measures
检疫措施

见*卫生与植物卫生措施(sanitary and phytosanitary measures)*。

Quint
5方

由澳大利亚、加拿大、日本和美国的农业部长及欧盟农业委员组成。在乌拉圭回合期间举行会议。

Quota: a restriction on the amount of a good that may be imported by a country or exported from it. *See also* ***import licensing***.

Quota-hopping: the transfer of production of products subject to an export quota from a country with a limited quota availability to one where a quota may be obtained more easily. *See also* ***rules of origin***.

Quota modulation: when a WTO member applies a ***safeguard*** on a product subject to ***import quotas***, the normal expectation would be that any restrictions on imports would more or less preserve the allocated shares. The ***Agreement on Safeguards*** makes it possible, however, to depart from this principle (i.e. to modulate a quota), but only in cases of ***serious injury***. Conditions are (a) that imports from certain members have increased disproportionately, (b) the departure can be justified, and (c) the change is equitable to all suppliers of the product concerned.

Quota right: the right granted to an importer or exporter to make use of the more favourable trading conditions available under a defined ***quota***.

QWERTY principle: not an accepted trade policy concept, but illustrative of the dangers of accepting uncritically established ideas. It was first proposed by the economic historian Paul Davis in 1982 and popularized greatly in the 1990s by Paul Krugman. The principle takes its starting point from the QWERTY layout of computer keyboards which dates back to the earliest manual typewriters. The latter apparently were likely to jam when the typing was too quick, and the QWERTY layout forced the typist to slow down (note that there is argument whether this is really true). Later mechanical improvements made the QWERTY layout unnecessary, but inertial thinking ensured its survival into the computer age, because it had become "locked in". More recently, the validity of the assertion that the QWERTY layout is an inferior solution has been questioned, and it may indeed be no more than a myth. Be that as it may, Krugman notes that the emergence of the QWERTY layout leads one to reject the idea that markets invariably lead the economy to a unique best solution, and that in fact the outcome of market competition often depends crucially on historical accident. The principle also stands for the idea that investigating the validity of long-held beliefs and practices is intrinsically worthwhile. *See also* ***conventional wisdom*** and ***vestigial thought***.

Quota

配额

一国可以进口或出口货物数量的限制。另见*进口许可(import licensing)*。

Quota-hopping

逃避配额

将受出口配额管辖产品的生产从配额有限的国家转移到更易获得配额的国家。另见*原产地规则(rules of origin)*。

Quota modulation

配额调整

如一WTO成员对进口配额管辖的产品实施保障措施，通常的期望会是，任何对进口的限制均会或多或少保留所分配的份额。而《保障措施协定》使背离这一原则(即调整配额)成为可能，但仅限于严重损害的情况。条件为：(a)自某些成员的进口增长不成比例；(b)偏离的理由是正当的；以及(c)变更对有关产品的所有供应商是公正的。

Quota right

配额权

给予进口商或出口商在规定配额项下利用更优惠贸易条件的权利。

QWERTY principle

QWERTY键盘原则

并非公认的贸易政策概念，但用以说明不加批判地接受既定想法的危险性。首先由经济历史学家保罗·戴维斯在1982年提出，在20世纪90年代由保罗·克鲁格曼推广。该原则源于计算机键盘的QWERTY布局，这种布局可追溯到以前的手动打字机，如果打字速度过快，手动打字机有可能卡住，而QWERTY布局迫使打字员放慢速度(这种说法的真实性存在争议)。后来的机械改进使QWERTY布局不再是必要的，但惯性思维使其延续到计算机时代，因为其已被“锁定”。最近，人们对QWERTY布局属于劣质解决方案的断言的有效性提出质疑，它可能只不过是一个神话。尽管如此，克鲁格曼指出，QWERTY布局的出现使人们拒绝这样一种观点，即市场必然会使经济找到独一无二的最佳解决方案，而事实上，市场竞争的结果往往很大程度取决于历史偶然。这一原则也代表调查长期持有的信仰和做法的有效性从本质上是值得的。另见*传统智慧(conventional wisdom)*、*残余思想(vestigial thought)*。

R

Race-to-the-bottom argument: expresses the fear that the need to compete with imports from countries with low labour costs and lower labour standards will reduce wages and labour conditions in the developed countries. This argument forms part of the rationale for discussions on a ***social clause*** and ***trade and labour standards***. A similar argument has been made in relation to environmental standards where it is thought that lower environmental requirements in some countries could give them a competitive advantage. *See also* ***core labour standards***, ***globalization***, ***social dumping***, ***trade and environment***, ***wage-differential argument*** and ***worker rights***.

Rapid Credit Facility: *see* ***Poverty Reduction and Growth Trust***.

Ratchet mechanism: refers to provisions on trade in services in some ***free-trade agreements*** whereby autonomous liberalization measures by a member between negotiating sessions are automatically included in that member's schedule of commitments under the agreement in question. *See also* ***non-conforming measures***.

Ratchet mechanism for non-conforming measures: free-trade agreements using negative lists for ***cross-border trade in services*** or ***investment*** usually contain a list of ***non-conforming measures*** (measures that for one reason or another do not yet conform to all the rules of the agreement). Such agreements sometimes contain a ***ratchet mechanism*** which has the effect of locking in any improvement or liberalization made after the agreement has entered into force. This process ensures that actual conditions prevail at any time, and that it is not necessary to wait for review sessions to achieve liberalization in these cases. Nor is it possible for the liberalization to be reversed easily.

Rational ignorance: a decision by voters not to spend time or money on getting to understand electoral matters not concerning them since the marginal cost of getting the information would be greater than the marginal benefit derived from it. [Dam 2001]

REACH: Registration, evaluation, authorization and restriction of chemicals. A European Union ***regulation*** which entered into force in 2007. Its aim is to improve the protection of human health and the environment through the better and earlier identification of the intrinsic properties of chemical substances. The regulation also calls for the progressive substitution of the most dangerous chemicals when suitable alternatives have been identified. *See also* ***Convention on Persistent Organic Pollutants***, ***Globally Harmonized System of Classification and Labelling of Chemicals*** and ***prior informed consent***.

R

Race-to-the-bottom argument

竞次论

表达这样一种担忧，即与来自低劳动力成本和低劳工标准国家的进口产品进行竞争的需要将降低发达国家的工资和劳动条件。这一观点构成了对社会条款、贸易与劳工标准开展讨论的部分理由。对环境标准也提出了类似观点，认为一些国家的较低环境要求会使这些国家拥有竞争优势。另见*核心劳工标准(core labour standards)*、*全球化(globalization)*、*社会倾销(social dumping)*、*贸易与环境(trade and environment)*、*工资差别理论(wage differential argument)*、*劳工权利(worker rights)*。

Rapid Credit Facility

快速信贷安排

见*减贫与增长信托基金(Poverty Reduction and Growth Trust)*。

Ratchet mechanism

棘轮机制

指一些自由贸易协定中的服务贸易条款，一成员在谈判中采取的自主自由化措施自动纳入该成员在所涉协定项下的承诺减让表中。另见*不符措施(nonconforming measures)*。

Ratchet mechanism for non-conforming measures

不符措施棘轮机制

对跨境服务贸易或投资使用负面清单的自由贸易协定，通常包含一份不符措施清单(因某种原因尚不符合协定所有规则的措施)。此类协定有时包含一种棘轮机制，效果在于锁定协定生效后的任何改进或自由化。这一过程可保证实际条件随时优先，而在这些情况下不必等待审议会议以实现自由化。自由化也不可能轻易逆转。

Rational ignorance

理性无知

选民决定不花时间或金钱去了解与他们无关的选举事务，因为获得信息的边际成本大于从中获得的边际收益。

REACH

化学品的注册、评估、授权和限制

2007年生效的欧盟条例。目的在于通过更好和更早识别化学物质内在特性改善对人类健康和环境的保护。该条例还呼吁在确定合适替代品的情况下，逐步替代最危险化学品。另见*关于持久性有机污染物的公约(Convention on Persistent Organic Pollutants)*、*全球化学品统一分类和标签制度(Globally Harmonized System of Classification and Labelling of Chemicals)*、*事先知情同意(prior informed consent)*。

Reasonable period of time: a term used in the WTO ***Dispute Settlement Understanding***. It denotes the time, generally a maximum of fifteen months, that may elapse between the adoption of a ***panel*** or ***Appellate Body*** report and the point when a trade regime found inconsistent with the WTO rules has to be brought into conformity with them. Where a WTO member refuses to take the necessary actions, the member notifying the dispute may impose the ***suspension of concessions or other obligations*** after the same reasonable period of time has passed. Three options are available for defining what may be a reasonable period of time. The first is the time proposed by the member itself, subject to the agreement of the ***Dispute Settlement Body***. If this does not work, the second option is for the parties to agree on a period of time within forty-five days of the adoption of the ruling. If there is still no agreement, an arbitrator will be appointed to settle on a period of no more than fifteen months from the adoption of a ***panel*** or ***Appellate Body*** report. The significance of this approach is that a WTO member has little opportunity or incentive to waste time over taking action in an adverse ruling since the clock starts when the Dispute Settlement Body adopts the panel or Appellate Body Report.

Rebuttable presumption: a legal term in common use in the United States meaning that an action is deemed to conform to the law until shown otherwise. Some say that the word "rebuttable" is redundant since any presumption can be challenged and, indeed, rebutted. The term is sometimes used in discussions of the ***precautionary principle***.

Recidivist dumping: sometimes used, especially by American negotiators, for companies that persist in ***dumping*** their products, and that allegedly see dumping as a way of doing business. *See also* ***anti-dumping measures*** and ***Persistent Dumping Clause***.

Reciprocal dumping: occurs when firms from two countries engage in ***dumping*** in each other's markets. Krugman and Brander have demonstrated that this can occur if monopoly profits exceed transport costs. [Krugman and Brander 1983]

Reciprocal free trade: the proposition that one should liberalize ***market access*** only to those who are prepared to open their markets in turn. There is no implication that this would necessarily lead to the condition usually defined as ***free trade***. *See also* ***reciprocity***.

Reciprocal free-trade area: *see* ***free-trade areas***.

Reciprocal retaliation: *see* ***mirror retaliation***.

Reciprocal trade agreement: a trade agreement which gives members equal rights and obligations. This form of agreement does not imply any particular content, but sometimes it may mean an agreement for reciprocal tariff reductions negotiated under the ***United States Reciprocal Trade Agreements Program***.

Reciprocal Trade Agreements Program: *see* ***United States Reciprocal Trade Agreements Program***.

Reciprocity: the practice in the WTO, but not a contractual requirement, by which governments extend similar ***concessions*** to each other, as when one

Reasonable period of time
合理期限

WTO《争端解决谅解》中用语。指从采纳专家组或上诉机构报告至使被认定不符合WTO规则的贸易政策符合规则可能需要的时间，通常最长为15个月。如果一WTO成员拒绝采取必要措施，提起争端的成员可在合理期限后中止减让或其他义务。定义合理期限有三种选择：第一种是成员自己提出的期限，需经争端解决机构同意。如不可行，则第二种选择是当事方在裁决通过后45天内议定一期限。如仍未达成一致，则指定一仲裁人确定期限，该期限不应超过自专家组或上诉机构报告通过后的15个月。这种方式的意义在于，由于争端解决机构通过专家组或上诉机构报告后即开始计算时间，WTO成员几无机会或动机在针对不利裁决采取行动方面浪费时间。

Rebuttable presumption
可反驳的推定

在美国常用的法律术语，意指一项行为被认为符合法律，除非另有反证。一些人认为"可反驳"一词是多余的，因为任何推定均可被质疑，即可被反驳。这一术语有时用于对预防原则的讨论中。

Recidivist dumping
倾销累犯

有时用于指持续倾销其产品、被外界视为将倾销作为作生意的一种方式的公司，特别是美国谈判人员如此使用。另见*反倾销措施(anti-dumping measures)*、*持续性倾销条款(Persistent Dumping Clause)*。

Reciprocal dumping
相互倾销

来自两国的企业在对方市场中进行倾销时发生此种情况。克鲁格曼和布兰德已经证明，如果垄断利润超过运输成本，此种情况即会发生。

Reciprocal free trade
互惠自由贸易

一种主张，指一方仅应在其他方也准备开放市场作为回应的情况下方可开放市场准入。这并不意味着必然产生通常被定义为自由贸易的条件。另见*互惠(reciprocity)*。

Reciprocal free-trade area
互惠自由贸易区

见*自由贸易区(free-trade areas)*。

Reciprocal retaliation
对等报复

见*镜像报复(mirror retaliation)*。

Reciprocal trade agreement
互惠贸易协定

给予成员相同权利和义务的贸易协定。此种形式的协定并不隐含任何特定内容，但有时可能意味着根据美国互惠贸易协定计划谈判达成的互惠关税减让协定。

Reciprocal Trade Agreements Program
互惠贸易协定计划

见*美国互惠贸易协定计划(United States Reciprocal Trade Agreements Program)*。

Reciprocity
互惠

WTO中的做法，但不是契约性要求，据此各成员政府相互给予相似减让，即

government lowers tariffs or other barriers impeding imports in exchange for equivalent concessions from a trading partner. This is also known as achieving a ***balance of concessions***. Concessions made as a result of reciprocal bargaining must be extended through the most-favoured-nation rule to all WTO members. *See also* ***mirror-image reciprocity*** and ***reciprocity at the margin***.

Reciprocity at the margin: a term meaning that the overall value of ***concessions*** offered to trading partners should roughly match the value of concessions received in turn. *See also* ***mirror-image reciprocity***.

Recognition: the act of recognizing by one country of the qualifications, standards, licence requirements or testing methods of another country. Such recognition can have a considerable impact on the conduct of trade. Under the ***General Agreement on Trade in Services***, recognition may be done unilaterally, mutually or through harmonization. If a country accords recognition to another country, it does not have to extend it to others, as ***most-favoured-nation treatment*** would require. It must, however, give others an opportunity to demonstrate that they, too, can meet the required standards. *See also* ***Agreement on Technical Barriers to Trade***, ***harmonization of standards and qualifications*** and ***mutual recognition arrangements***.

Recommendation: one of the means available to the ***European Union*** to influence the actions of member states, even though recommendations are not binding. Recommendations are also commonly used in the ***OECD***. *See also* ***European Union legislation***.

Recommendation for Further Combating Bribery of Foreign Public Officials in International Business Transactions: released by the ***OECD*** in 2009 to enhance the implementation of the ***Convention on Combating Bribery of Foreign Public Officials in International Business Transactions***. It recommends that member countries continue to take effective measures to deter, prevent and combat bribery and that each member country take concrete steps to examine its laws and regulations relevant to this area. Annex I to the Recommendation is a *Good Practice Guide on Implementing Specific Articles of the Convention on Combating Bribery of Foreign Public Officials in International Business Transactions*. *See also* **bribery** and **corruption**.

Rectifications: adjustments to a country's ***tariff schedule***, usually to remove errors made in its preparation. *See also* ***renegotiation of tariffs***.

Red-tape barriers: excessive requirements for documents as part of the process of importing as well as well as requests for the provision of information in minute detail. This can lead to considerable delays at entry points because someone presumably reads all the information that has been supplied. *See also* ***trade facilitation***.

Re-exports: goods brought into a country temporarily and destined ultimately for other markets, sometimes after some value has been added. *See also* ***entrepôt trade***, ***free-trade zones*** and ***remanufactured goods***.

Reference paper on telecommunications services: a set of definitions and principles concerning the regulatory framework for ***basic telecommunications***

一成员政府降低关税或阻碍进口的其他壁垒，以换取一贸易伙伴的同等减让。这也被称为实现减让平衡。作为互惠交易结果而作出的减让必须根据最惠国待遇规则适用于所有WTO成员。另见*镜像互惠(mirror-image reciprocity)*、*边际互惠(reciprocity at the margin)*。

Reciprocity at the margin
边际互惠

指向贸易伙伴提供的减让总价值应与相应所获减让的价值大致相当。另见*镜像互惠(mirror-image reciprocity)*。

Recognition
承认

一国承认另一国的资格、标准、许可要求或检验方法的行为。此种承认可以对开展贸易产生相当大影响。根据《服务贸易总协定》，承认可以单边实现、相互实现或通过协调实现。如一国给予另一国承认，不需要像最惠国待遇所要求的那样扩展到其他国家。但必须给其他国家证明也能达到所需标准的机会。另见*技术性贸易壁垒协定(Agreement on Technical Barriers to Trade)*、*标准和资格的协调(harmonization of standards and qualifications)*、*相互承认安排(mutual recognition arrangements)*。

Recommendation
建议

欧盟用于影响成员国行动的手段之一，但不具有约束力。经济合作与发展组织(OECD)也经常使用建议。另见*欧洲联盟立法(European Union legislation)*。

Recommendation for Further Combating Bribery of Foreign Public Officials in International Business Transactions
关于进一步打击国际商业交易中行贿外国公职人员行为的建议

经济合作与发展组织(OECD)于2009年发布，以加强《关于打击国际商业交易中行贿外国公职人员行为的公约》的执行。建议各成员国继续采取有效措施以遏制、预防和打击行贿行为，并建议每一成员国采取具体步骤，审查本国与这一领域相关的法律和法规。该建议的附件1为《关于执行<关于打击国际商业交易中行贿外国公职人员行为的公约>具体条款的良好实践指南》。另见*贿赂(bribery)*、*腐败(corruption)*。

Rectifications
更正

对一国关税减让表所作调整，通常为去除制定过程中的错误。另见*关税重新谈判(renegotiation of tariffs)*。

Red-tape barriers
繁文缛节壁垒

作为进口过程一部分的对单证的过度要求，且要求提供极为详细的信息。这可能导致在入境点的极大延迟，因为有人可能会阅读所有已经提供的信息。另见*贸易便利化(trade facilitation)*。

Re-exports
复出口

货物临时进入一国而最终被运往其他市场，有时是在增加部分价值后。另见*转口贸易(entrepôt trade)*、*自由贸易园区(free-trade zones)*、*再制造货物(remanufactured goods)*。

Reference paper on telecommunications services
电信服务参考文件

一套关于基础电信服务监管框架的定义和原则，WTO于1996年4月24日通过。

services, adopted by the WTO on 24 April 1996. The reference paper seeks to prevent anti-competitive practices, ensure interconnection under non-discriminatory terms, and to promote a transparent, non-discriminatory and competitively neutral universal service obligation. It makes the public availability of licensing criteria mandatory. It also postulates the existence of independent regulatory authorities. Allocation of scarce resources, including frequencies, numbers and rights of way, is to be done in an objective, timely, transparent and non-discriminatory manner. *See also* ***Agreement on Basic Telecommunications Services*** and ***competitive neutrality***.

Reference price: a benchmark for valuing goods adopted by some customs authorities to arrive at the amount of customs duties payable. Its main aim is to prevent ***under-invoicing*** as this would lead to a lower revenue collection. The reference is usually meant to reflect the market price for the goods, but it can be higher. *See also* ***customs valuation***.

Reform process/programme: The Uruguay Round ***Agreement on Agriculture*** starts a reform process for global agricultural trade. It sets out a first step in the process, i.e. a programme for reducing subsidies and production and other reforms. The negotiations launched under Article 20, now subsumed in the ***Doha Development Agenda***, are aimed at continuing the reform process. *See also* ***continuation clause***.

Refusal to deal: *see* ***boycott***.

Regatta approach: a term sometimes used in the context of ***enlargement*** of the ***European Union***. Under this approach, some applicant countries would start accession negotiations more or less at the same time, and those with the fewest adjustment difficulties to overcome would reach the finishing line first. They would then be admitted without awaiting equal progress by the others.

Regional Comprehensive Economic Partnership: RCEP. A proposed ***free-trade agreement*** between the ten members of ***ASEAN*** and Australia, China, India, Japan, Republic of Korea and New Zealand. ASEAN already has free-trade agreements with all of these countries. Negotiations were launched at the ***ASEAN Summit*** in November 2012. In November 2019 fifteen of the negotiators announced that had concluded text-based negotiations, and that they hoped to have a text ready for signature in 2020. At that time India had significant unresolved issues which precluded its joining in the consensus. The draft agreement covers trade in goods, rules of origin, customs procedures and trade facilitation, sanitary and phytosanitary measures, standards and conformity assessment, trade remedies, trade in services (including annexes on financial services, telecommunication services and professional services), movement of natural persons, investment, intellectual property, electronic commerce, competition, small and medium enterprises, economic and technical cooperation, government procurement and dispute settlement.

Regional Convention on pan-Euro-Mediterranean preferential rules of origin: entered into force in 2013. Lays down provisions on the origin of goods, i.e. ***rules of origin***, traded between the ***European Union***, ***EFTA***,

参考文件寻求防止限制竞争做法，保证根据非歧视条件进行互连，并促进透明、非歧视和竞争中立的普遍服务义务。参考文件将许可标准的公开可获得性作为强制性要求。还要求存在独立的管理者。稀缺资源的分配，包括频率、号码和通行权，应以客观、及时、透明和非歧视的方式进行。另见*基础电信协定(Agreement on Basic Telecommunications Services)*、*竞争中立(competitive neutrality)*。

Reference price

参考价格

一些海关为计算得出应缴关税税额而采用的货物估价基准。主要目的为防止会导致税收减少的低开发票。参考价格通常意味着反映货物的市场价格，但也可能会更高。另见*海关估价(customs valuation)*。

Reform process/programme

改革进程/计划

乌拉圭回合《农业协定》开启了全球农业贸易的改革进程。协定规定的进程第一步是"减少补贴和生产及其他改革的计划"。根据协定第20条启动的谈判现已纳入多哈发展议程，旨在继续改革进程。另见*继续谈判条款(continuation clause)*。

Refusal to deal

拒绝交易

见*抵制(boycott)*。

Regatta approach

帆船赛法

在欧盟扩盟背景下有时使用的词语。依照此种方法，一些申请国几乎同时开始加入谈判，那些需要克服最少调整困难的国家会首先到达终点线。它们随即被接纳为成员国而不必等待其他国家取得同样进展。

Regional Comprehensive Economic Partnership

区域全面经济伙伴关系协定

RCEP。指东盟10个成员国与澳大利亚、中国、印度、日本、韩国和新西兰之间拟议的自由贸易协定。东盟已经与所有这些国家签署自由贸易协定。谈判在2012年11月的东盟峰会上启动。2019年11月，15位谈判代表宣布已经结束基于文本的谈判，并表示希望在2020年形成一份可供签署的文本。当时印度存在重大未决问题而未加入共识。协定草案涵盖货物贸易、原产地规则、海关程序和贸易便利化、卫生与植物卫生措施、标准和合格评定程序、贸易救济措施、服务贸易(包括关于金融服务、电信服务和专业服务的附件)、自然人流动、投资、知识产权、电子商务、竞争、中小企业、经济技术合作、政府采购和争端解决。(2020年11月15日东盟10国与澳大利亚、中国、日本、韩国和新西兰签署RCEP，协定于2022年1月1日生效—译注)

Regional Convention on pan-Euro-Mediterranean preferential rules of origin

泛欧—地中海优惠原产地规则区域公约

2013年生效。规定了在欧盟、欧洲自由贸易联盟(EFTA)、土耳其、已签署《巴塞罗那宣言》的国家、西巴尔干半岛和法罗群岛之间所交易货物的原产地条

Turkey, the countries that have signed the ***Barcelona Declaration***, the Western Balkans and the Faroe Islands. It will replace about sixty bilateral protocols in force in the pan-Euro-Mediterranean zone. *See also* ***pan-Euro-Mediterranean cumulation***. [ec.europa.eu]

Regional Economic Communities: RECs. Proposed by the ***Lagos Plan of Action*** of 1980 as the basis for wider African integration. They have been incorporated into the work of the ***African Union***. The eight RECS in existence are: ***Arab Maghreb Union*** (AMU), ***Common Market for Eastern and Southern Africa*** (COMESA), ***Community of Sahel-Saharan States*** (CEN-SAD), ***East African Community*** (EAC), ***Economic Community of Central African States*** (ECCAS), ***Economic Community of West African States*** (ECOWAS), ***Inter-governmental Authority on Development*** (IGAD), and ***Southern African Development Community***. *See also* ***African Continental Free Trade Area*** and ***African regional economic integration***.

Regional economic integration organization: REIO. This is an omnibus term covering ***free-trade agreements***, ***common markets***, ***customs unions*** and other economic partnerships of various kinds.

Regional exhaustion: the doctrine that once a product embodying ***intellectual property rights*** has been sold in a regional market with the consent of the owner of these rights, the product can be resold or transferred within any of the countries or economies making up that regional market without the further consent of the owner of these rights. *See also* ***Community exhaustion***, ***exhaustion doctrine***, ***international exhaustion*** and ***parallel imports***. [Maskus 2000]

Regional integration arrangement: RIA. A bilateral or regional economic agreement that may go beyond the reach of a ***regional trade agreement***. RIAs typically seek to achieve a degree of economic integration based on, for example, ***harmonization*** of various national policies or the adoption of policies aimed at similar outcomes.

Regional International Organization for Plant Protection and Animal Health: RIOPPAH. Established in 1953 with the aim of coordinating among member countries on improved methods of investigation, prevention, control and eradication of plant and animal diseases and epidemics having international repercussions. Members are Belize, Costa Rica, Dominican Republic, El Salvador, Guatemala, Honduras, Mexico, Nicaragua and Panama. Located in San Salvador, El Salvador. *See also* ***International Plant Protection Convention***, ***sanitary and phytosanitary measures***, ***SPS Information Management System*** and ***World Organisation for Animal Health***.

Regionalism: actions by governments to liberalize or facilitate trade on a regional basis, sometimes through ***free-trade areas*** or ***customs unions***. Many see regionalism, which apparently is often no more than ***bilateralism***, as complementary to ***multilateralism*** because it appears to offer a quicker way to achieve results for the participating economies than the full multilateral process. This is not necessarily the case. Often, the perceived faster pace of regional liberalization, where this actually occurs, is due only to the fact that multilateral outcomes may take a long

款，即原产地规则。将取代泛欧—地中海地区实施的约60项双边协定。另见*泛欧—地中海累积(pan-Euro-Mediterranean cumulation)*。

Regional Economic Communities

区域经济共同体

RECs。由1980年《拉各斯行动计划》作为泛非洲一体化的基础提出，已纳入非洲联盟的工作之中。现有的8个区域经济共同体为：阿拉伯马格里布联盟(AMU)、东部和南部非洲共同市场(COMESA)、萨赫勒—撒哈拉国家共同体(CEN-SAD)、东非共同体(EAC)、中部非洲国家经济共同体(ECCAS)、西非国家经济共同体(ECOWAS)、东非政府间发展组织(IGAD)和南部非洲发展共同体。另见*非洲大陆自由贸易区(African Continental Free Trade Area)*、*非洲区域经济一体化(African regional economic integration)*。

Regional economic integration organization

区域经济一体化组织

REIO。涵盖自由贸易协定、共同市场、关税同盟和其他各种经济伙伴关系的统称。

Regional exhaustion

区域用尽

此种理论认为，一旦包含知识产权的产品经所有权人同意在区域市场中销售，该产品即可在组成该区域市场的任何国家或经济体中转售或转让，而无需经所有权人进一步同意。另见*共同体内权利用尽(Community exhaustion)*、*权利用尽原则(exhaustion doctrine)*、*国际用尽(international exhaustion)*、*平行进口(parallel imports)*。

Regional integration arrangement

区域一体化安排

RIA。可能超出区域贸易协定范围的双边或区域经济协定。RIAs通常寻求实现一定程度的经济一体化，采取的方式例如通过协调各种国家政策或采取旨在取得类似结果的政策。

Regional International Organization for Plant Protection and Animal Health

区域国际植物保护与动物卫生组织

RIOPPAH。1953年成立，旨在在成员之间协调改进调查、预防、控制和根除具有国际影响的动植物疾病和流行病的方法。成员包括伯利兹、哥斯达黎加、多米尼加、萨尔瓦多、危地马拉、洪都拉斯、墨西哥、尼加拉瓜和巴拿马。设在萨尔瓦多首都圣萨尔瓦多。另见*国际植物保护公约(International Plant Protection Convention)*、*卫生与植物卫生措施(sanitary and phytosanitary measures)*、*卫生与植物卫生信息管理系统(SPS Information Management System)*、*世界动物卫生组织(World Organisation for Animal Health)*。

Regionalism

区域主义

政府为实现区域性贸易自由化或便利化采取的行动，有时通过自由贸易区或关税同盟形式。许多人认为，区域主义——显然通常只是双边主义——是对多边主义的补充，因为与全面多边进程相比，能使参加的经济体更快取得成果。但情况并不一定如此。通常，区域自由化被认为速度更快，如果真正发生，

time to negotiate. Moreover, the apparently faster pace of regional negotiations is often balanced by extended phase-in arrangements or ***carve-outs*** for ***sensitive products***. The time difference in reaching the end-points may therefore be less than seems to be the case. *See also* ***APEC***, ***hub and spokes***, ***multilateralization of free-trade agreements***, ***open regionalism*** and ***spaghetti-bowl effect***.

Regionalization: in the field of ***sanitary and phytosanitary measures*** a recognition that an exporting region (part of a country or a border-straddling zone) is disease-free or has a lower incidence.

Regional trade agreement: RTA. A ***free-trade agreement***, ***customs union*** or ***common market*** consisting of two or more countries such as ***ANZCERTA***, ***NAFTA*** or the ***European Union***. Some analysts see RTAs as building blocks for a freer non-discriminatory multilateral trading system, others as agents for its undermining. John Whalley has listed six reasons why countries negotiate regional trade agreements. First, they can obtain the traditional gains of trade. Second, countries use legally binding agreements to strengthen domestic policy reform. Third, countries hope to increase their multilateral bargaining power in this way. Fourth, free-trade arrangements can offer guaranteed access to markets. Fifth, for some countries the possibility of strategic linkages is important. The sixth reason is that countries may be able to benefit from the multilateral and regional interplay by emphasizing their interest in bilateral negotiations at critical points in the multilateral negotiations. In early 1996 the WTO established a ***Committee on Regional Trade Agreements*** to examine further their effect on the global trading system. *See also* ***best practice for RTAs/FTAs in APEC***, ***first regionalism***, ***hub and spokes***, ***second regionalism***, ***substantially-all-trade criterion*** and ***transparency mechanism for RTAs***. [Crawford and Fiorentino 2005, Whalley 1996]

Regional trade and investment agreement: *see* ***bilateral investment treaties***, ***free-trade agreement***, ***international investment agreement*** and ***regional trade agreement***.

Regional trade and investment framework agreement: a type of agreement negotiated by the United States with groups of countries, aimed at addressing trade and investment issues and eliminating or reducing barriers to trade. *See also* ***trade and investment framework agreement***.

Regional value content: RVC. Also known as ***qualifying value content***. This is a concept used in the administration of ***rules of origin*** under ***preferential trade arrangements***, especially ***free-trade agreements***. The RVC is the share of the good exported from one partner to another that determines whether ***preferential market access*** will be given. It represents the value added to the good by one or more partners to the arrangement. The RVC is usually expressed as a percentage. If the RVC is below the prescribed threshold, the good will have to enter under a higher tariff, usually the ***most-favoured-nation tariff***. Various calculations have been devised to arrive at the RVC, such as the ***net cost value method*** and the ***FOB value method***. *See also* ***preferential rules of origin*** and ***substantial transformation***.

也只是由于多边成果需要更长时间进行谈判。此外，区域谈判明显更快，往往被延长的过渡安排或敏感产品例外所平衡。因此，实现最终结果的时间差可能比看起来的小。另见*亚太经济合作组织(APEC)*、*轮轴-辐条(hub and spokes)*、*自由贸易协定多边化(multilateralization of free-trade agreements)*、*开放的区域主义(open regionalism)*、*意大利面碗效应(spaghetti-bowl effect)*。

Regionalization

区域化

在卫生与植物卫生措施领域，承认一出口地区(一国的一部分或跨界区域)没有疾病或发病率较低。

Regional trade agreement

区域贸易协定

RTA。由两个或两个以上国家组成的自由贸易协定、关税同盟或共同市场，例如《澳大利亚与新西兰更紧密经济关系贸易协定》(ANZCERTA)、《北美自由贸易协定》(NAFTA)或欧盟。一些分析人士将区域贸易协定视为建立一个更加自由的、非歧视的多边贸易体制的组成部分，其他人则认为是破坏这一体制的推手。约翰·沃利列举了各国谈判区域贸易协定的6条原因。一是各国可以获得传统的贸易收益。二是各国利用具有法律约束力的协定加强国内政策改革。三是各国希望以此种方式增加多边讨价还价的能力。四是自由贸易安排可以保证市场准入。五是对于一些国家战略联系的可能性很重要。六是各国可在多边谈判的关键时刻强调它们在双边谈判中的利益，从而自多边和区域的相互影响中获益。1996年初，WTO设立区域贸易协定委员会以进一步审查这些协定对全球贸易体制的影响。另见*APEC区域贸易协定/自由贸易协定最佳实践(best practice for RTAs/FTAs in APEC)*、*第一次区域主义浪潮(first regionalism)*、*轮轴-辐条(hub and spokes)*、*第二次区域主义浪潮(second regionalism)*、*实质上所有贸易的标准(substantially-all-trade criterion)*、*区域贸易协定透明度机制(transparency mechanism for RTAs)*。

Regional trade and investment agreement

区域贸易投资协定

见*双边投资条约(bilateral investment treaties)*、*自由贸易协定(free-trade agreement)*、*国际投资协定(international investment agreement)*、*区域贸易协定(regional trade agreement)*。

Regional trade and investment framework agreement

区域贸易投资框架协定

美国与众多国家谈判达成的一种协定，旨在解决贸易和投资问题，消除或减少贸易壁垒。另见*贸易投资框架协定(trade and investment framework agreement)*。

Regional value content

区域价值成分

RVC。也称合格价值成分。用于优惠贸易安排、特别是自由贸易协定项下的原产地规则管理中。RVC为自一参加方向另一参加方所出口货物中能够确定是否给予优惠市场准入的比例。代表该安排的一个或多个参加方对该货物所增加的价值。RVC通常以百分比表示。如果RVC低于规定的最低值，该货物就要按较高关税进口，通常是最惠国关税。已经设计计算得出RVC的多种方法，例如净成本法和离岸价格法。另见*优惠原产地规则(preferential rules of origin)*、*实质性改变(substantial transformation)*。

Registered Exporter System: REX. A system of certification of origin established by the ***European Union*** on 1 January 2017 for its ***GSP*** (Generalized System of Preferences) The scheme is based on ***self-certification*** of ***economic operators*** who have to be registered on a database maintained by their competent authorities. Economic operators then have to prepare ***statements on origin***. The scheme eventually will apply to all preferential trade agreements of the European Union. [ec.europa.eu]

Registered geographical indication: a title of protection similar to ***protected appellation of origin***. The main difference is that protected appellations of origin are created by law or decree, whereas a registered geographical indication is usually created through registration of a ***geographical indication*** through a body established for this purpose. [WIPO SCT/8/4]

Registration, Evaluation and Authorization of Chemicals: *see* ***REACH***.

Regulated exports: goods that may be exported under certain conditions, such as ***export quotas*** or licensing requirements.

Regulation: an omnibus term covering all overt and covert actions or procedures instituted by governments with a view to influencing industry or customers of an industry in a particular manner. Government regulation may be imposed to correct perceived ***market failure*** or to redistribute income for the public good. Regulation may also refer to a system of rewards and penalties designed to influence the behaviour of firms and consumers. Other types of regulation include measures such as safety and environmental standards, market entry restrictions and price controls. Analysts of regulatory activities sometimes divide them into three categories: *economic regulation* (aimed at improving the efficiency of markets), *social regulation* (aimed at influencing the way companies approach social values and rights), and *administrative regulation* (aimed at improving the administrative efficiency of government agencies and to support governmental activities). In ***European Union legislation*** a regulation is an act binding all member states directly. *See also* ***deregulation***, ***privatization***, ***prudential regulation*** and ***re-regulation***.

Regulatory coherence: defined in Article 25.2 of the ***Trans-Pacific Partnership Agreement*** as "the use of good regulatory practices in the process of planning, designing, issuing, implementing and reviewing regulatory measures in order to facilitate domestic policy objectives, and in efforts across governments to enhance regulatory cooperation in order to further those objectives and promote international trade and investment, economic growth and employment". The term can also be found in other agreements.

Related rights: *see* ***neighbouring rights***.

Relative preferential margin: a preferential margin is usually assessed as the difference between the ***MFN tariff*** and the rate that may be available under a ***preferential trade arrangement***. Since, however, countries often conclude more than one free-trade agreement, the value of a preferential margin a particular country expects to enjoy may in fact be less than expected. The advantage gained by preferential access by one country is therefore tempered

Registered Exporter System

注册出口商制度

REX。欧盟于2017年1月1日为其普惠制(GSP)设立的原产地证书制度。该方案基于经营者自我认证，这些经营者必须在其主管部门维护的数据库中进行注册。经营者随后需要准备原产地声明。该方案最终将适用于欧盟的所有优惠贸易协定。

Registered geographical indication

注册地理标志

与受保护的原产地名称类似的保护权。主要区别在于，受保护的原产地名称是由法律或法令设立的，而地理标志的注册通常是通过在为此目的而设立的机构对地理标志进行注册后设立的。

Registration, Evaluation and Authorization of Chemicals

化学品的注册、评估和授权

见*化学品的注册、评估、授权和限制(REACH)*。

Regulated exports

受管制的出口

货物在某些条件下可以出口，例如出口配额或许可要求。

Regulation

管制

综合词语，涵盖政府为以一种特定方式影响产业或一产业的消费者而设立的所有公开或隐蔽的行动或程序。政府管制的实施可能是为纠正可觉察到的市场失灵，或为公共利益而重新分配收入。管制也可以指旨在影响企业和消费者行为的奖惩制度。其他类型的管制包括安全和环境标准、市场准入限制和价格控制等措施。管制活动的分析者有时将其分为三类：经济管制(旨在提高市场效率)、社会管制(旨在影响公司处理社会价值和权利的方式)和行政管制(旨在改善政府机构的行政效率并支持政府活动)。在欧洲联盟立法中，regulation(译为条例)是直接约束所有成员国的法令。另见*取消管制(deregulation)*、*私有化(privatization)*、*审慎监管(prudential regulation)*、*重新管制(re-regulation)*。

Regulatory coherence

监管一致性

《跨太平洋伙伴关系协定》第25.2条将其定义为“为便利本国政策目标的实现，在监管措施的计划、设计、发布、实施和审议过程中对良好监管实践的使用，以及各政府之间为深化这些目标及促进国际贸易和投资、经济增长和就业而加强监管合作努力过程中对良好监管实践的使用”。该词也出现在其他协定中。

Related rights

相关权利

见*邻接权(neighbouring rights)*。

Relative preferential margin

相对优惠幅度

优惠幅度通常估算为最惠国关税与优惠贸易安排项下可能获得的税率之间的差额。但是，由于各国往往缔结一项以上的自由贸易协定，一特定国家预期享受的优惠幅度的价值可能实际上低于预期。因此一国通过优惠准入获得的利

by the existing structure of preferences. Hence the relative preferential margin. [Nicita 2011]

Relative reciprocity: the expectation in a reciprocal arrangement that the partners would not have the same level of obligations towards each other. *See also* ***reciprocity at the margin***.

Relevant market: a concept used in the administration of ***competition policy***. When a competition authority investigates, for example, what the effect of a proposed merger between companies might be on competition in that industry, it has to consider what market might be affected by the merger. That determination is called the relevant market. It is not necessarily the same as the geographical area of the market of the companies concerned.

Remanufactured goods: these are goods made up from a combination of new parts and parts taken from used goods. They usually last as long as a new good of the same type, and they meet the same performance standards. *See also* ***Pathfinder on facilitating trade in remanufactured goods***.

Remedy: a legal term used to describe the action imposed or recommended by a court or tribunal in cases where a person has contravened a law.

Remissions: *see* ***border tax adjustments***.

Renegotiation of tariffs: most ***tariff*** negotiations are now conducted as part of ***multilateral trade negotiations*** or as sectoral negotiations like those resulting in the ***Information Technology Agreement***, but the GATT sets out several ways of renegotiating tariffs during other periods. The listing provided by John Jackson and William Davey in *Legal Problems of International Economic Relations* is particularly useful. First, GATT Article XXVIII:1 permits parties with a ***principal supplying interest*** or parties who have had earlier bilateral tariff negotiations to reopen these negotiations every three years. The period of three years originally reflected the United States practice of renewing the President's negotiating authority for three years at a time, and this was adopted as the period during which bindings could not be changed. Second, Article XXVIII:4 allows parties to request another party for special circumstance renegotiations. These would be small-scale negotiations confined to a few items resulting in a speedy conclusion, and they are meant to help countries relying on a relatively small number of primary commodities to diversify their economies. Third, Article XXVIII:5 envisages reserved renegotiations. This means that parties can reserve the right to modify their ***tariff schedules*** during the next three-year period in accordance with normal procedures, including the obligation to offer compensation to affected parties. Fourth, whenever two or more countries agree to form a ***customs union*** resulting in a ***common external tariff***, part of the tariff schedules of participating members must necessarily be changed. Tariff renegotiations are therefore required under Article XXIV:6 to ensure that the overall level of tariffs of the members of the customs area does not exceed the levels in force when there were separate tariffs. Fifth, developing countries have the right under Article XVIII:7 to change, under defined conditions, a tariff schedule as part of promoting an infant industry. Sixth,

益受到现有优惠结构的影响，即产生相对优惠幅度。

Relative reciprocity

相对互惠

互惠安排中的一种期望，即参加方对于彼此的义务水平不必相同。另见*边际互惠(reciprocity at the margin)*。

Relevant market

相关市场

竞争政策管理中使用的概念。当一竞争主管机关调查一拟议的公司并购可能对该行业的竞争产生何种影响时，必须考虑哪个市场可能受到并购影响。此种确定被称为相关市场。并不一定与有关公司所在市场的地理区域相同。

Remanufactured goods

再制造货物

由新零件和从旧货中提取的零件组合而成的货物。使用期限通常与同类型新产品相同，且满足相同性能标准。另见*促进再制造货物贸易探路者(Pathfinder on facilitating trade in remanufactured goods)*。

Remedy

救济

法律词语，用于描述法院或法庭一人违反法律时强制采取或建议采取的行动。

Remissions

免税

见*边境税调节(border tax adjustments)*。

Renegotiation of tariffs

关税重新谈判

大部分关税谈判目前作为多边贸易谈判的一部分进行，或作为像产生《信息技术协定》的部门谈判进行。而GATT规定了在其他期限内进行重新谈判关税的几种方式。约翰·杰克逊和威廉·戴维在《国际经济关系的法律问题》一书中提供的清单特别有用。第一，GATT第28条第1款，允许具有主要供应利益的各方或此前已经进行双边关税谈判的各方每3年重新开展关税谈判。3年期最初反映在美国当时每3年更新总统谈判授权的实践中，此点被采用因为在这一期限内约束是不能改变的。第二，第28条第4款，允许各方要求另一方在特殊情况下进行重新谈判。这些谈判是限于若干产品的小范围谈判，并迅速得出结果，旨在帮助依赖数量相对较少初级商品的国家实现经济多样化。第三，第28条第5款，设想了保留重新谈判的权利。这意味着各方可保留在下一3年期依照正常程序修改其关税减让表的权利，包括向受影响的各方提供补偿的义务。第四，如两个或两个以上国家同意组成形成共同对外关税的关税同盟，则参加关税同盟的各方的部分关税减让表必须进行修改。因此要求根据第24条第6款进行关税重新谈判，以保证关税同盟成员的总体关税水平不超过单独实施关税时的水平。第五，发展中国家根据第18条第7款有权在规定条件下作为促进幼稚产业的一部分而改变关税减让表。第六，第27条赋予各方改变与

Article XXVII gives parties the right to change a tariff concession negotiated with a country that either did not become a member of GATT or ceased to be one. Seventh, renegotiations of tariffs are possible also in the form of minor technical rectifications where clearly a mistake was made. WTO members tend to very careful to ensure that such technical changes do not amount to disguised substantive tariff increases which might entitle others to ***compensation***. *See also* ***tariff negotiations***. [Hoda 2018, Jackson and Davey 1986]

Renewed APEC Agenda for Structural Reform: RAASR. Adopted in 2015 with the aim of promoting structural reform in the APEC region, based on three pillars: (1) more open, well-functioning, transparent and competitive markets, (2) deeper participation in those markets by all segments of society, including MSMEs, women, youth, older workers and people with disabilities, and (3) sustainable social policies that promote pillars 1 and 2, enhance economic resilience, and are well targeted, effective and non-discriminatory. Each economy was then asked to prepare an action plan setting out its structural reform priorities up to 2020. RAASR supersedes the ***APEC New Strategy for Structural Reform*** (ANSSR). *See also* ***Leaders' Agenda to Implement Structural Reform***. [www.apec.org]

Repeat dumping: *see* ***recidivist dumping***.

Repression of unfair competition: *see* ***unfair competition***.

Request for consultations: the first step in the launching of a dispute case in the ***WTO***. Once this request has been lodged, the parties have an opportunity to resolve the matter through ***consultation***. If after sixty days the matter remains unresolved, the party requesting consultations (i.e. the complainant) can ask for the matter to be referred to a ***panel***. In practice, the majority of requests for consultations do not go beyond this stage. *See also* ***dispute settlement***.

Requests and offers: market access negotiations in the WTO for services usually proceed on the basis of bilateral requests and offers, except in the case of ***accession*** negotiations which are confined to requests by existing members. Requests are normally made by countries which have a significant interest in the traded service. Offers can be made in response to requests or concurrently. When two parties have reached agreement on the extent of new ***market access*** they are willing to give and accept, the result must be extended to all other WTO members on a most-favoured-nation basis. *See also* ***first-difference negotiations***, ***initial negotiating right***, ***most-favoured-nation treatment***, ***principal supplier right*** and ***principal supplying interest***.

Re-regulation: the institution of a new regulatory framework as part of the ***deregulation*** of an industry. This may seem contradictory at first glance, but it aims to ensure that competition feature in the deregulated market is genuine. Deregulation often takes away the ***monopoly*** function of service providers, but it tends to leave them as important players in the market which is now open to others. Because the former monopoly provider is well established, it may have sufficient dominance to retain a *de facto* monopoly. It may therefore be necessary to enact new ***competition laws*** to ensure that the former monopoly

一个未成为GATT缔约方或不再为GATT缔约方的国家谈判达成的关税减让的权利。第七，在存在明显错误的情况下，可以通过小的技术更正的方式进行关税重新谈判。WTO成员倾向于对此非常谨慎，以保证此类技术改变不会成为变相的实质性提高关税，如提高则其他成员有权获得补偿。另见*关税谈判(tariff negotiations)*。

Renewed APEC Agenda for Structural Reform

APEC结构性改革新议程

RAASR。2015年通过，旨在促进APEC区域的结构性改革，以三大支柱为基础：(1)更加开放、运行良好、透明和具有竞争力的市场；(2)社会各阶层更深入参与这些市场，包括中小微企业、妇女、青年、老年工人和残疾人；以及(3)促进支柱1和支柱2、可增强经济韧性、目标明确、有效和非歧视的可持续社会政策。要求每一经济体制定列出其到2020年的结构改革优先事项行动计划。RAASR取代APEC结构性改革新战略(ANSSR)。另见*领导人实施结构性改革议程(Leaders' Agenda to Implement Structural Reform)*。

Repeat dumping

重复倾销

见*倾销累犯(recidivist dumping)*。

Repression of unfair competition

制止不正当竞争

见*不正当竞争(unfair competition)*。

Request for consultations

磋商请求

在WTO中发起争端解决案件的第一步。一旦提出这一请求，各方即有机会通过磋商解决有关事项。如果60天后有关事项仍未解决，请求磋商的一方(即起诉方)可要求此事项提交专家组。实践中，大部分磋商请求不会超过这一阶段。另见*争端解决(dispute settlement)*。

Requests and offers

要价和出价

WTO中服务市场准入谈判通常在双边要价和出价基础上进行，仅限于现有成员提出要价的准入谈判除外。要价通常由对所涉服务贸易具有重要利益的国家提出，出价可针对要价提出或同时提出。在双方就它们愿意给予或接受的新市场准入的范围达成一致后，这一结果必须在最惠国待遇基础上适用于所有其他WTO成员。另见*第一差异谈判(first-difference negotiations)*、*最初谈判权(initial negotiating right)*、*最惠国待遇(most-favoured-nation treatment)*、*主要供应方权利(principal supplier right)*、*主要供应利益(principal supplying interest)*。

Re-regulation

重新管制

作为对一行业取消管制的一部分设立的新监管框架。初看起来这似乎是矛盾的，但其目的是保证取消管制的市场中的竞争特征是真实的。取消管制往往消除服务提供者的垄断功能，但往往使这些提供者在现在对其他人开放的市场上继续扮演重要角色。由于先前的垄断提供者已地位稳固，可能具有足够的支配地位以保持事实上的垄断，因此可能有必要制定新的竞争法以保证先

does not abuse its ***market power***, and that new entrants get a proper chance to establish their viability in the market.

Resale right: *see **droit de suite***.

Resentment, inefficiency, bureaucracy, and stupid signals: identified by Michael Aho as ingredients for the emergence of a series of regional trade blocs. [Aho 1990]

Reservation: an exemption from the obligations of an international agreement, such as a ***free-trade agreement*** or ***international investment agreement***, which applies to specified goods, services or investment activities. Reservations made under bilateral or regional trade and investment agreements are usually the result of negotiations between the parties. They may be permanent or time-bound. In the latter case they may be subject to a ***ratchet mechanism***. Some agreements do not allow any reservations. *See also **MFN exemption**, **non-conforming measures*** and ***two-annex method***.

Reserved list: in ***free-trade agreements*** using negative lists for investment laws, regulations, policies, etc., this is a list of sectors and activities for which the government retains complete flexibility of regulation. In other words, the government retains the right to make unilateral changes to its laws. Inscription of a sector in a reserved list does not necessarily mean that foreign investment in that sector is discouraged or even prohibited. *See also **national interest*** and ***non-conforming measures***.

Reserved negotiations: *see **renegotiation of tariffs***.

Residual quantitative restrictions: this normally refers to ***quantitative restrictions*** imposed to safeguard foreign exchange reserves, but which are still maintained after these difficulties have disappeared.

Residual rules of origin: an aspect of the administration of ***non-preferential rules of origin***. These rules must always result in a determination of the origin of a good so that, for example, it may be captured in import statistics. In a given case, a country may have chosen to use a ***change in tariff classification*** as its normal criterion. If that criterion is not met, possibly because the good went through some minor processing only in the country from which it was exported, the customs authorities then use additional criteria, known as residual rules. One of these might be determining the last country where the good underwent a ***substantial transformation***. Another residual rule in this case may be a value-added criterion. These rules are applied until the origin of the goods has been settled satisfactorily. An element of arbitrariness may be inevitable.

Residual tariffs: used by some to describe the low tariffs on industrial products that are now the rule in developed economies. Some see them as "left-overs" from the ***Uruguay Round*** that now should be eliminated completely. *See also **nuisance tariff***.

***Res judicata*:** the principle that once a matter has been dealt with by a court, it should not be reopened. [Brownlie 2019]

Resources diplomacy: national and intergovernmental actions and policies aimed at ensuring non-discriminatory and reliable access to supplies and remunerative

前的垄断者不会滥用其市场支配力，并保证新进入者获得在市场中形成其生存能力的适当机会。

Resale right

转售权

见*追续权(droit de suite)*。

Resentment, inefficiency, bureaucracy, and stupid signals

不满、低效、官僚和愚蠢信号

被迈克尔·阿霍确定为一系列区域贸易集团出现的因素。

Reservation

保留

对于适用于特定货物、服务或投资活动的国际协定义务的例外，例如自由贸易协定或国际投资协定。在双边或区域贸易和投资协定项下作出的保留通常是各方之间谈判的结果。可能是永久的，也可能是有时限的，后一种情况下可能受棘轮机制管辖。一些协定不允许任何保留。另见*最惠国待遇豁免(MFN exemption)*、*不符措施(non-conforming measures)*、*双附件法(two-annex method)*。

Reserved list

保留清单

在自由贸易协定中对投资法律、法规、政策等使用负面清单。这是一个政府保留全部监管灵活性的部门和活动的清单。换言之，政府保留单方面修改其法律的权利。将一部门列入保留清单并不一定意味着不鼓励或甚至禁止外国投资进入该部门。另见*国家利益(national interest)*、*不符措施(non-conforming measures)*。

Reserved negotiations

保留谈判

见*关税重新谈判(renegotiation of tariffs)*。

Residual quantitative restrictions

剩余数量限制

通常指为保护外汇储备而实施但在困难情况消失后仍然维持的数量限制。

Residual rules of origin

补足原产地规则

非优惠原产地规则管理的一个方面。这些规则必须始终能够对一货物的原产地进行确定，以便该货物可被纳入进口统计。在一特定情况下，一国可能选择使用税则归类改变作为其正常标准。如不符合该标准，可能由于货物仅在其出口国经过一些微小加工，海关因而会使用被称为补足规则的其他标准。其中之一可能是确定该货物在其中进行实质性改变的最后一个国家。另一个补足规则可能是增值标准。这些规则一直适用，直至货物的原产地得以满意解决。任意性因素可能难以避免。

Residual tariffs

剩余关税

一些人用于描述对工业品征收的低关税，这是目前发达经济体中的规则。有些人认为这些关税是乌拉圭回合的“残余”，现在应完全取消。另见*低率关税(nuisance tariff)*。

Res judicata

即决事项

一事项一旦经由法院处理即不应重新处理的原则。

Resources diplomacy

资源外交

旨在保证非歧视和可靠获得供应品和进入报酬丰厚的原材料市场的国家和政府间行动和政策。对于此问题和机制可见*农业与多边贸易体制(agriculture and*

markets for raw materials. For examples of issues and mechanisms *see* ***agriculture and the multilateral trading system***, ***Charter of Economic Rights and Duties of States***, ***commodity***, ***commodity cartels***, ***commodity policy***, ***commodity terms of trade***, ***Common Fund for Commodities***, ***Global Negotiations***, ***Integrated Programme for Commodities***, ***international commodity agreements***, ***international commodity bodies***, ***New International Economic Order***, ***Singer-Prebisch thesis*** and ***UNCTAD***.

Restrictive business practices: RBPs. Anti-competitive behaviour by private firms of the type dealt with by national ***competition laws*** and policies. These can include collusion, abuse of dominant position, refusals to deal, price discrimination, resale price maintenance, exclusive dealing, vertical and horizontal arrangements, etc. There is no accepted international standard on what constitutes RBPs or how they are to be dealt with. The ***Havana Charter*** included a chapter on them, but the Charter did not enter into force. In 1980, ***UNCTAD*** adopted the *Set of Multilaterally Agreed Equitable Principles and Rules for the Control of Restrictive Business Practices*, but it does not contain binding obligations. Much work has also been in the ***OECD*** on this subject. *See also* ***antitrust laws***, ***Arrangements for Consultations on Restrictive Business Practices***, ***competition policy*** and ***trade and competition***.

Results-based trade policy: an idea steeped in ***mercantilism*** based on the notion that certain benefits can be obtained through attacking carefully chosen targets. Advocates of such a policy usually expect the other side to make the ***concessions***. At the same time they defend their own trade regimes as being as perfect as might reasonably be expected in an imperfect world. The results, as always, tend to be mixed.

Retaliation: action taken by a country to restrain imports from a country that has increased a tariff or imposed other measures adversely affecting its exports. There are strict rules and procedures requiring exhaustion of ***dispute settlement*** under the WTO for retaliatory action, but countries sometimes are tempted to act outside these. In any case, the level of the retaliatory measures must not exceed the level of the measures they seek to deal with. Retaliation is also available to the United States under ***Section 301***. *See also* ***carousel legislation***, ***cross-retaliation*** and ***suspension of concessions or other obligations***.

Retaliatory tariff: a tariff aimed mainly at countering tariff increases by others, usually at a punitive level. Governments may feel satisfied that by imposing a retaliatory tariff they have defended the ***national interest***, but in reality they have also managed to raise costs for domestic producers and consumers alike. *See also* ***beggar-thy-neighbour policies***.

Retroactive anti-dumping duties: in most circumstances ***anti-dumping duties*** may be levied at the earliest from the time a ***preliminary determination of dumping*** was made and ***provisional anti-dumping duties*** were imposed. In some cases, however, it is possible to levy anti-dumping on goods imported up to ninety days before that determination. This can happen (a) when there is a history of dumping causing ***injury***, or (b) that the importer was aware, or should

the multilateral trading system)、*各国经济权利与义务宪章(Charter of Economic Rights and Duties of States)*、*商品(commodity)*、*商品卡特尔(commodity cartels)*、*商品政策(commodity policy)*、*商品贸易条件(commodity terms of trade)*、*商品共同基金(Common Fund for Commodities)*、*全球谈判(Global Negotiations)*、*商品综合方案(Integrated Programme for Commodities)*、*国际商品协定(international commodity agreements)*、*国际商品机构(international commodity bodies)*、*国际经济新秩序(New International Economic Order)*、*辛格-普雷维什命题(Singer-Prebisch thesis)*、*联合国贸易与发展会议(UNCTAD)*。

Restrictive business practices

限制性商业惯例

RBPs。国家竞争法和竞争政策所处理类型的私营企业反竞争行为。包括串通、滥用支配地位、拒绝交易、价格歧视、维持转售价格、排他性交易、垂直和水平安排等。对于限制性商业惯例的构成及如何处理，目前并无公认的国际标准。《哈瓦那宪章》包括关于该议题的一章，但宪章未生效。1980年，联合国贸易与发展会议(UNCTAD)通过了《一套多边协议的控制限制性商业惯例的公平原则和规则》，但不含具有约束力的义务。经济合作与发展组织(OECD)在这一问题上也作了很多工作。另见*反垄断法(antitrust laws)*、*关于限制性商业惯例磋商的安排(Arrangements for Consultations on Restrictive Business Practices)*、*竞争政策(competition policy)*、*贸易与竞争(trade and competition)*。

Results-based trade policy

基于结果的贸易政策

重商主义思想，所根据的理念为通过打击精心挑选的目标可以获得某些利益。该政策的支持者通常期望对方作出减让。同时他们维护自己的贸易制度，认为他们的制度是在一个不完美的世界中所能合理期望的完美制度。结果通常好坏参半。

Retaliation

报复

一国为限制自那些提高关税或实施对其出口产生不利影响的其他措施的国家的进口而采取的行动。有严格的规则和程序，要求采取报复行动首先穷尽WTO项下的争端解决，但是各国有时希望在这些规则之外采取行动。在任何情况下，报复性措施的水平不得超过它们寻求应对的措施的水平。根据301条款，美国也可以采取报复行动。另见*旋转木马立法(carousel legislation)*、*交叉报复(cross-retaliation)*、*中止减让或其他义务(suspension of concessions or other obligations)*。

Retaliatory tariff

报复性关税

实施的关税旨在抵制其他成员所提高的关税，通常为惩罚性水平。各政府可能为其征收报复性关税以捍卫国家利益而感到满意，但实际上，它们也同样提高了国内生产者和消费者的成本。另见*以邻为壑政策(beggar-thy-neighbour policies)*。

Retroactive anti-dumping duties

追溯性反倾销税

大多数情况下，反倾销税最早可自作出倾销初步裁定和征收临时反倾销税时起征收。但是在一些情况下，可对在作出确定前最长90天内进口的货物征收反倾销税。此种情况可能发生在(a)存在造成损害的倾销的记录；或(b)进口商

have been, that the exporter practises dumping causing injury, and (c) the injury is caused by massive dumped imports in a relatively short time which is likely to undermine the remedial effect of prospective ***definitive anti-dumping duties***. The importers must, however, be given a chance to comment on the proposed action.

Retroactive countervailing duties: normally countervailing duties cannot be imposed before a decision has been made, after an investigation, to impose ***preliminary countervailing duties***. It is possible, however, to levy countervailing duties on imports which were entered for consumption no more than ninety days before the application of provisional measures. This is the case when the investigating authority finds that the ***injury*** is difficult to repair because it is caused by massive imports in a relatively short time, and it concludes that retroactive duties are necessary to preclude the recurrence of injury.

Revealed comparative advantage: *see* ***comparative advantage***.

Revenue tariff: a ***tariff*** with a minimal protective function aimed mainly at producing a steady revenue stream for government. For some developing countries the tariff is one of the principal sources of income. They may therefore be reluctant to cut tariffs, unless another revenue source can be identified. *See also* ***nuisance tariff*** and ***residual tariffs***.

Reverse consensus: the principle that a report or decision is deemed adopted unless there is a ***consensus*** not to do so.

Reverse engineering: the controversial concept of acquiring a technological capacity through imitation of a product, generally by taking it apart to work out how it operates. The resulting product must not result in ***intellectual property right infringements***. *See also* ***decompilation***.

Reverse fast-track: a feature of the United States Trade Act of 1974. It gave Congress the option to reverse ***fast-track*** if it sensed that trade negotiations were not going in the right direction. *See also* ***Trade Promotion Authority***.

Reverse notification: the normal way to achieve transparency in the GATT, and now the WTO, is for governments to notify other members of trade measures they have taken or are about to take. A different approach was adopted at the end of the ***Tokyo Round*** when a database was established within the GATT Secretariat based on notifications made by governments of measures contained by others, i.e. through reverse notification. Reverse notification of course is also possible under other arrangements, such as the OECD ***national treatment instrument***. *See also* ***notification***.

Reverse preferences: preferences accorded by developing countries to developed countries.

Reverse special and differential treatment: a term devised by Jagdish Bhagwati to describe the proposition that developing countries should introduce measures to ensure minimum labour and environmental standards. The idea is that this would bring their costs into a more realistic relationship to those borne by developed countries already adhering to these standards. *See also* ***core labour standards*** and ***trade and environment***. [Bhagwati 1995]

已经知道或理应知道出口商进行造成损害的倾销；以及(c)损害是在相对较短时间内一产品的大量倾销进口造成的，有可能严重破坏预期的最终反倾销税的补救效果。但是，必须给予进口商对拟议行动发表意见的机会。

Retroactive countervailing duties

追溯性反补贴税

通常在调查后就征收最初反补贴税作出决定前不能征收反补贴税。但有可能对采取临时措施前不超过90天内进口供消费的产品征收反补贴税。在调查机关认为难以补救的损害是因为在相对较短时间内大量进口所造成的，并认为为防止损害再次发生有必要追溯征收反补贴税，即属此种情况。

Revealed comparative advantage

显性比较优势

见*比较优势(comparative advantage)*。

Revenue tariff

财政关税

具有最低保护功能的、主要旨在为政府提供稳定收入来源的关税。对于一些发展中国家，关税是主要收入来源之一。因此，它们可能不愿意削减关税，除非能找到另一个收入来源。另见*低率关税(nuisance tariff)*、*剩余关税(residual tariffs)*。

Reverse consensus

反向协商一致

除非协商一致予以反对，否则一报告或一决定即被视为获得通过。

Reverse engineering

逆向工程

一个有争议的概念，指通过模仿一产品，通常是拆解该产品以搞清其如何运作，以获得技术能力。由此产生的产品不得造成知识产权侵权。另见*反向编译(decompilation)*。

Reverse fast-track

反向快轨授权

美国《1974年贸易法》的一个特点。该法向国会提供了一个选项，即如果国会察觉到贸易谈判未能朝着正确方向发展，可以撤销快轨授权。另见*贸易促进授权(Trade Promotion Authority)*。

Reverse notification

反向通报

在GATT和现在的WTO中，实现透明度的通常方式是各成员政府向其他成员通报已经采取或即将采取的贸易措施。在东京回合结束时采取了一种不同的方式，在GATT秘书处根据各国政府所通报的其他国家维持的措施建立了一个数据库，即反向通报。当然，反向通报在其他安排项下也是可能的，例如经济合作与发展组织(OECD)国民待遇文件。另见*通报(notification)*。

Reverse preferences

反向优惠

指发展中国家给予发达国家的优惠。

Reverse special and differential treatment

反向特殊和差别待遇

贾格迪什·巴格瓦蒂发明的词语，用于描述发展中国家应采取措施保证最低劳动和环境标准的主张。想法是，这将使它们的成本与那些已经遵守这些标准的发达国家所承担的成本之间建立一种更加现实的关系。另见*核心劳工标准(core labour standards)*、*贸易与环境(trade and environment)*。

Reverse transfer of technology: a term used particularly in the ***United Nations*** system to describe the flow of scientists and highly trained specialists from developing countries to developed countries. This is the so-called brain drain. Numerous meetings on this subject have led neither to agreement on its causes nor on possible remedies. Suggestions by developing countries that recipient developed countries should pay some form of compensation have fallen on barren ground.

Revised Agreement on Government Procurement: the WTO ***plurilateral trade agreement*** which entered into force on 6 April 2014. It is the successor to the 1994 Agreement on Government procurement which became effective when the WTO was established on 1 January 1995. Accession is open to any WTO member. The Agreement applies to any measure regarding procurement for governmental purposes of goods and services or combinations of them. The exact coverage in respect of each member depends on the commitments made by that member. These are listed in an appendix to the Agreement. Annexes 1 to 3, respectively, list the central government authorities, sub-central government entities and all other entities covered by the Agreement. Goods and services bought by governments for commercial sale or resale or used in the production of goods and services for resale are not covered by the Agreement. Article I contains the definitions of terms used in the Agreement. Article II (Scope and Coverage) states that the Agreement applies to any measure regarding covered procurement, whether or not it is conducted exclusively or partially by electronic means. It also contains a list of exemptions, such as the acquisition or rental of land or buildings, public employment contracts and procurement for the specific purpose of international assistance, including development aid. Article III covers security and general exceptions. Article IV lists general principles: non-discrimination, use of generally available information technology systems and software, conduct of procurement in a transparent and impartial manner and use of the rules of origin used in the normal course of trade. Article V requires special consideration of the development, financial and trade needs of developing countries in accession negotiations and the implementation of the Agreement. Article VI requires prompt publication of any law, regulation, etc., pertaining to a member's procurement system. Article VII covers notices of intended procurement and notices of planned procurement. Article VIII requires that conditions for participation in a procurement must be limited to those needed to ensure that a supplier has the necessary legal and financial capacities and the commercial and technical abilities. Article IX sets out in detail the procedures applying to the qualification of suppliers. Article X deals with the requirements for technical specifications and tender documentation. Article XI requires that sufficient time be given to suppliers to prepare and submit requests for participation and tenders. Article XII permits procuring entities to enter into negotiation with prospective suppliers in certain circumstances, such as a situation where no tender is obviously the most advantageous in terms of the criteria. Article XIII permits the limitation of

Reverse transfer of technology
反向技术转让

联合国体制中专门使用的词语，用于描述科学家和训练有素的专家从发展中国家流向发达国家。此即所谓人才流失。关于这一议题的众多会议未能就其原因或就可能的补救措施达成一致。发展中国家关于作为接受方的发达国家应支付某种形式补偿的建议没有下文。

Revised Agreement on Government Procurement
政府采购协定修正版

2014年4月6日生效的WTO诸边贸易协定(GPA 2012—译注)。是1994年《政府采购协定》的后继协定，1994年协定(GPA 1994—译注)在1995年1月1日WTO建立时生效。协定加入对WTO任何成员开放。协定适用于有关为政府目的而采购的货物、服务或货物和服务组合的任何措施。对于每一参加方的确切涵盖范围取决于该参加方所作承诺，列入协定附录中。附件1至3分别列出协定涵盖的中央政府机关、次中央政府实体和所有其他实体。协定不涵盖政府用于商业销售或转售目的或用于供商业销售或转售的货物或服务的生产而进行的采购。第1条包含协定中使用术语的定义。第2条(适用范围和涵盖范围)规定，协定适用于有关涵盖采购的任何措施，无论采购是否全部或部分通过电子方式开展。该条含有一份例外清单，例如购买或租赁土地或建筑物、公共雇佣合同和为提供国际援助的特定目的而进行的采购，包括发展援助。第3条涵盖安全和一般例外。第4条列出一般原则：非歧视、使用可普遍获得的信息技术系统和软件、以透明和公正的方式开展采购以及使用正常贸易过程中适用的原产地规则。第5条要求在加入谈判和协定实施中，对发展中国家的发展、财政和贸易需要给予特殊考虑。第6条要求迅速公布与成员采购系统有关的任何法律法规等。第7条涵盖意向采购通知和计划采购通知。第8条要求采取参加条件必须限定在保证供应商具有法律、财务、商业和技术能力所必要的条件方面。第9条详细规定了适用于供应商资格的程序。第10条涉及技术规格和招标文件的要求。第11条要求给予供应商充足时间以准备和提交参加请求和投标。第12条允许采购实体在某些情况下与潜在供应商开展谈判，例如按照标准无投标具有明显优势。第13条允许在某些情况下对选定供应商进行限制性招标。

tendering to selected suppliers in some circumstances. If electronic auctions are used, Article XIV describes how they have to be conducted. Article XV covers the treatment of tenders and awarding of contracts. Article XVI deals with the transparency of procurement information once a contract has been awarded. Article XVII requires the prompt disclosure of any information necessary to determine whether a procurement was conducted fairly if another Party requests this. Article XVIII requires each party to have a timely, effective, transparent and non-discriminatory system of administrative or judicial review, and it sets out the relevant procedures. Article XIX sets out the procedures for modifications of rectification of coverage that a Party may wish to effect. Article XX states that the WTO ***Dispute Settlement Understanding*** applies to consultations and dispute settlement. Article XXI establishes a Committee on Government Procurement to consider matters relating to the operation of the Agreement. Article XXII (Final Provisions) deals with entry into force of the Agreement. It also states that no later than three years after entry into force the Parties will start further negotiations with a view to improving the Agreement.

Revised Treaty of Basseterre: *see* ***Organization of Eastern Caribbean States***.

Revised Treaty of Chaguaramas Establishing the Caribbean Community Including the CARICOM Single Market and Economy: *see* ***CARICOM Single Market and Economy***.

Right of establishment: the right to establish a commercial entity in another country for the purpose of producing for the local market or importing products from another economy and distributing them. Establishment normally entails some form of investment, including acquisitions, mergers and takeovers. *See also* ***commercial presence***, ***foreign direct investment***, ***joint venture***, ***post-establishment*** and ***pre-establishment***.

Right of non-establishment: the right to do business in another country without the need to establish a permanent operation there. This principle is often incorporated in the chapter on ***Cross-border trade in services*** in ***free-trade agreements***. *See also* ***commercial presence***.

Right of priority: a right available to signatories of the ***Paris Convention***. It means that a person filing for a ***patent*** in one country has a priority right to file for the same invention in another country within one year. In practical terms this means that once a company has filed for a patent in its home country and it then files for the same patent in another country, the patent will be protected from the date of the earlier application at home rather than the later one abroad. *See also* ***intellectual property***.

Right to Development: a declaration adopted by the United Nations General Assembly in Resolution 41/128 on 4 December 1986. Its ten articles, in abbreviated form, are: (1) The right to development is an inalienable human right entitling every human person and all peoples to participate in economic, social, cultural and political development. (2) The human person is the central subject of development and should be the active participant and beneficiary of the right to development. (3) States have the primary responsibility for the

第14条规定如何开展电子拍卖。第15条涵盖投标的处理和合同的授予。第16条涉及合同授予后采购信息的透明度问题。第17条要求应其他参加方请求，迅速披露确定采购是否公平进行所必需的任何信息。第18条要求每一参加方设立及时、有效、透明和非歧视的行政或司法审查制度，并规定了相关程序。第19条规定了一参加方可能希望实施的涵盖范围修改程序。第20条规定WTO《争端解决谅解》适用于协定项下的磋商和争端解决。第21条设立了政府采购委员会，以审议与协定运用有关的事项。第22条(最后条款)涉及协定生效问题。该条还规定不迟于协定生效后3年内，参加方将开始进一步谈判，以期改进协定。

Revised Treaty of Basseterre
经修订的巴斯特尔条约
见*东加勒比国家组织(Organization of Eastern Caribbean States)*。

Revised Treaty of Chaguaramas Establishing the Caribbean Community Including the CARICOM Single Market and Economy
经修订的关于建立包括加勒比共同体单一市场和经济在内的加勒比共同体的查瓜拉马斯条约
见*加勒比共同体单一市场和经济(CARICOM Single Market and Economy)*。

Right of establishment
设立权
在另一国设立商业实体的权利，目的在于为当地市场生产产品或自另一经济体进口并分销产品。设立通常需要某种形式的投资，包括收购、并购和接管。另见*商业存在(commercial presence)*、*外国直接投资(foreign direct investment)*、*合资企业(joint venture)*、*准入后(post-establishment)*、*准入前(pre-establishment)*。

Right of non-establishment
无需设立商业实体权
在另一国开展经营而无需在该国设立永久经营机构的权利。这一原则经常包含在自由贸易协定中的跨境服务贸易章节。另见*商业存在(commercial presence)*。

Right of priority
优先权
《巴黎公约》签署国可享有的权利。指在一国申请专利的人对在1年内在另一国就同一发明申请专利具有优先权。实践中这意味着，一旦一家公司在本国提出专利申请，随后在另一国对同一专利提出申请，对该专利的保证将自在本国提出的较早申请之日起获得而非自稍后在国外提出申请之日起获得。另见*知识产权(intellectual property)*。

Right to Development
发展权利宣言
联合国大会1986年12月4日在第41/128号决议中通过的宣言。10项条款可简述为：(1)发展权利是一项不可剥夺的人权，由于这种权利，每个人和所有各国人民均有权参与经济、社会、文化和政治发展。(2)人是发展的主体，应成为发展权利的积极参与者和受益者。(3)各国对创造有利于实现发展权利的国家

creation of national and international conditions favourable to the realization of the right to development. (4) States have the duty to take steps, individually and collectively, to facilitate the realization of the right to development. (5) States shall take resolute steps to eliminate massive and flagrant violations of human rights. (6) States should cooperate to promote, encourage and strengthen universal respect for the advancement of human rights. (7) States should promote the establishment, maintenance and strengthening of international peace and security. (8) States should undertake at the national level all necessary measures for the realization of the right to development. (9) All aspects of the right to development listed in the declaration are indivisible and interdependent. (10). Steps should be taken to ensure the full exercise and progressive enhancement of the right to development. This declaration is sometimes mentioned in discussions of ***trade and human rights*** and ***trade and labour standards***. [www.ohchr.org]

Rio Declaration on Environment and Development: a set of principles aimed at protecting the integrity of the global environmental and developmental systems adopted on 14 June 1992 at a meeting of ***UNCED*** (United Nations Conference on Environment and Development) in Rio de Janeiro. Principle 12 holds that "States should cooperate to promote a supportive and open international economic system that would lead to economic growth and sustainable development in all countries, to address better the problems of environmental degradation. ***Trade policy*** measures for environmental purposes should not constitute a means of ***arbitrary or unjustifiable discrimination*** or a ***disguised restriction on international trade***. Unilateral actions to deal with environmental challenges outside the jurisdiction of the importing country should be avoided. Environmental measures addressing transboundary or global environmental problems should, as far as possible, be based on an international consensus". This Principle is mentioned as a relevant text in the terms of reference for the WTO ***Committee on Trade and Environment***. *See also* ***Agenda 21***.

Rio Group: a group of Latin American and Caribbean countries established in 1983 in Rio de Janeiro with predominantly political and security aims. Superseded in 2010 by the ***Community of Latin American and Caribbean States***. *See also* ***Latin American regional integration arrangements***.

Risk assessment: members of the WTO may apply food safety, animal health and plant health regulations to their international trade, but they must not use them to discriminate arbitrarily or unjustifiably between members in similar conditions. The WTO ***Agreement on the Application of Sanitary and Phytosanitary Measures*** sets out rules for achieving this. It encourages members to harmonize measures and to base them on international standards, guidelines and recommendations where these are available. If members wish to maintain higher standards, they must carry out risk assessments. A risk assessment can be an evaluation of the likelihood of the introduction or spread of a pest or disease in the light of the sanitary and phytosanitary measures applied. It can also be an evaluation of the potential for adverse effects on human or animal health

和国际条件负有主要责任。(4)各国有义务单独地和集体地采取步骤，以促成实现发展权利。(5)各国应采取坚决步骤，消除大规模公然侵犯人权的行为。(6)各国应合作以促进、鼓励并加强对促进人权的普遍尊重。(7)各国应促进建立、维护并加强国际和平与安全。(8)各国应在国家一级采取一切必要措施实现发展权。(9)宣言规定的发展权利的所有各方面都是不可分割和相互依存的。(10)应采取步骤以保证充分行使和逐步增进发展权利。在讨论贸易与人权、贸易与劳工标准时，有时会提到这一宣言。

Rio Declaration on Environment and Development
里约环境与发展宣言

1992年6月14日在里约热内卢举行的联合国环境与发展会议(UNCED)的一次会议上通过的一套旨在保护全球环境与发展系统完整的原则。原则12认为："各国应进行合作以促进一个支持性的和开放的国际经济体系，这一体系将促成所有国家的经济增长和持续发展，更好地解决环境退化问题。为环境目的而采取的贸易政策措施不应成为一种任意或不合理的歧视的手段，或成为一种对国际贸易的变相限制。应避免采取单方面行动处理进口国家管辖范围以外的环境挑战。处理跨国界的或全球环境问题的环境措施应尽可能建立在国际一致的基础上。"这一原则在WTO贸易与环境委员会的职权范围中作为相关文本提及。*另见21世纪议程(Agenda 21)*。

Rio Group
里约集团

1983年在里约热内卢成立的拉丁美洲和加勒比国家集团，主要目标属政治和安全性质。2010年被拉丁美洲和加勒比国家共同体所取代。*另见拉丁美洲区域一体化安排(Latin American regional integration arrangements)*。

Risk assessment
风险评估

WTO成员可对其国际贸易适用食品安全、动物卫生和植物卫生规则，但不得在情形相同或相似的成员之间构成任意或不合理的歧视。WTO《实施卫生与植物卫生措施协定》规定了实现这一目标的规则。协定鼓励成员协调措施，并根据现有的国际标准、指南和建议制定这些措施。如果成员希望保持更高标准，他们必须进行风险评估。风险评估可以是根据所采取的卫生和植物卫生措施评估某种虫害或病害传入或传播的可能性。也可以是评估食品、饮料或饲料中所含添加剂、污染物、毒素或致病有机体对人类或动物的健康所产生的潜在不利影响。风险评估必须考虑可获得的科学证据、相关工序和生产方法、相关检查、抽样和检验方法、特定病害或虫害的流行、病虫害非疫区的存

arising from the presence of additives, contaminants, toxins or disease-causing organisms in food, beverages or feedstuffs. Risk assessment must take into account available scientific evidence, relevant ***processes and production methods***, relevant inspection, sampling and testing methods, prevalence of specific diseases or pests, existence of pest- or disease-free areas, relevant ecological and environmental conditions, and quarantine or other treatment. An assessment of the economic factors involved is also required with the objective of minimizing negative trade effects if measures are taken. This is balanced by a consideration of the damage to production if a disease enters the country, the cost of control and eradication and the cost-effectiveness of possible alternative measures. *See also* ***acceptable level of risk*** and ***sanitary and phytosanitary measures***.

Robinson-Patman Act: an amendment to paragraph 2 of the ***Clayton Act***. It prohibits price discrimination between different purchasers of goods of the same grade or quality. The Act essentially applies to commerce within the United States only. *See also* ***antitrust laws*** and ***competition policy***.

Rollback: multilateral or unilateral action taken to remove barriers to trade through the dismantling of existing measures. Often combined with a ***standstill***. *See also* ***trade liberalization***.

Rolling specificity: a term used in ***APEC*** to describe the process of developing action plans leading to free trade by 2010/2020. The idea is that countries will be able to be quite specific about their near-term plans, but less so about their medium- to long-term actions. Action plans will therefore be updated periodically and become more specific on a rolling basis. *See also* ***Bogor Declaration*** and ***APEC individual action plans***.

"Roll-up" principle: *see* ***absorption principle***.

Rome Convention: the *International Convention for the Protection of Performers, Producers of Phonograms and Broadcasting Organizations*. This Convention protects the rights of performers in performances. Phonogram producers have the right to authorize the reproduction of their phonograms, and broadcasting organizations have the rights concerning their broadcasts. The Convention is administered jointly by ***WIPO***, ***UNESCO***, and the ***International Labour Organization***. *See also* ***Agreement on Trade-Related Aspects of Intellectual Property Rights***, ***Beijing Treaty on Audiovisual Performances*** and ***neighbouring rights***.

Rotterdam Convention on the Prior Informed Consent Procedure for Certain Hazardous Chemicals and Pesticides in International Trade: *see* ***Convention on the Prior Informed Consent Procedure for Certain Hazardous Chemicals and Pesticides in International Trade***.

Round: *see* ***multilateral trade negotiations***.

RTA: *see* ***regional trade agreement***; sometimes regional trade arrangements.

Ruinous competition: *see* ***predatory pricing***.

Rule of reason: a method used in the administration of ***competition policy*** to ascertain whether an ostensibly anti-competitive business practice may have a

在、相关生态和环境条件以及检疫或其他处理方法。要求对相关经济因素进行评估，目的是将所采取措施对贸易的消极影响降到最低程度。同时应考虑病害传入该成员对生产所造成的损害、控制和根除病虫害的费用以及可能的替代方法的成本效益。另见*可接受的风险水平(acceptable level of risk)*、*卫生与植物卫生措施(sanitary and phytosanitary measures)*。

Robinson-Patman Act
罗宾逊帕特曼法

对《克莱顿法》第2款的修正。该法禁止在相同级别或质量的货物的不同购买者之间实行价格歧视。该法基本上只适用于美国国内的商业活动。另见*反垄断法(antitrust laws)*、*竞争政策(competition policy)*。

Rollback
回退

通过废除现有措施消除贸易壁垒的多边或单边行动。常与维持现状一并进行。另见*贸易自由化(trade liberalization)*。

Rolling specificity
滚动式明确性

APEC中使用的词语，用于描述制定到2010年/2020年促成自由贸易的行动计划的过程。该观点为各国对其近期计划十分明确，而对于其中长期行动则并非如此。因此行动计划将定期更新，在滚动基础上使之更加明确。另见*茂物宣言(Bogor Declaration)*、*APEC单边行动计划(APEC individual action plans)*。

"Roll-up" principle
总成原则

见*吸收原则(absorption principle)*。

Rome Convention
罗马公约

即《保护表演者、录音制品制作者和广播组织的国际公约》。公约保护表演者的演出权利。录音制品制作者有权授权复制他们的唱片，广播组织对其广播拥有权利。公约由世界知识产权组织(WIPO)、联合国教科文组织(UNESCO)和国际劳工组织(ILO)共同管理。另见*与贸易有关的知识产权协定(Agreement on Trade-Related Aspects of Intellectual Property Rights)*、*视听表演北京条约(Beijing Treaty on Audiovisual Performances)*、*邻接权(neighbouring rights)*。

Rotterdam Convention on the Prior Informed Consent Procedure for Certain Hazardous Chemicals and Pesticides in International Trade
关于在国际贸易中对某些危险化学品和农药采用事先知情同意程序的鹿特丹公约

见*关于在国际贸易中对某些危险化学品和农药采用事先知情同意程序的公约(Convention on the Prior Informed Consent Procedure for Certain Hazardous Chemicals and Pesticides in International Trade)*。

Round
回合

见*多边贸易谈判(multilateral trade negotiations)*。

RTA
区域贸易协定

见*区域贸易协定(regional trade agreement)*。有时称区域贸易安排。

Ruinous competition
破坏性竞争

见*掠夺性定价(predatory pricing)*。

Rule of reason
合理原则

管理竞争政策中使用的方法，用于确定一种表面上反竞争的商业惯例是否可

balancing pro-competitive impact. If this is the case, competition authorities may decide not to take action if the law gives them that flexibility. *See also* ***antitrust laws*** and ***per se conduct***.

Rules: an omnibus term for a group of WTO issues, including anti-dumping measures, subsidies and safeguards.

Rules of origin: ROOs. These are any laws, regulations, administrative rulings, etc., applied by governments to determine the country of origin of goods, services or investments. The origin of goods, services or investment is important because it may influence how they are treated in the receiving country. For example, some countries only permit investment in some activities if the investor is a national of a defined country. Similarly, permission to sell a service may depend on the origin of the seller. The origin of a good will determine the ***tariff*** applied to it. Another reason is that statistical authorities need to be able to ascribe an import to a supplying country. If a country maintains any administrative restrictions or ***tariff quotas***, it may need to know what country has filled its quota. If a country is a member of the ***Agreement on Government Procurement***, it may have obligations towards some supplying countries, but not to others. ROOs enable it to determine whether any goods it intends to buy are indeed the product of the country having the right to bid for contracts and to supply. The origin of a product thus can have a significant bearing on its cost in the import market or its access to it, and therefore on its ***competitiveness***. ROOs accordingly can be one of the considerations leading to an investment decision. ROOs for goods fall into two main categories. The first applies to goods traded under non-discriminatory conditions, i.e. ***non-preferential rules of origin*** or MFN rules of origin, where the main purpose is to establish the country of origin. This is easy in the case of basic commodities, such as wheat, sugar and iron ore, or products wholly manufactured in one country, such as paving bricks, carded wool, etc. More complex manufactures traded internationally may consist of components imported from several countries. A country may produce a car containing a Japanese gearbox, an Indonesian engine, a German ignition system, seats made with Australian leather and a Korean sound system. In this case the customs authorities would probably decide that the car is the product of the country where all of the components were assembled to make a product ready for the showroom. The situation would be more complicated if the car was assembled in one country and exported to another for cleaning and polishing and then re-exported it to its final destination. The country doing the polishing may deem the car as its product, but the customs authorities may decide that that the bulk of production occurred in the country of assembly. It is easy to see that, as ***globalization*** of production increases, the role of non-preferential ROOs in the administration of international trade rules will also increase. Work is now under way in the WTO and the ***World Customs Organization*** to harmonize ROOS for non-preferential trade. The second main category of ROOs applies to goods traded within ***free-trade areas*** under a ***preferential tariff***. Free-trade area partners usually will seek to ensure that only

能具有平衡性的有利于竞争的作用。如属此种情况，竞争主管机关在法律赋予其灵活性的情况下可能决定不采取措施。另见*反垄断法(antitrust laws)*、*固有行为(per se conduct)*。

Rules
规则

一组WTO问题的统称，包括反倾销措施、补贴和保障措施。

Rules of origin
原产地规则

ROOs。指政府实施的确定货物、服务或投资原产国的任何法律、法规和行政裁定等。货物、服务或投资的原产地之所以重要，是因为可以影响它们在接受国中的待遇。例如，如果投资者是一确定国家的国民，一些国家只允许投资某些活动。同样，服务销售许可可能取决于销售者的来源地。货物原产地将决定对其适用的关税。另一个原因是，统计机关需要能够将一件进口产品归属于某一供应国。如果一国维持任何行政限制或关税配额，可能需要知道哪个国家使用了配额。如果一国属《政府采购协定》参加方，可能对某些供应国有义务，但对其他国家则没有。原产地规则使一国能够确定准备购买的货物是否确实来自有权参与合同竞标和供应的国家。因此产品原产地对其在进口市场中的成本或进入市场的机会有重要影响，从而影响其竞争力。因此原产地规则是作出投资决定的一项考虑因素。货物原产地规则分为两类：第一种适用于非歧视条件下交易的货物，即非优惠原产地规则或最惠国原产地规则，主要目的是确定原产地。对于小麦、食糖和铁矿石等初级商品或地砖、粗梳羊毛等完全在一国制造的产品而言确定原产地很容易。国际贸易中更复杂的制成品可能由来自若干国家的进口部件构成。一国可制造包含日本变速箱、印度尼西亚发动机、德国点火系统、用澳大利亚皮革制作的座椅和韩国音响系统的汽车。此种情况下，海关可能决定汽车的原产地是在将所有部件进行组装成供销售成品的国家。如果汽车在一国进行组装后出口至另一国进行清洁和抛光，然后复出口至最终目的地，情形将更为复杂。进行抛光的国家可能将汽车视为其产品，但海关可能决定生产的主体部分发生在组装国。显然，随着全球化生产的不断增多，非优惠原产地规则在管理国际贸易规则中的作用也将提高。WTO和世界海关组织正在对非优惠贸易原产地规则进行协调。第二种原产地规则适用于自由贸易区内按照优惠关税进行贸易的产品。自由贸易区

products produced in one of the other partners will qualify for preferential treatment. The criteria for determining this consist of a set of ***preferential rules of origin***. Goods qualifying for preferential treatment are usually called ***originating goods***. Goods not receiving a preference are called ***non-originating goods***. Preferential ROOs differ from agreement to agreement. They can be complex though, in all fairness, in many cases this is no more than a perception. All the same, examples of unashamed protectionist intent can easily be found. Three main systems are used for deciding where a product originates regardless of whether trade is preferential or not. They all seek to establish whether ***substantial transformation*** has occurred in the exporting country. First, there is the ***change in tariff heading***, based on whether a product has been sufficiently transformed in the exporting country to be classified now under a different ***chapter***, ***heading*** or ***sub-heading*** in the national ***tariff schedule***. For example, a country may import dressed timber and export it as furniture ready for self-assembly. Second, an assessment can be made in terms of the value that may have been added to the product in the exporting country. Labour costs could be one factor. Third, the origin may be determined in terms of specific processing operations necessary to give the product its characteristics. Such rules often apply to dairy and textile products. In the case of services and investment, the most important criteria for determining the origin of the activity are the place of incorporation, the nationality of the owners, the location of the company head office and the place where business is actually conducted. *See also* ***Kyoto Convention*** and ***preferential rules of origin for least-developed countries***. [Estevadeordal and Suominen 2003, UNCTAD/ITCD/TSB/2, Vermulst, Waer and Bourgeois 1994, WTO WT/REG/W/45]

Rules of origin phase-in: *see* ***phase-in for rules of origin***.

参加方通常寻求保证在其中一个其他参加方中生产的产品方可享受优惠待遇。确定原产地的标准包含一套优惠原产地规则。有权享受优惠待遇的货物通常被称为原产货物。不享受优惠待遇的货物被称为非原产货物。优惠原产地规则因协定不同而不同。以上规则虽然复杂，但公平地讲，许多情况下只是一种感知而已。同样，无耻的保护主义意图的例子随处可见。无论是否属优惠贸易，有三种决定原产地的主要体制。这些体制均寻求确定是否在出口国中发生了实质性改变。第一，税目改变，基于产品是否在出口国中进行实质性改变而被归入一国关税税则中不同的章、税目或子目。例如一国可以进口刨光木材，制成可自行组装的家具出口。第二，可以对产品在出口国中增加的价值进行评估。劳动力成本可以成为一个因素。第三，原产地可以根据赋予产品特点的特定加工工序确定。此类规则经常适用于奶制品和纺织品。对于服务和投资，确定法律活动来源的最重要标准是企业注册地、所有者国籍、公司总部所在地和实际营业地。另见*京都公约(Kyoto Convention)*、*最不发达国家优惠原产地规则(preferential rules of origin for least-developed countries)*。

Rules of origin phase-in
原产地规则的分阶段实施

见*原产地规则分阶段实施(phase-in for rules of origin)*。

S

S&D: also S+D or SDT. "Special and differential treatment" provisions for developing countries contained in several agreements administered by the WTO. *See* ***special and differential treatment***.

S&D box: refers to Article 6.2 of the WTO ***Agreement on Agriculture*** which exempts from reduction commitments some government measures maintained by developing countries in support of agriculture. This includes (a) measures of assistance, whether direct or indirect, to encourage agricultural and rural development which are an integral part of development programmes, (b) investment subsidies generally available to agriculture, (c) agricultural subsidies generally available to low-income or resource-poor producers, and (e) support to producers to encourage diversification from growing illicit narcotic crops. *See also* ***amber box***, ***blue box*** and ***green box***.

SAARC: *see* ***South Asian Association for Regional Cooperation***.

SAARC Preferential Trading Arrangement: SAPTA. Signed in 1993. Now superseded by the South Asian Free Trade Agreement. *See also* ***South Asian Association for Regional Cooperation***.

SACU: the ***Southern African Customs Union*** which comprises Botswana, Eswatini, Lesotho, Namibia and South Africa.

SAFE Framework of Standards to Secure and Facilitate Global Trade: usually known the SAFE Framework. Adopted by the World Customs Organization in 2005 to act as a deterrent to international terrorism, secure revenue collections and promote ***trade facilitation*** worldwide. It prescribes baseline standards that have been tested in practice. The use of ***authorized economic operators*** is a key part of the Framework. *See also* ***Container Security Initiative***.

Safeguards: action taken to protect a specific industry from an unexpected build-up of imports causing, or threatening to cause, ***serious injury***. Safeguards measures usually refer to action taken under Article XIX (Emergency Action on Imports of Particular Products) of the GATT, the so-called ***escape clause***. However, safeguards action is possible also under Article XII (Restrictions to Safeguard the Balance of Payments) and Article XVIII (Governmental Assistance to Economic Development). A useful outline of the ways safeguards action may be instituted under the WTO rules has been devised by trade policy analysts within the ***World Bank***, but this approach is not necessarily accepted by all WTO members. According to this view, safeguards action may be taken in six different ways, all of which are subject to conditions ensuring that action

S

S&D

特殊和差别待遇

也写作S+D或SDT。"特殊和差别待遇"条款包含在WTO管理的多个协定中。另见*特殊和差别待遇(special and differential treatment)*。

S&D box

特殊和差别待遇箱

指WTO《农业协定》第6.2条，该条规定对发展中国家在农业支持方面保留的一些政府措施免于削减承诺。包括(a)作为发展计划的组成部分的直接或间接鼓励农业和农村发展的援助措施；(b)农业可普遍获得的投资补贴；(c)低收入或资源贫乏生产者可普遍获得的农业补贴；以及(d)鼓励对以生产多样化为途径停止种植非法麻醉作物而给予生产者的支持。另见*黄箱(amber box)*、*蓝箱(blue box)*、*绿箱(green box)*。

SAARC

南亚区域合作联盟

见*南亚区域合作联盟(South Asian Association for Regional Cooperation)*。

SAARC Preferential Trading Arrangement

SAARC优惠贸易安排

SAPTA。1993年签署。现被《南亚自由贸易协定》所取代。另见*南亚区域合作联盟(South Asian Association for Regional Cooperation)*。

SACU

南部非洲关税同盟

由博茨瓦纳、斯威士兰、莱索托、纳米比亚和南非组成。

SAFE Framework of Standards to Secure and Facilitate Global Trade

全球贸易安全与便利标准框架

通常称为 SAFE 框架。世界海关组织(WCO)于2005年通过该框架，以应对国际恐怖主义、确保税收征收和促进全球贸易便利化。框架规定了已经过实践检验的标准。使用经认证的经营者是框架一项主要内容。另见*集装箱安全倡议(Container Security Initiative)*。

Safeguards

保障措施

为保护一特定行业免受意外增加的进口造成的或威胁造成的严重损害而采取的行动。保障措施通常指根据GATT第19条(对某些产品进口的紧急措施)，即所谓的免责条款而采取的行动。但是，保障措施也可以根据第12条(为保障国际收支而实施的限制)和第18条(政府对经济发展的援助)实施。世界银行贸易政策分析专家制定了一份根据WTO规则采取保障措施的方式的有用框架，但这种方式并不一定为所有WTO成员接受。根据这一观点，保障措施可以按照6种方式采取，而所有方式均附有条件，即需保证措施仅在有正当理由时采取。

is taken only if valid reasons exist. There are also certain procedural steps which have to be followed in each case. First, Article VI of the ***GATT*** permits governments to take action if ***dumping*** occurs. The provisions of this article are refined further in the Agreement on Implementation of Article VI of the GATT 1994 (the ***Anti-Dumping Agreement***). Second, under Articles XII and, in the case of developing countries, XVIII:B, they may restrict imports in order to protect their external financial position and their ***balance of payments***. Third, Article XVIII:A and XVIII:C allow developing countries to provide governmental assistance to promote economic development. Fourth, Article XIX allows a country to suspend its obligations or to modify liberalizing commitments if there are ***unforeseen developments*** and if any product is being imported in such increased quantities or under such conditions as to cause or threaten serious ***injury*** to domestic producers of like or directly competitive products. Except in defined circumstances, safeguards action taken under Article XIX must be aimed at a particular product, regardless of its source. Discriminatory action aimed against the countries perceived to be the main problem is against the rules. If action is taken, there is an obligation to provide compensation to affected parties in the form of lower tariffs and/or better access conditions in other product lines. The ***Agreement on Safeguards*** establishes the detailed rules for the application of safeguard measures as provided for in Article XIX of the GATT. Fifth, it is possible to renegotiate commitments under GATT Article XXVIII with the aim of gaining relief from imports. Sixth, the ***general exceptions*** and the ***security exceptions*** under the ***General Agreement on Trade in Services*** and the GATT can also be viewed as a form of safeguards action. *See also* ***anti-dumping measures***, ***bilateral transitional safeguards***, ***Hatters' fur***, ***selectivity***, ***Transitional Product-Specific Safeguard Mechanism*** and ***transitional safeguard mechanism***. [Finger 1998, Lee 2003]

Safe-haven agreement: used by some commentators to describe a ***regional trade agreement*** to which a smaller country accedes in the expectation of obtaining secure access for its exports.

SAFTA: *see* ***South Asian Free Trade Area***.

Same-condition substitution duty drawback: a practice relating to trade in agricultural products prohibited under ***NAFTA***. It concerns the refund, waiving or reduction in the amount of customs duties owed on any agricultural good imported into the territory and substituted for an identical or similar good subsequently exported to the territory of another party. A similar prohibition applies to customs duties on manufactured products. *See also* ***maquiladora industries***.

Sanitary and phytosanitary measures: measures necessary to protect human health, animal or plant life or health. They are often called quarantine measures. The WTO ***Agreement on the Application of Sanitary and Phytosanitary Measures*** (the SPS agreement) defines them as any measure applied (a) to protect animal or plant life or health from risks arising from the entry, establishment or spread of pests, diseases, disease-carrying organisms or disease-causing

在每种情况下均需遵循某些程序性步骤。第一，GATT第6条允许政府在发生倾销时采取行动。该条在《关于实施1994年关税与贸易总协定第6条的协定》(《反倾销协定》)中得到进一步完善。第二，根据第12条，在涉及发展中国家的情况下，根据第18条B节，可以限制进口以保护其外部财政状况和国际收支。第三，第18条A节和C节允许发展中国家提供政府援助以促进经济发展。第四，第19条允许在因未预见的情况及任何产品的进口数量增加如此之大以至于对同类产品或直接竞争产品的国内生产者造成或威胁造成严重损害情况下，一国可中止其义务或修改自由化承诺。除特定情况外，根据第19条采取的保障措施必须针对一特定产品，而无论其来自何处。针对被视为主要问题来源的国家采取歧视性措施违反规则。如果采取行动，有义务以降低关税和/或提供对其他产品更优惠准入的形式向受影响的各方提供补偿。《保障措施协定》制定了GATT第19条中所规定的保障措施的详细实施规则。第五，可以根据GATT第28条重新谈判承诺，以期从进口产品中获得救济。第六，《服务贸易总协定》和GATT中的一般例外和安全例外也可视为一种保障措施。另见*反倾销措施(anti-dumping measures)*、*双边过渡性保障措施(bilateral transitional safeguards)*、*裘皮女帽案(Hatters' fur)*、*选择性(selectivity)*、*特定产品过渡性保障机制(Transitional Product-Specific Safeguard Mechanism)*、*过渡性保障机制(transitional safeguard mechanism)*。

Safe-haven agreement

避风港协定

一些评论家用于描述一较小国家期望为其出口产品获得安全准入而加入的区域贸易协定。

SAFTA

南亚自由贸易区

另见*南亚自由贸易区(South Asian Free Trade Area)*。

Same-condition substitution duty drawback

相同情形替代退税

《北美自由贸易协定》(NAFTA)所禁止的与农产品贸易有关的一种做法。涉及对进口至一参加方领土的农产品应缴关税税额的退还、豁免或削减，该农产品被替换为一种相同或类似的货物随后出口至另一参加方领土。类似的禁止适用于制成品的关税。另见*保税加工出口产业(maquiladora industries)*。

Sanitary and Phytosanitary measures

卫生与植物卫生措施

保护人类健康、动物或植物的生命或健康所必需的措施，通常称为检疫措施。WTO《实施卫生与植物卫生措施协定》(《SPS协定》)将其定义为为下列目的而实施任何措施：(a)保护动物或植物的生命或健康免受虫害、病害、带病有机体或致病有机体的传入、定居或传播所产生的风险；(b)保护人类或动物的

organisms, (b) to protect human or animal life or health from risks arising from additives, contaminants, toxins or disease-causing organisms in foods, beverages or foodstuffs, (c) to protect human life or health from risks arising from diseases carried by animals, plants or products thereof, or from the entry, establishment or spread of pests, or (d) to prevent or limit other damage form the entry, establishment or spread of pests. The Agreement sets out broadly the rights and obligations of WTO members in enforcing such measures. Among other things, they must be based on scientific principles, sufficient scientific evidence and on ***risk assessments***. Measures must not be applied in a manner which would constitute a means of ***arbitrary or unjustifiable discrimination*** between members where the same conditions prevail. Where international standards exist, these are to be used as the basis for national standards, but national standards may be higher if there is scientific justification for doing so. Sanitary and phytosanitary measures must not be used as a ***disguised restriction on international trade***. *See also* ***acceptable level of risk***, ***appropriate level of sanitary or phytosanitary protection***, ***International Plant Protection Convention***, ***SPS Information Management System***, ***Standards and Trade Development Facility*** and ***World Organisation for Animal Health***.

Santiago Initiative for Expanded Trade in APEC: a multi-year programme to promote further trade and investment liberalization among ***APEC*** economies and to intensify work on trade facilitation. It was adopted in November 2004 by the ***APEC Economic Leaders' Meeting***. [www.apec.org]

São Paulo Consensus: a statement adopted on 18 June 2004 at ***UNCTAD*** XI at São Paulo. It offers policy analysis and UNCTAD's response in four main areas: (a) development strategies in a globalizing world economy, (b) building productive capacities and international competitiveness, (c) assuring development gains from the international trading system and trade negotiations, and (d) partnership for development. The statement is essentially a broad outline of UNCTAD's work programme until UNCTAD XII. [UNCTAD TD/410]

SAPTA: the *SAARC Preferential Trading Arrangement*. Now superseded by the ***South Asian Free Trade Area***. *See also* ***South Asian Association for Regional Cooperation***.

Schedule: a WTO member's list of commitments on market access (bound tariff rates for goods, access to services markets). Goods schedules can include commitments on agricultural subsidies and domestic support. Services commitments include bindings on national treatment. *See also* ***additional commitments***, ***schedule of concessions*** and ***schedules of specific commitments on services***.

Schedule of concessions: a list of ***bound tariff rates*** negotiated under WTO auspices. It sets out the terms, conditions and qualifications under which goods may be imported. No additional duties or charges may be imposed at the border other than internal taxes also levied on similar domestic products, ***anti-dumping measures*** or countervailing duties or a fee-for-service charge. *See also* ***tariff***.

生命或健康免受食品、饮料或饲料中的添加剂、污染物、毒素或致病有机体所产生的风险；(c)保护人类的生命或健康免受动物、植物或动植物产品携带的病害或虫害的传入、定居或传播所产生的风险；或(d)防止或控制因虫害的传入、定居或传播所产生的其他损害。协定规定了WTO成员在执行此类措施方面的广泛权利和义务。其中要求，措施必须以科学原则、充分科学证据和风险评估为基础。措施的实施不得在情形相同的成员之间构成任意或不合理的歧视。在存在国际标准的情形下，它们将作为国内标准的基础，但如果有科学上的合理性，国内标准可以高于国际标准。卫生与植物卫生措施不得被用作对国际贸易的变相限制。另见*可接受的风险水平(acceptable level of risk)*、*适当的卫生与植物卫生保护水平(appropriate level of sanitary or phytosanitary protection)*、*国际植物保护公约(International Plant Protection Convention)*、*卫生与植物卫生信息管理系统(SPS Information Management System)*、*标准和贸易发展基金(Standards and Trade Development Facility)*、*世界动物卫生组织(World Organisation for Animal Health)*。

Santiago Initiative for Expanded Trade in APEC

促进APEC贸易发展的圣地亚哥倡议

多年期项目，旨在进一步促进APEC经济体之间贸易和投资自由化并加强贸易便利化工作。倡议于2004年11月在APEC经济领导人会议上通过。

São Paulo Consensus

圣保罗共识

2004年6月18日在圣保罗举行的联合国贸易与发展会议(UNCTAD)第11届大会上通过的声明。声明对四个主要领域进行了政策分析，并提出了UNCTAD的回应：(a)在全球化世界经济中的发展战略；(b)增强生产能力和国际竞争力；(c)保证自国际贸易体制和贸易谈判中获得发展收益；以及(d)发展伙伴关系。这一声明本质上是UNCTAD在第12届大会召开前的工作计划的概述。

SAPTA

南亚特惠贸易安排

现被南亚自由贸易区所取代。另见*南亚区域合作联盟(South Asian Association for Regional Cooperation)*。

Schedule

减让表

WTO成员关于市场准入的承诺清单(货物约束税率、服务市场准入)。货物减让表可以纳入农业补贴和国内支持的承诺。服务承诺包括关于国民待遇的约束。另见*附加承诺(additional commitments)*、*减让表(schedule of concessions)*、*服务贸易具体承诺减让表(schedules of specific commitments on services)*。

Schedule of concessions

减让表

在WTO主持下谈判达成的一份约束税率清单。其中列出货物进口依据的条款、条件和限定条件。除同样对国内类似产品征收的国内税、反倾销措施、反补贴税或服务费用外，不得在边境征收额外关税或费用。另见*关税(tariff)*。

Schedules of specific commitments on services: a requirement under the ***General Agreement on Trade in Services.*** They show what level of ***market access for services*** each WTO member is willing to accord other members. Similarly, they indicate whether ***national treatment*** is offered. These schedules perform a function similar to the ***tariff schedules*** for goods under the GATT.

Schengen Agreement: signed in 1985. Supplemented in 1995 by the Schengen Convention. Established the zone of free movement within the ***European Union*** and some of its neighbours. Ireland is not part of it. Nor was the United Kingdom during its membership of the European Union. ***Candidate countries*** must accept the whole of the Schengen provisions when they accede, but only after an evaluation that they can control their borders effectively. Iceland, Liechtenstein, Norway and Switzerland also take part in the Schengen area. *See also* ***Brexit***.

Schengen Convention: *see* ***Schengen Agreement***.

Scientific tariff: the ideal set of ***tariff*** rates sought over the years by many governments. Its aim would be to ensure that one's products can compete internationally on an equal basis with those of others, to promote employment at home and to offset perceived ***unfair trading practices*** by others. No country has yet succeeded in formulating a scientific tariff, though not for want of effort. In any case, even if it could be devised, it would be in direct conflict with the ideas of the ***international division of labour*** and ***comparative advantage***, and in this way negate the advantages of efficiencies available elsewhere. *See also* ***optimal-tariff argument***.

SCM Agreement: *see* ***Agreement on Subsidies and Countervailing Measures***.

Screwdriver **case:** dispute settlement proceedings initiated by Japan against the ***European Economic Community*** (EEC) in 1988 concerning ***anti-dumping measures*** taken by the EEC against Japanese products assembled or produced there from imported parts. The background was that the EEC had in the mid-1980s imposed anti-dumping duties on, among other things, hydraulic excavators, electronic weighing scales and electronic typewriters imported from Japan. EEC producers subsequently submitted that that although these duties were now applied, the prices of the relevant Japanese products had not increased, and in some cases they had even gone down. The producers alleged that this was possible because the Japanese companies, said to be multinationals with large financial resources at their disposal, were able to import the parts of the offending equipment at normal duty rates. They were then assembled within the EEC or third countries. EEC producers alleged that the cost of assembling these products by a "screwdriver" process was relatively low. In response to these complaints the EEC then proceeded to impose also anti-dumping duties on products made or assembled in the EEC of imported parts. It further sought undertakings from the enterprises concerned that they would limit the use of parts or materials originating in Japan. One of the arguments in the case by the EEC was that the anti-dumping duties on imported parts were justified as an ***anti-circumvention*** measure. The ***panel*** did not see it that way. It held that both

Schedules of specific commitments on services
服务贸易具体承诺减让表
《服务贸易总协定》项下的一项要求。减让表中显示每一WTO成员愿意给予其他成员的服务市场准入水平。同时表明是否提供国民待遇。减让表发挥的作用类似于GATT项下的货物关税减让表。

Schengen Agreement
申根协定
1985年签署。1995年经《申根公约》补充。协定在欧盟及其一些邻国之间建立自由流动区。爱尔兰未加入，英国在属欧盟成员国期间也未加入。候选国在加入欧盟时必须接受全部申根条款，但必须在对它们能够有效控制边界作出评估后。冰岛、列支敦士登、挪威和瑞士也加入了申根区。另见*英国脱欧(Brexit)*。

Schengen Convention
申根公约
见*申根协定(Schengen Agreement)*。

Scientific tariff
科学关税
许多政府多年来寻求的一套理想的关税税率。目的是保证一国的产品能够与其他国家的产品在平等的基础上进行国际竞争，促进国内就业，并抵消其他国家的不公平贸易做法。迄今尚无一国成功制定科学关税，虽然并不是由于缺乏努力。无论如何，即使能够设计出科学关税，也将与国际分工和比较优势的理念直接冲突，从而否定了其他地方的效率优势。另见*最优关税论(optimal-tariff argument)*。

SCM Agreement
补贴与反补贴措施协定
见*补贴与反补贴措施协定(Agreement on Subsidies and Countervailing Measures)*。

***Screwdriver* case**
日本诉欧共体改锥案
日本在1988年对欧洲经济共同体(EEC)发起的争端解决程序，涉及欧共体对日本使用进口零件组装或制造的产品采取的反倾销措施。背景是欧共体在20世纪80年代中期开始对自日本进口的液压挖掘机、电子秤和电子打字机等产品征收反倾销税。欧共体生产商随后提出，虽然现在征收了关税，但是相关日本产品的价格并未上涨，在一些情形下甚至下降了。生产商认为可能是因为这些日本公司——据说是拥有雄厚的可支配财力的跨国公司——能够以正常税率进口有关设备的零件。随后在欧共体境内或第三国组装。欧共体生产商认为，通过"螺丝刀"工序组装的这些产品成本相对较低。为回应这些质疑，欧共体随后开始对在欧共体境内使用进口零件生产或组装的产品征收反倾销税。欧共体进一步寻求有关企业作出关于限制使用原产于日本的零件或材料的承诺。欧共体在该案中的一项主张是，对进口零件征收反倾销税作为一项反规

of EEC's actions contravened the ***national treatment*** requirement of the GATT. [GATT BISD 37/S]

Screwdriver operations: a pejorative term for manufacturing operations concerned mainly with the assembly of components. This often involves little or no ***transfer of technology***. Screwdriver operations are more likely to be found where there is an adequate supply of comparatively inexpensive labour. They are partly a cause and a result of ***globalization*** driven by the need to find the most efficient production arrangement. They can also be due to ***preferential rules of origin*** which encourage firms to establish operations inside ***free-trade areas*** to get around ***market access*** impediments. *See also* ***delocalization***, ***export processing zones***, ***footloose industries***, ***maquiladora industries*** and ***rules of origin***.

Seasonal tariff: a tariff rate related to the seasonal supply of domestic agricultural products. Tariffs are low when domestic offerings are out of season and high when domestic production starts to reach the market. The imported product need not be exactly the same as the domestic product.

Seattle Ministerial Conference: the ***WTO Ministerial Conference*** held in Seattle from 30 November to 3 December 1999. *See also* ***Doha Ministerial Conference***.

Second Account: the finance programme established under the ***Common Fund for Commodities*** to fund commodity development measures aimed at improving the structural conditions in markets and enhancing the long-term competitiveness and prospects of particular commodities. *See also* ***First Account***.

Secondary dumping: the export of a product which incorporates components that have been landed at dumped prices. For example, the frame of a bicycle may have been imported by a firm in the exporting country at less than market price. Because of this, the firm enjoys a price advantage even if it is selling its completed bicycles at the market price prevailing in its own economy. The ***injury*** impact of secondary dumping is difficult to substantiate. *See also* ***anti-dumping measures***, ***dumping***, ***hidden dumping*** and ***indirect dumping***.

Second beer panel: a dispute in 1991 in the GATT between the United States and Canada. It concerned the import, distribution and sale of certain alcoholic drinks by Canadian provincial marketing agencies. There had been a case on the same issue in 1988, hence the name of this case. The Canadian marketing agencies ("liquor boards"), created by provincial laws, had a monopoly on the supply and distribution of alcoholic beverages within provincial boundaries. They also had a monopoly on the import of alcoholic beverages from other provinces or foreign countries. A provincial licence was needed for the brewing and selling of beer in a province, and most domestic beer had to be brewed in the province in which it was sold. All provinces operated government liquor stores, but they also allowed beer sales at privately-owned retail outlets and brewery stores. The 1988 ***panel*** had concluded that mark-ups on imported products that were higher than those on domestic products could only be justified in precisely defined circumstances, that the ***burden of proof*** in this

避措施是合理的。但专家组并不这样认为，而是认为欧共体的两项措施违反了GATT国民待遇要求。

Screwdriver operations

螺丝刀式经营

对于主要使用零件组装的制造过程的贬义词，通常很少包含或不包含技术转让。螺丝刀式经营更有可能在有相对廉价劳动力充足供应的地方出现。在一定程度上是寻找最有效率的生产安排所推动的全球化的起因和结果。也可能是由于优惠原产地规则鼓励企业在自由贸易区内开展经营，以避开市场准入障碍。另见*去本地化(delocalization)*、*出口加工区(export processing zones)*、*自由布局型产业(footloose industries)*、*保税加工出口产业(maquiladora industries)*、*原产地规则(rules of origin)*。

Seasonal tariff

季节性关税

一种与本国农产品的季节性供应有关的关税。当国内供应过季时，关税降低；当本国产品当季时，关税提高。进口产品不一定与本国产品完全相同。

Seattle Ministerial Conference

西雅图部长级会议

1999年11月30日至12月3日在西雅图举行的WTO部长级会议。另见*多哈部长级会议(Doha Ministerial Conference)*。

Second Account

第二账户

在商品共同基金下设立的为商品发展提供资金的融资项目，旨在改善市场的结构条件，提高特定商品的长期竞争力和前景。另见*第一账户(First Account)*。

Secondary dumping

二级倾销

包含以倾销价格进口的零件的一产品的出口。例如，自行车车架可能自出口国的一家企业以低于市场价格的价格进口。因此，即使该企业以其本国现行市场价格出售自行车整车也能享受价格优势。二级倾销的损害影响很难证明。另见*反倾销措施(anti-dumping measures)*、*倾销(dumping)*、*隐蔽倾销(hidden dumping)*、*间接倾销(indirect dumping)*。

Second beer panel

第二啤酒案专家组

1991年美国和加拿大在GATT中产生的争端。涉及加拿大省级销售机构对某些酒精饮料的进口、分销和销售。1988年曾发生相同问题的争端，故该案有此名称。根据省法律所设立的加拿大销售机构("酒类销售局")垄断省界内酒类饮料的供应和分销。还垄断自其他省或自国外进口的酒精饮料。在一省之内酿造和销售啤酒需要获得省级许可证，且大多数国产啤酒必须在销售啤酒的省份酿造。所有省份经营政府酒类商店，但是也允许在私营零售店和啤酒店销售啤酒。1988年专家组的结论是，对进口产品的加价高于本国产品的加价只有在严格限定的情况下方可证明合理，举证责任在加拿大，而对进口酒精饮料

regard lay with Canada, and that the listing requirements and the availability of points of sale discriminating against imported alcoholic beverages were restrictions made effective through state-trading operations contrary to Article XI (General Elimination of Quantitative Restrictions). In 1988, following the first panel, Canada concluded an agreement with the ***European Community*** aimed at resolving some of the points at issue. This agreement was to be implemented by the provinces on a most-favoured-nation basis. The panel concluded that, with the exception of one province, the United States had not substantiated its claim concerning Canadian listing and delisting practices. As to restrictions on access to points of sale, the panel considered that imported beer had access to fewer of them. It found that these restrictions were contrary to the provisions of the GATT. It concluded that the mere fact that imported and domestic beer were subject to different delivery systems was not in itself enough to establish inconsistency with the GATT since formally identical ***national treatment*** might leave the imported product worse off. The panel then considered the methods for assessing markups and taxes on imported beer and found that they were inconsistent with Article III:4 (National Treatment). The panel next turned to the question of minimum prices and concluded that the maintenance by an import monopoly of any minimum price for an imported product at a level at which a directly-competing, higher-priced domestic product was supplied was inconsistent with Article III:4. The panel considered that the taxes on beer containers had been dealt with as part of its consideration of restrictions on private delivery. It concluded that provincial notification procedures did not violate Article X (Publication and Administration of Trade Regulations). Finally, the panel concluded that Canada had failed to comply in several aspects of this case with its obligations under GATT Article XXIV:12 which enjoins GATT members to take reasonable measure to ensure compliance with the provisions of the Agreement by regional and local governments and authorities within its territories. *See also* ***implicit discrimination*** and ***second-level obligations***. [GATT BISD 39S]

Second High-Level United Nations Conference on South–South Cooperation: held in Buenos Aires in March 2019 with the objective of strengthening cooperation between developing countries, particularly in the context of a review of achievements on its fortieth anniversary of the adoption of the ***Buenos Aires Plan of Action for Promoting and Implementing Technical Co-operation among Developing Countries***. The first High-Level United Nations Conference on South–South Cooperation was held in Nairobi in 2009.

Second-level obligations: the obligations under the WTO agreements of central governments of federated states in respect of states or provinces constituting their jurisdictions. Two examples will suffice. The provisions of the ***GATT*** require WTO members to take such reasonable measures as may be available to them to ensure observance of GATT rules by regional and local governments and authorities within their territories. The ***General Agreement on Trade in***

的上市要求和销售点准入歧视是通过国营贸易经营有效实施的限制，违反第11条(普遍取消数量限制)。1988年，根据第一个专家组的主张，加拿大与欧洲共同体达成一项协议，旨在解决一些争议点。协议需由各省在最惠国基础上实施。专家组认为，除了一个省外，美国没有证明其关于加拿大上市和退市做法的主张。对于销售点的准入限制，专家组认为进口啤酒可以进入的销售点较少。认为这些限制与GATT条款不符。专家组得出结论认为，仅以进口啤酒和国产啤酒的运输体系不同这一事实本身并不足以证明与GATT的不一致性，因为形式上相同的国民待遇可能使进口产品的情况变得更糟。专家组随后审议了对进口啤酒的加价方法和国内税，认为与第3.4条(国民待遇)不一致。专家组接着审议了最低价格问题，认为进口垄断企业将进口产品的最低价格维持在直接竞争且定价较高的国产品的供应水平上，不符合第3.4条。专家组认为，对啤酒容器的国内税问题已经作为专家对私人运送限制问题审议的一部分加以处理。专家组认为省级通报程序未违反第10条(贸易法规的公布和实施)。最后，专家组认为，加拿大在本案中在几个方面未能遵守其在GATT第24.12条下的义务，该条要求GATT缔约方采取合理措施以保证领土内的地方政府和主管机关遵守GATT条款。另见*隐性歧视(implicit discrimination)*、*二级义务(second-level obligations)*。

Second High-Level United Nations Conference on South–South Cooperation
第二届联合国南南合作高级别会议

2019年3月在布宜诺斯艾利斯举行，目的为加强发展中国家之间的合作，特别是在审议《促进和实施发展中国家间技术合作的布宜诺斯艾利斯行动计划》通过40周年成就的背景下。第一届联合国南南合作高级别会议于2009年在内罗毕举行。

Second-level obligations
二级义务

联邦制国家的中央政府对于构成其管辖范围的州或省在WTO协定项下的义务。两个例子足以说明此点。GATT条款要求WTO成员采取其可采取的合理措施，以保证其领土内的地方政府及主管机关遵守GATT规则。《服务贸易总协定》

Services applies to measures taken by central, regional or local governments and authorities.

Second Protocol to the General Agreement on Trade in Services: the ***protocol*** giving effect to the commitments on trade in ***financial services*** made in the 1995 negotiations. It entered into force on 1 September 1996.

Second regionalism: a term used by Jagdish Bhagwati to describe the trend towards ***preferential trade arrangements*** that began in 1985 with the conclusion of the United States–Israel Free Trade Agreement. *See also* ***first regionalism***. [Bhagwati 1993]

Second United Nations Conference on the Least-Developed Countries: *see* ***SNPA***.

Secretariat of Central American Economic Integration: Secretaría de la Integracíon Económica Centroamericana (SIECA). It oversees the implementation of the Guatemala Protocol to the General Treaty on Central American Economic Integration. Its members are Costa Rica, El Salvador, Guatemala, Honduras, Nicaragua and Panama. SIECA is aiming to establish the Central American Customs Union. Its location is in Guatemala City. *See also* ***Central American Integration System*** and ***Central American Uniform Customs Code***.

Secretariat of the Pacific Community: an ***intergovernmental organization*** established in 1947 as the South Pacific Commission to give training and assistance in social, economic and cultural areas to the Pacific island countries. Its members are American Samoa, Australia, Cook Islands, Federated States of Micronesia, Fiji, France, French Polynesia, Guam, Kiribati, Marshall Islands, Nauru, New Caledonia, New Zealand, Niue, Northern Mariana Islands, Palau, Papua New Guinea, Pitcairn Islands, Samoa, Solomon Islands, Tokelau, Tonga, Tuvalu, United States, Vanuatu and Wallis and Futuna. Its secretariat is located at Noumea.

Section 22 waiver: refers to Section 22 of the United States Agricultural Adjustment Act which required the Administration to impose ***quantitative restrictions*** or surcharges (above normal tariffs) whenever agricultural imports interfered with a United States farm programme. In 1955, the United States was granted a ***waiver*** without a time limit to exempt this section of the Act from the GATT disciplines. Quotas imposed under Section 22 have been converted to tariff protection as a result of the ***Uruguay Round*** negotiations. *See also* ***agriculture and the multilateral trading system*** and ***tariffication***.

Section 201: a section, usually called the ***escape clause***, of the United States Trade Act of 1974 and subsequent versions of the Act. It gives American firms relief from imports that are considered causing, or threatening to cause, serious injury to an industry. It applies to products that are traded fairly. In other words, products are not considered subsidized or dumped. Relief may be brought about through temporary tariff increases, ***import quotas***, negotiated restraint arrangements or direct assistance to the industry concerned. *See also* ***safeguards*** and ***voluntary restraint arrangement***.

适用于中央、地区或地方政府及主管机关采取的措施。

Second Protocol to the General Agreement on Trade in Services
服务贸易总协定第二议定书

该议定书使1995年谈判中作出的金融服务贸易承诺得以生效。该议定书本身于1996年9月1日生效。

Second regionalism
第二次区域主义浪潮

贾格迪什·巴格瓦蒂使用该词描述随着1985年《美国—以色列自由贸易协定》缔结而开始的优惠贸易安排的趋势。另见*第一次区域主义浪潮(first regionalism)*。

Second United Nations Conference on the Least-Developed Countries
第二次联合国最不发达国家问题会议

见*20世纪80年代支援最不发达国家新的实质性行动纲领(SNPA)*。

Secretariat of Central American Economic Integration
中美洲经济一体化秘书处

秘书处负责监督《中美洲经济一体化总条约危地马拉议定书》的执行情况，成员国为哥斯达黎加、萨尔瓦多、危地马拉、洪都拉斯、尼加拉瓜和巴拿马。中美洲经济一体化的目标是建立中美洲关税同盟。秘书处设在危地马拉城。另见*中美洲一体化体系(Central American Integration System)*、*中美洲海关统一代码(Central American Uniform Customs Code)*。

Secretariat of the Pacific Community
太平洋共同体秘书处

1947年成立的政府间组织，作为南太平洋委员会向太平洋岛屿国家提供社会、经济和文化领域的培训和援助。成员为美属萨摩亚、澳大利亚、库克群岛、密克罗尼西亚联邦、斐济、法国、法属玻利尼西亚、关岛、基里巴斯、马绍尔群岛、瑙鲁、新喀里多尼亚、新西兰、纽埃、北马里亚纳群岛、帕劳、巴布亚新几内亚、皮特凯恩群岛、萨摩亚、所罗门群岛、托克劳、汤加、图瓦卢、美国、瓦努阿图、瓦利斯和富图纳。秘书处设在努美阿。

Section 22 waiver
22条豁免

指《美国农业调整法》第22节，该条要求联邦政府在农产品进口妨碍美国农业计划时采取数量限制或附加税(高于正常关税)。1955年，美国获得无时间限制的豁免，使该法中的此条不受GATT纪律约束。根据第22节实施的配额已经作为乌拉圭回合谈判的结果转为关税保护。另见*农业与多边贸易体制(agriculture and the multilateral trading system)*、*关税化(tariffication)*。

Section 201
201条款

美国《1974年贸易法》及该法修订版中的一节，通常称为免责条款。该条在进口产品被认为严重损害或威胁严重损害一产业时给予美国企业救济措施。该条适用于公平交易的产品。换言之，不被认为接受补贴或倾销的产品。救济措施可以通过临时提高关税、进口配额、谈判限制安排或对有关行业的直接援助提供。另见*保障措施(safeguards)*、*自愿限制安排(voluntary restraint arrangement)*。

Section 232 investigation: an investigation under Section 232 of the United States Trade Expansion Act of 1962, as amended, to determine the effects of imports on national security. Tariff reductions may not be made if this would affect national security.

Section 301: the section so numbered of the United States Trade Act of 1974. Section 301 is designed to enforce United States rights under trade agreements and to provide for responses to foreign unfair trading practices following petition and investigation. Unfair trading practices may take place in the United States, in the offending country itself or in third countries. Section 301 may also be used to obtain increased market access for United States goods and services, to secure fairer conditions for its investors abroad and to promote more effective protection in other countries for United States intellectual property rights. It also allows ***USTR*** to limit imports from countries that unfairly restrict United States trade in particular products. It is generally used for single product sectors. The threat of a Section 301 action is problematic to trade policy makers, not only because it may mean rethinking the rules in the targeted areas, but also because the defence requires much effort that is otherwise unproductive. Taking action is equally resource-intensive for the Americans, and USTR tends to pick cases it perceives as winnable to the extent that it has the choice. That flexibility has been eroded over the years. Some say that the history of Section 301 actions against the European Economic Community, Japan and Korea has shown that its imposition can be quite ineffectual if there is not already an inclination in the target country to reform access to the sector anyway. This is definitely an underestimate of its impact. Others say that the WTO ***Understanding on Rules and Procedures Governing Settlement of Disputes*** has taken the teeth out of Section 301. This is not the case. Section 301 is still available for retaliation if a WTO member does not act in accordance with the outcome of the dispute settlement process. Section 301 may also still be used as originally intended in all cases where there are no WTO rules covering an action perceived as unfair. *See also* ***Special 301*** and ***Super 301***.

Section-306 monitoring: a mechanism specified in the ***Omnibus Trade and Competitiveness Act***. It requires ***USTR*** to monitor the implementation of measures taken under ***Section 301***. If USTR considers that a foreign country is not implementing a measure or an agreement satisfactorily, it must determine what further action to take. Such a determination is considered to satisfy the requirements for further action under Section 301. In other words, no further investigation is necessary to justify additional action.

Section 337: a provision of the 1930 United States Tariff Act, also known as Smoot-Hawley Act, which allows the granting of fast-track relief from present or potential ***injury*** caused by unfair imports. Section 337 is quite broad in its application, but it has been used particularly for cases involving infringements of ***intellectual property rights***.

Section 1377 Review: an annual review of the operation and effectiveness of United States telecommunications trade agreements and the presence or

Section 232 investigation

232调查

根据经修正的美国《1962年贸易扩展法》第232节进行的调查，以确定进口产品对国家安全的影响。如果影响国家安全，则可以不实施关税削减。

Section 301

301条款

美国《1974年贸易法》第301节。301条款旨在执行美国在贸易协定项下的权利，并在提出申请和调查后对外国不公平贸易做法作出回应。不公平贸易做法可能发生在美国、违规国家或第三国。301条款也可用于为美国货物和服务争取更多市场准入，为其海外投资者争取更公平的条件，并促进在其他国家中更有效保护美国的知识产权。该条款还允许美国贸易代表办公室(USTR)对不公平限制美国特定产品贸易的国家采取进口限制措施。该条款通常用于单一产品部门。对贸易政策制定者而言，301条款的威胁是个麻烦，不仅因为这可能意味着重新考虑目标地区的规则，而且还因为采取防御措施需要付出大量努力，否则将无济于事。采取行动对美国人而言同样耗费资源，只要有选择的余地，USTR倾向于挑选其认为有胜算的案件。经过多年，这种灵活性已经逐渐消失。一些人认为，针对欧共体、日本和韩国的301措施的历史表明，如果目标国家没有改革有关部门市场准入的意向，那么实施措施可以说是相当无效的。这明显低估了该条款的影响。其他人则认为，WTO《关于争端解决规则与程序的谅解》已经把301条款的牙齿拔掉了。但情况并非如此。如果一WTO成员没有依照争端解决程序的结果采取行动，301条款仍然可以用于报复。在被认为不公平的措施未被WTO规则所涵盖时，301条款仍然可以如最初那样适用于所有案件。另见*特别301条款(Special 301)*、*超级301条款(Super 301)*。

Section-306 monitoring

306条款监控

美国《综合贸易与竞争法》中规定的机制。该机制要求美国贸易代表办公室(USTR)监督根据301条款采取措施的执行情况。如果USTR认为一外国未能令人满意地执行一措施或一协定，必须确定采取何种进一步措施。此种确定被认为满足根据301条款采取进一步措施的要求。换言之，不需要进一步调查以证明额外措施的合理性。

Section 337

337条款

美国《1930年关税法》中的条款，也称为《斯穆特-霍利法》，该法允许对因不公平进口所造成的现有或潜在损害给予快速救济。337条款的适用范围相当广泛，但主要适用于涉及侵犯知识产权的案件。

Section 1377 Review

1377审查

对美国电信贸易协定的运用和有效性的年度审查，并审查是否存在其他互利

absence of other mutually advantageous market opportunities. The review is required by Section 1377 of the ***Omnibus Trade and Competitiveness Act***.

Sectoral commitments: these are entries covering specific service sectors or subsectors in the schedules of commitments under the ***General Agreement on Trade in Services*** (GATS). Examples are accountancy, freight-forwarding or life insurance. A sectoral commitment attracts a higher level of GATS rights and obligations in relation to ***market access*** and ***national treatment***. Once a commitment has been made, the market access conditions applying to it may not be made more restrictive for at least three years. *See also* ***market access for services***.

Sectoral customs union: *see* ***sectoral free-trade area***.

Sectoral free-trade area: a ***free-trade area*** or a ***customs union*** covering some traded sectors only. This option is only available to developing countries under the ***Enabling Clause***. Developed countries may conduct ***sectoral trade negotiations***, but they must extend the benefits of sectoral trade liberalization on a most-favoured-nation basis.

Sectoral Initiative in Favour of Cotton: proposed by Benin, Burkina Faso, Chad and Mali in July 2003. It envisaged (a) the complete elimination of support for cotton production and export over three years, and (b) financial compensation for cotton-producing ***least-developed countries*** until support for cotton production had been phased out. In July 2004 this proposal became part of the WTO negotiations on agriculture. At the Nairobi ***WTO Ministerial Conference*** in 2015 it was agreed that developed-country members and developing-country members in a position to do so would give duty-free and quota-free access for cotton and cotton-related products from ***least-developed countries***.

Sectoral rules of origin: refers to ***rules of origin***, especially ***preferential rules of origin***, that apply to defined groups of goods only. Common examples of such goods are agricultural products, textiles, clothing, footwear, chemicals and cars.

Sectoral trade negotiations: the idea of achieving efficiencies in trade negotiations through tackling clusters of tariff items rather than through the item-by-item negotiations pursued in the early rounds of ***multilateral trade negotiations***. It was first attempted on a large scale during the ***Kennedy Round***. The main sectors so treated were aluminium, chemicals, cotton textiles, iron and steel, and pulp and paper. Though the results varied greatly, one thoughtful assessment of the Round considered that enough progress had been made for free trade between selected industry sectors to become a possible future means of tariff reductions. Canada then advocated during the ***Tokyo Round*** the sectoral reduction or elimination of tariff and non-tariff barriers. Canada argued that in some sectors it would be possible in this way to go beyond the trade liberalization resulting from the accepted negotiating techniques. In this way it would be feasible for all trade barriers from the raw-material stage to the finished product to be removed. Developing countries found this proposal attractive because it could have been adapted to the export products of main interest to them, and it might also have provided a solution to the problem of

的市场机会。审查为《综合贸易与竞争法》第1377节所要求进行。

Sectoral commitments

部门承诺

《服务贸易总协定》(GATS)项下承诺减让表中涵盖具体服务部门或子部门的条目。例如会计、货运代理或寿险。在市场准入和国民待遇方面，部门承诺赋予较GATS更高水平的权利和义务。一旦作出承诺，适用该承诺的市场准入条件在至少3年内限制性不得加严。另见*服务市场准入(market access for services)*。

Sectoral customs union

部门关税同盟

见*部门自由贸易区(sectoral free-trade area)*。

Sectoral free-trade area

部门自由贸易区

仅涵盖一些贸易部门的自由贸易区或关税同盟。这一选项仅限于发展中国家根据授权条款获得。发达国家可以进行部门贸易谈判，但是它们必须在最惠国基础上扩大部门贸易自由化利益的适用范围。

Sectoral Initiative in Favour of Cotton

棉花部门倡议

贝宁、布基纳法索、乍得和马里于2003年7月提出。倡议设想：(a)在3年内全部取消对棉花生产和出口的支持；及(b)在逐步取消棉花生产的支持之前，对生产棉花的最不发达国家给予财政补偿。2004年7月，这一提案成为WTO农业谈判的一部分。2015年在内罗毕举行的WTO部长级会议上，各方同意发达国家成员和宣布有此能力的发展中国家成员将为最不发达国家的棉花和棉花相关产品提供免关税和免配额市场准入。

Sectoral rules of origin

部门原产地规则

指原产地规则，特别是优惠原产地规则，适用于明确规定的货物类别。此类产品的常见例子为农产品、纺织品、服装、鞋类、化工品和汽车。

Sectoral trade negotiations

部门贸易谈判

通过处理一组关税税目而非通过多边贸易谈判早期回合中的逐税目谈判而实现贸易谈判效率的理念。在肯尼迪回合中，这一理论首次得到大规模尝试。采取这种方式处理的主要部门为铝、化工品、棉纺织品、钢铁、纸和纸浆。虽然结果差别很大，但是一项对该回合深入的评估认为，选定的产业部门之间的自由贸易已经取得足够进展，使之有可能成为关税削减的未来手段。加拿大随后在东京回合期间主张对关税和非关税壁垒进行部门削减或取消。加拿大认为，在一些部门采取这种方式有可能超越已接受的谈判技巧所产生的贸易自由化结果。通过这种方式，消除从原材料到制成品阶段的全部贸易壁垒是可行的。发展中国家认为这项建议具有吸引力，因为可以对它们具有主要利益的出口产品采用此种方式，而且可能还对关税升级提供解决办法。但是，

tariff escalation. However, resistance by others ensured that this proposal was not adopted. During the ***Uruguay Round*** sectoral trade negotiations took place at two levels. First, at a broad level, the negotiations on agriculture, textiles and services resulted, respectively, in the conclusion of the ***Agreement on Agriculture***, the ***Agreement on Textiles and Clothing*** and the ***General Agreement on Trade in Services***. All of these agreements achieved some trade liberalization, though not all that much in the case of services. Second, there were tariff negotiations in smaller sectoral groups. These eliminated among the main trading countries tariffs on pharmaceuticals, construction equipment, medical equipment, beer, farm machinery, wood and paper products, some fish products and toys. The United States and the ***European Community*** agreed in addition to reduce their tariffs on chemicals to about 3 per cent. An attempt to negotiate a ***Multilateral Steel Agreement*** was unsuccessful. Sectoral trade negotiations continued after the Uruguay Round in the financial services, telecommunications and maritime services. An outstanding example of what can be achieved through sectoral trade negotiations is the ***Information Technology Agreement***. A main reason why this Agreement succeeded so well is that it was supported by industry and government alike in all major producing and trading countries. The most recent example of trade negotiations in the WTO is the ***Doha Ministerial Conference*** mandate for negotiations on ***environmental goods and services***. ***APEC*** trade ministers decided in May 1997 to explore sectoral trade liberalization through the ***Early Voluntary Sectoral Liberalization*** initiative. Their intention was to identify sectors where all APEC economies could agree to reduce or eliminate tariffs and non-tariff barriers. This attempt was unsuccessful. Some see sector-by-sector negotiations as the best way to achieve trade liberalization. When they work, they achieve results efficiently. Their main drawback is that they put the burden of adjustment on a single industry which then sees itself as bearing all the costs. If the degree of resistance is too great, governments may decide not to push ahead. This is despite the fact that all trade liberalization results in gains for the economy. It is therefore likely that multilateral liberalization in agriculture, a ***sensitive sector*** in many countries, will for a long time only be possible in the setting of a round of ***multilateral trade negotiations***. These rounds allow governments to strike a balance between sectors in that they see "gains" here and "losses" there. Industries, too, can see that they have not been singled out for what they consider "sacrifices". *See also* ***zero-for-zero tariff reductions***.

Secure Trade in APEC Region: STAR. An initiative launched at the 2002 APEC Leaders' Meeting "to accelerate action on screening people and cargo for security before transit; increasing security on ships and airplanes while on route; and enhancing security in airports and seaports". The action plan to implement STAR has the following main elements: (a) identifying and examining high-risk containers, (b) implementing by 2005 common standards for electronic customs reporting, (c) cooperation to fight piracy in the region, (d) introducing new baggage screening procedures and equipment in all major

其他国家的抵制导致这一提案未被采纳。在乌拉圭回合期间，部门贸易谈判在两个层面进行。第一，在广泛的层面上，关于农业、纺织品和服务的谈判分别产生了《农业协定》、《纺织品与服装协定》和《服务贸易总协定》。所有这些协定都实现了一定程度的贸易自由化，尽管在服务贸易方面并非完全如此。第二，在较小的部门中进行了关税谈判，取消了主要贸易国对药品、建筑机械、医疗设备、啤酒、农业机械、木材和纸制品、部分鱼产品和玩具的关税。除此之外，美国和欧洲共同体同意将化工品关税降至3%左右。谈判一项多边钢铁协定的尝试没有成功。金融服务、电信和海运服务部门贸易谈判在乌拉圭回合之后继续进行。通过部门贸易谈判取得成果的一个突出例子是《信息技术协定》。该协定之所以如此成功的一个主要原因是，协定得到所有主要生产国和贸易国的产业界和政府的支持。WTO中贸易谈判的最新例子是多哈部长级会议授权的环境产品和服务谈判。1997年5月，APEC贸易部长决定通过部门提前自愿自由化倡议的方式探索部门贸易自由化。他们的目的是确定所有APEC经济体均愿意削减或取消关税和非关税壁垒的部门。这一尝试没有成功。一些人认为分部门谈判是实现贸易自由化的最佳途径。如果这种方式起作用，就能取得有效结果。主要缺点是，将调整的负担交由单一产业承担，而这一行业认为自身承担了所有成本。如果阻力过大，政府可能决定不推进。尽管事实上所有贸易自由化都会给经济带来收益。因此，对于农业这一许多国家的敏感部门的多边自由化在很长一段时间内很可能只有在举行一轮多边贸易谈判的背景下才能实现。这些回合允许政府在它们所认为的“得”与“失”的部门之间取得平衡。产业界也可以看到，他们并没有被单独挑出来成为他们认为的“牺牲品”。另见*零对零关税削减(zero-for-zero tariff reductions)*。

Secure Trade in APEC Region

APEC地区安全贸易倡议

STAR。在2002年APEC领导人会议上通过的倡议，旨在“加强旅客和货物在运输前的检查；改善轮船和飞机的航程安全；改善机场和港口的安全”。实施APEC地区安全贸易倡议行动计划的主要要素包括：(a)辨认和检查高风险集装箱；(b)最迟至2005年执行电子海关通报的共同标准；(c)开展区域合作打击盗版行为；(d)最迟至2005年，在所有主要APEC成员的机场采用新的行李检查程

APEC airports by 2005, (e) implementing a common global standard on advance passenger information, (f) adopting biometrics standards, and (g) reforming immigration service procedures. *See also* ***Container Security Initiative*** and ***SAFE Framework of Standards to Secure and Facilitate Global Trade***. [www.apec.org]

Security exceptions: the right of WTO members under the ***General Agreement on Trade in Services*** (Article XIVbis), the GATT (Article XXI) and Article 73 of the ***Agreement on Trade-Related Aspects of Intellectual Property Rights*** to suspend their obligations under these agreements if important national security issues are at stake. The circumstances when this might arise are (a) the right to refuse disclosure of information if this would be contrary to essential security interests, (b) the need to take action necessary for the protection of essential security interests relating to fissionable materials, traffic in arms, ammunition and implements of war, and in times of war or other international emergencies, and (c) the pursuit of action taken by the United Nations to preserve peace and security. These provisions are rarely used. *See also* ***general exceptions***.

SELA: Sistema Económico Latinoamericano, or Latin American Economic System. A regional organization, based in Venezuela, which includes twenty-seven Latin American and Caribbean countries. It aims to promote intra-regional cooperation to accelerate the economic and social development of its members, and to provide a permanent institutional structure for the adoption of unified strategies in international fora.

Selective safeguards: *see* ***selectivity***.

Selectivity: the imposition of ***import restrictions*** against one or more countries seen as the main threats to domestic producers rather than the use of non-discriminatory ***safeguard*** measures as required in most instances under WTO rules. Some selectivity is permitted in case of ***serious injury*** under Article 5.2 (b) of the ***Agreement on Safeguards*** if (i) it is clear that imports from certain countries have increased disproportionately in the period under consideration, (ii) all the other conditions for taking safeguard action have been satisfied, and (iii) if this would be equitable to other suppliers. *See also* ***escape clause*** and ***quota modulation***.

Self-certification: a method under some systems of ***rules of origin*** which allows, producers, exporters and/or importers to certify that the goods in question qualify for preferential treatment. Self-certification is easier and cheaper than obtaining a ***certificate of origin*** from a chamber of commerce or a governmental agency. *See also* ***Pathfinder Initiative for Self-Certification of Origin***.

Self-produced material: used to describe in the ***rules of origin*** of ***NAFTA*** a material that is produced by the producer of a good and used in the production of that good. *See also* ***intermediate material***.

Self-reliance: an economic development policy based on relying mainly on locally available natural resources, capital and skills. One of its characteristics is a profound disinclination to spend foreign exchange on factors of production

序和设备；(e)执行有关预报旅客信息的全球共同标准；(f)采纳生物特征识别标准；以及(g)改革移民服务程序。另见*集装箱安全倡议(Container Security Initiative)*、*全球贸易安全与便利标准框架(SAFE Framework of Standards to Secure and Facilitate Global Trade)*。

Security exceptions

安全例外

WTO成员根据《服务贸易总协定》第14.2条之二、GATT第21条以及《与贸易有关的知识产权协定》第73条，在重要的国家安全事项受到威胁时，有权暂停履行这些协定项下的义务。可能出现的情况包括：(a)有权拒绝披露其认为如披露会违背其基本安全利益的任何信息；(b)有权采取其认为对保护其基本国家安全利益所必需的任何行动，包括与裂变物质、武器、弹药和作战物资的交易相关的行动，以及在战时或国际关系其他紧急情况下采取的行动；以及(c)为履行其在《联合国宪章》项下的维护国际和平与安全的义务而采取的任何行动。上述条款很少使用。另见*一般例外(general exceptions)*。

SELA

拉丁美洲经济体系

区域组织，总部设在委内瑞拉，包括27个拉丁美洲和加勒比国家。旨在促进区域内合作，以加快成员经济和社会发展，并为在国际场合中采取统一策略提供常设机构。

Selective safeguards

选择性保障措施

见*选择性(selectivity)*。

Selectivity

选择性

针对被视为对国内生产者主要威胁的一个或多个国家实施进口限制，而不是使用WTO规则在大多数情形下所要求的非歧视性保障措施。根据《保障措施协定》第5.2条(b)项，在存在严重损害的情况下，允许一定程度的选择性，如果(1)在审查期内自某些成员进口的增长不成比例；(2)采取保障措施的所有其他条件均已满足；以及(3)对其他供应商是公正的。另见*免责条款(escape clause)*、*配额调整(quota modulation)*。

Self-certification

自我认证

一些原产地规则制度中的方法，允许生产商、出口商和/或进口商证明所涉货物符合优惠待遇。自我认证比自商会或政府机构获得原产地证书更容易且费用低。另见*APEC原产地自我认证探路者倡议(Pathfinder Initiative for Self-Certification of Origin)*。

Self-produced material

自产材料

在《北美自由贸易协定》(NAFTA)的原产地规则中用于描述由一货物生产商自己制造并用于该货物生产的材料。另见*中间材料(intermediate material)*。

Self-reliance

自力更生

主要依靠本地可获自然资源、资本和技术的经济发展政策。特点之一为极不情愿将外汇用在不会立即和直接产生更多外汇流入的生产要素上。产生的一

that do not immediately and directly result in greater inflows of foreign exchange. A consequence is that domestic enterprises and research institutes spend much of their time and funds on re-inventing products and processes already available elsewhere, but they never seem to catch up. Outward-looking economies avoid this trap and seek instead to find their place in the system of international specialization through international trade and foreign investment. *See also* ***autarky***, ***comparative advantage***, ***self-sufficiency*** and ***techno-nationalism***.

Self-sufficiency: an economic policy under which a country aims to produce to the greatest extent what it consumes itself. Foreign trade does occur in countries practising such policies, but it tends to be confined to importing essential raw materials not available locally and the export of raw materials and other products not needed on the local market. Such a policy disregards the gains to be made from international specialization, and it acts therefore as a brake on the expansion of trade and the economy more broadly. *See also* ***autarky***, ***comparative advantage***, ***food security***, ***international division of labour***, ***self-reliance*** and ***techno-nationalism***.

Semi-conductor*:** a dispute with the United States and Japan brought before the GATT Council by the ***European Economic Community (EEC) in 1986. The case made by the EEC stemmed from an arrangement made between the United States and Japan in 1986 concerning trade in semi-conductors. This provided for better market access for imported semi-conductors in Japan and the monitoring of export prices by the Government of Japan to prevent ***dumping*** in the United States. The provisions on monitoring and dumping were applicable to third-country markets. Japan used its ***COCOM*** enforcement mechanism to monitor export prices which caused delays in the granting of export approvals. The EEC claimed that (a) the Japanese monitoring measures, especially those applied to third-country markets, contravened Articles VI (Anti-dumping) and XI (General Elimination of Quantitative Restrictions), (b) the provisions for access to the Japanese market contravened Article I (General Most-Favoured-Nation Treatment), and (c) the lack of transparency surrounding the whole issue contravened Article X (Publication and Administration of Trade Regulations). It argued that third-country monitoring was aimed at ensuring, now that the arrangement had increased prices in the United States, that United States companies would not be disadvantaged in these markets. The ***panel*** first considered the claims concerning Article XI and found that the request to Japanese companies not to export semi-conductors at prices below company-specific costs to GATT members other than the United States, combined with the complex system of monitoring price, was inconsistent with Article XI, as was the system of administering export licences. It also found that the evidence submitted did not demonstrate preferential market access to Japan by United States firms in contravention of the most-favoured-nation clause. The panel held that Article VI was silent on actions by exporting countries to prevent dumping, and that it was therefore not a justification for export restrictions or

个结果是，国内企业和研究机构将大部分时间和资金花费在重新发明其他地方已有的产品和工艺上，而它们似乎从未追赶上。外向型经济避免了这种陷阱，而是寻求通过国际贸易和外国投资在国际专业化体系中找到自己的位置。另见*经济闭关自守(autarky)*、*比较优势(comparative advantage)*、*自给自足(self-sufficiency)*、*技术民族主义(techno-nationalism)*。

Self-sufficiency

自给自足

一国最大限度地生产本国消费产品的经济政策。在实行此类政策的国家中，对外贸易确实发生，但往往限于进口本地无法获得的基本原材料，出口本地市场不需要的原材料和其他产品。此种政策忽视从国际专业化中获得的利益，因此限制了更广泛的贸易和经济发展。另见*经济闭关自守(autarky)*、*比较优势(comparative advantage)*、*粮食安全(food security)*、*国际劳动分工(international division of labour)*、*自力更生(self-reliance)*、*技术民族主义(techno-nationalism)*。

Semi-conductor

半导体案

1986年欧洲经济共同体(EEC)针对美国和日本向GATT理事会提起的争端。该案源于1986年美国和日本之间达成的关于半导体贸易的安排。该安排为日本进口半导体提供了更好的市场准入，并使日本政府能够监测出口价格，以防止对美国倾销。关于监测和倾销的条款适用于第三国市场。日本通过多边出口管制协调委员会(COCOM)执行机制监测出口价格，此举导致出口许可发放的延误。欧共体主张，(a)日本的监测措施，特别是适用于第三国市场的监测措施，违反了第6条(反倾销)和第11条(普遍取消数量限制)；(b)对日本市场的准入条款违反了第1条(普遍最惠国待遇)；以及(c)整个问题缺乏透明度，违反了第10条(贸易法规的公布和实施)。欧共体认为，第三国监测旨在保证该安排提高了在美国的价格，使美国公司不会在这些市场上处于不利地位。专家组首先审查了与第11条有关的主张，认为要求日本公司不得对除美国外的GATT缔约方以低于公司特定成本的价格出口半导体，加之复杂的价格监测系统，与第11条不符，出口许可管理制度也同样如此。专家组还认为，提交的证据并未表明美国企业对日本的优惠市场准入违反最惠国待遇条款。专家组认为，第6条未涉及出口国采取的防止倾销的措施，因此不能成为采取出口限制或出

export price measures. It also noted that Article VI was silent on the right of exporting countries to impose ***anti-dumping measures*** on their exports. [GATT BISD 35S]

Semi-generic geographical indications: names widely used to describe some wines and other products not necessarily produced in the place where the name originated. Examples for wine are *Burgundy* and *Chablis*. The use of such names is permitted in some jurisdictions if the correct place of origin is also indicated on the product. A hypothetical example of permitted use would be "Chablis, product of Iceland". In other jurisdictions this kind of labelling may be illegal. *See also* ***geographical indications*** and ***generic geographical indications***.

Semi-tradables: goods and services that exhibit features putting them in the category of ***tradables*** and others that may make them ***non-tradables***. The distinction between these categories can be difficult to make in practice.

Sensitive products: these are products more likely than others to encounter ***import restrictions***. Typical examples are many agricultural products, textiles, clothing and footwear, passenger motor vehicles, chemicals and, sometimes, steel. The reasons for the sensitivity surrounding these products are complex. It may be the perceived need to protect the traditional occupation of a national minority, as is the case with Japanese tanneries. In other cases, technological changes and new investment may lead to lower-cost foreign competitors and an inability by domestic producers to adjust quickly. Agriculture, as shown by the European and American examples, is particularly complicated. Traditional political power combined with a vague community perception that the rural population expresses the national spirit and must therefore be preserved, may render any reform of the rural sector a delicate matter. Sensitive products were also proposed as a modality for a flexible tariff reduction treatment in the ***Doha Development Agenda*** agriculture negotiations where market access was expected to be offered through a combination of tariff reduction and tariff rate quotas rather than the full tariff cut. *See also* ***Japanese measures on leather*** and ***sensitive sectors***.

Sensitive sectors: parts of the domestic economy posing special challenges to trade policy makers for various reasons, including relative technological backwardness, cultural factors, over-production or political clout. Among them are agriculture, audiovisual services and cultural activities more generally, defence-related industries, financial services, shipbuilding, textiles and footwear. In fact, almost any industry can turn itself into a sensitive sector if it feels the pressure of imports, and if it is willing to organise itself. The long-term solutions for dealing with the problems caused by sensitive sectors are usually found through ***structural adjustment*** or, if nothing else is done, through accidental obsolescence and the disappearance of some of the sector as players. *See also* ***cultural identity***, ***sectoral trade negotiations*** and ***sensitive products***.

Seoul Declaration: the declaration on ***APEC*** objectives made at the November 1991 APEC Ministerial Meeting in Seoul. The four objectives are: (i) to sustain

口价格措施的理由。专家组同时指出，第6条未涉及出口国对其出口产品采取反倾销措施的权利。

Semi-generic geographical indications

半通用地理标志

广泛用于描述一些葡萄酒和其他产品的名称，这些产品不一定产自该名称的起源地。葡萄酒的例子为勃艮第和夏布利。在一些管辖范围，如果产品上同时标明正确原产地，也允许使用此类名称。允许使用的假设例子为“夏布利，冰岛产品”。在其他管辖范围，此种标签可能是非法的。另见*地理标志(geographical indications)*、*通用地理标志(generic geographical indications)*。

Semi-tradables

半贸易品

货物和服务所显示的特征可将其归入贸易品，而其他特征可使其归入非贸易品。这些类别在实践中可能是难以区分的。

Sensitive products

敏感产品

这些产品较其他产品更容易遭受进口限制。典型的例子为许多农产品、纺织品、服装和鞋类、乘用车、化工品，有时还包括钢铁。这些产品具有敏感性的原因是复杂的。可能是为保护少数民族的传统职业的需要，如日本的制革业。在其他情况下，技术变革和新投资可能带来低成本的外国竞争者，而国内生产者缺乏快速调整能力。欧洲和美国的例子表明，农业特别复杂。传统政治势力与模糊社会观念加在一起认为，农村人口展示了民族精神，因此必须予以维护，这可能使农业部门的任何改革成为一个很微妙的问题。在多哈发展议程农业谈判中，还提出将敏感产品作为灵活关税削减待遇的一种模式，期望通过关税削减和关税配额相结合的方式提供市场准入而非全面关税削减。另见*日本皮革措施案(Japanese measures on leather)*、*敏感部门(sensitive sectors)*。

Sensitive sectors

敏感部门

由于各种原因，包括技术相对落后、文化因素、生产过剩或政治影响，国内经济的一部分对贸易政策制定者构成特殊挑战。包括农业、视听服务和更广泛的文化活动、国防相关产业、金融服务、造船、纺织品和鞋类。事实上，如果一产业感受到进口压力且愿意自行组织起来，那么几乎任何一个产业都可以把自己变成一个敏感部门。对于敏感部门所产生问题的长期解决办法通常通过结构性调整获得，或在不采取任何措施的情况下，则通过意外淘汰和部分部门参与者消失而获得。另见*文化特性(cultural identity)*、*部门贸易谈判(sectoral trade negotiations)*、*敏感产品(sensitive products)*。

Seoul Declaration

汉城宣言

1991年11月在韩国汉城举行的APEC部长会议发布关于APEC目标的宣言。四

the growth and development of the region for the common good of its peoples and, in this way, to contribute to the growth and development of the world economy, (ii) to enhance the positive gains, both for the region and the world economy, resulting from increasing economic interdependence, including by encouraging the flow of goods, services, capital and technology, (iii) to develop and strengthen the open multilateral trading system in the interest of Asia-Pacific and all other economies, and (iv) to reduce barriers to trade in goods and services and investment among participants in a manner consistent with GATT principles, where applicable, and without detriment to other economies. *See also* ***Bogor Declaration*** and ***Osaka Action Agenda***.

Separate Arbitration Agreement: *see* ***Model Arbitration Clause***.

Sequencing: refers to a problem that can arise in proceedings under the WTO ***Dispute Settlement Understanding***: whether Article 21.5 covering compliance proceedings or Article 22.2 covering suspension of obligations has priority. The question is whether the complainant can request authorization to suspend obligations before a ***panel*** or the ***Appellate Body*** has established that there has been a failure to comply with rulings and recommendations of a panel. The problem has not yet been solved. *See also* ***compliance panel***.

Sequential foreign direct investment: defined by ***UNCTAD*** as ***foreign direct investment*** by firms that are already established in the market. In most cases, such investment consists of reinvested earnings. *See also* ***associated foreign direct investment***.

Serious damage: the condition that has be satisfied, for example, to justify action under the ***specific transitional safeguard mechanism*** to restrain the import of textiles and clothing. The ***Agreement on Textiles and Clothing*** does not define "serious damage", but it explains that the claim of serious damage can be assessed by the effect of the imports of the product in question on the particular industry, as reflected, for example, in changes of output, productivity, utilization of capacity, inventories, market share, exports, wages, employment, domestic prices, profits and investment. *See also* ***injury***.

Serious injury: defined in the WTO ***Agreement on Safeguards*** as "a significant overall impairment in the position of a domestic industry". The term is not further defined, but authorities investigating whether serious injury exists are required to "evaluate all relevant factors of an objective and quantifiable nature". These include the rate and amount of the increase in imports of the product concerned in absolute and relative terms, the share of the domestic market taken by increased imports, changes in the level of sales, production, productivity, capacity utilization, profits and losses, and employment. *See also* ***injury***.

Serious prejudice: this exists under the WTO ***Agreement on Subsidies and Countervailing Measures*** when subsidies have certain effects on the interests of other members. Broadly, this arises in cases (a) when the total subsidy on a product exceeds 5 per cent, (b) when subsidies are awarded to cover the operating losses of an industry, (c) of subsidies covering operating losses to allow the development of long-term solutions and to avoid acute social

项目标为：(1)为本地区的人民的共同利益保持经济增长和发展，并以此为世界经济增长和发展作出贡献；(2)通过鼓励货物、服务、资本和技术流动等方式，促进相互依存，使本地区和世界经济获得积极成果；(3)为亚太地区和所有其他经济体的利益，发展和加强开放的多边贸易体制；以及(4)以与GATT原则相一致的方式，在不损害其他经济体的情况下，减少参加方之间的货物、服务及投资壁垒。另见*茂物宣言(Bogor Declaration)*、*大阪行动议程(Osaka Action Agenda)*。

Separate Arbitration Agreement

独立仲裁协议

见*示范仲裁条款(Model Arbitration Clause)*。

Sequencing

适用顺序问题

指在根据WTO《争端解决谅解》的程序中可能出现的问题：涵盖遵守程序的第21.5条和涵盖中止义务的第22.2条的优先顺序问题。存在的问题是起诉方是否可以在专家组或上诉机构已经确定未能遵守专家组的裁决和建议之前请求授权中止义务。该问题尚未解决。另见*执行之诉专家组(compliance panel)*。

Sequential foreign direct investment

连续外国直接投资

联合国贸易与发展会议(UNCTAD)将其定义为已经在市场上建立的公司进行的外国直接投资。在大多数情况下，此种投资由进行再投资的收益组成。另见*关联外国直接投资(associated foreign direct investment)*。

Serious damage

严重损害

证明根据过渡性特殊保障机制限制纺织品和服装进口属合理而需要满足的条件。《纺织品与服装协定》未定义“严重损害”，但协定说明，确定严重损害可以通过有关产品的进口对特定产业状况的影响加以评估，例如反映在产量、生产率、开工率、库存、市场份额、出口、工资、就业、国内价格、利润和投资等方面的变化。另见*损害(injury)*。

Serious injury

严重损害

WTO《保障措施协定》将其定义为“对一国内产业状况的重大全面减损”。协定对该词未进一步定义，但是主管机关在确定是否存在严重损害时，需要“评估所有相关的客观和可量化的因素”。这些因素包括有关产品按绝对值和相对值计算的进口增加的比率和数量、增加的进口所占国内市场的份额、销售、产量、生产率、产能利用率、利润和亏损以及就业等水平的变化。另见*损害(injury)*。

Serious prejudice

严重侵害

根据WTO《补贴与反补贴措施协定》，如补贴对其他成员的利益产生特定影响，即存在严重侵害。一般而言，出现的情况包括：(a)对一产品从价补贴的总额超过5%；(b)用以弥补一产业承受的经营亏损的补贴；(c)为制定长期解决办法和避免严重社会问题，用以弥补经营亏损而发放的补贴；以及(d)直接免

problems, and (d) direct forgiveness of debt owed to government. The member country must take appropriate action in these cases. The Agreement also describes a range of situations in which serious prejudice may, rather than will, arise. Different rules apply to agricultural subsidies under the WTO ***Agreement on Agriculture***. *See also* ***actionable subsidies***, ***prohibited subsidies*** and ***subsidies***.

Service dumping: said to result from the use of subsidized or discriminatory pricing arrangements in the provision of shipping services. The resulting freight at less than cost is thought to give the exporter an advantage that may be reflected in the landed price of the product. The product itself may have been landed at ***normal value***, but the freight reduction could still lead to a charge of dumping. This concept was discussed during the drafting of the ***Havana Charter***, but it is not reflected in the current anti-dumping rules. *See also* ***anti-dumping measures***.

Service mark: a ***trademark*** uniquely associated with the provision of a service. It can be a mark, word, name or symbol, or a combination of them.

Services: these include key economic activities such as telecommunications, banking, insurance, land and water transport, aviation, accountancy, law, engineering, entertainment, etc., which can be produced in their own right or as a component of some product or another service. Services account for about 60–75 per cent of GDP in most countries. The variations can be explained partly by structural factors and partly because of the use of different statistical methods. The importance of services was not always recognized. Adam Smith's view was that "the labour of some of the most respectable orders in the society is, like that of menial servants, unproductive of any value, and does not fix or realize itself in any permanent subject, or vendible commodity, which endures after that labour is past, and for which an equal quantity of labour could afterwards be procured ... In the same class must be ranked, some both of the gravest and most important, and some of the most frivolous professions: churchmen, lawyers, physicians, men of letters of all kinds; players, buffoons, musicians, opera-singers, opera-dancers, etc." If this view of services was not consciously held by later generations, there was nevertheless frequently a tendency to underplay their role in the economy. There is no universally accepted definition of services. Several approaches have been tried, but none has received full approval. First, services are often characterized as intangible, invisible, incapable of storage and therefore requiring simultaneous production and consumption. These characteristics are already implicit in Adam Smith's remarks. Technological advances have, however, made this an obsolescent definition. Second, the institutional approach assumes that anything not classified as primary or secondary industry must be a service or a service occupation. Third, there is the functional approach, pioneered by T. P. Hill in 1977 when he defined services as "a change in the condition of a person or of a good belonging to some economic unit, which is brought about as the result of the activity of some other economic unit with the prior agreement of the former

除政府持有债务。在这些情况下，成员国必须采取适当措施。协定还描述了一系列严重侵害可能出现但并非必然出现的情况。根据WTO《农业协定》，对农业补贴适用不同的规则。另见*可诉补贴(actionable subsidies)*、*禁止性补贴(prohibited subsidies)*、*补贴(subsidies)*。

Service dumping

服务倾销

据说产生于提供运输服务时使用补贴或歧视性定价安排。由此产生的低于成本的运费被认为给予出口商利益，并可能反映在产品的到岸价上。产品本身可以正常价值到岸，但减少的运费仍然可能引发倾销的指控。这一概念曾在《哈瓦那宪章》起草过程中进行过讨论，但是并未反映在现行反倾销规则中。另见*反倾销措施(anti-dumping measures)*。

Service mark

服务标志

与提供一项服务惟一相关的商标。可以是标志、词语、名称或符号，或上述各项的组合。

Services

服务

包括电信、银行、保险、水陆运输、航空、会计、法律、工程、娱乐等关键经济活动，这些活动可以独立生产，也可以作为产品或其他服务的组成部分。大多数国家的服务占国内生产总值约60—75%。这种差异部分可归因于结构性因素，部分由于使用不同的统计方法。服务的重要性并不总被认可。亚当·斯密的观点是"社会上有一些最受尊敬的劳动，也像仆人的劳动一样，不生产任何价值，不固定或体现在任何永久性的劳动对象或可贩卖商品上，这些东西在劳动过去以后还能存在，随后还能获得等量的劳动。……在这一类中，必须列入某种最庄严、最重要的职业，以及某些最不重要的职业：牧师、律师、医生、各种文人；演员、滑稽剧演员、音乐家、歌剧歌唱家、歌剧舞蹈家，等等。"如果对服务业的这种看法不为后代所自觉持有，那么人们往往倾向于低估服务在经济中的作用。目前没有普遍接受的关于服务的定义。已经尝试了若干方式，但其中没有一种方式得到完全认可。第一，服务通常被描述为无形的、看不见的、无法存储的，因此需要同时生产和消费。这些特点已经隐含在亚当·斯密的评论中。但是，技术进步使之成为过时的定义。第二，制度分析法假设任何不归为第一产业或第二产业的活动必须是服务或服务性职业。第三，1977年，T. P. 希尔首先采用了功能法，他将服务定义为"属于一些经济单位的个人或货物的状态改变，此种改变因其他经济单位根据与前述个人或单位的先前协议而开展的活动所致"。一些人认为这一定义存在缺陷，因为未能涵

person or economic unit". Some have argued that this definition is deficient because it does not cover, for example, security services or preventive medicine. The United States Office of Technology Assessment has proposed classification into two types: (a) knowledge-based services (insurance, professional and technical services, certain banking services, information technology services, etc.), and (b) tertiary services (leasing, shipping, distribution, franchising, retail trade, travel, etc.). In its prohibition of restrictions on the freedom to provide services within the ***European Union***, the ***Treaty on the Functioning of the European Union*** notes "services" normally means services provided for remuneration, and it particular it refers to (a) activities of an industrial character, (b) activities of a commercial character, (c) activities of craftsmen, and (d) activities of professions. In the *Work of Nations*, Robert Reich offers three different categories of services according to occupations. The first is routine production services entailing repetitive tasks guided by standard procedures and codified rules, much in the way assembly work is done by blue-collar occupations. These services can be traded globally. The second category he calls in-person services, also entailing simple and repetitive tasks, but they must be provided person-to-person. He notes that these providers often must have a pleasant demeanour, and they must smile and exude confidence and good cheer even when they feel morose. His third category is symbolic-analytic services. This covers problem-solving, problem-identifying and strategic-brokering activities. These services can be traded internationally, but they are not standardized. They include many business, professional, financial and engineering services. This list of classification systems is by no means exhaustive. Version 2.1 of the ***United Nations Central Product Classification*** has a comprehensive listing of services. *See also* ***trade in services statistics***. [Hill 1977, Reich 1991, Smith 1991 (1776)]

Services Trade Barometer: a WTO indicator which highlights turning points and illustrates changing patterns in world services trade. It combines six component indices into an overall composite index. The Services Trade Barometer is issued twice a year. *See also* ***Goods Trade Barometer***.

Set-aside programmes: instituted particularly by the United States and the European Union, but also Japan, to take agricultural land out of production as one way to reduce agricultural over-production. Farmers receive financial compensation for participating in these programmes.

Set of Multilaterally Agreed Equitable Principles and Rules for the Conduct of Restrictive Business Practices: *see* ***restrictive business practices***.

Seventh-freedom cargo services: the right of an airline to operate cargo services between countries entirely outside its home country. *See also* ***freedoms of the air*** and ***Multilateral Agreement on the Liberalization of International Air Transportation***.

Shallow free-trade agreement: a ***free-trade agreement*** basically confined to reduction of ***tariffs*** and ***non-tariff barriers***, usually supported by other provisions related to trade in goods. *See also* ***deep free-trade agreement***.

盖安全服务或预防医学等服务。美国技术评估局建议将服务分为两类：(a)基于知识的服务(保险、专业和技术服务、某些银行服务、信息技术服务等)；及(b)第三产业服务(租赁、运输、分销、特许经营、零售贸易、旅游等)。《欧洲联盟运行条约》禁止在欧盟内部限制提供服务的自由，指出“服务”通常指为获得报酬而提供的服务，特指(a)工业性质的活动；(b)商业性质的活动；(c)工匠的活动；以及(d)专业活动。在《国家的作用》一书中，罗伯特·赖克根据职业将服务分为三类：第一种是日常生产性服务，涵盖按照标准程序和成文规则进行的重复性工作，很像蓝领职业从事的装配工作。这些服务可以在全球范围内进行交易。第二类服务被称为“面对面服务”，也涵盖简单和重复性任务，但此类服务必须通过个人接触提供。他指出，这些提供者通常必须举止优雅，面带微笑，充满自信，心情愉悦，即使在他们心情不好的时候。第三类是符号分析服务。涵盖问题解决、问题识别和战略经纪活动。这些服务可以在国际上进行交易，但并未标准化。其中包括许多商业、专业、金融和工程服务。这一分类体系清单决不是详尽无遗的。联合国中央产品分类2.1版有一个全面的服务清单。另见*服务贸易统计(trade in services statistics)*。

Services Trade Barometer

服务贸易晴雨表

WTO发布的一项指标，突出显示世界服务贸易的拐点，并说明变化趋势。将6个指数组合成一个综合指数，每年发布两次。另见*货物贸易晴雨表(Goods Trade Barometer)*。

Set-aside programmes

休耕计划

主要由美国和欧盟以及日本制定，作为减少农业生产过剩的一种方式使农田退出生产的做法。参与这些计划的农民可获得财政补偿。

Set of Multilaterally Agreed Equitable Principles and Rules for the Conduct of Restrictive Business Practices

一套多边协议的控制限制性商业惯例的公平原则和规则

见*限制性商业惯例(restrictive business practices)*。

Seventh-freedom cargo services

货运第七航权

航空公司在完全位于其母国之外的国家之间从事货运服务的权利。另见*航空自由(freedoms of the air)*、*国际航空运输自由化多边协定(Multilateral Agreement on the Liberalization of International Air Transportation)*。

Shallow free-trade agreement

浅层自由贸易协定

基本上限于削减关税和非关税壁垒的自由贸易协定，通常得到其他与货物贸易有关条款的辅助。另见*深度自由贸易协定(deep free-trade agreement)*。

Shallow integration: a situation in which economies pursue economic policies sharing some characteristics, but each economy is free to pursue its own ends. An example of this occurs under free-trade arrangements or when economies adopt the results of ***multilateral trade negotiations***. *See also* ***deep integration***.

Sham litigation: *see* ***non-price predation*** and ***trade harassment***.

Shanghai Accord: an appendix to the statement issued after the 2001 Shanghai ***APEC Economic Leaders' Meeting***. The Shanghai Accord consists of five elements. The first is a commitment to broadening and updating the ***Osaka Action Agenda***. It covers in particular the ***e-APEC strategy*** and APEC's work on strengthening the functioning of markets. Second, member economies agreed to the pathfinder approach to promote progress towards the goals listed in the ***Bogor Declaration***. Third, they will promote the adoption of appropriate trade policies for the ***new economy***. Fourth, members will aim to reduce trade transaction costs by 5 per cent through implementing the APEC Trade Facilitation Principles. Fifth, members will pursue the implementation of the APEC transparency principles.

Shanghai Cooperation Organization: known until June 2001 as the "Shanghai Five". It consists of China, India, Kazakhstan, Kyrgyz Republic, Pakistan, Russia, Tajikistan and Uzbekistan. Its main goals are (a) strengthening mutual trust and neighbourliness among the member states, (b) promoting their effective cooperation in politics, trade, the economy, research, technology and culture, education, energy, transport, tourism, environment and other areas, (c) making joint efforts to maintain and ensure peace, security and stability in the region, and (d) moving towards the establishment of a democratic, fair and rational new international political and economic order. Its secretariat is Beijing.

Shared competence: where responsibility for a policy or an activity is shared by two or more agencies. In the ***European Union***, for example, competence is shared between the Union and the member states in the following areas as outlined in Article 4 of the ***Treaty on the Functioning of the European Union***: (a) internal market, (b) social policy, for the aspects defined in the ***Treaties***, (c) economic, social and territorial cohesion, (d) agriculture and fisheries, excluding the conservation of marine biological resources, (e) environment, (f) consumer protection, (g) transport, (h) trans-European networks, (i) energy, (j) area of freedom, security and justice, and (k) common safety concerns in public health matters, for the aspects defined in the Treaty. In the areas of research, technological development and space as well as development cooperation and humanitarian aid the Union has competence to carry out activities and conduct a common policy, but this does not prevent member states from carrying out their own. Agreements relating to trade in cultural and audiovisual services, educational services and social and human services are subject to shared competence under the ***common commercial policy***. *See also* ***competence*** and ***subsidiarity***.

Shelf-life restrictions: usually public health regulations covering especially food items, chemicals, pharmaceuticals, etc., to ensure that a product only remains

Shallow integration

浅度一体化

各经济体推行具有一些共同特点的经济政策，但每一经济体均可以自由追求各自目标的情况。例如发生在达成自由贸易安排的情况下，或各经济体通过多边贸易谈判结果的情况下。另见*深度一体化(deep integration)*。

Sham litigation

虚假诉讼

见*非价格掠夺(non-price predation)*、*贸易干扰(trade harassment)*。

Shanghai Accord

上海共识

2001年上海APEC领导人会议所发表声明的附录。共识由5个要素组成：第一个要素是承诺扩展和更新《大阪行动议程》。特别涵盖数字APEC战略和APEC关于加强市场功能的工作。第二个要素是成员经济体同意采取探路者方式，促进实现《茂物宣言》中所列目标。第三个要素是他们将为新经济采取适当的贸易政策。第四个要素是成员将致力于通过实施APEC贸易便利化原则，将贸易成本降低5%。第五个要素是成员将实施APEC透明度原则。

Shanghai Cooperation Organization

上海合作组织

2001年6月前称为“上海五国”。由中国、印度、哈萨克斯坦、吉尔吉斯斯坦、巴基斯坦、俄罗斯、塔吉克斯坦和乌兹别克斯坦组成。主要目标为：(a)加强成员国之间相互信任与睦邻友好；(b)促进成员国在政治、贸易、经济、研究、技术和文化、教育、能源、交通、旅游、环境等领域的有效合作；(c)共同努力维护和加强本地区的和平、安全与稳定；以及(d)推动建立民主、公平、合理的国际政治经济新秩序。秘书处设在北京。

Shared competence

共享权限

一项政策或一项活动的责任由两个或两个以上机构共同承担。例如，在欧盟中，如《欧洲联盟运行条约》第4条所述，欧盟与成员国在下列领域共享权限：(a)内部市场；(b)条约中所规定方面的社会政策；(c)经济、社会和地域凝聚；(d)农业和渔业，不含海洋生物资源保护；(e)环境；(f)消费者保护；(g)运输；(h)跨欧洲网络；(i)能源；(j)自由、安全和司法领域；以及(k)公共健康事务中的共同安全关注。在研究、技术发展和太空以及发展合作和人道主义援助领域，欧盟有权开展活动和执行共同政策，但不妨碍成员国执行自己的政策。与文化和视听服务、教育服务、社会和公共服务贸易有关的协定在共同商业政策下受共享权限管辖。另见*权限(competence)*、*辅助原则(subsidiarity)*。

Shelf-life restrictions

保质期限制

通常为专门涵盖食品、化学品、药品等的公共健康法规，以保证一产品仅在

on sale in the shops as long as its quality and safety can be maintained and assured. If the shelf-life of a product is declared artificially short, ***market access*** by foreign suppliers may be impeded since the time needed for transport and customs clearance has to be allowed for. This reduces the time the product can be left on the shelf, and it increases the importer's costs because there might be greater wastage. It may even deter shops from stocking the product. Shelf-life restrictions then become ***technical barriers to trade***. Motivations for shelf-life restrictions vary. They can be based on a desire to protect local manufacturers, a genuine belief that shelf-life should not exceed a certain period for health and safety reasons, a reluctance to accept the efficiency of certain types of packaging and hesitation to accept the validity of new testing methods.

Sheltered industries: industries benefiting from a ***protective tariff*** which ensures that they are not exposed to full international competition.

Sherman Act: a United States law passed in 1890 with the aim of prohibiting monopolies and restraints in interstate commerce as well as foreign trade. It remains the basis of the American system of ***antitrust laws*** and policies. The United States Supreme Court said of it in 1958: "The *Sherman Act* was designed to be a comprehensive charter of economic liberty aimed at preserving free and unfettered competition as the rule of trade". Section 1 of the Act states that "Every contract, combination in the form of trust or otherwise, or conspiracy, in restraint of trade or commerce among the several States, or with foreign nations, is hereby declared to be illegal". In the early days this was interpreted literally, but a 1911 Supreme Court judgment held that only unreasonable or undue restraints of trade were to be covered. Section 2 of the Act states that "Every person who shall monopolize, or attempt to monopolize, or combine and conspire with any other person or persons, to monopolize any part of the trade or commerce among the several States, or with foreign nations, shall be deemed guilty of a felony . . ." *See also* ***Webb-Pomerene Act*** and ***Wilson Tariff Act***.

Sherpa: in the ***G7*** and ***G8*** the personal representative of a head of government who is responsible, together with the sherpas from the other member countries, for preparing the Economic Summit. Each sherpa is normally assisted by two sous-sherpas drawn from the foreign and finance ministries. The term is apparently drawn from the Nepali word for a person who guides climbers to Himalayan summits.

Shortage clause: a provision sometimes included in ***free-trade agreements*** to enable a party to impose export restrictions because of a shortage of a commodity on the internal market. The free-trade agreement between the ***European Union*** and Mexico, for example, states that a party may adopt export restrictions or export customs duties if major difficulties arise, or are likely to arise, for the exporting party because of (a) a critical shortage, or threat thereof, of foodstuffs or other products essential to the exporting party, or (b) a shortage of essential quantities of domestic materials to a domestic processing industry when prices are held below the world market price as part of a governmental

其质量和安全得以维持和保证的情况下才能在商店中销售。如果一产品的保质期人为申报较短，外国供应商的市场准入可能会受到阻碍，因为需要考虑运输和清关所需时间。这就缩短了产品的保质期，且因为可能出现更多损耗而增加进口商的成本。甚至妨碍商店储存此种产品。保质期限制因而成为技术性贸易壁垒。保质期限制的动机各不相同。可能基于保护本地制造商的愿望、出于健康和安全原因考虑保质期不应超过特定期限的真实看法、不愿接受特定类型包装的效率以及对新测试方法有效性的怀疑。

Sheltered industries
受保护产业

受益于保护性关税的产业，此种关税保证产业不会面临全面的国际竞争。

Sherman Act
谢尔曼法

美国于1890年通过的法律，旨在禁止垄断和限制州际贸易以及对外贸易。该法仍然是美国反垄断法和政策体系的基础。美国最高法院在1958年指出："《谢尔曼法》被设计成为一部关于经济自由的综合性宪章，旨在维护以自由和不受限制的竞争为基础的贸易规则"。该法第1条规定，"任何契约、以托拉斯形式或其他形式的联合、共谋，用来限制州际间或与外国之间的贸易或商业，是非法的"。在早期，这一规定按照字面意思加以解释，但1911年最高法院的一项判决认为，该节仅适用于不合理或过度的贸易限制。该法第2条规定，"任何人垄断或企图垄断，或与他人联合、共谋垄断州际间或与外国间的商贸和贸易，是严重犯罪……"另见*韦布-波默林法(Webb-Pomerene Act)*、*威尔逊关税法(Wilson Tariff Act)*。

Sherpa
协调人

在7国集团和8国集团中政府首脑的私人代表，负责与其他成员国的协调人共同筹备经济峰会。每位协调人通常由来自外交部和财政部的两名副协调人协助。该词显然取自尼泊尔语，指带领攀登者登上喜马拉雅山的向导。

Shortage clause
短缺条款

自由贸易协定中有时包括的一项条款，使一参加方能够因国内市场中一商品短缺而实施出口限制。例如，欧盟与墨西哥自由贸易协定规定，如果因以下原因，出口参加方出现或可能出现重大困难，则该参加方可以实行出口限制或征收出口税：(a)出口参加方的食品或其他必需品严重短缺或出现严重短缺威胁；或(b)如作为政府稳定计划的一部分，价格压低于国际市场价格，或向出

stabilization plan, or re-export to a third country against which the exporting party maintains export customs duties or export prohibitions or restrictions. If such measures are taken, they must not be arbitrarily or unjustifiably discriminatory, and they must not be used to protect the domestic industry.

Short-supply products: Article XI of the GATT prohibits, with some defined exceptions, import and export quotas. One of these exceptions is that it permits ***export quotas*** if they are needed temporarily to prevent or relieve critical shortages of foodstuffs or other products essential to the exporting country.

Short-supply regulations: a framework of regulations under discussion in 1997 in the context of amended United States legislation on ***anti-dumping measures***. The argument for such regulations was that some manufacturing operations are dependent on a competitive supply of components to maintain sales of their products. Sometimes these components are temporarily in short supply from domestic sources, but they may at the same time be subject to anti-dumping procedures. In such a situation, the anti-dumping action should in the view of importers be disregarded. This would allow firms to continue to benefit from lower prices charged for imported components and this way maintain their competitiveness. This argument was in the end rejected by the legislators.

Short-Term Arrangement Regarding International Trade in Cotton Textiles: an arrangement under the GATT between large textile exporters and importers to manage trade in these products through selective quantitative restrictions. It entered into force in 1961 for one year and was replaced in 1962 by the ***Long-Term Arrangement Regarding International Trade in Cotton Textiles*** which in turn was superseded in 1973 by the ***Multi-Fibre Arrangement***. *See also* ***Agreement on Textiles and Clothing*** which brought the textiles trade again under the normal rules of the WTO.

Sideswipe problem: an expression used particularly by Canadian trade analysts to describe any negative effects on Canada by United States actions aimed primarily at third countries.

Similar goods: defined in the ***Customs Valuation Agreement*** as "goods which, although not alike in all respects, have like characteristics and like component materials which enable them to perform the same functions and to be commercially interchangeable". The quality of the goods, their reputation and the existence of a trademark are among the factors to be considered in determining whether products are similar. Among other conditions, goods are not regarded as "similar goods" unless they were produced in the same country as the goods being valued. *See also* ***accordion of likeness***, ***fungible goods***, ***identical goods*** and ***like product***.

Simplified balance-of-payments consultations: consultations in the WTO after the invocation by a ***least-developed country*** member of the WTO provisions permitting measures to safeguard its external financial position. They are distinguished from the ***full balance-of-payments consultations*** normally used in the case of other WTO members. *See also* ***balance-of-payments consultations***.

口参加方维持出口税或出口禁止或限制的第三国复出口，从而导致国内加工业所必需的国内原材料数量严重短缺。如果采取此类措施，这些措施不得以任意或不合理歧视的方式实施，也不得用于保护国内产业。

Short-supply products

短缺产品

GATT第11条禁止实行进口配额和出口配额，一些规定的例外情况除外。其中一项例外是，如果为暂时防止或缓解出口国的粮食或其他必需品的严重短缺，则允许实行出口配额。

Short-supply regulations

短缺供应法规

1997年在美国关于反倾销措施的修正立法背景下讨论的法规框架。支持此类法规的理由是，一些制造业务依赖于有竞争力的部件供应以维持产品销售。有时，这些部件的国内供应会出现临时短缺，而同时可能受反倾销程序的约束。在此种情况下，从进口商的角度看，不应采取反倾销措施。这会使企业继续受益于对进口部件收取的较低价格，从而保持其竞争力。最后立法者拒绝接受这一论点。

Short-Term Arrangement Regarding International Trade in Cotton Textiles

国际棉纺织品贸易短期安排

在GATT中，纺织品出口大国和进口大国之间通过选择性数量限制管理此类产品贸易的安排。1961年生效，为期1年，随后在1962年被《国际棉纺织品贸易长期安排》所取代，后者于1973年被《多种纤维协定》所取代。另见将纺织品贸易纳入WTO正常规则框架的*《纺织品与服装协定》(Agreement on Textiles and Clothing)*。

Sideswipe problem

殃及问题

加拿大贸易分析人士专门用于描述美国主要针对第三国的行动对加拿大造成的任何消极影响的一种表述。

Similar goods

类似货物

在《海关估价协定》中定义为"虽然不是在所有方面均相同，但具有相似的特性和相似的组成材料，从而使其具有相同功能，且在商业上可以互换的货物"。货物的质量、声誉和商标的存在是确定产品是否相似的考虑因素。在其他条件中，除非货物与被估价货物在相同国家生产，否则不应视为"类似货物"。另见*符合同类性(accordion of likeness)*、*可替代产品(fungible goods)*、*相同货物(identical goods)*、*同类产品(like product)*。

Simplified balance-of-payments consultations

国际收支简化磋商程序

最不发达国家成员援引WTO允许采取措施保障对外金融地位的条款后，在WTO中进行的磋商。此种磋商不同于WTO其他成员通常使用的国际收支全面磋商。另见*国际收支磋商(balance-of-payments consultations)*。

Singapore issues: so named because they entered the WTO work programme through the declaration issued by the ***Singapore WTO Ministerial Conference***. The issues are ***trade and investment***, ***trade and competition***, ***transparency*** in ***government procurement*** and ***trade facilitation***.

Singapore Treaty on the Law of Trademarks: a revision adopted in 2006 of the ***Trademark Law Treaty***. Entered into force in 2009. It allows the registration of two-dimensional and three-dimensional ***trademarks***, including hologram marks, colour marks and marks consisting of non-visible signs, such as sound and taste marks. It also establishes an assembly of contracting parties to deal with matters arising from the treaty. [www.wipo.int]

Singapore WTO Ministerial Conference: the first of the biennial WTO meetings at ministerial level, held in December 1996. *See also* ***Cancún Ministerial Conference***, ***Doha Ministerial Conference***, ***Seattle Ministerial Conference*** and other ***WTO Ministerial Conferences***, such as the ***Buenos Aires WTO Ministerial Conference*** and the ***Nairobi WTO Ministerial Conference***.

Singer-Prebisch thesis: refers to the proposition advanced in 1950 by the economists Hans Singer and Raúl Prebisch that the ***terms of trade*** of commodity-producing developing countries in their trade with developed countries will deteriorate over time. Singer and Prebisch arrived at the proposition independently of each other and from different assumptions. The proposition is known also as Prebisch-Singer thesis. The reason that Singer is often mentioned first is that apparently Prebisch was able to make good use of analytical work performed by Singer. On the other hand, the eventual popularity of the thesis owed much to its advocacy by Prebisch first as Secretary-General of ***ECLA*** and later as the first Secretary-General of ***UNCTAD***. The starting point for Prebisch appears to have been the role of the labour market in developed and developing countries. He argued that because trade unions in developed countries, i.e. the countries producing manufactures, were strong, wages there tended to rise quickly in good times, but wage reductions in bad times were much slower. He saw this as an important factor in maintaining the price of manufactures. In developing countries, the weakness of trade unions meant that wages rose less quickly in good times and fell more quickly in bad times. This situation, according to Prebisch, meant that the gap between the cost of commodities and that of manufactures was increasing. Singer, on the other hand, was concerned more with price and income elasticities. He said that the demand for primary commodities had a relatively low income elasticity, and this meant that a rise in income tended to lower demand, and therefore the price, of commodities more than was the case for manufactures. He also held that technological improvements tended to reduce the demand for raw materials through, for example, the production of man-made substitutes and more efficient use of existing raw materials. This meant over time a lower growth in demand for primary commodities than for manufactures. Both Singer and Prebisch agreed that the solution for commodity-producing developing countries was to encourage industrialization. The Singer-Prebisch thesis became an

Singapore issues

新加坡议题

之所以如此命名，是因为这些议题通过新加坡WTO部长级会议发表的宣言进入了WTO工作计划。包括贸易与投资、贸易与竞争、政府采购透明度和贸易便利化。

Singapore Treaty on the Law of Trademarks

商标法新加坡条约

2006年通过的对《商标法条约》的修订，于2009年生效。条约允许二维和三维商标进行注册，包括全息商标、颜色商标以及由声音和味觉标志等不可见标志组成的商标。条约还设立了一个缔约方大会，以处理由条约所产生的事项。

Singapore WTO Ministerial Conference

WTO新加坡部长级会议

1996年12月举行的WTO首届部长级会议，部长级会议每2年召开一次。另见*坎昆部长级会议(Cancún Ministerial Conference)*、*多哈部长级会议(Doha Ministerial Conference)*、*西雅图部长级会议(Seattle Ministerial Conference)*及其他*WTO部长级会议(WTO Ministerial Conferences)*，例如*WTO布宜诺斯艾利斯部长级会议(Buenos Aires WTO Ministerial Conference)*、*WTO内罗毕部长级会议(Nairobi WTO Ministerial Conference)*。

Singer-Prebisch thesis

辛格-普雷维什命题

1950年，经济学家汉斯·辛格和劳尔·普雷维什提出的命题，即生产初级产品的发展中国家在与发达国家开展贸易过程中的贸易条件将随着时间的推移而恶化。辛格和普雷维什是从不同的假设出发，各自独立提出了这一观点。这一观点也被称为普雷维什-辛格命题。辛格之所以经常先被提到，显然是因为普雷维什能够很好地利用辛格的分析工作。另一方面，这一命题最终受到欢迎，在很大程度上归功于普雷维什的提倡，他先后担任拉丁美洲经济委员会(ECLA)秘书长和联合国贸易与发展会议(UNCTAD)首任秘书长。普雷维什的出发点似乎是发达国家和发展中国家劳动力市场的作用。他认为，由于发达国家和制成品生产国中的工会强大，工资在经济景气时往往快速上涨，而在萧条时工资削减要慢得多。他将此视为维持制成品价格的一个重要因素。在发展中国家中，工会的弱小意味着工资在经济景气时上涨较慢，在萧条时下降较快。在普雷维什看来，此种情况意味着商品成本和制成品成本之间的差距正在拉大。另一方面，辛格更关注价格和收入弹性。他指出，对初级商品的需求具有相对低的收入弹性，而这意味着收入的增加往往使需求下降，从而使商品价格降低的幅度大于制成品价格降低的幅度。他还认为，技术进步往往会减少对原材料的需求，例如通过生产人造替代品和更有效利用现有原材料。这意味着从长期看，对初级商品的需求增长低于对制成品的需求增长。辛格和普雷维什均认为，对于生产初级商品的发展中国家而言，解决办法是鼓励工业化。辛格-普雷维什命题成为发展经济学的一个重要方面，但一直存在

important aspect of development economics, but it has always been controversial, partly because it appeared to encourage ***protectionism*** by developing countries. Certainly, one of its effects in Latin America especially was the widespread resort to ***import substitution*** policies. Additionally, the statistical evidence for a long-term deterioration of commodity terms of trade does not appear conclusive. It is always possible to find periods during which the terms of trade for commodity-producing developing countries decline, but equally other periods can be found to show the opposite. The heyday of the thesis spanned two decades beginning with the early 1960s. Today few economics textbooks discuss it in any depth. Its influence, however, is continuing in the ***GSP*** (Generalized System of Preferences), the ***Integrated Programme for Commodities***, the concept of ***special and differential treatment***, the ***Enabling Clause***, the ***GSTP*** (Global System of Trade Preferences Among Developing Countries), etc. All of these are aimed at promoting increased participation by developing countries in world trade. *See also* ***core–periphery thesis*** and ***export pessimism***. [Cuddington, Ludema and Jayasuria 2002, Prebisch 1950, Prebisch 1963, Singer 1950, Toye and Toye 2003]

Single-column tariff: a ***tariff schedule*** under which all trading partners are treated in the same way. The schedule does not allow preferences, and it permits importers to seek the best possible suppliers. A single-column tariff represents the ideal state of the ***multilateral trading system***. *See also* ***multi-column tariff***.

Single commodity producers: refers mainly to developing countries that rely on one or two commodities for a large part of their exports. Such economies can experience large fluctuations in export income as demand and supply rise and fall.

Single-desk selling: the practice in some countries of marketing abroad and exporting agricultural commodities through ***marketing boards***. Often, these have a monopoly on exporting and, sometimes, for imports also. In ***market economies*** at least, they usually operate on commercial principles in response to market signals. *See also* ***state trading***.

Single economic space: an imprecise term which can mean anything from a ***free-trade area*** to a ***common market***. *See also* ***common economic space*** and ***Eurasian Economic Community***.

Single entry point: *see* ***Single Window***.

Single European Act: an amendment in 1987 to the ***Treaty of Rome*** with the aim of transforming relations among European Community member states into a European Union, and to contribute to making concrete progress towards European unity. The content of the Act is, however, mainly economic. It extended the Community's competence to include the internal market, monetary policy, social policy, economic and social cohesion, research and technology, and the environment. It made possible the ***European Single Market***. The *Single European Act* also contains important institutional changes, such as making a formal linkage between the ***European Communities***

争议，部分原因是这一命题似乎鼓励发展中国家的保护主义。可以肯定的是，这一命题在对拉丁美洲的影响之一是广泛采用进口替代政策。此外，关于商品贸易条件长期恶化的统计学证据似乎并不确凿。总是可以找到生产初级商品的发展中国家的贸易条件恶化的时期，但同样可以找到出现相反情况的其他时期。这一命题从20世纪60年代初起盛行了20年。今天，很少有经济学教科书对此有任何深入的讨论。但是，这一命题的影响继续存在于普惠制(GSP)、商品综合方案、特殊和差别待遇、授权条款、发展中国家全球贸易优惠制(GSTP)等方面。所有这些均旨在促进发展中国家更多参与世界贸易。另见*核心-外围理论(core–periphery thesis)*、*出口悲观主义(export pessimism)*。

Single-column tariff

单栏关税

以相同方式对待所有贸易伙伴的关税税则。该税则没有优惠，且允许进口商寻求最佳可能的供应商。单栏关税代表了多边贸易体制的理想状态。另见*多栏关税(multi-column tariff)*。

Single commodity producers

单一商品生产国

主要指大部分出口依赖一种或两种商品的发展中国家。此类经济体的出口收入会随着需求和供给的增加和减少而出现大幅波动。

Single-desk selling

专责销售

一些国家通过销售局在国外销售和出口农产品的做法。通常涉及对出口的垄断，有时还包括进口。至少在市场经济体中，通常根据市场信号，按照商业原则经营。另见*国营贸易(state trading)*。

Single economic space

单一经济空间

一个不确切的词语，可以指从自由贸易区到共同市场的任何情形。另见*共同经济空间(common economic space)*、*欧亚经济共同体(Eurasian Economic Community)*。

Single entry point

单一接入点

见*单一窗口(Single Window)*。

Single European Act

单一欧洲法

1987年对《罗马条约》的修正，旨在将欧洲共同体成员国之间的关系转变成为一个欧洲的联盟，并在促进欧洲一体化方面作出实质贡献。但是，该法的内容主要为经济方面。该法将共同体的权限扩展至内部市场、货币政策、社会政策、经济和社会凝聚力、研究和技术以及环境。使欧洲单一市场成为可能。《单一欧洲法》还包含重要的制度性变革，例如在欧洲共同体与欧洲政治合

and European Political Cooperation. *See also* ***European Union*** and ***European Union treaties***.

Single-firm behaviour: an aspect of company behaviour usually regulated under ***antitrust laws*** or ***competition laws***. Its main manifestations are ***predatory pricing***, price discrimination and fidelity rebates.

Single Market: *see* ***European Single Market***.

Single Payment Scheme: the single payment, independent of production, which was available to ***European Union*** agricultural producers from 2007 to 2013. It was replaced by the ***Basic Payment Scheme***.

Single undertaking: a guiding principle in the framework of multilateral trade negotiations. The Doha Ministerial Declaration states that "the conduct, conclusion and entry into force of the outcome of the negotiations shall be treated as part of a single undertaking". The Punta del Este Declaration, which launched the ***Uruguay Round***, also said that the conduct of the negotiations, their conclusion and entry into force were to be treated as a single process. "Single undertaking" has also been used to refer to the requirement that WTO members must join all the agreements administered by it, except for the two plurilateral agreements. Membership of these remains optional. Before the WTO was established, GATT members could elect to a large extent which of the agreements under the purview of the GATT, other than the GATT itself, they wanted to join. *See also* ***early harvest***.

Single Window: either a physical or an electronic point which permits traders to lodge all the documentation required for importing or exporting in one action. This is seen as an important way to reduce the regulatory burden on business, partly because the creation of a Single Window often leads to a review and simplification of the actual documentation requirements. Article 10 of the WTO ***Agreement on Trade Facilitation*** requires the establishment of a Single Window where documents can be lodged and which is also used to notify applicants. Wherever possible, members should use information technology to support the Single Window. Other international organizations are doing work to support the more widespread use of the Single Window, including the United Nations ***Economic Commission for Europe*** and ***APEC*** through the ***APEC Single Window Strategic Plan***. *See also* ***trade facilitation***.

SITC: Standard International Trade Classification. A ***United Nations*** classification which covers transportable goods. Services and non-traded sectors are not included. SITC is the most commonly used statistical classification for measuring trade in goods. *See also* ***Harmonized Commodity Description and Coding System***, ***International Standard Industrial Classification of All Economic Activities*** and ***United Nations Central Product Classification***.

Sliding-scale tariff: a ***tariff schedule*** which sets tariff rates according to the value of the imported products. In most cases, the rates rise as the value of the goods increases.

Slippery slope: has roughly the same meaning as the ***thin edge of the wedge***. It refers to the beginning of a process that will almost inevitably lead to

作之间建立正式联系。另见*欧洲联盟(European Union)*、*欧洲联盟主要条约(European Union treaties)*。

Single-firm behaviour

单一企业行为

公司行为的一个方面，通常受到反垄断法或竞争法规范，主要表现为掠夺性定价、价格歧视和忠诚回扣。

Single Market

单一市场

见*欧洲单一市场(European Single Market)*。

Single Payment Scheme

单一支付计划

2007年至2013年期间适用于欧盟农业生产者的单一支付，与生产无关。已被基本支付方案所取代。

Single undertaking

一揽子承诺

多边贸易谈判框架中的一项指导原则。《多哈部长宣言》指出，“谈判的进行、结束以及谈判结果的生效应被视为一揽子承诺”。启动乌拉圭回合的《埃斯特角城宣言》还指出，谈判的进行、结束和生效应被视为一个单一进程。“一揽子承诺”也用于指WTO成员必须加入WTO所管理的所有协定，两项诸边协定除外。诸边协定的参加是选择性的。在WTO建立之前，除了GATT本身之外，GATT缔约方可以在很大程度上选择它们希望加入GATT范围内的协定。另见*早期收获(early harvest)*。

Single Window

单一窗口

实体或电子接入点，允许贸易商一次性提交进口或出口所需的所有单证。被认为是减少商业监管负担的一个重要途径，部分原因是单一窗口的创设往往促成对实际单证要求的审查和简化。WTO《贸易便利化协定》第10条要求建立一个可以提交单证的单一窗口，也用于向申请人进行通报。如可能，成员应使用信息技术支持单一窗口。其他国际组织正在开展工作以支持更广泛地使用单一窗口，包括联合国欧洲经济委员会和APEC通过APEC单一窗口战略计划。另见*贸易便利化(trade facilitation)*。

SITC

国际贸易标准分类

涵盖可运输货物的联合国分类系统。不包括服务和非贸易部门。SITC是衡量货物贸易最常用的统计分类。另见*商品名称及编码协调制度(Harmonized Commodity Description and Coding System)*、*全部经济活动国际标准行业分类(International Standard Industrial Classification of All Economic Activities)*、*联合国中央产品分类(United Nations Central Product Classification)*。

Sliding-scale tariff

滑准税

根据进口产品的价值确定税率的关税税则。在大多数情况下，税率随着货物价值的增加而提高。

Slippery slope

滑坡谬误

与坏事的端倪的含义大致相同。指一个进程的开端，这一进程几乎不可避免

undesirable results from the point of view of those who do not wish to be anywhere near it.

Small economies: a WTO work programme established at the ***Doha Ministerial Conference*** which aims at the fuller integration of small, vulnerable economies into the ***multilateral trading system***.

Small island developing states: SIDS. A group of thirty-eight countries and territories recognized by the United Nations as having unique problems and special vulnerabilities in achieving ***sustainable development***. The Alliance of Small Island States (AOSIS) operates within the group as a lobby and negotiating voice, but not all AOSIS members are part of SIDS. AOSIS pays attention especially to the vulnerability of SIDS to the effects of ***climate change***.

Small vulnerable economies: an imprecise term sometimes used to cover economies sharing several or all of the following characteristics: (a) domestic markets of a limited size, (b) limited diversification in export structure, both in terms of products and markets, (c) vulnerability to internal and external shocks, such as natural disasters or rapid increases in prices for imported energies, (d) long distance from markets and high transport costs, (e) shortage of suitably qualifies human resources, and (f) shortfalls in institutional and administrative capacities. In the WTO this is also a group of developing countries seeking flexibility and enhanced ***special and differential treatment*** in the negotiations. [www.wto.org]

Smoot-Hawley Tariff Act: the 1930 United States *Tariff Act*. It was passed at the onset of the Great Depression and is chiefly remembered for having raised tariffs to the highest level in United States history. The tariff rates specified by this Act, like those of its predecessor, the *Tariff Act* of 1909, were fixed and could not be reduced through negotiation. It was amended in 1934 by the *Reciprocal Trade Agreements Act*. This launched the Reciprocal Trade Agreements Program which permitted negotiated tariff reductions. The effect on international trade of the Smoot-Hawley tariff is still being debated. There is a widespread belief, expressed in many economic histories, that it was one of the major causes of the deepening recession. Countries for whom the United States was a major market were of course very much affected by the higher rates. Regardless of the effect of the Act on trade, it was symptomatic of the ***beggar-thy-neighbour policies*** pursued by many countries in the inter-war years. The Smoot-Hawley tariff rates are still in force, and they apply to products from countries not receiving ***most-favoured-nation treatment*** by the United States, i.e. countries with which the United States does not have ***normal trade relations***. This Act also bans the import into the United States of goods produced by ***prison labour***, forced or indentured labour. *See also* ***autonomous tariff quota***, ***Section 337*** and ***United States Reciprocal Trade Agreements Program***.

Smuggling: taking goods illegally across borders. If the goods could be imported legally into the country after the payment of applicable ***customs duties***, the main motivation may simply be the avoidance of these duties. If the import of

地会导致那些不想靠近此事的人所不期望的结果。

Small economies

小经济体

多哈部长级会议制定的WTO工作计划，旨在使弱小经济体更充分融入多边贸易体制。

Small island developing states

小岛屿发展中国家

SIDS。由38个国家和地区组成的集团，这些国家和地区被联合国认为在实现可持续发展方面存在独特问题和特殊脆弱性。小岛屿国家联盟(AOSIS)在该集团中作为一个游说组织和谈判的声音存在，但并非所有AOSIS成员均为小岛屿发展中国家的一部分。联盟特别关注小岛屿发展中国家面临气候变化影响的脆弱性。

Small vulnerable economies

弱小经济体

一个不确切的词语，有时用于统称具有下列若干或全部特征的经济体：(a)国内市场规模有限；(b)产品和市场的出口结构多样化有限；(c)容易受到内部和外部冲击，例如自然灾害或进口能源价格迅速上涨；(d)市场距离远且运输成本高；(e)缺乏适当的人力资源；以及(f)体制和行政能力不足。在WTO中，这也是在谈判中寻求灵活性及加强特殊和差别待遇的一组发展中国家。

Smoot-Hawley Tariff Act

斯穆特-霍利关税法

美国《1930年关税法》。该法在大萧条时期获得通过，使人印象最深刻的是该法将关税提高至美国历史最高水平。与其前身《1909年关税法》一样，该法规定的关税税率是固定的，不能通过谈判削减。该法经《1934年互惠贸易协定法》修正，启动了通过谈判降低关税的互惠贸易协定计划。《斯穆特-霍利关税法》对国际贸易的影响仍然存在争议。普遍认为，这是衰退加剧的主要原因之一，这一观点在许多经济史上都有所表述。对于那些以美国为主要市场的国家而言，较高的关税当然对它们会产生很大影响。无论该法对贸易产生何种影响，都反映了许多国家在两次世界大战之间奉行以邻为壑政策的征兆。斯穆特-霍利关税税率目前仍然有效，且适用于未获得美国最惠国待遇的国家的产品，即与美国未建立正常贸易关系的国家。该法还禁止美国进口由监狱劳役、强迫劳动或契约劳工生产的产品。另见*自主关税配额(autonomous tariff quota)*、*337条款(Section 337)*、*美国互惠贸易协定计划(United States Reciprocal Trade Agreements Program)*。

Smuggling

走私

非法携带货物跨越边境。如果这些货物在缴纳适用关税后可以合法进口到该国，那么其主要动机可能仅为逃避关税。如果进口货物首先是非法的，那么

the good is illegal in the first place, other motivations of course come into play. *See also* ***trafficking***.

Snapback provision: a mechanism sometimes built into preferential trade agreements or other trade agreements which allows an importing country to increase temporarily the ***tariff*** on a specified good or limit the quantities of that good that may be imported at the preferential tariff if its value at the border drops below a certain point. *See also* ***safeguards***.

SNPA: the *Substantial New Programme of Action for the 1980s for the Least-Developed Countries*. Adopted in Paris on 14 September 1981 by the United Nations Conference for the Least-Developed Countries to promote the advancement of ***least-developed countries***. Progress on the implementation of the SNPA was reviewed and new targets set for it at the Second United Nations Conference for the Least-Developed Countries held in September 1990, also in Paris. *See also* ***Programme of Action for the Least-Developed Countries for the Decade 2011–2020.***

Social Chapter: *see* ***European Social Charter***.

Social Charter: *see* ***European Social Charter***.

Social clause: short for the question of whether trade penalties in the form of WTO measures should be able to be applied to member countries found in breach of internationally agreed labour practices. The aim of a social clause would be to improve labour conditions in exporting countries by permitting sanctions against exporters who fail to observe certain minimum labour standards formulated by the ***International Labour Organization*** (ILO). There is no agreement yet on its feasibility or desirability, though similar measures have been discussed for well over a century in other fora. It was discussed in December 1996 at the ***Singapore WTO Ministerial Conference*** where ministers agreed that labour standards were a matter for the ILO. It is worth recalling, though, that the 1954 international sugar and tin agreements contained, for example, a "fair labour standards" clause which sought to ensure that labour engaged in the production of the commodity concerned would enjoy fair remuneration, social security benefits and other satisfactory conditions. The 1976 World Employment Conference held that the competitiveness of imports from developing countries should not be achieved at the expense of fair labour standards. Four years later, the first ***Brandt Report*** also recommended that fair labour standards should be internationally agreed to facilitate trade liberalization. The ***International Coffee Agreement*** of 2011 contains a clause promoting improved standards of living for populations engaged in the coffee sector. *See also* ***child labour***, ***Convention Concerning the Prohibition and Immediate Action for the Elimination of the Worst Forms of Child Labour***, ***democracy clause***, ***human rights clause***, ***international commodity agreements, trade and labour standards*** and ***worker rights***.

Social conditionality: the attachment of social objectives to trade rules and making adherence to these rules conditional on the observance of certain social practices. *See also* ***social clause***, ***trade and human rights*** and ***trade and labour standards***.

当然就是出于其他动机。另见*非法交易(trafficking)*。

Snapback provision

回弹条款

有时纳入优惠贸易协定或其他贸易协定的机制，允许进口国在一规定货物的边境价格低于某一点时，临时提高该货物的关税或限制该货物按优惠关税进口的数量。另见*保障措施(safeguards)*。

SNPA

20世纪80年代支援最不发达国家新的实质性行动纲领

1981年9月14日，在巴黎召开的联合国最不发达国家问题会议上通过，以促进最不发达国家的发展。1990年9月在巴黎举行的联合国第二次最不发达国家问题会议对这一行动纲领的执行情况进行了审议，并为其确定了新目标。另见*2011—2020年十年期支援最不发达国家行动纲领(Programme of Action for the Least-Developed Countries for the Decade 2011–2020)*。

Social Chapter

社会章节

见*欧洲社会宪章(European Social Charter)*。

Social Charter

社会宪章

见*欧洲社会宪章(European Social Charter)*。

Social clause

社会条款

关于以WTO措施为形式的贸易惩罚能否适用于被认定违反国际议定劳工措施成员的问题的简称。社会条款的目的在于通过允许针对不遵守国际劳工组织(ILO)制定的某些最低劳工标准的出口商实行制裁，从而改善出口国的劳动条件。尽管类似的措施已经在其他场所中讨论了超过一个世纪，但是对于措施的可行性和可取性未达成一致。在1996年12月的新加坡WTO部长级会议上，部长们一致认为劳工标准应由国际劳工组织负责。不过，值得回忆的是，1954年的国际糖和锡协定包含"公平劳工标准"条款，该条款旨在寻求保证从事有关商品生产的劳工享有公平报酬、社会保障福利和其他令人满意的条件。1976年世界就业会议认为，来自发展中国家的进口产品的竞争力不应以牺牲公平劳工标准为代价。4年后，第一份《勃兰特报告》也建议公平劳工标准应在国际上达成一致，以促进贸易自由化。2011年的《国际咖啡协定》包含一项旨在提高咖啡行业从业人员生活水平的条款。另见*童工(child labour)*、*禁止和立即行动消除最恶劣形式的童工劳动公约(Convention Concerning the Prohibition and Immediate Action for the Elimination of the Worst Forms of Child Labour)*、*民主条款(democracy clause)*、*人权条款(human rights clause)*、*国际商品协定(international commodity agreements)*、*贸易与劳工标准(trade and labour standards)*、*劳工权利(worker rights)*。

Social conditionality

社会制约性

将社会目标附加在贸易规则之上，使规则的遵守以符合某些社会惯例为前提。另见*社会条款(social clause)*、*贸易与人权(trade and human rights)*、*贸易与劳工标准(trade and labour standards)*。

Social dimension of the liberalization of international trade: *see* ***World Commission on the Social Dimension of Globalization***.

Social dumping: an imprecise term for actions assumed to occur when goods produced by prison or sweated labour are exported at very low prices. It was one of the putative categories of dumping identified by some participants in the ***Havana Charter*** negotiations. No rules were drafted for this type of alleged dumping, and it is not an accepted ***trade policy*** concept. The GATT contains a ***general exception*** in Article XX(e) covering goods made by ***prison labour***. More recently, the term "social dumping" has also been used for products allegedly produced and exported under conditions that do not reflect standards, other than technical ones, prevailing in developed economies. *See also* ***dumping***, ***pauper-labour argument***, ***social clause***, ***trade and labour standards*** and ***worker rights***.

Social labelling: the practice of attaching a label or a mark to a product to indicate that it has been made under conditions of ***fair labour standards***. There are no international rules on this, and many fear that compulsory social labelling would be the first step towards discriminatory treatment of ***sensitive products*** to protect some domestic industries. Proponents of the idea say that such is not their intent. *Rugmark* is an example of voluntary labelling. Products bearing this label are made without ***child labour***. *See also* ***eco-labelling***, ***genetic labelling*** and ***social clause***.

Socially-responsible investing: the practice of taking into account ethical and economic criteria when making a decision to invest. *See also* ***Corporate Social Responsibility***.

Social regulation: *see* ***regulation***.

Social subsidies: some claim that these occur when governments permit the existence particularly in export industries of labour standards lower than those applied internationally, or if they do not enforce their own standards. The perceived resulting lower operating costs of enterprises benefiting from these practices are seen as an indirect export subsidy. Analysis tends to indicate, however, that lower labour standards have little effect on export competitiveness and, indeed, that they may impede it. Nor is the concept of social subsidies an accepted part of the ***trade policy*** vocabulary. *See also* ***core labour standards***, ***pauper-labour argument*** and ***social clause***.

Social tariff: a ***tariff*** intended to take into account social conditions in the importing country. For example, an industry may be given higher tariffs if it can show that it satisfies certain employment conditions, etc. The social tariff is best seen as an argument for ***protectionism***. *See also* ***Australian argument for protection***.

Soft law: in ***trade policy*** parlance, international arrangements that do not require parties to them to enforce the ***measures*** contained in them. In other words, they are hortatory arrangements. Examples of instruments entailing soft law are the Set of Multilaterally Agreed Equitable Principles and Rules for the Control of Restrictive Business Practices negotiated under ***UNCTAD*** auspices, the ***OECD***

Social dimension of the liberalization of international trade
国际贸易自由化的社会内涵

见*全球化社会问题世界委员会(World Commission on the Social Dimension of Globalization)*。

Social dumping
社会倾销

一个不确切的词语，指监狱劳役或血汗劳动生产的货物以非常低的价格出口时假定发生的行为。在《哈瓦那宪章》谈判中，一些谈判者所确定的一个推定的倾销类别。对此类被指控的倾销行为并未制定任何规则，而且也不是一个被接受的贸易政策概念。GATT第20条(e)款包含涵盖监狱劳役产品的一般例外。近期，"社会倾销"一词也被用于指在发达经济体中普遍存在的技术标准以外的条件下所生产和出口的产品。另见*倾销(dumping)*、*贫民劳动论(pauper-labour argument)*、*社会条款(social clause)*、*贸易与劳工标准(trade and labour standards)*、*劳工权利(worker rights)*。

Social labelling
社会标签

在产品上加贴标签或标记以表明产品是在公平劳工标准的条件下生产的做法。对此并无国际规则，许多人担心强制性社会标签将是对敏感产品实行歧视待遇以保护一些国内产业的第一步。这一设想的支持者认为，这并不是他们的意图。地毯标签就是一个自愿标签的例子。带有这一标签的产品在制造过程中不使用童工。另见*生态标签(eco-labelling)*、*基因标签(genetic labelling)*、*社会条款(social clause)*。

Socially-responsible investing
社会责任投资

在作出投资决定时考虑道德和经济准则的做法。另见*企业社会责任(Corporate Social Responsibility)*。

Social regulation
社会管制

见*管制(regulation)*。

Social subsidies
社会补贴

一些人认为，社会补贴出现在政府允许，特别是在出口产业，存在低于国际适用标准的劳工标准时，或出现在政府不执行它们自已的标准时。从这些做法中获益的企业的低运营成本被认为是一种间接出口补贴。但是，分析往往表明，较低的劳工标准对出口竞争力几无影响，实际上，它们可能会阻碍出口竞争力。社会补贴的概念也不是一个为人所接受的贸易政策用语。另见*核心劳工标准(core labour standards)*、*贫民劳动论(pauper-labour argument)*、*社会条款(social clause)*。

Social tariff
社会关税

旨在考虑进口国社会条件的关税。例如，如果一产业能够证明满足一定就业条件等，即可能被设定更高的关税。社会关税可被视为保护主义的论点。另见*澳大利亚保护论(Australian argument for protection)*。

Soft law
软法

在贸易政策术语中，指不要求参加方执行其中所含措施的国际安排。换言之，它们属于劝励性安排。例如包含软法的法律文件有联合国贸易与发展会议

Guidelines for Multinational Enterprises and the ***APEC Non-Binding Principles on Government Procurement***. *See also* ***hard law***.

Soft loan: a loan made by a government or a ***multilateral development bank*** at interest rates that are lower than commercial rates and possibly extended repayment periods.

SOLVIT: a ***European Community*** mechanism for ***alternative dispute resolution***. It can be used by natural or legal persons that have run into problems resulting from the possible misapplication of internal market rules by another member state. The target deadline for finding a solution is ten weeks.

Sous-sherpa: *see* ***sherpa***.

South: *see* ***developing country***.

South American Community of Nations: SACN. Launched in 2004 with an expectation that it would lead to a convergence between ***Mercosur*** and the ***Andean Community*** as well as Chile, Suriname and Guyana. The target clearly was deep integration since its proponents envisaged a common currency, parliament and passport. At this stage it is not clear whether these aims will be achieved. *See also* ***Latin American regional integration arrangements***.

South Asian Association for Regional Cooperation: SAARC. It was established on 8 December 1985. Members are Afghanistan, Bangladesh, Bhutan, India, Maldives, Nepal, Pakistan and Sri Lanka. Among the objectives of SAARC are accelerated economic growth in the region and active collaboration in the economic field. As part of this, members have established the ***South Asian Free Trade Area***. The Association's secretariat is located at Kathmandu.

South Asian Free Trade Area: SAFTA. The successor to the ***SAARC Preferential Trading Arrangement***. Entered into force on 1 January 2006. It covers trade in goods. Members are Afghanistan, Bangladesh, Bhutan, India, Maldives, Nepal, Pakistan and Sri Lanka.

South-East Europe Free Trade Area: SEEFTA. This was formed in June 2001. Eventually Albania, Bosnia and Herzegovina, Bulgaria, Croatia, Moldova, North Macedonia, Romania, and Serbia and Montenegro all became members. SEEFTA was replaced on 1 January 2007 by ***CEFTA 2006***. At the same time Bulgaria and Romania joined the ***European Union***. Croatia did so in 2013.

Southern African Customs Union: SACU. A customs union originally established in 1910 and relaunched in 1969. The current SACU was formed in 2002 with the objectives, among others, of facilitating the cross-border movement of goods, promote conditions for fair competition and substantially increase investment opportunities in the SACU area. Its members are Botswana, Eswatini, Lesotho, Namibia and South Africa. Its secretariat is located in Windhoek, Namibia. *See also* ***African regional economic integration***.

Southern African Development Community: SADC. An association of fifteen southern African states (Angola, Botswana, Democratic Republic of Congo, Eswatini, Lesotho, Madagascar, Malawi, Mauritius, Mozambique, Namibia, Seychelles, South Africa, Tanzania, Zambia and Zimbabwe) established in

(UNCTAD)主持下谈判达成的《一套多边协议的控制限制性商业惯例的公平原则和规则》、经济合作与发展组织(OECD)《跨国企业行为准则》以及APEC《政府采购非约束性原则》。另见*硬法(hard law)*。

Soft loan

软贷款

政府或多边开发银行提供的贷款，利率低于商业利率并可能延长还款期。

SOLVIT

非诉讼争端解决机制

欧洲共同体机制，如自然人或法人因另一成员国可能滥用内部市场规则而遇到问题时可以使用这一机制。找到解决方案的目标期限为10周。

Sous-sherpa

副协调人

见*协调人(sherpa)*。

South

南方

见*发展中国家(developing country)*。

South American Community of Nations

南美洲国家共同体

SACN。2004年成立，期望促成南方共同市场(Mercosur)与安第斯共同体以及智利、苏里南和圭亚那之间的融合。目标显然是深度融合，因为支持者设想建立共同的货币、议会和护照。在现阶段，还不清楚这些目标是否能够实现。另见*拉丁美洲区域一体化安排(Latin American regional integration arrangements)*。

South Asian Association for Regional Cooperation

南亚区域合作联盟

SAARC。1985年12月8日成立。成员包括阿富汗、孟加拉国、不丹、印度、马尔代夫、尼泊尔、巴基斯坦和斯里兰卡。SAARC的目标包括加快本地区经济增长和促进在经济领域的积极合作。作为目标的一部分，成员国已经建立南亚自由贸易区。联盟秘书处设在加德满都。

South Asian Free Trade Area

南亚自由贸易区

SAFTA。《南亚区域合作联盟优惠贸易安排》的后继安排，于2006年1月1日生效，涵盖货物贸易。成员包括阿富汗、孟加拉国、不丹、印度、马尔代夫、尼泊尔、巴基斯坦和斯里兰卡。

South-East Europe Free Trade Area

东南欧自由贸易区

SEEFTA。2001年6月成立。最终，阿尔巴尼亚、波斯尼亚和黑塞哥维那、保加利亚、克罗地亚、摩尔多瓦、北马其顿、罗马尼亚以及塞尔维亚和黑山均成为会员。2007年1月1日SEEFTA被《2006年中欧自由贸易协定》所取代。同期，保加利亚和罗马尼亚加入欧盟。克罗地亚于2013年加入欧盟。

Southern African Customs Union

南部非洲关税同盟

SACU。关税同盟最初于1910年成立，1969年重新启动。目前的SACU成立于2002年，目标包括便利货物跨境流动、促进公平竞争条件以及实质增加SACU地区的投资机会。成员包括博茨瓦纳、斯威士兰、莱索托、纳米比亚和南非。秘书处设在纳米比亚温得和克。另见*非洲区域经济一体化(African regional economic integration)*。

Southern African Development Community

南部非洲发展共同体

SADC。由南部非洲15国组成的联盟，15国为安哥拉、博茨瓦纳、刚果(金)、斯威士兰、莱索托、马达加斯加、马拉维、毛里求斯、莫桑比克、纳米比亚、塞舌尔、南非、坦桑尼亚、赞比亚和津巴布韦，1992年作为南部非洲发展协

1992 as the successor to the Southern African Development Co-ordination Conference. Members signed a free-trade protocol in 1996. A ***free-trade area*** was established by 2008. This was to be followed by a ***customs union*** by 2013 and a ***common market*** by 2015. This was an ambitious plan, and it has not yet been realized. A longer-term aim is an economic union including monetary union with a single currency. SADC's headquarters is at Gabarone, Botswana.

South Pacific Commission: *see* ***Secretariat of the Pacific Community***.

South Pacific Forum: *see* ***Pacific Islands Forum***.

South Pacific Regional Trade and Economic Cooperation Agreement: *see* ***SPARTECA***.

South–South cooperation: cooperation between developing countries. *See also* ***Buenos Aires Plan of Action for Promoting and Implementing Technical Co-operation among Developing Countries***, ***developing country***, ***ECDC***, ***G-15***, ***Group of 77***, ***GSTP*** and ***Second High-Level United Nations Conference on South–South Cooperation***.

South–South trade: trade between developing countries and the attendant ***trade policy*** issues. *See also* ***ECDC*** and ***GSTP***.

Southern Common Market: *see* ***Mercosur***.

Sovereign immunity: the principle in ***public international law*** that a sovereign government cannot be sued without its consent.

Soybean **case:** *see* ***Oilseeds***.

Spaghetti-bowl effect: a term used by Jagdish Bhagwati to describe the complexity of trade rules resulting from a proliferation of ***free-trade areas***. A typical example of this is the existence of different ***rules of origin*** for each free-trade area. Countries that are members of more than one arrangement of this kind will have to administer different rules for each of them. [Bhagwati and Panagariya 1996]

SPARTECA: *South Pacific Regional Trade and Economic Cooperation Agreement*. This Agreement, which entered into force on 1 January 1981, gives countries located in the South Pacific preferential non-reciprocal access to Australia and New Zealand. Access for sugar to the Australian market is excluded. *See also* ***asymmetrical trade agreements***, ***Pacific Agreement on Closer Economic Relations*** and ***Pacific Agreement on Closer Economic Relations (PACER) Plus.***

Special 301: part of the United States Trade Act of 1974, as amended. It requires ***USTR*** to make investigations every year of foreign countries that deny adequate and effective protection to United States ***intellectual property rights*** or that deny fair and equitable market access for persons that rely on intellectual property protection. Countries that have the most onerous or ***egregious*** conditions and whose conditions have the greatest adverse actual or potential impact on relevant United States products must be designated as ***priority foreign countries***. This is done through the priority watch list. Placement on this list results in increased USTR attention. There is also a watch list. Countries on it

调会议的后继组织成立。成员在1996年签署了一份自由贸易议定书，2008年建立了自由贸易区。此后2013年建立关税同盟，2015年建立共同市场。这是一个雄心勃勃的计划，但目前还未实现。更长期的目标是建立一个使用单一货币的经济联盟。SADC总部设在博茨瓦纳哈博罗内。

South Pacific Commission
南太平洋委员会
见*太平洋共同体秘书处(Secretariat of the Pacific Community)*。

South Pacific Forum
南太平洋论坛
见*太平洋岛国论坛(Pacific Islands Forum)*。

South Pacific Regional Trade and Economic Cooperation Agreement
南太平洋区域贸易经济合作协定
见*南太平洋区域贸易经济合作协定(SPARTECA)*。

South–South cooperation
南南合作
发展中国家之间的合作。另见*促进和实施发展中国家间技术合作的布宜诺斯艾利斯行动计划(Buenos Aires Plan of Action for Promoting and Implementing Technical Co-operation among Developing Countries)*、*发展中国家(Developing Countries)*、*发展中国家间经济合作(ECDC)*、*15国集团(G-15)*、*77国集团(Group of 77)*、*全球贸易优惠制(GSTP)*、*第二届联合国南南合作高级别会议(Second High-Level United Nations Conference on South–South Cooperation)*。

South–South trade
南南贸易
发展中国家之间的贸易和伴随的贸易政策事务。另见*发展中国家间经济合作(ECDC)*、*全球贸易优惠制(GSTP)*。

Southern Common Market
南方共同市场
见*南方共同市场(Mercosur)*。

Sovereign immunity
主权豁免
国际公法中关于未经一主权政府同意不能起诉该主权政府的原则。

***Soybean* case**
大豆案
见*油籽案(Oilseeds)*。

Spaghetti-bowl effect
意大利面碗效应
贾格迪什·巴格瓦蒂用于描述因自由贸易区激增而导致贸易规则复杂化的词语。一个典型的例子是每一自由贸易区存在不同的原产地规则。属一个以上此类安排成员的国家不得不针对每一安排管理不同的原产地规则。

SPARTECA
南太平洋区域贸易经济合作协定
协定于1981年1月1日生效，给予南太平洋国家的产品进入澳大利亚和新西兰的非互惠优惠准入待遇。食糖不在澳大利亚市场准入清单中。另见*非对称贸易协定(asymmetrical trade agreements)*、*太平洋更紧密经济关系协定(Pacific Agreement on Closer Economic Relations)*、*太平洋更紧密经济关系协定(PACER Plus)(Pacific Agreement on Closer Economic Relations (PACER) Plus)*。

Special 301
特别301条款
经修正的美国《1974年贸易法》的一部分。要求美国贸易代表办公室(USTR)每年对拒绝为美国知识产权提供充分和有效保护或拒绝为依赖知识产权保护的人提供公平和公正市场准入的外国进行调查。条件最繁琐复杂或最恶劣的

are thought to pose problems, but not of a sufficient nature to require action. Investigations initiated as a result of Special 301 are fast-track. Unfairness and retaliation determinations must be made within six months of initiating an investigation. A particular feature of Special 301 is that, following amendment through the *Uruguay Round Agreements Act*, it can be applied to countries denying adequate and effective intellectual property protection even if they are in compliance with their obligations under the WTO ***Agreement on Trade-Related Aspects of Intellectual Property Rights***. In contrast to ***Super 301***, Special 301 does not have to be renewed at fixed intervals. A *Special 301 Review* is published annually. *See also* ***Section 301***.

Special Agreement on Commodity Arrangements: SACA. A proposal emerging in early 1955 among GATT contracting parties for an agreement to deal outside normal market forces with the disequilibrium between production and consumption of primary commodities, particularly agricultural commodities. The proposal had lapsed by the end of the year. *See also* ***agriculture and the multilateral trading system*** and ***GATT review session***.

Special agricultural safeguards: a mechanism available under the WTO ***Agreement on Agriculture*** to members who have converted ***non-tariff measures*** to ***tariff*** protection. It allows members to impose additional tariffs on agricultural products if import volumes exceed defined trigger levels or import prices fall below defined ***trigger prices***. Special safeguards therefore provide a safety net for importing countries that are also producers in the event of a surge in imports. They are meant to be introduced in a transparent manner. *See also* ***safeguards, selectivity***, ***tariffication*** and ***transitional safeguards***.

Special agricultural safeguards for developing countries: refers to proposals made by some developing countries in the ***Doha Development Agenda*** negotiations for the creation of a special safeguards mechanism for agricultural products. It would deal with cases where import volumes of specified agricultural products are rising rapidly and import prices fall below a fixed reference price. The special agricultural safeguards would only be available to developing countries meeting some defined conditions. The proposal is still under discussion. Increasingly ***free-trade agreements*** seem to make use of special agricultural safeguards. *See also* ***safeguards***.

Special and differential treatment: often referred to as S&D or S+D. It is the concept that exports of developing countries should be given preferential access to markets of developed countries, that developing countries participating in trade negotiations need not reciprocate fully the ***concessions*** they receive, and that they should be able to restrict access to their markets to promote, for example, infant industries. Under S+D developing countries also enjoy longer timeframes for phasing in new rules and lower levels of obligations for adherence to the rules. The term is drawn from the ministerial declaration launching the ***Tokyo Round*** which raised the possibility of differential measures in favour of developing countries by giving them special and more favourable treatment. *See also* ***developing countries and the multilateral***

国家和条件对相关美国产品产生最大实际或潜在不利影响的国家，必须被指定为重点国家。此点通过重点观察名单实现。USTR将增加对列入此名单国家的关注。还有一个观察名单。这一名单上的国家被认为造成了问题，但其性质不足以要求采取行动。因特别301条款而启动的调查必须快速处理。必须在启动调查后6个月内作出不公平和报复决定。特别301条款的一个特点是，在经过《乌拉圭回合协定法》进行修正后，即使一国遵守了WTO《与贸易有关的知识产权协定》项下义务，这一条款仍可对拒绝提供充分和有效知识产权保护的国家适用。与超级301条款相对比，特别301条款不需要定期更新。《特别301报告》每年发布。另见*301条款(Section 301)*。

Special Agreement on Commodity Arrangements

商品安排特别协定

SACA。1955年初，GATT缔约方中提出的一项提案，就处理正常市场力量之外的初级商品生产和消费之间的不平衡问题达成协议，特别是农产品。该提案在当年年末即不再被提及。另见*农业与多边贸易体制(agriculture and the multilateral trading system)*、*GATT审议会议(GATT review session)*。

Special agricultural safeguards

农业特殊保障条款

WTO《农业协定》项下对于已将非关税措施转化为关税保护的成员可使用的一种机制。允许成员在进口量超过规定的触发水平或进口价格低于规定的触发价格时对农产品征收额外关税。因此，特殊保障条款在进口激增时为同时属生产国的进口国提供了一个安全网。这些措施应以透明的方式采用。另见*保障措施(safeguards)*、*选择性(selectivity)*、*关税化(tariffication)*、*过渡性保障措施(transitional safeguards)*。

Special agricultural safeguards for developing countries

发展中国家农产品特殊保障机制

指一些发展中国家在多哈发展议程谈判中提出的关于建立农产品特殊保障机制的提案。该机制将用于处理规定农产品进口量快速增长和进口价格低于固定参考价格的情况。农产品特殊保障机制只适用于满足一些规定条件的发展中国家。提案仍在讨论中。越来越多的自由贸易协定似乎使用了农产品特殊保障机制。另见*保障措施(safeguards)*。

Special and differential treatment

特殊和差别待遇

通常称为“S&D”或“S+D”。应给予发展中国家的出口产品对发达国家市场的优惠准入，参加贸易谈判的发展中国家不需要对其所获减让作出完全对等的减让，且它们应有权为促进幼稚产业而限制对其市场的准入。按照特殊和差别待遇，发展中国家还可在更长的时间内逐步实施新规则，且在遵守规则方面享受较低的义务水平。该词取自启动东京回合的部长声明，该声明通过给予发展中国家特殊和更优惠的待遇，提高了给予有利于发展中国家的差别措施的可能性。另见*发展中国家与多边贸易体制(developing countries and the multilateral trading system)*、*发展箱(development box)*、*授权条款(Enabling*

trading system*, *development box*, *Enabling Clause*, *GSP*, *infant-industry argument*, *least-developed countries*, *Part IV of the GATT*, *reciprocity and ***S&D box***. [Gallagher 2000, Keck and Low 2004]

Special products: refers to a proposal in the WTO by developing countries that they should be able to exempt some agricultural products from tariff reductions and liberalization of ***tariff rate quotas***. A ceiling would apply to the number of ***tariff lines*** that could be treated in this way, but developing countries would be able to decide what products would be included. *See also* ***Alliance for Strategic Products and Special Safeguard Mechanism***.

Special protection: seen by some Canadians as a peculiarly American phenomenon. It means that some industries that are especially powerful in a political sense may not have to settle for ***trade remedies*** to keep foreign competitors at bay. Instead, they are said to be able to secure "special protection" through an executive branch reinforced by powerful congressional pressure.

Special session: meeting of the WTO Council and committees focusing only on negotiations.

Special-structure countries: a name for Australia, Canada, New Zealand and South Africa in the ***Kennedy Round*** of ***multilateral trade negotiations***. The four claimed, and were accorded, a different status in the ***linear tariff cut*** negotiations on the basis that their industries had not developed to the point where they would be able to compete with low-tariff imports of manufactures, and that the linear approach would not reduce protection for agriculture in their main export markets. In the event, they followed largely the item-by-item approach in the tariff negotiations.

Specialty air services: defined in ***NAFTA*** as aerial mapping, aerial surveying, aerial photography, forest fire management, fire fighting, aerial advertising, glider towing, parachute jumping, aerial construction, helilogging, aerial sightseeing, flight training, aerial inspection and surveillance, and aerial spraying services.

Specific commitments: *see* ***schedules of specific commitments on services***.

Specificity: a concept embodied in Article 2 of the WTO ***Agreement on Subsidies and Countervailing Measures***. It is a test to determine whether a ***subsidy*** is available only to an enterprise or industry, or group of enterprises or industries. A subsidy is considered specific when the granting authority, or the legislation on which it operates, explicitly limits access to it to certain enterprises. A subsidy may also be considered specific when there is use of a subsidy programme by a limited number of enterprises, predominant use by certain enterprises, the granting of disproportionately large amounts of subsidy to certain enterprises, and the manner in which discretion has been exercised by the granting authority in the decision to grant a subsidy. Depending on the type of subsidies and the impact they have, they may be ***prohibited subsidies***, ***actionable subsidies*** or ***non-actionable subsidies***. Subsidies dependent on export performance are also considered specific. They are always prohibited. *See also* ***but for test***.

Clause)、*普惠制(GSP)*、*幼稚产业论(infant-industry argument)*、*最不发达国家(least-developed countries)*、*GATT第四部分(Part IV of the GATT)*、*互惠(reciprocity)*、*特殊和差别待遇箱(S&D box)*。

Special products
特殊产品

指发展中国家在WTO中提出的一项提案，即这些国家应有权将一些农产品免于进行关税削减和放开关税配额。按此处理的税目数量应有上限，但发展中国家能够决定纳入哪些产品。另见*战略产品与特殊保障机制联盟(Alliance for Strategic Products and Special Safeguard Mechanism)*。

Special protection
特殊保护

一些加拿大人将此视为一种特有的美国现象。指一些产业在政治方面特别强大，而不需要通过贸易救济阻止外国竞争者。相反，据说它们能够通过一个强大国会压力所加强的行政部门获得"特殊保护"。

Special session
特别会议

专门负责谈判的WTO理事会和委员会的会议。

Special-structure countries
特殊结构国家

在肯尼迪回合多边贸易谈判中对澳大利亚、加拿大、新西兰和南非的称呼。这4个国家要求并获得了在线性关税削减谈判中的不同地位，根据是它们的产业尚未发展到能够与低关税进口制成品进行竞争的程度，而线性方式不能减少其主要出口市场对农业的保护。在此种情况下，它们在关税谈判中主要采取逐税目方式。

Specialty air services
专业航空服务

在《北美自由贸易协定》(NAFTA)中定义为航空测绘、航空测量、航空拍摄、森林火灾管理、消防、航空广告、滑翔机牵引、跳伞、高空作业、直升机采木、航空观光、飞行训练、航空检查和纠察以及飞机喷雾服务。

Specific commitments
具体承诺

见*服务贸易具体承诺减让表(schedules of specific commitments on services)*。

Specificity
专向性

WTO《补贴与反补贴措施协定》第2条中所含概念。是一种测试方法，以确定一项补贴是否只给予一企业或产业，或一组企业或产业。如补贴授予机关或其运作所依据的立法明确将补贴限定于某些企业，该项补贴即被认为具有专向性。如由于有限数量的某些企业使用补贴计划、某些企业主要使用补贴、给予某些企业不成比例的大量补贴以及授予机关在作出给予补贴的决定时行使酌量权的方式等因素，一项补贴也可被视为具有专向性。根据补贴的类型和所产生的影响，可以是禁止性补贴、可诉补贴或不可诉补贴。取决于出口实绩的补贴也被认为具有专向性，是被禁止的。另见*若非测试(but for test)*。

Specific process criterion: a concept sometimes used in the administration of ***rules of origin*** under preferential trade agreements. It means that a good has to have been processed in a certain way to qualify for preferential customs tariffs. *See also* ***change in tariff classification***, ***substantial transformation*** and ***value-added criterion***.

Specific reciprocity: *see* ***mirror-image reciprocity***.

Specific rules of origin: a system of ***rules of origin*** which prescribes the process each product must undergo to qualify as an originating product.

Specific subsidy: *see* ***specificity***.

Specific tariff: a ***tariff*** expressed as a specific charge on the particular item to be imported. A hypothetical example of a specific tariff would be a rate of one dollar per item regardless of its value. *See also* ***ad valorem tariff***.

Specific transitional safeguard mechanism: a mechanism available under the WTO ***Agreement on Textiles and Clothing*** during the transition period (i.e. the period ending on 1 January 2005 when trade in textiles and clothing had to be liberalized). The agreement has now expired. *See also* ***safeguards***, ***selectivity*** and ***Transitional Product-Specific Safeguard Mechanism***.

Specified risk material: SRM. A term used in the administration of ***sanitary and phytosanitary measures***. This is a material associated with an identified or defined risk. In the case of ***BSE***, for example, SRMs are often defined as the tissues from BSE-affected cattle which have been shown to contain the infective agent and able to transmit the disease. Such tissues cannot be used for producing goods for human consumption.

Split sub-heading: the ***Harmonized Commodity Description and Coding System*** is divided into two-digit entries (chapters), four-digit entries (headings) and six-digit entries (sub-headings). These entries are the same for all economies using this system. They cannot be altered. Countries may, however, divide headings further into split sub-headings. The definitions of split sub-headings and the number of digits vary from country to country, though there must be at least seven digits. The following is an example from the Australian tariff. Sub-heading 900130 is contact lenses. This is divided into split sub-headings 900130.10 (ophthalmic powered contact lenses) and 900130.90 (other contact lenses).

Sporadic dumping: a form of ***dumping*** said to occur when a firm decides from time to time to sell surplus stocks internationally at prices lower than it charges it home.

Springboarding: *see* ***generic springboarding***.

SPS Information Management System: SPS IMS. A database maintained by the ***WTO*** which allows users to obtain information on measures that WTO members have supplied to the WTO Committee on Sanitary and Phytosanitary Measures. It also contains committee documents and information on relevant enquiry points. [spsims.wto.org]

SPS regulations: sanitary and phytosanitary regulations. These are government standards to protect human, animal and plant life and health. They help ensure

Specific process criterion
特定工序标准

有时用于管理优惠贸易协定项下原产地规则的概念。指一货物必须以某种特定方式进行加工，方可有资格享受优惠关税。另见*税则归类改变(change in tariff classification)*、*实质性改变(substantial transformation)*、*增值标准(value-added criterion)*。

Specific reciprocity
专向互惠

见*镜像互惠(mirror-image reciprocity)*。

Specific rules of origin
特定原产地规则

一种原产地规则体系，其中规定每种产品成为原产地产品所必须经过的工序。

Specific subsidy
专向性补贴

见*专向性(specificity)*。

Specific tariff
从量关税

以对特定进口产品所征收的具体费用表示的关税。例如，对每件产品征收1美元而无论其价值如何即为从量关税。另见*从价关税(ad valorem tariff)*。

Specific transitional safeguard mechanism
过渡性特殊保障机制

WTO《纺织品与服装协定》项下过渡期内可使用的一种机制。该过渡期于2005年1月1日结束，此后纺织品与服装贸易实现自由化。协定现已失效。另见*保障措施(safeguards)*、*选择性(selectivity)*、*特定产品过渡性保障机制(Transitional Product-Specific Safeguard Mechanism)*。

Specified risk material
特定风险物质

SRM。管理卫生与植物卫生措施方面使用的词语。指一种与已识别或确定的风险相关的物质。例如，对于疯牛病(BSE)，特定风险物质通常被定义为已被证明含有具有传染性病原体且能够传播疾病的受疯牛病影响的牛的组织。此类组织不能用于生产供人类消费的产品。

Split sub-heading
分列税目

商品名称及编码协调制度分为2位编码条目(章)、4位编码条目(税目)和6位编码条目(子目)。这些条目对于使用该制度的所有经济体均相同，不能改变。但是各国可以将税目进一步拆分为分列子目。虽然各国的分列子目在定义和数量上各不相同，但至少要有7位编码。下面是澳大利亚关税的一个例子。子目900130是隐形眼镜，分列子目为900130.10(眼科隐形眼镜)和900130.90(其他隐形眼镜)。

Sporadic dumping
偶然性倾销

一种倾销形式，发生在一公司偶尔决定以低于其在国内所收取价格的价格在国际市场上出售剩余库存之时。

Springboarding
跳板

见*仿制药跳板(generic springboarding)*。

SPS Information Management System
卫生与植物卫生措施信息管理系统

SPS IMS。由WTO维护的数据库，允许用户获得WTO成员向WTO卫生与植物卫生措施委员会提供的措施信息。还包含委员会的文件和相关咨询点的信息。

SPS regulations
卫生与植物卫生法规

保护人类、动物和植物生命与健康的政府标准。有助于保证食品可以安全消

that food is safe for consumption. *See also* ***Agreement on the Application of Sanitary and Phytosanitary Measures***.

Spurious dumping: a term used by Jacob Viner in *Dumping: A Problem in International Trade* to describe situations where differences in price applied to different markets are the result of varying order sizes, length of credit terms and extent of credit risks, method of selling or freight and packaging requirements peculiar to the market, rather than conscious price discrimination. The charge of ***dumping*** could accordingly not be sustained in these cases. [Viner 1921]

Square brackets: *see* ***bracketed language***.

STABEX: System for the Stabilization of Export Earnings. A scheme established under the ***Lomé Convention*** which sought to stabilize the export earnings of developing countries associated with the ***European Community*** through the Convention. It aimed at compensating them for export earnings shortfalls in their trade with the European Community if they derived a large part of their total earnings from a single commodity. Conditionality was limited and aimed at ensuring that funds were used in the sector causing the difficulties. STABEX was not renewed in the ACP-EC Partnership Agreement, now the ***ACP-EU Partnership Agreement***, which replaced the Lomé Convention. *See also* ***Common Fund for Commodities***, ***compensatory financing arrangements*** and ***SYSMIN***.

Stabilization and Association Agreements: negotiated by the ***European Union*** with Western Balkan countries. Their emphasis is on fostering respect for key democratic values and to promote the disciplines of the ***European Single Market***. The aim of such agreements is to allow partner countries to achieve full association with the European Union. *See also* ***Association Agreements*** and ***Europe Agreements***.

Stacking: the use of two or more trade measures at the same time in respect of one good, e.g. the concurrent imposition of a ***non-tariff barrier*** and a ***tariff***. [United Nations Conference on Trade and Development 2003]

Staging: also known as phasing. The introduction of tariff reductions or other trade-liberalizing measures according to a unilateral or an internationally agreed timetable. For example, many developed countries phased in their ***Uruguay Round*** commitments to cut tariffs over five years, starting on 1 January 1995. The tariff eliminations under the ***Information Technology Agreement*** occurred in four stages, beginning on 1 July 1997 and ending on 1 January 2000. Staging is also a feature of many free-trade arrangements. ***NAFTA***, for example, has five different staging categories: (a) goods receiving duty-free treatment before entry into force of the Agreement, (b) goods for which tariffs have been eliminated from the day of entry into force, (c) goods on which tariffs are eliminated in five equal annual stages, (d) goods on which tariffs are eliminated in ten equal annual stages, and (e) goods on which tariffs are eliminated in fifteen equal annual stages. In the case of the latter three categories, the first stage occurred on entry into force of the Agreement.

费。另见*实施卫生与植物卫生措施协定(Agreement on the Application of Sanitary and Phytosanitary Measures)*。

Spurious dumping

虚假倾销

是雅各布·瓦伊纳在《倾销：国际贸易中的一个问题》一书中使用的词语，用于描述由于订单大小、信用期限和信用风险程度、销售或运输方法以及市场特有的包装要求不同，而造成适用于不同市场的价格存在差异的情况，而非有意识的价格歧视。因此，倾销的指控在这些情况下不能成立。

Square Brackets

方括号

见*方括号内文字(bracketed language)*。

STABEX

出口收入稳定机制

根据《洛美协定》建立的机制，寻求通过该协定稳定与欧洲共同体有联系的发展中国家的出口收入。目的在于，如果发展中国家出口收入的很大部分来自单一商品，该机制将补偿这些国家与欧洲共同体贸易中产生的出口收入不足。条件是有限的，目的在于保证将资金用于产生困难的部门。出口收入稳定机制(STABEX)在取代《洛美协定》的《非加太地区国家与欧共体伙伴关系协定》中未得到更新，即现在的《非加太地区国家与欧盟伙伴关系协定》。另见*商品共同基金(Common Fund for Commodities)*、*补偿性融资安排(compensatory financing arrangements)*、*矿产生产及出口促进制度(SYSMIN)*。

Stabilization and Association Agreements

稳定与联系协定

由欧盟与西巴尔干半岛国家谈判达成，重点是促进尊重关键民主价值观和促进欧洲单一市场的纪律。此类协定的目的在于允许伙伴国实现与欧盟的完全联合。另见*洛美协定(Lomé Convention)*、*欧洲协定(Europe Agreements)*。

Stacking

叠加

对一种货物同时使用两种或两种以上贸易措施，例如同时实施非关税壁垒和关税。

Staging

降税期

也称分阶段实施。根据单边或国际议定的时间表，引入关税削减或其他贸易自由化措施。例如，许多发达国家在自1995年1月1日起的5年内，分阶段履行乌拉圭回合关税削减承诺。《信息技术协定》项下的关税取消分4个阶段完成，自1997年7月1日起至2000年1月1日结束。降税期也是许多自由贸易协定的特征。例如，《北美自由贸易协定》(NAFTA)有5个不同的降税期类别：(a)在协定生效前享受免税待遇的货物；(b)自协定生效之日起取消关税的货物；(c)分5次年度均等削减取消关税的货物；(d)分10次年度均等削减取消关税的货物；以及(e)分15次年度均等削减取消关税的货物。对于后3类，第一次阶段削减在协定生效之日进行。

Standard International Trade Classification: *see* ***SITC***.

Standards: methods to ensure uniform specifications or attributes of a product or a service. They are divided broadly into technical standards (e.g. minimum or maximum size, colour, composition, etc.) or performance standards (the product or service must have at least a certain capability). Additionally, standards may be compulsory or voluntary. The WTO ***Agreement on Technical Barriers to Trade***, which applies to goods only, defines a standard as a "document approved by a recognized body that provides, for common and repeated use, rules, guidelines or characteristics for products or related processes and production methods, with which compliance is not mandatory. It may also include or deal exclusively with terminology, symbols, packaging, marking or labelling requirements, as they apply to a product, process or production method". *See also* ***conformity assessment***, ***International Electrotechnical Commission***, ***International Organization for Standardization***, ***ISO 9000***, ***ISO 14000*** and ***technical barriers to trade***.

Standards and Trade Development Facility: STDF. A mechanism established jointly by the ***Food and Agriculture Organization***, ***World Bank***, the World Health Organization and the WTO after the ***Hong Kong Ministerial Conference***. It supports developing countries needing help to develop their expertise and capacity to implement sanitary and phytosanitary standards, especially for agricultural products intended for export markets. The STDF secretariat is located in the WTO, Geneva. *See also* ***sanitary and phytosanitary measures***. [www.standardsfacility.org]

Standards code: *see* ***Tokyo Round agreements*** and ***Agreement on Technical Barriers to Trade***.

Standards of treatment: the quality of treatment afforded by parties to trade and investment agreements to goods, services, investors and investments from the other parties. Agreements usually provide for ***most-favoured-nation treatment*** or MFN (non-discrimination between foreign suppliers of goods and services, investors and their investments, as the case may be). Many agreements also provide for ***national treatment*** (non-discrimination between imported and domestic goods and services, or between foreign and domestic investors and their investments). Both of these standards are variable between countries. One country, for example, may have high agricultural tariffs. Another may have rather low ones. Yet each applies its own standard to all foreign suppliers and their products under the MFN principle. In the case of national treatment, one country may insist on strict product standards in some manufactures, but another may be more flexible. Neither breaches its legal obligations by insisting on its own standards as long as it does not discriminate against imported products. A standard of treatment different to MFN and national treatment is the ***minimum standard of treatment*** contained in ***NAFTA Chapter 11***. According to Article 1105 "each party shall accord to investments of investors of another party treatment in accordance with international law". The minimum

Standard International Trade Classification
国际贸易标准分类

见*国际贸易标准分类(SITC)*。

Standards
标准

保证产品或服务具有统一规格或属性的方法。大致分为技术标准(例如最小或最大尺寸、颜色、成分等)或性能标准(产品或服务必须至少具备的特定性能)。此外，标准可以是强制性的，也可以是自愿的。WTO《技术性贸易壁垒协定》将标准界定为“经公认机构批准的、规定非强制执行的、供通用或重复使用的产品或相关工序和生产方法的规则、指南或特性的文件。该文件还可包括或专门关于适用于产品、工序或生产方法的专门术语、符号、包装、标志或标签要求”。该协定仅适用于货物。另见*合格评定(conformity assessment)*、*国际电工委员会(International Electrotechnical Commission)*、*国际标准化组织(International Organization for Standardization)*、*ISO 9000质量管理体系(ISO 9000)*、*ISO 14000环境管理体系(ISO 14000)*、*技术性贸易壁垒(technical barriers to trade)*。

Standards and Trade Development Facility
标准和贸易发展基金

STDF。在香港WTO部长级会议举行后，由粮农组织(FAO)、世界银行、世界卫生组织和WTO共同建立的机制。支持需要帮助的发展中国家发展其专业技术和能力，以执行卫生和植物卫生标准，特别是针对供出口市场的农产品。STDF秘书处设在位于日内瓦的WTO。另见*卫生与植物卫生措施(sanitary and phytosanitary measures)*。

Standards code
标准守则

见*东京回合协定(Tokyo Round agreements)*、*技术性贸易壁垒协定(Agreement on Technical Barriers to Trade)*。

Standards of treatment
待遇标准

贸易和投资协定参加方对来自其他参加方的货物、服务、投资者和投资所给予待遇的质量。协定通常规定最惠国待遇(对外国货物和服务提供者、投资者及其投资视情提供非歧视待遇)。许多协定还规定了国民待遇(对进口和国产货物和服务，或对外国和国内投资者及其投资提供非歧视待遇)。这些标准因国家不同而不同。例如，一国可能有很高的农产品关税，另一国的关税可能很低。然而两国均按照最惠国待遇原则，将其自身标准适用于所有外国供应商及其产品。对于国民待遇，一国可能会要求对一些制成品实施严格的产品标准，而另一国可能更灵活。只要不歧视进口产品，两国都不会因要求实施本国标准而违反其法律义务。与最惠国待遇和国民待遇不同的待遇标准是《北美自由贸易协定》第11章所含最低待遇标准。根据第1105条，“每一缔约方应给予另一缔约方的投资者的投资与国际法相一致的待遇”。因此，最低待遇标准

standard of treatment is therefore sometimes called an absolute standard. ***Fair and equitable treatment*** is yet another undefined standard of treatment.

Stand-by Credit Facility: *see **Poverty Reduction and Growth Trust**.*

Standing of industry to apply for anti-dumping or countervailing duties investigations: describes the minimum industry participation which is needed for an application for an investigation of alleged ***dumping*** to be accepted by the relevant authorities. The formula given by the ***Anti-Dumping Agreement*** and the ***Agreement on Subsidies and Countervailing Measures*** is this. The agreements assume that domestic producers of the ***like product*** will either support an application, oppose it or not express a view either way. These producers together make up the total production of the like product produced by the domestic industry. The share of production by the producers not expressing a view is then set aside. This leaves those who support or oppose an application. An application is then considered successful and to have been made "by or on behalf of the industry" if producers representing at least 50 per cent of the production made by this group support the application. However, no investigation may be launched if this group in fact represents less than 25 per cent of the total production of the like product produced by domestic industry. The following example may help. Assume that the domestic industry producing the like product consists of 100 firms each accounting for 1 per cent of the total output of the like product. It now is evident that 20 per cent of these firms (20 per cent of the total output of the like product) have no view on whether alleged dumping should be investigated. That leaves 80 firms accounting for 80 per cent of total production. If 60 of these firms (i.e. three-quarters of them) support the call for an investigation, the application will be successful since they account for 60 per cent of total domestic production of the like product. In practice, calculating industry support for an investigation isn't anywhere near this simple.

Standstill: an undertaking not to impose new or more restrictive trade measures after a certain date, usually the date on which the undertaking was made. Often combined with ***rollback***. *See also **moratorium on customs duties on electronic transmissions*** and ***trade pledge***.

STAR: *see **Secure Trade in APEC Region**.*

Stare decisis*:** the principle that a tribunal should follow its own previous decisions and those of other tribunals of equal or greater authority. *See also **obiter dictum. [Brownlie 2019]

State aids: the term for ***subsidies*** used in the ***Treaty on the Functioning of the European Union***. According to Article 107 of the Treaty, member states of the ***European Union*** may not grant any aids to firms that would distort or threaten to distort competition. Exceptions deemed compatible with the provisions of the Treaty include non-discriminatory aids of a social character granted to individual consumers and aids intended to remedy damage caused by natural calamities or other extraordinary events. State aids which may be compatible with the Treaty include, among others, those intended to promote regional

有时也被称为一项绝对标准。公平和公正的待遇是另一项未定义的待遇标准。

Stand-by Credit Facility

备用信贷机制

见*减贫与增长信托基金(Poverty Reduction and Growth Trust)*。

Standing of industry to apply for anti-dumping or countervailing duties investigations

申请反倾销或反补贴调查的产业代表性

指相关机构受理被指控的倾销调查申请所需的最低行业参与程度。《反倾销协定》和《补贴与反补贴措施协定》所规定的公式为：协定认为同类产品的国内生产商要么支持一项申请，要么反对申请，要么不发表支持或反对申请的意见。这些生产商共同构成同类产品国内总产量。那些无意见的生产商的产量份额不予考虑，只考虑支持或反对申请的生产商。如果代表该集团生产量至少50%的生产商支持该申请，则申请成功，申请应被视为"由国内产业或代表国内产业"提出。但是，如果这一群体所占国内生产的同类产品总产量不足25%，则不得开展调查。下面的例子可能有助于理解这一概念。假设生产同类产品的国内产业由100家企业组成，每家企业产量占同类产品总产量的1%。现在这些企业中20%的企业(占同类产品总产量的20%)对是否应当对指控的倾销开展调查不发表意见，余下的80家公司占总产量的80%。如果这些公司中有60家(即四分之三)支持开展调查，则申请成功，因为它们代表了同类产品国内总产量的60%。但在实践中，计算产业对申请的支持并非如此简单。

Standstill

维持现状

关于在某一日期后不采取新的或更具限制性贸易措施的承诺，该日期通常为作出该承诺的日期。通常伴随着回退。另见*电子传输暂免关税(moratorium on customs duties on electronic transmissions)*、*贸易保证(trade pledge)*。

STAR

APEC地区安全贸易倡议

见*APEC地区安全贸易倡议(Secure Trade in APEC Region)*。

Stare decisis

遵循先例

关于法庭应遵循自身或其他拥有同等或更大权力的法庭以往裁决的原则。另见*判决附带意见(obiter dictum)*。

State aids

政府援助

在《欧洲联盟运行条约》中用于指补贴的词语。根据条约第107条，欧盟成员国不得向企业提供扭曲或威胁扭曲竞争的任何援助。视为符合条约规定的例外包括：给予消费者个人的具有社会性的非歧视性援助、补偿因自然灾害或其他特殊事件所造成损失的援助。视为符合条约规定的政府援助包括旨在促

economic development where the standard of living is abnormally low, important projects or to remedy serious economic disturbances and aid to promote culture and heritage conservation.

Statements on origin: used under the Registered Exporter (REX) System, a ***self-certification*** scheme of the European Union. A statement of origin is a specific declaration on the invoice that or another commercial document identifying the exported products. [ec.europa.eu]

State-owned enterprise: SOE. A business entity in which the government has a significant degree of ownership, possibly full ownership. Such enterprises are often large. The long-term trend in many countries has been to subject them to ***privatization***, but in some countries this trend has some way to go. *See also* ***public body***.

State secrets doctrine: also called state secrets privilege. It is the basis for a refusal by a state to disclose documents or information of vital interest to the security of the state.

State trading: there are two basic types of state trading. First, there is international trade conducted by state-owned, state-controlled or state-licensed private enterprises in market economies, sometimes with exclusive rights over certain products. These enterprises trade like normal commercial firms and respond to market signals. Second, state trading is a feature of ***non-market economies*** where price may not be the only or the dominant consideration in making import or export decisions. In this case, there is significant potential for market distortions and little ***transparency***. State trading should be distinguished from ***government procurement*** which covers purchases by governments for their own use. *See also* ***centrally-planned economies***, ***marketing boards*** and ***single-desk selling***.

State-trading dumping: *see* ***dumping***.

State-trading enterprises: commercial entities usually owned by the state which are authorized to conduct international trade. Often they have a ***monopoly*** or a near-monopoly on the import or export of a good. *See also* ***marketing boards*** and ***single-desk selling***.

Statism: theories and policies which stress the importance of the state in the promotion of national economic development. Statism is not synonymous with excessive ***regulation***, but it often leads in that direction.

Steel: *see* ***Davignon Plan***, ***Global Forum on Steel Excess Capacity***, ***international steel cartel***, ***Multilateral Specialty Steel Agreement*** and ***Multilateral Steel Agreement***.

Stockholm Convention on Persistent Organic Pollutants: *see* ***Convention on Persistent Organic Pollutants***.

Stolper-Samuelson theorem: a proposition put forward in 1941 by the economists Wolfgang Stolper and Paul Samuelson. It holds that under certain assumptions (importantly that land and labour are the only factors of production) a move from no trade to free trade results in increasing income going to the factor of production used intensively in the export industry experiencing

进生活水平异常低地区的经济发展、重要项目或补救严重经济动荡以及促进文化和遗产保护的援助。

Statements on origin
原产地声明
在注册出口商体系(REX)下使用的欧盟自我认证机制。原产地声明是发票上的一个具体声明，或识别出口产品的另一个商业单证。

State-owned enterprise
国有企业
SOE。政府拥有相当大所有权的商业实体，可能拥有完全所有权。此类企业通常是大型的。许多国家的长期趋势是将此类企业私有化，但在一些国家这种趋势还有一段路要走。另见*公共机构(public body)*。

State secrets doctrine
国家机密原则
又称国家机密特权，是一国拒绝披露对其国家安全至关重要的文件或信息的根据。

State trading
国营贸易
国营贸易有两种基本类型：第一种，在市场经济中，国有、国家控制或国家授权经营的私营企业进行国际贸易，有时对某些产品拥有专有权。这些企业像普通商业企业一样开展贸易，并对市场信号作出反应。第二种，国营贸易是非市场经济体的特征，价格可能不是作出进出口决定的惟一或决定因素。在此种情况下，市场扭曲的可能性很大且缺乏透明度。国营贸易应该与政府采购加以区分，后者涵盖政府为自用目的而进行的采购。另见*中央计划经济体(centrally-planned economies)*、*销售局(marketing boards)*、*专责销售(single-desk selling)*。

State-trading dumping
国营贸易倾销
见*倾销(dumping)*。

State-trading enterprises
国营贸易企业
国家拥有并授权开展国际贸易的商业实体。通常对一货物的出口或进口中实行垄断或近乎垄断。另见*销售局(marketing boards)*、*专责销售(single-desk selling)*。

Statism
国家主义
强调国家在促进国家经济发展中的重要性的理论和政策。国家主义不是过度管制的同义词，但它往往引向这一方向。

Steel
钢铁
见*达维央计划(Davignon Plan)*、*钢铁产能过剩全球论坛(Global Forum on Steel Excess Capacity)*、*国际钢铁卡特尔(international steel cartel)*、*多边特种钢协定(Multilateral Specialty Steel Agreement)*、*多边钢铁协定(Multilateral Steel Agreement)*。

Stockholm Convention on Persistent Organic Pollutants
关于持久性有机污染物的斯德哥尔摩公约
见*关于持久性有机污染物的公约(Convention on Persistent Organic Pollutants)*。

Stolper-Samuelson theorem
斯托尔珀-萨缪尔森定理
经济学家沃尔夫冈·斯托尔珀和保罗·萨缪尔森在1941年提出的观点。该定理认为，在一定假设条件下(重要的是土地和劳动力是惟一生产要素)，从无贸

rising prices. Conversely, such a move would result in decreasing returns for the factor used intensively in the industry subject to falling prices. *See also* ***comparative advantage***, ***Heckscher-Ohlin theorem*** and ***new trade theory***.

Strasbourg Agreement Concerning the International Patent Classification: concluded on 24 March 1971 and amended on 28 September 1979. It establishes the International Patent Classification (IPC). This is a common classification for patents for invention, inventors' certificates, utility models and utility certificates. The eight IPC categories for patents are: (a) human necessities, (b) performing operations; transporting, (c) chemistry; metallurgy, (d) textiles; paper, (e) fixed constructions, (f) mechanical engineering; lighting; heating; weapons; blasting, (g) physics, and (h) electricity. The Agreement is administered by ***WIPO***.

Strategic business alliances: SBAs. Cooperative arrangements between firms requiring them to work towards common goals. Typically, partners to such alliances do not invest in the other partner. If they do, they may confine themselves to holding very small stakes. The aim in all cases is to improve the competitive standing of all the partners. The formation of SBAs may be subject to national ***competition policy*** or ***antitrust laws***.

Strategic dumping: *see* ***dumping***.

Strategic exports: goods and services thought to have an actual or potential effect on the military balance in a given region. *See also* ***COCOM***, ***dual-purpose exports*** and ***Wassenaar Arrangement on Export Controls for Conventional Arms and Dual-Use Goods and Technologies***.

Strategic Products and Special Safeguard Mechanism: *see* ***Alliance for Strategic Products and Special Safeguard Mechanism***.

Strategic trade policy: *see* ***strategic trade theory.***

Strategic trade theory: often used interchangeably with strategic trade policy. It is the idea that governments can adopt, or threaten to adopt, domestic policies promoting the emergence and development of industries likely to become significant exporters. The theory appears to take its name from the recognition that actions by government can alter the strategic relationship between firms. The implementation of this theory is almost always based on ***subsidies*** or ***protection*** of one kind or another, though its proponents on the whole have not advocated such crude action. The theory shows satisfactorily that in closely defined circumstances such actions could bring net benefits to an economy. It is worth remembering, however, that the constraints and the rigour academic economists bring to their work soon disappears when an attempt is made by governments to translate a theory into a policy. *See also* ***comparative advantage***, ***competitive advantage***, ***national champions***, ***new trade theory*** and ***picking winners***. [Brander 1995, Dam 2001, Krugman 1986]

Stresa Convention: the *International Convention for the Use of Appellations of Origin and Denominations of Cheeses*, concluded on 1 June 1951 at Stresa, Italy. Founding members were Austria, Denmark, France, Italy, Netherlands and Switzerland. The Convention seeks to reserve the names of certain cheeses

易转变为自由贸易会使增加的收入流向经历价格上涨的出口产业中所集中使用的生产要素。相反，此种转变会导致受价格下跌影响的产业所集中使用的生产要素的收益减少。另见*比较优势(comparative advantage)*、*赫克舍尔-奥林定理(Heckscher-Ohlin theorem)*、*新贸易理论(new trade theory)*。

Strasbourg Agreement Concerning the International Patent Classification
国际专利分类斯特拉斯堡协定

于1971年3月24日缔结，1979年9月28日修正。协定创设了国际专利分类法(IPC)。这是一种涵盖发明专利、发明人证书、实用新型和实用证书的通用分类系统。IPC将专利分为8类：(a)生活必需品；(b)各种操作、运输；(c)化学和冶金；(d)纺织和造纸；(e)永久性构筑物；(f)机械工程、照明、加热、武器、爆破；(g)物理学；以及(h)电学。协定由世界知识产权组织(WIPO)管理。

Strategic business alliances
战略性商业联盟

SBAs。要求企业朝着共同目标努力的企业之间的合作安排。通常，此类联盟的合作伙伴不会对其他伙伴进行投资。如果进行投资，他们会自行控制只持有很少股份。任何情况下，目标都是提高所有伙伴的竞争地位。SBAs的成立可能要受国家竞争政策或反垄断法管辖。

Strategic dumping
战略性倾销

见*倾销(dumping)*。

Strategic exports
战略性出口

被认为对特定地区的军事平衡具有实际或潜在影响的货物和服务。另见*多边出口管制协调委员会(COCOM)*、*两用物品出口(dual-purpose exports)*、*关于常规武器和两用物品及技术出口管制的瓦森纳安排(Wassenaar Arrangement on Export Controls for Conventional Arms and Dual-Use Goods and Technologies)*。

Strategic Products and Special Safeguard Mechanism
战略产品与特殊保障机制联盟

见*战略产品与特殊保障机制联盟(Alliance for Strategic Products and Special Safeguard Mechanism)*。

Strategic trade policy
战略性贸易政策

见*战略性贸易理论(strategic trade theory)*。

Strategic trade theory
战略性贸易理论

经常与战略性贸易政策互换使用。该理论表达这样一种设想，即政府可以采取或威胁采取国内政策，以促进有可能成为重要出口来源的产业的出现和发展。这一理论的名称可能源于这样一种认知，即政府所采取的行动可以改变企业之间的战略关系。理论的实施几乎总是依靠这样或那样的补贴或保护，尽管理论的支持者总体上并不主张这种粗暴的行动。这一理论可以令人满意地显示，在严格界定的情况下，此类行动可以给经济带来净收益。但是要记住的是，当政府试图将一项理论转化为一项政策时，经济学家们在理论研究中设定的严苛约束条件很快即消失。另见*比较优势(comparative advantage)*、*竞争优势(competitive advantage)*、*国家龙头企业(national champions)*、*新贸易理论(new trade theory)*、*挑选赢家(picking winners)*。

Stresa Convention
斯特雷萨公约

《乳制品产地俗称使用和命名国际公约》，1951年6月1日在意大利斯特雷萨缔结。创始成员为奥地利、丹麦、法国、意大利、荷兰和瑞士。公约寻求保

for the use of member countries. It distinguishes between ***appellations of origin*** and denominations. The former refers to cheese made or manufactured in traditional regions and which have special qualities by virtue of long usage, etc. Such names are always reserved for the region giving rise to the name. *Roquefort* (France) is one of them. The characteristics of the latter are defined in terms of shape, weight, size, type and colour of the rind and curd by the party first using the name. Other parties may use these denominations provided that they describe the cheeses in accordance with the terms of the Convention. These cheeses include *Provolone* (Italy) and *Emmental* (Switzerland).

Structural adjustment: the continuous process experienced by all industries of needing to adjust to new economic and commercial conditions brought about by changes in consumer preferences, technological innovation, tariff reductions, subsidy phase-outs, long-term changes in the cost of components and raw materials, etc. Sometimes this results in the rapid disappearance of a complete sector, such as has occurred in slide-rule production when the electronic calculator appeared. Structural adjustment can be accompanied by government support for the retraining of workers and other measures. Whether governments are prepared to pay up often depends on the political clout of the industry. Since the mid-1980s, the term has also come to refer to a particular set of policy prescriptions requested of developing countries by international financial institutions such as the ***World Bank*** and the ***IMF***. The granting of assistance packages by these institutions is typically conditional on a tightening of fiscal policies and the achievement of macroeconomic stability through tough anti-inflationary policies. *See also* ***protectionism***.

Structural impediments: structural features of an economy seen as impeding the emergence of fully competitive markets. These can result from inappropriate or excessive ***regulation***, widespread use of ***subsidies***, the existence of private or government monopolies, rigid labour markets, inadequate disciplines on ***restrictive business practices*** and other similar factors.

Structural Impediments Initiative: SII. A 1989 United States initiative aimed at opening the Japanese market to American firms. It was based on the proposition that the removal of traditional barriers to trade was not enough, and that meaningful changes had to be brought about through changes to Japanese domestic policies and practices. Japanese market and distribution systems were a target, as was the relationship between government and business. Few now would claim that the SII had been a success, possibly because the target was not understood well enough. *See also* ***keiretsu relationships***, ***Market-Oriented Sector-Specific talks*** and ***United States–Japan Framework for a New Economic Partnership***.

Structuralism: *see* ***structural trade theory***.

Structural trade theory: a contentious theory emerging in the 1950s which held that structural forces in international trade impeded the development of countries dependent on the production and export of primary commodities and raw materials. Its proponents argued that there was a persistent bias against

留成员国所使用的某些奶酪的名称。公约对原产地名称和命名加以区分。原产地名称指在传统地区制造或生产，并具有保质期长等特性的奶酪。此类名称通常保留给该名称起源的地区。如“洛克福羊乳奶酪”(法国)就是其中之一。命名的特点是由首先使用的一方根据产品外皮和凝乳的形状、重量、大小、类型和颜色进行定义。其他各方也可以使用这些名称，只要他们依照公约条款描述这些奶酪，包括“波萝伏洛干酪”(意大利)和“埃曼塔尔干酪”(瑞士)。

Structural adjustment

结构性调整

所有产业所经历的需要调整适应因消费者偏好变化、技术革新、关税削减、补贴逐步取消、零部件和原材料成本长期变化所带来的新的经济和商业条件的持续过程。有时这会导致一个部门迅速全部消失，例如电子计算器出现后计算尺生产所出现的情况。结构性调整可以辅以政府对工人再培训和其他支持措施。政府肯不肯付钱往往取决于产业的政治影响力。自20世纪80年代中期以来，这一词语也用来指世界银行和国际货币基金组织(IMF)等国际金融机构要求发展中国家采取的一系列特定政策处方。这些机构提供一揽子援助的条件通常为紧缩财政政策和通过强硬的反通货膨胀政策实现宏观经济稳定。另见*保护主义(protectionism)*。

Structural impediments

结构性障碍

被视为阻碍完全竞争性市场出现的经济结构性特征。原因可以是不当或过度管制、广泛使用补贴、存在私人或政府垄断、劳动力市场僵化、对限制性商业惯例缺乏约束和其他类似因素。

Structural Impediments Initiative

日美结构协议会

SII。1989年美国发起的一项倡议，旨在要求日本市场向美国公司开放。所依据的主张是，仅仅消除传统的贸易壁垒是不够的，必须通过改变日本的国内政策和做法以实现有意义的改变。日本市场和销售系统是目标，政府与企业关系也是目标。现在很少有人称 SII 取得了成功，可能是因为对目标没有很好的理解。另见*经连关系(keiretsu relationships)*、*市场导向型的多领域谈判方案(Market-Oriented Sector-Specific talks)*、*美日新经济伙伴关系框架(United States–Japan Framework for a New Economic Partnership)*。

Structuralism

结构主义

见*结构贸易理论(structural trade theory)*。

Structural trade theory

结构贸易理论

20世纪50年代出现的一种有争议的理论，认为国际贸易中的结构性力量阻碍了依赖初级商品和原材料生产和出口的国家的发展。该理论的支持者认为，由于这些生产者的贸易条件长期恶化，导致对他们存在持续偏见。提出的解

such producers because of a long-term deterioration in their ***terms of trade***. The proposed solutions included the promotion of preferential ***South–South trade*** (trade among developing countries). It was thought that in this more limited environment developing countries would be relatively more competitive and able to get ready to supply industrialized countries once their industries had developed sufficiently. Preferential access to developed countries for products of export interest to developing countries through a ***GSP*** was also advocated. Few of the resulting preferential trade areas became effective enough to make a practical difference, but the structuralists had succeeded in drawing attention to the important issue of trade and development. *See also* ***GSTP*** and ***UNCTAD***.

Stumbling blocks: a term coined by Jagdish Bhagwati. It is used to describe ***free-trade areas*** that impede the development of multilateral ***trade liberalization***. *See also* building-block approach. [Bhagwati 1991]

Sub-heading: a six-digit entry in the ***Harmonized Commodity Description and Coding System***. Examples are 030110 (ornamental fish), 450310 (corks and stoppers) and 900130 (contact lenses). *See also* ***chapter*** and ***heading***.

Sub-national obligations: *see* ***second-level obligations***.

Sub-regional economic zones: *see* ***growth triangles***.

Subrogation: a term found in many ***investment promotion and protection agreements***. It means that in cases where investors have received payments from their national investment insurance agency against the covered risks, the home country of these investors or its insurance agency takes over the rights or claims of the investors against the home state.

Sub-Saharan Africa: a geographic area encompassing forty-nine countries: Angola, Benin, Botswana, Burkina Faso, Burundi, Cameroon, Cape Verde, Central African Republic, Chad, Comoros, Congo, Côte d'Ivoire, Democratic Republic of Congo, Djibouti, Equatorial Guinea, Eritrea, Eswatini, Ethiopia, Gabon, The Gambia, Ghana, Guinea, Guinea-Bissau, Kenya, Lesotho, Liberia, Madagascar, Malawi, Mali, Mauritania, Mauritius, Mozambique, Namibia, Niger, Nigeria, Rwanda, Sao Tome and Principe, Senegal, Seychelles, Sierra Leone, Somalia, South Africa, South Sudan, Sudan, Tanzania, Togo, Uganda, Zambia and Zimbabwe. *See also* ***African Growth and Opportunity Act***.

Subsidiarity: a concept which postulates that the ***European Community*** should only take action in areas where it does not have exclusive competence if the envisaged objective cannot be sufficiently achieved by the member states acting alone. The subsidiarity principle may have implications for the formulation of European Union policy on aspects of ***trade in services***, especially in areas where no fully developed common policy exists as yet. *See also* ***competence***, ***European Union legislation*** and ***shared competence***.

Subsidies: financial or in-kind assistance by governments to producers or exporters of commodities, manufactures and services. There are two general types of subsidies: export and domestic. An export subsidy is a benefit contingent on exports conferred on a firm by the government. A domestic subsidy is a benefit not directly linked to exports. Subsidies are paid for many reasons, including

决方案包括促进优惠的南南贸易(发展中国家之间的贸易)。人们认为，在这种更为有限的环境中，发展中国家将相对更具竞争力，一旦其产业充分发展，这些国家就能够准备向工业化国家提供产品。还有人倡导通过普惠制(GSP)使发展中国家具有出口利益的产品获得对发达国家的优惠准入。由此产生的优惠贸易区中很少实现足以产生实际差异的效果，但结构主义者成功地引起人们对贸易和发展这一重要问题的关注。另见*全球贸易优惠制(GSTP)*、*联合国贸易与发展会议(UNCTAD)*。

Stumbling blocks
绊脚石

由贾格迪什·巴格瓦蒂创造的词语，用于描述阻碍多边贸易自由化发展的自由贸易区。另见*积木法(building-block approach)*。

Sub-heading
子目

商品名称及编码协调制度中的6位编码条目。例如030110(观赏鱼)、450310(软木塞和塞子)和900130(隐形眼镜)。另见*章(chapter)*、*税目(heading)*。

Sub-national obligations
次中央级义务

见*二级义务(second-level obligations)*。

Sub-regional economic zones
次区域经济区

见*增长三角(growth triangles)*。

Subrogation
代位求偿权

许多投资促进与保护协定中出现的词语，指如果投资者从国家投资保险机构收到针对承保风险的付款，这些投资者的母国或其保险机构将接管投资者对母国的权利或索赔。

Sub-Saharan Africa
撒哈拉以南非洲

由49个国家组成的地理区域：安哥拉、贝宁、博茨瓦纳、布基纳法索、布隆迪、喀麦隆、佛得角、中非共和国、乍得、科摩洛、刚果(布)、科特迪瓦、刚果(金)、吉布提、赤道几内亚、厄立特里亚、斯威士兰、埃塞俄比亚、加蓬、冈比亚、加纳、几内亚、几内亚比绍、肯尼亚、莱索托、利比里亚、马达加斯加、马拉维、马里、毛里塔尼亚、毛里求斯、莫桑比克、纳米比亚、尼日尔、尼日利亚、卢旺达、圣多美和普林西比、塞内加尔、塞舌尔、塞拉利昂、索马里、南非、南苏丹、苏丹、坦桑尼亚、多哥、乌干达、赞比亚和津巴布韦。另见*非洲增长与机遇法(African Growth and Opportunity Act)*。

Subsidiarity
辅助原则

这一概念的假设是，欧洲共同体只有在成员国单独行动不能充分实现预想目标时，方可在其无专属权限的领域采取行动。辅助原则可能影响欧盟制定服务贸易方面的政策，特别是在尚未完全制定共同政策的领域。另见*权限(competence)*、*欧洲联盟立法(European Union legislation)*、*共享权限(shared competence)*。

Subsidies
补贴

政府对商品、制成品和服务的生产商或出口商给予的财政或实物援助。有两大类补贴：出口补贴和国内补贴。出口补贴是政府视出口情况而授予企业的利益。国内补贴是不与出口直接关联的利益。给予补贴的原因很多，包括需

the need to prop up an inefficient production structure, the wish to raise the income of one sector, the wish to promote regional development, the aim to develop export markets, etc. Broadly, the WTO ***Agreement on Subsidies and Countervailing Measures*** defines subsidies as financial contributions by a government or public body, direct transfer of funds or potential transfer of funds (e.g. grants, loans, equity infusions), government revenue foregone or not collected, government provision of goods and services other than general infrastructure, payments to a funding mechanism or a private body to perform these functions, income or price support if they also confer a benefit. The 2006 *World Trade Report* covers questions related to subsidies in some detail. ***Agricultural subsidies*** are covered by the ***Agreement on Agriculture***. *See also* ***bounty***, ***countervailing measures***, ***specificity*** and ***state aids***.

Subsidies Code: *see* ***Agreement on Subsidies and Countervailing Measures*** and ***Tokyo Round agreements***.

Substantial cause: under some of the trade agreements negotiated by the United States, such as the ***free-trade agreement*** with Jordan, safeguards action may be taken when increased quantities of imports are a substantial cause of ***serious injury***, or ***threat of serious injury***, to domestic industries. A substantial cause is defined as “important and not less than any other cause”.

Substantial interest: *see* ***interested third parties***.

Substantially-all-discrimination criterion: the ***General Agreement on Trade in Services*** (GATS) permits the establishment of ***free-trade areas*** in services under certain conditions. One of these is that the other partners to the arrangement must be given ***national treatment*** in substantially all the sectors covered by the agreement. The term “substantial” is not defined further in the GATS.

Substantially-all-trade criterion: Article XXIV of the ***GATT*** sets out the conditions under which ***customs unions*** and ***free-trade areas*** may be regarded as consistent with the Agreement. It requires that substantially all trade between the parties to a preferential agreement must be covered as part of qualifying under the rules. The GATT does not say how this is to be understood or calculated. Two schools of thought have emerged on what the criterion means. The first adopts a quantitative approach, and it defines “substantially all trade” in terms of the value of total trade. A broad assumption among WTO members has been that this should be about 80–90 per cent of total trade. Under this approach, agriculture or other ***sensitive sectors*** might not be covered by an agreement, but the remainder of trade might be enough to satisfy the criterion. The second approach is qualitative. It says that all sectors must be covered, and that leaving out agriculture, for example, would automatically violate the criterion. Agreement on which school should prevail is not in sight, even though WTO members have agreed during the ***Uruguay Round*** that the contribution of a ***free-trade agreement*** to world trade would be diminished if any major sector of trade was excluded. A trend has developed more recently to make a start at least in the sectors that one or more parties find difficult to liberalize. Article V of the ***General Agreement***

要支持低效率的生产结构、希望提高一部门的收入、希望促进区域发展和拓展出口市场等。广义而言，WTO《补贴与反补贴措施协定》将补贴定义为，政府或公共机构的财政资助、资金的直接转移或潜在的资金转移(例如赠款、贷款、投股)、放弃或未予征收的政府税收、政府提供的一般基础设施外的货物和服务、向筹资机构或私营机构付款以履行这些职能以及收入或价格支持(如授予利益)。《世界贸易报告2006》较为详细地讨论了与补贴有关的问题。农业补贴由《农业协定》所涵盖。另见*津贴(bounty)*、*反补贴措施(countervailing measures)*、*专向性(specificity)*、*政府援助(state aids)*。

Subsidies Code
补贴守则

见*补贴与反补贴措施协定(Agreement on Subsidies and Countervailing Measures)*、*东京回合协定(Tokyo Round agreements)*。

Substantial cause
实质性原因

根据美国谈判达成的一些贸易协定，例如与约旦的自由贸易协定，如果进口数量增加是对国内产业造成严重损害或严重损害威胁的实质性原因，则可以采取保障措施。实质性原因被定义为“重要且不亚于其他任何原因的原因”。

Substantial interest
实质性利益

见*利害关系第三方(interested third parties)*。

Substantially-all-discrimination criterion
实质上所有歧视的标准

《服务贸易总协定》(GATS)允许在特定条件下建立服务自由贸易区。条件之一是相关安排的其他参加方必须在协定所涵盖的实质上所有部门中获得国民待遇。GATS未对“实质上”进一步定义。

Substantially-all-trade criterion
实质上所有贸易的标准

GATT第24条规定了关税同盟和自由贸易区可被视为符合GATT的条件。要求优惠协议参加方之间实质上所有贸易都必须包含在规则适用范围内。GATT没有说明如何理解或计算。对这一标准的含义出现两种看法：第一种采用定量法。以总贸易值定义“实质上所有贸易”。在WTO成员中的广泛假设是，应为全部贸易的80—90%。根据这一方法，农业或其他敏感部门可能不在协定范围内，但余下的贸易量可能足以满足这一标准。第二种为定性法。要求所有部门都必须涵盖在内，如果不包括农业即会自动违反这一标准。就使用哪种方法还没有达成一致，尽管WTO成员在乌拉圭回合期间议定，如果将任何主要贸易部门排除在外，自由贸易协定对世界贸易的贡献即会减少。最近出现的一种趋势是，至少应自一个或多个参加方难以自由化的部门开始。《服务贸易总协定》第5条涵盖服务贸易自由化协定，也有一个实质上所有贸易的的标准。

on Trade in Services, which covers free-trade agreements in services, also has a substantially-all-trade criterion. It is divided into the need for substantial sectoral coverage of services and the absence or elimination of substantially all discrimination in terms of ***national treatment***. "Substantial sectoral coverage" is to be understood in terms of number of sectors, volume of trade affected and ***modes of services delivery***. Additionally, no mode of supply should be excluded *a priori*.

Substantial New Programme of Action for the 1980s for the Least-Developed Countries: *see* ***SNPA***. *See also* ***Programme of Action for the Least-Developed Countries for the Decade 2011–2020***.

Substantial sectoral coverage: a criterion preferential ***economic integration agreements*** in ***trade in services*** must meet to qualify under Article V of the ***General Agreement on Trade in Services*** for an exemption from the most-favoured-nation requirement. The word "substantial" is not defined in quantitative terms, but a footnote to the Article states that it is to be understood in terms of number of sectors, volume of trade affected and ***modes of services delivery***. No mode of supply should be excluded *a priori*.

Substantial supplying interest: under the rules for the negotiation of tariff reductions set out in Article XXVIII of the GATT, negotiations are normally conducted with the party having a ***principal supplying interest***. The same Article says that the interests of a party with a substantial interest in trade in that product have to be considered. An explanatory note says that the expression "substantial interest" is not capable of a precise definition, but that it is intended to be construed as a significant market share or the expectation of such a share. *See also* ***renegotiation of tariffs***.

Substantial transformation: a term used by customs authorities in the administration of ***rules of origin*** to determine what the origin of a good is. In the case of goods originating entirely in the exporting country, so-called ***wholly obtained goods***, this is easy. Many goods entering the export trade, however, are made up of imported materials or contain imported components. They may also have undergone ***transshipment*** through a third country. One of the criteria customs officers can use to determine the origin of a good is to ascertain the place where the good acquired its current form through having been substantially reworked from another form. A simple example of a substantial transformation is the case of a stepladder made in China from Canadian aluminium lengths. The ladder would be considered a Chinese product because it acquired its form in China, and that form is substantially different to aluminium lengths. On the other hand, simply repackaging a good or painting it would not be considered a substantial transformation since the good had all of its essential characteristics before it was painted or repackaged. Another way to ascertain whether substantial transformation has occurred is to measure the value added to it in the exporting country. This is the ***regional value content***, expressed as a percentage of the total value of the good. *See also* ***change in tariff heading***, ***last substantial transformation*** and ***preferential rules of origin***.

该条分为涵盖众多服务部门的需要和去除或取消国民待遇方面的实质上所有歧视。"涵盖众多部门"应从部门数量、受影响的贸易量和服务提供模式加以理解。此外，不应预见先排除任何提供模式。

Substantial New Programme of Action for the 1980s for the Least-Developed Countries

20世纪80年代支援最不发达国家新的实质性行动纲领

见*20世纪80年代支援最不发达国家新的实质性行动纲领(SNPA)*。另见*2011—2020年十年期支援最不发达国家行动纲领(Programme of Action for the Least-Developed Countries for the Decade 2011-2020)*。

Substantial sectoral coverage

涵盖众多部门

服务贸易的优惠经济一体化协定必须满足的标准，以符合《服务贸易总协定》第5条规定的免除最惠国要求的标准。"众多"一词按数量进行定义，但该条的脚注指出，应以部门数量、受影响的贸易量和服务提供模式加以理解。不应预先排除任何提供模式。

Substantial supplying interest

实质供应利益

根据GATT第28条中所规定的关税减让谈判规则，谈判通常与拥有主要供应利益的成员进行。该条规定，应考虑对该产品贸易具有实质利益的成员的利益。解释性注释指出，"实质利益"并不能精确定义，但可被解释为占有或可合理预期占有重要份额。另见*关税重新谈判(renegotiation of tariffs)*。

Substantial transformation

实质性改变

海关在管理原产地规则时用于确定货物原产地的词语。对于完全来自出口国的货物，即所谓的完全获得的货物，确定原产地很容易。但是，进行出口贸易的许多货物由进口材料构成或包含进口部件。也可能通过第三国转运。海关官员用于确定货物原产地的标准之一，是确定货物通过从另一种形态进行实质性重新加工而获得其当前形态的地点。实质性改变的一个简单例子是使用加拿大铝材在中国制造的梯子。梯子会被认为是中国产品，因为是在中国获得其形态，而这种形态实质上不同于铝材。另一方面，对货物进行简单重新包装或上色不被认为属实质性改变，因为货物在上色或重新包装前已经具有了其所有基本特点。另一种确定是否属实质性改变的方法是测量其在出口国中所增加的价值，即区域价值成分，以货物总价值的百分比表示。另见*税目改变(change in tariff heading)*、*最后实质性改变(last substantial transformation)*、*优惠原产地规则(preferential rules of origin)*。

Sufficiently worked or processed: a criterion used in the administration especially of ***preferential rules of origin*** under ***free-trade agreements***. It has a meaning similar to ***substantial transformation***. Suppose that economy B imports steel rods from economy A. It then transforms these steel rods into fencing wire. This action makes the imported good into a different good. Hence, when economy B exports the fencing wire to economy C, the customs authority there will consider it a product of economy B. If, however, economy B had done no more than cutting the steel rods into shorter lengths and perhaps painting them, economy C would probably still consider them as products of economy A.

Sufficient transformation: a transformation that meets the requirements of a set of ***preferential rules of origin***.

Sui generis* right:** a type of ***intellectual property protection used often as a form of ***copyright*** protection. It treats the matter to be protected as unique and requiring specific protection on that basis. *Sui generis* protection is used especially for computer software and related subject matter. *See also* ***layout-designs of integrated circuits*** and ***plant breeders' rights***.

Sullivan Principles: a set of six principles proposed by the Reverend Leon Sullivan, a director of General Motors, in 1977 for the conduct of the company's operations in South Africa under the apartheid system. The principles quickly gained widespread acceptance. They are concerned especially with equal and fair employment policies for all workers and the improvement of their conditions inside and outside the workplace. *See also* ***trade and environment*** and ***trade and labour standards***.

Sunrise industries: emerging industries, often with a high ***intellectual property*** content which, through the use of innovative methods and technological advances, succeed in doing things more efficiently or in creating entirely new classes of products. Information technology in particular has spawned sunrise industries. ***Trade policy*** interest in sunrise industries partly derives from issues related to the protection of ***intellectual property rights*** and from the fact that governments sometimes wish to promote them by ***picking winners*** or through the adoption of actions based on ***strategic trade theory***, both of which may have the effect of distorting trade. *See also* ***knowledge-based industry***, ***national champions***, ***new economy*** and ***sunset industries***.

Sunset clause: a provision in an agreement under which a measure taken by a government expires automatically once a certain time has elapsed, or unless some specified action has been taken. The WTO agreements dealing with ***anti-dumping measures*** and countervailing duties contain sunset clauses under which relevant measures expire after five years unless a review finds that they should continue. The ***United States–Mexico–Canada Agreement*** will terminate sixteen years after its entry into force unless the parties agree to renew it. *See also* ***Manufacturing Clause*** for a dispute arising because of a sunset clause in United States legislation.

Sunset industries: industries considered moribund because of technological advances in other sectors of the economy or changes in consumer preferences.

Sufficiently worked or processed

充分制造或加工

特别用于管理自由贸易协定项下优惠原产地规则的标准。含义类似于实质性改变。假设经济体B从经济体A进口钢筋。随后将钢筋变成铁丝网。这一动作使进口货物变成另一种货物。因此，当经济体B向经济体C出口铁丝网时，经济体C的海关会将其视为经济体B的产品。但是，如果经济体B只将钢筋切短和上色，经济体C可能仍然将其视为来自经济体A的产品。

Sufficient transformation

充分改变

满足一套优惠原产地规则要求的改变。

***Sui generis* right**

特殊权利

知识产权保护的一种类型，常用作版权保护的一种形式。将受保护事项视为独一无二的，并在此基础上要求进行特殊保护。特殊权利保护主要用于计算机软件和相关主题事项。另见*集成电路布图设计(layout-designs of integrated circuits)*、*植物育种者权利(plant breeders' rights)*。

Sullivan Principles

苏利文原则

1977年由通用汽车董事莱昂·苏利文牧师提出的一套六项原则，用于指导该公司在南非种族隔离制度下的业务运营。这些原则很快得到广泛接受，特别关注所有工人的平等和公平就业政策，以及改善工作场所内外的条件。另见*贸易与环境(trade and environment)*、*贸易与劳工标准(trade and labour standards)*。

Sunrise industries

朝阳产业

新兴产业，通常具有高知识产权含量，通过使用创新方法和技术进步，成功提高工作效率或创造全新产品类别。信息技术特别催生了朝阳产业。对朝阳产业的贸易政策利益部分源自与保护知识产权有关的问题，及政府有时希望通过挑选赢家的方法或采取基于战略性贸易理论的行动以促进这些产业的发展，这两种做法都可能产生扭曲贸易的效果。另见*知识型产业(knowledge-based industry)*、*国家龙头企业(national champions)*、*新经济(new economy)*、*夕阳产业(sunset industries)*。

Sunset clause

日落条款

协议中的一项条款，据此政府采取的一项措施在某一时间过后即自动失效，除非已经采取一些特定行动。WTO处理反倾销措施和反补贴税的协定中包含日落条款，据此相关措施在5年后失效，除非审议认为应继续实施。《美国—墨西哥—加拿大协定》将在生效16年后终止，除非各方同意展期。另见因美国立法中的日落条款而引发争端的*制造条款案(Manufacturing Clause)*。

Sunset industries

夕阳产业

因其他经济部门的技术进步或消费者偏好改变而被认为是行将消失的产业。

Such industries are sometimes exemplified by unprofitable old-style steel mills whose closure would lead to widespread local unemployment. Some new steel mills could of course be classified as ***sunrise industries***. Attaining the status of a sunset industry may be a matter of months, as happened among the slide-rule producers when the electronic pocket calculator made its appearance. In other cases, it may be a drawn-out process as industries produce insufficient returns to be able to modernize and are unable to attract new investment, but are earning enough to carry on through cost-saving measures and gradual staff reductions. This is often the time when governments are asked to alleviate an industry's discomfiture through ***protection*** in the form of ***local content requirements***, ***import restrictions***, measures designed to promote ***structural adjustment***, ***subsidies***, ***voluntary restraint arrangements***, etc.

Sunshine rule: the practice of conducting open hearings to examine proposed or existing governmental policies.

Super 301: the name commonly given to Section 1302 of the 1988 ***Omnibus Trade and Competitiveness Act***. It requires ***USTR*** (the United States Trade Representative) to prepare a report annually on United States trade expansion priorities which identifies "***priority foreign country*** practices, the elimination of which is likely to have the most significant potential to increase United States exports, either directly or through the establishment of a beneficial precedent". This original Super 301 also required the identification of priority foreign countries, but this was changed to priority foreign country practices alone in the *Uruguay Round Agreements Act*. In practice, the effect is the same. At the same time, USTR was authorized to report on foreign country practices that may in the future warrant identification as priority foreign country practices. Super 301 differs from ***Section 301*** in that it concentrates on systemic unfair trade practices. Super 301 was originally enacted for the years 1989 and 1990. It requires periodic renewal by the President. The provision is dormant at present. *See also* ***Special 301***.

Superfund*:** a case launched in the GATT in 1987 by Canada, Mexico and the European Community against the United States. It dealt with a tax to be levied under the United States *Superfund Amendments and Reauthorization Act* of 1986. The tax had not become effective at the time the dispute was launched. It imposed, *inter alia*, a new tax on certain imported substances produced or manufactured from taxable feedstock chemicals. The tax to be levied on imported substances equalled in principle the tax that would have been payable on chemical components if these chemicals had been sold in the United States for the same use. A penalty rate could be levied if importers supplied insufficient information regarding the chemical components of the imported substance. The complainants argued that the tax on the imported products was higher than the tax on the like domestic product, and that it therefore contravened the ***national-treatment principle. The ***panel*** considered that the imported and domestic products were ***like products*** within the meaning of the GATT, that there was a difference in the prospective treatment of domestic and

人们有时以无利可图的老式钢铁厂作为此类行业的例子，这些钢铁厂的关闭会导致当地大范围失业。一些新型钢铁厂当然可以归为朝阳产业。沦为夕阳产业可能仅需几个月，就像袖珍电子计算器出现后计算尺生产商所经历的那样。在其他情况下，可能是一个漫长的过程，因为产业的利润不足以支持现代化改造，也无法吸引新的投资，但通过成本节约措施和逐步裁员，收入可足以维持生产。通常是政府被要求通过以当地含量要求、进口限制、旨在促进结构性调整的措施、补贴、自愿限制安排等为形式的保护，缓解这些产业的困境。

Sunshine rule

阳光规则

举行公开听证会以审查拟议的或现有的政府政策的做法。

Super 301

超级301条款

对美国1988年《贸易与竞争综合法》第1302节的常用名称。该节要求美国贸易代表办公室(USTR)每年编写一份关于美国贸易扩展优先事项的报告，确定"重点国家的做法，消除这些做法即有极大的可能直接或通过建立有益先例增加美国的出口"。最初的超级301条款还要求确定重点国家，但在《乌拉圭回合协定法》中改为仅确定重点国家的做法。在实践中，效果是一样的。与此同时，USTR被授权报告未来可能需要确定为重点国家做法的外国做法。超级301条款与301条款的区别在于，超级301条款专注系统性不公平贸易做法，这一条款最初在1989年—1990年有效，需要总统定期更新。该条款目前处于休眠状态。另见*特别301条款(Special 301)*。

Superfund

超级基金案

1987年加拿大、墨西哥和欧洲共同体在GATT中对美国发起的争端案件。该案针对美国根据1986年《美国超级基金修正及再授权法》征收的国内税。在争端发起时该国内税尚未生效。除其他影响外，该国内税成为对使用应税化工原料生产或制造的某些进口物质征收的新税。对进口物质拟征税原则上与这些化学原料如果在美国国内销售用于相同用途所应付税相同。如果进口商对进口物质的化学原料未能提供充足信息，则可按惩罚税率征税。起诉方称，进口产品所征税高于国内同类产品所征税，因此违反了国民待遇原则。专家组认为，进口产品和本国产品属GATT范围内的同类产品，本国产品和进口产品

imported products, and that the tax to be levied by the United States was inconsistent with the obligations the United States had under the GATT. It found at the same time that, as the Act gave the authorities discretion to impose the tax, the existence of penalty rates as such did not constitute a violation of the GATT. [GATT BISD 34S]

Supervised exports: goods which may be exported freely when they are in normal supply, but which may be limited when they are becoming more scarce at home and their price rises.

Support prices: a device to give producers of primary commodities in particular an assured minimum return. This can be done through, for example, a ***floor price***, the ***loan rate***, ***subsidies*** and ***variable levies***, sometimes aided by ***import restrictions***. Support prices may be related to the market price in that they respond to price signals to some extent. Determining the market price itself becomes problematical under such conditions. Support prices may be unrelated to market prices. Their purpose then simply is to give producers a guaranteed income. The domestic consumer and efficient producers in other countries share the bill between them.

Surrogate country: *see* ***analogue country***.

Surtax: *see* ***import surcharge*** and ***primage***.

Surveillance: regular monitoring by members of the WTO of national trade policies of other members to ensure that they are in conformity with the rules of the ***multilateral trading system*** and that they reflect the ***commitments*** made by individual member states. One mechanism that can be used for this purpose is the ***Trade Policy Review Mechanism***, but many of the agreements administered by the WTO contain provisions requiring notification of changes to policies or action taken under the terms of the specific agreement. *See also* ***notification***, ***reverse notification*** and ***transparency***.

Suspension of concessions or other obligations: if a WTO member fails to act on a recommendation or ruling by a ***panel*** or the ***Appellate Body***, the member bringing the complaint may ask the ***Dispute Settlement Body*** to suspend the application of ***concessions*** or other obligations to the member failing to take action. This may be done twenty days after the expiry of a ***reasonable period of time*** (usually no more than fifteen months after the adoption of the origin panel or Appellate Body report). The following main principles apply to the selection of concessions or other obligations to be suspended. First, the suspensions should be in the sector where a violation of the rules occurred. Second, if this is not effective or practicable, other sectors covered by the same agreement may be chosen (i.e. if the matter concerns GATT rules, the suspensions should apply to matters covered by the GATT). Third, if this is not a satisfactory way to proceed, suspensions may made under another agreement covered by the ***Dispute Settlement Understanding*** (i.e. it would be possible to suspend ***commitments*** under the ***General Agreement on Trade in Services*** or the ***Agreement on Trade-Related Aspects of Intellectual Property Rights*** even though the original matter may have arisen under the GATT). Members suspending concessions are asked to take into account the importance of the trade to the other party and the

的预期待遇存在不同，美国拟征国内税不符合美国在GATT项下的义务。专家组同时认为，该法案赋予主管机关征税的酌量权，惩罚税率本身的存在并不构成对GATT的违反。

Supervised exports

出口监管

货物在正常供应时可以自由出口，而在国内变得稀缺且价格上涨时，其出口可能受到限制。

Support prices

支持价格

为特别是初级商品的生产者提供有保证的最低回报保证的工具。可通过最低价格、基准贷款价格、补贴和差价税等实现，有时也辅以进口限制。支持价格可能与市场价格有关，因为这些价格在一定程度上会对价格信号作出反应。在此种情况下，确定市场价格本身就成了问题。支持价格也可能与市场价格无关。目的仅为给予生产者有保障的收入。国内消费者和其他国家的高效生产者共同分担由此产生的费用。

Surrogate country

替代国

见*类比国(analogue country)*。

Surtax

附加税

见*进口附加税(import surcharge)*、*关税附加税(primage)*。

Surveillance

监督

WTO成员对其他成员贸易政策的定期监测，以保证这些政策符合多边贸易体制的规则，并反映各成员所作承诺。为此目的可使用的机制是贸易政策审议机制，但WTO所管理的多个协定包含要求对政策变化情况或根据具体协定条款所采取行动进行通报的条款。另见*通报(notification)*、*反向通报(reverse notification)*、*透明度(transparency)*。

Suspension of concessions or other obligations

中止减让或其他义务

如果一WTO成员未能按照专家组或上诉机构的建议或裁决采取行动，则提出起诉的成员可请求争端解决机构对未能采取行动的成员中止减让或其他义务。可在合理期限(通常不超过原专家组或上诉机构报告通过后15个月)届满20天后进行。下列主要原则适用于拟中止的减让或其他义务：第一，中止应在发生违反情况的部门；第二，如不可行或无效，可以选择同一协定下的其他部门(即有关事项涉及GATT规则，中止即应适用于GATT所涵盖的事项)；第三，如不能令人满意，中止可针对《争端解决谅解》所涵盖的另一项协定进行(即可以中止《服务贸易总协定》或《与贸易有关的知识产权协定》项下的承诺。即使有关事项在GATT项下产生)。中止减让或其他义务的成员应考虑贸易对另一方的重要性，及中止减让或其他义务所引发的更广泛的经济后果。另见*第*

broader economic consequences of suspending concessions or obligations. *See also* ***Article 21.5 panel***, ***Article 22.6 arbitration*** and ***retaliation***.

Sustainability Impact Assessment: SIA. A trade-specific mechanism of the ***European Union*** to support major trade negotiations. It provides an analysis of the potential economic, social, human rights and environmental impacts of trade negotiations.

Sustainability Toolkit for Trade Negotiators: prepared by ***UN Environment Programme*** to assist trade negotiators of regional trade and investment agreements. It enables to become more fully aware of the impact of trade provisions and environmental protection provisions when negotiating such agreements. [iisd.org]

Sustainable development: defined by the ***World Commission on Environment and Development*** as ensuring that development meets the needs of the present without compromising the ability of future generations to meet their own needs. *See also* ***World Summit on Sustainable Development***.

Sustainable Development Goals: SDGs. Part of the ***United Nations 2030 Agenda for Sustainable Development***. Adopted by the ***United Nations*** in 2015. They build on the ***Millennium Development Goals***. The seventeen goals are: (1) end poverty in all its forms everywhere, (2) end hunger, achieve food security and improved nutrition and promote sustainable agriculture, (3) ensure healthy lives and promote well-being for all at all ages, (4) ensure inclusive and equitable quality education and promote lifelong learning opportunities for all, (5) achieve gender equality and empower all women and girls, (6) ensure availability and sustainable management of water and sanitation for all, (7) ensure access to affordable, reliable, sustainable and modern energy for all, (8) promote sustained, inclusive and sustainable economic growth, full and productive employment and decent work for all, (9) build resilient infrastructure, promote inclusive and sustainable industrialization and foster innovation, (10) reduce inequality within and among countries, (11) make cities and human settlements inclusive, safe, resilient and sustainable, (12) ensure sustainable consumption and production patterns, (13) take urgent action to combat climate change and its impacts, (14) conserve and sustainably use the oceans, seas and marine resources for sustainable development, (15) protect, restore and promote sustainable use of terrestrial ecosystems, sustainably manage forests, combat desertification, and halt and reverse land degradation and halt diversity loss, (16) promote peaceful and inclusive societies for sustainable development, provide access to justice for all and build effective, accountable and inclusive institutions at all levels, and (17) strengthen the means of implementation and revitalize the global partnership for sustainable development. The United Nations Statistics Division prepares an annual *Sustainable Development Goals Report*. *See also* ***Investment Policy Framework for Sustainable Development***.

Sustainable trade policy: a trade policy which seeks to balance the aim of trade opening with the aim of promoting ***sustainable development*** while at the same time guaranteeing social development.

21.5条专家组(Article 21.5 panel)、*第22.6条仲裁(Article 22.6 arbitration)*、*报复(retaliation)*。

Sustainability Impact Assessment

可持续发展影响评估

SIA。欧盟支持重大贸易谈判的特定贸易机制。对贸易谈判的经济、社会、人权和环境潜在影响提供分析。

Sustainability Toolkit for Trade Negotiators

贸易谈判人员可持续发展工具包

由联合国环境规划署编制，以协助区域贸易和投资协定的贸易谈判人员。可在谈判此类协定时，更充分意识到贸易条款和环境保护条款的影响。

Sustainable development

可持续发展

世界环境与发展委员会对可持续发展的定义为：保证发展既满足当代人的需求，又不危及后代人满足自身需求的发展。另见*可持续发展问题世界首脑会议(World Summit on Sustainable Development)*。

Sustainable Development Goals

可持续发展目标

SDG。《联合国2030年可持续发展议程》的一部分，于2015年由联合国通过，建立在千年发展目标基础之上。17项目标为：(1)在全世界消除一切形式的贫困；(2)消除饥饿，实现粮食安全，改善营养状况和促进可持续农业；(3)保证健康的生活方式、促进各年龄段人群的福祉；(4)确保包容和公平的优质教育，让全民终身享有学习机会；(5)实现性别平等，增强所有妇女和女童的权能；(6)为所有人提供水和环境卫生并对其进行可持续管理；(7)确保人人获得负担得起、可靠和可持续的现代能源；(8)促进持久、包容和可持续的经济增长，促进充分的生产性就业和人人获得体面工作；(9)建造具备抵御灾害能力的基础设施，促进具有包容性的可持续工业化，推动创新；(10)减少国家内部和国家之间的不平等；(11)建设包容、安全、有抵御灾害能力的可持续的城市和人类住区；(12)采用可持续的消费和生产模式；(13)采取紧急行动应对气候变化及其影响；(14)保护和可持续利用海洋和海洋资源以促进可持续发展；(15)保护、恢复和促进可持续利用陆地生态系统，可持续管理森林，防治荒漠化，制止和扭转土地退化，遏制生物多样性的丧失；(16)创建和平、包容的社会以促进可持续发展，让所有人都能诉诸司法，在各级建立有效、负责和包容的机构；以及(17)加强执行手段，重振可持续发展全球伙伴关系。联合国统计司编制年度《可持续发展目标报告》。另见*可持续发展投资政策框架(Investment Policy Framework for Sustainable Development)*。

Sustainable trade policy

可持续贸易政策

旨在寻求平衡贸易开放目标与促进可持续发展目标同时保证社会发展的贸易政策。

Sweated labour: describes workers suffering abuse and exploitation through, for example, inadequate working conditions and the payment of wages that are as low as possible. *See also* ***social dumping*** and ***trade and labour standards***.

Sweatshop-labour argument: *see* ***pauper-labour argument***, ***trade and human rights***, ***trade and labour standards*** and ***wage-differential argument***.

Swing mechanism: this refers to an interpretation by some WTO members of the right to use export subsidies for agricultural products. The ***Agreement on Agriculture*** sets annual limits on the level of export subsidies members may apply. Some now say that if a country does not use up its ceiling level in any year, it should be able to use the unused amount in another year, provided that the total permissible amount is not exceeded. This proposition does not enjoy widespread support. The swing mechanism was an accepted method under the ***Agreement on Textiles and Clothing***. The Agreement permitted swing (transfer of part of an export quota for one product to quota for another product), subject to certain established guidelines and practices.

Swiss-Army-knife approach to tariff negotiations: creating a family of modified ***Swiss formulas*** in which the coefficient is adjusted to increase the reductions in lower tariffs. The standard Swiss formula produces large reductions when tariffs are high and tiny reductions when they are low. [Francois and Martin 2003]

Swiss formula: a compromise formula for achieving ***linear tariff cuts*** proposed by Switzerland during the ***Tokyo Round***. It was intended to reduce higher tariffs by a greater proportion than lower tariffs. The formula reads:

$$Z = AX/(A + X)$$

where X represents the initial tariff rate, and A is a coefficient to be agreed on. Z is the resulting lower tariff rate. The ***European Economic Community***, the ***Nordic countries*** and Australia used the coefficient 16, the United States, Japan and Switzerland 14. New Zealand used the item-by-item technique. *See also* ***truncated Swiss formula***.

Symbolic deals: a term used by Bernard Hoekman in *Trade Laws and Institutions: Good Practices and the World Trade Organization* to describe agreed negotiating outcomes that are apparently or patently not substantive. Such deals can occur in situations where the negotiators realize that agreement on the substantive issues is not possible for the time being, but to leave the table without any agreement at all might be worse presentationally. To do otherwise might also make it more difficult to restart the negotiations. Such deals sometimes are called political outcomes. [Hoekman 1995]

SYSMIN: System for the Promotion of Mineral Production and Exports, or sometimes System for Safeguarding and Developing Mineral Production. A commodity stabilization mechanism established by the ***European Economic Community*** in 1980 under the umbrella of Lomé-II as an alternative to bringing minerals under ***STABEX***. It aimed at protecting ***ACP states*** against reductions in mine output and consequent export earnings shortfalls. SYSMIN was not

Sweated labour
血汗劳工

描述因恶劣工作环境和极低工资报酬等原因而遭受虐待和剥削的工人。另见*社会倾销(social dumping)*、*贸易与劳工标准(trade and labour standards)*。

Sweatshop-labour argument
血汗工厂劳工论

见*贫民劳工论(pauper-labour argument)*、*贸易与人权(trade and human rights)*、*贸易与劳工标准(trade and labour standards)*、*工资差别理论(wage-differential argument)*。

Swing mechanism
调用机制

指一些WTO成员对农产品出口补贴使用权的解释。《农业协定》对成员可以实施的出口补贴水平设定了年度限制。一些成员认为，如果一成员在任何一年内未达到上限水平，则可在任何一年使用未使用的金额，只要不超过所允许的总量。这一主张并未得到广泛支持。调用机制是《纺织品与服装协定》项下的一种被接受的方法。协定允许调用(将一产品的部分出口配额转至另一种产品的配额上)，但需要遵守某些既定准则和惯例。

Swiss-Army-knife approach to tariff negotiations
瑞士军刀法关税谈判

创建一系列改进的瑞士公式，通过调整系数以增加低关税的削减幅度。标准瑞士公式对高关税的削减幅度大，对低关税的削减幅度小。

Swiss formula
瑞士公式

东京回合期间为实现线性关税削减由瑞士提出的折中公式。旨在使对高关税的削减幅度大于对低关税的削减幅度。公式如下：

$$Z = AX/(A + X)$$

其中X代表最初关税税率，A为有待议定的系数，Z为降低后的关税税率。欧洲经济共同体、北欧国家和澳大利亚的系数为16，美国、日本和瑞士的系数为14。新西兰采用逐税目法。另见*缩减瑞士公式(truncated Swiss formula)*。

Symbolic deals
象征性协议

伯纳德·霍克曼在《贸易法律与制度：良好做法与世界贸易组织》一书中用于描述明显或显然无实质意义的谈判达成结果的词语。此类协议发生的情况是，谈判者意识到就实质问题达成一致暂时不可能，而空手离开谈判桌又看上去更糟糕。如果不这样作会使重启谈判更加困难。此类协议有时称为“政治成果”。

SYSMIN
矿产生产及出口促进制度

有时称为保障及发展矿产生产制度。欧洲经济共同体在1980年根据《第二个洛美协定》建立的商品稳定机制，作为将矿产品纳入出口收入稳定机制(STABEX)的替代方案。旨在保护非加太地区国家不受矿产减产和由此造成的

renewed in the ACP-EC Partnership Agreement, now the ***ACP-EU Partnership Agreement***, which replaced the ***Lomé Convention***.

Systemic issues: matters pertaining to the functioning or the broad rules of the ***multilateral trading system***. Issues usually included under this heading include, for example, ***dispute settlement*** provisions, ***safeguards*** mechanisms, ***transparency*** rules, etc.

出口收入不足的影响。SYSMIN未在《非加太地区国家与欧共体伙伴关系协定》中得到展期，该协定取代《洛美协定》，现为《非加太地区国家与欧盟伙伴关系协定》。

Systemic issues

系统性问题

与多边贸易体制运作或广泛规则有关的事项。通常包括在这一标题下的问题有：争端解决条款、保障措施机制、透明度规则等。

T

TAFTA: Trans-Atlantic Free Trade Agreement. A proposal at one time for a ***free-trade area*** between the United States and the ***European Union***. It is not on a formal negotiating agenda. *See also* New Transatlantic Agenda and ***Transatlantic Trade and Investment Partnership***.

Tailor-made tariffs: *see* ***made-to-measure tariffs***.

Takeover principle: another name for the ***absorption principle*** or "roll-up" principle. This principle permits the use of ***non-originating materials*** that have acquired origin through processing to retain that status when they are used in a further transformation. *See also* ***preferential rules of origin*** and ***rules of origin***.

Taking of property: *see* ***expropriation***.

Targeted dumping: dumping concentrated in sales to certain regions, customers, or time periods. *See also* ***anti-dumping measures***. [WTO WT/DS219/AB/R]

Targeting: *see* ***picking winners*** and ***strategic trade theory***. In United States trade law, targeting by others may give rise to an action under ***Section 301***.

TARIC: Tariff Intégré Communautaire. *See* ***Integrated Tariff of the European Union***.

Tariff: a customs duty on merchandise imports. Levied either as an ***ad valorem tariff*** (percentage of value) or as a ***specific tariff*** (e.g. $7 per 100 kg regardless of its value). Less often, a ***compound tariff*** made up of both of these elements applies. Tariffs give a price advantage to similar locally-produced goods and raise revenues for the government. Tariffs are mostly levied on imports, but there are cases of ***export tariffs***. For economists, a tariff is the equivalent of the imposition concurrently of a consumption tax and a production subsidy. Although governments often understand this clearly, they may be reluctant to reduce tariffs since this may have important fiscal implications in cases where they rely on ***customs duties*** as a predictable source of revenue. It is worth noting, however, the view expressed in the ***Brigden Report*** that the "popularity of a tariff among Treasuries and Governments is due to the fact that it is a means of 'painless extraction', the indirectness of the method acting as an anaesthetic". *See also* ***ad valorem tariff***, ***binding***, ***Lerner's symmetry theorem***, ***seasonal tariff*** and ***specific tariff***.

Tariff anomaly: used by some to refer to what is commonly known as ***tariff escalation***, i.e. the tariff rate on raw materials or semi-finished products is lower than on the finished product made of these materials in order to encourage domestic manufacturing. For others, a tariff anomaly is precisely the opposite,

T

TAFTA
跨大西洋自由贸易协定

曾经提议的美国与欧盟之间的自由贸易区。未列入正式谈判议程。另见*新跨大西洋议程(New Transatlantic Agenda)*、*跨大西洋贸易与投资伙伴关系协定(Transatlantic Trade and Investment Partnership)*。

Tailor-made tariffs
定制关税

见*定制关税(made-to-measure tariffs)*。

Takeover principle
接管原则

吸收原则或"总成"原则的别称。该原则允许使用通过加工已经获得原产地资格的非原产材料在用于进一步改变过程中保留这一地位。另见*优惠原产地规则(preferential rules of origin)*、*原产地规则(rules of origin)*。

Taking of property
没收财产

见*征收(expropriation)*。

Targeted dumping
目标倾销

集中对某些地区、客户或时间段开展销售而进行的倾销。另见*反倾销措施(anti-dumping measures)*。

Targeting
目标策略

见*挑选赢家(picking winners)*、*战略性贸易理论(strategic trade theory)*。在美国贸易法中，其他国家采取的目标策略可能引发根据301条款采取的行动。

TARIC
欧盟关税数据库

见*欧盟关税数据库(Integrated Tariff of the European Union)*。

Tariff
关税

对制成品进口征收的关税。按从价关税(价值的百分比)或按从量关税(如每100公斤7美元，无论价值如何)征收。少数情况下，按由从价关税和从量关税组合而成的混合关税征收。关税为本地生产的类似货物提供了价格优势，并为政府增加收入。关税主要对进口产品征收，但也有出口关税。对于经济学家而言，关税相当于同时征收消费税和实行生产补贴。尽管各国政府通常明白这一点，但在政府依赖关税作为可预测税收来源的情况下，可能不愿意削减关税，因为这样作可能产生重要的财政影响。但是，值得注意的是，《布里格登报告》所表达的一种观点为，"关税受到财政部门和政府的欢迎，是因为这是一种'无痛提取'手段，这种方法的间接性起到了麻醉剂作用"。另见*从价关税(ad valorem tariff)*、*约束(binding)*、*勒纳对称性原理(Lerner's symmetry theorem)*、*季节性关税(seasonal tariff)*、*从量关税(specific tariff)*。

Tariff anomaly
关税异常

一些人用于指通常所说的关税升级，即为鼓励国内制造，原材料或半制成品

i.e. the tariff rate on raw materials and semi-finished products is higher than the rate levied on the finished product.

Tariff binding: a commitment not to increase a rate of duty beyond an agreed level. Once a rate of duty is bound, it may not be raised without compensating the affected parties.

Tariff classification: a method for listing systematically nearly every good that is traded internationally. Its main purpose is to assist customs authorities in assessing the correct rate of duty, but it can also be used for the presentation of statistics and other purposes. The classification used by WTO members is the ***Harmonized Commodity Description and Coding System***.

Tariff code: a number assigned to a good or group of goods in a ***tariff classification***.

Tariff concession: the same as a ***tariff binding***. This is a contractual undertaking, usually as the result of negotiations, not to exceed the tariff level on a good as entered in that country's ***tariff schedule***.

Tariff Conference: the formal name for the first four rounds of ***multilateral trade negotiations*** under the GATT. These were the Geneva 1947, Annecy, Torquay and Geneva 1955–56 tariff conferences.

Tariff equivalent: a calculation based on an agreed formula of what the impact of a ***non-tariff measure*** would be if it were converted into a ***tariff***. Such calculations are complex, but they add considerably to the ***transparency*** of trade regimes. *See also* ***tariffication***.

Tariff escalation: higher import duties on semi-processed products than on raw materials, and higher still on finished products. This practice protects domestic processing industries and discourages the development of processing activity in the countries where the raw materials originate. *See also* ***effective rate of assistance***.

Tariff evasion: the action of avoiding the payment of ***customs duties*** altogether or of seeking to pay less than should be the case. Main ways of achieving this are seeking to have the goods classified in a category with lower or no tariffs, or having an invoice made out that understates the value of the goods. Sometimes goods are also imported free of duty into ***free-trade zones*** and then re-exported illegally into the domestic market. Preventing tariff evasion is one of the reasons for adopting ***preshipment inspection***. *See also* ***circumvention***, ***customs valuation*** and ***smuggling***.

Tariff-Free World: a proposal for the elimination of all tariffs on consumer and industrial goods by WTO members by 2015. It was made by the United States in November 2002 in the negotiations under the ***Doha Development Agenda***. Members did not react favourably.

Tariffication: procedures relating to the agricultural market-access provision in the ***Agreement on Agriculture*** under which all non-tariff measures are converted into tariffs. *See also* ***minimum access tariff quotas*** and ***water in the tariff***.

的关税低于由这些材料制作的制成品的关税。对于其他人，关税异常恰恰相反，即原材料或半制成品的关税高于制成品的关税。

Tariff binding

关税约束

不将关税税率提高至超出一议定水平的承诺。一旦税率受到约束，即在未补偿受影响各方的情况下不得提高。

Tariff classification

关税分类

系统列出国际贸易中几乎所有货物的方法。主要目的是协助海关核定正确税率，但也可用于显现统计数字和其他目的。WTO成员使用的分类方法是商品名称及编码协调制度。

Tariff code

关税代码

关税分类中分配给一货物或一组货物的编码。

Tariff concession

关税减让

与关税约束相同。一种契约承诺，通常为谈判结果，承诺不超过一货物在该国关税减让表中的关税水平。

Tariff Conference

关税会议

GATT下进行的前4轮多边贸易谈判的正式名称。即1947年日内瓦、安纳西、托奎和1955年至1956年日内瓦关税会议。

Tariff equivalent

关税等值

根据议定公式计算一非关税措施转换为关税后的影响。此类计算很复杂，但可以大大提高贸易制度的透明度。另见*关税化(tariffication)*。

Tariff escalation

关税升级

半制成品的进口关税高于原材料的进口关税，制成品的进口关税更高。这一做法可以保护国内加工业，阻碍原材料的原产国中加工活动的发展。另见*有效援助率(effective rate of assistance)*。

Tariff evasion

逃税

全部逃避关税或设法少缴关税的行为。实现这一目标的主要途径是设法将货物归入关税较低或无关税的类别，或开具发票低报货物价值。有时，货物也可以先免税进入自由贸易园区，随后再非法复出口至国内市场。防止逃税是采用装运前检验的原因之一。另见*规避(circumvention)*、*海关估价(customs valuation)*、*走私(smuggling)*。

Tariff-Free World

零关税世界

关于WTO成员在2015年前取消所有消费品和工业品关税的倡议。美国在2002年11月在多哈发展议程谈判中提出。成员未积极回应。

Tariffication

关税化

与《农业协定》中关于农产品市场准入条款有关的程序，根据这一程序，所有非关税措施均转化为关税。另见*关税配额最低准入(minimum access tariff quotas)*、*关税水分(water in the tariff)*。

Tariff-jumping investment: investment in a production facility in another country in order to overcome high tariff barriers or other border measures. Views differ whether trade and investment in such cases are complementary, or whether tariff-jumping replaces trade. A view held by many is that trade and investment are now integrated in nearly all cases, and that the distinction can in practical terms easily be overdrawn. *See also* ***tariff escalation***.

Tariff line: a product as defined in lists of tariff rates. Often a six-digit entry in the ***Harmonized Commodity Description and Coding System*** is used, but these descriptions can be subdivided to the level of detail required.

Tariff negotiations: a key function of the WTO. From the entry into force of the GATT on 1 January 1948 until the ***Dillon Round*** of 1960–61, tariffs were negotiated item by item or product by product under the ***requests and offers*** system. The principal supplier of a product to another GATT member had the right to request tariff reductions. From the ***Kennedy Round*** onwards, ***linear tariff cuts*** became the dominant method. Whole sections of the tariff were thereby reduced uniformly according to an agreed formula. In the ***Tokyo Round***, the ***Swiss formula*** for linear tariff cuts was used as a working hypothesis under which higher tariffs were reduced by a greater proportion than low ones. Tariff negotiations in the ***Uruguay Round*** were partly of the product-by-product type and partly ***zero-for-zero tariff reductions*** under which tariffs are reduced to zero for whole classes of products. *See also* ***banded formula***, ***blended formula***, ***harmonized tariff reductions***, ***Information Technology Agreement***, ***principal supplier right***, ***renegotiation of tariffs***, ***sectoral trade negotiations*** and ***Swiss formula***.

Tariff-only regime: a trade regime where ***tariffs*** are the only border measures. Import licences, quotas, etc., are not used. Standards, sanitary and phytosanitary measures and so on would of course still apply.

Tariff peaks: relatively high tariffs, usually on so-called ***sensitive products***, amidst generally low tariff levels. For industrialized countries, tariffs of 15 per cent and above would generally be recognized as tariff peaks, but lower tariffs might also be recognized as tariff peaks in some cases.

Tariff preferences: the fundamental assumption under the agreements administered by the WTO is that countries give each other ***most-favoured-nation treatment*** in their administration of their ***tariff*** regimes. It is, however, possible under certain conditions to accord lower tariff rates or zero tariffs to selected trading partners. The principal means are preferential rates by developed countries for developing countries under ***GSP*** schemes, and zero-tariff rates between members of ***customs unions*** or ***free-trade areas***. Developing countries may also accord each other preferential rates, for example, under ***Part IV of the GATT*** and the ***Enabling Clause***. One occurrence of this is the ***GSTP***. *See also* ***imperial preferences arrangement***.

Tariff quota: in common usage this term is a synonym for a ***tariff rate quota***, but in its specialized meaning it is a tariff that increases, discreetly, at a certain level or levels of quantity imported. [Deardorff and Stern 1997]

Tariff-jumping investment

跳越关税投资

为免受高关税壁垒或其他边境措施影响而对另一国的生产设施进行投资。对于贸易和投资在此种情况下是否互补的问题，或逃避关税是否取代了贸易，人们看法不同。许多人持有的观点是，现在贸易和投资几乎在所有情况下都是互相结合的，这种区别在实际中很容易被夸大。另见*关税升级(tariff escalation)*。

Tariff line

税目

关税税率表中定义的一产品。通常使用商品名称及编码协调制度中的6位编码条目，但这些描述可以细分为所需要的详细程度。

Tariff negotiations

关税谈判

WTO的重要职能。自GATT在1948年1月1日生效至1960年至1961年狄龙回合，关税根据要价和出价制度进行逐项或逐产品谈判。一GATT缔约方一产品的主要供应方有权提出关税削减要价。自肯尼迪回合起，线性关税削减成为主要方法。因此关税整体按照议定公式进行统一削减。在东京回合中，瑞士公式作为工作假设用于线性关税削减，据此高关税削减比例大于低关税削减比例。乌拉圭回合中的关税谈判部分采用逐项产品方法，部分采用零对零关税削减，据此将整类产品的关税降为零。另见*分层公式(banded formula)*、*混合公式(blended formula)*、*协调关税削减(harmonized tariff reductions)*、*信息技术协定(Information Technology Agreement)*、*主要供应方权利(principal supplier right)*、*关税重新谈判(renegotiation of tariffs)*、*部门贸易谈判(sectoral trade negotiations)*、*瑞士公式(Swiss formula)*。

Tariff-only regime

单一关税制度

将关税作为惟一边境措施的贸易制度，不使用进口许可证、配额等措施，但标准和卫生与植物卫生措施等仍然适用。

Tariff peaks

关税高峰

在总体上低关税水平中相对较高的关税，通常对所谓的敏感产品适用。对于工业化国家，15%及以上的关税通常被视为关税高峰，但在一些情况下较低的关税也可被视为关税高峰。

Tariff preferences

关税优惠

WTO所管理的各项协定项下的一个基本假设为，各成员在管理其关税制度时相互给予最惠国待遇。但在某些条件下，可以给予部分贸易伙伴较低关税税率或零关税。主要手段为发达国家根据普惠制(GSP)方案给予发展中国家优惠税率，及关税同盟或自由贸易区成员之间的零关税税率。发展中国家还可以相互给予优惠税率，例如根据GATT第四部分和授权条款。其中一个例子是全球贸易优惠制(GSTP)。另见*帝国特惠安排(imperial preferences arrangement)*。

Tariff quota

关税配额

在通常用法中，该词与关税配额同义。但其专门含义指，在进口数量的某一水平或多个水平上谨慎提高的关税。

Tariff quota expansion: increases in quantities that may be imported within a ***tariff quota***.

Tariff rate quota: TRQ. The application of a reduced ***tariff*** rate for a specified quantity of imported goods. Imports above this specified quantity face a higher tariff rate. Some claim that tariff quotas liberalize trade since, in contrast to ***import quotas***, there is no ceiling on imports under this system. This assumption can be quite erroneous. The difference between the in-quota tariff and the out-of-quota tariff is often so large as to preclude any trade at the higher rate. *See also* ***current access tariff quotas***, ***minimum access tariff quotas*** and ***Understanding on tariff rate quota administration provisions of agricultural products***.

Tariff redundancy: that part of a ***tariff*** which does not have any effect on trade because it is above the point where the tariff would have the desired impact. An example would be where the government decides that a tariff of 10 per cent on a given good would suit its purposes, but for some reason it then sets the tariff at 15 per cent. The difference of 5 per cent would be the redundant tariff. [Corden 1971]

Tariff schedule: the document setting out the tariff rates a country applies to imports and, sometimes, to exports. *See also* ***applied tariff rates***, ***bound tariff rates***, ***multi-column tariff***, ***schedule of concessions*** and ***single-column tariff***.

Tariff stabilization: a result of the practice in the ***GATT*** and the WTO of accepting a legally binding obligation not to raise a bound tariff except in accordance with the rules. This has made the tariffs of most member countries stable and predictable.

Tariff wall: popularly used for a tariff maintained by an importing country at a sufficiently high level to make importing difficult or even preventing it.

Tariff wedge: under conditions of ***tariff escalation***, the difference between the tariff of the more processed product and the tariff on the less processed products that are transformed into the more processed product.

Task Force on International Trade Statistics: *see* ***Inter-Agency Task Force on International Trade Statistics***.

Taxes occultes: literally, hidden taxes. Cumulative indirect taxes a firm incurs in making a product, such as taxes in embodied in capital equipment used in the production process. Taxes on advertising, energy, machinery and transport are the main examples. It does not include taxes on components incorporated in the product. [GATT BISD 18]

TBT: technical barriers to trade. Regulations, standards, testing and certification procedures which may obstruct trade. The WTO ***Agreement on Technical Barriers to Trade*** aims to ensure that these do not create unnecessary obstacles to trade.

TBT Agreement: the WTO ***Agreement on Technical Barriers to Trade***.

TBT Information Management System: *see* ***Agreement on Technical Barriers to Trade***.

TCDC: *see* ***technical cooperation among developing countries***.

Tariff quota expansion
关税配额扩大

扩大可在一关税配额内进口的数量。

Tariff rate quota
关税配额

TRQ。对规定数量的进口货物适用削减后的关税税率。超过规定数量的进口产品征收较高税率。一些人称关税配额可以开放贸易，因为与进口配额相比，这一体系下对进口没有上限。这种假设可能是非常错误的。配额内税率和配额外税率之间的差距非常之大，足以阻碍任何较高税率的贸易。另见*关税配额现行准入(current access tariff quotas)*、*关税配额最低准入(minimum access tariff quotas)*、*关于农产品关税配额管理规定的谅解(Understanding on tariff rate quota administration provisions of agricultural products)*。

Tariff redundancy
关税冗余

关税中对贸易没有任何影响的部分，因为此部分高于关税能够发挥预期影响的值。例如，政府决定对一指定货物征收10%的关税即可达到目的，但出于某种原因，政府随后将关税定为15%。5%的差额就是冗余关税。

Tariff schedule
关税税则/关税减让表

规定一国对进口产品、有时对出口产品适用的关税税率的文件(通常译为关税税则，指一国在GATT/WTO中的关税承诺时译为关税减让表—译注)。另见*实施税率(applied tariff rates)*、*约束税率(bound tariff rates)*、*多栏关税(multi-column tariff)*、*减让表(schedule of concessions)*、*单栏关税(single-column tariff)*。

Tariff stabilization
关税稳定

GATT和WTO中接受不提高约束关税的法定义务所产生的实践结果，除非按规则提高。这一做法使大多数国家的关税稳定和可预见。

Tariff wall
关税墙

常指一进口国维持造成进口困难或甚至阻碍进口的足够高的关税水平。

Tariff wedge
关税分岔

在关税升级的情况下，加工程度较高产品的关税与由加工程度较低产品转变为加工程度较高产品的关税之间的差额。

Task Force on International Trade Statistics
国际贸易统计特别工作组

见*国际贸易统计机构间特别工作组(Inter-Agency Task Force on International Trade Statistics)*。

Taxes occultes
隐性税

字面意思为隐藏税，即一企业在生产一产品过程中发生的间接税，例如用于生产过程的资本设备所含税，对广告、能源、机械和交通所征税。不包括对产品所含部件所征税。

TBT
技术性贸易壁垒

可能阻碍贸易的法规、标准、测试和认证程序。WTO《技术性贸易壁垒协定》旨在保证这些壁垒不对贸易造成不必要的障碍。

TBT Agreement
技术性贸易壁垒协定

即WTO《技术性贸易壁垒协定》。

TBT Information Management System
技术性贸易壁垒信息管理系统

见*技术性贸易壁垒协定(Agreement on Technical Barriers to Trade)*。

TCDC
发展中国家间技术合作

见*发展中国家间技术合作(technical cooperation among developing countries)*。

Technical barriers to trade: refers to the impact ***standards*** and ***conformity assessment*** systems may have on trade flows. Many of these measures in fact have little impact because of ***mutual recognition arrangements*** as well as ***harmonization of standards and qualifications***. Some standards are seen as essential, for example, for reasons of health and safety. The WTO ***Agreement on Technical Barriers to Trade*** contains provisions for the harmonization, reduction and elimination of such barriers. The 2005 ***World Trade Report*** has a detailed analysis of standards, including ***sanitary and phytosanitary measures***, in the multilateral trading system. *See also* ***Code of Good Practice for the Preparation, Adoption and Application of Standards***, ***ePing SPS and TBT notification alert system***, ***International Electrotechnical Commission*** and ***International Organization for Standardization***.

Technical Committee on Rules of Origin: established through the WTO ***Agreement on Rules of Origin***, but under the auspices of the ***World Customs Organization***, to conduct technical work for the harmonization of ***non-preferential rules of origin***. *See also* ***rules of origin***.

Technical cooperation among developing countries: *see* ***Buenos Aires Plan of Action for Promoting and Implementing Technical Co-operation among Developing Countries***, ***ECDC***, ***Second High-Level United Nations Conference on South–South Cooperation*** and ***South–South Cooperation***.

Technical dumping: occurs when goods are imported under conditions that satisfy the ***dumping*** criterion (i.e. they are sold for export at a price that is below the price at which they are sold in the exporting market), but the reason for that pricing is meeting the price of the domestic competition in the import market.

Technical regulation: this is defined in Annex 1 of the WTO ***Agreement on Technical Barriers to Trade*** as a document which lays down product characteristics or their related ***processes and production methods***, including the applicable administrative provisions, with which compliance is mandatory. Such a document may also include or deal exclusively with terminology, symbols, packaging, marking or labelling requirements as they apply to a product, process or production method.

Technical test method: a method used in the ***rules of origin*** of some ***free-trade agreements*** to describe under what conditions goods may receive ***tariff preferences***. Such methods usually prescribe that the good must have gone through a defined production process, such as a chemical reaction, or that the materials used must satisfy certain conditions in respect of their origin.

Techno-nationalism: this has two main meanings. First, it is the idea that technological advances are useful only if they are achieved through domestic efforts even if they already exist elsewhere. These advances are normally achieved at much greater cost than if the technology was imported commercially. The results are often inferior to the best available elsewhere. Reasons for this type of technonationalism include a shortage of foreign exchange, the need to nurture national self-esteem, defence considerations and the "not-made-here" syndrome. Second, it also refers to policies aimed at keeping technological

Technical barriers to trade
技术性贸易壁垒

指标准和合格评定制度可能对贸易流动产生的影响。由于相互承认安排及标准和资格的协调，这些措施中许多事实上影响甚微。一些标准被视为是必不可少的，例如出于健康和安全原因。WTO《技术性贸易壁垒协定》包含协调、减少和消除此类壁垒的条款。《世界贸易报告2005》详细分析了多边贸易体制中的标准，包括卫生与植物卫生措施。另见*关于制定、采用和实施标准的良好行为规范(Code of Good Practice for the Preparation, Adoption and Application of Standards)*、*TBT/SPS ePing通报提醒系统(ePing SPS and TBT notification alert system)*、*国际电工委员会(International Electrotechnical Commission)*、*国际标准化组织(International Organization for Standardization)*。

Technical Committee on Rules of Origin
原产地规则技术委员会

通过WTO《原产地规则协定》设立，但由世界海关组织管理，为协调非优惠原产地规则开展技术工作。另见*原产地规则(rules of origin)*。

Technical cooperation among developing countries
发展中国家间技术合作

见*促进和实施发展中国家间技术合作布宜诺斯艾利斯行动计划(Buenos Aires Plan of Action for Promoting and Implementing Technical Co-operation among Developing Countries)*、*发展中国家间经济合作(ECDC)*、*第二届联合国南南合作高级别会议(Second High-Level United Nations Conference on South–South Cooperation)*、*南南合作(South–South Cooperation)*。

Technical dumping
技术倾销

发生在进口货物满足倾销标准的条件下(即产品出口价格低于在出口市场中的销售价格)，但定价理由是为达到进口国市场中的国内竞争价格。

Technical regulation
技术法规

WTO《技术性贸易壁垒协定》附件1中的定义为，规定强制执行的产品特性或其相关工序和生产方法，包括适用的管理规定在内的文件。该文件还可包括或专门关于适用于产品、工序或生产方法的专门术语、符号、包装、标志或标签要求。

Technical test method
技术检验方法

一些自由贸易协定的原产地规则中用于描述在什么条件下货物可以获得关税优惠的方法。此类方法通常规定，货物必须经过规定的生产过程，例如化学反应，或所使用的材料必须满足有关其原产地的某些条件。

Techno-nationalism
技术民族主义

有两个主要含义：第一是这样一种想法，即技术进步只有在通过国内努力实现的情况下才是有用的，即使它们已经存在于其他地方。实现这些进步的成本通常大大高于商业化引进的技术。结果也往往不如其他地方可获得的那样好。造成这种技术民族主义的原因包括外汇短缺、需要培养民族自尊、国防方面的考虑以及“非本地制造”综合征。第二是指那些旨在将技术进步留在原产国的政策，以期借此拥有竞争优势。另见*经济闭关自守(autarky)*、*比较优势*

advances within the originating country in the hope that this will lead to a ***competitive advantage***. *See also* ***autarky***, ***comparative advantage***, ***national champions***, ***self-reliance*** and ***self-sufficiency***.

Telecommunications: defined in the ***Annex on Telecommunications*** to the ***General Agreement on Trade in Services*** as "the transmission and reception of signals by any electromagnetic means". *See also* ***accounting rate***, ***Agreement on Basic Telecommunications Services***, ***Fourth Protocol to the General Agreement on Trade in Services***, ***reference paper on telecommunications services*** and ***Section 1377 Review***.

Telecommunications termination services: services provided by one telecommunications network to another to allow a caller in one network to talk to a caller in another network. This is done through interconnection. Calls between two networks consist of three stages: (a) transporting the call to the terminating or destination network, (b) providing an entry point or gateway to the terminating network, and (c) forwarding the call to its final destination. The latter two make up the termination service. The price charged by the second network for this service is called the ***accounting rate***.

Temporary admission of goods: conditional permission to import goods free or partially free of import duties and taxes into a customs territory. The goods must brought into the customs territory for a specific purpose, such as displays at trade fairs or demonstrations at the premises of potential customers. The goods must be destined for re-export within a specific period, and they must not undergo any changes except normal depreciation and wear and tear because of use made of them. *See also* ***Customs Convention on the ATA Carnet for the Temporary Admission of Goods*** and ***trade facilitation***.

Temporary entry for business persons: in trade agreements this usually refers to business persons entering the territory of another party for a limited time for the purpose of engaging in trade in goods, trade in services or investment activities. This category excludes natural persons seeking access to the employment market of another party, and it does not apply to measures regarding citizenship, nationality, residence or employment on a permanent basis.

Temporary normal trade relations: a term used by the United States to indicate that giving ***most-favoured-nation treatment*** to a given country is subject to periodic renewal. *See also* ***normal trade relations*** and ***permanent normal trade relations***.

Temporary tariff suspension: when a component or finished good is not produced or supplied within the ***European Union***, manufacturers or importers may apply for it to enter free of duty. If a temporary tariff suspension is granted, the good may be imported free of duty in unlimited quantities until the tariff suspension is revoked. Other economies employ similar systems. *See also* ***autonomous tariff quota***.

Termination services: *see* ***telecommunications termination services***.

Terms of trade: an expression for the relative price of one good in terms of another, usually originating from different countries. The terms of trade move

(comparative advantage)、*国家龙头企业(national champions)*、*自力更生(self-reliance)*、*自给自足(self-sufficiency)*。

Telecommunications

电信

《服务贸易总协定》的《关于电信服务的附件》中的定义为“以任何电磁方式传送和接收信号”。另见*结算价(accounting rate)*、*基础电信协定(Agreement on Basic Telecommunications Services)*、*服务贸易总协定第四议定书(Fourth Protocol to the General Agreement on Trade in Services)*、*电信服务参考文件(reference paper on telecommunications services)*、*1377审查(Section 1377 Review)*。

Telecommunications termination services

电信终端服务

一电信网络向另一电信网络提供的服务，允许一网络的呼叫者与另一个网络的呼叫者进行通话。以上通过互连完成。两网络之间的通话包括三个阶段：(a)将呼叫传输至终端网络或目的地网络；(b)为终端网络提供入口点或网关；以及(c)将呼叫转接至其最终目的地。后两者构成终端服务。第二网络对这一服务收取的费用称为结算价。

Temporary admission of goods

货物暂准进口

有条件地允许免税或部分免税进口货物进入一关税领土。货物进入一关税领土必须有特定目的，例如在商品交易会上展览或在潜在客户的场所展示。货物必须在一规定期限内复出口，且除正常折旧或因使用而磨损外，不得有任何变化。另见*关于货物暂准进口的ATA报关单证册海关公约(Customs Convention on the ATA Carnet for the Temporary Admission of Goods)*、*贸易便利化(trade facilitation)*。

Temporary entry for business persons

商务人员临时入境

在贸易协定中，商务人员临时入境通常指商务人员为从事货物贸易、服务贸易或投资活动而在有限时间内进入另一方领土。这一类别不包括寻求进入另一方就业市场的自然人，且不适用于有关公民身份、国籍、长期居住或就业的措施。

Temporary normal trade relations

临时正常贸易关系

美国用于表示给予一国的需经定期展期的最惠国待遇的词语。另见*正常贸易关系(normal trade relations)*、*永久正常贸易关系(permanent normal trade relations)*。

Temporary tariff suspension

暂免关税

不在欧盟境内生产或供应的一部件或制成品可申请暂免关税而免税进入。如果给予暂免关税待遇，该货物可免税进口而无数量限制，直至暂免关税取消。其他经济体采用类似制度。另见*自主关税配额(autonomous tariff quota)*。

Termination services

终端服务

见*电信终端服务(telecommunications termination services)*。

Terms of trade

贸易条件

该措辞指一货物以另一货物表示的相对价格，通常货物源自不同国家。如果A国为获得B国生产的物品而需要提供更多自己的物品，则贸易条件对A国不利。

against country A if it has to offer more of its products for the article produced by country B. The reverse is true if the terms of trade move in favour of country A. *See also* ***commodity terms of trade***.

Territorial waters: defined by the ***United Nations Convention on the Law of the Sea*** as extending at most twelve nautical miles from the shore of a coastal state. A priority issue in the ***WTO*** negotiations on fisheries is whether disciplines on subsidized fishing activity should apply to fishing in territorial waters or beyond them. *See also* ***Exclusive Economic Zone***.

Textiles and the multilateral trading system: *see* ***Short-Term Arrangement Regarding International Trade in Cotton Textiles*** (1961), ***Long-Term Arrangement Regarding International Trade in Cotton Textiles*** (1962–73), ***Multi-Fibre Arrangement*** (1974–94) and ***Agreement on Textiles and Clothing*** (1995).

Textiles Monitoring Body: TMB. A body established under the WTO ***Agreement on Textiles and Clothing*** to supervise the implementation of the Agreement. *See also* ***Multi-Fibre Arrangement***.

Textile Surveillance Body: TSB. The body supervising and administering the ***Multi-Fibre Arrangement***.

Thai cigarettes**:** a dispute brought before the GATT in 1990 by the United States over Thailand's import regime for cigarettes. *Background.* Thailand at that time prohibited all imports and exports of tobacco and tobacco products except where a licence had been granted. This had happened only three times since 1966, and then only to the Thai Tobacco Monopoly. Thailand also applied an excise tax, a business tax and municipal taxes to sales of tobacco products. *Claims.* Thailand's main claims were (a) that its restrictions on imports were justified because cigarettes were an agricultural product within the meaning of Article XI, and that Thailand had acted to limit the area in which tobacco could be planted and the production of cigarettes, (b) the restrictions on "imports were also justified under Article XX(b) because measures which could only be effective if cigarette imports were prohibited had been adopted by the government to control smoking and because chemical and other additives contained in United States cigarettes might make them more harmful than Thai cigarettes", (c) the excise, business and municipal taxes on imported cigarettes were no higher than those on domestic ones, and (d) the measures were justified because they predated Thailand's ***accession*** to the GATT and because they were mandatory in their intent. The United States asked the ***panel*** to find that (a) the restrictions on imports of cigarettes were inconsistent with Article XI because cigarettes were not an agricultural or fisheries product within the meaning of that Article, and the restriction was therefore an import prohibition not accompanied by domestic supply restrictions, (b) the same restrictions could not be justified under Article XX(b) since, as applied by Thailand, they were not necessary to protect human health, (c) the excise, business and municipal taxes on imported cigarettes were applied at a higher rate than for domestic cigarettes, and (d) that

如果贸易条件对A国有利，则情况正好相反。另见*商品贸易条件(commodity terms of trade)*。

Territorial waters
领水

《联合国海洋法公约》定义为，自一沿海国家的海岸延伸不超过12海里。WTO渔业谈判中的一个优先问题是，关于补贴渔业活动的纪律是否应适用于在领水或领水之外水域的捕捞。另见*专属经济区(Exclusive Economic Zone)*。

Textiles and the multilateral trading system
纺织品与多边贸易体制

见*国际棉纺织品贸易短期安排(1961年)(Short-Term Arrangement Regarding International Trade in Cotton Textiles (1961))*、*国际棉纺织品贸易长期安排(1962年至1973年)(Long-Term Arrangement Regarding International Trade in Cotton Textiles (1962–73))*、*多种纤维协定(1974年至1994年)(Multi-Fibre Arrangement (1974–94))*、*纺织品与服装协定(1995年)(Agreement on Textiles and Clothing (1995))*。

Textiles Monitoring Body
纺织品监督机构

TMB。根据WTO《纺织品与服装协定》设立的机构，负责监督该协定的执行情况。另见*多种纤维协定(Multi-Fibre Arrangement)*。

Textile Surveillance Body
纺织品监督机构

TSB。该机构负责监督和管理《多种纤维协定》。

Thai cigarettes
泰国香烟案

美国1990年在GATT中对泰国香烟进口制度提起的争端。背景：当时泰国禁止全部烟草和烟草制品的进口和出口，除非已经颁发许可证。自1966年以来，许可证只颁发过三次，且只发给泰国烟草专卖局。泰国还对烟草产品销售征收消费税、营业税和市政税。诉求：泰国的主要诉求为：(a)其对进口的限制是合理的，因为香烟属于第11条范围内的农产品，且泰国已经采取行动限制烟草种植面积和香烟生产；(b)"同时根据第20条(b)款对进口的限制也是合理的，因为只有在禁止香烟进口的情况下，政府采取的控烟措施才有效，而且还因为美国香烟中所含化学和其他添加剂可能使其比泰国香烟危害更大"；(c)对进口香烟征收的消费税、营业税和市政税并不高于对国内香烟征收的税；以及(d)这些措施是合理的，因为这些措施的出台早于泰国加入GATT，而且措施的意图是强制性。美国请专家组认定：(a)对香烟进口的限制不符合第11条规定，因为香烟不属该条范围内的"农产品"或"渔业产品"，因而此种限制是一种无国内供应限制的进口禁令；(b)泰国实施相同的限制并不能根据第20条(b)款证明合理，这些措施并非保护人类健康所必需；(c)对进口香烟征收的消费税、营业税和市政税高于对国产香烟征收的税率；以及(d)泰国《加入议定书》不适

Thailand's ***Protocol of Accession*** did not apply because the relevant act did not impose mandatory import restrictions. The panel sought advice from the World Health Organization (WHO) on the technical aspects of the case. *Findings*. The panel found that Thailand had acted inconsistently with GATT Article XI (General Elimination of Quantitative Restrictions) in maintaining a virtual import prohibition on cigarettes. It had also acted inconsistently with Article XI:2 which permits import restrictions on agricultural or fisheries products in an early stage of processing when they are still perishable, if this is done to enforce governmental measures to restrict production and selling of the like domestic product. Cigarettes could not be described as "leaf tobacco in an early stage of processing" because they had already undergone extensive processing and were not intended for further processing. The panel further considered that various measures consistent with the GATT were reasonably available to Thailand to control the quality and quantity of cigarettes smoked which could achieve the health policies pursued by the Thai government through import restrictions. The practice of permitting the sale of domestic cigarettes while not permitting the import of foreign cigarettes was an inconsistency with the GATT not "necessary" within the meaning of Article XX(b). Concerning the question of the Protocol of Accession, the panel found that the relevant Thai law did not impose on Thai authorities a requirement to restrict imports that could not be modified by executive action. Indeed, the law explicitly gave the Thai authorities the power to grant import licences. Hence the clause concerning existing legislation in the Protocol did not exempt restrictions on the import of cigarettes. Finally, the panel found that the rates of applicable taxes were broadly consistent with the requirement for ***national treatment*** (Article III). Thailand's regime for the import of cigarettes remains under pressure. A complaint initiated by the Philippines more than ten years ago remains unresolved. *See also* GATT-consistency of national legislation. [GATT BISD 37S]

Theory of hegemonic stability: a proposition first developed by Charles Kindleberger and adapted and widened by others since. In his analysis of the reasons for the Great Depression of the 1930s and its persistence, he suggested that the main lesson of the inter-war years could be summed up as: "that for the world economy to be stabilized, there has to a stabilizer, one stabilizer". In the view of those who subscribe to this theory, its correctness was demonstrated by the dominant role the United States assumed in the creation of the ***multilateral trading system*** exemplified by the ***GATT***. [Kindleberger 1973]

Theory of second-best: a theory in international economics which assumes that the first-best solution for optimal trade lies in ***free trade*** not encumbered by distorting factors such as taxes, monopolies or tariffs. The theory of second-best postulates that it is still possible to aim for the optimality goal in trade by taking certain measures which, however, may not lead to the best possible outcome. What the measures likely to produce the second-best outcome are, assuming the first-best is not possible, depends on a case-by-case analysis. Others see

用，因为相关措施未实行强制性进口限制。专家组向世界卫生组织寻求该案技术层面的意见。调查结果：专家组认为，泰国维持对香烟的实质进口的做法与GATT第11条(普遍取消数量限制)不一致。同时也与第11条第2款不一致，该款允许对仍属易腐性质的处于早期加工阶段的农产品和渔业产品进行限制，如果限制措施是为了执行限制国产同类产品的生产和销售。香烟不能被称为“处于早期加工阶段的烟叶”，因为它们已经经过深加工，且无进一步加工需要。专家组进一步认为，泰国可合理使用多项符合GATT的措施，用于控制香烟的质量和数量，从而实现其通过进口限制所实行的健康政策。允许国产香烟销售而不允许进口外国香烟的做法不符合GATT，不属第20条(b)款范围中的“必需”范围。关于《加入议定书》的问题，专家组认为，泰国相关法律未要求泰国主管机关采取不能通过行政措施修改的限制进口措施。事实上，法律明确赋予泰国主管机关颁发进口许可证的权力。因此，议定书中有关现行法律的条款并未免除对进口香烟的限制。最后专家组认为，适用国内税的实施税率大体上与国民待遇(第3条)的要求相一致。泰国进口香烟制度面临压力。菲律宾在此前十多年提起的诉讼一直未决。另见*国家立法与GATT一致性(GATT-consistency of national legislation)*。

Theory of hegemonic stability

霸权稳定论

查尔斯·金德尔伯格最早提出的理论，后被其他人采用和拓展。在他对1930年代经济大萧条的原因及其持久性的分析中，他指出两次世界大战之间的主要教训可以概括为：“要稳定世界经济，就必须有稳定器，必须有一个稳定器”。在赞同这一理论的人看来，美国在创设以GATT为代表的多边贸易体制过程中所发挥的主导作用证明了这一理论的正确性。

Theory of second-best

次优理论

国际经济学中的理论，认为最佳贸易的最优解决办法在于自由贸易，不受税收、垄断或关税等扭曲因素的限制。次优理论假定，通过采取某些措施仍然有可能实现贸易中的最佳目标，尽管这些措施可能不会产生最佳的可能结果。假设最优结果不可能，那么有可能产生次优结果的措施取决于个案分析。其

preferential trade arrangements as an aspect of second-best. Theories of second-best of course are used in many other areas of economics.

Thin end of the wedge: the first step towards an outcome one wishes to avoid. Much effort is therefore spent in ensuring that the wedge does not gain a hold. *See also* ***slippery slope***.

Third-country dumping: the alleged practice of ***dumping*** by competitors in third markets in which one also has an interest. The WTO rules on ***anti-dumping measures*** do not cover so-called third-country dumping.

Third-country problem: a name for a putative trade effect of particular concern during the ***Kennedy Round*** negotiations on ***linear tariff cuts***. The problem is based on the assumption that countries have few export interests in products on which they maintain a high tariff. Hence they are not too concerned if the low-tariff country does not cut its tariffs on these products in the same proportion. This may have the effect, at least in modelling exercises, of shifting the main burden of the resulting trade regime on third countries, forcing them to make adjustments to their tariffs. The problem is therefore concerned with the relative ranking of a country's tariff rate in a given range of products. Any attempt to understand this problem from the perspective of economic sense probably will be fruitless.

Third-generation free-trade agreements: used by some to describe ***free-trade agreements*** that include, in addition to trade in goods and services, provisions concerning investment, competition, labour and environmental standards, etc. *See also* ***next-generation free-trade agreements***.

Third-line forcing: a term used in the administration of ***antitrust laws***. It describes the practice of supplying goods or services only if the buyer at the same time agrees to buy products from a third source. If the buyer does not agree, the supplier in question refuses to deal with him altogether. *See also* ***boycott***.

Third parties: also known as interested third parties. In proceedings under the WTO ***Dispute Settlement Understanding*** these are members who are not directly involved in the launch of a dispute, but who participate in the proceedings because they have a substantial interest in the matter. A mere interest in the proceedings is not enough. Members wishing to become third parties must show that they have an interest at stake. Third parties may appear before the ***panel***. They may also make written submissions. In turn, they receive the submissions to the first panel meeting of the parties in dispute. Third parties may not appeal against panel reports or decisions. In cases where a third party considers that the subject of a dispute has adverse effects on it, it may resort to the normal dispute settlement procedures. Where possible, the original panel will hear this submission also.

Third Protocol to the General Agreement on Trade in Services: the ***protocol*** giving effect to the new commitments on the ***movement of natural persons*** which resulted from the 1995 negotiations on this subject. It entered into force on 30 January 1996.

他人认为优惠贸易安排是次优贸易安排的一个方面。次优理论也被应用于经济学的许多其他领域。

Thin end of the wedge

坏事的端倪

朝着想要避免出现的结果迈出的第一步。因此需要付出大量努力以保证楔子不要入槽(字面义为“楔子的细端”，引申义为“导致大问题的小问题”“开头无所谓而实则严重的苗头”“重大问题的前兆”等—译者注)。另见*滑坡谬误(slippery slope)*。

Third-country dumping

第三国倾销

被在一国具有利益的第三国市场中的竞争者所指控的倾销做法。WTO关于反倾销措施的规则不涵盖所谓的第三国倾销。

Third-country problem

第三国问题

肯尼迪回合谈判中对线性关税削减引起特别关注的假定贸易影响的名称。这一问题基于一种假设，即各国对于维持高关税的产品几无出口利益。因此它们并不关心低关税国家未按相同比例削减这些产品的关税。此点至少在模型模拟中可能会产生这样的效果：将由此产生的贸易制度的主要负担转移至第三国，迫使它们调整其关税。这一问题因此与一国关税税率在指定产品范围内的相对排名有关。任何从经济意义上理解这一问题的尝试都可能是徒劳的。

Third-generation free-trade agreements

第三代自由贸易协定

一些人用于描述除包含货物贸易和服务贸易外，还包括有关投资、竞争、劳工和环境标准等条款的自由贸易协定。另见*下一代自由贸易协定(next-generation free-trade agreements)*。

Third-line forcing

第三方捆绑销售

反垄断法管理中使用的词语。用于描述只有在购买者同时同意购买第三方产品的情况下才提供商品或服务的做法。如果购买者不同意，则所涉供应商拒绝与其进行交易。另见*抵制(boycott)*。

Third parties

第三方

也称利害关系第三方。在WTO《争端解决谅解》程序中，第三方不直接发起争端，但参与诉讼程序，因为他们对该事项具有实质利益。仅对诉讼程序感兴趣并不够。希望成为第三方的成员必须证明他们的利益受到威胁。第三方可以出席专家组会议。第三方也可以提交书面意见。作为回应，他们可收到争端方向专家组第一次会议提交的陈述。第三方不得对专家组报告或裁决提起上诉。如果第三方认为争端议题对其有不利影响，可诉诸正常的争端解决程序。如可能，原专家组也将听取陈述。

Third Protocol to the General Agreement on Trade in Services

服务贸易总协定第三议定书

该议定书使1995年就自然人流动议题谈判所产生的关于自然人流动的新承诺得以生效。该议定书本身于1996年1月30日生效。

Third-wave free-trade agreements: also ***third-generation free-trade agreements***. Refers to the ***free-trade agreements*** concluded since the late 1990s. Some say that what distinguishes them from earlier agreements is that in many cases they are provisions on ***competition policy***, protection of ***intellectual property rights***, ***government procurement***, etc.

Third World: a translation of the French word *tiers-monde* (apparently coined by the French sociologist Maurice Duverger in the 1960s). It is no longer in common use in the English language where it has long given way to "developing countries". It generally was understood to include the countries that were not included in the group of industrialized democracies (the first world) or the communist countries (the second world). Like many such umbrella terms, it represents a useful first approach to the subject, but it masks a considerable diversity of economic progress and political views among the countries included in the group. *See also* ***developing countries and the multilateral trading system***.

Thirty:ten formula: the first proposal for a formula leading to ***linear tariff cuts*** made by the ***European Economic Community*** (EEC) during the ***Kennedy Round***. The idea initially was that there would be a comparison of the tariff rates of each participant, later modified to mean the EEC, Japan, the United States and the United Kingdom as the largest traders. Whenever the high tariff was more than 30 per cent *ad valorem* and the difference with the low tariff was more than 10 percentage points, it would have been subject to the linear reduction formula yet to be elaborated. The formula was abandoned because it was thought to lead to incongruous results when applied to actual trade flows. It was succeeded by the ***double écart formula***. *See also* ***écrêtement*** and ***peak tariffs***.

Threat of injury: *see* ***injury***.

Threat of serious injury: a term used in the WTO ***Agreement on Safeguards*** to mean ***serious injury*** that is clearly imminent. The Agreement states that the existence of a threat of serious injury "shall be based on facts and not merely on allegation, conjecture or remote possibility". *See also* ***injury*** and ***safeguards***.

Three pillars: in ***APEC*** this refers to trade and investment liberalization, business facilitation and economic and technical cooperation. The pillars were formed through the ***Osaka Action Agenda*** and are intended to help implementing the ***Bogor Declaration***.

Three pillars of agriculture: the framework for commitments under the WTO ***Agreement on Agriculture***. They are domestic support, market access, and export subsidies and related issues (export competition).

Tied aid: the granting of ***official development assistance*** in the form of loans to developing countries on condition that some of the funds are used in a certain way, often the purchase of capital goods or services from the donor country. *See also* ***mixed credits*** and trade and aid.

Tied loan: a loan extended by a government to another country on condition that it is spent in a prescribed way, usually through purchasing goods and services from the lender country.

Third-wave free-trade agreements

第三波自由贸易协定

也称第三代自由贸易协定。指自20世纪90年代末以来缔结的自由贸易协定。一些人认为，这些协定与先前协定的不同之处在于，在许多情况下，它们是关于竞争政策、保护知识产权、政府采购等方面的规定。

Third World

第三世界

法语单词tiers-monde的翻译(显然是由法国社会学家路易·迪维尔在20世纪60年代创造的)。这个词在英语中不再通用，因为它早已让位于“发展中国家”。人们普遍认为，它包括那些不属于工业化民主国家集团(第一世界)或共产主义国家(第二世界)的国家。与许多此类笼统用语一样，它是处理这一问题的首选用词，但它掩盖了该集团所包括的国家之间经济进步和政治观点的巨大差异。另见*发展中国家与多边贸易体制(developing countries and the multilateral trading system)*。

Thirty:ten formula

30:10公式

欧洲经济共同体(EEC)在肯尼迪回合期间最初提出的第一个产生线性关税削减公式的建议。最初的想法是对每一参加方的关税税率进行比较，后改为欧共体、日本、美国和英国作为最大贸易方。一旦高关税超过从价税率30%，且同时与低关税相差超过10个百分点以上，即需要进行有待细化的线性削减公式。这一公式被放弃，因为它被认为如果适用于实际贸易流动会产生不协调的结果。被双差公式所取代。另见*关税削平(écrêtement)*、*关税高峰(peak tariffs)*。

Threat of injury

损害威胁

见*损害(injury)*。

Threat of serious injury

严重损害威胁

WTO《保障措施协定》中使用的词语，指明显迫近的严重损害。协定规定，严重损害威胁的存在“应根据事实，而非仅凭指控、推测或极小的可能性”。另见*损害(injury)*、*保障措施(safeguards)*。

Three pillars

三大支柱

在APEC中，指贸易和投资自由化、商业便利化以及经济技术合作。三大支柱通过《大阪行动议程》形成，旨在帮助实施《茂物宣言》。

Three pillars of agriculture

农业三大支柱

WTO《农业协定》项下的承诺框架。它们是国内支持、市场准入、出口补贴及相关问题(出口竞争)。

Tied aid

附条件援助

以贷款形式向发展中国家提供官方发展援助，条件是部分资金以某种特定方式使用，通常是自捐助国购买资本货物或服务。另见*混合信贷(mixed credits)*、*贸易与援助(trade and aid)*。

Tied loan

附条件贷款

一国政府向另一国发放的贷款，条件是以规定方式使用，通常是自贷款国购买货物和服务。

Tiered formula: a method for cutting higher ***tariffs*** or high ***subsidies*** more steeply than they would be for low tariffs or subsidies. *See also* ***Swiss formula***.

Time-consistency problem: a government decides to implement a certain policy at some future time, but finds that the time is no longer opportune when the moment for its implementation arrives. [WTO 2009]

TiVA: Trade in Value Added. *See* ***value-added***.

TMB: *see* ***Textiles Monitoring Body***.

Tokyo Declaration: the declaration adopted by the GATT Ministerial Meeting on 14 September 1973 in Tokyo. It launched what became known as the ***Tokyo Round*** of ***multilateral trade negotiations***.

Tokyo International Conference on African Development: TICAD. A conference initiated by Japan in 1993 and held every three to four years. Its aims are (a) to raise awareness of African development issues, (b) to promote ownership of Africa and partnership in the international community, and (c) to mobilize an expanded partnership. *See also* ***one-stop border post***.

Tokyo Round: the seventh round of GATT ***multilateral trade negotiations*** which took place between 1973 and 1979. 102 countries participated in this round. Both from the point of view of participation and the breadth of the negotiating agenda, this was the biggest round up to that time. The Tokyo Round was launched on 14 September 1973 at a Ministerial Meeting in Tokyo, but the negotiations were conducted largely in Geneva. The Ministerial declaration setting out the ambit for the negotiations foresaw work aimed at (a) ***tariff*** negotiations using the formula method, (b) reducing or eliminating ***non-tariff measures***, (c) examining the possibility of reducing or eliminating all barriers in selected sectors, (d) examining the adequacy of the multilateral ***safeguard*** system, (e) negotiations in agriculture, taking into account the special characteristics and problems in this sector, and (f) treating ***tropical products*** as a special and priority sector. Ministers intended that the negotiations should be concluded in 1975. The Tokyo Round negotiations were dominated by events within the United States, the European Economic Community (EEC), Japan and the relations between them. The President did not have any negotiating authority until January 1975 when the Trade Act of 1974 became law. This negotiating authority was due to expire on 3 January 1980. The situation was complicated by the fact that 1976 was a presidential election year in the United States. The EEC had expanded its membership to nine on 1 January 1973 and was preoccupied with making the enlarged system work. Its internal coordinating system accordingly became much more complex. Japan had achieved its transformation into a first-rate economic and trading power and had become the cause of protectionist pressures in many economies. The various negotiating groups, in which the specialized negotiations would take place, were only established in February 1975. The developing countries were drawn into the negotiating process much more than during the ***Kennedy Round***. This was the time of heightened developing-country expectations in that it coincided with preparations for the ***New International Economic Order*** initiative and the

Tiered formula

分层公式

一种比低关税或补贴更大幅度削减高关税或高补贴的方法。另见*瑞士公式(Swiss formula)*。

Time-consistency problem

时间一致性问题

一政府决定在未来某时执行某项政策，但等到实施之时却发现时机已不适当。

TiVA

增加值贸易

见*增值(value-added)*。

TMB

纺织品监督机构

见*纺织品监督机构(Textiles Monitoring Body)*。

Tokyo Declaration

东京宣言

GATT部长级会议于1973年9月14日在东京通过的宣言。宣言启动了称为东京回合的多边贸易谈判。

Tokyo International Conference on African Development

东京非洲发展国际会议

TICAD。日本在1993年倡议发起的会议，每3至4年举行一次。旨在(a)提高对非洲发展问题的认识；(b)促进非洲的自主权和国际社会的伙伴关系；以及(c)动员扩大伙伴关系。另见*一站式边境口岸(one-stop border post)*。

Tokyo Round

东京回合

GATT第7轮多边贸易谈判，1973年至1979年举行。102个国家参加了这一回合谈判。无论从参加的角度还是从谈判议程的广度来看，是截至那时为止的最大一轮谈判。东京回合于1973年9月14日在东京举行的部长级会议上启动，但是谈判主要在日内瓦进行。部长宣言规定了谈判范围，预计开展如下工作：(a)使用公式法进行关税谈判；(b)减少或取消非关税措施；(c)在选定部门审查减少或取消所有壁垒的可能性；(d)审查多边保障措施制度的适当性；(e)农业谈判，同时考虑该部门的特殊性质和问题；以及(f)将热带产品视为特殊和优先部门。部长们希望谈判应在1975年完成。东京回合谈判受到美国、欧共体、日本内部事件及三者之间关系的影响。美国总统没有任何谈判授权，直到1975年1月《1974年贸易法》成为法律。谈判授权定于1980年1月3日到期。由于1976年是美国总统大选年，情况变得更加复杂。欧共体在1973年1月1日将成员扩大到9个国家，全部精力用在使扩大后的系统运转上。其内部协调系统也因而变得更为复杂。日本实现成为第一流经济贸易大国的转型，成为许多经济体中贸易保护主义压力的根源。开展专门谈判的各谈判小组直到1975年2月才设立。与肯尼迪回合相比，更多发展中国家加入了谈判进程。此时发展中国家的期望值大大提高，因为正好赶上国际经济新秩序倡议的准备工作和南北对话

intensification of the ***North–South dialogue***. Much necessary preparatory work of a substantive nature was done between 1973 and early 1977, but no real developments in the negotiations were possible until the new United States administration had formulated its policies and appointed its negotiating team. Negotiations began in earnest in July 1977 following a meeting between the United States and the EEC which ironed out some of their major differences on policy and procedure. The two reached agreement that there should be an accelerated timetable consisting of four phases to be concluded by January 1978. The first phase would consist of a general tariff plan, including a tariff-cutting formula using the ***Swiss formula*** as a working hypothesis, and specific directives for the treatment of agriculture. The second phase would cover the tabling of requests for tariff cuts and the removal of non-tariff measures. Phase three would see the tabling of draft texts for the codes on ***non-tariff measures***, and in the fourth phase participants would respond to the requests by tabling offers. By July 1978 a large group of developed countries was able to put forward a "Framework of Understanding" which set out the principal elements they considered necessary for a balanced outcome to the negotiations. The developing countries objected to this package on substantive and procedural grounds. They objected particularly to what they saw as an attempt to leave them at the periphery of the negotiations. The package nevertheless was an important factor in maintaining momentum as agreement emerged to conclude the negotiations by 15 December 1978. A major obstacle then turned up in the form of a section of the United States Trade Act which allowed the President to waive a requirement that countervailing duties be imposed on subsidized imports over the four-year period ending on 3 January 1979. If the existing waiver lapsed, countervailing duties would become automatic. Congress appeared reluctant to renew the waiver, but it did so once the EEC declared that it could not conclude the negotiations unless the United States first solved its internal problems. This happened in late March 1979, and the Tokyo Round negotiations ended formally on 12 April 1979. The negotiations resulted in average cuts of tariffs by developed countries for industrial products of about 35 per cent, and average tariffs were reduced to about 4.7 per cent, to be phased in over eight years. The Tokyo Round resulted in nine separate agreements (six of which were called "codes") and four understandings on the aims and operation of the GATT. These agreements and understandings added considerably to GATT law. Most of them were adapted further in the ***Uruguay Round*** and incorporated in the formal overall outcome for that round. Little progress was made on systemic issues in trade in agricultural products. There was agreement that negotiations should be continued after the round on the development of a ***Multilateral Agricultural Framework*** aimed at avoiding continuing political and commercial confrontations in this highly ***sensitive sector***. In reality this was little more than a device enabling the conclusion of the round as a whole and, as many expected, it did not lead anywhere once negotiations resumed. Achievements in the negotiations on tropical products were uneven, but reductions in tariffs and non-tariff

增强之时。1973年至1977年初之间，进行了许多必要的实质性筹备工作，但在谈判中不可能取得真正进展，直到美国新政府制定其政策并任命谈判队伍。1977年7月美国和欧共体举行会议，消除了双方在政策和程序上的一些主要分歧，开始进行认真的谈判。双方一致认为应有一个加快的时间表，由4阶段组成，在1978年1月前完成。第一阶段由一个总的关税计划组成，包括作为使用瑞士公式作为工作假设的关税削减公式和处理农业问题的具体指示。第二阶段涵盖提交关税削减和取消非关税措施的要价。第三阶段提出关于非关税措施守则的文本草案。在第四阶段，参加方通过提交出价对要价作出回应。到1978年7月，大批发达国家得以提出"谅解框架"，其中列出了它们认为谈判达成平衡结果所必需的主要要素。发展中国家以实质性和程序性理由反对这一揽子方案。它们特别反对看似企图将其在谈判中边缘化的内容。尽管如此，随着达成在1978年12月15日前结束谈判的协议，一揽子计划成为保持势头的一个重要因素。随后出现一个主要障碍，美国贸易法中的一节允许总统豁免在1979年1月3日结束的4年期内对补贴进口产品征收反补贴税的要求。如果现有豁免失效，反补贴税将自动生效。国会似乎不愿意对豁免进行延期，但在欧共体宣布除非美国首先解决其内部问题，否则谈判将不会结束之后，国会对豁免进行了延期。此事发生在1979年3月底，东京回合谈判于1979年4月12日正式结束。谈判结果为，发达国家工业品关税平均削减约35%，平均关税降至约4.7%，将在8年内分阶段实施。东京回合达成9个单独协定(其中6个称为"守则")和4个关于GATT目标和运行的谅解。这些协定和谅解大大丰富了GATT法律。它们中的大多数在乌拉圭回合中得到进一步改进，并被纳入该回合的正式全面成果中。在农产品贸易的体制性问题上几无进展。各方一致认为，本轮回合后应在发展多边农业框架方面继续谈判，旨在避免在这一高度敏感部门的政治和商业冲突。实际上，这只不过是使整个回合能够结束的一种手段，正如许多人所预期的，恢复谈判后并未取得进展。热带产品谈判的成果并不平均，但对于所有这些产品进行了关税和非关税措施削减。对于多边保障制度未达成

measures occurred across the full range of these products. No agreement was reached concerning a multilateral safeguard system. Negotiations were continued after the round, though without much success. One outcome developing countries saw as particularly important for them was the ***Enabling Clause***. It was aimed at promoting an increased participation by developing countries in the global trading system, and it allowed developed GATT members to accord differential treatment in favour of developing countries in the tariff and non-tariff areas. *See also* ***linear tariff cuts***, ***special and differential treatment*** and ***Tokyo Round agreements***. [GATT Secretariat 1979, Glick 1984]

Tokyo Round agreements: the collective name for the six codes on ***non-tariff measures***, three sectoral agreements and four decisions, sometimes referred to as ***framework agreements***, concluded as part of the ***Tokyo Round*** negotiations. Governments were able to choose to a large extent which of the agreements they would join. The codes are (a) the *Agreement on Technical Barriers to Trade*, usually referred to as the "standards code" which seeks to ensure that technical regulations, standards, testing and certification do not become impediments to trade, (b) the *Agreement on Government Procurement*, aimed at bringing non-discrimination, competition and transparency into purchases made by governments, (c) the *Agreement on Interpretation and Application of Articles VI, XVI and XXIII*, usually known as the "subsidies code", aimed at ensuring that subsidies do not harm the interests of other trading partners, (d) the *Agreement on Implementation of Article VII*, also known as the "customs valuation code" which seeks a fair, uniform and neutral system for the valuation of goods for customs purposes, (e) the *Agreement on Import Licensing Procedures*, aimed at ensuring that import licensing requirements are not in themselves restrictions on trade, and (f) the *Agreement on Implementation of Article VI*, usually known as the "anti-dumping code", a revised version of the anti-dumping code negotiated during the ***Kennedy Round***. The three sectoral agreements are (a) the *Agreement Regarding Bovine Meat*, aimed at expanding, liberalizing and stabilizing trade in meat and livestock, (b) the *International Dairy Arrangement* which sought to do the same for world trade in dairy products, and (c) the ***Agreement on Trade in Civil Aircraft*** under which participants eliminated customs duties on civil aircraft and parts. The four decisions concerned differential treatment for developing countries, trade measures taken for balance-of-payments purposes, greater flexibility for developing countries in taking trade measures for development purposes, and an understanding concerning improved dispute settlement measures. *See also* ***WTO plurilateral trade agreements*** and ***WTO Agreement***.

Tokyo Round codes: *see* ***Tokyo Round agreements***.

Tolerance rules: a component of many systems of ***rules of origin*** used in ***free-trade agreements***. Such rules permit the inclusion of some ***non-originating materials*** that would otherwise not be allowable. The tolerance seldom exceeds 10 per cent of the value of the final product. *See also* ***de minimis***.

协议。谈判在该轮回合后继续进行，但也没有太多进展。发展中国家认为对它们特别重要的一项成果是授权条款。该条款旨在促进发展中国家更多地参与全球贸易体系，且允许GATT发达缔约方在关税和非关税领域给予发展中国家差别待遇。另见*线性关税削减(linear tariff cuts)*、*特殊和差别待遇(special and differential treatment)*、*东京回合协定(Tokyo Round agreements)*。

Tokyo Round agreements

东京回合协定

对作为东京回合谈判一部分而缔结的6个非关税措施守则、3个部门协定和4个决定(有时称为框架协定)的统称。各国政府在很大程度上可以选择加入哪些协定。守则包括：(a)《技术性贸易壁垒协定》，通常称为"标准守则"，寻求保证技术法规、标准、检验和认证不会成为贸易障碍；(b)《政府采购协定》，旨在将非歧视、竞争和透明度引入政府所进行的采购活动；(c)《关于解释和适用第6条、第16条和第23条的协定》，通常称为"补贴守则"，旨在保证补贴不损害其他贸易伙伴的利益；(d)《关于实施第7条的协定》，也称"海关估价守则"，旨在寻求一个公平、统一和中立的货物海关估价制度；(e)《进口许可程序协定》，旨在保证进口许可要求本身不构成对贸易的限制；以及(f)《关于实施第6条的协定》，通常称为"反倾销守则"，是对肯尼迪回合中谈判达成的反倾销守则的修订版本。3个部门协定为：(a)《牛肉协定》，旨在扩大、开放和稳定肉类和牲畜贸易；(b)《国际奶制品安排》，寻求世界奶制品贸易的扩大、开放和稳定；以及(c)《民用航空器贸易协定》，参加方根据协定取消对民用航空器及其零部件的关税。4个决定涉及发展中国家的差别待遇、为国际收支目的所采取的贸易措施、发展中国家为发展目的所采取贸易措施的更大灵活性以及关于改进争端解决措施的谅解。另见*WTO诸边贸易协定(WTO plurilateral trade agreements)*、*WTO协定(WTO Agreement)*。

Tokyo Round codes

东京回合守则

见*东京回合协定(Tokyo Round agreements)*。

Tolerance rules

容忍规则

自由贸易协定中所使用的许多原产地规则制度的组成部分。此类规则允许包含一些原本不允许的非原产材料。容忍水平很少超过最终产品价值的10%。另见*微量(de minimis)*。

Top-down approach: a preference in preparing an agenda for trade negotiations to define the overall shape of the agenda and then to proceed to consider how to deal with individual components. The term is also used to describe the use of negative lists for services and investment commitments in ***free-trade agreements***. *See also* ***bottom-up approach***.

Torquay Tariff Conference: held at Torquay, United Kingdom, from September 1950 to April 1951. The work programme consisted of ***accession*** negotiations with six countries (Austria, Federal Republic of Germany, Republic of Korea, Peru, Philippines and Turkey) as well as some tariff negotiations among the participants themselves. This is now deemed to have been the third round of ***multilateral trade negotiations***. In the end, Korea acceded to the GATT only in 1967 and the Philippines in 1979.

Total Aggregate Measurement of Support: a term used in the WTO ***Agreement on Agriculture***. It means the sum of all domestic support provided to agricultural producers. It is the total of all ***aggregate measurements of support*** for ***basic agricultural products***, all aggregate measurements of support not aimed at a specific product and all equivalent measurements of support for agricultural products. Formulas like these do a lot to explain why agricultural negotiations consume so much time. *See also* ***amber box***.

TPP: *see* ***Trans-Pacific Partnership Agreement***.

TPP-11: the ***Trans-Pacific Partnership Agreement*** without the United States. *See* ***Comprehensive and Progressive Agreement for Trans-Pacific Partnership***.

TPRB: the ***Trade Policy Review Body*** is the ***General Council*** operating under special procedures for meetings to review trade policies and practices of individual WTO members under the ***Trade Policy Review Mechanism*** and the trade-monitoring reports of the entire WTO membership.

TPRM: *see* ***Trade Policy Review Mechanism***.

Traceability: the ability to trace, for example, meat sold in retail shops back to an abattoir and thence to the farm where the animal was raised. Traceability has become an important part of efforts to raise and enforce food safety standards. The ***European Union*** has established a system to trace products containing or produced from ***genetically modified organisms*** (GMOs). The system permits control and verification of labelling claims, monitoring of potential effects on the environment and withdrawing relevant products in cases of unforeseen health or environment risks.

Tradables: goods and services that can be traded on international markets. In the case of services, this includes, for example, air travel, telecommunications and management consulting, but haircutting would not normally be considered a tradable service. *See also* ***non-tradables*** and ***semi-tradables***.

Trade: usually refers to the sale and distribution of goods and services across international borders. There are many different ways of doing this, but there must be a commercial element for a transaction to qualify as trade. *See also* ***barter trade***, ***commerce***, ***compensation trade*** and ***countertrade***.

Top-down approach
自上而下方式

在制定贸易谈判议程时，倾向于确定议程的总体框架，随后考虑如何处理各组成部分的方法。该词也用于描述在自由贸易协定中对服务和投资承诺使用负面清单的情况。另见*自下而上方式(bottom-up approach)*。

Torquay Tariff Conference
托奎关税会议

1950年9月至1951年4月在英国托奎举行。工作计划包括6国(奥地利、联邦德国、韩国、秘鲁、菲律宾和土耳其)加入谈判，以及在参加方之间的一些关税谈判。现在被视为第3轮多边贸易谈判。最终韩国在1967年加入GATT和菲律宾在1979年加入GATT。

Total Aggregate Measurement of Support
综合支持总量

WTO《农业协定》中使用的词语。指对向农业生产者提供的所有国内支持的总和。为基本农产品的所有综合支持量、所有非特定产品综合支持量以及所有农产品支持等值的总和。像这样的公式可以说明为什么农业谈判如此耗费时间。另见*黄箱(amber box)*。

TPP
跨太平洋伙伴关系协定

见*跨太平洋伙伴关系协定(Trans-Pacific Partnership Agreement)*。

TPP-11

没有美国参加的《跨太平洋伙伴关系协定》。另见*全面与进步跨太平洋伙伴关系协定(Comprehensive and Progressive Agreement for Trans-Pacific Partnership)*。

TPRB
贸易政策审议机构

贸易政策审议机构是总理事会按照特殊程序召开会议，在贸易政策审议机制项下审议WTO各成员的贸易政策和实践，并审议全体成员的贸易监督报告。

TPRM

见*贸易政策审议机制(Trade Policy Review Mechanism)*。

Traceability
可追溯性

可以追溯的能力，例如零售店中出售的肉类可以追溯到屠宰场，再到饲养动物的农场。可追溯性已经成为提高和执行食品安全标准努力的重要组成部分。欧盟已经建立含有或产自转基因生物(GMOs)产品的追溯系统。该系统允许对标签要求进行控制和核实、监测对环境的潜在影响以及在出现不可预见的健康或环境风险时召回相关产品。

Tradables
贸易品

可以在国际上交易的货物和服务。对于服务，例如包括航空运输、电信和管理咨询，但理发一般不被认为属可交易的服务。另见*非贸易品(non-tradables)*、*半贸易品(semi-tradables)*。

Trade
贸易

通常指跨越国际边界的货物和服务的销售和分销。开展贸易有许多不同方式，但必须包括一个开展交易的商业因素才能有资格成为贸易。另见*易货贸易(barter trade)*、*商业(commerce)*、*补偿贸易(compensation trade)*、*对销贸易(countertrade)*。

Trade adjustment assistance: support, such as training or relocation grants, given by governments to individuals or companies to enable them to adapt more easily to changed circumstances in their area of activity. *See also* ***structural adjustment***.

Trade agreement: *see* ***bilateral trade agreement***.

Trade and aid: this refers to the range of policy issues subsumed in the aim of promoting the economic growth of developing countries through a greater harmonization of trade policies and aid policies of developed countries. Frequently, this is done through the provision of ***tied aid*** or ***mixed credits*** for the funding of projects that are not commercially viable in themselves, but which can make a contribution to the export performance of the recipient country. Some point out that there can, however, be an inherent contradiction between the aim of fostering the economic development of developing countries and the willingness of donor countries to open their markets to the newly emerging production and export capacity. There is therefore a view that the concept of trade and aid is no more than a way to subsidize exporters in donor countries. *See also* ***official development assistance***.

Trade and competition: one of the so-called ***new trade issues***, but already a negotiating subject at the time of the ***Havana Charter***. As an OECD report notes, the liberalization of trade and investment stimulates healthy competition. There are two main reasons for an examination of the relationship between trade and competition. First, there is an increasing recognition that the benefits of international trade liberalization may be negated by domestic measures inimical to an open, competitive market environment. Such barriers may take the form of private anti-competitive behaviour, abuse of monopoly and dominant supplier powers or inappropriate governmental regulatory frameworks. In some countries, the problem is made worse by a weak ***competition policy*** or its inadequate coverage of domestic economic activity. Sometimes competition laws explicitly allow companies to behave in other markets in ways which would be illegal in the domestic market. Second, there are cases where the use of either ***trade policy*** or competition policy could lead to differing results, depending on which policy was given priority. A frequently used example is that tests for action under competition laws tend to be harder to satisfy than those applying to ***anti-dumping measures***. However, the two sets of laws do not necessarily try to solve the same sets of problems. A bilateral solution found between Australia and New Zealand is that neither country takes anti-dumping action against the other, but each has the right to pursue through the courts anti-competitive behaviour giving rise to dumping. This solution probably is feasible only in cases where each side understands fully the court procedures of the other side and has full confidence in the way they work. Many ***free-trade agreements*** have chapters on competition, but for the most part these are limited to information and staff exchanges, etc. The ***Singapore WTO Ministerial Conference*** established in December 1996 a ***Working Group on the Interaction between Trade and Competition Policy*** to examine this issue. Exploratory work on trade and competition is continuing under the declaration

Trade adjustment assistance

贸易调整援助

由政府给予个人或公司的援助，例如培训或重新安置补助等，以使其更容易适应它们所处活动领域内的情况变化。另见*结构性调整(structural adjustment)*。

Trade agreement

贸易协定

见*双边贸易协定(bilateral trade agreement)*。

Trade and aid

贸易与援助

指通过更加协调的贸易政策和发达国家的援助政策，促进发展中国家经济增长的目标所包含的一系列政策问题。这常常通过提供附条件援助或混合信贷的方式，对商业上不可行但可对受援助国出口实绩作出贡献的项目提供资金。但是一些人指出，在促进发展中国家的经济发展目标与援助国对新兴的生产和出口能力开放其市场的意愿之间存在矛盾。因此有观点认为，贸易与援助之间的关系只不过是对援助国出口商的一种补贴而已。另见*官方发展援助(official development assistance)*。

Trade and competition

贸易与竞争

所谓的新贸易议题，但在谈判《哈瓦那宪章》时就已经是一个谈判议题。正如经济合作与发展组织(OECD)发布的报告所指出的，贸易和投资自由化刺激了健康的竞争。审查贸易与竞争之间的关系有两个主要原因。第一，人们越来越认识到，国际贸易自由化利益可能会被不利于开放和竞争的市场环境的国内措施所抵消。此类壁垒可能会采取私人反竞争行为、滥用垄断地位和支配性供应商地位或不适当的政府监管框架等形式。在一些国家，由于较弱的竞争政策或竞争政策对国内经济活动的涵盖范围不足，这一问题变得更加严重。有时竞争法明确允许公司在其他市场采取在本国市场属违法的行为。第二，有些情况是，使用贸易政策或使用竞争政策可能会导致不同结果，取决于优先使用哪种政策。一个常用的例子是，根据竞争法采取行动的测试往往比适用于反倾销措施的测试更难满足。但是，两套法律并不一定是要解决相同的问题。在澳大利亚和新西兰之间的双边解决方法是，两国均不针对对方采取反倾销措施，但均有权通过法院程序追究导致倾销的反竞争行为。这种解决办法可能仅在每一方充分了解对方法院程序且充分信任法院工作方式的情况下才可行。许多自由贸易协定都包含竞争章节，但大多数情况下这些章节仅限于信息和工作人员交流。1996年12月，新加坡WTO部长级会议设立了贸易与竞争政策相互关系工作组以审查这一问题。关于贸易和竞争的探索性工作

made by the ***Doha Ministerial Conference***. A decision was to be made at the fifth ***Cancún Ministerial Conference*** in 2003 on whether to start negotiations, but no agreement was reached. *See also* ***antitrust laws***, ***competition policy***, ***international contestability of markets*** and ***restrictive business practices***. [Hope and Maeleng 1998, OECD 2001]

Trade and corruption: *see* ***trade and illicit payments***.

Trade and culture: one of the possible ***new trade issues***, but not yet on any negotiating agenda. It is concerned with the impact international trade has on ***cultural identity***. In a narrow sense, the subject covers trade in audio and audiovisual material and the governmental measures, such as local content rules, that are applied to it. Some see it as covering in a wider sense the impact of international trade and investment on the cultural identity of a country. A subset of this concern is represented by ideas making up the theory of cultural imperialism which holds that trade and investment threaten to destroy local traditions and to submerge the cultural heritage of other countries. Understood in this way, the issue may provide the excuse for protectionist actions that otherwise would not be available. *See also* ***audiovisual services***, ***Canadian periodicals***, ***cultural industries*** and ***globalization***.

Trade and debt: the question of the relationship between a country's ***trade policy***, the impediments it faces to its export aims, and need to service or repay borrowings obtained sometimes a long time ago. Progress on this question is likely to be slow, partly because it would force trade ministries and finance ministries to cooperate more closely than they sometimes seem to like.

Trade and Development Act of 2000: a United States act which includes, among many other provisions, the ***African Growth and Opportunity Act***, the ***Caribbean Basin Initiative***, the ***carousel legislation*** and the aim of eliminating the ***worst forms of child labour***.

Trade and Development Board: TDB. The executive body of ***UNCTAD*** between the quadrennial conferences. It meets once a year in a regular session and deals with the international implications of macroeconomic policies, monetary and finance matters, trade issues, trade policies, structural adjustment and economic reform and related matters. There is also provision for up to three one-day executive sessions a year to deal mainly with management and institutional matters.

Trade and Development Report: TDR. An annual ***UNCTAD*** publication which analyses current economic trends and major policy issues of international concern. It also makes suggestions for addressing these issues at various levels. Each year the TDR focuses on a major issue. In the past decade these have been: 2009 *Economic outlook in the context of the global financial and economic crisis*, 2010 *Employment, globalization and development*, 2011 *Post-crisis policy challenges in the world economy*, 2012 *Policies for inclusive and balanced growth*, also in 2012: *1982–2011: Three decades of thinking development*, 2013 *Adjusting to the changing dynamics of the world economy*, 2014 *Global governance and policy space for development*, 2015 *Making the*

根据多哈部长级会议所作宣言继续开展。在2003年第5届坎昆部长级会议上准备作出关于是否启动谈判的决定，但未达成协议。另见*反垄断法(antitrust laws)*、*竞争政策(competition policy)*、*市场的国际竞争性(international contestability of markets)*、*限制性商业惯例(restrictive business practices)*。

Trade and corruption
贸易与腐败

见*贸易与违法付款(trade and illicit payments)*。

Trade and culture
贸易与文化

可能的新贸易议题，但尚未出现在任何谈判议程上。该议题关注国际贸易对文化特性的影响。狭义讲，议题涵盖音像材料贸易及适用的本地内容规则等政府措施。一些人认为这一议题涵盖了更广泛意义上的国际贸易和投资对一国文化特性的影响。这一关注的一个子集由构成文化帝国主义理论的思想所代表，该理论认为贸易和投资威胁破坏当地传统，侵蚀其他国家的文化遗产。按此方式理解，这一问题可能为其他情况下不能采取的保护主义行动提供借口。另见*视听服务(audiovisual services)*、*加拿大期刊案(Canadian periodicals)*、*文化产业(cultural industries)*、*全球化(globalization)*。

Trade and debt
贸易与债务

关于一国贸易政策、其出口目标所面临障碍以及对早期借款付息或偿还的关系问题。这一问题上的进展似乎很慢，部分由于这将迫使贸易部门和财政部门进行比从表面看更为密切的合作。

Trade and Development Act of 2000
2000年贸易与发展法

美国法案，其中包括《非洲增长与机遇法》、《加勒比盆地倡议》及旋转木马立法以及消除最恶劣形式的童工劳动的目标。

Trade and Development Board
贸易与发展理事会

TDB。联合国贸易与发展会议(UNCTAD)每4年一次大会休会期间的执行机构。每年举行一次例会，负责处理宏观经济政策、货币和金融事务、贸易问题、贸易政策、结构性调整和经济改革及相关事项的国际影响。另规定，每年可最多举办3次为期1天的执行会议，主要处理管理和机构事项。

Trade and Development Report
贸易与发展报告

TDR。联合国贸易与发展会议(UNCTAD)的年度出版物，分析现行经济趋势和国际关注的主要政策议题。报告还提出在不同层级处理这些问题的建议。报告每年专注于一个主要议题。过去10年的主要议题分别为：2009年全球金融和经济危机背景下经济展望；2010年就业、全球化和发展；2011年危机后世界经济政策挑战；2012年包容性和平衡增长政策，2012年另一议题为：1982—2011年—30年思维发展；2013年适应不断变化的世界经济动态；2014年促进发展的全球治理和政策空间；2015年使国际金融架构为发展服务；2016年促进

international financial architecture work for development, 2016 *Structural transformation for inclusive and sustained growth*, 2017 *Beyond austerity: towards a global new deal*, 2018 *Power, platform and the free trade delusion* and 2019 *Financing a Global Green New Deal*. *See also* ***World Development Report***, ***World Investment Report*** and ***World Trade Report***.

Trade and economic agreement: TEA. An imprecise term for an agreement between two or more countries, intended to cover part or all of their trade and economic relations. TEAs frequently have treaty status. The contents and structure of TEAs vary greatly. The simpler ones sometimes contain little more than assurances of ***most-favoured-nation treatment*** and ***best-endeavour undertakings*** to promote the expansion of trade and economic relations with the other party or parties or to consider sympathetically any trade issue that may arise between them. More complex TEAs can commit the partners to adopt ***trade facilitation*** measures, to engage in a regular structured dialogue and to work towards solutions to specific trade issues. TEAs do not normally contain free-trade provisions, but there would be no impediment to including a ***free-trade agreement*** in the framework of a TEA. *See also* ***trade and investment framework agreement***.

Trade and employment: one of the items on the agenda of the 1947–48 ***United Nations Conference on Trade and Employment*** and its preparatory meetings. Its inclusion stemmed from a recognition that pre-war unemployment exacerbated by ***beggar-thy-neighbour policies*** had been one of the reasons for the outbreak of the war. From the start of the Conference, there was a division between those who wanted to write effective employment provisions into what became the ***Havana Charter*** and those who were equally desirous of full employment, but who saw ***ECOSOC*** as the proper organization to deal particularly with cyclical unemployment and the coordination of measures to combat it. The Havana Charter imposed the following principal obligations on its members: (a) to achieve and maintain full employment in their territories, (b) to make measures to sustain employment consistent with other provisions of the Charter, (c) to avoid measures which would create balance-of-payments difficulties in other countries, (d) to take appropriate and feasible action to eliminate unfair labour conditions, (e) to act jointly with others that may be involved to eliminate persistent balance-of-payments problems, and (f) to participate in activities sponsored by ECOSOC to promote employment. The ***WTO Agreement*** and the ***GATT*** list the objective of ensuring full employment in their preambles. Some claim that this gives the WTO a mandate for an examination of trade and labour issues, but this argument probably goes too far.

Trade and environment: this is concerned with the issues arising from the interaction between measures to expand international trade and those aimed at protecting the environment. There is a view that virtually all trade–environment issues fall within one of the following categories: (i) the trade effects of environmental regulation of protection, (ii) the trade effects of environmentally-related product standards, (iii) the use of trade measures to secure international

包容性和可持续增长的结构转型；2017年超越紧缩—迈向全球新政；2018年能源、平台和自由贸易错觉；2019年为全球绿色新政提供资金。另见*世界发展报告(World Development Report)*、*世界投资报告(World Investment Report)*、*世界贸易报告(World Trade Report)*。

Trade and economic agreement

贸易经济协定

TEA。对两个或两个以上国家间旨在涵盖它们部分或全部贸易和经济关系的协定的不精确称呼。TEA通常具有条约地位。TEA的内容和结构差异很大。较简单的协定有时只包含确认最惠国待遇和促进扩大与一个或多个参加方的经济贸易关系的最佳努力承诺，或同情考虑它们之间可能产生的任何贸易问题。更复杂的TEA可以包含贸易伙伴承诺采取贸易便利化措施，参与定期结构性对话，并致力于解决具体贸易问题的内容。TEA通常不包含自由贸易条款，但在TEA框架内包含自由贸易协定不存在任何障碍。另见*贸易与投资框架协定(trade and investment framework agreement)*。

Trade and employment

贸易与就业

1947年至1948年联合国贸易与就业会议及其筹备会议议程中的议题之一。纳入议程的原因源自人们认识到，以邻为壑政策所加剧的战前失业是二战爆发的原因之一。从会议一开始即出现分歧，一些人希望将有效就业条款写入后来的《哈瓦那宪章》，而一些人同样希望实现充分就业，但认为联合国经社理事会(ECOSOC)才是专门处理周期性失业问题和协调应对措施的适当组织。

《哈瓦那宪章》对其成员规定了下列主要义务：(a)在各成员领土内实现和维持充分就业；(b)维持就业的措施应与宪章其他条款相一致；(c)避免采取使其他国家产生国际收支困难的措施；(d)采取适当和可行的行动以消除不公平劳动条件；(e)与其他成员共同努力以消除国际收支的持续失调；以及(f)参与联合国经社理事会主持的活动以促进就业。《WTO协定》和GATT的序言中均列出保证充分就业的目标。一些人称此即授予WTO审查贸易与劳工问题的授权，但这一论点可能走得太远了。

Trade and environment

贸易与环境

涉及扩大国际贸易的措施与旨在保护环境的措施之间的互相关系所产生的问题。有观点认为，几乎所有贸易-环境问题均可以归入以下其中一类：(1)环境保护法规的贸易影响；(2)与环境有关的产品标准的贸易影响；(3)采用贸易措

environmental objectives, and (iv) the environmental effects of trade and trade liberalization. Hoekman and Kostecki list four main reasons offered by its proponents for the inclusion of this issue in the WTO agenda. First, production and consumption activities in one country may have a detrimental environmental impact on other countries. Second, some environmentalist groups have propounded the view that trade itself is bad for the environment because of its potential to spread pollution. Third, some consider that environmental measures and policies are bad for trade because they might allow countries with low environmental standards to be more competitive than those that have to bear the cost of higher standards. Fourth, environmental policies may unnecessarily restrict trade as shown in the tuna cases. Schoenbaum notes that criticism of the impact of trade on the environment tends to be based on the following propositions: (a) free trade is generally bad for the environment, (b) the rules of the ***multilateral trading system*** can make implementation of ***multilateral environment agreements*** difficult, (c) the rules of the multilateral trading system impede attempts to protect resources and the environment outside of national jurisdictions, (d) the rules of the multilateral trading system prevent countries from adopting measures to protect their domestic environment, and (e) the rules of the multilateral trading system obstruct efforts to compel other countries to adopt high environmental standards. These propositions contain in part some misunderstandings about the working of the multilateral trading system. They also contain some deliberate obfuscation of the issues. The multilateral trading system as exemplified by the WTO rules has not prevented any country from instituting environmental measures it deems appropriate. In principle it requires, however, that domestic measures are implemented in the least trade-restrictive manner, that there is no ***arbitrary or unjustifiable discrimination*** and that the measures must not be a ***disguised restriction on international trade***. There is much argument about the possibility that differences in environmental standards might lead to cost differentials which could be exploited by those enjoying lower costs. Extensive academic analysis of this problem has not yielded credible evidence that trade and environment cannot coexist or that trade has a detrimental effect on the environment. The proposition that trade measures ought to be used in support of environmental objectives generally, usually by way of amendment of Article XX (General Exceptions) of the GATT, is not on the whole favoured by trade-policy makers because it might lead to a whole new array of protectionist measures only tenuously connected with the aim of environmental protection. A work programme is now under way on these issues in the WTO ***Committee on Trade and Environment***. The Committee covers goods and services. *See also* ***Agenda 21***, ***Basel Convention***, ***CITES***, ***Convention on the Prior Informed Consent Procedure for Certain Hazardous Chemicals and Pesticides in International Trade***, ***environmental goods and services***, ***environmental rules under the WTO***, ***general exceptions***, ***London Guidelines for the Exchange of Information on Chemicals in International Trade***, ***Montreal Protocol***, ***pollution-haven hypothesis***, ***prior informed consent***,

施保证国际环境目标实现；以及(4)贸易和贸易自由化的环境影响。霍克曼和科斯特奇列出了将这一问题纳入WTO议程的支持者的4个主要理由。第一，一国的生产和消费活动可能会对其他国家的环境产生不利影响。第二，一些环保主义团体提出的观点是，贸易本身对环境有害，因为贸易有传播污染的可能性。第三，一些人认为，环境措施和政策不利于贸易，因为它们可能使环境标准低的国家比那些必须承担更高环境标准的成本的国家更具竞争力。第四，如“金枪鱼案”所表明的，环境政策可能会产生对贸易不必要的限制。肖恩鲍姆指出，贸易对环境影响的批评往往基于以下理由：(a)自由贸易通常不利于环境；(b)多边贸易体制的规则可能使多边环境协定的实施变得困难；(c)多边贸易体制的规则阻碍在国家管辖范围之外保护资源和环境的努力；(d)多边贸易体制的规则阻碍一国采取措施保护其国内环境；以及(e)多边贸易体制的规则阻碍一国迫使其他国家采用高环境标准的努力。这些主张在一定程度上包含对多边贸易体制运作的误解。也含有一些故意混淆问题的内容。以WTO规则为代表的多边贸易体制并未阻止任何国家制定其认为适当的环境措施。但是，原则上WTO规则要求国内措施应以贸易限制作用最小的方式实施，无任意或不合理的歧视，且这些措施不得构成对国际贸易的变相限制。对于环境标准差异导致成本差异的可能性存在很多争论，这可能被那些享受较低成本的人利用。对此议题的大量学术分析并没有得出贸易和环境不能共存或贸易对环境产生不利影响的可信证据。对于贸易措施应总体上用于支持环境目标的观点，通常通过修正GATT第21条(一般例外)，总体上未受到贸易政策制定者的青睐，因为这可能会导致一系列新的保护主义措施，而这些措施与环境保护目标只有微弱的联系。WTO贸易与环境委员会正在就这些问题制定工作计划。委员会涵盖货物和服务。另见*21世纪议程(Agenda 21)*、*巴塞尔公约(Basel Convention)*、*濒危野生动植物种国际贸易公约(CITES)*、*关于在国际贸易中对某些危险化学品和农药采用事先知情同意程序的鹿特丹公约(Convention on the Prior Informed Consent Procedure for Certain Hazardous Chemicals and Pesticides in International Trade)*、*环境产品和服务(environmental goods and services)*、*WTO环境规则(environmental rules under the WTO)*、*一般例外(general exceptions)*、*关于化学品国际贸易资料交换的伦敦准则(London Guidelines for the Exchange of Information on Chemicals in International Trade)*、*蒙特利尔议定书(Montreal Protocol)*、*污染天堂假说(pollution-haven hypothesis)*、*事先知情同*

race-to-the-bottom argument, ***Rio Declaration on Environment and Development*** and ***United Nations Framework Convention on Climate Change***. [Birnie and Boyle 2002, Hoekman and Kostecki 1995, Schoenbaum 2002]

Trade and foreign exchange: suggested by some for consideration in the WTO as a ***new trade issue***. It concerns the relationship between international trade and the ***exchange rate*** system. Proponents tend to subscribe to the view that the system of floating exchange rates is one of the causes of protectionist pressures on the trading system. Others claim that it was the fixed exchange rate system that led to protectionism. Few seem to be keen to start early negotiations.

Trade and gender: refers to international flows of trade and their impact especially on the female population. Often the subject is understood in terms of the existence or otherwise of gender equality. An ***UNCTAD*** study notes that trade can affect gender equality in several ways: (a) a positive or negative impact on growth and employment opportunities, (b) competitive pressures, which may reduce or encourage gender discrimination, in particular wage differentials, (c) facilitating or raising barriers to access by women to resources and services, and (d) multilateral trading rules which may facilitate or constrain governments in applying policies or regulations that address gender inequality. Trade and gender is often seen as an aspect of ***trade and poverty*** because the burden of coping daily with poverty appears to fall disproportionately on women in many developing countries. Most analysts of this issue accept that income increases and advances in development brought about by trade, and also by implication trade liberalization, will benefit women. Goal 5 of the ***Sustainable Development Goals*** seeks to achieve gender equality and to empower all women and girls. The Buenos Aires ***WTO Ministerial Conference*** in 2017 issued a ***Joint Declaration on Trade and Women's Economic Empowerment*** aimed at a better understanding of policies and practices needed to enable women to participate more fully in national and international economic activities. [UNCTAD/EDM/2004/2]

Trade and human rights: this expression embraces a set of three broad issues. They have in common the thought that international trade can have an effect on the enjoyment or exercise of ***human rights*** in all countries. First, there is the pessimistic assumption that ***trade liberalization*** by developing countries nearly always entails a social cost to them which outweighs its economic benefits. It also assumes that the benefits of trade liberalization go almost exclusively to privileged urban minorities, and that other groups fall further behind in their living standards. Trade liberalization always entails some ***structural adjustment***, but it is not of course the only cause of it. Some occupations will be affected adversely by the need for structural adjustment, but the evidence overall points to an improvement in the observance of human rights as economic well-being increases. Second, trade and human rights stands for the proposition that trade measures should be used to promote or enforce human rights. Often this is aimed at a better observance of ***core labour standards***. Indeed, some commentators use *human rights* and *labour standards*

意(prior informed consent)、*竞次论(race-to-the-bottom argument)*、*里约环境与发展宣言(Rio Declaration on Environment and Development)*、*联合国气候变化框架公约(United Nations Framework Convention on Climate Change)*。

Trade and foreign exchange
贸易与外汇

一些人建议在WTO中将这一议题作为新贸易议题进行审议。这一议题关注国际贸易和汇率系统之间的关系。支持者倾向于认为，浮动汇率制是产生对贸易体制的保护主义压力的原因之一。其他人则认为，是固定汇率制导致了保护主义。几乎无人愿意启动早期谈判。

Trade and gender
贸易与性别

指国际贸易流动及其特别对女性人口的影响。这一议题经常从性别平等的存在或其他方面加以理解。联合国贸易与发展会议(UNCTAD)的一项研究指出，贸易可通过若干方式影响性别平等：(a)对增长和就业机会的积极或消极影响；(b)竞争压力，可能减少或鼓励性别歧视，特别是工资差别；(c)便利妇女获得资源和服务或增加这方面的壁垒；(d)可以促进或限制政府实施处理性别不平等问题政策或法规的多边贸易规则。贸易与性别问题经常被视为贸易与贫困的一个方面，因为每日应付贫穷的负担在许多发展中国家似乎大部分落在女性身上。这一议题的大多数分析人士认为，贸易所带来的收入增长和发展进步，以及贸易自由化影响，将会使女性受益。可持续发展目标中的第5目标寻求实现性别平等，赋予所有女性和女孩权利。2017年布宜诺斯艾利斯WTO部长级会议发表了《贸易与妇女经济赋权联合宣言》，旨在更好地理解使妇女能够更充分参与国内和国际经济活动的政策和做法。

Trade and human rights
贸易与人权

这一表述包括三大问题。它们的共同点在于，国际贸易可以对所有国家享有或行使人权产生影响。第一，有一种悲观的假设，认为发展中国家的贸易自由化几乎总是给它们带来超过其经济利益的社会成本。还假设贸易自由化的好处几乎完全属于享有特权的城市少数人口，而其他群体的生活水平进一步落后。贸易自由化总是需要一些结构性调整，但它当然不是惟一的原因。一些职业将因需要进行结构性调整而受到不利影响，但总体证据表明，随着经济福利的增加，尊重人权的情况将得到改善。第二，贸易与人权代表着贸易措施应用于促进或执行人权的观点。这通常是为了更好地遵守核心劳工标准。事实上，一些评论人士交替使用人权和劳工标准。持有这一观点的人士倾向于支

interchangeably. Holders of this view tend to support the use of ***GSP*** schemes for this purpose since these are unilateral instruments that can be made conditional on a range of factors. The relationship between the country offering the GSP and a country using it is that of a donor and a beneficiary. The donor can within reason impose conditions on the use of the scheme. The ***European Union***'s GSP scheme, for example, can be suspended in case of human rights violations in beneficiary countries. Its standard scheme is supplemented by ***GSP+*** which offers additional trade incentives to eligible countries that maintain and implement effectively fifteen core human and labour rights UN/ILO conventions and twelve conventions related to environment and governance principles. The United States ***African Growth and Opportunity Act*** is another example of a trade law requiring beneficiaries to observe the protection of human rights. A third strand is the thought that non-observance of human rights in the form of core labour standards gives the exporting country an unfair advantage because its exporters supposedly incur fewer costs. This is the ***pauper-labour argument*** in some other form. Empirical studies cast doubt on the validity of this proposition. Advocates of this view usually argue that importing countries ought to be able to use trade measures to defend themselves against unfair practices of this sort. This is the basis of calls for rules against so-called ***social dumping***. Some of the proponents of the view that trade measures should be used to promote the observance of human rights go a step further to argue that the WTO framework of rules could be used for the purpose. They seem to have in mind especially the WTO dispute settlement mechanism which leads to binding decisions on the parties. Several objections have been raised to this proposition. One is that the ***Dispute Settlement Understanding*** requires ***panels*** to examine disputed matters in the light of the ***covered agreements***, to preserve the rights and obligations of members under these agreements and to clarify "the existing provisions of those agreements in accordance with customary rules of interpretation of public international law". As the WTO framework of rules makes no mention of human rights or any international human rights instrument, panels cannot make their findings against a member's observance of such rights or instruments. Panels examining a case with a human rights aspect could seek advice from competent bodies charged with the promotion of human rights on the nature of these rights. However, one can assume that because of the limit of their jurisdiction to WTO law only, they would seek such advice in an effort to ascertain whether the responding member would have been able to draw on other means to achieve its human rights aims. This, at any rate, is how panels have approached the question of ***trade and environment***. Basing one's view on the jurisdictional limitations imposed on panels of course is to some extent a circular argument. WTO members could, if they so wished, decide to amend their rules to introduce a ***human rights clause***. The prospects for this appear to be small. Many of them fear, especially developing countries, that a human rights clause in the WTO rules would be open to abuse for protectionist purposes. A further question is what human rights would be

持为此目的使用普惠制(GSP)方案，因为这些方案是以一系列因素为条件的单边手段。提供普惠制的国家和使用普惠制的国家之间的关系是捐助方和受益方之间的关系。捐助者有理由对方案的使用附加条件。例如，欧盟的普惠制方案可以在受益国中人权受到侵犯的情况下暂停执行。欧盟的标准方案得到普惠制附加(GSP+)的补充，普惠制附加对有效维护和实施联合国/国际劳工组织(ILO)15项核心人权和劳工权利公约及与环境和治理原则有关的12项公约的符合条件的国家给予额外贸易刺激。美国《非洲增长与机遇法》是贸易法要求受益方遵守人权保护的另一例。第三种观点是，不遵守以核心劳工标准为形式的人权会使出口国获得不公平利益，因为其产品被认为成本更低。这是贫民劳动论的另一种形式。实证研究对这一说法的有效性提出了质疑。这种观点的支持者通常认为，进口国应该能够使用贸易措施以保护自己免受这种不公平做法的侵害。这就是呼吁制定反对所谓社会倾销规则的基础。一些持有贸易措施应用于促进遵守人权观点的人进一步认为，WTO的规则框架可用于此目的。他们似乎特别想到了WTO争端解决机制，这一机制可以产生对各方具有约束力的裁决。对这一观点提出了多种反对意见。其中之一是，《争端解决谅解》要求专家组根据适用协定审查争端事项，以维护成员在这些协定项下的权利和义务，并澄清“依照关于解释国际公法的习惯规则解释这些协定的相关条款”。由于WTO的规则框架从未提及人权或任何国际人权文件，专家组不能针对一成员遵守此类权利或文件的情况提出调查结果。专家组在审查涉及人权问题的案件时，可以向负责人权促进的机构寻求有关这些权利性质的咨询意见。但是，可以假设的是，由于专家组的管辖权仅限于WTO法律，它们将会征求此种咨询意见以确定作出回应的成员是否能够采取其他手段实现其人权目标。无论如何，这就是专家组处理贸易与环境问题的方法。将观点建立在专家组管辖权限制基础上的观点当然在某种程度上是一种循环论证。WTO成员可以决定修正其规则以引入人权条款，如果他们愿意的话。但这样作的可能性似乎很小。他们中的许多人，特别是发展中国家，担心WTO规则中的人权条款会被滥用于保护主义目的。更深入问题是，何种人权应以这种

protected in this way. Some of the proponents are limiting themselves to the issues covered by ***trade and labour standards***. Others see matters in a more expansive way. They see little reason why instruments such as the ***Universal Declaration of Human Rights*** or the ***International Covenant on Economic, Social and Cultural Rights*** could not be part of the rules panels routinely consult in their examinations. They argue that, after all, WTO members are already parties to many of these conventions. Moreover, they argue, that the duty of panels to interpret the rules in accordance with the customary rules of international law requires them to go beyond the WTO rules proper. This view is fiercely contested. Opponents point out that the WTO panels and the ***Appellate Body*** are not international judicial bodies of the kind of the ***International Court of Justice*** or the European Court of Justice. Some also point to a lack of practicality. Panels are not usually composed of jurists, though some members will have had legal training. The Appellate Body, on the other hand, argues its cases with legal rigour. How such a two-tier system would cope with the added burden of human rights law, some of which is far removed from the WTO's role of promoting freer international trade, is difficult to assess. *See also* ***anti-globalization***, ***European Social Charter***, ***wage-differential argument*** and ***World Commission on the Social Dimension of Globalization***. [Howse 2002, Lim 2001, Marceau 2002]

Trade and illicit payments: one of the ***new trade issues***. It is concerned with bribery, corruption and lack of transparency in ***government procurement***. The main proponent of negotiations on this issue has been the United States. The aim of such negotiations would be to promote measures to discourage illicit payments in line with its own legislation which makes such payments an offence under the ***Foreign Corrupt Practices Act***. The entry into force on 15 February 1999 of the ***Convention on Combating Bribery of Foreign Public Officials in International Business Transactions***, negotiated in the ***OECD***, and the conclusion of the ***United Nations Convention Against Corruption*** have greatly reduced calls for similar action in the WTO. *See also* ***African Union Convention on Preventing and Combating Corruption***, ***Draft International Agreement on Illicit Payments***, ***G20 Anti-Corruption Action Plan*** and ***Recommendation for Further Combating Bribery of Foreign Public Officials in International Business Transactions***.

Trade and investment: one of the ***new trade issues***, even though some rudimentary rules on ***investment*** formed part of the ***Havana Charter***. The issue is concerned with the relationship between trade and investment as factors in ***international economic relations*** and the emergence of investment as a ***market access*** issue. Broadly speaking, for a long time trade and investment tended to be regarded as separate policy issues. Today, the two are increasingly regarded as complementing each other. In a situation of declining border protection, investment flows can stimulate new trade patterns and strengthen older ones. In other cases, firms are more or less forced to invest and produce in target markets because high tariffs make importing an unrealistic option. The ***Singapore WTO***

方式加以保护。一些支持者将自己局限于贸易与劳工标准所涵盖的问题上。其他人则以更为开放的方式看待问题。他们认为，《世界人权宣言》或《经济、社会和文化权利国际公约》等文件不能成为专家组在审查时通常参考的规则的一部分是毫无依据的。他们认为，无论如何，WTO成员已经是这些公约中许多公约的缔约方。此外，他们认为，专家组依照解释国际公法的习惯规则解释规则的责任要求他们超越WTO规则本身。这种观点饱受争议。反对者指出，WTO专家组和上诉机构不是国际法院或欧洲法院之类的国际司法机构。一些人还指出，这种做法缺乏实用性。尽管一些专家组成员接受过法律培训，但专家组通常不由法学家组成。另一方面，上诉机构以严苛的法律标准方式处理案件。很难评估这样一个两级体系将如何应对人权法所带来的额外负担，因为一些人权法的内容与WTO促进更自由的国际贸易的作用相去甚远。另见*反全球化(anti-globalization)*、*欧洲社会宪章(European Social Charter)*、*工资差别理论(wage-differential argument)*、*全球化社会问题世界委员会(World Commission on the Social Dimension of Globalization)*。

Trade and illicit payments

贸易与违法付款

新贸易议题。涉及贿赂、贪腐和政府采购缺乏透明度等问题。关于这一问题谈判的主要倡导者是美国。此类谈判的目标是促进采取措施，根据将此类付款定为《反海外腐败法》项下犯罪行为的本国立法阻止违法付款。在经济合作与发展组织(OECD)中谈判达成的《关于打击国际商业交易中行贿外国公职人员行为的公约》于1999年2月15日生效，《联合国反腐败公约》的缔结，在很大程度上减少了在WTO中采取类似行动的呼声。另见*非洲联盟预防和惩治腐败公约(African Union Convention on Preventing and Combating Corruption)*、*关于违法付款的国际协定草案(Draft International Agreement on Illicit Payments)*、*20国集团反腐败行动计划 (G20 Anti-Corruption Action Plan)*、*关于进一步打击国际商业交易中行贿外国公职人员行为的建议(Recommendation for Further Combating Bribery of Foreign Public Officials in International Business Transactions)*。

Trade and investment

贸易与投资

新贸易议题，尽管关于投资的一些初步原则构成《哈瓦那宪章》的一部分。这一问题涉及贸易与作为国际经济关系因素的投资的关系和投资作为市场准入问题出现的情况。概括地讲，在很长时间里贸易和投资往往被视为独立的问题。当前，这两个问题被认为具有互补性。在边境保护减弱的情况下，投资流动可以刺激新贸易模式并巩固原有模式。在其他情况下，企业或多或少被迫在目标市场中进行投资和生产，因为高关税使进口成为不现实的选择。新加

Ministerial Conference established in December 1996 a ***Working Group on the Relationship between Trade and Investment*** to examine this issue. The ***Doha Ministerial Conference*** authorized exploratory work on trade and investment. The ***Cancún Ministerial Conference*** in 2003 had been expected to make a decision on whether to start negotiations, but agreement was not possible. The ***July package*** of 2004 means that no negotiations in this area will be undertaken under the ***Doha Development Agenda***. *See also* ***globalization***, ***investment facilitation***, ***Multilateral Agreement on Investment*** and ***tariff-jumping investment***.

Trade and investment facilitation agreement: TIFA. Such agreements are aimed at promoting trade and investment between the partners through making the existing rules and regulations work more smoothly.

Trade and investment framework agreement: TIFA. An agreement outlining the broad principles and aims for the conduct of trade and investment activities between the parties. It can be accompanied by more detailed subsidiary instruments for issues that require more detailed treatment.

Trade and labour standards: this is concerned with the question whether trade rules should be used to promote minimum labour standards, or ***core labour standards***, in exporting countries. Like others of the new trade issues, it has actually been around for some time. Some trace it back to the anti-slavery campaigns of the nineteenth century. The 1919 constitution of the ***International Labour Organization*** had the adoption and promotion of labour standards as a main objective. Some consider that the concept of "fair labour standards" derives from Article 23(a) of the Covenant of the ***League of Nations*** in which members endeavoured "to secure and maintain fair and humane conditions of labour for men, women and children both in their own countries and in all the countries to which their commercial and industrial relations extend". The ***Atlantic Charter*** of 1941 sought to secure "for all, improved labour standards, economic advancement and social security". In 1943, the International Labour Office recommended that "wherever existing conditions are unsatisfactory, there should be arrangements to ensure that labour employed in the production of controlled commodities receive fair remuneration and adequate social security protection and that other conditions of employment are satisfactory". The link between international trade and labour standards was made more explicit in Article 7(1) of the ***Havana Charter*** which noted that "unfair labour conditions, particularly in production for export, create difficulties in international trade, and, accordingly, each Member shall take whatever action may be appropriate and feasible to eliminate such conditions within its territory". Some of the international commodity arrangements also contain provisions exhorting members to promote fair labour standards. The ***GSP*** scheme of the ***European Union*** has a special incentive arrangement for countries whose national legislation incorporates ***International Labour Organization*** conventions covering the abolition of forced labour, the freedom of association and the right to collective bargaining, non-discrimination in respect

坡WTO部长级会议在1996年12月设立贸易与投资关系工作组，以审议此问题。多哈部长级会议授权对贸易和投资开展探索性工作。人们曾期望2003年的坎昆部长级会议对是否启动谈判作出决定，但未能达成一致。2004年7月工作计划意味着在多哈发展议程中不会在此领域开展任何谈判。另见*全球化(globalization)*、*投资便利化(investment facilitation)*、*多边投资协定(Multilateral Agreement on Investment)*、*跳越关税投资(tariff-jumping investment)*。

Trade and investment facilitation agreement

贸易投资便利化协定

TIFA。此类协定旨在通过使现有规章制度更流畅运行从而促进参加方之间的贸易和投资。

Trade and investment framework agreement

贸易投资框架协定

TIFA。列出参加方之间开展贸易和投资活动的总原则和目标的协定。对于需要详细处理的问题可辅以更为详细的附属文件。

Trade and labour standards

贸易与劳工标准

这一问题涉及贸易规则是否应被用于促进出口国中最低劳工标准或核心劳工标准的问题。与其他新贸易议题一样，这一议题实际上已经提出一段时间。有些人追溯到19世纪的反奴隶制运动。国际劳工组织(ILO)1919年章程将采用和促进劳工标准作为一项主要目标。一些人认为，“公平劳工标准”的概念源自《国际联盟盟约》第23条(a)款，其中要求成员“勉力设法为男女及儿童在其本国及其工商关系所及之各国确保公平、人道的劳动条件”。1941年的《大西洋宪章》寻求“促进所有国家的劳动水平、经济进步和社会保障”。1943年，国际劳工局建议，“在现有条件不能令人满意的情况下，应作出安排，以保证从事管制商品生产所雇佣的劳工获得公平报酬和充分社会保障，并保证其他就业条件令人满意”。《哈瓦那宪章》第7条第1款更明确规定了国际贸易与劳工标准之间的联系，指出“不公平劳工条件，特别是在供出口的生产方面，对国际贸易造成了困难，因此每一成员应采取在其领土内消除此类条件的任何适当和可行的行动”。一些国际商品协定也包含鼓励成员促进公平劳工标准的条款。欧盟的普惠制(GSP)方案包含一种特殊激励安排，针对国内立法纳入关于消除强迫劳动、结社自由和集体谈判权、消除就业职业方面的歧视以及废除童工

of employment and occupation, and the abolition of child labour. *See also* ***child labour***, ***social clause***, ***social dumping***, ***social subsidies*** and ***trade and human rights***. [Addo 2002]

Trade and poverty: this subject forms the background to many trade initiatives. It is concerned particularly with the contribution international trade can make to the alleviation of pervasive ***poverty*** or how poorer countries can achieve greater, and shared, prosperity among their populations. Many studies have drawn attention to the fact that alleviation of poverty goes beyond economic and trade policy. Rather, the entire range of government responsibilities and policies come into play when solutions to this problem are sought. The 2030 Agenda for Sustainable Development which contains the seventeen ***Sustainable Development Goals*** is illustrative of the range of activities involved. The past two or three decades have shown that poor countries equipped with the right policies and a determination to overcome poverty can succeed, sometimes spectacularly so. The same period, however, has also shown that countries well-endowed with natural resources and located near major markets can rapidly descend into economic decline by promoting inappropriate policies. The search for ***autarky***, for example, will inevitably lead to a reduction in gross domestic income even if some segments of the population are not excessively affected by them. A report prepared jointly prepared in 2015 by the ***WTO*** and the ***World Bank*** noted strengthened evidence that "trade has played a critical role in poverty reduction and that the further integration of developing countries into an open global economy will be essential for achieving the goal of ending extreme poverty by 2030". The report identified five policy options that governments can take individually or collectively to better the conditions of the poor: (1) lowering trade costs for deeper integration of markets by tackling policy and infrastructure barriers, (2) improving the enabling environment, including policies related to human and physical capital, access to finance, governance and macroeconomic stability, (3) intensifying the poverty impact of integration policies by tackling remoteness from markets at the sub-national level and facilitating the activities of poor traders, (4) managing and mitigating risks faced by the poor, and (5) improving data and analysis to inform policy. A follow-up report by the World Bank Group and the World Trade Organization of 2018 notes that "reducing barriers for the goods that the poor consume, facilitating access to external markets for the goods that the poor produce, and connecting the poor to global markets by overcoming international and domestic trade-related costs are all central to maximizing the potential benefits of trade for poverty reduction". It also highlights that trade reforms can create new opportunities, but they also can involve adjustment costs for the poor. Additionally, the effects of international trade on the poor will depend on where they live and where they work. The report lists three conclusions on policy priorities and issues for deeper analysis: (1) a focus on high trade transaction costs faced by poor workers and consumers in developing countries to realize potential trade gains, (2) ensuring

的国际劳工组织公约的国家。另见*童工(child labour)*、*社会条款(social clause)*、*社会倾销(social dumping)*、*社会补贴(social subsidies)*、*贸易与人权(trade and human rights)*。

Trade and poverty

贸易与贫困

这一议题构成许多贸易倡议的背景。特别关注国际贸易能够对减少普遍贫困所作的贡献，或较为贫穷的国家如何能够使民众实现更大的共同繁荣。许多研究提请注意这样一个事实，即减少贫困超出了经济和贸易政策的范畴。相反，当寻求对此问题的解决办法时，所有的政府责任和政策都要发挥作用。2030年可持续发展议程包含17个可持续发展目标，列出了所涉及的活动范围。过去的二三十年已经表明，贫穷国家如果拥有正确政策和克服贫穷的决心就能够取得成功，有时甚至是惊人的成功。但是，同一时期也表明，即便拥有丰富自然资源且临近主要市场的国家也可能因推行不适当的政策而迅速陷入经济衰退。例如，寻求经济闭关自守将不可避免地导致国内总收入的减少，即使部分人口并未受到过大的影响。WTO和世界银行于2015年联合编写的一份报告指出，有更多证据表明，“贸易在减少贫困方面发挥了关键作用，发展中国家进一步融入开放的全球经济对于到2030年实现消除赤贫的目标至关重要”。报告确定了政府选择可用于改善贫困人口条件的单独或联合采取的5种政策：(1)通过处理政策和基础设施障碍降低更深层次市场一体化的贸易成本；(2)改善有利环境，包括与人力和物质资本、融资渠道、治理和宏观经济稳定性有关的政策；(3)通过解决次国家级行政区远离市场的问题和便利贫穷贸易者的活动，加强一体化政策对贫穷的影响；(4)管理和减轻贫困人口面临的风险；以及(5)改进数据和分析，为政策提供信息。世界银行集团和WTO在2018年提出的一份后续报告指出，“减少贫困人口消费商品的壁垒，便利贫困人口生产的商品进入外部市场，以及通过克服国际和国内贸易相关成本，将贫困人口与全球市场联系在一起，这些都是最大限度发挥贸易对减贫的潜在利益的关键”。报告还强调，贸易改革可以创造新机会，但也会涉及贫困人口的调整成本。此外，国际贸易对贫困人口的影响取决于他们在哪里生活和工作。报告列出了关于政策优先事项和需要进一步分析的问题的三个结论：(1)重点关注发展中国家贫困工人和消费者为实现潜在贸易收益而所面临的高交易成本；(2)保证在国内分销网络中提供服务方面的竞争和效率；以及(3)更加关注减轻贫困生产者和工人面临的进口竞争增加的风险。多个国际货币基金组织(IMF)融资机

competition and efficiency in the provision of services along domestic distribution networks and (3) more attention to mitigating the risks that poor producers and workers face from increased import competition. Several ***IMF financing facilities*** are aimed specifically at short-term and longer-term needs of low-income countries with balance of payments problems. *See also* ***Aid for Trade***, ***Everything But Arms***, ***globalization***, ***GSP***, ***GSTP***, ***Integrated Framework for Trade-Related Assistance to Least-Developed Countries***, ***least-developed countries***, ***Poverty Reduction and Growth Trust***, ***Programme of Action for the Least-Developed Countries for the Decade 2011–2020***, ***trade facilitation*** and ***Vienna Programme of Action for Landlocked Developing Countries for the Decade 2014–2024***. [Bartley Johns et al. 2015, World Bank Group and World Trade Organization 2018]

Trade and social conditions: *see* ***child labour***, ***core labour standards***, ***human rights***, ***Millennium Development Goals***, ***social clause***, ***social labelling***, ***Sustainable Development Goals***, ***trade and labour standards*** and ***worker rights***.

Trade and sustainable development: this is used to refer in general to the promotion and pursuit of international trade and its intersection with sustainability or sustainable development. Following the release of the United Nations ***Sustainable Development Goals*** (SDGs) a discussion of trade and sustainability often tends to be conducted within the framework of the seventeen SDGs. *See also* ***Investment Policy Framework for Sustainable Development***.

Trade and taxation: an issue proposed by some for inclusion in the agenda of a future round of ***multilateral trade negotiations***. It is based on a perception that taxation regimes could be used to distort a country's international trade. The prospective complexities of this issue are such that even most of those who concede a direct relationship between trade and taxation measures have shown little desire to start a discussion of what might be done. *See also* ***new trade issues*** and ***transfer pricing***.

Trade and transfer of technology: *see* ***Working Group on Transfer of Technology***.

Trade-balancing measure: a requirement that the investor use earnings from exports to pay for imports.

Trade-balancing requirement: a requirement that an investor use earnings from exports to pay for imports. It is based essentially on ***mercantilism***. Such a condition always puts a limit on the growth of the firm concerned, and in this way also on the economic growth of host countries. Trade-balancing requirements contravene the provisions of the WTO ***Agreement on Trade-Related Investment Measures***.

Trade Barriers Regulation: a ***European Union*** instrument first entering into force in 1995 and amended on 15 May 2014. Its aims are (a) to respond to breaches by third countries of international trade rules which affect the European Union's interests, with a view to seeking a satisfactory solution that restores benefits for the European Union's ***economic operators***, and (b) to

制专门针对有国际收支问题的低收入国家的短期和长期需求。另见*促贸援助(Aid for Trade)*、*除武器外的所有产品(Everything But Arms)*、*全球化(globalization)*、*普惠制(GSP)*、*发展中国家全球贸易优惠制(GSTP)*、*针对最不发达国家的与贸易有关的技术援助综合框架(Integrated Framework for Trade-Related Assistance to Least-Developed Countries)*、*最不发达国家(least-developed countries)*、*减贫与增长信托基金(Poverty Reduction and Growth Trust)*、*2011—2020年十年期支援最不发达国家行动纲领(Programme of Action for the Least-Developed Countries for the Decade 2011-2020)*、*贸易便利化(trade facilitation)*、*内陆发展中国家2014—2024年十年维也纳行动纲领(Vienna Programme of Action for Landlocked Developing Countries for the Decade 2014-2024)*。

Trade and social conditions
贸易与社会条件

见*童工(child labour)*、*核心劳工标准(core labour standards)*、*人权(human rights)*、*千年发展目标(Millennium Development Goals)*、*社会条款(social clause)*、*社会标签(social labelling)*、*可持续发展目标(Sustainable Development Goals)*、*贸易与劳工标准(trade and labour standards)*、*劳工权利(worker rights)*。

Trade and sustainable development
贸易与可持续发展

用于指促进和追求国际贸易及其与发展的可持续性或可持续发展的交集。在联合国可持续发展目标(SDGs)发布后，关于贸易与可持续发展的讨论往往在17项可持续发展目标的框架内进行。另见*可持续发展投资政策框架(Investment Policy Framework for Sustainable Development)*。

Trade and taxation
贸易与税收

一些人建议纳入未来回合多边贸易谈判议程的议题。所基于的理念是，税收制度可用于扭曲一国的国际贸易。这一议题可预见的复杂性在于即使那些承认贸易和税收措施存在直接关系的人也不愿意就可能采取的行动进行讨论。另见*新贸易议题(new trade issues)*、*转让定价(transfer pricing)*。

Trade and transfer of technology
贸易与技术转让

见*技术转让工作组(Working Group on Transfer of Technology)*。

Trade-balancing measure
贸易平衡措施

投资者使用出口收益支付进口费用的要求。

Trade-balancing requirement
贸易平衡要求

投资者使用出口收益支付进口费用的要求。主要基于重商主义。此种条件常常限制有关企业的发展，并以此限制东道国的经济增长。贸易平衡要求违反WTO《与贸易有关的投资措施协定》。

Trade Barriers Regulation
贸易壁垒条例

欧盟文件，最初于1995年生效，2014年5月15日修正。旨在：(a)应对第三国违反影响欧盟利益的国际贸易规则的行为，以期寻求令人满意的解决办法，恢复欧盟经济运营者的利益；及(b)在与第三国的贸易关系中，当给予来自欧盟

rebalance concessions or other obligations in the trade relations with third countries, when the treatment accorded to goods from the European Union is altered in a way that affects its interests. It applies (a) when the European Union has been authorized to suspend concessions or other obligations following a WTO ***Dispute Settlement Understanding*** decision, (b) following the adjudication of trade disputes under international trade agreements where the European Union has the right to suspend concessions or other obligations, (c) for the rebalancing of concessions or other obligations if a third country has applied ***safeguards***, and (d) where concessions by a WTO member have been modified, and no compensatory adjustments had been agreed. Remedies include suspension of tariff concessions or imposition of new tariffs, introduction or increase of ***quantitative restrictions*** or suspension of concessions regarding goods, services or suppliers in the area of public procurement. *See also* ***suspension of concessions or other obligations***. [Regulation (EU) 654/2014]

Trade bloc: used popularly to describe a group of countries that cooperate, often formally, on trade matters, possibly through a ***free-trade agreement***.

Trade-chill effect: the result of an action, such as ***trade harassment***, which engenders a contraction in the exports of a given product to a defined country. *See also* ***trade war***.

Trade control measures: an omnibus term for ***tariffs***, ***para-tariffs*** and ***non-tariff measures***.

Trade coverage: a term used in ***tariff negotiations*** to denote how much of a country's trade is liberalized by the tariff reductions under discussion.

Trade creation: a criterion used for the assessment of the impact of ***free-trade areas*** and ***customs unions*** on others. Trade theory holds that the reduction or elimination of barriers to trade will lead to increased trade between members and non-members if external barriers are not raised at the same time. The experience of the GATT system and the expansion of trade under it would indicate that this theory is underpinned by evidence. In practice, the validity of the argument is quite difficult to demonstrate for any given area because of the interplay of other factors, particularly secular changes such as technological advances, changing investment patterns, etc. *See also* ***trade diversion***. [Viner 1950]

Trade defence instruments: *see* ***contingent protection***.

Trade deficit: this occurs when the value of one's imports exceeds the value of one's exports over a given period. Often, only merchandise trade is considered for this calculation. Taken in isolation, the existence of a trade deficit does not yield any useful insights about a country's economic health. However, it may be that a persistent trade deficit reflects some deficiencies in prevailing economic settings which need to be corrected. Sometimes the anxiety induced by a trade deficit simply reflects symptoms of ***mercantilism***. *See also* ***balance of trade*** and ***trade surplus***.

Trade deflection: *see* ***trade diversion***.

Trade deviation: a term sometimes used to describe a situation arising from the fact that a country may be a member of two ***free-trade areas***. Unless there are

货物的待遇发生变化而影响其利益时，重新平衡减让或其他义务。在下列情况下适用：(a)根据WTO《争端解决谅解》项下的裁决，授权欧盟中止减让或其他义务；(b)根据国际贸易协定项下的贸易争端裁决，欧盟有权中止减让或其他义务；(c)在第三国实施保障措施的情况下，为重新平衡减让或其他义务；以及(d)如一WTO成员已对减让作出修改，且未能达成补偿性调整。救济措施包括中止关税减让或征收新的关税、采用或增加数量限制或中止公共采购领域对货物、服务或供应商的减让。另见*中止减让或其他义务(suspension of concessions or other obligations)*。

Trade bloc

贸易集团

用于描述可能通过签署自由贸易协定而就贸易事项开展合作的一组国家。

Trade-chill effect

贸易冷却效应

一项行动的结果，例如贸易干扰，会导致一给定产品对一特定国家出口的减少。另见*贸易战(trade war)*。

Trade control measures

贸易控制措施

对关税、准关税和非关税措施的统称。

Trade coverage

贸易范围

关税谈判中使用的词语，指讨论中的关税削减使一国贸易实现自由化的程度。

Trade creation

贸易创造

用于评估自由贸易区和关税同盟对其他国家影响的标准。贸易理论认为贸易壁垒减少或消除会在外部壁垒不同时提高的情况下，使成员与非成员之间的贸易增长。GATT体制的经验和这一体制下的贸易扩张表明这一理论是以证据为基础的。在实践中，由于其他因素的相互作用，特别是技术进步、不断改变的投资模式等长期变化，该论点的有效性对于一给定地区很难得到证明。另见*贸易转移(trade diversion)*。

Trade defence instruments

贸易防御工具

见*紧急保护(contingent protection)*。

Trade deficit

贸易逆差

这一情况发生在一给定时期一国进口值超过其出口值之时。通常，这一计算只考虑商品贸易。如果独立地看，贸易逆差的存在并不能提供关于一国经济健康的任何有用的见解。但是，持续的贸易逆差可以反映主流经济环境中需要纠正的一些缺陷。有时，贸易逆差所引发的焦虑仅仅反映了重商主义的症状。另见*贸易平衡(balance of trade)*、*贸易顺差(trade surplus)*。

Trade deflection

贸易偏转

见*贸易转移(trade diversion)*。

Trade deviation

贸易偏移

有时用于形容一国同属两个自由贸易区成员所引发的情况。除非存在适当的

appropriate ***rules of origin***, goods originating in one of these free-trade areas may in this way circulate freely to the other free-trade area once they have entered the ***customs territory*** of the first country. *See also* ***hub and spokes***.

Trade diversion: also known as trade deflection. One of the criteria used for the assessment of the impact of ***free-trade areas*** and ***customs unions***. The creation of such bodies normally leads to the expansion of trade between its members, but economic theory postulates that a share of the increased trade experienced by participants is merely due to a redirection of their trade, and not increased trade due to the arrangement. This effect can be demonstrated convincingly in models. In practice, trade diversion has always been very difficult to isolate because of other factors. These include technological innovation, global reduction in tariffs, changes in investment policies, etc. *See also* ***trade creation***. [Viner 1950]

Trade effect: a change in trade flows resulting from a change in laws, regulations, consumer preferences, technological changes, etc.

Trade Efficiency Programme: an ***UNCTAD*** programme aimed at increasing the international awareness and effective application of information technologies to trade, and to promote the use of models capable of reducing procedural costs in international trade. *See also* ***electronic commerce*** and ***World Trade Point Federation***.

Trade embargo: a ban on trade with a specified country, usually imposed through a United Nations decision, but sometimes based on unilateral or regional action. An example of a justification for a trade embargo can be found in the ***security exceptions*** written into the GATS and GATT which specifically allow the suspension of obligations under the agreements if this is necessary for conforming with United Nations decisions. *See also* ***United Nations economic sanctions***.

Trade-expanding policies: policies requiring or calling on trading partners to increase their imports from one's economy, often through schemes for ***voluntary import expansion***.

Trade Expansion Act: *see* ***Kennedy Round*** and ***United States trade agreements legislation***.

Trade facilitation: activities aimed at making it easier to import and export. Several definitions are available. They tend to have four principles in common: transparency, simplification, harmonization and standardization. The ***UN/CEFACT*** definition is "the simplification, standardization and harmonization of procedures and associated information flows required to move goods from seller to buyer and to make payment". The ***European Commission*** defines it as "simplification, modernization and automation of international trade procedures, particularly import and export procedures, transit requirements and procedures applied by Customs and other agencies" with the overarching goal of making trade transactions easier, quicker, more efficient and less costly, thereby easing trade flows. In the ***World Customs Organization*** trade facilitation "means the avoidance of unnecessary trade restrictiveness. This can be

原产地规则，否则原产于其中一个自由贸易区的货物一旦进入第一个国家的关税领土后即可自由流动至另一个自由贸易区。另见*轮轴-辐条(hub and spokes)*。

Trade diversion

贸易转移

用于评估自由贸易区和关税同盟影响的标准之一。此类组织的创设通常促成其成员之间贸易的扩大，但是经济理论认为，参加方所经历的贸易增长的份额只是因为它们的贸易方向发生了改变，并非因相关安排而增加的贸易。这种效果可以在模型中得到令人信服的证明。在实践中，贸易转移总是很难区分出来，原因是存在其他因素。这些因素包括技术创新、全球关税削减、投资政策变化等。另见*贸易创造(trade creation)*。

Trade effect

贸易效应

因法律、法规、消费者偏好、技术变化等方面的变化而引起的贸易流的变化。

Trade Efficiency Programme

贸易效率计划

联合国贸易与发展会议(UNCTAD)的一项计划，旨在提高对信息技术的国际认识及其在贸易中的有效应用，并促进使用能够降低国际贸易程序成本的模式。另见*电子商务(electronic commerce)*、*世界贸易网点联盟(World Trade Point Federation)*。

Trade embargo

贸易禁运

对于与一特定国家开展贸易的禁令，通常通过联合国的决议实施，但有时也会根据单边或区域行动。实行贸易禁运理由的例子可在《服务贸易总协定》和GATT的安全例外条款中找到，规定如果为符合联合国决议所必需，允许中止实施协定项下的义务。另见*联合国经济制裁(United Nations economic sanctions)*。

Trade-expanding policies

贸易扩张政策

要求或呼吁贸易伙伴增加自一经济体进口的政策，经常通过自愿扩大进口计划实现。

Trade Expansion Act

贸易扩张法

见*肯尼迪回合(Kennedy Round)*、*美国贸易协定立法(United States trade agreements legislation)*。

Trade facilitation

贸易便利化

旨在使进口和出口更为容易的活动。存在多个定义。这些定义往往有四项原则是共同的：透明度、简化、协调和标准化。联合国贸易便利化与电子商务中心(UN/CEFACT)的定义为："货物自卖方向买方流动的和支付所需程序及相关信息流的简化、标准化和协调"。欧盟委员会定义为："国际贸易程序，特别是进出口程序、过境要求和海关及其他机构所实施程序的简化、现代化和自动化"，总体目标是使贸易交易更容易、更快、更有效和成本更低，从而便利贸

achieved by applying modern techniques and technologies, while improving the quality of controls in an internationally harmonized manner". The ***WTO*** refers to the "simplification, modernization and harmonization of export and import processes". ***Free-trade agreements*** usually contain a chapter on trade facilitation. The ***United States–Mexico–Canada Agreement***, for example, states in Article 7.1 that "With a view to minimizing the costs incurred by traders thorough the importation and exportation, and transit of a good, each Party shall administer customs procedures in a manner that facilitates the importation, exportation, and transit of a good, and supports compliance with its laws". Global trade means that imports and exports have to cross borders, sometimes several times, and there is potential for consignments to be held up for a shorter or longer time for inspection purposes, but sometimes simply because there is large backlog of goods to be processed. In the case of perishable goods or goods needed for downstream manufacturing, such delays can have greatly adverse consequences. Examples of reasons for delays include assessments of goods for customs duties or compliance with ***sanitary and phytosanitary measures***, but other possibilities include faulty or incomplete documentation, late submission of documents, etc. Trade facilitation dos not remove the government's right to decide under what conditions goods may be admitted, but it seeks to make their impact as small as possible to permit a free flow of trade. The benefits available from trade facilitation are considerable. The *World Trade Report 2015* estimates that the full implementation of the WTO ***Agreement on Trade Facilitation*** could reduce trade costs by an average of 14.3 per cent and boost global trade by up to $1 trillion per year. It notes that the biggest benefits would be experienced by the poorest counties. The adoption of the Agreement on Trade Facilitation brought trade facilitation to the fore in the WTO, though the subject has always been there through various articles of the GATT and other agreements administered by the WTO. The WTO Trade Facilitation Agreement Facility was launched in 2014 with the aim of ensuring that developing countries and ***least-developed countries*** can benefit fully from this Agreement. Other organizations have long worked in this area. Among them are UN/CEFACT and ***UN/EDIFACT***, both of which are located within the United Nations ***Economic Commission for Europe*** (UN-ECE). Their work has been particularly productive in electronic data interchange and electronic business. ECE has also prepared a ***Trade Facilitation Implementation Guide***, available at http://tfig.unece.org. ***UNCTAD*** has a very active technical assistance programme in this area. It runs, for example, an ***Empowerment Programme for National Trade Facilitation Bodies*** and supports a broad range of ***National Trade Facilitation Committees***. The World Bank Trade Facilitation Agenda, an umbrella name for its extensive trade facilitation programme of wpractical assistance and analytical support, has long been one of the principal proponents of global work on trade facilitation, partly through the use of its Trade Facilitation Facility. The ***OECD*** has done a great deal of analytical work, and it has developed the ***OECD Trade Facilitation Indicators*** to help governments

易流动。在世界海关组织中，贸易便利化“意味着避免不必要的贸易限制。此点可以通过应用现代技术和科技实现，同时以国际协调的方式提高控制的质量。”WTO的定义为：“进出口流程的简化、现代化和协调”。自由贸易协定通常包含贸易便利化章节，例如《美国—墨西哥—加拿大协定》第7.1条规定：“为尽量减少贸易商在货物进出口和过境过程中产生的费用，每一参加方应以便利货物进出口和过境的方式管理海关程序，并支持对其法律的遵守。”全球贸易意味着进出口必须跨越边境，有时还需要多次跨越，且有可能装运货物为检查目的而滞留或长或短的时间，而有时仅因为待处理货物大量积压。对于易腐货物或下游制造业所需货物，此类延误会产生严重不利后果。造成延误的原因包括对评定货物关税或卫生与植物卫生措施合规情况，而其他可能性还包括单证有误或不完整、迟交单证等。贸易便利化并不完全剥夺政府决定在什么条件下可以允许货物进入的权利，但寻求尽可能减少这些条件的影响，以允许贸易自由流动。贸易便利化可带来的好处是可观的。《世界贸易报告2015》估计，WTO《贸易便利化协定》全面实施可使贸易成本平均降低14.3%，并使全球贸易每年增长高达1万亿美元。WTO指出，最不发达国家将获得最大利益。《贸易便利化协定》的通过使贸易便利化问题成为WTO的重要议题的，尽管这一议题因GATT多个条款和WTO所管理的其他协定而一直存在。WTO在2014年推出《贸易便利化协定》基金，旨在保证发展中国家和最不发达国家能够从协定中充分受益。其他组织长期在这一领域开展工作。包括UN/CEFACT和联合国行政、商业和运输用电子数据交换规则(UN/EDIFACT)，均设在联合国欧洲经济委员会(UN-ECE)内。两组织的工作在电子数据交换和电子商务方面卓有成效。欧洲经济委员会还制定了一份《贸易便利化实施指南》，可在http://tfig.unece.org网站上查阅。联合国贸易与发展会议(UNCTAD)在这一领域有一个非常积极的技术援助项目。例如，它运行国家贸易便利化机构赋权计划，并支持多个国家贸易便利化委员会。世界银行贸易便利化议程是其实际援助和分析支持的大量贸易便利化方案的统称，长期以来是贸易便利化全球工作的主要支持者之一，部分通过使用其贸易便利化基金。经济合作与发展组织(OECD)进行了大量分析工作，并制定了OECD贸易便利化指数，以帮助各国政府通过贸易便利化获得更大利益。全球贸易便利化联盟是一个由国际组织、政府和商业机构组成的合作组织，开展的项目旨在处理边境延误和不必要延误的问题。长期以来，国际商会一直是有效贸易便利化的大力倡导者。APEC已形成两项贸易便利化行动计划，每项计划的目标均为减

obtain greater benefits through trade facilitation. The ***Global Alliance for Trade Facilitation***, a collaboration of international organizations, governments and business, runs programmes designed to address delay and unnecessary delays at borders. The ***International Chamber of Commerce*** also has long been a strong advocate of effective trade facilitation. ***APEC*** has concluded two trade facilitation action plans, each of which aimed to reduce trade transaction costs by 5 per cent. *See also* ***APEC Principles on Trade Facilitation***, ***APEC Second Trade Facilitation Action Plan***, ***Asia-Pacific Trade Facilitation Forum***, ***Buy-Ship-Pay Model***, ***Compendium of Trade Facilitation Recommendations***, ***Container Security Initiative***, ***Empowerment Programme for National Trade Facilitation Bodies***, ***Framework Agreement on Facilitation of Cross-border Paperless Trade in Asia and the Pacific***, ***one-stop border post***, ***red-tape barriers***, ***SAFE Framework of Standards to Secure and Facilitate Global Trade***, ***Single Window*** and ***Trade Facilitation Agreement Database***.

Trade Facilitation Agreement: *see* ***Agreement on Trade Facilitation***.

Trade Facilitation Agreement Database: TFAD. A database maintained by the ***WTO*** Secretariat to report on the implementation of the ***Agreement on Trade Facilitation***. [tfadatabase.org]

Trade facilitation barriers: seen by some as a subset of ***non-tariff measures***. They include excessive documentation requirements, refusal to accept electronic versions of documents, lack of administrative transparency, little use of risk assessment procedures by customs authorities which means that they inspect every consignment, customs delays, and many more. *See also* ***Agreement on Trade Facilitation***.

Trade Facilitation Implementation Guide: a website maintained by the United Nations ***Economic Commission for Europe*** to explain the methods and benefits of a programme of ***trade facilitation***. It uses the ***Buy-Ship-Pay Model*** developed by ***UN/CEFACT*** as a simplified way of demonstrating a supply chain. It stresses the importance of information flows accompanying the physical movement of goods through the chain. [tfig.unece.org]

Trade finance: the financing of trade, usually through short-term instruments. Forms of finance include letters of credit, bank guarantees, loans, trade credit insurance, factoring, etc. A 2019 WTO-IFC study found that up to 80 per cent is financed by credit or credit insurance. [WTO-IFC 2019]

Trade – finance – currency linkage: an element of the Ministerial declaration made at Marrakesh in April 1994 at the conclusion of the ***Uruguay Round***. It envisages cooperation between the WTO, the ***IMF*** and the ***World Bank*** to achieve greater global coherence of policies in the fields of trade, money and finance. *See also* ***trade and foreign exchange*** and ***trade and taxation***.

Trade harassment: the use of overt and covert domestic measures as a device to make the import of products intentionally difficult. Overt measures include the aggressive use of ***anti-dumping measures***, ***safeguards*** actions or ***countervailing measures***. Sometimes the mere threat of such an action is sufficient to cause importers to reduce or stop purchases from abroad. At other times, the effect of

少5%的贸易交易成本。另见*APEC贸易便利化原则(APEC Principles on Trade Facilitation)*、*APEC第二个贸易便利化行动计划(APEC Second Trade Facilitation Action Plan)*、*亚太贸易便利化论坛(Asia-Pacific Trade Facilitation Forum)*、*购买-运输-支付模型(Buy-Ship-Pay Model)*、*贸易便利化建议汇编(Compendium of Trade Facilitation Recommendations)*、*集装箱安全倡议(Container Security Initiative)*、*国家贸易便利化机构赋权计划(Empowerment Programme for National Trade Facilitation Bodies)*、*亚洲及太平洋跨境无纸贸易便利化框架协定(Framework Agreement on Facilitation of Cross-border Paperless Trade in Asia and the Pacific)*、*一站式边境站(one-stop border post)*、*繁文缛节壁垒(red-tape barriers)*、*全球贸易安全与便利标准框架(SAFE Framework of Standards to Secure and Facilitate Global Trade)*、*单一窗口(Single Window)*、*贸易便利化协定数据库(Trade Facilitation Agreement Database)*。

Trade Facilitation Agreement

贸易便利化协定

见*贸易便利化协定(Agreement on Trade Facilitation)*。

Trade Facilitation Agreement Database

贸易便利化协定数据库

TFAD。由WTO秘书处维护的数据库，用于报告《贸易便利化协定》的实施情况。

Trade facilitation barriers

贸易便利化壁垒

一些人视之为非关税措施的子集。包括过多单证要求、拒绝接受单证电子版、缺乏行政透明度、海关很少使用风险评估程序，这意味着对每一批货物进行检查，海关延误以及其他很多做法。另见*贸易便利化协定(Agreement on Trade Facilitation)*。

Trade Facilitation Implementation Guide

贸易便利化实施指南

联合国欧洲经济委员会维护的网站，旨在说明贸易便利化计划的方法和好处。使用由联合国贸易便利化和电子商务中心(UN/CEFACT)开发的购买-运输-支付模型，作为显示供应链的简化方式。指南强调伴随货物沿着供应链进行物理移动的信息流的重要性。

Trade finance

贸易融资

指对贸易的融资，通常是通过短期工具。融资方式包括信用证、银行担保、贷款、贸易信用保险、保理融资等。WTO与国际金融公司(IFC)2019年的研究显示，高达80%是通过信贷或信贷保险获得融资的。

Trade – finance – currency linkage

贸易-财政-货币联系

1994年4月乌拉圭回合结束时发表的马拉喀什部长宣言中的内容。宣言设想WTO、国际货币基金组织、世界银行进行合作，在贸易、货币和财政领域实现全球决策更大一致性。另见*贸易与外汇(trade and foreign exchange)*、*贸易与税收(trade and taxation)*。

Trade harassment

贸易干扰

使用公开或隐蔽的国内措施作为故意刁难进口产品的手段。公开措施包括大量使用反倾销措施、保障措施或反补贴措施。有时仅是威胁采取此类措施即足以使进口商减少或停止自国外购买产品。在其他情况下，价格承诺可使进

price undertakings may make importing less attractive. Trade harassment can also occur through sham litigation. *See also* ***non-price predation***.

Trade in cultural property: *see* ***Beirut Agreement***, ***Convention on the Means of Prohibiting and Preventing the Illicit Import, Export and Transfer of Ownership of Cultural Property***, ***Florence Agreement*** and ***UNIDROIT Convention on Stolen or Illegally Exported Cultural Objects***. Under Article XX(f) of the GATT, WTO members may take trade measures necessary to protect national treasures of artistic, historic or archaeological significance. *See also* ***trade and culture***.

Trade-induced competition: a situation of enhanced competition on domestic markets caused by imported products. The extent to which trade-induced competition occurs depends on the level of market access foreign firms and their products have. *See also* ***import discipline hypothesis*** and ***international contestability of markets***.

Trade in services: the supply of ***services*** on commercial terms to residents of another country, either through ***cross-border trade*** or through ***commercial presence***. *See also* ***data protection in trade in services***, ***General Agreement on Trade in Services***, ***modes of services delivery***, ***services***, ***tradable*** and ***transactions in services***.

Trade in Services Agreement: TiSA. A proposal for the negotiation of a new agreement on ***trade in services*** launched in 2012. It builds on the ***General Agreement on Trade in Services***, (GATS), but it is independent of it. It also seeks to include elements of existing ***free-trade agreements***. One important difference from the GATS is that market access commitments are made through positive lists, but ***national treatment*** is done through negative lists. Negotiations are conducted in Geneva, but not under the auspices of the World Trade Organization. Some twenty-three parties are participating. No timetable for the end of the negotiations is available.

Trade in services statistics: in all countries statistics for trade in ***services*** are much less detailed than they are for trade in goods. International financial statistics offer the only reliable way for recording the value of traded services since any service bought from another country eventually has to be paid for through the use of foreign exchange. Successive editions of the ***IMF Balance of Payments Manual*** have made services statistics much more informative, and further improvements no doubt will be made. The sixth edition of the IMF Manual, published in 2010, classifies them in the following categories: manufacturing services on physical inputs owned by others, maintenance and repair services n.i.e. (not included elsewhere), transport, travel, construction, insurance and pension services, financial services, charges for the use of intellectual property n.i.e., telecommunications, computer and information services, other business services, personal, cultural and recreational services, and government goods and services n.i.e. Many governments now publish their services trade statistics using the sixth edition or in even more detailed form. Others continue to adhere to the less detailed fifth edition of 1993. This

口的吸引力下降。贸易干扰也可通过虚假诉讼发生。另见*非价格掠夺(non-price predation)*。

Trade in cultural property
文化财产贸易

见*贝鲁特协定(Beirut Agreement)*、*关于禁止和防止非法进出口文化财产和非法转让其所有权的方法的公约(Convention on the Means of Prohibiting and Preventing the Illicit Import, Export and Transfer of Ownership of Cultural Property)*、*佛罗伦萨协定(Florence Agreement)*、*国际统一私法协会关于被盗或非法出口文物的公约(UNIDROIT Convention on Stolen or Illegally Exported Cultural Objects)*。根据GATT第20条(f)款，WTO成员为保护具有艺术、历史或考古价值的国宝可以采取必要的贸易措施。另见*贸易与文化(trade and culture)*。

Trade-induced competition
贸易引发的竞争

进口产品造成国内市场竞争加剧的情况。贸易引发竞争的程度取决于外国公司及其产品的市场准入水平。另见*进口纪律假说(import discipline hypothesis)*、*市场的国际竞争性(international contestability of markets)*。

Trade in services
服务贸易

以商业条件向另一国居民提供服务，可通过跨境贸易或通过商业存在提供。另见*服务贸易中的数据保护(data protection in trade in services)*、*服务贸易总协定(General Agreement on Trade in Services)*、*服务提供模式(modes of services delivery)*、*服务(services)*、*贸易品(tradable)*、*服务交易(transactions in services)*。

Trade in Services Agreement
服务贸易协定

TiSA。2012年启动的谈判一项关于服务贸易的新协定的提案。协定以《服务贸易总协定》(GATS)为基础，但独立于该协定。还寻求纳入现有自由贸易协定的要素。与GATS的重要不同之处在于，市场准入承诺通过正面清单体现，而国民待遇通过负面清单体现。谈判在日内瓦举行，但不是在WTO主持下进行。约23个参加方参加谈判。目前无结束谈判的时间表。

Trade in services statistics
服务贸易统计

在所有国家中，服务贸易统计均不如货物贸易详细。国际金融统计数据提供了记录服务贸易价值的惟一可靠方法，因为自其他国家购买的任何服务最终均要通过使用外汇进行支付。连续多版国际货币基金组织(IMF)的《国际收支手册》使服务统计数字可以提供更多信息，且毫无疑问将得到进一步改进。2010年出版的IMF手册第6版将服务分为以下类别：对他人拥有的有形投入的制造服务；别处未包括的保养和维修；运输；旅行；建筑；保险和养恤金服务；金融服务；别处未包括的知识产权使用费；电信、计算机和信息服务；其他商业服务；个人、文化和娱乐服务以及别处未包括的政府货物和服务。许多国家政府现在使用第6版手册或更详细的表格公布其服务贸易统计。其他国家政府继续使用不那么详细的1993年版本。该版本将服务分为交通运输、旅行、通信服务、建设、计算机和信息服务、特许权使用费及许可费以及其他商业服务。

disaggregates services into transportation, travel, communication services, construction services, computer and information services, royalties and license fees, and other business services. The *World Trade Statistics Review,* published annually by the WTO, also provides detailed trade in services statistics and a dataset on trade in services by mode of supply. *See also* ***Inter-Agency Task Force on Statistics of International Trade in Services***. [www.imf.org]

Trade Integration Mechanism: TIM. A mechanism established by the ***IMF*** in 2004 to help member countries in meeting balance of payments shortfalls that might be caused by multilateral trade liberalization. It is not a specific lending facility, but rather a policy designed to make resources available under other IMF lending facilities more predictable. Member countries can apply for consideration under this mechanism if they expect a net balance of payments shortfall because of measures implemented by other countries that lead to more open market access for goods and services. [imf.org]

Trade intensity: a measure of the importance of trade to a given economy. It is the proportion of imports and exports of goods and services in relation to the total economy.

Trade is good, but imports are bad: *see* ***balance of trade***.

Trade liberalization: a general term for the gradual or complete removal of existing impediments to trade in goods and services. ***Free trade*** may be its ultimate aim, but more likely it is freer trade. Investment restrictions may also be covered by this term if investment in the target market is necessary for effective market access. *See also* ***trade facilitation***.

Trademark Law Treaty: a treaty negotiated in 1994 under ***WIPO*** auspices aimed at making national and regional ***trademarks*** systems easier to use. It seeks to do this through the simplification and harmonization of procedures. The Treaty entered into force on 1 August 1996. *See also* ***Madrid Agreement for the Repression of False or Deceptive Indications of Source on Goods***, ***Nice Agreement Concerning the International Classification of Goods and Services for the Purposes of the Registration of Marks*** and ***Singapore Treaty on the Law of Trademarks***.

Trademarks: words, names, symbols, devices or combinations of these, used by manufacturers and merchants to identify their goods and to distinguish them from the products of their competitors. *See also* ***Agreement on Trade-Related Aspects of Intellectual Property Rights***, ***famous mark***, ***intellectual property***, ***service mark***, ***Singapore Treaty on the Law of Trademarks***, ***Trademark Law Treaty*** and ***well-known mark***.

Trade measures: laws, regulations or rules adopted by a government which influence the way goods are traded across borders. ***Tariffs***, ***non-tariff measures*** and ***trade remedies*** are the main ones. However, domestic regulations not framed primarily with foreign trade in mind, such as health, safety and licensing regulations, can also have more or less pronounced effects on trade. *See also* ***sanitary and phytosanitary measures*** and ***technical barriers to trade***.

WTO每年出版的《世界贸易统计》还提供了详细的服务贸易统计数据和按供应模式分列的服务贸易数据。另见*国际服务贸易统计机构间特别工作组(Inter-Agency Task Force on Statistics of International Trade in Services)*。

Trade Integration Mechanism
贸易一体化机制

TIM。国际货币基金组织(IMF)在2004年设立的机制，旨在帮助成员国解决多边贸易自由化可能引起的国际收支差额问题。不是专项贷款，而是一项旨在使IMF其他贷款措施项下的资源更具可预测性的政策。成员国如果预期因其他国家实施更为开放的货物和服务市场准入而出现国际收支差额，可以申请在这一机制下得到审议。

Trade intensity
贸易强度

衡量贸易对一指定经济体的重要性的指标。为进口和出口的货物和服务占经济总量的比例。

Trade is good, but imports are bad
贸易是好的，但进口是坏的

见*贸易平衡(balance of trade)*。

Trade liberalization
贸易自由化

逐渐或全部取消货物贸易和服务贸易现有障碍做法的统称。自由贸易可能是贸易自由化的最终目标，但更有可能是更自由的贸易。如果投资在目标市场中是实现有效市场准入所必需的，那么投资限制也可为这一词语所涵盖。另见*贸易便利化(trade facilitation)*。

Trademark Law Treaty
商标法条约

在世界知识产权组织(WIPO)主持下于1994年谈判的条约，旨在使国家和区域商标体系更易使用。条约寻求通过简化和协调程序实现这一目标。于1996年8月1日生效。另见*制止商品来源虚假或欺骗性标记马德里协定(Madrid Agreement for the Repression of False or Deceptive Indications of Source on Goods)*、*商标注册用商品和服务国际分类尼斯协定(Nice Agreement Concerning the International Classification of Goods and Services for the Purposes of the Registration of Marks)*、*商标法新加坡条约(Singapore Treaty on the Law of Trademarks)*。

Trademarks
商标

生产商和商人用于识别其货物并与其竞争者的产品相区别而使用的文字、名称、符号、图案或以上各项的组合。另见*与贸易有关的知识产权协定(Agreement on Trade-Related Aspects of Intellectual Property Rights)*、*著名商标(famous mark)*、*知识产权(intellectual property)*、*服务标志(service mark)*、*商标法新加坡条约(Singapore Treaty on the Law of Trademarks)*、*商标法条约(Trademark Law Treaty)*、*驰名商标(well-known mark)*。

Trade measures
贸易措施

一国政府所采取的影响跨境货物交易方式的法律、法规或规定。主要包括关税、非关税措施和贸易救济。但是，国内规章在制定时并未考虑对外贸易因素，例如健康、安全与许可制度等，也可以或多或少对贸易产生显著影响。另见*卫生与植物卫生措施(sanitary and phytosanitary measures)*、*技术性贸易壁垒(technical barriers to trade)*。

Trade negotiations between developing countries: in November 1971 GATT members agreed to a ***waiver*** from the most-favoured-nation rule to permit developing countries to accord each other preferential treatment. Some fifteen developing countries availed themselves of this opportunity. These trade negotiations, conducted under GATT auspices, led to modest results. *See also* ***Asia-Pacific Trade Agreement***, ***developing countries and the multilateral trading system***, ***ECDC*** and ***GSTP***.

Trade Negotiations Committee: TNC. A committee usually established at the start of a multilateral round of trade negotiations. It consists of all participants and acts mainly as a transparency and stocktake mechanism. Its size makes it unwieldy for actual negotiations. *See also* ***multilateral trade negotiations***.

Trade-neutral measures: measures taken by governments for reasons unrelated to the regulation of international trade which do not have any effect on the flow of trade.

Trade openness: denotes the extent to which a country is receptive to imports and international competition. *See also* ***indicators of market competition***, ***OECD Services Trade Restrictiveness Index***, ***Overall Trade Restrictiveness Index***, ***Trade Restrictiveness Index*** and ***World Bank Services Trade Restrictiveness Index***.

Trade pledge: a name sometimes used for the idea of a ***standstill***. The term was apparently first used in 1974 by the ***OECD***.

Trade Policies for a Better Future*:** *see* ***Leutwiler Report.

Trade policy: the complete framework of laws, regulations, international agreements and negotiating stances adopted by government to achieve legally binding market access for domestic firms. Trade policy also seeks to develop rules providing predictability and security for firms. Fundamental components of trade policy are ***most-favoured-nation treatment***, ***national treatment***, ***transparency*** and ***exchange of concessions***. To be effective, trade policy needs to be supported by domestic policies to foster innovation and international competitiveness, and it needs to be conducted with flexibility and pragmatism. It is worth bearing in mind the observation by Bernard Hoekman and Michael Kostecki in *The Political Economy of the World Trading System* that trade policy is by definition a nationalistic policy in that it discriminates against foreign producers. Put differently, it represents the international dimension of national policies adapted for domestic reasons. *See also* ***commercial policy***, ***common commercial policy*** and ***four pillars of trade liberalization***. [Hoekman and Kostecki 1995]

Trade Policy Committee: the ***European Union*** body charged with assisting the ***European Commission*** in its conduct of the ***common commercial policy***. Article 207 of the ***Treaty on the Functioning of the European Union*** states that the Commission will be assisted by a special committee appointed by the ***European Council*** to conduct negotiations of agreements falling under the purview of Article 207. That special committee is the Trade Policy Committee.

Trade Policy Framework Review: a programme offered by ***UNCTAD*** to assist countries in a systematic manner. The focus of the review is on identifying key

Trade negotiations between developing countries
发展中国家间贸易谈判

GATT缔约方在1971年11月同意给予最惠国待遇豁免，以允许发展中国家相互给予优惠待遇。约15个发展中国家利用了这一机会。这些在GATT主持下开展的谈判成果有限。另见*亚太贸易协定(Asia-Pacific Trade Agreement)*、*发展中国家与多边贸易体制(developing countries and the multilateral trading system)*、*发展中国家间经济合作(ECDC)*、*全球贸易优惠制(GSTP)*。

Trade Negotiations Committee
贸易谈判委员会

TNC。在多边贸易谈判回合开始时通常设立的委员会。由所有参加方组成，主要作为透明度和盘点机制。其规模使实际谈判尾大不掉。另见*多边贸易谈判(multilateral trade negotiations)*。

Trade-neutral measures
贸易中立措施

政府采取的措施，采取原因与国际贸易规定无关，对贸易流动不会产生影响。

Trade openness
贸易开放度

表示一国对进口和国际竞争的接受程度。另见*市场竞争度指标(indicators of market competition)*、*OECD服务贸易限制目录(OECD Services Trade Restrictiveness Index)*、*总体贸易限制指数(Overall Trade Restrictiveness Index)*、*贸易限制指数(Trade Restrictiveness Index)*、*世界银行服务贸易限制指数(World Bank Services Trade Restrictiveness Index)*。

Trade pledge
贸易保证

有时用于表达维持现状想法的词语。这一词语显然首次是经济合作与发展组织(OECD)在1974年首次使用的。

Trade Policies for a Better Future
促进更美好未来的贸易政策

见*路特威勒报告(Leutwiler Report)*。

Trade policy
贸易政策

政府采用的一套包括法律、法规、国际协定和谈判立场的完整框架，旨在为国内企业实现具有法律约束力的市场准入。贸易政策还寻求制定为企业提供可预测和安全的规则。贸易政策的基本构成包括最惠国待遇、国民待遇、透明度和交换减让。为产生效果，贸易政策需要国内政策的支持以提高创新和国际竞争力，同时也需要灵活且现实的方式实施。值得注意的是，伯纳德·霍克曼和迈克尔·科斯特基在《世界贸易体制的政治经济学》一书中提到，贸易政策从定义上讲是民族主义政策，即歧视外国生产商。换言之，贸易政策代表着为国内原因而采用的国内政策的国际方面。另见*商业政策(commercial policy)*、*共同商业政策(common commercial policy)*、*贸易自由化四大支柱(four pillars of trade liberalization)*。

Trade Policy Committee
贸易政策委员会

欧盟机构，负责协助欧盟委员会执行共同商业政策。《欧洲联盟运行条约》第207条规定，委员会将得到由欧洲理事会指定的一个特别委员会的协助，以开展属第207条范围的协定的谈判。特别委员会即贸易政策委员会。

Trade Policy Framework Review
贸易政策框架审议

联合国贸易与发展会议(UNCTAD)提供的系统协助各国的方案。审议的重点

sectors for diversification, matching trade policies with development priorities and making sure of effective implementation. [www.unctad.org]

Trade policy review: a review conducted at fixed intervals in the WTO under the ***Trade Policy Review Mechanism***. Its main aim is a smoother functioning of the ***multilateral trading system***.

Trade Policy Review Body: TPRB. The WTO ***General Council*** when it exercises its responsibilities under the ***Trade Policy Review Mechanism***.

Trade Policy Review Mechanism: TPRM. A ***WTO*** review mechanism established in December 1988 at the Montreal Ministerial Meeting which conducted a midterm review of the ***Uruguay Round***. It is managed by the ***Trade Policy Review Body***. The TPRM is aimed at a smoother functioning of the ***multilateral trading system*** through greater domestic and international ***transparency*** in the trade regime of individual WTO members. The review is supported by a report prepared by the member under review and a report prepared by the WTO Secretariat under its own responsibility. The Secretariat can also draw on the trade monitoring reports of the entire WTO membership. Issues may be raised regardless of whether they are covered by WTO rules, though there is an understanding that they should be related to the ***trade policy*** of the country being examined. Reviews are conducted according to a fixed timetable. The frequency of reviews is related to the share of world trade, with large traders being reviewed more often. The TPRM is not used for the enforcement of specific WTO obligations or for ***dispute settlement*** procedures. *See also* ***surveillance***.

Trade promotion: activities designed to increase a firm's or a country's export trade. It includes participation in trade fairs, trade missions, publicity campaigns, etc. *See also* ***trade facilitation***.

Trade Promotion Agreement: TPA. A type of ***free-trade agreement*** the United States has concluded with Colombia (2012), Panama (2012) and Peru (2009). Together with Bolivia these countries had previously preferential trade treatment by the United States under the Andean Trade Promotion and Drug Eradication Act of 2002.

Trade Promotion Authority: TPA. The name adopted in the US Trade Act of 2002 for the negotiating authority given by the United States Congress to the President. Before that it had been known as ***fast-track***. It defines United States negotiating objectives and priorities for trade agreements and establishes consultation and notification requirements for the President to follow during the negotiating process. At the end of the negotiations Congress either votes for against the agreement. Amendments are not possible. In this way the TPA reaffirms the overall constitutional role of Congress in the development and management of United States trade policy. The current TPA came into force in 2015 for three years and an extension to 1 July 2021 if neither part of Congress objects to doing so. Extension duly happened on 2 July 2018. Overall trade negotiating objectives (in abbreviated form) are (1) more open, equitable and reciprocal market access, (2) reduction or elimination of barriers and distortions

是确定关键的多元化部门，使贸易政策与发展优先事项相匹配，并保证有效实施。

Trade policy review

贸易政策审议

在贸易政策审议机制下，在WTO中以固定时间间隔进行的审议。主要目的是使多边贸易体制的运行更为顺畅。

Trade Policy Review Body

贸易政策审议机构

TPRB。行使贸易政策审议机制项下职责时的WTO总理事会。

Trade Policy Review Mechanism

贸易政策审议机制

TPRM。WTO审议机制，最初在1988年12月对乌拉圭回合进行中期审评的蒙特利尔部长级会议上设立。该机制由贸易政策审议机构管理。TPRM旨在通过提高WTO各成员贸易制度的国内和国际透明度，使多边贸易体制的运行更加顺畅。审议得到接受审议成员起草的报告和WTO秘书处自负其责起草的报告的支持。秘书处还可参考WTO全体成员的贸易监督报告。问题无论是否为WTO规则所涵盖均可提出，但共识是，所提问题应与接受审议国家的贸易政策有关。审议根据固定时间表开展。审议的频率与世界贸易份额相关联，较大贸易方接受审议的频率较高。TPRM并不用于执行WTO具体义务或争端解决程序。*另见监督(surveillance)*。

Trade promotion

贸易促进

旨在增加一公司或一国出口贸易的活动。包括参加贸易展览会、贸易代表团、宣传活动等。*另见贸易便利化(trade facilitation)*。

Trade Promotion Agreement

贸易促进协定

TPA。美国与哥伦比亚(2012年)、巴拿马(2012年)和秘鲁(2009年)缔结的一种自由贸易协定。这些国家与玻利维亚均根据2002年《安第斯贸易促进与毒品根除法》享受美国的优惠贸易待遇。

Trade Promotion Authority

贸易促进授权

TPA。美国《2002年贸易法》中采用的名称，指美国国会赋予总统的谈判授权，此前称为快轨授权。TPA规定了美国贸易协定的谈判目标和优先事项及总统在谈判过程中遵循的磋商和通报要求。在谈判结束时，国会会投票选择支持或反对协定，不能进行修正。通过此种方式，TPA重申了国会在制定和管理美国贸易政策方面的总体宪法地位。现行TPA于2015年生效，有效期3年，此后如果国会两院均不反对，即延长至2021年7月1日。延期应在2018年7月2日按期进行。贸易谈判总目标(简略而言)为：(1)更加开放、公正和互惠的市场准入；(2)减少或消除与贸易和投资及美国市场机会相关的壁垒和扭曲；(3)加强国际

directly related to trade and investment and the market opportunities for the United States, (3) strengthen international trade and investment disciplines and procedures, including dispute settlement, (4) foster economic growth, raise living standards, enhance the competitiveness of the United States and promote full employment, (5) ensure that trade and environmental policies are mutually supportive, (6) promote respect for worker rights and the rights of children consistent with core labour standards of the International Labour Organization (ILO), (7) provisions in trade agreements that do not weaken or reduce the protections available under domestic and environmental laws as an encouragement for trade, (8) equal access for small business to international markets, (9) promote universal ratification and full compliance with ILO Convention No. 182 concerning the Prohibition and Immediate Action for the Elimination of the Worst Forms of Child Labour, (10) ensure that trade agreements reflect the increasingly interrelated multi-sectoral nature of trade and investment activity, (11) recognize the growing significance of the Internet as a trading platform in international commerce, (12) take into account other legitimate United States domestic objectives, such as health or safety, essential security and consumer interests, and (13) take into account conditions relating to religious freedom of any party to negotiations for a trade agreement with the United States. *See also* ***United States trade agreements legislation***.

Trade protection: a term sometimes used by the ***European Union*** and others instead of ***trade remedies***.

Trade-related antitrust principles: the term used by Bernard Hoekman for the ***competition policy*** issues that might be covered in a future multilateral agreement on ***trade and competition***. [Hoekman 1996]

Trade-related aspects of competition law and policy: TRACLAP. A term used by some scholars to denote ***trade and competition***. *See also* ***Working Group on the Interaction between Trade and Competition Policy***.

Trade-related aspects of economic development: describes the WTO provisions concerning the participation of developing countries in the world trading system, particularly the ***Enabling Clause*** and ***Part IV of the GATT***.

Trade-related aspects of electronic commerce: a subject proposed by some WTO members for future negotiations in the WTO. Not yet on any negotiating agenda. *See also* ***electronic commerce***.

Trade-related aspects of intellectual property rights: TRIPS. *See* ***Agreement on Trade-Related Aspects of Intellectual Property Rights***.

Trade-related aspects of monetary measures: an expression used by some to refer to the provisions contained in GATT Article XV concerning exchange arrangements.

Trade-related capacity-building: *see* ***capacity-building***.

Trade-related human rights: *see* ***trade and human rights*** and ***trade and labour standards***.

Trade-related investment measures: TRIMs. *See* ***Agreement on Trade-Related Investment Measures***.

贸易和投资纪律及程序，包括争端解决；(4)促进经济增长，提高生活水平，提高美国的竞争力，并促进充分就业；(5)保证贸易和环境政策相互支持；(6)根据国际劳工组织(ILO)的核心劳工标准，促进对工人权利和儿童权利的尊重；(7)贸易协定条款作为鼓励贸易的手段不削弱或减少国内法和环境法；(8)小企业平等进入国际市场；(9)推动对国际劳工组织第182号公约,即《禁止和立即行动消除最恶劣形式的童工劳动公约》的普遍认同和充分遵守；(10)保证贸易协定反映贸易和投资活动中日益关联多部门的性质；(11)认识到互联网作为国际商业中贸易平台的日益增加的重要性；(12)考虑美国其他合法国内目标，例如健康或安全、基本安全和消费者利益；以及(13)考虑与美国进行贸易协定谈判的任何一方与宗教自由相关的条件。另见*美国贸易协定立法(United States trade agreements legislation)*。

Trade protection
贸易保护

欧盟和其他国家有时用于替代贸易救济的词语。

Trade-related antitrust principles
与贸易有关的反垄断原则

伯纳德·霍克曼对未来关于贸易与竞争的多边协定中可能涵盖的竞争政策问题的用语。

Trade-related aspects of competition law and policy
与贸易有关的竞争法与政策

TRACLAP。一些学者用于表示贸易与竞争的词语。另见*贸易与竞争政策相互关系工作组(Working Group on the Interaction between Trade and Competition Policy)*。

Trade-related aspects of economic development
与贸易有关的经济发展

指WTO条款中有关发展中国家参与世界贸易体制的条款，特别是授权条款和GATT第四部分。

Trade-related aspects of electronic commerce
与贸易有关的电子商务

一些WTO成员为WTO中未来谈判提出的议题，该议题尚未列入任何谈判议程。另见*电子商务(electronic commerce)*。

Trade-related aspects of intellectual property rights
与贸易有关的知识产权

TRIPS。见*与贸易有关的知识产权协定(Agreement on Trade-Related Aspects of Intellectual Property Rights)*。

Trade-related aspects of monetary measures
与贸易有关的货币措施

一些人用于指GATT第15条中所含关于外汇安排的条款。

Trade-related capacity-building
与贸易有关的能力建设

见*能力建设(capacity-building)*。

Trade-related human rights
与贸易有关的人权

见*贸易与人权(trade and human rights)*、*贸易与劳工标准(trade and labour standards)*。

Trade-related investment measures
与贸易有关的投资措施

TRIMs。见*与贸易有关的投资措施协定(Agreement on Trade-Related Investment Measures)*。

Trade-related technical assistance: TRTA. Assistance given to developing countries through bilateral, regional or multilateral schemes to promote their integration into the global system. Such schemes usually aim to improve the competitiveness of receiving countries as well as enabling them to operate more effectively within the multilateral rules. *See also* ***capacity-building*** and ***Doha Development Agenda Global Trust Fund***.

Trade relief: the easing of competitive pressures on domestic firms through the use of ***trade remedies***.

Trade remedies: usually refers to ***anti-dumping measures***, countervailing duties and ***safeguards*** to deal with the effects of trade actions by others. The selection of the available trade remedy depends on the section of the trade law applicable to each case. It can include ***tariff*** increases, ***import quotas***, ***countervailing measures***, ***retaliation***, etc. *See also* ***Section 201***, ***Section 301***, ***Special 301*** and ***Super 301***.

Trade-restrictive environmental measures: measures to protect the environment which have a restrictive impact on trade. The impact may be direct and intended, as in the case of United States measures to protect dolphins, or it may be incidental. *See also* ***trade and environment***, ***Tuna (Canada–United States, 1982)***, ***Tuna I*** and ***Tuna II***.

Trade-restrictive measures: the set of essential measures, such as health and safety provisions, and discretionary actions aimed at influencing trade flows. Many trade-restrictive measures are permitted, subject to various conditions, by a range of WTO agreements. *See* further ***Agreement on Safeguards***, ***Agreement on Technical Barriers to Trade***, ***Agreement on the Application of Sanitary and Phytosanitary Measures***, ***anti-dumping measures***, ***APEC Cross-Cutting Principles on Non-Tariff Measures***, ***non-tariff measures***, ***OECD Services Trade Restrictiveness Index***, ***Overall Trade Restrictiveness Index***, ***red-tape barriers***, ***safeguards*** and ***Trade Restrictiveness Index***.

Trade Restrictiveness Index: TRI. A way to measure the extent to which a traded good or service encounters obstacles from the time it leaves the exporter until it reaches the importer. Since Neery and Anderson devised their pioneering method, several broad-based indices have become available, including the ones listed here. ***UNCTAD*** uses the Tariff Trade Restrictiveness Index (TTRI) to measure the average level of trade restrictions imposed on imports and the Market Access-Tariff Trade Restrictiveness (MA-TTRI) which measures the average level of tariff restrictions imposed on exports. The ***World Bank*** maintains an ***Overall Trade Restrictiveness Index*** (OTRI) to calculate the weighted average tariff of a given country. The OECD ***Services Trade Restrictiveness Index*** (STRI) analyses services trade barriers in twenty-two sectors across forty-four countries. The World Bank also offers Services Trade Restrictiveness Index which covers telecommunications, transport, financial services, retail and professional services in 103 countries.

Trade reversal: a term used by Max Corden to describe the situation whereby a country has traditionally been an importer of a good and which, through the

Trade-related technical assistance
与贸易有关的技术援助

TRTA。通过双边、区域或多边方案给予发展中国家的援助，以促进其融入全球体制。此类方案通常旨在提高受援国的竞争力，并使其能够在多边规则中更有效运转。另见*能力建设(capacity-building)*、*多哈发展议程全球信托基金(Doha Development Agenda Global Trust Fund)*。

Trade relief
贸易救济

通过使用贸易救济缓解国内企业的竞争压力。

Trade remedies
贸易救济

通常指为应对其他国家贸易措施影响而实施的反倾销措施、反补贴税和保障措施。对可使用的贸易救济措施的选择取决于对每种情况适用的贸易法章节。可以包括提高关税、进口配额、反补贴措施、报复等。另见*201条款(Section 201)*、*301条款(Section 301)*、*特别301条款(Special 301)*、*超级301条款(Super 301)*。

Trade-restrictive environmental measures
限制贸易的环境措施

对贸易有限制性影响的环境保护措施。影响可能是直接和有意的，例如美国保护海豚的措施，或可能是无意的。另见*贸易与环境(trade and environment)*、*1982年加拿大-美国金枪鱼案(Tuna (Canada–United States, 1982))*、*第一个金枪鱼案(Tuna I)*、*第二个金枪鱼案(Tuna II)*。

Trade-restrictive measures
贸易限制措施

旨在影响贸易流动的一套基本措施，例如健康和安全规定，及自由裁量行动。许多贸易限制措施在遵守不同条件的情况下可被一系列WTO协定所允许。另见*保障措施协定(Agreement on Safeguards)*、*技术贸易壁垒协定(Agreement on Technical Barriers to Trade)*、*实施卫生与植物卫生措施协定(Agreement on the Application of Sanitary and Phytosanitary Measures)*、*反倾销措施(anti-dumping measures)*、*APEC非关税措施交叉原则(APEC Cross-Cutting Principles on Non-Tariff Measures)*、*非关税措施(non-tariff measures)*、*OECD服务贸易限制性指数(OECD Services Trade Restrictiveness Index)*、*总体贸易限制指数(Overall Trade Restrictiveness Index)*、*繁文缛节壁垒(red-tape barriers)*、*保障措施(safeguards)*、*贸易限制指数(Trade Restrictiveness Index)*。

Trade Restrictiveness Index
贸易限制指数

TRI。衡量所交易的货物或服务自离开出口商时起至抵达进口商时止所遇阻碍程度的一种方法。自从尼尔力和安德森发明了这一开创性方法起，出现过多个宽基指数，包括：联合国贸易与发展会议(UNCTAD)使用关税贸易限制指数(TTRI)衡量对进口实施的贸易限制平均水平，使用市场准入-关税贸易限制指数(MA-TTRI)衡量对出口实施的关税限制平均水平。世界银行使用总体贸易限制指数(OTRI)以计算一指定国家的加权平均关税。经济合作与发展组织(OECD)使用服务贸易限制性指数(STRI)分析44个国家中22个部门的服务贸易壁垒。世界银行还提供涵盖103个国家的电信、运输、金融服务、零售和专业服务的服务贸易限制指数。

Trade reversal
贸易逆转

马克斯·科登用于描述一国传统上是一货物的进口国，通过征收进口关税和

imposition of an import tariff and an export subsidy, becomes an exporter. [Corden 1971]

Trade secrets: information deriving its value from not being known to the public, competitors or other parties who may gain benefits from its disclosure or use. *See also* ***Agreement on Trade-Related Aspects of Intellectual Property Rights, data protection in trade in services*** and ***material transfer agreement***.

Trade suppression: a term introduced by Jacob Viner and popularized by Max Corden. It describes the replacement, following the formation of a ***customs union*** or a ***free-trade area***, of a cheaper production source outside the union or area by a more expensive source within the newly formed preferential area. The more expensive source could now be more competitive because it could benefit from the absence of tariffs. *See also* ***trade creation*** and ***trade diversion***. [Corden 1985]

Trade surplus: this comes about when in a given period the value of one's exports exceeds that of one's imports. It is a goal pursued by most governments, but particularly stubbornly and sometimes mindlessly, by adherents of ***mercantilism*** who tend to look, in any case, at ***merchandise trade*** only. One should not assume that a trade surplus is intrinsically good and a ***trade deficit*** automatically bad. A meaningful assessment of the significance of a trade surplus can only be made by looking at the overall state of the economy. *See also* ***balance of trade***.

Trade war: a period of major trade disputes between often important trading partners. Usually those involved in such disputes seek a negotiated outcome acceptable to both sides and in conformity with the applicable trade rules. This can be a difficult task when, for example, large tariff increases are imposed to secure an outcome in a quite different area, such as intellectual property. When the dispute is between two large trading partners of about equal importance in the trading system, the matter can become intractable over an extended period since neither side will want to be seen to be backing down. One certainty is that producers and consumers in the affected countries will pay the price, though this may be mitigated to some extent if alternative sources of supply and markets are available. In addition, there probably will be consequences for third parties. Greg Mastel in *American Trade Laws after the Uruguay Round* notes that "a trade war is only a shade more rational than a nuclear war, harder to launch and nearly as unpalatable". That view may now not reflect adequately the ease with which a trade war may be launched, and how hard it can be to stop it. *See also* the 2018 UNCTAD ***Trade and Development Report*** for a detailed analysis of one scenario for a trade war. *See also* ***Chicken War*** and ***Ploughshares War***. [Mastel 1996]

Trade-weighted average tariffs: a method of calculating the average impact of a tariff regime through weighting tariffs according to the amount of trade in a given tariff line. Items traded in high volumes therefore have a greater impact on the calculation of the ***average tariff*** than items less or rarely traded. The major problem with this analytical approach is that high tariffs discourage trade

实施出口补贴而变为出口国的情况的词语。

Trade secrets

商业秘密

因不为公众、竞争对手或可能从其披露或使用中获益的其他方所知而产生价值的信息。另见*与贸易有关的知识产权协定(Agreement on Trade-Related Aspects of Intellectual Property Rights)*、*服务贸易中的数据保护(data protection in trade in services)*、*材料转让协定(material transfer agreement)*。

Trade suppression

贸易抑制

雅各布·韦纳提出并由马克斯·柯登推广的词语。描述在形成关税同盟或自由贸易区后，在同盟或自贸区之外的较便宜的生产来源被新建立的优惠区域内的较昂贵的来源所取代。更昂贵的来源因得益于取消关税而更具竞争力。另见*贸易创造(trade creation)*、*贸易转移(trade diversion)*。

Trade surplus

贸易顺差

指在一指定时期内一国出口额超过进口额的情况。这是大多数政府所追求的目标，但也是重商主义的追随者的非常固执、有时盲目追求的目标，他们在任何情况下只关注商品贸易。不应该认为贸易顺差本质上是好的，而贸易逆差就是坏的。对贸易顺差重要性的评估只有通过观察一国经济的总体状况才能作出。另见*贸易平衡(balance of trade)*。

Trade war

贸易战

重要贸易伙伴之间发生严重贸易争端的时期。通常此类争端所涉及的国家寻求一个双方均能接受并符合适用贸易规则的谈判结果。这可能是一项艰巨任务，例如大幅提高关税的目的是为了在知识产权等完全不同的领域取得结果。如果争端发生在贸易体制中同样重要的两个大型贸易伙伴之间，这一问题可能会在很长一段时间内变得棘手，因为任何一方都不希望被视为作出让步。可以确定的情况是，受影响国家中的生产者和消费者将付出代价，然后如果可以获得替代供应来源和市场，这种代价可能会在一定程度上得到减轻。此外，可能会对第三方产生影响。格雷格·马斯特尔在《乌拉圭回合后的美国贸易法》一书中指出，“贸易战只比核战争理性一点，更难以发动，而几乎同样难以接受。”这种观点可能现在不能充分反映贸易战发动的容易程度和阻止贸易战的难度。另见联合国贸易与发展会议(UNCTAD) 2018年《贸易与发展报告》中关于贸易战一种情况的详细分析。另见*鸡肉战(Chicken War)*、*犁铧战(Ploughshares War)*。

Trade-weighted average tariffs

贸易加权平均关税

通过按照一指定关税税目的贸易量对关税进行加权计算得出的关税制度平均影响的方法。贸易量大的商品因而在计算平均关税时比贸易量少或无交易的商品具有更大的影响。这种分析方法的主要问题是，高关税从一开始即阻碍

in the first place, and an average tariff calculated in this way is always likely to understate the actual level of tariff protection. Nevertheless, its general usefulness as an indicator of the overall incidence of tariff rates is not in doubt.

Trading rights: the right, accorded to selected firms, to import and export, particularly in ***centrally-planned economies*** or those in transition to ***market economies***. Trading rights may be limited to the export of goods or to trade in certain product categories. Firms need not be owned by the state to enjoy trading rights. *See also* ***state trading***.

Traditional comity: *see* ***negative comity***.

Traditional cultural expressions: used by many with largely the same meaning as expressions of ***folklore***, but seen as being more neutral than the term "folklore". They are a subset of ***traditional knowledge***. Traditional cultural expressions cover a wide variety of customs, traditions, forms of artistic expression, knowledge, beliefs, products, and so on. [WIPO/GRTKF/IC/5/3]

Traditional expressions: a term used in the administration of ***intellectual property rights*** as it may relate particularly to the quality, colour or type of wine, spirits and food. Examples of traditional expressions for wine are Spätlese, Qualitätswein, Grand Cru, vin primeur, vino generoso de licor, denominazione di origine controllata, etc. Such expressions may qualify for ***intellectual property protection*** under bilateral agreements. *See also* ***appellations of origin*** and ***geographical indications***.

Traditional knowledge: a new subject in discussions concerning the protection of ***intellectual property rights***. ***WIPO*** says that there is no agreed definition, but it is seen as encompassing medicinal, agricultural and ecological knowledge, music and dance, stories and poetry (folklore), the production of artefacts and spiritual expressions. Traditional knowledge is transmitted from generation to generation orally and by example. It is subject to collective responsibility and ownership, and it keeps on evolving. All of these characteristics make the development of a framework of protection a difficult task because intellectual property rights are best suited for codified and documented materials. WIPO also says that protection of intellectual property for traditional knowledge may take three main forms: (a) protection extended to the content, substance or idea of knowledge and culture, (b) protection extended to the form, expression or representation of traditional cultures, and (c) protection extended to the reputation and distinctive character of signs, symbols, indications, patterns and styles associated with traditional cultures. The ***Convention on Biological Diversity*** enjoins its parties to respect, preserve and maintain knowledge, innovations and practices of indigenous and local communities embodying traditional lifestyles relevant for the conservation and sustainable use of biological diversity. ***See*** also ***farmers' rights*** and ***folklore*** which raise similar considerations. [WIPO/GRTKF/IC/5/8]

Traditional speciality guaranteed: TSG. Part of the ***European Union*** system for protecting the name of a product originating in a specific region. This designation was previously known as ***certificate of specific character***. TSG

了贸易，以这种方式计算的平均关税常常有可能低估关税保护的实际水平。尽管如此，作为关税税率总体指数的普遍实用性是毋庸置疑的。

Trading rights

贸易权

给予选定企业进口和出口的权利，特别是在中央计划经济体或向市场经济体过渡的国家中。贸易权可能仅限于货物出口或某些产品类别的贸易。享受贸易权的企业不一定是国有企业。另见*国营贸易(state trading)*。

Traditional comity

传统礼让

见*消极礼让(negative comity)*。

Traditional cultural expressions

传统文化表现形式

许多人使用的词语，与民间文学艺术这一表述的含义大致相同，但被认为比“民间文学艺术”更为中性。属传统知识的一个子集。传统文化表达方式涵盖了种类繁多的习俗、传统、艺术表现形式、知识、信仰、产品等等。

Traditional expressions

传统表达方式

知识产权管理中使用的词语，可特别与葡萄酒、烈酒和食品的质量、颜色或种类相关。葡萄酒的传统表达方式的例子包括(德国)晚摘酒(Spätese)、(德国)优质葡萄酒(Qualitätswein)、(法国)特级园酒(Grand Cru)、(法国)期酒(primeur)、(西班牙)列性高度酒(generoso de licor)、(意大利)法定产区葡萄酒(denominazione di originalcontrollata)等。此类表达方式可以根据双边协定获得知识产权保护的资格。另见*原产地名称(appellations of origin)*、*地理标志(geographical indications)*。

Traditional knowledge

传统知识

正在讨论中的关于知识产权保护的新话题。世界知识产权组织(WIPO)表示，对此没有议定的定义，但可视为包括医学、农业和生态学知识、音乐和舞蹈、故事和诗歌(民间文学艺术)、手工艺品的生产和精神表达。传统知识通过口头和实例代代相传。服从于集体责任和所有权，并且不断演进。所有这些特征使制定保护框架任务艰巨，因为知识产权最适用于编纂成文的材料。WIPO还表示，对传统知识产权的保护可以采取三种主要形式：(a)将保护扩大到知识和文化的内容、实质或想法；(b)将保护扩大到传统文化的形式、表达方式或代表；以及(c)将保护扩大到与传统文化有关的标志、符号、指示、图案和样式的声誉和独特特征。《生物多样性公约》要求缔约方尊重、保存和维持土著和地方社区体现传统生活方式而与生物多样性保护和持久利用相关的知识、创新和做法。另见提出类似考虑的*农民权利(farmers' rights)*、*民间文学艺术(folklore)*。

Traditional speciality guaranteed

注册传统特色产品

TSG。欧盟保护源自一特定区域的产品名称制度的一部分，以往称为特定品

emphasizes the traditional aspects of a product, such as the way it is made or its composition. It is not linked to a specific area, but registration as a TSG product protects it against falsification or misuse. A label indicating TSG is mandatory for all products so registered. *See also* ***appellations of origin***, ***geographical indications***, ***protected designation of origin*** and ***protected geographical indication***.

Trafficking: the original meaning of this word was trading or engaging in commerce. It now tends to be used for unsavoury or illegal trading activities, such as the illegal drug trade. *See also* ***smuggling***.

Traffic light approach: a procedural framework adopted during the ***Uruguay Round*** negotiations on the reduction or elimination of subsidies. Negotiators agreed to a system which ultimately led them to categorize ***prohibited subsidies*** as red, ***actionable subsidies*** (i.e. subsidies that may be subject to ***countervailing measures*** because they are causing to harm to producers in other countries) as amber, and ***non-actionable subsidies*** (on which no countervailing measures may be taken) as green. Agricultural subsidies did not fall into this framework, and separate rules were negotiated on them as part of the ***Agreement on Agriculture***. It uses the ***green box***, ***blue box*** and ***amber box***. The traffic light approach had been tried unsuccessfully in the ***Tokyo Round*** and, indeed, in the early stages of the negotiations for the United States–Canada Free-Trade Agreement. ***UNCTAD*** has developed the concept of "red light" ***host country operational measures*** (HCOMs) denoting investment measures explicitly prohibited through multilateral agreements, such as the ***Agreement on Trade-Related Investment Measures***. "Yellow light" measures are additionally prohibited, conditioned or discouraged by inter-regional, regional or bilateral agreements. "Green light" HCOMs are the remaining measures not regulated by ***international investment agreements***.

Traffic rights: *see* ***freedoms of the air***.

Transaction-based definition of investment: *see* ***investment***.

Transactions in services: preferred by some analysts as an alternative to ***trade in services*** because they see it as emphasizing that much international activity in services is dependent on foreign direct investment, and that it is not simply cross-border trade. Trade in services, its competitor, appears to have won the day in ***trade policy*** formulation. *See also* ***cross-border trade in services*** and ***General Agreement on Trade in Services***.

Transaction value: a method for valuing goods to be imported for the purpose of assessing the ***customs duties*** payable. Under the WTO ***Customs Valuation Agreement***, it is the price actually paid or payable for the goods when sold under competitive conditions for export to the country of import. This method is based on the ***Brussels Definition of Value*** developed under the auspices of the Customs Cooperation Council, now the ***World Customs Organization***. *See also* ***customs valuation***.

Transaction value method: one of the methods used to establish whether a good imported from another party to a ***free-trade agreement*** qualifies for the

质证书。TSG强调一产品的传统特性，例如制作方法或构成。并不与特定地区相关联，但是注册为TSG的产品可以保护其不被仿制或滥用。按此注册的所有产品必须加贴TSG标签。另见*原产地名称(appellations of origin)*、*地理标志(geographical indications)*、*原产地命名保护(protected designation of origin)*、*地理标志保护(protected geographical indication)*。

Trafficking

非法交易

该词的最初含义是交易或从事商业活动。现在往往被用于不光彩或非法交易活动，例如非法毒品交易。另见*走私(smuggling)*。

Traffic light approach

交通灯法

乌拉圭回合谈判期间通过的关于减少或取消补贴的程序性框架。谈判方同意使用一种制度，最终将禁止性补贴列为红色，可诉补贴(即可能因对其他国家的生产者造成损害而被采取反补贴措施的补贴)列为黄色，并将不可诉补贴(不得采取反补贴措施的补贴)列为绿色。农业补贴不属于这一框架，就此谈判了单独的规则，作为《农业协定》的一部分。《农业协定》使用绿箱、蓝箱和黄箱。“交通灯法”在东京回合及《美国—加拿大自由贸易协定》谈判的初期均未成功。联合国贸易与发展会议(UNCTAD)制定了“红灯”东道国执行措施(HCOMs)的概念，用于表示由例如《与贸易有关的投资措施协定》等多边协定所明确禁止的投资措施，“黄灯”措施在区域间、区域或双边协定中受到禁止、限制或不予鼓励，“绿灯” HCOMs是国际投资协定所不管理的剩余措施。

Traffic rights

航权

见*航空自由(freedoms of the air)*。

Transaction-based definition of investment

基于交易的投资定义

见*投资(investment)*。

Transactions in services

服务交易

一些分析人士喜欢使用的服务贸易的替代词语，因为他们认为该词所强调的是服务业中许多国际活动依赖于外国直接投资，且不是简单的跨境贸易。服务贸易作为该词的竞争对手，似乎在贸易政策制定过程中获胜。另见*跨境服务贸易(cross-border trade in services)*、*服务贸易总协定(General Agreement on Trade in Services)*。

Transaction value

成交价格

为审定应付关税目的而对拟进口货物进行估价的方法。根据WTO《海关估价协定》，此种价格为在竞争条件下出口销售至进口国时的实付或应付价格。此种方法是根据海关合作理事会(CCC)，即现在的世界海关组织主持下制定的布鲁塞尔估价定义制定。另见*海关估价(customs valuation)*。

Transaction value method

成交价格法

用于确定自一自由贸易协定另一参加方进口的货物是否符合优惠关税资格的

preferential tariff. In the free-trade agreement between Canada and Chile the formula is:

$$RVC = \frac{TV - VNM}{TV} \times 100$$

where RVC is the ***regional value content***, expressed as a percentage (in this case 35 per cent), TV is the ***transaction value*** of the good adjusted to an ***FOB*** (free on board) basis, and VNM is the value of ***non-originating materials*** used by the producer in the production of the good. *See also* ***FOB value method***.

Transatlantic Business Dialogue: a mechanism established in 1995 involving European and United States business leaders to discuss trade and commercial issues of common interest and to propose solutions for the removal of obstacles to trade and investment across the Atlantic. *See also* ***New Transatlantic Agenda*** and ***New Transatlantic Marketplace***.

Transatlantic Free Trade Agreement: *see* ***TAFTA***.

Transatlantic Trade and Investment Partnership: TTIP. A proposed ***free-trade agreement*** being negotiated between the United States and the ***European Union***. Negotiations began in 2013. Current indications are that, once completed, TTIP will be a very comprehensive arrangement. *See also* ***New Transatlantic Agenda*** and ***Positive Economic Agenda***.

Transfer of technology: defined in the ***Draft International Code of Conduct on the Transfer of Technology*** as the transfer of systematic knowledge for the manufacture of a product, for the application of a process or for the rendering of a service. It does not extend to transactions involving the mere sale or mere lease of goods. The WTO ***Doha Ministerial Conference*** adopted a work programme on trade and transfer of technology. *See also* ***forced technology transfer***.

Transfer pricing: the practice of using pricing policies that are not based on market prices in order to achieve savings in taxation payments, to optimize the use of foreign exchange or for other reasons. The reference price used to ascertain whether transfer pricing has occurred is the arm's-length price. This is the price that would obtain between completely unrelated parties. Intra-corporate transactions and transactions between related parties are generally thought to be more at risk of exposure to transfer pricing. Articles 33 and 34 of the ***Draft United Nations Code of Conduct on Transnational Corporations*** seek to minimize its occurrence. *See also* ***arm's-length pricing*** and ***OECD Transfer Pricing Guidelines for Multinational Enterprises and Tax Administration***.

Transgenic product: a product containing a ***genetically modified organism*** or made of materials containing such an organism.

Transit fees: fees levied by countries for the handling of goods in transit. Such fees are in addition to freight charges, etc.

Transitional dumping: defined by some as the pricing of products below marginal cost in order to maximize sales and expand market share. There is room

方法。在加拿大与智利的自由贸易协定中，公式如下：

$$RVC = \frac{TV - VNM}{TV} \times 100$$

其中RVC为区域价值成分，以百分比表示(本例中为35%)，TV为按离岸价格(FOB)调整后的产品成交价格，VNM为生产商在生产货物中使用的非原产地材料的价值。另见*离岸价格法(FOB value method)*。

Transatlantic Business Dialogue
跨大西洋商业对话

1995年建立的机制，欧洲和美国商业领袖参加，讨论共同关心的贸易和商业问题，并提出消除跨大西洋贸易和投资障碍的解决办法。另见*新跨大西洋议程(New Transatlantic Agenda)*、*新跨大西洋市场(New Transatlantic Marketplace)*。

Transatlantic Free Trade Agreement
跨大西洋自由贸易协定

见*跨大西洋自由贸易协定(TAFTA)*。

Transatlantic Trade and Investment Partnership
跨大西洋贸易与投资伙伴关系协定

TTIP。美国和欧盟之间正在谈判的拟议自由贸易协定。谈判始于2013年。目前的迹象表明，一旦谈判完成，TTIP将是一个非常全面的贸易协定。另见*新跨大西洋议程(New Transatlantic Agenda)*、*积极经济议程(Positive Economic Agenda)*。

Transfer of technology
技术转让

《国际技术转让行动守则草案》将技术转让定义为为制造产品、应用工序或提供服务而转让系统性知识。不包含涉及仅销售或仅租赁货物的交易。WTO多哈部长级会议通过了一项关于贸易与技术转让的工作计划。另见*强制技术转让(forced technology transfer)*。

Transfer pricing
转让定价

使用不以市场价格为基础的定价政策以实现节省税款、优化外汇使用或其他目的的做法。参考价格用于确定转让定价是否为公平定价，该价格为在完全无关联方之间获得的价格。公司内部交易和关联方之间的交易通常被认为更容易受到转让定价的影响。《联合国跨国公司行为守则草案》第33条和第34条寻求尽量减少此种情况的发生。另见*公平定价(arm's-length pricing)*、*OECD跨国企业与税务机关转让定价指南(OECD Transfer Pricing Guidelines for Multinational Enterprises and Tax Administration)*。

Transgenic product
转基因产品

含有转基因生物或由含有转基因生物的材料制作的产品。

Transit fees
过境费

各国因处理过境货物而收取的费用。此类费用在运费等费用之外征收。

Transitional dumping
过渡性倾销

一些人将其定义为以低于边际成本对产品进行定价，以实现销售最大化和扩大市场份额。此种做法是否属掠夺性定价的一种形式仍存争议，特别是在此

for argument that such a practice would be a form of ***predatory pricing***, especially if it were to continue for an extended period. *See also* ***anti-dumping measures*** and ***dumping***.

Transitional economies: *see* ***economies in transition***.

Transitional measures: measures usually associated with the implementation of a new trade agreement when the old and new systems often exist side by side. Such measures are time-bound. Sometimes transitional measures have the purpose of giving developing countries more time to adjust to the new regime.

Transitional Product-Specific Safeguard Mechanism: a safeguard mechanism established in 2001 under the protocol for China's ***accession*** to the WTO and to terminate after twelve years, i.e. December 2013. It dealt with the possibility that Chinese products may cause or threaten to cause market disruption to domestic producers in other WTO members of directly competitive products. In such cases, WTO members could seek consultations aimed at finding a satisfactory solution, including possible recourse to the ***Agreement on Safeguards***. The protocol says that disruption shall exist whenever imports of an article, like or directly competitive with an article produced by the domestic industry, are increasing rapidly, either absolutely or relatively, so as to be a significant cause of material injury, or threat of material injury, to the domestic industry. *See also* ***Transitional Review Mechanism***.

Transitional Review Mechanism: a mechanism established in 2001 under the protocol for China's ***accession*** to the WTO to review annually for eight years progress made by China in bringing its trade regime into conformity with the WTO rules. The final review was specified to be made after ten years. Information to be provided by China included economic data, economic policies, its framework for making and enforcing policies, policies affecting trade in goods and services, and its trade-related intellectual property regime. *See also* ***Transitional Product-Specific Safeguard Mechanism***.

Transitional safeguard mechanism: Article 6 of the ***Agreement on Textiles and Clothing*** (expired on 1 January 2005) established a ten-year transition period for members to bring their trade in textiles and clothing under the normal WTO rules. During that transition period WTO members could impose restrictions against individual export countries if the importing country could show that both overall imports and of a product and imports from the individual countries were entering the country in such increased quantities as to cause, or threaten to cause, serious damage to the relevant domestic industry.

Transitional safeguards: many ***free-trade agreements*** permit the use of safeguards when ***tariffs*** are being phased out. This mechanism can no longer be used when the tariff for a product reaches zero. *See* ***bilateral transitional safeguards***.

Transition Report: published annually by the European Bank for Reconstruction and Development (EBRD). It contains detailed assessments of the progress made on economic liberalization by the ***economies in transition*** in Central

种做法持续很长一段时间的情况下。另见*反倾销措施(anti-dumping measures)*、*倾销(dumping)*。

Transitional economies

转型经济体

见*转型经济体(economies in transition)*。

Transitional measures

过渡性措施

通常与实施一项新贸易协定相关的措施，往往新旧体制同时存在。此类措施有时间限制。有时，过渡性措施的目的在于给予发展中国家更多时间以适应新制度。

Transitional Product-Specific Safeguard Mechanism

特定产品过渡性保障机制

根据中国加入WTO议定书在2001年设立的保障措施机制，在12年后即2013年12月终止。旨在处理中国产品可能造成或威胁造成对其他WTO成员中直接竞争产品的市场扰乱的情况。在此种情况下，WTO成员可以寻求进行磋商，以期找到双方满意的解决办法，包括可以援用《保障措施协定》。议定书规定，如果一项产品的进口快速增长，无论是绝对增长还是相对增长，从而构成对生产同类产品或直接竞争产品的国内产业造成或威胁造成实质损害，则存在市场扰乱。另见*过渡性审议机制(Transitional Review Mechanism)*。

Transitional Review Mechanism

过渡性审议机制

根据中国加入WTO议定书在2001年设立的机制，在8年内每年审议中国在使其贸易制度符合WTO规则方面取得的进展。最后一次审议是在加入10年后。中国提供的信息包括经济数据、经济政策、制定和执行政策的框架、影响货物和服务贸易的政策以及与贸易有关的知识产权制度。另见*特定产品过渡性保障机制(Transitional Product-Specific Safeguard Mechanism)*。

Transitional safeguard mechanism

过渡性保障机制

《纺织品与服装协定》(2005年1月1日终止)第6条为成员设立了将其纺织品和服装贸易纳入正常WTO规则的10年过渡期。在过渡期内，如果进口国能够证明一产品的总进口量及来自各国进口量增加，对相关国内产业造成或威胁造成严重损害，则WTO成员可以对个别出口国采取限制措施。

Transitional safeguards

过渡性保障措施

许多自由贸易协定允许在关税逐步取消过程中使用保障措施。这一机制在一种产品的关税降至零时不再使用。另见*双边过渡性保障措施(bilateral transitional safeguards)*。

Transition Report

转型报告

欧洲复兴开发银行(EBRD)每年出版。包含对中欧、东欧的转型经济体和独立

and Eastern Europe and the members of the ***Commonwealth of Independent States***.

Transit trade: goods passing through at least one other country between manufacture and reaching their final destination. This occurs, for example, when a country is landlocked and needs access to a sea port. *See also* ***transshipment***.

Transit zone: a place to which goods may be shipped temporarily pending their departure to their final destination. Usually, no further transformation of the goods takes place in a transit zone, and they are admitted free of duties other than applicable port or handling charges. *See also* ***entrepôt trade***.

Transnational corporations: TNCs. Also called multinational corporations (MNCs) or multinational enterprises (MNEs). They are large and very large corporations and conglomerates with production facilities and sales offices in many countries established as branches, subsidiaries or other units. Individual units usually report to a head office which may be a holding company. It can be quite difficult to establish where effective control over a unit within a TNC in a particular case lies. Their ownership can be diversified, and component units may have much autonomy in the conduct of their business. Units of a TNC may even compete with each other in world markets. Nevertheless, TNCs are often thought of as having a single nationality despite their appearance in many places. In many cases, such companies first rose to prominence in a single market, and their nationality was clear-cut then. In some circles TNCs, because of their ***market power*** and ability to influence production patterns, have been treated with great suspicion. Calls for greater controls over their activities have led, for example, to a ***Draft United Nations Code of Conduct on Transnational Corporations*** which, however, remains contentious and is unlikely to enter into force in the near future. More recently, TNCs have met a much more welcoming climate in potential host countries and in international organizations concerned with development issues because of their ability to mobilize investment funds, promote the ***transfer of technology*** and create employment. A main focus for analysis of issues relating to TNCs is the ***UNCTAD Commission on Investment, Enterprise and Development***, located within ***UNCTAD***, which also publishes the ***World Investment Report***. The ***OECD*** countries have adopted the ***OECD Guidelines for Multinational Enterprises*** as one instrument governing their handling of TNCs. *See also* ***dependence theory***, ***intra-firm trade*** and ***multi-domestic corporation***.

Transnationality index: a method developed by ***UNCTAD*** to measure the degree to which a ***transnational corporation*** (TNC) or a country (host economy) is actually transnational. In the case of TNCs, it does this by comparing home-country assets, sales and employment of a TNC with its assets, sales and employment abroad. The greater the weight of the foreign numbers, the more transnational a company is thought to be. In the case of countries, the index is calculated as the average of FDI inflows as a share of gross fixed capital formation, FDI inward stock as a percentage of GDP, value-added of foreign affiliates as a percentage of total national value-added, and employment of

国家联合体成员国经济自由化方面取得进展的详细评估。

Transit trade

过境贸易

货物在生产和抵达最终目的地之间经过至少一个其他国家的情况。例如，此种情况发生在一内陆国需要使用一海港时。另见*转运(transshipment)*。

Transit zone

过境区

货物在运往最终目的地之前可以暂时运到的一个地点。通常，货物在过境区内不会发生进一步改变，可以免税入境，除适用的港口或手续费外。另见*转口贸易(entrepôt trade)*。

Transnational corporations

跨国公司

TNCs。也称多国公司(MNCs)或多国企业(MNEs)。它们是在许多国家以分支机构、子公司或其他实体的形式建立生产设施和销售办事处的大型和超大型企业和企业集团。个体实体通常向总公司报告，总公司可能是一家控股公司。在特定情况下，很难确定跨国公司内部一实体的有效控制权在哪里。其所有权可以是多样化的，组成实体可以在开展业务方面有很大自主权。跨国公司的实体甚至可以在世界市场上相互竞争。但是，跨国公司常被视为拥有单一国籍，尽管它们在许多地方出现。在许多情况下，此类公司首先在一单一市场上暂露头角，其国籍此时是明确的。在某些圈子里，跨国公司因其市场支配力和影响生产模式的能力，受到极大质疑。例如，由于呼吁加强对跨国公司活动的控制而产生了《联合国跨国公司行为守则草案》，但其仍存争议，近期不太可能生效。最近，跨国公司在潜在的东道国和关注发展问题的国际组织中更加受到欢迎，因为它们有能力调动投资资金，促进技术转让和创造就业。分析与跨国公司有关问题的一个重点部门是设在联合国贸易与发展会议(UNCTAD)内的投资、企业和发展委员会，该委员会还出版《世界投资报告》。经济合作与发展组织(OECD)成员国已经采纳OECD《跨国企业行为准则》作为管理其处理跨国公司事务的文件。另见*依附理论(dependence theory)*、*公司内部贸易(intra-firm trade)*、*多国化公司(multi-domestic corporation)*。

Transnationality index

跨国指数

联合国贸易与发展会议(UNCTAD)制定的一种方法，以衡量一跨国公司(TNC)或一国(东道国经济)实际的跨国程度。对于跨国公司而言，指数通过比较一跨国公司的母国资产、销售和就业情况与其国外资产、销售和就业情况得出。国外数字的权重越大，一公司被认为具有的跨国性就越大。对于国家而言，指数计算为外国直接投资流入占固定资本形成总额份额、外国直接投资流入存量占国内生产总值百分比、外国子公司增加值占全国增加值总额百分比以及外

foreign affiliates as a percentage of total employment. The transnationality index of TNCs and countries is usually published in the ***World Investment Report***.

Trans-Pacific Partnership Agreement: TPP. Negotiations for this ***free-trade agreement*** began in 2008 in the context of a possible expansion of the ***Trans-Pacific Strategic Economic Partnership Agreement*** of 2005. In 2016 twelve countries (Australia, Brunei, Canada, Chile, Japan, Malaysia, Mexico, New Zealand, Peru, Singapore, United States and Viet Nam) signed the completed draft agreement. In January 2017 the United States announced its withdrawal from the Agreement. The remaining eleven countries decided to keep the Agreement alive, and this led to the ***Comprehensive and Progressive Agreement for Trans-Pacific Partnership*** which incorporates the TPP. The TPP has provisions outlining how it would enter into force, but these remain inoperative. It is one of the most comprehensive ***free-trade agreements***. It has thirty chapters covering trade in goods, textiles and apparel, rules of origin, customs administration and trade facilitation, sanitary and phytosanitary measures, technical barriers to trade, trade remedies, investment, trade in services, financial services, temporary entry, telecommunications, electronic commerce, government procurement, competition policy, state-owned enterprises, intellectual property, labour, environment, capacity-building and development, business facilitation, small- and medium-sized enterprises, regulatory coherence, transparency and anti-corruption and dispute settlement. The investment and trade in services chapters use negative lists for commitments. The financial services chapter uses a negative list. Submissions on dispute settlement would be made public, hearings would usually be open to the public and non-governmental bodies located in the territory of disputing party would be able to make submissions. The TPP attracted much negative comment in the course of its negotiation, not all of it based on either an understanding of the concepts or a close inspection of the draft text. As the ***Comprehensive and Progressive Agreement for Trans-Pacific Partnership*** entered into force on 30 December 2018, a more detailed description of the Agreement is given under that item.

Trans-Pacific Strategic Economic Partnership Agreement: a ***free-trade agreement*** between Brunei, Chile, New Zealand and Singapore. It entered into force on 28 May 2006. It gave impetus to the negotiation of the ***Trans-Pacific Partnership Agreement***.

Transparency: the degree to which trade policies and practices, and the process by which they are established, are open and predictable. The transparency obligation is spelt out in Article X of the ***GATT***, Article III of the ***General Agreement on Trade in Services*** and other provisions of the agreements administered by the WTO. Members are required to publish any laws, regulations, judicial decisions, ***administrative rulings of general application*** and international agreements pertaining to trade in goods and services. They must also administer these instruments reasonably and impartially. *See also* ***APEC principles on transparency standards***, ***notification***, ***surveillance*** and ***Trade Policy Review Mechanism***.

国子公司就业占总就业百分比。跨国公司和国家的跨国指数通常发表在《世界投资报告》中。

Trans-Pacific Partnership Agreement

跨太平洋伙伴关系协定

TPP。关于这一自由贸易协定的谈判始于2008年，在对2005年《跨太平洋战略经济伙伴关系协定》可能扩大的背景下。2016年，12个国家(澳大利亚、文莱、加拿大、智利、日本、马来西亚、墨西哥、新西兰、秘鲁、新加坡、美国和越南)签署完整的协定草案。2017年1月，美国宣布退出协定。其余11个国家决定保留协定，由此产生《全面与进步跨太平洋伙伴关系协定》，其中包含TPP。TPP中包含规定如何生效的条款，但这些条款仍未生效。TPP是最全面的自由贸易协定之一。共30章，涵盖货物贸易、纺织品和服装、原产地规则、海关管理和贸易便利化、卫生与植物卫生措施、技术性贸易壁垒、贸易救济、投资、服务贸易、金融服务、临时入境、电信、电子商务、政府采购、竞争政策、国有企业、知识产权、劳工、环境、能力建设和发展、商业便利化、中小型企业、监管一致性、透明度和反腐败以及争端解决。投资和服务贸易章节使用负面清单作出承诺。金融服务章节使用负面清单形式。关于争端解决的陈述将予以公开，听证会通常向公众开放，设在争端方领土内的非政府组织可以提交陈述。TPP在谈判过程中受到了许多负面评论，但并非所有评论都是基于对概念的理解或对案文草案的仔细审查作出的。《全面与进步跨太平洋伙伴关系协定》已于2018年12月30日生效，在该词条下对协定作了更为详细的说明。

Trans-Pacific Strategic Economic Partnership Agreement

跨太平洋战略经济伙伴关系协定

文莱、智利、新西兰和新加坡之间的自由贸易协定。协定于2006年5月28日生效，推动了《跨太平洋伙伴关系协定》的谈判。

Transparency

透明度

贸易政策和做法及其制定过程的开放和可预测程度。透明度义务载于GATT第10条、《服务贸易总协定》第3条以及WTO管理的其他协定条款。要求成员公布与货物服务和服务贸易有关的任何法律、法规、司法裁决、普遍适用的行政裁定以及国际协定。成员还必须合理和公正地管理这些文件。另见*APEC透明度标准原则(APEC principles on transparency standards)*、*通报(notification)*、*监督(surveillance)*、*贸易政策审议机制(Trade Policy Review Mechanism)*。

Transparency mechanism for RTAs: established through a decision taken by the ***General Council*** in December 2006 which further clarifies rules for ***WTO*** members to notify the WTO of new ***regional trade agreements*** (RTAs) and for procedures to be followed by the committee which considers RTAs. This would normally be the ***Committee on Regional Trade Agreements***. The mechanism sets out the timing of the notification and the type of information that members must provide to enable the WTO Secretariat to prepare a factual presentation on the RTA. Members consider the notified RTA on the basis of the factual presentation. The mechanism also requires members to notify changes to existing RTAs and to submit a report at the end of implementation of the RTA. It also encourages members to provide information on RTA negotiations. The transparency mechanism is implemented on a provisional basis. Members are to review and, if necessary, modify the decision and replace it by a permanent mechanism adopted as part of the overall results of the ***Doha Development Agenda***.

Transparent: sharing information, in this case so all members know what is happening in smaller group meetings. In ***WTO*** negotiations, and other decision-making, ideas are tested and issues are discussed in a variety of meetings, many of them with only some members present. Members approve of this process so long as information is shared. They also want the process to ensure that they can have input into it ("inclusive"). The final decision can only be taken by a formal meeting of the full membership. *See also* ***concentric circles*** and ***inclusive***.

Trans-Regional EU-ASEAN Trade Initiative: TREATI. A trade action plan adopted by the ***European Union*** on 9 July 2003 to expand trade and investment flows. Initial focus of activities was on trade facilitation, investment facilitation and promotion, sanitary and phytosanitary standards, industrial product standards and technical barriers to trade, intellectual property rights, and trade and the environment as well as tourism and forestry products. Negotiations for a free-trade agreement began in 2007, but progress was slow, and negotiations were suspended and replaced by bilateral negotiations between the European Union and individual ASEAN countries. Several free-trade agreements have been concluded.

Transshipment: the shipment of goods through an intermediary port in another country where they may have to be unloaded and reloaded. This is its main meaning. Another meaning refers to the practice of producing a good in one country, shipping it to another country that is part of a ***free-trade area***, attaching a new label to it and then forwarding it to its final destination, also a member of that free-trade area. In this way, the original producer and the importer are able to evade the payment of some ***customs duties***. As transshipment entails a cost, the production cost in the producing country would have to be low enough to absorb these and still leave a margin of profit. Opinions differ sharply on how prevalent this practice may be. In any case, ***free-trade agreements*** usually have detailed provisions to counter it. *See also* ***certificate of non-manipulation***, ***preferential rules of origin*** and ***tariff evasion***.

Transparency mechanism for RTAs

区域贸易协定透明度机制

根据总理事会2006年12月所作决定建立，该决定进一步澄清了WTO成员向WTO通报新的区域贸易协定(RTAs)的规则及委员会审议区域贸易协定应遵循的程序。通常由区域贸易协定委员会承担。该机制规定了通报的时间和成员必须提供的信息类型，以使WTO秘书处能够编写关于区域贸易协定的事实陈述。成员根据事实陈述审议通报的区域贸易协定。该机制还要求成员通报现有区域贸易协定的变更情况，并在区域贸易协定实施结束后提交报告。该机制也鼓励成员提供关于区域贸易协定谈判的信息。透明度机制在临时性基础上实施。成员将审议并在必要时修改该决定，使其成为一个常设机制作为多哈发展议程总体成果一部分获得通过。

Transparent

透明

分享信息，在此种情况下，所有成员均知道在小范围会议上所发生的事情。在WTO谈判和其他决策过程中，各种会议讨论不同想法和问题，许多会议只有部分成员出席。只要能够共享信息，成员即同意这一进程。他们也希望这一进程能够保证自己能够参与其中(“包容性”)。最终决定只能通过全体成员出席的正式会议作出。另见*同心圆(concentric circles)*、*包容性(inclusive)*。

Trans-Regional EU-ASEAN Trade Initiative

跨地区欧盟—东盟贸易倡议

TREATI。欧盟于2003年7月9日通过的贸易行动计划，旨在扩大贸易和投资流动。活动的最初重点是贸易便利化、投资便利化和促进、卫生和植物卫生标准、工业产品标准和技术性贸易壁垒、知识产权、贸易和环境以及旅游和林产品。自由贸易协定的谈判始于2007年，但进展缓慢，谈判已中止，取而代之的是欧盟与各东盟国家之间的双边谈判，已经缔结若干自由贸易协定。

Transshipment

转运

装运货物通过另一国家的中间港口，在该港口可能需要卸载和重新装载。这是该词的主要含义。另一个含义指在一国生产一货物，将其运至属自由贸易区一部分的另一国，加贴新标签后将其转至最终目的地的做法，该目的地也属该自由贸易区成员。通过这种方式，原生产商和进口商可以避免缴纳部分关税。由于转运需要成本，因而在生产国中的生产成本必须足够低以吸收这些成本，而仍然留有利润空间。人们对于这种做法可能有多普遍众说纷纭。在任何情况下，自由贸易协定通常包含详细的条款以应对此种情况。另见*未再加工证明(certificate of non-manipulation)*、*优惠原产地规则(preferential rules of origin)*、*逃税(tariff evasion)*。

Trans-Tasman Mutual Recognition Arrangement: TTMRA. An arrangement between Australia and New Zealand which enables the sale of goods originating in either country in the other country without the need for further testing or other conformance assessment. The TTMRA also covers skilled personnel. It enables a person registered to practise in either country to seek registration in the other without any need for further testing or the vetting of qualifications. The TTMRA entered into force on 1 January 1997. *See also* ***ANZCERTA***, ***mutual recognition arrangements*** and ***technical barriers to trade***.

Travaux préparatoires: the records produced by preparatory committees, expert groups, negotiating groups, etc., in the negotiations for a treaty or a convention. These records can give valuable guidance to the intentions of the drafters when ambiguous language has to be interpreted later, but this only works properly with consensus documents. Individual members of an agreement may make use of other, not agreed, *travaux préparatoires* to support their case in a dispute, but they still have to demonstrate that their interpretation is to be preferred. Article 32 of the ***Vienna Convention on the Law of Treaties*** sees *travaux préparatoires* as something to be employed with discretion and in the main only when the treaty text itself is not sufficiently clear to allow a single interpretation or when it would lead to a manifestly absurd or unreasonable result.

Treaties, the: in the context of the ***European Union*** the ***Treaty on European Union*** and ***Treaty on the Functioning of the European Union***.

Treaties of friendship, commerce and navigation: usually known as FCN treaties. A bilateral treaty form now obsolete. It sets out the terms under which bilateral trade and shipping are conducted, and it describes the rights of persons from one state conducting business in the other state or establishing a commercial presence there, including ownership of property. Main subjects covered by FCN treaties usually are rights of entry for business and residence, protection of individuals and companies, practice of professions, acquisition of property, ***patents***, taxes, remittance of earnings and capital, trade measures, expropriation and nationalization, etc. Earlier versions of FCN treaties also contained consular and customs provisions. FCN treaties are considered by some as a form of ***preferential trade arrangements***.

Treaty: defined in the ***Vienna Convention on the Law of Treaties*** as "an international agreement concluded between States in written form and governed by international law, whether embodied in a single instrument or in two or more related instruments and whatever its particular designation". Other names often used for a treaty are convention, covenant, ***protocol*** and exchange of letters, the latter two often being concluded as part of a treaty or to supplement a treaty after it has entered into force. Treaties are legal instruments under which the parties establish mutual rights and obligations. Through acceding to a treaty, the parties undertake to become obliged to behave in accordance with it, and to face the possibility of sanction if they do not. Treaties usually have to be ratified, sometimes through a constitutionally defined process, before they enter into

Trans-Tasman Mutual Recognition Arrangement
跨塔斯曼互认安排

TTMRA。澳大利亚和新西兰之间的一项安排，允许原产于两国的货物在另一国销售，无需进一步测试或其他合格评定。TTMRA也涵盖技术人员。使在两国中任一国注册执业的人员可在另一国注册执业，无需进一步测试或资格审查。TTMRA于1997年1月1日生效。另见*澳大利亚与新西兰更紧密经济关系贸易协定(ANZCERTA)*、*相互承认安排(mutual recognition arrangements)*、*技术性贸易壁垒(technical barriers to trade)*。

Travaux préparatoires
准备工作文件

筹备委员会、专家组、谈判组等在谈判条约或公约时所产生的记录。当日后必须对含义模糊的文字进行解释时，这些记录可以提供关于起草者意图的有价值的指导，但仅适用于协商一致的文件。协定各成员可以利用未经议定的其他准备工作文件以支持其在争端中的立场，但他们仍然需要证明他们的解释是可取的。《维也纳条约法公约》第32条将准备工作文件视为应慎重使用的材料，基本上是在条约文字本身意义仍属不明或难解，或所获结果显属荒谬或不合理时。

Treaties, the
条约

对于欧盟，指《欧洲联盟条约》和《欧洲联盟运行条约》。

Treaties of friendship, commerce and navigation
友好通商航海条约

通常称为FCN条约。现在已经过时的双边条约形式。规定开展双边贸易和航运的条件，并阐述一国的人在另一国开展商业活动或在该另一国建立商业存在的权利，包括财产所有权。FCN条约所涵盖的主要主题通常是商务和居住入境权、对个人和公司的保护、执业、获得财产、专利、税收、收入和资本汇出、贸易措施、征收和国有化等。早期版本的FCN条约还包含领事和海关条款。FCN条约被一些人认为是一种形式的优惠贸易安排。

Treaty
条约

《维也纳条约法公约》将其定义为“国家间所缔结而以国际法为准之国际书面协定，不论其载于一项单独文书或两项以上相互有关之文书内，亦不论其特定名称如何”。通常使用的表示条约的其他名称有公约、盟约、议定书和换文，后两者通常作为条约的一部分缔结，或在条约生效后作为条约的补充缔结。条约是参加方据此建立共同权利和义务的法律文书。通过加入条约，参加方承诺依照条约行事的义务，并承诺如不如此行事即面临制裁的可能。条约通

effect. *See also* ***good faith***, ***memorandum of understanding*** and ***pacta sunt servanda***.

Treaty establishing the European Community: *see* ***European Union treaties***.

Treaty establishing the European Economic Community: *see* ***European Union treaties*** and ***Treaty of Rome***.

Treaty of Abuja: *see* ***African Economic Community***.

Treaty of Amsterdam: formally *Treaty of Amsterdam Amending the Treaty on European Union, the Treaties establishing the European Communities and Certain Related Acts*. Signed in Amsterdam on 2 October 1997. Entered into force on 1 May 1999. It amends the ***Treaty on European Union*** (the ***Treaty of Maastricht***), the *Treaty establishing the European Community*, the *Treaty establishing the* ***European Coal and Steel Community*** and the Treaty establishing the European Atomic Energy Community and simplifies many of their provisions. *See also* ***European Union treaties***.

Treaty of Lisbon: amends the ***Treaty of Maastricht*** and the *Treaty establishing the European Community* (also known as the ***Treaty of Rome***) which became the Treaty on the Functioning of the European Community. Signed in Lisbon on 13 December 2007 and entered into force on 1 December 2009. This Treaty gives the European Union full legal personality. It also gives in what became Article 50 of the *Treaty on the Functioning of the European Community* the procedure to be followed by member countries who wish to withdraw. *See also* ***Brexit***.

Treaty of Maastricht: formally ***Treaty on European Union***, signed on 7 February 1992. Entered into force on 1 November 1993. It formally established the ***European Union*** (the Union) and defined its powers. Article C states that the "Union shall be served by a single institutional framework which shall ensure the consistency and continuity of the activities carried out in order to attain its objectives while respecting and building on the ***acquis communautaire***". The Treaty extensively amends the ***Treaty of Rome*** and it replaces the term ***European Economic Community*** by European Community. The treaty also created citizenship of the European Union extended to every citizen of a member state. It established a common foreign and security policy and provided for cooperation in the fields of justice and home affairs, and it set in train the creation of single European currency. The powers of the European Parliament were enlarged. *See also* ***European Union treaties***.

Treaty of Montevideo: *see* ***ALADI***.

Treaty of Nice: formally *Treaty of Nice Amending the Treaty on European Union, the Treaties establishing the European Communities and Certain Related Acts*. Signed on 26 February 2001. Entered into force on 1 February 2003. Its objective was to prepare the ***European Union*** for the expected ***enlargement*** over the next several years and to put in place appropriate decision-making procedures for the institutions of the European Union, such as the ***European Council*** and the composition of the European Parliament. The working of the ***common commercial policy*** was clarified, and agreements relating to trade in

常在生效前须经批准，有时是通过宪法规定的程序。另见*善意(good faith)*、*谅解备忘录(memorandum of understanding)*、*条约必须遵守(pacta sunt servanda)*。

Treaty establishing the European Community
建立欧洲共同体条约

见*欧洲联盟主要条约(European Union treaties)*。

Treaty establishing the European Economic Community
建立欧洲经济共同体的条约

见*欧洲联盟主要条约(European Union treaties)*、*罗马条约(Treaty of Rome)*。

Treaty of Abuja
阿布贾条约

见*非洲经济共同体(African Economic Community)*。

Treaty of Amsterdam
阿姆斯特丹条约

正式名称为《修正欧洲联盟条约、建立欧洲共同体的各项条约和若干有关文件的阿姆斯特丹条约》。1997年10月2日在阿姆斯特丹签署。1999年5月1日生效。条约对《欧洲联盟条约》(《马斯特里赫特条约》)、《建立欧洲共同体条约》、《建立欧洲煤钢共同体条约》和《建立欧洲原子能共同体条约》进行了修正，并简化了其中多个条款。另见*欧洲联盟主要条约(European Union treaties)*。

Treaty of Lisbon
里斯本条约

对《马斯特里赫特条约》和《建立欧洲共同体条约》(又称《罗马条约》)进行了修正，后者成为《欧洲共同体运行条约》。2007年12月13日在里斯本签署，2009年12月1日生效。条约赋予欧盟完全的法律人格。还在后成为《欧洲共同体运行条约》第50条中规定了希望退出的成员国应遵循的程序。另见*英国脱欧(Brexit)*。

Treaty of Maastricht
马斯特里赫特条约

正式名称为《欧洲联盟条约》，1992年2月7日签署。1993年11月1日生效。条约正式建立欧盟并确定其权力。C条规定，“联盟由一个单一的组织系统为之服务，该组织系统应在尊重和基于欧盟现行法的同时确保为达到目标所进行的活动的一致性和连续性”。该条约对《罗马条约》进行了大幅修正，并以欧洲共同体取代欧洲经济共同体一词。条约还创设了给予各成员国每一公民的欧盟公民身份。公约制定了共同的外交和安全政策，规定在司法和内政领域进行合作，并启动建立单一欧洲货币，欧洲议会的权力得到扩大。另见*欧洲联盟主要条约(European Union treaties)*。

Treaty of Montevideo
蒙得维的亚条约

见*拉丁美洲一体化协会(ALADI)*。

Treaty of Nice
尼斯条约

正式名称为《修正欧洲联盟条约、建立欧洲共同体的各项条约和若干有关文件的尼斯条约》。2001年2月26日签署。2003年2月1日生效。目标是使欧盟对其后若干年内预期的扩盟作好准备，并为欧盟的机构建立适当决策程序，例如欧洲理事会和欧洲议会的组成。共同商业政策的运作得到澄清，且规定与

audiovisual services, educational services and social and human services were defined as being subject to ***shared competence***. *See also* ***European Union treaties***.

Treaty of Rome: the instrument creating the ***European Economic Community***. It was signed on 25 March 1975 in Rome and entered into force on 1 January 1958. Initial members were Belgium, Federal Republic of Germany, France, Italy, Luxembourg and the Netherlands (the EEC-6). The Treaty created a ***common market*** based on the free movement of goods, people, services and capital. It also established a ***customs union*** with a ***common external tariff*** applying to imports and a ***common commercial policy***. The Treaty was amended in substantial ways several times. Its current form is the ***Treaty on the Functioning of the European Community***. Another treaty signed in Rome on 25 March 1975 was the one establishing the European Atomic Energy Community (Euratom). This Dictionary is not further concerned with Euratom, and "Treaty of Rome" in these pages always refers to treaty establishing the European Economic Community. *See also* ***European Union treaties*** and ***Treaty on European Union***.

Treaty on European Union: one of the two basic texts governing the working of the ***European Union*** (the Union). Entered into force in 2009. Title I (Articles 1–8) establishes the European Union and sets out the values governing it. The objectives of the European Union in simplified form are: (a) promotion of peace, its values and the well-being of its peoples, (b) an area of freedom, security and justice without internal frontiers, (c) an internal market with sustainable development, a highly competitive social market economy and promotion of scientific and technological advance, (d) absence of social exclusion and discrimination, (e) economic, social and territorial cohesion, (f) respect for cultural and linguistic variety, (g) economic and monetary union whose currency is the ***euro***, and (h) upholding and promoting the Union's values in its relations with the wider world. Title II (Articles 9–12) contains the provisions on democratic principles. It creates Union citizenship in addition to national citizenship and states that the functioning of the Union is founded on representative democracy. Title III (Articles 13–19) contains the provisions on Union institutions. These are the European Parliament, the ***European Council***, the Council, ***European Commission***, ***Court of Justice of the European Union***, European Central Bank and the Court of Auditors. The European Parliament exercises legislative and parliamentary functions jointly with the Council. The European Commission has the task of ensuring the application of the European Union Treaties (this Treaty and the ***Treaty on the Functioning of the European Union***) and of measures adopted by the institutions pursuant to the Treaties. Title IV (Article 20) contains provisions on enhanced cooperation between the member states. Title V contains general and specific provisions on the Common Foreign and Security Policy. Article 21 lists the guiding principles the Union will seek to advance in the wider world: democracy, the rule of law, the universality and indivisibility of human rights and fundamental freedoms,

视听服务、教育服务以及社会和人类服务贸易相关的协定应受共享权限管辖。*另见欧洲联盟主要条约(European Union treaties)*。

Treaty of Rome
罗马条约

建立欧洲经济共同体的文件。1957年3月25日在罗马签署，1958年1月1日生效。最初成员为比利时、德意志联邦共和国、法国、意大利、卢森堡和荷兰(EEC-6)。条约建立基于货物、人员、服务和资本自由流动的共同市场。条约还建立关税同盟，对进口实行共同对外关税，并制定共同商业政策。条约多次经过实质性修正。条约目前的形式为《欧洲共同体运行条约》。在1957年3月25日在罗马签署的另一项条约建立了欧洲原子能共同体(Euratom)。本辞典不再涉及欧洲原子能共同体，“罗马条约”即指建立欧洲经济共同体的条约。*另见欧洲联盟主要条约(European Union Treaties)*、*欧洲联盟条约(Treaty on European Union)*。

Treaty on European Union
欧洲联盟条约

管辖欧盟运行的两个基本文本之一。2009年生效。第一章(第1至8条)建立欧盟，并规范了管理联盟的价值观。欧盟的目标简单表述为：(a)促进和平、其价值观及其人民的福祉；(b)无内部边界的自由、安全和正义的地区；(c)可持续发展的内部市场、高度竞争的社会市场经济和促进科学技术进步；(d)没有社会排斥和歧视；(e)经济、社会和领土凝聚力；(f)尊重文化和语言多样性；(g)以欧元为货币的经济和货币联盟；以及(h)在与更广大的世界的关系中维护和促进欧盟价值观。第二章(第9至12条)包含关于民主原则的条款。在国家公民身份基础上创设联盟公民身份，并规定联盟的运行建立在代议制民主基础上。第三章(第13至19条)包含关于联盟机构的条款。这些机构包括欧洲议会、欧洲理事会、理事会、欧盟委员会、欧洲法院、欧洲中央银行和欧洲审计院。欧洲议会与理事会共同行使立法和议会职能。欧盟委员会的任务是保证欧盟各项条约(本条约及《欧洲联盟运行条约》)得到适用，并保证各机构根据这些条约采取措施。第四章(第20条)包含关于成员国之间加强合作的条款。第五章包含关于共同外交和安全政策的一般和具体条款。第21条列出欧盟寻求在更广大的世界推进的指导原则：民主、法治、人权和基本自由的普遍性和不可分割性，尊重人的尊严、平等和团结的原则以及尊重《联合国宪章》和国际法的

respect for human dignity, the principles of equality and solidarity, and respect for the principles of the United Nations Charter and international law. Articles 24 to 46 outline the Union's ***competence*** in matters of common foreign and security policy (all areas of foreign policy and all questions relating to the Union's security). Title VI contains the final provisions. Article 49 outlines the basic steps leading to European Union membership. Article 50 states that any member state may decide to withdraw from the Union in accordance with its own constitutional requirements. To do so, a member has to notify the European Council of its intention. Negotiations towards a withdrawal agreement are then initiated. Union membership ceases from the date of entry into force of the withdrawal agreement. If there is no agreement, membership will cease two years after notification of the intent of withdrawal unless the European Council and the member state concerned unanimously decide to extend the period. Article 53 states that this Treaty is concluded for an unlimited period.

Treaty on Intellectual Property in Respect of Integrated Circuits: one of the treaties which contains the standards of protection to be applied under the ***Agreement on Trade-Related Aspects of Intellectual Property Rights***. It was concluded in Washington, DC, on 26 May 1992 under ***WIPO*** auspices, but it is not yet in force. Each party must afford intellectual property protection to original ***layout-designs of integrated circuits*** (topographies) whether or not the integrated circuit is incorporated in an article. Parties to the Treaty must also accord ***national treatment*** to natural persons and legal entities of all other parties. Protection of integrated circuits must be for at least eight years. As a minimum, the reproduction of the layout-design, and the import, sale or other distribution for commercial purposes of the layout-design or its incorporation in an article must be deemed illegal if it is done without the authorization of the holder of the ***intellectual property rights***. *See also* ***sui generis right***.

Treaty on the Functioning of the European Union: one of the two basic texts governing the working of the ***European Union***. The other is the ***Treaty on European Union***. It is in substance a much amended and enlarged version of the ***Treaty of Rome***. It organizes the functioning of the (European) Union and determines the categories and areas of Union competences. Part One, Title I (Articles 2–6) deals with these matters. Where the Union has exclusive ***competence*** in a specific area, only the Union may legislate and adopt legally binding acts. Article 3 states that these areas are (a) customs union, (b) establishment of competition rules necessary for the functioning of the internal market, (c) monetary policy for the member states whose currency is the ***euro***, (d) conservation of maritime biological resources under the ***common fisheries policy***, and (e) ***commercial policy***. The Union also has exclusive competence for some aspects of conclusion of international agreements. ***Shared competence*** applies to a range of other areas. Title II, Part 1 (Articles 7–17) contains provisions of general application. These include consistency policies and activities, elimination of inequalities and promotion of equality between men and women. Environmental protection and consumer protection requirements must

原则。第24至46条列出欧盟在共同外交和安全政策事务(所有外交政策的领域和所有与欧盟安全有关的问题)中的权限。第六章包含最后条款。第49条列出成为欧盟成员国的基本步骤。第50条规定，任何成员国均可以依照自己的宪法要求决定退出欧盟。为此，成员国必须向欧洲理事会通报其意图。随后启动关于退出协定的谈判。欧盟成员资格自退出协定生效之日起终止。如未能达成协议，成员资格将在作出退出意向通报后2年终止，除非欧洲理事会和有关成员国一致决定延长该期限。第53条规定，条约的缔结期不受限制。

Treaty on Intellectual Property in Respect of Integrated Circuits
关于集成电路知识产权的条约

包含《与贸易有关的知识产权协定》项下适用的保护标准的条约之一。1992年5月26日在世界知识产权组织(WIPO)主持下在华盛顿特区签署，但尚未生效。每一缔约方必须对原始集成电路布图设计(拓扑图)提供知识产权保护，无论集成电路是否结合在一产品中。条约缔约方还必须对其他缔约方的所有自然人和法律实体给予国民待遇。集成电路的保护期必须至少为8年。作为最低要求，未经知识产权权利人授权而复制布图设计及为商业目的进口、销售或其他方式分销布图设计或将其结合在一产品中必须视为非法。另见*特殊权利(sui generis right)*。

Treaty on the Functioning of the European Union
欧洲联盟运行条约

管辖欧盟运行的两个基本文本之一。另一个是《欧洲联盟条约》。实质上，条约是《罗马条约》的大幅修正和扩充版本。条约安排了(欧洲)联盟的运行，并确定了欧盟权限的类别和领域。第一部分，第一章(第2至6条)处理这些事项。如果欧盟在一特定领域拥有专属权限，只有欧盟可以立法和通过具有法律约束力的法案。第3条规定，这些领域包括：(a)关税同盟；(b)制定国内市场运行所需的竞争规则；(c)货币使用欧元的成员国的货币政策；(d)根据共同渔业政策养护海洋生物资源；以及(e)商业政策。欧盟还对缔结国际协定的某些方面拥有专属权限。共享权限适用于一系列其他领域。第二部分第二章(第7至17条)包含普遍适用的条款。包括一致性政策和活动、消除不平等和促进男女平等。环境保护和消费者保护要求必须在欧盟政策和活动中予以考虑。每个人有权

be taken into account in Union policies and activities. Everyone has the right to the protection of personal data concerning them (Article 16). Title II, Part 2 (Articles 18–25) deals with non-discrimination and citizenship of the Union. Part Three of the Treaty covers Union policies and internal actions. Title I (Articles 26 and 27) covers the functions of the internal market. Title II (Articles 28 and 29) deals with the free movement of goods. Article 28 declares that the Union comprises a ***customs union*** covering trade in all goods. No customs duties or other charges with equivalent effect may be imposed between member states, and a common customs tariff applies to trade with third countries. Articles 30 to 32 deal with the operation of the customs union. Article 33 promotes customs cooperation. Articles 34 and 35 prohibit quantitative import and export restrictions between member states. Title III (Articles 38–44) covers agriculture and fisheries, including the ***common agricultural policy*** and the ***common fisheries policy***. Title IV deals with the free movement of persons, services and capital. Workers may move freely within the Union. Restrictions on the ***right of establishment*** of nationals of another member state are prohibited. Restrictions on freedom to provide services within the Union are prohibited in respect of nationals and member states. Restrictions on the movement of capital between member states and member states and third countries are prohibited. Title V (Articles 67–76) makes the Union an area of freedom, security and justice with respect for fundamental rights. Articles 77 to 80 cover policies on border checks, asylum and immigration, Article 81 judicial cooperation in civil matters, Articles 82 to 86 judicial cooperation in criminal matters and Articles 87 to 89 police cooperation. Title VI concerns matters to be pursued within a common transport policy. Title VII governs common rules on competition, taxation and approximation of laws. Title VIII covers economic and monetary policy. Articles 136 to 138 list provisions specific to member states whose currency is the ***euro***. Title IX deals with employment, Title X with social policy, Title XI with the European Social Fund, Title XII with education, vocational training, youth and sport, Title XIII with culture, Title XIV with public health, Title XV with consumer protection, Title XVI with trans-European networks, Title XVII with industry, Title XVIII with economic, social and territorial cohesion, Title XIX with research and technological development and space, Title XX with environment, Title XXI with energy, Title XXII with tourism, Title XXIII with civil protection, and Title XXIV with administrative cooperation. Part Four covers association with overseas countries and territories. Part Five of the Treaty deals with external action by the Union. Title I contains general provisions on them. Title II (Articles 206 and 207) details the functioning of the ***common commercial policy***. Article 207 states that it is to "be based on uniform principles, particularly with regard to changes in tariff rates, the conclusion of tariff and trade agreements relating to goods and services, and the commercial aspects of intellectual property, foreign direct investment, the achievement of uniformity in measures of liberalization, export policy and measures to protect trade such as those to be taken

保护自己的个人信息(第16条)。第二部分第二章(第18至25条)处理非歧视和欧盟公民权。条约第三部分涵盖欧盟政策和内部行动。第一章(第26条和第27条)涵盖内部市场的职能。第二章(第28条和第29条)处理货物的自由流动。第28条宣布，欧盟组成涵盖所有货物贸易的关税同盟。成员国之间不得实施关税和具有同等效力的其他费用，并对与第三国的贸易适用共同关税。第30至32条处理关税同盟的运行。第33条规定促进海关合作。第34条和第35条禁止成员国之间的进出口数量限制。第三章(第38至44条)涵盖农业和渔业，包括共同农业政策和共同渔业政策。第四章处理人员、服务和资本的自由流动。工人可以在欧盟内自由流动。禁止对另一成员国国民设立权进行限制。禁止对国民和成员国在欧盟内提供服务的自由进行限制。禁止对成员国之间和成员国与第三国之间的资本流动进行限制。第五章(第67至76条)规定，欧盟是一个尊重基本权利的自由、安全和公正的地区。第77至80条涵盖边境检查、庇护和移民政策、第81条涵盖民事司法合作、第82至86条涵盖刑事司法合作，第87至89条涵盖警务合作。第六章涉及在共同交通政策范围内需要解决的问题。第七章管辖关于竞争、税收和法律接近的共同规则。第八章涵盖经济和货币政策。第136至138条列出了针对货币使用欧元的成员国的具体条款。第九章处理就业问题，第十章处理社会政策，第十一章处理欧洲社会基金，第十二章处理教育、职业培训、青年和体育，第十三章处理文化，第十四章处理公共卫生，第十五章处理消费者保护，第十六章处理跨欧洲网络，第十七章处理产业，第十八章处理经济、社会和地域凝聚，第十九章处理研究和技术发展及空间，第二十章处理环境，第二十一章处理能源，第二十二章处理旅游，第二十三章处理民事保护，第二十四章处理行政合作。第四部分涵盖与海外国家和领土的联系。条约第五部分处理欧盟的对外行动。第一章包含关于这些条款的一般规定，第二章(第206条和第207条)详细规定共同商业政策的运作。第207条规定，这一政策应“以统一原则为基础，特别是关税税率的变化、缔结与货物和服务有关的关税和贸易协定、知识产权的商业方面、外国直接投资、实现自由化措施的统一、出口政策以及在倾销和补贴情况下采取的保护贸易的措施”。国际

in the event of dumping or subsidies". International negotiations are to be conducted by a special committee (in the Treaty of Rome this was the ***Article 113 Committee***, later the ***Article 133 Committee*** and now the ***Trade Policy Committee***). Title III covers cooperation with third countries and humanitarian aid. This includes development cooperation, economic, financial and technical cooperation. Title IV covers restrictions that may become necessary. Title V authorizes the Union to conclude international agreements. Title VI deals with the Union's relations with international organizations, third countries and Union delegations. Title VII is a solidarity clause applicable in the case of a terrorist attack or a natural or man-made disaster. Part Six of the Treaty deals with institutional and financial provisions. It also lists the legal acts of the Union. These are regulation (general application and binding on all members), directive (binding on the member to which it is addressed), decision (binding in its entirety) and recommendation and opinion (no binding force). Part Seven of the Treaty (Articles 335–358) contains general and final provisions. Article 356 states that the Treaty is concluded for an unlimited period.

Treble damages: under Section 77 of the ***Wilson Tariff Act*** of 1894 and Section 4 of the ***Clayton Act*** of 1914, which are part of the United States framework of ***antitrust laws***, the person injured because of a prohibited practice may recover through the courts three times the damages sustained. There is no upper limit on the damages that may be payable. The original antitrust law, the ***Sherman Act***, only set maximum fines or prison terms for guilty parties. *See also* ***clawback provisions*** and ***Anti-Dumping Act of 1916***.

Trends in International Trade**:** *see* ***Haberler Report***.

Triadization: the recognition, described by the Group of Lisbon, that the process of technological, economic and socio-cultural integration is much more advanced among the three most developed regions of the word. The three regions are Japan plus the Asian newly industrializing countries, Western Europe and North America. *See also* ***tripolarization***. [Group of Lisbon 1995]

Trigger price: a price level fixed in domestic support arrangements, particularly for agriculture, or international agreements which, once reached, will automatically authorize, and sometimes make mandatory, the taking of prescribed action. *See also* ***buffer stocks***, ***international commodity agreements***, ***peril points*** and ***safeguards***.

TRIMs: Trade-Related Investment Measures. These include export targets, import limitations, local purchase requirements or ***local content requirements***, research and development requirements and similar conditions imposed on an enterprise as part of receiving permission to invest in another country. *See also* ***Agreement on Trade-Related Investment Measures*** and ***export performance requirements***.

Tripartite Free Trade Area: TFTA. A proposal for a free-trade area comprising the ***Common Market for Eastern and Southern Africa***, the ***Southern African Development Community*** and the ***East African Community***. An agreement to this effect was signed in 2017. TFTA would cover twenty-seven countries. It

谈判将由一个特别委员会开展(在《罗马条约》中，此为第113条委员会，后为第133条委员会，现为贸易政策委员会)。第三章涵盖与第三国的合作和人道主义援助。包括发展合作、经济、金融和技术合作。第四章涵盖可能需要采取的限制。第五章授权欧盟缔结国际协定。第六章处理欧盟与国际组织、第三国和欧盟代表团的关系。第七章是适用于恐怖袭击或自然或人为灾难情况下的团结条款。条约第六部分处理机构和财务条款，还列出欧盟的法律行为。即条例(对所有成员普遍适用并具有约束力)、指令(对所涉成员具有约束力)、决定(整体具有约束力)以及建议和意见(无约束力)。条约的第七部分(第335至358条)包含一般条款和最后条款。第356条规定，条约的缔结期不受限制。

Treble damages

三倍赔偿

根据1894年《威尔逊关税法》第77条和1914年《克莱顿法》第4条，即美国反垄断法框架的一部分，因被禁止的做法而受到伤害的人可通过法院获得三倍于所受损害的赔偿。没有规定可支付的损害赔偿金的上限。最初的反垄断法，即《谢尔曼法》，只对有罪一方规定了最高的罚款或刑期。另见*回拨条款(clawback provisions)*、*1916年反倾销法(Anti-Dumping Act of 1916)*。

Trends in International Trade

国际贸易趋势

见*哈伯勒报告(Haberler Report)*。

Triadization

三区域化

里斯本集团将此种认识描述为，世界上三个最发达区域之间的技术、经济和社会文化一体化进程更为先进。这三个区域为日本加上亚洲新兴工业化国家、西欧和北美。另见*三极化(tripolarization)*。

Trigger price

触发价格

在国内支持安排、特别是农业国内支持安排中，或国际协定中确定的价格水平，一旦达到这一水平即自动授权采取规定行动，有时是强制性采取。另见*缓冲储存(buffer stocks)*、*国际商品协定(international commodity agreements)*、*危险点(peril points)*、*保障措施(safeguards)*。

TRIMs

与贸易有关的投资措施

包括作为获准在另一国投资的一部分而对一企业施加的出口目标、进口限制、本地采购要求或当地含量要求、研究与开发要求以及类似条件。另见*与贸易有关的投资措施协定(Agreement on Trade-Related Investment Measures)*、*出口实绩要求(export performance requirements)*。

Tripartite Free Trade Area

三方自由贸易区

TFTA。建立自由贸易区的提案，以包含东部和南部非洲共同市场、南部非洲发展共同体和东部非洲共同体。为此目的达成的协定于2017年签署。TFTA将

will enter into force once fourteen countries have signed it. *See also* ***African regional economic integration***.

Triple transformation: occurs when a good undergoes three ***substantial transformations*** in succession. An example would be the transformation of bauxite into alumina, then smelting the alumina into aluminium and finally producing intermediate or final goods made of aluminium. Another example would be spinning raw fibres into yarn, then weaving the yarn into a fabric and finally cutting and sewing the fabric into garments. *See also* ***double transformation***.

Tripolarization: a term descriptive of the fact that much international economic activity is caused or influenced by actions originating in Western Europe, East Asia or North America. Every now and then a breathless work appears postulating that the world is about to break up into three trading areas centred around these regions, and this almost certainly will lead to a ***trade war***. So far, all of these predictions have been premature. *See also* ***triadization***.

TRIPS: Trade-related aspects of intellectual property rights. *See* ***Agreement on Trade-Related Aspects of Intellectual Property Rights***.

Troika: a consultative or fact-finding body with three members (after a Russian word for a carriage drawn by three horses) established by some ***intergovernmental organizations***. Another of its aims can be ensuring continuity of policy. In the ***Black Sea Economic Cooperation Organization***, for example, it consists of the present, past and future chairs of the Council of Ministers. Similarly, in the ***Southern African Development Community*** the Troika is made up of the Chair, Incoming Chair and the Outgoing Chair of the Community. At one time it was used in the ***European Union*** for a group consisting of a representative each of the ***European Commission***, the actual presidency and the incoming presidency. A more recent use of the word has been for the European Commission, the IMF and the European Central Bank in their efforts to deal with the crisis in the ***Eurozone*** following the ***global financial crisis***. Other examples can be found.

Trophy agreement: a colloquial description of an agreement ostensibly aimed at achieving a defined result, but which in fact is devoid of real obligations. Such agreements are often negotiated quite hastily, sometimes to ensure that ministers visiting other countries can point to an achievement on their return home.

Tropical products: this is not a clearly defined group of products; various products or product groups of interest to developing countries were included in the trade negotiations in the past to deal with problems affecting trade in such products. Over time, an indicative list of seven product groups including tropical beverages, spices, certain oilseeds, tobacco, tropical fruits and nuts, tropical wood and rubber and jute and hard fibres emerged. Tropical products received priority attention in the various GATT rounds of negotiations starting more specifically from the ***Kennedy Round***. Liberalization of trade in tropical products also received special attention in the ***Uruguay Round***, where participants agreed to engage in negotiations on tropical beverages (coffee, cocoa and tea, and products based on them), spices, cut flowers, tropical plants and plant

覆盖27个国家。待经14国签署后，协定即生效。另见*非洲区域经济一体化(African regional economic integration)*。

Triple transformation

三重改变

发生在一货物经过连续三次实质性改变后。例如铝土矿转化成氧化铝，然后将氧化铝熔化成铝，最后生产出由铝制成的中间产品或最终产品。另一个例子是将原纤维纺成纱线，然后将纱线编织成织物，最后将织物裁剪并缝制成服装。另见*双重改变(double transformation)*。

Tripolarization

三极化

描述许多国际经济活动是由源自西欧、东亚或北美的活动所引起或影响的事实的词语。不时会出现令人吃惊的著作假设称，世界即将分裂成以这些地区为中心的三个贸易区，且这几乎肯定会引发贸易战。目前为止，所有这些预测均为时过早。另见*三区域化(triadization)*。

TRIPS

与贸易有关的知识产权协定

见*与贸易有关的知识产权协定(Agreement on Trade-Related Aspects of Intellectual Property Rights)*。

Troika

三巨头

由一些政府间组织建立的由三名成员组成的咨询或事实调查机构，得名于一个俄语单词，意为三驾马车。另一个目标是保证政策连续性。例如，在黑海经济合作组织中，三巨头由现任、卸任和候任的部长理事会主席组成。同样，在南部非洲发展共同体，三巨头由主席、候任主席和卸任主席组成。三巨头在欧盟中曾用于指由欧盟委员会、现任主席和候任主席各一名代表组成的小组。此词的最新用法指欧盟委员会、国际货币基金组织和欧洲央行在应对全球金融危机之后的欧元区危机中共同作出努力的情况。还可以找到其他例子。

Trophy agreement

战利品协定

对表面上旨在实现规定结果而实际无真正义务的协定的通俗描述。此类协定仓促达成，有时是为保证访问其他国家的部长在回国时带回一项成果。

Tropical products

热带产品

并非一个明确界定的产品类别；在以往贸易谈判中包括对发展中国家具有利益的各种产品或产品组，以处理影响此类产品贸易的问题。随着时间的推移，出现了包括7个产品组的指示性清单，即热带饮料、香料、某些油籽、烟草、热带水果和坚果、热带木材和橡胶以及黄麻和硬质纤维。准确地讲，自肯尼迪回合起，热带产品在GATT各轮回合谈判中得到优先关注。热带产品的贸易自由化在乌拉圭回合中也受到特别关注，参加方同意就下列产品开展谈判：热带饮料(咖啡、可可和茶及其制品)、香料、切花、热带植物和植物产品、油籽、

products, oilseeds, vegetable oils and oilcake, tobacco, rice, manioc and other tropical roots, tropical fruits and nuts, tropical wood and rubber, jute, sisal and other hard fibres. Tropical products also form part of the market access discussions in the ongoing ***Doha Development Agenda*** agriculture negotiations where a linkage with the issue of preference erosion has been acknowledged.

TRQ: *see* ***tariff rate quota***.

Truncated Swiss Formula: a method of reducing tariffs by applying ***linear tariff cuts*** up to a level nominated by the user and then switching to the ***Swiss formula.***

TSE: transmissible spongiform encephalopathy, a disease related to ***BSE***.

Tuna (Canada–United States, 1982): a dispute in the GATT between Canada and the United States. The facts were that on 31 August 1979 the United States prohibited imports from Canada of tuna and tuna products after some United States fishing vessels had been seized by Canadian authorities for fishing without authorization in waters regarded by Canada to be under its jurisdiction. The United States, on the other hand, regarded these waters to be outside the tuna fisheries jurisdiction of any state. The United States action was based on Section 205 (Import Prohibitions) of the *Fishery Conservation and Management Act* of 1976 which required mandatory action in case of violation. The prohibition was lifted one year later following the conclusion of an arrangement with Canada, but before the dispute had been adjudicated in the GATT. The ***panel*** noted that the dispute was part of a wider disagreement on fisheries matters between the United States and Canada, and that the trade aspects had to be seen in that context. It found that the United States prohibition on the import of tuna from Canada constituted a prohibition in terms of GATT Article XI:1. The panel also found that the requirements of Article XX(g) had not been satisfied in that the alleged conservation measures had not been coupled with restrictions on domestic production or consumption. *See also* ***general exceptions***, ***Herring and salmon***, ***Tuna I*** and ***Tuna II***.

Tuna I: a dispute brought before the GATT in 1991 by Mexico against the United States. The background to this case was, as noted in the ***panel*** report, that studies monitoring catch levels had shown that tuna fish and dolphins were found together in a number of areas around the world, and that this could lead to incidental taking of dolphins during fishing operations. This is especially the case in the Eastern Tropical Pacific Ocean where tuna and dolphins often occur together, the former under water, the latter near or on the surface. This association between tuna and dolphins leads fishermen to finding and chasing dolphins on the surface and encircling them with nets to catch the tuna underneath. Once dolphins and tuna are surrounded, it is possible to exclude or eliminate the catch of dolphins through following certain procedures. In 1972 the United States enacted the Marine Mammal Protection Act (MMPA) aimed at reducing to insignificant levels approaching zero incidental kill or serious injury of marine mammals during commercial fishing. It imposed a general prohibition of "taking" (harassment, hunting, capture, killing or

植物油及油饼、烟草、大米、木薯和其他热带根、热带水果及坚果、热带木材和橡胶、黄麻、剑麻及其他硬纤维。热带产品也是正在进行的多哈发展议程农业谈判中关于市场准入讨论的一部分，其中承认与优惠侵蚀问题存在关联。

TRQ

关税配额

见*关税配额(tariff rate quota)*。

Truncated Swiss Formula

截断瑞士公式

一种降低关税的方法，通过使用线性关税削减至使用者指定的水平，随后切换至瑞士公式。

TSE

传染性海绵状脑病

一种与疯牛病有关的疾病。

Tuna (Canada–United States, 1982)

1982年加拿大-美国金枪鱼案

加拿大和美国在GATT中的争端。案情为，在一些美国渔船被加拿大当局以在加视为属其管辖水域内进行未经许可的捕捞为由进行扣押后，美国于1979年8月31日禁止自加拿大进口金枪鱼和金枪鱼产品。另一方面，美国认为这些水域不属于任何国家的金枪鱼渔业管辖范围。美国的行动根据1976年《渔业养护和管理法》第205条(进口禁止)采取，该条要求对于违反行为采取强制行动。禁令在与加拿大达成一项安排1年后解除，但此时争端在GATT中尚未裁决。专家组指出，该争端是美国和加拿大在渔业问题上更大分歧的一部分，贸易问题必须在这一背景下看待。专家组认为，美国禁止自加拿大进口金枪鱼构成了GATT第11条第1款范围内的禁止。专家组还认为，第20条(g)款的要求没有得到满足，因所称的保护措施未与对国内生产或消费的限制同时实施。另见*一般例外(general exceptions)*、*鲱鱼和鲑鱼案(Herring and salmon)*、*第一个金枪鱼案(Tuna I)*、*第二个金枪鱼案(Tuna II)*。

Tuna I

第一个金枪鱼案

1991年墨西哥在GATT中对美国发起的争端。如专家组报告所指出的，该案的背景是，监测渔获量的研究表明，在世界范围内的许多地区，金枪鱼和海豚同时出现，这可能导致在捕捞作业时会非有意捕获海豚。此种情况特别会在热带东太平洋发生，在那里金枪鱼和海豚经常同时出现，前者在水下，后者临近水面或在水面。金枪鱼和海豚之间的这种关联使渔民在水面发现和追逐海豚，用网围住它们以捕捞水下的金枪鱼。一旦海豚和金枪鱼被包围，即有可能通过某种程序不去捕捞海豚。1972年，美国颁布了《海洋哺乳动物保护法》(MMPA)，旨在将商业捕捞期间非有意杀害或严重伤害海洋哺乳动物降至接近零的非常低的水平。该法实施了一项关于海洋哺乳动物“捕获”(侵扰、狩猎、捕捞、杀害或此类企图)和进口至美国的普遍禁令，除非给予明确授权。MMPA

attempting to do so) and the import into the United States of marine mammals, except where an explicit authorization had been given. The MMPA also required the Secretary of Commerce to require any intermediary nation from which yellowfin tuna or tuna products were to be exported to the United States to certify that it had acted to prohibit the import of such products from countries not meeting the MMPA standards. If satisfactory assurances were not given, imports into the United States of yellowfin tuna and tuna products from intermediary countries were to be prohibited. This is the "intermediary nation embargo". In early 1991 such an embargo went into effect against Mexico. The embargo on imports of yellowfin tuna and tuna products could be strengthened by the use of the "Pelly Amendment", part of the 1967 *Fishermen's Protective Act*, which gave the President discretionary authority to order a prohibition of imports of all fish products from designated countries. The panel, in considering the evidence offered by the parties, noted that the MMPA regulated the domestic harvesting of yellowfin tuna to reduce the incidental taking of dolphins. As these regulations did not apply to tuna products as such, they would not directly regulate the sale of tuna and could not possibly affect tuna as a product. The panel considered that GATT Article III (National Treatment) called for a comparison of the treatment of imported tuna *as a product* with that of domestic tuna *as a product* (emphasis in the original). The United States was therefore obliged to accord treatment to Mexican tuna no less favourable than that accorded to United States tuna, no matter whether the incidental taking of dolphins differed. The panel also found that the import prohibition was inconsistent with Article XI, and it therefore saw no need to make a finding on the consistency of the United States action with Article XII. The panel then turned to Article XX (General Exceptions). It noted that the broad interpretation of Article XX(b) [measures necessary to protect human, animal or plant life or health] sought by the United States would mean, if accepted, that each GATT member could impose its own policies on other members, and that the GATT would then no longer be a multilateral trade framework for all of its members. The panel noted that Article XX(g) allowed each member to adopt its own conservation policies, subject to the limitation that measures taken under this Article must be related to the conservation of exhaustible natural resources, and this condition had not been satisfied by the United States action. Considering the possible use of the Pelly Amendment, the panel decided to follow previous rulings which held that legislation merely giving executive authorities discretionary power to act inconsistently with the GATT was not, in itself, inconsistent with it. In its concluding remarks, the panel noted that the provisions of the GATT impose few constraints on a member's ability to implement domestic environmental policies. On the other hand, a member may not restrict imports of a product merely because it originates in a country with environmental policies different from its own. *See also* ***GATT-consistency of national legislation***, ***general exceptions***, ***Herring and salmon***, ***trade and environment***, ***Tuna (Canada–United States, 1982)*** and ***Tuna II***. [GATT BISD 39]

还规定商务部长应要求出口至美国的黄鳍金枪鱼或金枪鱼产品的任何中间国需证明，已采取行动禁止自未达到MMPA标准的国家进口此类产品。如果未得到令人满意的保证，禁止自中间国将黄鳍金枪鱼和金枪鱼产品进口至美国。此即“中间国家禁运”。1991年初，此种禁运对墨西哥实施。对黄鳍金枪鱼和金枪鱼产品的进口禁运可以通过使用《培利修正案》得以增强，该修正案为1967年《渔民保护法》的一部分，赋予总统自由裁量权以下令禁止自指定国家进口所有鱼类产品。专家组在审议双方提供的证据后指出，MMPA管辖国内捕捞黄鳍金枪鱼以减少非有意捕捞海豚的情况。由于这些规定不适用于金枪鱼产品本身，它们也不能直接管辖金枪鱼的销售，不能影响作为一种产品的金枪鱼。专家组认为，GATT第3条(国民待遇)要求将进口金枪鱼作为产品的待遇与国内金枪鱼作为产品的待遇进行比较(划线处为原文强调)。美国因此有义务给予墨西哥金枪鱼不低于给予美国金枪鱼的待遇，无论非有意捕获海豚的情况是否不同。专家组还认为，禁止进口不符合GATT第11条，因此认为没有必要就美国的行动是否符合第12条作出裁决。专家组随后提到第20条(一般例外)，指出美国所寻求的对第20条(b)款[保护人类、动物或植物生命或健康所必需的措施]的广泛解释如予以接受，即意味着每一GATT缔约方都可以将自己的政策强加于其他缔约方，那么GATT将不再是其所有缔约方的多边贸易框架。专家组指出，第20条(g)款允许每一缔约方采取自己的保护政策，但需要遵守的限制条件是，根据该条采取的措施必须与保护可用尽的自然资源相关，而美国的行动并未满足这一条件。考虑到援引《培利修正案》的可能性，专家组决定遵循以往的裁决，即该法仅给予行政当局以不符合GATT规则行事的自由裁量权，立法本身不与GATT相抵触。在其结论中，专家组指出，GATT条款对一缔约方为实施国内环境政策的能力几无限制。另一方面，一缔约方为不能仅为一产品原产自与其本国环境政策不同的国家而限制其进口。另见*国家立法与GATT一致性(GATT-consistency of national legislation)*、*一般例外(general exceptions)*、*鲱鱼和鲑鱼案(Herring and salmon)*、*贸易与环境(trade and environment)*、*1982年加拿大-美国金枪鱼案(Tuna (Canada–United States, 1982))*、*第二个金枪鱼案(Tuna II)*。

Tuna II: a dispute brought before the GATT in 1992 by the ***European Economic Community*** (EEC), and separately the Netherlands on behalf of the Netherlands Antilles, against the United States. The background to this case was that in the Eastern Tropical Pacific Ocean, but not in other waters, schools of tuna often swim below visible herds of dolphin. Fishermen in these waters therefore often use herds of dolphin to locate schools of tuna. The use of purse seine nets (two boats using one net to encircle a school) to catch the tuna then leads to the incidental killing and injury of many dolphins. The United States had long been a leader in promoting international efforts to reduce dolphin mortality from this cause. In 1972 it also passed the Marine Mammal Protection Act (MMPA) which, among other things, prohibited the import into the United States of any commercial fish or fish products harvested by a method resulting in the incidental kill or serious injury of marine mammals in excess of United States standards. This was known as the "primary nation embargo". Countries able to demonstrate that they had a regulatory programme and a rate of incidental "taking" (harassment, hunting, capture, killing or attempts to do so) of dolphins comparable to that of the United States were not affected by this rule. The MMPA also required proof from countries exporting yellowfin tuna or yellowfin tuna products to the United States that they had not imported yellowfin tuna that would not have been allowed into the United States under conditions of direct export. This was known as the "intermediary nation embargo". In 1991 and 1992 several countries, including some members of the EEC and separately the Netherlands Antilles, were identified as "intermediary nations". This list was, however, shortened later in 1992. The panel did not report on this dispute until May 1994 because of various procedural delays sought by the parties. It found that "Article III calls for a comparison between the treatment accorded to domestic and imported ***like products***, not for a comparison of the policies or practices of the country of origin with those of the country of importation". In other words, Article III applied to the product as is, not how it became that product. The panel then said that the embargoes imposed by the United States were "prohibitions or restrictions" in terms of Article XI since the act banned imports of tuna or tuna products from any country not meeting certain policy conditions. The panel found that the policy pursued by the United States to conserve dolphins in the Eastern Tropical Pacific Ocean fell within the range of policies covered by Article XX(g). However, because it was not accompanied by restrictions on domestic production or consumption, the import prohibitions on tuna and tuna products also maintained inconsistently with Article XI were not justified by Article XX(g). The same inconsistency also meant that the import prohibitions were not justified by Article XX(b) (measures necessary to protect human, animal or plant life or health) and Article XX(d) (measures necessary to comply with laws or regulations not inconsistent with the GATT). In its final observations, the panel noted that the validity of the United States environmental objectives to protect and conserve dolphins was not the issue in this dispute. Rather, it was whether

Tuna II
第二个金枪鱼案

1992年欧洲经济共同体(EEC)针对美国在GATT提起的争端，荷兰另代表荷属安的列斯群岛向美国提起争端。该案背景为，在热带东太平洋(不在其他水域)，金枪鱼群经常在肉眼可见的海豚群下游弋。这些水域的渔民因此经常利用海豚群定位金枪鱼群。使用拖网(两船用一张网围住鱼群)捕捉金枪鱼，因而使许多海豚非有意死亡和受伤。美国长期以来是促进减少海豚因此原因死亡的国际努力的领导者。1972年，美国还通过了《海洋哺乳动物保护法》(MMPA)，该法中除其他内容外，禁止将使用导致海洋哺乳动物意外死亡或严重伤害超过美国标准的方法所捕捞的鱼类进口至美国。此称"主要国家禁运"。能够证明制定监管方案且偶然"捕获"(侵扰、狩猎、捕捞、杀害或此类企图)海豚的比率与美国的比率相当的国家不受该规定影响。MMPA还要求向美国出口黄鳍金枪鱼或黄鳍金枪鱼产品的国家提供证明，未进口在直接出口条件下不允许进入美国的黄鳍金枪鱼。此称"中间国家禁运"。1991年和1992年，包括欧共体一些成员国和荷属安的列斯群岛在内的几个国家被确定为"中间国家"。但这一清单在1992年稍后期缩短了。由于各方所要求的各种程序上的延误，专家组直至1994年5月才对这一争端提出报告。专家组认为，"第3条要求对给予国内同类产品和进口同类产品的待遇进行比较，而非比较原产国和进口国的政策或做法"。换言之，第3条适用于产品本身，而非成为产品的方式。专家组随后指出，美国实施的禁运属第11条范围的"禁止或限制"，因该法禁止自任何不符合某些政策条件的国家进口金枪鱼或金枪鱼产品。专家组认为，美国在东热带太平洋推行的保护海豚的政策属第20条(g)款所涵盖的政策范围。但是，由于未与国内生产或消费的限制一同实施，因而对金枪鱼和金枪鱼产品所维持的不符合第11条的进口禁止不能被第20条(g)款证明合理。同样的不一致性还意味着，进口禁止也不能被第20条(b)款(保护人类、动物或植物生命或健康所必需的措施)和第20条(d)款(为保证与GATT条款不相抵触的法律或法规得到遵守所必需的措施)证明合理。在其最终意见中，专家组指出，美国保护和养

the United States could impose trade embargoes designed to achieve policy changes in other jurisdictions. The panel therefore had to resolve whether the parties to the GATT had given each other the right to impose trade embargoes for this purpose. It considered that Article XX could not be interpreted in this way. *See also* ***extraterritoriality***, ***general exceptions***, ***Tuna (Canada–United States, 1982)*** and ***Tuna I***.

Two-annex method: a way to schedule commitments for services and investment laws and policies in a ***free-trade agreement*** when a negative list is used. The two annexes to the agreement usually are (a) the list of ***non-conforming measures*** (i.e. measures that are not in full compliance with the agreement but are expected to be brought into conformity over time) and (b) a ***reserved list*** containing sectors or activities for which a party may maintain existing restrictions that do not conform to the provisions of the agreement or make them more restrictive. *See also* ***positive listings***.

护海豚的环境目标的有效性不属本争端中的问题。相反，问题在于美国是否可以实施旨在实现其他管辖范围政策变化的贸易禁运。专家组因此必须决定GATT 缔约方是否相互给予为此目的而实施贸易禁运的权利。专家组认为第20条不能以此种方式加以解释。另见*治外法权(extraterritoriality)*、*一般例外(general exceptions)*、*1982年加拿大-美国金枪鱼案(Tuna (Canada–United States, 1982))*、*第一个金枪鱼案(Tuna I)*。

Two-annex method

双附件法

在自由贸易协定中使用负面清单时，将服务和投资方面的法律及政策列入承诺的一种途径。协定的两个附件通常为：(a)不符措施清单(即不完全符合协定但预计随着时间的推移将实现一致的措施)和(b)保留清单，其中包含一参加方可能维持的不符合协定条款的或使之更具限制性的部门或活动。另见*正面清单(positive listings)*。

U

UDEAC: Union douanière et économique de l'Afrique centrale. *See* ***Central African Customs and Economic Union***.

Unbound commitments: commitments under the ***General Agreement on Trade in Services*** (GATS) which can be changed unilaterally by the country making them. They give the listing country complete flexibility to change its trading regime in the affected activity without the need to offer ***compensation***. Unbound commitments are therefore much less valuable than ***binding commitments***, though they may in some cases assist ***transparency***.

UNCED: United Nations Conference on Environment and Development, held from 3 to 14 January 1992 in Rio de Janeiro. This conference adopted the ***United Nations Framework Convention on Climate Change***, the ***Convention on Biological Diversity***, ***Agenda 21***, the ***Rio Declaration on Environment and Development*** and the Statement on Forest Principles.

UN/CEFACT: United Nations Centre for Trade Facilitation and Electronic Business. A subsidiary of the United Nations ***Economic Commission for Europe***. It serves as focal point within ***ECOSOC*** for ***trade facilitation*** recommendations and electronic business standards.

UN/CEFACT Recommendation No. 4: *see* ***PRO Committees***.

UNCITRAL: United Nations Commission on International Trade Law. Established in 1966 for the purpose of reducing or removing legal obstacles to the flow of international trade and the progressive harmonization and unification of the law of international trade. UNCITRAL has thirty-six members who are selected by the ***United Nations General Assembly***. It is the core legal body within the United Nations system in the field of international trade law. UNCITRAL has pursued an extensive work programme on subjects covering particularly international commercial arbitration and conciliation and the international transport and sale of goods. It is located in Vienna. *See also* ***United Nations Convention on the Use of Electronic Communications in International Contracts***. [uncitral.org]

UNCITRAL Arbitration Rules: adopted on 15 December 1976. These rules are aimed at helping to settle disputes arising in the context of international commercial relations. Parties to a contract first have to agree in writing that disputes concerning the contract should be referred to ***arbitration*** under the UNCITRAL Arbitration Rules. Disputes will then be settled in accordance with these rules. One or three arbitrators may be appointed depending on the circumstances of the case. This instrument also contains a ***Model Arbitration Clause***.

U

UDEAC

中部非洲关税与经济同盟

见*中部非洲关税与经济同盟(Central African Customs and Economic Union)*。

Unbound commitments

非约束承诺

可以由作出承诺的国家单方面改变的《服务贸易总协定》项下的承诺。这些承诺给予作出承诺的国家充分灵活性，以改变受影响活动的贸易制度，而无需提供补偿。因此，非约束承诺的价值远低于约束承诺，尽管在一些情况下这些承诺可以有助于提高透明度。

UNCED

联合国环境与发展会议

1992年1月3日至14日在里约热内卢举行。会议通过了《联合国气候变化框架公约》、《生物多样性公约》、《21世纪议程》、《里约环境与发展宣言》和《关于森林原则的声明》。

UN/CEFACT

联合国贸易便利化与电子商务中心

联合国欧洲经济委员会附属机构。作为联合国经社理事会(ECOSOC)贸易便利化建议和电子商务标准的协调中心。

UN/CEFACT Recommendation No. 4

联合国贸易便利化与电子商务中心建议第4号

见*贸易便利化委员会(PRO Committees)*。

UNCITRAL

联合国国际贸易法委员会

1966年成立，目的在于减少或消除国际贸易流动的法律障碍，并逐步协调和统一国际贸易法。UNCITRAL有36个成员，由联合国大会选出。是联合国系统内国际贸易法领域的核心法律机构。UNCITRAL推行一项广泛的工作计划，特别涵盖国际商事仲裁和调解及国际货物运输和销售方面等议题。委员会设在维也纳。另见*联合国国际合同使用电子通信公约(United Nations Convention on the Use of Electronic Communications in International Contracts)*。

UNCITRAL Arbitration Rules

联合国国际贸易法委员会仲裁规则

1976年12月15日通过。规则旨在帮助解决在国际商业关系中产生的争议。合同当事人首先必须书面同意，有关合同的争议应根据仲裁规则提交仲裁。争议随后依照这些规则加以解决。可指定1名或3名仲裁人，数量取决于案情。该一文件还包含一项示范仲裁条款。

UNCITRAL model law on electronic commerce: adopted on 16 December 1996. Its purpose is to give legislators a way to remove legal obstacles to the wider use of electronic messages in the conduct of international transactions. The model law does not define the meaning of ***electronic commerce***, but it applies to all kinds of data messages that might be generated, stored or communicated. Chapter II deals with the application of the legal requirements to data messages, such as the treatment of signatures, the admissibility of data messages in evidence and the retention of data messages. Chapter III covers the communication of data messages, especially the formation and validity of contracts. A separate chapter deals with actions related to contracts of carriage of goods.

UNCITRAL model law on procurement of goods, construction and services: a model law adopted by ***UNCITRAL*** in 1994 for use by national legislatures that are considering adopting new or revised ***government procurement*** legislation. Its main objectives are economy and efficiency in government purchasing, maximizing participation of bidders and competition among them, fairness in the treatment of bidders, objectivity in decision-making, and transparency of regulations and process.

UNCLOS: *see* ***United Nations Convention on the Law of the Sea*** and ***Exclusive Economic Zone***.

UN Commodity Trade Statistics Database: *see* ***COMTRADE database***.

UNCPC: *see* ***United Nations Central Product Classification***.

UNCTAD: United Nations Conference on Trade and Development. Established in 1964 through ***United Nations General Assembly*** resolution (XIX) 1995 to promote a greater participation by developing countries in the global trading system and thereby promote their economic development. In October 2004 it had 192 members. UNCTAD describes itself as the primary forum for analysis, discussion and consensus-building on policies designed to achieve ***sustainable development*** in all regions to accelerate growth in weaker economies. The reasons leading to the formation of UNCTAD were broadly the difficulties developing countries appeared to experience in furthering their economic development, and the absence of any specialized international organization which might have assisted them in this challenge. Pressure for adequate attention to their problems increased as many colonies became independent in the early 1960s. In 1961, the Second Committee of ***ECOSOC*** asked the United Nations Secretary-General to consult on the possibility of holding a world conference on international trade problems, and in 1962 the United Nations General Assembly decided to hold the conference in Geneva in 1964. This conference became known as UNCTAD I. One of its early effects was the formation of the ***Group of 77*** which quickly seized the initiative in formulating the UNCTAD agenda. Many of the issues that would ultimately make up UNCTAD's work programme were discussed at this conference, including commodities trade and arrangements, manufactures, transfer of capital and shipping. Later additions to the work programme included debt, insurance, ***ECDC*** (economic cooperation between developing countries), ***restrictive***

UNCITRAL model law on electronic commerce
联合国国际贸易法委员会电子商务示范法

1996年12月16日通过。目的在于为立法者提供一种消除在国际交易中更广泛使用电子信息的法律障碍的方法。示范法没有界定电子商务的含义，但适用于可能生成、储存或传递的各种数据电文。第二章处理对数据电文适用法律要求的问题，例如签名的处理、数据电文作为证据的可接受性和数据电文的留存。第三章涵盖数据信息的传递，特别是合同的订立和有效性。一个单独章节处理与货物运输合同有关的行动。

UNCITRAL model law on procurement of goods, construction and services
联合国国际贸易法委员会货物、工程和服务采购示范法

联合国国际贸易法委员会(UNCITRAL)1994年通过的示范法，供正在考虑通过新的或经修改的政府采购法的国家立法机构使用。主要目标为政府采购中的经济和效率、投标人的参与和竞争最大化、公平对待投标人、决策的客观性以及法规和程序的透明度。

UNCLOS
联合国海洋法公约

见*联合国海洋法公约(United Nations Convention on the Law of the Sea)*、*专属经济区(Exclusive Economic Zone)*。

UN Commodity Trade Statistics Database
联合国商品贸易统计数据库

见*商品贸易统计数据库(COMTRADE database)*。

UNCPC
联合国中央产品分类

见*联合国中央产品分类(United Nations Central Product Classification)*。

UNCTAD
联合国贸易与发展会议

根据联合国大会第1995(XIX)号决议于1964年建立，旨在促进发展中国家更多参与全球贸易体系，从而促进其经济发展。2004年10月，UNCTAD有192个成员。UNCTAD自称是就在所有地区实质可持续发展从而加快较弱经济体增长的政策进行分析、讨论和形成共识的主要场所。促成UNCTAD建立的原因主要是发展中国家在促进自身经济发展方面遇到的困难，而缺乏任何专门的国际组织可以协助它们应对这一挑战。随着许多殖民地在20世纪60年代初独立，对它们的问题给予充分关注的压力增大。1961年，联合国经社理事会(ECOSOC)第二委员会请联合国秘书长就举行一个国际贸易问题世界会议的可能性进行磋商，联合国大会于1962年决定于1964年在日内瓦举行会议。此次会议成为UNCTAD一大。此次会议的早期影响之一是77国集团的成立，这一集团迅速掌握了制定UNCTAD议程的主动权。此次会议上讨论了最终构成UNCTAD工作计划的许多问题，包括商品贸易和安排、制成品、资本转移和航运。后来加入工作计划的议题包括债务、保险、发展中国家间经济合作(ECDC)、限制性

business practices, ***transfer of technology***, and the problems of ***least-developed countries***, among others. Despite the contribution UNCTAD has made to the development of developing countries, it has on the whole not been able to achieve the role its proponents expected it to have. UNCTAD has been particularly active in the development of the ***GSP*** and international commodity arrangements. The secretariat prepares many high-class reports, particularly the ***World Investment Report***, the *International Investment Agreement Issues Papers*, the ***Digital Economy Report***, the ***Least-Developed Countries Report*** and the ***Trade and Development Report***, which do not always attract adequate discussion by the UNCTAD membership. The executive body of UNCTAD is the ***Trade and Development Board*** which meets once a year in a regular session. UNCTAD's substantive work is done under the auspices of the ***UNCTAD Trade and Development Commission*** and the ***UNCTAD Commission on Investment, Enterprise and Development***. UNCTAD is also the name used for the ministerial conference held every four years under its auspices. UNCTAD I was held in Geneva. The other conferences were held at New Delhi (UNCTAD II, 1968), Santiago de Chile (UNCTAD III, 1972), Nairobi (UNCTAD IV, 1976), Manila (UNCTAD V, 1979), Belgrade (UNCTAD VI, 1983), Geneva (UNCTAD VII, 1987), Cartagena (UNCTAD VIII, 1992), Midrand (UNCTAD IX, 1996), Bangkok (UNCTAD X, 2000), São Paulo (UNCTAD XI, 2004), Accra (UNCTAD XII, 2008), Doha (UNCTAD XIII, 2012) and Nairobi (UNCTAD XIV, 2016. UNCTAD XV will be held in August 2020 in Bridgetown, Barbados. *See also* ***ASYCUDA***, ***Common Fund for Commodities***, ***GSP***, ***Integrated Programme for Commodities*** and ***Trade Efficiency Programme***.

UNCTAD Automated System for Customs Data: *see* ***ASYCUDA***.

UNCTAD BioTrade Initiative: BTI. The objective of BTI is to contribute to the conservation and sustainable use of ***biodiversity*** through the promotion of trade and investment in ***BioTrade products*** and services in line with the objectives and principles of the ***Convention on Biological Diversity***. BioTrade includes activities related to the collection or production, transformation and commercialization of goods and services derived from native diversity (genetic resources, species and ecosystems) according to criteria of environmental, social and economic sustainability. The BTI is organized along seven principles, and criteria have been developed for assessments under each of the principles. The principles are (1) conservation of biodiversity, (2) sustainable use of diversity, (3) fair and equitable sharing of benefits derived from the use of biodiversity, (4) socio-economic sustainability (productive, financial and market management), (5) compliance with national and international regulations, (6) respect for the rights of actors involved in BioTrade activity, and (7) clarity about land tenure, use of and access to natural resources and knowledge. One of the activities under this Initiative is the BioTrade Facilitation Programme which focuses on enhancing sustainable bio-resources management, product development, value-adding processing and marketing. *See also* ***Blue BioTrade*** and ***sustainable development***. [www.unctad.org]

商业惯例、技术转让以及最不发达国家问题等等。尽管UNCTAD对发展中国家的发展作出了贡献，但总体上未能发挥其支持者所期望的作用。UNCTAD在发展普惠制(GSP)和国际商品安排方面特别积极。秘书处编写了许多高级别报告，特别是《世界投资报告》、《国际投资协定问题文件》、《数字经济报告》、《最不发达国家报告》和《贸易与发展报告》，这些报告并不总能吸引UNCTAD成员进行充分讨论。UNCTAD的执行机构是贸易与发展理事会，每年召开一次例会。UNCTAD的实质性工作是在UNCTAD贸易与发展委员会和UNCTAD投资、企业与发展委员会主持下完成的。UNCTAD也用于指在其主持下每4年举行一次的部长级会议。第1届大会在日内瓦举行。其他会议分别在新德里(第2届大会，1968年)、智利圣地亚哥(第3届大会，1972年)、内罗毕(第4届大会，1976年)、马尼拉(第5届大会，1979年)、贝尔格莱德(第6届大会，1983年)、日内瓦(第7届大会，1987年)、卡塔赫纳(第8届大会，1992年)、米德兰 (第9届大会，1996年)、曼谷 (第10届大会，2000年)、圣保罗(第11届大会，2004年)、阿克拉(第12届大会，2008年)、多哈(第13届大会，2012年)、内罗毕(第14届大会，2016年)。第15届大会定于2020年8月在巴巴多斯的布里奇顿举行。另见*海关数据自动化系统(ASYCUDA)*、*商品共同基金(Common Fund for Commodities)*、*普惠制(GSP)*、*商品综合方案(Integrated Programme for Commodities)*、*贸易效率计划(Trade Efficiency Programme)*。

UNCTAD Automated System for Customs Data

UNCTAD海关数据自动系统

见*海关数据自动化系统(ASYCUDA)*。

UNCTAD BioTrade Initiative

UNCTAD生物贸易倡议

BTI。BTI的目标是按照《生物多样性公约》的目标和原则，通过促进生物贸易产品和服务的贸易和投资，为生物多样性的维护和可持续利用作出贡献。生物贸易包括根据环境、社会和经济可持续性标准，收集或生产、转化和商业化源自本地多样性(遗传资源、物种和生态系统)的商品和服务的活动。BTI 按照七项原则进行组织，并制定根据每一原则进行评估的标准。这些原则为：(1)保护生物多样性；(2)可持续利用生物多样性；(3)公平和公正分享利用生物多样性所产生的收益；(4)社会经济可持续性(生产、财务和市场管理)；(5)遵守国家和国际法规；(6)尊重参与生物贸易活动的行为者的权利；以及(7)明确土地保有权、自然资源和知识的使用和获取。该倡议下的活动之一是生物贸易便利化计划，其重点是加强可持续生物资源管理、产品开发、增值加工和销售。另见*蓝色生物贸易(Blue BioTrade)*、*可持续发展(sustainable development)*。

UNCTAD Coding System of Trade Control Measures: a comprehensive classification system divided into more than 100 different types of trade measures, maintained by the ***UNCTAD*** Secretariat. Its main components are (a) tariff measures (statutory customs duties, MFN duties, GATT ***ceiling duties***, seasonal duties, temporary reduced duties, temporary increased duties and preferential duties under trade agreements, (b) para-tariff measures (customs surcharges, additional charges, internal taxes and charges levied on imports and decreed customs valuation), (c) price control measures (administrative price fixing, voluntary export restraint, anti-dumping measures, anti-dumping investigations, anti-dumping duties, anti-dumping price undertakings, countervailing measures, countervailing investigations, countervailing duties and countervailing undertakings), (d) finance measures (advance payment requirements, multiple exchange rates, restrictive official foreign exchange allocation, regulations concerning terms of payments for imports, transfer delays, queues, etc.), (e) automatic licensing measures and import monitoring, (f) quality control measures (non-automatic licensing, quotas, prohibitions, export restraint arrangements and enterprise-specific restrictions), (g) monopolistic measures (single channel for imports and compulsory national services), and (h) technical measures (technical regulations, preshipment inspection, special customs formalities and obligation to return used product). The coding system also lists environmental, sanitary and phytosanitary measures under relevant sub-headings. The ***UNCTAD TRAINS*** database makes extensive use of this coding system. [www.unctad.org]

UNCTAD Commission on Investment, Enterprise and Development: meets annually for discussions of issues related to investment, investment facilitation, investment promotion and technology. [www.unctad.org]

UNCTAD Global Action Menu for Investment Facilitation: issued in a revised version in May 2017. It defines investment facilitation as "the set of policies and actions aimed at making it easier for investors to establish and expand their investments, as well as to conduct their day-to-day business in host countries". The Menu has ten Action Lines: (1) promote accessibility and transparency in investment policies and regulations and procedures relevant to investors, (2) enhance predictability and consistency in the application of investment policies, (3) improve the efficiency of investment administrative procedures, (4) build constructive stakeholder relationships in investment policy practice, (5) designate a lead agency, focal point or investment facilitator with a mandate to take relevant action, (6) establish monitoring and review mechanisms for investment facilitation, (7) enhance international cooperation on investment facilitation, (8) strengthen investment facilitation efforts in developing-country partners through support and technical assistance, (9) enhance investment policy and proactive investment attraction in developing-country partners through capacity-building in a broad range of areas, and (10) complement investment facilitation by enhancing international cooperation for investment promotion for development, including through

UNCTAD Coding System of Trade Control Measures

UNCTAD贸易管制措施编码系统

将贸易措施分为100多种不同类型的综合分类系统，由联合国贸易与发展会议(UNCTAD)秘书处维护。主要组成部分为：(a)关税措施(法定关税、最惠国关税、GATT上限税率、季节性关税、临时减税、临时加税和贸易协定项下优惠关税)；(b)准关税措施(关税附加费、附加费用、国内税和进口收费以及法定海关估价)；(c)价格控制措施(行政定价、自愿出口限制、反倾销措施、反倾销调查、反倾销税、反倾销价格承诺、反补贴措施、反补贴调查、反补贴税和反补贴承诺)；(d)金融措施(预付款要求、多重汇率、限制性官方外汇分配、有关进口付款条件、转让延迟、排队等候等的规定)；(e)自动许可措施和进口监测；(f)数量控制措施(非自动许可程序、配额、禁止、出口限制安排和特定企业限制)；(g)垄断措施(单一进口渠道和强制性国家服务)；以及(h)技术措施(技术法规、装运前检验、特殊海关手续和退货义务)。编码系统还在相关子目下列出环境、卫生和植物卫生措施。UNCTAD TRAINS数据库广泛使用了这一编码系统。

UNCTAD Commission on Investment, Enterprise and Development

UNCTAD投资、企业和发展委员会

每年举行会议，讨论与投资、投资便利化、投资促进和技术有关的问题。

UNCTAD Global Action Menu for Investment Facilitation

UNCTAD全球投资便利化行动清单

2017年5月发布修订版。清单将投资便利化定义为“旨在使投资者更容易设立和扩大其投资以及在东道国中开展日常业务的一套政策和行动”。清单有10条行动方针：(1)促进与投资者相关的投资政策、法规和程序的可获性和透明度；(2)提高投资政策实施的可预测性和一致性；(3)提高投资管理程序的效率；(4)在投资政策实践中建立利益攸关方建设性关系；(5)指定一负责采取相关行动的牵头机构、协调中心或投资促进者；(6)建立投资便利化监测和审查机制；(7)加强投资便利化方面的国际合作；(8)通过支持和技术援助加强发展中国家伙伴中的投资便利化的努力；(9)通过在广泛领域的能力建设加强发展中国家伙伴的投资政策水平和积极吸引投资的能力；以及(10)通过加强促进发展投资

provisions in ***international investment agreements***. *See also* ***investment facilitation***. [investmentpolicy.unctad.org]

UNCTAD Investment Policy Framework for Sustainable Development: *see* ***Investment Policy Framework for Sustainable Development***.

UNCTAD Investment Policy Review: *see* ***Investment Policy Review***.

UNCTAD Liner Code: *see* ***Convention on a Code of Conduct for Liner Conferences***.

UNCTAD Set of Multilaterally Agreed Equitable Principles and Rules for the Control of Restrictive Business Practices: *see* ***restrictive business practices***.

UNCTAD's Reform Package for the International Investment Regime: a proposal by the ***UNCTAD*** Secretariat issued in revised form in 2018 intended to improve the international investment regime and its benefits. It focuses particularly on ***international investment agreements*** (IIAs), and it proposes a work programme consisting of three phases. The proponents note that the use of "phases" does not imply a time sequence (a phase is more like a grouping of issues), and that the reform package should be considered a "living document". The reform package is informed by six guidelines: (i) harness IIAs for sustainable development, (ii) focus on critical reform areas, (iii) act at all levels, (iv) sequence properly for concrete solutions, (v) ensure an inclusive and transparent reform process, and (vi) strengthen the multilateral supportive structure. Phase 1 concerns the substance of IIAs with five priority areas: (i) safeguarding the right to regulate in the public interest while providing protection, (ii) reforming investment dispute settlement, (iii) promoting and facilitating investment, (iv) ensuring responsible investment, and (v) enhancing the systemic consistency of the IIA regime. Phase 2 envisages the modernization of existing treaties through amendments, replacement of "outdated" treaties, abandoning unratified old treaties, terminating existing old treaties, etc. Phase 3 focuses on improving coherence, consistency and interaction between different levels and types of policymaking. *See also* ***Investment Policy Framework for Sustainable Development*** and ***UNCTAD Global Action Menu for Investment Facilitation***. [investmentpolicy.unctad.org]

UNCTAD Trade and Development Commission: established at UNCTAD XII in 2008. Its mandate covers trade in goods, trade in services, and commodities. Meets annually.

UNCTAD TRAINS: Trade Analysis and Information System. A database containing trade control measures (tariffs, para-tariffs and non-tariff measures), as well as import flows, for more than 100 countries at the six-digit level of the ***Harmonized Commodity Description and Coding System***.

UNCTAD Virtual Institute on Trade and Development: Vi. Launched at UNCTAD XI in 2004. Its aim is to help developing countries design evidence-based policies resulting in inclusive and sustainable development. The mechanism is the involvement of academic institutions. Institutional membership is open to universities and research centres involved in the teaching and

的国际合作补充投资便利化，包括通过国际投资协定中的条款。另见*投资便利化(investment facilitation)*。

UNCTAD Investment Policy Framework for Sustainable Development

UNCTAD可持续发展的投资政策框架

见*可持续发展投资政策框架(Investment Policy Framework for Sustainable Development)*。

UNCTAD Investment Policy Review

UNCTAD投资政策审议

见*投资政策审议(Investment Policy Review)*。

UNCTAD Liner Code

UNCTAD班轮守则

见*班轮公会行动守则公约(Convention on a Code of Conduct for Liner Conferences)*。

UNCTAD Set of Multilaterally Agreed Equitable Principles and Rules for the Control of Restrictive Business Practices

UNCTAD一套多边协议的控制限制性商业惯例的公平原则和规则

见*限制性商业惯例(restrictive business practices)*。

UNCTAD's Reform Package for the International Investment Regime

UNCTAD关于国际投资制度的一揽子改革方案

联合国贸易与发展会议(UNCTAD)秘书处于2018年发布该提案的修订版，旨在改进国际投资制度和提升其利益。改革方案特别关注国际投资协定(IIAs)，提出一个由三阶段组成的工作计划。提案方指出，"阶段"一词并非意味着时间顺序(一阶段更像是一组问题)，应将改革方案视为一份"活文件"。改革方案遵循6项指导方针：(1)利用国际投资协定促进可持续发展；(2)聚焦关键改革领域；(3)在各级采取行动；(4)为具体解决方案合理排序；(5)保证包容和透明的改革进程；以及(6)加强多边支持结构。第1阶段涉及国际投资协定的实质内容，包含5个优先领域：(1)在提供保护的同时，保障为公共利益而进行监管的权利；(2)改革投资争端解决；(3)促进和便利投资；(4)保护负责任的投资；(5)增强国际投资协定体制的系统一致性。第2阶段设想通过修正使现行条约实现现代化，替代"过时"条约，废止未批准的旧条约、终止现行旧条约等。第3阶段聚焦改进不同级别和类型决策之间的连贯性、一致性和互动性。另见*可持续发展投资政策框架(Investment Policy Framework for Sustainable Development)*、*UNCTAD全球投资便利化行动清单(UNCTAD Global Action Menu for Investment Facilitation)*。

UNCTAD Trade and Development Commission

UNCTAD贸易与发展委员会

在2008年联合国贸易与发展会议(UNCTAD)第12届大会上设立。任务包括货物贸易、服务贸易和商品。每年举行会议。

UNCTAD TRAINS

UNCTAD贸易分析与信息系统

包含100多个国家的贸易控制措施(关税、准关税和非关税措施)及进口流量的数据库，以商品名称及编码协调制度6位编码列出。

UNCTAD Virtual Institute on Trade and Development

UNCTAD贸易与发展虚拟学院

Vi。在2004年联合国贸易与发展会议(UNCTAD)第11届大会上启动。旨在帮助发展中国家设计产生包容性和可持续发展的循证政策。该机制由学术机构参

research of trade and development topics. Vi has more than 100 members in 52 countries. [vi.unctad.org]

Under-invoicing: preparing or presenting an invoice giving a price for goods or services that is lower than the price actually paid for them. The motivation may be to reduce the amount of customs duties payable in the case of goods, or to reduce the amount of internal taxes payable in the case of goods and services. *See also* ***over-invoicing***.

Understanding on Commitments in Financial Services: an adjunct to the ***General Agreement on Trade in Services*** (GATS) adopted by developed WTO members only. It defines further how fair trade in ***financial services*** should be understood in GATS terms. The Understanding forms the basis for ***negative listings*** in the schedules of commitments.

Understanding on Rules and Procedures Governing the Settlement of Disputes: usually known as the ***Dispute Settlement Understanding*** or simply DSU. It contains the rules WTO members must follow when they become party to a dispute that involves their rights and obligations under the WTO disciplines.

Understanding on tariff rate quota administration provisions of agricultural products: adopted at the Bali ***WTO Ministerial Conference*** in 2013. The Understanding deems tariff quota administration of scheduled tariff quotas an instance of "import licensing" within the WTO ***Agreement on Import Licensing Procedures***, and that Agreement applies in full to such quotas. The Understanding also introduces a range of more specific transparency and administration provisions.

Understanding on the Balance-of-Payments Provisions of the GATT: one of the ***Uruguay Round*** outcomes. Its purpose is to clarify the rules on the imposition of measures available to WTO members under GATT Articles XII and XVIII:B to improve their balance-of-payments conditions. In particular, it seeks to achieve greater ***transparency*** through an improved system of ***notifications*** and ***consultations***.

Undertakings: the WTO ***Agreement on Subsidies and Countervailing Measures*** allows the investigating authority to suspend or terminate its proceedings if it receives a satisfactory voluntary undertaking that would remove the effect of that part of the ***subsidy*** causing ***injury***. Two options are available. First, the exporter's government can agree to eliminate or limit the subsidy or otherwise deal with its effects. Second, the exporter can undertake to raise the price sufficiently to remove the injury caused by the subsidy. Undertakings may only be made or accepted if there has been a ***preliminary affirmative determination of subsidization*** and injury so caused.

Undisclosed information: the ***Agreement on Trade-Related Aspects of Intellectual Property Rights*** requires WTO members to protect some types of undisclosed information. This protection is available as long as the information is (a) secret in the sense that it is not, in its entirety or in parts, generally known among or readily accessible to persons who normally deal with this kind of

与，机构成员资格向参与教学和研究的大学和研究中心开放，在52个国家拥有100多名成员。

Under-invoicing

低开发票

制备或出具显示货物或服务价格低于实际支付价格的发票。动机可能是为减少货物应付关税税额，或减少货物和服务的国内税税额。另见*高开发票(over-invoicing)*。

Understanding on Commitments in Financial Services

关于金融服务承诺的谅解

《服务贸易总协定》(GATS)附件，仅由WTO发达成员采用。谅解进一步规定如何从GATS条款的角度理解金融服务中的公平贸易。谅解构成承诺减让表中的负面清单的基础。

Understanding on Rules and Procedures Governing the Settlement of Disputes

关于争端解决规则与程序的谅解

通常称为《争端解决谅解》或DSU。包含WTO成员作为涉及其在WTO纪律项下权利和义务的争端方时必须遵守的规则。

Understanding on tariff rate quota administration provisions of agricultural products

关于农产品关税税率配额管理规定的谅解

2013年巴厘岛WTO部长级会议通过。谅解将列入减让表的关税配额的管理视为WTO《进口许可程序协定》范围内的"进口许可"，《进口许可程序协定》应全部适用。谅解还引入了一系列更具体的透明度和管理规定。

Understanding on the Balance-of-Payments Provisions of the GATT

关于1994年关税与贸易总协定国际收支条款的谅解

乌拉圭回合成果。目的是澄清WTO成员根据GATT第12条和第18条B节规定为改善其国际收支状况采取措施的规则。特别是，谅解寻求通过改进的通报和磋商制度实现更大的透明度。

Undertakings

承诺

WTO《补贴与反补贴措施协定》允许调查机关在收到关于可消除造成损害的补贴的令人满意的自愿承诺后可以中止或终止其程序。有两种选择。一是出口商的政府可以同意取消或限制补贴，或以其他方式处理其影响。二是出口商可以承诺提高价格，足以消除补贴造成的损害。承诺只有在作出补贴初步肯定裁定且已经造成损害的情况下方有可能作出或接受。

Undisclosed information

未披露信息

WTO《与贸易有关的知识产权协定》要求WTO成员保护某些类型的未披露信息。只要此类信息属下列情况即提供保护：(a)属秘密，即作为一个整体或就其各部分的精确排列和组合而言，该信息尚不为通常处理所涉及信息范围内的人所普遍知晓，或不易为其所获得；(b)因属秘密而具有商业价值；以及(c)

information, (b) has commercial value because it is secret, and (c) and the person lawfully in control of the information has taken reasonable steps to protect it. Members who require testing of new pharmaceuticals or agricultural chemical products before they are put on the market have to protect data supplied against unfair commercial use. *See also* ***in a manner contrary to honest commercial practices*** and ***trade secrets***.

UNDP: *see* ***United Nations Development Programme***.

UN/EDIFACT: United Nations Rules for Electronic Data Interchange for Administration, Commerce and Transport. They are maintained by the United Nations ***Economic Commission for Europe***. UN/EDIFACT provides a set of syntax rules to structure data. It is a UN-recommended standard used in business and government. *See also* ***trade facilitation***. [unece.org]

UNEP: *see* ***United Nations Environment Programme***.

UNESCO: *see* ***United Nations Educational, Scientific and Cultural Organization***.

Unfair business practices: *see* ***restrictive business practices***.

Unfair competition: defined in Article 10bis of the ***Paris Convention*** as any act "contrary to honest practices in industrial or commercial matters". The Convention prohibits (1) all acts of such a nature as to create confusion by any means whatever with the establishment, the goods, or industrial or commercial activities, of a competitor, (2) false allegations in the course of trade of such a nature as to discredit the establishment, the goods, or industrial or commercial activities, of a competitor, and (3) the use of indications or allegations which in the course of trade is liable to mislead the public as to the nature, the manufacturing process, the characteristics, the suitability for their purpose, or the quantity of the goods. Many competition and consumer protection laws also deal with unfair competition. *See also* ***passing off***, ***restrictive business practices*** and ***WIPO Model Provisions on Protection Against Unfair Competition***.

Unfair pricing practices: a term used by some to mean ***dumping***.

Unfair-trade remedies: *see* ***trade remedies***.

Unfair trading practices: refers to the improper or illegal use of ***subsidies*** or the export of products at dumped prices. *See also* ***anti-dumping measures***, ***countervailing measures*** and ***dumping***.

Unfavourable balance of trade: *see* ***balance of trade*** and ***mercantilism***.

Unforeseen developments: GATT Article XIX allows WTO members to impose safeguard action if a "product is being imported in such increased quantities as to cause or threaten serious ***injury***" to domestic producers of the ***like product***, but only if the increased imports are due to unforeseen developments and the effect of trade liberalization. The article does not define what an unforeseen development might be. In 1950 the Working Party considering ***Hatters' fur*** noted that "the term 'unforeseen developments' should be interpreted to mean developments occurring after the negotiation of the relevant ***concession*** which it would not be reasonable to expect that the negotiators of the country seeking the concessions could and should have foreseen at the time when the

信息的合法控制人采取合理的步骤加以保护。要求新药或农用化学品在投放市场前进行试验的成员必须保护所提交的数据，以防止不正当的商业使用。另见*以违反诚实商业惯例的方式(in a manner contrary to honest commercial practices)*、*商业秘密(trade secrets)*。

UNDP

联合国开发计划署

见*联合国开发计划署(United Nations Development Programme)*。

UN/EDIFACT

联合国行政、商业和运输用电子数据交换规则

由联合国欧洲经济委员会维护。UN/EDIFACT提供了一套构造数据的语法规则，是联合国建议用于商业和政府的标准。另见*贸易便利化(trade facilitation)*。

UNEP

联合国环境规划署

见*联合国环境规划署(United Nations Environment Programme)*。

UNESCO

联合国教育、科学及文化组织

见*联合国教育、科学及文化组织(*United Nations Educational, Scientific and Cultural Organization*)*。

Unfair business practices

不正当商业做法

见*限制性商业惯例(restrictive business practice)*。

Unfair competition

不正当竞争

《巴黎公约》第10条之二中将其定义为，“凡在工商业事务中违反诚实的习惯做法”。公约禁止(1)具有不择手段地对竞争者的营业所、商品或工商业活动造成混乱性质的一切行为；(2)在经营商业中，具有损害竞争者的营业所、商品或工商业活动商誉性质的虚伪说法；以及(3)在经营商业中使用会使公众对商品的性质、制造方法、特点、用途或数量易于产生误解的表示或说法。许多竞争和消费者保护法也处理不正当竞争。另见*假冒商品(passing off)*、*限制性商业惯例(restrictive business practices)*、*WIPO反不正当竞争示范条款(WIPO Model Provisions on Protection Against Unfair Competition)*。

Unfair pricing practices

不公平定价行为

一些人所用词语，意为倾销。

Unfair-trade remedies

不公平贸易救济措施

见*贸易救济(trade remedies)*。

Unfair trading practices

不公平贸易做法

指不适当或非法使用补贴或以倾销价格出口产品。另见*反倾销措施(anti-dumping measures)*、*反补贴措施(countervailing measures)*、*倾销(dumping)*。

Unfavourable balance of trade

贸易逆差

见*贸易平衡(balance of trade)*、*重商主义(mercantilism)*。

Unforeseen developments

未预见的情况

GATT第19条允许WTO成员在一种产品“进口数量增加如此之大且情况如此严重，以至于对同类产品或直接竞争产品的国内生产者造成或威胁造成严重损害”的情况下采取保障措施，但条件是进口增长是因未预见的情况和贸易自由化的影响。该条未定义未预见的情况可能是什么。1950年，审议“裘皮女帽案”的工作组指出，“‘未预见的情况’一词应解释为在相关减让谈判之后发生

concession was negotiated". The ***Agreement on Safeguards***, which interprets and amplifies Article XIX, does not list "unforeseen developments" among the conditions enabling safeguards action. Many then assumed that this criterion was no longer applicable. They were too hasty. In *Argentina – Safeguard Measures on Imports of Footwear* and *Korea – Definite Safeguard Measure on Imports of certain Dairy Products* the ***Appellate Body*** held that the two provisions were part of the one treaty, and that they had to be read "harmoniously" and as "an inseparable package of rights and disciplines". [GATT/CP/106, WT/DS/98/AB/R, WT/DS/121/AB/R, Mueller 2003]

UNGASS: United Nations General Assembly Special Session. *See* ***United Nations General Assembly***.

UNIDO: *see* ***United Nations Industrial Development Organization***.

Unidroit Convention on Stolen or Illegally Exported Cultural Objects: adopted in Rome on 24 June 1995. The Convention requires the owner of a cultural object which has been stolen, unlawfully excavated or lawfully excavated but unlawfully retained, to return it. A party to the Convention (contracting state) may request the courts of another party to order the return of a cultural object illegally exported from the requesting party. Claims generally have to be made within fifty years from the time of the theft. Compensation may be payable in some circumstances. *See also* ***Convention on the Means of Prohibiting and Preventing the Illicit Import, Export and Transfer of Ownership of Cultural Property***.

Uniform tariff: a tariff schedule in which the rates are the same, or nearly the same, for all products. The best-known example of a uniform tariff is that of Chile which applies a most-favoured-nation rate of 6 per cent for nearly all products. Most of its bound rates were set at 25 per cent. *See also* ***dispersed tariff rates*** and ***flat-tariff structure***.

Unilateralism: this term has two quite different meanings in ***trade policy***. The first is the policy or action of lowering tariffs or removing other impediments to trade unilaterally without the expectation of reciprocal action by others. The second meaning is the desire to impose one's view of the desirable features of global trade policy or trade in a particular product on others, and have it accepted by them. Unilateralism of this kind only works if one has the advantage of overwhelming economic dominance, but success is not assured even then. It can achieve some of one's objectives, but it usually leads to a prolonged adversarial atmosphere. For most countries, the cost exacted in terms of resources to be used and the likely benefits to be gained would not make it an option anyway. *See also* ***bilateralism***, ***multilateralism***, ***reciprocity***, ***Section 301***, ***Special 301*** and ***Super 301***.

Unilateral preferential agreements: also called ***asymmetrical trade agreements***. These are preferential trade agreements under which a party receives preferential treatment without being expected to requite this treatment.

Unilateral preferential rules of origin: *see* ***autonomous preferential rules of origin***.

Union du Maghreb Arabe: UMA. *See* ***Arab Maghreb Union***.

的情况，此种情况期望寻求减让的国家在谈判减让时能够和应该预见到是不合理的。”解释和详述第19条的《保障措施协定》未将“未预见的情况”列入采取保障措施的条件之中。因而许多人认为，这一条件不再适用。但他们过于草率了。在“阿根廷-对进口鞋类保障措施案”和“韩国-奶制品进口最终保障措施案”中，上诉机构认为，两条款均为一个条约组成部分，应“以协调的方式”加以理解，并作为“不可分割的一揽子权利与纪律”。

UNGASS

联合国大会特别会议

见*联合国大会(United Nations General Assembly)*。

UNIDO

联合国工业发展组织

见*联合国工业发展组织(United Nations Industrial Development Organization)*。

Unidroit Convention on Stolen or Illegally Exported Cultural Objects

国际统一私法协会关于被盗或者非法出口文物的公约

1995年6月24日在罗马通过。公约要求，被盗、非法发掘或合法发掘但非法占有的文物的占有人应返还该文物。公约的参加方(缔约国)可以请求另一参加方的法院命令归还自请求国非法出口的文物。归还请求通常必须在被盗时起50年内提出。某些情况下可以支付补偿。另见*关于禁止和防止非法进出口文化财产和非法转让其所有权的方法的公约(Convention on the Means of Prohibiting and Preventing the Illicit Import, Export and Transfer of Ownership of Cultural Property)*。

Uniform tariff

统一关税

所有产品的税率相同或几乎相同的关税税则。统一关税的著名例子是智利，几乎所有产品均实行6%的最惠国税率，大部分约束关税定在25%。另见*分散型税率(dispersed tariff rates)*、*单一关税结构(flat-tariff structure)*。

Unilateralism

单边主义

该词在贸易政策中有两个截然不同的含义：第一个含义是单方面降低关税或取消其他贸易障碍而不期望其他各方采取互惠行动的政策或行动。第二个含义是期望将自己对全球贸易政策或对一特定产品贸易所期望拥有特点的观点强加于其他人，并要求其他人接受。这种单边主义只有在该成员具有压倒性经济优势时才能起作用，但即使如此也不能保证成功。这种做法能够实现一方的部分目标，但常常会导致漫长的敌对气氛。对大多数国家而言，使用资源方面的成本和可能获得的利益不会使之成为一种选项。另见*双边主义(bilateralism)*、*多边主义(multilateralism)*、*互惠(reciprocity)*、*301条款(Section 301)*、*特别301条款(Special 301)*、*超级301条款(Super 301)*。

Unilateral preferential agreements

单边优惠协定

也称非对称贸易协定。指一参加方获得优惠待遇而并不要求对此种待遇作出回报的优惠贸易协定。

Unilateral preferential rules of origin

单边优惠原产地规则

见*自主优惠原产地规则(autonomous preferential rules of origin)*。

Union du Maghreb Arabe

阿拉伯马格里布联盟

见*阿拉伯马格里布联盟(Arab Maghreb Union)*。

Union Économique et Monétaire Ouest Africaine: UEMOA. *See* ***West African Economic and Monetary Union***.

Union for the Mediterranean: an intergovernmental organization consisting of the twenty-seven members of the ***European Union*** and fifteen countries of the Southern and Eastern Mediterranean. Its three objectives are stability, human development and integration. Its secretariat is in Barcelona.

Union of South American Nations: UNASUR. Established on 11 March 2011. At one time its members are Argentina, Bolivia, Brazil, Chile, Colombia, Ecuador, Guyana, Paraguay, Peru, Suriname, Uruguay and Venezuela. In April 2018 Argentina, Brazil, Chile, Colombia, Paraguay and Peru suspended their membership. Colombia later withdrew altogether. At this stage the prospects for UNASUR are unclear. Its secretariat is in Quito, Ecuador. *See also* ***Latin American regional integration arrangements***.

United Nations: UN. The United Nations Charter, the constituting document of the organization, was signed on 26 June 1945 by fifty countries, and the United Nations came into existence on 24 October 1945 after ratification by the required number of countries. The Charter created six main organs: the General Assembly, the Security Council, the Economic and Social Council (often known as ***ECOSOC***), the Trusteeship Council, the ***International Court of Justice*** and the Secretariat, Its main deliberative organ is the General Assembly (GA or UNGA). The United Nations body most concerned with trade-related matters is ***UNCTAD*** (United Nations Conference on Trade and Development), but many other agencies and bodies have work programmes dealing with various aspects of trade and commodity policies. Among these are the ***United Nations regional commissions***, and the ***United Nations specialized agencies***, such as the ***Food and Agriculture Organization*** (FAO), the ***International Labour Organization***, the ***International Telecommunication Union*** and ***WIPO*** (World Intellectual Property Organization). The ***WTO*** is not part of the United Nations agencies, but it cooperates closely with them in many areas. *See also* ***United Nations specialized agencies***.

United Nations 2030 Agenda for Sustainable Development: the resolution adopted by the ***United Nations General Assembly*** on 25 September 2015 which contains the seventeen ***Sustainable Development Goals***. *See also* ***Millennium Development Goals***.

United Nations Central Product Classification: UNCPC. It covers products that are an output of economic activities, including transportable goods, non-transportable goods and services. An earlier version of UNCPC was used as the basis for the original listings in the GATS schedules of commitments. Version 2.1 of 2015 with a much expanded services section is now current. *See also* ***W/120***. [www.unstats.un.org]

United Nations Centre for Trade Facilitation and Electronic Business: *see* ***UN/CEFACT***.

United Nations Code of Conduct on Transnational Corporations: *see* ***Draft United Nations Code of Conduct on Transnational Corporations***.

Union Économique et Monétaire Ouest Africaine
西非经济货币联盟

UEMOA。见*西非经济与货币联盟(West African Economic and Monetary Union)*。

Union for the Mediterranean
地中海联盟

由欧盟27个成员国与地中海东部和南部15个国家组成的政府间组织。三个目标为稳定、人类发展和一体化。秘书处设在巴塞罗那。

Union of South American Nation
南美洲国家联盟

UNASUR。2011年3月11日成立。成员国曾经包括阿根廷、玻利维亚、巴西、智利、哥伦比亚、厄瓜多尔、圭亚那、巴拉圭、秘鲁、苏里南、乌拉圭和委内瑞拉。2018年4月，阿根廷、巴西、智利、哥伦比亚、巴拉圭和秘鲁中止成员资格，哥伦比亚后完全退出。目前阶段，UNASUR的前景不明。秘书处设在厄瓜多尔基多。另见*拉丁美洲区域一体化安排(Latin American regional integration arrangements)*。

United Nations
联合国

UN。1945年6月26日，50个国家签署该组织的构成文件——《联合国宪章》。在经所需数量的国家批准后，联合国于1945年10月24日成立。宪章创设6个主要机构：大会、安全理事会、联合国经社理事会(ECOSOC)、托管理事会、国际法院及秘书处。联合国主要议事机构是联合国大会(GA或UNGA)。最关注贸易事务的联合国机构是联合国贸易与发展会议(UNCTAD)，但许多其他部门和机构有处理贸易和商品政策各个方面的工作计划。包括联合国区域委员会和联合国专门机构，如粮农组织(FAO)、国际劳工组织(ILO)、国际电信联盟和世界知识产权组织(WIPO)。WTO不是联合国机构，但在很多领域与这些机构进行密切合作。另见*联合国专门机构(United Nations specialized agencies)*。

United Nations 2030 Agenda for Sustainable Development
联合国2030年可持续发展议程

2015年9月25日联合国大会通过的决议，包含17个可持续发展目标。另见*千年发展目标(Millennium Development Goals)*。

United Nations Central Product Classification
联合国中央产品分类

UNCPC。涵盖经济活动产出的产品，包括可运输货物、不可运输货物和服务。早期版本的UNCPC用作 GATS 承诺减让表中最初清单的基础。现行版本为2015年的2.1版，服务部分作了很大扩充。另见 *W/120文件(W/120)*。

United Nations Centre for Trade Facilitation and Electronic Business
联合国贸易便利化与电子商务中心

见*联合国贸易便利化与电子商务中心(UN/CEFACT)*。

United Nations Code of Conduct on Transnational Corporations
联合国跨国公司行为守则

见*联合国跨国公司行为守则草案(Draft United Nations Code of Conduct on Transnational Corporations)*。

United Nations Conference on Environment and Development: UNCED. The Earth Summit. *See* ***Rio Declaration on Environment and Development*** and ***World Summit on Sustainable Development***.

United Nations Conference on the Least-Developed Countries: *see* ***SNPA***.

United Nations Conference on Trade and Development: *see* ***UNCTAD***.

United Nations Conference on Trade and Employment: the conference held in Havana from November 1947 to March 1948 which considered the draft ***Havana Charter*** and made further amendments to it. The conference was preceded by three preparatory committee meetings. The first meeting, the first preparatory session for the Havana Conference, held in London in 1946, considered a draft of a Charter for an International Trade Organization (ITO). The second, a meeting of the drafting committee, at Lake Success, New York, in January–February 1947, resulted in the first full draft of a ***GATT***, with language drawn mainly from the draft Charter. The third meeting, the second preparatory session for the Havana Conference, held in Geneva from April to August 1947, completed a further draft of the Charter for transmission to the Havana Conference. It also completed the GATT, and it conducted some tariff negotiations. *See also* ***GATT 1947***, ***ITO*** and ***trade and employment***.

United Nations Convention Against Corruption: adopted by the United Nations General Assembly on 31 October 2003. Entered into force on 14 December 2005. The Convention does not attempt to define ***corruption*** precisely. It leaves that task to the parties. However, the Convention applies to the various forms of corruption now existing, and it aims to be capable of being applied to new forms also. It requires the parties to make corruption a criminal offence. It also enables the recovery of funds. Other parts of the Convention concern prevention of corruption and international cooperation to fight corruption. *See also* ***trade and illicit payments***.

United Nations Convention on a Code of Conduct for Liner Conferences: *see* ***Convention on a Code of Conduct for Liner Conferences***.

United Nations Convention on the Law of the Sea: UNCLOS. Adopted on 10 December 1982 and entered into force on 16 November 1994. The Convention creates a framework for the protection of the sea, the seabed and subsoil as well as the airspace above it. It is intended to promote the peaceful uses of the seas and oceans, the equitable and efficient utilization of their resources, and the study, protection and preservation of the marine environment. Part V of the Convention is of greatest interest to ***trade policy***. It creates the ***Exclusive Economic Zone*** (EEZ) not extending beyond 200 nautical miles from the baseline, normally the low-water line along the coast. In the EEZ the coastal state has sovereign rights for the purpose of exploring and exploiting, conserving and managing the natural resources of the sea and the seabed. It has the same right for the economic exploitation and exploration of the EEZ, such as the production of energy from the water, current and winds. *See also* ***territorial waters***.

United Nations Conference on Environment and Development
联合国环境与发展会议

UNCED。地球峰会。见*里约环境与发展宣言(Rio Declaration on Environment and Development)*、*可持续发展问题世界首脑会议(World Summit on Sustainable Development)*。

United Nations Conference on the Least-Developed Countries
联合国最不发达国家问题大会

见*20世纪80年代支援最不发达国家新的实质性行动纲领(SNPA)*。

United Nations Conference on Trade and Development
联合国贸易与发展会议

见*联合国贸易与发展会议(UNCTAD)*。

United Nations Conference on Trade and Employment
联合国贸易与就业会议

会议于1947年11月至1948年3月在哈瓦那召开，讨论了《哈瓦那宪章》(草案)，对宪章进行了进一步修正。此次会议前举行了三次筹备委员会会议：第一次会议，即1946年在伦敦举行的哈瓦那会议第一次筹备会议，讨论了国际贸易组织(ITO)的宪章草案。第二次会议，即1947年1月至2月在纽约成功湖举行的起草委员会会议，产生了第一份GATT完整草案，文字主要取自宪章草案。第三次会议，即哈瓦那宪章第二次筹备会议，于1947年4月至8月在日内瓦举行，完成了宪章草案起草，准备提交哈瓦那会议，还完成了GATT起草及一些关税谈判。另见*1947年关税与贸易总协定(GATT 1947)*、*国际贸易组织(ITO)*、*贸易与就业(trade and employment)*。

United Nations Convention Against Corruption
联合国反腐败公约

联合国大会2003年10月31日通过，2005年12月14日生效。公约并未尝试精确定义腐败，而将这一任务留给各缔约国完成。但是，公约适用于现存的各种形式的腐败，并旨在能够适用于新形式腐败。公约要求缔约国将腐败定为犯罪行为，同时使追回资金成为可能。公约其他部分涉及预防腐败和反腐败国际合作。另见*贸易与违法付款(trade and illicit payments)*。

United Nations Convention on a Code of Conduct for Liner Conferences
联合国班轮公会行动守则公约

见*班轮公会行动守则公约(Convention on a Code of Conduct for Liner Conferences)*。

United Nations Convention on the Law of the Sea
联合国海洋法公约

UNCLOS。1982年12月10日通过，1994年11月16日生效。公约为保护海洋、海床和底土及其上方空域创设了框架，旨在促进海洋的和平利用、海洋资源的公平有效利用以及海洋环境的研究、保护和养护。公约第五部分与贸易政策关系最密切。公约创立了“专属经济区(EEZ)”的概念，即不超过基线200海里的范围，基线通常为沿海岸的低潮线。在专属经济区内，沿岸国家拥有对海洋和海床自然资源勘探、开发、保护和管理的主权，同时对专属经济区的经济勘探和开发拥有相同权利，例如利用水、潮汐和风力发电。另见*领水(territorial waters)*。

United Nations Convention on the Recognition and Enforcement of Foreign Arbitral Awards: *see* ***New York Convention***.

United Nations Convention on the Use of Electronic Communications in International Contracts: signed on 23 November 2005. Entered into force on 1 March 2013. It applies to the use of electronic communications in connection with the formation or performance of a contract between parties where the businesses are in different states. It also provides that communication or a contract cannot be denied validity or enforceability solely on the grounds that it is in the form of an electronic communication. In other words, contracts in electronic form have the same legal standing as contracts in paper form. Communications or contracts do not have to be in any particular form. *See also* ***electronic commerce***. [uncitral.org]

United Nations Development Programme: UNDP. It acquired its present name on 1 January 1966, but many of its aims and functions date back to the establishment of the ***United Nations***. UNDP administers and coordinates almost all technical assistance provided to developing countries through the United Nations system. Its main programme areas are democratic governance, poverty reduction, crisis prevention and recovery, energy and environment, and HIV/AIDS. It also promotes the achievement of the ***Millennium Development Goals*** and the ***Sustainable Development Goals***. UNDP publishes annually the ***Human Development Report***. [undp.org]

United Nations Economic and Social Commission for Western Asia: *see* ***Economic and Social Commission for Western Asia***.

United Nations Economic and Social Council: *see* ***ECOSOC***.

United Nations Economic Commission for Africa: *see* ***Economic Commission for Africa***.

United Nations Economic Commission for Europe: *see* ***Economic Commission for Europe***.

United Nations Economic Commission for Latin America and the Caribbean: *see* ***Economic Commission for Latin America and the Caribbean***.

United Nations economic sanctions: Under Article 39 of the Charter of the ***United Nations***, the ***United Nations Security Council*** can determine the existence of any threat to the peace, breach of the peace or act of aggression and make recommendations. It may also, under Article 41, decide on measures not involving the use of armed force to give effect to its decisions, and to call upon members of the United Nations to apply these measures. This may include complete or partial interruption of economic relations and of rail, sea, air, postal, telegraphic, radio and other means of communication, as well as the severance of diplomatic relations. The effectiveness of ***economic sanctions*** as a foreign policy tool has been hotly debated for many years. In many cases, it is impossible to ensure that all United Nations members with a significant interest in the matter participate. This is partly because it can be difficult to convince countries that their exporters will not suffer equally or more than the industry in the country against which sanctions are directed. One of the ***security exceptions***

United Nations Convention on the Recognition and Enforcement of Foreign Arbitral Awards

联合国承认及执行外国仲裁裁决公约

见*纽约公约(New York Convention)*。

United Nations Convention on the Use of Electronic Communications in International Contracts

联合国国际合同使用电子通信公约

2005年11月23日签署，2013年3月1日生效。公约适用于与营业地设在不同国家的当事人之间订立或履行合同有关的电子通信的使用。关于电子通信形式，公约规定对于一项通信或一项合同，不得仅以其为电子通信形式为由而否定其效力或可执行性。换句话说，电子合同与纸质合同具有相同法律地位。不要求一项通信或一项合同以任何特定形式作出。另见*电子商务(electronic commerce)*。

United Nations Development Programme

联合国开发计划署

UNDP。1966年1月1日改为现名，但计划署目标和职能中的很多内容可以追溯到联合国成立之初。UNDP管理和协调几乎所有通过联合国系统向发展中国家提供的技术援助。主要项目领域为民主治理、减少贫困、危机预防和恢复、能源和环境以及艾滋病毒/艾滋病。此外UNDP还促进实现千年发展目标和可持续发展目标。UNDP每年出版《人类发展报告》。

United Nations Economic and Social Commission for Western Asia

联合国西亚经济社会委员会

见*西亚经济社会委员会(Economic and Social Commission for Western Asia)*。

United Nations Economic and Social Council

联合国经济及社会理事会

见*联合国经济及社会理事会(ECOSOC)*。

United Nations Economic Commission for Africa

联合国非洲经济委员会

见*非洲经济委员会(Economic Commission for Africa)*。

United Nations Economic Commission for Europe

联合国欧洲经济委员会

见*欧洲经济委员会(Economic Commission for Europe)*。

United Nations Economic Commission for Latin America and the Caribbean

拉丁美洲和加勒比经济委员会

见*拉丁美洲和加勒比经济委员会(Economic Commission for Latin America and the Caribbean)*。

United Nations economic sanctions

联合国经济制裁

根据《联合国宪章》第39条，联合国安全理事会可判定是否存在对和平的任何威胁、破坏和平的行为或侵略行为，并提出建议。安全理事会还可根据第41条决定采用非武力措施以执行其决定，并吁请联合国成员国实施这些措施。这些措施可能包括完全或部分中断经济关系、中断铁路、海运、航空、邮政、电报、无线电和其他通信手段，以及断绝外交关系。经济制裁作为外交政策工

listed in each of Article XXI of the GATT, Article XIVbis of the ***General Agreement on Trade in Services*** and Article 73 of the ***Agreement on Trade-Related Aspects of Intellectual Property Rights*** allows WTO members to suspend their obligations under these agreements to the extent necessary to comply with a United Nations decision.

United Nations Educational, Scientific and Cultural Organization: UNESCO. One of the ***United Nations specialized agencies***. Several agreements and conventions with an actual or potential trade effect have been negotiated under its auspices. The more important ones include the ***Beirut Agreement***, ***Convention on the Means of Prohibiting and Preventing the Illicit Import, Export and Transfer of Ownership of Cultural Property***, ***Florence Agreement*** and the ***Universal Copyright Convention***. UNESCO is located in Paris.

United Nations Environment Programme: UNEP. Established in 1972. It is the body within the United Nations system with responsibility for the global environmental agenda and the implementation of the environmental dimension of sustainable development within the United Nations. Its work is done in seven thematic areas: climate change, disasters and conflicts, ecosystem management, environmental governance, chemicals and waste, resource efficiency and environment under review. See also multilateral environment agreements. [www.unenvironment.org].

United Nations Forum on Sustainability Standards: UNFSS. A forum for decision makers in developing countries to find the right information on ***Voluntary Sustainability Standards***. It is coordinated by steering committee consisting of the ***Food and Agriculture Organization***, ***International Trade Centre***, ***UNCTAD***, ***UN Environment*** and the ***United Nations Industrial Development Organization***. [unfss.org]

United Nations Framework Convention on Climate Change: UNFCC. Adopted on 9 May 1992. Entered into force on 21 March 1994. Its objective is to achieve the stabilization of greenhouse gas concentrations in the atmosphere at a level that would prevent dangerous anthropogenic interference with the climate system. Such a level should be achieved within a timeframe to allow ecosystems to adapt naturally to ***climate change***, to ensure that food production is not threatened and to enable economic development to proceed in a sustainable manner. Parties to the Convention are guided by five principles: (1) protecting the climate system for the benefit of past and future generations, (2) giving full consideration to the special needs of developing countries, (3) taking precautionary measures, (4) to promote ***sustainable development***, and (5) measures taken to combat climate change should not constitute a means of arbitrary or unjustifiable discrimination or a disguised restriction on international trade. The Convention divides its members into ***Annex I countries*** (OECD countries, Russia and some East European countries), ***Annex II*** countries (OECD members) and the remaining group (mainly developing countries).

具的有效性多年来备受争议。在许多情况下，不可能保证所有具有相关重大利益关系的联合国成员国参与其中。这部分是由于很难说服各国其出口商不会遭受与制裁所针对的国家的产业同等或更大程度的损失。GATT第21条、《服务贸易总协定》第14条之二以及《与贸易有关的知识产权协定》第73条列出的安全例外允许WTO成员在遵守联合国决定所必需的限度内终止履行其在这些协定项下的义务。

United Nations Educational, Scientific and Cultural Organization
联合国教育、科学及文化组织

UNESCO。联合国专门机构。在其主持下，谈判达成多个具有实际或潜在贸易影响的协定和公约。其中较为重要的包括《贝鲁特协定》、《关于禁止和防止非法进出口文化财产和非法转让其所有权的方法的公约》、《佛罗伦萨协定》和《世界版权公约》。UNESCO总部设在巴黎。

United Nations Environment Programme
联合国环境规划署

UNEP。1972年成立。联合国系统内负责全球环境的机构，并负责联合国内可持续发展的环境问题。主要工作涉及7个专题领域：气候变化、灾害和冲突、生态系统管理、环境治理、化学品和废物、资源效率和环境审议。另见*多边环境协定(multilateral environment agreements)*。

United Nations Forum on Sustainability Standards
联合国可持续发展标准论坛

UNFSS。为发展中国家中决策者找到关于自愿可持续性标准的正确信息的论坛。论坛由粮农组织(FAO)、国际贸易中心、联合国贸易与发展会议、联合国环境规划署和联合国工业发展组织组成的指导委员会进行协调。

United Nations Framework Convention on Climate Change
联合国气候变化框架公约

UNFCC。1992年5月9日通过，1994年3月21日生效。目标是将大气温室气体浓度维持在一个稳定水平，在该水平上人类活动对气候系统的危险的干扰不会发生。此种水平应在一个时间框架内达到，使生态系统能够自然地适应气候变化，保证食品生产不受到威胁，并使经济发展以可持续的方式进行。公约缔约方应遵循五项原则：(1)为了人类当代和后代的利益保护气候系统；(2)充分考虑发展中国家的特殊需要；(3)采取预防措施；(4)促进可持续发展；以及(5)应对气候变化而采取的措施不得构成任意或不合理的歧视或对国际贸易的变相限制。公约将其成员分为附件1国家(OECD成员国、俄罗斯和一些东欧国家)、附件2国家(OECD成员国)及其他国家集团(主要为发展中国家)。另见*温室气*

See also ***greenhouse gases***, ***Kyoto Protocol***, ***Paris Agreement***, ***precautionary principle*** and ***trade and environment***. [unfccc.int]

United Nations General Assembly: UNGA. The main deliberative assembly of the ***United Nations***. It usually meets from September to December. Special sessions, abbreviated to UNGASS, are conducted from time to time to discuss particular topics.

United Nations Industrial Development Organization: UNIDO. Established in 1966 as an autonomous organization within the United Nations. It became a specialized agency in 1986. Its mandate is to promote and accelerate industrial development and modernization in developing countries, and to promote cooperation and development at the global, regional and national level as well as in individual industrial sectors. UNIDO also coordinates all activities in the United Nations system relating to industrial development. It is located in Vienna. *See also* ***United Nations specialized agencies***.

United Nations Millennium Declaration: *see* ***Millennium Declaration***.

United Nations Monetary and Financial Conference: *see* ***Bretton Woods agreements***.

United Nations regional commissions: bodies established under the United Nations system to promote the economic development of their member countries and to strengthen and improve economic relations between them. Some also have work programmes on social issues. They are not usually engaged in the elaboration of binding trade rules. Their immediate parent body is ***ECOSOC***. The regional commissions are ***Economic Commission for Africa*** (established in 1958), ***Economic Commission for Europe*** (1947), ***Economic Commission for Latin America and the Caribbean*** (1948), ***ESCAP*** (1947) and ***Economic and Social Commission for Western Asia*** (1973).

United Nations Rules for Electronic Data Interchange for Administration, Commerce and Transport: *see* ***UN/EDIFACT***.

United Nations Security Council: UNSC. One of the principal organs of the ***United Nations***. Its main responsibility is maintaining international peace and security. The UNSC has fifteen members. China, France, Russia, United Kingdom and United States are permanent members. The other ten are elected for two years. In some cases, a UNSC decision may result in the invocation of ***security exceptions*** by WTO members.

United Nations specialized agencies: these are intergovernmental agencies constituted as separate and autonomous organizations related to the ***United Nations***. They have their own legislative and executive bodies, membership and budgets. They work with each other and the United Nations through ***ECOSOC***. The specialized agencies are the ***Food and Agriculture Organization*** (FAO), ***World Bank*** (International Bank for Reconstruction and Development or IBRD), ***IMF*** (International Monetary Fund), International Civil Aviation Organization (ICAO; *see* ***Chicago Convention***), ***International Fund for Agricultural Development*** (IFAD), ***International Labour Organization***

体(greenhouse gases)、*京都议定书(Kyoto Protocol)*、*巴黎协定(Paris Agreement)*、*预防原则(precautionary principle)*、*贸易与环境(trade and environment)*。

United Nations General Assembly

联合国大会

UNGA。联合国的主要审议大会。通常在9月至12月召开会议。不定期召开联合国特别会议(UNGASS)，以讨论特定主题。

United Nations Industrial Development Organization

联合国工业发展组织

UNIDO。1966年建立，联合国系统内的自治组织，1986年成为专门机构。其授权为，促进发展中国家的工业发展和现代化，并促进全球、区域和国家层面以及具体工业部门的合作与发展。UNIDO还协调联合国系统内与工业发展相关的所有活动。该机构设在维也纳。另见*联合国专门机构(United Nations specialized agencies)*。

United Nations Millennium Declaration

联合国千年宣言

见*千年宣言(Millennium Declaration)*。

United Nations Monetary and Financial Conference

联合国货币与金融会议

见*布雷顿森林协定(Bretton Woods agreements)*。

United Nations regional commissions

联合国区域委员会

指联合国系统内设立的机构，目的为促进其成员国经济发展，加强和改善它们之间的经济关系。一些机构还有针对社会问题的工作计划。通常它们不参与制定具有约束力的贸易规则。此类机构的直接上级机构是联合国经社理事会(ECOSOC)。区域委员会包括：非洲经济委员会(1958年成立)、欧洲经济委员会(1947年)、拉丁美洲和加勒比经济委员会(1948年)、亚洲及太平洋经济社会理事会(ESCAP)(1947年)以及西亚经济社会委员会(1973年)。

United Nations Rules for Electronic Data Interchange for Administration, Commerce and Transport

联合国行政、商业和运输用电子数据交换规则

见*联合国行政、商业和运输用电子数据交换规则(UN/EDIFACT)*。

United Nations Security Council

联合国安全理事会

UNSC。联合国主要机构。主要职能是维持国际和平与安全。UNSC有15个成员。中国、法国、俄罗斯、英国和美国是常任理事国。其他10个非常任理事国每2年选举一次。在某些情况下，UNSC的决定可能导致WTO成员援引安全例外条款。

United Nations specialized agencies

联合国专门机构

由政府间机构组成的与联合国有关的独立和自治组织。这些机构拥有自己的立法和执行部门、成员资格和预算。这些机构通过联合国经社理事会(ECOSOC)相互合作，并与联合国合作。专门机构有粮农组织(FAO)、世界银行(国际复

(ILO), ***International Maritime Organization*** (IMO), ***International Telecommunication Union*** (ITU), ***United Nations Educational, Scientific and Cultural Organization*** (UNESCO), ***United Nations Industrial Development Organization*** (UNIDO), Universal Postal Union (UPU), World Health Organization (WHO), ***WIPO*** (World Intellectual Property Organization), World Meteorological Organization (WMO) and World Tourism Organization (WTO).

United Nations Sustainable Development Goals: *see* ***Sustainable Development Goals***.

United States Agricultural Trade and Development Act: *see* ***PL 480***.

United States Anti-Dumping Act of 1916: *see* ***Anti-Dumping Act of 1916***.

United States–Caribbean Basin Trade Partnership Act: *see* ***Caribbean Basin Initiative***.

United States–Central American Free Trade Agreement: CAFTA. A comprehensive ***free-trade agreement*** consisting of Costa Rica, El Salvador, Guatemala, Honduras, Nicaragua, Dominican Republic and the United States. It entered into force on 1 January 2009.

United States–Japan financial services agreement: Concluded in February 1995 following United States complaints about closed financial markets in Japan. The main components of the Agreement are that Japan undertook to (a) provide unrestricted access to its public pension fund market by investment advisory companies, (b) eliminate balanced funds requirements, thus enabling more firms to compete,(c) move towards market value accounting for pension liabilities, (d) permit dual licensing of investment trust businesses and discretionary investment management businesses, (e) liberalize restrictions on the introduction of new financial instruments, (f) introduce a domestic asset-backed securities market in Japan, and (g) eliminate restrictions on the offshore securitization of Japanese assets.

United States–Japan Framework for a New Economic Partnership: concluded in July 1993 to create more avenues of entry for United States firms into Japan. Japan committed itself to address five major areas: (a) ***government procurement***, (b) regulatory reform and competitiveness, (c) other major sectors, including cars and car parts, (d) economic harmonization, aimed at correcting macroeconomic imbalances in the Japanese market, and especially its low inflow of foreign investment, and (e) implementation of existing arrangements and measures. *See also* ***Market-Oriented Sector-Specific talks***, ***Structural Impediments Initiative*** and ***United States–Japan financial services agreement***.

United States–Jordan free-trade agreement: entered into force on 17 December 2001. In most respects this is a standard bilateral ***free-trade agreement***, but it has strong provisions on labour and environment. In Articles 5 and 6 the parties recognize that it is inappropriate to encourage trade by relaxing domestic environmental and labour laws. Each party may establish its own level of domestic environmental protection and labour standards, though these are expected to be high. The parties agree to enforce their environmental and

兴开发银行或IBRD)、国际货币基金组织(IMF)、国际民用航空组织(ICAO；另见*《芝加哥公约》(Chicago Convention)*)、国际农业发展基金(IFAD)、国际劳工组织(ILO)、国际海事组织(IMO)、国际电信联盟(ITU)、联合国教科文组织(UNESCO)、联合国工业发展组织(UNIDO)、万国邮政联盟(UPU)、世界卫生组织(WHO)、世界知识产权组织(WIPO)、世界气象组织(WMO)以及世界旅游组织(WTO)。

United Nations Sustainable Development Goals
联合国可持续发展目标

见*可持续发展目标(Sustainable Development Goals)*。

United States Agricultural Trade and Development Act
美国农业贸易发展与援助法

见*480号公法(PL480)*。

United States Anti-Dumping Act of 1916
1916年美国反倾销法

见*1916年反倾销法(Anti-Dumping Act of 1916)*。

United States–Caribbean Basin Trade Partnership Act
美国—加勒比盆地贸易伙伴关系法

见*加勒比盆地倡议(Caribbean Basin Initiative)*。

United States–Central American Free Trade Agreement
美国—中美洲自由贸易协定

CAFTA。全面自由贸易协定，成员为哥斯达黎加、萨尔瓦多、危地马拉、洪都拉斯、尼加拉瓜、多米尼加和美国。协定于2009年1月1日生效。

United States–Japan financial services agreement
美国—日本金融服务协定

在美国抱怨日本金融市场封闭后，于1995年2月达成。协定主要内容是日本承诺：(a)向投资咨询公司提供进入其公共年金市场的无限制准入；(b)取消平衡基金要求，以允许更多的公司参与竞争；(c)在年金负债方面，向市场价值会计方法过渡；(d)允许颁发投资信托业务和任意投资管理业务双项许可；(e)取消引进新金融工具方面的限制；(f)在日本建立以国内资产为依托的证券市场；以及(g)取消对日本资产海外证券化的限制。

United States–Japan Framework for a New Economic Partnership
美国—日本新经济伙伴关系框架协定

1993年7月达成，为美国企业进入日本创造更多途径。日本在5个主要领域作出承诺：(a)政府采购；(b)规制改革和竞争性；(c)其他主要部门，包括汽车和汽车零部件；(d)经济协调，旨在调整日本市场中的宏观经济失衡，特别是在低水平的外国投资流入方面；以及(e)实施现有安排和措施。另见*市场导向型的多领域谈判方案(Market-Oriented Sector-Specific talks)*、*日美结构协议会(Structural Impediments Initiative)*、*美国—日本金融服务协定(United States–Japan financial services agreement)*。

United States–Jordan free-trade agreement
美国—约旦自由贸易协定

2001年12月17日生效。从很多方面讲，是一个标准的双边自由贸易协定，但在劳工和环境方面订有强有力的条款。在第5条和第6条中，双方认识到通过放

labour laws effectively. In Article 6 the parties also reaffirm their obligations under the ILO ***Declaration on Fundamental Principles and Rights at Work***. Environmental laws are defined as statutes or regulations with the primary purpose to protect the environment, or to prevent danger to human, animal, or plant life or health, through (a) the prevention, abatement or control of the release, discharge or emission of pollutants or environmental contaminants; (b) the control of environmentally hazardous or toxic chemicals, substances, materials and wastes, and the dissemination of information related to this; or (c) the protection or conservation of wild flora or fauna, including endangered species, their habitat, and specially protected natural areas. Labour laws are defined as (a) the right of association, (b) the right to organize and bargain collectively, (c) a prohibition on the use of any form of forced or compulsory labour, (d) a minimum age for the employment of children, and (e) acceptable conditions of work with respect to minimum wages, hours of work, and occupational safety and health. *See also* ***core labour standards***.

United States Marine Mammal Protection Act: *see* ***Tuna I*** and ***Tuna II***.

United States Merchant Marine Act: *see* ***Jones Act***.

United States–Mexico–Canada Agreement: USMCA. A ***free-trade agreement*** adopted by the United States, Mexico and Canada on 30 September 2018 to succeed ***NAFTA***. It will enter into force two months after the last of the members has notified the others of its acceptance. The Agreement retains many of the NAFTA provisions, but some have undergone significant changes. Some chapters are new. The following is a basic introduction to the Agreement. Chapter 1 establishes a free-trade area consistent with Article XXIV (Customs Unions and Free Trade Areas) of the ***GATT*** and Article V of the ***General Agreement on Trade in Services*** (Economic Integration). It also contains a list of definitions. Chapter 2 requires the parties to accord ***national treatment*** and ***most-favoured-nation treatment*** to goods of another party. As a general rule the parties may not maintain any import or export restrictions for any good destined to another party. This also applies to ***remanufactured goods***. Chapter 3 covers agriculture. The background to this Chapter is the WTO ***Agreement on Agriculture***. ***Export subsidies*** may not be used within the free-trade area. Export restrictions may be maintained under defined conditions. The United States gains additional market access for dairy, milk, poultry and egg products in Canada. Chapter 4 sets out the ***rules of origin***. The basic method is the ***change in tariff classification***, but the net-cost method and the ***transaction value method*** are also applied to assess ***regional value content***. The ***USMCA rules of origin for automotive products*** have changed considerably from those applicable in NAFTA. Chapter 5 lists the procedures for applying the rules of origin. Chapter 6 covers textiles and apparel goods. Chapter 7 deals with customs administration and ***trade facilitation***. Relevant information must be available online, and a ***Single Window*** must be established. In Chapter 8 the parties confirm their recognition of the Mexican State's direct, inalienable and imprescriptible ownership of hydrocarbons. Chapter 9 sets out the applicable

松国内环境和劳动法鼓励贸易是不适当的。每一方可以确定自身的国内环境保护和劳工标准的水平，尽管这些标准预计会很高。双方同意有效实施其环境和劳动法。在第6条中，双方还重申它们在国际劳工组织(ILO)《关于工作中基本原则和权利宣言》项下的义务。环境法定义为以保护环境或通过以下方式防止对人类、动物、植物的生命或健康造成危害为首要目的的法令或法规：(a)防止、减少或控制污染物或环境污染物的释放、排出或排放；(b)控制对环境有害或有毒的化学品、物质、材料和废物，以及传播与此相关的信息；或(c)保护或养护野生动植物，包括濒危物种及其栖息地，特别是受保护的自然区域。劳动法的定义为：(a)结社权利；(b)组织和集体谈判权；(c)禁止使用任何形式的强迫或强制劳动；(d)雇佣儿童的最低年龄；以及(e)关于最低工资、工作时间和职业安全及健康的可接受的工作条件。另见*核心劳工标准(core labour standards)*。

United States Marine Mammal Protection Act
美国海洋哺乳动物保护法

见*第一个金枪鱼案(Tuna I)*、*第二个金枪鱼案(Tuna II)*。

United States Merchant Marine Act
美国商船法案

见*琼斯法案(Jones Act)*。

United States–Mexico–Canada Agreement
美国—墨西哥—加拿大协定

USMCA。美国、墨西哥和加拿大于2018年9月30日通过的自由贸易协定，取代《北美自由贸易协定》(NAFTA)。协定在最后一缔约方通知其他缔约方其已接受协定的2个月后生效。协定保留了NAFTA的许多条款，但一些条款作了重大改变。一些章节是新增的。以下是对协定的基本介绍。第1章规定建立符合GATT第24条(关税同盟和自由贸易区)、《服务贸易总协定》第5条(经济一体化)的自由贸易区，还包含一份定义清单。第2章要求各缔约方对另一缔约方的货物给予国民待遇和最惠国待遇。作为一般规则，各缔约方不得对运往另一缔约方的任何货物维持任何进口或出口限制。这一规定也适用于再制造货物。第3章涵盖农业。该章的背景是WTO《农业协定》。出口补贴不得在自由贸易区内使用。出口限制可以在规定条件下维持。美国获得奶制品、牛奶、家禽和蛋品对加拿大的额外市场准入。第4章规定了原产地规则。基本方法是税则归类改变，但净成本法和成交价格法也用于评估区域价值成分。USMCA汽车产品原产地规则与NAFTA中的规则相比变化很大。第5章列出适用原产地规则的程序。第6章涵盖纺织品和服装。第7章处理海关管理和贸易便利化。相关信息需要在线提供，且需要建立单一窗口。在第8章中，缔约方确认承认墨西哥政府对碳氢化合物的直接、不可剥夺和不可侵犯的所有权。第9章规定了适用的卫生与植物卫生措施。第10章涵盖贸易救济。一般而言，缔约方保留其在

sanitary and phytosanitary measures. Chapter 10 covers ***trade remedies***. In general the parties retain their rights and obligations under Article XIX of the GATT and the WTO ***Agreement on Safeguards***. They also retain their rights and obligations under Article VI of the GATT (Anti-Dumping and Countervailing Duties), the WTO ***Anti-Dumping Agreement*** and the ***Agreement on Subsidies and Countervailing Measures***. Specific rules apply for the review and dispute settlement in anti-dumping and countervailing duty matters between the United States and Canada. Chapter 11 has comprehensive provisions on ***technical barriers to trade***. Chapter 12 contains sectoral annexes on chemical substances, cosmetic products, information and communication technologies, energy performance standards, medical devices and pharmaceuticals. Chapter 13 on ***government procurement*** only applies as between Mexico and the United States (Mexico is not a party to the WTO ***Agreement on Government Procurement***). Chapter 14 is the investment chapter. It requires the parties to accord each other national treatment and most-favoured-nation treatment, including that given to non-parties. ***Cross-border trade in services*** is dealt with in Chapter 15. Again, national treatment and most-favoured-nation treatment applies. Chapter 16 covers ***temporary entry for business persons***. It does not apply to persons seeking employment, or to measures regarding citizenship, nationality, residence or permanent employment. Chapters 17 and 18 cover financial services and telecommunications, respectively. Chapter 19 on ***digital trade*** is entirely new. It seeks to promote consumer confidence in digital trade and to avoid unnecessary barriers to its use and development. No party may impose customs duties, fees or other charges on the import or export of digital products transmitted electronically. ***Intellectual property rights*** are covered in Chapter 20. The parties affirm their commitment to the ***Declaration on the TRIPS Agreement and Public Health***. The term of protection for ***copyright*** and related rights is not less than the life of the author and 70 years after the author's death. Chapter 21 deals with ***competition law***. Chapter 22 covers ***state-owned enterprises*** and ***designated monopolies***. It does not apply to regulatory or supervisory activities, such as monetary or exchange rate policy. Chapter 23 makes labour a chapter in its own right (in NAFTA it was covered by the ***North American Agreement on Labor Cooperation***). Similarly, environment, previously covered by the North American Agreement on Environmental Cooperation, has been elevated to Chapter 24. Chapter 25 promotes the economic competitiveness of small and medium-sized enterprises (SMEs). Chapter 26 establishes a North American Competitiveness Committee to discuss and develop cooperation activities and enhance a predictable and transparent regulatory environment. In Chapter 27 the parties take steps to prevent and combat ***bribery*** and ***corruption*** in international trade and investment. Chapter 28 deals with publication and administration, such as the publication of laws, and review and appeals against administrative proceedings. It contains rules for transparency and procedural fairness for pharmaceutical products and medical devices. Chapter 29 covers transparency. Section B of this Chapter has rules for

GATT第19条和WTO《保障措施协定》项下的权利和义务。缔约方还保留其在GATT第6条(反倾销税和反补贴税)、WTO《反倾销协定》和《补贴与反补贴措施协定》项下的权利和义务。美国和加拿大之间对反倾销税和反补贴税问题的复审和争端解决适用特定规则。第11章对技术性贸易壁垒作出全面规定。第12章包含关于化学物质、化妆品、信息和通信技术、能源性能标准、医疗设备和药品的部门附件。第13章关于政府采购，仅适用于墨西哥与美国之间(墨西哥不是WTO《政府采购协定》参加方)。第14章是投资章节，要求缔约方给予其他缔约方货物国民待遇和最惠国待遇，包括给予非缔约方的待遇。第15章处理跨境服务贸易，国民待遇和最惠国待遇同样适用于本章。第16章涵盖商务人员临时入境，不适用于寻求就业的人员，也不适用于有关公民身份、国籍、居住或永久就业的措施。第17章和第18章分别涵盖金融服务和电信。第19章关于数字贸易，是全新章节，旨在提高消费者对数字贸易的信心，并避免对其使用和发展的不必要障碍。任何缔约方不得对以电子方式传输的进口或出口的数字产品征收关税、规费或其他费用。第20章涵盖知识产权。各缔约方确认其对《关于<与贸易有关的知识产权协定>与公共健康的宣言》的承诺。版权和相关权的保护期限不少于作者生前加作者死亡后70年。第21章处理竞争法。第22章涵盖国有企业和指定垄断。不适用于监管或监督活动，例如货币或外汇政策。第23章将劳工独立成章(在NAFTA中，劳工由《北美劳工合作协定》所涵盖)。同样，先前由《北美环境合作协定》所涵盖的环境问题升级为第24章。第25章涵盖中小企业(SMEs)经济竞争力促进。第26章设立北美竞争力委员会，以讨论和发展合作活动，并增强可预测和透明的监管环境。在第27章中，各缔约方采取措施防止和打击国际贸易和投资中的贿赂和腐败。第28章处理公布和行政管理，例如法律的公布、对行政程序的审查和上诉。该章包含医药产品和医疗的透明度及程序公平的规则。第29章涵盖透明度，该章B节对医药产品和医疗设备的透明度和程序公平性作出规定。第30章包含管理和机

transparency and procedural fairness for pharmaceutical products and medical devices. Chapter 30 contains the administrative and institutional provisions, including the establishment of a Free Trade Commission to oversee the functioning of the Agreement. Chapter 31 covers ***dispute settlement***. Parties can exercise a choice of forum where this is available, but the dispute cannot then be taken elsewhere. Chapter 32 deals with ***general exceptions*** and ***security exceptions***. It exempts taxation measures from the purview of the Agreement. Parties may adopt or maintain measures to fulfil their obligations to indigenous peoples. This Chapter also requires a party to notify the other parties if it intends to start free-trade agreement negotiations with a non-market country. A non-market country is a country that at least one of the parties has defined a non-market country under its trade laws. If such an agreement enters into force, the other two parties have the right to terminate USMCA and turn it into a bilateral agreement. Chapter 33 on macroeconomic policies and exchange rate matters is also new. It requires the parties to avoid manipulating exchange rates or the international monetary system. Chapter 34 contains the final provisions. This contains a ***sunset clause***. The Agreement will be terminated sixteen years after entry into force unless the parties confirm that they wish it to continue for another sixteen-year term.

United States–Middle East Free Trade Area: a long-term project first proposed in 2003 which could lead step by step to a regional free-trade agreement.

United States – prohibition of imports of tuna and tuna products from Canada: *see **tuna (Canada–United States, 1982)***.

United States Reciprocal Trade Agreements Program: established by the *Reciprocal Trade Agreements Act* of 1934 which is an amendment to the *Tariff Act* of 1930, known also as the ***Smoot-Hawley Tariff Act***. It authorized the President to enter into trade agreements with foreign governments and to modify existing duties, ***import restrictions*** and customs or excise treatment as necessary to carry out the agreements made with them. There was no sense, however, that tariffs on agricultural products would be included in the programme of prospective reciprocal tariff reductions. It should be noted that some of the earlier tariff acts had contained provisions permitting reciprocal tariff reductions, but these were not used, either because the conditions were too strict, or because there was no inclination anyway to reduce tariffs. Until the passing of the *Reciprocal Trade Agreements Act*, the tariff levels prescribed by the 1930 *Tariff Act* were mandatory, and they could only be changed with the consent of Congress. The Reciprocal Trade Agreements Program's importance for the ***multilateral trading system*** partly stems from the language included in some of the thirty-two bilateral agreements negotiated under it between 1934 and 1945. For example, all of the seventeen general clauses contained in the United States–Mexico bilateral trade agreement of December 1942 are reflected to a greater or lesser extent in the GATT. These include a most-favoured-nation clause, ***national treatment***, agreed rules for the non-discriminatory application of ***quantitative restrictions***, ***customs valuation***,

构条款，包括设立自由贸易委员会以监督协定的运行。第31章涵盖争端解决。缔约方可以在有条件的情况下行使法院选择权，但争端不能随之转至他处。第32章处理一般例外和安全例外。免除了协定范围内的税收措施。缔约方可采取或维持措施履行其对土著人民的义务。该章还要求，如一缔约方拟与一非市场国家启动自由贸易协定谈判，应通知其他缔约方。非市场国家指至少一缔约方根据其贸易法定义为非市场国家的国家。如此类协定生效，其他两缔约方有权终止USMCA并将其转为双边协定。第33章关于宏观经济政策和外汇事务，也是全新的，要求各缔约方避免操纵汇率或国际货币体系。第34章包含最后条款，其中包含日落条款，协定将在生效后16年终止，除非缔约方确认希望将协定再延长16年。

United States–Middle East Free Trade Area
美国—中东自由贸易区

2003年首次提出的长期项目，可逐步形成区域自由贸易协定。

United States – prohibition of imports of tuna and tuna products from Canada
美国-禁止自加拿大进口金枪鱼和金枪鱼制品案

见*1982年加拿大-美国金枪鱼案(tuna (Canada–United States, 1982))*。

United States Reciprocal Trade Agreements Program
美国互惠贸易协定计划

根据《1934年互惠贸易协定法》制定，该法是对《1930年关税法》、即《斯穆特-霍利关税法》的修正。该计划授权美国总统与外国政府签订贸易协定，并为实施与外国政府签订的协定而对现行关税、进口限制和海关待遇或消费税待遇进行必要修改。但是，将农产品的关税纳入可能的互惠关税削减计划是没有意义的。应该注意的是，一些较早的关税法已经包含允许互惠关税削减的条款，但未被使用，或是由于条件过于严格，或是由于根本没有削减关税的意愿。在《1934年互惠贸易协定法》获得通过前，《1930年关税法》所制定的关税水平是强制性的，且只有经国会批准才能改变。互惠贸易协定计划对多边贸易体制的重要性，部分源自在1934年至1945年根据该计划谈判的32个双边协定的文本，例如1942年12月《美国—墨西哥双边贸易协定》所含17个一般条款或多或少反映在GATT中，包括最惠国条款、国民待遇、关于数量限制的非歧视管理、海关估价、透明度和保障措施等议定规则。保障措施条款的主旨

transparency, ***safeguards***, etc. The tenor of the safeguards clause was changed considerably by a strengthened element of consultation. Other GATT articles drawing on this agreement contain additional principles reflecting the views of other trading countries. The 1934 *Reciprocal Trade Agreements Act*, as amended, was superseded by the *Trade Expansion Act* of 1962. *See also* ***United States trade agreements legislation***.

United States – restrictions on imports of tuna: *see* ***Tuna I***.

United States Tariff Act of 1930: *see* ***Smoot-Hawley Tariff Act***.

United States – taxes on petroleum and certain imported substances: *see* ***Superfund***.

United States trade agreements legislation: like other countries, the United States has a range of legislation covering its import and export trade, but the influence of the United States in the world economy, the GATT and the WTO, and the role Congress has in the formulation of external economic relations have always meant that its trade legislation is viewed as particularly important by other countries. This entry mainly deals with the legislation enabling the United States to participate in ***multilateral trade negotiations***. The starting point for such legislation is the *Reciprocal Trade Agreements Act* of 1934 which authorized the President to enter into trade agreements with other governments and to modify the United States tariff regime for the entry of goods. This Act was extended with minor changes in 1937, 1940, 1943 and 1945. On the expiry of the 1945 extension on 1 June 1948, it was extended for one year with the significant inclusion of ***peril points***. The 1949 extension, to 30 June 1951, repealed this change. The *Trade Agreements Extension Act* of 1955 permitted the President to make limited tariff reductions, a measure which, with some minor changes, was carried forward into the 1958 extension, due to expire in 1962. It reintroduced the idea of peril points. This limited negotiating authority was a major reason for the meagre results of the ***Dillon Round***. Until 1962 the President did not have the authority to deal with ***systemic issues***. The passage of the *Trade Expansion Act* of 1962 extended the presidential authority considerably, largely because of a realization of what the economic and trade potential of the ***European Economic Community*** (EEC), now that Europe had fully recovered from the damage caused by the war, might mean to United States trading interests. The Act allowed a reduction of existing tariffs by 50 per cent and even to zero if they were less than 5 per cent, but leaving it to the President how this might be achieved. This allowed experimentation with the ***linear tariff cut*** formula. Some prospective reductions to zero were conditional on an agreement with the EEC. There was provision in the Act for retaliatory action if foreign governments harmed the trade of the United States. Industries and workers injured by increased imports became eligible for direct assistance. Finally, this Act also created the Office of the Special Representative for Trade Negotiations, the forerunner of the ***USTR***. When the 1962 negotiating authority expired in 1967, it was not renewed until the Trade Act of 1974 which gave the President authority to participate in the ***Tokyo Round*** negotiations until

由于增加了磋商的内容而变化较大。取自这一协定的其他GATT条款包含反映其他贸易国观点的额外原则。经修正的《1934年互惠贸易协定法》被《1962年贸易扩展法》所取代。另见*美国贸易协定立法(United States trade agreements legislation)*。

United States – restrictions on imports of tuna

美国-限制金枪鱼进口案

见*第一个金枪鱼案(Tuna I)*。

United States Tariff Act of 1930

美国1930年关税法

见*斯穆特-霍利关税法(Smoot-Hawley Tariff Act)*。

United States – taxes on petroleum and certain imported substances

美国-石油和某些进口物质征税案

见*超级基金案(Superfund)*。

United States trade agreements legislation

美国贸易协定立法

与其他国家一样，美国有一系列立法涵盖其进口和出口贸易，但由于美国在世界经济、GATT和WTO中的影响以及美国国会在对外经济关系制定过程中的作用，美国贸易立法被认为对其他国家特别重要。本词条主要涉及使美国能够参与多边贸易谈判的立法。此类立法的起点是《1934年互惠贸易协定法》，该法授权美国总统与其他国家政府签署贸易协定，并有权修改美国进口货物的关税制度。该法先后在1937年、1940年、1943年和1945年延长，只经细微修改。1945年的延期在1948年6月1日到期后再延长1年，包含了重要的危险点条款。1949年的延长至1951年6月30日，取消了这一变化。《1955年贸易协定延长法》允许总统进行有限的关税削减，这一措施在经细微修改后，在1958年延长中得以保留，并应在1962年到期。协定再次引入"危险点"的概念。这一有限的谈判授权是狄龙回合成果不显著的主要原因。直到1962年，总统没有处理体制性问题的授权。《1962年贸易扩展法》的通过大大扩展了总统的授权，很大程度上是由于美国认识到欧洲经济共同体(EEC)的经济和贸易潜力，此时欧洲已经从战争造成的破坏中全面恢复，可能对美国意味着贸易利益。该法允许将当时的关税降低50%，5%以下的关税可以降至零，但由总统决定如何实现。此即允许尝试使用线性关税削减公式。一些可能的零关税削减以与欧洲经济共同体所达成的一项协定为条件。该法中还包含在外国政府损害美国贸易的情况下采取报复行动的条款。受进口增加损害的产业和工人有权获得直接援助。最后，该法还创设了特别贸易谈判代表办公室，即美国贸易代表办公室(USTR)的前身。1962年谈判授权在1967年到期后，直至《1974年贸易法》才得到更新，该法给予总统参加东京回合谈判的授权，直至1980年1月5日。

5 January 1980. This was the first appearance of ***fast-track***. This Act also formalized the retaliatory power of the United States Government in cases of illegal or unfair action by foreign governments through ***Section 301***. This section became part, in amended form, of all subsequent trade legislation. The *Trade Agreements Act* of 1979 adopted the Tokyo Round outcomes. The next act, the *Trade and Tariffs Act* of 1984, did not give the President new negotiating authority. That had to wait until 1988 with the passing of the ***Omnibus Trade and Competitiveness Act***. This was also the first time since the end of the Second World War that a major trade act did not emanate from the executive. President Clinton failed to obtain fast-track authority when the *Uruguay Round Agreements Act* became law in December 1994. He appeared to have regained the initiative when he tabled the *Export Expansion and Reciprocal Trade Agreements Act* in September 1997. There appears to be some intended symbolism in the choice of the title in that it harks back to the great trade acts passed during the presidencies of Franklin Delano Roosevelt and John F. Kennedy. In the end, Congress did not act on the bill. When in early 2001 the new administration again sought fast-track authority, it renamed it the ***Trade Promotion Authority***. The latest version of it was enacted in 2015 with a six-year mandate. *See also* ***Jackson-Vanik amendment***, ***Smoot-Hawley Tariff Act*** and ***United States Reciprocal Trade Agreements Program***.

United States Trade Representative: *see* ***USTR***.

Universal Copyright Convention: administered by the ***United Nations Educational, Scientific and Cultural Organization*** (UNESCO). Many of its basic principles are the same as those contained in the ***Berne Convention***, except for the requirement of a copyright notice on the copyright work itself. *See also* ***copyright***.

Universal Declaration of Human Rights: adopted by the ***United Nations General Assembly*** on 10 December 1948. It has established a framework for all discussion of, and progress in, ***human rights*** since the end of the Second World War. Some parts of it are directly relevant to the debate on ***trade and labour standards***. Article 23 states everyone has the right to work, to free choice of employment, just and favourable conditions of work and to protection against unemployment, the right to equal pay for equal work, the right to just and favourable remuneration and the right to form and join trade unions for the protection of his interests. Article 24 grants everyone the right to rest and leisure, including reasonable limitation of working hours and periodic holidays with pay. *See also* ***International Covenant on Economic, Social and Cultural Rights***.

Universal service: a term used for services, such as telecommunications or postal services, which are available to all prospective users at a guaranteed level of quality and at affordable prices. *See also* ***basic telecommunications***.

Unrecorded trade: trade flows not recorded in statistical summaries prepared by the customs or revenue authorities. No duties are paid on unrecorded trade, and the country therefore suffers a revenue shortfall. *See also* ***smuggling***.

这是快轨授权首次出现。该法还通过301条款将美国政府对外国政府非法或不公正行为的报复权正式化。经修正的301条款成为所有后续贸易法的一部分。《1979年贸易协定法》通过了东京回合结果。接下来的《1984年贸易与关税法》未给予总统新的谈判授权，这要等到1988年《综合贸易与竞争法》通过之后。这也是第二次世界大战后第一个不是由行政部门发起的主要贸易法。克林顿总统未能在1994年12月《乌拉圭回合协定法》成为法律时获得快轨授权。他似乎在1997年9月提交《出口扩张和互惠贸易协定法案》时重新提出了这一倡议。该法标题的选择似乎想体现一种象征意义，使人们想起富兰克林·罗斯福和约翰·肯尼迪总统任期内通过的重要贸易法。最终，国会没有对法案采取行动。在2001年年初，新一届政府再次寻求快轨授权，将之更名为"贸易促进授权"。这一授权的最新版本在2015年授予，期限为6年。另见*杰克逊-瓦尼克修正案(Jackson-Vanik amendment)*、*斯穆特-霍利关税法(Smoot-Hawley Tariff Act)*、*美国互惠贸易协定计划(United States Reciprocal Trade Agreements Program)*。

United States Trade Representative

美国贸易代表办公室

见*美国贸易代表办公室(USTR)*。

Universal Copyright Convention

世界版权公约

由联合国教科文组织(UNESCO)管理。公约许多基本原则与《伯尔尼公约》所含原则相同，除关于对版权作品本身进行版权通知的要求外。另见*版权(copyright)*。

Universal Declaration of Human Rights

世界人权宣言

1948年12月10日联合国大会通过。宣言确立了自第二次世界大战结束时起所有关于人权的讨论和人权方面进展的框架。其中部分内容与贸易与劳工标准的讨论直接相关。第23条规定，人人有权工作、自由选择职业、享受公正和合适的工作条件并享受免于失业的保障，人人有同工同酬的权利，有权享受公正和合适的报酬以及人人有为维护其利益而组织和参加工会的权利。第24条给予人人有享受休息和闲暇的权利，包括工作时间有合理限制和定期带薪休假的权利。另见*经济、社会和文化权利国际公约(International Covenant on Economic, Social and Cultural Rights)*。

Universal service

普遍服务

用于服务的词语，例如电信或邮政服务，所有潜在使用者均可在质量有保障和价格可承受的情况下获得此类服务。另见*基础电信(basic telecommunications)*。

Unrecorded trade

未记录贸易

未记录在海关或财政部门制定的统计摘要中的贸易流。未记录贸易不缴税，因此国家遭受税收损失。另见*走私(smuggling)*。

UPOV: Union internationale pour la protection des obtentions végétales. *See* ***International Convention for the Protection of New Varieties of Plants***.

Upper-middle-income economies: a group of sixty economies classified in this way by the ***World Bank***. In July 2018 these countries had a per capita GNI (gross national income) ranging from $3,996 to $12,375. *See also* ***high-income economies***, ***low-income economies*** and ***lower-middle-income economies***.

Upstream subsidy: a ***subsidy*** paid to a producer of a product that is incorporated into the final product.

Upward harmonization: harmonization of standards on the principle that participants in a harmonization arrangement will meet the highest standard prevailing among them. *See also* ***harmonization of standards and qualifications***.

Uruguay Round: the eighth round of ***multilateral trade negotiations***. It was launched at Punta del Este, Uruguay, on 25 September 1986. Negotiations concluded in Geneva on 15 December 1993, and it was signed by Ministers in Marrakesh, Morocco, on 15 April 1994. The objectives of the negotiations were (i) further liberalization and expansion of world trade, (ii) strengthening the role of the GATT and improving the ***multilateral trading system***, (iii) increasing the responsiveness of the GATT to the international economic environment, and (iv) fostering international cooperative economic action. Participants agreed to a ***standstill*** on trade-restrictive measures during the negotiations and a ***rollback*** provision. The subjects for negotiations, the widest of any GATT round, were ***tariffs***, ***non-tariff measures***, ***tropical products*** as a priority area, ***natural resource-based products***, textiles and clothing, agriculture, review of GATT articles, ***safeguards***, ***Tokyo Round*** agreements and arrangements, subsidies and countervailing measures, ***dispute settlement***, ***trade-related aspects of intellectual property rights***, trade-related investment measures and the Functioning of the GATT System (FOGS). Each of these subjects was managed by a negotiating group established for the purpose. Negotiations on ***trade in services*** were to be held on a legally separate track at the insistence of a group of developing countries who did not accept that services should be covered by the GATT. Ministers agreed that negotiations would conclude within four years. The negotiations can be divided into three stages: (a) from the launch at Punta del Este to the Montreal mid-term review in December 1988, (b) the period from then on up the Brussels Ministerial Meeting in December 1990 which was supposed to mark the end of the negotiations, and (c) the events leading up to the Marrakesh Ministerial Meeting in April 1994. Substantive negotiations ended on 15 December 1993 when the second extension to the United States negotiating authority, the ***fast-track*** authority, expired. The Uruguay Round was therefore by far the longest round of ***multilateral trade negotiations***. It would be wrong, however, to view it as a continuous set of negotiations. Long stretches of its seven-and-a-half years were spent waiting for this or that participant or group of participants to come to terms with the need for a change in its negotiating position. This was the case especially in the third period when the ***Blair House Accord*** was negotiated and then renegotiated. The text of the

UPOV

国际植物新品种保护联盟

见*国际植物新品种保护公约(International Convention for the Protection of New Varieties of Plants)*。

Upper-middle-income economies

中等偏上收入经济体

由世界银行如此分类的60个经济体组成的国家组。2018年7月，这些国家的人均国民总收入(GNI)在3,996美元至12,375美元之间。另见*高收入经济体(high-income economies)*、*低收入经济体(low-income economies)*、*中等偏下收入经济体(lower-middle-income economies)*。

Upstream subsidy

上游补贴

给予最终产品加工过程中所使用产品的生产商的补贴。

Upward harmonization

向上协调

一协调安排的参加方按照满足它们之间流行的最高标准的原则对标准进行协调。另见*标准和资格的协调(harmonization of standards and qualifications)*。

Uruguay Round

乌拉圭回合

指第8轮多边贸易谈判。谈判于1986年9月25日在乌拉圭埃斯特角城启动，1993年12月15日在日内瓦结束，参加方部长于1994年4月15日在摩洛哥马拉喀什签署最后文件。谈判的目标为：(1)进一步放宽和扩大世界贸易；(2)加强GATT的作用，改善多边贸易体制；(3)增强GATT体制对国际经济环境的适应能力；以及(4)加强国际经济合作。参加方同意在谈判期间对贸易限制措施维持现状，并同意逐步回退条款。谈判的议题是所有GATT回合中最广泛的，包括关税、非关税措施、作为优先领域的热带产品、自然资源产品、纺织品和服装、农业、GATT条款审议、保障措施、东京回合协定和安排、补贴和反补贴措施、争端解决、与贸易有关的知识产权、与贸易有关的投资措施以及GATT体制的作用谈判小组(FOGS)。每项议题均由专门设立的谈判小组管理。因一组发展中国家坚持不接受GATT应涵盖服务，服务贸易谈判在法律上分开的轨道上进行。部长们同意谈判应在4年内结束。谈判可以分为三个阶段：(a)自埃斯特角城启动至1988年12月蒙特利尔中期审评；(b)此后至1990年12月布鲁塞尔部长级会议，该次会议本应标志着谈判结束；以及(c)直至1994年4月马拉喀什部长级会议所发生的事件。实质性谈判于1993年12月15日结束，当时美国的谈判授权，即快轨授权的第二次延长到期。因此乌拉圭回合是迄今为止时间最长的多边贸易谈判。但是，如将其视为一系列连续谈判是不对的。这漫长的7年半时间都花在等待这个或那个参加方或一组参加方对其谈判立场作出必要改变上了。第三阶段尤其如此。当时就《布莱尔宫协议》进行了谈判，随后又进行了谈

"first approximation to the Final Act" of the Uruguay Round, submitted by the Director-General of the GATT to the Brussels Ministerial Meeting in December 1990, was in fact very close to the agreement finally adopted at Marrakesh in April 1994. The main achievements of the Uruguay Round included a ***trade-weighted average tariff*** cut of 38 per cent, conclusion of the ***Agreement on Agriculture*** which brought agricultural trade for the first time under full ***GATT*** disciplines, adoption of the ***General Agreement on Trade in Services***, the ***Agreement on Trade-Related Aspects of Intellectual Property Rights*** and the ***Agreement on Trade-Related Investment Measures***, the creation of a unified and predictable ***dispute settlement*** mechanism, adoption of the ***Trade Policy Review Mechanism***, and the establishment of the World Trade Organization (***WTO***) which administers fifteen multilateral and four plurilateral trade agreements. Other results of the round were strengthened provisions on anti-dumping, subsidies and safeguards. The new ***Agreement on Textiles and Clothing*** brought this sector under the GATT rules by replacing the ***Multi-Fibre Arrangement***. *See also* ***Cairns Group***, ***Leutwiler Report*** and ***WTO Agreement***.

Uruguay Round acquis: a term used particularly by the ***European Union*** for the agreements and decisions that make up the ***Uruguay Round*** outcome. *See also* ***acquis communautaire*** and ***WTO Agreement***.

US–EU aircraft agreement: *see* ***EU–US aircraft agreement***.

USMCA rules of origin for automotive products: these are listed in Annex 4-B to the Agreement. They cover advanced technology vehicles (electric vehicles, fuel cell vehicles, vehicles with autonomous driving capacity, etc.), passenger vehicles, light trucks and heavy trucks. The requirements are quite detailed, but in summary they entail for passenger vehicles and light trucks (a) in addition to a prescribed ***change in tariff classification*** a 66 per cent ***regional value content*** (RVC) using the net-cost method (NC) on the later date of the entry into force of the Agreement or 1 January 2020, 69 per cent a year later, 72 per cent another year later and 75 per cent on 1 January 2023 or three years after the entry into force. Strong content requirements also apply to parts such as engines and transmissions. For heavy trucks the top rate will be 60 per cent using the NC method or 70 per cent using the ***transaction value method*** on 1 January 2027 or seven years after the entry into force of the Agreement, whichever is later. A 70 per cent North American steel and aluminium requirement will apply, as well as a ***labour value content*** requirement of a production wage rate of at least US$16 an hour.

USTR: refers both to the Office of the United States Trade Representative and the person of cabinet rank in charge of it. First created in 1962 as Special Representative for Trade Negotiations and upgraded to cabinet rank in 1974. It was renamed USTR in 1980. USTR is the principal United States locus for ***trade policy*** coordination and negotiations, including commodity negotiations. In ***financial services***, USTR has responsibility for insurance, but Treasury handles banking, funds management and securities. USTR publishes annually the

判。乌拉圭回合"最后文本的第一份草案"由GATT总干事提交1990年12月的布鲁塞尔部长级会议，这一文本实际上与1994年4月在马拉喀什最终通过的文本非常相近。乌拉圭回合主要成果包括贸易加权平均关税削减 38％；达成《农业协定》，首次将农产品贸易纳入全面GATT纪律；通过《服务贸易总协定》、《与贸易有关的知识产权协定》、《与贸易有关的投资措施协定》；建立统一和可预测的争端解决机制；通过贸易政策审议机制；以及建立世界贸易组织(WTO)，管理15个多边贸易协定和4个诸边贸易协定。该回合的其他成果包括，加强了反倾销、反补贴和保障措施条款，新的《纺织品与服装协定》将该部门纳入GATT规则，取代《多种纤维协定》。另见*凯恩斯集团(Cairns Group)*、*路特威勒报告(Leutwiler Report)*、*WTO 协定(WTO Agreement)*。

Uruguay Round acquis

乌拉圭回合谈判结果

欧盟用于指构成乌拉圭回合结果的协定和决定的词语。另见*欧盟现行法(acquis communautaire)*、*WTO协定(WTO Agreement)*。

US–EU aircraft agreement

美国—欧盟航空器协定

见*欧美航空器协定(EU–US aircraft agreement)*。

USMCA rules of origin for automotive products

USMCA汽车产品原产地规则

列入《美国—墨西哥—加拿大协定》(USMCA)附件4-B。规则涵盖先进技术汽车(电动汽车、燃料电池汽车、自动驾驶车辆等)、客车、轻型卡车和重型卡车。要求十分详细，但总而言之，要求客车和轻型卡车在规定的税则归类改变基础上，在协定生效之日或2020年1月1日(以较晚者为准)，使用净成本法(NC)计算的区域价值成分(RVC)应为66%，1年后应为69%，2年后应为72%，2023年1月1日或生效3年后应为75%。严格的含量要求也适用于发动机和变速箱等零件。对于重型卡车，在2027年1月1日或协定生效后7年(以较晚者为准)，采用净成本法的最高比例应为60%，或采用成交价格法的最高比例应为70%。适用70%的北美钢铁和铝要求及生产工资至少为每小时16美元的劳动价值含量要求。

USTR

美国贸易代表办公室

同时指美国贸易代表办公室和负责这一办公室的内阁级别官员。1962年最初以特别贸易谈判代表的名义设立，1974年提升为内阁级别，1980年更名为USTR。USTR是美国专门负责贸易政策协调和谈判(包括商品谈判)的主要机构。在金融服务中，USTR负责保险，财政部负责银行、基金管理和证券。USTR

National Trade Estimate Report on Foreign Trade Barriers, an inventory of the perceived most important barriers affecting United States exports of goods and services, ***foreign direct investment*** by United States persons, and protection of ***intellectual property*** rights. *See also* ***Section 301***, ***Section-306 monitoring***, ***Special 301***, ***Super 301*** and ***United States trade agreements legislation***. [Dryden 1995]

每年发布《对外贸易壁垒国家贸易评估报告》，详细列出被认为影响美国货物和服务出口、美国人进行的外国直接投资、保护知识产权方面的主要壁垒。另见*301条款(Section 301)*、*306条款监控(Section-306 monitoring)*、*特别301条款(Special 301)*、*超级301条款(Super 301)*、*美国贸易协定立法(United States trade agreements legislation)*。

Vaduz Convention: *see* ***EFTA Convention 2001***.

Value-added: the amount by which the value of a product increases at each stage of its production. Value-added, for example, can be used to determine whether a product has access to a market under a preferential trade agreement through the application of ***rules of origin***. Import statistics for goods imported under ***most-favoured-nation treatment*** often do not reflect the countries or customs territories where the bulk of the value has been added. They simply list the country or customs territory where the good was obtained. Statisticians therefore strive to obtain a better understanding of value added to products in the international production process which can assist government policy formulation. The OECD and the WTO, for example, are working on a Trade in Value Added (TiVA) database. This will give policy makers a clearer picture of the nature of trade flows.

Value-added criterion: a concept used in the administration of ***rules of origin*** under preferential trade agreements. It means that a specified amount of transformation or processing, usually expressed as a percentage of the total value of the good, has to have occurred in the country exporting the good if the good is to benefit from preferential tariff treatment. *See also* ***change in tariff classification***, ***regional value content*** and ***substantial transformation***.

Value-added tax: a ***consumption tax*** levied ***ad valorem*** on goods and services at the point of retail sale.

Value-added telecommunications: also called enhanced services. It includes services such as electronic mail, voice mail, enhanced facsimile services, including store-and-forward services. *See also* ***basic telecommunications***.

Variable geometry: sometimes flexibility in geometry, flexible geometry, etc. A term suggesting that a departure from the standards norms for an agreement may be achievable or even on offer, such as those governing ***asymmetrical trade agreements***. An example of variable geometry sometimes given is that of the ***Information Technology Agreement*** where some members accept deeper obligations which they then make available to the other members without a reciprocal obligation.

Variable levies: customs duty rates which vary in response to domestic criteria. They are intended to ensure that the price of a product on the domestic market remains unchanged regardless of price fluctuations in world markets and always well above world prices. *See also* ***Chicken War*** and ***Oilseeds*** for examples of trade tension caused by the introduction of variable levies.

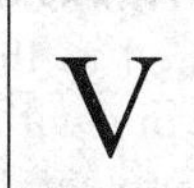

Vaduz Convention

瓦杜兹公约

见*2001年欧洲自由贸易联盟公约(EFTA Convention 2001)*。

Value-added

增值

一产品在每一生产阶段所增加价值的数量。例如，增值可用于确定一产品通过适用原产地规则是否可以根据一优惠贸易协定进入一市场。最惠国待遇项下进口货物的进口统计数字往往不能反映大部分增值所发生的国家或关税领土，而只是简单列出获得货物的国家或关税领土。统计学家因此尝试更好地理解在国际生产过程中对产品所增加的价值，这有助于政府制定政策。例如，经济合作与发展组织(OECD)和WTO正在建立一个增加值贸易(TiVA)数据库，有助于政策制定者更清晰地理解贸易流动的基本特征。

Value-added criterion

增值标准

优惠贸易协定项下原产地规则管理中使用的概念。指如果一货物想要享受优惠关税待遇，该货物必须在出口国中完成规定数量的改变或加工，通常以占货物总价值的百分比表示。另见*税则归类改变(change in tariff classification)*、*区域价值成分(regional value content)*、*实质性改变(substantial transformation)*。

Value-added tax

增值税

在零售环节对货物和服务征收的从价消费税。

Value-added telecommunications

增值电信

又称"增强服务"，包括电子邮件、语音邮件、增强传真服务(包括储存和发送服务)。另见*基础电信(basic telecommunications)*。

Variable geometry

可变几何

又称几何灵活性、灵活几何等。该词指对协定标准规范的偏离可以实现甚至可以提供，例如管辖非对称贸易协定的标准规范。可变几何的例子为《信息技术协定》，其中一些成员在没有互惠义务的情况下向其他成员提供更深层次的义务。

Variable levies

差价税

根据国内标准而变化的关税税率。意在无论国际市场价格如何波动，保证产品在国内市场中的价格不变，且总是高于国际市场价格。因采用差价税而引发的贸易紧张局势的例子如"鸡肉战"和"油籽案"。

Variable tariff: a ***tariff*** that is adjusted according to the relationship between the domestic price and the ***world market*** price for a ***commodity***. It is lowered when the domestic price is high compared to the world price and raised when the domestic price is low. The purpose of a variable tariff therefore is partly to bring stability to a market and partly to protect domestic producers.

VAT: *see* ***value-added tax***.

VER: voluntary export restraint. *See* ***voluntary restraint arrangement***.

Vertical arrangements: *see* ***competition policy***.

Vertical foreign direct investment: this refers to ***foreign direct investment*** by a firm either upstream or downstream of its own production activity. For example, a cloth manufacturer might invest in a wool processing plant or in a garment factory.

Vertical *keiretsu*: *see* ***keiretsu relationships***.

Vestigial thought: the term used by Robert Reich in his *Work of Nations* to describe economic analysis based on conditions that no longer apply, or that now apply to a limited extent only. It follows that vestigial thinking offers a fair prospect of leading to the wrong conclusions. *See also* **conventional wisdom** and ***QWERTY principle***. [Reich 1991]

VIE: *see* ***voluntary import expansion***.

Vienna Convention on the Law of Treaties: entered into force on 27 January 1980. It applies to treaties between states. Part II of the Convention contains provisions concerning the conclusion of treaties, the formulation of reservations, and the entry into force and provisional application of treaties. Part III is concerned with the observance, application and interpretation of treaties, Part IV with amendments and modifications, and Part V with invalidity, termination and suspension of the operation of treaties. Part VI deals with problems arising from the succession of states, hostilities and severance of diplomatic and consular relations. Part VII covers depositaries, modifications, corrections and registration of treaties. An annex deals with procedures for conciliation. The Convention is drafted in unusually clear language, and it is in fact an excellent introduction to the main elements and principles of international treaties law. *See also* ***pacta sunt servanda*** and ***treaty***.

Vienna Programme of Action for Landlocked Developing Countries for the Decade 2014–2024: adopted in November 2014 under the auspices of the United Nations. It has six priorities. Broadly they are: (1) *Fundamental transport policy issues*: to improve travel time, to allow transit cargos to move faster and reduce the time spent at land borders, (2) *Infrastructure development and maintenance* for transport, as well as energy and information and communications technology, (3) *International trade and trade facilitation*: increase significantly the participation of landlocked developing countries in global trade with a focus on increasing exports, (4) *Regional integration and cooperation* by, *inter alia*, strengthening regional trade, transport and communications and energy networks, (5) *Structural economic transformation*: increase value addition in the manufacturing and agricultural sectors, increase economic and

Variable tariff
可变关税

根据一商品的国内价格和世界市场价格的关系进行调整的关税。国内价格高于国际价格时，降低可变关税；国内价格低时，提高可变关税。因而可变关税的目的部分在于稳定市场，部分在于保护国内生产商。

VAT
增值税

见*增值税(value-added tax)*。

VER
自愿出口限制

见*自愿限制安排(voluntary restraint arrangement)*。

Vertical arrangements
纵向安排

见*竞争政策(competition policy)*。

Vertical foreign direct investment
纵向外国直接投资

指一企业对其生产活动的上游或下游进行的外国直接投资。例如，布料制造商可能会投资羊毛加工厂或投资服装厂。

Vertical *keiretsu*
纵向经连

见*经连关系(keiretsu relationships)*。

Vestigial thought
残余思想

罗伯特·莱赫在其所著《国家工作》一书中所用词语，描述根据不再适用的条件或目前仅有限适用的条件进行的经济分析。因此残余思想有可能产生错误结论。另见*传统智慧(conventional wisdom)*、*QWERTY键盘原则(QWERTY principle)*。

VIE
自愿扩大进口

见*自愿扩大进口(voluntary import expansion)*。

Vienna Convention on the Law of Treaties
维也纳条约法公约

1980年1月27日生效，适用于国家之间的条约。公约第二部分包含关于条约缔结、保留的制定以及条约生效和临时适用的条款。第三部分关于条约的遵守、适用和解释。第四部分关于修正和修改。第五部分关于条约运用的失效、终止和中止。第六部分处理因国家继承、敌对及外交和领事关系断绝所产生的问题。第七部分涵盖条约的交存、修改、更正和登记。附件处理调解程序。公约使用非常明确的文字起草，且实际上是对国际条约法的主要要素和原则的绝佳介绍。另见*条约必须遵守(pacta sunt servanda)*、*条约(treaty)*。

Vienna Programme of Action for Landlocked Developing Countries for the Decade 2014–2024
内陆发展中国家2014—2024年十年维也纳行动纲领

2014年11月在联合国主持下通过。有6项优先事项。分别为：(1)基本运输政策问题：改善旅行时间，允许过境货物更快移动，缩短在陆地边界所花时间；(2)运输基础设施的发展和维护，以及能源及信息和通信技术的发展和维护；(3)国际贸易和贸易便利化：大幅增加内陆发展中国家对全球贸易的参与，重点为增加出口；(4)区域一体化和合作，特别通过加强区域贸易、运输和通信以

export diversification and encourage the inflow of foreign direct investment in high-value-added sectors, and (6) *Means of implementation*. *See also* ***Almaty Programme of Action***. [unohrlls.org]

Violation cases: dispute settlement proceedings in the WTO in which a party alleges that another party is in direct breach of its obligations under one or more of the agreements administered by the WTO. *See also* ***non-violation***.

Virtual Institute on Trade and Development: *see* ***UNCTAD Virtual Institute on Trade and Development***.

Virtuous circle: used in many policy areas to describe a beneficial sequence of events. One frequently mentioned in ***trade policy*** consists of economic development, the growth of trade and social progress. *See also* ***World Commission on the Social Dimension of Globalization***.

Visegrád countries: Czech Republic, Hungary, Poland and Slovakia. The name for these countries had its origin in the Declaration of Visegrád, made on 15 February 1991 by Hungary, Poland and the then Czechoslovakia. This declaration marked the first sign that these countries would seek closer cooperation with the ***European Community***. Visegrád is a small town on the Danube not far from Budapest. *See also* ***CEFTA 2006***, ***Central European Free Trade Agreement*** and ***enlargement***.

Vitamin B12*:** a case brought by the ***European Economic Community (EEC) against the United States in 1981 on the grounds that the United States was not honouring one of its ***Tokyo Round*** commitments. The United States had agreed to abolish the ***American Selling Price*** (ASP) as part of the Tokyo Round outcome. Imports of both Vitamin B12 feedgrade and pharmaceutical quality were subject to the ASP at a bound rate negotiated in the ***Kennedy Round***. At the time of the binding, the United States had reserved the right the change the tariff rate for goods in the event that the ASP was abolished, as seemed possible at the time. Between 1976 and 1980 Vitamin B12 of pharmaceutical quality entered the United States at a higher rate than Vitamin B12 of feedgrade quality. When the Customs Valuation Code, one of the ***Tokyo Round agreements***, entered into force on 1 July 1980, the two rates were combined at the weighted average of the actual charges collected for both rates, which meant that Vitamin B12 feedgrade was now subject to a higher duty. In an understanding dated 2 March 1979 the EEC and the United States had agreed to consult on differences arising from the conversion of ASP rates. The ***panel*** held that the United States had no obligation to maintain a tariff rate differentiation for feedgrade quality and pharmaceutical quality Vitamin B12. The EEC could have foreseen that the ASP conversion would in some cases result in higher tariff rates, but not to the extent that it actually affected its trade. The panel therefore felt that the United States should be invited to advance the tariff reductions envisaged in the implementation of the Tokyo Round commitment on feedgrade Vitamin B12 at a rate that would allow imported vitamins to regain their traditional competitive position in the United States. [GATT BISD 29S]

及能源网络；(5)结构性经济转型：增加制造业和农业部门的附加值，增强经济和出口多样化，鼓励外国直接投资流入高附加值部门；以及(6)实施手段。另见*阿拉木图行动纲领(Almaty Programme of Action)*。

Violation cases

违反案件

在WTO的争端解决程序中，其中一争端方声称另一争端方直接违反WTO所管理的一个或多个协定项下的义务。另见*非违反(non-violation)*。

Virtual Institute on Trade and Development

贸易与发展虚拟学院

见*UNCTAD贸易与发展虚拟学院(UNCTAD Virtual Institute on Trade and Development)*。

Virtuous circle

良性循环

用于很多政策领域以形容一个有利的事件序列。在贸易政策中经常提及的良性循环包括经济发展、贸易增长和社会进步。另见*全球化社会问题世界委员会 (World Commission on the Social Dimension of Globalization)*。

Visegrád countries

维谢格拉德国家

捷克、匈牙利、波兰和斯洛伐克。这些国家的名称源自1991年2月15日由匈牙利、波兰和当时的捷克斯洛伐克发表的《维谢格拉德宣言》。宣言是标志着这些国家将寻求与欧洲共同体开展更紧密合作的第一个象征。维谢格拉德是距离布达佩斯不远的多瑙河边小镇。另见*2006年中欧自由贸易协定(CEFTA 2006)*、*中欧自由贸易协定(Central European Free Trade Agreement)*、*扩盟(enlargement)*。

Vitamin B12

维生素B12案

欧洲经济共同体(EEC)1981年以美国未履行其一项东京回合承诺为由针对美国提起的案件。美国作为东京回合成果的一部分，已经同意取消美国销售价格(ASP)。饲料用和药用维生素B12的进口需按美国销售价格适用肯尼迪回合谈判达成的约束税率。在进行关税约束时，美国保留了在美国销售价格取消情况下更改货物关税税率的权利，当时看似可能发生。在1976年至1980年期间，药用维生素B12进口至美国的税率高于饲料用维生素B12的税率。1980年7月1日东京回合协定之一的《海关估价守则》生效时，上述两税率按两税率实际收取税额加权平均后合并，这意味着需对饲料用维生素B12征收较高税率。在1979年3月2日欧共体与美国达成的谅解中，双方同意就美国销售价格税率转换过程中产生的分歧进行磋商。专家组认为，美国无义务对饲料用和药用维生素B12维持不同关税税率。欧共体本应可以预见到美国销售价格转换会在一些情况下导致关税税率提高，但不会达到实际影响其贸易的程度。专家组因此认为，应该邀请美国继续进行关税削减，如其在东京回合中所承诺的将饲料用维生素B12的税率降至可使进口维生素重获美国传统竞争地位的水平。

Voluntarism: one of the principles pervading the activities of ***APEC***. By and large, participation in many APEC sub-programmes and working groups is voluntary, as long as the end-dates for full trade liberalization expressed in the ***Bogor Declaration*** are met. In practice, however, member economies find that it can be quite difficult to opt out of an activity when most of the others are willing to pursue it. *See also* ***APEC Pathfinders***.

Voluntary export restraint: VER. *See* ***voluntary restraint arrangement***.

Voluntary import expansion: VIE. A mechanism under a bilateral arrangement under which a country agrees, ostensibly voluntarily, to adopt measures promoting the use of imported products of particular export interest to the other country. Some fear that such arrangements could be taking the place of the ***grey-area measures*** which are now illegal under WTO rules.

Voluntary restraint arrangement: VRA. A bilateral arrangement whereby an exporting country (government or industry) agrees to reduce or restrict exports so that the importing country does not have to use quotas, raise tariffs or impose other import controls. VRAs have been used for steel, cars, semi-conductors and other products in so-called ***sensitive sectors***. These arrangements are voluntary only to the extent that the exporting country wishes to avert an even greater threat to its trade and therefore chooses the lesser of two evils. VRAs not only deny the benefits of ***comparative advantage*** to efficient suppliers. They can also lead to an inefficient allocation of resources because industries affected by them may be forced to invest in less efficient markets to retain access to them. Another possible outcome is that they give exporters and importers windfall profits because of lessened competition. The WTO ***Agreement on Safeguards*** makes new VRAs illegal, and all those in existence on 1 January 1995, when the WTO was established, had to be phased out within five years.

Voluntary Sustainability Standards: VSS. Usually non-government initiatives, but often supported by government, at the local, regional or international level. They respond to environmental and social concerns in the production, processing and marketing of products by promoting sustainable production and business practices. They also help buyers in selecting products produced under sustainable conditions. The development and implementation of such standards is assisted by the ***United Nations Forum on Sustainability Standards***. [unfss.org]

Voting rights in the WTO: each WTO member is entitled to one vote regardless of its ranking as a trading nation. The ***European Union*** is entitled to a number of votes equalling the number of its member states, but the member states themselves do not vote. *See also* ***amendments to WTO agreements***, ***common commercial policy***, ***consensus*** and ***decision-making in the WTO***.

VRA: *see* ***voluntary restraint arrangement***.

Vulnerability: the extent to which a country, household or person is likely to suffer harm from adverse developments, or the extent to which it is exposed to the risk of such events occurring. This is a concept sometimes used in the study of problems facing ***least-developed countries***. *See also* ***small vulnerable economies*** and ***trade and poverty***.

Voluntarism

自愿主义

普遍适用于APEC活动的一项原则。总体而言，许多APEC子项目和工作组的参与属自愿，只要满足《茂物宣言》中所述的充分贸易自由化的最终日期。但是实际上，成员经济体发现，很难选择退出一项其他大多数成员经济体愿意参与的活动。另见*APEC探路者(APEC Pathfinders)*。

Voluntary export restraint

自愿出口限制

VER。见*自愿限制安排(voluntary restraint arrangement)*。

Voluntary import expansion

自愿扩大进口

VIE。双边安排项下的机制，根据这一机制，一国表面上同意自愿采取措施以促进对另一国具有特殊出口利益的进口产品的使用。一些人担心此类安排可能取代灰色区域措施，后者根据WTO规则现属非法。

Voluntary restraint arrangement

自愿限制安排

VRA。双边安排，其中一出口国(政府或产业)同意减少或限制出口，从而使进口国不再需要使用配额、提高关税或施加其他进口控制。自愿限制安排曾使用在钢铁、汽车、半导体和所谓敏感部门的其他产品上。此类安排所谓自愿仅仅是在出口国希望避免其贸易受到更大威胁的意义上，因此只是两害相权取其轻。自愿限制安排不仅抹杀了有效供应方的比较优势利益，而且导致了资源的低效率分配，因为受其影响的产业可能被迫投资于低效率的市场，以便保留对此类市场的准入。另一个可能的结果是，由于竞争减少而带给出口商和进口商不劳而获的利润。WTO《保障措施协定》规定，新的自愿限制安排属非法，在1995年1月1日WTO建立时已经存在的措施需要在5年内逐步取消。

Voluntary Sustainability Standards

自愿可持续性标准

VSS。通常为在地方、区域或国际层面的非政府倡议，但往往得到政府的支持。通过促进可持续生产和商业惯例以回应产品生产、加工和销售中的环境和社会问题。还帮助购买者选择在可持续条件下生产的产品。联合国可持续发展标准论坛协助制定和实施此类标准。

Voting rights in the WTO

WTO中的投票权

每一WTO成员有权获得一票，无论其作为贸易国的排名如何。欧盟拥有的票数与其成员国数相等，但成员国本身不进行投票。另见*WTO协定的修正(amendments to WTO agreements)*、*共同商业政策(common commercial policy)*、*协商一致(consensus)*、*WTO决策机制(decision-making in the WTO)*。

VRA

自愿限制安排

见*自愿限制安排(voluntary restraint arrangement)*。

Vulnerability

脆弱性

一国、一家庭或一个人有可能因不利发展因素而遭受损害的程度，或其面临此类事件发生风险的程度。有时用在研究最不发达国家所面临问题方面的概念。另见*弱小经济体(small vulnerable economies)*、*贸易与贫困(trade and poverty)*。

W/120: a services sectoral classification list prepared by the GATT Secretariat in 1991 to support the ***Uruguay Round*** negotiations on trade in services. It was issued as document MTN.GNS/W/120.

Wage-differential argument: the proposition that countries with low wages are able to undercut countries with high wages, and that they therefore enjoy a competitive advantage. Economists have been satisfied for 150 years that this is not the case, and that the difference in wages can be accounted for by a gap in productivity. In ***trade policy*** the argument lives on, and it underlies part of the debate on ***trade and labour standards*** and the alleged need for a ***social clause***. *See also* ***pauper-labour argument*** and ***race-to-the-bottom argument***.

Waiver: a dispensation granted by WTO members to another member freeing it from the obligation to apply a particular provision to a defined aspect of its international trade. Under WTO rules, waivers must be approved by three-quarters of WTO members. Once granted, they are subject to periodic review. *See also* ***LDC services waiver*** and ***Section 22 waiver***.

Washington Consensus: a much-misunderstood term coined by John Williamson in 1990. He uses it for a set of eleven principles that he considered embodied the "lowest common denominator" of reforms the Washington-based financial institutions, including the ***IMF*** and the ***World Bank***, could agree on in 1989 as suitable for Latin America. The principles were: fiscal discipline, redirection of public expenditure towards high economic returns and better income distribution, tax reform, interest rate liberalization, competitive exchange rate, trade liberalization, liberalization of inward direct investment, privatization, deregulation and secure property rights. Though Williamson saw merit in many of these principles individually, he was critical of what he saw as a tendency by the Washington-based institutions to apply this set of principles as a universal remedy. He later became particularly displeased that the term "Washington Consensus" had been appropriated by those who advocated "market fundamentalism". [Williamson 2000]

Washington Treaty on Intellectual Property in Respect of Integrated Circuits: *see* ***Treaty on Intellectual Property in Respect of Integrated Circuits***.

Wassenaar Arrangement on Export Controls for Conventional Arms and Dual-Use Goods and Technologies: this arrangement entered into force on 1 November 1996 as the successor to ***COCOM***. Its purpose is to promote transparency, exchange of views and information and greater responsibility in transfers of conventional arms and dual-use goods and technologies. The

W/120

W/120文件

GATT秘书处1991年编制的支持乌拉圭回合服务贸易部门分类清单。以MTN.GNS/W/120号文件发布。

Wage-differential argument

工资差别理论

该主张认为，低工资国家可以与高工资国家进行低价竞争，因而享受竞争优势。但150年来，经济学家一直认为情况并非如此，认为工资差别可以通过生产效率差异弥补。在贸易政策方面，此种观点一直存在，同时也是构成贸易与劳工标准争论的部分内容，且成为所谓的对社会条款的需要。另见*贫民劳动论(pauper-labour argument)*、*竞次论(race-to-the-bottom argument)*。

Waiver

豁免

WTO成员给予另一成员的豁免，免除该成员对于其一国际贸易的具体方面无需适用一特定条款的义务。根据WTO规则，豁免必须经WTO成员的四分之三多数批准。一旦给予，豁免需经阶段性审议。另见*最不发达国家服务豁免(LDC services waiver)*、*22条豁免(Section 22 waiver)*。

Washington Consensus

华盛顿共识

约翰·威廉姆森1990年创造的一个经常被误解的词语，他用这一词语指一套11项原则，他认为这些原则包含了对设在华盛顿的金融机构(包括国际货币基金组织和世界银行)改革的"最小公分母"，可以在1989年取得一致而适用于拉美国家。这些原则为：财政纪律、把政府开支的重点转向经济效益高和有利于改善收入分配的领域、税制改革、利率自由化、具有竞争力的汇率制度、贸易自由化、对内直接投资自由化、私有化、放松政府管制和保护产权。虽然威廉姆森认为这些原则中许多原则各有优点，但是他对总部设在华盛顿的机构将这套原则作为普遍补救措施的趋势持批评态度。后来，他对"华盛顿共识"一词被那些主张"市场原教旨主义"的人所盗用而感到非常不满。

Washington Treaty on Intellectual Property in Respect of Integrated Circuits

集成电路知识产权华盛顿条约

见*关于集成电路知识产权的条约(Treaty on Intellectual Property in Respect of Integrated Circuits)*。

Wassenaar Arrangement on Export Controls for Conventional Arms and Dual-Use Goods and Technologies

关于常规武器和两用物品及技术出口管制的瓦森纳安排

该安排于1996年11月1日生效，取代多边出口管制协调委员会(COCOM)。协定旨在促进常规武器和两用物品及技术转让方面的透明度、观点和信息的交流

Arrangement is not directed against any state or group of states. Each member country enforces its own export control laws. Members are Argentina, Australia, Austria, Belgium, Bulgaria, Canada, Croatia, Czech Republic, Denmark, Estonia, Finland, France, Germany, Greece, Hungary, India, Ireland, Italy, Japan, Latvia, Lithuania, Luxembourg, Malta, Mexico, Netherlands, New Zealand, Norway, Poland, Portugal, Republic of Korea, Romania, Russia, Slovakia, Slovenia, South Africa, Spain, Sweden, Switzerland, Turkey, Ukraine, United Kingdom and the United States. Its secretariat is in Vienna. *See also* ***dual-purpose exports***. [www.wassenaar.org]

Watch list: *see* ***priority foreign country*** and ***Special 301***.

Water in the tariff: an expression used in the ***Uruguay Round*** negotiations on ***tariffication*** (the conversion of ***non-tariff measures*** into ***tariff equivalents***), but of much earlier origin. Negotiators accept that such conversions can never be completely accurate because of legitimate differences about the impact of these measures and the methods to be adopted. There were cases, however, where countries offered tariff equivalents that were obviously inflated. The difference between what would be seen as a defensible tariff conversion and the one actually offered was described as "water in the tariff" or "dirty tariffication". The term "water" or tariff overhang is also understood as the difference between members' bound and applied tariffs.

WCO: *see* ***World Customs Organization***.

Webb-Pomerene Act: a United States law adopted in 1918 which permits American companies to combine within certain limits for the purpose of engaging in export trade. Firms may not, as a result of combining, restrain trade in the United States or restrain the export trade of competitors. That would still be illegal under the ***Sherman Act*** and other ***antitrust laws***. *See also* ***competition policy***.

Weighted average tariff: *see* ***trade-weighted average tariffs***.

Well-known mark: a ***trademark*** registered in one country which, under Article 6bis of the ***Paris Convention***, may qualify for protection in another by virtue of having a reputation as such even though it is not registered there. Using a confusingly similar mark would often be considered ***unfair competition***. *The WIPO Joint Recommendations Concerning Provisions on the Protection of Well-Known Marks*, adopted in September 1999, list the following criteria which may assist in determining whether a mark is well known: (a) the degree of knowledge or recognition in the relevant sector of the public (i.e. not the public at large), (b) duration, extent and geographical area of any use of the mark, (c) duration, extent and geographical area of any promotion of the mark, (d) duration and geographical area of any registration and/or applications for registration of the mark, (e) record of successful enforcement of rights in the mark, and (f) the value associated with the mark.

West African Economic and Monetary Union: WAEMU or Union Économique et Monétaire Ouest Africaine – UEMOA. Members are Benin, Burkina Faso, Guinea Bissau, Côte d'Ivoire, Mali, Niger, Senegal and Togo. Established in

以及更大的责任。安排不针对任何一个国家或一组国家。每一成员国实施各自的出口管制法律。成员国为阿根廷、澳大利亚、奥地利、比利时、保加利亚、加拿大、克罗地亚、捷克、丹麦、爱沙尼亚、芬兰、法国、德国、希腊、匈牙利、印度、爱尔兰、意大利、日本、拉脱维亚、立陶宛、卢森堡、马耳他、墨西哥、荷兰、新西兰、挪威、波兰、葡萄牙、韩国、罗马尼亚、俄罗斯、斯洛伐克、斯洛文尼亚、南非、西班牙、瑞典、瑞士、土耳其、乌克兰、英国和美国。秘书处设在维也纳。另见*两用物品出口(dual-purpose exports)*。

Watch list

观察名单

见*重点国家(priority foreign country)*、*特别301条款(Special 301)*。

Water in the tariff

关税水分

乌拉圭回合关税化谈判中使用的表述，关税化即将非关税措施转换为关税等值，但这一表述的起源更早。谈判者承认此种转换永远无法作到完全精确，原因在于这些措施的影响与拟采用的方法之间存在合理差异。但是，出现的情况是，一些国家提出的关税等值明显夸大。看似防守性的关税转换与实际出价的关税转换之间的差异被称为“关税水分”或“肮脏的关税化”。“水分”或关税超出的表述也被理解为成员约束关税与实施关税之间的差异。

WCO

世界海关组织

见*世界海关组织(World Customs Organization)*。

Webb-Pomerene Act

韦布-波默林法

1918年通过的一项美国法律，允许美国公司为参与出口贸易而在某些限度内进行合并。作为合并结果，公司不能限制美国国内的贸易或限制竞争者的出口贸易。否则根据《谢尔曼法》和其他反垄断法属违法行为。另见*竞争政策(competition policy)*。

Weighted average tariff

加权平均关税

见*贸易加权平均关税(trade-weighted average tariffs)*。

Well-known mark

驰名商标

根据《巴黎公约》第六条之二，在一国注册的商标在未进行注册的另一国可凭借其自身声誉而有资格获得保护。使用一易混淆的类似商标通常被视为属不正当竞争。1999年9月通过的世界知识产权组织(WIPO)《关于驰名商标保护规定的联合建议》列举了以下标准，可协助用于确定一商标是否属驰名：(a)在相关公众(即不是全部公众)中的了解和认知程度；(b)该商标任何使用的持续时间、程度和地理范围；(c)该商标任何宣传的持续时间、程度和地理范围；(d)任何注册或任何注册申请的持续时间和地理范围；(e)成功实施商标权的记录；以及(f)该商标的相关价值。

West African Economic and Monetary Union

西非经济与货币联盟

WAEMU或UEMOA。成员为贝宁、布基纳法索、几内亚比绍、科特迪瓦、马

1994. Its aims are (a) strengthening economic and financial competitiveness of member states, (b) secure convergence in their economic the presentations and policies, (c) create a common market based on the free movement of persons, goods, services and capital, the right of establishment of self-employed or salaried persons, as well as a common external tariff and a common market policy, (d) coordinate national sector-based policies, and (e) harmonize, to the extent necessary, the smooth running of the common market, the legislative system of member states, and particularly the taxation system. Its secretariat is in Ouagadougou, Burkina Faso. *See also* ***African regional economic integration***.

West African Economic Community: established in 1967. Its membership included Benin, Côte d'Ivoire, Dahomey (now Burkina Faso), Liberia, Mali, Mauritania, Niger, Senegal and Sierra Leone. It was succeeded in 1975 by the ***Economic Community of West African States***.

Western European Union: established in 1948 as the Western Union under the *Treaty of Economic, Social and Cultural Cooperation and Collective Self-Defence* and renamed Western European Union in 1954. It is mainly concerned with political and security matters and organizationally distinct from the ***European Union***. It is located in Brussels.

Western Hemisphere Free Trade Agreement: *see* ***FTAA***.

Westinghouse Uranium*:** a case brought in the mid-1970s by Westinghouse, a manufacturer of nuclear power stations, under United States ***antitrust laws against twenty-nine domestic and foreign uranium suppliers. Much of the case against the foreign companies had to be conducted under ***extraterritoriality*** provisions. The matters raised by this case were eventually settled, partly because the foreign companies were loath to lose their access to the United States market. One of its longer-term effects was, however, the emergence of ***blocking statutes*** and ***clawback provisions***.

Wheat flour*:** a case brought in 1982 by the United States before the GATT against the ***European Economic Community (EEC) on the grounds the EEC did not honour its commitments under the ***Tokyo Round*** Subsidies Code, one of the ***Tokyo Round agreements***. Much of the case was concerned with the meaning of ***equitable share of the market***, and whether the EEC had acquired more than it should have. The ***panel*** concluded that (a) EEC export refunds for wheat flour were a subsidy in terms of Article XVI (Subsidies) of the GATT, (b) the EEC share of world exports of wheat flour had increased considerably, and that the share of the United States and others had decreased, (c) in the light of the many factors to be considered, a ruling on whether this had resulted in "more than an equitable share" was not possible, (d) market displacement in the sense of Article 10:2(a) of the Subsidies Code, under which the effect of an export subsidy has to be taken into account, was not evident, (e) there was insufficient evidence concerning price undercutting, (f) the EEC export refunds had caused undue disturbance to the normal commercial interests of the United States, and (g) the EEC should make greater efforts to limit the use of subsidies on the

里、尼日尔、塞内加尔和多哥，于1994年建立。目标为：(a)加强成员国经济和金融竞争力；(b)保证经济表现和政策的一致性；(c)建立基于人员、货物、服务和资本自由流动、个体经营者或受薪人士的设立权以及共同对外关税和共同市场政策的共同市场；(d)协调国家的部门政策；以及(e)在必要的限度内协调共同市场、成员国立法制度、特别是税收制度的顺利运行。秘书处设在布基纳法索乌加度古。另见*非洲区域经济一体化(African regional economic integration)*。

West African Economic Community

西非经济共同体

于1967年建立。成员包括贝宁、科特迪瓦、达荷美共和国(现布基纳法索)、利比里亚、马里、毛里塔尼亚、尼日尔、塞内加尔和塞拉利昂。1975年被西非国家经济共同体所取代。

Western European Union

西欧联盟

1948年根据《经济、社会、文化合作和集体防御条约》建立西部联盟，1954年更名为“西欧联盟”。主要涉及政治和安全问题，在组织上区别于欧盟。联盟设在布鲁塞尔。

Western Hemisphere Free Trade Agreement

西半球自由贸易协定

见*美洲自由贸易区(FTAA)*。

Westinghouse Uranium

西屋铀案

核电站制造商西屋公司于20世纪70年代中期根据美国反垄断法针对29个国内外铀供应商提起的案件。针对外国公司的大部分案件必须根据治外法权条款进行。该案引发的问题最终得到解决，部分由于外国公司不愿失去进入美国市场的机会。但是一个长远影响是阻断法和回拨条款的出现。

Wheat flour

小麦面粉案

1982年美国在GATT起诉欧洲经济共同体(EEC)的案件，理由是欧共体未遵守其在东京回合协定之一的东京回合《补贴守则》项下的承诺。该案大部分内容涉及公正市场份额的含义，及欧共体所获份额是否超过其应得份额。专家组的结论为：(a)欧共体的小麦面粉出口退税根据GATT第16条(补贴)属于补贴；(b)欧共体小麦面粉的世界出口份额大幅增加，而美国和其他国家的份额下降；(c)由于有许多因素需要考虑，不可能对此种做法是否导致“超出公正份额”作出裁决；(d)对于评估出口补贴影响需要考虑的《补贴守则》第10条第2款(a)项范围内的市场替代并不明显；(e)削低价格的证据不足；(f)欧共体出口退税对美国正常商业利益造成不适当干扰；以及(g)欧共体应作出更大努力限制小麦

exports of wheat flour. The panel also expressed concern, from a broader economic and trade policy perspective, about the effectiveness of the legal provisions regarding export subsidies and other aspects of trade in wheat flour. It found it anomalous that the EEC, which would not be able to export substantial quantities of wheat flour without subsidies, had become the world's largest exporter. It suggested that a clearer understanding of the concept of "more than an equitable share" was needed to make the concept more operational. It also questioned whether international understandings on sales on non-commercial terms adequately complemented the intended disciplines on export subsidies. [GATT SCM/42]

White Paper: a public document, originally with a white cover, which sets out actual or proposed government policy. The practice of governments in their use varies considerably. The annual White Papers issued by Japanese ministries and agencies are rather like annual reports, though they often examine in detail new policies adopted by the Government. ***European Union*** White Papers contain proposals for Community action in a specific area which, if received favourably, may in time be adopted as policy. Many governments issue White Papers infrequently, and then to indicate their broad policy aims in a given area. *See also* ***Green Paper***.

Wholly obtained goods: the ***rules of origin*** under ***free-trade agreements*** always distinguish between goods that were made or produced (obtained wholly) in the territories of the partners to the agreement and those that were made partly in them. Goods made or obtained wholly within these territories always enjoy preferential tariff treatment, but those made there partly have to undergo some test to ascertain their eligibility for preferential treatment. This is to ensure that preferences do not leak to third countries. The definition of wholly obtained goods varies between arrangements. The United States–Singapore Free Trade Agreement, for example, defines them as: (a) a mineral extracted from the soil, waters, seabed, or beneath the seabed; (b) a vegetable good harvested or gathered there [i.e. the party exporting the good]; (c) a live animal born and raised there; (d) a good obtained from live animals born and raised there; (e) a good obtained from hunting, trapping, fishing or aquaculture conducted there; (f) a good of sea fishing and other marine goods taken outside its waters by vessels registered or recorded there; (g) a good processed and/or made on board factory ships registered or recorded there exclusively from products taken by vessels registered there; (h) a good taken by a Party, or a person of a Party, from the seabed or beneath the seabed outside territorial waters, provided that the Party has the right to exploit that seabed; (i) waste and scrap derived from production there; (j) waste and scrap derived from used articles, provided that the articles are fit only for the recovery of raw materials; (k) recovered goods, parts left over after cleaning, inspecting, testing, etc., of the goods; and (l) a good produced exclusively from the goods listed above. *See also* ***non-originating goods***, ***originating goods*** and ***preferential rules of origin***.

面粉出口补贴。专家组还从更广泛的经济和贸易政策角度，对有关小麦面粉贸易的出口补贴和其他方面的法律条款的有效性表达了关注。指出，欧共体已经成为世界上最大的小麦面粉出口方，而如果没有补贴，欧共体即无法大量出口小麦面粉，这是不正常的。专家组建议，需要对“超出公正份额”的概念进行更为明确的理解，从而使这一概念更具操作性。专家组还质疑关于非商业条款销售的国际谅解是否能够充分补充关于出口补贴的拟议纪律。

White Paper

白皮书

列出实际的或拟议的政府政策的公共文件，最初使用白色封面。各国政府对白皮书的使用在做法上差别很大。日本各部和机构发布的年度白皮书更像是年度报告，尽管这些白皮书经常详细审查政府采取的新政策。欧盟白皮书包含共同体在特定领域采取行动的建议，如果得到好评，这些建议适时可以作为政策予以采纳。许多政府偶尔发布白皮书，以表明在一指定领域的广泛政策目标。另见*绿皮书(Green Paper)*。

Wholly obtained goods

完全获得的货物

自由贸易协定项下的原产地规则通常对全部在协定参加方领土内制造或生产的产品(完全获得)和部分在此类领土内生产的产品加以区分。完全在这些领土内制造或获得的货物通常享受优惠关税待遇，而那些部分在这些领土内生产的货物需要进行一些测试以确定是否有资格获得优惠待遇。这样作是为保证优惠不会漏给第三国。各项安排对完全获得的货物的定义各有不同。例如《美国—新加坡自由贸易协定》将其定义为：(a)自土壤、水域、海床或海床下底土提取的矿物质；(b)在该参加方(即出口该货物的参加方)收获或采摘的蔬菜；(c)在该参加方出生和饲养的活动物；(d)自在该参加方出生和饲养的活体动物中获得的货物；(e)在该参加方通过狩猎、诱捕、捕捞或内水养殖获得的货物；(f)海洋捕捞的产品及由在该参加方注册的船舶在其水域外捕捞的其他海货；(g)由在该参加方注册或登记的捕鱼加工船全部使用在该参加方注册的船舶获得的产品加工和/或制造的货物；(h)一参加方或一参加方的个人自领海外的海床或海床下底土获得的货物，只要该参加方有权开发该海床；(i)源自在该参加方的生产过程的废碎料；(j)源自旧货的废碎料，只要这些货物仅适合原材料回收；(k)回收货物、货物清洗、检验、测试后遗留零件；以及(l)全部使用以上所列货物生产的货物。另见***非原产货物****(non-originating goods)*、***原产货物****(originating goods)*、***优惠原产地规则****(preferential rules of origin)*。

Wider competition policy: this deals with the approach of governments to the promotion of competition in sectors currently benefiting from regulation now seen as inappropriate or the opening of so-called natural monopolies to competition. *See also* ***antitrust laws***, ***competition policy***, ***deregulation***, ***narrow competition policy*** and ***re-regulation***.

Wilson Tariff Act: a United States Act of 1894. Apart from its provisions on tariffs, now entirely superseded, it prohibits "every combination, conspiracy, trust, agreement or contract" made by two or more persons or corporations engaged in importing goods into the United States, where the agreement is intended to restrain trade or increase the market price of the goods. Violation may result in a fine, a prison term or seizure of the imported goods. *See also* ***antitrust*** and ***antitrust guidelines for international enforcement and cooperation***.

Wine: *see* ***Agreement on Mutual Acceptance of Oenological Practices***, ***Agreement on Trade-Related Aspects of Intellectual Property Rights***, ***appellation d'origine contrôlée***, ***appellations of origin***, ***International Organisation of Vine and Wine***, ***Organisation internationale de la vigne et du vin*** and ***World Wine Trade Group***.

Wine gallon assessment: the United States practice, now terminated, of assessing spirits imported at less than 100 proof as though they were 100 proof since the same rule would have applied to domestic spirits of less than 100 proof if withdrawn from bond. The importer could get around this by purchasing spirits at 100 proof or more and diluting them later. This meant importing in bulk and bottling in the United States. Customers, however, generally preferred spirits bottled in the country of origin. This rule therefore disadvantaged foreign products even though there was no difference with the treatment of similar domestic products. The wine gallon assessment is often used to show how formally identical ***national treatment*** can in fact be discriminatory. *See also* ***implicit discrimination***.

Wine lake: the name given in popular parlance to the wine surplus created in Europe through the ***common agricultural policy***. *See also* ***butter mountain***.

Wingspread Declaration: a version of the ***precautionary principle***, adopted by participants in an environmental seminar at the Wingspread Conference Center, University of Wisconsin, in January 1998. It states in part that "when an activity raises threats of harm to human health or the environment, precautionary measures should be taken even if some cause and effect relationships are not established scientifically. In this context the proponent of the activity, rather than the public, should bear the burden of proof. The process of applying the Precautionary Principle must be open, informed and democratic and must include potentially affected parties. It must also involve an examination of the full range of alternatives, including no action."

WIPO: World Intellectual Property Organization, one of the ***United Nations specialized agencies***. It is the main ***intergovernmental organization*** responsible for the protection of ***intellectual property rights*** and, through it, the

Wider competition policy
广义竞争政策

这一政策涉及政府在目前得益于现在看似不适当的管制的部门促进竞争的方式，或开放所谓自然垄断进行竞争的方式。另见*反垄断法(antitrust laws)*、*竞争政策(competition policy)*、*取消管制(deregulation)*、*狭义竞争政策(narrow competition policy)*、*重新管制(re-regulation)*。

Wilson Tariff Act
威尔逊关税法

美国1894年法案。其中除目前全部废止的关税条款外，该法禁止参与将货物进口至美国的由两个或两个以上个人或公司进行的任何“合并、共谋、托拉斯、协议或合同”行为，如所订立的协议旨在限制贸易或提高该货物的市场价格。违反该法可能导致罚款、监禁或进口货物被没收。另见*反垄断(antitrust)*、*国际执法与合作反垄断指导原则(antitrust guidelines for international enforcement and cooperation)*。

Wine
葡萄酒

见*关于相互接受酿酒方法的协定(Agreement on Mutual Acceptance of Oenological Practices)*、*与贸易有关的知识产权协定(Agreement on Trade-Related Aspects of Intellectual Property Rights)*、*原产地命名控制(appellation d'origine contrôlée)*、*原产地名称(appellations of origin)*、*国际葡萄与葡萄酒组织(International Organisation of Vine and Wine)*、*国际葡萄与葡萄酒组织(Organisation internationale de la vigne et du vin)*、*世界葡萄酒贸易集团(World Wine Trade Group)*。

Wine gallon assessment
葡萄酒加仑评估法

美国评估葡萄酒的做法，现已废止，将低于100标准酒精度的进口烈酒评估为100标准酒精度，因为相同规则也适用于提取自监封酒库的100标准酒精度以下的国产烈酒。进口商可以通过购买100标准酒精度或以上的烈酒再稀释而绕过这一规定。这意味着批量进口后在美国国内装瓶。但是，顾客通常喜欢在原产国装瓶的烈酒。因此，这一规定实际上对外国产品不利，即使与类似国产品的待遇并无不同之处。葡萄酒加仑评估法常用于说明形式上相同的国民待遇实际上可能存在歧视。另见*隐性歧视(implicit discrimination)*。

Wine lake
葡萄酒湖

对共同农业政策所导致的欧洲葡萄酒过剩的俗称。另见*黄油山(butter mountain)*。

Wingspread Declaration
温斯布雷德宣言

预防原则的一个版本，1998年1月由在威斯康星大学温斯布雷德会议中心举行的环境研讨会参加方通过。宣言指出“当一项活动对人类健康或环境产生危害威胁时，即使在科学上还没有充分地建立因果关系，也应当采取风险预防措施。在此种情况下，应当由活动的发起人，而非大众，承担举证责任。适用预防原则的程序应当公开、信息充分及民主，并且应当包括潜在受影响的当事人，包括不采取行动。”

WIPO
世界知识产权组织

联合国专门机构。主要负责保护知识产权的政府间组织，并通过保护知识产

encouragement of innovation and economic development. The two most important agreements administered by WIPO are the ***Paris Convention*** for the Protection of Industrial Property and the ***Berne Convention*** for the Protection of Literary and Artistic Works. The WIPO secretariat is located in Geneva. *See also* ***Beijing Treaty on Audiovisual Performances***, ***Budapest Treaty on the International Recognition of the Deposit of Microorganisms for the Purposes of Patent Procedure***, ***folklore***, ***Geneva Act of the Lisbon Agreement on Appellations of Origin and Geographical Indications***, ***Geneva Convention***, ***Joint Recommendation Concerning Provisions on the Protection of Well-Known Marks***, ***Lisbon Agreement***, ***Locarno Agreement Establishing an International Classification for Industrial Designs***, ***Madrid Agreement Concerning the International Registration of Marks***, ***Madrid Agreement for the Repression of False or Deceptive Indications of Source on Goods***, ***moral rights***, ***Patent Cooperation Treaty***, ***Rome Convention***, ***Singapore Treaty on the Law of Trademarks***, ***Strasbourg Agreement Concerning the International Patent Classification***, ***Trademark Law Treaty***, ***WIPO Copyright Treaty*** and ***WIPO Performances and Phonograms Treaty***.

WIPO Copyright Treaty: entered into force on 6 March 2002. It updates the ***Berne Convention*** by, for example, giving ***copyright*** protection to computer programs and databases (but not the material making up the database). It also covers rental rights and legal protection against the circumvention of effective technological measures used by authors. *See also* ***Agreement on Trade-Related Aspects of Intellectual Property Rights*** and ***parallel imports***.

WIPO Internet treaties: a name sometimes given to the ***WIPO Copyright Treaty*** and the ***WIPO Performances and Phonograms Treaty*** because they offer some ***copyright*** protection for digital products delivered electronically, for example, through the Internet.

WIPO Model Provisions on Protection Against Unfair Competition: produced by the International Bureau of WIPO in 1996. They represent an effort to show how Article 10bis of the ***Paris Convention*** could be given effect. This Article prohibits acts of ***unfair competition*** in matters covered by the Convention.

WIPO Performances and Phonograms Treaty: entered into force on 20 May 2002. It gives performers (actors, singers, musicians, dancers and others who perform literary or artistic works or expressions of folklore) ***moral rights*** (the right to claim to be identified as the performer of performances), economic rights in unfixed performances (the right to authorize the broadcasting, etc., of unrecorded performances), right of reproduction (the right to authorize direct and indirect reproduction of recordings), right of distribution and the right to make available to the public recordings of performances. These rights are balanced by rights to producers of phonograms (the person responsible for the first recording of a performance), including the right of reproduction, right of distribution, right of rental, and the right of making available phonograms. *See also* ***neighbouring rights*** and ***WIPO***.

权鼓励创新和经济发展。WIPO管理的两个最重要的协定为《保护工业产权巴黎公约》和《保护文学艺术作品伯尔尼公约》。WIPO秘书处设在日内瓦。另见*视听表演北京条约(Beijing Treaty on Audiovisual Performances)*、*国际承认用于专利程序的微生物保存布达佩斯条约(Budapest Treaty on the International Recognition of the Deposit of Microorganisms for the Purposes of Patent Procedure)*、*民间文学艺术(folklore)*、*原产地名称和地理标志里斯本协定日内瓦文本(Geneva Act of the Lisbon Agreement on Appellations of Origin and Geographical Indications)*、*日内瓦公约(Geneva Convention)*、*关于生产驰名商标保护规定的联合建议(Joint Recommendation Concerning Provisions on the Protection of Well-Known Marks)*、*里斯本协定(Lisbon Agreement)*、*建立工业品外观设计国际分类洛迦诺协定(Locarno Agreement Establishing an International Classification for Industrial Designs)*、*商标国际注册马德里协定(Madrid Agreement Concerning the International Registration of Marks)*、*制止商品来源虚假或欺骗性标记马德里协定(Madrid Agreement for the Repression of False or Deceptive Indications of Source on Goods)*、*精神权利(moral rights)*、*专利合作条约(Patent Cooperation Treaty)*、*罗马公约(Rome Convention)*、*商标法新加坡条约(Singapore Treaty on the Law of Trademarks)*、*国际专利分类斯特拉斯堡协定(Strasbourg Agreement Concerning the International Patent Classification)*、*商标法条约(Trademark Law Treaty)*、*WIPO组织版权条约(WIPO Copyright Treaty)*、*WIPO表演和录音制品条约(WIPO Performances and Phonograms Treaty)*。

WIPO Copyright Treaty

WIPO版权条约

于2002年3月6日生效。公约对《伯尔尼公约》进行了更新，例如对计算机程序和数据库(不延及数据或资料本身)给予版权保护。同时涵盖出租权和对规避作者使用的有效技术措施提供法律保护。另见*与贸易有关的知识产权协定(Agreement on Trade-Related Aspects of Intellectual Property Rights)*、*平行进口(parallel imports)*。

WIPO Internet treaties

WIPO互联网条约

有时对《WIPO版权条约》和《WIPO表演和录音制品条约》使用的名称，因为两条约为通过互联网等电子手段交付的数字产品提供部分版权保护。

WIPO Model Provisions on Protection Against Unfair Competition

WIPO反不正当竞争示范条款

世界知识产权组织(WIPO)知识产权国际局于1996年编撰。代表着为使《巴黎公约》第十条之二生效所作努力。该条禁止对公约所涵盖事项的不正当竞争行为。

WIPO Performances and Phonograms Treaty

WIPO表演和录音制品条约

2002年5月20日生效。条约赋予表演者(演员、歌唱家、音乐家、舞蹈家及其他方式表演文学或艺术作品或民间文学艺术作品的其他人员)精神权利(有权承认其系表演的表演者的权利)、对未录制表演的经济权利(授权对尚未录制的表演进行广播等)、复制权(授权直接和间接复制录音制品)、发行权和向公众传播录音制品的权利。这些权利是由录音制品制作者(负责首次录制表演者)的权利相平衡的，包括录音制品的复制权、发行权、出租权和传播权。另见*邻接权(neighbouring rights)*、*世界知识产权组织(WIPO)*。

Withdrawal of trade benefits: an expression meaning the imposition of trade sanctions or resort to ***retaliation***. *See also* ***suspension of concessions or other obligations*** and ***trade war***.

Without prejudice: used to signify in negotiations that although one is willing to examine a proposition made by the other side, or that one is prepared to propose a course of action, this is done on the understanding that one's options remain open. That is, one declares that although one may be ready to consider or propose something, this is done without commitment to a specific outcome. *See* ***ad referendum agreement*** and ***bracketed language***.

Women and trade: *see* ***Joint Declaration on Trade and Women's Economic Empowerment*** and ***trade and gender***.

Worker rights: an issue identified by sections of the United States Congress as relevant to the emergence of more equitable trade practices and policies. It is partly based on the view that some governments gain a competitive advantage by denying their workforces the conditions considered normal in the United States. The issue also has a more general human rights dimension. In practice the two strands are difficult to disentangle, but for many the human rights aspect is more important. The ***Trade Promotion Authority*** seeks to promote respect for worker rights defined as (a) the right of association, (b) the right to organize and bargain collectively, (c) a prohibition on the use of any form of forced or compulsory labour, (d) a minimum age for the employment of children, and (e) acceptable conditions of work with respect to minimum wages, hours of work, and occupational health and safety. ***Section 301*** requires ***USTR*** to take action if a foreign country shows a persistent pattern of conduct of denying worker rights. *See also* ***core labour standards***, ***social clause***, ***trade and human rights***, and ***trade and labour standards***.

Working Group on the Interaction between Trade and Competition Policy: established in December 1996 at the ***Singapore WTO Ministerial Conference*** to study issues related to the interaction between ***trade policy*** and ***competition policy***, including anti-competitive practices. Its task is to identify any areas that need to be considered further in the WTO framework. Work on this issue has been suspended during the ***Doha Development Agenda*** negotiations. *See also* ***trade and competition***.

Working Group on the Relationship between Trade and Investment: established in December 1996 at the ***Singapore WTO Ministerial Conference*** to examine the relationship between ***trade and investment***. Work on this issue has been suspended during the ***Doha Development Agenda*** negotiations.

Working Group on Transfer of Technology: established at the WTO ***Doha Ministerial Conference*** to examine the relationship between trade and the transfer of technology from developed to developing countries, and to increase flows of technology to developing countries.

Working Group on Transparency in Government Procurement: established at the December 1996 ***Singapore WTO Ministerial Conference*** to conduct a

Withdrawal of trade benefits
贸易利益的撤销

该表述意为施加贸易制裁或采取报复手段。另见*中止减让或其他义务(suspension of concessions or other obligations)*、*贸易战(trade war)*。

Without prejudice
无损我方权益

用于表示在谈判中尽管一方愿意考虑另一方所提建议，或一方准备提出一行动方案，但是这样作是在一方的选择仍然开放的理解基础上进行的。即一方声明，尽管一方可能准备好考虑或提出某事，但这样作并不承诺达到某一特定结果(without prejudice通常标在纸质文件的首页—译注)。另见*待核准协定(ad referendum agreement)*、*方括号内文字(bracketed language)*。

Women and trade
女性与贸易

见*贸易与妇女经济赋权联合宣言(Joint Declaration on Trade and Women's Economic Empowerment)*、*贸易与性别(trade and gender)*。

Worker rights
劳工权利

被美国国会各委员会认定为与更公正的贸易做法和政策的出现相关的问题。在一定程度上基于以下观点，即一些国家政府通过拒绝给予本国工人在美国看来属正常的工作条件而获得竞争优势。这一问题还具有在更广泛的人权层面的含义。在实践中这两个问题难以拆分，但对于许多人，人权问题更为重要。贸易促进授权寻求促进对工人权利的尊重，指(a)结社权；(b)组织与集体谈判权；(c)禁止任何形式的强迫或强制劳动；(d)受雇佣儿童的最低年龄；以及(e)可接受的工作条件如最低工资、工作时间和职业健康与安全。如果一国表现出持续拒绝给予劳工权利的行为方式，301条款即要求美国贸易代表办公室(USTR)采取行动。另见*核心劳工标准(core labour standards)*、*社会条款(social clause)*、*贸易与人权(trade and human rights)*、*贸易与劳工标准(trade and labour standards)*。

Working Group on the Interaction between Trade and Competition Policy
贸易与竞争政策相互关系工作组

1996年12月在新加坡WTO部长级会议上设立，负责研究贸易政策与竞争政策之间相互关系有关的问题，包括反竞争做法。任务是确定需要在WTO框架内得到进一步考虑的任何领域。关于这一问题的工作已经在多哈发展议程谈判中暂停。另见*贸易与竞争(trade and competition)*。

Working Group on the Relationship between Trade and Investment
贸易与投资关系工作组

1996年12月在新加坡WTO部长级会议上设立，负责审查贸易与投资之间的关系。关于这一问题的工作已经在多哈发展议程谈判中暂停。

Working Group on Transfer of Technology
技术转让工作组

在WTO多哈部长级会议上设立，负责审查贸易与自发达国家向发展中国家的技术转让之间的关系，并增加向发展中国家的技术流动。

Working Group on Transparency in Government Procurement
政府采购透明度工作组

1996年12月在新加坡WTO部长级会议上设立，负责研究政府采购做法的透明

study on ***transparency*** in ***government procurement*** practices. It has developed elements for inclusion in an appropriate agreement, but it does not have a negotiating mandate. Work on this issue has been suspended during the ***Doha Development Agenda*** negotiations.

Working Group on WTO Reform: the name of two groups. First, in July 2018 the European Union and the United States agreed to set up a working group to address WTO reform issues. The working group would discuss topics such as "unfair trading practices, including intellectual property theft, forced technology transfer, industrial subsidies, distortions caused by ***state-owned enterprises***, and over-capacity". The working group would be open to like-minded countries. Second, the European Union and China also launched a working group on WTO reform. Part of the motivation for the establishment of these working groups clearly is a degree of dissatisfaction with the WTO negotiating process. Another is search for a mechanism for rising tensions in international trade over the use of ***intellectual property rights***.

Working party (accession): a group of WTO members, sometimes nearly every-one, negotiating multilaterally with a country applying to join the ***WTO***.

Working Party on Domestic Regulation: established by the WTO on 26 April 1999 to develop disciplines aimed at ensuring that licensing requirements, technical standards and qualification requirements do not become unneces-sary barriers to trade in services. The mandate for this Working Party also reflects to a large extent Article VI:4 of the ***General Agreement on Trade in Services***. *See also* ***domestic regulation*** and ***Working Party on Professional Services***.

Working Party on Professional Services: WPPS. A WTO working party estab-lished in 1995 to examine the extent to which qualifications, licensing and standards requirements are impediments to trade in professional services, and to develop appropriate multilateral disciplines. It produced the ***Guidelines for Mutual Recognition Agreements or Arrangements in the Accountancy Sector***. The WPPS was abolished on 26 April 1999 and the ***Working Party on Domestic Regulation*** established instead. *See also* ***mutual recognition arrangements***.

Working Party on the Social Dimension of Globalization: established in March 2002 by the ***International Labour Organization*** to continue and broaden its work on the social dimension of trade liberalization. *See also* ***World Commis-sion on the Social Dimension of Globalization***.

Working party report (accession): the final document passed to the ***General Council*** for approval which covers the applicant country's commitments on opening its markets and on applying to the WTO rules.

Work programme: a more or less detailed schedule or list of tasks, often accompanied by objectives, in a defined subject area. Open-ended discussions in the preparation of a work programme ensure that it is reasonably acceptable to all parties. Work programmes may have time limits or regular review points. Establishment of a work programme does not in itself solve a problem, but it

度问题。工作组制定了纳入有关协定的要素，但没有谈判授权。关于这一问题的工作已经在多哈发展议程谈判中暂停。

Working Group on WTO Reform

WTO改革工作组

两个小组的名称。第一个小组是2018年7月欧盟和美国同意设立的一个工作组，以处理WTO改革问题。工作组将讨论例如"不公平贸易做法，包括知识产权盗窃、强制技术转让、产业补贴、国有企业造成的扭曲和产能过剩"等议题。工作组将向所有志同道合的国家开放。第二个小组是欧盟和中国成立的一个WTO改革工作组。设立这些工作组的部分动机显然是在一定程度上对WTO谈判进程的不满，另一个动机是寻找一种机制，以应对国际贸易中因知识产权使用而日益紧张的局势。

Working party (accession)

(加入)工作组

与申请加入WTO的国家进行多边谈判的一组WTO成员，有时几乎包括所有WTO成员。

Working Party on Domestic Regulation

国内规制工作组

WTO于1999年4月26日设立的工作组，制定规则以保证许可要求、技术标准和资格要求不对服务贸易构成不必要的壁垒。工作组的授权还在很大程度上体现了《服务贸易总协定》第6条第4款。另见*国内规制(domestic regulation)*、*专业服务工作组(Working Party on Professional Services)*。

Working Party on Professional Services

专业服务工作组

WPPS。WTO于1995年设立的工作组，负责审查资格要求、许可要求和标准要求对专业服务贸易构成壁垒的程度，并制定适当多边纪律。工作组制定了《关于会计部门相互承认协定或安排的指导原则》。工作组于1999年4月26日被撤销，进而设立国内规制工作组。另见*相互承认安排(mutual recognition arrangements)*。

Working Party on the Social Dimension of Globalization

全球化社会问题工作组

国际劳工组织(ILO)2002年3月设立的工作组，旨在继续并扩大其关于贸易自由化的社会问题的工作。另见*全球化社会问题世界委员会(World Commission on the Social Dimension of Globalization)*。

Working party report (accession)

(加入)工作组报告书

总理事会通过的涵盖申请加入国关于开放市场和适用WTO规则的承诺的最后文件。

Work programme

工作计划

规定议题领域的详细或简单的时间表或任务清单，通常附目标。在起草工作计划过程中的开放式讨论可保证所有各方可以合理接受工作计划。工作计划可以包含时限或定期审议节点。制定工作计划本身并不解决某一问题，但可

ensure that there is a good common understanding of the nature of the tasks before more detailed discussions or negotiations begin.

Work Programme on Small Economies: a work programme established at the ***Doha Ministerial Conference*** "to frame responses to the trade-related issues identified for the fuller integration of small, vulnerable economies into the multilateral trading system".

Workshop economies: refers to economies which produce large quantities of labour-intensive products for export. [Trade and Development Report 2003]

World Association of Investment Promotion Agencies: WAIPA. A non-governmental organization established in 1995. Its objectives are: (a) promote and develop understanding and cooperation among investment promotion agencies, (b) strengthen information-gathering systems, promote the efficient use of information and facilitate access to data sources, (c) share country and regional experiences in attracting foreign investment and enhancing outward investment, (d) assist investment promotion agencies in advising their respective governments on the formulation of appropriate investment promotion policies and strategies, and (e) facilitate access to technical assistance and promote training of investment promotion agencies. It has about 170 members from 130 countries. Its secretariat is in Geneva. *See also* ***investment facilitation***. [waipa.org]

World Bank: the International Bank for Reconstruction and Development (IBRD). One of the organizations established at the 1944 United Nations Monetary and Financial Conference held at Bretton Woods. One of its main functions is to promote the development of economically less advanced member countries. It does this through the financing of projects for which private capital is not available on reasonable terms. It obtains most of its capital on international bond markets. The World Bank publishes annually the ***World Development Report*** which always contains trade policy analysis of topical interest. Among its operating agencies are the ***International Development Association***, ***International Finance Corporation*** and the ***Multilateral Investment Guarantee Agency***. *See also* ***Bretton Woods agreements***, ***Facility for Investment Climate Advisory Services***, ***ICSID***, ***high-income economies***, ***low-income economies***, ***lower-middle-income economies***, ***Poverty Reduction and Growth Trust***, ***upper-middle-income economies***, ***World Bank Guidelines on the Treatment of Foreign Direct Investment*** and ***World Bank Services Trade Restrictiveness Index***.

World Bank Doing Business Report: an annual report issued by the ***World Bank***. It measures aspects of business regulation affecting small and medium-sized firms based on standardized case scenarios and located in the largest business city of each economy. Its foundation is the notion that economic activity benefits from clear and coherent rules that set out and clarify property rights and facilitate the resolution of disputes. [www.doingbusiness.org]

World Bank Group: consists of the International Bank for Reconstruction and Development (IBRD or ***World Bank***), ***International Development Association***

以保证在更详细的讨论或谈判开始前对任务的性质有良好共识。

Work Programme on Small Economies

小经济体工作计划

在多哈部长级会议上设立的工作计划，旨在“对于使脆弱的小经济体更加充分地融入多边贸易体制过程中所确定的与贸易有关的问题制定应对措施”。

Workshop economies

车间经济体

指生产大量供出口的劳动密集型产品的经济体。

World Association of Investment Promotion Agencies

世界投资促进机构协会

WAIPA。1995年成立的非政府组织。目标为：(a)促进和发展投资促进机构之间的理解和合作；(b)加强信息收集系统，促进信息有效利用和便利数据源获取；(c)分享国家和地区吸引外国投资和增强对外投资的经验；(d)帮助投资促进机构向各自政府建议制定适当的投资促进政策和战略；以及(e)便利技术援助的获得和促进投资促进机构的培训。现拥有来自130个国家的170个成员。秘书处设在日内瓦。另见*投资便利化(investment facilitation)*。

World Bank

世界银行

国际复兴开发银行(IBRD)。1944年在美国布雷顿森林召开的联合国货币与金融会议所建立的组织之一。一项主要职能为促进经济欠发达成员国的发展，实现途径为向无法以合理条件获得私人资本的项目提供资金。世界银行在国际债券市场上获得其大部分资本。世界银行每年发布《世界发展报告》，报告通常包含热门话题的贸易政策分析。运营机构包括国际开发协会、国际金融公司和多边投资担保机构。另见*布雷顿森林协定(Bretton Woods agreements)*、*外国投资咨询服务中心(Facility for Investment Climate Advisory Services)*、*国际投资争端解决中心(ICSID)*、*高收入经济体(high-income economies)*、*低收入经济体(low-income economies)*、*中等偏下收入经济体(lower-middle-income economies)*、*减贫与增长信托基金(Poverty Reduction and Growth Trust)*、*中等偏上收入经济体(upper-middle-income economies)*、*世界银行外国直接投资待遇指南(World Bank Guidelines on the Treatment of Foreign Direct Investment)*、*世界银行服务贸易限制指数(World Bank Services Trade Restrictiveness Index)*。

World Bank Doing Business Report

世界银行营商环境报告

世界银行发布的年度报告。报告根据标准化案例情境和位于每个经济体最大商业城市的中小企业衡量商业监管对中小企业的影响程度。报告的基本理念为，经济活动得益于规定和澄清产权及便利解决争议的清晰和一致的规则。

World Bank Group

世界银行集团

由国际复兴开发银行(IBRD或世界银行)、国际开发协会、国际金融公司(IFC)、

(IDA), ***International Finance Corporation*** (IFC), ***Multilateral Investment Guarantee Agency*** (MIGA) and the International Centre for Settlement of Investment Disputes (***ICSID***). [worldbank.org]

World Bank Guidelines on the Treatment of Foreign Direct Investment: a set of voluntary principles adopted in September 1992 to address governmental treatment of good-faith foreign investors. The Guidelines do not deal with the conduct of foreign investors. The broad aim of the Guidelines is to encourage foreign investment because of its benefits in terms of improving the long-term efficiency of the host country through greater competition, transfer of capital, technology and managerial skills, enhancement of market access and expansion of international trade. Article I states that the Guidelines are based on the general premise that equal treatment of investors in similar circumstances and free competition among them are prerequisites of a positive investment environment, and that there is no suggestion that foreign investors should receive better treatment than national investors. Article II seeks an open environment for the admission of investment. Article III exhorts states to extend to investments by nationals of any other state fair and equitable treatment. Article IV deals with expropriation and unilateral alterations or terminations of contract. Article V seeks to promote the orderly settlement of disputes, either through national courts or through other agreed mechanisms. *See also* ***investment*** and ***Multilateral Investment Guarantee Agency***.

World Bank Services Trade Restrictiveness Index: a ***World Bank*** tool for identifying policy measures that restrict trade. It uses a Services Trade Restrictions Database covering 103 countries in all regions and income groups. For each country it covers financial services, (retail banking and insurance), telecommunications (fixed line and mobile), retail distribution, transport (air passenger, maritime shipping, road trucking and railway freight) and professional services (accounting, auditing and legal services). *See also* ***OECD Services Trade Restrictiveness Index***. [https://datacatalog.worldbank.org/dataset/services-trade-restrictions-database]

World Commission on Environment and Development: established in 1983 by the ***United Nations General Assembly*** to work out an action plan for long-term environmental strategies and to strike a balance between the aims of development and the protection of natural resources. It was chaired by Gro Harlem Brundtland, Prime Minister of Norway. The Commission's report, *Our Common Future*, was completed in 1987. The final chapter of the report called for an international conference to review progress and to create a follow-up structure. This became the ***United Nations Conference on Environment and Development***.

World Commission on the Social Dimension of Globalization: established by the ***International Labour Organization*** in February 2002 to examine and report on all major aspects of ***globalization***. It was chaired jointly by Ms Tarja Halonen, President of Finland, and Mr Benjamin Mkapa, President of Tanzania. Its report was issued in February 2004 under the title *A Fair Globalization: Creating Opportunities for All*. The report made many detailed

多边投资担保机构(MIGA)和国际投资争端解决中心(ICSID)组成。

World Bank Guidelines on the Treatment of Foreign Direct Investment

世界银行外国直接投资待遇指南

1992年9月通过的一套自愿原则，以处理针对善意外国投资者的政府待遇问题。指南不处理外国投资者的行为。指南的总体目标是鼓励外国投资，因为外国投资有利于通过提高竞争力、资本转移、技术和管理技能转让、增强市场准入和扩大国际贸易，提高东道国的长期效率。第1条规定，指南所根据的总的前提是，在相似条件下给予投资者平等待遇和投资者之间的自由竞争是积极投资环境的前提，并不建议应给予外国投资者比国内投资者更好的待遇。第2条寻求开放的投资准入环境。第3条敦促各国将公平和公正待遇给予任何其他国家国民的投资。第4条处理征收和单方变更或终止合同的问题。第5条寻求通过国家法院或通过各方议定的其他机制促进有序解决争端。另见*投资(investment)*、*多边投资担保机构(Multilateral Investment Guarantee Agency)*。

World Bank Services Trade Restrictiveness Index

世界银行服务贸易限制指数

世界银行用于确定限制贸易的政策措施的工具。所使用的服务贸易数据库涵盖来自所有区域和所有收入组的103个国家。对于每一国家，数据库涵盖金融服务(银行零售服务和保险)、电信(固话和移动电话)、零售分销、运输(航空客运、海运、公路货运和铁路货运)和专业服务(会计、审计和法律服务)。另见*OECD服务贸易限制指数(OECD Services Trade Restrictiveness Index)*。

World Commission on Environment and Development

世界环境与发展委员会

联合国大会于1983年设立，旨在制定一个长期环境战略的行动计划，并在发展和保护自然资源的目标之间寻求平衡。委员会主席由挪威首相格罗·哈莱姆·布伦特兰担任。委员会的报告——《我们共同的未来》于1987年完成。报告的最后一章呼吁召开国际会议以审议进展情况和设立后续框架。后来形成联合国环境与发展会议。

World Commission on the Social Dimension of Globalization

全球化社会问题世界委员会

国际劳工组织(ILO)2002年2月设立。旨在审查和报告全球化的所有主要方面。委员会主席由芬兰总统塔里娅·哈洛宁和坦桑尼亚总统本杰明·姆卡帕共同担任。委员会的报告于2004年2月发布，题为《一个公平的全球化：为所有的

recommendations, but in essence it sought (a) a process of globalization based on universally shared values which require all actors to assume their individual responsibilities, (b) an international commitment to ensure the basic material and other requirements of human dignity for all, (c) a sustainable path of development which provides opportunities for all, expands sustainable livelihoods and employment, promotes gender equality, and reduces disparities between countries and people, and (d) a more democratic governance of globalization, which allows for greater participation, ensures accountability while fully respecting the authority of institutions of representative democracy and the rule of law.

World Customs Organization: WCO. Previously known as the Customs Cooperation Council (CCC). Based in Brussels. It is the principal body for international cooperation to simplify and rationalize customs procedures. It developed and administers the ***Harmonized Commodity Description and Coding System***, and it administers the ***Istanbul Convention*** and the ***Kyoto Convention***.

World Development Report: WDR. A report issued annually by the ***World Bank*** on issues of particular relevance to the development process. Each year the WDR focuses on a major issue. In the past decade these have been: 2010 *Development and climate change*, 2011 *Conflict, security and development*, 2012 *Gender equality and development*, 2013 *Jobs*, 2014 *Risk and opportunity (risk management, development and poverty reduction)*, 2015 *Mind, society and behaviour*, 2016 *Digital dividends*, 2017 *Governance and the law*, 2018 *Learning to realize education's promise*, 2019 *The changing nature of work* and 2020 *Global Value Chains: Trading for Development. See also* ***Trade and Development Report***, ***World Investment Report*** and ***World Trade Report***. [worldbank.org]

World Economic Forum: an independent non-profit organization founded in 1971 and located in Geneva. It aims to bring together people in politics, business, academia and other circles to explore current political, social and economic issues. Its major annual gathering is held in Davos, Switzerland.

World Food Programme: WFP. A body established in 1961 by the United Nations. It began operations on 1 January 1963. Its mission is to manage food aid to low-income food-deficit countries as well as to victims of natural disasters. The WFP also runs programmes aimed at economic and social development of these countries. It cooperates closely with the ***Food and Agriculture Organization***. Its administration is located in Rome.

World Integrated Trade Solution: WITS. A database of trade measures and tariffs developed jointly by ***UNCTAD*** and the ***World Bank***. It contains data on many countries contributed by several international agencies. The database aims to help policy makers engaged in identifying trade and negotiating options through, for example, letting them do simulations.

World Investment Report: WIR. An annual publication by ***UNCTAD***. It covers the latest trends in foreign investment and analyses in depth a selected topic

人创造机遇》。报告提出了许多详细建议，但主要寻求：(a)一个基于要求所有行动者承担各自责任的普遍接受的价值观的全球化进程；(b)一个保证所有人的基本物质和全人类尊严所需其他要求得以满足的国际承诺；(c)一个为所有人提供机遇、扩大可持续生计和就业、促进性别平等、减少国家和人民之间不平等的可持续发展道路；以及(d)允许更多参与、保证问责制的全球化的更民主治理，同时充分尊重代议制民主和法治机构的权威。

World Customs Organization
世界海关组织

WCO。前身为海关合作理事会(CCC)，设在布鲁塞尔，是就简化和精简海关程序开展国家间合作的主要机构。制定和管理商品名称及编码协调制度，并管理《伊斯坦布尔公约》和《京都公约》。

World Development Report
世界发展报告

WDR。世界银行每年发布的与发展进程特别相关问题的报告。每年世界发展报告聚焦一个主要问题。过去10年里的主要议题分别为：2010年发展与气候变化；2011年冲突、安全与发展；2012年性别平等与发展；2013年就业；2014年风险和机遇(风险管理、发展和减少贫困)；2015年思维、社会和行为；2016年数字红利；2017年治理和法律；2018年学习以实现教育诺言；2019年正在改变的工作性质；2020年全球价值链：贸易促发展。另见*贸易与发展报告(Trade and Development Report)*、*世界投资报告(World Investment Report)*、*世界贸易报告(World Trade Report)*。

World Economic Forum
世界经济论坛

独立的非盈利组织，1971年成立，设在日内瓦。论坛旨在聚集来自政界、商界、学术界及其他各界人士探讨现行政治、社会和经济议题。论坛年会在瑞士达沃斯举办。

World Food Programme
世界粮食计划署

WFP。联合国1961年设立的机构，1963年1月1日开始运营。任务是管理提供给低收入粮食短缺国家及遭受自然灾害国家的粮食援助。WFP也运营旨在促进这些国家经济和社会发展的项目。WFP与粮农组织(FAO)密切合作。管理机构设在罗马。

World Integrated Trade Solution
世界综合贸易方案

WITS。联合国贸易与发展会议(UNCTAD)和世界银行联合建立的贸易措施和关税数据库。包含由多个国际机构提供的多国数据。数据库旨在帮助政策制定者通过进行模拟等方式确定贸易和谈判选项。

World Investment Report
世界投资报告

WIR。联合国贸易与发展会议(UNCTAD)年度出版物。报告涵盖最新外国投

related to foreign direct investment and development. In the past decades these topics have been: 2009 *Transnational corporations, agricultural production and development*, 2010 *Investing in a low-carbon economy*, 2011 *Non-equity modes of international production and development*, 2012 *Towards a new generation of investment policies*, 2013 *Global value chains: investment and trade for development*, 2014 *Investing in the Sustainable Development Goals: an action plan*, 2015 *Reforming international investment governance*, 2016 *Investor nationality: policy challenges*, 2017 *Investment and the digital economy*, 2018 *Investment and new industrial policies*, and 2019 *Special Economic Zones*. *See also* ***Trade and Development Report***, ***World Development Report*** and ***World Trade Report***. [www.unctad.org]

World market: an imprecise term denoting more or less the largest possible market for a good or a service. In some cases, this may well be something close to the world. In practice, however, consumer tastes, licensing agreements, distribution arrangements, levels of development, etc., mean that the actual market is rather smaller.

World Organisation for Animal Health: OIE. Its main objectives are to (a) ensure transparency in the global animal disease situation, (b) collect, analyse and disseminate veterinary scientific information, (c) encourage international solidarity in the control of animal diseases, (d) safeguard world trade by publishing health standards for international trade in animals and animal products, (e) improve the legal framework and resources of national veterinary services, and (f) provide a better guarantee of food of animal origin and to promote animal welfare through a science-based approach. OIE cooperates closely with the members of the WTO in the administration of the ***Agreement on the Application of Sanitary and Phytosanitary Measures***. OIE was founded in 1924 as the Office International des Epizooties (International Office of Epizootics). In 2003 it changed its name to World Organisation for Animal Health, but it retains the acronym OIE. Its secretariat is located in Paris. [www.oie.int]

World Summit for Social Development: *see* ***Copenhagen Declaration and Programme of Action***.

World Summit on Sustainable Development: WSSD. This summit was held in Johannesburg, South Africa, from 26 August to 4 September 2002. Its purpose was to review progress in the implementation of the work programme of the ***United Nations Conference on Environment and Development*** of 1992, now renamed WSSD. The summit produced the Johannesburg Declaration on Sustainable Development, a political statement. It commits participants to the Johannesburg Plan of Implementation, an unusually long action plan which, partly because of its many checks and balances, defies easy summing-up. Its chapters deal with poverty eradication, changing unsustainable patterns of consumption and production, protecting and managing the natural resource base of economic and social development, sustainable development in a globalizing world, health and sustainable development, sustainable development of small island developing states, and sustainable development for Africa and

资趋势和对与外国直接投资和发展相关的选定主题的深入分析。过去10年的主题分别为：2009年跨国公司、农业生产和发展；2010年低碳经济投资；2011年国际生产和发展的非股权模式；2012年迈向新一代投资政策；2013年全球价值链：投资和贸易促发展；2014年投资可持续发展目标行动计划；2015年改革国际投资治理；2016年投资者国籍：政策挑战；2017年投资和数字经济；2018年投资和新产业政策；2019年特殊经济区。另见*贸易与发展报告(Trade and Development Report)*、*世界发展报告(World Development Report)*、*世界贸易报告(World Trade Report)*。

World market

世界市场

一个不精确的词语，大致表示货物或服务的最大可能市场。在一些情况下，这很可能接近于指整个世界。但在实际中，消费者喜好、许可协议、分销安排、发展水平等意味着实际市场要小得多。

World Organisation for Animal Health

世界动物卫生组织

OIE。该组织主要目标为：(a)实现全球动物疫情透明化；(b)收集、分析和传播兽医科学信息；(c)鼓励动物疫病防控国际合作；(d)通过发布动物和动物产品国际贸易卫生标准以保障世界贸易；(e)提高各国兽医服务法律框架和资源；以及(f)通过科学方式提高动物源性食品安全和动物福利。OIE与WTO在管理《实施卫生与植物卫生措施协定》过程中密切合作。OIE于1924年建立，原名为国际兽疫局，2003年改为世界动物卫生组织，但仍保留OIE的英文缩写。秘书处设在巴黎。

World Summit for Social Development

社会发展问题世界首脑会议

见*哥本哈根宣言和行动纲领(Copenhagen Declaration and Programme of Action)*。

World Summit on Sustainable Development

可持续发展世界首脑会议

WSSD。首脑会议于2002年8月26日至9月4日在南非约翰内斯堡举行，旨在审议1992年联合国环境与发展会议工作计划的实施进度，现更名为WSSD。首脑会议通过了一份政治宣言。即《约翰内斯堡可持续发展宣言》。宣言中参加方承诺参与《约翰内斯堡实施计划》，这是一个非常长的行动计划，部分由于其中的许多制约和平衡而难以简单概括。各章节内容涉及消除贫困、改变不可持续的消费和生产模式、保护和管理作为经济和社会发展资源基础的自然资源、在全球化世界中的可持续发展、健康和可持续发展、发展中小岛屿国可

other regions. *See also* ***Agenda 21***, ***Rio Declaration on Environment and Development*** and ***Sustainable Development Goals***.

World Tariff Profiles: a comprehensive statistical yearbook published jointly by the ***WTO***, ***ITC*** and ***UNCTAD***. It contains tariff profiles for all WTO members and some other countries and customs territories. Bound and applied tariffs are listed. [www.wto.org, www.intracen.org, www.unctad.org]

World Trade Organization: *see* ***WTO***.

World Trade Outlook Indicator: *see* ***Goods Trade Barometer*** and ***Services Trade Barometer***.

World Trade Point Federation: established by ***UNCTAD*** to enhance the participation of developing countries and ***economies in transition*** in international trade, to reduce transaction costs and to allow them better access to trade-related information and global networks. Some 100 national Trade Points now exist. They are connected electronically. They act as ***trade facilitation*** centres where all necessary formalities can be transacted under one roof, and they provide information to traders on export opportunities. In November 2002 the programme was transferred from UNCTAD to the World Trade Point Federation, located in Geneva. *See also* ***electronic commerce*** and ***Trade Efficiency Programme***.

World Trade Report: WTR. An annual publication by the ***WTO*** that aims to deepen understanding about trends trade, trade policy issues and the ***multilateral trading system***. Each year the WTR focuses on a major issue. For the past decade the issues analysed in this way have been: 2009 *Trade policy commitments and contingency measures*, 2010 *Trade in natural resources*, 2011 *The WTO and preferential trade agreements*, 2012 *Trade and public policies: a closer look at non-tariff measures in the 21st century*, 2013 *Factors shaping the future of world trade*, 2014 *Trade and development: recent trends and the role of the WTO*, 2015 *Speeding up trade: benefits and challenges of implementing the WTO Trade Facilitation Agreement*, 2016 *Levelling the trading field for SMEs*, 2017 *Trade, technology and jobs*, 2018 *The future of world trade: how digital technologies are transforming global commerce* and 2019 *The future of services trade*. *See also* ***Trade and Development Report***, ***World Development Report*** and ***World Investment Report***. [www.wto.org]

World Wine Trade Group: WWTG. A group of government and industry representatives from the wine-producing countries of Argentina, Australia, Canada, Chile, Georgia, New Zealand, South Africa, the United States and Uruguay. In 2001 it adopted an Agreement on Mutual Acceptance on Oenological Practices to facilitate trade in wine. The 2007 Agreement on Requirements for Wine Labelling enables wine exporters to sell wine into WWTG countries by using the same label for all markets. In 2017 WWTG members adopted an Agreement on Information Exchange, Technical Cooperation and Counterfeiting. *See also* ***geographical indications***.

Worst forms of child labour: defined in the ***Convention Concerning the Prohibition and Immediate Action for the Elimination of the Worst Forms of Child***

持续发展以及非洲和其他区域的可持续发展。另见*21世纪议程(Agenda 21)*、*里约环境与发展宣言(Rio Declaration on Environment and Development)*、*可持续发展目标(Sustainable Development Goals)*。

World Tariff Profiles

世界关税概况

WTO、国际贸易中心(ITC)和联合国贸易与发展会议(UNCTAD)联合出版的全面数据年鉴。包括所有WTO成员和其他一些国家和关税领土的关税概况，其中列出约束税率和实施税率。

World Trade Organization

世界贸易组织

见*WTO(世界贸易组织)*。

World Trade Outlook Indicator

世界贸易展望指标

见*货物贸易晴雨表(Goods Trade Barometer)*、*服务贸易晴雨表(Services Trade Barometer)*。

World Trade Point Federation

世界贸易网点联盟

联合国贸易与发展会议(UNCTAD)建立，旨在提高发展中国家和转型经济体对国际贸易的参与，减少交易成本并使这些国家更好地获得与贸易相关的信息和全球网络。现有约100个国家的贸易网点通过电子方式实现互连。这些网点发挥贸易便利化中心的作用，在网点中所有必要手续可以在一个屋檐下完成，并向贸易商提供有关出口机会的信息。2002年11月，该项目从UNCTAD转至世界贸易网点联盟，总部设在日内瓦。另见*电子商务(electronic commerce)*、*贸易效率计划(Trade Efficiency Programme)*。

World Trade Report

世界贸易报告

WTR。WTO年度出版物，旨在深化对贸易趋势、贸易政策问题和多边贸易体制的理解。报告每年聚焦一个主要议题。过去10年分析的议题分别为：2009年贸易政策承诺和应急措施；2010年自然资源贸易；2011年WTO与优惠贸易协定；2012年贸易和公共政策：21世纪非关税措施近观；2013年塑造未来世界贸易的因素；2014年贸易和发展：趋势和WTO的作用；2015年贸易提速：实施WTO《贸易便利化协定》的收益和挑战；2016年为中小企业提供公平贸易平台；2017年贸易、技术与就业；2018年世界贸易的未来：数字技术如何改变全球商务；2019年服务贸易的未来。另见*贸易与发展报告(Trade and Development Report)*、*世界发展报告(World Development Report)*、*世界投资报告(World Investment Report)*。

World Wine Trade Group

世界葡萄酒贸易集团

WWTG。由来自葡萄酒生产国的政府和产业界代表组成的集团，主要生产国包括阿根廷、澳大利亚、加拿大、智利、格鲁吉亚、新西兰、南非、美国和乌拉圭。2001年集团通过了《关于相互接受酿酒方法的协定》，以便利葡萄酒贸易。2007年《葡萄酒标签要求协定》使葡萄酒出口商能够对所有市场使用相同标签而向WWTG国家销售葡萄酒。2017年WWTG成员通过《关于信息交流、技术合作和假冒的协定》。另见*地理标志(geographical indications)*。

Worst forms of child labour

最恶劣形式的童工劳动

在国际劳工组织(ILO)通过的《禁止和立即行动消除最恶劣形式的童工劳动公

Labour (known as ILO Convention No. 182) adopted by the ***International Labour Organization*** as (a) all forms of slavery or practices similar to slavery, such as the sale and trafficking of children, debt bondage and serfdom and forced or compulsory labour, including forced or compulsory recruitment of children for use in armed conflict, (b) the use, procuring or offering of a child for prostitution, for the production of pornography or for pornographic performances, (c) the use, procuring or offering of a child for illicit activities, in particular for the production and trafficking of drugs as defined in the relevant international treaties, and (d) work which, by its nature or the circumstances in which it is carried out, is likely to harm the health, safety or morals of children. The promotion of ratification and full compliance with this Convention is one of the objectives of the United States ***Trade Promotion Authority***.

WTO: World Trade Organization, established on 1 January 1995 as the successor to the ***GATT*** (*General Agreement on Tariffs and Trade*) and its secretariat. Among the agreements it manages are the ***General Agreement on Trade in Services*** (GATS) and the ***Agreement on Trade-Related Aspects of Intellectual Property Rights***. In August 2019 the WTO had 164 members. The WTO is an organization for the discussion, negotiation and resolution of trade issues covering goods, services and intellectual property. Its essential functions are administering and implementing the multilateral and plurilateral trade agreements that constitute it, acting as a forum for ***multilateral trade negotiations***, seeking to resolve trade disputes, overseeing national trade policies and cooperating with other international institutions involved in global economic policy-making. *See also* ***WTO Agreement***.

WTO Agreement: formally the Marrakesh Agreement Establishing the World Trade Organization. Adopted on 15 April 1994 at the Marrakesh Ministerial Meeting. It established the ***WTO***. It also sets out, in four annexes, the multilateral and plurilateral agreements under its jurisdiction. These are described at the end of this entry. The WTO Agreement entered into force on 1 January 1995. Article I establishes the WTO. Article II makes all of the agreements contained in Annexes 1, 2 and 3 binding on all members. The agreements listed in Annex 4 are binding only on those that have accepted them. Article III outlines the functions of the WTO. These are administering and operating the multilateral and plurilateral trade agreements, providing a forum for negotiations among members and to administer the dispute settlement mechanism. Article IV requires the ***WTO Ministerial Conference*** to meet at least once every two years. In the intervals the ***General Council*** carries out these functions. The General Council also convenes as the ***Dispute Settlement Body*** and the ***Trade Policy Review Body***. Below the General Council are the ***Council for Trade in Goods***, the ***Council for Trade in Services*** and the Council for Trade-Related Aspects of Intellectual Property Rights. Article V charges the General Council with making arrangements for effective cooperation and consultation with intergovernmental and non-governmental organizations with related responsibilities. Article VI establishes the WTO Secretariat headed by the Director-

约》(ILO第182号公约)定义为：(a)所有形式的奴隶制或类似奴隶制的做法，如出售和贩卖儿童、债务劳役和奴役，以及强迫或强制劳动，包括强迫或强制招募儿童用于武装冲突；(b)使用、招收或提供儿童卖淫、生产色情制品或进行色情表演；(c)使用、招收或提供儿童从事非法活动，特别是生产和贩卖有关国际条约中界定的毒品；以及(d)在可能对儿童健康、安全或道德有伤害性的环境中工作。促进批准和全面遵守该公约是美国贸易促进授权目标之一。

WTO

世界贸易组织

1995年1月1日作为GATT及其秘书处的后继组织建立。所管理的协定包括《服务贸易总协定》(GATS)和《与贸易有关的知识产权协定》。截至2019年8月，WTO共有164个成员(截至2024年8月，WTO共有166个成员—译注)。WTO中讨论、谈判和解决涵盖货物、服务和知识产权的贸易问题的组织。基本职能是管理和实施多边和诸边贸易协定，作为多边贸易谈判的场所，寻求解决贸易争端，监督各国贸易政策以及与涉及全球贸易政策制定的其他国际组织开展合作。另见*WTO协定(WTO Agreement)*。

WTO Agreement

WTO协定

正式名称为《马拉喀什建立世界贸易组织协定》。1994年4月15日在马拉喀什部长级会议上通过。WTO根据这一协定建立。协定在其4个附件中列出了所管辖的多边和诸边协定，这些协定在本词条最后部分列出。《WTO协定》于1995年1月1日生效。第1条规定建立WTO。第2条规定附件1、2、3对所有成员具有约束力，附件4中的协定只对接受协定的成员具有约束力。第3条概述了WTO的职能，即管理和实施多边和诸边贸易协定、为成员谈判提供场所和管理争端解决机制。第4条要求WTO部长级会议至少每2年召开一次，休会期间由总理事会行使上述职能；总理事会还作为争端解决机构和贸易政策审议机构召开会议。总理事会下设货物贸易理事会、服务贸易理事会和与贸易有关的知识产权理事会。第5条要求总理事会就与职责相关的政府间组织和非政府间组织开展有效合作协商作出安排。第6条规定设立秘书处，由总干事领导。第7

General. Article VII sets out broadly the procedures to be followed for the establishment of the budget and the financial contributions to be paid by members. Article VIII gives the WTO legal personality with privileges and immunities as necessary. Article IX states that the WTO follows the practice of making decisions by ***consensus*** as was done under the GATT. Where a decision by consensus is not possible, the matter is decided by voting as outlined in this Article. Article X deals with amendments to the agreements administered by the WTO. Under Article XI all contracting parties of the GATT become original members of the WTO. Accession is possible under Article XII for any state or separate customs territory having full autonomy to conduct its external economic relations. Terms of the accession have to be negotiated between the applicant and existing members. Article XIII states the Agreement does not apply between two members only in the case where one member, at the time the other becomes a member, does not consent to the accession. Article XIV sets out the procedures to be followed for accepting the terms of accession to this Agreement either as an original member of the WTO or through a later accession. Article XV says that withdrawal from the Agreement becomes effective six months after the Director-General has received written notice of the intention to withdraw. Article XVI contains some miscellaneous provisions. Among these are that the WTO is to be guided by the decisions, procedures and practices followed by the GATT. If there is a conflict between the provisions of this Agreement and a provision in any of the multilateral agreements, this Agreement prevails. No reservations are possible in respect of any provision of this Agreement. Annex 1 contains the following multilateral agreements: ***GATT 1994***, ***Agreement on Agriculture***, ***Agreement on the Application of Sanitary and Phytosanitary Measures***, ***Agreement on Technical Barriers to Trade***, ***Agreement on Textiles and Clothing***, ***Agreement on Trade-Related Investment Measures***, ***Agreement on Implementation of Article VI of the General Agreement on Tariffs and Trade 1994***, ***Agreement on Implementation of Article VII of the General Agreement on Tariffs and Trade [Customs Valuation] 1994***, ***Agreement on Preshipment Inspection***, ***Agreement on Rules of Origin***, ***Agreement on Import Licensing Procedures***, ***Agreement on Subsidies and Countervailing Measures***, the ***Agreement on Safeguards*** and the ***Agreement on Trade Facilitation***. Annex 2 consists of the ***General Agreement on Trade in Services***. Annex 3 is the ***Agreement on Trade-Related Aspects of Intellectual Property Rights***. Annex 4 consists of the ***Understanding on Rules and Procedures Governing the Settlement of Disputes***, the ***Trade Policy Review Mechanism*** and the ***WTO plurilateral trade agreements***. [Gallagher 2005]

WTO Analytical Index: a guide to the interpretation of the agreements administered by the WTO It reflects the decisions taken by the various WTO bodies, the ***panels*** and the ***Appellate Body***. Like its predecessor, the ***GATT Analytical Index***, it is indispensable for the study and analysis of WTO law. It is available in electronic format via the WTO website.

条总体规定了预算编制和成员会费分担所遵循的程序。第8条给予WTO法律人格及所必需的特权和豁免。第9条规定WTO在决策时应遵循GATT中的协商一致原则。如一决定无法经协商一致作出，有关事项将按本条所规定的进行投票决定。第10条规定对WTO所管理协定的修正问题。根据第11条，所有GATT缔约方成为WTO创始成员。根据第12条，任何国家和在处理其对外贸易关系方面拥有完全自主权的单独关税区可以加入WTO。加入条件需要在申请方和现有成员之间进行谈判。第13条规定多边贸易协定只有当一成员在另一成员成为成员时不同意该成员加入，方可在该两成员间互不适用。第14条规定接受作为WTO创始成员或后期加入的申请方接受加入协定的条款应遵循的程序。第15条规定在WTO总干事收到书面退出通知之日起6个月期满时退出生效。第16条包含一些杂项条款，其中包括WTO应以GATT所遵循的决定、程序和惯例为指导。如本协定的条款与任何多边贸易协定的条款产生冲突，应以本协定的条款为准。不得对本协定的任何条款提出保留。附件1A(英文误为附件1—译注)包含下列多边贸易协定：《1994年关税与贸易总协定》(GATT 1994)、《农业协定》、《实施卫生与植物卫生措施协定》、《技术性贸易壁垒协定》、《纺织品与服装协定》、《与贸易有关的投资措施协定》、《关于实施1994年关税与贸易总协定第6条的协定》、《关于实施1994年关税与贸易总协定第7条的协定》(海关估价)、《装运前检验协定》、《原产地规则协定》、《进口许可程序协定》、《补贴与反补贴措施协定》、《保障措施协定》和《贸易便利化协定》。附件1B(英文误为附件2—译注)包含《服务贸易总协定》。附件1C(英文误为附件3—译注)包含《与贸易有关的知识产权协定》。附件2(英文误为附件4—译注)为《关于争端解决规则与程序的谅解》。附件3为《贸易政策审议机制》。附件4为WTO诸边贸易协定。

WTO Analytical Index

WTO分析索引

解释WTO所管理协定的指南。反映了WTO各机构、专家组和上诉机构所作决定。与其前身《GATT分析索引》一样，是学习和分析WTO法律不可或缺的工具。通过WTO官方网站以电子方式提供。

WTO Basic Instruments and Selected Documents: the successor to the ***GATT Basic Instruments and Selected Documents***. It is the official collection of legal documents, protocols and reports adopted by the WTO, including the ***Protocols of Accession*** to the WTO since 1995.

WTO-beyond: measures in ***regional trade agreements*** or ***free-trade agreements*** that do not have any precedents under the ***WTO*** rules, such as ***bribery*** or ***corruption***. *See also* ***WTO-plus***. [Lajárraga 2014]

WTO built-in agenda: *see* ***built-in agenda***.

WTO-consistency: being in conformity with the rules and disciplines of the WTO. All members of the WTO have to ensure that their laws, regulations, practices, etc., meet this criterion. *See also* ***GATT-consistency of national legislation***.

WTO Enabling Regulation: a ***regulation*** adopted by the ***European Union*** on 11 March 2015 concerning the measures the European Union may take following an adverse report adopted by the WTO ***Dispute Settlement Body*** on anti-dumping and anti-subsidy matters. It enables the European Union either to repeal or amend the disputed measure, or to adopt any other special implementing measure deemed to be appropriate in the circumstances in order to bring the Union in conformity with the recommendations and rulings contained in the report. The ***European Commission*** may also decide to initiate a review of the disputed measure. This enabling regulation has nothing to do with the WTO ***Enabling Clause***. [Regulation (EU) No 2015/476]

WTO Environmental Database: EDB. A listing of all environment-related notifications submitted by WTO members as well as environmental measures and policies referred to in ***trade policy reviews*** of WTO members. [edb.wto.rg]

WTO membership: since July 2016 the WTO has 164 members. The ***European Union*** has been a member from the start. Its twenty-seven members are also WTO members in their own right. *See also* ***voting rights in the WTO***.

WTO Ministerial Conference: a conference composed of the representatives of all WTO members at ministerial level which is to meet at least once every two years. It has authority to take decisions on all matters under any of the multilateral trade agreements under its jurisdiction. The Ministerial Conferences so far have been Singapore 1996, Geneva 1998, Seattle 1999, Doha 2001, Cancún 2003, Hong Kong 2005, Geneva 2009, Geneva 2011, Bali 2013, Nairobi 2015, and Buenos Aires 2017. *See also* ***Doha Ministerial Conference***, ***Seattle Ministerial Conference*** and ***Singapore WTO Ministerial Conference***.

WTO plurilateral trade agreements: these are the: ***Agreement on Trade in Civil Aircraft***, ***Agreement on Government Procurement***, ***International Dairy Agreement***, ***International Bovine Meat Agreement*** and the ***Information Technology Agreement***. They are included in Annex 4 to the ***WTO Agreement***. These agreements were originally negotiated as so-called "codes" during the ***Tokyo Round***. They contain additional disciplines for each of the sectors they cover. Membership of these agreements is not a precondition of WTO membership. The *International Bovine Meat Agreement* and the *International Dairy*

WTO Basic Instruments and Selected Documents
WTO基本文件资料选编
《GATT基本文件资料选编》的后继出版物，是WTO通过的法律文件、议定书和报告的官方汇编，包括自1995年以来的WTO加入议定书。

WTO-beyond
超越WTO
区域贸易协定或自由贸易协定中在WTO规则下无任何先例的措施，例如贿赂或腐败。另见*超WTO(WTO-plus)*。

WTO built-in agenda
WTO既定议程
见*既定议程(built-in agenda)*。

WTO-consistency
WTO一致性
符合WTO规则和纪律。所有WTO成员必须保证其法律、法规、实践等符合这一标准。另见*国家立法与GATT一致性(GATT-consistency of national legislation)*。

WTO Enabling Regulation
WTO授权条例
欧盟于2015年3月11日通过的条例，涉及欧盟在WTO争端解决机构就反倾销和反补贴事项所作不利报告后可以采取的措施。条例授权欧盟可以撤销或修正争议措施，或采取在当时情况下被认为适当的特别实施措施，从而使欧盟遵守报告中所含建议和裁决。欧盟委员会也可以决定启动对争议措施的审议。这一授权条例与WTO授权条款无关。

WTO Environmental Database
WTO环境数据库
EDB。WTO成员提交的所有与环境相关的通报及在WTO成员贸易政策审议中提及的环境措施和政策列表。

WTO membership
WTO成员资格
截至2016年7月，WTO共有164个成员(截至2024年8月，WTO共有166个成员—译注)。欧盟自WTO建立即为成员，27个成员国同为WTO成员，各自拥有权利。另见*WTO中的投票权(voting rights in the WTO)*。

WTO Ministerial Conference
WTO部长级会议
由所有WTO成员的部长级官员作为代表参加的会议，至少每2年召开一次。会议有权对WTO管辖范围内的多边贸易协定项下所有议题作出决定。截至目前部长级会议先后在下列时间和地点举办：1996年新加坡、1998年日内瓦、1999年西雅图、2001年多哈、2003年坎昆、2005年香港、2009年日内瓦、2011年日内瓦、2013年巴厘岛、2015年内罗毕、2017年布宜诺斯艾利斯。另见*多哈部长级会议(Doha Ministerial Conference)*、*西雅图部长级会议(Seattle Ministerial Conference)*、*新加坡部长级会议(Singapore WTO Ministerial Conference)*。

WTO plurilateral trade agreements
WTO诸边贸易协定
指《民用航空器贸易协定》、《政府采购协定》、《国际奶制品协定》、《国际牛肉协定》和《信息技术协定》。前4个协定包含在《WTO协定》附件4中，最初在东京回合作为所谓“守则”进行谈判，包含对所涵盖部门的附加规定。

Agreement were terminated on 31 December 1997, and they have been deleted from Annex 4. *See also* ***Tokyo Round agreements***.

WTO-plus: provisions, for example, in ***regional trade agreements*** or ***free-trade agreements*** that are based on the rules of the WTO, but that go beyond them in their ambit. Although this expression is often used with great conviction by proponents of free-trade agreements as an indication of their ambition, one wonders whether such agreements would be worth doing if they simply restated the WTO provisions. *See also* ***WTO-beyond***.

WTO reform: sometimes WTO modernization. A debate inside and outside the ***WTO*** on the extent to which the current system of trading rules and their supervision, including dispute settlement, meet the requirements of WTO members and their importers and exporters. For example, in June 2019 the ***G20*** trade ministers committed to "work constructively with other WTO members to undertake necessary WTO reform with a sense of urgency". *See also* ***Appellate Body*** and ***Working Group on WTO Reform***.

加入诸边协定不是获得WTO成员资格的前提。《国际牛肉协定》和《国际奶制品协定》已于1997年12月31日终止，并从附件4中删除。另见*东京回合协定(Tokyo Round agreements)*。

WTO-plus

超WTO

例如区域贸易协定或自由贸易协定中的条款以WTO规则为基础，但又超出原有规则范围。尽管这一表述经常被自由贸易协定支持者信心十足地使用于表明他们的雄心，但有人怀疑如果协定只是重述WTO规则，此类协定是否值得签署。另见*超越WTO(WTO-beyond)*。

WTO reform

WTO改革

有时称WTO现代化。即在WTO内外进行的关于现行贸易规则和规则监督制度，包括争端解决，在多大程度上符合WTO成员及其进出口商要求的辩论。例如，在2019年6月，20国集团贸易部长承诺"与其他WTO成员建设性地合作，带着紧迫感来推进必要的WTO改革"。另见*上诉机构(Appellate Body)*、*WTO改革工作组(Working Group on WTO Reform)*。

X-ing out: this can mean either a ***carve-out*** or a decision to leave an aspect of negotiations aside until some other problems have been solved.

X-ing out

搁置

可指例外或指关于将谈判中某个问题放在一边直至其他一些问题得到解决。

Yaoundé Convention: an agreement of association between the ***European Economic Community*** and eighteen African developing countries giving them a range of trade and economic benefits. It was concluded on 20 July 1963 and superseded in 1975 by the ***Lomé Convention***. *See also* ***ACP-EU Partnership Agreement***.

Yarn forward rule: a ***rule of origin*** in ***NAFTA*** and other ***free-trade agreements*** (FTAs) concluded by the United States. It says that yarns, threads, cordage, twine and similar products are deemed to originate in the country where they are spun from their constituent fibres, or, in the case of synthetic filaments produced by extrusion, in the country where they are extruded. This means, in the case of free-trade agreements, that the yarns for the component conferring the essential character of a garment must originate within one of the FTA partners to qualify for preferential treatment. *See also* ***fabric-forward rule*** and ***fibre-forward rule***.

Yaoundé Convention
雅温得公约

欧洲经济共同体与18个非洲发展中国家签订的联合协定，协定给予这些非洲国家一系列贸易和经济利益。协定于1963年7月20日缔结，1975年被《洛美协定》所取代。另见*非加太地区国家与欧盟伙伴关系协定(ACP-EU Partnership Agreement)*。

Yarn forward rule
自纱线开始规则

《北美自由贸易协定》(NAFTA)和美国缔结的其他自由贸易协定(FTAs)中的原产地规则。规定纱、线、绳、麻和其他类似产品被视为源自组成纤维纺成的国家，或对于挤压生产的合成长丝，为原挤压成型的国家。这意味着，对于自由贸易协定，给予服装基本特征的组成纱线必须源自自由贸易协定的参加方之一方可有资格享受优惠待遇。另见*自织物开始规则(fabric-forward rule)*、*自纤维开始规则(fibre-forward rule)*。

Z

Zanzibar Declaration: a statement adopted at a meeting in Zanzibar in July 2001 of trade ministers representing ***least-developed countries*** in preparation for the ***Doha Ministerial Conference***. It calls on WTO members to make a range of greater efforts to promote increased integration of least-developed countries into the multilateral trading system. Among these are cancellation of debts, increased ***official development assistance*** and duty-free and quota-free access for products from these countries.

Zero binding: a legally binding undertaking in the WTO to eliminate ***customs duties*** altogether on defined products.

Zero-for-zero tariff reductions: a request/offer system for the achievement of ***tariff*** reductions in which the parties involved aim at reducing tariffs to zero (i.e. at eliminating tariffs) on a reciprocal basis in complete sectors, such as pharmaceuticals or wood products. The ***Information Technology Agreement*** is an example of this approach. *See also* ***requests and offers*** and ***sectoral trade negotiations***.

Zeroing: an investigative authority in anti-dumping cases usually calculates that dumping margins by getting the average of the differences between the export prices and the home market prices of the product in question. When it chooses to disregard or put a value of zero on instances where the export is price is higher than the home market price, the practice is called "zeroing". Critics claim that this practice artificially inflates dumping margins.

Zeroing negative margins of dumping: when a group of closely related products is subject to a single anti-dumping investigation, some of the individual products may show a ***positive margin of dumping*** (i.e. they are deemed to have been dumped). Others may show a ***negative margin of dumping*** (i.e. they are deemed not to have been dumped). Once the pricing of the individual products in the group has been investigated, the relevant authority has to make an assessment for the group of products as a whole. Some of the positive and negative margins will then cancel each other out. Some investigating authorities have, however, adopted the practice of allocating any negative value a zero value. This means that only positive margins count for the assessment of the extent of dumping. Obviously, the result will always err in favour of a finding of dumping. The ***Appellate Body*** found in *EC – Bed Linen* that zeroing violates the WTO Anti-Dumping Agreement. [Lindsey and Ikenson 2002, WTO/DS141/AB/R]

Zero-margin harmonization: a situation in which there is complete harmonization of laws, regulations, standards, etc., in one or more areas of economic activity.

Z

Zanzibar Declaration

桑给巴尔宣言

2001年7月由代表最不发达国家的贸易部长为准备多哈部长级会议在桑给巴尔召开的会议上通过的宣言。宣言呼吁WTO成员通过一系列更大的努力促进最不发达国家进一步融入多边贸易体制。其中包括免除债务、增加官方发展援助以及给予这些国家产品免关税和免配额准入。

Zero binding

零关税约束

WTO中取消规定产品关税的具有法律约束力的承诺。

Zero-for-zero tariff reductions

零对零关税削减

实现关税削减的要价和出价制度，参加方旨在在互惠基础上将整个部门的关税削减至零(即取消关税)，例如药品或林产品。《信息技术协定》即属此例。*另见要价和出价(requests and offers)、部门贸易谈判(sectoral trade negotiations)*。

Zeroing

归零

调查机关在反倾销案件中通常通过取得一所涉产品的出口价格和本国市场价格的差额的平均值计算倾销幅度。如果在出口价格高于本国市场价格时，调查机关选择忽略或将价值定为零，此种做法即称为“归零”。批评者认为此种做法人为扩大了倾销幅度。

Zeroing negative margins of dumping

负倾销幅度归零

如一组关联度高的产品接受一单一的反倾销调查，一些单个产品可能显示正倾销幅度(即被视为存在倾销)，其他产品可能显示负倾销幅度(即不被视为存在倾销)。一旦此组产品中的单个产品的价格接受调查，相关主管机关需要对对整组产品进行评估。一些正倾销幅度和负倾销幅度即会相互抵消。但是一些调查机关采用将所有负值定为零的做法。此即意味着，在评估倾销幅度时只计算正倾销幅度。显然，结果将总是错误地偏向于认定存在倾销。上诉机构在“欧共体床单案”中裁决，归零方法违反WTO《反倾销协定》。

Zero-margin harmonization

零差别协调

在一个或多个经济活动领域，法律、法规、标准等完全协调的情况。

Zero option: this usually refers to a United States proposal early in the ***Uruguay Round*** negotiations on agriculture to the effect that all subsidies distorting agricultural trade or production should be eliminated within ten years.

Zero-price knowledge: a concept used as part of the justification of protection for ***intellectual property***. If knowledge always is free, i.e. available at a zero price, there will be less incentive to add to the stock of knowledge since adding will not be rewarded. Granting the originator of knowledge the right to profit from it through the protection of ***intellectual property rights*** provides this incentive.

Zero rating: said to be attracted by goods that enter a country free of any ***customs duties***.

Zero risk: in the use of ***sanitary and phytosanitary measures***, a judgement made in identifying the appropriate level of risk for a given product that not taking any risk is justified by the facts. In practice this usually means a complete ban on imports of that product.

Zero-sum nationalism: the view that in the conduct of international trade and economic relations countries only have a choice between winning and not winning. A win by another country, however temporary, is considered a loss by the country making the comparison. This is essentially a broader, more political, restatement of the idea underpinning ***mercantilism*** which sees the aim of trade as the accumulation of specie and foreign exchange, the maximization of manufacturing exports and the minimization of manufacturing imports. It completely ignores the benefits available through the ***international division of labour*** and the effect of ***globalization*** on the international economy.

Zero tolerance: used in the same sense as ***zero risk***.

Zollverein: *Ger.* customs union. Established under Prussian leadership in 1834 through unifying several local customs unions. Its growth continued through the adhesion of other German states until 1871 when it was subsumed in the newly formed German Empire. The Zollverein is given credit for much of Germany's economic progress in the first half of the nineteenth century. However, as its early years coincided with the industrial revolution in Germany, its exact contribution to economic development, though clearly substantial, is difficult to assess. *See also* ***customs union***.

Zero option

零选择

通常指美国乌拉圭回合农业谈判早期提出的提案，要求所有扭曲农业贸易或生产的补贴应在10年内取消。

Zero-price knowledge

零价格知识

用于保护知识产权的部分理由的概念。如果知识总是免费的，即可以零价格获得，就会减少对增加知识存量的激励，因为增加并不能获得回报。通过知识产权保护，给予知识创造者获利权即可以提供此种激励。

Zero rating

零税率

货物免税进入一国。

Zero risk

零风险

在实施卫生和植物卫生措施时，在确定一指定产品风险的适当水平时根据事实有理由作出不承担任何风险的判断。在实践中，这通常意味着完全禁止该产品进口。

Zero-sum nationalism

零和民族主义

此种观点认为，在处理国际经贸关系时，国家在赢输之间只有一个选择。另一国赢，即使是暂时的，也被作出比较的国家视为输。该观点本质上是对重商主义所含理念的一种更广泛和更政治化的重述，重商主义认为贸易的目的是积累货币和外汇，制成品出口最大化和制成品进口最小化。完全忽略了通过国际分工所带来的利益及全球化对国际经济的影响。

Zero tolerance

零容忍

与零风险同义。

Zollverein

关税同盟

德语关税同盟。1834年在普鲁士人领导下通过统一多个当地关税同盟组建而成。随着其他德国州加入而不断扩大，直至1871年并入新成立的德意志帝国。19世纪上半叶德国的大部分经济进步可以归功于关税同盟。但是，关税同盟早期恰逢德国工业革命，对经济发展的确切贡献，即使具有实质贡献的话，也难以评估。*另见关税同盟(customs union)*。

ABBREVIATIONS USED IN INTERNATIONAL TRADE RELATIONS
国际贸易关系常用缩略语

~ A ~

AA	Association Agreement 联系协定
AACP	Alleged Anti-Competitive Practice 被指控的反竞争行为
AATPO	Association of African Trade Promotion Organizations 非洲贸易促进组织协会
ABAC	APEC Business Advisory Council APEC工商咨询理事会
ABTC	APEC Business Travel Card APEC商务旅行卡
ACCAS	Economic Community of Central African States 中部非洲国家经济共同体
ACDS	APEC Communications and Database System APEC交流与数据库系统
ACFTA	ASEAN-China Free Trade Area 中国—东盟自由贸易区
ACIA	ASEAN Comprehensive Investment Agreement 东盟全面投资协定
ACP	African, Caribbean and Pacific [States] 非加太地区[国家]
ACTA	Anti-Counterfeiting Trade Agreement 反假冒贸易协定
ACV	Agreement on Customs Valuation 海关估价协定
ACWL	Advisory Centre on WTO Law WTO法律咨询中心
AD	Anti-Dumping 反倾销
ADP	Anti-Dumping Practices 反倾销做法
ADR	Alternative Dispute Resolution 非诉讼争端解决
AEC	African Economic Community 非洲经济共同体
AEC	ASEAN Economic Community 东盟经济共同体

AECF Asia-Europe Cooperation Framework 2000
亚欧合作框架2000

AEM ASEAN Economic Ministers
东盟经济部长

AEO Authorized economic operator
经认证的经营者

AfCFTA African Continental Free Trade Area
非洲大陆自由贸易区

AFL-CIO American Federation of Labor and Congress of Industrial Organizations
美国劳工联合会-产业工会联合会

AFTA ASEAN Free Trade Area
东盟自由贸易区

AGCI African Global Competitiveness Initiative
非洲全球竞争力倡议

Ag-IMS Agriculture Information Management System
农业信息管理系统

AGOA African Growth and Opportunity Act
非洲增长与机遇法

AGP Agreement on Government Procurement
政府采购协定

AIA Advance Informed Agreement
预先知情同意

AIA ASEAN Investment Area
东盟投资区

AICO ASEAN Industrial Cooperation [Scheme]
东盟产业合作[计划]

AIJV ASEAN Industrial Joint Venture [Scheme]
东盟产业合资[计划]

AIS Andean Integration System
安第斯一体化体系

AISP ASEAN Integration System of Preferences
东盟一体化优惠体系

AIT Agreement on international trade
国际贸易协定

AITIC Agency for International Trade Information and Cooperation
国际贸易信息与合作署

AJCEP ASEAN–Japan Comprehensive Economic Partnership
东盟—日本全面经济伙伴关系协定

ALADI Asociación Latinoamericana de Integración (Latin American Integration Association)
拉丁美洲一体化协会

ALOP	Acceptable Level of [Sanitary or Phytosanitary] Protection 可接受的[卫生与植物卫生]保护水平
AM	Additive manufacturing 增材制造
AMAD	Agricultural Market Access Database 农产品市场准入数据库
AMIS	Agricultural Market Information System 农产品市场信息系统
AMS	Aggregate Measure of Support 综合支持量
AMU	Arab Maghreb Union 阿拉伯马格里布联盟
ANSSR	APEC New Strategy for Structural Reform APEC结构性改革新战略
ANZCERTA	Australia New Zealand Closer Economic Relations Trade Agreement 澳大利亚与新西兰更紧密经济关系贸易协定
AOC	Appellation d'Origine Contrôlée 原产地命名控制
AOSIS	Alliance of Small Island States 小岛屿国家联盟
AP	Administrative Protection 行政保护
APEC	Asia Pacific Economic Cooperation 亚太经济合作组织
APECTR	APEC Trade Repository APEC贸易资料库
APRG	Advance Payment Refund Guarantee 预付款还款担保
APTFF	Asia-Pacific Trade Facilitation Forum 亚太贸易便利化论坛
ARCAM	APEC Regulatory Cooperation Advanced Mechanism [on Trade-Related Standards and Technical Regulation] APEC监管合作高级机制[与贸易有关的标准和技术法规]
ARMS	Actions Reporting and Monitoring System (APEC) 行动报告和监控系统(APEC)
ARO	Agreement on Rules of Origin 原产地规则协定
ASCF	APEC Services Cooperation Framework APEC服务合作框架
ASCR	APEC Services Competitiveness Roadmap APEC服务竞争力路线图
ASEAN	Association of South-East Asian Nations 东南亚国家联盟

ASEM Asia-Europe Meeting
亚欧会议

ASP American Selling Price
美国销售价格

ASYCUDA Automated System for Customs Data (UNCTAD)
海关数据自动化系统(UNCTAD)

ATC Agreement on Textiles and Clothing
纺织品与服装协定

ATCA Agreement on Trade in Civil Aircraft
民用航空器贸易协定

ATIGA ASEAN Trade in Goods Agreement
东盟货物贸易协定

ATL Accelerated Tariff Liberalization
加速关税自由化

ATPA Andean Trade Preference Act
安第斯贸易优惠法

ATPC Association of Tin Producing Countries
锡生产国协会

ATPDEA Andean Trade Promotion and Drug Eradication Act
安第斯贸易促进与毒品根除法

ATR ASEAN Trade Repository
东盟贸易资料库

AV Adjusted Value
调整价格

AV Audiovisual [Services]
视听[服务]

AVE Ad Valorem Equivalent
从价税等值

AVMSD Audiovisual Media Services Directive
视听媒体服务指令

~ B ~

BAA	Buy American Act 购买美国货法
BDV	Brussels Definition of Value 布鲁塞尔估价定义
BEM	Big Emerging Market 新兴大市场
BFTA	Bilateral Free-Trade Agreement 双边自由贸易协定
BIA	Built-In Agenda (World Trade Organization) 既定议程(世界贸易组织)
BIMP-EAGA	Brunei-Indonesia-Malaysia East ASEAN Growth Area 东盟东部增长区
BIMST-EC	Bangladesh India Myanmar Sri Lanka Thailand Economic Cooperation 孟加拉国—印度—缅甸—斯里兰卡—泰国经济合作
BISD	Basic Instruments and Selected Documents 基本文件资料选编
BIT	Bilateral Investment Treaty 双边投资条约
BOB	Balance of Benefits 利益平衡
BOP	Balance of Payments 国际收支
BOT	Balance of Trade 贸易平衡
BPO	Business Process Outsourcing 业务流程外包
BRICS	Brazil, Russia, India, China and South Africa 金砖国家(巴西、俄罗斯、印度、中国和南非)
BSEC	Black Sea Economic Cooperation Organization 黑海经济合作组织
BTA	Bilateral Trade Agreement 双边贸易协定
BTA	Border Tax Adjustment 边境税调节
BTFP	BioTrade Facilitation Programme [UNCTAD] 生物贸易便利化计划[UNCTAD]
BTN	Brussels Tariff Nomenclature 布鲁塞尔关税税则
BTS	Basic Telecommunications Services 基础电信服务

~ *C* ~

CAA Clean Air Act (United States)
清洁空气法(美国)

CABEI Central American Bank for Economic Integration
中美洲经济一体化银行

CACEU Central African Customs and Economic Union
中部非洲关税与经济联盟

CACM Central American Common Market
中美洲共同市场

CACO Central Asian Cooperation Organization
中亚合作组织

CAFTA [United States–] Central American Free Trade Agreement
[美国—]中美洲自由贸易协定

CAFTA China–ASEAN Free-Trade Agreement
中国—东盟自由贸易协定

CAN Andean Community of Nations
安第斯国家共同体

CAP Collective Action Plan (APEC)
集体行动计划(APEC)

CAP Common Agricultural Policy
共同农业政策

CAREC Central Asia Regional Economic Cooperation
中亚区域经济合作组织

CARICOM Caribbean Community and Common Market
加勒比共同体和共同市场

CARIFTA Caribbean Free Trade Association
加勒比自由贸易协会

CAUCA Central American Uniform Customs Code
中美洲统一海关代码

CBD Convention on Biodiversity
生物多样性公约

CBERA Caribbean Basin Economic Recovery Act
加勒比盆地经济复苏法

CBI Caribbean Basin Initiative
加勒比盆地倡议

CBTPA [United States–] Caribbean Basin Trade Partnership Act
[美国—]加勒比盆地贸易伙伴关系法

CBTS Cross-Border Trade in Services
跨境服务贸易

CCC Commodity Credit Corporation (United States)
商品信贷公司(美国)

CCC	Customs Cooperation Council 海关合作理事会
CCFF	[IMF] Compensatory and Contingency Financing Facility [IMF]补偿与应急贷款
CCP	Common Commercial Policy 共同商业政策
CCT	Common Customs Tariff 共同关税
CDDC	Commodity-Dependent Developing Country 依赖初级商品的发展中国家
CDSOA	Continued Dumping and Subsidy Offset Act [United States] 持续倾销与补贴抵消法[美国]
CE	Council of Europe 欧洲理事会
CEAO	West African Economic Community 西非经济共同体
CEC	Commission of the European Community 欧洲共同体委员会
CECA	Comprehensive Economic Cooperation Agreement 全面经济合作协定
CEEC	Central and East European Countries 中东欧国家
CEFTA	Central European Free Trade Agreement 中欧自由贸易协定
CELAC	Comunidad des Estados Latinoamericanos y Caribeños (Community of Latin American and Caribbean States) 拉丁美洲和加勒比国家共同体
CEMAC	Communauté économique et monétaire de l'Afrique centrale 中部非洲经济与货币同盟
CEN-SAD	Community of Sahel-Saharan States 萨赫勒—撒哈拉国家共同体
CEP	Comprehensive Economic Partnership 全面经济伙伴关系
CEPAL	Comisión Económica de las Naciones Unidas para América Latina y el Caribe [ECLAC] 拉丁美洲和加勒比经济委员会
CEPT	Common Effective Preferential Tariff (ASEAN) 共同有效特惠关税安排(东盟)
CER	[Australia New Zealand] Closer Economic Relations [澳大利亚与新西兰]更紧密经济关系
CERDS	Charter of Economic Rights and Duties of States 各国经济权利与义务宪章
CET	Common External Tariff 共同对外关税

CETA	Comprehensive Economic and Trade Agreement 全面经济贸易协定
CF	Common Fund 共同基金
CFC	Chlorofluorocarbons 氟氯碳化合物
CFF	Compensatory Financing Facility 出口波动补偿贷款
CFP	Common Fisheries Policy 共同渔业政策
CG-18	Consultative Group of Eighteen (GATT) 18国咨询小组(GATT)
CGIAR	Consultative Group on International Agricultural Research 国际农业研究磋商组织
CHOGM	Commonwealth Heads of Government Meeting 英联邦政府首脑会议
CHOGRM	Commonwealth Heads of Government Regional Meeting 英联邦政府首脑区域会议
CI	Consular Invoice 领事发票
CIEC	Conference on International Economic Cooperation 国际经济合作会议
CIF	Cost, Insurance and Freight 到岸价格
CIS	Commonwealth of Independent States 独立国家联合体
CISFTA	Commonwealth of Independent States Free Trade Area 独立国家联合体自由贸易区
CITES	Convention on International Trade in Endangered Species of Wild Fauna and Flora 濒危野生动植物种国际贸易公约
CLMV	Cambodia, Laos, Myanmar and Vietnam 柬埔寨、老挝、缅甸和越南
CM	Common Market 共同市场
CMEA	Council for Mutual Economic Assistance 经济互助委员会
CNM	Certificate of non-manipulation 未再加工证明
CNUCED	Conférence des Nations unies sur le commerce et le développement 联合国贸易与发展会议

COCOM	Co-ordinating Committee for Multilateral Export Controls 多边出口管制协调委员会
COMESA	Common Market for Eastern and Southern Africa 东部和南部非洲共同市场
COREPER	Committee of Permanent Representatives (EC) 常驻代表委员会(欧共体)
CP	Contracting Party (GATT) 缔约方(GATT)
CPE	Centrally Planned Economy 中央计划经济体
CPTPP	Comprehensive and Progressive Agreement for Trans-Pacific Partnership 全面与进步跨太平洋伙伴关系协定
CRTA	Committee on Regional Trade Agreements (WTO) 区域贸易协定委员会(WTO)
CSC	Committee on Specific Commitments (WTO) 具体承诺委员会(WTO)
CSD	Commission on Sustainable Development 可持续发展委员会
CSE	Consumer Subsidy Equivalent 消费者补贴等值
CSI	Container Security Initiative 集装箱安全倡议
CSME	CARICOM Single Market and Economy 加勒比共同体单一市场和经济
CSR	Corporate Social Responsibility 企业社会责任
CSSD	Consultative Sub-Committee on Surplus Disposal 剩余产品处理磋商小组委员会
CTD	Committee on Trade and Development (WTO) 贸易与发展委员会(WTO)
CTE	[WTO] Committee on Trade and Environment [WTO]贸易与环境委员会
CTH	Change in Tariff Heading 税目改变
CTI	[APEC] Committee on Trade and Investment [APEC]贸易与投资委员会
CTS	Consolidated Tariff Schedule 合并关税减让表
CU	Customs Union 关税同盟
CUSTA	Canada–United States Trade Agreement 加拿大—美国贸易协定

CVAL Customs valuation
海关估价
CVD Countervailing Duties
反补贴税
CXT Common External Tariff
共同对外关税

~ D ~

DA	Development Assistance 发展援助
DAE	Dynamic Asian Economy 充满活力的亚洲经济
DDA	Doha Development Agenda 多哈发展议程
DDAGTF	Doha Development Agenda Global Trust Fund 多哈发展议程全球信托基金
DEIP	Dairy Export Incentive Program 奶制品出口激励计划
DEQF	Duty-free and quota-free [market access] 免关税和免配额[市场准入]
DG	Directorate-General (European Commission) 总司长(欧盟委员会)
DIAC	Draft International Antitrust Code 国际反垄断法典草案
DISC	Domestic International Sales Corporation (United States) 本国国际销售公司(美国)
DME	Developed Market Economy 发达市场经济体
DPG	Domestically Prohibited Goods 国内禁止货物
DSB	Dispute Settlement Body 争端解决机构
DSM	Dispute Settlement Mechanism 争端解决机制
DSP	Dispute Settlement Procedures 争端解决程序
DTIS	Diagnostic Trade Integration Studies 诊断性贸易一体化研究

~ *E* ~

EAC	East African Cooperation 东非合作
EADB	East African Development Bank 东非开发银行
EAEU	Eurasian Economic Union 欧亚经济联盟
EAFRD	European Agricultural Fund for Rural Development 欧洲农村农业发展基金
EAFTA	East Asia Free Trade Agreement 东亚自由贸易协定
EAGA	East ASEAN Growth Area 东盟东部增长区
EAGGF	European Agricultural Guidance and Guarantee Fund 欧洲农业指导和担保基金
EAI	Enterprise for ASEAN Initiative 东盟企业倡议
EAI	Enterprise for the Americas Initiative 美洲企业倡议
EALAF	East Asia Latin America Forum 东亚—拉美论坛
EAS	East Asia Summit 东亚峰会
EBA	Everything But Arms 除武器外的所有产品
EBOPS	Extended Balance of Payments Services Classification [IMF] 国际收支服务扩展分类[IMF]
EBRD	European Bank for Reconstruction and Development 欧洲复兴开发银行
EC	European Community 欧洲共同体
ECA	Economic Cooperation Agreement 经济合作协定
ECABS	Economic Cooperation Area of Black Sea Countries 黑海国家经济合作区
ECAFE	[United Nations] Economic Commission for Asia and the Far East [联合国]亚洲及远东经济委员会
ECCAS	Economic Community of Central African States 中部非洲国家经济共同体
ECDC	Economic Cooperation between Developing Countries 发展中国家间经济合作

ECE	[United Nations] Economic Commission for Europe [联合国]欧洲经济委员会
ECF	Extended Credit Facility 中期贷款
ECJ	European Court of Justice 欧洲法院
ECLAC	[United Nations] Economic Commission for Latin America and the Caribbean [联合国]拉丁美洲和加勒比经济委员会
ECO	Economic Cooperation Organization 经济合作组织
ECOSOC	[United Nations] Economic and Social Council [联合国]经济及社会理事会
ECOTA	Economic Cooperation Organization Trade Agreement 经济合作组织贸易协定
ECOTECH	[APEC] Economic and Technical Cooperation [APEC]经济与技术合作
ECOWAS	Economic Community of West African States 西非国家经济共同体
ECSC	European Coal and Steel Community 欧洲煤钢共同体
ECT	Energy Charter Treaty 能源宪章条约
ECU	European Currency Unit 欧洲货币单位
ECWA	Economic Commission for Western Africa (United Nations) 西非经济委员会(联合国)
EDB	Environmental Database 环境数据库
EDI	Electronic Data Interchange 电子数据交换
EDIFACT	Electronic Data Interchange for Administration, Commerce and Transport 行政、商业和运输用电子数据交换
EEA	European Economic Area 欧洲经济区
EEC	European Economic Community 欧洲经济共同体
EEP	Export Enhancement Program 出口增强计划
EEZ	Exclusive Economic Zone 专属经济区
EFTA	European Free Trade Association 欧洲自由贸易联盟

EIA　Economic Integration Agreement
经济一体化协定

e-IAP　Electronic Individual Action Plan
电子版单边行动计划

EIF　Enhanced Integrated Framework
综合增强框架

EIT　Economies in Transition
转型经济体

ELS　Eco-Labelling Scheme
生态标签方案

EMDC　Emerging Market and Developing Countries
新兴市场和发展中国家

EME　Emerging Market Economy
新兴市场经济体

EMEA　Euro-Mediterranean Economic Area
欧盟—地中海经济区

EMFTA　Euro-Mediterranean Free Trade Area
欧洲—地中海自由贸易区

EMR　Exclusive Marketing Right
专有销售权

EMS　Equivalent Measure of Support
支持等值

ENP　European Neighbourhood Policy
欧洲睦邻政策

EPA　Economic Partnership Agreement
经济伙伴协定

EPC　European Political Cooperation
欧洲政治合作

EPG　Eminent Persons Group
知名人士小组

EPR　Export Performance Requirement
出口实绩要求

EPZ　Export Processing Zone
出口加工区

ERA　Effective Rate of Assistance
有效援助率

ERA　Export Restraint Arrangement
出口限制安排

ERP　Effective Rate of Protection
有效保护率

ESAP　Environmental Services Action Plan (APEC)
环境服务行动计划(APEC)

ESCAP [United Nations] Economic and Social Commission for Asia and the Pacific
[联合国]亚洲及太平洋经济社会理事会

ESCWA [United Nations] Economic and Social Commission for Western Asia
[联合国]西亚经济社会委员会

ESM Emergency Safeguard Mechanism (or Measures)
紧急保障机制(或措施)

EST Environmentally sound technologies
环境友好型技术

EU European Union
欧洲联盟

EURASEC Eurasian Economic Community
欧亚经济共同体

EUROSTAT Statistical Office of the European Communities
欧洲共同体统计局

EVSL Early Voluntary Sectoral Liberalization
部门提前自愿自由化

~ F ~

FAC	Food Aid Convention 粮食援助公约
FAO	[United Nations] Food and Agriculture Organization [联合国]粮食及农业组织
FCCC	[United Nations] Framework Convention on Climate Change [联合国]气候变化框架公约
FCN	[Treaties of] Friendship, Commerce and Navigation 友好通商航海[条约]
FCPA	Foreign Corrupt Practices Act (United States) 反海外腐败法(美国)
FDI	Foreign Direct Investment 外国直接投资
FEALAC	Forum for East Asia and Latin American Cooperation 东亚—拉丁美洲合作论坛
FEOGA	Fonds européen d’orientation et de garantie agricole 欧洲农业指导和保证基金
FIAS	Facility for Investment Climate Advisory Services 外国投资服务咨询中心
FIFD	Friends of Investment Facilitation for Development 投资便利化之友
FIG	Food-Importing Group 粮食进口集团
FIPA	Foreign Investment [Promotion and] Protection Agreement 外国投资[促进和]保护协定
FIPs	Five Interested Parties 利害关系5方
FIRA	Foreign Investment Review Act [or Agency] (Canada) 外国投资审查法[或机构](加拿大)
FMO	Framework of Mutual Obligations 共同义务框架
FOB	Free on Board 离岸价格
FOGS	Functioning of the GATT System GATT体制运行谈判组
FPTA	Full Preferential Trade Agreement 全面优惠贸易协定
FSB	Financial Stability Board 金融稳定委员会
FSC	Foreign Sales Corporation (United States) 外国销售公司(美国)

FTA	Free-Trade Area, Free-Trade Agreement, Free-Trade Arrangement 自由贸易区、自由贸易协定、自由贸易安排
FTAA	Free Trade Area of the Americas 美洲自由贸易区
FTAAP	Free Trade Area of the Asia-Pacific 亚太自由贸易区
FTZ	Free-Trade Zone 自由贸易园区
FVNM	Focused value of non-originating material method 非原产材料价格法

~ *G* ~

GAAP Generally Accepted Accounting Principles
公认会计原则

GAFTA Greater Arab Free Trade Area
大阿拉伯自由贸易区

GAL Guaranteed Access Level (textiles)
保证准入水平(纺织品)

GATS General Agreement on Trade in Services
服务贸易总协定

GATT General Agreement on Tariffs and Trade
关税与贸易总协定

GBT Group on Basic Telecommunications
基础电信谈判组

GCC Gulf Cooperation Council
海湾合作委员会

GDP Gross Domestic Product
国内生产总值

GDPR General Data Protection Regulation
通用数据保护条例

GEF Global Environment Facility
全球环境基金

GFC Global Financial Crisis
全球金融危机

GFSEC Global Forum on Steel Excess Capacity
钢铁产能过剩全球论坛

GHS Globally Harmonized System of Classification and Labelling of Chemicals
全球化学品统一分类和标签制度

GI Geographical Indication
地理标志

GII Global Information Infrastructure
全球信息基础设施

GLP Good Laboratory Practice
良好实验室规范

GMM Genetically Modified Micro-Organism
转基因微生物

GMO Genetically Modified Organism
转基因生物

GMP Good Manufacturing Practice
良好生产规范

GNG Group of Negotiations on Goods
货物谈判组

GNI Gross National Income
国民总收入

GNS Group of Negotiations on Services
服务谈判组

GPA Government Procurement Agreement
政府采购协定

GPT General preferential tariff
普遍优惠关税

GRULAC Group of Latin American and Caribbean Countries
拉丁美洲与加勒比国家集团

GSA Global Sugar Alliance
全球糖业联盟

GSP Generalized System of Preferences
普遍优惠制

GSTP Global System of Trade Preferences
全球贸易优惠制

GTC Grains Trade Convention
谷物贸易公约

GTPN Global Trade Point Network (UNCTAD)
全球贸易点网络(UNCTAD)

GVC Global Value Chain
全球价值链

~ H ~

HACCP Hazard Analysis and Critical Control Points [Program]
危害分析与关键控制点[计划]

HCOM Host Country Operational Measures
东道国执行措施

HGP Hormone Growth Promotant
激素增长促进剂案

HIC High-Income Country
高收入国家

HIPC Heavily Indebted Poor Countries
重债穷国

HKSAR Hong Kong Special Administrative Region
香港特别行政区

HLM High-Level Meeting
高级别会议

HS Harmonized [Commodity Description and Coding] System
[商品名称及编码]协调制度

HST Hegemonic Stability Theory
霸权稳定论

HTS Harmonized Tariff Schedule
协调关税税则

~ I ~

IAC Industrially Advanced Country
工业发达国家

IAJJP International Agreement on Jute and Jute Products
国际黄麻和黄麻制品协定

IAS International Accounting Standards
国际会计准则

IASC International Accounting Standards Committee
国际会计准则委员会

IATTC Inter-American Tropical Tuna Commission
美洲间热带金枪鱼委员会

IBA International Bauxite Association
国际铝土协会

IBMA International Bovine Meat Agreement
国际牛肉协定

IBRD International Bank for Reconstruction and Development
国际复兴开发银行

ICA International Commodity Agreement
国际商品协定

ICAC International Cotton Advisory Council
国际棉花咨询委员会

ICAO International Civil Aviation Organization
国际民航组织

ICB International Commodity Body
国际商品机构

ICC International Chamber of Commerce
国际商会

ICCA International Cocoa Agreement
国际可可协定

ICCEC Intergovernmental Council of Copper Exporting Countries
铜出口国政府间委员会

ICCICA Interim Co-ordinating Committee for International Commodity Arrangements (ECOSOC)
国际商品安排临时协调委员会(ECOSOC)

ICCO International Cocoa Organization
国际可可组织

ICDR International Commercial Dispute Resolution
国际商事纠纷解决

ICFA International Coffee Agreement
国际咖啡协定

ICFO International Coffee Organization
国际咖啡组织

ICGFI International Consultative Group on Food Irradiation
国际食品辐照咨询组

ICIDI Independent Commission on International Development Issues
国际发展问题独立委员会

ICJ International Court of Justice
国际法院

ICPM Interim Commission on Phytosanitary Measures
植物卫生措施临时委员会

ICREA International Commodity-Related Environment Agreement
与商品有关的国际环境协定

ICSG International Copper Study Group
国际铜业研究组织

ICSID International Centre for Settlement of Investment Disputes
国际投资争端解决中心

ICT Information and Communication(s) Technology
信息通信技术

ICTSD International Centre for Trade and Sustainable Development
国际贸易与可持续发展中心

IDA International Development Association
国际开发协会

IDL International Division of Labour
国际劳动分工

IE Independent Entity
独立实体

IEA International Energy Agency
国际能源署

IEC International Electrotechnical Commission
国际电工委员会

IFA Interregional Framework Agreement
区域间框架协定

IFAD International Fund for Agricultural Development
国际农业发展基金

IFAP Investment Facilitation Action Plan
投资便利化行动计划

IFC International Finance Corporation
国际金融公司

IFDI Inward Foreign Direct Investment
外国直接投资

IFI International Financial Institution
国际金融机构

IFIA International Federation of Inspection Agencies
国际检验机构联盟

IGAD Intergovernmental Authority on Development
政府间发展组织
IGC Intergovernmental Conference (European Union)
欧盟政府间会议
IGC International Grains Council
国际谷物理事会
IGO Indication of Geographical Origin
原产地地理标志
IIA International Investment Agreement
国际投资协定
IIT Intra-Industry Trade
产业内贸易
IJO International Jute Organization
国际黄麻组织
IJSG International Jute Study Group
国际黄麻研究小组
ILO International Labour Organization
国际劳工组织
ILP [Agreement on] Import Licensing Procedures
进口许可程序[协定]
ILSA Iran–Libya Sanctions Act (United States)
伊朗与利比亚制裁法(美国)
ILZSG International Lead and Zinc Study Group
国际铅锌研究小组
IMC International Meat Council
国际肉类理事会
IMF International Monetary Fund
国际货币基金组织
IMO International Maritime Organization
国际海事组织
INBAR International Network on Bamboo and Rattan
国际竹藤组织
INR Initial Negotiating Right
最初谈判权
INRA International Natural Rubber Agreement
国际天然橡胶协定
INRO International Natural Rubber Organization
国际天然橡胶组织
INSG International Nickel Study Group
国际镍研究小组
IOOA International Olive Oil Agreement
国际橄榄油协定
IOOC International Olive Oil Council
国际橄榄油理事会

IOR	Indian Ocean Rim 环印度洋
IORA	Indian Ocean Rim Association 环印度洋联盟
IOR-ARC	Indian Ocean Rim Association for Regional Cooperation 环印度洋地区合作联盟
IORI	Indian Ocean Regional Initiative 印度洋区域计划
IOSCO	International Organization of Securities Commissions 国际证券委员会组织
IoT	Internet of Things 物联网
IP	Intellectual Property 知识产权
IPAP	Investment Protection Action Plan 投资保护行动计划
IPC	Integrated Programme for Commodities 商品综合方案
IPC	International Patent Classification 国际专利分类
IPE	International Political Economy 国际政治经济学
IPEC	International Program for the Elimination of Child Labour 国际消除童工计划
IPGRI	International Plant Genetic Resources Institute 国际植物遗传资源研究所
IPIC	Treaty on Intellectual Property in Respect of Integrated Circuits 集成电路知识产权条约
IPPA	Investment Promotion and Protection Arrangement 投资促进与保护协定
IPPC	International Plant Protection Convention 国际植物保护公约
IPR	Intellectual Property Right 知识产权
IPR	Investment Policy Review 投资政策审议
IRA	Import Risk Assessment 进口风险评估
IRE	Independent Review Entity 独立审查实体
IRSG	International Rubber Study Group 国际橡胶研究小组

IRTM	Investment-Related Trade Measure 与投资有关的贸易措施
ISA	International Sugar Agreement 国际糖协定
ISCO	International Standard Classification of Occupations 国际标准职业分类
ISD	Investment Services Directive (European Community) 投资服务指令(欧共体)
ISIC	International Standard Industrial Classification 国际标准行业分类
ISO	International Organization for Standardization 国际标准化组织
ISO	International Sugar Organization 国际糖组织
ISONET	International Organization for Standardization Information Network 国际标准化信息网络组织
ISPM	International Standard for Phytosanitary Measures 国际植物卫生标准
ITA	Information Technology Agreement 信息技术协定
ITA	International Tea Agreement 国际茶协定
ITA	International Tin Agreement 国际锡协定
ITC	International Trade Centre (UNCTAD/WTO) (UNCTAD/WTO)国际贸易中心
ITC	International Trade Commission (United States) 国际贸易委员会(美国)
ITCB	International Textiles and Clothing Bureau 国际纺织服装局
ITO	International Trade Organization 国际贸易组织
ITPA	International Tea Promotion Association 国际茶叶促进协会
ITRC	International Tripartite Rubber Council 国际三国橡胶联盟理事会
ITSG	International Tin Study Group 国际锡研究小组
ITTA	International Tropical Timber Agreement 国际热带木材协定
ITTO	International Tropical Timber Organization 国际热带木材组织
ITU	International Telecommunication Union 国际电信联盟

IUCN	International Union for the Conservation of Nature and Natural Resources 保护自然和自然资源国际联盟
IUU	Illegal, Unreported and Unregulated [fishing] 非法、未报告和无管制的[捕捞]
IVANS	International Value-Added Network Services 国际增值网络服务
IWA	International Wheat Agreement 国际小麦协定
IWC	International Wheat Council 国际小麦理事会

~ J ~

JITAP Joint Integrated Technical Assistance Programme
技术援助共同综合方案

JTC Joint Trade Committee
联合贸易委员会

JUSCANZ Japan, United States, Canada, Australia, New Zealand [plus Switzerland, Norway and Turkey]
日美加澳新集团[加瑞士、挪威和土耳其]

JV Joint Venture
合资企业

~ *K* ~

KPCS	Kimberley Process Certification Scheme 金伯利进程证书制度

~ L ~

LAC	Latin America(n) and Caribbean 拉丁美洲和加勒比地区
LAC	Less-Advantaged Countries 弱势国家
LAES	Latin American Economic System 拉丁美洲经济体系
LAFTA	Latin American Free Trade Association 拉丁美洲自由贸易协会
LAIA	Latin American Integration Association 拉丁美洲一体化协会
LAISR	Leaders' Agenda to Implement Structural Reform (APEC) 领导人实施结构性改革议程(APEC)
LASU	Large Aircraft Sector Understanding 民用航空器行业谅解
LCA	Life Cycle Assessment 生命周期评估
LCR	Local Content Requirement 当地含量要求
LDC	Least-Developed Country 最不发达国家
LDC	Less-Developed Country 欠发达国家
LIBOR	London Interbank Offered Rate 伦敦同业拆借利率
LLDC	Land-Locked Developing Country 内陆发展中国家
LMG	Like-Minded Group 志同道合国家
LMICs	Low-Middle-Income Countries 中等偏下收入国家
LMO	Living Modified Organism 改性活生物体
LTA	Long-Term Arrangement Regarding International Trade in Cotton Textiles 国际棉纺织品贸易长期安排
LTFV	Less than Fair Value 低于公允价值
LVC	Labour Value Content 劳动价值含量

~M~

MAC	Multilateral Agreement on Competition 多边竞争协定
MAI	Multilateral Agreement on Investment 多边投资协定
MALIAT	Multilateral Agreement on the Liberalization of International Air Transportation 国际航空运输自由化多边协定
MAPA	Manila Action Plan for APEC APEC马尼拉行动计划
MA-TTRI	Market Access-Tariff Trade Restrictiveness Index 市场准入-关税贸易限制指数
MAV	Minimum Access Volume 最低准入量
MCA	Monetary Compensation Amount 货币补偿金额
MCC	Millennium Challenge Corporation 千年挑战公司
MCF	Multilateral Competition Policy Framework 多边竞争政策框架
MCM	Ministerial Council Meeting (OECD) 部长理事会会议(OECD)
MCO	Manufacturer's Certificate of Origin 制造商原产地证书
MDB	Multilateral Development Bank 多边开发银行
MEA	Multilateral Environment Agreement 多边环境协定
MEFTA	Middle East Free Trade Area [Initiative] 中东自由贸易区[倡议]
METI	Ministry of Economy, Trade and Industry (Japan) 经济产业省(日本)
MFA	Multi-Fibre Arrangement 多种纤维协定
MFN	Most-Favoured-Nation [Treatment] 最惠国[待遇]
MIGA	Multilateral Investment Guarantee Agency 多边投资担保机构
MIP	Minimum Import Price 最低进口价格
MITI	Ministry of International Trade and Industry (Japan) 通商产业省(日本)

MMPA	Marine Mammal Protection Act (United States) 海洋哺乳动物保护法(美国)
MNC	Multinational Corporation 跨国公司
MNE	Multinational Enterprise 跨国企业
MOFTEC	Ministry of Foreign Trade and Economic Cooperation (China) 对外贸易经济合作部(中国)
MOP	Margin of Preference 优惠幅度
MOSS	Market-Oriented Sector-Selective [talks] 市场导向型的多领域[谈判方案]
MOU	Memorandum of Understanding 谅解备忘录
MRA	Mutual Recognition Agreement 相互承认协定
MRU	Mano River Union 马诺河联盟
MSA	Multilateral Steel Agreement 多边钢铁协定
MSAP	Manufacturing Related Services Action Plan 制造业相关服务行动计划
MSMEs	Micro, small and medium enterprises 中小微企业
MSO	Manufacturer's Statement of Origin 制造商原产地声明
MSSA	Multilateral Specialty Steel Arrangement 多边特种钢协定
MTA	Material Transfer Agreement 材料转移协议
MTA	Mini-Trading Area 小型贸易区
MTA	Multilateral Trade Agreement 多边贸易协定
MTN	Multilateral Trade Negotiations 多边贸易谈判
MTO	Multilateral Trade Organization 多边贸易组织
MTS	Multilateral Trading System 多边贸易体制

~N~

NAALC	North American Agreement on Labour Cooperation 北美劳工合作协定
NAFTA	New Zealand–Australia Free Trade Agreement 新西兰—澳大利亚自由贸易协定
NAFTA	North American Free Trade Agreement 北美自由贸易协定
NAM	Non-Aligned Movement 不结盟运动
NAMA	Non-Agricultural Market Access 非农产品市场准入
NBIP	Non-Binding Investment Principles (APEC) 投资非约束性原则(APEC)
NCPI	New Commercial Policy Instrument 新商业政策机制
NEAFTA	North East Asia Free-Trade Area 东北亚自由贸易区
NEPAD	New Partnership for Africa's Development 非洲发展新伙伴关系计划
n.e.s.	Not elsewhere specified 其他处未列明
NFIC	Net Food-Importing Country 粮食净进口国
NFIDC	Net Food-Importing Developing Country 粮食净进口发展中国家
NGBT	Negotiating Group on Basic Telecommunications 基础电信谈判组
NGMA	Negotiating Group on Market Access 市场准入谈判组
NGMTS	Negotiating Group on Maritime Transport Services 海运服务谈判组
NGO	Non-Governmental Organization 非政府组织
NGTF	Negotiating Group on Trade Facilitation 贸易便利化谈判组
NIC	Newly-Industrializing Country 新兴工业化国家
NIDL	New International Division of Labour 新国际分工
NIE	Newly-Industrializing Economy 新兴工业化经济体

n.i.e.	Not included elsewhere 别处未包括
NIEO	New International Economic Order 国际经济新秩序
NIP	New Industrial Policy 新产业政策
NIS	Newly Independent States 新独立国家
NLC	Newly Liberalizing Country 新自由化国家
NRA	Nominal Rate of Assistance 名义援助率
NRBP	Natural Resource-Based Product 自然资源产品
NRP	Nominal Rate of Protection 名义保护率
NT	National Treatment 国民待遇
NTA	New Trade Agenda 新贸易议程
NTA	New Transatlantic Agenda 新跨大西洋议程
NTB	Non-Tariff Barrier 非关税壁垒
NTE	National Trade Estimate [Report] (United States) 对外贸易壁垒国家贸易评估[报告] (美国)
NTFB	National Trade Facilitation Bodies 国家贸易便利化机构
NTFC	National Trade Facilitation Committees 国家贸易便利化委员会
NTI	National Treatment Instrument 国民待遇文件
NTM	New Transatlantic Marketplace 新跨大西洋市场
NTM	Non-Tariff Measure 非关税措施
NTR	Normal Trade Relations 正常贸易关系
NTT	New Trade Theory 新贸易理论
NWO	New World Order 世界新秩序

~ O ~

OAA	Osaka Action Agenda (APEC) 大阪行动议程(APEC)
OAS	Organization of American States 美洲国家组织
OAU	Organization of African Unity 非洲统一组织
ODA	Official Development Assistance 官方发展援助
OECD	Organisation for Economic Co-operation and Development 经济合作与发展组织
OECS	Organization of Eastern Caribbean States 东加勒比国家组织
OEEC	Organisation for European Economic Cooperation 欧洲经济合作组织
OFDI	Outward Foreign Direct Investment 对外直接投资
OIC	Organization of Islamic Cooperation 伊斯兰合作组织
OIE	Office International des Epizooties 国际兽疫局
OIF	Organisation Internationale de la Francophonie 法语国家组织
OIV	Office international de la Vigne et du vin 国际葡萄与葡萄酒组织
OMA	Orderly Marketing Arrangement 有序销售安排
OMC	Organisation Mondiale du Commerce [WTO] 世界贸易组织[WTO]
OPEC	Organization of Petroleum Exporting Countries 石油输出国组织
OPTAD	Organization of Pacific Trade and Development 太平洋贸易与发展组织
ORIGIN	Organisation for an International Geographical Indications Network 国际地理标志网络组织
ORRC	Other Restrictive Regulations of Commerce 其他限制性贸易法规
OTC	Organization for Trade Cooperation 贸易合作组织
OTCA	Omnibus Trade and Competitiveness Act 综合贸易与竞争法

OTDS Overall trade-distorting domestic support
扭曲贸易的国内支持总量

OTDS Overall trade-distorting support
扭曲贸易的支持总量

OVOP One Village, One Product
一村一品

~ *P* ~

PACER	Pacific Agreement on Closer Economic Relations 太平洋更紧密经济关系协定
PAFTA	Pacific Free Trade Area 太平洋自由贸易区
PBEC	Pacific Basin Economic Conference 太平洋盆地经济理事会
PBR	Plant Breeders' Right 植物育种者权利
PDO	Protected Designation of Origin [European Community] 原产地命名保护[欧洲共同体]
PECC	Pacific Economic Cooperation Council 太平洋经济合作理事会
PFC	Priority Foreign Country 重点国家
PFP	Partners for Progress (APEC) 进步伙伴(APEC)
PGE	Permanent Group of Experts 常设专家小组
PGI	Protected Geographical Indication [European Community] 地理标志保护[欧洲共同体]
PIC	Prior Informed Consent 事先知情同意
PICTA	Pacific Island Countries Trade Agreement 太平洋岛国贸易协定
PIF	Pacific Islands Forum 太平洋岛国论坛
PITs	Partners in Transition (OECD) 转型合作伙伴(OECD)
PL480	Public Law 480 (United States) 480号公法(美国)
PMD	Processing, Marketing and Distribution [of Commodities] [商品]加工、市场营销和分销
PMV	Passenger Motor Vehicle 乘用车
PNTR	Permanent Normal Trade Relations 永久正常贸易关系
PPA	Protocol of Provisional Application 临时适用议定书
PPM	Processes and Production Methods 工序和生产方法

PPTA	Partial Preferential Trade Agreement 部分优惠贸易协定
PRA	Pest Risk Assessment 有害生物风险评估
PRGF	Poverty Reduction and Growth Facility 减贫与增长贷款
PRSP	Poverty Reduction Strategy Paper 减贫战略文件
PSE	Production Subsidy Equivalent 生产补贴等值
PSI	Preshipment Inspection 装运前检验
PTA	Preferential Trade Agreement (or Area) 优惠贸易协定(或区)
PTA	Preferential Trade Area for Eastern and Southern African States 东部和南部非洲国家优惠贸易区

~ *Q* ~

QR Quantitative Restriction
数量限制

~ R ~

RA	Risk Assessment 风险评估
RAM	Recently acceded member 新加入成员
RBPs	Restrictive Business Practices 限制性商业惯例
REI	Regional Economic Integration 区域经济一体化
REIO	Regional Economic Integration Organization 区域经济一体化组织
REPA	Regional Economic Partnership Agreement 区域经济伙伴关系协定
RHQ	Regional Headquarters 地区总部
RIA	Regional Integration Arrangement 区域经济一体化安排
RIOPPAH	Regional International Organization for Plant Protection and Animal Health 区域国际植物保护与动物卫生组织
ROOs	Rules of Origin 原产地规则
RTA	Regional Trade Agreement 区域贸易协定
RTAA	Reciprocal Trade Agreements Act (United States) 互惠贸易协定法(美国)
RTIA	Regional Trade and Investment Agreement 区域贸易投资协定
RVC	Regional Value Content 区域价值成分

~S~

S+D Special and Differential [Treatment]
特殊和差别[待遇]

SAARC South Asian Association for Regional Cooperation
南亚区域合作联盟

SACA Special Agreement on Commodity Arrangements
商品安排特别协定

SACU Southern African Customs Union
南部非洲关税同盟

SADC Southern African Development Community
南部非洲发展共同体

SAFTA South American Free Trade Agreement
南美自由贸易协定

SAP Structural Adjustment Programme
结构性调整计划

SAPTA South Asian Preferential Trade Area
南亚优惠贸易区

SBA Strategic Business Alliance
战略性商业联盟

SBCD Second Banking Coordination Directive (European Community)
第二银行协作指令(欧洲共同体)

SCM Subsidies and Countervailing Measures
补贴与反补贴措施

SCU Sectoral Customs Union
部门关税同盟

SDPC State Development and Planning Commission (China)
国家发展计划委员会(中国)

SDR Special Drawing Right
特别提款权

SEA Single European Act
单一欧洲法

SEE State Economic Enterprise
国有经济企业

SEEFTA Southeast European Free Trade Agreement
东南欧自由贸易协定

SELA Sistema Económico Latinoamericano (Latin American Economic System)
拉丁美洲经济体系

SEM Single European Market
单一欧洲市场

SFPR Strategic Framework for Poverty Reduction
减贫战略框架

SFTA	Sectoral Free-Trade Area 部门自由贸易区
SIA	Sustainability Impact Assessment 可持续发展影响评估
SICA	Sistema de la Integración Centroamericana 中美洲一体化体系
SIDS	Small Island Developing States 小岛屿发展中国家
SIECA	Secretaría de Integración Económica Centroamericana ([Permanent] Secretariat of the General Treaty on Central American Economic Integration) 中美洲经济一体化总条约[常设]秘书处
SII	Structural Impediments Initiative 日美结构协议会
SITC	Standard International Trade Classification 国际贸易标准分类
SMC	Singapore Ministerial Conference 新加坡部长级会议
SNPA	Substantial New Programme of Action[for the 1980s for the Least-Developed Countries] [20世纪80年代支援最不发达国家]新的实质性行动纲领
SOM	Senior Officials' Meeting 高级别官员会议
SPARTECA	South Pacific Regional Trade and Economic Cooperation Agreement 南太平洋区域贸易经济合作协定
SPF	South Pacific Forum 南太平洋论坛
SPM	Sanitary and Phytosanitary Measures 卫生与植物卫生措施
SPS	Sanitary and Phytosanitary [Measures] 卫生与植物卫生[措施]
SPS	Single Payment Scheme 单一支付计划
SPS	Special Preferential Sugar Agreement (ACP-EC) 食糖特惠协定(非加太地区国家与欧共体)
SREZ	Sub-Regional Economic Zone 次区域经济区
SRM	Specified Risk Material 特定风险物质
SSG	Special Safeguard 特殊保障措施
SSP	Special Safeguard Provisions 特殊保障条款

STA	Semiconductor Trade Arrangement 半导体贸易安排
STA	Short-Term Arrangement Regarding International Trade in Cotton Textiles 国际棉纺织品贸易短期安排
STABEX	[System for the] Stabilization of Export Earnings (European Community) 出口收入稳定[机制](欧洲共同体)
STDF	Standards and Trade Development Facility 标准和贸易发展基金
STE	State-Trading Enterprise 国营贸易企业
STIC	Sustainable Trade and Innovation Centre 可持续贸易与创新中心
STO	Specific trade obligation 特定贸易义务
STO	State Trading Organization 国营贸易组织
STR	Special Trade Representative 特别贸易代表
SVE	Small, vulnerable economy 弱小经济体
SYSMIN	System for the Promotion of Mineral Production and Exports (European Community) 矿产生产及出口促进制度(欧洲共同体)

~ T ~

TABD Trans-Atlantic Business Dialogue
跨大西洋商业对话

TAFTA Trans-Atlantic Free Trade Area
跨大西洋自由贸易区

TARIC Tarif intégré de l'Union européenne (Integrated Tariff of the European Community)
欧洲共同体综合税则

TBT Technical Barriers to Trade
技术性贸易壁垒

TCDC Technical Cooperation between Developing Countries
发展中国家间技术合作

TCF Textiles, Clothing and Footwear
纺织品、服装和鞋

TCRO Technical Committee on Rules of Origin
原产地规则技术委员会

TDB Trade and Development Board
贸易与发展理事会

TDR Trade and Development Report
贸易与发展报告

TE Traditional Expression
传统表达方式

TEA Trade and Economic Agreement
贸易经济协定

TEA Trade Expansion Act (United States)
贸易扩张法(美国)

TECA Trade and Economic Cooperation Agreement
贸易经济合作协定

TEL Temporary Exclusion List (AFTA)
临时例外清单(AFTA)

TEU [Maastricht] Treaty of European Union
[马斯特里赫特]欧洲联盟条约

TFA Trade Facilitation Alliance
贸易便利化联盟

TFAP Trade Facilitation Action Plan
贸易便利化行动计划

TICAD Tokyo International Conference on African Development
东京非洲发展国际会议

TIDDB Trade and Investment Data Database (APEC)
贸易与投资数据库(APEC)

TIFA Trade and Investment Facilitation Agreement
贸易投资便利化协定

TIFA　Trade and Investment Framework Agreement
贸易投资框架协定
TILF　Trade and Investment Liberalization and Facilitation (APEC)
贸易投资自由化便利化(APEC)
TIS　Trade in Services
服务贸易
TLT　Trademark Law Treaty (WIPO)
商标法条约(WIPO)
TMB　Textiles Monitoring Body
纺织品监督机构
TNC　Trade Negotiations Committee
贸易谈判委员会
TNC　Transnational Corporation
跨国公司
TOT　Transfer of Technology
技术转让
TPA　Trade Promotion Agreement
贸易促进协定
TPA　Trade Promotion Authority
贸易促进授权
TPF　Trade Policy Framework
贸易政策框架
TPM　Trigger Price Mechanism
触发价格机制
TPRB　Trade Policy Review Body
贸易政策审议机构
TPRM　Trade Policy Review Mechanism
贸易政策审议机制
TPSEPA　Trans-Pacific Strategic Economic Partnership Agreement
跨太平洋战略经济伙伴关系协定
TQ　Tariff Quota
关税配额
TRACLAP　Trade-Related Aspects of Competition Law and Policy
与贸易有关的竞争法和政策
TRAINS　[UNCTAD] Trade Analysis and Information System
[UNCTAD]贸易分析与信息系统
TRAPs　Trade-Related Antitrust Principles
与贸易有关的反垄断原则
TREATI　Trans-Regional EU-ASEAN Trade Initiative
跨地区欧盟—东盟贸易倡议
TREM　Trade-Restrictive Environmental Measure
限制贸易的环境措施

TREPS	Trade-Related Aspects of Environmental Policies 与贸易有关的环境政策
TRIMs	Trade-Related Investment Measures 与贸易有关的投资措施
TRIPS	Trade-Related Aspects of Intellectual Property Rights 与贸易有关的知识产权
TRQ	Tariff Rate Quota 关税配额
TRTA	Trade-Related Technical Assistance 与贸易有关的技术援助
TSB	Textile Surveillance Body 纺织品监督机构
TSG	Traditional speciality guaranteed 注册传统特色产品
TSSC	Textiles-Specific Safeguard Clause 纺织品特殊保障条款
TSUS	Tariff Schedule of the United States 美国关税税则
TTMRA	Trans-Tasman Mutual Recognition Arrangement 跨塔斯曼互认安排

~ *U* ~

UAP	Unprocessed Agricultural Products 未加工农产品
UDEAC	Union douanière et économique de l'Afrique centrale (see CACEU) 中部非洲关税与经济同盟(见CACEU)
UN	United Nations 联合国
UNCAC	United Nations Convention Against Corruption 联合国反腐败公约
UNCED	United Nations Conference on Environment and Development 联合国环境发展大会
UNCITRAL	United Nations Commission on International Trade Law 联合国国际贸易法委员会
UNCLOS	United Nations Convention on the Law of the Sea 联合国海洋法公约
UNCPC	United Nations Central Product Classification 联合国中央产品分类
UNCTAD	United Nations Conference on Trade and Development 联合国贸易与发展会议
UNECA	United Nations Economic Commission for Africa 联合国非洲经济委员会
UNECWA	United Nations Economic Commission for Western Asia 联合国西亚济委员会
UNEP	United Nations Environment Programme 联合国环境规划署
UNESCO	United Nations Educational, Scientific and Cultural Organization 联合国教育、科学及文化组织
UNFCCC	United Nations Framework Convention on Climate Change 联合国气候变化框架公约
UNGA	United Nations General Assembly 联合国大会
UNGASS	United Nations General Assembly Special Session 联合国大会特别会议
UNIDO	United Nations Industrial Development Organization 联合国工业发展组织
UNISTE	United Nations International Symposium on Trade Efficiency 联合国贸易效率国际研讨会
UNSC	United Nations Security Council 联合国安全理事会
UNSD	United Nations Statistics Division 联合国统计司

UPOV	International Union for the Protection of New Varieties of Plants (Fr. Union internationale pour la protection des obtentions végétales) 国际植物新品种保护联盟
UR	Uruguay Round 乌拉圭回合
URAA	Uruguay Round Agreements Act (United States) 乌拉圭回合协定法(美国)
USITC	United States International Trade Commission 美国国际贸易委员会
USTR	United States Trade Representative 美国贸易代表办公室
UTL	Unilateral Trade Liberalization 单边贸易自由化

~ *V* ~

VCLT	Vienna Convention on the Law of Treaties 维也纳条约法公约
VER	Voluntary Export Restraint 自愿出口限制
VIE	Voluntary Import Expansion [Programme] 自愿扩大进口[计划]
VNM	Value of Non-originating Materials 非原产材料价格
VOM	Value of Originating Materials 原产材料价格
VRA	Voluntary Restraint Agreement 自愿限制协定

~ W ~

WAEC	West African Economic Community 西非经济共同体
WAEMU	West African Economic and Monetary Union 西非经济与货币联盟
WAIPA	World Association of Investment Promotion Agencies 世界投资促进机构协会
WCED	World Commission on Environment and Development 世界环境与发展委员会
WCO	World Customs Organization 世界海关组织
WDPR	Working Party on Domestic Regulation 国内规制工作组
WDR	World Development Report 世界发展报告
WEF	World Economic Forum 世界经济论坛
WEU	Western European Union 西欧联盟
WFP	World Food Programme 世界粮食计划署
WHFTA	Western Hemisphere Free Trade Agreement 西半球自由贸易协定
WIPO	World Intellectual Property Organization 世界知识产权组织
WIR	World Investment Report 世界投资报告
WITS	World Integrated Trade Solution 世界综合贸易方案
WPPS	Working Party on Professional Services 专业服务工作组
WPPT	WIPO Performances and Phonograms Treaty WIPO组织表演和录音制品条约
WSSD	World Summit on Sustainable Development 可持续发展世界首脑会议
WTO	World Trade Organization 世界贸易组织
WWTG	World Wine Trade Group 国际葡萄酒贸易集团

~ *Z*~

ZFZ	Zero-for-Zero [Tariff Reductions] 零对零[关税削减]

BIBLIOGRAPHY
参考书目

Abbott, Frederick, Thomas Cottier and Francis Gurry (1999), *The International Intellectual Property System: Commentary and Materials*, Kluwer Law International, The Hague

Addo, Kofi (2002), "The Correlation between Labour Standards and International Trade: Which Way Forward?", *Journal of World Trade*, 36(2): 285–303

Addor, Felix and Alexandra Grazioli (2002), "Geographical Indications beyond Wines and Spirits: A Roadmap for a Better Protection for Geographical Indications in the WTO TRIPs Agreement", *Journal of World Intellectual Property*, 5(6): 865–97

Aho, C. Michael (1990), "A Recipe for RIBS – Resentment, Inefficiency, Bureaucracy and Stupid Signals", in Richard S. Belous and Rebecca S. Hartley, eds., *The Growth of Regional Trading Blocs in the Global Economy*, National Planning Association, Washington, DC

APEC (2000), *Towards Knowledge-Based Economies in APEC*, APEC Secretariat, Singapore

Areeda, Phillip and Donald F. Turner (1975), "Predatory Pricing and Related Practices under Section 2 of the Sherman Act", *Harvard Law Review*, 88(4): 697–733

Asian Development Bank (2002), *Asian Development Outlook 2002*, Manila

Atlantic Council of the United States (1976), *GATT-plus – Proposal for Trade Reform*, Praeger Publishers, New York

Audier, J. (2000), *TRIPs Agreement: Geographical Indications*, Office for Official Publications, European Communities, Luxembourg

Aust, Anthony (2000), *Modern Treaty Law and Practice*, Cambridge University Press, Cambridge

Bal, Salman (2001), "International Free Trade Agreements and Human Rights: Reinterpreting Article XX of the GATT", *Minnesota Journal of Global Trade*, 10(1): 62–108

Baldwin, Richard (1993), *A Domino Theory of Regionalism*, NBER Working Paper No. 4465, National Bureau of Economic Research, Cambridge, MA

Bartley Johns, Marcus, Paul Brenton, Massimiliano Cali, Mombert Hoppe and Roberta Piermartini (2015), *The Role of Trade in Ending Poverty*, World Trade Organization, Geneva

Bayard, Thomas O. and Kimberley Ann Elliott (1994), *Reciprocity and Realisation in U.S. Trade Policy*, Institute for International Economics, Washington, DC

Bergsten, C. Fred (1996), *Competitive Liberalization and Global Free Trade: A Vision for the Early 20th Century*, Working Paper 96-15, Institute for International Economics, Washington, DC

Bertrand, Trent J. and Jaroslav Vanek (1971), "The Theory of Tariffs, Taxes, and Subsidies: Some Aspects of the Second Best", *American Economic Review*, 61: 925–31

Bhagwati, Jagdish N. (1988), *Protectionism*, MIT Press, Cambridge, MA

(1991), *The World Trading System at Risk*, Harvester Wheatsheaf, London

(1993), "Regionalism and Multilateralism: An Overview", in Jaime de Melo and Arvind Panagariya, eds., *New Dimensions in Regional Integration*, Cambridge University Press

(1995), "The Demands to Reduce Domestic Diversity among Trading Nations", in Jagdish Bhagwati and Robert E. Hudec, eds., *Fair Trade and Harmonization*, vol. 1, MIT Press, Cambridge, MA

(2002a), *Free Trade Today*, Princeton University Press, Princeton, NJ

(2002b), *Going Alone: The Case for Relaxed Reciprocity in Freeing Trade*, MIT Press, Cambridge, MA

Bhagwati, Jagdish N. and Robert E. Hudec, eds. (1995), *Fair Trade and Harmonization: Prerequisites for Free Trade*, 2 vols., MIT Press, Cambridge, MA

Bhagwati, Jagdish N. and Arvind Panagariya, eds. (1996), *The Economics of Preferential Trade Agreements*, AEI Press, Washington, DC

Birnie, P. W. and A. E Boyle (2002), *International Law and the Environment*, 2nd edn., Oxford University Press, Oxford

Brander, James A. (1995), *Strategic Trade Policy*, NBER Working Paper No. 5020, National Bureau of Economic Research, Cambridge, MA

Brandt Commission (1980), *North–South: A Programme for Survival*, Pan Books, London

(1983), *Common Crisis North–South: Cooperation for World Recovery*, Pan Books, London

Brenton, Paul, Henry Scott and Peter Sinclair (1997), *International Trade: A European Text*, Oxford University Press, Oxford

Brown, William Adams (1950), *The United States and the Restoration of World Trade*, Brookings Institution, Washington, DC

Brownlie, Ian (2019), *Principles of Public International Law*, 9th edn., Clarendon Press, Oxford

Butler, Nicholas (1983), "The Ploughshares War between Europe and America", *Foreign Affairs*, 62(1): 105–22

Chang, Sea-Jin (2003), *Financial Crisis and Transformation of Korean Business Groups: The Rise and Fall of Chaebols*, Cambridge University Press, Cambridge

Cho, Sungjoon (1998), *GATT Non-Violation Issues in the WTO Framework: Are they the Achilles Heel of the Dispute Settlement Process?*, Jean Monnet Working Paper No. 9/98, New York University School of Law, New York

Cline, William R., ed. (1983), *Trade Policy in the 1980s*, Institute for International Economics, Washington, DC

Coats, A. W (1987), *Mercantilism: Economic Ideas, History, Policy*, University of Newcastle, Australia

Corden, W. Max (1971), *The Theory of Protection*, Clarendon Press, Oxford

(1974), *Trade Policy and Economic Welfare*, Clarendon Press, Oxford

(1985), *Protection, Growth and Trade*, Basil Blackwell, London

Cossy, Mireille (2006), *Determining Likeness under the GATS: Squaring the Circle*, Staff Working Paper ERSD-2006-08, World Trade Organization, Geneva

Cowhey, Peter F. and Jonathan D. Aronson (1993), "A New Trade Order", *Foreign Affairs*, 72(1): 183–95

Crawford, James (2000), *Third Report on State Responsibility*, International Law Commission, United Nations General Assembly document A/CN.4/507

Crawford, Jo-Anne and Roberto V. Fiorentino (2005), *The Changing Landscape of Regional Trade Agreements*, WTO Staff Discussion Paper No. 8, World Trade Organization, Geneva

Croome, John (1995), *Reshaping the World Trading System*, World Trade Organization, Geneva

(1999), *Guide to the Uruguay Agreements*, Kluwer Law International, The Hague

Cuddington, John T., Rodney Ludema and Shamila A. Jayasuria (2002), *Prebisch-Singer Redux*, Central Bank of Chile Working Papers, No. 140, Santiago

Curzon, Gerard (1965), *Multilateral Commercial Diplomacy*, Michael Joseph, London

Dabbah, Maher, M. (2003), *The Internationalisation of Antitrust Policy*, Cambridge University Press, Cambridge

Dam, Kenneth W. (1970), *The GATT: Law and International Economic Organisation*, University of Chicago Press, Chicago

(2001), *The Rules of the Global Game: A New Look at US International Policymaking*, University of Chicago Press, Chicago and London

Deardorff, Alan V. (1990), "Economic Perspectives in Anti-Dumping Law", in John H. Jackson and E. A. Vermulst, eds., *Antidumping Law and Practice: A Comparative Study*, Harvester Wheatsheaf, London

(2003), "What Might Globalisation's Critics Believe?", *World Economy*, 26(5): 639-58

Deardorff, Alan V. and Robert M. Stern (1997), *Measurement of Non-Tariff Barriers*, Economics Department Working Papers No. 179, OECD, Paris

Dent, Christopher M. (2006), *New Free Trade Agreements in the Asia-Pacific*, Palgrave Macmillan, Basingstoke

Destler, I. M. (1993), *American Trade Politics*, 3rd edn., Institute for International Economics, Washington, DC

Dollar, Davi (2002), "Global Economic Integration and Global Inequality", in David Gruen, Terry O'Brien and Jeremy Lawson, eds., *Globalisation, Living Standards and Inequality: Recent Progress and Continuing Challenges*, Reserve Bank of Australia and Australian Treasury, Canberra

Dressler, Andreas (2018), *Investment Facilitation: A Practical Perspective*, EIS Initiative, International Centre for Trade and Sustainable Development (ICTSD) and World Economic Forum, Geneva

Dryden, S. (1995), *Trade Warriors: USTR and the American Crusade for Free Trade*, Oxford University Press, Oxford and New York

Durling, James P. and Matthew R. Nicely (2002), *Understanding the WTO Anti-Dumping Agreement: Negotiating History and Subsequent Interpretation*, Cameron May, London

Estevadeordal, Antoni and Kati Suominen (2003), "Rules of Origin in the World Trading System", Paper prepared for the Seminar on Regional Trade Agreements and the WTO, 14 November, World Trade Organization, Geneva

Esty, Daniel C. (1994), *Greening the GATT: Trade, Environment and the Future*, Institute for International Economics, Washington, DC

Evans, John W. (1972), *The Kennedy Round in American Trade Policy*, Harvard University Press, Cambridge, MA

Fikentscher, Wolfgang and Ulrich Immenga (1995), *Draft International Antitrust Code: Kommentierter Entwurf eines internationalen Wettbewerbsrechts*, Nomos, Baden-Baden

Finger, J. Michael, ed. (1993), *Antidumping: How it Works and Who Gets Hurt*, University of Michigan Press, Ann Arbor

Finger, J. Michael (1998) *GATT Experience with Safeguards: Making Economic and Political Sense of the Possibilities that the GATT Allows to Restrict Imports*, World Bank Policy Research Working Papers WPS2000, Washington, DC

Francois, Joseph and Will Martin (2003), "Formula Approaches for Market Access Negotiations", *The World Economy*, 26(1): 1–23

Frankel, Jeffrey A. and Andrew K. Rose (2002), *Is Trade Good or Bad for the Environment? Sorting out the Causality*, NBER Working Paper 9201, National Bureau of Economic Research, Cambridge, MA

Galbraith, John Kenneth (1958), *The Affluent Society*, Hamish Hamilton, London

(1981), *A Life in Our Times*, Houghton Mifflin Company, Boston

Gallagher, Peter (2000), *Guide to the WTO and Developing Countries*, Kluwer Law International, The Hague, and World Trade Organization, Geneva

(2005), *The First Ten Years of the WTO*, Cambridge University Press and World Trade Organization, Cambridge and Geneva

Ganne, Emanuelle (2018), *Can Blockchain Revolutionize International Trade?*, World Trade Organization, Geneva

GATT documents:

GATT/CP/106, Report of the Intersessional Working Party on the Complaint of Czechoslovakia Concerning the Withdrawal by the United States of a Tariff Concession under the Terms of Article XIX

SCM/42, European Economic Community – Subsidies on Exports of Wheat Flour

SCM/43, European Economic Community – Subsidies on Export of Pasta Products

GATT Secretariat (1952–94), *General Agreement on Tariffs and Trade: Basic Instruments and Selected Documents*, GATT, Geneva

(1959), *Trends in International Trade: Report by a Panel of Experts*, GATT, Geneva

(1979), *The Tokyo Round of Multilateral Trade Negotiations*, GATT, Geneva

(1985), *Trade Policies for a Better Future: Proposals for Action*, GATT, Geneva

Gervais, Daniel (2003), *The TRIPS Agreement: Drafting History and Analysis*, 2nd edn., Sweet & Maxwell, London

Gilpin, Robert (1987), *The Political Economy of International Relations*, Princeton University Press, Princeton, NJ

Glick, Leslie Alan (1984), *Multilateral Trade Negotiations: World Trade after the Tokyo Round*, Rowman & Allanheld, Totowa, NJ

Godek, Paul E. (1986), "The Politically Optimal Tariff: Tariff Levels of Trade Restrictions across Developed Countries", *Economic Inquiry*, 24(4): 587–93

Goode, Walter (2009), *Negotiating Free-Trade Agreements: A Guide*, Department of Foreign Affairs and Trade, Canberra

Green, Roy E., ed. (2003), *The Enterprise for the Americas Initiative*, Praeger Publishers, Westport, CT

Group of Lisbon (1995), *Limits to Competition*, MIT Press, Cambridge, MA

Harrison, Mark (2001), "'Pop Mercantilism?' Staff and Student Attitudes in Economics at Warwick", www.warwick.ac.uk/economics/harrison/comment/mercantilism.pdf

Hill, T. P. (1977), "On Goods and Services", *Review of Income and Wealth*, 23: 315–38

Hoda, Anwarul (2018), *Tariff Negotiations and Renegotiations under the GATT and the WTO*, 2nd revised edn, World Trade Organization and Cambridge University Press, Geneva and Cambridge

Hoekman, Bernard (1995), *Trade Laws and Institutions: Good Practices and the World Trade Organization*, World Bank Discussion Papers No. 282, World Bank, Washington, DC

(1996), *Trade and Competition Policy in the WTO System*, Centre for Economic Policy Research Discussion Paper No. 1501, London

Hoekman, Bernard and Michael Kostecki (1995), *The Political Economy of the World Trading System: From GATT to WTO*, Oxford University Press, Oxford

Hope, Einar and Per Maeleng, eds. (1998), *Competition and Trade Policies: Coherence or Conflict?*, Routledge, London and New York

Howse, Robert (2002), "Human Rights in the WTO: Whose Rights, What Humanity? Comment on Petersmann", *European Journal of International Law*, 13(3): 651–60

Hudec, Robert E. (1999), *Essays on the Nature of International Trade Law*, Cameron May, London

Hudec, Robert E., Daniel L. M. Kennedy and Mark Sgarbossa (1993), "A Statistical Profile of GATT Dispute Settlement Cases: 1948–1989", *Minnesota Journal of Global Trade*, 2(1): 1–113

Hufbauer, Gary Clyde, Jeffrey J. Schott and Kimberley Ann Elliott (1990), *Economic Sanctions Reconsidered: History and Current Policy*, Institute for International Economics, Washington, DC

Inama, Stefano (2000), "Non-Preferential Rules of Origin", in *A Positive Agenda for Developing Countries: Issues for Future Trade Negotiations*, United Nations Conference on Trade and Development, New York and Geneva

Ingco, Merlinda D., John D. Nash and Kevin M. Cleaver (2004), *Agriculture and the WTO: Creating a Trading System for Development*, World Bank, Washington, DC

International Labour Office (2003), *Fundamental Rights at Work and International Labour Standards*, International Labour Organization, Geneva

International Trademark Association (2000), *Issue Brief: Lisbon Agreement for the Protection of Appellations of Origin: Violation of the* TRIPS *Agreement*, New York

Irwin, Douglas A. (1996), *Against the Tide: An Intellectual History of Free Trade*, Princeton University Press, Princeton, NJ

Jackson, John H. (1969), *World Trade and the Law of the GATT*, Bobbs-Merrill Company, Indianapolis, IN

(1997), *The World Trading System: Law and Policy of International Economic Relations*, MIT Press, Cambridge, MA

(2000), *The Jurisprudence of the GATT and the WTO*, Cambridge University Press, Cambridge

Jackson, John H. and William A. Davey (1986), *Legal Problems of International Economic Relations*, 2nd edn., West Publishing, St Paul, MN

Jackson, John H. and E. A. Vermulst, eds. (1990), *Antidumping Law and Practice: A Comparative Study*, Harvester Wheatsheaf, London

Johnson, Harry G. (1968), "Tariffs and Economic Development: Some Theoretical Issues", in J. D. Theberge, ed., *Economics of Trade and Development*, John Wiley & Sons, New York

Josling, Timothy E., Stefan Tangermann and T. K. Warley (1996), *Agriculture in the GATT*, St. Martin's Press, New York

Jung, Youngjin and Sun Hyeong Lee (2003), "The Legacy of the Byrd Amendment Controversies: Rethinking the Principle of Good Faith", *Journal of World Trade*, 37(5): 921–58

Kahneman, D. and A. Tversky (1979) "Prospect Theory: An Analysis of Decision Under Risk", *Econometrica*, 47(2): 263–91

Kasahara, Shigehisa (2004), *The Flying Geese Paradigm: A Critical Study of its Application to East Asian Regional Development*, Discussion Paper No. 169, United Nations Conference on Trade and Development, Geneva

Keck, Alexander and Patrick Low (2004), *Special and Differential Treatment in the WTO: Why, When and How?*, Staff Working Paper ERSD-2004-03, World Trade Organization, Geneva

Kindleberger, Charles P. (1973), *The World in Depression 1929–1939*, Allen Lane, The Penguin Press, Harmondsworth

Kjeldsen-Kragh, Søren (2001), *International Trade Policy*, Copenhagen Business School Press, Copenhagen

Kohl, Richard, ed. (2003), *Globalization, Poverty and Inequality*, OECD, Paris

Krugman, Paul R. (1986), *Strategic Trade Policy and the New International Economics*, MIT Press, Cambridge, MA

(1990), *Rethinking International Trade*, MIT Press, Cambridge, MA

(1991), "The Move Toward Free Trade Zones". Symposium sponsored by the Federal Reserve Board of Kansas City on Policy Implications of Free Trade and Currency Zones

(1998), "Ricardo's Difficult Idea: Why Intellectuals Don't Understand Comparative Advantage", in Gary Cook, ed., *The Economics and Politics of International Trade: Freedom and Trade*, vol. II, Routledge, London and New York

Krugman, Paul R. and James Brander (1983), "A 'Reciprocal Dumping' Model of International Trade", *Journal of International Economics*, 15: 313–21. Reprinted in Paul R. Krugman (1990)

Laird, S. and R. Vossenar (1991), "Porqué nos preocupan las bareras no arancelarias?", *Informacion Comercial Española*, Special Issue: 31–54

Leclerc, Jean-Marc (1999), "Reforming Anti-Dumping Law: Balancing the Interests of Consumers and Domestic Industries", *McGill Law Journal*, 44: 111–40.

Lee Yong-shik (2003), *Safeguard Measures in World Trade: The Legal Analysis*, Kluwer Law International, The Hague

Lejárraga, I. (2014), "Deep Provisions in Regional Trade Agreements: How Multilateral-Friendly? An Overview of OECD Findings", *OECD Trade Policy Papers*, No. 168, OECD Publishing, Paris, https://doi.org.10.18166873

Lerner, A. P. (1936), "The Symmetry between Import and Export Taxes", *Economica*, 3(11): 306–13. Reprinted in American Economic Association, *Readings in International Economics*, vol. XI, George Allen & Unwin, London

Lim, Hoe (2001), "Trade and Human Rights: What's at Issue?", *Journal of World Trade*, 35(2): 275–300

Lindsey, Brink and Dan Ikenson (2002), *Antidumping 101: The Devilish Details of "Unfair Trade" Law*, Trade Policy Analysis Paper No. 20, Cato Institute, Washington, DC

López, Ramó and Arvind Panagaryia (1992), "On the Theory of Piecemeal Tariff Reform: The Case of Pure Imported Intermediate Inputs", *American Economic Review*, 82(3): 615–25

Magnusson, Lars (1994), *Mercantilism: The Shaping of an Economic Language*, Routledge, London and New York

Maneschi, Andrea (1998), *Comparative Advantage in International Trade*, Edward Elgar, Cheltenham

Marceau, Gabrielle (1994), *Anti-Dumping and Anti-Trust Issues in Free Trade Areas*, Clarendon Press, Oxford

(2002), "WTO Dispute Settlement and Human Rights", *European Journal of International Law*, 13(4): 753–814

Marceau, Gabrielle and Joel P. Trachtman (2002), “The Technical Barriers to Trade Agreement, the Sanitary and Phytosanitary Measures Agreement, and the General Agreement on Tariffs and Trade: A Map of the World Trade Organization Law of Domestic Regulation of Goods”, *Journal of World Trade*, 36(5): 811–81

Maskus, Keith E. (2000), “Parallel Imports”, *The World Economy*, 23(9): 1269–84

Mastel, Greg (1996), *American Trade Laws after the Uruguay Round*, M. E. Sharpe, Armonk, NY

Mavroidis, Petros C. (2000), “Remedies in the WTO Legal System: Between a Rock and a Hard Place”, *European Journal of International Law*, 11(4): 763–813

(2001), *Amicus Curiae Briefs before the WTO: Much Ado about Nothing*, Jean Monnet Working Paper 2/01, New York University School of Law, New York

Mayer, Jörg (2002), “The Fallacy of Composition: A Review of the Literature”, *The World Economy*, 25(6): 875–94

Meade, J. E. (1955), *Trade and Welfare*, Oxford University Press, London

Mendoza, Miguel Rodriguez (2012), *Free Trade Agreements in South America: Trends, Prospects and Challenges*, Banca de Desarollo de América Latina, Caracas

Messenger, Gregory (2017), “The Public-Private Distinction at the World Trade Organization: Fundamental Challenges to Determining the Meaning of ‘Public Body’”, *International Journal of Constitutional Law* 15: 60–83

Ministry of Economic Development (2002), *Bioprospecting in New Zealand: Discussing the Options*, Wellington, New Zealand

Moon, Bruce E. (2000), *Dilemmas of International Trade*, Westview Press, Boulder, CO

Mueller, Felix (2003), “Is the General Agreement on Tariffs and Trade Article XIX ‘Unforeseen Developments Clause’ Still Effective under the Agreement on Safeguards?”, *Journal of World Trade*, 37(6): 1119–51

Neufeld, Inge Nora (2001), *Anti-Dumping and Countervailing Procedures – Use or Abuse? Implications for Developing Countries*, Policy Issues in International Trade and Commodities Study Series No. 9, United Nations Conference on Trade and Development, New York and Geneva

(2014), *The Long and Winding Road: How WTO Members Finally Reached a Trade Facilitation Agreement*, WTO Staff Working Paper ERSD-2014-06, Geneva

Nicita, Alessandro (2011), *Measuring the Relative Strength of Preferential Market Access*, Policy Issues in Trade and Commodities Study Series No. 47, UNCTAD, Geneva

Nicolaïdis, Kalypso (1997), “Managed Mutual Recognition: The New Approach to the Liberalization of Professional Services”, in OECD, *Liberalization of Trade in Services*, Paris

OECD (2000), *International Trade and Core Labour Standards*, OECD, Paris

(2001), *Trade and Competition: Options for a Greater Coherence*, OECD, Paris

(2003), *Multifunctionality: The Policy Implications*, OECD, Paris

(2017), *OECD Transfer Pricing Guidelines for International Enterprises and Tax Administrations 2017*, OECD, Paris

(2018), *Trade Facilitation and the Global Economy*, OECD, Paris

C(98)35/FINAL, *Recommendation of the Council Concerning Effective Action Against Hard Core Cartels*

Ohmae, Kenichi (1991), *The Borderless World: Power and Strategy in the International Economy*, Fontana, London

Pauwelyn, Joost (2002), *The Nature of WTO Obligations*, Jean Monnet Working Paper 1/02, New York University School of Law, New York

(2004), "The Puzzle of WTO Safeguards and Regional Trade Agreements", *Journal of International Economic Law*, 7(1): 109–42

(2007), "Legal Avenues to 'Multilateralizing Regionalism': Beyond Article XXIV", Paper presented at the Conference on Multilateralizing Regionalism, WTO-HEI, Geneva

Petersmann, Ernst-Ulrich (2001), *Time for Integrating Human Rights into the Law of Worldwide Organizations: Lessons from European Integration Law for Global Integration Law*, Jean Monnet Working Paper 7/01, New York University School of Law, New York

Pierce, Richard J. Jr (2000), "Antidumping Law as a Means of Facilitating Cartelization", *Antitrust Law*, 67(3): 725–43.

Porter, Michael E. (1990), *The Competitive Advantage of Nations*, Free Press, New York

Prebisch,Raúl (1950), "The Economic Development of Latin America", United Nations Department of Economic Affairs, Economic Commission for Latin America (ECLA), New York. Reprinted in *Economic Bulletin for Latin America*, 7(1)(1962): 1–22

(1963), "Development Problems of the Peripheral Countries and the Terms of Trade", in *Towards a Dynamic Development Policy for Latin America*, United Nations, New York. Reprinted in J. D. Theberge (ed.), *Economics of Trade and Development*, John Wiley & Sons, New York, 1968

Preeg, Ernest H. (1970), *Traders and Diplomats: An Analysis of the Kennedy Round of Negotiations under the General Agreement on Tariffs and Trade*, Brookings Institution, Washington, DC

(1995a), *Trade Policy Ahead: Three Tracks and One Question*, Center for Strategic and International Studies, Washington, DC

(1995b), *Traders in a Brave New World: The Uruguay Round and the Future of the International Trading System*, University of Chicago Press, Chicago

Rangnekar, Dwijen (2003), *Geographical Indications: A Review of Proposals at the TRIPS Council: Extending Article 23 to Products other than Wines and Spirits*, UNCTAD/ICTSD, Geneva

Reich, Robert R. (1991), *The Work of Nations*, Simon & Schuster, London

Ricardo, David (1960) [1817], *The Principles of Political Economy and Taxation*, Every- man Library, London

Robinson, Joan (1947), "Beggar-My-Neighbour Remedies for Unemployment". American Economic Association, *Readings in the Theory of International Trade*, vol. IV, George Allen & Unwin, London

Rodrik, Dani (2012), *The Globalization Paradox: Why Global Markets, States and Democracy Can't Co-exist*, Oxford University Press, Oxford

Ruggie, John Gerard (1982), "International Regimes, Transactions, and Change: Embedded Liberalism in Postwar Economic Order", *International Organization*, 36(2): 379–415

Russell, Brian R. (1999), "How Long Can You Tread Water? The Anti-Economics of Trade Remedy Law", in Miguel Rodríguez Mendoza, Patrick Low and Barbara Kotschwar, eds., *Trade Rules in the Making: Challenges in Regional and Multilateral Negotiations*, Organization of American States, Brookings Institution Press, Washington, DC

Salvatore, Dominick (1987), *The New Protectionist Threat to World Welfare*, North-Holland, New York

Schiff, Maurice and L. Alan Winters (2003), *Regional Integration and Development*, The International Bank for Reconstruction and Development / World Bank, Washington, DC

Schoenbaum, Thomas J. (2002), "International Trade and Environmental Protection", in P. W. Birnie and A. E. Boyle, *International Law and the Environment*, 2nd edn., Oxford University Press, Oxford

Schroeder, Werner (2003), *European Union and European Communities*, Jean Monnet Working Paper 9/03, New York University School of Law, New York

Schumpeter, Joseph A. (1982) [1954], *History of Economic Analysis*, Allen & Unwin, London

Seid, Sherif H. (2002), *Global Regulation of Foreign Direct Investment*, Ashgate Publishing, Aldershot

Shaw, Malcolm N. (2014), *International Law*, 7th edn., Grotius Publications, Cambridge

Singer, H. W. (1950), "U.S. Foreign Investment in Underdeveloped Areas: The Distribution of Gains between Investing and Borrowing Countries", *American Economic Review*, 40: 473–85

Smith, Adam (1991) [1776], *The Wealth of Nations*, Everyman Library, London

Starke, J. G. (1989), *Introduction to International Law*, Butterworths, London

Steele, Keith, ed. (1996), *Anti-Dumping under the WTO: A Comparative Review*, Kluwer Law International and International Bar Association, London

Stiglitz, Joseph E. (2002), *Globalization and its Discontents*, W. W. Norton, New York

Stoever, William A. (2002), "Attempting to Resolve the Attraction-Aversion Dilemma: A Study of the FDI Policy of the Republic of Korea", *Transnational Corporations*, 11(1): 49–76

Sykes, Alan O. (1998), "Antidumping and Antitrust: What Problems Does Each Address?", in Robert Z. Lawrence, ed., *Brookings Trade Forum 1998*, Brookings Institution, Washington, DC

Taubman, Antony, Hannu Wager and Jayashree Watal, eds. (2012), *A Handbook on the WTO TRIPS Agreement*, Cambridge University Press, Cambridge

Toye, John and Richard Toye (2003), "The Origins and Interpretation of the Prebisch-Singer Thesis", *History of Political Economy*, 35(3): 437–67

United Mexican States v. Metalclad (2001), British Columbia Supreme Court (Tysoe J.), 2001 B.C.D. Civ. J. 1708

United Nations (2015), *The Millennium Development Goals Report*, United Nations, New York

United Nations Conference on Trade and Development (1985), *The History of UNCTAD*, United Nations, New York and Geneva

(2003), *Back to Basics: Market Access Issues in the Doha Agenda*, United Nations, New York and Geneva

(2004), *Beyond Conventional Wisdom in Development Policy: An Intellectual History of UNCTAD 1964–2004*, United Nations, New York and Geneva

(2005), *Investor-State Disputes Arising from Investment Treaties: A Review*, United Nations, New York and Geneva

(2015), *Investment Policy Framework for Sustainable Development*, United Nations, New York and Geneva

(2018a), *Creative Economy Outlook: Trends in International Trade in Creative Industries*, United Nations, New York and Geneva

(2018b), *Trade and Development Report 2018: Power, Platforms and the Free Trade Delusion*, United Nations, New York and Geneva

(2018c), *UNCTAD's Reform Package for the International Investment Regime*, United Nations, New York and Geneva

(Annually), *E-Commerce and Development Report*, United Nations, New York and Geneva

(Annually), *The Least Developed Countries Report*, United Nations, New York and Geneva

(Annually), *Trade and Development Report*, United Nations, New York and Geneva

(Annually), *World Investment Report*, United Nations, New York and Geneva

United Nations Conference on Trade and Development (UNCTAD) documents:

UNCTAD/EDM/2004/2, *Trade and Gender: Opportunities and Challenges for Developing Countries*

UNCTAD/ITCD/TSB/2, 24 March 1998, *Globalization and the International Trading System: Issues Relating to Rules of Origin*

United Nations Conference on Trade and Development and World Bank (2018), *The Unseen Impact of Non-Tariff Measures*, United Nations, New York and Geneva

United Nations Development Programme (2003), *Human Development Report 2003: Millennium Development Goals: A Compact among Nations to end Human Poverty* Oxford University Press, New York and Oxford

Vermulst, Edwin A. (1990), "The Antidumping Systems of Australia, Canada, the EEC and the USA: Have Antidumping Laws Become a Problem in International Trade?", in John H. Jackson and Edwin A. Vermulst, eds., *Antidumping Law and Practice*, Harvester Wheatsheaf, London

Vermulst, Edwin A., Paul Waer and Jacques Bourgeois (1994), *Rules of Origin in International Trade: A Comparative Study*, University of Michigan Press, Ann Arbor

Vernon, Raymond (1966), "International Investment and International Trade in the Product Cycle", *Quarterly Journal of Economics*, 80: 190–207

Viner, Jacob (1921), *Dumping: A Problem in International Trade*. Reprinted in A. M. Kelley (ed.), *Reprints of Economic Classics*, New York, 1966

(1950) [1923], *The Customs Union Issue*, Stevens & Sons, London

Wessel, Ramses A. (2003), *The Constitutional Relationship between the European Union and the European Community: Consequences for the Relationship with the Member States*, Jean Monnet Working Paper 9/03, New York University School of Law, New York

Whalley, John (1996), *Why Do Countries Seek Regional Trade Agreements?*, NBER Working Paper 5552, National Bureau of Economic Research, Cambridge, MA

Williamson, John (1990), "What Washington Means by Policy Reform", in John Williamson, ed., *Latin American Adjustment: How Much Has Happened?*, Institute for International Economics, Washington, DC

(2000), "What Should the World Bank Think about the Washington Consensus?", *The World Bank Research Observer*, 15(2): 251–64

Willig, Robert D. (1998), "Economic Effects of Antidumping Policy," in Robert Z. Lawrence, ed., *Brookings Trade Forum 1998*, Brookings Institution, Washington, DC

Winham, Gilbert R. (1986), *International Trade and the Tokyo Round Negotiations*, Princeton University Press, Princeton, NJ

Winters, L. Alan, Neil McCulloch and Andrew McKay (2004), "Trade Liberalization and Poverty: The Evidence So Far", *Journal of Economic Literature*, 42: 72–115

WIPO documents:

SCT/5/3, Standing Committee on the Law of Trademarks, Industrial Designs and Geographical Indications, Geneva, 11–15 September 2000, *Possible Solutions for Conflicts between Trade and Geographical Indications and for Conflicts between Homonymous Geographical Indications*

SCT/8/4, Standing Committee on the Law of Trademarks, Industrial Designs and Geographical Indications, Geneva, 27–31 May 2002, *Geographical Indications: Historical Background, Nature of Rights, Existing Systems for Protection and Obtaining Protection in Other Countries*

SCT/9/4, Standing Committee on the Law of Trademarks, Industrial Designs and Geographical Indications, Geneva, 11–15 November 2002, *The Definition of Geographical Indications*

WIPO/GRTKF/IC/5/3, Intergovernmental Committee on Intellectual Property and Gen- etic Resources, Traditional Knowledge and Folklore, Geneva, 7–15 July 2003, *Consolidated Analysis of the Legal Protection of Traditional Cultural Expressions*

WIPO/IPTK/MCT/02/INF.4, WIPO International Forum on "Intellectual Property and Traditional Knowledge: Our Identity, Our Future", Muscat, 21–22 January 2002, *The Protection of Traditional Knowledge, Including Expressions of Folklore*

Wolf, Martin (2004), *Why Globalization Works*, Yale University Press, New Haven, CT

World Bank Group and World Trade Organization (2018), *Trade and Poverty Reduction: New Evidence of Impacts on Developing Countries*, World Trade Organization, Geneva

World Commission on the Social Dimension of Globalization (2004), *A Fair Globalization: Creating Opportunities for All*, International Labour Office, Geneva

World Trade Organization (1995a), *Analytical Index: A Guide to GATT Law and Practice*, updated 6th edn., Geneva

(1995b), *Regionalism and the World Trading System*, Geneva

(1996–), *Dispute Settlement Reports*, Cambridge University Press, Cambridge

(1999), *The Legal Texts: Results of the Uruguay Round of Multilateral Trade Negotiations*, Cambridge University Press, Cambridge

(2001), *The WTO Dispute Settlement Procedures: A Collection of the Relevant Legal Texts*, 2nd edn., Cambridge University Press, Cambridge

(2009), *World Trade Report 2009: Trade Policy Commitments and Contingency Measures*, Geneva

(2015), *World Trade Report 2015: Speeding Up Trade: Benefits and Challenges of Implementing the WTO Trade Facilitation Agreement*, Geneva

(2018a), *GATT Disputes: 1948–1995*, Volume 1: *Overview and One-Page Case Summaries*, Geneva

(2018b), *GATT Disputes: 1948–1995*, Volume 2: *Dispute Settlement Procedures*, Geneva

(2018c), *World Trade Report 2018: The Future of World Trade: How Digital Technologies Are Transforming Global Commerce*, Geneva

WTO documents:

TN/MA/S/2, *Data Availability and Software Tools for Tariff Negotiations*

WT/DS/98/AB/R, *Korea – Definitive Safeguard Measure on Imports of Certain Dairy Products*

WT/DS/121/AB/R, *Argentina – Safeguard Measures on Imports of Footwear*

WT/DS/141/AB/R – *European Communities – Anti-Dumping Duties on Imports of Cotton-Type Bed Linen from India*

WT/DS/217/AB/R, WT/DS234/AB/R, *United States – Continued Dumping and Subsidy Offset Act of 2000*

WT/DS6/AB/R, *Japan – Taxes on Alcoholic Beverages*

WT/DS26ARB, *European Communities – Measures Concerning Meat and Meat Products (Hormones) – Original Complaint by the United States – Recourse to Arbitration by the European Communities under Article 22.6 of the DSU*

WT/DS27/AB/R, *European Communities – Regime for the Importation, Sale and Distribution of Bananas*
WT/DS44/R, *Japan – Measures Affecting Consumer Photographic Film and Paper*
WT/DS58/R, *United States – Import Prohibition of Certain Shrimp and Shrimp Products*
WT/DS75/AB/R, WT/DS84/AB/R, *Korea – Taxes on Alcoholic Beverages*
WT/DS98/R, *Korea – Definitive Safeguard Measure on Imports of Certain Dairy Products*
WT/DS135/R, *European Communities – Measures Affecting Asbestos and Asbestos Related Components*
WT/DS136/AB/R, *United States – Anti-Dumping Act of 1916*
WT/DS136/ARB, *United States – Anti-Dumping Act of 1916 – Original Complaint by the European Communities – Recourse to Arbitration by the United States under Article22.6 of the DSU*
WT/DS136/R, *United States – Anti-Dumping Act of 1916*
WT/DS160/R, *United States – Section 110(5) of the US Copyright Act*
WT/DS161/AB/R, WT/DS169/AB/R, *Korea – Measures Affecting Imports of Fresh, Chilled or Frozen Beef*
WT/DS219/AB/R, *European Communities – Anti-Dumping Duties on Malleable Cast Iron Tube or Pipe Fittings from Brazil*
WT/DS243/R, *United States – Rules of Origin for Textiles and Apparel Products: Report of the Panel*
WT/DS257/R, *United States – Final Countervailing Duty Determination with Respect to Certain Softwood Lumber from Canada*
WT/REG/W/45, Rules of Origin Regimes in Regional Trade Agreements (5 April 2002)

World Trade Organization and International Finance Corporation (2019), *Trade Finance and the Compliance Challenge*, Geneva and Washington, DC

World Trade Organization and UN Environment (2018), *Making Trade Work for the Environment, Prosperity and Resilience*, Geneva and Nairobi

Zeiler, Thomas W. (1999), *Free Trade, Free World: The Advent of GATT*, University of North Carolina Press, Chapel Hill

Zonnekeyn, Geert A. (2002), "The *Bed Linen* Case and its Aftermath: Some Comments on the European Community's World Trade Organization Enabling Regulation", *Journal of World Trade*, 36(5): 993–1003